Bisexuality in the United States

A SOCIAL SCIENCE READER

Between Men ~ Between Women

Lesbian and Gay Studies

Lillian Faderman and Larry Gross, Editors

D1451189

Bisexuality in the United States

A Social Science Reader

Paula C. Rodríguez Rust

Columbia University Press

New York

Columbia University Press
Publishers Since 1893
New York   Chichester, West Sussex
Copyright © 2000 Columbia University Press
All rights reserved
Copyright acknowledgments for previously
published material appear following index
Library of Congress Cataloging-in-Publication Data
Bisexuality in the United States : a social science reader / edited by Paula C. Rodríguez Rust.
p.   cm.— (Between men—between women)
Includes bibliographical references and index.
ISBN 0–231–10226–7 (cloth: alk. paper)—ISBN 0–231–10227–5 (pbk.: alk. paper)
1. Bisexuality—United States. 2. Bisexuals—United States. I. Rust, Paula C., 1959– II. Series.

99–058484
HQ74.2.U5 B55 2000
306.76'5—dc21

∞
Casebound editions of Columbia University Press books are printed on permanent and durable
acid-free paper.
Printed in the United States of America

c 10 9 8 7 6 5 4 3 2 1
p 10 9 8 7 6 5 4 3 2 1

Dedicated

to the most important people in my world,
my mother, my life partner, and my children

Mildred D. Rust
Lorna Rodríguez Rust
Mykelti Antonio Rodríguez Rust
Saraiah Raquel Rodríguez Rust
Etienne J. J. Rodríguez Rust

Live long, live fully, live free, respect all, and be happy

Contents

Preface

As a society, we are fascinated by sexuality. We pretend that sexuality is a taboo subject, but the taboo only makes it more exciting to talk about. The number of "sex surveys" and articles about sexuality in popular magazines is a testament to our curiosity. We want to know what other people are doing and how; we want to know if our sexual habits are "normal" and we are mesmerized by others' unusual sex habits. But even though we are curious about others' sexuality, we have historically looked askance at the people who collect sexual information and bring it to us. Until recently, the study of sexuality was stigmatized; anyone who undertook research in this area risked their career and their personal reputation. As a result, research on sexuality was scarce and value laden. Before the 1970s most researchers who trod this dangerous ground aimed to discover a "cure" for undesirable sexual practices, and the few researchers who were sympathetic toward sexual diversity wrote about their findings in overly technical jargon to discourage sensationalization and maintain scientific credibility.

The field of sex research changed dramatically in the 1960s, 1970s, and 1980s. The stigma surrounding sex research abated as sexuality entered the political arena in the form of debates about birth control and abortion, pornography, prostitution, sexual coercion, sex in the media, and sexual orientation. Both the feminist movement and the lesbian and gay movements helped legitimize sexuality as a political —not just a personal—issue. The removal of "homosexuality" from the Diagnostic and Statistical Manual of the American Psychiatric Association opened the door for research on sexual orientation that treated lesbians and gay men as the psychological, social, and moral equivalents of heterosexuals. Changes in the social and political climate also made it possible for lesbians and gay men in the social and psychological sciences to come out and begin studying our own communities from our own points of view. Finally, socially constructed and actual crises such as the "breakdown of the family," rising rates of unwed teenage pregnancy, and the AIDS pandemic forced us to realize that our ignorance about sexuality was costing us dearly. Sexual knowledge became vital to our economic, social, and even personal survival. The field of sexuality grew rapidly; the floodgates had finally opened.

As the field of sexuality grew, colleges and universities expanded their curricular offerings on sexuality. The basic "general human sexuality" course, previously the only one that was offered, became an introductory course followed by advanced courses on specific topics in sexuality. Some universities developed programs or departments for the study of human sexuality or, more specifically, lesbian and gay studies. When I went to college in the late 1970s I had trouble finding any academic literature on lesbian and gay issues, let alone a college course on the subject; now I teach the course that I would like to have taken.

But there is a gaping hole in the scientific literature, and in most curricular offerings, on human sexuality. In the midst of the explosion of research on sexuality in the 1970s and early 1980s, few people noticed the absence of research on bisexuality. For the most part researchers had adopted the popular conception of sexuality as dichotomous, that is, as composed of two opposite and opposing forms of sexuality known as homosexuality and heterosexuality. In this conceptualization bisexuality is either nonexistent or a transitory state or transitional phase. At best, it is an unstable mixture of homosexual and heterosexual elements. Researchers typically excluded bisexuals from their research, if they detected their existence at all; more commonly, they classified them as homosexuals because they believed they were really lesbians or gay men in the process of coming out or because, in a heterosexist culture, "one drop" of same-sex interest or experience makes a person homosexual.

Theorists repeatedly admonished researchers for their neglect of bisexuality and proposed new models of sexuality capable of incorporating bisexuality as an authentic form of sexuality. But despite growing evidence that bisexual behavior might be more prevalent than exclusively homosexual behavior, most researchers clung to a dichotomous or "binary" model of sexuality and ignored the pleas of the theorists. Even those researchers who acknowledged the neglect of bisexuality and the inadequacy of the dichotomous model usually paid lip service to these concerns and then proceeded to commit the same errors in their own research. It was not until the mid 1980s, when the public and health officials became alarmed at the possibility that bisexuals might be the "gateway" through which HIV could spread from the gay population into the heterosexual population, that many researchers took the message to heart. At last they realized— even if for the wrong reasons— that if knowledge of sexuality in general is vital to our survival, knowledge about bisexuality is no less vital.

In addition to the AIDS crisis the growth of a bisexual community and movement in the late 1980s led to increasing interest and opportunities for research on bisexuality, just as the growth of the lesbian and gay movements in the 1970s had encouraged research on homosexuality. Today's students, who have grown up with new concepts of gender in an age of queer politics, are demanding courses that reflect a sophisticated understanding of sexual diversity, just as I wished for courses on lesbian and gay topics when I was in college. It is now time to incorporate bisexuality into our courses on human sexuality and to develop courses that are specifically focused on bisexuality wherever our curricula provide the opportunity to do so.

This book is designed to facilitate the effort to incorporate bisexuality into our teaching and research. It is a collection of the important theoretical and empirical publications on the study of bisexuality in the United States, including examples of each of the major genres of research on bisexuality. Although sexology in general, and the study of bisexuality in particular, owes much to early European research, a comprehensive review of the history of European sexology is outside the scope of this book. Social scientific research on bisexuality in the United States has its own history, and this book is dedicated to documenting that history.

Toward that end, *Bisexuality in the United States* is organized chronologically to illustrate the development of research on bisexuality. Each section represents a genre of research on bisexuality and begins with a discussion of the historical and scientific context of the genre and a review of the literature in it, followed by reprinted publications illustrating the genre. Some reprinted works are theoretical, and some are empirical. Some are easily understood by the nontechnical reader, whereas others use technical jargon or advanced statistical analysis. Most are scholarly, but the volume ends with a look at the images of bisexuality portrayed by popular national magazines. This volume may be used as a reader for college or graduate level courses on sexuality or by the serious student of sexuality who wishes to obtain a thorough knowledge of the scope and texture of social scientific literature on bisexuality and its place in the field of sexology.

Bisexuality in the United States is also useful as a reference book and annotated bibliography to the literature on bisexuality in the United States from before 1970 through 1999. Within its pages are references to approximately one thousand articles, books, and book chapters that either focus on or refer to bisexuality, however briefly. These citations include, with few exceptions, every scholarly journal article listed in sociological and psychological databases whose title or abstract includes the word *bisexual*[1] that was either published in the United States or based on research conducted in the United States, plus works cited in these articles. The citations also include many other articles and chapters from books that cannot be found via the usual literature search methods, dozens of works published before 1970, and relevant scholarly journal articles on bisexuality in countries other than the United States.

Finally, this book will also be of interest to bisexual people, whether they are involved in academia or not. In particular, bisexual readers might be interested in information about the prevalence of bisexuality in the United States, the history of bisexual politics, and the differences between bisexuals, heterosexuals, lesbians, and gay men. Although we still have a great deal to learn about bisexuality, the flood of information about the subject has begun. This book documents the first wave of the flood.

Terminology

That there are many ways to understand sexuality is one theme of this book. Because each way of understanding sexuality has its own terminology, presenting different ways of understanding sexuality means working with several different sets of terms. These different terminologies overlap and differ from each other; sometimes it is not clear which term should be used in a given instance, and sometimes there is no one term that accurately and clearly conveys the intended meaning. For example, should the attraction of a woman for another woman be described as homosexual, bisexual, same-sex, or same-gender? Often the answer depends on the context in which the attraction is being described, so the attraction might be described as "same-sex" for one purpose, but "same-gender" for another. Even the term *bisexual* itself is problematic because it incorporates a dualistic understanding of sexuality, in which bisexuality is composed of parts of heterosexuality and homosexuality, that many bisexuals reject.

Throughout this book I have struggled with terminology. So that readers can best use the book, they need to know something about the choices I've made. When describing another author's theoretical or empirical work, I generally use the terms used by that author in order to remain as true as possible to the original. In the case of empirical work, I describe the author's methodology so that the meanings of the terms the author uses will be clear. When the author's terminology differs so greatly from generally accepted contemporary terminology as to cause confusion—often the case in work done before the 1970s—I either explain the author's usage or substitute more widely accepted equivalent terms. In some cases an entire genre of research and theory tends toward particular usage; so as to avoid shifting terms, even when I am not directly discussing a particular author's work, I tend toward usages that are typical for the body of research I am discussing.

When referring to individuals—for example, other authors, historical figures, or research subjects—whose sexual self-identities are known and relevant to the point being made, I use the terms they use to describe themselves. For example, if a woman calls herself "bisexual" I will refer to her as bisexual, and if a man calls himself "gay" or "homosexual," I will refer to him as such. Sometimes, if clarification is needed, for example, if their behavior would generally be considered inconsistent with their self-identity, I might also describe their attractions or behaviors using other terms. I use the term *self-identity* rather than simply *identity* when referring to individuals' descriptions of themselves, even when reporting the work of authors who use the shortened term *identity*. In social psychological literature *identity* can refer to any identification, whether by oneself or by another; I adopt this convention here. Unless otherwise noted or implied by the context, *self-identity* refers to one's *sexual orientation* self-identity.

When writing in my own voice I choose terminology based on context and meaning. Throughout the book I use the word *bisexual* as an adjective to describe sexual behavior when it involves sex acts with both same-sex/gender and other-sex/gender partners during a given period of time. I also use *bisexual* to describe sexual attractions to both sexes or both genders, and to describe individuals who engage in bisexual behavior, have bisexual attractions, or identify as bisexual. Sometimes I use *behavioral bisexual* to refer to someone who has engaged in sexual acts with both sexes/genders, especially when they do not identify themselves as bisexual or when their sexual self-identity is unknown or unspecified. I discuss the drawbacks to the term *bisexual,* but I use it myself because it is the widely recognized term that describes the various forms of sexuality covered in this book.

I use the word *homosexual* to refer to sexual behavior or attraction when it occurs exclusively with or toward people of the same sex/gender or to refer specifically to same-sex/gender behaviors or attractions when the existence of accompanying other-sex/gender behaviors or attractions is unspecified or irrelevant to the point being made. In the former case I sometimes use *exclusively homosexual* for additional clarity. In general, except when I am conveying another author's work or when an individual calls her or himself homosexual, I do not use the term *homosexual* to refer to individuals or their identities. To refer to individuals with exclusively same-sex/gender attractions or behaviors I prefer the terms *lesbian* for women and *gay* for men.

Although I use the term *homosexual* under certain circumstances, I find the term personally offensive because of its historical use by researchers seeking a cure for homosexuality. Therefore, whenever possible I use the descriptors *same-sex* or *same-gender* instead of *homosexual.* However, these terms can be awkward for at least two reasons. First, they bring up the problematic distinction between sex and gender and necessitate either a choice between the two or the unattractive conjunction *sex/gender.* Second, using these terms to refer to sexual behaviors or attractions produces language that superficially appears to be redundant, for example, *same-sex sexual behavior.* When I do use these terms, the choice between *sex* and *gender* again depends on context. For example, when in section 4, chapter 14, I discuss "homosexual behavior" among prisoners, I address the various gender roles that exist in prison sexual subculture. Among male prisoners the partners in a sex act are generally of different gender although both are male. In this context, therefore, *same-sex* is accurate whereas *same-gender* is not. In other contexts *same-gender* would be more accurate.

Sex refers not only to biological sex but also to the act of having sex. Although it is common parlance to refer to individuals' *sexual partners,* I use *sex partners* instead. One's sex partners are not necessarily particularly sexual; the adjective refers not to the sexuality or sexiness of the partner, or to any other characteristic of the partner, but to the type of act in which she or he is one's partner. I do, however, use the term *sexual act;* here the adjective *sexual* is appropriate because the act itself is sexual.

Although the use of so many different terms might be disconcerting to some readers, it is necessary for accuracy. Sexuality is complex; pretending it is not complex will not make it so, nor will it promote a deeper understanding of sexuality. Failure to acknowledge the complexity of sexuality is, in large part, responsible for past social and scientific neglect of bisexuality. The goal of this book is to redress that neglect.

Note

1. With the following exceptions: psychiatric and social work case studies, case studies of organizations or communities, dissertations and theses, articles written in languages other than English, research on bisexual behavior among nonhuman animals, and articles in which the term *bisexuality* is used to refer to what is otherwise known as hermaphroditism or intersexuality rather than to a form of sexuality or a sexual orientation.

Acknowledgments

THIS book began in the mind of Ann Miller, editor at Columbia University Press, who called to ask if I could produce an anthology of previously printed works representing the best of social scientific research on bisexuality in the United States. Quickly. I replied that I would love to and that I would like to write some additional chapters discussing the history and present state of social scientific research on bisexuality so that the book would also be useful as a course textbook and reference work. She has been extremely patient, waiting for her "quick" book on bisexuality for four years while I gave full expression to my compulsion to be inclusive and exhaustive. As I traced others' citations and performed literature search after literature search to make sure I hadn't missed anything, I told her, over and over again, "I'm almost done." Finally, I am done.

Many people have helped along the way. First of all, I am indebted to the authors, publishers, and other copyright holders who allowed me to include previously published works. Many did so at a fraction of their usual permission fees because they recognized the academic need for a review of work on bisexuality. I am also deeply grateful to Andrew Lane, who tirelessly and meticulously helped with the most intellectually challenging—and the most intellectually dulling—aspects of the production of this book. Andy proofread text, checked facts, ordered articles, photocopied hundreds of pages, and reminded me to eat and sleep.

The support of Hamilton College has been invaluable to me as I put together this book. As an out, self-identified queer scholar whose research and teaching focuses primarily on sexual and gender diversity, I always expected an uphill battle in the academic world. At Hamilton my fears were allayed by the enthusiastic support of my department, faculty in other departments, the students, and several members of the administration. In particular, I would like to thank Dan Chambliss, Dennis Gilbert, and Gwen Dordick of the Department of Sociology, President Eugene Tobin, and Dean Bobby Fong. I was able to complete this book in four years, instead of eight—despite becoming a mother thrice during that period—because of Hamilton's leave policy, which encompasses domestic partners on an equal basis with married spouses, and because of the generosity of my department and the administration in agreeing to let me teach part time. A special thanks goes to the wonderful reference librarians at Burke Library whose ability to locate obscure bits of writing repeatedly amazed me, to the librarians at the circulation desk who sent me polite reminder notices asking if I *still* needed the two dozen books I had checked out over a year earlier, and to the librarians at the interlibrary loan desk who, I am told, maintained three order card boxes—one for all students, one for all other faculty, and one for me.

In 1997 I left Hamilton for family reasons and the last stages in the preparation of this book were completed with the support of the State University of New York, Geneseo campus. Thanks go to the administration and the Sociology Department at Geneseo and to the State of New York United University Professions (UUP) Affirmative Action Committee for providing me with leave time and to Harriet Sleggs and Judy Bushnell of the SUNY-Geneseo Library for rushing me numerous articles and bits of information so I could complete my last-minute fact checking.

Thanks also go to all the friends whose cheerful inquiries ("So how's the book coming?") were as often as not met with a blank stare and a change of subject. Lois Hartsough, Ellen Yacknin, and Cathy Mazzotta have been especially steadfast— remembering my name and continuing to call despite my long social hibernation.

On many days, as I worked at my computer in my study at home, I could hear my children laughing and playing downstairs. I am grateful to Wilma Cotto for the warmth and tenderness she has given Mykelti, Saraiah, and Etienne over the last three years. I was able to work, enjoying their laughter from a distance, only because I knew that they were safe, happy, and growing under her care. Thanks also to her husband, David, and her best friend, Jamilette, for their help. My sons and my daughter are happy children because they know that they are loved and respected by all the adults in their lives.

Writing, like everything else in life, is easier with the support of a loving family. I remember my paternal grandparents, my maternal grandfather, and especially my mother's deeply loved partner Lou, all of whom passed away during the writing of this book. I discuss teaching strategies with my sister, Lynn, and I see the smile on my father's face as he enjoys his grandchildren's fascination with the toys he makes for them. I deny feeling jealous when Saraiah falls asleep only at the foot of Abuela Raquel's bed or in the arms of Titi Pinti or Aunt Lynn, and I work in the attic study and relax in the basement exercise room built by Abuelo Paco after my second-floor study became the nursery. My mother is a source of strength for many people, including me, and I have always known that I couldn't begin to understand the depth of her gift to me. She gave me not only life itself but the freedom and ability to enjoy that life to the fullest. One of the reasons I longed for motherhood was to acquire a better understanding of her side of our relationship. Our bond has a new and wonderful dimension, and birthdays have acquired a whole new meaning. This book is dedicated in part to her.

Finally, my deepest gratitude and love go to my closest family member and most enthusiastic supporter, Lorna Rodríguez Rust, who has been with me through everything for the last fifteen years and who will be with me through everything to come in the future.

PART ONE

Paving the Way for Research on Bisexuality

1
Wherefore Art Thou, Bisexuality?

As Thomas S. Kuhn (1970) pointed out in *The Structure of Scientific Revolutions*, scientific research tends to proceed within the theoretical and empirical boundaries established by previous research. New fields of study and novel approaches to research that challenge these boundaries are usually met with skepticism. This scientific inertia results because experienced researchers have vested interests in preserving the paradigms within which they made their reputations, because the creativity of new researchers is channeled by their training in existing theories and by dependence on their mentors, and because those who lack vested interests or mentors usually also lack the means to acquire the respect of the scientific community for their innovative ideas. Therefore, new topics like bisexuality usually receive serious scientific attention only after repeated criticism has undermined confidence in existing scientific approaches, and only after some theoretical and empirical groundwork has been laid for research in the new area. The three sections in part 1 examine the process by which such a foundation was established for research on bisexuality. Section 1 examines the criticisms that undermined the legitimacy of simplistic approaches to sexuality, approaches that led to the neglect of bisexuality. Section 2 examines the theoretical advances that provided a framework for more sophisticated understandings of sexuality, including a conceptual basis for research on bisexuality. Section 3 reviews research findings pertaining to the prevalence of bisexuality, empirical findings that were used by researchers studying bisexuality as evidence of the moral and practical importance of their topic.

1

Criticisms of the Scholarly Literature on Sexuality for Its Neglect of Bisexuality

Paula C. Rodríguez Rust

IN the early 1980s several scholars urged their colleagues in sexology to acknowledge the existence of bisexuality as an authentic form of sexuality. Before this time many researchers had, in fact, recognized the existence of bisexual experience, but they had generally conceptualized it as a lesser degree of "homosexual" experience, as the intermediate range on a heterosexual-homosexual continuum, or as a matter of "diversity among homosexuals."[1] Critics of this approach argued that bisexuality should be distinguished from homosexuality and studied in its own right. They provided statistics indicating that bisexuality is at least as common as homosexuality, and therefore as deserving of scientific attention, and showed how failure to distinguish bisexuality had compromised the quality of previous research on homosexuality. Most, including Jay P. Paul (1985) and A. P. MacDonald Jr. (1983), whose critiques are reprinted in this section, attributed the lack of attention to scientists' uncritical acceptance of a belief popular in contemporary English-speaking and European-derived cultures that there are only two authentic forms of sexual orientation, that is, heterosexuality and homosexuality (cf. Coleman 1998). This belief in a sexual dichotomy leads to the conclusion that bisexuality either does not exist at all, or exists only as an unstable hybrid combination of heterosexuality and homosexuality, an intermediate sexual variation, or as a watered down version of homosexuality, and that bisexuality per se therefore does not merit serious scientific study.

The content of the belief that there are only two authentic forms of sexuality, now recognized as one of many possible ways to conceptualize sexuality, has been analyzed by several authors. John P. De Cecco and Michael G. Shively (1984) pointed out that the distinction between homosexuality and heterosexuality is based on the biological distinction between the sexes because homosexuality and heterosexuality are defined in terms of the similarity or difference in the genitalia of the partners in sexual relationships (see also Coleman 1998; Richardson 1984). Marilyn J. Freimuth and Gail A. Hornstein (1982), in an article reprinted in the next section, argued, somewhat differently, that the concept of sexual orientation is based on the concept of gender and on the assumption that the components of gender—which include but are not limited to biological sex—are dichotomous and perfectly correlated with each other such that all people fall clearly into one of two gender categories (see also Ault 1996; Birke 1982; Fausto-Sterling 1993; Haeberle and Gindorf 1998; Kaplan and Rogers 1984; Lorber 1994, 1996; Ross 1983a, 1983b, 1984; Ross and Paul 1992; Schwartz and Blumstein 1998). In this "sex/gender system" (Rubin 1976), if all people are clearly either biologically female or male, and correspondingly women or men, then all sexual relationships are clearly between either same-sexed/gendered or other-sexed/gendered people and hence clearly either homosexual or heterosexual, thus producing dichotomous sexual orientation.

Despite the definitional reference to sexual relationships, however, homosexuality and heterosexuality are viewed not merely as descriptions of sexual relationships or sexual behavior *between people* but as "essential" characteristics, that is, core, enduring, and intrinsic characteristics *of individuals* or individual "states of being" (e.g., Richardson 1984). There are, therefore, not only two forms of sexual orientation but two distinct types of sexual people—homosexuals and heterosexuals—and a person can be a homosexual without knowing it. De Cecco and Shively (1984; see also McIntosh 1968) commented that such a view enabled Derrick Sherwin Bailey (1955) to refer to "true" homosexuals and John Boswell (1980:109) to write of "homosexual acts committed by apparently heterosexual persons." John C. Gonsiorek (1982; see also Salzman 1965) attributed the concepts of "latent homosexuality" and "pseudohomosexuality" to efforts to fit human sexual diversity into these two simplistic categories. The view that sexual orientation is essential also enabled historians to search transhistorically and anthropologists to search crossculturally for evidence of homosexual[2] people and communities in the cultures of the past and present, cultures that often did not or do not themselves ascribe sexual orientations to their members or distinguish people from each other based on the genitalia of their sex partners.[2]

The historical and cultural roots of the dichotomous conceptualization of sexuality, in particular the concept of the homosexual as a type of person, have been traced by several authors.[3] Briefly, these authors tell "origin stories" (King 1986) in which descriptions of sexual behavior were replaced by a focus on categories of sexual persons within European scientific, legal, and popular thought,[4] in a process Eli Coleman (1998) described as the first "paradigm shift" in the modern conceptualization of sexual orientation. This shift occurred because of larger cultural changes and because theorists, in an effort to explain why individuals would engage in "deviant" sexual behaviors such as homosexuality, invented the "homosexual person" and mused instead over the question of why some people are homosexual. The answers they gave tended to attribute homosexuality to congenital abnormalities of the sex organs or to "inversion" of the sexual impulse in which male homosexuals possessed a female sexual impulse and vice versa (e.g., Ellis

[1897] 1915, 1928; Hirschfeld [1896] 1938; Kertbeny 1869; Ulrichs 1864; Westphal 1870). The concept of homosexuality gave rise to its complement, heterosexuality—although the term *heterosexual* was, ironically, once used to refer to persons with "inclinations to both sexes" (Katz 1997:178; see also Katz 1990). Later, Freud explained both homosexuality and heterosexuality as derivatives of a universal bisexual potential arising from universal embryologic hermaphrodism;[5] he and other theorists built their arguments by confounding biological hermaphrodism with bisexual attractions or sexual orientation.[6] More recently, geneticists, physicians, anatomists, neurologists, and sociobiologists search for differences in the genes, brains, prenatal environments, and hormone levels of homosexuals and heterosexuals,[7] further essentializing the concept of sexual orientation by linking one's sexuality causally to one's biology. By 1956, with the distinction between essential homosexuality and heterosexuality firmly in hand, Edmund Bergler ([1956] 1962) was able to describe bisexuality as "a state that has no existence beyond the word itself" and an "out-and-out fraud" (80).

The two articles reprinted in this section, "Bisexuality: Reassessing Our Paradigms of Sexuality," by Jay P. Paul, and "A Little Bit of Lavender Goes a Long Way: A Critique of Research on Sexual Orientation," by A. P. MacDonald Jr., show how the hegemony of the dichotomous conception of sexuality among scientific researchers leads to a neglect of bisexuality. Paul (1985) examined the historical development of the concepts of the homosexual and the heterosexual person, including the role of gay politics in essentializing and reifying homosexuality, and argued that the use of this simplistic model of sexuality in scientific research leads to flaws and inconsistencies as scientists attempt to force it to fit the complexity of human sexuality. MacDonald (1983) reviewed the existing literature on bisexuality, demonstrating how the imposition of a dichotomous model of sexuality not only suppressed evidence of bisexuality but contaminated our knowledge of lesbianism and gayness as well. The seeds of MacDonald's 1983 article can be found in an earlier article (1981), in which MacDonald not only cited examples of researchers who lumped bisexuals together with homosexuals or considered bisexuality a form of homosexual denial but also covered such widely divergent topics as "Is bisexual behavior increasing?" and "Problems faced by bisexuals." The generality and breadth of this article, as well as the fact that MacDonald was unable to cite published research to support many assertions, reflects the prenatal state of modern research on bisexuality at the time.

Charles E. Hansen and Anne Evans (1985), in an article not included here, attributed the lack of research attention not only to the hegemony of the dichotomous model of sexuality but also to cultural erotophobia and to "The Law of the Excluded Middle" (Bergler [1956] 1962). Observing that bisexuals are stereotyped as promiscuous, they asserted that researchers' mishandling of bisexuality stems partially from erotophobia, that is, cultural anxiety over sexual enjoyment unrestrained by cultural norms such as normative fidelity. "The Law of the Excluded Middle" describes the way in which individuals are classified sexually; they are presumed heterosexual in the absence of evidence to the contrary, but an individual who engages in one homosexual act is classified as homosexual. Classification as a homosexual is maintained because any heterosexual behavior is thereafter considered "counterfeit." This process of classification explains how complex sexual experience is forced to fit into dichotomous—that is, binary—notions of sexuality, thereby rendering the coexistence of authentic heterosexuality and homosexuality within an individual—that is, bisexuality—conceptually impossible. Hansen and Evans also pointed out that the assumption that the various components of gender and sexuality—including biological sex, sexual affections and behavior, and sexual orientation self-identity—are perfectly correlated with each other has become increasingly problematic. The rise of the gay liberation movement, which has produced social pressures that influence sexual self-identification, has weakened the correspondence between sexual behaviors or feelings, on the one hand, and sexual self-identities, on the other hand.

Other authors criticized researchers not only for their neglect of bisexuality in particular but for their simplistic treatment of sexual orientation in general. For example, in the preface to *Two Lives to Lead: Bisexuality in Men and Women*, previously published as a special issue on bisexuality of the *Journal of Homosexuality* in which the articles by Paul (1985) and by Hansen and Evans (1985) appeared, *JH* editor John P. De Cecco characterized the concept of sexual orientation as "biological reductionism." Arguing that the allegedly psychological and social concept of sexual orientation "genitalizes" human sexuality by defining an individual's sexuality in terms of the genitalia of that individual's sex partners, De Cecco criticized the practice of identifying individuals not only as heterosexual or homosexual but also as bisexual. He argued that current concepts "[render] bisexuals as lame females or males and self-deceived or conniving heterosexuals or homosexuals" (1985:xi) and that replacing a dichotomy with a trichotomy would be only a marginal improvement (1981).[8] One year earlier, in the same journal, De Cecco and coauthors Michael G. Shively and Christopher Jones (Shively, Jones, and De Cecco 1983/84) had systematically reviewed the literature on sexual orientation, documenting the ways in which researchers conceptually and operationally defined sexual orientation. They found that sexual orientation was conceptually defined in only 12.3 percent of studies, indicating that most researchers had not engaged in any discussion of the concept of sexual orientation but instead had allowed their methods to operationally define the concept. For example, in 86.0 percent of studies researchers had assumed the sexual orientations of their subjects based on the settings in which the subjects were found, often with no corroborating evidence. The authors concluded that researchers paid little attention to the complexity of human sexuality and the assumptions about sexuality that underlay their research.

These criticisms of research practices paved the way for other authors to propose alternatives to the dichotomous model of sexuality in the hope that researchers would adopt these models and produce more theoretically informed research. The next section, "Now You Don't See It, Now You Do," explores the many different models of sexuality proposed by various authors, many of whom cite Jay P. Paul and A. P. MacDonald Jr. for having pointed out the need for more sophisticated models of sexuality.

Notes

1. The concept of degrees of homosexuality is strongest among researchers working in the Kinseyan tradition. For example, Bell (1975) criticized other researchers for their failure to carefully attend to problems of definition and diversity among "homosexuals," arguing that homosexuals "differ with respect to the degree to which they are exclusively homosexual in their sexual arousal and behavior" (423). Predating other criticisms that became popular in the late 1980s and 1990s, Bell also argued that homosexuals differ along dimensions other than gender-based arousal and behavior, including degree of intimacy desired, frequency of sexual contacts, and degree of overtness. Bell characterized previous research as "an incredible waste of time," and wrote, "If it were up to me, I would declare a moratorium on the usual conduct of research in homosexuality . . . [to allow researchers to go] back to the drawing board" to examine their conceptualizations of and methods for assessing homosexuality (422). These ideas were put into practice in Bell and Weinberg's *Homosexualities*, published in 1978.

Coons (1972) is a notable exception to the statement that bisexuality was generally conceptualized by pre-1980s critics as a lesser degree of homosexuality. Preferring the term *ambisexuality*, Coons argued that "when we as a society and as professionals dichotomize human sexuality into homosexual versus heterosexual, we contribute to the misery and alienation of millions" (142). Coons's view was consistent with the sexual liberatory "bisexual chic" atmosphere of the 1970s (see section 9) and, as director of the psychiatric division of a student health center, his goal was not to establish an additional category of sexuality but to increase professional acceptance of "personal and perhaps unique sexual adaptations" that would increase the "quality and depth of (students clients') human relationships with both sexes" (144). As early as 1968 Mary McIntosh also argued against the construction of a third sexual orientation category.

2. De Cecco and Shively (1984) cited Bullough (1976) and Boswell (1980) as examples of transhistorical applications of the concept of homosexual essence and Trumbach (1977) and Bray (1982) for their efforts to unearth the historical origins of the modern "gay community." For a carefully and self-consciously constructed example of the historicization of lesbianism, see Faderman (1981). For additional discussion of nineteenth-century romantic friendships and their construction as the predecessors of modern lesbian relationships, see Smith-Rosenberg (1975) and Jeffreys (1985); see Donoghue (1993) on the seventeenth and eighteenth centuries; for a discussion of bisexuality in the ancient world, see Cantarella (1992). See Duberman (1997), Duberman, Vicinus, and Chauncey (1989), and Vicinus (1992) for a variety of essays in "gay and lesbian history" in a variety of cultural contexts, from the ancient world through the present. Even the social constructionist authors cited in notes 3 and 4 of this chapter who critique the concept of a transhistorical essential homosexuality and tell origin stories of the birth of the modern concept of the "homosexual" engage in an effort to discover the historical roots of this concept, thus constructing a historical link between premodern and modern concepts of homosexuality. See Vicinus (1992) and Ferguson (1981) for discussion and critique of efforts to construct a history of lesbianism and a transhistorical definition of lesbianism, respectively, and Rust (1995a) for a discussion of the implications of this constructivist project for the development of lesbian/gay quasi-ethnicity. See Whitehead (1981) for a critique of the anthropological practice of analogizing Native American concepts of "two-spirited" people to non-Native concepts of gay, lesbian, transsexual, or transgendered people. See Williams (1993) on cultural biases introduced when Western (heterosexual) anthropologists study Native American constructions of gender and sexuality. See also Jacobs and Cromwell (1992), Murray (1984).

3. For example, Adam (1979, 1987); Altman (1982); Bray (1982); Boswell (1980, 1982, 1990); Bullough (1976, 1979, 1990); Chauncey (1982); Coleman (1998); De Cecco (1981); Foucault (1979); Haeberle and Gindorf (1998); Halperin (1993); Herdt (1988); Katz (1976, 1983, 1990, 1995, 1997); McIntosh (1968); Miller (1995); Murray (1984); Padgug (1979); Paul

(1983/1984); Plummer (1975, 1981a, 1981b); Richardson (1984); Somerville (1996); Trumbach (1977); and Weeks (1977, 1981a, 1981b, 1982, 1985, 1986).

4. See Boswell (1990) for a succinct critique of some of the premises of these origin stories, Trumbach (1977) for an argument that the concept of the homosexual person arose earlier than argued by other historians, and Halperin (1993) on the social construction of a history of sexuality. See also Coleman (1998) for an argument that three, rather than two, sexual orientations were essentialized during the late nineteenth and early twentieth centuries.

Coleman (1998) also pointed out that the use of biological sex to distinguish sexual orientations was based on the nineteenth-century assumption that normal sexuality is motivated by a drive toward procreation. Katz (1990), however, pointed out that the procreative assumption was not determinative; procreation also underlay nineteenth-century concepts of proper womanhood and manhood prior to the advent of concepts of persons as *erotic* beings.

Hoffman (1984) presented an argument regarding the origins of attitudes toward homosexuality that could also be applied to the development of sexual categories in European thought. Hoffman contrasted polytheistic cosmology, which is characterized by a continuity of creation, a fluid and interconnected universe, and gender blurring in the realm of the supernatural, with monotheistic cosmology, which is characterized by strict separations and distinctions such as between the natural and supernatural and between the male and female. Hoffman argued that monotheistic cosmologies reject ambiguity as an abomination and maintain purity via the establishment and strict maintenance of categories. He suggested that this explains the greater rejection of homosexuality in monotheistic as compared to polytheistic cultures. Applying Hoffman's argument to the question of the shift from homosexuality as an act to homosexuality as a state of being suggests that this shift occurred to enable monotheistic European cultures to defend themselves against sexual ambiguity by creating "pure" categories of sexual people. Such a theory would be consistent with the resistance of the dichotomous model of sexuality toward concepts of bisexuality.

5. As described by Wolff, Freud argued that "all human beings are bisexual by nature, in accordance with their phylogenetic and ontogenetic history. . . . In other words, in early foetal life human beings are potentially double-sexed creatures, and they retain rudiments of the opposite sex . . . which points to the naturalness of bisexuality and thus of homosexuality" (1971:20–21). See note 7 in chapter 4 of this volume for a fuller description of Freud's theories of the origin of homosexuality and sexuality and references to other discussions of psychoanalytic treatments of bisexuality.

6. Gonsiorek (1982). Diamond (1998) discussed the distinction—and relationship—between "structural" bisexuality (i.e., biological bisexuality or hermaphrodism) and behavioral bisexuality and reviewed the evidence of each among nonhuman species. See also Herdt and Boxer (1995); Rado (1965); and the discussion of bisexuality and biology in chapter 23, this volume.

7. For reviews, discussions, and critiques of this literature, see note 8 in chapter 23. See also discussion of bisexuality and biology in that chapter.

8. A related point was made by Hansen and Evans (1985), who argued that sexologists did recognize the social and psychological dimensions of sexuality when they discussed heterosexuality and homosexuality but returned to a reductionist focus on genitalia when discussing bisexuality.

2

Bisexuality: Reassessing Our Paradigms of Sexuality

Jay P. Paul

THE confluence of heterosexual and homosexual desire in individuals is a reality discrepant with many of our formulations of sexuality. Treating bisexuality as a discrete entity rather than subsuming it in discussions of homosexuality presents a set of definitional and conceptual problems that highlight the gaps between theoretical representations and the realities of human sexuality. There is far more variability and fluidity in many people's sexual patterns than theoretical notions tend to allow, suggesting that researchers have imparted an artificial consistency to an inchoate sexual universe.

It is not that science has ignored the indisputable fact that the sexual biographies of many include sexual experiences with both men and women, but rather the theoretical *meanings* given to those experiences. The tendency is to deny the legitimacy of one's erotic responsiveness to either males or females; thereby, one assumes that all people are either basically heterosexual or homosexual. This refusal to allow for an equivalent basic bisexuality in some portion of the population leads to a variety of explanations for bisexual patterns.

MacDonald (1981) notes three interpretations that reinforce the heterosexual/homosexual dichotomy. First, bisexuality can be viewed as a transitory phenomenon; the individual eventually comes to re-establish his or her "true" orientation. In this case, the bisexual phase may be seen as a wish to be "chic" or "trendy," or as an indication of disturbed interpersonal relations. Second, bisexuality can be viewed as a transitional state, with the individual shifting from one sexual pole to the other—this is primarily noted in cases where the shift is from heterosexuality to exclusive homosexuality. In this instance, the person who attempts to maintain any bisexual lifestyle is seen as "fence-sitting," avoiding a true commitment to anyone (Masters and Johnson, 1979), or as a "pathetic creature" suffering from arrested development and identity confusion (Cory and LeRoy, 1963). And third, bisexuality is perceived as a denial of one's fundamental homosexual orientation due to internalized homophobia, or one's fears of being either socially stigmatized or socially isolated (Blair, 1974; Harry and Lovely, 1979; Schafer, 1976).

If one can ignore bisexuality, conceiving sexuality dichotomously is attractively simple. Such a binary division is rooted in the basic biological dichotomy of male/female, and assumes a similarly clear distinction between those fundamentally homosexual and those fundamentally heterosexual, based on the gender of one's sexual partners. Where there has been both heterosexual and homosexual activity, various assumptions guide the observer in the detection of the person's "true" orientation by one or two "fundamental" signs, i.e., sexual fantasies or dreams. Proposed etiologies for sexual orientation vary but tend to assume that such qualities are fixed by early childhood and possess an immutability and temporal constancy analogous to that of gender identity. This lends weight to notions of an individual's sexuality being a primary organizing principle of personality and lifestyle, bypassing the social/historical context. While the impact of social forces on the construction of specific sexual labels and roles may be acknowledged, this factor is undercut by attempts to view heterosexual and homosexual orientations as entities that both transcend a specific historical context and deal with much more than erotic and affectional desires.

Such a system is neat and clear cut in its categorization of exclusively heterosexual or homosexual persons, but it demands the grafting on of a host of assumptions to deal with the facts of bisexuality. Those who prefer the precision of such a model to the muddle of real life transfer blame from the theory to the person eroticizing both men and women. Such a person is seen as disturbed or confused. To those willing to examine the facts more critically, the strained reasoning used to dismiss bisexuality is one additional token of the inadequacy and unscientific nature of such a sexual paradigm.

This article will point out some of the critical questions that have arisen both in the attempt to fit bisexuality into current constructs of sexuality, and in current re-examinations of the issue of sexual identity. These questions emerge out of an attempt to understand the nature of sexuality and the divisions of homosexuality, heterosexuality, and bisexuality. A primary issue is the essentiality of the given sexual categories and identities, an assumption which leads to notions that sexuality and sexual desire as fixed and static in individuals. It is vital to identify our criteria for the current elements in our organization of sex. What determines the leap from behavior to identity? Furthermore, what is the justification for embellishing such an identity with non-erotic components? How appropriate are these labels as personal, integrative constructs?

In looking at this, we must be careful to disentangle the scientific construct from the idiomatic usage of these labels peculiar to our given culture and time. The difficulty of this is pointed out by Blumstein and Schwartz (1977):

> We take the simple position that personal views about sexuality in the abstract reflect wider cultural understandings, and affect, in turn, the concrete constructions people place on their own feelings and experiences, and thereby affect their

behavior. So it is essential to accept cultural understandings of sexuality as crucial data, while at the same time rejecting the scientific validity of their underlying premise. (p. 31)

It is clear that acknowledging the power of the terms homosexual, bisexual, and heterosexual as *social* labels does not indicate a validity to our constructions of sexuality, which tend to be reifications of popular myths of sexuality. A review of historical conceptualizations of sexual identity highlights the culture-bound nature of our scientific understandings.

Historical Perspectives

To speak of early formulations of sexual orientation is to refer to a relatively recent scientific perspective on the basis of homosexual behavior. The 19th century saw the transformation of homosexuality from a vice (by Judaeo-Christian moral standards) into a "condition"—one that shifted focus from the act itself to the actor, from a specific point in time to a life history. Our attention has been fixed upon the person ever since.

The last century's transformation of socially censured sexual acts into signs of medical illness or pervasive biological anomalies led to the emergence of the "homosexual person," who differed constitutionally from the "normal" population. This was an extension of the then-popular concept of psychophysical parallelism, which posited a simple congruence between character and physiological traits. Socially sanctioned forms of sexual expression were reinforced by science's assertion that they were biological norms. Notions of the naturalness of the male-female configuration (justified by reproductive necessity) led to an immediate categorization of erotic desires by the biological sex of the pairing. Simplistic assumptions led to a confusion and confounding of sexual orientation, social sex-roles, and gender identity. Bisexuality was termed "psychic hermaphroditism," while those actively homosexual were labeled "inverts," the "third sex," and the "intersexes." Scientists probed, measured, and examined, expecting to find signs of physiological masculinization accompanying an assumed psychological masculinization of female homosexuals, and signs of feminization in male homosexuals. Although some physicians initially saw homosexuality as a product of moral or nervous degeneration, the primary theoretical focus was on the so-called "invert."

The simplistic notion that the homosexually active person suffered from some form of gender inversion, given the eroticizing of others of the same sex, runs into problems in dealing with the fundamentals of non-exclusive homosexuality or bisexuality. Various attempts were made to differentiate the "congenital" from the "acquired" in sexual behavior. The tendency, as in much writing on sex since then, has been to view homosexual behavior as innate and heterosexual behavior as an overlay of the homosexual substratum (Ellis, 1972). The emphasis on fundamental differences between the heterosexual and homosexual groupings led to some ludicrous ascriptions by sexologists as distinguished as Havelock Ellis (1972):

> Male inverts are sometimes unable to whistle. In both sexes a notable youthful-
> ness of appearance is often preserved into adult age. The love of green (which is
> normally a preferred color chiefly by children and especially girls) is frequently
> observed. (p. 232)

The concept of the homosexual as intrinsically distinct from the rest of the population was a notion initially widely accepted and approved of by those open about
their homoeroticism. It was the basis for arguments for decriminalization of homosexuality, since this theory could be used as a defense against charges of moral cul-
pability for homosexual behavior, and against the apparently groundless fear of
homosexuals seducing and "converting" others. The Scientific Humanitarian
Committee, led by Magnus Hirschfeld, combined goals of scientific study and
social and political activism (Lauritsen and Thorstad, 1974). However, it was not
recognized until later what power this construct unwittingly gave the medical
profession: power to act as agents of social control under the guise of treating illness.

Freud switched the focus of etiological theories for homosexuality from biological to psycho-social developmental factors, declaring that initially the sexual in-
stinct exists independent of a sexual object (Freud, 1905), and that the debate over
"inherited" versus "acquired" forms of homosexuality was thus inappropriate
(Freud, 1922). His concept of an innate bisexual disposition acting as a primary unconscious force was based upon fallacious assumptions current at the time regarding the biological bisexuality of the fetus. This pointed to his own difficulties in escaping the biological determinism and psychophysical parallelism of the period.
Innate bisexuality was conceptualized as nothing more than an initial biological
potential for sexual attraction to both men and women; rather than expecting it to
be expressed behaviorally, it was hypothesized to be an unconscious driving force
for certain psychological processes. Freud assumed a normal course of development must lead to a heterosexual object-choice; only a series of vicissitudes could
lead the libido astray to a homosexual object-choice. Bisexual activity, rather than
proceeding naturally from an innate bisexual disposition, was construed as a kind
of inversion, of either the "amphigenic" or "contingent" variety (Freud, 1905).
Although object-choice was not assumed to be innate, it was seen as established
and invariant by early childhood.

These early formulations of heterosexual and homosexual patterns were based
on the assumption that homosexual behavior appears in only a very small and distinct subgroup of the population. Such behavior was taken as stemming from a
basic and fixed aspect of the person. As Richardson (1983/1984) points out, the
publication of the Kinsey group studies of male and female sexual behavior in 1948
and 1953 posed a major definitional crisis for these scientific formulations of homosexuality. The data showed a high incidence of homosexual behavior and response
(especially in the male sample), as well as apparent fluctuations of all kinds in respondents' sexual orientations.

A host of new terms emerged to safeguard the theoretical construct of a "real" homosexuality, differentiating "genuine" from "incidental," "situational," or "temporary" homosexuals. Whereas earlier formulations identified an internal state on the basis of observable behavior, the new distinctions demanded the concept of an internal state that could be in direct contradiction to behavioral signs. In a perversion of Freud's concept of latent homosexuality, it was generally assumed that practicing heterosexuals could be "latent homosexuals." Paradoxically, this apparent blurring of boundaries *maintained* the essential homosexual/heterosexual distinction. It thus seemed that only medical experts or a retrospective analysis could determine one's "true self." This perspective left no room for the notion of someone being a "real" bisexual, as science could discredit behavioral evidence and claim to know the person better than the person could know himself or herself.

The last 20 years have led to a new set of ideas about sexual orientation, broadening the concept to that of "sexual identity." Richardson (1983/1984) sees these ideas as a consequence of an infusion of sociological research and theory in the area, the emergence of the gay liberation movement, and the increasing acceptance of homosexuality in our society. Sociological theory emphasized the social impact of labeling and deviant status, leading to the gay liberation movement's appropriation of the labeling function to create a nonpathologizing (and nonpathological) nomenclature. The emergence of the notion of the gay identity as distinct from the homosexual identity was part of this process. (The lesbian/gay distinction emerged later out of other considerations, so "gay" will be treated initially in this discussion as a genderless term, in line with historical events.)

The notion of the gay identity developed within a formulation of the "homosexual" along sociological rather than psycho(patho)logical lines. The problems facing the homosexual person were not fundamentally a product of personality or internal organization, but of society's punitive treatment of homosexuals as deviates (Weinberg, 1973). An awareness of the power of the labeling process led homosexuals to relabel themselves with a term that was positive and free of perjorative associations (Morin, 1977).

Being "gay" was initially an idealized reversal of connotations attached to being "homosexual." The individual could accept and enjoy homosexuality, while dismissing the negative societal stereotypes and attitudes about homosexuals:

> At its best it means not limiting oneself to a stereotype—a model of some previous homosexual—for one's personality, at work, at parties, with a lover. . . . It means being able to investigate one's preferences and desires in sexual roles where one chooses. . . . In essence, it means being convinced that any erotic orientation and preference may be housed in any human being. (Weinberg, 1973, p. 71)

> Homosexual is the label that was applied to Gay people as a device for separating us from the rest of the population. . . . *Gay* is a descriptive label we have assigned to ourselves as a way of reminding ourselves and others that awareness of our sexuality facilitates a capability rather than creating a restriction. It means that we are *capable* of fully loving a person of the same gender. . . . But the label

does not limit us. We who are Gay can still love someone of the other gender. (Clark, 1977, pp. 103– 106)

Although it might be seen as another instance of the bisexual identity being subsumed under the homosexual identity, Clark's use of "Gay" to include non-exclusively homosexual persons was in keeping with the early aspirations of the Gay Liberation movement. One of its initial ideals was the sexual liberation of all people, freeing them from categories of gender and sexual orientation to act and love as they chose (Orlando, 1984). It was anticipated that the categories of hetero-sexuality and homosexuality would lose their power to polarize actions, feelings and people (Altman, 1971).

Just as the emphasis of the Gay Liberation movement shifted over the course of its first decade (Altman, 1982), so did the implications of the "gay" label. Initially, it was used in a self-conscious counteracting effort to posit a healthy alternative to the sullied "homosexual" tag. The slogan "Gay is Good" was meant to offset the conventional perception of homosexuals as "sick." But "gay" soon acquired a new, more concrete meaning as an identity encompassing far more than the sexual and affectional aspects of self. In part, this reflected a shift in political tactics, as the goal of massive changes in the general population's attitudes about sex seemed unreal-istic. "Gay people" were redefined in terms of being another disadvantaged mi-nority in our society, and the image of the "gay world" of secretive sexually tinged assemblages was replaced by the "gay community" with its own culture, history, social organizations, and politics. Within that community a far more differentiated picture of the "gay identity" emerged. As a consequence, popular perceptions of homosexuality have undergone a great deal of change. In the midst of this, it is sometimes difficult to remember that the homosexual-as-an-entity is a notion that has existed in our culture only about 120 years, and is alien to most societies in which homosexuality is common (Altman, 1982; Ford and Beach, 1951).

Politics of the Gay Identity

From the assumption that the "gay identity" represented a positive counterpoise to the "homosexual identity" came a set of criteria for the "truly gay" person, based both on values espoused in the gay community, and research on what factors promote a healthy integration of one's homosexuality into one's self-concept. This research has concerned itself with the "coming out" process and the developmen-tal stages hypothesized in the formation of a "gay identity," and is reflective of the values and assumptions of certain arbiters of health and self-actualization from the ranks of "public gays" (Lee, 1977). A primary criterion is one's sense of affiliation with the gay community "in a cultural and sociable sense" (Warren, 1974, p. 149), which can be measured in as simplistic a manner as comparing the relative num-bers of one's homosexual and heterosexual friends (Harry and Lovely, 1979). Being exclusively homosexual in one's sexual and affectional relationships has also been assumed to be indicative of one's "commitment" to the "gay community." Such measures place the person who is not exclusively homosexual at an immediate disadvantage. Ironically, "choosing" to keep what may be a more constricted social life is valued as emotionally and morally superior, and as politically purer.

In the process of reconstructing the homosexual as a member of a distinct minority group, not only has a positive value been placed on separatist lifestyles, but also on old beliefs in the essentiality of homosexuality. Articles on "coming out" and homosexual identity formation hint at a basic inner state of homosexual desire (almost equivalent to antiquated notions of a "homosexual sex drive") that is fixed at an early age (Berzon in Giteck, 1984; Malyon, 1981) and seems to emerge at various points in a person's life only because it has been denied, repressed, or too emotionally "loaded" to be acknowledged (Bozett, 1980; Malyon, 1981; Ross, 1971; Voeller and Walters, 1978). The idea of the emergence of homosexual feelings as indicating a belated recognition of the "true self" (Coleman, 1982; De Monteflores and Schultz, 1978; McDonald, 1982) is a recrudescence of the old invariant-inner-state/variable-behavior explanation for the Kinsey data's contradiction of biologically based theories of sexuality. The search for biological bases for homosexuality remind one of the third-sex notions of the last century; the investment in such ideas by some in the gay and lesbian communities may be similarly politically motivated.

The problem of the intrusion of political considerations into the manner in which scientists interpret data is exemplified by the arguments of Whitam (1981), who has strongly resisted any theories positing a socially constructed "homosexual role." He distinguishes homosexual activity from a biologically determined "homosexual orientation." To justify his viewpoints, he makes sweeping assertions about the universality of "basic elements appearing in homosexual subcultures," and of early appearing nonsexual "complex behavioral elements" of the homosexual orientation (p. 68). (One of these universal behavioral elements of a homosexual orientation is "the tendency toward entertainment and the arts.") Furthermore, he attacks the theoretical basis of Goode's notions of a "homosexual role" by pointing out purely political considerations:

> While sociologists may lament the misuse of sociological concepts by homophobic elements it nevertheless is true that the view that homosexuality as an orientation is a superficial, learned, flexible aspect of one's personality feeds the primordial fears of the Anglo-Saxons that homosexuals are dangerous people and that homosexual orientations can be taught to others. . . . Such [judicial] rulings favorable to blacks and other ethnic groups, women, and the handicapped have frequently proceeded on the legal principle of "immutable characteristics," an advantage which gays will never achieve as long as the social scientific formulation of their sexuality proceeds along the lines of "sexual preference," "choice," "role," "alternative life style," and "social learning." (pp. 70–71)

Whereas the evidence of political and patently unscientific concerns intruding upon the scientific judgments of someone such as Whitam is clear, much of the influence of social and political factors in this area is far less overt because of the rudimentary level of our understanding of sexuality, especially outside of a specific familiar (and constrictive) cultural context. As a brief example of this, we can continue to examine the interpretations made by some gay-identified authors of heterosexuality comingling with homosexuality. It is not that the people singled out need to be criticized any more than any others in this field, but that owing to the large political component grafted onto the idea of homosexual or gay identity, it is easier to examine the political and social assumptions that undergird their scholarly work.

The Bisexual and the Homosexual Communities

Many authors have tried to adopt a more constructionist approach to the concept of homosexual identity, emphasizing the individual as an active participant in the development of meanings for homoerotic feelings or behavior and the creation of an identity based on those meanings (Cass, 1979; Minton and McDonald, 1983/1984; Troiden, 1979; Troiden and Goode, 1980; Weinberg, 1978). However, these authors focus more on the consequences relabeling these experiences have on personal identity than they do on the interactions between the individual's understanding of his or her (1) potential for homosexual relations, (2) potential for heterosexual relations, (3) actual relationships, and (4) self-labeling. Part of the decision to adopt a homosexual identity, as opposed to a bisexual identity or a heterosexual identity, involves not only the personal significance or value one attaches to one's homosexual experience and perceived potential, but also one's simultaneous evaluation of one's heterosexuality. The authors may mention someone who went through a period of seeing himself (in these studies) as bisexual; however, there is no parallel investigation of the factors that may have led to such an identification or the need to change it. That lapse leads to an implicit discounting of the bisexual identity and to treating it as a potential intermediate identity, but not as a real option if one is to fully integrate homosexuality into one's sense of self.

Given that the self-identified bisexual can expect hostility and rejection both from the mainstream heterosexual hegemony and from self-identified homosexuals, and that social context is a powerful determinant in how one interprets behaviors and feelings (a reiterated point in these models of identity formation), there is tremendous pressure on the individual to identify as homosexual. Once one identifies as homosexual, there is then further pressure to be exclusively homosexual (especially among a subgroup of lesbian feminists) in order to be accepted (Blumstein and Schwartz, 1977). Thus, the adoption of a label for political purposes, as described in Lee (1977) and by a quoted statement in Blumstein and Schwartz (1976), may later impinge upon actual behavior. Sagarin (1973) points to that by labeling themselves as homosexual, people who are homosexually active "become entrapped in a false consciousness. They believe that they discover what they are (and by implication, since this is a discovery, they must have been this way all along). Learning their 'identity' they become . . . boxed into their own biographies" (p. 10). Altman (1982) suggests that there may be a "new style emerging among younger 'gays,' in which more will behave bisexually, but will continue to identify as homosexual 'for political reasons'" (pp. 15–16). He then goes on to undercut that identification as continuing solely for political reasons by negating the discriminatory value of sexual behavior, implying both that bisexually active "gays" will be unlikely to find significant emotional involvements with opposite-sex partners, and that the non-sexual aspects of a homosexual identification would assume greater significance.

The attempt to render the homosexual identity as a higher order construct than the bisexual identity by emphasizing its meaning for non-sexual aspects of self necessitates a belief in a biological or fixed basis for these non-erotic components. Otherwise, it requires an explanation of why the bisexual identity could not, allowed to develop alongside specifically bisexual social institutions, assume many of the non-sexual trappings the homosexual identity has taken on in the last decade. When we look longitudinally, we can see the tremendous change in the social power of the "gay community." We have no evidence to counter that a hypothetical "bisexual community" could not similarly emerge, developing its own set of personal attributions for "the bisexual." Just as the content implied by the gay label has changed over the course of a decade, so could the content of the bisexual label.

The issue of marginality for "the bisexual," caught between two sexual categories that define a clear social identity, has been outlined elsewhere (Paul, 1983/1984). The confusion between scientific and popularized meanings for sexual identity is highlighted by this conflict. The bisexual has neither a clear social identity nor a strong political voice, which results in bisexually active people not gaining appropriate recognition in scientific theory, given the history of social and political intrusions into an ostensibly scientific study of sexuality.

The Utility of the Sexual Identity Construct in Research

Articles reviewing the use of various terms of sexual identity in studies argue, with a great deal of confirmatory evidence, that research in the area of sexuality has been consistently flawed by theoretical inconsistencies and simplistic determinations of homosexual and heterosexual samples (De Cecco, 1981; De Cecco and Shively, 1983/1984; MacDonald, 1981; Paul and Weinrich, 1982). Researchers have rarely bothered with conceptual definitions of the terms gay, lesbian, homosexual, heterosexual, straight, ambisexual, or bisexual. Operational definitions have been ridiculously crude and demonstrate a serious naiveté about sexuality. As Shively, Jones, and De Cecco (1983/1984) note: "Sexual orientation was treated as if it were a palpable, unitary phenomenon although it was conceived in divergent and sometimes contradictory ways" (p. 134).

Studies may have used sexual behavior, sexual fantasy, physical location, self-report, or any number of divergent cues. When the Kinsey scale was used, it was usually reduced from a continuum to a set of categories—primarily heterosexual and homosexual (Weinberg and Williams, 1974). MacDonald (1981) points to a number of studies ostensibly of "homosexuals" which covered a range of persons who were actively homosexual and, to some degree, also heterosexually responsive. Blumstein and Schwartz (1977) point out the lack of correspondence between self-described sexual identity and the sexual biographies of those in their study sample who did not have exclusively heterosexual or exclusively homosexual histories. Part of that inconsistency appears to be a reflection of the variety of meanings attached to these labels beyond that of the biological sex of one's sexual partners: Some are perjorative and associated with social sex-role, others political in content, or diverging; from the simple consideration of erotic desire.

Despite the divergent meanings given to the labels "gay" and "homosexual"—with the gay (or lesbian) identity presumably reflecting a greater political and social involvement with the so-called gay community, a higher valuation placed on one's homosexuality, and the extent to which awareness of one's homosexuality is seen as an organizing principle in various areas of one's life—it is unclear how often individuals (respondents or researchers) make the necessary distinctions between the terms. Furthermore, there is evidence that people may decide that more than one term is applicable to them (Kooden, Morin, Riddle, Rogers, Song, and Strassburger, 1979). These labels have been most often used in defining and differentiating groups in a study, a practice that still can mean tremendous variability either of subjects within a group or between studies supposedly of the same target population. Given their different meanings for the same labels, it is important for researchers to recognize the focus of their research and to look at the issues they want to examine as those between *people* rather than between categories in an artificially imposed dichotomy or trichotomy of sexuality. If one is interested in studying homosexual behavior, it is clear that studying individuals who identify as gay, lesbian, homosexual, or even bisexual will represent only a small group of those who embody homosexual desire. A common complaint is that, because "bisexuals" covers such a vast range of individuals with such varying histories and potentials, to talk about them as a unity is to invite ridicule. But that is also something that we are discovering in study after study about "homosexuals" and "heterosexuals." Given that these categories both fail to represent the total population engaged in a particular form of sexual behavior one might be studying, and also provide no clear consistency within their groupings, it is hard to understand their benefit. They tend to reduce individuals and relationships into populations about whom researchers make all sorts of assumptions. Rather than being meaningful terms for categorizing various types according to erotic and affectional factors, they tend to be merely instrumental in determining how others will initially react to and think about those individuals as *social* rather than sexual beings.

Yet an alternative is not immediately obvious. There is wisdom in stepping back from the individual and focusing instead on the various kinds of relationships individuals may form, as suggested by DeCecco and Shively (1983/1984). Rather than imposing identities on people that presumably dictate how they interact with others, researchers need to articulate a descriptive language of relationships. Authors and researchers have pointed out that it is not possible to attach a single meaning to homosexual behavior, but that it acquires its personal meaning for the participants through the relational context in which it occurs (Weinberg, 1978; Troiden, 1979; Cass, 1983/1984; Minton and McDonald, 1983/1984). Any given relationship is unique; it is not simply a summation of fixed or static qualities in the individual, but a reflection of the relationship's history, anticipated future, aims, and rules for each member. In addition, studied relationships can have an immediacy and palpability that categorized individuals do not.

Conclusion

The field of sexuality research is at a point where it has the resources to compare critically the current model of sexuality in western society with differing cross-cultural and trans-historical perspectives. Research theory must undergo a transition in which it sheds the accretions of folk mythologies and politically determined assumptions about sex so as to be able to reach new levels of understanding. In such research, those involved must be careful to separate out constructs that are popular from those that provide scientific insight. As Jonathan Katz said:

> The words *heterosexual* and *homosexual* represent a particular conjunction of a gender category and an erotic category. Because of the reigning heterosexual hegemony, we're only beginning to understand that there were other basic ways of thinking about, and institutionalizing, sexuality in the past. That opens up the possibility that in the future we can have a completely different social organization of sex. (Hall, 1983, p. 41)

REFERENCES

Altman, D. (1982). *The homosexualization of America, the Americanization of the homosexual.* New York: St. Martin's Press.

Altman, D. (1971). *Homosexual oppression and liberation.* New York: Avon Books.

Blair, R. (1974). Counseling concerns and bisexual behavior. *The Homosexual Counseling Journal,* 1(2), 26–30.

Blumstein, P. W., and Schwartz, P. (1976). Bisexuality in men. *Urban Life,* 5, 339–358 .

Blumstein, P. W., and Schwartz, P. (1977). Bisexuality: Some social-psychological issues. *Journal of Social Issues,* 33, 30–45.

Bozett, F. W. (1980). Gay fathers: How and why they disclose their homosexuality to their children. *Family Relations,* 29, 173–179.

Cass, V. C. (1983/1984). Homosexual identity: A concept in need of definition. *Journal of Homosexuality,* 9(2/3), 105–126.

Cass, V. C. (1979). Homosexual identity formation: A theoretical model. *Journal of Homosexuality,* 4, 219–235.

Clark, D. (1977). *Loving someone gay.* New York: Signet Books.

Coleman, E. (1982). Developmental stages of the coming-out process. In W. Paul, J. D. Weinrich, J. C. Gonsiorek, and M. E. Hotvedt (Eds.), *Homosexuality: Social, psychological, and biological issues* (pp. 149–158). Beverly Hills, CA : Sage Publications.

Cory, D. and LeRoy, J. P. (1963). *The homosexual and his society.* New York: Citadel Press.

De Cecco, J. P. (1981). Definition and meaning of sexual orientation. *Journal of Homosexuality,* 6(4), 51–67 .

DeCecco, J. P., and Shively, M. G. (1983/1984). From sexual identity to sexual relationships: A contextual shift. *Journal of Homosexuality,* 9(2/3), 1–26 .

De Monteflores, C., and Schultz, S. J. (1978). Coming out: Similarities and differences for lesbians and gay men. *Journal of Social Issues*, 34, 59–72.

Ellis, H. (1972). The psychology of sex: A manual for students. New York: Emerson Books. (Originally published 1938)

Ford, C. S., and Beach, F. A. (1951). *Patterns of sexual behavior*. New York: Harper and Row.

Freud, S. (1961). Three essays on the theory of sexuality. In J. Strachey (Ed. and Trans.), *The standard edition of the complete psychological works of Sigmund Freud* (Vol. 7). London: Hogarth Press. (Original work published 1905)

Freud, S. (1961). Psychogenesis in of a case of homosexuality in a woman. In J. Strachey (Ed. and Trans.), *The standard edition of the complete psychological works of Sigmund Freud* (Vol. 18). London: Hogarth Press. (Original work published 1922)

Giteck, L. (1984, October 2). The gay theory of relativity: Family by design. *The Advocate*, pp. 28, 33, 56.

Hall, R. (1983 , June 23). Historian Jonathan Katz: A new documentary for a minority in question. *The Advocate*, pp. 37–41, 79.

Harry, J. and Lovely, R. (1979). Gay marriages and communities of sexual orientation. *Alternative Lifestyles*, 2,177– 200.

Kooden, H. D., Morin, S. F., Riddle, D. I., Rogers, M., Sang, B. E., and Strassburger, F. (1979) *Removing the stigma: Final report, task force on the status of lesbian and gay male psychologists*. Washington, D.C.: American Psychological Association.

Lauritsen, J., and Thorstad, D. (1974). *The early homosexual rights movement (1864–1935)*. New York: Times Change Press.

Lee, J. A. (1977). Going public: A study in the sociology of homosexual liberation. *Journal of Homosexuality*, 3, 49–78.

MacDonald, A. P., Jr. (1981). Bisexuality: Some comments on research and theory. *Journal of Homosexuality*, 6(3), 21–33.

Malyon, A. (1981/1982). Psychotherapeutic implications of internalized homophobia in gay males. *Journal of Homosexuality*, 7(2/3), 59–69.

Malyon, A. (1981). The homosexual adolescent: Developmental issues and social bias. *Child Welfare*, 60, 321–330.

Masters, W. M., and Johnson, V. E. (1979). *Homosexuality in perspective*. Boston: Little, Brown .

McDonald, G. J. (1982). Individual differences in the coming-out process for gay men: Implications for theoretical models. *Journal of Homosexuality*, 8(1), 47–60.

Minton, H. L., and McDonald, G. J. (1983/1984). Homosexual identity formation as a developmental process. *Journal of Homosexuality*, 9(2/3), 91–104.

Morin, S. F. (1977). Heterosexual bias in psychological research on lesbianism and male homosexuality, *American Psychologist*, 32, 629–637.

Orlando, L. (1984, February 25). Loving whom we choose: Bisexuality and the lesbian/gay community. Where we stand. *Gay Community News*, 11.

Paul, J. P. (1983/1984). The bisexual identity: An idea without social recognition. *Journal of Homosexuality*, 9(2/ 3), 45–63.

Paul, W., and Weinrich J. D. (1982). Whom and what we study: Definition and scope of sexual orientation. In W. Paul, J. D. Weinrich, J. C. Gonsiorek, and M. E. Hotvedt (Eds.), *Homosexuality: Social, psychological, and biological issues* (pp. 23–28). Beverly Hills, CA: Sage.

Richardson, D. (1983/1984). The dilemma of essentiality in homosexual theory. *Journal of Homosexuality*, 9(213), 79–90.

Ross, H. L. (1971). Modes of adjustment of married homosexuals. *Social Problems*, 18, 385–393.

Sagarin, E. (1973). The good guys, the bad guys and the gay guys. *Contemporary Sociology*, 2(1), 3–13.

Schafer, S. (1976). Sexual and social problems of lesbians. *Journal of Sex Research*, 12, 50–69.

Shively, M. G., Jones, C., and De Cecco, J. P. (1983/1984). Research on sexual orientation: Definitions and methods. *Journal of Homosexuality*, 9(2/3), 127–136.

Troiden, R. R. (1979). Becoming homosexual: A model of gay identity acquisition. *Psychiatry*, 42, 362–373.

Troiden, R. R., and Goode, E. (1980). Variables related to the acquisition of a gay identity. *Journal of Homosexuality*, 5, 383–392.

Voeller, B., and Walters, J. (1978). Gay fathers. *The Family Coordinator*, 27, 149–157.

Warren, C. A. B. (1974). *Identity and community in the gay world*. New York: John Wiley and Sons.

Weinberg, G. (1973). *Society and the healthy homosexual*. New York: Anchor Books.

Weinberg , M. S., and Williams, C. J. (1974). *Male homosexuals: Their problems and adaptations*. New York: Penguin Books.

Weinberg, T. S. (1978), On "doing" and "being" gay: Sexual behavior and homosexual male self-identity. *Journal of Homosexuality*, 4, 143–157.

Whitam, F. L. (1981). A reply to Goode on "The homosexual role." *Journal of Sex Research*, 17, 66–72 .

3

A Little Bit of Lavender Goes a Long Way: A Critique of Research on Sexual Orientation

A. P. MacDonald Jr.

Dr. Evelyn Hooker stated in the final report of the National Institute of Mental Health's Task Force on Homosexuality (Livingood, 1972): "Thus it is clear that 'Who is homosexual?' and 'What is homosexuality?' are very complex questions, clarification of which would be a lasting contribution to social science" (p. 11). She was referring to definitions that include psychic arousal vs. those which emphasize overt experience, etc. I propose that the confusion is even greater than that. I argue that we have little knowledge concerning homosexuality because the research reviewed by the Task Force and subsequent research is thoroughly confounded by the inclusion of large numbers of bisexuals as "homosexuals."

Over three decades ago, Alfred Kinsey recognized diversity in sexual orientations. Kinsey, Pomeroy, Martin and Gebhard (1953) argued that, although some people are exclusively homosexual, whereas others are exclusively heterosexual, there are "a considerable number of persons who include both homosexual and heterosexual responses and/or activities in their histories. . . . This group of persons is identified in the literature as bisexual" (p. 468). However, Kinsey et al. pointed out that bisexuals are considered to be homosexual in the public mind; i.e., anyone known to have had *any* homosexual experience at all is labeled homosexual. Kinsey and his colleagues remarked that "it would be as reasonable to rate all individuals heterosexual if they have any heterosexual experience, and irrespective of the amount of homosexual experience which they may be having" (p. 469).

Kinsey proposed a homosexual-heterosexual continuum, with exclusive homosexuality on the one end, exclusive heterosexuality on the other end, and bisexuality in the middle. Accordingly, he introduced the 7-point (0–6) Kinsey Scale.[1] Five

This study was partially supported by a Faculty Research Grant (FRG 203191) from the University of Massachusetts.

of the seven points (1–5) of the scale represent various degrees of bisexuality, perhaps suggesting that bisexuals constitute a large segment of the population. Indeed, Kinsey, Pomeroy, and Martin (1948) concluded from their study of males that "since only 50 percent of the population is exclusively heterosexual throughout its adult life, and since only 4 percent of the population is exclusively homosexual throughout its life, it appears that nearly half (46 percent) of the population engages in both heterosexual and homosexual activities, or reacts to persons of both sexes, in the course of their adult lives" (p. 656).

One should be careful to avoid making inferences about proportions of bisexuals in cohorts from such longitudinal claims. The estimates of the number of bisexuals will also vary depending on the definition used. The numbers will be large if one counts bisexual behavior over the life span; larger still if one includes bisexual desires (fantasies). A considerably smaller number will be obtained if only those presently engaged in a bisexual lifestyle are counted. For example, many might find it difficult to affix the bisexual label to an adult who had but one preadolescent homosexual experience.

Even those who accept bisexuality as a valid sexual orientation find themselves in heated debate over definitional issues: What role should self-identification play?[2] Should erotic fantasy be considered or should only overt behaviors be considered? Is it legitimate to identify all who have had sexual relations with both genders as bisexual even if sex with one gender took place in early childhood and was never repeated as an adult? Must one have engaged in overt genital sex with members of both genders to be identified as bisexual? These and many more questions need to be resolved. The purpose of this paper is not to attempt to resolve these issues. All of these questions rest on one common assumption: that bisexually oriented people do exist. Rather, the purpose of this paper is to point out that this is a reasonable assumption, as well as to persuade the reader that research on bisexuality is needed. Also, a major point made in this paper is that the failure to recognize bisexuals as a separate group has resulted in the confounding of homosexual study samples.

In his book, *The Bisexual Option*, Klein (1978, p. 117) claims that between 30 to 45 percent of the male population are definable on the Kinsey Scale as bisexual, and 15 to 35 percent of the female population fit that description; i.e., there are about 30 to 40 million bisexuals in the United States. Therefore, (though he presents no explicitly supporting data) if Klein is correct, bisexually oriented people constitute a rather sizable proportion of the population; a proportion at least considerably larger than the exclusively homosexual population. A number of sex researchers agree with him (e.g., Blumstein and Schwartz, 1974), and the famed Margaret Mead proposed that bisexually inclined human beings are "probably a majority" (Mead, 1975, p. 29). However, the actual percentages of bisexuals need yet to be documented.

Despite the claims that bisexuals constitute a large segment of the population there is a paucity of research on the subject. Blumstein and Schwartz (1974, 1976a, 1976b, 1977; Schwartz and Bumstein, 1976) have reported their qualitative analyses of intensive interviews done with 78 male and 78 female bisexuals. Few conclusions are drawn and no comparisons with exclusively homosexual or heterosexual individuals were made. I have found only two studies in which bisexuals, heterosexuals, and homosexuals have been compared (Ellis, 1962; Kenyon, 1968).

Ellis (1962) compared 19 bisexuals, 33 confirmed homosexuals who maintained their own sex roles, and 14 "inverts" (those who were exclusively homosexual, but who had adopted the role of the opposite sex), and 150 "highly heterosexual" patients on creativity. It was found that a higher percentage of heterosexuals (61 percent) and bisexuals (63 percent) than homosexuals (54 percent) and "inverts" (53 percent) became more creative during the course of treatment.

Kenyon (1968) compared 77 bisexual women (1–5 on the Kinsey Scale), 46 exclusively homosexual (Kinsey 6), and 123 exclusively heterosexual (Kinsey 0) women. The three groups were found to be significantly different from one another in many ways too numerous to report here. A few examples are: (all statistically significant) (a) bisexuals (48 percent) began menstruation earlier (before 13 years of age) than the lesbians (22 percent) or heterosexuals (39 percent), whereas lesbians were overrepresented among those who began menstruation after 13 years of age (lesbians, 42 percent; bisexuals, 31 percent; and heterosexuals, 34 percent), (b) premenstrual oedema was experienced by only 34 percent of the lesbians, but was experienced by over 50 percent of the bisexuals and heterosexuals, (c) 67 percent of the lesbians said they resented menstruation, as compared to 42 percent of the bisexuals and 15 percent of the heterosexuals, (d) more bisexuals (30 percent) attended universities than lesbians (21 percent) or heterosexuals (15 percent) (though bisexuals were significantly different from lesbians and heterosexuals, the latter two groups did not differ from each other), (e) bisexuals tended to be more religious than lesbians, (f) more bisexuals (22 percent) than lesbians (7 percent) felt guilty about their homosexuality, and (g) only 13 percent of the lesbians compared to 40 percent of the bisexuals said they felt fully feminine. Overall, Kenyon's study shows that bisexual females differ from both lesbians and heterosexual women and, therefore, should not be included as "homosexuals" in homosexual study samples.

In a more recent study of homosexuality, Bell and Weinberg (1978) had black and white male and female subjects rate themselves on the Kinsey Scale twice; once for their behaviors and once for their feelings (desires). Roughly one-third of the respondents indicated bisexual behavior and approximately 40 percent indicated bisexual desires. The authors inform us (pp. 60–61) that the inclusion of such high percentages of bisexuals is not unusual in surveys of this kind, where deliberate attempts are made to recruit only homosexuals. Their observation is confirmed in another study of 2,437 "homosexual" males in three cultures (the United States, the Netherlands, and Denmark) (Weinberg and Williams, 1974). The investigators report (p. 209) that 49.4 percent of the American sample reported some degree of bisexuality on the Kinsey Scale. Many of these men were heterosexually married. However, apart from a chapter on bisexuality, these bisexuals were treated as homosexuals in the major analyses reported throughout the book. Bell and Weinberg (1978) also included their bisexual subjects (one-third behaviorally so and about 40 percent by desire) in their analyses of black and white male and female "homosexuals." This was done despite the fact that the investigators accepted the self-ratings on the Kinsey Scale as valid:

> Respondents' ratings of themselves on the homosexual-heterosexual continuum were in agreement with their sexual histories. Those who rated themselves as exclusively homosexual were less apt to have engaged in sexual activity with persons of the opposite sex or ever to have been sexually aroused in a heterosexual context than were those respondents who scored in more of a heterosexual direction. As one moves from point to point along the seven-point Kinsey Scale (from 6 to 0), increasingly larger percentages reported more heterosexual experiences. At the very least, it would appear that respondents' self-ratings were valid reflections of their sexual whereabouts. (p. 60)

Bell and Weinberg make no statistical comparisons between their homosexual and bisexual respondents. However, in two tables (pp. 291 and 293) they report on the heterosexual behavior of their subjects. The data are broken down by sex and race and are presented for separate ratings on the Kinsey Scale. The data are reported in percentages, with total numbers indicated. By computing the frequencies from the percentages I performed chi-square analyses. I compared the responses of the exclusively homosexual subjects (Kinsey 6) to the responses of the bisexual subjects (Kinsey 3–5 combined). As one would expect, bisexuals report significantly more heterosexual behavior than exclusive homosexuals. One might argue that such differences are tautological, as well they may be, but they both address the claim that most "homosexuals" have heterosexual experiences and the validity of the claim that bisexuals do exist as a group apart from homosexuals.[3]

Bell and Weinberg also report (pp. 292 and 294) on the heterosexual feelings of their subjects, broken down in the same way as described above. They report the percentages of subjects' responses to questions pertaining to their heterosexual feelings (i.e., sex dreams, masturbatory fantasies, and sexual arousal). My chi-square analyses of these data once again show that the bisexuals are significantly more heterosexually oriented than the homosexuals.[4]

Also, it should be noted that Weinberg and Williams (1974) present data (pp. 212–215) that show that (in their sample from the United States) their bisexual males differed significantly (p < .001) from their homosexual males in the 18 comparisons that were made (primarily having to do with relating to the homo- and heterosexual worlds). But, again, the differences are what one would expect if one accepted bisexuals as a group apart from homosexuals.

The limited findings reported above indicate that bisexuals differ in significant ways from homosexuals and, therefore, should not be combined with homosexuals in homosexual study samples. The practice of including bisexuals as homosexuals is not peculiar to the productive researchers at the Kinsey Institute; rather, it is standard procedure among sex researchers. Witness the following examples.

Twenty male and 20 female Kinsey 3 (i.e., equally homosexual and heterosexual) subjects were selected as members of the homosexual study-subject population (Masters and Johnson, 1979, p. 144).[5]

Twenty-eight percent of the homosexual subjects were bisexual, some of whom had had sustained heterosexual relationships (in some instances, marriage and children) while at the same time engaging in clandestine homosexual relationships (Bieber, Dain, Dince, Drellich, Grand, Gundlach, Kremer, Rifkin, Wilbur, and Bieber, 1962).

Consequently, even sophisticated sex researchers obscure meaningful differences between bisexuals and homosexuals while presenting data that show that bisexuals constitute large proportions of their "homosexual" study samples. One cannot help but draw a parallel between this behavior and the behavior of the prejudiced person who upon discovering that a white person has a black ancestor decides that that person is therefore a "Nigger." It has often been said that a little bit of black goes a long way. My review of the literature on sexual orientation indicates that a little bit of lavender also goes a long way.[6] Apart from the impropriety of labeling bisexuals "homosexuals," this practice has sufficiently confounded the literature on homosexuality to make it possibly misleading. And, it leaves us with no knowledge of bisexuality .

Inclusion of bisexuals as homosexuals may come about as a result of the belief that sexual orientations are truly dichotomous; i.e., either homo- or heterosexual. Therefore, bisexuals are *really* homosexuals who are engaging in homosexual denial. The most blatant example of this belief can be found in a study by Harry and Lovely (1979). These investigators operationalized exclusive homosexuals (also, most or all of their friends were gay) as "homosexuals with a high commitment to the gay community," and bisexuals (most or all friends were heterosexual) as "heterosexuals with a low commitment to the gay community." They justified their procedure as follows:

> It might be argued that our operationalization of commitment to a community of sexual orientation is largely a distinction between exclusive homosexuals and bisexuals, and that an analysis of the correlates of commitment should be performed only among those who are exclusive or near-exclusive homosexuals. This argument assumes that those men who place themselves in the middle-bisexual ranges of the Kinsey Scale are in fact accurately reporting their erotic predispositions. However, we believe that the vast majority of such persons are not bisexuals, but use this label as a means of avoiding the full stigma of a homosexual label. (pp. 182–183)

It is curious that Harry and Lovely propose that homosexuals take on bisexual identities to avoid the full stigma of a homosexual identity. Even a cursory examination of the literature indicates that bisexuals are themselves stigmatized, especially by homosexuals. For example, Cory (cited in Warren, 1974) comments that the gay community does not accept men married to women: "The submerged group life accepts with hesitance and deep reservation the married man. He is not one of them" (p. 133). Blumstein and Schwartz (1974) remark: "The lesbian community cannot deny the existence of bisexual behavior, but its members do not encourage it, and they do not easily accept women with a bisexual identification" (p. 292). "Bisexuality meets with antagonism and suspicion in most, although not all, Lesbian Communities" (p. 290). These are but a few of many examples.

Perhaps bisexuals are better accepted by heterosexuals. I know of no research on the issue. However, considering the above, it doesn't appear that people can successfully avoid stigma by assuming a bisexual rather than a homosexual identity. Rather, self-identification as either bisexual or homosexual seems to result in becoming the object of prejudice and discrimination. Therefore, it seems that Bell and Weinberg (1978, p. 60) are correct in their claim that respondents' self-ratings of their bisexual orientations are, for the most part, valid, and not merely indicative of homosexual denial.

The practice of treating bisexuals as homosexuals must stop if we are to learn anything about sexual orientations. We seem to know nothing much about bisexuality, and, considering the inclusion of bisexuals in homosexual study samples, how much do we know about homosexuals? We need to conduct studies that compare bisexuals, heterosexuals, and homosexuals. Also, those who do research on homosexuality must be careful when they select their samples. It is no longer legitimate to identify a person as a homosexual simply on the basis of *any* homosexual experience. Further, journal editors and reviewers, as well as funding agencies, should be alert to this problem and take deliberate steps to correct it.

Notes

1. The Kinsey Scale is well known and doesn't require a detailed description here. For a detailed description see Churchill (1967, chap. 2) and Kinsey et al. (1953, pp. 471–472). Simply, 0 = Exclusively heterosexual, 1 = Predominantly heterosexual, 2 = Predominantly heterosexual, but significantly homosexual, 3 = Equally homosexual and heterosexual, 4 = Predominantly homosexual, only insignificantly heterosexual, and 6 = Exclusively homosexual. For criticism of the Kinsey Scale, especially when it is used report orgasms with each gender, see Gagnon (1977, pp. 260–262).

2. The degree to which self-identification should be considered is a complex issue. As mentioned elsewhere in this paper, Bell and Weinberg (1978, p. 60) found a direct match between respondents' ratings of themselves on the Kinsey Scale and the respondents' sexual histories. In sharp contrast, Blumstein and Schwartz (1976b) report: "We have encountered many women whose behavior immediately evokes in us the label bisexual, but who adamantly claim to be either homosexual or heterosexual, also women who claim to be bisexual, but whose behavior seems not to support such self-definition" (p. 155). It may be that these apparent contradictory findings can be resolved through close examination of the different methodologies that were used. It is clear, however, that the role of self-identification in the definition of sexual orientation needs to be scrutinized.

3. The details of these statistical re-analyses can be obtained by writing the author.

4. My calculations from data collected for research on homosexuality and bisexuality indicate that (a) Kinsey 3 bisexuals constitute approximately 20 percent of all bisexuals, (b) more female than male bisexuals claim to have no preference for either sex, and (c) black females are more likely than white females to claim no preference (44 percent vs. 20 percent, respectively, in the Bell and Weinberg study). Therefore, the majority of bisexuals have a preference for one sex over the other. However, these estimates must be viewed with caution since (apart from the dated work of Kinsey) no study of the distributions of the various sexual orientations in the general population has been done.

5. "Many homosexuals, like their heterosexual counterparts, believe that for most people 'one drop' of homosexual behavior makes one totally homosexual" (Blumstein and Schwartz, 1976a, p. 349).

6. The color lavender has long been associated with homosexuals, particularly lesbians.

References

Bell, A. P., and Weinberg, M. S. *Homosexualities: A study of diversity among men and women.* New York: Simon and Schuster, 1978.

Bieber, I., Dain, H. J., Dince, P. R., Drellich, M. G., Grand, H. G., Gundlach, R. H., Kremer, M. W., Rifkin, A. H., Wilbur, C. B., and Bieber, T. B. *Homosexuality: A psychoanalytic study.* New York: Basic Books, Inc., 1962.

Blumstein , P. W., and Schwartz, P. Lesbianism and bisexuality. In E. Goode and R. R. Troiden (Eds.), *Sexual deviance and sexual deviants.* New York: William Morrow and Co., 1974.

Blumstein, P. W., and Schwartz, P. Bisexuality in men. *Urban Life,* 1976, 5, 339–358. (a)

Blumstein, P. W., and Schwartz, P. Bisexual women. In J. P. Wiseman (Ed.), *The social psychology of sex.* New York: Harper and Row, 1976.(b)

Blumstein, P. W., and Schwartz, P. Bisexuality: Some social psychological issues. *The Journal of Social Issues,* 1977, 33, 30–45.

Churchill, W. *Homosexual behavior among males: A cross-cultural and cross-species investigation.* New York: Hawthorn Books, 1967.

Ellis, A. Are homosexuals really creative? *Sexology,* 1962, 29, 88–93.

Gagnon, M. H. *Human sexualities.* Glenview, Illinois: Scott, Foresman and Company, 1977.

Harry, J., and Lovely, R. Gay marriages and communities of sexual orientation. *Alternative Lifestyles,* 1979, 2, 177–200.

Kenyon, F. E. Studies in female homosexuality, VI: The exclusively homosexual group. *Acta Psychiatrica Scandinavica,* 1968, 44, 224–237.

Kinsey, A. C., Pomeroy, W. B., and Martin, C. E. *Sexual behavior in the human male.* Philadelphia: W. B. Saunders, 1948.

Kinsey, A. C., Pomeroy, W. B., Martin, C. E., and Gebhard, P. H. *Sexual behavior in the human female.* Philadelphia: W. B. Saunders, 1953.

Klein, F. *The bisexual option: A concept of one hundred percent intimacy.* New York: Arbor House, 1978.

Livingood, J M. (Ed.). *National Institute of Mental Health Task Force on Homosexuality: Final report and background papers* (DHEW Publication No. HSM 72–9116). Washington, D.C.: U.S. Government Printing Office, 1972.

Masters, W. H., and Johnson, V. E. *Homosexuality in perspective.* Boston: Little, Brown and Company, 1979.

Mead, M. Bisexuality: What's it all about? *Redbook,* January, 1975, pp. 29 and 31.

Schwartz, P. and Blumstein, P. Bisexuality: Where love speaks louder than labels. *Ms.,* November, 1976, 5, 80–81.

Warren, C. A. B. *Identity and community in the gay world.* New York: John Wiley and Sons, 1974.

Warren, C. Homosexuality and stigma. In J. Marmor (Ed.), *Homosexual behavior: A modern reappraisal.* New York: Basic Books, Inc., 1980.

Weinberg, M. S., and Williams, C. J. *Male homosexuals: Their problems and adaptations.* New York: Oxford University Press, 1974.

2

Now You Don't See It, Now You Do

4

Alternatives to Binary Sexuality: Modeling Bisexuality

Paula C. Rodríguez Rust

As pointed out in the chapters in section 1, through the mid-1980s modern research on sexuality was dominated by a dichotomous model of sexuality in which hetero-sexuality and homosexuality were considered the only authentic forms of sexual-ity. Research conducted under this model either excluded bisexuals, grouped them with homosexuals or, at best, distinguished them as "secondary homosexuals."[1] Hoping to destroy the hegemony of the dichotomous model of sexuality by insti-gating a "paradigm shift" (Coleman 1998; Firestein 1996; Kuhn 1970), beginning in the mid-twentieth century, several theorists proposed alternative models of sexu-ality that were capable of incorporating a concept of authentic bisexuality.[2] The best-known alternative model is the Kinsey scale (K-scale), a seven-point scale ranging from 0 (exclusively heterosexual) to 6 (exclusively homosexual), proposed and used by Alfred C. Kinsey and his co-researchers (Kinsey, Pomeroy, and Martin 1948; Kinsey, Pomeroy, Martin, and Gebhard 1953). As documented by critics (e.g., Hansen and Evans 1985; Paul 1985; Robinson 1976), however, the Kinsey scale is often misused by researchers who assess subjects' K-scale scores only to dichot-omize them, lumping Kinsey 1's through 5's with either heterosexuals or homo-sexuals or excluding them from analysis altogether. The scale is also used by lay people in a way contrary to Kinsey and his associates' intentions. Instead of dis-couraging the use of *homosexual* and *heterosexual* as nouns representing groups and as the bases for essentialist self-identities, the Kinsey scale has become a new basis for the self-identities of individuals who now refer to themselves as "a Kinsey 4" or "a Kinsey 6" (Cass 1990; De Cecco 1990; Kinsey, Pomeroy, and Martin 1948). Nevertheless, the work of Kinsey and his associates helped weaken the view that there is only one form of natural sexual expression, introducing the concept of normal and natural variation in sexuality as the "second paradigm shift" in modern understandings of sexuality (Coleman 1998).

Later theorists built on the Kinsey scale. For example, Alan P. Bell and Martin S. Weinberg (1978) asked their respondents to rate themselves on the Kinsey scale twice, once regarding their sexual behaviors and once regarding their sexual feelings. Similarly, Michael G. Shively, James R. Rudolph, and John P. De Cecco (1978) asked respondents to rate themselves on three scales representing physical sexual activity, close relationships, and erotic fantasies. Martin S. Weinberg, Colin J. Williams, and Douglas Pryor (1994) also used three scales, representing sexual feelings, sexual behavior, and romantic feelings. Richard E. Whalen, David C. Geary, and Frank Johnson (1990) proposed a model that includes nine dimensions, including hetero- and homosexual activities, hetero- and homosocial activities, sexual fantasies, degree of sexual arousability, and relationship stability as well as one's own and one's partner's degrees of masculinity and femininity.

Such expansions of the Kinsey scale allow behavior, feelings, and other aspects of sexuality to vary independently of one another. For example, an individual might be more sexually attracted to and fantasize more frequently about members of her or his own gender than members of the other gender but, because of cultural proscriptions against homosexual behavior, confine her or himself to heterosexual behavior and relationships. Under the dichotomous model such a person would be forced into either a homosexual or heterosexual category by discrediting either their behavioral or their emotional experience. Or, two people might have identical ratios of homosexual to heterosexual behavior but differ in the quality or overall frequency of their sexual behavior. Under the original Kinsey scale these two people would receive identical scores, as would "an exclusively homosexual drill sergeant, a full-time gynemimetic impersonator in the entertainment industry, a gay transvestophile, [and] a preoperative male-to-female transexual" (Money 1990b:56), if they all had exclusively male sex partners. However, under Bell and Weinberg's two-scale model, or Shively, Rudolph and De Cecco's or Weinberg, Williams, and Pryor's three-scale models, or Whalen, Geary, and Johnson's nine-scale model these individuals' sexualities can be more completely and accurately described and distinguished from each other. Taywaditep and Stokes (1998) have demonstrated the utility of such multidimensional descriptions of sexuality; their cluster analysis of three dimensions of sexuality produced eight "subtypes" of bisexual men whose demographic, psychosocial, and health characteristics differed in ways that could not have been predicted by any one dimension.

Fritz Klein, Barry Sepekoff, and Timothy J. Wolf (1985) expanded the Kinsey scale in a different direction by adding the dimension of time. Klein, Sepekoff, and Wolf's subjects rated themselves three times on each of seven seven-point scales. The seven scales represent sexual attraction, sexual behavior, sexual fantasies, emotional preference, social preference, self-identification, and sexual lifestyle, and the three ratings on each scale represent the subject's past, present, and "ideal" positions on the scale. This Klein Sexual Orientation Grid (KSOG) therefore recognizes not only the distinction between different dimensions of sexuality, including the fact that one's sexual self-identity bears no necessary relationship to one's actual sexual experience, but also the fact that one's sexuality can change over time.[3] Using the KSOG, an individual need not discredit or ignore her or his past sexual experiences if they differ from her or his current experiences, but can describe the variety in her or his sexual history.

The KSOG was introduced by Klein (1978) in the first edition of his classic *The Bisexual Option: A Concept of One Hundred Percent Intimacy,* modified for publication in the "Bisexualities: Theory and Research" issue of the *Journal of Homosexuality,*[4] and appeared in its final form in the revised edition of *The Bisexual Option* (1993). It is currently the most well-known modification to the original K-scale; it has been used by other researchers (e.g., Bhugra and De Silva 1998; Coleman, Bockting, and Gooren 1993; Gooren and Cohen-Kettenis 1991; Snyder, Weinrich, and Pillard 1994; Weinrich et al. 1993) and has achieved some recognition among clinical psychologists. Paula C. Rust (1996) observed that the KSOG can be a useful therapeutic tool for clients who are confused by their simultaneous attractions to both women and men because it frees them from having to decide which aspects of their sexuality to discredit to fit themselves into either a homosexual or a heterosexual category, thereby enabling them to examine their experiences and feelings honestly.

The concept of sexual continua is not universally accepted among theorists; some defend the dichotomous model of sexuality. Kenneth Z. Altshuler (1984), for example, argued that if sexuality were scalar, then perfect Kinsey 3's should exist. If such people do not exist, Altchuler argued, sexuality is dichotomous and not scalar. Reviewing twenty-five years of clinical practice and interviews with thirteen self-identified bisexuals recruited from a gay political caucus, Altshuler reported that not one patient or interviewee had convinced him that they obtained equal pleasure from men and from women, displayed a random pattern of male and female partners, and were psychologically healthy. He therefore concluded that Kinsey 3's—and therefore bisexuals—do not exist, and that those who claimed to be bisexual were doing so to save face. Similarly, Van Wyk and Geist (1984) recalculated Kinsey data and claimed that their results were not continuously distributed and therefore supported the view that heterosexuality and homosexuality are polar extremes. Richard C. Pillard and J. Michael Bailey (1995), although not rejecting the concept of a continuum altogether, implicity attributed greater authenticity to its endpoints. They reported that "survey respondents who currently label themselves 'bisexual' (or fall in the Kinsey mid-range 2–4) tend to be relatively few and to be adolescents or younger adults who move toward either end of the Kinsey continuum as they get older" (73).[5] Using individuals' tendency to move toward either end of the Kinsey scale as they grow older to characterize bisexuality as rare, the authors constructed bisexuality as an immature "phase" and implied that as individuals grow older they gravitate toward their "true" sexual orientation.

Nathaniel McConaghy (1987) and Rust (1993a, 1996d) flatly rejected the conclusion that sexuality tends toward dichotomy. McConaghy pointed out that Paul H. Van Wyk and Chrisann S. Geist's own calculations did not show a dichotomous distribution. Also commenting on Altshuler's search for perfect Kinsey 3's as evidence of the existence of bisexuality, McConaghy wrote, "The naivety of this viewpoint is astonishing. It is equivalent to arguing that for a person to like herrings and caviar equally he or she must eat equal quantities of both" (1987:419). McConaghy's stance is supported by the findings of Lee Ellis, Donald Burke, and

M. Ashley Ames (1987) who found that some individuals do occupy the middle range of the Kinsey scale, pointed out that cutting the scale to produce dichotomous categories would produce different estimates of the proportion of the population that is homosexual depending on where in the scale the cuts were made, and recommended that researchers thenceforth measure sexual orientation as a continuous, and not a dichotomous, variable. Blackford, Doty, and Pollack (1996), upon finding that self-identified bisexual women, unlike self-identified lesbian and heterosexual women, were strongly aroused by video depictions of both female-female and male-female sexual contact, argued that bisexuality is a "unique orientation." Rust (1993a, 1996d) rejected Pillard and Bailey's (1995) assumption that self-identity is more likely to reflect one's "true" sexual orientation as one grows older. In fact, the aging process might be one in which an individual increasingly interprets their experiences in terms of socially authenticated sexual categories, i.e., one of increasing social conformity rather than one in which the individual's self-identity becomes a more accurate reflection of their true sexuality. Weinrich and colleagues (1993) took a more conciliatory stance; on the basis of factor analysis of KSOG results from two very different samples of respondents they concluded that both the "lumpers"—those who want to reduce sexual classifications to as few categories as possible—and the "splitters"—those who prefer intricate classification schemes that highlight individual and group differences—have an empirical basis for their theoretical preferences.

Other objections to the concept of a Kinsey-type heterosexual-homosexual continuum were raised by theorists who, far from advocating a return to a simplistic dichotomous model of sexuality, offered more complex models of sexuality. For example, in an argument reminiscent of Sandra L. Bem's (1974) critique of unidimensional bipolar models of gender,[6] Michael G. Shively and John P. De Cecco (1977; see also Storms 1978, 1980; Whalen, Geary, and Johnson 1990) questioned the assumption implicit in unidimensional bipolar Kinsey-type scales that heterosexuality and homosexuality are opposing forms of sexuality. They argued that sexual orientation is composed of two independent continua representing degree of heterosexuality and degree of homosexuality. Similarly, Michael D. Storms (1978) distinguished "gynoeroticism" and "androeroticism." Shively and De Cecco also argued that sexual orientation has two aspects, physical preference and affectional preference, each of which consists of separate heterosexual and homosexual continua. Physical and affectional preferences can be expressed through behavior and fantasy, both of which must be taken into account in a full assessment of an individual's sexual orientation. Sexual orientation, in turn, is only one of four components of sexual identity, which also includes biological sex, gender identity, and social-sex role identity.

John C. Gonsiorek, Randall L. Sell, and James D. Weinrich (1995) went even farther; the Sell Scale of Sexual Orientation recognizes three separate dimensions: homosexuality, heterosexuality (or androphilia, gynephilia), and bisexuality. For example, the Sell Scale assesses sexual self-identity with four "I consider myself" questions; one asks for self-ratings on a seven-point unidimensional homosexual-heterosexual scale and the other three ask for self-ratings of one's degrees of, respectively, homosexuality, heterosexuality, and bisexuality. The Sell Scale also assesses frequency and strength of sexual interests and frequency of sexual contacts using both unidimensional homosexual-heterosexual scales and separate androphilic and gynephilic scales.

Gary A. Zinik (1985), whose article "Identity Conflict or Adaptive Flexibility?" is reprinted as chapter 5 in this section, also questioned the need to conceptualize heterosexuality and homosexuality as opposing forms of sexuality. Zinik proposed reconceptualizing bisexuality as a form of "adaptive flexibility" rather than a sexuality plagued by inherent contradictions. In proposing this reconceptualization of bisexuality, Zinik (1985) drew loosely on Sigmund Freud's ([1905] 1962, [1920] 1955, [1937] 1964) concept of inherent bisexuality. Freud's immediate intellectual heirs in the psychological disciplines had chosen to focus their attention on the notion of heterosexuality as the outcome of normal psychosexual development, relegating homosexuality to the world of immaturity and bisexuality to the world of the unformed or undeveloped where it served as the source of neuroses.[7] Recent theorists like Zinik (1985), however, have reclaimed Freud's more affirming concept of bisexuality as a potential inherent in all humans (see also Money 1987, 1998; Elise 1997, 1998). In Zinik's view, far from being a derivative combination of homosexuality and heterosexuality as implied by the dichotomous model of sexuality, bisexuality is the original condition from which heterosexuality and homosexuality are derivatives (see also Money 1987, 1990b; cf. Valverde 1985).

In contrast to Shively and De Cecco (1977), who conceptualized heterosexuality and homosexuality as separate continua in order to remove the implication that they are opposite forms of sexuality, Derek Evan and Antonette M. Zeiss, in a prime example of the "identity conflict" model described by Zinik (1985), separated them for the express purpose of conceptualizing them as opposing forces. Noting that previous research had shown that few people were able to "sustain a lifestyle in which regular, concurrent sexual contact with both sexes occurred" (1985:236), these authors asserted that most bisexuals display "behavioral discontinuity" because they have male and female partners serially. Taking this discontinuity as evidence of "orientation shifts," they set out to explain why bisexuals "shift" from heterosexuality to homosexuality. They hypothesized two sets of opposing factors, one set favoring a homosexual orientation and the other favoring a heterosexual orientation. Then, applying mathematical catastrophe theory, they argued that a person's choice of a male or female partner at any given point in time reflects the relative strength of these two sets of factors. At the moment one set of forces becomes stronger than the other, the individual would presumably leave their current partner to take on a partner of the other sex. Thus, although the strength of each set of factors varies continuously, their combination produces abrupt—not continuous or gradual—changes in behavior. This model, contrary to the efforts of other contemporary sexological theorists, reifies rather than deconstructs traditional notions of dichotomous sexuality and reinforces the notion of bisexuality as an unstable and inauthentic hybrid form of sexuality. This, plus the fact that it was published in a British journal, guaranteed that it would be ignored by sexological theorists in the United States.[8]

Eli Coleman (1987, 1990) offered another variation on the concept of sexuality as a set of continua that is much more in keeping with the current theoretical climate in sexology. In an effort to create a measure of sexual orientation with even greater clinical utility than the KSOG, he synthesized ideas from Klein, Sepekoff, and Wolf's KSOG, Bell and Weinberg (1978), and Shively and De Cecco (1977) with his own ideas about the structure of sexual orientation to form a nine-dimensional model. Only two of Coleman's dimensions take the form of Kinsey-type scales; current and ideal sexual self-identification are assessed using five-point scales ranging from exclusively homosexual to exclusively heterosexual, plus a sixth response category for individuals who are "unsure" of their self-identity—an option not available in the KSOG. Physical, gender, sex-role, and sexual orientation identities are all assessed via blank circles instead of scales. Subjects are asked to transform each circle into a two-area pie chart to indicate the relative proportions of male and female elements they perceive themselves as having or wish to have. This procedure retains the concept of a bipolar scale in that male and female elements are assumed to be mutually exclusive and exhaustive—and therefore opposing—categories, but the circle graphic allows subjects to treat the scale as a continuous one rather than as an ordinal scale with a predetermined number of permitted responses. Two other dimensions assess aspects of sexuality that were not included in previous scalar models: comfort with one's sexual orientation and one's current relationship status, the latter measured using an expanded version of the traditional "marital status" question.

Coleman (1987, see also 1998) pointed out that, like the essentialist dichotomous model, most alternative models of sexuality—including his own—define sexual orientation in terms of dichotomous biological sex or gender. However, in what Coleman labeled the "third paradigm shift" in modern understandings of sexuality, some contemporary theorists question the central role that biological sex and gender play in the definition of sexual orientation. After all, as Eve Kosofsky Sedgwick argued, it is "amazing" that "of the very many dimensions along which the genital activity of one person can be differentiated from that of another . . . precisely one, the gender of object choice, emerged from the turn of the century, and has remained, as *the* dimension denoted by the now ubiquitous category of 'sexual orientation'" (1990:8). Most theorists would not eliminate the reference to sex and gender but instead advocate incorporating more complex nonbinary concepts of sex and gender, more complex relationships between sex, gender, and sexuality, and/or additional nongendered dimensions into models of sexuality (cf. Hemmings 1993).

For example, Gisela T. Kaplan and Lesley J. Rogers (1984) deemed the emphasis on biological sex appropriate because biological sex is in fact an important factor in sexual attraction but argued that its importance derives from the social emphasis placed on this characteristic rather than from any intrinsic role in sexual attraction. Furthermore, because genitalia themselves are not immediately observable, they argued that other gender-related characteristics are important influences on sexual attraction because of their socially assumed, rather than their actual, relationship to biological sex. Anne Fausto-Sterling (1993) posited that there are at least five biological sexes, and, in "A Critical Examination of the Concept of Gender," chapter 6 of this section, Marilyn J. Freimuth and Gail A. Hornstein (1982) argued that gender has five distinct aspects, each of which forms a continuous dimension rather than a dichotomy. Like Kaplan and Rogers (1984), Freimuth and Hornstein (1982) argued that genitals are only one of the many gender-related characteristics that influence people's choices of romantic and sexual partners (see also Hansen and Evans 1985). Examining the historical use of the concepts of biological and psychological bisexuality, with special attention to the work of Freud, Freimuth and Hornstein outlined the implications of viewing gender as continuous and multidimensional for the conceptualization of sexual orientation or, as they referred to it because they considered it one of the five aspects of gender, gender preference.

Also addressing the question of the relationship between gender and sexual orientation, Richard C. Pillard and James D. Weinrich (1987) suggested viewing variations in sexual orientation, gender identity, and gender role as gender transpositions. Similarly, John Money (e.g., 1990b), who has also used the term *gender transposition*, considers *gender* more inclusive than *sex*, with the former being an umbrella term covering all sex difference including the sex-genital, sex-erotic, and sex-procreative components of sex difference. Judith Lorber considers gender an overarching category or social institution that "organizes almost all areas of social life" (1996:146, see also 1994), specifically including sexuality; sexuality is, therefore, "gendered." Similarly, Weinberg, Williams, and Pryor (1994) argued that individuals of all sexualities—even bisexuals—learn gender schemas and experience gendered attractions. Conversely, Whalen, Geary, and Johnson (1990), in their model, which is described earlier in this chapter, posited femininity and masculinity as dimensions of sexuality. In other words, whereas Freimuth and Hornstein (1982) perceived a complex model of gender as the basis for a definition of gender preference that is itself one of the five aspects of gender, Pillard and Weinrich perceived heterosexuality and homosexuality as forms of gender, Money subsumed sex under gender, Lorber and Weinberg, Williams, and Pryor saw sexuality as organized by gender, and Whalen, Geary, and Johnson perceived gender as an aspect of sexuality. Eli Coleman, Louis Gooren, and Michael Ross (1989) soundly criticized Pillard and Weinrich's attempt to subsume sexual orientation under the rubric of gender transposition. Perhaps anticipating Coleman, Gooren, and Ross's criticisms, Weinrich (1988), in an article titled "The Periodic Model of the Gender Transpositions: Part II," chapter 7 of this section, distinguished two types of sexual attraction. "Lusty" sexual attractions arise from imprinting experiences and are, therefore, usually associated with stimuli of a particular sex or gender, whereas "limerent" sexual attractions are less likely to be sex- or gender-specific. Limerent attractions are, therefore, more likely to be bisexual; in this usage bisexuality is defined as an attraction that might arise independent of gender.

The concept of bisexuality as a form of gender-independent sexual attraction received sophisticated and detailed treatment in the hands of Michael W. Ross and Jay P. Paul, whose article "Beyond Gender: The Basis of Sexual Attraction in Bisexual Men and Women" (1992) appears in this section as chapter 8. Based on research with bisexual men and women, Ross and Paul argued that "gender is not a critical variable in sexual attraction in bisexual individuals" (1992:1283), an idea advanced earlier by Ross (1984; see also Paul 1996).[9] Although the fact that sexual response depends on factors other than partner gender has long been recognized in other branches of sexology, for example, sexual physiology, in the study of *sexual orientation* Ross and Paul's finding poses a direct challenge to the dichotomous model in which heterosexuality and homosexuality are distinguished from each other on the basis of partner gender and bisexuality is conceptualized as either nonexistent or as a hybrid combination of these two gender-based forms of sexuality.

Ross and Paul's finding also suggests a new distinction to replace that between homosexuality and heterosexuality, i.e., the distinction between gender-specific sexuality (homosexuality and heterosexuality) and nongender-specific sexuality (bisexuality). Ross and Paul (1992) modeled this distinction as a scale representing degrees of importance of gender. Fourteen years earlier, in *The Bisexual Option* (1978), Klein drew a similar distinction between homosexuality and heterosexuality on one hand and bisexuality on the other. Klein described homosexuality and heterosexuality as sexualities characterized by limitations, and bisexuality as a sexuality reflecting a tolerance for ambiguity, a potential for "one hundred percent intimacy," and a "wholeness of behavior" (1978:14). As viewed by Ross and Paul or by Klein, bisexuality is not a hybrid combination of two gender-exclusive forms of sexuality, as suggested by the dichotomous model of sexuality, but a qualitatively different form of sexuality. The distinction between gender-specific and nongender-specific sexuality is embodied in, and essentialized by, the new concept of the "monosexual" who, unlike the "bisexual," restricts her or his sexuality to partners of only one sex or the other. The concept of monosexuality as a counterpoint to bisexuality has gained considerable currency among bisexual activists; the politics of this distinction and its relationship to the reality of bisexual experience are explored in chapters 23 and 27.[10]

Having removed the blinders of an exclusive focus on gender as a basis for sexual attraction, in their 1992 article Ross and Paul began the work of discovering which other personality and physical characteristics play a role in sexual attraction.[11] Ross and Paul's model of sexuality as a scale representing degrees of gender importance does not do justice to the theoretical sophistication of their own argument and findings. The authors argued that gender is only one of a number of characteristics that might influence or describe sexual attraction, but in the end retain a focus on gender by defining all sexual orientations in terms of their relationship to gender; heterosexuality and homosexuality are defined in terms of their emphasis of gender and bisexuality is defined in terms of its deemphasis of gender. Rust (1995b) has argued that such research might eventually lead to a model in which the importance of gender is only one of a number of such scales, each representing a characteristic discovered to influence or describe attractions.

As has been argued by several authors including Ross (1984; see also Blumstein and Schwartz 1977), bisexuals will play an important role in this research because, although characteristics other than gender influence sexual attraction among nonbisexuals as well as bisexuals, among bisexuals these other characteristics are not overshadowed by gender exclusivity and can therefore be more readily identified and studied. Of particular interest are de facto bisexuals who do not identify as bisexual because they choose instead to base their sexual self-identities on the characteristics that do matter to them. For example, some individuals who enjoy sadomasochism and identify as sadomasochists do not identify as bisexual although they have, or could have, both male and female sex partners. Their sadomasochistic self-identity—and their lack of bisexual self-identity—reflect the fact that finding a partner who is interested in sadomasochism is more important to them than finding a partner of a particular gender. As Pat Califia put it, "I identify more strongly as a sado-masochist than as a lesbian. . . . If I had a choice between being shipwrecked on a desert island with a vanilla lesbian and a hot male masochist, I'd pick the boy" ([1979] 1994:158). Whereas earlier researchers who viewed bisexuality as a hybrid combination of heterosexuality and homosexuality assumed that bisexuality could be understood through the study of heterosexuality and homosexuality, this new approach suggests conversely that the study of bisexuality—de facto or otherwise—holds the key to a deeper understanding of sexual attraction in general, including that classified as heterosexual or homosexual.[12]

De Cecco and Shively (1983/1984) took a different approach to resolving the limitations imposed by defining an individual's sexual orientation in terms of their actual or potential partners' genders. Writing nearly a decade before Ross and Paul (1992), and before the crest of the deconstructionist tidal wave, they proposed a radical shift in the focus of analysis rather than a degendering of the concept of sexual orientation. Seeking to resolve the irony implicit in defining individual sexual orientation in terms of the characteristics of others, in their oft-cited article, "From Sexual Identity to Sexual Relationships: A Contextual Shift," chapter 9 in this section, they argued that researchers should shift to a focus on the sexual relationship instead of the sexual individual as the unit of analysis. Focusing on the sexual individual implicitly treats sexual orientation as an essential characteristic of the individual that is somehow independent of the actual or potential relationships that were used to infer it; focusing on the sexual relationship itself would be not only more appropriate but also a fruitful basis for research. Research on sexual relationships of the type advocated by De Cecco and Shively has been conducted, and Letitia Anne Peplau and Susan D. Cochran (1990) provided a review of this literature including Philip Blumstein and Pepper Schwartz's (1983) classic comparison of lesbian, gay, and heterosexual relationships entitled *American Couples: Money, Work, Sex.*

The suggestion that researchers shift toward studying the sexual relationship rather than the sexual individual is only radical within the context of a sexology that has essentialized sexual orientation in the individual. Recall that the terms *homosexual* and *heterosexual* were originally defined in terms of the similarity or difference between the biological sexes or genders of partners in a relationship; i.e., the original unit of analysis for these concepts was, in fact, the relationship. The terms for these concepts were retained even as the concepts were essentialized and relocated to the sexual individual. De Cecco and Shively's recommendation constitutes a shift back to the original unit of analysis, which would restore consistency between terminology and conceptualization. An alternative route to restoring this consistency would be to replace the terminology. Some authors, for example, Louis Gooren (1990) and Milton Diamond (1998; see also 1995), use the terms *gynephile* to refer to woman-loving, i.e., to describe the condition of those who would be called male heterosexuals or female homosexuals using heterosexual/homosexual terminology, and *androphile* to refer to man-loving as practiced by male homosexuals and female heterosexuals. Recall also Storms's (1978) use of "gynoeroticism" and "androeroticism." Whereas the terms *heterosexual* and *homosexual* as nouns applied to persons confound the distinction between biological sex, gender, and sexual object choice that so many theorists—who nevertheless continue to use these terms as nouns—struggle to maintain, the terms *gynephile/gynoeroticism* and *androphile/androeroticism* succeed in reflecting these conceptual distinctions. The latter terms also suggest different bases for grouping sexual individuals for comparison to each other, i.e., instead of suggesting similarities between heterosexual men and women and between homosexual men and women, and comparisons of heterosexuals of both genders to homosexuals of both genders, they suggest that there might be similarities among all woman-lovers and among all man-lovers, and reasons to compare woman-lovers of both genders to man-lovers of both genders. Research based on this reconceptualization would produce new findings about the empirical relationship between gender status and sexuality (cf. the concept of inversion).[13]

Studying sexual relationships is a more sociological approach to sexuality than is the study of sexual individuals. More sociological still are Mary McIntosh's classic analysis (1968) of homosexuality as a social role rather than an essential condition and John Gagnon and William Simon's sexual scripting theory (Gagnon and Simon 1973; Gagnon 1990a, 1990b; Laumann, Gagnon, Michael, and Michaels 1994; Simon and Gagnon 1987). Briefly, scripting theory focuses on the sociocultural processes that "play a fundamental role in determining what we perceive to be 'sexual' and how we construct and interpret our sexual fantasies and thoughts. . . . Sexual scripts specify with whom people have sex, when and where they should have sex, what they should do sexually, and why they should do sexual things" (Laumann, Gagnon, Michael, and Michaels 1994:5–6). Different scripts exist for different people in different cultures, at different times, places, and situations, and individuals can improvise on the basis of these scripts, thereby changing the "sexual culture" of their society. By focusing attention on the scripts that guide a particular sexual encounter, scripting theory emphasizes the cultural context of the sex act rather than the sexual individuals or sexual couple engaging in the act.

Blumstein and Schwartz (1977; cf. Schwartz and Blumstein 1998) also criticized research on sexuality for its focus on the individual. Blumstein and Schwartz, however, suggested a shift in a different direction, toward a focus on the specific sexual behaviors engaged in by individuals. Research instruments that focus on behavior do exist and have been used by researchers.[14] For example, the Clarke Sexual History Questionnaire (Paitich et al. 1977), the Sexual Activity and Preference Scale (Nurius and Hudson 1988; Nurius 1983), the Sex Inventory (Thorne 1966), and the interview questionnaires used by Kinsey and his associates (Kinsey, Pomeroy, and Martin 1948; Kinsey, Pomeroy, and Martin, and Gebhard 1953), Bell and Weinberg (1978), Weinberg, Williams, and Pryor (1994), and Edward O. Laumann, John H. Gagnon, Robert T. Michael, and Stuart Michaels (1994) collect extensive and detailed information on specific sexual behaviors. Weinberg, Williams, and Pryor (1994) reported having asked each respondent a total of 541 questions, most of which concerned sexuality, and Laumann, Gagnon, Michael, and Michaels (1994) included the text of their questionnaire as an appendix; the questions pertaining to sex fill more than sixty book pages.

Many of these instruments include numerous questions pertaining to aspects of sexual behavior without reference to the sexes or genders of the individuals involved in the behavior. For example, the Clarke Sexual History Questionnaire (SHQ), developed for clinical use, is a 225-item scale that assesses, in addition to heterosexual and homosexual behavior, cross-dressing, masturbation fantasies, obscene telephone calls, voyeurism, exhibitionism, pedophilia, rape, and contact with various sexualized body parts and distinguishes between preferred and actual sexual behaviors. The Sexual Activity and Preference Scale (SAPS) is a 78-item scale with six dimensions including, in addition to heterosexual and homosexual dimensions, autosexual, anal, location, and multiple partners dimensions, each assessed once with regard to subjects' actual experiences and a second time with regard to subjects' expressed preferences. The Sex Inventory is a 200-item inventory assessing sexual interest and personality factors that D. R. Laws described as "one of the most extensively researched instruments in this area" (1984:188). The Kinsey questionaire includes questions about the number and types of respondents' sex partners as well as their genders and about specific sexual activities and statuses including masturbation techniques, petting, sexual contact with animals, nocturnal emissions, virginity, use of contraception, content of sex dreams, and sexual positions, to name a few.[15] Bell and Weinberg (1978), in addition to asking respondents to rate their feelings and behaviors on Kinsey-style scales, assessed specific sexual feelings and behaviors such as masturbation fantasies, sex dreams, cruising locales, and oral sex. They also questioned respondents about their sexual techniques, sexual problems such as lack of orgasm, degree of overtness about homosexuality, numbers of sex partners, lengths of sexual relationships, levels of sexual interest and activity, and feelings about their sexuality.

Recent epidemiological research on HIV also focuses on specific sexual behaviors rather than sexual individuals. In HIV research the unit of analysis is typically the individual, but behavioral data is usually used in its own right instead of as a vehicle for the classification of that individual's sexual orientation. The findings of this research are reviewed in chapters 11 and 22, but a couple examples here will serve to illustrate the approach. In a study of the correlation of risk behaviors with seropositivity and HIV disease progression, Heino F. L. Meyer-Bahlburg and colleagues (1991) used a modification of a SERBAS-A scale (Meyer-Bahlburg et al 1988) to assess twenty-eight different sexual practices (e.g., receptive fellatio without a condom, urinating into partner's mouth), the gender, number, and locations of respondents' sex partners and sexual acts, and the context of their sexual acts (e.g., whether sex was exchanged for money or drugs), in addition to Kinsey self-ratings. Mary Jane Rotheram-Borus et al. (1994) used a variation of the same scale designed for youth, and similar types of information were collected by David J. McKirnan, Joseph P. Stokes, Lynda Doll, and Rebecca G. Burzette (1995) on a sample of 536 bisexually active men. The focus on specific sexual behaviors rather than on individual sexual orientation is generally seen as appropriate in HIV research because it is specific behaviors, not sexual orientation, that determines risk of infection (cf. DeHart and Birkimer 1997).

Blumstein and Schwartz's (1977) opinion that focusing on specific sexual behaviors is a step forward for sexology is not universally shared; Gilbert H. Herdt (1990), an anthropologist, criticized research that emphasizes discrete sex acts for not giving proper weight to the "whole person" and the cultural context in which those acts take place. Even in recent research on HIV epidemiology the concept of the *sexual person*, or the *sexual career*, is being reintroduced, following recognition of the epidemiological importance of social constructions of the self in mediating exposure and responses to safer sex messages.

Finally, at the opposite extreme from the gross categories of the dichotomous model of sexuality are individualized models of sexuality such as Money's concept of "lovemaps" (1984, 1986) and Harry Brierley's (1984) description of sexuality as a homeostatic system. Money described a lovemap as analogous to native language, "a developmental representation or template, synchronously functional in the mind and the brain, depicting the idealized lover, the idealized love affair, and the idealized program of sexuoerotic activity with that lover, projected in imagery and ideation, or in actual performance" (Money and Lamacz 1989:43). Each individual has their own unique lovemap resulting from the interplay of congenital and environmental influences. Brierley (1984), reprinted as the last chapter of this section, suggested viewing sexuality as an integrated system in which numerous psychological and behavioral dimensions tend toward individualized homeostasis in the "well-integrated personality." The relationships between identity, behavior, and various other dimensions are, therefore, the result of systematic adaptation producing highly individualized solutions. There might be some individuals whose adaptations conform closely to our notions of the heterosexual and the homosexual, but humanity is not divided into groups of people with particular behavior patterns. Brierley offered a schematic diagram of his model and illustrated it using case studies.

Models like Money's and Brierley's provide maximum freedom in modeling sexual orientation because they permit individualized variation. By the same token, however, they have limited potential as a basis for large scale or social scientific research because they cannot be used to classify or rank subjects for purpose of comparison to each other. At best, they can be used clinically to analyze individual cases, as Money and Brierley themselves demonstrate. Whereas the hegemonic dichotomous model of sexuality is inadequate to describe human sexual diversity, individualistic models are inadequate to detect social and cultural patterns amid this diversity.

A Critical Look at the Process of Modeling and the Social Construction of Essence

As can be seen by the progression from the essentialist dichotomous model of sexuality, through scalar models of sexuality, to Money's lovemaps and Brierley's homeostatic model of sexuality, as models of sexuality become more complex, they become more useful in describing actual human sexual diversity but less useful for social research purposes. One might ask, Why don't we bypass this time-consuming process of slowly increasing theoretical complexity and diminishing social scientific utility by discovering once and for all what sexuality is really like, and then developing a model that is perfectly accurate? Such a model is impossible because the process of developing a model is a process of giving tangible form to something, such as sexuality, that is intangible. A more familiar example of an intangible thing is the economy. One cannot see or touch the economy, but economists use computerized models of the economy to understand the real economy and predict how it will behave under certain circumstances. One assesses the quality of the model not by comparing the model itself to the real economy—that cannot be done because the economy itself cannot be seen, touched, or otherwise measured—but by comparing the model's *predictions* to certain measurable *characteristics* of the real economy such as unemployment rates and stock market behavior. No model, whether it is a model of the economy or a model of sexuality, can be perfect because the process of modeling is a process of giving form to something that does not have a particular form of its own.

Two implications follow from the fact that no model is perfect. First, it follows that each model highlights certain aspects of the thing being modeled while concealing others. When I teach, I illustrate this point with a classroom desk chair. You can look at the chair from many different angles, and from each angle you can see certain aspects of the chair whereas others are hidden from you. For example, if you look at the front of the chair, you can see the color of the front of the chair but you cannot see the color of the back of the chair. You might guess that the back of the chair is the same color as the front, but you do not know what color the back is unless you look at the back. When you look at the back, you can see the color of the back, but now you cannot see the front. However, because you previously saw the front, and you have a memory, you do not have to guess the color of the front—you know its color. By looking at the chair from many different angles, learning what you can by looking at it from each angle, and then putting all that information together, you get a more complete understanding of what the chair as a whole looks like than you would have if you looked at the chair from only one angle.

Using models is like looking at a chair from different angles. Every model contains assumptions that are analogous to the guesses you must make when viewing the chair from a single angle; we are usually unaware of the assumptions we are making, and the only way to discover these assumptions and replace them with observation is to use more than one model, each of which reveals the assumptions made by the others. Therefore, when comparing models to each other, as you will do while reading the chapters in this section, the proper question to ask is not which model is correct, nor whether a given model is accurate, but what you can discover about sexuality by using each model and how you can use multiple models to gain a more complete understanding of sexuality than you would have if you had used only one model. True theoretical sophistication, therefore, is not in a model itself but in the mind of the person who complements it with other models.

Second, the fact that no model is perfect suggests that the process of modeling can be subject to critical examination. Like models themselves, the process of modeling contains assumptions. Most important, the process of modeling something such as sexuality assumes that that something exists independently of our attempt to model it, i.e., that there *is* a thing that existed before we began to study it, whose nature we are attempting to *discover* and represent via our models. This assumption—that things have an existence independent of our ability to perceive and understand them—is known as essentialism, and the independently extant thing is known as essence. For example, as discussed in chapter 1, in the dichotomous model of sexuality people are assumed to *be* homosexual or heterosexual, that is, to have a homosexual or heterosexual essence. The scientific perspective known as social constructionism questions the essentialist assumption. Social construction-ists do not necessarily maintain that there is no essence—social constructionism and essentialism, except in their extreme forms, can be compatible and compli-mentary rather than mutually exclusive or conflicting perspectives—but they question the assumption that there is essence. Social constructionists are not inter-ested in discovering essence, nor even in the question of *whether* there is essence, but rather in the ways in which others' attempts to discover essence actually give shape to, and thereby *create,* that which those others assume is essential.[16]

For example, researchers using a dichotomous model of sexuality before more complex models of sexuality were developed often assumed that there were in fact two distinct forms of sexuality, heterosexuality and homosexuality. In other words, they confused their model with the thing it was intended to represent. Today, with the benefit of the vision provided by other models of sexuality, we can see that the dichotomy is only one way of conceptualizing sexuality and that people are either heterosexual or homosexual only if we overlook considerable variation among those classified within either category as well as the distinctions between the vari-ous dimensions of sexuality such as behavior, attraction, identity, etc. Lay people and some scientists, however, continue to act as if there really are two distinct types of sexual people; for the most part, this strategy works because their belief in a di-chotomy is shared by most other people who have, as a result, conveniently classified themselves as either heterosexual or homosexual, thereby creating the very dichotomy that they believe already existed in essence. As Gagnon wrote, "Most individuals with same-gender erotic experiences actually [live] in terms of . . . social types" (1990a:191). In effect, a model becomes a self-fulfilling prophecy that creates the essence we think it is reflecting. This does not mean, of course, that we should scrap the model, only that we should remember its limitations and avoid confusing it with the thing it is intended to represent (Blumstein and Schwartz 1990). As Zvi Lothane wrote, "Words die hard; the labels will not go away. Besides, we need such descriptive adjectives as homosexual, bisexual, heterosexual . . . to refer to people who practice sex a certain way, the same way we need the adjective schizophrenic, even though there is no such essence as schizophrenia to be found anywhere, only people labeled schizophrenic" (1992:19). Similarly, even if, as J. Michael Bailey (1995) asserted, essentialists are those whom the social constructionists have labeled as such and are, therefore, the social creation of social constructionists—the label *essentialist* is useful and social constructionists would undoubtedly be the last to give up using the term as a descriptive adjective.

The distinction between essentialism and social constructionism is frequently misunderstood as being analogous to the distinction between nature and nurture. The nature vs. nurture debate involves the question of whether our sexual orientations, or any other personal characteristics, are determined by nature, that is, biology or genetics, or by nurture, i.e., the socialization process we experience because of the environment in which we grow up. The distinction between essentialism and social constructionism, on the other hand, involves the question of whether the existence of an essence—which might be the result of either nature or nurture— is to be assumed or questioned. The relationship between cultural constructs and individual outcomes is arguably mediated by socialization, but it is not the psychological learning process of socialization that is the focus of social constructionist inquiry. Another misconception about social constructionism is that the notion that sexuality is constructed is equivalent to the notion that it is chosen—in fact, we have no more control over the social constructs in our cultural inheritance than we do over our genetic inheritance, even though the effects of both are subject to our influence within narrow limits. Something that is not inborn is not necessarily chosen nor necessarily mutable; as Money (1990b) analogized, "You do not choose your native language . . . even though you are born without it" (43). Social constructionism focuses not on the ways in which a person is socialized into, or chooses, a particular sexuality but on the cultural factors that create a concept of that form of sexuality that individuals can use to describe themselves and their experiences and on the ways those individuals use social constructs to create their selves.

Social constructionists want to know not what our models reveal about sexuality but about what our modeling reveals about us. *How* do we give tangible shape to something that is intangible? What factors determine which aspects of a phenomenon we will codify in our models and which we will overlook? For example, why does the dichotomous model of sexuality classify a person's sexual orientation by the gender of their (potential) sex partner(s) instead of some other characteristic such as their partner's eye color? By what historical and cultural process did sexual orientation come to have this particular gender-based meaning in English-speaking, European-derived societies, and by what process does it come to have this meaning—or any other—for each individual in these societies? By what historical and cultural process did we come to have a concept of sexual orientation at all—or even a concept of sexuality, for that matter (e.g., Weeks 1986; Foucault 1979)?

The chapters that appear in this section are all social constructionist to the extent that they question the process by which the models they seek to replace were developed, recognize that models are social constructions, and avoid assuming that sexuality is essential—although Weinrich's concept (1988) of lust can be characterized as an acquired essence. The use of the social constructionist perspective is most explicit in Freimuth and Hornstein (1982) and De Cecco and Shively (1984). Citing Suzanne J. Kessler and Wendy McKenna (1978), Freimuth and Hornstein pointed out that even biological sex is not independent of social construction and De Cecco and Shively explicitly criticized the popular notion of sexual identity for its basis in the biological concept of genital sex. Studying the sexual relationship rather than the sexual individual, as they suggest, would avoid the assumption that individuals have sexual essences and encourage sensitivity to the social and historical contexts within which these relationships take place, i.e., to social constructive processes.

Modeling Bisexuality

What are the implications of the various models of sexuality discussed in this chapter for the conceptualization of bisexuality? Each model is capable of accounting for bisexuality, but each—with the exception of De Cecco and Shively's (1983/1984) and Brierley's (1984) models—produces a different concept of bisexuality. The Kinsey scale and modified versions of the Kinsey scale such as the KSOG produce a concept of bisexuality as a combination of varying degrees of heterosexuality and homosexuality. Zinik (1985) conceptualized bisexuality as a form of sexual flexibility, and Evan and Zeiss (1985) conceptualized bisexuality as a behavioral pattern consisting of alternating same- and other-gender sex partners. In contrast, Freimuth and Hornstein's (1982) assertion that gender is a continuous rather than a categorical characteristic produces a concept of bisexuality not as a sexuality whose object might be either male/masculine or female/feminine but as a sexuality whose object might possess varying degrees of maleness/masculinity and femaleness/femininity. Whereas Evan and Zeiss could conceive of bisexuality only where there are multiple sex partners, some male and some female, Freimuth and Hornstein could conceive of bisexuality within a single monogamous relationship involving persons who are each individually themselves both male and female. Weinrich (1988) and Ross and Paul (1992) conceptualized bisexuality as a form of gender-independent or nongender-based sexuality, in contrast to homosexuality and heterosexuality, which are forms of gender-based sexuality.

Brierley's (1984) model and De Cecco and Shively's (1983/1984) model encompass that which would be considered bisexuality under another model, but they do not produce concepts of bisexuality. One of the elements in Brierley's model is an individual's "sex object," which Brierley defined as the person or object on whom the individual's sexual arousal is centered. Brierley did not discuss the characteristics that might make this object attractive to the individual. Given, however, that one of these characteristics could be gender, the combined heterosexuality and homosexuality that constitutes Kinseyan bisexuality, Zinik's sexual flexibility, Evan and Zeiss's serial bisexual behavior, and Freimuth and Hornstein's hermaphroditic relationships are all possible within Brierley's model, but none of them would be *called* bisexuality. Given, alternatively, that one of these characteristics might not be gender, Brierley's model also accounts for Weinrich/Ross- and Paul-style bisexuality in which gender is explicitly deemphasized but, again, does not call it bisexuality. By not discussing whether gender is one of these characteristics, Brierley went even farther than Ross and Paul in deemphasizing gender as a basis for the conceptualization of sexual orientation, with the result that bisexuality per se is left undescribed by the model. De Cecco and Shively's model focuses on the sexual relationship rather than the sexual individual. Insofar as serial bisexuality such as conceived by Evan and Zeiss can be observed only by focusing on an individual's consecutive relationships and not by observing a single relationship, this kind of bisexuality is outside the scope of De Cecco and Shively's model. But, insofar as a single relationship might involve people with varying degrees of maleness/masculinity and femaleness/femininity, that relationship might be bisexual by Freimuth and Hornstein's standards. Again, however, under De Cecco and Shively's model neither this nor any other phenomenon is defined as bisexuality. Thus, both Brierley's model and De Cecco and Shively's model account for what we would otherwise call bisexuality, but neither produces a concept of bisexuality.

The fact that some models of sexuality do not produce concepts of bisexuality means that within these models, bisexuality does not exist. Recall that one criticism of the traditional dichotomous model of sexuality is that it denies the existence of bisexuality. But models like De Cecco and Shively's or Brierley's are not subject to the same criticism because the way in which bisexuality does not exist in these models is different from the way in which it does not exist in the dichotomous model. In the dichotomous model, a *concept* of bisexuality exists; bisexuality is conceptualized as a combination of (equal parts of) heterosexuality and homosexuality. But the model also implies that this form of sexuality exists in theory only; it does not, or can not, actually occur in real life because in real life there are only two distinct forms of sexuality—homosexuality and heterosexuality. A prime example of this is Altshuler (1984), who conceptualized the bisexual person as a perfect Kinsey 3 and then argued that there are no such people. Altshuler *denied* the existence of bisexuality. In contrast, in models like De Cecco and Shively's or Brierley's, sexuality itself is conceptualized in such a fundamentally different way as to render our usual concept of sexual orientation meaningless. These models do not *deny* the existence of bisexuality; instead, by not producing a concept of bisexuality they fail to *create* bisexuality. The concepts of sexuality they do produce cannot be described by the label *bisexual*—or the labels *homosexual* or *heterosexual*. In these models, therefore, bisexuality does not exist—and neither do heterosexuality and homosexuality.

The fact that some models do *not* create bisexuality highlights the fact that bisexuality exists within other models not because it is a real, or essential, phenomenon but because these other models *do* create bisexuality. Bisexuality—the concept that

forms the basis of the book you hold in your hands—is, therefore, socially constructed. Specifically, it exists as bisexuality only within models that take the individual as the focus of attention and that either emphasize or explicitly deempha-
size gender as a criterion of sexual orientation; it does not exist in models that focus
attention on sexual relationships or any other unit of analysis or in models that
truly disregard gender. By the same token, bisexuality does not exist in cultures in
which sexuality is not conceptualized as individual and gender-based. This is not
to say that people in other cultures don't engage in both heterosexual and homosexual behavior or feel attracted to both genders—nothing could be further from
the truth—but that in some other cultures these behaviors and feelings are, in a
very real sense, not "bisexual." But popular conceptions of sexuality in the United
States and in European Western culture in general are individual and gender-
based, and in these cultures heterosexuals, homosexuals, and bisexuals do exist.
The fact that they exist as a result of a process of social construction neither denies
the possibility of a bisexual essence nor makes them any less real. To maintain
otherwise is, as McConaghy (1987) put it, simply "naive," and, in an era in which a
full understanding of sexuality is of vital social, political, moral, and medical importance, dangerously so.

Having examined some of the ways in which bisexuality can be conceptualized,
I turn in the next section to the equally problematic question of how many people
are bisexual. The answer to this question, of course, depends on how bisexuality is
conceptualized.

Notes

1. Feldman and MacCulloch (1971) defined primary homosexuals as those who have
never experienced heterosexual arousal at any point in their lives, although they might have
engaged in heterosexual behavior for the sake of social appearance, and secondary homosexuals as those who have experienced heterosexual arousal and activity. Feldman (1984)
suggested that primary homosexuals and primary heterosexuals correspond closely to
Kinsey 6's and Kinsey 0's, whereas secondary homosexuals inhabit positions 1–5 and are expected to display much more sexual fluidity, vacillating within this midrange during a lifetime. Secondary homosexuals are, therefore, the equivalent of Kinseyan bisexuals.
Similarly, Burch (1993) defined "primary lesbians" as women whose self-identity and sexual object choice are both lesbian, in contrast to self-identified lesbian women who are bisexual in orientation. See also Golden (1987) and Ponse (1978).

2. Sell (1997), criticizing researchers for lack of standardization and attention to the
models of sexual orientation used in empirical work, reviewed models that are already
available and implored researchers to incorporate them into empirical research.

Theorists differ on the proper use of the term *model*. Some authors use the term *model* to
refer to etiological theories of sexuality, i.e., to theories of the factors that influence or determine an individual's sexual orientation. In chapter 10, this section, for example, Harry
Brierley wrote about the "psychodynamic model" and the "biological model." He criticized
what he referred to as "classificatory models," i.e., typologies, for not being "proper
models" because they do not "have implications for action, provide an identification of origins and dynamics and have some reliable basis for predictions" (1984:67). In direct disagreement with Brierley, Money (1990b) argued against references to etiology in the
construction of typologies. Money pointed out that etiology can be discovered only as a

result of time-consuming empirical research and asserted that it is presumptuous to attribute causality a priori by incorporating it into our classification systems.

Here I use the term *model* to refer to ways of conceptualizing sexual orientation and not to theories of its etiology or development. My definition of *model* includes, but is not limited to, typologies. I do not, however, review typological models of sexuality in chapter 4 because they are categorical and therefore do not offer ways of conceptualizing sexuality that differ fundamentally from the dichotomous model.

The distinction between primary and secondary homosexuals mentioned in the beginning of this chapter is one example of a typology. Other examples include Bell and Weinberg's classification of "homosexuals" into five categories: close-coupleds, open-coupleds, functionals, dysfunctionals, and asexuals. Weinberg, Williams, and Pryor outlined nine categories of people, five of which are types of bisexuals, based on their scores on three Kinsey-type scales: the Pure Type, Mid Type, Heterosexual-Leaning Type, Homosexual-Leaning Type, and Varied Type Bisexual, and the Pure Heterosexual Type, the Pure Homosexual Type, and the Somewhat Mixed Heterosexual and Homosexual Types. Ponse (1980) distinguished between overt, or political, and covert, or secretive, lesbians and Herdt (1990) proposed that homosexuality takes four forms cross-culturally: age-structured homosexuality, gender-reversed homosexuality, role-specialized homosexuality, and the modern gay movement. Burch presented a model combining both the classificatory and etiological elements by classifying sexual orientations in terms of their origins. She referred to "the diversity of sexual orientations," by which she meant the diversity in origins: "either lesbianism or heterosexuality may have different psychological meanings from one woman to another. Lesbianism may be an expression of love/longing for the mother or fear/rejection of the father; it may reflect discomfort with traditional gender roles, or some alliance with feminist interests. Likewise, heterosexuality may express love/longing for the father or fear/rejection of the mother; it may reflect identification with traditional gender roles, or a need to conform to social norms" (1993:85).

See Laws (1984) for a brief discussion and review of typological modeling; see chapter 23 for a brief review of typologies of bisexuals; see McWhirter, Sanders, and Reinisch (1990) for a differently organized and differently motivated review of perspectives on sexuality than that given in this chapter; and see Ellis (1996a) for a brief interdisciplinary review of the major etiological "theories of homosexuality."

3. For research findings that sexual expression and self-identity change over time, see chapters 17 and 23. Herdt (1990) discussed discontinuities in sexuality over the life course from a cross-cultural perspective.

4. This entire issue of the *Journal of Homosexuality* was reprinted as *Two Lives to Lead: Bisexuality in Men and Women*, edited by Fritz Klein and Timothy J. Wolf. The article in this issue is the above-cited 1985 article by Klein, Sepekoff, and Wolf. The KSOG is also described in Klein (1990).

5. This statement itself is without direct citation, but in the next sentence Pillard and Bailey cited Diamond (1993) and agreed with his conclusion, based on a review of empirical literature, that "exclusive or predominantly exclusive homosexual activities are more common than bisexual activities" (1995:73). The source of Pillard and Bailey's claim that bisexual *identity* is rare could be their own research. In a study of the familiality of sexual orientation, Pillard reported that efforts on the part of a graduate student to redress the absence of bisexuals aged over twenty-five in the sample were unsuccessful because "most of the self-identified bisexual men he found were in their late adolescence . . . or had a single woman sexual partner but serial male partners with predominately homoerotic fantasies or identified themselves as "in transition" from heterosexuality to homosexuality. Also of interest is the fact that many of these subjects who were self-identified as bisexuals were rated by us as Kinsey 5s and even Kinsey 6s" (1990:92).

6. See also Reinisch (1976); Reinisch and Sanders (1987); and Spence, Helmreich, and Stapp (1974) for discussion of femininity and masculinity as orthogonal dimensions, and

Pillard and Weinrich (1987); Whalen (1974); and Whalen, Geary, and Johnson (1990) for characterization of "feminization-defeminization" and "masculinization-demasculinization" as distinct dimensions for the description of prenatal and postnatal biological sexual differentiation.

7. Discussions of the historical use of the concept of bisexuality by sexologists and psychoanalysts, including Freud, can be found in Burch (1993; see also 1997); Butler (1990); Deb (1979); Friedman (1986); Karlen (1971); Money (1990a, 1998); Murphy (1983/1984); Paul (1983/1984); and Wolff (1971). Money (1990a, 1998), for example, discussed the concepts of the "primordial hermaphrodite" and "sexual bipotentiality," including usage of the former as an explanation for the latter, e.g., by Freud and Ulrichs. Karlen (1971) reviewed and discussed Freudian thought in several chapters of *Sex and Homosexuality,* including a critique of the concept of bisexual potential as arising from physical hermaphrodism and explaining manifest bisexuality and homosexuality (397). Murphy (1983/1984) analyzed and critiqued Freud's use of the concept of bisexuality. Friedman (1986) critically discussed psychoanalytic views of male homosexuality as they began with Freud and developed in subsequent years, and Burch (1997) critically discussed and reworked psychoanalytic theory pertaining to lesbianism and female bisexuality. Deb (1979) provided a wholly uncritical look at the psychoanalytic use of the concept of bisexuality as an explanation for neuroses; drawing directly on Freud, Deb argued that "it is palpably obvious that the repression and the formation of neurosis is originated out of the conflict between masculine and feminine tendencies, that is out of bisexuality" (53) and that "anorexia, difficulty in breathing, certain paralytic limb malfunctioning have got roots in settlement difficulties of bisexual tendencies" (56).

In brief, Freud and Ulrichs argued that humans are originally hermaphroditic, therefore containing within them both male and female sexual impulses (see also Wolff 1971, whose ideas are briefly described in note 1 in chapter 20). The male impulse is directed toward female sexual objects, and the female impulse toward male sexual objects, such that all humans are therefore potentially bisexual in orientation. Either the male impulse or the female impulse or both might be expressed by a given individual. Actual heterosexuality, bisexuality, and homosexuality are, therefore, all explained by hermaphroditic physiology. Note that this explanation is based on an assumption of heterosexuality; homosexuality, for example, is explained by positing a male sexual impulse within a woman or a female sexual impulse within a man, such that the sexual impulse itself is always heterosexual. This argument, in effect, apparently explains homosexuality, bisexuality, and heterosexuality, while in fact doing little more than shifting "bisexuality" from the realm of sexual behavior to the realm of physiology and leaving heterosexuality unquestioned. Butler characterized Freud's concept of bisexuality as *"the coincidence of two heterosexual desires within a single psyche"* (1990:61).

8. Evan and Zeiss (1985) has been cited only once in an academic journal, according to a search of the periodical literature via a social sciences citation database, and that citation (Guastello 1987) occurred in a review article on a topic other than sexuality.

9. The concept of a sexuality not based on gender is not new. However, its earlier incarnations carry connotations so different from those carried by Ross and Paul's concept of bisexuality as to render the similarity virtually undetectable. For example, the concept of fetishism is usually defined *without reference* to gender and invokes the specter of mental illness, as in, "Fetishism may be defined as a form of behaviour wherein sexual activity or sexual fantasy focuses to an unusual extent upon a body part or an inanimate object rather than on a person as a whole. The question as to when such behaviour should be regarded as pathological has occupied classical writers on the subject" (Gosselin and Wilson 1984). Herdt offered a definition with reference to gender that makes the genderlessness of fetishism recognizable: "Specific forms of anatomy, adornments, and behavioral acts may thus become stimulating and attractive *regardless of the sex of the object*" (Herdt 1984:58). Other paraphiliac sexual diagnoses, such as voyeurism, are also typically defined in the Diagnostic and Statistical Manual of Mental Disorders (DSM-IV, American Psychiatric

Association 1994) without reference to the gender of the sexual object. In other words, non-gendered forms of sexuality in which other characteristics of the sexual object, e.g., age, dress, or species, take precedence over gender have typically been cast as pathological; Ross and Paul's contribution is not so much the concept of nongendered sexuality as it is the concept of nonpathological nongendered sexuality. Taken to an extreme, this process might end in the reconceptualization of heterosexuality and homosexuality as forms of gender fetishism.

10. Kauth and Kalichman (1995) incorporated both the heterosexual-homosexual and the bisexual-monosexual distinctions into their model, which consists of a circle with the North, East, South, and West poles representing mono- , homo- , bi- , and heterosexuality, respectively.

Evans (1993) cited Gagnon (1977) for a different use of the term *monosexual*: "Indeed, the only 'bisexual' script seriously considered by him is one that is literally not bisexual at all, being the rationalizations of those who have sex with both men and women regardless of any specific gender or sexual interests in either. . . . To this type Gagnon gives the label 'monosexual' bisexual" (1993:158). Note that Evans constructed this type as "not bisexual."

11. Califia (1983) also noted that, for some people, gender might be less important than other characteristics of the sex partner or situation, and lists some of these characteristics, including age, race, socioeconomic background, group sex, or particular sexual techniques.

The fact that many factors affect sexual attractions, including external circumstances (social situation, setting) and state of mind as well as characteristics of the potential sexual partner including but not limited to gender, is also recognized by researchers in the field of sexual physiology (e.g., Rowland 1995).

12. For a different reason Herdt (1990) also suggested that research on bisexuals holds the key to a deeper understanding of sexuality. Interested in expectations regarding changes in sexual practice over the life course in varying cultures, Herdt asserted that "we would do well . . . to study the 'bisexuals' more, for they, in their sense of themselves and their sexual practice, may more closely approximate developmental continuity through the life cycle. If this is true—and if it is experienced consciously as such in the fact of differential social pressures and stigma that should have forced them to 'make a choice' on either side—we are presented with a great opportunity to understand the biopsychological and cultural factors that constrain developmental continuity and discontinuity in human sexuality" (1990:224).

13. The concept of homosexuality as gender or sex *inversion* also leads to a search for similarities among woman-lovers and among man-lovers, and to comparisons between woman-lovers and man-lovers of both genders. However, the concept of inversion differs from the conceptualizations of sexuality underlying the terms *gynephile* and *androphile*. Under the concept of inversion, traditionally gendered heterosexual individuals are constructed as the norm, and then lesbians and gay men are likened to, respectively, "men" and "women." Under the concepts of gynephile and androphile, gender and sexual orientation are distinct such that lesbians and heterosexual men—and gay men and heterosexual women—are likened *to each other*, with neither honored as the prototype of the *gender* categories man and woman.

14. For a more complete review of methods of assessing sexual diversity, including types of assessment not reviewed here such as projective methods, see Laws (1984). Among the sex inventories, questionnaires, and rating scales reviewed by Laws are the Sex Knowledge and Attitude Test (SKAT), the Sexual Orientation Method (SOM; Feldman et al. 1966), Harbison et al.'s variation on the SOM (1974), and Bentler's Guttman-type scale for assessing changes in behavior (1968). Laws joined Blumstein and Schwartz (1977) in stressing the importance of assessing specific sexual behaviors.

15. As Laws (1984) noted, the original Kinsey volumes (1948, 1953) do not contain great detail about the methodology used in the Kinsey research. Later, Pomeroy (1972; Pomeroy, Flax, and Wheeler 1982) published details of the interview procedure.

16. For other brief and accessible explanations of the distinction between essentialism and social constructionism, of the distinction between weak and strong constructionism, and of the history of social constructionist thought, written by authors with differing theoretical preferences themselves, see Bailey (1995); Blumstein and Schwartz (1990); Hart and Richardson (1981); Kitzinger (1995); Koertge (1990); LeVay (1996); Plummer (1981b, 1984); Suppe (1984); and Weeks (1981a, 1985, 1986).

5

Identity Conflict or Adaptive Flexibility? Bisexuality Reconsidered

Gary Zinik

The Bisexual Debate

Both clinicians and sex researchers have engaged in a long-standing controversy over bisexuality. Emerging from this debate are two theories explaining the nature of bisexuality. I have called them the "conflict model" and the "flexibility model." The conflict model views bisexuality as inherently characterized by conflict, confusion, ambivalence, and the inability to decide one's sexual preference. The alternative view is the flexibility model. This view explains bisexuality as characterized by cognitive and interpersonal flexibility and, for some people, the desire for personal growth and fulfillment. The conflict model portrays bisexuals as anxious "fence-sitters," while the flexibility model describes bisexuals as experiencing the "best of both worlds."

The Conflict Model of Bisexuality

Underlying the conflict model of bisexuality is the notion that sexual orientation is a dichotomy: One is either heterosexual or homosexual. This dichotomous notion derives from the following logic. Since men and women are viewed as opposite sexes, it appears contradictory that anyone could eroticize two opposite things at the same time. Attraction to one sex would logically rule out attraction to the other, or else lead to psychological dissonance and conflict. It follows that people claiming to be bisexual are: (1) experiencing identity conflict or confusion; (2) living in an inherently temporary or transitional stage which masks the person's true underlying sexual orientation (presumably homosexual); and (3) employing the label as a method of either consciously denying or unconsciously defending against one's true homosexual preference.

In 1956, Edmund Bergler denounced bisexuality with surprising vehemence. He declared that bisexuality is an "out-and-out fraud," but conceded that male homosexuals can occasionally have "lustless mechanical sex" with women. Ruitenbeek (1973) wrote that the "mask of bisexuality" may even be "dangerous" since it prevents people from coming to terms with their own sexuality. When questioned about bisexuality, Irving Bieber (1971) stated, "A man is homosexual if his behavior is homosexual. Self-identity is not relevant" (p. 63). Some authorities admit that bisexuals exist but have weak heterosexual potency. Stern (1961) reported that people claiming to be bisexual are highly disturbed individuals with identity problems and conflicts coupled with guilt feelings. Cory and Leroy (1963) described bisexuals as "overgrown adolescents" who are confused, lack a sense of group identity, and "whose inability to differentiate one form of sexuality from another has never developed" (p. 89).

The conflict model of bisexuality is based on general assumptions about human sexuality that deserve examination. First is the notion that homosexual interests eradicate heterosexual responsiveness. Since one would cancel out the other, they cannot exist side-by-side without creating irreconcilable conflict. As mentioned earlier, this follows from the notion (based on principles of formal logic) that men and women represent opposite sexual poles; eroticizing one sex precludes eroticizing the other. Once homosexual behavior begins, subsequent heterosexual behavior is seen as hiding or denying one's homosexuality. Indeed, even heterosexual relations prior to the initial homosexual behavior are retrospectively rendered invalid by some as early instances of denial.

The second assumption underlying the conflict model is the "one drop" notion of homosexuality which states that since homosexuality is not something one would choose voluntarily in this culture in light of the social costs involved, the slightest evidence of it must indicate a deep, predispositional feature of the individual. Thus "one drop" of homosexual behavior (i.e., even one contact) is taken as evidence of an underlying homosexual orientation.

In the field of sex research, many psychological and sociological studies group bisexuals together with homosexuals; rarely are differences between the two examined (MacDonald, 1983). The common practice for sex researchers is to define people as homosexual who have had, according to the Kinsey scale (1948), "more than incidental homosexual experience" regardless of the amount of heterosexual experience.

Bisexuality is also viewed with skepticism and suspicion by the general public. This is the case in both the heterosexual and homosexual communities (Blumstein and Schwartz, 1974, 1976a, 1976b; Klein, 1978; *Playboy*, 1983; Tripp, 1975). In fact, skepticism by both heterosexuals and homosexuals is congruent with the conflict model of bisexuality; members of both groups may view claims to bisexuality as a failure to adjust to a homosexual orientation.

From the point of view of conventional heterosexual society, bisexuality may be considered the same as homosexuality (MacDonald, 1983; Money, 1980).

Homosexuality continues to be stigmatized, and bisexuality considered just as "bad" ("Gay America," 1983). Indeed, bisexuality may even appear more threatening than homosexuality since it disrupts the conventional belief that people can be classified into two distinct sexual groups.

From the viewpoint of gay subculture, bisexuality is sometimes seen as an attempt to have one's cake and eat it too. Some gay activists view bisexuality as an act of political betrayal. Bisexuals are seen as enjoying the privileges of heterosexual society while at the same time avoiding the stigma of homosexuality. The same is also true in the lesbian subculture.

Thus, members of both straight and gay communities often disbelieve the individual's assertions of bisexuality and attribute such claims to the inability to come to grips with a homosexual label. For this reason, a self-identified bisexual may be required to possess ample heterosexual "credentials" before a homosexual label can be avoided. Moreover, bisexuals can find themselves in a "double closet"; they hide their heterosexual activities from their homosexual peers while at the same time hiding their homosexual activities from their heterosexual peers. Bisexuals thus make an effort to appear either homosexual or heterosexual, depending on the social context, to avoid embarrassment or ostracism.

The Flexibility Model of Bisexuality

There is growing academic and clinical support for the validity of a bisexual orientation and lifestyle. The flexibility model portrays the bisexual as somewhat of a chameleon, capable of moving easily between the heterosexual and homosexual worlds. Bisexuality is characterized as the coexistence of heteroerotic and homoerotic feelings and behaviors, and an integration of homosexual and heterosexual identities. Both homosexual and heterosexual attractions and sexual experiences are considered genuine. Such dual experience may require a form of perceptual/cognitive flexibility which allows one to "see" seemingly opposite sexual objects as erotic and arousing. Qualities such as androgyny (sex-role flexibility) and interpersonal flexibility would aid such individuals in conducting sexually and emotionally intimate relationships in a comfortable manner (Klein, 1978).

The flexibility model has important conceptual differences from the conflict model. Rather than considering homosexual and heterosexual responses as mutually exclusive, the flexibility model posits that these two can coexist in the form of bisexual eroticism (Kinsey, Pomeroy, and Martin, 1948; Saliba, 1982; Zinik, 1983). In one sense, this is possible if males and females are no longer regarded as "opposite" sexes, hence resolving the apparent logical contradiction that one cannot eroticize two opposite sexual objects at the same time. If men and women are not considered opposites but, as it were, "variations on a theme," then sexual attraction to one sex would not necessarily preclude sexual attraction to the other. Indeed, many self-identified bisexuals report that they are attracted to qualities of particular people rather than aspects of gender per se (Bode, 1976; Coons, 1972; MacInnes, 1973; Zinik, 1983).

Unlike the conflict model, which is characterized by "either/or" thinking (one must be either heterosexual or homosexual), the flexibility model is characterized by "both/and" thinking: one can be both heterosexual and homosexual—that is, bisexual. The rationale behind the flexibility model makes it possible for homosexual and heterosexual interests to exist side-by-side without producing conflict.

The flexibility model does not, however, imply that bisexuality never produces ambivalence. Psychological confusion may accompany bisexuality, but not inevitably. Rather, the model posits that some individuals can maintain a psychologically harmonious bisexual orientation. This is in contrast to the conflict model, which views bisexuality as inherently problematic, as always characterized by confusion and conflict. Claims to bisexuality likewise do not necessarily signify a failure to adjust to an exclusive homosexual preference, though this may be true in some cases. Rather, it is possible to conceptualize bisexuality as the successful adjustment to a dual homosexual and heterosexual preference.

Sigmund Freud believed that all human beings possess bisexual potential at birth (Freud, 1953; Stoller, 1972). Steckel (1922), one of Freud's early followers, extended the bisexual period beyond the Oedipal phase of early childhood, claiming that "normal persons show a distinct bisexual period up to the age of puberty" (p. 39).

Money and Tucker (1975) also stated that all humans are born with bisexual potential, and that it is fallacious to dichotomize individuals as "pure" homosexuals or heterosexuals. During his joint research with Tucker, Money stated:

> In reality people are infinitely varied along the spectrum in between, all capable of bisexual behavior. In fact, it is safe to say that every adult human being has, in fantasy, engaged in some form of bisexual behavior, if not physical contact, to some degree at some time in his or her life. "Ambisexual" describes the human race more accurately than "heterosexual," "homosexual," or even "bisexual," although the degree of ambisexuality varies in intensity from one person to the next. (p. 16)

Klein (1978) observed that bisexuality is a relatively new term in our vocabulary, and not until recently did people even have the option of thinking of it as a way of life. Childs (1976), reporting the platform statement on women's sexuality of the Association for Women in Psychology, listed four sexual options: celibacy, lesbianism, heterosexuality, and bisexuality. Earlier, Coons (1972) and Kelly (1974), both staff clinicians at university counseling centers, had discussed the emergence of bisexuality among the youth culture as an "alternative adaptation."

Churchill (1967) described how bisexuality is discouraged by western society even more than exclusive homosexuality due to the conventional trend to dichotomize people into two sexual groups. Money and Tucker (1975) speculated that bisexuality would be much more common if encouraged, as it was in ancient Greece, by role models and cultural stereotypes.

However, society's attitude toward bisexuality appears to be changing in the 1980s. Gossip columns in newspapers, magazines, and other pop culture media leave the occasional impression that it is fashionable to be bisexual among those who live in the fast lane. More than a few celebrities and jet-setters have come out of the closet to declare their bisexuality, including singers Janis Joplin, Joan Baez, and Mick Jagger, writer Dorothy Thompson, tennis star Billy Jean King, and feminist Kate Millet (see "Bisexual Chic," 1974; Brody, 1974; Carroll, 1974; Knox, 1974; "The New Bisexuals," 1974).

Summary of the Models

It should be emphasized that the foregoing discussion of the flexibility model is not meant to imply that bisexuality is somehow superior or more highly evolved than heterosexuality or homosexuality. Neither are heterosexuals or homosexuals perceived to be less generally flexible than bisexuals. While psychological and interpersonal flexibility are considered desirable traits in this culture, obviously it is not necessary to be bisexual to attain these qualities. On the other hand, to be bisexual as here defined (eroticizing and having sex with both genders and self-identifying as bisexual) may require a reasonable degree of psychological or interpersonal flexibility, as hypothesized by the model.

The terms "conflict model" and "flexibility model" were chosen because they encapsulate the opposing views on the issues of choice and decision-making: the conflict model explains bisexuality as characterized by indecision and the inability to choose a sexual/gender preference; the flexibility model characterizes bisexuality as the conscious decision to adopt a dual orientation, as a free choice.

REFERENCES

Bergler, E. (1956). *Homosexuality: Disease or way of life?* New York: Hill and Wang.

Bieber. I. (1971, April). Playboy Panel: Homosexuality. *Playboy Magazine*, pp. 63–67.

Bisexual chic: Anyone goes. (1974, May 27). *Time Magazine*, p. 90.

Blumstein, P. W., and Schwartz, P. (1974). Lesbianism and bisexuality. In E. Goode and R. R. Troiden (Eds.), *Sexual divorce* [*sic*] *and sexual deviants* (pp. 278–295). New York: William Morrow.

Blumstein, P. W., and Schwartz, P. (1976a). Bisexuality in men. *Urban Life*, 5, 339–358.

Blumstein, P. W., and Schwartz, P. (1976b). Bisexuality in women. *Archives of Sexual Behavior*, 5, 171–181.

Bode, J. (1976). *View from another closet: Exploring bisexuality in women*. New York: Hawthorn.

Brody, J. (1974, March 24). Bisexual life-style appears to be spreading and not necessarily among swingers. *New York Times*, p. 37.

Carroll, J. (1974, February). Bisexual chic. *Oui Magazine*, pp. 115–120.

Childs, E. K. (1976). Women's sexuality: A feminist view. In S. Cox (Ed.), *Female psychology: The emerging self*. Chicago: Science Research Associates.

Churchill, W. (1967). *Homosexual behavior among males: A cross-cultural and cross-species investigation*. New York : Hawthorn Books.

Coons, F. W. (1972). Ambisexuality as an alternative adaptation. *Journal of the American College Health Association*, 21, 142–144.

Cory, D. W., and Le Roy, J. P. (1963). *The homosexual and his society*. New York: Citadel Press.

Freud, S. (1953). Three essays on the theory of sexuality. In J. Strachey (Ed. and Trans.) *The standard edition of the complete psychological works of Sigmund Freud* (Vol. 7, pp. 125–245). London: Hogarth Press. (Original work published 1901)

Gay America. (1983, August 8). *Newsweek Magazine*, pp. 30–36.

Kelly, G. F. (1974). Bisexuality and the youth culture. *Homosexuality Counseling Journal*, 1(2), 16–25.

Kinsey, A. C., Pomeroy, W. B., and Martin, C. E. (1948). *Sexual behavior in the human male*. Philadelphia: W. H. Saunders.

Klein, F. (1978). *The bisexual option*. New York: Arbor House.

Knox, L. (1974, July). The bisexual phenomena. *Viva Magazine*, pp. 42–45, 88, 94.

MacDonald, A. P. (1983). A little bit of lavender goes a long way: A critique of research on sexual orientation. *Journal of Sex Research*, 19, 94–100.

MacInnes, C. (1973). *Loving them both: A study of bisexuality and bisexuals*. London: Martin, Brian and O'Keefe.

Money, J. (1980). *Love and love sickness: The science of sex, gender differentiation and pairbonding*. Baltimore: Johns Hopkins Press.

Money, J., and Tucker, P. (1975). *Sexual signatures: On being a man or a woman*. Boston: Little, Brown.

The new bisexuals. (1974, May 13). *Time Magazine*, p. 79.

Playboy readers sex survey. (1983, May). *Playboy Magazine*, pp. 126–128, 136 , 210–220.

Ruitenbeek, H. M. (Ed.). (1973). *Homosexuality: A changing picture*. London: Souvenir.

Saliba, P. (1982). Research project on sexual orientation. *The Bi-monthly Newsletter of the Bisexual Center of San Francisco*, 6(5), pp. 3–6.

Stekel, W. (1922). *Bisexual love*. New York: Emerson Books.

Stern, J. (1961). *The Sixth Man*. New York: Doubleday.

Stoller, R. J. (1972). The "bedrock" of masculinity and femininity: Bisexuality. *Archives of General Psychiatry*, 26, 207–212.

Tripp, C. A. (1975). *The homosexual matrix*. New York: McGraw-Hill.

Zinik, G. (1983). The relationship between sexual orientation and eroticism, cognitive flexibility, and negative affect. Unpublished doctoral dissertation, University of California, Santa Barbara, CA.

6

A Critical Examination of the Concept of Gender

Marilyn J. Freimuth and Gail A. Hornstein

THE relationship between an individual's gender and his/her personality and behavioral repertoire has interested psychologists for a long time. Judging by the number of recent studies in areas such as sex differences, gender identity, and sex role, interest in these topics seems to be increasing. However, a number of important conceptual problems, central to all of this research, have not been addressed by most investigators. Until these issues are clarified and resolved, it will be difficult to make sense of the empirical findings or, more generally, to have a clear idea of what is being studied in gender-related research.

The central problem has to do with the definition and conceptualization of gender. Traditionally, gender has been conceptualized at the psychological level in terms of two dichotomous categories (masculine/feminine). This conceptualization derives from two assumptions: (a) There are clear differences between males and females on the biological level, and (b) these differences are paralleled by similar differences on the psychological level. Thus, the traditional assumption has been that just as individuals are biologically either male or female, psychologically, they are either masculine or feminine.

Several writers (e.g., Bem, 1974, 1976; Constantinople, 1973; Jung, 1953; Money and Ehrhardt, 1972; Spence and Helmreich, 1978) have already pointed out that one major problem with defining gender in terms of dichotomous categories is that such a view rules out the possibility that some individuals manifest a combination of both masculine and feminine characteristics. The work of Money and Ehrhardt (1972) on hermaphroditism has demonstrated that such "intermediate cases" exist on the biological level; and work by Bem (1974, 1976) and Spence and Helmreich (1978) on androgyny has shown that combinatory cases also exist on the psychological level. These writers have suggested, at least implicitly, that to take these findings into account, the concept of gender should be reformulated to include a third category to cover combinations. This would mean that most individuals would still be categorized as masculine or feminine, but a relatively small number of individuals would be described as being androgynous or hermaphroditic.

While this kind of reformulation is clearly a step in the right direction, it does not begin to address most of the problems inherent in the traditional conceptualization of gender. For example, in suggesting that we add a third category (androgynous) to the two we already have (masculine and feminine), writers such as Bem and Spence have failed to consider a more basic question, namely, whether specifying gender in terms of discrete categories makes sense in the first place. If, as we shall argue, individuals always manifest some combination of masculine and feminine characteristics, adding a third category to cover obviously androgynous cases only serves to obscure the fact that what we really need to do is reformulate the whole concept of gender in a fundamental way.

The necessity for a fundamental reformulation becomes even more apparent when we look at the way gender terms are typically employed. Different criteria (some biological, some psychological) are used to determine whether an individual is masculine or feminine. For example, an individual may be labeled feminine because she has a vagina and a uterus, because she likes to play with dolls, or because she is dependent in her relations with others. Unfortunately, these criteria are rarely made explicit and, even when they are, there is no general agreement about which criteria are most appropriate. Given this ambiguity, it is not surprising that difficulties arise in trying to make sense of empirical findings in the area of gender research—the conceptual categories themselves are unclear.

One preliminary step toward trying to clarify this issue has been to distinguish sex from gender (Unger, 1979; Vaughter, 1976). In this view, "sex" refers to biological factors such as genes, hormones, and anatomical/reproductive structures which are assumed to clearly differentiate between the two dichotomous categories of "male" and "female." In contrast, "gender" is used to refer to psychological characteristics which are socially construed as "masculine" and "feminine" and which are nondichotomous (i.e., individuals typically manifest a combination of both).

While distinguishing between "sex" and "gender" clarifies some issues, important problems remain. First, such a distinction obscures the fact that our *perceptions* of biological characteristics, and not merely the characteristics themselves, are important. Such perceptions need to be included as part of the psychological concept of gender. Second, the "male/female" dichotomy assumed at the biological level does not always hold (e.g., both "males" and "females" have androgens as well as estrogens; some individuals have both testes and a vagina). Finally, this view assumes "sex" to be a given which is independent of social construction. Kessler and McKenna (1978) have provided a detailed critique of this assumption, and we will not review all the complexities of this issue here. Their analysis describes clearly how, having socially constructed the categories of "male" and "female," we implicitly deny that such categories are constructions and take them to be givens in the "natural world."

Our goal in writing this article is to begin to address some of the problems inherent in existing conceptions of gender. We will try to show that (a) if the term gender is taken to refer to a set of biological and psychological variables which are related to one another in a complex way, and (b) if gender differences are treated as differences in degree and not in kind, then the concept of gender can be used in a meaningful way to make sense of the things we observe about people.

We want to stress that in arguing against a dichotomous conceptualization of gender, we are not trying to dispute the fact that most people, including gender researchers, believe that there are two groups, "males" and "females," who can be clearly and dichotomously distinguished from one another. If we look carefully at the basis for this belief, we find that it rests on the assumed dichotomy between "male" and "female" genitals and reproductive structures. Now, as Kessler and McKenna (1978) point out, we are not usually in a position to know the genital/reproductive structure of people we meet, so what we actually do is "attribute" a certain set of genitals to a person on the basis of the masculinity/femininity of his/her appearance, behavior, personality characteristics, etc. In the discussion which follows, we are not trying to claim that there are no "males" and "females," if what is meant by these terms is people with genital/reproductive structures of one type versus those with another type. What we will try to show is that gender includes a great deal more than genital or reproductive structure, and that once we include the variety of other variables which are part of gender (including aspects of physical appearance which are not dichotomous), we no longer have two conceptually distinct categories of "male" and "female."

To maintain consistency throughout our discussion, we have used the terms "male" or "men" and "female" or "women" *only* in those instances where we want to distinguish between people with genital/reproductive structures of one type versus those with an other type (i.e., we have used the terms "male" and "female" in the way that most people really mean them). In most of our discussion, we use the terms "masculine" and "feminine," because we want to stress that if gender is taken to include a variety of physical and psychological characteristics, many of which are *not* dichotomous, these terms are more appropriate. Throughout the article, we are focusing on the concept of gender itself, rather than on the ways in which people typically think about gender. We hope that by clarifying this concept on a theoretical level, we can begin to move toward more productive ways of thinking about gender in our everyday lives.

The view of gender we propose differs in certain important ways from the views of most current writers; however, there are historical precedents for the approach we take. Freud's work on bisexuality (Freud, 1905/1953, 1954, 1920/1955, 1923/1961a, 1925/1959, 1925/1961b, 1930/1961c, 1931/1961d; 1932/1964a, 1937/1964b), provides one such precedent. We have, therefore, chosen to begin our discussion by reviewing his work in this area, because it seems to us that in proposing that all individuals are bisexual to some degree, Freud was suggesting an alternative to the view that gender be conceptualized in terms of dichotomous categories. Further, by arguing that there are both biological and psychological aspects to bisexuality and that these various aspects interact with each other in a complex way, Freud was providing us with the kind of conceptual model we need to think about gender more generally. For these reasons, Freud's work serves to provide both an historical context and a logical introduction to the ideas we want to develop in the rest of this article.

Freud's Concept of Bisexuality

Bisexuality was originally a biological concept that was widely used by nineteenth-century embryologists in describing the initial state of the embryo prior to full sexual differentiation. Freud's contribution to this viewpoint was to recognize that a state of early biological bisexuality might have consequences for later biological and psychological functioning. As we will indicate, Freud relied on existing medical evidence as well as his own clinical observations in formulating his claims about both psychological and biological bisexuality.

Although Freud came to view bisexuality as a factor of fundamental importance, he never clarified the exact conceptual status of this notion, and he talked about it in a number of different ways. This scattered treatment, combined with the skepticism which now surrounds many of Freud's biologically based concepts, probably account for the fact that many feminists (e.g., Frieze, Parsons, Johnson, Ruble, and Zellman, 1978) and most contemporary analytic theorists (e.g., Rado, 1940; Stoller, 1972, 1974) have either criticized the concept of bisexuality or tended to ignore it. In our review of the concept, we will try to clarify the differences between Freud's various usages, in addition to pointing out certain relationships which exist among them.

BIOLOGICAL BISEXUALITY

Freud's first discussions of bisexuality focused on the structure of the reproductive organs (Freud, 1905/1953, 1920/1955, 1932/1964a). Having read a number of medical studies in which the original state of fetal internal reproductive organs was described as hermaphroditic (i.e., as having both male and female characteristics), Freud concluded that the commonsense view of genital structure as dichotomous (i.e., as either male or female) was incorrect. In contrast, he argued that genital structure is always bisexual to some extent because in every normal adult, "traces are found of the apparatus of the opposite sex. These either persist without function as rudimentary organs or become modified and take on other functions" (1905/1953, p. 141).

By making the point that each individual is anatomically bisexual to some extent, Freud cast hermaphroditism in a new light. Hermaphroditism no longer seemed to represent an unusual melding of two separate sets of reproductive organs; rather, it exemplified the manifest form of the natural bisexual state which is characteristic of all individuals. By conceptualizing hermaphroditism in this way, Freud was arguing that, as in the case of neuroses, an abnormal instance is merely an exaggeration of a normal instance, differing only in degree, not in kind.

Thus, Freud was suggesting that no individual has a genital structure that represents a "pure" case of maleness or femaleness. Instead, each individual falls somewhere on a continuum of anatomical bisexuality, conceptualized as ranging from predominantly masculine structure at one end to predominantly feminine structure at the other, with actual hermaphroditism at the midpoint.[1]

In addition to discussing bisexuality with respect to reproductive anatomy, Freud also considered the bisexual nature of male and female physiology (which he called "sexual chemistry"). Basing his conclusions on current medical evidence, Freud (1905/1953, 1954) argued that there are distinct male and female chemical substances, and each sex both produces and responds to each kind of chemical (these chemicals have now been identified as the hormones androgen and estrogen). For example, to support the claim that each sex is responsive to both chemicals, he cited the case of a man whose testes did not function properly, and who, as a result, developed a more feminine appearance (e.g., change in body hair and fat distribution) and began to act in a passive manner. According to the hypothesis of bisexual physiology, there is a quantitative, but not a qualitative, physiological difference between males and females. Each individual is physiologically bisexual in the sense of responding to and producing both male and female chemical substances; however, males have a higher amount of and greater sensitivity to the male substance, and females have a higher amount of and greater sensitivity to the female substance.[2]

PSYCHOLOGICAL BISEXUALITY

Freud's interest in bisexuality was not limited to biological variables; he was equally concerned with the question of whether psychological variables could be considered bisexual in their own right. One of the issues he discusses has to do with personality organization; that is, whether an individual's constellation of personality traits is typically made up of both masculine and feminine characteristics (Freud, 1905/1953, 1920/1955, 1925/1961b, 1930/1961c, 1932/1964a). Such a view seemed to make sense on the basis of his clinical observations that women invariably had some traits that were "active" or "masculine"; men invariably had some traits that were "passive" or "feminine"; and even homosexuals, who were often thought to have only opposite-sex traits, typically showed a mixture of both male and female characteristics (Freud, 1905/1953).

From these observations, Freud concluded that "all human individuals . . . combine in themselves both masculine and feminine characteristics, so that pure masculinity and femininity remain theoretical constructions of uncertain content" (Freud, 1925/1961b, p. 258). His claim here is of the same form as his claims about anatomy and physiology; men and women do not fall neatly into dichotomous categories, but each individual's personality represents a mixture of masculine and feminine characteristics. Thus, here again, men and women are seen to differ in a quantitative, but not a qualitative, sense.

In addition to discussing bisexuality with respect to personality characteristics, Freud also examined the concept as it relates to "object choice" (now more commonly termed "sexual preference"). His claim was that all individuals have libidinal cathexes, or attractions, to both males and females; however, in most cases, only one of these cathexes is expressed overtly (Freud, 1920/1955, 1937/1964b). Like the notion of bisexual trait organization, the idea of bisexual object choice arose from Freud's clinical observations. Three observations in particular seem to have been important to the development of this idea. First, it was clear to Freud that while most individuals restrict their choice of sexual partners to either males or females, they have important affective relationships with both. Second, with regard to sexual behavior, he observed that any individual could develop either a homosexual or a heterosexual object choice. In addition, Freud noted that some individuals are literally bisexual with respect to object choice (i.e., they engage in sexual relationships with both males and females).

Since Freud always assumed that superficially different patterns of behavior may have essentially the same dynamics, he tried to formulate a single principle to explain heterosexual, homosexual, and bisexual object choices. Making the assumption that a general bisexuality is involved in all patterns of object choice seemed to be a step toward this goal. On this view, all individuals form libidinal cathexes to both males and females, but they differ with respect to which of these cathexes is manifest and which is latent. In individuals labeled "bisexual," both kinds of cathexis are manifest. Homosexuals and heterosexuals, on the other hand, show a pattern in which one cathexis is manifest, but the other is latent. That is, some feelings of attraction are repressed and are all owed expression only in an attenuated form, as friendship (Freud, 1920 /1955).

These hypotheses about bisexual object choice, like those about bisexual trait organization, have implications for the psychoanalytic view of development. To be consistent with the rest of psychoanalytic theory, it must be assumed that adults would have a combination of masculine and feminine traits and cathexes to both males and females only if they developed these patterns of behavior during childhood.

This kind of reasoning apparently led Freud to go back and revise his formulations about the Oedipal period (Freud, 1925/1959, 1923/1961a, 1925/1961b), taking into account two factors that had been ignored in his original description of Oedipal dynamics: (a) the constitutional anatomical and physiological bisexuality of the child and (b) the psychological bisexuality of the child's parents.

The inclusion of these two factors led Freud to posit that two opposing sets of dynamics—the so-called positive and negative complexes—are involved in the Oedipal conflict (Freud, 1923/1961a). He assumed that both boys and girls have to deal with one conflict derived from the masculine aspect of their personalities, and a second conflict derived from the feminine aspect of their personalities.

Freud argued that these conflicts could be resolved in a variety of ways. The particular resolution which is achieved is assumed to depend upon the relative strength of the child's constitutionally derived masculine and feminine aspects, as well as the relative strength of the respective masculine and feminine characteristics of the parents. Since Freud maintained that none of these factors exists in a "pure" form, he concluded that no matter how the child resolved the Oedipal conflicts, (s)he would necessarily develop both masculine and feminine traits and cathexes (either manifest or latent) to both males and females.

Implications of Freud's Work on Bisexuality

For our purposes, the relevance of Freud's work is found in the fact that he questioned the common assumption that individuals could be purely male or female, masculine or feminine. In attempting to develop a more adequate conception of gender, Freud introduced ideas which seem to us to have interesting implications. The two most important implications we have drawn from his work are these:

1. Gender cannot be designated adequately on the basis of any one criterion. Since a person can be clearly bisexual with respect to one variable (e.g., physiology) but less clearly so with respect to others (e.g., object choice), the whole set of variables—both biological and psychological—must be taken into account in designating gender. In other words, there are distinct aspects to gender, each of which is important in its own right and in terms of its potential relationship to other aspects.
2. Each aspect of gender can be conceptualized as a continuous dimension. Since each individual manifests characteristics typical of both males and females, and since individuals differ from one another in terms of the degree to which these kinds of characteristics are manifest, no aspect of gender can be described adequately in terms of two dichotomous categories.

While several authors (e.g., Constantinople, 1973; Kessler and McKenna, 1978; Money and Ehrhardt, 1972; Unger, 1979; Vaughter, 1976) make use of either one or both of these assumptions in their discussions of gender (albeit without reference to Freud), they rarely do so explicitly. As a consequence, the implications of these assumptions for a systematic conceptualization of gender are not elaborated. In the following sections, we try to address this problem by sketching the outlines of a reformulated view of gender based on these assumptions. Drawing on some of the specifics of Freud's discussion of bisexuality, as well as more recent work on the social construction of gender, we discuss gender in terms of five aspects, showing how each of these can be conceptualized as a continuous dimension. We then present some preliminary ideas about organizing relationships among these five aspects and outline some of the empirical implications of this approach.

Aspects of Gender

GENDER-RELATED HORMONES

Biological differences between "males" and "females" are typically taken to be dichotomous; thus, it is not surprising that we tend to talk about androgen as the male hormone and estrogen and progestin as the female hormones. However, as Freud argued and as has become common knowledge in light of recent research (see Gadpaille, 1972; Money and Ehrhardt, 1972), differentiating male and female physiology in terms of the presence or absence of these hormones oversimplifies the complexity of gender-related physiology, because in actuality all three hormones are present in the bloodstream of all individuals. What differentiates "males" and "females" is not the kind of hormone, but the relative amounts of each hormone. Thus, physiologically, "males" are characterized by an androgen level that is much higher than their estrogen/progestin level; "females" are characterized by estrogen/progestin levels that far exceed their androgen level.

Once we realize that the difference between "males" and "females" is really one of degree, we can see that some individuals (i.e., those for whom the relative amounts of each hormone differ from normative levels) would constitute intermediate cases, physiologically speaking. By taking this into account, we are led to think of gender-related hormonal patterns as lying along a continuum, which ranges from a masculine pattern at one end to a feminine pattern at the other.

GENDER-RELATED PHYSICAL CHARACTERISTICS

Gender-related physical differences are almost always described in terms of dichotomous categories. This is not surprising, since at least with respect to genital and reproductive structure, most individuals fall into one category or the other. However, by focusing only on genital and reproductive structure (cf. Freud, 1905/1953; Stoller, 1972, 1974), we cast the issue of gender-related physical differences in a way that limits the possibilities of thinking about intermediate cases. We thereby end up in the same position as Freud; if we want to consider such cases, we are left with only hermaphrodites to discuss.

A focus on anatomical structures to the exclusion of other physical characteristics also makes it seem as if, in ordinary circumstances, we judge a person's gender on the basis of the appearance of his/her genitals or internal organs. This is obviously not the case; in fact, we typically have no information about such structures. Yet we have little difficulty in making gender attributions (Kessler and McKenna, 1978) and do so frequently every day. Clearly, in making such judgements, we are relying on the fact that there are gender-related physical differences besides the obvious ones.

Aside from genital/reproductive structures, there are other physical characteristics which are used in making gender attributions. Some of these, typically called "secondary sex characteristics," are partially linked to the balance of gender-related hormones in the body. these characteristics (e.g., facial hair, breast and hip size, general body build, voice quality) provide a significant amount of information about an individual's gender. Although such characteristics are biologically based, it is important to note that sociocultural factors influence which of these characteristics are taken to be most relevant in a given culture. For example, in our culture, femininity is marked by little or no body hair; in Europe this is not so clearly the case. There is also another set of physical characteristics, not clearly linked to hormonal levels, which are used in making gender attributions; these are characteristics which are arbitrarily defined by a particular culture at a particular time as being masculine or feminine (e.g., in our culture at the present time, long hair and long eyelashes are taken to be feminine). These "culturally defined" characteristics provide additional information about an individual's gender over and above that provided by "secondary sex characteristics" and genital/reproductive structure.

Once we broaden our conceptualization of gender-related physical characteristics, it becomes apparent that individuals can vary in how masculine or feminine they appear to be. For example, a person who has a great deal of facial hair, rough skin, and short hair is likely to appear more masculine than a person with little facial hair, soft skin, and long hair. Similarly, a person who has a delicate build, long eyelashes, and soft facial features is likely to appear more feminine than a person with a more angular build, short eyelashes, and rough facial features (Darden, 1972; Thompson and Bentler, 1971; Hornstein and Freimuth, 1981).

Thus, when we observe an individual's physical appearance and draw conclusions about his/her gender, we are doing more than just deciding whether (s)he is "male" or "female"; we are also comparing him/her to a prototype of physical masculinity or femininity. Gender-related physical characteristics, when taken to include the variety of characteristics we have distinguished, therefore constitute a continuous dimension, ranging from clear cases of masculinity at one end to clear cases of femininity at the other.

GENDER ROLE

Typically defined in the literature as behaviors and traits culturally specified as feminine or masculine, gender role has received more theoretical and empirical examination than other psychological aspects of gender. Since our conceptualization differs from certain views which are currently popular in the literature, we think it is important to discuss this aspect of gender in some detail.

Unlike other variables considered in this article, gender role has typically been conceptualized (at least since the work of Terman and Miles, 1936) as a continuum ranging from masculine characteristics at one end to feminine characteristics at the other. This is not surprising, since aside from a few biologically based limitations (e.g., women cannot donate sperm, and men cannot serve as wet nurses) people can enact the same behaviors. Any individual can have in his/her repertoire some behaviors which are commonly considered masculine and some which are commonly considered feminine.

In most current discussions, a broad range of characteristics is included within the category of gender role (e.g., appearance, activities, attitudes, skills, interests, sexual preference). From the diversity of these characteristics, it seems that any psychological characteristic or behavior which defines someone as masculine or feminine is being included in the category of gender role. In light of evidence suggesting a lack of correlation between either appearance (Montemayor, 1978) or sexual preference (Storms, 1978) and behavioral/trait aspects of gender role, it seems that a more differentiated view is necessary. As a step toward thinking about psychological gender in a more differentiated manner, we have narrowed the breadth of this category (e.g., by including appearance within gender-relevant physical characteristics and by viewing sexual preference as a facet of gender preference—see below).

In recent years, several investigators (Bem, 1974; Spence and Helmreich, 1978) have constructed inventories to assess this more limited behavioral/trait aspect of gender role. Although these writers also base their view of gender on cultural norms, our conceptualization differs in certain important respects from theirs.

In opposition to the traditional continuum view of gender role, Bem and Spence, among others (e.g., Constantinople, 1973), have argued that masculinity and femininity constitute two orthogonal dimensions (i.e., the two types of gender are qualitatively distinct). The assumption behind this "dualistic view" is that predictions about an individual's masculinity cannot be made from information about his/her femininity. In other words, just because an individual is not masculine does not mean that (s)he is feminine.

In contrast, in keeping with the traditional view, we are arguing that masculinity and femininity represent the poles of a continuous dimension. In this view, statements about an individual's masculinity inherently imply something about his/her femininity; saying that an individual is very masculine is the same as saying that (s)he is not very feminine. Bem and Spence reject this bipolar view on both empirical and theoretical grounds.

On an empirical level, they point to the fact that the negative correlation between masculine and feminine scores which is predicted by the bipolar view has not been observed on traditional scales. Bem and Spence also fail to find a negative correlation, but this is not surprising, given that their scales are constructed with two independent monopolar dimensions. However, even the lack of such a correlation on traditional bipolar scales does not require rejection of the bipolar view. The negative correlation may be masked by response biases (see Russell, 1979) or the inclusion of diverse components of gender role (e.g., appearance, sexual preference) which more appropriately belong to different dimensions of gender. Thus, while masculine and feminine scores may correlate negatively within a single dimension, an overall negative correlation would be masked by the fact that people can be at different points along the continuum for different components. Constantinople (1973) has discussed at length the need to assess gender in terms of distinct dimensions in order to rule out such problems.

Theoretically, Bem and Spence reject a bipolar view because it does not allow for the possibility that some individuals are very masculine *and* very feminine (androgynous), while others are *neither* very masculine nor very feminine (undifferentiated gender role). We do not dispute the fact that if masculine and feminine characteristics are scored separately (as they are on the Bem and Spence scales), some individuals will end up with these response patterns. In our view, the dualistic conceptualization, not the assessment technique, is problematic. Simply put, we disagree with the assumption that gender-role characteristics can be defined in the abstract as either masculine or feminine. To the extent that masculine traits such as aggressiveness are defined in our culture in terms of a contrast with feminine traits such as passivity, conceptual independence between masculine and feminine characteristics is not possible. Applying this logic, if a person says (s)he is happy at a particular time, (s)he is also saying something about not feeling sad. Likewise, with gender, if a person describes him/herself as "never aggressive," we can conclude that in some sense (s)he is saying that (s)he is passive, given the way that we typically use these words. Thus, in our view, it does not follow conceptually to define some gender-role characteristics as masculine and others as feminine. Each characteristic represents a continuum which ranges from clear masculinity at one end to clear femininity at the other.

With a bipolar view of the kind being proposed, some individuals will undoubtedly fall at the midpoint on individual items or in terms of the sum for a number of characteristics. While some (e.g., Berzins, Welling, and Wetter, 1978) have taken this midpoint on bipolar scales to be gender neutral, we believe it is better thought of as a relatively equal mix of masculinity and femininity and thus could well be labeled "androgynous." It is true that if an inventory were to be constructed from the bipolar perspective, it would not be possible to distinguish between the so-called androgynous and undifferentiated types. However, this does not seem to constitute a real limitation of the bipolar view, since the conceptual status of the "undifferentiated" group is unclear. To imagine what it would mean for an individual to be neither feminine, masculine, or androgynous is difficult; and given that these people have relatively low self-esteem (Spence and Helmreich, 1978), their failure to find many gender-relevant terms applicable might possibly reflect a more general sense of depression.

In sum, it is important to emphasize that by conceptualizing gender role as a bipolar continuum, we do not advocate the return to more traditional gender-role scales such as those reviewed by Constantinople (1973). The assumptions that gender role be limited to behavioral/trait characteristics and be defined as a social construction are not met by these scales.

Gender Preference

Ordinarily, we define an individual's sexual preference in terms of whether his/her genital anatomy is the same or different from the genital anatomy of his/her sexual partners. That is, we distinguish heterosexuals, who choose partners with different genitals, from homosexuals, who choose partners with the same genitals. With this kind of view, bisexuals represent a kind of intermediate case, in that they choose some partners with the same and some with different genital anatomy (Kinsey, Pomeroy, Martin, and Gebhard, 1953). What is striking about this whole conceptualization of sexual preference is that it relies solely on genital structure to define the nature of an individual's affectional choices.

There is no doubt that genitals are clearly a significant factor in sexual preference. Nevertheless, by conceptualizing the issue solely in these terms, we are ignoring the fact that other gender-related characteristics influence the choice of sexual/romantic partners. We are talking here about physical and behavioral characteristics which are related to the relative masculinity or femininity of the individual and his/her partner. The preference of a "masculine male" for a "feminine female" is not the same as the preference of an equally "masculine male" for a "masculine female." In discussions of homosexuality, this potential variability in terms of gender role and identities of partners has been recognized (Bell and Weinberg, 1978), but the implications of these observations have not been applied to heterosexuality or sexual preference more generally.

To highlight the fact that the basis for selecting sexual and romantic partners includes, but is not limited to, genital structure, we use the term "gender preference" as an alternative to "sexual preference." According to this view, an individual is more or less heterosexual, homosexual, or bisexual, depending on (a) the degree of difference between his/her own relative masculinity/femininity and that of his/her partners, and (b) the relative frequency of his/her choice of such partners. Gender preference then becomes a continuum like the others we have described, in the sense that it ranges from relative heterosexuality at one end (i.e., frequent clear difference between the gender of partners with different genitals) to relative homosexuality at the other end (i.e., frequent clear similarity in the gender of partners with the same genitals).

That this potential variability among people has been ignored is interesting. The singular focus on genitals to define sexual preference may rest on the long-standing assumption of a one-to-one relationship between genitals and psychological facets of gender. The gender "inversion" theory of homosexuality reflects this thinking in that, for example, homosexual men are presumed to have feminine identities and gender roles. As recently demonstrated by Storms (1978), this theory is clearly inadequate—heterosexuals, homosexuals, and bisexuals (as typically defined) all showed varying combinations of masculinity and femininity. To extend these findings, the conceptualization of gender preference described above emphasizes the potential variability among partners. By not homogenizing such differences, we may begin to understand more fully the bases for sexual/romantic attractions.

SUBJECTIVE GENDER IDENTITY

Some theorists have noted that one of the most basic and perhaps primary outcomes of the process of gender development is that the individual comes to have a stable concept of him/herself as male or female (Kohlberg, 1966; Money and Ehrhardt, 1972; Stoller, 1972, 1974). Since this concept is typically assumed to be a reflection of the individual's genital structure (transsexuals, of course, provide the exception), most writers have discussed subjective aspects of gender identity in dichotomous terms. That is, they have focused only on whether an individual psychologically accepts or rejects his /her genital anatomy.

An individual's identification of him/herself as male or female is clearly a basic part of subjective gender identity. However, as we have been indicating all along, gender is not a unitary concept; it has distinct aspects. Consequently, one would expect that a person's sense of his/her own gender is not constituted solely by a perception of genital structure; rather, this concept represents an integrated conception of a variety of continuously distributed physical and psychological characteristics which (s)he takes to be gender relevant.

In other words, to the extent that gender identity is a statement about one's relative masculinity or femininity and not just one's maleness or femaleness, it is likely to vary across individuals—even among those who have the same genital anatomy. Thus, like the other variables we have discussed, subjective gender identity can be thought of as a continuum, ranging from clear masculinity at one end to clear femininity at the other. Preliminary empirical support for this bipolar view of subjective gender identity is found in Storms' (1978) study as well as in Gaudreau's (1977) finding of a strong negative correlation (r = -.91) between individuals' self-ratings on the terms "masculine" and "feminine."

Relations Among Aspects of Gender

In the discussion thus far, we have outlined what we take to be five distinct aspects of gender, each of which can be conceptualized as a continuous dimension. One implication of viewing gender in terms of distinct aspects is that the gender of a particular individual is described in terms of a profile. In other words, from our perspective, an individual's gender cannot be adequately characterized in terms of only one or two of the five aspects; rather, each of these aspects needs to be taken into account. To the extent that this is the case, it becomes important to know whether an individual's position on one dimension can be predicted from information about his/her position on another. That is, we need to know something about relations among the different aspects of gender.

Most of those who are writing on sex roles and gender differences have not addressed this issue, and those who have, have not found the sorts of relations typically expected. For example, Maccoby and Jacklin's (1974) extensive review of studies examining the relation between "sex" of subject (presumably defined in terms of attributed genital structure) and some specific aspect of gender role (e.g., assertiveness, empathy) indicated that there was little evidence for relations of this type. Given the absence of data, our expectations regarding various forms of relation among the different aspects of gender must be speculative.

We would, however, expect some relation between gender hormones and gender-relevant physical characteristics because secondary sex characteristics, one component of gender-relevant physical characteristics, are influenced by hormonal balance. In addition, gender-relevant physical characteristics, both biologically and culturally determined, may influence some aspects of gender role. For example, a strong stocky "female" is likely to be more capable of performing some traditionally defined masculine activities than a small delicately built "female" is. Of course, this relation may not always be in a positive direction; Biller and Liebman (1971) demonstrated that feminine-appearing boys have highly masculine interests, perhaps in part to compensate for the femininity of their appearance. To the extent that subjective gender identity represents a global perception of one's masculinity/femininity, we would also expect it to show some correlation with individual components of gender and to be strongly related to a composite of all the individual components.

Although we would expect some correlation among the components of gender, there are several reasons why we would not expect this relation to take the form of a one-to-one correspondence. First, some components should be more closely related than others. For example, biological and physical aspects of gender are likely to be more highly correlated to one another than either would be to the purely psychological components of gender. Second, various cultural and interpersonal factors may have independent effects on the different psychological components of gender, further limiting their covariation. For example, strong parental encouragement may lead a child to undertake activities that are atypical for people with his/her physical build (e.g., a delicately built "female" doing construction work). Finally, an individual's developmental status may affect the degree of relation among aspects of gender such that there is greater differentiation between components at more advanced stages. For example, during adolescence, when appearance and sexual attractiveness are central concerns, gender-relevant physical characteristics are likely to have a strong effect on gender role and subjective gender identity. In contrast, changes in appearance or gender role in middle age are less likely to be associated with a change in subjective gender identity.

The model of gender we have proposed would lead to different kinds of questions being posed in research. For example, Money (1975) reports the case of a "male" infant who was surgically, hormonally, and socially reassigned as a "female" after irreparable damage had occurred to his penis. Money claims that this child subsequently developed a feminine gender and is a "normal girl." While we would expect that this child would have a primarily feminine subjective gender identity, we would argue that with increasing age, her sterility, her slight degree of physical masculinization relative to other girls, and her own (probably limited and somewhat confused) knowledge of the reassignment would necessarily affect the way she views herself, especially with respect to gender-relevant physical characteristics. In other words, a global assessment of gender across varied components and across age may be inadequate in conceptualizing gender.

Clearly, these examples are only speculative. In order to talk about relations among aspects of gender with any certainty, a great deal of empirical research is necessary. Before such work can be initiated, we need to clarify further each dimension of gender, translate these claims into empirical terms, and articulate more clearly the ways in which we expect the various aspects to covary. The ideas presented in this article are intended to serve as stimuli for research, for the development of alternative models, and for more careful thought about the concept of gender.

Notes

This article is based in part on a symposium entitled "Psychosexual Development and the Nature of Androgyny" presented at the annual meeting of the Association for Women in Psychology, Pittsburgh, March 1978. Since both authors contributed equally to the conceptualization and writing of this paper, the order of authorship was determined by the toss of a coin. The authors would like to thank James Laird, Dennis Wixon, and Roger Bibace, Clark University, who read and commented on an earlier draft of this paper, and several anonymous reviewers whose comments helped us to clarify our presentation. Correspondence should be sent to Gail A. Hornstein, Department of Psychology and Education, Mount Holyoke College, South Hadley, Massachusetts 01075.

1. In relation to this claim that rudimentary structures of the opposite sex exist in each normal individual, Freud (1905/1953, 1925/1961b) argued that the clitoris is a biological "homologue" to the penis. Many writers interpreted Freud to be claiming that all embryos are initially male and that the clitoris is a "vestigial" penis. They have countered this position by arguing either that the fetus is originally female (Sherfey, 1972; Stoller, 1972) or undifferentiated (Hampson and Hampson, 1961; Money and Ehrhardt, 1972).

These remarks may be misdirected, since in describing the clitoris as a "homologue" to the penis, Freud may have been taking note of a functional, rather than a structural, similarity between the two (i.e., both organs are easily manipulable and become erect when stimulated). Regardless of whether Freud was making a structural or a functional observation, it is important to recognize, as many feminists have noted, that anatomical bisexuality is the basis for Freud's misinterpretation of female sexuality and more general devaluation of women. While acknowledging the inaccuracies in his theoretical account, our interest here is in highlighting the assumptions underlying this account which may be useful in conceptualizing gender.

2. In discussions of biological bisexuality, Freud seems at some points to make a direct case for a one-to-one correspondence between biological and psychological facets of bisexuality. Although Stoller (1972, 1974) has rejected the whole concept of bisexuality based on certain examples of this type, it is clear from Freud's discussion of Oedipal dynamics (1905/1953) and his more general discussions of biological determinants of behavior (1920/1955) that he saw the biological as merely one of many factors determining gender.

REFERENCES

Bell, A. P., and Weinberg, M. S. *Homosexualities: A study of diversity among men and women.* New York: Simon and Schuster, 1978.

Bem, S. L. The measurement of psychological androgyny. *Journal of Consulting and Clinical Psychology,* 1974, 42, 155–162.

Bem, S. L. Probing the promise of androgyny. In A. Kaplan and J. Bean (Eds.), *Beyond sex-role stereotypes: Readings toward a psychology of androgyny.* Boston: Little, Brown, 1976.

Berzins, J. I., Welling, M. A., and Wetter, R. A. A new measure of psychological androgyny based on the Personality Research Form. *Journal of Consulting and Clinical Psychology,* 1978, 46, 126–138.

Biller, H. B., and Liebman, D. A. Body build, sex-role preference, and sex-role adoption in junior high school boys. *Journal of Genetic Psychology,* 1971, 118, 81–86.

Constantinople, A. Masculinity-femininity: An exception to a famous dictum? *Psychological Bulletin,* 1973, 80, 389–407.

Darden, E. Masculinity-femininity body rankings by males and females. *Journal of Psychology,* 1972, 80, 205–212.

Freud, S. Three essays on the theory of sexuality. In J. Strachey (Ed. and trans.), *The standard edition of the complete psychological works of Sigmund Freud* (Vol. 7). London: Hogarth Press, 1953. (Originally published, 1905.)

Freud, S. Letters to Wilhelm Fliess. In M. Bonaparte, A. Freud, and E. Kris (Eds.), *The origins of psychoanalysis: Letters to Wilhelm Fliess 1887–1902*. New York: Basic Books, 1954.

Freud, S. The psychogenesis of a case of female homosexuality. In J. Strachey (Ed. and trans.), *The standard edition of the complete psychological works of Sigmund Freud* (Vol. 18). London: Hogarth Press, 1955. (Originally published, 1920.)

Freud, S. An autobiographical study. In J. Strachey (Ed. and trans.), *The standard edition of the complete psychological works of Sigmund Freud* (Vol. 20). London: Hogarth Press, 1959. (Originally published 1925.)

Freud, S. The ego and the id. In J. Strachey (Ed. and trans.), *The standard edition of the complete psychological works of Sigmund Freud* (Vol. 19). London: Hogarth Press, 1961. (Originally published, 1923.) (a)

Freud, S. Some psychical consequences of the anatomical distinction between the sexes. In J. Strachey (Ed. and trans.), *The standard edition of the complete psychological works of Sigmund Freud* (Vol. 19). London: Hogarth Press, 1961. (Originally published, 1925.) (b)

Freud, S. Civilization and its discontents. In J. Strachey (Ed. and trans.), *The standard edition of the complete psychological works of Sigmund Freud* (Vol. 21). London: Hogarth Press, 1961. (Originally published, 1930.) (c)

Freud, S. Female sexuality. In J. Strachey (Ed. and trans.), *The standard edition of the complete psychological works of Sigmund Freud* (Vol. 21). London: Hogarth Press, 1961. (Originally published, 1931.) (d)

Freud, S. Femininity. In J. Strachey (Ed. and trans.), *The standard edition of the complete psychological works of Sigmund Freud* (Vol. 22). London: Hogarth Press, 1964. (Originally published, 1932.) (a)

Freud, S. Analysis terminable and interminable. In J. Strachey (Ed. and trans.), *The standard edition of the complete psychological works of Sigmund Freud* (Vol. 23). London: Hogarth Press, 1964. (Originally published, 1937.) (b)

Frieze, I. H., Parsons, J. E., Johnson, P. B., Ruble, D. N., and Zellman, G. L. *Women and sex roles: A social psychological perspective*. New York: Norton, 1978.

Gadpaille, W. J. Research into the physiology of maleness and femaleness. *Archives of General Psychiatry*, 1972, 26, 193–206.

Gaudreau, P. Factor analysis of the Bem Sex Role Inventory. *Journal of Consulting and Clinical Psychology*, 1977, 45, 299–302.

Hampson, J. L., and Hampson, J. G. The ontogenesis of sexual behavior in man. In W. C. Young (Ed.), *Sex and internal secretions* (3rd ed.). Baltimore: Williams and Wilkins, 1961.

Hornstein, G. A., and Freimuth, M. J. 1981. Perceiving physical masculinity and femininity in oneself and others. Paper presented at the meeting of the Eastern Psychological Association, New York, April.

Jung, C. G. Anima and animus. In *Two essays on analytical psychology* (R. F. C. Hull, trans.). London: Routledge and Kegan Paul, 1953.

Kessler, S., and McKenna, W. *Gender: An ethnomethodological approach*. New York: Wiley, 1978.

Kinsey, A. C., Pomeroy, W. B., Martin, C. E., and Gebhard, P. H. *Sexual behavior in the human female*. Philadelphia: Saunders, 1953.

Kohlberg, L. A. A cognitive-developmental analysis of children's sex-role concepts and attitudes. In E. E. Maccoby (Ed.), *The development of sex differences*. Stanford: Stanford University Press, 1966.

Maccoby, E. E., and Jacklin, C. N. *The psychology of sex differences*. Stanford: Stanford University Press, 1974.

Money, J. Ablatio penis: Normal male infant sex-reassigned as a girl. *Archives of Sexual Behavior*, 1975, 4, 65–71.

Money, J., and Ehrhardt, A. A. *Man and woman, boy and girl.* Baltimore: Johns Hopkins University Press, 1972.

Montemayor, R. Men and their bodies: The relationship between body type and behavior. *Journal of Social Issues,* 1978, 34, 48–64.

Rado, S. A critical examination of the concept of bisexuality. *Psychosomatic Medicine,* 1940, 2, 459–467.

Russell, J. A. Affective space is bipolar. *Journal of Personality and Social Psychology,* 1979, 37, 345–356.

Sherfey, M. J. *The nature and evolution of female sexuality.* New York: Random House, 1972.

Spence, J. T., and Helmreich, R. *Masculinity and femininity: Their psychological dimensions, correlates and antecedents.* Austin: University of Texas Press, 1978.

Stoller, R. J. The "bedrock" of masculinity and femininity: Bisexuality. *Archives of General Psychiatry,* 1972, 26, 207–212.

Stoller, R. J. Facts and fancies: An examination of Freud's concept of bisexuality. In J. Strouse (Ed.), *Women and analysis.* New York: Grossman, 1974.

Storms, M. D. Sexual orientation and self-perception. In P. Pliner, K. R. Blanstein, I. M. Spigel, P. Alloway, and L. Krames (Eds.), *Advances in the study of communication and affect: Vol. V. Perception of emotion in self and others.* New York: Plenum, 1978.

Terman, L., and Miles, C. C. *Sex and personality.* New York: McGraw-Hill, 1936.

Thompson, S. K., and Bentler, P. M. The priority of cues in sex discrimination by children and adults. *Developmental Psychology,* 1971, 5, 181–185

Unger, R. K. Toward a redefinition of sex and gender. *American Psychologist,* 1979, 34, 1085–1094.

Vaughter, R. M. Review essay: Psychology. *Signs,* 1976, 2, 120–146.

7

The Periodic Table Model of the Gender Transpositions: Part II. Limerent and Lusty Sexual Attractions and the Nature of Bisexuality

James D. Weinrich

THE notion that there are different kinds of sexual attraction is not a new one. The ancient Greeks, for example, distinguished between *eros, philia,* and *agape* (Boswell, 1980, pp. 46–48), and modern English distinguishes between love and lust. I believe that these distinctions merit further study and have thus constructed a theory that puts the notion of at least two sexual attractions into a precise, testable form.

I was first moved to investigate this area by a puzzling irregularity in the distribution of the gender transpositions: the fact that bisexuality among women is apparently more common (relatively, and probably absolutely) than it is among men (Gebhard, 1972; Gebhard and Johnson, 1979; Haynes and Oziel, 1976; Kinsey, Pomeroy, and Martin, 1948; Kinsey, Pomeroy, Martin, and Gebhard, 1953; Saghir and Robins, 1973; Schäfer, 1976, 1977). All the other gender transpositions are more common among men, as are the fetishes and paraphilias.

A second puzzling irregularity concerns the pattern of social attitudes toward homosexuality. Male homosexuality is typically more severely condemned than lesbianism is (Carrier, 1980; Cory, 1967; Kinsey et al., 1953, pp. 483–487; Millham, San Miguel, and Kellogg, 1976). But there is a sex difference: Typical heterosexual men often show less hostility toward lesbianism than heterosexual women do. And heterosexual women often show far less hostility toward male homosexuality than heterosexual men do (Hatfield, Sprecher, and Traupmann, 1978, Fig. 1; Steffensmeier and Steffensmeier, 1974, p. 62).

This research was supported in part by Grant 32,170 from the National Institute of Mental Health. The author thanks John Boswell, John Gonsiorek, Ralph Hexter, John Kirsch, Charles Moser, and Richard Pillard for comments on versions of the manuscript.

A third motivation was the current controversy about the definition, prevalence, and scientific importance of bisexuality (Klein, 1978; MacDonald, 1983). Defined in a certain way, bisexuality may be rare or absent among men (Freund, 1974), but it is certainly not rare among women.

A fourth motivation was the weakness of certain sociological and social psychological theories of development of the gender transpositions. For example, how may we explain the apparently higher incidence of male than female homosexuality in the light of the fact that male homosexuality is more negatively sanctioned than is lesbianism? If male homosexuality is more negatively sanctioned, then one might expect that it would be rarer. It is not. Indeed, the fact that female-female relations are less taboo is one that has been known for over a century, and this seemed to validate the common belief that lesbianism was more common than male homosexuality (see Kinsey et al., 1953, pp. 475–476)! After the Kinsey group showed that the facts are different, explanations were reworked, but at the cost of requiring more intricate hypotheses to explain the facts.

Finally, I noted Tripp (1975, pp. 94–97 and chap. 8) argued that many bisexual men experience attractions, that they describe as entirely different, to men and to women. This point is now common in the bisexuality literature; sexual attraction to men and sexual attraction to women are not opposites and are not necessarily incompatible. (I agree in part with this argument; indeed, such a two-dimensional point of view should be familiar to readers of Pillard and Weinrich, 1987.) But in an entirely different passage, Tripp made a point about promiscuity and pair-bonding.

> Consider, for instance, the man who has had perhaps a hundred brief encounters, a number of short-range affairs, and one profound relationship which lasts for years or for the rest of his life. This combination of experiences is not at all unusual and it lends itself to three correct statements about the man: that he is highly promiscuous, that most of his relationships do not last, and that he clearly can and does maintain an important and substantial ongoing relationship. (Tripp, 1975, p. 160)

This passage suggests that desire for a long-term relationship and desire for short-term relationships are not opposites and are not necessarily incompatible. Either desire can arise autonomously, not "caused" by any obvious environmental stimulus, and either might arise only in reaction to certain stimuli. If they are distinct, a given person might be especially responsive to both of them, neither of them, or just one of them and not the other. (This two-dimensional point of view, also, should be familiar to readers of Pillard and Weinrich, 1987.)

In the present paper, I weave the above threads into a general theory of sexual attraction. This theory begins independently of the periodic table model described in Part I but eventually meshes with that model. The result is a synthetic theory of sexual orientation and sexual response that explains most of the features of sexual orientation in humans, including bisexuality, with a remarkably small number of hypotheses.

Definitions

My first distinction is between *reactions* and *autonomous desires*. I use these terms in a special sense and so will first define them, then capitalize them in use.

A *Reaction* is a behavior elicited by stimuli reliably related to that behavior—a behavior, moreover, that makes logical sense in the light of the stimuli eliciting it. Individuals can (loosely speaking) be said to have or possess a Reaction if they perform it with some regularity after the appropriate stimuli have occurred.

For example, take a group of people and show them a sexually explicit film. Presumably, many of the penises of the men in this group will become erect, and many of the women's vaginas will lubricate. These events are logical in the light of the stimulus and would occur fairly reliably, and so they constitute Reactions—in particular, sexual Reactions.

An *Autonomous Desire* is either (a) that mental state associated with seeking out the stimuli eliciting a particular behavior—that is, seeking out opportunities to perform a Reaction—or (b) a readiness to perform a behavior which arises without first being elicited by particular stimuli. Individuals can be said to have an Autonomous Desire if they seek out stimuli which elicit particular Reactions or perform behaviors in the absence of stimuli that would logically be expected to elicit them. For brevity, I will often drop the adjective *autonomous*, although it is considered implicit in the term.

For example, consider a group of people who simply want to see a film and are deciding which one to go see. Some of these people, even without consulting the film listings, may decide that they would like to see a sexually explicit film. Although this is not a strange desire, aspects of it are not directly explainable in the light of the stimulus ("Let's go see a movie"). This kind of behavior constitutes evidence of a Desire—in particular, a sexual Desire.

Thus, both Reactions and Autonomous Desires are readinesses to perform particular sets of behaviors. The first occurs only under a particular set of circumstances logically related to the elicited behavior, whereas the second reflects the readiness to perform the behavior even in the absence of a particular stimulus. Another way to phrase this distinction is that the threshold for eliciting a behavior is high or specific for a Reaction, but it is low, random, or nonexistent for a Desire.

I will now define two different kinds of autonomous sexual Desires and sexual Reactions. In choosing names for them, I wanted to avoid problems of hierarchy (such as would arise by naming them with numbers or letters) and wanted to be scientifically precise without being jargonistic. Hence, I call them *limerent* and *lusty*.

The *limerent Desire* and the *limerent Reaction* (Tennov, 1979) are those involved in eroticizing the physical and/or personality characteristics of a particular Limerent Object (abbreviated LiO). That is, limerence is involved when someone "falls in love" with someone they have met or are getting to know, and whose particular traits (physical or mental) are eroticized over a period of time. It is often inhibited when the LiO is a new stimulus (e.g., a stranger), although with some people this period of inhibition is short.

The *lusty Desire* and the *lusty Reaction* are involved with erotic response to novel objects. That is, lustiness is involved when someone "falls in lust" with someone they are not previously acquainted with soon after first seeing or meeting them. It is characteristically facilitated when the Lusty Object (LuO) is a stranger, and in some people is inhibited when the LuO is familiar (i.e., a friend).

A convenient way to summarize these definitions is as follows: If your love is blind, then it's limerence; if your love is blond, then it's lust.

Finally, a sexual *attraction* is the general term used to describe both sexual Reactions and autonomous sexual Desires. It is convenient in two situations: when we are uncertain whether a particular behavior arose in response to a particular stimulus, and when we need to refer to both Reactions and Desires at once.

The Three Hypotheses

Next I present three hypotheses that can account for many aspects of sexual orientation. I follow each hypothesis with a brief discussion, and present an extended discussion of the third and most controversial hypothesis.

THE HYPOTHESES

1. *Limerence and lustiness are experienced by both sexes; there is, however, an average sex difference in the ease with which each can be elicited in a particular sex.* In particular, *limerence is experienced by most women in our culture as an Autonomous Desire,* whereas lustiness, when it occurs, is experienced as a Reaction. On the other hand, *lustiness is experienced by most men in our culture as an Autonomous Desire,* whereas limerence, when it occurs, is experienced as a Reaction. (Notice that these hypotheses are independent of any particular discipline or theoretical outlook.)

This is the key hypothesis of the theory, as I have put it as gender-neutrally as I believe the evidence will permit. Both sexes are capable of responding in both modes. Men fantasize about falling in love (Friday, 1980) and do so often (Tennov, 1979). When women are placed in sexually stimulating environments, they can and do respond with sexual arousal—and to about the same extent as men do when placed in corresponding environments (Symons, 1979, p. 170 summarized this position). The theory presumes both sorts of impulse to be "sexy," rejecting the notion that lustiness is "real" sexiness and limerence is "mere" love, or that limerence is an "acceptable" sexiness and lustiness a "bad" one.

The definition of limerence states that it is dependent upon friendship and familiarity. This suggests the second hypothesis:

2. *In some people limerent attractions can be indifferent (or nearly so) to the sex or gender of the LiO.* This hypothesis is unproven but very reasonable, as many people know they can be friends with both men and women, and so they can imagine that some people would be able to fall in love with both men and

women. In these cases, the limerent attraction would be a bisexual one, and the LiO's genitalia and/or gender would be less important than their personality or character would be in eliciting it. (However, there may be some people whose friendships occur among one sex alone; there is nothing preventing the limerent attractions felt by these people from being unisexual.)

In contrast, lusty attractions would be very unlikely to be bisexual, if it is the case that they key into a particular "type" of Lusty Object in which visual factors (and hence, usually, genitalia) are important. I believe this is so and formalize this belief in the following hypothesis:

> 3. *Most men and women are capable of undergoing an eroticization/imprinting/ critical-period experience before adulthood that imprints an image of the Lusty Object into the developing brain*—an image which typically is discovered to be the sexually attractive object when the child's sexual impulses are turned on by the hormonal changes of puberty or later life.

Discussion of Hypothesis 3

This last hypothesis requires documentation and amplification. In animals, eroticization/imprinting/critical-period experiences (henceforth, "EICP experiences") are very well described (Lorenz, 1937, as corrected by Scott, 1978, pp. 82–83; Alcock, 1984, pp. 99–101), although species vary in their "imprintability" (Lorenz). In imprinting, a newborn or juvenile sees an image prominent in its environment, usually its mother or other adult members of its species (but sometimes an atypical object such as a colored paper cutout or a human being) and learns its characteristics in a permanent and inflexible way. Typically, it follows the object it has imprinted upon and runs to it when it is distressed. (There can be other equivalent or related behaviors dependent upon the species.) Falling short of "true" imprinting, but still included in my hypotheses above, are critical-period learning experiences, in which the time period for learning certain associations is developmentally limited.

I include eroticization in the definition of an EICP experience because sometimes the imprinted-upon object becomes the image at which courtship is directed beginning in adolescence. For example (Lorenz, 1937):

Portielje, of the Amsterdam Zoological Gardens, raised a male of the South American Bittern (*Tigrisoma*) who, when mature, courted human beings. When a female [bittern] was procured, he first refused to have anything to do with her but accepted her later when left alone with her for a considerable time. The birds then successfully reared a number of broods, but even then Portielje had to refrain from visiting the birds too often, because the male would, on the appearance of the former foster-father, instantly rush at the female, drive her roughly away from the nest and, turning to his keeper, perform the ceremony of nest-relief, inviting Portielje to step into the nest and incubate! What is very remarkable in all this is that while all the bird's instinctive reactions pertaining to reproduction had been repeatedly and successfully performed with the female and not once

had been consummated with a human being for their object, they yet stayed irreversibly conditioned to the latter in preference to the biologically proper object.
(p. 263)

This male bird, in short, regarded human beings—Portielje in particular—as the
"real thing" when it came to courtship. This phenomenon is now well-accepted
among animal breeders and zookeepers, sometimes with amusing results (McNulty,
1983).

One cannot help but be struck by the apparent similarity between these phenomena and those found in human eroticism (Money, 1980):

> The hormones of puberty mature the body and activate in the mind the erotic sex-
> ualism that is already programed [*sic*] therein. . . . The protruding shape of girls'
> nipples, for example, may be heavily weighted as an erotic turn-on in a particu-
> lar boy, so that it enters imperatively into his erotic fantasies. . . . This boy will
> classify himself as a "tit man," . . . [and] persuade himself that he prefers or
> selects breast imagery as an erotic turn-on, and even persuade himself that his
> preference is a voluntary choice, whereas in point of fact it is an option that was
> pre-programed [*sic*] into him without his informed consent, perhaps as early as
> the age of three, when he was still unweaned and suckling at his mother's nip-
> ples. (p. 37)

Margaret Mead held a similar view (Mead, 1961, p. 1456): "Both male and female
infants learn in infancy something about the mother's breasts which will be part of
the adult pattern of foreplay."

Of course, animal examples cannot be used to conclude that EICP mechanisms
must or even probably exist in humans; such an argument would be by way of
phylogeny (evolutionary relatedness or descent), and the phylogenetic occurrence
of such experience is not continuous. But it can be used to suggest that it would not
be surprising to find such mechanisms in humans, because the mechanism is phy-
logenetically widespread. Even if it does exist, it might exist in only one sex; in
many animals, for example, sexual objects attractive to males are determined by
imprinting, but those attractive to females are genetically preset (Alcock, 1984, pp.
99–100). In other species, the sexually attractive objects in adulthood are genetically preprogrammed for both sexes (Lorenz, 1937). And there may be, for all I
know, various environmental or genetic conditions which make EICP experiences
more likely in particular individuals.

There have been challenges to the notion that some aspects of human sexual
preference or orientation could be based upon imprinting or critical-period learning. For example, although Singer (1985, p. 244) admitted that "an ethological
mechanism" such as imprinting "fits . . . well" the data that "children do seem to
form early attachments to people or even to objects," he claimed that "there are no
clear implications for sexual orientation." That remains to be seen. Hypothesis 3 is
only a hypothesis.

THE THREE HYPOTHESES, RESTATED

I will now restate and slightly extend the three hypotheses in the light of the above discussion (in reverse order):

3. Lusty sexual Desires (and probably also lusty sexual Reactions) are directed at particular members of a class of LuOs for which the individual has previously undergone an EICP experience. One's attraction to such an object begins (for humans) with visual arousal at a distance. A logical consequence of this hypothesis is that the lusty attractions are unlikely to be bisexual, since male and female roles, genitalia, and outward appearances (in every culture known to anthropology, not to mention in our own!) are significantly different from each other.

2. Limerent Desires and Reactions are directed not at a particular class of objects but at a particular kind of relationship with an LiO—an eroticized particular friendship. One's attraction to such an object—a person—begins with getting acquainted with his or her particular characteristics, whether they be physical or mental. A logical consequence of this hypothesis is that the limerent Desire/Reaction is capable of being bisexual, at least in some people—perhaps most people.

1. Most women (at least in our culture and probably in many others) experience limerence as an autonomous Desire and experience lustiness as a Reaction to particular stimuli, whereas most men experience lustiness as an autonomous Desire and limerence as a Reaction to particular stimuli. For example, many men are aware of their attraction to visual erotica, but both men and women can be aroused by viewing it. Likewise, many women are aware of their attraction to romance novels (Radway, 1984), but both women and men can be aroused by reading them.

Taken together, all this suggests that when talking about "their sexuality," women and men will often be talking about different things—limerence and lust, respectively, for the most part. This fact may explain much of the miscommunication across the gender gap, as I will now show.

BISEXUALITY IN MEN AND WOMEN: THREE PREDICTIONS

The key to understanding sexual orientation is understanding precisely the nature of bisexuality, or more precisely, the nature of the various bisexualities definable in the light of lustiness and limerence. In this section, let us consider the implications of the three hypotheses for the theory of bisexuality, stopping just short of those implications which require application of the periodic-table theory of the gender transpositions (Pillard and Weinrich, 1987).

1. The first consequence is that *bisexuality will be more common in women than in men, although the bisexualities experienced in the two sexes would often be different.* Speaking in generalities, women experience their sexuality as a

limerent Desire, which can in its nature be bisexual. Hence, a substantial number of women will notice bisexual attractions in themselves. Men in general, on the other hand, experience their sexuality as a lusty Desire, which in its nature is rarely bisexual. Hence, few men will notice bisexual attractions in themselves.

2. Many men who do notice bisexual attractions within themselves will find their heterosexual responses occurring in entirely different contexts (limerent contexts) from many or most of their homosexual ones (lusty contexts). Bisexual women, on the other hand, will often find their heterosexual responses occurring in nearly identical contexts as their homosexual ones (limerent contexts in both cases). In short, *many bisexual men will find their homosexual and heterosexual attractions to be entirely different, and many bisexual women will find the two to be very much the same.*

3. On average, *the sexes will differ in the extent to which heterosexuals are emotionally predisposed to understand and/or accept homosexuality among members of their own sex.* Many heterosexual women who do not consider themselves bisexual will be able to understand why a woman might fall in love with a woman because they have women friends and can understand how someone might eroticize any friendship. Many heterosexual men with intense friendships with other men will nevertheless find it incomprehensible that a man could be sexually aroused by another man, because in their own experience sexual arousal is not connected with friendship.

Moreover, it should be much easier for a heterosexual woman to understand (on the basis of her own experience) why someone might fall in love with a man than for a heterosexual man to do so, so acceptance of male homosexuality ought to be higher among heterosexual women than among heterosexual men. But it should be only somewhat easier for a heterosexual man to understand why someone might be sexually aroused by a woman than for a heterosexual woman to do so, so acceptance of female homosexuality ought to be only somewhat higher among heterosexual men than among heterosexual women.

EMPIRICAL EVIDENCE FOR THE THREE PREDICTIONS

I believe that aspects of these predictions are amply confirmed. Much evidence for prediction 1 has already been cited (see the Introduction). Prediction 1 also strongly suggests that bisexuality should be especially rare in lusty Desires, a suggestion for which there is a great deal of support. Besides the work of John Money (cited above), it is also supported by the ethologically motivated work of Kurt Freund, who employed the penile plethysmograph, a direct genital measurement device (Bancroft, Jones, and Pullan, 1966; Freund, Diamant, and Pinkava, 1958; Freund, Sedlacek, and Knob, 1965; Geer, 1975). Freund (1974) defined a male bisexual as a man who is significantly sexually aroused in adulthood by the sight of the nude body shape of sexually mature individuals of both sexes. Such a man would, under my definition, exhibit bisexuality in his lusty, autonomous sexual Desires.

Freund (1974) has conducted an extensive search for such men and has found none, except those who are predominantly attracted sexually to very underage partners (Freund, Scher, Chan, and Ben-Aron, 1982). (The theory does not account for pedophilia, and hence I will ignore this complication. Note, however, that the body types of underage males and females do not differ from each other as much as do the body types of adult women and men.) I take Freund's finding to be a confirmation that lusty-Desire bisexuality is rare. However, for some conflicting data, see McConaghy (1978).

Pillard and I have also gathered data suggesting that bisexuality of a particular type is rare among men in our culture. We conducted a study which recruited samples of men through newspaper advertisements in gay and general audience newspapers (Pillard and Weinrich, 1986). Potential subjects were given a detailed sex history interview, from which a Kinsey rating was derived (Pillard, Pouma-dere, and Carretta, 1981). This interview identified only a handful of men who could be considered neither predominantly homosexual nor predominantly het-erosexual; the only individual who seemed clearly to fall into this category judging by his report of his fantasy life had not yet engaged in sexual behavior to orgasm with a partner. It is our impression that our subjects are typical of young men in general in the sense that they implicitly used a lusty-Desire definition to describe their orientation, and thus rarely thought of themselves as bisexual.

When it comes to women, the evidence is quite different. Pillard, Greenfield, and I are conducting a study of women parallel to the study of men cited above, and it has not been difficult to find clearcut examples of bisexuality among women. In many other studies, even those of lesbian women who do not consider them-selves bisexual, significant levels of bisexual behavior and fantasy are encountered in the sample. For example, lesbians as a group have lower ages at first heterosex-ual coitus than heterosexual women do (Bell, Weinberg, and Hammersmith, 1981, p. 159; Saghir and Robins, 1973; Schäfer, 1977) and report much higher frequencies of heterosexual fantasy and behavior than homosexual men do (e.g., Schäfer, 1976, 1977).

Evidence for prediction 2 as it applies to men is admittedly sparse (see the quo-tation from Tripp, 1975, in the Introduction). As applied to women the evidence is likewise sparse, but I believe it is consistent with my theory For example, Abbott and Love (1972, p. 101) stated that "Lesbians, like women generally, respond pri-marily to a combination of physical and psychic attributes, to a manner, a personal-ity." They approvingly cited other authorities who suggested that women's attrac-tions to men and women are similar—in particular, one saying that some lesbians "acknowledged a liking for some males but based their liking entirely on the indi-vidual's charm, wit and intellect—not specifically masculine attributes" (p. 140) and another stating that the sex of the love partner is relatively unimportant in fe-male sexuality (p. 145).

For prediction 3 I have likewise cited the evidence in the Introduction. For the most part these studies concur that many heterosexual men are highly aroused by fantasies of lesbian lovemaking and (perhaps as a direct result) are more accepting of lesbians than they are of male homosexuals. On the other hand, heterosexual women are less disapproving of female homosexuality than heterosexual men are of male homosexuality. Future researchers would do well to distinguish between *arousal* and *approval* and between attitudes toward homosexual *acts* and toward homosexual *persons*, for such distinctions are relevant to the predictions.

Further Predictions When Meshed with the Periodic Table Model

I now proceed to mesh the limerent and lusty model with the previously described model of the gender transpositions (Pillard and Weinrich, 1987).

The model's main tenet is easily stated. Human brains exhibit sexual dimorphism in neural circuits relevant to sexual behavior and feelings, and the various aspects of this sexual dimorphism can be classified into two groups on developmental grounds: those that differ between the sexes because a male fetal brain undergoes a biobehavioral masculinization process in its prenatal development, and those that differ between the sexes because a male fetus's or child's brain undergoes a biobehavioral defeminization process in pre- or postnatal development. The key insight is that brain masculinization and brain defeminization are two distinct processes that sometimes can proceed independently of each other. In particular, Pillard and I suggested that male homosexuals and some female homosexuals have neural substrates that have been masculinized but not defeminized, that male heterosexuals have neural substrates that have been both masculinized and defeminized, and that female heterosexuals have neural substrates that have been neither masculinized nor defeminized. Masculinizing and/or defeminizing agents could be genetic, hormonal, psychological and/or social.

Figure 7.1 diagrams one way in which masculinization and defeminization might affect tendencies to respond to the limerent and lusty attractions. By comparing Figure 7.1 with the appropriate figures in the previous paper (Pillard and Weinrich, 1987, Figures 1 and 2), readers can deduce the following predictions.

4. People with masculinized neural substrates—most heterosexual and homosexual men, and some lesbian women—should possess lusty sexual Desires directed towards a particular "type" of LuO. People with intermediately masculinized neural substrates—most crossdressers, and most bisexual women—might also have such Desires, perhaps to a lesser degree.

5. Fetishists—people who in some sense have lusty sexual Desires directed toward an inanimate LuO—would likewise be expected to have masculinized neural substrates. If so, this would account for the predominance of fetishism among men, and for the fact that in those rare cases when women display fetishes, the women always have homosexual fantasies (K. W. Freund, personal communication, May, 1985; Stoller, 1982). Fetishism in men occurs in both heterosexuals and homosexuals.

6. People with neural substrates placing them in the lower right-hand quadrant of Figure 7.1 ought to have a special situation pertain when it comes to sex and friendship. These people could find themselves with autonomous

Figure 7.1 *Meshing the Limerent/Lusty Theory with the Periodic Table Theory*

Unmasculinized and Defeminized	Masculinized and Defeminized
Lusty sexual Reaction Erotic Reaction to novelty Erotic visual Reactions Less aware of erotic "type"	Lusty sexual Desire Autonomous seeking of erotic novelty Autonomous seeking of visual erotica Highly aware of erotic "type"
Limerent sexual Reaction Capacity to eroticize particular friendship Little aware of romantic "type" Fewer romantic fantasies	Limerent sexual Reaction Capacity to eroticize particular friendship? Little aware of romantic "type" Fewer romantic fantasies
Unmasculinized and Undefeminized	Masculinized and Undefeminized
Lusty sexual Reaction Erotic Reaction to novelty Erotic visual Reactions Less aware of erotic "type"	Lusty sexual Desire Autonomous seeking of erotic novelty Autonomous seeking of visual erotica Highly aware of erotic "type"
Limerent sexual Desire Autonomous eroticization of particular friendship Highly aware of romantic "type" More romantic fantasies	Limerent sexual Desire Autonomous eroticization of particular friendship Highly aware of romantic "type" More romantic fantasies

Defeminization (vertical axis, pointing up)

Masculinization (horizontal axis, pointing right)

Desires for both limerent and lusty stimuli (in comparison with the more ordinary individuals in the upper-right and lower-left corners): a Desire for
eroticizing particular friendships, and also a Desire for sexual relationships
without friendship. It is in that quadrant, then, that one would find the most
intense competition, co-existence, conflict, or confusion about sex with
friends versus sex with acquaintances (depending upon the individual's
socialization and capacity to handle cognitive dissonance). Walt Whitman's
homoerotic poetry, for example, exalts the love of companions, and Sappho's
shows a familiarity with sexual arousal at a distance. Some romance novels
are now directed at lesbian readers and others at homosexual men. Much
visually explicit erotica is now directed at homosexual men and some other
erotica at lesbian women.

7. The distinction between Reactions and Autonomous Desires probably
is related to the distinction some people make between their sexual orientation as an unchangeable "given" and their sexual preference as a "choice."
There are women who state that they have chosen to be lesbian, for example—a statement that some other lesbians and many homosexual men find
difficult to understand based on their own experience. This emphasis on
choice may be especially important for women—who for so many centuries
have been given no choice at all in sexual matters, or only the option to veto
marital partners, not the option to choose them themselves. But it may also be
true—as the theory suggests—that this choice is related to the greater salience of friendship eroticization in women's sexuality. After all, one cannot
choose whom one is lustily aroused by, but one can to some extent choose
one's friends, and one can certainly choose *not* to be someone's friend.

Discussion and Qualifications

The parallel between limerent and lusty attractions is the main reason I have allowed the objects of both to have similar abbreviations (LiO and LuO). Sorting out precisely which kind of attraction is involved in particular instances is a useful exercise for anyone and is especially important clinically for people confused about their sexual attractions.

Limerent and lusty attractions need not be uniform across the lifespan. In particular, it would not be surprising if the lusty ones in men behave as erectile responses in general do—that is, lusty Desires in men probably lessen with age in frequency and intensity. If so, then the (absolute or relative) importance of limerence in men may well increase with age.

Cultures and subcultures differ in the significance attached to various forms of sexual attraction, and these differences can complicate the statement of my conclusions. For example, in some locales or subcultures, people readily have casual or recreational sex with friends or strangers, and the existence of bisexuality in this kind of sex (even of the lusty variety) is not of the same significance as its existence would be in a subculture in which a recreational sex ethic is absent or very uncommon.

Social and biological conditions interact in subtle ways when it comes to the matter of sexual identity. Consider those male-to-female transsexuals who happen to have, contrary to the usual rule, some sexual attraction to women. In a society which prescribes a rigid differentiation of male and female gender roles, such individuals might well repress the sexual attraction portion of the psyche and present to clinicians as men who want to become heterosexual women by way of a sex-change operation (Blanchard, 1985). Perhaps such transsexuals overlook their sexual attraction to women or honestly believe that it will disappear as a result of the operation. These people would probably identify themselves as "real women" who happen to be trapped in a man's body. In another kind of society—one which allows a role for women who love women—such people might be less likely to repress their sexual attraction to women and present as people born male but who want to have a sex-change operation. These people would sometimes identify themselves as lesbians.

This example illustrates how important socialization and culture are in the social construction of sexual realities and how these social constructions are, in turn, important in people's identities. The same so-called "biological" givens in an individual might cause someone entirely different consequences in different societies.

Finally, in this paper I implicitly adopt a point of view about the relationship between theory and data in sexology. I believe that in the study of sexual orientation, we are now at a point where we can begin to use some hypothetico-deductive methods in addition to the more tried and true empirical ones. Theories must of course be judged by their usefulness in generating hypotheses that can be tested and by the results of those tests. But theories can also be judged by their simplicity, their elegance, and their efficiency in explaining a large number of observations with a small number of hypotheses. It is a fact that in many other disciplines, the most elegantly simple (but not simplistic) theories often turn out to be the correct ones. It is in that spirit that I offer the limerent and lusty theory to the empiricists in the sexological community.

References

Abbott, S., and Love, B. (1972). *Sappho was a right-on woman. A liberated view of lesbianism.* New York: Stein and Day.

Alcock, J. (1984). *Animal behavior: An evolutionary approach* (3rd ed.). Sunderland, MA: Sinauer Associates.

Bancroft, J. H., Jones, H. G., and Pullan, B. P. (1966). A simple transducer for measuring penile erection, with comments on its use in the treatment of sexual disorders. *Behaviour Research and Therapy,* 4, 239–241.

Bell, A. P., Weinberg, M. S., and Hammersmith, S. K. (1981). *Sexual preference: Its development in men and women.* Statistical appendix. Bloomington, IN: Indiana University Press.

Blanchard, R. (1985). Typology of male-to-female transsexualism. *Archives of Sexual Behavior,* 14, 247–261.

Boswell, J. E. (1980). *Christianity, social tolerance, and homosexuality: Gay people in Western Europe from the beginning of the Christian era to the fourteenth century.* Chicago: University of Chicago Press.

Carrier, J. M. (1980). Homosexual behavior in cross-cultural perspective. In J. Marmor (Ed.), *Homosexual behavior: A modern reappraisal* (pp. 100–122). New York: Basic Books.

Cory, D. W. (1967). Homosexuality. In A. Ellis and A. Abarbanel (Eds.), *The encyclopedia of sexual behavior* (pp. 485–493). New York: Hawthorn.

Freund, K. W. (1974). Male homosexuality: An analysis of the pattern. In J. A. Loraine (Ed.), *Understanding homosexuality: Its biological and psychological bases* (pp. 25–81). New York: American Elsevier.

Freund, K. W., Diamant, J., and Pinkava, V. J. (1958). On the validity and reliability of the phalloplethysmographic (Php) diagnosis of some sexual deviations. *Review of Czechoslovak Medicine,* 4, 145–151.

Freund, K. W., Scher, H., Chan, S., and Ben-Aron, M. (1982). Experimental analysis of pedophilia. *Behavior Research and Therapy,* 20, 105–112.

Freund, K. W., Sedlacek, F., and Knob, K. (1965). A simple transducer for mechanical plethysmography of the male genital. *Journal of the Experimental Analysis of Behavior,* 8, 169–170.

Friday, N. (1980). *Men in love, men's sexual fantasies: The triumph of love over rage.* New York: Delacorte.

Gebhard, P. H. (1972). Incidence of overt homosexuality in the United States and Western Europe. In J. M. Livingood (Ed.), *National Institute of Mental Health Task Force on Homosexuality: Final report and background papers* (pp. 22–29). Washington, DC: Government Printing Office. (DHEW publication #HSM 72–9116).

Gebhard, P. H., and Johnson, A. B. (1979). *The Kinsey data: Marginal tabulations of the 1938–1963 interviews conducted by the Institute for Sex Research.* Philadelphia: Saunders.

Geer, J. H. (1975). Direct measurement of genital responding. *American Psychologist,* 30, 415–418.

Hatfield, E., Sprecher S., and Traupmann, J. (1978). Men's and women's reactions to sexually explicit films: A serendipitous finding. *Archives of Sexual Behavior,* 7, 583–592.

Haynes, S. N., and Oziel, L. J. (1976). Homosexuality: Behaviors and attitudes. *Archives of Sexual Behavior,* 4, 283–289.

Kinsey, A. C., Pomeroy, W. B., and Martin, C. E. (1948). *Sexual behavior in the human male.* Philadelphia: Saunders.

Kinsey, A. C., Pomeroy, W. B., Martin, C. E., and Gebhard, P. H. (1953). *Sexual behavior in the human female*. Philadelphia: Saunders.

Klein, F. (1978) *The bisexual option: A concept of one hundred percent intimacy*. New York: Arbor House.

Lorenz, K. Z. (1937) The companion in the bird's world. *The Auk*, 54, 245–273.

MacDonald, A. P., Jr. (1983). A little bit of lavender goes a long way: A critique of research on sexual orientation. *The Journal of Sex Research*, 19, 94–100.

McConaghy, N. (1978). Heterosexual experience, marital status, and orientation of homosexual males. *Archives of Sexual Behavior*, 7, 575–581.

McNulty, F. (1983, January 17). Our far-flung correspondents: Peeping in the shell. *The New Yorker*, 58, pp. 88–97.

Mead, M. (1961). Cultural determinants of sexual behavior. In W. C. Young (Ed.), *Sex and internal secretions* (3rd ed., pp. 1433–1479). Baltimore, MD: Williams and Wilkins.

Millham, J., San Miguel, C. L., and Kellogg, R. (1976). A factor-analytic conceptualization of attitudes toward male and female homosexuals. *Journal of Homosexuality*, 2, 3–10.

Money, J. (1980). *Love and love sickness: The science of sex, gender difference, and pair-bonding*. Baltimore, MD: Johns Hopkins University Press.

Pillard, R. C., Poumadere, J., and Carretta, R. A. (1981). Is homosexuality familial? A review, some data, and a suggestion. *Archives of Sexual Behavior*, 10, 465–475.

Pillard, R. C., and Weinrich, J. D. (1986). Evidence of familial nature of male homosexuality. *Archives of General Psychiatry*, 42, 808–812.

Pillard, R. C., and Weinrich, J. D. (1987). The periodic table model of the gender transpositions: Part I. A theory based on masculinization and defeminization of the brain. *The Journal of Sex Research*, 23, 425–454.

Radway, J. A. (1984). *Reading the romance: Women, patriarchy, and popular literature*. Chapel Hill, NC: University of North Carolina Press.

Saghir, M. T., and Robins, E. (1973). *Male and female homosexuality: A comprehensive investigation*. Baltimore, MD: Williams and Wilkins.

Schäfer, S. (1976). Sexual and social problems of lesbians. *The Journal of Sex Research*, 12, 50–69.

Schäfer, S. (1977). Sociosexual behavior in male and female homosexuals: A study in sex differences. *Archives of Sexual Behavior*, 6, 355–364.

Scott, J. P. (1978). Editor's comments on papers six through nine. In J. P. Scott (Ed.), *Benchmark papers in animal behavior* (Vol. 12, p. 82–84). Stroudsburg, PA: Dowden, Hutchinson and Ross.

Singer, B. (1985). A comparison of evolutionary and environmental theories of erotic response: Part I: Structural features. *The Journal of Sex Research*, 21, 229–257.

Steffensmeier, D., and Steffensmeier, R. (1974). Sex differences in reactions to homosexuals: Research continues and further developments. *The Journal of Sex Research*, 10, 52–67.

Stoller, R. J. (1982). Transvestism in women. *Archives of Sexual Behavior*, 11, 99–115.

Symons, D. (1979). *The evolution of human sexuality*. New York/Oxford: Oxford University Press.

Tennov, D. (1979). *Love and limerence—The experience of being in love*. New York: Stein and Day.

Tripp, C. A. (1975). *The homosexual matrix*. New York: McGraw-Hill.

8

Beyond Gender: The Basis of Sexual Attraction in Bisexual Men and Women

Michael W. Ross and Jay P. Paul

THE construct of sexual orientation has typically emphasized a partner's gender as the most important single feature in the typology of desire. This is true whether one treats sexual orientation as a categorical variable or a continuous variable. It seems evident that those who are either exclusively heterosexual or exclusively homosexual *do* react to gender-based determinants of sexual and emotional attraction. What is not so clear, however, is whether a sexual partner's gender similarity transcends all other factors for everyone. Just as the exploration of bisexuality has forced us to reconsider other aspects of our paradigms of sexuality, sexual orientation, and identity (Paul, 1985), it may be that the study of bisexuality may call into question some of our notions regarding gender as critical in cueing sexual response. As bisexual persons have both male and female sexual partners, it is possible to explore the extent to which sexual partners are differentiated along gender-linked versus nongender-specific dimensions.

The focus on gender as the key variable in sexual attraction is probably a product of an unduly restrictive focus on sexual behavior in terms of its biological function of reproduction. Sexually dimorphic mating behavior must involve a process conducive to male/female pairing. Along these lines, behavioral endocrinologists have tried to link not only mating behavior, but all sexual behavior, to hormonal influences in men and women. But in humans, sexual behavior is far more varied and complex, serving many more ends than that of the continuation of the species (Ross, 1984). Extrapolating from that, Ross has argued that it may be that gender-specific characteristics are one set of factors that kindle sexual interest or desire— and not necessarily the predominant class of variables.

Reproduced with permission of authors and publisher from Ross, M. W and Paul, J. P. Beyond Gender: the basis of sexual attraction in bisexual men and women. *Psychological Reports*, 1992, 71, 1283–1290. © Psychological Reports 1992.

Sexual partners' gender preference may be determined by variables not linked to gender, such as emotional and personality-based features (Ross, Rogers, and McCulloch, 1978). More recently, Kaplan and Rogers (1984) have also argued that concepts of sexuality based upon the physical sex of partners limit the way in which human sexuality is conceptualized and investigated. To examine the basis of sexual attraction to partners, it is necessary to investigate an amalgam of both mental and physical nongender-specific characteristics.

Treating gender as the critical variable tends to foster dichotomous thinking with regard to our concepts of sexual attraction and sexual orientation. Sexual attraction is typically associated with genitalia (male or female), secondary sexual characteristics (male or female), or other culturally determined sex-typed characteristics (e.g., clothing). Some theories of human sexuality presume that sexual attraction to one gender implies the inverse—sexual aversion—to the other. Given this presumed polarity, bisexuality patterns of behavior are often dismissed as situationally determined, transitory phenomena, or simply transitional, rather than being of a stable, fundamental disposition. If bisexuality is treated as an enduring orientation, it may be viewed as the midpoint of a continuum with exclusive homosexuality at one end and exclusive heterosexuality at the other. Ross (1984, 1987) has argued that this emphasis on gender or preferred sexual partners may be inappropriate. Research into bisexuality may more appropriately identify bisexual individuals as those for whom a sexual partner's gender is immaterial, in contrast to both homosexual and heterosexual individuals, for whom gender is a critical consideration. This implicit continuum is defined at the poles by gender-critical choice of partner and gender-immaterial choice of sexual partner (with homosexuals and heterosexuals together at one end of the continuum and bisexuals at the other).

This paradigm of sexual responsiveness receives some support by the findings on "ambisexuals" by Masters and Johnson (1979). They used this term to describe individuals seen in their laboratory who enjoyed, solicited, or responded to overt sexual opportunity without discriminating between male or female sexual partners. However, Masters and Johnson provided an additional criterion for inclusion in their "ambisexual" sample that leads the sample to diverge and perhaps to be a subgroup of the "gender-immaterial" bisexuals described here. Their "ambisexuals" had to have no interest in any ongoing relationship with a sexual partner, which suggests that their responsiveness to others was limited to their genitals.

No previous investigation of bisexual individuals has examined the nature of their preferences for a sexual partner or the dimensions by which they conceptualize their sexual partners. This paper describes an examination of whether sexual partners would be seen as similar to one another (which would support the gender-immaterial paradigm) and what the conceptual dimensions of choice of sexual partner might be. There is an alternative hypothesis to be examined as well: that the determinants of male or female choice of a sexual partner by bisexual individuals may be highly variable, with little agreement across individuals. As a preliminary investigation of this theory, we carried out a repertory grid analysis of the elements of choice of sexual partner in nine bisexual women and men.

From a scientific point of view, if we can demonstrate that one or more bisexuals select sexual partners based on variables unrelated to gender, then we will be able to confirm that there are some bisexual individuals for whom gender is apparently immaterial in selection of partners. It is impossible to use a control group, as any possible controls (homosexual or heterosexual) would by definition select sexual partners based upon gender.

Method

The sample consisted of nine respondents (three women, six men) recruited by the second author from a bisexual organization in San Francisco in 1984. The participants were not intended to be a representative sample. They were white, ranged in age from 25 to 81 years (median age of 31), and all educated beyond high school. All described themselves as equally heterosexual and homosexual in preference for sexual partners, utilizing a Kinsey scale (Kinsey, Pomeroy, and Martin, 1978).

The repertory grid technique (Kelly, 1955) utilized in this research provides a means of eliciting the cognitive categories used by an individual to organize personal perceptions, as well as formal mathematical procedure for relating these constructs to individuals or categories (known as "elements"). Elements were self, parents, most and least preferred male and female sexual partners, and best nonsexual male and female friends. Grids were administered by the second author. Respondents were asked to choose specific persons in their lives who fitted the categories for sexual partners and friends. Constructs were all elicited from respondents with the exception of the final construct-contrast pair (masculine-feminine), which was provided. Subjects were given the following instructions, which are typical of repertory grid studies:

> We want to know how people conceptualize a number of individuals, including sexual partners. On this grid, you will see a number of individuals along the top line. On the next line, and for the subsequent lines, there are three circles for each line. The first line has the circles under Self, Mother, and Father. Now, think of a way in which two of these people are similar and one different. [The polar constructs "Happy-Sad" might be elicited, that is, an individual may believe that two of these people were happy and one sad]. Write these characteristics in the space on the right, one under "1" and the other under "5." Now go back to the beginning of the line and rate each person (including the ones with the circles in the boxes) on a scale of 1 to 5, where "1" is "Happy" and "5" is "Sad," for example, "2" would be "Moderately Happy." Then do the same for the next line, looking at the way that two of the Most Preferred Male Partner, Most Preferred Female Partner, and Best Nonsexual Male Friend are the same or different; rate each of the boxes in the line; and continue until you reach the end.

Each respondent was interviewed separately and had the grid explained individually to them by the second author, with the first lines being filled out in his presence to ensure that the respondents understood the task. Readers unfamiliar with repertory grid theory and technique are referred to Kelly (1955) for a more detailed description.

Since each numerical entry fixes an element in relation to a construct, the entry is a precise representation of cognition and an efficient way of presenting a personal construct system. However, this representation is complex, and in this format it is difficult to grasp the salient features of an individual's system of cognitive classification.

Data reduction by means of principal components analysis is used to accomplish the necessary simplification. Standard repertory grid computer programs (*INGRID* and *PREFAN*: Slater, 1976, 1977) were used to analyze the data. A decision as to the number of factors considered significant was based on the scree method of Tsujioka and Cattell (1965). While this method is subjective, it provides a means of reducing a complex situation into an abbreviated set of apparently meaningful factors.

Briefly, principal components analysis creates linear combinations of the variables or constructs. A principal components analysis can indicate how these constructs are related to one another and proved a means of reducing the respondent's set of constructs to a minimal number of unique and descriptive dimensions. The first principal component is the combination of personal constructs that accounts for the largest proportion of variance in the respondent's "view" of the elements (the individuals rated). The second principal component is the combination of constructs for the next largest amount of variance and is uncorrelated with the first. Successive components explain progressively smaller amounts of the total variance and are each independent of one another.

By examination of the construct content of each independent component, it is possible to measure the relevance of each construct in an individual's classification system for a sexual partner as represented by the repertory grid. As the construct of masculine-feminine was provided in the grid, we can evaluate the extent to which the dimensions extracted from the respondent's elicited constructs are associated with gender. In addition, by looking at the loading of each element (each individual listed at the top of the grid) on each respective principal component, we can evaluate the extent to which each dimension "characterizes" a particular element (see Table 8.2 below). The greater the absolute value of the loading, the stronger the relationship between that principal component and the element.

In a combined analysis, the relative distance of each element (or person) was computed from the angular distances between elements for each respondent. Constructs and elements were plotted in terms of Cartesian coordinates against principal components 1 and 2. Where components are described in Tables 8.3 and 8.4 below, they are presented not as bipolar constructs, but in terms of the poles of the constructs which maximally separate and are parallel to most preferred male and female sexual partners. Thus, the highest positive loading may be "athletic" and the highest negative loading "dishonest," so that the component would be described as "athletic vs dishonest."

Results and Discussion

Results are presented in Tables 8.1 to 8.4. Although an exploratory analysis based on a small sample and idiographic data, some interesting interpretations can be made. First, it is apparent that, even with the provided construct pair of masculine-feminine, the majority of the dimensions which distinguish these individuals are based on interactive rather than gender-based characteristics. These data do suggest that for some bisexual persons, the dimensions on which male and female sexual partners are conceptualized are nongender-based.

Second, preferred sexual partners are conceptualized as being closer to "self" (the respondent) than to any other individual listed as an element (Table 8.1). These data suggest that people who are acceptable as sexual partners are those seen as being like oneself on a number of personality dimensions. These preferred sexual partners were closer to self over the sum of the nine grids than were the best nonsexual friends. This is illustrated in Table 8.2, where it is evident that preferred male and female sexual partners are almost identical in loadings on the first two components extracted, while other pairings (e.g., parents and least preferred sexual partners) have widely discrepant loadings with opposite signs. This last point suggests that, although gender-based distinctions can be made, *they are not made for preferred sexual partners.*

Third, when the distances and dimensions along which preferred male and female sexual partners occur are examined for each grid individually, it is apparent that the dimensions which maximally separate most preferred sexual partners are not gender-based in seven of the nine grids (see Table 8.3). These data offer the strongest suggestion that it may be appropriate to conceptualize some bisexual

TABLE 8.1 *Distances of Elements from Preferred Partners*

Element	Preferred Male		Preferred Female	
	Loading	Rank	Loading	Rank
Self	0.832	1	.841	1
Mother	1.106	8	0.987	6
Father	1.026	7	1.130	8
Most Preferred Male Partner			0.896	3
Most Preferred Female Partner	0.896	2		
Least Preferred Male Partner	1.018	6	1.069	7
Least Preferred Female Partner	1.003	5	0.948	5
Best Nonsexual Male Friend	0.904	3	0.898	4
Best Nonsexual Female Friend	0.959	4	.885	2

TABLE 8.2 *Element Loadings on First Three Components Extracted*

Element	Component		
	1	2	3
Self	−9.6	2.0	−0.2
Mother	−2.3	−7.0	8.8
Father	17.5	2.4	−2.1
Most Preferred Male Partner	−4.8	−0.1	−3.6
Most Preferred Female Partner	−4.7	−1.4	3.4
Least Preferred Male Partner	−7.8	−9.6	−5.5
Least Preferred Female Partner	11.1	1.7	0.8
Best Nonsexual Male Friend	−3.4	0.3	−1.2
Best Nonsexual Female Friend	0.1	4.7	−0.4

people as making choices not on the basis of gender, but on the basis of personality or physical attributes not necessarily associated with gender.

Finally, from Table 8.4 it is apparent that the three female respondents saw minimal separation in distance between most preferred male and female sexual partners, while there was considerably more separation between these partners for male respondents. This may reflect gender-based differences in how respondents perceive sexual partners or what they seek in sexual partners. Further research in this area is warranted.

Further work is necessary to examine the implicit assumption here: that the cognitions tapped by the descriptive categories these respondents used to differentiate the grid's elements are related to the dimensions that determine sexual attraction for them. Another possible means of exploring what constitutes sexual attraction would be to look at the similarities and differences among a number of previous sexual partners for any individual respondent.

This analysis was an exploration of whether there may be any support for the hypothesis that, for bisexual people, choice of sexual partner may not be based on

TABLE 8.3 *Constructs Used Within Each Respondent's Personal Belief System*

Respondent		Construct
1 (female)	1	Sexual/Accepting vs Dependent/Thin
	2	Obese/Potent vs Feminine
2 (female)	1	Athletic/Spontaneous vs Dishonest/Does not depend on me
	2	Honest/Open vs Nondrinker
3 (female)	1	Liberal/Masculine vs Quiet/Unathletic
	2	Workaholic/Reflective vs Radical/Unconventional
4 (male)	1	Sexually inhibited/Conservative vs Couple-oriented/Close
	2	Open/Indifferent vs Flamboyant/Experimental
5 (male)	1	Demanding vs Relaxed/Not verbally expressive
	2	Physically playful/Physically fit vs Unconventional/Nonmonogamous
6 (male)	1	Feels rejected/Narrow-minded vs Lazy
	2	Egotistical/Irascible vs Extravagant
7 (male)	1	Manipulative vs Inhibited/Nonempathic
	2	Frolicsome/Congenial vs Genuine/Introspective
8 (male)	1	Honest/Intimate friendship vs Noncreative/Intolerant
	2	Nonplayful/No sense of humor vs Nonneurotic/Nonuptight
9 (male)	1	Nonmusical/Patient vs Not self-centered
	2	Not self-centered/Practical vs Not sensual/Uncuddly

TABLE 8.4 *Constructs on Which Respondents Differentiated Male and Female Partners*

Respondent	Construct
1 (female)	Potent vs Feminine*
2 (female)	Spontaneous vs Not Cuddly*
3 (female)	Radical vs Lazy
4 (male)	Dark Hair vs Indifferent
5 (male)	Nonconventional vs Physically Playful
6 (male)	Pushy vs Feminine
7 (male)	Calm vs Establishment
8 (male)	Nonneurotic vs Sense of Humor
9 (male)	Unsentimental vs Practical

* Minimal separation between elements.

gender but on other dimensions of person perception. The data provide some support for this paradigm. They suggest that the notion of bisexuals making relatively gender-free choices of sexual partners in contrast to those for whom sexual partner's gender is a major dimension of choice (those exclusively heterosexual or homosexual) is warranted.

References

Kaplan, G. T., and Rogers, L. J. (1984) Breaking out of the dominant paradigm: A new look at sexual attraction. *Journal of Homosexuality*, 10, 71–75.

Kelly, G. A. (1955) *The psychology of personal constructs*. Vol. 1. New York: Norton.

Kinsey, A. C., Pomeroy, W., and Martin, C. E. (1978) [*sic*] *Sexual behavior in the human male*. Philadelphia, PA: Saunders.

Masters, W. H., and Johnson, V. E. (1979) *Homosexuality in perspective*. Boston, MA: Little, Brown.

Paul, J. P. (1985) Bisexuality: Reassessing our paradigms of sexuality. *Journal of Homosexuality*, 11, 21–34.

Ross, M. W. (1984) Beyond the biological model: New directions in bisexual and homosexual research. *Journal of Homosexuality*, 10, 63–70.

Ross, M. W. (1987) Theory of normal homosexuality: A critique and redefinition of homosexual contacts. In L. Diamant (Ed.), *Male and female homosexuality: psychological approaches*. Washington, DD: Hemisphere. Pp. 237–259.

Ross, M. W., Rogers, L. J. and McCulloch, H. (1978) Stigma, sex and society: A new look at gender differentiation and sexual variation. *Journal of Homosexuality*, 3, 315–330.

Slater, P. (1976) *The measurement of interpersonal space by grid technique*. Vol. 1. London: Wiley.

Slater, P. (1977) *The measurement of interpersonal space by grid technique*. Vol. 2. London: Wiley.

Tsujioka, B., and Cattell, R. B. (1965) Constancy and difference in personality structure and mean profile in the questionnaire medium after applying the 16 PF test in America and Japan. *British Journal of Social and Clinical Psychology*, 4, 287–297.

9

From Sexual Identity to Sexual Relationships: A Contextual Shift

John P. De Cecco and Michael G. Shively

A SEXUAL relationship can be defined by its structure, the constituent elements of which are the attitudes of partners that inform their treatment of each other. These attitudes may, for example, include beliefs about biological sex, femininity and masculinity, complementarity, exclusivity, sensuosity, intimacy, and permanency. The structure of a sexual relationship consists of the implications or consequences of partners' having various attitudes. For example, partners may view a relationship as a network of externally prescribed obligations or they may view it as consisting of both negotiated and personal choices. These differing views of relationships would probably have sharply contrasting structural implications or consequences. As such, the structure is unknown to the partners because it is the conceptualization of the social scientist who notes the implications of partners' holding similar or dissimilar sets of beliefs. As noted by F. A. Hayek (1952/1979): "It is important to observe that . . . the various types of individual attitudes are not themselves the object of our [the social scientists'] explanation, but merely the element from which we build up the structure of possible relationships between individuals" (p. 68).

Still unanswered is the question of what distinguishes a relationship that is *sexual* from one that is not sexual. A relationship can be considered sexual from two vantage points: that of a shared moral tradition and that of the individual. Because traditional sexual morality has been chiefly concerned with regulating physical contact between individuals, particularly when it involves the genitalia, a relationship can be viewed as sexual whenever it falls within the purview of strictures placed on such conduct.

Sexual conduct, however, is not a static reality. Although the Judaeo-Christian tradition proscribed forms of sexual conduct such as sodomy and bestiality, it did little to elucidate what particular behavior was forbidden. The institutional fear of fostering the forbidden sexual conduct resulted in only elliptical references to specific behavior. The individual, therefore, was the unwitting heir of the freedom to determine which specific acts were forbidden.

Therefore, a relationship can also be considered sexual because of the individual's understanding of traditional morality and independent beliefs about what constitutes sexual conduct. Moral principles are not ingested or applied by individuals as irreducible substances. They are ideas that are modified by the individual on the basis of conscious and unconscious knowledge and are applied as the individual deems necessary or appropriate. . . .

From Identity to Relationships

There are distinct advantages, we believe, in shifting the discourse on sexual identity, in its historical, bisexual, homosexual, and biological contexts, to an inquiry about the structure of sexual relationships. These advantages may be categorized as conceptual, moral, and methodological.

The initial conceptual advantage is that the focus of inquiry is shifted from isolated individuals to their mutual associations. The emphasis on individuals outside of their historical and social contexts is probably an unfortunate import by the social sciences from medicine and natural science. In biology, as well as medicine, a picture of the whole phenomenon is usually developed through a detailed analysis of its parts. In psychotherapy the attitudinal and behavioral structures of clients are probed for the purpose of individual insight and possible change. Social scientists, we believe, should be curious about the mental attitudes of the individuals they observe. However, the focus of their inquiry should not be isolated individuals but the structure of social relationships, be they economic, political, or sexual.

The second and, perhaps, major advantage would be to allow social scientists the opportunity to explore aspects of sexual relationships other than the biological. The chief conceptual difficulty posed by the idea of sexual identity is that it rivets attention on the biological aspects of sexual relationships almost to the exclusion of other considerations.

Sexual identity is basically a biological concept that makes the an atomical differences between females and males the pivotal analytical distinction. The biological penumbra that hangs over the idea of sexual identity ultimately leads to viewing sexual relationships as grounded in the genitalia of the partners. These simple anatomical differences are then symbolically elaborated as psychological properties of individuals, such as feminine and masculine attitudes, or as socio-cultural properties of sexual collectivities, such as the "straight lifestyle" or the "gay community." It may be asserted, perhaps rather boldly, that the long discourse on sexual identity has been essentially an exercise in exhaustively symbolizing the myriad ways in which sexual relationships can be described as extensions of the biological sex of partners.

Investigations of sexual relationships from other than a biological stance may discover structures based on motivations, attitudes, and expectations of partners that are unrecognized because there are no taxonomies or theories with which to describe or explain them. Since the eighteenth century Enlightenment bequeathed to individuals the ideology of personal choice, to be exercised in selecting partners or in sustaining or ending relationships, it is difficult to believe that these choices can be understood simply in terms of biological characteristics. The idea of sexual identity, with its aura of biological determinism, hardly provides a context broad enough to account for the complexity and consequences of choices that are conceived and exercised in sexual relationships.

A third conceptual advantage pertains to our definition of sexual relationships as a structure that is described by the social scientist who notes the consequences of partners holding particular sexual attitudes. Because these attitudes are unique amalgams of personal and societal knowledge and meanings, the shift in focus from sexual identity to sexual relationships capitalizes on the advantages but avoids the shortcomings of both psychoanalytic theory and symbolic interactionism (i.e., social constructionism). Psychoanalytic theory is exquisitely sensitive to the fact that individuals create personal meanings out of the vicissitudes of experience rather than simply importing them from the social milieu. It tends, however, to lose the individual in a world of private meanings that are only vaguely tied to historical or social contexts. Symbolic interactionism is acutely aware that the personal and social categories to which individuals assign themselves and others are largely imports from meanings handed down through society and history. However, it tends to surrender the individual to a world of social meanings that are minimally subject to personal criticism and interpolation. The structure of sexual relationships, as conceived here, exists as an intersection of both the uniquely personal meanings of the individual partners and a locus in history and society.

The moral injunctions implied by the scientific discourse on sexual identity have been essentially a perpetuation of Judaeo-Christian strictures. Relationships had to have an extrinsic, "higher," purpose, if not procreation and rearing of family, then some transcendental reembodiment of the individual in, for example, romantic love, poetry, painting, or altruism. In the discourse on sexual identity there has been the lingering note of discomfort with sexual relationships that are formed perhaps exclusively for the purpose of the happiness and satisfaction of the partners alone.

Judaeo-Christian doctrine had warned against sexual relationships that were formed outside of prescribed boundaries as seriously jeopardizing the individual's soul and salvation. Under the banner of science, medicine also warned people about the dangers of errant sexual behavior. If the warning was not heeded, the proscribed behavior constituted a serious threat to physical and mental health. Lust, the Church Fathers had sternly cautioned, could drive men and women to perdition. Their successors in the nineteenth and twentieth centuries, the fathers of medicine and the social sciences, zealously warned individuals that lustful indulgence could drive them to insanity, perversion, and loss of identity.

There are advantages in moral clarity that could be gained in shifting the discourse from sexual identity to a focus on the structure of sexual relationships. The underlying assumption has been that permissible relationships are prescribed for individuals rather than by them. The scientific discourse on sexual identity, because it has embodied the Judaeo-Christian morality, overshadowed the view of human relationships propounded by the philosophers of the eighteenth century Enlightenment. Their philosophy bequeathed moral choice to the individual where previously there had been only the moral authority of Church and State (Gay, 1954). Peter Gay (1954) drew this contrast between Christian and Enlightenment views of sexual morality:

> Whatever the rationalism of some Christian theologians, fundamental to Christianity was the enmity of passion and salvation: a sense of guilt was to hold back desire—the Fall of man at once created lust and gave man a weapon against it. In the Enlightenment, the dichotomy of lust versus guilt was softened into the opposition of reason to emotion, and with this softening rose the opportunity of achieving a view of man in which these opposites would be reconciled. (p. 154)

These moral prescriptions have been perpetuated in their biological, psychological, or sociological avatars. Biology prescribed the fundamental structure of sexual relationships because it was based on the anatomical differences between the two sexes. By extension, however, bisexual and homosexual relationships were conceived as adaptations within the design rather than basic modifications. Because psychiatry and, later, psychology, as the sciences of mental and behavioral processes, and sociology, as the science of collective processes, were modeled in part after evolutionary biology, it was possible to express the biological design for sexual relationships in psychological and sociological metaphors.

The awesome inevitability of biological, psychological, and social processes, presumably working in concert, placed most responsibility for sexual relationships well beyond the grasp of the partners involved in them. If any responsibility was left for the individual, then it was the "choice" to form relationships that were harmonious with the requirements of a stern reality. To ignore or flout this reality was to risk "punishment," visited in the form of biological incapacity, mental suffering, or social rejection.

The structural implications of individuals replacing a morality of obligation with a morality of choice in their sexual relationships has scarcely been explored in the social sciences. It is possible to theorize, however, about the changes that would transpire. First, and perhaps most obviously, decision-making within the relationship would be viewed as the prerogative of the partners themselves. Power would be exercised as if it resided in the relationship rather than in some authority external to it. Second, rules governing the relationship and establishing its boundaries would be created and modified through a process of negotiation in which each partner had a voice. Third, the structure of the relationship would reflect the attitudes and values of the individuals who comprised it regardless of how accurately or inaccurately these incorporated the prevailing morality.

There are important methodological advantages for historiography and the social sciences in shifting to a focus on sexual relationships. For one thing, the taxonomies and theories for describing and explaining relationships would be derived from the consequences of partners exercising particular choices as a reflection of personal attitudes and expectations. The proper subject matter of the social sciences, according to Hayek (1952/1979), is the mentality of the individuals whose relationships the investigator hopes to decipher. Furthermore, it would be possible to study a broad spectrum of relationships without prejudging them as natural, normal, or morally right. The structural similarities of particular sexual relationships, heterosexual and homosexual, for example, may go unrecognized because it is assumed that the sexual identity of partners requires dissimilar structures.

The uncharted territory in sexual relationships are those feelings, motivations, attitudes, intentions, and expectations held by the partners themselves. Approaching relationships as if they are governed by lawful forces, in the manner in which the physical universe is organized, the social scientist is blinded to the boundless ingenuity individuals can exercise in forming, maintaining, and even ending sexual relationships and to the fortuitous consequences that the reformulation of past relationships has for future ones. Projected against these possible discoveries, the concern with the sexual identity of partners appears to be a narrow preoccupation.

REFERENCES

Gay, P. 1954. *The party of humanity: Essays on the Enlightenment.* New York: Alfred A. Knopf.
Hayek, F. A. 1979 [1952]. *The counter-revolution of science: Studies on the abuse of reason.* Indianapolis, IN: Liberty Press.

10

Gender Identity and Sexual Behaviour

Harry Brierley

Problems of Definition

In common parlance the terms "sex" and "gender" are virtually synonymous. However, is necessary to make a distinction between them if we are to understand sexual behaviour of differing varieties. "Sex" itself is a concept capable of very wide meanings from, for instance, psychoanalytic polymorphous and latent sexuality, to the narrow euphemistic sense of "having sex." Sex is, of course, the distinction between man and woman, and an individual is ascribed male or female sexuality. This is fairly clearly and indelibly stated on the birth certificate. It is determined by the doctor attending the birth, in almost all cases no doubt by a fairly cursory examination of the physical organs of reproduction. The assumption is made that these organs represent appropriate internal structures and reproductive instincts. The diagnosis of sex is, therefore, relatively crude but almost irrevocable.

Behaviour connected with the physical organs and reproductive mechanisms, especially with a physiological erotic arousal, is sexual behaviour. Courtship may be called sexual behaviour; putting the shot, spitting and coal-mining in most cultures are characteristic of one sex rather than the other but are not sexual behaviour.

Behaviours which are not sexual in this sense but are associated with one sex rather than the other are genderal. That is to say, needlework and flower-arrangement are feminine occupations, whilst rugby football and gambling are masculine. This is not to say that females do not gamble but only that when they do so in this culture they are exhibiting genderal behaviour which is masculine. The only implication is that genderal behaviours are those which are most commonly found amongst men or women in a particular culture. At first sight this appears obvious, and a woman who spits may well be doing something regarded as masculine or unfeminine but certainly not sexual. However, we cannot understand sexual variations without appreciating that there is an area of confusion. If a man seeks a feminine occupation or dresses in a feminine manner a dissonance occurs which results in the interpretation of the behaviour as sexual when it may well be entirely genderal.

The origins of sex and gender are not, of course, unconnected, even though a female may be masculine and a male feminine. Their origins do involve morphological sex to a considerable degree. Thus when we meet a stranger in the street we note certain badges of gender: hair length, adornments, cosmetics, and so on. We make confident predictions about the way the stranger will behave in terms of norms of masculine and feminine behaviour. We note also body features, breasts, arm length, waist, hip width, beard and other more subtle factors like smell and we make confident predictions about the individual's sexual instincts and the possession of reproductive sexual organs. One does not predict the other only in a hazardous way. If a woman chooses to wear trousers and drive a bus there may be a confused response and she may be identified not simply as a female enjoying a masculine occupation but as one who is sexually different from the norm. If a transvestite chooses to wear the clothes of the opposite sex, he or she is perceived as a sexual threat and provokes a call for legal sanctions.

Looked at in these broad terms the meanings of sex and gender ought to be clear and rational, but the consensus is not solid and usage continues to be confused. The gender concept owes a great deal to the work of Money (Money et al. 1957) and his colleagues. However, Money's meaning tends to be confused by the way his argument has developed. It has been necessary for him to look at two components of gender: "role" and "identity." Identity in Money's view is established in the early years of life and role is fixed later. In reality it is clear that there is no such dichotomy; it can only be some components of gender which are acquired earlier than others. Nevertheless Money does give what he calls the "Official definitions" (Money and Ehrhardt 1972):

Gender Identity: The sameness, unity, and persistence of one's individuality as male, female, or ambivalent, in greater or lesser degree, especially as it is experienced in self awareness and behaviour; gender identity is the private experience of gender role, and gender role is the public expression of gender identity.

Gender Role: Everything that a person says and does, to indicate to others or to the self the degree that one is either male, or female, or ambivalent; it includes but is not restricted to sexual arousal and response.

Complex though these definitions are they do not seem consistent with Money's general thesis. For example, how, if gender identity is "the private experience of gender role," does it become fixed, as Money asserts, by the age of two to three years whereas gender role is not fixed until much later? Why also does Money include sexual arousal as an aspect of gender role?

Stoller (1968) has a rather more simple approach:

Gender is a term that has psychological and cultural rather than biological connotations; if the proper terms for sex are "male" and "female," the proper terms for gender are "masculine" and "feminine"; these latter may be quite independent of (biological) sex. Gender is the amount of masculinity or femininity found in a person, and, obviously, while there are mixtures of both in many humans, the normal male has a preponderance of masculinity and the normal female a preponderance of femininity.

The latter fact is actuarial rather than biological, of course, and some would prefer the use of "average" rather than "normal."

Oakley (1972) comments on the fact that in different cultures the same distinctions prevail between the sexes but there are great variations in gender roles. She points out that where "intersex" cases have been studied they may be just as masculine or feminine as those who are biologically normal. She concludes, "If proof is needed that sex and gender are two separate entities then this is it."

"Deviant" Sexual Behaviour

Research in sexual behaviour is difficult because, on the one hand, of the private nature of sexual instincts and, on the other, of social pressures. Sexual responsiveness, being "sexy" or even promiscuous, carries a social value—although some groups affect to deny this. Vague beliefs of normality in sexual behaviour exist, e.g., frequency of intercourse, and "sex" at an early age being an indicator of normality. Such themes, although belonging more to folklore than fact, become foci for the neurotic anxieties of some people. These social pressures to conform to what is decreed as "normal" are immense and must necessarily influence behaviour. An individual's erotic fantasies and sexual behaviour are liable to be classified as "abnormal" or "deviant," because society has not recognized the normality of a wide variation of sexual behaviours.

Arbitrary lines are drawn, as exemplified by the well-known scale of homosexuality devised by Kinsey; but who is deviant on such a scale? A fetishist earns the title if there is a belief, usually on the part of a doctor, that the individual is dependent on his fetish to obtain orgasm—an unlikely limitation. There is evidence that fetishism is the norm rather than the deviation, and indeed social norms have changed somewhat over the last 20 years. It seems that a fetish for black nighties has become a part of normal sexual behaviour but a fetish for black plastic macs has not. The inconsistency is remarkable.

In the final analysis an individual's sexual behaviour becomes "deviant" when he seeks help, usually medical, allowing his discomfort to be attributed to his sexual behaviour. The exchange between Green and Bancroft (Crown 1979) puts this succinctly in reference to homosexuality: "Green: Homosexuality may be the sole condition which is a mental disorder only if you go to a psychiatrist for it! Bancroft: The treatment then is to get rid of all psychiatrists." Unfortunately Green understates the situation since much the same is true of many aspects of sexual behaviour.

Models of Sexual Deviance

Vast changes in social awareness of sexual behaviour have occurred since the second world war, exposing its complexity. To avoid pejorative terms like "deviance," the term "variation" can be used (or "diversity"—see Introduction). A number of models of sexual variation are in use. All these, however, minimize the wholeness of human behaviour and depict the variant as variant only in his biological sexuality and the consequent behaviour. The principal models are as follows:

THE CLASSIFICATORY MODEL

The traditional medical approach has been to gather together parcels of behaviour into diagnostic categories. Symptoms are linked together, often on tenuous grounds; importance is attached to a diagnosis; then a "treatment of choice" is assumed to follow. Discussion of the symptoms of, say, transsexualism are copious in the literature. To such workers it seems important to resolve what constitutes the "true transsexual." Whether he stands or sits to urinate are matters for solemn evaluation (Wallinder 1975). In reality it is usually, if not always, the case that there are no obvious reliable sequelae from such diagnoses (Laub and Fisk 1974). Such diagnostic categories appear as discrete paragraphs both in text-books and in the International Classification of Diseases.

Criticism of this approach usually evokes the comment that "the medical model has not been properly understood." While this may be so, it seems rarely to have been properly explained. It must surely stand on more than a grouping together of behaviours which seem related. A proper model should have implications for action, provide an identification of origins and dynamics and have some reliable basis for predictions.

There are a very large number of such categories of sexual variation as postulated diagnoses. Cross-dressing alone provides 56 at a conservative estimate (Brierley 1979).

THE PSYCHODYNAMIC MODEL

The psychodynamic approach conceives of sexual variations as perversions. Normal sexual urges are channelled into unusual forms by the accidents of nurture and experience. Perversion in this context, as with much psychoanalytic usage, does not have quite the same meaning as in day-to-day usage. Within a psychodynamic framework, diagnostic categories are inappropriate because of the individuality of the process. The dynamics of a specific case are seen as appropriate to that case only and the dynamics of the case may well not be those of similar behaviour in others. In fact, many analytical writers are seduced, presumably by the medical model, into making general applications of the dynamics of single cases, as if dealing with diagnostic categories. Fenichel's (1930) analysis of a case which included transvestite behaviour of a fetishistic kind concluded that the dynamics elicited in analysis did not account for the transvestite behaviour. Moreover, he confessed that similar dynamics were to be found in many different kinds of sexual behaviour. Nevertheless Fenichel's analysis has quite commonly been taken as an authoritative explanation of all cross-dressing behaviour—and quite wrongly so.

Freud based his thinking on the concept of infantile polymorphous sexuality, which became channelled into individual forms in maturity. Psychotherapy is thus directed towards initiating a rechannelling of the sexual urges. "Change therapy" is often used as a derogatory term for such a general approach, implying that society directs the therapist to guide the change towards some "socially desirable" goal. Whilst this ought not to be so, it is sometimes not clear that this has been grasped by the therapist. This is sometimes true of behaviour therapy, where concentration on the symptom avoids an analysis of the goals which the therapist may be inferring in the client.

Hypotheses such as that of McGuire et al. (1965) that sexual behaviour patterns are learned by contiguous masturbation have a close similarity to those of psychoanalysis. Based loosely on learning principles, McGuire's suggestion is that patterns of sexual behaviour are shaped around fantasies and objects by the concomitant erotic reinforcement in masturbation. This assumes, as did Freud, a polymorphic sexuality constrained by learning.

The Biological Model

The biological approach contests the notion of undifferentiated sexuality at birth (e.g. Diamond 1965). From this viewpoint, animal studies are interpreted as showing that sexual behaviour is not dependent on post-natal learning. Thus sexual behaviour is seen as a product of physiological and genetic influences which can be adjusted by physical methods such as hormone therapy, brain surgery, and reassignment of sex.

The Sociological Model

This approach regards sexual diversity as a matter primarily of statistical variation. From this viewpoint it is stressed that all societies breed members with widely differing sexual behaviour, sometimes approved in one society, honoured in another and despised in a third. This being so, it is argued that the ideal society is not one in which the sexual behaviour of all is closely similar but one which can cater for, and value, a wide range of sexual variation. Western society is clearly not such a society, struggling as it does to contain sexual variations by exclusion, imprisonment, hospitalization, ghettos, etc. Glover (1960) expresses this view in respect of homosexuality: "the answer to this problem, if it be a problem, is in the development of greater tolerance amongst sections of the community which at present tend to make a scapegoat of homosexuality. In this sense the treatment of homosexuality as a whole should be directed as much at the 'diseased' prejudices of society as at the 'diseased' propensities of the individual homosexual."

The Human Rights Model

The minority groups look at the problems of sexual variation from a different perspective. Like sociologists, members of such groups may point to the occurrence and acceptance of the same "deviant" sexual variations in other cultures and at other times. They argue that the problem is thus of society's creation and that it is society which violates the rights of the minorities. From this viewpoint, the failure of a society to tolerate those who differ in their sexual behaviour is a mark of its fundamental unjust nature.

The Value of the Models

I suggest that none of these ways of thinking about sexual variation does a great deal to further the understanding of human sexual behaviour. The major obstacles are the attention to biological sex alone and the misconception of some behaviours as solely sexual. Thus the homosexual becomes for Money (1970) a person with a propensity for same-sex copulation, without reference to the mass of non-sexual qualities which seem to characterize the total person who is homosexual (Willmott and Brierley 1983). Even more marked is the assumption that all cross-dressing and cross-gender behaviour is sexual. Nowhere can this be more farcically expressed than in Karpman (1947), who says that all cross-dressing is fetishistic in that it is followed in the next few hours by masturbation—or urination, which is the psychic equivalent!

Goode (1981) is one of the many who have entered the debate about whether homosexuality should be defined as a role or as a form of sexual behaviour. Essentially the debate is abortive since it assumes the homogeneity of the homosexual role, ignoring the fact that there are as many roles as there are homosexuals.

I contend that it is essential to look at the total personality organization of the individual to understand his or her sexual behaviour, not just to examine the person's biological needs. Freud in 1905 recognized this full well and wrote in his "Three essays on sexuality" of the impossibility of understanding homosexuality on the basis of physical sex alone and turned to some concept of "mental sex," which seems, at least, to have elements which foreshadow the concept of gender as Stoner defines it.

The gender concept has its origins in the work of Money and the Hampsons (1955 and 1957). They found that where sex at birth was in some doubt in hermaphrodite children, the "sex" of rearing was almost always adopted. The rearing pattern appeared to transcend the biological factors. A child who should be regarded as female according to, say, chromosomal criteria but who was reared as a boy would acquire a belief that she/he was masculine like other boys. She/he would acquire the usual cultural characteristics of a boy. Moreover if an attempt was made to reverse the rearing pattern after two or three years it would not succeed and a masculine gender identity would be retained. Thus it seemed that the gender identity or sense of "I am a boy" became established in this early critical period whilst the acquisition of the gender role, or style of behaving like a boy, would follow on.

Clearly such issues of gender identity and role are vastly important in understanding the gender dysphorias, transvestism, transsexualism and homosexuality. It seems clear that the transsexual's claim is "I am feminine (or masculine) but my body is male (or female)—change my body and I will be a coherent whole."

A Model of Sexual Behaviour

Bancroft (1972) proposed a model of the functional aspects of sexual behaviour in terms of cognitive consistency principles. Figure 10.1 is an attempt to elaborate on Bancroft's model using personal construct theory. The figure has three main parts. Firstly, the personal construct system, covering the range of self concepts or elements, exemplified by "Me as I really am," "Me as I wish I was," and "Me as others would see the real me." In personal construct terms it is hypothesized that the individual's construct system, which is highly personalized and can only be loosely described, as it is in this example, serves as the structure on which the individual can best perceive his world as secure and predictable. Personal constructs are tools which allow the individual to anticipate events reliably.

In ideal circumstances, and in the well-integrated personality, separate elements of the type shown in figure 10.1 would be closely related. The individual would construe his real self very much as he construes the way others see him, and how he would like to be. The example illustrates, of course, a highly dissonant personality whose perception of his role relationships would be very complex and uncertain. He would be fundamentally insecure because of his inability to make general confident predictions about his world, an important aspect of which would be his sexual roles. Kelly suggests that it is the need to make sound predictions of events which primarily reinforces behaviour rather than pleasure *per se*.

Secondly, in the area of interpersonal perceptions gender role is, like other roles, not a self concept as much as a persistent pattern of behaviour which arises from the expectations of how those about the individual will construe him. Thus the role is played without great dependency on cues. The gender identity, on the other hand, is a core role and is determined by the most firmly established and least flexible constructs. It goes without saying that both role and identity are expectations of how the individual will be seen by others, not necessarily of how he is actually seen by them.

The sex object is the person, or perhaps object, on whom sexual arousal is centred in the broad sense. In this model, the sex object, as perceived by the individual, is adopted by the application of his personal construct system to reality, that is, the person seeks the best realistic fit to maximize the predictive capacity of his construct system, in a sexual sense. It will be increasingly difficult to determine an adequate sex object the more disparate the set of self concepts becomes. The sex object would need to be construed in terms of the individual's true self as much as in terms of the way others are predicted to construe him or her. The sex object must

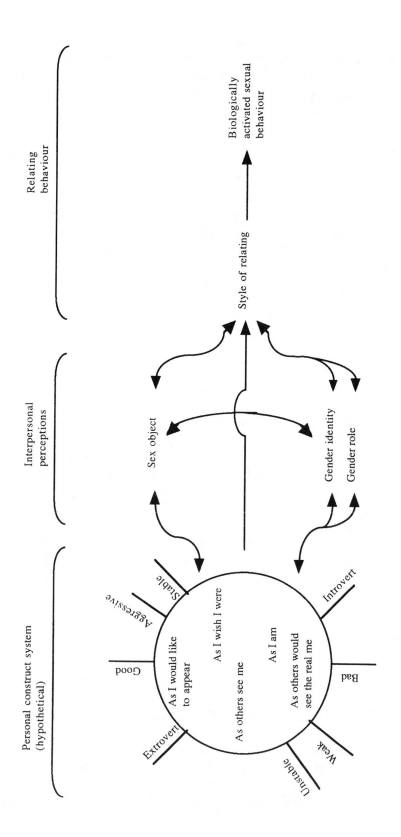

Figure 10.1: Model - Origins of Sexual Behaviour

clearly be in a relationship with the gender identity and role. This relationship is described as the "style of relating," which is, in effect, the behavioural solution to the maintenance of an equilibrium in the system. This style of relating, when biologically activated, gives rise to the individual's style of sexual behaviour and forms the third part of the system.

The separate elements of the system are in a state of homeostatic balance. That is to say, the system adjusts as far as possible to maintain stability and to oppose external constraints. Core constructs and gender identity are themselves resistant to change and the sex object appears moderately so. The style of relating is fairly fluid and, as is implicit in personal construct theory, the construct system itself, is in a constant state of modification and testing, to maximize its predictive efficiency. The system functions as a whole to maintain the best working compromise and determines the style of relating and consequently sexual behaviour itself.

The model represents only the psychological aspect of the system. Other forces produce constraints on this system. The law and social conventions in particular limit the resultant sexual behaviour. Biological and endocrine factors play some part, it seems, in determining gender. Family structures, occupational roles and environmental issues are similarly involved in determining the construct system itself.

IMPLICATIONS OF THE MODEL

The immediate implication of such a model is the unacceptability of conceptualizing sexual variations as discrete entities. It may be possible to say that an individual conforms to some degree to some hypothetical concept of, say, a homosexual or a heterosexual but not that he or she belongs to a distinct group of people with a common circumscribed behaviour pattern. Rationally one can make sense of sex-related patterns of behaviour only as varying modes of adaptation within a fairly delicately balanced system.

An obstacle to change in such a system may well be that, unlike the neuroses, which are essentially maladaptive, sexual patterns may be adaptive and valued by the individual. It is often only the secondary factors, like law or social disapproval, which cause pain and motivate change.

THE MODEL APPLIED TO CROSS-DRESSING

A consideration of cross-dressing behaviour illustrates some points about the model and its implications for all aspects of the individual's functioning. It is possible, using this model, to see the relationship between three conditions, fetishism, transvestism and transsexualism, a relationship which undoubtedly exists despite the usual assumption that the three are separate "syndromes."

Conventionally fetishism is seen as the use of an inanimate object for sexual gratification. One large class of fetishistic objects is clothing of the opposite sex, often of a bizarre kind, such as rubber or leather garments. In one form of fetishism a heterosexual partner may wear the fetishistic article. Indeed clothing fashion often seems to involve elements of common fetishes. Alternatively the fetishism may be autosexual and the individual handles, fantasizes or wears the garment himself, promoting erotic arousal centred upon his own body. Not infrequently the fetishistic transvestite examines himself in a mirror and is aroused by the fantasy of being the sort of person he sees there. More often than not his cross-dressing is unconvincing as a portrayal of a person of the opposite sex, deliberately dressed as he is in unusual, garish articles. Fetishism of this kind is rarely exclusive, and is usually private, outside an otherwise heterosexual existence—even if he sometimes attempts to involve a partner in the fetish. There are thus two alternative sex objects to which the individual relates and, hypothetically, the two are related to different aspects of his self concept. The heterosexual object is associated with how he would hope to be perceived, and the image he sees in the mirror with how he really experiences himself.

Asexual transvestism represents a partial resolution of this situation. Transvestism is often misunderstood as being solely fetishistic—a confusion of a gender problem with a purely sexual one. Many transvestites report a development from a fetishistic phase, although by no means all clothing fetishists develop to the transvestite position. The fetishistic element declines until the individual finds the cross gender role rewarding in its own right, and is then no longer materially involved in an erotic experience. Instead of the fantasy relationship with the second sex-object, he incorporates that object and modifies his own gender identity. The asexual transvestite often describes his two selves as "my brother and sister," feeling that they are different people with different characteristics. Still the "brother" seems to maintain an ordinary heterosexual existence. Occasionally the "sister" experiments with alternative sex objects, but they almost invariably prove unsatisfactory. However, the "sister" role resolves difficulties by providing a means of sporadic flight into an idealized world where there are no sexual obligations and all is just "lace curtains, tea cups, and feminine chat."

Like many of the "minorities," transsexuals find themselves in a position where they must conform to the concept of a distinct disease entity to press their point. Thus almost invariably they strenuously deny the previous existence of any fetishistic or transvestite phase. Nevertheless, the idea of the transsexual as a person with a fixed cross-gender identity from the earliest days of consciousness rarely fits the individual in reality. The path of the development of a conviction that life in a cross-sex role is necessary is usually clear and more often than not passes through transvestite or homosexual phases. The solution is, therefore, not unlike that adopted by the transvestite, except that the demands of the strongly atypical gender identity require a more radical assumption of a whole-time cross-gender role. In fact he takes refuge in the new role and, as Stoller (1968) points out, the situation is eased by the obliteration of his sexual drives resulting from oestrogen therapy. He may attempt to create a new form of sex object in relation to his idealized new role but, of course, this attempt is weakly motivated at a sexual level.

These three patterns of sexual behaviour are, therefore, three modes of adaptation or states of equilibrium within the system the model attempts to outline. They are solutions for the individual rather than fixed prescribed roles to which the individual conforms. To place, for instance, the transsexual (defined only in terms of his wish for reassignment) in such a hypothetical strait-jacket as a condition for meeting his demands is clearly putting the cart before the horse.

Gender Role and Identity

Gender is perhaps the most contentious part of the model just described. It has to be admitted that in Money's concept of gender identity as immutable after the early years of life it hardly seems appropriate to a homeostatic system at all. Despite Money's later denials, it seems fairly clear that he initially thought of gender as wholly or almost wholly learned. At one stage (Money 1970) he argued for the imprinting of gender. The argument has been put forward that gender is genetically and physiologically determined, hence equally immutable. Hutt (1972) seems inclined to this view and sums up her assessment of Money's work by saying, "the evidence to date has made such a view untenable." It is therefore important to look at the question of gender development and assess the extent to which it needs to be involved in a consideration of sexual variations.

Bancroft (1972) remarks, "as far as gender identity is concerned, it is how the individual sees himself rather than how others see him that is most important." This is implicit in the model, but few researches have endeavoured to link self concepts of gender with biological factors. In Money's own work so little seems to have been done to determine gender identity in an objective manner that his conclusions are laid open to much doubt and criticism. Evidence is at best tenuously inferred from studies of the gender dysphorias and animal studies of copulatory behaviour.

Order seems to dictate that strict sexual dimorphism be the rule. There should be male and female: the remainder are "errors" or "experiments of nature." In a High Court judgement in 1983 Mr. Justice Parker declared that this was "a matter of common sense." However, it does seem beyond biological science to define sex in clear-cut, unarguable terms, and the law has to resort to an operational definition that sex is simply what is written on the birth certificate, despite any evidence to the contrary. It could be said that the sex-differentiation process is such that "errors" are a direct and predictable result, and therefore not errors at all but part of the normal pattern of things.

Polani (1972) lists four "components of sex." The first three are reasonably clear physical issues: gonads, hormones and internal genital tracts, and external genitalia. The fourth is simply "a variety of attributes"; some are anatomical and physiological, like skin texture, whilst others are "cultural and socio-psychological attributes not specifically sexual." Admitting, or finding it necessary to include such a diverse group of attributes as part of a definition of sex immediately suggests that a concept of distinct groups of males and females is indeed no matter of common sense but considerably idealized.

Chromosomal Aspects

The sex chromosome complex, male XY and female XX, has become an accepted key to sexual differentiation. There are, however, a substantial number of individuals showing sex chromosome complexes which do not conform. They are the first of two categories of unusual sex-determination. Hutt (1972) stresses the rarity of these cases, but, rare or not, they represent a real part of humanity which does not fit in with the dimorphic model. In addition we have those sexually intermediate states which result from the process of intrauterine differentiation itself.

In its initial stages the human foetus is female in form, and only at about the third month do male features begin to appear. This differentiation from female form is believed to be associated with the presence of the Y chromosome characterizing the male.

Perhaps the major anomaly in this process is that of the XX male who is born "masculinized" in anatomy with testes and yet does not appear to possess a Y chromosome. More common are the Klinefelter syndrome cases whose genetic make-up is of the XXY type, but XXXY and XXYY also occur. The Klinefelter cases are sterile, possess small male genitalia, weak secondary hair and sometimes small breasts. As with many of the genetic "errors' it is not clear why these cases are regarded as male with an extra X chromosome rather than female with a Y. This could be a curious convention or predisposition to ascribe to people the benefits of being male if at all possible! The Klinefelter has been quoted in older textbooks as sometimes transvestite, fetishistic and sometimes homosexual. Of course, such sexual behaviours are likely to be sought out in the examination of individuals seen at the outset as having sexual problems and they merit no wide generalization. Certainly they do not indicate a genetic basis to the gender dysphorias.

There are many other genetic patterns including the "mosaics" who possess body cells of both XX and XY types. Armstrong and Marshall (1964) published a report on a case of this kind who lived as a female, had a male appearance but possessed both ovaries and testes. Some chromosome patterns like the triple X female seem to be of no consequence, the individual being a seemingly normal female.

Studies of chromosome structures, therefore, throw up intermediate states or hermaphrodites classified as male or female to fit the birth certificate and convention but who are effectively sexually indeterminate. Looked at from the other angle no studies of gender dysphorias, homosexuality or transsexuality give any indication of genetic "errors" being relevant.

Curious results have occurred in the study of inheritance in homosexual groups. Brother/sister ratios have been found to be atypical. In the general population the ratio of brothers to sisters of male probands is 106:100. Darke (1948) found a similar ratio for male homosexuals but Kallman (1952) found a ratio of 125:100 in a highly regarded study. Lang (1940) found a ratio of 121:100 rising to 128:100 amongst homosexuals over 25 years. Of course such patterns are as likely to be related to rearing patterns as they are to inheritance.

More complex family patterns were shown by Martensen-Larsen (1957). Again more brothers than expected were found and the male homosexuals came more frequently from the younger third of the family. Slater (1958, 1962) confirmed this and the rather obvious corollary that homosexuals tend to have older mothers. This, for Martensen-Larsen, seemed to indicate that the important variable was that of rearing, but he strengthened the inheritance hypothesis when he found a preponderance of males in the sibs of fathers and grandfathers whilst there was a preponderance of sisters amongst mothers and grandmothers. Lesbians on the other hand had a preponderance of female sibs. More recent studies have tended not to confirm many of the older findings about the family relationships of homosexuals (e.g., Siegelman 1981) but it does appear that the more recent studies involve more heterogeneous populations and it is hard to dismiss replicated previous findings.

Kallman's (1952) studies of twins showed virtually 100 percent concordance for homosexuality in monozygotic twins but a concordance rate for dizygotics in line with Kinsey's findings for the incidence of homosexual behaviour in the general population. However, too much has, perhaps, been made of Kallman's study and he himself was at pains to point out in his original paper the grave limitations imposed on his work by prevailing social and legal forces.

If the Y chromosome initiates the differentiation process, a male child may not result for a number of other reasons. Also, the absence of a Y chromosome may not result in a strictly female child. A male foetus castrated *in utero* will be born with external genitalia which appear female. The effect has been produced experimentally in animals only but the administration of hormones which suppress androgens during pregnancy may produce the same result. Despite the apparent external female organs in the genetic male, the female internal organs would not be present and there would be testes.

Analogues in humans are found in the testicular feminization syndrome and the 5-a reductase deficiency. In these cases genetic XY males appear female at birth as a result, in the former, of a foetal insensitivity to androgen and, in the latter, of an absence of an enzyme responsible for the production of an androgen derivative. These cases are often unrecognized at birth and are reared as females until there are problems at adolescence in the failure to menstruate, masculinization, or other features which bring them to medical attention. The conventional approach has been to feminize the individual by oestrogens, removing the undescended testes, and perhaps to carry out some surgical modification. These "girls" are reported to be strongly feminine in appearance with emphatically female psychosexual orientation and strong maternal feelings. However, such cases have rarely been examined in any depth psychologically and the cases described at the end of this chapter conflict with this view. There is always a tendency for clinical judgement of matters as difficult to determine as gender identity to support the medical course already chosen.

In genetic females the adrenogenital syndrome produces male-like development in the foetus. In these cases there is a high secretion of androgens in the absence of a Y chromosome in the foetus, which develops a penis but no testes and has female ovaries. There is no vagina. A similar phenomenon has been found in the children of mothers treated with hormones to prevent miscarriages. The medical convention has been to carry out surgery to remove the internal female organs and to administer androgens to masculinize the individual further. The few studies that exist report male appearance and psychosexual disposition.

Ehrhardt and his colleagues (1967, 1968) examined cases of adrenogenital syndrome where the masculinization had been corrected soon after birth. He reported that they were tomboyish, chose boys' games, rejected dolls, did not have homosexual feelings but were uninterested in the male sex. Here it seems that there were no remaining male features of a physical kind to affect the postnatal learning of masculine gender roles or to suppress the feminine behaviour.

Dörner's Work

Dörner (1979) presents a complex series of investigations purporting to demonstrate a relationship between physiological processes and gender. His fundamental hypothesis is of a closed-loop endocrine system. Changes in the environment, external and internal, affect neurotransmitter metabolism. In turn the neurotransmitters affect fundamental processes of reproduction and metabolism as well as information processing. In turn the cycle is completed by the environment being affected. Usually such a loop is reversible but Dörner suggests that this is not so at critical periods of sex-differentiation of the foetus.

One aspect of sex-differentiation is the gonadotrophin secretion mechanism. Neurotransmitters influence the hypothalamus to secrete a gonadotrophin-release hormone and under this influence the pituitary secretes gonadotrophins. Sex hormones exert either a male inhibitory or female stimulatory influence on the secretion and this sex difference is a feature of foetal differentiation (Dörner et al. 1976). Animal studies support this argument and Dörner claimed that the higher the androgen level during sex-differentiation at the stage of foetal differentiation the more masculine the sexual behaviour of both sexes. On this basis he argues that hyposexuality, bisexuality and homosexuality represent the influence of increasing androgen deficiency at the foetal differentiation of males and androgen excess for females.

Many workers seem to have failed to find evidence of hormonal differences between heterosexuals and homosexuals but Dörner claimed to find that "effeminate homosexuals" and "transsexuals" showed raised luteinizing hormone and follicle-stimulating hormone as well as low free plasma testosterone. In two papers (1972 and—with his colleagues—1975) Dörner examined the feedback associated with the administration of oestrogens in homosexuals and transsexuals. He claimed to have found female patterns of +ve feedback, i.e., increased gonadotrophin levels. His conclusion was that these groups "possess at least in part a predominantly female differentiated brain."

Some support comes from Seyler et al. (1978) who found that the gonadotrophin release in female to male transsexuals and lesbians was more typical of males than females. Otherwise attempts to replicate this part of Dörner's work seems to have been unfruitful. Haslam (personal communication, 1982) reports a continuing

attempt to examine the feedback response to conjugated oestrogens in male transsexuals. Some preliminary results showed a female pattern in some transsexuals,
though a fair proportion of control subjects showed the same result.

There are many weak points in Dörner's work. For Dörner, environmental influences refer to very fundamental processes such as the effects of bottlefeeding. His
concept of "effeminacy" appears very vague and is dependent on superficial cultural factors such as adornments. He nevertheless gives it a crucial position in his
argument. He does not seem to appreciate the radical difference between "effeminacy" and "femininity." Most importantly, the statistical appraisal of his results
seems, at best, vague.

Of great concern are Dörner's enthusiastic extrapolation of his findings to suggest monitoring the amniotic fluid so as to detect "potential permanent disorders
of mating and non-mating behaviour" and his hopes for intervention. He cites
Roeder and Muller (1969) and their effective suppression of homosexual behaviour
by the use of stereotaxic lesions of the hypothalamic ventromedial nucleus. The
suggestion is as naive as it is abhorrent but it is by no means without precedent.
Lukianowicz (1959) expressed a similar notion: "all the horrors of the reassignment
of transsexuals can be avoided by a simple brain operation"! The view is based on
the false assumption that homosexuals and transsexuals "suffer." It is of importance in the context of work like Dörner's to realize that such "suffering," if it exists
at all, is imposed solely by society. In particular, transsexuals, even more than
homosexuals, uniformly reject attempts to coerce them into an acceptance of their
genetic sex. Further more it is facile to assume that suppression of sexual behaviour in a homosexual constitutes the "normalization" of the whole person—it may
simply create an impotent homosexual.

Dörner's stance is clearly one in which sex and gender are determined largely
by biological processes and partly by elementary environmental ones which have
gross physiological consequences of a particular kind. Research by Imperato-
McGinley and co-workers (1974, 1979) and the report by Savage et al. (1980) on
5-a reductase deficiency appear to conflict with important aspects of both Money's
and Dörner's work, which both envisage the establishment of a fixed gender identity.

Imperato-McGinley investigated a village community in the Dominican Republic. Thirty-eight cases were studied intensively. These people were diagnosed
as suffering from the 5-a reductase enzyme deficiency. The function of the enzyme
is to promote the conversion of testosterone into dihydrotestosterone during the
period of foetal sex-differentiation. Testosterone and dihydrotestosterone have different functions. Testosterone is believed to effect the development of male internal
structures whilst dihydrotestosterone governs the external organ development. At
puberty testosterone governs voice changes, muscle mass, and increases in phallic
size, whilst dihydrotestosterone governs prostate growth, facial hair and recession
of hair-line, as well as acne. The cases studied were genetic males born with apparently female genitalia who were reared as girls until puberty. At that time there was
a spontaneous morphological change with testicles appearing and penile development. Imperato-McGinley reports that, in addition, the initially acquired feminine

gender identity was relinquished and a masculine identity adopted. Imperato-McGinley was quickly taken to task in letters to the *New England Medical Journal* by supporters of the school regarding learning as the major source of gender identity. It seemed that the reversal of gender at puberty indicated that learning played little part. However, Imperato-McGinley responded by pointing out that the acquisition of an early feminine identity was strong support for the learning hypothesis, although the reversal of the learned role suggested that it could be overridden by the androgen influence. Such is the ambiguity of much of the existing biological evidence.

Social Learning Effects and Gender Role

It seems fair to say that some aspects of gender identity are learned, even though they may be less crucial aspects. Money does seem to have modified his stance over the years in favour of a greater contribution from biological influences. If gender identity is the sense of belonging to one group, boy or girl, there can be little doubt that simple cognitive components can be acquired by learning. The biological fact of morphological differences is also relevant. Thus at this simple level it must be the case that gender is determined by a biological predisposition and a process of learning. The extent to which the finer attributes of gender are acquired by learning or biological predisposition is more uncertain. The biological influences may well be a great deal more subtle than the influence of simple morphology but it is necessary to appreciate that there is no exact one-to-one relationship between sex and gender. The lack of such relationship is shown by transsexuals and probably by homosexuals. As Bancroft (1972) says "the homosexual, if he is to achieve stability, usually needs to produce a special type of gender identity—'I am a homosexual.'"

There is also evidence from other cultures. Mead (1950) gives a classic account of how the masculine and feminine models of gender differ dramatically in different cultures. Although males usually acquire in all cultures the gender identity appropriate to their sex, what being a male or being a female amounts to in terms of, say, aggression, child-care, adornment and styles of courtship behaviour is infinitely variable. Such variety can hardly be attributable to biological processes alone.

Biological differences can underlie learning of course. It has been suggested that birth is more traumatic for boys on purely physical grounds and this alone may lead to differences in nursing. To this the greater irritability of boys has been attributed. They respond less to stress but relax less easily, they cry more and sleep less, even in very early days of life. The maternal respondent behaviour follows suit. Moss (1970) showed that at three weeks mothers held male babies half an hour longer in each eight-hour period than girls. Mothers respond to children according to what they believe is the sex of the child and, if misled, will behave inappropriately. Mother's soothing of the boy gives way to toleration. She expects him to oppose her and to assert himself against her. The girl she regards as an extension of herself, sharing in the things she does and being in emotional harmony with her.

Hartley (1966) classified such parental actions under four principal headings. A mother manipulates the female child a great deal, she examines her closely, combs her hair at length, dresses her attentively and continually praises her looks. Parents canalize the child's play by presenting toys and regulating play by approval and disapproval so that it is appropriate to the child's sex. They prescribe for the children boxing-gloves, tea-sets, guns and doll's houses, which foreshadow what they expect of the child in later life. Both parents employ specific verbal appellations, e.g., "big strong boy" or "pretty little girl." The fact that in some dialects there is a pronounced difference between masculine and feminine speech suggests that parental speech style to boy and girl might also differ. In the speech-training of transsexuals it is usually more important to modify the speech rhythm, inflections and usages than the pitch. Finally, the child is exposed to real-life activities which are again gender-appropriate. The boy is encouraged to help dad with the car and the girl to lay tables and bake cakes with mum. Of course, such parental actions are almost entirely culturally determined but it is significant that on the whole it is easier for the girl to respond than the boy. A young girl can realistically help in the home whilst a boy of the same age can do very little to assist repairing the car. Admiration of the girl is easily accepted by her but counter-balanced by the challenges to the boy to be bigger and stronger.

Between three and eight years children become quite clear about the toys appropriate to their sex but it is curious that their choices are more emphatic when observed than when playing alone. If the children deviate from appropriate play forms they are constrained ; boys especially are ridiculed as "soft" or "sissy."

Institutions, be they "bonny baby" competitions or schools, propagate gender stereotypes. Sexton (1970) emphasizes the feminizing effect of education conducted mostly by female teachers. Male teachers for boys and female teachers for girls was a cause espoused by a whole teachers' union. However, the argument is simplistic since the acquisition of gender is not simple global imitation of whole figures. Freud (1933) recognized that the child finds its models not just in single individuals but in the functions exercised by many individuals around him. The child's model of father will include the extent to which mother also exerts a paternal role.

Bandura (1963) and others have shown the importance of resource control in identifying the degree to which a child imitates one parent or another. Grinder and Judith (1965) also found that boys tended to see fathers as resource controllers and that girls saw mothers in that role. Again Bandura comments on the complexity of the gender models: "Children are not simply junior-sized replicas of one or the other model—rather they exhibit a relatively novel amalgam of elements from both . . . parents' response repertoires."

There is evidence too of the relationship between parent's rearing behaviour and the child's gender. Thus highly masculine males see their fathers as more punitive but also more caring than less masculine males do. Maternal dominance tends to be associated with more feminine and non-aggressive boys on the one hand and aggressive girls on the other.

In adolescence and later life society enforces very many genderal features quite rigidly. The badges of gender may change but the gender line is kept starkly defined. A young man may wear two ear-rings in one ear and demonstrate his aggressive masculinity but also assert with conviction that he would look "a bloody fool" with one ear-ring in each ear. A male may not wear clothing of certain colours or certain classes of perfume without becoming generally suspect. He may not stand in a particular way or make particular gestures or he may be labelled with some contempt. At all costs he must keep his voice in a low register. He must profess high aspirations and climb mountains "just because they are there." He must demonstrate financial success and independence.

These qualities are reflected in parental expectations. Aberle and Naegele (1952) showed that American middle-class fathers became concerned if their sons did not take responsibility and if they lacked initiative. They needed to have athletic prowess and academic achievement from them. The fathers were most concerned if their sons were over-conforming, excitable, fearful or showed what they believed to be homosexual traits. On the other hand girls were expected to marry and to be affectionate and "sweet," but their roles were less emphatically laid down.

In adult life roles are enforced by ridicule and law. Professions and occupations are either closed to generally non-conforming males or else society classes as "queer" the man in an occupation which is seen as not conforming to the masculine role. Women appear to be less restricted, although feminist movements deny this. Obstructions to women in generally atypical roles may be very positive but they do not contain the same ruthless sanctions of ridicule and, in the extreme, fear. Lesbians are not, it seems, "security risks" as male homosexuals are accused of being. The male teacher who is convicted of a sexual offense is by law reported to the Department of Education and "black-listed" whether or not his offence is related to children. The male "streaker" is prosecuted and heavily fined on the basis one supposes of a presumed sexual motivation. The female "streaker" becomes something of a television personality as a sort of liberated feminist!

Illustrative Case

In the following case the identities of the two women concerned are of course disguised, owing to the delicate nature of their problem. The relevant facts are nonetheless substantially correct.

Anne was an 18-year-old member of the sixth form of a girl's public school. She attended a routine medical examination and without explanation was referred by the doctor to an endocrinologist. Naturally the matter of the referral was discussed by the family and her older sister Beverly, aged 20, a law student, went to see her general practitioner asking that she could be similarly referred.

Both girls were intellectually bright and excelled in sports. The younger was a member of a girl's football team whilst the older played squash for her county. Both were outgoing, sociable and popular. Both had good health records. They had casual boyfriends but neither had had any heterosexual relationships of any intensity. They gave the impression of being substantially unaware of sexual feelings.

Physically they were tall, almost six feet. They had large hands and noticeably long arms. Their body contours and faces were rounded. Their skins were clear, with no unusual hair growth apparent. However, they had male proportions in rather wide shoulders, little or no waist and smaller hips than one would expect of women. Their voices were rather deep by female standards but soft with feminine intonation. Their mannerisms were neither distinctly masculine nor feminine.

They were the only children of parents in early middle age when they were born. The family was a close-knit group and the home life was happy and stable. The parents were proud of their children and they stated categorically that they were unaware of any medical problems which Anne and Beverly might have. They did not know of any family history of health problems. They were surprised by the mysterious referral of Anne and by Beverly's initiative but they were placid people and accepted that, what ever it was about, the medical attention was for the best. Questioning of the parents revealed no abnormality in the rearing pattern of the girls and their sex had never been in question as far as family and friends were concerned. Neither had their success in sport at a fairly high level been seen as unusual.

The endocrinologist who examined the girls reported that they were both masculine, so much so that he had difficulty in treating them as female. He felt they were like men dressed up. This seemed strikingly at variance with their general acceptance as girls. The psychiatrist found Anne but not Beverly to be very masculine. I, on the other hand, who spent considerable time with both girls, found Anne to be quite attractively feminine, despite being aware of her rather male body-build. I found Beverly less feminine, but not outstandingly masculine, and attributed this to her much more assertive manner and obvious achievement needs. It seemed possible that the different impressions were determined by the orientation and attitudes which the three professions brought to the problem.

The school doctor had noted three features in the examination of Anne: little or no breast development, failure to menstruate, and a somewhat enlarged clitoris. Beverly also showed these features when examined. The endocrinological investigations showed that both were genetic males with the positive symptoms of 5-a reductase deficiency, but it should be noted that there was no evidence of gross spontaneous masculinization, which has been reported particularly in more recent literature, and certainly no changes of gender.

The principal results of the psychological investigations were as follows: Terman-Miles Attitude Interest Test (see Brierley 1979): Anne scored –27 and Beverly –22. Both these suggest normal femininity of attitudes. The responses were remarkably similar. On six of the seven subtests they did not differ by more than two points. On the seventh they differed by seven points on 105 items. This subtest emphasizes strong emotional reactions, fear, anger, etc., and here Beverly had the higher score.

Cattell 16 PF Questionnaire: The same striking similarity was found here. Beverly was more tense and less emotionally stable to a minor degree. Anne was rather more guarded and suspicious but had less self-conflict. The small differences could be attributed to age: Beverly had had to deal with her problems for longer and had reached a level of doubt and discouragement. Both girls were bright and practically minded with strong social needs. There were no features which might have suggested that they were other than perfectly normal females.

Repertory grid (details of this particular application of the technique are given in Brierley 1979): Beverly's grid showed that she construed herself as quite removed from all other elements including "the person I would most like to be." She could not see herself becoming like other people, only as becoming increasingly sensitive and submissive. Anne's grid was more complex; she saw herself as gathering qualities which were more masculine. Both girls construed themselves as tense, insecure and rather ill-controlled. They wanted to acquire stability and self-confidence.

Personal Questionnaire (PQRST—Mulhall 1976): This technique, based on interview, evaluates the relative strength of the patients' problem areas. Anne showed that her major dissatisfactions were to do with her body, especially insofar as she was physically different, which isolated her from other girls so that she had to lie about her periods and obscure her lack of breast development. This distressed her a great deal. She expressed pleasure in her "feminine feelings." Beverly was very unhappy about her body which she felt was "freakish." She was discontented about feeling like "a boy gone wrong" and being "tomboyish." Instinctively her athletic and sporting ability was enjoyable but at the same time she regretted it as unfeminine. She was very much concerned that she could not get "a straight answer" (although she never asked the question!) and she very much disliked discussing her problems.

Discussion by a multidisciplinary gender dysphoria committee became centred around the objectives of hormonal and surgical procedures and subsequent counselling. The core issue from which no escape seemed possible was that of whether the girls should be treated in a way to make them conform better to the male or female stereotype. It seemed impossible to maintain the view that they would never adequately conform to either. The impasse can be illustrated by the fact that a prolonged discussion ended with the resolution to leave counselling to a female psychiatrist who was neither present nor had any previous experience in counselling people with gender problems! In the event continued semi-ignorance seemed to be the best policy. Anne was informed that she suffered from a malformation of her internal reproductive organs. This information distressed her a great deal. Beverly had a similar explanation but an operation to remove her "ovaries" was carried out whilst in reality her testes were removed.

The two girls exemplified a clear and continued acceptance of a feminine gender identity and role. Neither expressed any desire to be more masculine in any way; in fact they were apparently rather guilty about their tomboyishness. Certainly neither would readily have adopted a male role. This was clear in early tentative counselling. Indeed to attempt to initiate a gender-role change would have been socially disastrous to both. Their problems were in no way resolved and it is clear that they were trapped by a social, and to some extent medical, demand that they conform to one of the two proper sexes. They were neither men nor women but this was a fact that they themselves would have found hard to accept and society would have refused to accept. It is questionable whether several years of medical intervention left them any happier.

Conclusions

I began by pointing out the way in which concepts of "sexual deviance" tend to be framed in terms of a diseased sexuality. This approach does not lead to an understanding of sexual variations. I then attempted to define what is meant by sex and gender. Some variations in what are often regarded as sexual behaviour, such as transsexualism, are more correctly variations in gender identity.

I have argued that sex itself is not as clearly defined as the convention of a sexual dichotomy assumes. Apart from the small but not insignificant group who do not conform biologically but are nevertheless assigned to male and female groups, there seems to be a need to include non-biological characteristics in the concept of sex which considerably confuse the issue of what is labelled male and female.

The biological investigations of the basis of sex and gender do not produce other than ambiguous answers. Rather, they blur the male-female dichotomy. However, there can be no doubt that both biology and learning are important in the development of gender identity. It thus seems important to appreciate that, in the understanding of sexual behaviour, an adherence to strict dichotomies of male/female and masculine/feminine is obstructive. Sex, gender and sexual behaviour are highly individual matters.

Kessler and McKenna (1978) describe experiments which lead them to conclude that the prime concept is gender and that it is a social concept at that. Sex, they argue, is simply the accumulation of social and scientific data which support a social dichotomy of gender. The present argument is not so extreme but emphasizes that both sex and gender are not as well defined and distinct as social "commonsense" dictates.

The study of two "sisters" with a hermaphrodite condition shows clearly the adoption of a strong feminine gender identity in genetic males. This was strongly in conflict with their awareness of masculine physical characteristics. Difficulty in dealing with such a problem lies in the intensity of the social demand for conformity to the male-female dichotomy. Society finds it hard to accept that some people simply do not conform to these hypothetical and ubiquitous sex stereotypes.

References

Aberle, D. F., and Naegele, K. D. (1952). Middle-class fathers' occupational role and attitudes toward children. *American Journal of Orthopsychiatry*, 22, 366–78.

Armstrong, C. N., and Marshall, A. J. (1964). *Intersexuality*. London: Academic Press.

Bancroft, J. (1972). The relationship between gender identity and sexual behaviour. In C. Ounsted and D. C. Taylor (eds), *Gender Differences*. Edinburgh: Churchill Livingstone.

Bandura, A., Ross, D., and Ross, S. A. (1963). A comparative test of the status envy, social power, and secondary reinforcement theories of identification learning. *Journal of Abnormal and Social Psychology*, 67, 6, 527–34.

Brierley, H. (1979). *Transvestism: A Handbook.* London: Pergamon.

Crown, S. (1979). Male homosexuality: perversion, deviation or variant? In *Ciba Foundation Symposium 62,* New York: Excerpta Medica.

Darke, R. A. (1948). Heredity as an etiological factor in homosexuality. *Journal of Nervous and Mental Disease,* 107, 251–68.

Diamond, M. (1965). A critical evaluation of the ontogeny of human sexual behaviour. *Quarterly Review of Biology,* 40, 147–75.

Dörner, G. (1972); Auslösung eines positiven Östrogenfeedback-Effect bei homosexuellen Männern. *Endokrinologie,* 60, 297–301.

Dörner, G. (1979). Hormones and sexual differentiation of the brain. In *Ciba Foundation Symposium 62,* New York: Excerpta Medica.

Dörner, G., Hecht, K., and Hinz, G. (1976). Teratopsychogenic effect apparently produced by non-physiological neurotransmettir concentrations during brain differentiation. *Endokrinologie,* 68, 1–5.

Dörner, G., Rohde, W., Stahl, F., Krell, L., and Masius, W. (1975). Neurendocrine conditioned predisposition for homosexuality in men. *Archives of Sexual Behaviour,* 4, 1–8.

Ehrhardt, A. A., Evers, K., and Money, J. (1968). Influence of androgen and some aspects of sexually dimorphic behaviour in women with late treated adrenogenital syndrome. *Johns Hopkins Medical Journal,* 123, 115–22.

Ehrhardt, A. A., and Money, J. (1967). Projestin-induced hermaphroditism: I.Q. and psychosexual identity in a study of ten girls. *Journal of Sex Research,* 3, 83–100.

Fenichel, O. (1930). The psychology of transvestism. *International Journal of Psycho-Analysis,* 11, 211.

Freud, S. (1905). Three essays on the theory of sexuality. The sexual aberrations. In *Complete Works of Sigmund Freud.* London: Hogarth.

Freud, S. (1933) *New Introductory Lectures on Psychoanalysis.* London: Hogarth.

Glover, E. (1960). The problem of male homosexuality. In *The Roots of Crime.* London: Imago.

Goode, E. (1981). Comments on the homosexual role. *Journal of Sex Research,* 17, 1, 54–65.

Grinder, R. E., and Judith, C. S. (1965). Sex differences in adolescents' perceptions of parental resource control. *Journal of Genetic Psychology,* 106, 337–44.

Hartley, R. E. (1966). A developmental view of female sex-role identification. In B. J. Biddle and E. J. Thomas (eds), *Role Theory.* New York: Wiley.

Hutt, C. (1972). *Males and Females.* Harmondsworth: Penguin.

Imperato-McGinley, J., Guerrero, L., Gautier, T. and Peterson, R. E. (1974). Steroid 5*a*-reductase deficiency in man. An inherited form of male pseudohermaphroditism. *Science,* 186, 1213–15.

Imperato-McGinley, J., Peterson, R. E., Gautier, T., and Sturla, E. (1979). Androgens and the evolution of male gender identity among male pseudohermaphrodites with 5*a*-reductase deficiency. *New England Medical Journal,* 300, 22, 1232–37.

Kallman, F.J. (1952). A comparative twin study on the genetic aspects of male homosexuality. *Journal of Nervous and Mental Disease,* 115, 283–89.

Karpman, B. J. (1947). Dream life in a case of transvestism. *Journal of Nervous and Mental Disease,* 106, 292.

Kessler, S. J., and McKenna, W. (1978). Gender: An Ethnomethodological Approach. New York: Wiley.

Lang, W. (1940). Studies on the genetic determination of homosexuality. *Journal of Nervous and Mental Disease,* 92, 55–64.

Laub, D. R., and Fisk, N. (1974). A rehabilitation program for gender dysphoria syndrome by surgical sex change. *Plastic Reconstructive Surgery,* 53, 388–403.

Lukianowicz, N. (1959). Survey of various aspects of transvestism in the light of our present knowledge. *Journal of Nervous and Mental Disease,* 128, 36–64.

McGuire, R. J., Carlisle, J. M., and Young, B. G. (1965). Sexual deviation as conditioned behaviour. *Behaviour Research and Therapy*, 2, 185–90.

Martensen-Larsen, O. (1957). The family constellation and homosexualism. *Acta Genetica et Statistica Medica*, 7, 445–46.

Mead, M. (1950). *Male and Female*. Harmondsworth: Penguin.

Money, J. (1970). Sexual dimorphism and homosexual gender identity. *Psychological Bulletin*, 74, 425–40.

Money, J., and Ehrhardt, A. (1972). *Man and Woman, Boy and Girl*. Baltimore: Johns Hopkins University Press.

Money, J., Hampson, J. G., and Hampson, J. L. (1955). An examination of some basic sexual concepts. The evidence of hermaphroditism. *Bulletin of Johns Hopkins Hospital*, 97, 301–57.

Money, J., Hampson, J. G., and Hampson, J. L. (1957). Imprinting and the establishment of the gender role. *A.M.A. Archives of Neurological Psychiatry*, 77, 333–36.

Moss, H. A. (1970). Sex, age and state as determinants of mother-infant interaction. In K. Danziger (ed.), *Readings in Child Socialisation*. Oxford: Pergamon.

Mulhall, D. J. (1976). Systematic self-assessment by PQRST (Personal Questionnaire Rapid Scaling Technique). *Psychological Medicine*, 6, 591–97.

Oakley, A. (1972). *Sex, Gender and Society*. London: Temple Smith.

Polani, P. E. (1972). Errors of sex determinance and sex chromosome anomalies. In C. Ounsted and D. C. Taylor (eds), *Gender Differences*. Edinburgh: Churchill Livingstone.

Roeder, F., and Muller, D. (1969). Zur stereotaktischen Heilung der pädophilen Homosexualität. *Deutsch Medizinisch Wochenschrift*, 94, 409–15.

Savage, M. O., Preece, M. A., Jeffcoate, S. L., Ransley, P. G., Rumsby, G., Mansfield, M. D., and Williams, D. I. (1980). Familial male pseudohermaphroditism due to deficiency of 5a-reductase. *Clinical Endocrinology*, 12, 397–406.

Sexton, P. (1970). *Feminised Male: Classrooms, White Collars and the Decline of Manliness*. New York: Random.

Seyler, L. E., Canalis, E., Spare, S., and Reichlin, S. (1978). Abnormal gonadotrophin secretory responses to LRH in transsexual women after diethyl stlboestrol [sic] priming. *Journal of Clinical Endocrinology and Metabolism*, 47, 176–83.

Siegelman, M. (1981). Parental background of homosexual and heterosexual men: a cross-national replication. *Archives of Sexual Behavior*, 10, 6, 505–13.

Slater, E. (1958). The sibs and children of homosexuals. In D. R. Smith and W. A. Davidson (eds), *Symposium on Nuclear Sex*. London: Heineman.

Slater, E. (1962). Birth order and maternal age of homosexuals. *Lancet*, 1, 69–71.

Stoller, R. J. (1968). *Sex and Gender*. London: Hogarth.

Wallinder, J. (1975). *A Social-Psychiatric Follow-up Study of 24 Sex-reassigned Transsexuals*. Goteburg: Scandinavian University Books.

Willmott, M., and Brierley, H. (1984). Cognitive characteristics and homosexuality. *Archives of Sexual Behavior*, in press.

3
How Many Bisexuals Are There?

11

Review of Statistical Findings About Bisexual Behavior, Feelings, and Identities

Paula C. Rodríguez Rust

THE contemporary wave of theory and research on bisexuality began as a trickle in the early 1980s and swelled dramatically in the late 1980s. Many authors, especially those whose works were published before widespread recognition of the need to study bisexuality, had to justify their focus on bisexuality to an audience that barely acknowledged its existence. To do so, these authors often pointed to evidence of the prevalence of bisexual feelings and behavior in the United States; research reports and theoretical articles published in the early 1980s typically began with a litany of statistics designed to convince the reader of the importance of bisexuality by impressing her or him with the large size of the bisexual population. The truth is, however, that evidence of the prevalence of bisexual behavior and feelings has existed since publication of the first Kinsey report in 1948; if the scientific importance of bisexuality actually lay in its prevalence, the upsurge in scientific attention to bisexuality would have begun in the early 1950s, not the 1980s. In fact, the upsurge in attention was motivated by social and political changes brought about by AIDS and increased bisexual visibility. Conversely, the source of scientific and public interest in the question of prevalence probably has more to do with the political implications of these numbers than with their scientific implications. But whatever the reason, both scientists and the general public seem fascinated by the question of prevalence, and several recent studies of sexual behavior in the United States, for example, *The Janus Report on Sexual Behavior* (1993) and Edward O. Laumann, John H. Gagnon, Robert T. Michael, and Stuart Michaels's *The Social Organization of Sexuality: Sexual Practices in the United States* (1994), have received widespread attention not only outside sexological circles but also outside scientific circles.

Despite popular and scientific interest, because of the challenges involved in studying stigmatized behavior, such as the difficulty of obtaining funding for sex research and the impossibility of drawing representative samples of hidden populations, we have only recently begun to acquire comprehensive data on the prevalence of various types of sexual feelings and behaviors in the United States as a whole.[1] The data we have now come from a few national surveys on sexuality and from smaller studies focusing on the sexualities of specific populations within the United States. Each study must be interpreted carefully, because findings produced by any research study are heavily influenced by how subjects were recruited to participate in the study, what questions they were asked, and how these questions were asked.

Taking the Spin Out of Sex: A Short Primer on the Critical Interpretation of Sex Statistics

The method of subject recruitment is important because it determines what types of people were included in a study and therefore what types of people are described by the study's findings and how accurately they are described. For example, if a study includes only white European Americans, then the findings reliably describe only white European Americans; they tell us nothing about African Americans or Asian Americans. But a study does not have to include everyone of a particular type in order to tell us something about people of that type in general. For example, we would not have to ask all white European Americans about their sex lives in order to find out something about the sex lives of white European Americans in general. In fact, scientists rarely study everyone in a population, because doing so would be prohibitively expensive and equally valid results can be obtained from a sample of people—if the sample is chosen using scientific probability sampling techniques.

The process of scientific probability sampling is as reliable as drawing a sample of blood for a medical test; it would be neither necessary nor desirable to take all of a person's blood to get an accurate test result.[2] Statisticians and survey researchers generally agree that if probability sampling methods are used, and if a sufficiently large percentage of the people chosen by these methods agree to participate in the study, then the sample is a microcosm of the larger population and findings based on that sample can be generalized to the larger population from which the sample was drawn with a known degree of certainty. However, if a substantial percentage of the people chosen refuse to participate in the study, then the representativeness of the sample is compromised because of the possibility that those individuals who refused to participate differ from those who did participate in a way that could affect the study's findings. For example, in a study by B. W. Dixon and colleagues of HIV risk behaviors among men, 16 percent of the men selected using probability sampling methods refused to participate (Dixon et al. 1991). The researchers conducted a second study of the men who had refused, and found that 16.8 percent of them had engaged in male-male sex since 1978, as compared to only 5.1 percent of the men who had consented to participate in the first study. In other words, the findings of the first study regarding the incidence of male-male sex were biased by the fact that men who had had male-male sex were less likely to agree to participate in the study than men who had not had male-male sex were. The interested reader can refer to any textbook on social statistics or survey methodology for an explanation of the theory and procedure behind probability sampling, and for techniques to estimate bias introduced by respondent refusal and other forms of "nonresponse."[3]

If probability sampling techniques are not used, then the potential for biased findings is even higher. Nonprobability samples usually over- or underrepresent certain types of people, and the degree of this misrepresentation can be difficult to estimate. Therefore, conclusions about the larger population based on findings from nonprobability samples must be drawn very carefully. For example, Janet Lever and colleagues (1992; reprinted as chapter 12) drew their sample from among the readers of *Playboy*. Although *Playboy* readers live all across the United States, this sample is undoubtedly not representative of the general population of the United States because certain types of people are more likely to read *Playboy* than others. In particular, the sample probably overrepresents people with strong—or particular—sexual interests, and if we want to draw conclusions about the sexual behavior of all people in the United States based on this sample we would have to be extremely careful indeed. In fact, Lever and colleagues' sample is probably not even representative of *Playboy* readers because certain types of readers—those who do read the articles, for example, as opposed to those who only look at the photos—were probably more likely to choose to participate in the survey than other readers.

It is also important to know exactly what questions a researcher asked her or his subjects about their sexuality. As discussed in sections 1 and 2, we tend to think simplistically that people are either heterosexual, lesbian or gay, or bisexual, and that heterosexuals are attracted to and have sex only with members of the other sex, that lesbians and gay men are attracted to and have sex only with members of their own sex, and that bisexuals are attracted to and have sex with members of both sexes. We assume, for example, that if a woman says she is a lesbian she is attracted to women and that if she is sexually active she is active with women. In fact, as suggested by the various models of sexuality discussed in section 2, sexuality is far more complex than most people realize and different people—including different researchers—define heterosexuality, homosexuality, and bisexuality differently. For example, it is quite possible for a woman who identifies as a lesbian to feel attracted to both women and men and to engage in sexual contact with men, or for a heterosexually married man to identify as heterosexual even though he no longer has sexual relations with his wife and dates men instead. Each of these people would be classified variously as heterosexual, bisexual, or lesbian/gay depending on whether they were asked about their sexual self-identity, their feelings of sexual attraction, or their behavior. Moreover, people's sexual behavior often changes over the life course, so the time frame of the question is also important; a woman who left a heterosexual marriage at age forty-seven and began a lesbian relationship would be classified as lesbian if only current behavior were taken into account and as bisexual if lifetime behavior were considered. The question of what anyone "really" is sexually is a philosophical question that assumes the existence of a sexual essence, not a scientific question. Scientifically, research findings about subjects' sexualities can be interpreted only if the questions those subjects were asked are known. Thus, there is no single answer to the question of what percentage of the population is bisexual because bisexuality, like sexuality in general, is composed of multiple and independently varying dimensions such that measurement of each dimension yields a different percentage.

Finally, it is important to know how the researchers asked their questions of the subjects. Although question wording and interview environment are always important in survey research, they are especially important when the questions pertain to such sensitive and controversial topics as sexual feelings and behaviors because these circumstances can affect subjects' honesty. For example, it is important that questions use nonjudgmental and clear language. Aside from being offensive, the question "Have you ever engaged in any deviant sexual practices?" would not elicit useful information because it stigmatizes the behavior in question and thus discourages respondents from reporting it. The question "Have you ever had sexual contact with a member of your own sex?" is also problematic because it does not explain what is meant by "sexual contact." Does any intimate touching count, or is the question asking about genital contact, or contact to the point of orgasm? In the absence of clarification different respondents will interpret the question differently, yielding a useless mixture of answers.

The environment in which questions about sexuality are asked is as important as the wording of the questions themselves. For example, asking a man whether he has engaged in same-gender sexual activity since becoming married is more likely to elicit an honest answer if asked in private than if asked in front of his wife, who might be unaware of his extramarital activity. In fact, even the presence of an interviewer might cause some respondents to be dishonest. Therefore, more accurate findings are probably obtained when sensitive questions are asked using self-administered questionnaires rather than orally by an interviewer. But even self-administered questionnaires do not necessarily elicit completely honest answers. Edward McGuire III and colleagues (1992) administered a questionnaire on sexual behavior to 204 urban college students, 43 of whom—more than one out of five—disagreed with the statement "I have answered all questions honestly."[4] This finding indicates that the error introduced into survey-based estimates of the prevalence of sexual behaviors is likely to be substantial, and, because most surveys on sexual behavior do not include questions asking respondents whether they have answered truthfully, usually not estimable.

The context of each question within the interview or questionnaire can also affect respondents' interpretation of a question and willingness to answer it honestly. To avoid context effects, researchers have to think carefully about the order in which they ask questions, and even about whether to ask certain questions at all. For example, in a study of HIV risk behavior among women, Patricia E. Stevens (1994) chose not to ask respondents whether they identified as lesbian, gay, or bisexual out of concern that, having claimed a sexual self-identity, subjects would avoid reporting sexual behavior that might seem incongruent.

Although the findings of any research on sexuality must be interpreted carefully, and different studies often produce apparently conflicting findings because of differences in methodology, by triangulating the many studies that have been done to date we can achieve an overall picture of sexuality in the United States. Taken together, these studies provide us with a rough estimate of the prevalence of bisexual behaviors, feelings, and identities in the United States. The findings suggest that bisexual behaviors and feelings are more common than exclusively same-gender behaviors and feelings, that bisexual self-identity is less common than lesbian or gay self-identity, that at any given point in time the capacity for bisexual arousal is more common than actual bisexual behavior, and that bisexual self-identity is less common than either bisexual behavior or the capacity for bisexual arousal, presumably because of the lack of social support for bisexual self-identity.

The Kinsey Reports and the Downfall of the Famous 10 Percent

Although the findings of Kinsey and his associates have been heavily critiqued and superseded by more recent and reliable research findings, it is important to examine them because they were, for a long time, the best—in fact, the only—quantitative information available about the sexual behavior of people in the United States. As such, they formed the basis for much popular knowledge about sexuality that persists today, knowledge that played a role in shaping the politics of the lesbian and gay movements and, to a lesser extent, the bisexual movement.

At the time of their publication in 1948 and 1953 the Kinsey reports surprised a sexually conservative society by reporting that same-gender sexual behavior was much more common than previously believed.[5] Heterosexuals were shocked; "homosexuals" discovered that they were not alone and, armed with this knowledge and with social connections forged during World War II, formed the homophile organizations of the 1950s. Later lesbian and gay activists took the figure "10 percent of the population is gay" from the Kinsey reports and used it to emphasize the size and clout of the lesbian and gay population. Overlooked amid the reaction to the news that homosexuality is not rare was the fact that the Kinsey findings suggested that sexual difference is a matter of degree and that degrees of bisexual behavior and erotic capacity are much more common than exclusively same-gender sexual behavior and erotic capacity. Kinsey and his associates (Kinsey, Pomeroy, and Martin 1948; Kinsey, Pomeroy, Martin, and Gebhard 1953) reported that 0.3 percent to 3.0 percent of women (aged twenty to thirty-five and depending on marital status) and 4 percent of postadolescent men were exclusively homosexual, whereas 28 percent of women had responded erotically to another woman and 50 percent of men had either had sexual experience with another man to the point of orgasm after the onset of adolescence (37 percent) or responded erotically to another man (13 percent). This leads to the conclusion that 25 to 28 percent of women and 46 percent of men are capable of erotic response to both women and men, suggesting that the capacity for bisexual response is much more common than the capacity for exclusively homosexual response. Kinsey, Pomeroy, Martin, and

Gebhard (1953) also reported that 4 to 8 percent of unmarried women had had more than incidental sexual experiences with or erotic responses to both women and men.

But how reliable are these statistics, which both encouraged political action and were interpreted through a political lens? As with any research on sexuality, an accurate interpretation of the Kinsey statistics requires knowledge of the methods used by Kinsey and his associates. Several other authors have analyzed the effects of these methods—particularly the use of nonprobability sampling methods—on the Kinsey findings, and the interested reader is referred to their writings.[6] For present purposes it is necessary to discuss the implications of two aspects of Kinseyan methodology on the interpretation of Kinsey findings. The first pertains to the questions Kinsey and his associates asked of their subjects. They asked subjects about their capacity for erotic response and their actual sexual behavior. They did not ask questions regarding how they felt about or perceived these sexual capacities and experiences, nor did they ask questions about sexual self-identity, affiliation with sexual minority communities, or political beliefs. The fact that 25–28 percent of the Kinsey researchers' women subjects were capable of responding erotically to both women and men, therefore, tells us nothing about whether these women identified themselves as bisexual; most probably considered themselves heterosexual. Whether they "are" bisexual depends on your definition of bisexuality. If you define bisexuality as the mere capacity to be erotically responsive to both women and men, whether or not one has ever actually so responded or acted on that response, then these 25–28 percent of the Kinsey researchers' women subjects were bisexual. If you would not consider a person bisexual unless they had experienced more than incidental attractions to both women and men, then you would consider 4–8 percent of the Kinsey researchers' women subjects bisexual. If you consider a person bisexual if they consider themselves bisexual, then the Kinsey statistics provide you with no estimate of the percentage of the population that is bisexual.

The second aspect of Kinseyan methodology that is relevant here pertains to the methods Kinsey and his associates used to recruit subjects. For reasons of feasibility they did not use probability sampling methods that would have produced samples representative of the national population. Instead, they recruited subjects through snowball sampling and through contacts with professional and community organizations, colleges and universities, penal and other correctional institutions, and social networks. Because of the nature of some of the social networks and institutions sampled for the purpose of securing a sexually diverse sample, the sample overrepresented the sexually active portion of the population and produced inflated estimates of the prevalence of all types of sexual behavior and erotic response—heterosexual as well as bisexual and homosexual. Therefore, we cannot generalize particular rates found in the Kinsey samples to the general population. For example, the fact that 37 percent of the Kinsey researchers' men subjects had had sexual contact after the onset of adolescence with another man to the point of orgasm does not mean that 37 percent of men in the United States have had such sexual contact; the rate of such sexual behavior among men in general is probably somewhat lower than the rate among the men in the Kinsey sample. Morton Hunt (1974), on the basis of knowledge of the sampling methods used by the Kinsey researchers, estimated that a more accurate figure would be 25 percent. Supporting this revised estimate, more recent researchers, whose findings will be described later in this chapter, have consistently reported rates substantially lower than those reported in the Kinsey studies.

Although particular rates cannot be generalized, comparisons between rates tend to be more robust. If we could assume that rates of heterosexuality, bisexuality, and homosexuality were all equally inflated among the Kinsey respondents, we could accept at face value the finding that the capacity for bisexual response is more common than the capacity for exclusively homosexual response in the general population of the United States. In fact, this assumption is tenuous because Kinsey researchers made special efforts to recruit subjects from gay communities and prisons. But if those portions of the Kinsey samples that overrepresent people with same-gender sexual attractions or experiences are excluded, comparative rates can be calculated. Paul H. Van Wyk and Chrisann S. Geist (1984) did just that, arriving at estimates that 94.1 percent of females and 85.7 of males were virtually exclusively heterosexual, 1.8 percent of females and 4.7 percent of males were predominantly homosexual (K-scores of 4.01 to 6), and 4.1 percent of females and 9.6 percent of males had bisexual K-scores of 0.005 to 4.00, thus confirming the finding that bisexual erotic capacity is more common than exclusively homosexual erotic capacity, although both are less common than reported by Kinsey and his associates (see also Gagnon and Simon 1973).[7] More recent research has also confirmed the findings that same-gender sexual behavior (although not necessarily erotic capacity) is more common among men than among women, that bisexual behavior is more prevalent than exclusively homosexual behavior (e.g., Diamond 1993; Hunt 1974; Laumann, Gagnon, Michael, and Michaels 1994; Rogers and Turner 1991; Smith 1991) and that bisexual erotic capacity is even more common than overt bisexual behavior (e.g., Bell and Weinberg 1978). The findings of these more recent studies will be examined in detail later in this chapter.

Bearing in mind this information about the Kinsey methods, consider the popular understanding of the oft-quoted statistic "10 percent of the population is gay." There are two stories about the route by which this statistic was lifted from the Kinsey findings and given political meaning. One story holds that this statistic does not appear in either the 1948 or the 1953 volumes but was calculated by Bruce Voeller, an academic and nascent political activist, using data from both volumes. Voeller's calculations were confirmed in a letter by Paul Gebhard of the Kinsey Institute for Sex Research.[8] Voeller recalls (1990; see also Laumann, Gagnon, Michael, and Michaels 1994:289, note 7) that he produced this statistic for the express purpose of demonstrating that gay men and lesbians are numerous and therefore politically important. In fact, a 10 percent statistic does appear in the 1948 volume; it refers to the percentage of the male population who are "more or less exclusively homosexual (i.e., rate 5 or 6) for at least three years between the ages of 16 and 55" (1948:651), and some authors cite this as the source of the politicized 10 percent statistic (e.g., Harry 1990:92).

Whatever its origin, in nonscientific contexts this statistic is often used as an indication of the size of the lesbian and gay population, usually in conjunction with the assertion that everyone (read: every heterosexual) probably knows at least one lesbian or gay person even if they don't realize it or the assertion that such a large lesbian and gay population merits attention to its needs or wields considerable social or political power. These assertions imply that if a heterosexual asked ten of her or his friends if they were lesbian or gay, on average she or he would hear one "yes" answer, or that politicians should pay attention to lesbian and gay needs because one in ten of their constituents votes according to their stance on lesbian and gay issues. In other words, the statistic is usually taken to mean that one in ten people are not only attracted to members of their own sex but identify as lesbian or gay, consider themselves part of a "lesbian and gay population," and organize their social and political lives around this affiliation.

This is a gross misinterpretation of the original Kinsey finding. First, because the Kinsey sample was not a representative one and because all Kinseyan findings regarding the prevalence of specific sexual behaviors—especially those concerning same-gender sexual behavior—are likely to be overestimates, the 10 percent figure is probably an overestimate of the percentage of men who are more or less exclusively homosexual for at least three years.[9] For a more detailed argument and supporting statistics, see Milton Diamond's review (1993). Second, even if 10 percent of men were more or less exclusively homosexual for three years of their lives, these three years would occur at different points in time for different men and many of these men would behave heterosexually at other times in their lives. Thus, the percentage of the male population that is more or less exclusively homosexual at any given point in time is probably substantially smaller than 10 percent, and a substantial portion of these men are probably more accurately described as bisexual. Gebhard (1972:27) revised the Kinseyan 10 percent figure downward; excluding subjects without college educations because of the high rate of prison experience among grade-school educated subjects, he estimated that "about 4 percent of the white college-educated adult males are predominantly homosexual." Third, the Kinsey figure refers to sexual behavior and erotic response only; it has nothing to do with sexual self-identification or political affiliation. Many men who engage in same-gender sexual behavior neither identify as gay nor vote gay. Fourth, the finding is based on a sample of men and therefore does not represent women who do, after all, make up half the national population.[10] Kinsey, Pomeroy, Martin, and Gebhard (1953) found that rates of same-gender sexual behavior and erotic capacity among women were generally half the rates found among men (1948).

Despite their methodological flaws, the Kinsey reports are invaluable for their historical significance. Perhaps their most important contribution to modern sexology was not the findings themselves but the legitimacy they helped bestow on the study of sexuality. The Kinsey studies demonstrated that sexuality could be studied scientifically and broke the ground within a profession and a public that tends to look upon sex researchers with suspicion. They are, therefore, not to be criticized for having produced unreliable findings but applauded for having paved the way for other researchers to conduct studies that have since produced reliable findings.

Bell and Weinberg, Hunt, Playboy, Janus and Janus, and Hite: Findings from Post-Kinsey Nonrepresentative Studies

After publishing the *Male* and *Female* volumes Kinsey had planned to conduct a third study, one that would focus on homosexuality, but died before completing this project (Gebhard 1978). Several years later Kinsey's idea became a reality when the Institute for Sex Research (later, the Kinsey Institute for Sex Research, and, more recently, the Kinsey Institute for Research in Sex, Gender, and Reproduction) supported work that resulted in the 1978 publication of Alan P. Bell and Martin S. Weinberg's oft-cited study, *Homosexualities: A Study of Diversity Among Men and Women*, and the 1981 publication of Alan P. Bell, Martin S. Weinberg, and Sue Kiefer Hammersmith's *Sexual Preference: Its Development in Men and Women*. A few pages in *Sexual Preference* are devoted to bisexuals. However, *Homosexualities* is of greater relevance to the study of bisexuality because its purpose was to explore, for the first time, diversity *among* "homosexuals," including diversity with respect to degree of exclusivity of same-gender sexual behavior and feelings.

Both *Homosexualities* and *Sexual Preference* report findings based on interviews with nearly one thousand homosexual men and women and a comparison group of nearly five hundred heterosexual men and women. The homosexual sample was drawn from the population of the San Francisco Bay Area by recruiting potential subjects through public advertising, bars, personal contacts, gay baths, organizations, mailing lists, and public places, and then by selecting subjects to fill quotas based on their sex, race, age, educational level, and method of recruitment.[11] Bell and Weinberg noted the nonrepresentative character of the sample, emphasizing that conclusions cannot be drawn regarding the proportion of the homosexual population that exhibits a given characteristic. Nor can conclusions be drawn about the proportion of the general population of the United States that is homosexual or has homosexual characteristics, because the homosexual and heterosexual samples were drawn separately and their relative sizes determined by the researchers and not by their proportions in the general population. However, as Bell and Weinberg noted, relationships between variables are more resistant to sampling bias and can be more reliably generalized to the population of the United States. Therefore, they reported their findings as relationships between sexual characteristics and demographic characteristics, namely, sex and race.

For example, Bell and Weinberg (1978) reported that, among "homosexuals," 74 percent of white men, 68 percent of white women, 62 percent of Black men, and 61 percent of Black women rated themselves as exclusively homosexual (Kinsey 6) in current behavior; that 21 percent, 24 percent, 34 percent, and 22 percent, respectively, rated themselves as Kinsey 4's or 5's; and that 5 percent, 8 percent, 4 percent, and 17 percent rated themselves as Kinsey 0–3's.[12] Unfortunately, the authors did not distinguish Kinsey 0's from Kinsey 1–3's, so it is impossible to tell exactly what percentage of subjects described themselves as "bisexual" in behavior. If, however, it is assumed either that there are virtually no Kinsey 0's in this "homosexual sample"—an assumption implicitly shared by the authors who defined a "bisexual" rating as "a score of 4 or less" (59)—or that the percentage of Kinsey 0's does not differ substantially by race or sex, then Bell and Weinberg's findings suggest that, among "homosexuals," bisexual behavior is most common among Black women, less common among Black men and white women, and least common among white men. Some additional information about bisexuality in this homosexual sample is given by Bell, Weinberg, and Hammersmith, who reported that 8 percent of white males and 13 percent of white females had average Kinsey behavior and feelings scores of 2–4, whereas 55 percent and 45 percent, respectively, were exclusively homosexual (Kinsey 6's) in both their behavior and their feelings.

Bell and Weinberg noted that subjects' self-reported behavioral Kinsey scores were consistent with their reports of heterosexual contact. Rates of heterosexual coitus were higher among Blacks than among whites and higher among women than among men. Specifically, 22 percent of Black men and 14 percent of white men had engaged in heterosexual coitus within the past year and 73 percent and 64 percent, respectively, had done so ever in their lives. Thirty-three percent of Black women and 24 percent of white women had engaged in heterosexual coitus in the past year, and 88 percent and 83 percent, respectively, had done so ever in their lives.

Consistent with the Kinsey finding that bisexual erotic capacity is more common than bisexual behavior, Bell and Weinberg (1978) found that, with the exception of Black women, fewer subjects rated themselves as Kinsey 6's with regard to feelings than with regard to behavior: 62 percent of Black women, 58 percent of white men, 50 percent of white women, and 45 percent of Black men rated themselves as Kinsey 6's. Rates of exclusivity were even lower when subjects were asked whether they had ever experienced heterosexual arousal; 72–84 percent of each race-sex group reported having been aroused by someone of the other gender. Bell and Weinberg offered the explanation that feelings are less likely than behavior to be exclusively homosexual because they cannot be controlled as well as can behavior.

Homosexualities still enjoys fame as one of the notable studies in the history of sexology in the United States. In sexological memory it overshadows *Sexual Behavior in the 1970s,* published four years earlier by Morton Hunt, even though the Hunt study involved a larger and more geographically diverse sample drawn by probability sampling methods. Commissioned by the Playboy Foundation, the Hunt study was conducted by an independent research organization, Research Guild, Inc., that chose subjects through random selection of names in twenty-four cities in the United States. Despite the use of this probability sampling procedure, the fact that only approximately one in five people contacted agreed to participate seriously compromised the study's representativeness. The 2,026 people who did participate resembled the United States population in terms of demographic variables such as race (Black and white), marital status, age, and education, but there is no way to know whether they differed sexually from the much larger group of people who were selected but refused to participate and therefore no way of knowing how accurately respondents' sexual behavior reflected the sexual behavior of the United States population in general. Hunt himself believed the sample underrepresented "committed homosexuals," because they "live somewhat outside the cultural mainstream" (1974:310) and therefore were not as accessible through standard sampling techniques.

Primarily interested in the extent to which sweeping changes in sexual attitudes had resulted in changes in sexual behavior during the 1960s, Hunt reported that little change had occurred in the incidence of homosexual behavior since the Kinsey studies. Although he found rates considerably lower than did Kinsey and his associates, he attributed much of the difference to the Kinsey researchers' oversampling and the Research Guild, Inc.'s undersampling of people with homosexual experiences. Seven percent of males and 11 percent of females in the Hunt study had masturbated to homosexual fantasies, 17–18 percent of males had homosexual experiences after the onset of adolescence, 1 percent of males and 0.5 percent of females rated themselves as "mainly" or "totally" homosexual, and similar percentages rated themselves as "equally heterosexual and homosexual" (1974:310). Aside from this last statistic, Hunt did not report incidence data for bisexuality. However, as with the Kinsey data, subtracting the percentage of subjects who were exclusively homosexual from the percentage with homosexual experience yields a rough estimate of the percentage who might be described as having bisexual experience. Discounting his own findings, Hunt cited several sources such as the Mattachine Society and an interview with William Simon (Karlen 1971:456) to support his estimate that more or less exclusive homosexuals make up 2–3 percent of the population. Subtracting this from his 17–18 percent figure (comparable to Kinsey, Pomeroy, and Martin's 37 percent, which Hunt adjusted downward to 25 percent), Hunt's findings suggest that 14–16 percent of men have had homosexual experiences since the onset of adolescence but do not live exclusively homosexual lifestyles. Alternatively, we can look at Hunt's figures for homosexual behavior among heterosexually married women and men. He found that 9 percent of married women had had at least one homosexual experience; adjusted for the age distribution of the sample, this yields a 10–11 percent lifetime cumulative incidence. The comparable adjusted figure for married men is 12–13 percent. If we assume that these married women and men have had heterosexual experiences, then these percentages reflect the percentages of married women and men with bisexual experience. Either way, Hunt's findings concur with Kinsey findings that bisexual behavior is more common than exclusively homosexual behavior over the lifetime.

A decade after commissioning the Hunt study, in January 1982 the publishers of *Playboy* published a survey questionnaire in the magazine itself. Part 3 of the report, released sixteen months later in May 1983, carried the teaser "Do bisexuals really double their chances of getting a date on Saturday night?" (Cook et al. 1983). With a total response of over 100,000 the findings reported in *Playboy* in 1983 contained an unprecedented number of bisexuals: 2,786 bisexual men and 948 bisexual women, and a more scholarly treatment of the results of this survey appears in this section as chapter 12 (Lever et al. 1992). There were approximately three times as many bisexuals as there were gay men (932) or lesbians (247) in the sample described in *Playboy* in 1983. Although the authors of the *Playboy* article did not explicitly indicate the basis on which they classified respondents into these categories, the facts that they characterized the article as pertaining to "sexual identity" and reported the percentages of respondents in each category who had had same-sex and other-sex experience suggest that these statistics reflect self-identity.

Consistent with other studies, the findings reported by *Playboy* in 1983 indicate that bisexual experience is not limited to "bisexuals." Eight percent of the "heterosexual" men and women in the *Playboy* study had had adult homosexual experiences, and one-third of men and nearly one-fifth of women had had adolescent homosexual experiences. In all, 35 percent of male respondents, regardless of sexual identity, reported ever having had homosexual experiences; the authors noted that this statistic is very close to the 37 percent reported by Kinsey, Pomeroy, and Martin (1948). Among "bisexual" men and women in the survey heterosexual experience predominated; only 16 percent of the men and 12 percent of the women reported that their current experience was primarily homosexual, although 63 percent of the men and 61 percent of the women reported that they were having same-sex contact at least rarely. One-third of the "bisexual" men and 40 percent of the women reported being married. The predominance of heterosexual experience in this sample might well be the result of sampling bias; bisexuals with stronger same-sex interests might be underrepresented in the readership of *Playboy*.

In the 1980s and 1990s sexuality research caught the attention of a public fearful of AIDS and conflicted over sexual morality and changing gender roles. Touted as a "startling revelation of how women in America today feel about love"[13] (read: heterosexual love) and geared toward a nonacademic audience, Shere Hite's *Women and Love: A Cultural Revolution in Progress* (1987) received publicity as a documentation of women's dissatisfactions in their relationships with men. Drawn using nonprobability sampling methods designed to reach a variety of women and involving the distribution of questionnaires through women's rights organizations, counseling centers, professional groups, church groups, voting and political groups, and other clubs and organizations, the sample nevertheless resembles the national female population on demographic variables such as race, education, income, age, marital status, geographic region, occupation, religion, and political affiliation. The fact that the sample is demographically representative of the national population is somewhat reassuring but does not guarantee that it is representative of national sexual behavior. Hite reported that out of over three thousand respondents 9 percent identified themselves as bisexual or had had experiences with both men and women but did not answer the question about their sexual preference. Eight percent preferred sex with women, and 11 percent "have love relationships only with other women. An additional 7 percent sometimes have relationships with women" (1987:542). In the appendicized statistical data Hite described this 7 percent as bisexual. Hite also commented on the number of older women who, once married, were now in relationships with women; 61 percent of women over age forty in lesbian relationships had been previously married.

When it was published in 1993 *The Janus Report on Sexual Behavior* by Samuel S. Janus and Cynthia L. Janus caused considerable debate within the lesbian, gay, and bisexual communities because it was the first well-publicized evidence that the popular belief "10 percent of the population is gay" might be incorrect. The study was based on a sample of 2,765 adults living in the forty-eight contiguous states. Because of limited funding the sample was not drawn using probability sampling methods, and the authors did not provide details about how questionnaires were distributed. However, they did provide a comparison of the distribution of demographic characteristics in their sample to national census data. The sample closely resembles the national population in terms of sex, age, and geographic region. It underrepresents people with less than a high school education, overrepresents single women and underrepresents widowed women, overrepresents people with incomes over $20,000, and underrepresents Protestants while overrepresenting those of Jewish and "other" religions. The researchers reported that 22 percent of men and 17 percent of women answered "yes" to the question "Have you had homosexual experiences?"—including 23 percent of "career women" and 10 percent of homemakers—and that 5 percent of women and 9 percent of men described these experiences as "frequent" or "ongoing" in response to a follow-up question. Unfortunately, these data were not cross-tabulated with data on heterosexual experiences to yield statistics on rates of bisexual experience. The researchers did report, however, that 2 percent of women and 4 percent of men identified themselves as homosexual whereas 3 percent of women (5 percent among career women) and 5 percent of men identified themselves as bisexual. Thus, in this sample, bisexual self-identity is more common than homosexual, lesbian, or gay self-identity.

A National Picture Finally Emerges: Recent Reliable Findings from National Probability Surveys

Since the mid 1980s the quality of our information about Americans' sex habits has been increased dramatically by a few national probability surveys focusing on sexual behavior and by the inclusion of questions on sexual behavior and identity in national probability surveys on other topics. National surveys on sexuality include the National Health and Social Life Survey (NHSLS), the National AIDS Behavioral Survey (NABS), and the Project HOPE Center for Health Affairs' International Survey of AIDS-Risk Behaviors. National surveys on other topics that have included questions on sexuality include the National Opinion Research Center's (NORC) annual General Social Survey (GSS), the 1991 National Survey of Men (NSM), and an American Broadcasting Company–Washington Post opinion poll (ABC-WP poll).[14] Because the sample used in each study was selected using probability sampling methods and the findings are therefore accurate with a known degree of certainty, these findings can be combined and compared to each other—and to the findings of other, more limited, studies—to yield even greater insight than any one study can provide. Diane Binson and colleagues Stuart Michaels, Ron Stall, Thomas J. Coates, John H. Gagnon, and Joseph A. Catania (1995), for example, compared the 1988–1991, 1993, and 1994 GSSs and the NHSLS to the NABS. Tom W. Smith (1991) compared the 1988 and 1989 GSSs. Robert

E. Fay, Charles F. Turner, Albert D. Klassen, and John H. Gagnon (1989) compared the 1988 GSS to a national probability sex survey undertaken in 1970 under the direction of the Kinsey Institute for Sex Research, and Susan M. Rogers and Charles F. Turner (1991) compared the 1988, 1989, and 1990 GSSs to each other, to the 1970 Kinsey Institute Survey, and to a pretest for a proposed National Household Seroprevalence Survey (NHSS pretest) done in Dallas County, Texas.[15]

Among sexologists the National Health and Social Life Survey (NHSLS) is perhaps best known for its embroilment in political struggles over the funding of research on sexuality during the Reagan and Bush presidencies.[16] Originally formed in 1987 in response to a call for proposals by the United States Department of Health and Human Services' (DHHS) National Institute for Child Health and Human Development (NICHD), the NHSLS research team was awarded and then denied federal funding and eventually proceeded in 1992 with private funds and the help and support of NORC, which also conducts the annual GSS. The NHSLS survey assessed sexual behavior, desire, and self-identity using interviews and a self-administered questionnaire. Potential respondents were selected using multistage area probability sampling of the English-speaking United States residential population aged eighteen to fifty-nine. Seventeen percent of those selected refused to participate, and the final sample numbered 3,432 women and men. Meanwhile, during the battle over NHSLS funding the NORC began including self-administered questions on sexual behavior in the GSS in 1988.[17] Because the GSS is conducted using a nationally representative sample and because the questions on sexual behavior comprise only a small portion of a questionnaire covering many topics that would therefore not cause people with homosexual feelings to disproportionately decline to participate in the survey, GSS samples are probably sexually representative of the United States population. Questions about sexual behavior are asked using a self-administered questionnaire within the context of a face-to-face interview. The GSS annually includes approximately 1,500 English-speaking adults aged eighteen and older. GSS survey response rates ranged from 73.9–77.6 percent for the 1988–1990 surveys, and 18.6 percent of respondents in the combined 1989–1990 GSSs did not respond to the question regarding adult same-gender contact (Rogers and Turner 1991).

Two books have been published by NHSLS researchers based on the NHSLS and GSS data, and the reader who is not satisfied by the summary below is referred to either book for a detailed report of the findings. *The Social Organization of Sexuality* by Edward O. Laumann, John H. Gagnon, Robert T. Michael, and Stuart Michaels (1994) is intended for a professional readers, and *Sex in America* by Robert T. Michael, John H. Gagnon, Edward O. Laumann, and Gina Kolata (1994) is intended for a more general audience. Binson and colleagues (1995) also provided a concise report of NHSLS and GSS findings on the prevalence and correlates of same-gender sexual behavior among men.

Findings of the NHSLS, the GSSs, and the Center for Health Affairs Survey regarding the prevalence of total same-gender sexual behavior, exclusively same-gender behavior, and bisexual behavior are very similar to each other, whereas the NSM generally yielded lower prevalence estimates. Describing NHSLS findings,

Laumann, Gagnon, Michael, and Michaels (1994) reported that 4.3 percent of women and 9.1 percent of men have engaged in one or more specific sexual activities with a member of the same gender since puberty; the authors pointed out that the latter number is dramatically smaller than the 37 percent reported by Kinsey, Pomeroy, and Martin (1948). Laumann, Gagnon, Michael, and Michaels further reported that 4.1 percent of women and 4.9 percent of men reported same-gender sexual behavior since age eighteen, and that 1.3 percent of sexually active women and 2.7 percent of sexually active men reported having engaged in same-gender sexual behavior within the past year.[18] These findings are consistent with the Center for Health Affairs Survey, in which 3.6 percent of women and 6.2 percent of men had had sexual contact with a member of their own sex within the previous five years, and 6.7 percent of women and 12.1 percent of men had engaged in same-sex sexual activity since age fifteen (Sell, Wells, and Wypij 1995).[19] Findings from both studies indicate that, as would be expected, the longer the time period in question, the greater the percentage of people who have engaged in same-gender sexual behavior during that period.

Also as would be expected, the longer the time period in question, the greater the percentage of people who have had bisexual experience during that period. Laumann, Gagnon, Michael, Michaels (1994) found that among NHSLS respondents who had had same-gender partners, the percentage of women and men who had had partners of both genders was, respectively, 90.7 percent and 94.9 percent since puberty, 62.9 percent and 51.6 percent within the past five years, and 25.0 percent and 25.3 percent within the past year—rates comparable to the rates of heterosexual coitus in the past year and in one's lifetime found by Bell and Weinberg in their "homosexual" sample.[20] Also consistent with these findings, among NSM respondents who had had same-gender sexual contact in the previous ten years approximately 57 percent of those aged twenty-five to twenty-nine and 82 percent of those aged thirty to thirty-four had had heterosexual contact during that period as well (Billy, Tanfer, Grady, and Klepinger 1993).[21] The NHSLS findings show that when lifetime sexual behavior is taken into account the vast majority of people with same-gender experiences in fact have had bisexual experience. In terms of the entire NHSLS sample, 5.8 percent of all men and 3.3 percent of all women had had both men and women partners since puberty, whereas only 0.6 percent of men and 0.2 percent of women had been exclusively homosexual since puberty. In contrast, in the short term, rates of exclusive homosexuality are higher than rates of bisexual behavior; 0.7 percent of all men and 0.3 percent of all women had had both men and women partners in the past year, whereas 2.0 percent of men and 1.0 percent of women had had only same-gender sex partners. Intermediate rates are provided by the Center for Health Affairs Survey, which found five-year rates of bisexual behavior of 5.4 percent among men and 3.3 percent among women compared to rates of 0.8 percent and 0.3 percent, respectively, for exclusively homosexual behavior, and by John O. G. Billy, Koray Tanfer, William R. Grady, and Daniel H. Klepinger (1993), who found lower rates of exclusive homosexuality (1.1 percent) and bisexual behavior (1.2 percent) over the course of a ten-year period among men in the NSM.

After adjusting for possible biases introduced by missing data, Smith (1991) concluded from the 1988 and 1989 GSS datasets that 3 percent of adults have not been sexually active since age eighteen, whereas 91 percent have been exclusively heterosexual, 5.6 percent have been bisexual, and 0.7 percent have been exclusively homosexual. He found higher rates of homosexuality among men than women in the 1988 data, but no gender difference in the 1989 data. Rogers and Turner (1991) cross-tabulated the numbers of male and female partners reported by men since age eighteen in the 1989 and 1990 datasets. Weighted to adjust for the fact that NORC household sampling methods give adults living in households with other adults a lower probability of being selected than adults who live alone, this cross-tabulation indicates that 4 percent of men have not had a sex partner since age eighteen, 90.5 percent of men have had female but no male partners since age eighteen, and that among men who have had at least one male partner since age eighteen, 88 percent (4.8 percent of all men) have also had female partners and 12 percent (0.7 percent of all men) have been exclusively homosexual; these figures are substantially in agreement with Smith's (1991) and with NHSLS findings.[22] Rogers and Turner (1991) further reported that within the past year 0.3 percent of men have had both female and male partners and 0.9 percent have had only male partners.[23] Thus, as in NHSLS findings, the shorter time period produces lower estimates of bisexual behavior and higher estimates of exclusively homosexual behavior, leading Rogers and Turner (1991) to conclude that there is a small but stable population of men whose adult sexual contacts are exclusively homosexual and a larger population with episodic or sporadic homosexual contact in addition to heterosexual contact. The former group comprises a majority of the men who are homosexually active at any given point in time but a minority of men who have ever had a homosexual experience.[24]

To what extent are rates of homosexual and bisexual behavior affected by social changes? The 1970s and 1980s saw dramatic changes in sexual attitudes, the advent of the AIDS pandemic, and the "ethnicization" of lesbians and gay men as they adopted the political model provided by racial and ethnic political movements and created quasi-ethnic lesbian and gay identities;[25] any of these factors could conceivably affect individuals' inclinations to express same-gender sexual attractions through same-gender sexual behavior, thereby affecting overall rates of same-gender sexual behavior. Comparisons of NHSLS and GSS data to data from the 1970 Kinsey Institute Survey, although complicated by differences in methodology, suggest that the prevalence of lifetime same-gender sexual behavior among men decreased during the 1970s and 1980s whereas rates of recent same-gender sexual behavior increased. Fieldwork for the 1970 study was done by the NORC under the direction of the Kinsey Institute for Sex Research. Although the sample of 3,018 women and men was drawn via scientific sampling methods, results pertaining to men might be affected by the fact that 15 percent of men did not answer questions about same-gender sexual experiences, 6 percent did not answer these questions fully, and an unknown number of potential respondents refused to participate.[26] By imputing values for missing data, Fay, Turner, Klassen, and Gagnon (1989) estimated that 20.3 percent of the 1,450 men aged over twenty-one surveyed in 1970 had had at least one homosexual experience, that 11.9 percent had had their last such experience at age fifteen or older, and that 6.7 percent had had their last such experience at age twenty or older. These figures are substantially higher than the rates of same-gender sexual behavior since puberty and since age eighteen that were obtained in the NHSLS and GSS two decades later; the different findings are not explained by the difference in the lengths of the time periods in question. In contrast, Fay and colleagues (1989) found twelve-month incidence rates in the 1970 Kinsey study to be slightly lower than those in the 1988 GSS; weighting to correct for differential selection probabilities for members of households of different sizes, they calculated from 1988 GSS data that 2.4 percent of men had had same-gender sexual experiences in the past year whereas the 1970 Kinsey survey had found that 1.6–2.0 percent had had same-gender sexual experiences within the past year.

Although these differences in the findings of the 1970 Kinsey study on one hand and the NHSLS and GSS on the other hand might be attributable to differences in methods rather than actual changes in rates of same-gender sexual behavior between 1970 and the late 1980s/1990s, the fact that at each point in history similar findings were obtained by different researchers lends credence to the latter explanation. Regarding the late 1980s/1990s, the fact that NHSLS and GSS findings are similar to each other increases our confidence in the accuracy of the findings of each study. Similarly, our confidence in the 1970 Kinsey findings is increased by their similarity to the contemporaneous findings of Hunt (1974). For example, as mentioned earlier in this chapter, Hunt (1974) found that 17–18 percent of men had had a homosexual experience since the onset of adolescence, a finding that is consistent with 1970 Kinsey findings that 20.3 percent of men have ever had a same-gender sexual experience and that 11.9 percent have had one since age fifteen.

If it is indeed true that lifetime prevalence rates decreased whereas short-term prevalence rates increased slightly between 1970 and the early 1990s, the explanation might lie in changing behavior patterns. For example, such findings would be expected if same-gender sexual behavior was more common in the early 1970s but less likely to lead to a stable gay self-identity and a "homosexual career" than it would be two decades later. Given the ethnicization of gayness that took place during the 1970s and 1980s, a process that created a stronger cultural connection between same-gender sexual behavior and gay self-identity and a clearer cultural distinction between heterosexuals as a group and gay men and lesbians as a group, it is quite possible that men were more likely to engage in same-gender sexual behavior in 1970 but, having once engaged, less likely to establish a self-identity or a long-term sexual behavior pattern based on that experience than they were in the 1990s. In other words, because of the solidification of gay self-identity and the heightening of the distinction between the gay and straight worlds, men's sexual behavior might have become more exclusive—and, conversely, less likely to be bisexual—during the 1970s and 1980s.

Although comparing data from the 1970s to data from the late 1980s/1990s suggests that patterns of same-gender sexual behavior might have become more exclusive during the 1970s and 1980s, nonexclusive same-gender sexual behavior—

that is, bisexual behavior—is still more common than exclusive same-gender sexual behavior. Fay, Turner, Klassen, and Gagnon noted that both the 1970 and the 1988 datasets "point to a particularly significant contribution of currently married men to homosexual activity" (1989:344). For example, in the 1970 sample approximately half of the men who had had homosexual contact in the past year were currently or previously married, 4.8 percent of currently married men had had homosexual contact at or since their age at their first marriage, and "the reporting of heterosexual contact among never married men" was also "substantial" (1989: 345). These results suggest that much homosexual activity occurs among men who also engage in heterosexual activity, i.e., men who are behaviorally bisexual.

Statistics on the prevalence of exclusively homosexual and bisexual behavior in the National AIDS Behavioral Survey (NABS) as reported by Binson and colleagues (1995) are surprisingly similar to those found in the GSS by Smith (1991) and Rogers and Turner (1991), surprising because of differences in methodology and sampling between the two surveys. The NABS was a random-digit dialing telephone survey that included an urban oversampling of Black and Hispanic respondents; this urban oversample is the source of the findings reported by Binson and colleagues (1995). Of 2,664 men aged eighteen to forty-nine in the NABS urban oversample, 6.5 percent of all men had had sex with another man in the past five years and, of these, 67.2 percent (4.4 percent of all men) had had sex only with men and 32.8 percent (2.1 percent of all men) had also had sex with a woman in the past five years.[27] The similarity with NHSLS and GSS findings is probably a result of two opposing factors. The difference in the length of the time period in question — since age eighteen in the GSS versus the past five years in NABS—would tend to produce higher rates of both heterosexual and homosexual activity in the GSS. On the other hand, the difference in population—a general national population in the GSS versus an urban population in the NABS—would tend to produce higher rates of same-gender activity in the NABS because, as we will see later in this chapter, there is evidence that the prevalence of same-gender sexual behavior is higher among urban than nonurban residents.

How does the prevalence of same-gender and bisexual feelings of attraction compare to the prevalence of same-gender and bisexual behavior? One study that assessed feelings of sexual attraction was the American Broadcasting Company–Washington Post poll described by Joseph Harry (1990). Like the GSS, the ABC–WP poll provided information about American sexuality based on a national probability sample drawn for purposes other than the study of sexuality—in this case, to assess opinions on political and social issues. Therefore, it is unlikely that the results of this poll are biased by lower participation rates among individuals hoping to conceal their stigmatized sexual feelings. The ABC-WP poll was conducted via telephone interviews with respondents in all fifty states in 1985. At the end of the telephone interview, after a series of questions on AIDS and prefaced with a reassurance of confidentiality, male respondents were asked, "Would you say that you are sexually attracted to members of the opposite sex or members of your own sex?" Harry noted that the question did not provide for the response "bisexual" and offered the following revealing thoughts:

The fact that the alternative of "bisexual" was not offered may be a deficiency in the question asked. Many people will take the middle alternative in survey questions when it is offered (Converse and Presser, 1986). However, it is unclear that the inclusion of this alternative would have increased accuracy by identifying more truly bisexual persons. Some homosexuals may choose a "bisexual" label because they believe it is less stigmatizing while either homosexuals or heterosexuals may choose that label because they believe on theoretical grounds that all persons are by nature bisexual. Such responses would decrease the accuracy of the information gathered. (1990:95)

In other words, Harry thought that, like the midpoint on a Likert Scale, the response option bisexual would allow respondents to take the easy way out by giving a nonanswer; he preferred to encourage respondents to classify themselves as either heterosexually or homosexually attracted. Clearly, Harry did not consider "bisexual" an authentic sexual identity on a par with monosexual identities; he thought that those who would label themselves bisexual were not choosing a bisexual label but instead avoiding the choice between heterosexual and homosexual identities.

Of 663 male respondents in the ABC-WP poll, 16 said they were homosexually attracted, 5 described themselves as bisexual, and 15 refused to answer the question. Weighting the data to correct for demographic sampling bias produced the estimate that 3.7 percent of males are homosexual or bisexual in their attractions, one-quarter of whom are sufficiently resistant to classification as homosexual to supply their own bisexual label. If all the 15 respondents who refused to answer the question did so to avoid admitting to stigmatized homosexual attractions, the 3.7 percent figure would be 5.7 percent, a figure that Harry points out is substantially lower than the famous Kinseyan 10 percent.

NHSLS respondents were also asked about their feelings of sexual attraction, but the question used was very different from that used in the ABC-WP poll. In the NHSLS respondents were asked to rate their feelings of sexual attraction on a five-point scale and thus offered opportunities not only to indicate bisexual attraction but to indicate the "degree" of that bisexual attraction. Some degree of attraction to both women and men was reported by 4.1 percent of women and 3.9 percent of men, although in each case approximately two-thirds of these reported that they were "mostly" attracted to the other gender. Exclusive same-gender sexual attraction was reported by 0.3 percent of women and 2.4 percent of men, indicating that both women and men were more likely to report bisexual than exclusively homosexual feelings of attraction.[28] This pattern was particularly strong among women, few of whom claimed to be exclusively attracted to other women (Laumann, Gagnon, Michael, and Michaels 1994). In general, these rates of same-gender sexual attraction are substantially higher than the rates of recent same-gender sexual behavior found in the same sample.[29] These findings indicate that, at any given point in time, same-gender sexual attraction is much more common than same-gender sexual behavior. In particular, bisexual attraction is seven times as common as recent bisexual behavior among women and five times as common as recent bisexual behavior among men.

Comparing Laumann, Gagnon, Michael, and Michaels's (1994) findings to those obtained by Harry (1990) indicates that male NHSLS respondents were nearly twice as likely to indicate same-gender sexual attractions, and four times more likely to report bisexual attractions, as ABC-WP poll respondents. In fact, whereas Harry (1990) found fewer bisexual than homosexual respondents, NHSLS researchers found fewer exclusively homosexual than bisexual respondents. The lower rates of overall same-gender attraction and the lower rates of bisexuality found by Harry (1990) are most likely due to the absence of an available bisexual response category; respondents who were mostly attracted to the other gender probably chose to classify themselves as heterosexually attracted and respondents who were equally attracted to both genders probably fit themselves into either the heterosexual or homosexual response categories.

Despite indications that bisexual attractions are more common than exclusively homosexual attractions, NHSLS respondents were more likely to report a homosexual than a bisexual self-identity; 0.5 percent of women and 0.8 percent of men identified themselves as bisexual and 0.9 percent of women and 2.0 percent of men identified themselves as homosexual, gay, or lesbian (Laumann, Gagnon, Michael, and Michaels 1994). The authors pointed out that the ratio of homosexual to bisexual self-identity is similar to the ratio of exclusively homosexual to bisexual behavior within the past year, suggesting that individuals might base their sexual self-identity primarily on their recent sexual behavior even if that behavior differs from their earlier behavior. Note also that the figures for bisexual self-identity are substantially lower than the figures for bisexual attraction, by a factor of eight among women and a factor of five among men. In other words, most individuals who currently feel sexually attracted to both women and men do not identify as bisexual, and the discrepancy between attractions and self-identity is greater among women than among men. Low rates of bisexual self-identification, similar to those found in national surveys like the NHSLS, have also been found in some representative surveys of particular cities and counties, and weaker links between sexual behavior, attractions, and self-identities among women than men have also been found in nonprobability samples (e.g., Pillard 1990) and several studies of specific populations (e.g., Golden 1987; Nichols 1985, 1990; Storms 1978; Weinberg, Williams, and Pryor 1994) that are reviewed later in this chapter.[30] The social and political factors responsible for generally low rates of bisexual self-identification and for the greater "internal inconsistency" in women's than men's sexuality are explored in chapter 23.

The fact that different estimates of the prevalence of bisexuality and homosexuality are obtained depending on whether respondents are asked about their sexual behavior, attractions, or identities provides suggestive evidence that these components of sexuality can vary independently of each other, but more direct evidence is provided by the cross-tabulation of these components with each other. Laumann, Gagnon, Michael, and Michaels's (1994) multivariate Venn diagrams and pie charts show that individuals can display homosexuality in any one or two of these three areas without necessarily displaying it in all three areas. The most prevalent combination is homosexual desire without adult homosexual behavior or self-identity, which includes 59 percent of women and 44 percent of men who express homosexual desire; the least likely combination is self-identity without desire or behavior.

In summary, a coherent picture of the prevalence of exclusively same-gender and bisexual behavior, attractions, and identities is beginning to emerge from the findings of recent studies using representative samples. Bisexual feelings of attraction are usually found to be more prevalent than exclusively homosexual feelings of attraction, but bisexual self-identity is less common than lesbian or gay self-identity and less common than bisexual feelings of attraction. In other words, a majority of individuals with same-gender sexual attractions also have other-gender sexual attractions, i.e., they have bisexual feelings, and a substantial proportion of individuals with bisexual feelings do not identify as bisexual. Whether or not bisexual and exclusively homosexual behavior are more or less prevalent than bisexual or lesbian/gay attractions and identities depends on the length of the time period during which the incidence of same- and other-gender sexual behavior is assessed. Reported rates of same-gender sexual attraction are similar to rates of total same-gender sexual behavior since puberty, with bisexual attraction and behavior more common than exclusively same-gender attraction and behavior among both women and men. In contrast, the prevalences of bisexual and lesbian/gay identities are similar to the rates of bisexual and exclusively same-gender sexual behavior in the past year, with bisexual self-identity and behavior substantially less common than homosexual self-identity and behavior among both women and men.

Who is Most Likely to Be Bisexual? Findings from National Probability Surveys on the Demographic Correlates of Bisexuality and Homosexuality

In addition to providing estimates of the prevalence of bisexuality and exclusive homosexuality in the general United States population as a whole, national probability surveys provide information about sexual differences between people with different demographic characteristics. A number of popular beliefs about the demographic characteristics of lesbians, gay men, and bisexuals can be tested using data from these surveys. For example, it is widely believed that younger people are more sexually liberal and liberated; national probability sex surveys can tell us whether younger people are in fact more likely to engage in same-gender or bisexual behavior than older people. Popular belief also has it that lesbians, gay men, and bisexuals tend to congregate in cities, either because cities provide a safer environment for the expression of same-gender desire among those already living in them or because people with same-gender desires living elsewhere migrate to cities in the hope of finding a supportive community. Beliefs like these can be confirmed or disproven by testing to see whether sexual characteristics such as sexual behaviors, feelings, and identities are correlated with demographic characteristics such as age, residence, marital status, income, education, and race.

Knowing the demographic correlates of sexual differences is also useful in estimating the representativeness of samples not drawn via probability methods. In one of the last segments of this chapter I will review nonprobability samples of specific populations such as samples of lesbians and gay men. Compared to the national population, samples of lesbians and gay men typically include disproportionately high percentages of adults in their twenties to forties who are white and well educated. Without knowing the demographic correlates of same-gender sexuality, it is impossible to determine the degree to which these samples reflect the general population of lesbians and gay men. If white, well-educated, young adults are more likely to have same-gender sexual interests than People of Color, the less educated, and older adults, then such samples might in fact be a true reflection of the lesbian and gay population. But if people of different races, educational levels, and ages are all equally likely to have same-gender sexual interests, then the fact that such a variety of people does not appear in samples of lesbians and gay men indicates that these samples do not reflect the demographic diversity of the lesbian and gay population.

Harry (1990), Laumann, Gagnon, Michael, and Michaels (1994), Rogers and Turner (1991), Billy, Tanfer, Grady, and Klepinger (1993), and Binson and colleagues (1995) looked for demographic differences between homosexual, bisexual, and heterosexual men. Unfortunately, Harry (1990), Laumann, Gagnon, Michael, and Michaels (1994), and Rogers and Turner (1991) did not distinguish homosexual from bisexual men in their analyses—a procedure that Laumann, Gagnon, Michael, and Michaels explained would have produced unreliable findings because of the small numbers of respondents involved—so only Billy, Tanfer, Grady, and Klepinger (1993) and Binson and colleagues (1995) provided information about demographic differences between homosexual and bisexual men. In comparing the findings of these five sets of authors, it is important to remember that in Harry's study sexual orientation classifications were based on respondents' self-reported feelings of sexual attraction, with reports of bisexual attraction discouraged, whereas in the GSS, NSM, and NABS surveys described by Rogers and Turner (1991), Billy, Tanfer, Grady, and Klepinger (1993), and Binson and colleagues (1995) respondents were classified according to their same- and other-gender sexual experiences, and in the NHSLS respondents' sexual behaviors, feelings of attraction, and self-identity were all assessed. Any differences in demographic correlates, therefore, might well be because of the fact that these different surveys explored different aspects of sexual orientation. Further, the GSS data presented by Rogers and Turner (1991) reflects adult sexual behavior, whereas the NSM data pertain to sexual behavior in the past ten years among respondents aged twenty to thirty-nine, and the NABS data presented by Binson and colleagues (1995) reflects sexual behavior in the past five years among respondents aged eighteen to forty-nine, so comparisons of findings from these different studies must take into account differences in the length of the time periods in question and in the ages of the respondents.

Despite the difference in their operational definitions of homosexuality/ bisexuality, Harry (1990), Rogers and Turner (1991), and Binson and colleagues (1995) all reported no substantial difference in age between homosexual/bisexual and heterosexual men, suggesting conversely that men of different ages, i.e., different generations, are equally likely to be homosexual/bisexual, whether sexual orientation is defined in terms of sexual attraction or actual sexual behavior and whether sexual behavior is assessed since attainment of adulthood or only within the past five years.[31] Billy, Tanfer, Grady, and Klepinger (1993) found higher rates of same-gender sexual behavior in the past ten years among men in their twenties than among men in their thirties, but this difference weakened when marital status was controlled. Binson and colleagues (1995) further compared homosexual to bisexual men and found that, in the NABS urban subsample, although the overall percentage of men who had had sex with men remained constant across age groups, among men who had had sex with men (MSM) rates of exclusive homosexuality increased and rates of bisexual behavior decreased with age; MSM aged eighteen to twenty-nine were as likely to have had sex with women as not in the past five years, whereas only one in five MSM aged forty to forty-nine had also had sex with women in the past five years. Undoubtedly, the fact that the time period in question was limited to the past five years allowed this finding to emerge; in statistics on sexual activity since age eighteen age differences in behavior would be obscured because older respondents' differential rates of bisexual behavior during different periods of their lives would, in effect, be averaged together, thus reducing the difference between their behavior and that of currently younger men. Binson and colleagues' (1995) finding suggests that as men grow older they become more gender exclusive in their sexual behavior. This would be the case if as men grow older they are more likely to be involved in monogamous relationships. Alternatively, the finding could reflect a cohort effect in which older generations of men were more gender exclusive even in their younger years, whereas younger men today are less likely to limit their partners to one gender.

The experiences of the youngest generation were studied by Gary Remafedi, Michael Resnick, Robert Blum, and Linda Harris (1992) and Freya L. Sonenstein, Joseph H. Pleck, and Leighton C. Ku (1989). In a representative sample of 34,706 junior and senior high school students in Minnesota, Remafedi and colleagues found that the percentage reporting same-sex attractions increased with age; 2 percent of twelve year olds compared to 6 percent of eighteen year olds reported predominantly same-sex attractions—although the prevalence of bisexual attractions decreased with age. Bisexual attractions were more common among males than females (0.8 percent vs. 0.5 percent), whereas homosexual attractions were more common among females (5.2 percent vs. 3.7 percent). Among males, the percentage with same-sex experience also increased with age; less than 1 percent of twelve year olds and almost 3 percent of eighteen year olds had engaged in homosexual behavior. Same-sex fantasies were reported by almost 3 percent of respondents of all ages, and among all respondents 0.4 percent identified as mostly or totally homosexual and 0.7 percent identified as bisexual, although an additional 10.7 percent said they were "unsure" of their sexual orientation. Those who said they were unsure were younger and more likely to report bisexual attractions than other students were. Sonenstein, Pleck, and Ku (1989) reported similar statistics on adolescent male same-sex behavior from the 1988 National Survey of Adolescent Males; of 1,880 never-married males aged fifteen to nineteen residing in the contiguous United States and recruited via area probability sampling, 3 percent had engaged in homosexual activity. Additional research findings regarding the sexual identities and behaviors of adolescents, as they pertain to the experience of coming out, are explored in chapter 23.

Not surprisingly, findings of national surveys show a correlation between marital status and homosexual or bisexual experience. For example, Harry (1990) found that 42 percent of homosexual/bisexual men, compared to 60 percent of heterosexual men in the ABC-WP poll, were married; a difference of only 18 percent. Harry pointed out that the former figure is much higher than the 2–7 percent figures found in nonprobability samples taken from gay populations, suggesting that gay and bisexual men are much more likely to be married than would be concluded from these samples. The underrepresentation of married gay and bisexual men in "gay" samples is probably because they are more likely than single men to be closeted and less likely to be socially connected to the gay organizations and social networks through which nonprobability samples of gay and bisexual men are recruited. Therefore, they are less likely to be included in samples drawn via nonprobability methods. The difference in the marital status of homosexual and bisexual men as compared to heterosexual men might explain Harry's related finding that homosexual and bisexual men were more likely to live alone than heterosexual men (33 percent versus 18 percent), even though they were no less likely to have school age children.

Conversely, Rogers and Turner (1991), Billy, Tanfer, Grady, and Klepinger (1993), and Binson and colleagues (1995) found that unmarried or never married men were more likely to have engaged in same-gender sexual activity than married men. In the NSM, among men aged twenty to thirty-nine currently married men were less likely (0.6 percent) to have had same-gender sexual contact in the past ten years than never-married men (4.9 percent, Billy, Tanfer, Grady, and Klepinger 1993). Combining the 1989 and 1990 GSSs also yields the finding that, among men aged twenty-one years and older, married men were less likely (3.4 percent) than never married men (9.4 percent) to have had adult homosexual contact (Rogers and Turner 1991).[32] Reversing the GSS percentages to make them comparable to Harry's, we find that 43.3 percent of men with homosexual contact and 64.1 percent of exclusively heterosexual men were married in the late 1980s, figures that are virtually identical to those obtained by Harry (1990) using 1985 data.[33] In the 1970 Kinsey Institute Survey, among men aged twenty-one years and older currently married men were again less likely (6.0 percent) than never married men (12.2 percent) to have had adult homosexual contact (Rogers and Turner 1991).[34] Reversing the 1970 Kinsey percentages yields estimates that 71.5 percent of men with homosexual contact and 80.6 percent of exclusively heterosexual men were currently married in 1970. In the NABS urban subsample, among men aged eighteen to forty-nine years, 0.4 percent of married men, 10.6 percent of never married men, and 20.9 percent of cohabiting men had had sex with men in the past five years (Binson and colleagues 1995); reversed, 2.6 percent of men with same-gender sexual contact in the past five years and 45.1 percent of men without such experience were married.[35]

Laumann, Gagnon, Michael, and Michaels's (1994) data show similar patterns among women; never married women, like men, were more likely to have had same-gender sexual experiences, to feel same-gender sexual attractions, and to identify as homosexual (lesbian/gay) or bisexual. Using NHSLS data only, they found that 11.8 percent and 5.6 percent of never married men and women, respectively, as compared to 4.1 percent and 2.6 percent of married men and women, have had same-gender sexual contact since puberty. They also found that 7.1 percent and 3.7 percent of never married men and women, respectively, identified as either homosexual (lesbian/gay) or bisexual, compared to 0.6 percent and 0.1 percent of married men and women.

Comparing the 1970 Kinsey marriage statistics to Harry's 1985 and to the GSS's 1989 and 1990 marriage statistics reveals two historical trends regarding marriage among men. First, there is a decreasing marriage rate among men in general and, second, there is an increasing difference in marriage rates between homosexually experienced and inexperienced men (see also Hewitt 1998). Apparently, whereas men in general are becoming less likely to marry, this rejection of marriage is most dramatic among men with homosexual experience who probably, in earlier decades, felt greater pressure to marry for the sake of appearance. The fact that marriage rates in the NABS survey are substantially lower than marriage rates in the GSSs, especially among men with same-gender sexual experience, even though the surveys were conducted during the same time period, probably reflects the urbanicity of the NABS sample and the fact that GSS rates of same-gender activity include all adult contact whereas the NABS rates refer to same-gender activity within the past five years.

If homosexual and bisexual men are less likely to be married than heterosexual men, how do the marriage rates of homosexual and bisexual men compare to each other? Among men who have had sex with men within the past five years, those who have also had sex with women are, not surprisingly, more likely to be married than those who have not. Conversely, those who are married are more likely to have been bisexually active as opposed to exclusively homosexually active in the past five or ten years than those who never married. Binson and colleagues (1995) reported that among ever married men who had had sex with men in the past five years 55.2 percent had also had sex with women, whereas among never married men who had had sex with men only 35.6 percent had also had sex with women.[36] Similarly, in the NSM, 100 percent of currently married men and 43 percent of never married men who had had sex with men had also had sex with women in the past ten years.[37]

Rogers and Turner (1991), Laumann, Gagnon, Michael, and Michaels (1994), and Binson and colleagues (1995) found an association between same-gender sexual behavior and urban residence. In both the 1970 Kinsey Institute Survey and the 1989 and 1990 GSSs men in cities/towns with populations of twenty-five thousand plus were more likely to have had same-gender sexual experiences than men in less populous areas (Rogers and Turner 1991). Combining the GSS and NHSLS data, Binson and colleagues (1995) reported that men aged eighteen to forty-nine in the central cities of the twelve largest metropolitan areas were more likely to have had same-gender sex partners since age eighteen (14.4 percent), in the past five years (11.1 percent), and in the past year (7.8 percent) than men living in less urban areas, with the prevalence of same-gender sexual experience decreasing steadily with urbanicity and reaching a low of 2.1 percent, 1.8 percent, and 0.9 percent, respectively, in counties comprised of towns with less than ten thousand people.

Laumann, Gagnon, Michael, and Michaels (1994) also found that urban residents were more likely than suburban or rural residents to report same-gender sexual attractions or homosexual or bisexual identities; among people living in the top twelve central cities 15.8 percent of men and 5.9 percent of women reported same-gender sexual attractions and 9.2 percent of men and 2.6 percent of women identified as homosexual or bisexual. In comparison, among rural residents 4.4 percent of men and 0.5 percent of women reported same-gender sexual attractions and 1.3 percent of men and 0 percent of women identified as homosexual or bisexual. The findings pertaining to sexual attraction conflict with Harry's (1990) finding that homosexual and bisexual men are no more likely to live in large cities, a discrepancy that might be due to the small numbers of respondents involved in the ABC-WP poll or to differences in question wording. The fact that ABC-WP respondents were forced to choose between reporting same- and other-gender sexual attractions undoubtedly suppressed the reporting of same-gender attractions among those with bisexual attractions, possibly masking urban-rural differences.[38]

Findings regarding educational differences are also contradictory. Whereas Harry (1990) found an insignificant tendency for homosexuals and bisexuals to be overrepresented in the lowest educational category,[39] Rogers and Turner (1991) found no significant difference in education, Billy, Tanfer, Grady, and Klepinger (1993) and Binson and colleagues (1995) reported that men with high levels of education were significantly more likely to report same-gender sexual activity than those with less education, and Laumann, Gagnon, Michael, and Michaels (1994) found that rates of homosexual behavior, self-identity, and attraction were positively correlated with education, more strongly among women than among men. For example, among women 9.3 percent of college graduates compared to 1.6 percent of high school graduates reported some degree of same-gender sexual attraction. In the NABS urban subsample 8.8 percent of men with more than a high school education reported having had same-gender sex within the past five years, compared to only 2.4 percent of men with less than a high school education. However, among men who had had sex with men in the past five years Binson and colleagues (1995) found no significant difference in rates of bisexual activity between men with more and less education. This finding suggests that more highly educated men are more likely to have had sex with men, with rates of homosexual and bisexual behavior equally elevated in comparison to less educated men.[40]

Racial and ethnic differences in sexuality are complex. Harry (1990) classified subjects into "white" and "non-white" categories, a common procedure that ignores the fact that there is no reason to think that racial and ethnic groups lumped together by virtue of their "nonwhiteness" have anything in common with each other—and the fact that "whites" also have diverse ethnic heritages. Because non-white is not a meaningful category, comparisons between whites and nonwhites have no meaningful interpretation. The problem is, however, that because racial and ethnic groups other than whites each constitute a small fraction of the general United States population, national survey samples typically contain too few members of any given racial or ethnic group other than white to produce either reliable estimates of the prevalence of same- and other-gender sexual activity within that racial or ethnic group, or statistically significant findings regarding differences between racial/ethnic groups. Findings regarding racial and ethnic differences are, therefore, to be handled with caution.

Notwithstanding this problem, Rogers and Turner (1991) reported an insignificant trend toward higher rates of same-gender sexual experience among whites than Blacks in the 1970 Kinsey study and the NHSS, and Binson and colleagues (1995) reported a significant difference in the same direction in the NABS data. In contrast, Laumann, Gagnon, Michael, and Michaels (1994)—who presented tabulated statistics on the sexual characteristics of respondents of different racial-ethnic groups but drew no conclusions about racial differences in their main text—found higher rates of same-gender sexual experience among Blacks than whites, depending on gender and the length of time in question, in the combined NHSLS and GSS data.[41] Although suggestive, Laumann, Gagnon, Michael, and Michaels's findings are statistically insignificant. Billy, Tanfer, Grady, and Klepinger (1993) reported that Hispanic men were more likely than non-Hispanic men to have had same-gender contact (4.8 percent versus 2.0 percent), exclusively same-gender contact (2.0 percent versus 1.0 percent), and bisexual contact (2.8 percent versus 1.0 percent). In their study of Minnesota junior and high school students, Remafedi, Resnick, Blum, and Harris (1992) found that same-sex attractions were more common among Hispanic (9.3 percent) females than among Asian/ Pacific (5.1 percent) and white (4.5 percent) females, and least common among Native American (2.6 percent) and Black (1.7 percent) females. Overall, bisexual attractions were more common among nonwhite males and females (1.9 percent) than among whites (0.6 percent); these findings are compromised by the fact that nonwhite students were less likely than white students to answer the questions about sexuality.

Despite these suggestive findings, before we can draw any conclusions about whether there are racial or ethnic differences in sexuality in the United States, let alone describe these differences, we need samples containing larger numbers of African American, Latino/a, and other People of Color. Better representation of particular racial and ethnic groups in probability survey samples can be obtained only by drawing a very large sample or by oversampling these racial and ethnic groups. The NABS urban subsample includes such an oversampling of Black and Hispanic respondents. Binson and colleagues (1995) reported that 9.1 percent of white men, 3.1 percent of Black men, 2.7 percent of Hispanic men, and 2.2 percent of "Asian/other" men had had sex with a man in the past five years.[42] Among men who had had sex with a man (MSM) in the past five years Blacks were more likely (56.9 percent) than either Hispanics (34.1 percent) or whites (29.0 percent) to also have had sex with a woman in the past five years ($p < .05$; cf. Wold 1998). These last statistics, however, are based on small numbers of respondents; despite the over-sampling of Black and Hispanic men, the proportion of men who had had sex with men within each racial or ethnic group is so small that the NABS dataset includes only nineteen Black MSM and twelve Hispanic MSM. In another study that used random and quota sampling to obtain approximately equal numbers of Black and white women and men in four cities in the United States for a study of cardio-vascular risk factors (CARDIA), Krieger and Sidney (1997) reported that white women and men were more likely to have had sex partners of both sexes (12.3 per-cent, 10.6 percent) and more likely to have had only same-sex partners (1.8 percent, 5.7 percent) in their lifetimes than Black women and men (5.8 percent, 5.4 percent; 0.7 percent, 0.5 percent). Findings regarding racial/ethnic differences in rates of bi-sexual and homosexual experience might be complicated by racial differences in nonresponse. In a study based on a subset of the CARDIA sample, for example, Blacks had substantially lower response rates (48 percent among Black men) than whites (Berrios et al. 1992). Saewyc and colleagues (1998) found that nonresponse was more common among Native American adolescents than Anglo adolescents (17.2–26.7 percent versus 4.1–11.3 percent). In this study of 12,978 Native American adolescents and 11,356 Anglo adolescents, Native Americans were more likely to self-label as bisexual (1.1 percent versus 0.8 percent) or homosexual (0.5 percent versus 0.3 percent) and to report attractions to both sexes (17.4 percent versus 11.3 percent) and fantasies about both sexes (women: 8.1 percent versus 2.0 percent, men: 3.2 percent versus 1.4 percent). There have also been several studies involv-ing samples of MSM only, quite a few of which include sufficient numbers of racial and ethnic minority respondents. The results of these studies, which are discussed in chapter 22, confirm findings that bisexuality, relative to exclusive homosexual-ity, is more common among African Americans and Latinos than among whites.

Ethnographic research also provides insight into racial and ethnic differences in sexuality. This research suggests that members of different racial and ethnic groups interpret their sexual feelings and behaviors differently and assign these experi-ences differential importance. Thus, any racial or ethnic differences in sexuality are far more complex than simple estimates of the prevalence of same-gender sexual attractions or behaviors—categories of sexual experience that are themselves based on European American sexual concepts—can reveal. Even with sufficient numbers of racial and ethnic minority respondents survey research would be un-likely to detect racial or ethnic differences in the qualitative interpretation of sexual experiences. For a review of literature on cultural differences between racial and ethnic groups that might lead to racial or ethnic differences in sexual expression and self-perception, including findings suggesting that bisexual self-identity might be more common or more acceptable among African Americans than among whites, see Rust (1996a) and chapters 22 and 23 of this volume.

A Closer Look at Specific Populations

In addition to large-scale national sex surveys, there have been a number of smaller studies of sexual feelings, behaviors, and identities within specific segments of the United States population. Typically, such studies are done on specific populations for whom sexuality is medically or socially problematic, populations that are expected to differ sexually from the general population of the United States, or populations that are too small to be represented in sufficient numbers in a national probability sample. These studies are useful because they provide more detailed information about the sexuality of these particular populations than large national surveys do.

For example, since the modern political lesbian and gay movement turned scientific attention away from questions pertaining to the cause and "cure" of homosexuality and toward issues of interest to lesbians and gay men, a number of studies have focused on specific lesbian or gay populations. Because it is impossible to use probability sampling methods to draw a sample of a population many of whose members are hidden, these samples are typically drawn by recruiting respondents from lesbian or gay organizations, at lesbian or gay events, or through publicity within lesbian and gay social networks. An example is Bell and Weinberg's (1978) study, described earlier in this chapter. Samples drawn in this way are not representative of the general lesbian and gay population; as mentioned earlier in this chapter, they typically overrepresent individuals who are open about their sexual orientation, aged in their twenties, thirties, or forties, white, and highly educated; see Harry (1990) for a discussion of the nature and reasons for these sample biases. Most of these studies of lesbian or gay populations are not undertaken with the goal of providing estimates of the prevalence of various sexual patterns such as bisexuality but incidentally produce such estimates in the process of exploring other research questions.

These studies indicate a high degree of bisexuality among individuals recruited via lesbian and gay networks. Previous heterosexual behavior is very common, although current heterosexual behavior is rare. Heterosexual attractions are also common, and 10–30 percent of individuals in "lesbian, gay (and bisexual)" samples typically self-identify as bisexual. One must conclude that bisexuality is prevalent within what is commonly referred to as the "lesbian and gay community." In contrast to the findings of studies using representative general population samples, in which bisexuality and homosexuality are more common among men than women, in "lesbian, gay, and bisexual" samples bisexuality is typically more common among women than among men; the reasons for this are explored in chapter 23.

Regarding current heterosexual experience among samples of "gay" men, 4.8 percent of Marcel T. Saghir and Eli Robins's (1973) male homosexual subjects were currently engaging in heterosexual intercourse.[43] Other studies found rates of "recent" heterosexual experience among men recruited in gay settings to be higher and to depend on the length of time considered "recent" as well as the specific gay settings used for recruitment. For example, a survey of 1,776 men entering gay bars in sixteen U.S. cities, 92 percent of whom were white, found that 10.4 percent of those who reported at least one male partner in the previous two months had also had at least one female partner within that time period (Heckman et al. 1995). Heino F. L. Meyer-Bahlburg and colleagues (1991) found that 4.4 percent of a predominantly white (87 percent) sample of 205 "gay and bisexual men" in New York City, recruited through advertising in the gay community, had had both male and female partners within the previous six months. A sample of 250 African American men recruited in gay and African American settings in three California cities who identified as either gay or bisexual found that 65 percent rated their sexual experience over the past two years as exclusively homosexual, whereas 21 percent described their experiences as more homosexual than heterosexual, 8 percent as equally homosexual and heterosexual, and 6 percent as more heterosexual than homosexual (Peterson et al. 1992).[44] Lower rates are found among men recruited from gay settings but claiming "gay" self-identity. For example, a survey of male readers of the gay and lesbian newsmagazine the *Advocate*, 90 percent of whom were white, found that 2 percent of those saying they were gay had had vaginal intercourse within the previous twelve months (Lever 1994).[45]

Higher rates of recent heterosexual activity are typically found in "lesbian" samples than in "gay" samples. A study of 529 Black lesbians recruited through the mailing lists of Black gay organizations, fliers in lesbian bars, press releases to gay newspapers, and lesbian-oriented businesses found that 12 percent had had heterosexual coitus in the past year (Cochran and Mays 1988). Jack H. Hedblom (1973) found that 15.6 percent of a sample of 65 lesbians, all but one of whom were white, recruited through "homosexual" bars, friends, or acquaintances, reported having had "sexual relations" with a man in the previous year. In a San Francisco Department of Public Health Study, among 483 self-identified lesbian and bisexual women who were recruited at street fairs, film festivals, and sex clubs where lesbian and bisexual women were known to congregate, 65 percent were Caucasian, 11 percent African American, 11 percent Latina, and 9 percent Asian or Pacific Islander. Of these women 17 percent had had sex with one man in the past three years, 12 percent had had sex with two or three men, and 7 percent had had sex with four or more men in that time period—a total of 36 percent. Eighteen percent had had primary relationships with men during the previous three years. Among those who self-identified as lesbian, 22 percent had had sex with both women and men in the previous three years, and an additional 3 percent had had sex with men only during that time—yielding the finding that 25 percent of self-identified lesbians had had recent heterosexual experience (SFDPH 1993a). Among 1,056 women entering gay bars in sixteen cities, 90 percent of whom were European American, Ann Duecy Norman and colleagues (1996) found that 1 percent of women who described themselves as "exclusively homosexual" on a five-point scale, and 9.4 percent of the entire sample, reported having had male sex partners during the previous two months.

When lifetime sexual behavior is considered, rates of heterosexual experience among "gay" and "lesbian" samples increase; again, rates of heterosexual experience are higher among lesbians than among gay men. Recall, for example, that Bell and Weinberg (1978) found that 64 to 73 percent of "homosexual" men and 83 to 88 percent of "homosexual" women, depending on race, had ever engaged in heterosexual coitus. Weinberg and Williams (1974) found that 51 percent of male homosexuals who rated themselves as Kinsey 5's or 6's and 80.1 percent of those who rated themselves as Kinsey 2's to 4's had had heterosexual intercourse.[46] Saghir and Robins (1973) found the rate among their male homosexual subjects to be 48 percent. George F. Lemp and colleagues (1995) recruited a sample of 498 women in San Francisco and Berkeley who had had sex with women since 1978 or who self-identified as lesbian or bisexual, via street locations, dance clubs, bars, and cafes catering to a lesbian and bisexual clientele. Although most of the sample was white (53.8 percent), substantial percentages were African American (16.7 percent), Latina (14.7 percent), or Asian/Pacific Islander (12.4 percent). Lemp and colleagues (1995) found that 75.9 percent had had both male and female sex partners and that 5.4 percent had had only male sex partners since 1978. Regarding self-identified lesbians, based on predominately white samples, Hedblom (1973), Ralph H. Gundlach and Bernard F. Riess (1968),[47] Schäfer (1976),[48] and Saghir and Robins (1973) found that 50 to 80 percent had ever had heterosexual intercourse. June Machover Reinisch, Stephanie A. Sanders, and M. M. Ziemba-Davis (1988, see also 1995) found that 75 percent had had heterosex since age eighteen—including 43 percent of those who had "always identified themselves as lesbian"[49]—and Susan D. Cochran and Vickie Mays (1988) found that 90 percent of Black self-identified lesbians had ever had heterosexual intercourse and that 12 percent had done so within the previous year.

The percentage of lesbians and gay men with lifetime heterosexual experience is even larger when sexual activity other than intercourse is considered or when questions about sexual activity allow respondents to use their own definitions of "sexual activity" that might or might not be limited to intercourse. Beata E. Chapman and JoAnn C. Brannock (1987) found that 85 percent of 197 self-identified lesbians had had heterosexual contact and Lena Einhorn and Michael Polgar (1994) found that 53 percent of self-identified lesbians reported having heterosexual contact since 1978.[50] Meyer-Bahlburg and colleagues (1991) found that 72.1 percent of gay and bisexual men in New York City had had both male and female partners in their lifetimes and Saghir and Robins (1973) found that 73 percent of homosexual men had been aroused to erection by heterosexual stimuli. Schäfer (1976) found that 97 percent of lesbians had dated heterosexually, and Saghir and Robins (1973) found that 95 percent of homosexual women and 87 percent of homosexual men had dated heterosexually. Paula C. Rust (1992) reported that 90 percent of her self-identified lesbian respondents had ever been involved in a heterosexual relationship (including dating relationships), and half of these women described their heterosexual relationships as having been serious or marital. One might argue that these heterosexual relationships took place before these women came out as lesbian and hence have no bearing on their current sexual orientations. However, Rust also found that 43 percent of self-identified lesbians had been involved with men after they first came out as lesbians, although only a handful (less than 2 percent) were currently heterosexually involved.

Whereas previous heterosexual behavior is common among lesbians and gay men, one need not look back into history to find evidence of heterosexual attraction among lesbians and gay men. Substantial numbers—especially among lesbians—report that they are currently attracted to members of the other gender as well as members of their own gender. For example, Weinberg, Williams, and Pryor (1994) found that one half of "homosexual" women and one third of "homosexual" men reported that their feelings were not exclusively homosexual, and research by Margaret Nichols (1985, 1990) also suggests that "incongruent" attractions are more common among lesbians than gay men. As reported earlier in this chapter, 38 percent to 55 percent of Bell and Weinberg's "homosexual" Black and white men and women rated their sexual feelings as 5 or lower on the Kinsey scale. William H. Masters and Virginia E. Johnson (1979) found that heterosexual fantasies were the third most common fantasy among lesbians and among gay men (conversely, lesbian and gay fantasies were the fifth and fourth most common fantasies among heterosexual women and men). One in seven male readers of the *Advocate* reported some attraction to women (Lever 1994). Angela Pattatucci and Dean Hamer (1995) found that among women whose Kinsey scores indicated predominant or exclusive lesbianism, 45.3 percent reported ever being romantically or sexually attracted to men. Two-thirds of Rust's (1992) self-identified lesbian respondents indicated on an eleven-point scale that 10–60 percent of their feelings of sexual attraction were toward men, i.e., that they were bisexually attracted.

In Rust's study many self-identified lesbians reconciled their bisexual feelings with their lesbian or gay identities by conceptualizing sexual orientation in terms of the gender to which one is more strongly attracted. That is, one can have heterosexual feelings and be lesbian or gay as long as one's same-gender feelings are stronger than one's other-gender feelings. Other individuals defined sexual orientation in terms of sexual behavior, such that one's sexual attractions to the other gender are irrelevant as long as one has sex only with members of their own gender. For further findings about and discussion of lesbians' varied definitions of sexual orientation and the cultural meanings that permit lesbian and gay identities to subsume what could be considered bisexual experience, see Rust (1995a). For further findings regarding the prevalence and variation of bisexual feelings and behaviors among self-identified lesbians and gay men—and for findings regarding bisexuality among self-identified heterosexuals—see chapters 22 and 23.

Besides the fact that many self-identified lesbians and gay men have had heterosexual experiences and feel sexually attracted to members of the other gender, some individuals who participate in lesbian and gay communities—and who are, therefore, included in "lesbian and gay" samples recruited through these communities—identify themselves as bisexual or rate themselves as bisexual on five- or seven-point scales. The results of several different research studies, most of which used predominantly white samples, suggest that the percentage of such individuals tends to be approximately 20 percent among women, and less than 10 percent among men; percentages are higher in samples with greater representation of African Americans and Latinos and vary depending on recruitment strategies, although the greater preponderance of bisexual self-identity among women is a fairly consistent finding that has been noted by others (e.g., Pattatucci and Hamer 1995; Pillard 1990).

Among "lesbian and bisexual" women, for example, the San Francisco Department of Public Health (SFDPH 1993a; see also SFDPH 1993b) study found that 19 percent of self-identified lesbian and bisexual women recruited from "street and community locations" (8) identified as bisexual; 77 percent identified as lesbian, and 4 percent as heterosexual or as having "no" sexual orientation. In a survey of 1,086 women recruited through women's festivals, bars, and organizations Einhorn and Polgar (1994) found that 6.5 percent self-identified as bisexual, 8.6 percent "resisted a label" (516), and 84.9 percent identified as lesbian. Pattatucci and Hamer (1995) asked women recruited from homophile organizations in Washington, D.C. to rate themselves on four Kinsey scales; 36.9 percent had average Kinsey scores between 1.5 and 5.49 and were classified as bisexual whereas 61.3 percent were classified as lesbian. Among women entering gay bars in sixteen cities, Norman and colleagues (1996) found that 6.5 percent identified themselves on a five-point scale as bisexual, and an additional 17.3 percent and 5.1 percent rated themselves as primarily homosexual or primarily heterosexual, respectively; 57.1 percent rated themselves exclusively homosexual and 14 percent rated themselves exclusively heterosexual.

Among men, Meyer-Bahlburg and colleagues (1991) found that 7.4 percent of "gay and bisexual" men recruited via gay community advertising in New York City identified as bisexual; 91.1 percent identified as gay and 1.5 percent identified as straight. Lever and colleagues (1994) found that 3 percent of male readers of the *Advocate* said they were bisexual. Dean Hamer and colleagues Stella Hu, Victoria Magnuson, Nan Hu, and Angela Pattatucci (1993a) found that less than 10 percent of men recruited from HIV clinics and homophile organizations in Washington, D.C. rated their self-identities as Kinsey 2–4 and that only 5 percent rated their attractions and fantasies as Kinsey 2–4. In a study of AIDS knowledge and concern among older men, using a predominantly white sample recruited largely from the membership of a social organization for gay and bisexual men over age fifty in the United States, Canada, and Australia, Leonard Kooperman (1994) found that 12 percent self-identified as bisexual and 88 percent as gay.

Studies including both men and women also typically find higher rates of bisexual self-identification among women. D'Augelli and Hershberger (1993) recruited youths from gay-identified community centers in fourteen cities. After excluding those who described themselves as bisexual but predominantly heterosexual, they found that females were more likely to say that they were bisexual (14 percent versus 3 percent) although males were more likely to describe themselves as bisexual but mostly lesbian/gay (22 percent versus 12 percent). Some studies find similar rates of bisexual identification among men and women, however. In a study of the relationship between satisfaction with one's coming out process and the personality trait called "self-monitoring," Lynn R. Anderson and Lori Randlet (1993, 1994) asked their subjects, who were members of lesbian and gay organizations and 63 percent of whom were white, to classify themselves on a seven-point scale ranging from "exclusively heterosexual" (7) to "exclusively homosexual" (1), on which the intermediate points were labeled "bisexual."[51] Of those who rated themselves 1–5, 20 percent of the women (sixteen out of eighty) and 18.7 percent of the men (fourteen out of seventy-five) described themselves as 3, 4, or 5 and were therefore classified by the authors as bisexual.[52] In Pepper Schwartz and Philip Blumstein's study of men and women with "more than incidental sexual experience as adults with both men and women" (1998:187), conducted in the 1970s, men and women were equally likely to identify themselves as bisexual: 41 percent. Women were only slightly more likely than men to identify as heterosexual (24 percent versus 18 percent) or to refuse to choose an identity (7 percent versus 4 percent).

Some research teams conduct separate but comparable studies of men and women. For example, in a study of lesbian and bisexual women with co-twins or genetically unrelated (adopted) sisters recruited via ads in lesbian-oriented publications in several cities in the United States, J. Michael Bailey, Richard C. Pillard, Michael C. Neale, and Yvonne Agyei (1993) found that 14.3 percent identified themselves as bisexual, with fantasy and behavior Kinsey scores averaging 4.8.[53] In a similar study of gay and bisexual men J. Michael Bailey and Richard C. Pillard (1991) found that 6.8 percent identified as bisexual, with average Kinsey fantasy and behavior scores of 5.4.

In some studies of "lesbians and gay men," men and women are not distinguished from each other in the presentation of statistics on self-identity, although sufficient information is sometimes given to calculate rates of bisexual self-identification separately for men and women. James M. Croteau and Mark von Destinon (1994), for example, surveyed 249 student affairs professionals of unspecified race and ethnicity.[54] Of those respondents who identified as lesbian, gay, or bisexual, 34 percent identified as lesbians, 49 percent as gay men, and 18 percent as bisexual; 84 percent of those identifying as bisexual were women; calculations by the current author indicate that approximately 30 percent of women and 5 percent of men identified as bisexual. Curtis D. Proctor and Victor K. Groze (1994) surveyed 221 males and females aged 21.1 or younger via gay, lesbian, and bisexual youth groups in the United States and Canada. The sample is 71.9 percent male, 28.1 percent female, and 69 percent white; 13.6 percent identified as bisexual, 23.5 percent as lesbian, and 62.9 percent as gay. Assuming all self-identified lesbians are female and all self-identified gays are male, these findings indicate that 16.1 percent of female youths and 12.6 percent of male youths in this study self-identified as bisexual.[55] Higher rates of bisexual identification were reported by Koch and Schockman (1998), who found that 87 percent of 7,210 users of an internet access service provided by the Los Angeles Gay and Lesbian Community Services Center were male and that 19.5 percent identified themselves as bisexual, 7 percent as lesbian, and 55 percent as gay.

Rates of bisexual self-identification appear to vary between racial and ethnic groups, and the patterns of racial or ethnic differences in self-identity might be different for men and women. Compared to the 20 percent typically found in predominantly white samples of women, Cochran and Mays (1988) found that 11 percent of 594 Black women recruited through mailings to the memberships of the National Coalition of Black Lesbians and Gays and local organizations in Los Angeles identified themselves as bisexual; the rest identified as lesbian.[56] In contrast, in comparison to the less than 10 percent typically found in predominantly white samples of men, a study of HIV risk among Black (62.7 percent) and Hispanic (36.1 percent) men recruited from local chapters of the National Association of Black and White Men Together found a 20 percent rate of bisexual self-identification (Thomas and Hodges 1991). Among HIV seropositive MSM Lynda S. Doll and colleagues (1992; see also 1990) found that bisexual self-identity was more common among Black than white men; 44 percent of Black men, 25 percent of white men, 17 percent of Hispanic men rated themselves as 3–5's on a "Kinsey-like" 1–7 scale, which the authors interpreted as bisexual self-identification. Whites tended to identify as homosexual (54 percent), whereas both homosexual (49 percent) and heterosexual (34 percent) self-identities were common among Hispanics. Similarly, David J. McKirnan, Joseph P. Stokes, Lynda Doll, and Rebecca G. Burzette (1995) found that, among men who had had sex with both women and men, Black men were more likely to identify as bisexual. Recall that Bell and Weinberg (1978), whose findings are reviewed earlier in this chapter, found that among "homosexuals" white men were more likely than Black men to describe their feelings as exclusively homosexual, and that bisexual behavior was more common among Blacks than whites for both men and women; 22 percent of Black men and 33 percent of Black women, compared to 14 percent of white men and 24 percent of white women, had engaged in heterosexual intercourse in the previous year. Recall also Binson and colleagues' (1995) findings that Black men who had had sex with men were more likely than white MSM to have also had sex with a woman, i.e., to be behaviorally bisexual.

Evidence of racial and ethnic differences in sexual self-identity shows up in studies of gay and bisexual youths as well. Rates of bisexual self-identification are higher in samples of youth containing larger proportions of African Americans and Latinos than in predominantly white samples. In predominantly white (75–82 percent) samples Gary Remafedi, James A. Farrow, and Robert W. Deisher (1991) found a 12 percent bisexual self-identification rate among male youths in the U.S. Midwest and Pacific Northwest, and Remafedi (1994a, 1994b) found that 9 percent of "gay and bisexual" male adolescents aged thirteen to twenty-one years old and recruited via ads in gay publications, gay social groups, events, and referrals described themselves as "bisexual." Among 83 "gay and bisexual male youths" aged seventeen to twenty-three, only 16 percent of whom were racial or ethnic minorities and who were recruited through class lectures and ads in local bars, restaurants, and newspapers for a study on "growing up as a gay or bisexual male in the 1980s," Ritch C. Savin-Williams (1995a) found that 14 percent rated themselves as Kinsey 2–4's. These figures are similar to the 13.6 percent rate found by Proctor and Groze among predominantly white (69.1 percent) male and female youths in the United States and Canada. In contrast, Mary Jane Rotheram-Borus and colleagues, (Rotheram-Borus, Reid, Rosario, and Kasen 1995; see also Rotheram-Borus, Rosario, Reid, and Koopman 1995; and Rotheram-Borus, Hunter, and Rosario 1994) found that of 136 predominantly Black (29 percent) and Hispanic (53 percent) male adolescents aged fourteen to nineteen who sought services at the Hetrick-Martin Institute, a "gay identified social service agency" (Rotheram Borus, Reid, Rosario, and Kasen 1995:3) in New York City, 66 percent "reported their sexual orientation as gay (homosexual), 25% as bisexual, 3% as straight (heterosexual) and 6% as other" (Rotheram-Borus, Reid, Rosario, and Kasen 1995:6). Ten percent reported heterosexual activity in the past three months.[57] Among homosexual and bisexual men aged seventeen to twenty-two years old recruited from street corners, bars, and parks in San Francisco and Berkeley, 49 percent of whom were white and 22 percent of whom were Latino, Lemp and colleagues (1994) found that 23.3 percent identified as bisexual, 66.8 percent as homosexual, and 9.9 percent as "other." In a study of male and female youths aged fourteen to twenty-one recruited from community-based and college organizations for lesbian and gay youths in New York City, 35 percent of whom were Black and 37 percent of whom were Hispanic, Margaret Rosario and colleagues including Heino F. L. Meyer-Bahlburg (1996) found that 31 percent of males and 32 percent of females identified as bisexual; the rest identified as gay or lesbian.[58] However, within their own sample Rosario and colleagues (1996) found no ethnic differences in sexual self-identity in a sample of male and female gay, lesbian, and bisexual youths in New York City that was 35 percent Black, 37 percent Hispanic, and 22 percent white. These findings indicate the need for further research into racial and ethnic differences in sexual self-identity and sexual behavior. Some research, motivated by concerns about the spread of HIV among bisexuals and People of Color, has been undertaken using samples of men; findings of this research regarding the possibility of racial and ethnic differences in sexual self-identity among men, and the relationship between sexual self-identity and sexual behavior among men, are discussed in chapter 22.

In the wake of the AIDS crisis another specific population that has received considerable attention is "men who have had sex with men" (MSM), particularly "men who have had sex with men since 1977."[59] The descriptor *MSM* is gradually replacing the phrase *homosexual and bisexual men* in the literature on the epidemiology of HIV infection, a transition that reflects increasing recognition that HIV risk is related to behavior, not social or psychological identity. Because it refers to behavior rather than identity, the term *MSM* defines a different population than does the phrase *homosexual and bisexual men*. MSM includes self-identified heterosexual men who behave homosexually or bisexually and who are not in touch with the organized gay community, a population of critical importance in HIV epidemiology because it is not reached by safer sex messages promulgated by and in the gay community. HIV-related research on MSM is reviewed in detail in chapter 22; findings of this research are described here briefly only insofar as they provide estimates of the prevalences of and relationship between bisexual self-identity and bisexual behavior within this specific population.

In a study of Latino MSM who had had at least one male partner within the previous year, Alex Carballo-Diéguez and Curtis Dolezal (1994) found that 20 percent identified themselves as bisexual or as *hombres modernos*, 10 percent identified as heterosexual, 65 percent as gay, and 4 percent as drag queens. In the Pitt Men's Study, part of the Multi-Center AIDS Cohort Study, 32 percent of a predominantly white (93 percent) sample of MSM recruited through ads, posters, and informal networks described themselves as bisexual (Silvestre et al. 1986). In another predominantly white (96 percent) sample consisting of men who visited a health center in Boston during a six-month period, had had recent same-sex contact, and displayed no symptoms of AIDS or ARC, Jane McCusker, Jane G. Zapka, Anne M. Stoddard, and Kenneth H. Mayer (1989) found that 17 percent identified their "sexual orientation" as bisexual and 83 percent identified as homosexual. Among participants in Project ARIES, a safer sex counseling program for MSM, Latinos were more likely to identify as bisexual (23.7 percent) than European Americans (19.1 percent) or African Americans (16.1 percent; Ryan, Longres, and Roffman 1996). Among 466 MSM recruited via community-based methods in Boston who had been sexually active during the previous six months, 10 percent had had sex with both men and women in the previous six months, 18 percent in the past year, and 58 percent in their lifetimes (Wold et al. 1998). Among 619 men recruited via a media campaign in several states in the United States and Vancouver, British Columbia who reported at least three instances of unprotected sex with men during the previous three months, 82 percent of whom were white, 23 percent had also had sex with a female partner during the previous year (Kalichman, Roffman, Picciano, and Bolan 1998).

Research on MSM concurs with research on more general populations in demonstrating that sexual behaviors and sexual self-identities are not necessarily congruent. Many MSM are behaviorally bisexual, but many such men do not self-identify as bisexual. Lynda Doll, Lyle R. Peterson, and Carol R. White (1990) found that among 129 men who had had sex with both men and women since 1978 30 percent self-identified as homosexual, 34 percent as bisexual, and 36 percent as heterosexual. Similarly, using data systematically collected by the AIDS Prevention Project of the Seattle-King County Department of Public Health on individuals seeking HIV counseling and testing in 1987–1991, Robert W. Wood, Leigh E. Krueger, Tsilke Pearlman, and Gary Goldbaum (1993) found that among 5,480 men who had had sex with men since 1977, 77 percent identified as gay, 13 percent identified as bisexual, and 8.4 percent identified as straight.[60] Among 451 HIV-negative subjects who had had both female and male partners in the past year, 61 percent identified as bisexual, 19 percent as gay, and 16 percent as straight. McKirnan, Stokes, Doll, and Burzette (1995) found that 59 percent of behavioral bisexuals identified as bisexual; 29 percent identified as gay, 10 percent as straight, and 2 percent claimed no self-identity. They also found that 66 percent of behavioral bisexuals rated their "overall sexual orientation" as falling in the middle three categories of a seven-point scale; 23 percent rated themselves primarily or exclusively homosexual, and 11 percent rated themselves primarily or exclusively heterosexual. Weatherburn and colleagues (1998) found that only 43.9 percent of men in the United Kingdom who had had sex with men and women (MSMW) in the previous five years, recruited for anonymous telephone interviews via ads in the "contact" sections of selected newspapers and magazines, described themselves as bisexual "even after describing their own sexual behaviour in considerable detail" (1998:465).

Conversely, self-identity does not necessarily predict sexual behavior; not all self-identified bisexual MSM are currently or recently bisexually active, and some

MSM who identify as gay or heterosexual are bisexually active. Recalculating data from Wood, Krueger, Pearlman, and Goldbaum's (1993) tables yields estimates that 44.5 percent of self-identified bisexual seronegative men had been bisexually active in the past year, compared to 2.8 percent of self-identified gay men and 16.6 percent of self-identified straight men.[61] The sample used in this study can be considered reasonably representative of all individuals who seek HIV testing in that geographic area.[62] Maria L. Ekstrand and colleagues (1994) found that only 26 percent of 119 self-identified bisexual men in the San Francisco Men's Health Study had had both same- and other-sex contact during the year 1984–1985, and only 7 percent did so five years later in 1988–1989. Among 105 men responding to an advertisement targeting "bisexuals" Joseph P. Stokes, David J. McKirnan, and Rebecca G. Burzette (1993) found that about half had had both male and female partners in the previous six months. Studying HIV+ MSM, Doll et al. (1992) found that of the 45 percent of their respondents who identified as homosexual, 6 percent had had sex with women and 11 percent had been celibate during the prior year; of the 30 percent who identified as bisexual, 34 percent had had sex only with men, 5 percent only with women, and 10 percent had been celibate; of the 25 percent who identified as heterosexual, 6 percent had had sex only with men, 23 percent with both men and women, and 17 percent had been celibate.[63]

In the Carballo-Diéguez and Dolezal (1994) study, of those who identified as bisexual 80 percent had had sex with a woman in the past year—a greater proportion than among those who identified as heterosexual (63 percent). Of those who identified as gay, about three-fifths had ever had sex with a woman, and 8 percent had done so within the previous year. The fact that self-identified bisexuals were more likely than self-identified heterosexuals to be heterosexually active was interpreted by the authors as an indication that these men used their previous heterosexual experience to support their claim to bisexual identity because they were more comfortable with that label. An alternative explanation is that self-identified bisexual men are more sexually active and adventurous in general and this attitude leads to both bisexuality and high rates of heterosexual experience. The term *hombres modernos*, which the men choose for themselves, suggests such a spirit of adventure and open-mindedness.

Women who have had sex with women (WSW) have received much less attention from researchers than MSM. Pamela Jean Bevier, Mary Ann Chiasson, Richard T. Heffernan, and Kennth G. Castro (1995), in a New York City Department of Health study of 4,585 women attending a sexually transmitted disease clinic, found that 9 percent had had sex with women since 1978, whereas 91 percent had sex only with men during that time. In a study of 511 women, all of whom had had sex with women since 1978, who were recruited from both sexually transmitted disease clinics and women's health clinics, Scott B. McCombs and colleagues (1992) found different rates of bisexuality among women attending the different types of clinics. Among STD clinic clients 95 percent of WSW had also had male partners since 1978, compared to 78 percent among WSW attending women's health clinics. The sample was composed of predominantly white (46 percent) and Black (41 percent) respondents. Rebecca M. Young, Gloria Weissman, and Judith

B. Cohen (1992) studied WSW and non-WSW who were participants in the Association for Women's AIDS Research and Education (AWARE) program in San Francisco and Alameda counties. Forty-six percent had had sex with a woman since 1980, but on a seven-point scale 76 percent described themselves as exclusively heterosexual and 21 percent described themselves as "preferring some combination of both genders" (176).

In addition to lesbians, gay men, and MSM, another population for whom sexuality is socially problematic is runaway teenagers. Many teenagers run away for reasons pertaining to sexuality, such as an abusive family member or a family unaccepting of their sexual orientation, and some engage in survival sex after running away. Rotheram-Borus and colleagues (1992) collected detailed sexual history information from a sample of 88 male and 118 female runaways consecutively admitted to residential shelters in New York City. The sample is 62 percent Black and 26 percent Hispanic. Asked, "When you think about sex, do *you* think of yourself as gay, bisexual, or straight?" 98 percent of females and 94 percent of males identified themselves as straight even though "only" 77 percent of females and 90 percent of males had been heterosexually active. Only two males and one female chose "gay" and three males and one female chose "bisexual." But 9 percent and 6 percent of males and females, respectively, had engaged in sexual activity with same-gender partners, most of whom had also engaged in heterosexual activity.[64] This gender difference is not significant, and no significant differences were found in the numbers of same-gender partners or the types of same-gender sexual activities experienced by males and females.[65] These figures are very similar to those found in national probability surveys such as the NHSLS and higher than those found in national surveys of nonrunaway adolescents,[66] suggesting that patterns of sexual self-identity and same- and other-gender sexual behavior among teenage runaways resemble patterns found among adults rather than other teenagers. The authors suggest that the discrepancy between gay or bisexual self-identity and same-gender experience among teenage runaways is due to the experimental nature of some adolescents' same-gender experiences.

Other studies are conducted on specific populations not because the populations are of particular sexological interest but simply because they are convenient and readily available to the researcher; nevertheless, these studies can provide useful preliminary insights. In a study of psychiatrists at five medical schools, Klitzman, Bodkin, and Pope (1998) reported that 3.5 percent self-identified as "predominantly heterosexual," 1.4 percent as "bisexual," 1.6 percent as "predominantly homosexual," and 2.6 percent as "exclusively homosexual" and suggested that gay and bisexual medical students' experience of marginalization might attract them to the study of psychiatry. In another study Lee Ellis, Donald Burke, and M. Ashley Ames (1987) drew an eclectic sample of 171 males and 257 females from among the students at the State University of North Dakota (54 percent), a support group for people with autoimmune diseases (13 percent), an organization for parents with "homosexual" children (5 percent), audiences at the authors' public appearances (5 percent), and persons listed in telephone directories (22 percent). They asked respondents to estimate the percentage of their fantasies about sexual relationships that involved members of the other, versus the same, sex and the percentage of persons with whom they had had climactic and nonclimactic sexual relations who were of the other versus their own sex. Because the sample cannot be considered even vaguely representative of any particular population, no weight can be put on the specific prevalence rates found in it. For example, Ellis, Burke, and Ames found prevalence rates of same-gender behavior nearly twice those found among women and three times those found among men in the NHSLS, suggesting that the Ellis, Burke, and Ames rates are gross overestimates. However, specific rates can be compared to each other to yield rough estimates of the relative prevalence of bisexual fantasy and behavior. These comparisons indicate that among men rates of same-gender sexual behavior (27 percent) and rates of same-gender sexual fantasy (28 percent) are nearly identical to each other, whereas women are far more likely to engage in same-gender fantasies (27 percent) than same-gender behavior (7 percent); apparently many women envision same-gender sexual experiences that they have never had. Ellis, Burke, and Ames also reported that both men and women were more likely to have bisexual (18 percent, 25 percent) than homosexual (10 percent, 2 percent) fantasies, and that women, compared to men, were less likely to engage in bisexual behavior (4 percent versus 13 percent) but more likely to engage in bisexual fantasy (25 percent versus 18 percent).

Many studies using convenience samples are studies of college students because students are easily accessible to researchers who hold college faculty positions. For example, Erich Goode and Lynn Haber (1977) studied sexual behavior among women college students. They discovered that women who had had sexual contact with other women were more heterosexually experienced—more likely to have had other-sex experiences and to have had more other-sex partners—than women who had not had sexual contact with another woman (cf. Gundlach and Riess 1968; Haynes and Oziel 1976). This is consistent with a finding by Saghir and Robins (1973) that 79 percent of "homosexual women," compared to 58 percent of "heterosexual women" had ever had heterosexual intercourse,[67] and complements Carballo-Diéguez and Dolezal's (1994) finding regarding higher rates of heterosexual behavior among self-identified bisexual, compared to self-identified heterosexual, Latino MSM.[67] Such findings fly in the face of simplistic assumptions about the relationship between sexual self-identity and sexual behavior and about the opposing nature of same-sex and other-sex activities. Unlike Carballo-Diéguez and Dolezal, who implied that at least some self-identified bisexual men are not really bisexual but using their heterosexual experience to justify a bisexual identity, Goode and Haber studiously avoided the question of whether their subjects were "really" heterosexual or homosexual, and they did not use the word *bisexual* once in the article. However, their findings amount to evidence that women with same-gender experience have usually had bisexual experience.

In a study mentioned earlier in this chapter for its findings on dishonesty among sex survey respondents, McGuire and colleagues (1992) administered a survey on sexual behavior to a convenience sample of urban college students who had received class release time to voluntarily attend an educational session on AIDS in

1987. Those who attended comprised 35 percent of all first-year students at the institution. Of the 158 nonforeign students who did not admit to answering questions dishonestly and whose answers were internally consistent, half (51 percent) reported never having been sexually active, 47 percent reported heterosexual activity only, 1 man reported same-gender activity only, and 1 man reported both same- and other-gender activity. Although one would expect rates of same-gender behavior to be higher among students voluntarily attending an educational session on AIDS than among the general student population, the rates found were lower than those found in probability samples of the general United States population. This is probably largely due to the young age and sexual inexperience of the students sampled.[68] If accurate, these findings provide a context for the interpretation of the above-mentioned findings on teenage runaways; compared to the McGuire college students, the Rotheram-Borus (1992) runaways have high rates of both same- and other-gender sexual activity.

Paula S. Nurius (1983) studied preferences for specific sexual activities as well as actual sexual experiences among 685 graduate and upperclass undergraduate college students (46 percent Caucasian, 30 percent Japanese) recruited from social science courses in Hawaii and several other states. Using the Sexual Activity and Preference Scale (SAPS), she concluded on the basis of subjects' expressed preferences for specific sexual activities that 74.2 percent were heterosexual, 1.2 percent were homosexual, 8.2 percent had no substantial preferences for either heterosexual or homosexual activities, and 16.5 percent (20 percent of men and 15 percent of women) had substantial preferences for both heterosexual and homosexual activities; she called this last group *ambisexual,* a term that was also preferred by Blumstein and Schwartz, by Masters and Johnson, and by Frederick W. Coons (1972). Ronald A. LaTorre and Kristina Wendenburg (1983) discovered that, among 125 women recruited from a campus women's center and four psychology courses, 68 percent self-identified as heterosexual, 17.6 percent as bisexual, and 14.4 percent as lesbian or homosexual. Among the self-identified heterosexuals 3 reported that they preferred sex with women over sex with men, and 5 reported no preference for either gender over the other. One self-identified lesbian also reported no preference.

Michael D. Storms (1978) tested a two-dimensional measure of sexual fantasy on seventy college students, finding that 30 percent of men and 23 percent of women scored above the overall medians for both gynoeroticism and androeroticism, and that 10.7 percent of the men and 14.4 percent of the women labeled themselves bisexual. Storms also explored the correlation between fantasy and self-identity, finding that, among homoerotics 100 percent of the men and 80 percent of the women self-identified as gay, whereas among heteroerotics 100 percent of the men and 98 percent of the women self-identified as straight. Ambierotics chose a variety of labels, with a greater prevalence of bisexual self-identity among women than among men. Among men 23.7 percent identified as bisexual, and 15.8 percent and 60.5 percent identified as straight or as gay, whereas among women 33.3 percent identified as bisexual and 45.5 percent and 21.2 percent identified as straight or as gay. Carla Golden (1987), who interviewed women college students, found a high degree of incongruence between women's sexual behavior and sexual self-identities.

Nurius's findings are consistent with national probability studies showing that bisexual responsiveness is more common among men than women, and Storms's and Golden's findings are consistent with national probability studies indicating that the prevalence of bisexual responsiveness is greater than the prevalence of bisexual self-identification. Storms's and Golden's findings are also consistent with studies done on probability samples (e.g., Laumann, Gagnon, Michael, and Michaels 1994), nonprobability samples (e.g., Pillard 1990), and "lesbian and gay" samples (e.g., Weinberg, Williams, and Pryor 1994; Nichols 1985, 1990) that find weaker correlations between self-identity and other aspects of sexuality among women than among men.

In summary, different rates of homosexual and bisexual behavior, sexual behavior in general, feelings of sexual attraction, and self-identity are found within different specific populations in the United States including college students, runaways, MSM, lesbians and gay men, the very young, the elderly, Blacks, Latinos/as, and members of other racial/ethnic groups. Most of these differences were not detected in national probability surveys because these populations, and other populations that have not yet been studied, are too small to appear in sufficient numbers in such surveys. Whereas national surveys are a necessary source of reliable data on the overall prevalence of various sexual patterns in the United States, we also need more focused research into the sexualities of different specific populations to gain a complete understanding of sexuality in the United States.

Summary

Recent national probability surveys of American sexuality, in addition to a number of smaller studies of specific populations, have greatly improved the quality of our knowledge about Americans' sexual behaviors, feelings, and self-identities. The Kinsey reports and other early studies, valuable for their historical role in the development of the field of sexology and for their documentation of the diversity of American sexuality, have been superseded by the more reliable findings of studies like the NHSLS and the GSS. Although the specific figures regarding the prevalence of same-gender and bisexual behavior and erotic response obtained by Kinsey and his associates are generally recognized as overestimates, Kinsey findings regarding the relative prevalence of exclusively same-gender and bisexual response have been upheld. Specifically, when lifetime experience is taken into consideration bisexual behavior is indeed more prevalent than exclusively homosexual behavior, although in the short term the reverse is true, and bisexual erotic response or feelings of attraction are indeed more common than exclusively homosexual response or feelings of attraction. Recent studies have also, unlike the Kinsey studies, assessed sexual self-identity and generally found that bisexual self-identity is less common than lesbian or gay self-identity, less common than lifetime bisexual behavior, and less common than bisexual feelings of attraction. The rarity of bisexual self-identity in comparison to the prevalence of bisexual behavior and feelings is commonly attributed to the lack of social validation of bisexual identity that encourages individuals to identify as either lesbian/gay or heterosexual despite their bisexual experience.[69] The social factors that encourage lesbian/gay or heterosexual self-identification, and the cultural constructions of sexuality that underlie these social factors, are explored in chapter 23.

In addition to confirming Kinsey findings regarding the relative prevalence of various sexual behavior patterns, recent probability studies provide us with reliable estimates of the absolute prevalence of particular patterns of sexual behavior, feelings, and self-identities. Our faith in the accuracy of these statistics derives not only from the fact that they have been obtained from representative national samples but also from the fact that different studies have produced consistent estimates. This consistency, of course, can only be observed by taking into account the differences in the questions asked of respondents in the different studies. For example, questions about sexual behavior vary in terms of the length of time and the life stage about which they inquire, and these differences necessarily affect the rates of same-gender and bisexual behavior produced by these questions. The longer the time period in question, and the earlier the age at which that time period starts, the higher the percentage of respondents who report having had same-gender sexual experiences during that time period. Thus, more respondents have engaged in same-gender sexual behavior in the past five years than have done so in the past year, and more respondents have engaged in same-gender sexual behavior since puberty than since age eighteen. Estimates varying in terms of the length of the time period in question range from the NHSLS and NABS findings that 4.1–6.5 percent of men have engaged in same-gender sexual behavior in the past five years (Lauman, Gagnon, Michael, and Michaels 1994; Binson et al. 1995) to the NHSLS, GSS, and 1970 Kinsey findings that 1.2–2.7 percent of men have done so in the past year (Fay, Turner, Klassen, and Gagnon 1989; Laumann, Gagnon, Michael, and Michaels 1994; Rogers and Turner 1991). Estimates varying in terms of the age at which the time period in question starts range from the 1970 Kinsey finding that 20.3 percent of men have ever had a same-gender sexual experience (Fay, Turner, Klassen, and Gagnon 1989), to NHSLS estimates that 9.1 percent have had such experiences since puberty (Laumann, Gagnon, Michael, and Michaels 1994), to estimates that 4.9 percent to 6.7 percent have had such experiences since age eighteen (Laumann, Gagnon, Michael, and Michaels 1994; Rogers and Turner 1991; Smith 1991) or age twenty (Fay, Turner, Klassen, and Gagnon 1989).[70] Comparable rates for women are 1.3 percent within the past year, 2.2 percent within the past five years, 4.1 percent since age eighteen, and 4.3 percent since puberty. The former pattern is statistically inevitable because cumulative rates can only increase (or remain constant) as the length of the time period in question increases; they cannot decrease. The latter reflects the fact that a substantial proportion of people with same-gender sexual experiences had those experiences before adulthood; the inclusion of these youthful experiences increases the rate of same-gender sexual experience.

Among those with same-gender sexual experience rates of bisexual experience increase as the length of the time period increases and as the age in question decreases. This is illustrated nicely by NHSLS and GSS data; among female NHSLS respondents with same-gender experiences heterosexual experience in the last year was reported by 25 percent, in the last five years by 62.9 percent, and since puberty by 90.7 percent (Laumann, Gagnon, Michael, and Michaels 1994). Among male GSS respondents with same-gender experiences 25 percent had also had heterosexual experiences in the last year but 88 percent had had such experiences since age eighteen. This pattern, too, is statistically inevitable; given a population with same-gender experience, the percentage of that population that has also had heterosexual experience can only increase with time.

Whereas survey questions about sexual behavior differ greatly in terms of the length of the time period in question, thus producing divergent estimates of the prevalence of different sexual behaviors, questions about sexual attraction and self-identity generally ask for current assessments only. However, different question wordings can nevertheless produce different estimates of the prevalence of homosexual and bisexual attractions and self-identities. A scale on which respondents are allowed to indicate not only bisexual attraction but degrees of bisexual attraction produces higher estimates of bisexuality than does a forced choice between homosexual and heterosexual self-descriptions; assuming that the former produces more accurate findings, approximately 4 percent of men and women in the United States describe themselves as bisexually attracted.

In the general United States population the percentage of individuals who identify as bisexual is minuscule—less than 1 percent of both women and men. However, within lesbian and gay populations the percentage of individuals that identify as bisexual appears to be approximately 20 percent among women and 3–30 percent among men, depending on age and racial or ethnic identity. Although the 20 percent figure is derived from research involving nonprobability samples, it is found so consistently by different researchers studying different "lesbian" populations that it merits some confidence, at least insofar as predominantly white populations are concerned.

Homosexual and bisexual experiences are not distributed evenly within the United States population; some types of people are more likely than others to have had same-gender sexual contacts and/or to have gay or bisexual self-identities. For example, urban dwellers are more likely than the residents of towns or rural areas to be homosexually experienced; whether they are also more likely to be bisexually experienced is a question that awaits further research. It is also likely that there are racial and ethnic differences in rates of homosexual and bisexual behaviors, attractions, and self-identities, although what these differences are is still unclear. National probability surveys contain too few respondents belonging to any given racial or ethnic minority to produce reliable descriptions of the sexual diversity to be found within these populations. However, the findings of ethnographic research and studies of specific populations suggest that European American men who have sex with men are more likely than African American and Hispanic men who have sex with men to be exclusively homosexual in their behavior. If racial/ethnic differences in sexuality do exist, they are likely to result from complex cultural factors affecting not only objective prevalence rates of particular sexual behaviors and feelings but, more important, individuals' interpretations of their own behaviors and feelings.

The question "How many people are bisexual?" is deceptively complex. The answer depends on whether bisexuality is defined in terms of behavior, feelings of attraction, or self-identity and, if in terms of behavior, exactly which behaviors—and at what ages—count. Recent research findings indicate that, at most, 5.8 percent of men and 3.3 percent of women are bisexual if behavior since puberty is considered. At minimum, 0.7 percent of men and 0.3 percent of women are bisexual if behavior in the past year is considered, or 0.8 percent of men and 0.5 percent of women are bisexual if self-identity is considered. Given a national population of over 260 million, the latter figures lead to the conservative estimate that there are well over 1 million males and 650,000 females in the United States who are either self-identified bisexual adults or children who will become bisexual adults. Self-identified bisexual individuals might be a small percentage of the total United States population, but they are a large number of people. The real point, however, is that the importance of bisexuality lies not in its prevalence but in what we can learn about the nature of sexuality in general by studying bisexuality. The rest of this volume is dedicated to that pursuit.

Selected Readings

The articles included in this section were both chosen because they report findings derived from unique research methodologies. Chapter 12, by Lever and colleagues (1992), reported the results of the 1982 *Playboy* magazine survey. The readers of *Playboy* are not representative of the United States population, but, with a sample size of 6,982 men who had had sexual experiences with both men and women during adulthood, this survey is one of the largest sex surveys ever conducted in the United States and Lever and her colleagues' treatment of the data is theoretically sophisticated and comprehensive. Their article is one of the few large-scale research reports on bisexuality to acknowledge the distinction between behavior and self-identity and to carry this acknowledgment through data analysis. The authors reported data on the incidence of bisexual self-identity and bisexual behavior and on the relationship between the two. They also compared the demographic characteristics of men with bisexual, heterosexual, and homosexual experience.

Sophie Freud Loewenstein (1984/85), in chapter 13, drew a large convenience sample of women from her classes, lecture audiences, and friendship networks. The brilliance of her research lies in her measurement technique. Instead of asking respondents about their romantic or sexual feelings, she asked about their "passions." By doing so, she was able to overcome her respondents' socially constructed interpretations of their feelings for others and elicit descriptions of passions for both women and men from self-identified heterosexual and lesbian women as well as self-identified bisexual women. Standard measurement techniques would not have elicited these responses as successfully because by the time an individual recognizes her own feelings of sexual attraction such that she can verbalize them to a researcher, she has already unconsciously eliminated many feelings that are inconsistent with her sexual self-identity by interpreting them as nonsexual. Loewenstein's research suggests that bisexual feelings might be even more common than individuals themselves are able to recognize because individuals typically interpret their feelings in a manner consistent with their self-identities, and these self-identities are rarely bisexual.

Notes

1. See, for example, Lever et al. (1992; chapter 12, this volume) for comments on the difficulty of drawing a representative sample of lesbian and gay, or of bisexual, individuals. This difficulty arises not only because these populations are largely hidden but also because their boundaries are not clearly defined; as is evident from the discussion in chapter 4 of this volume, a given person might or might not belong to this population depending on how "sexual orientation" is defined. Herek, Kimmel, Amaro, and Melton (1991) wrote that "in the past, researchers often have assumed that lesbians, gay men, and bisexuals could not be sampled through probability methods because of their status as "hidden" minorities in the United States. Recently, however, survey items about sexual behavior and orientation have been successfully administered to probability samples" (959). The probability samples Herek and coauthors refered to are, however, samples of the general population that necessarily include lesbian, gay, and bisexual individuals as well as heterosexual individuals; they are not samples of the lesbian, gay, and/or bisexual population. Although it is true that if one eliminated the nonlesbian, nongay, and nonbisexual subjects from these samples one would be left with a representative sample of the lesbian, gay, and bisexual population, as discussed later in this chapter because of the small percentage of the population that is lesbian, gay, or bisexual one would have had to draw an extremely large general sample to extract an adequately sized sample of lesbian, gay, and/or bisexual respondents. Such a procedure is prohibitively expensive, if one's goal is to produce a sample of the lesbian, gay, and/or bisexual population. See also note 3 in this chapter.

2. Credit for the blood sample analogy goes to Herbert S. Shalom (personal communication with his daughter, Gwen Dordick).

3. Also refer to Watters and Biernacki (1989); Heckathorn (1997); and Sudman and Kalton (1986) for discussion of sampling procedures for hidden and other unenumerated populations; to Berk (1983) for discussion of the effects of sampling bias on internal validity; and to Martin and Dean (1990) for a brief review of literature pertinent to the validity of quantitative analysis of data gathered from nonprobability samples with a focus on recruiting a sample of gay men. See Bancroft (1997) for a comprehensive examination of sampling methodologies pertinent to research on sexuality.

4. These figures exclude foreign students who also participated in the survey.

5. See Gagnon (1990a) and Pomeroy (1972) for discussions of the social context, history, and historical import of Kinsey and his work.

6. See, for example, Gagnon and Simon's (1987) comments on the nonrepresentativeness of the Kinsey samples; Wallis's (1949) comments on Kinsey et al.'s sample size, sample composition and inadequate estimation of sampling bias and crosschecking, and failure to clarify the empirical bases of the conclusions drawn; Terman (1948) on the lack of information given in the 1948 volume about the sampling methods used and the sample obtained, the probable oversampling of sexually active populations, and Kinsey et al.'s interview and questioning techniques; and Cochran, Mosteller, and Tukey (1953) on Kinsey et al.'s statistical methodology. See also Turner, Miller, and Moses (1989) for a brief discussion of Kinsey et al.'s interviewing and sampling techniques; and Pomeroy (1972) for details of the methodology used by Kinsey and his associates.

7. Gagnon and Simon (1973) found that among Kinsey respondents who were interviewed while in college or graduate school, a subsample less biased by self-selection than other portions of the Kinsey sample, "30 percent had undergone at least one homosexual experience in which either the interviewee *or* his male partner was stimulated to the point of orgasm" (131). Of these, half (16 percent of total) had homosexual experience only prior to age fifteen, and one-third (9 percent of total) had all homosexual acts in adolescense, or only incidentally prior to age twenty. Of the remainder, half (3 percent of total) had had only homosexual experiences, and half (3 percent) had substantial homosexual histories as well as heterosexual histories. Thus, depending on whether bisexuality is defined in terms of substantial adult bisexual experience, experience since puberty, or lifetime experience, 3 percent, 12 percent, or 28 percent of men have bisexual histories, compared to 3 percent with exclusively homosexual histories.

8. In a letter dated March 18, 1977, Gebhard wrote: "In the 1948 and 1953 studies, it was stated that 13 percent of the male and 7 percent of the female population had more homosexual experience or psychological response for at least three years between the ages of 16 and 55, for a combined percentage of 10 percent for the total population. These figures have been criticized for including psychological response along with overt experience. However, I have been recently reworking the 1938 to 1963 data to include only 'experience' (defined as deliberate physical contact intended by at least one of the participants to produce sexual arousal).

"Tabulations based on these criteria indicate that 13.95 percent of males and 4.25 percent of females, or a combined average of 9.13 percent of the total population had either extensive (21 or more partners or 52 or more experiences) or more than incidental (5–20 partners or 21–50 experiences) homosexual experience. I wish to point out that although the Institute did interview members of homosexual groups and organizations as part of its research, all such persons were excluded from the above tabulation." Letter to the National Gay Task Force reprinted in Voeller (1990:34).

9. If those respondents recruited from homosexual groups and organizations are excluded from the calculation, the degree of this overestimation is reduced.

10. If Voeller (and Gebhard) is the source of the 10 percent statistic, then this criticism doesn't apply because Voeller obtained his 10 percent by averaging Kinsey statistics for women and men.

11. The heterosexual sample was drawn via a combination of random probability sampling (of census tracts and city blocks) and quota sampling (of individuals within blocks). See Suppe (1981) for an extensive discussion of Bell and Weinberg's methods and findings and a balanced evaluation of the contributions and weaknesses of *Homosexualities*.

12. Bell and Weinberg assessed exclusivity by asking respondents to classify themselves "as you see yourself right now" twice on the seven-point Kinsey scale, once with regard to their sexual behavior and once again with regard to their sexual feelings. The researchers also asked subjects other questions about specific sexual behaviors and feelings; the interested reader is referred to Bell and Weinberg (1978) for details regarding these findings, and for details regarding findings on diversity among homosexuals along other dimensions.

13. From the cover flap.

14. Methodological information about the NHSLS is given in the text.

The NABS was a random-digit dialing telephone survey that included an urban oversampling of Black and Hispanic respondents, with a total of 10,630 respondents. For details regarding NABS methodology, see Catania et al. (1992).

The Center for Health Affairs, with Harris and Associates, conducted national surveys of AIDS risk behaviors and knowledge, using representative samples stratified by region and by urban/nonurbanicity in the United States, the United Kingdom, and France. Data were collected via interviews and self-administered questionnaires.

The NSM consists of a sample of 3,321 men, representing 70 percent of men aged 20–39 living in the coterminous United States selected via stratified, clustered, disproportionate area probability sampling. Black households were oversampled and the final sample weighted.

15. The GSS datasets are available from the Roper Center at the University of Connecticut.

16. See Laumann, Gagnon, Michael, and Michaels (1994) for detailed historical and methodological information about the NHSLS. For further information about the politics of the funding of sex research, particularly with respect to the NHSLS, see William Booth, "U.S. probe meets resistance," *Science* (April 1989), vol. 244, p. 419, or "Senate Action: Social Science Triumphs in Congress after Setback on American Teenage Study," *Footnotes* (September 1991), vol. 19, no. 7, pp. 1, 12; reprinted from *COSSA Washington Update,* August 5, 1991.

17. See Davis and Smith (1994) for detailed information about the methods used in the GSS.

18. Laumann, Gagnon, Michael, and Michaels's figures for sexual behavior since puberty and since age eighteen are not entirely comparable to each other because they were obtained via different methods of questioning; see Laumann, Gagnon, Michael, and Michaels (1994) for details.

19. The last pair of statistics were not presented by Sell, Wells, and Wypij but were calculated on the basis of other presented findings. The authors reported that 20.8 percent of males reported some homosexual attraction or homosexual behavior since age fifteen, and that 8.7 percent of males reported homosexual attraction but no homosexual behavior since age fifteen, indicating that 20.8 percent - 8.7 percent = 12.1 percent had engaged in homosexual behavior since age fifteen. Comparable figures for females are 17.8 percent and 11.1 percent.

20. Laumann, Gagnon, Michael, and Michaels's (1994) rates for bisexual behavior since puberty are higher than Bell and Weinberg's (1978) lifetime rates for heterosexual coitus among "homosexuals," and Laumann, Gagnon, Michael, and Michaels did not find the gender differences Bell and Weinberg found wherein women were more likely than men to have engaged in heterosexual coitus. Note that Bell and Weinberg's rates for heterosexual coitus among homosexuals are not directly interpretable as rates of bisexual behavior, because not all subjects recruited via Bell and Weinberg's methods were necessarily homosexually experienced.

21. These statistics are labeled approximations because they are recalculations based on findings reported by Billy et al. (1993). For example, Billy et al. reported that 2.8 percent of sexually active men aged 25–29 had had same-gender sexual contact in the previous ten years and that 1.2 percent of sexually active men aged twenty-five to twenty-nine had had exclusively same-gender sexual activity in the previous ten years. Subtracting the latter from the former yields the finding that 1.6 percent of sexually active men had had both same- and other-gender contact during the previous ten years. Dividing that percentage by 2.8 percent yields the finding that 57 percent of men who had had sex with men had also had sex with women in the previous ten years. This is an approximation because it is likely to include a measurable amount of rounding error; more accurate calculations are not possible based on the tabulated data presented by Billy et al. because the authors did not provide cell frequencies.

Approximate rates of bisexual activity among men who had had sex with men aged twenty to twenty-four and thirty-five to thirty-nine based on Billy et al.'s findings are 23 percent and 38 percent, respectively. These statistics are not reported in the main text of this volume because the rates for men aged twenty to twenty-four are affected by the fact that the ten-year time span probably includes years prior to the beginning of sexual activity for most men, and the rates for men aged thirty-five to thirty-nine exclude adolescent and young adult sexual experiences, which, as shown later in this chapter, are disproportionately likely to be same-gender. Were these youthful experiences included, the NSM findings for men aged thirty-five to thirty-nine might, as the findings for men aged twenty to twenty-four and twenty-five to twenty-nine do, support the NHSLS findings that *lifetime* sexual behavior is more likely to be bisexual than exclusively same-gender. The fact that excluding them produces a substantially lower statistic (38 percent) indicates the importance of youthful same-gender and other-gender experience in producing the finding that lifetime sexual behavior is more likely to be bisexual than exclusively same-gender.

22. Rogers and Turner (1991) also provided a cross-tabulation of data on men's male and female partners from the NHSS pretest. The NHSS pretest, which assessed HIV risk behaviors, included 1,446 noninstitutionalized adults aged eighteen to fifty-four, representing 84 percent of persons randomly selected from households in Dallas County, Texas. The weighted response rate was 88 percent. For further methodological information about the NHSS pretest see Dixon et al. (1991). In this survey men were asked for their total number of male and female partners since 1978 (unlike the GSS, which asks about partners since age eighteen). Four and a half percent reported no male or female partners, 85.5 percent reported only female partners, 5.3 percent reported only male partners, and 4.7 percent reported both male and female partners (Rogers and Turner 1991). Note that the rate of bisexual behavior is similar to national rates derived from the GSS but that the rate of homosexual behavior is substantially higher, a difference the authors attribute to the urban character of the NHSS sample.

23. Michael, Laumann, Gagnon, and Smith (1988) reported that the rate of homosexual contact within the past twelve months for all sexually active men (men aged eighteen or older who had at least one sexual partner during the 12 months) in the 1988 GSS was 3.2 percent (which includes 0.4 percent with both homosexual and heterosexual experience). Fay et al. (1989) reported that "when men reporting no partners are included in the denominator, the rate for all men 21 years or older becomes 3.0 percent" (343–344). Adjusting for differing probabilities of selection for people in households of differing sizes, Fay et al. (1989) offered a revised estimate based on the 1988 data of 2.4 percent. Rogers and Turner (1991) reported comparable figures of 1.2 percent and 1.9 percent for the 1989 and 1990 GSS samples.

24. Incidentally, much lower rates of homosexual activity were found in a comparable study done in France in 1991–1992 than were found in the NHSLS or the GSS in the United States. In a national probability telephone sample of 20,055 in which an introductory letter sent to selected households did not mention the survey's focus on sexual behavior, only 4.1 percent of men and 2.6 percent of women reported having had same-gender intercourse at least once in their lifetimes, most of whom (82 percent and 78 percent, respectively) had also had intercourse with other-gender partners (Spira et al. 1992).

Data for a stratified random sample of males in Calgary, Canada were presented by Bagley and Tremblay (1998). Fourteen percent of their subjects had had sex with another man since age twelve. Of these 27.6 percent identified themselves as bisexual and 41.9 percent identified themselves as homosexual. In the whole sample 6.1 percent identified themselves as bisexual and 9.2 percent had had sex with a male during the previous six months, including the 4.9 percent who had had sex with at least one male and one female during this period.

25. Here, *ethnic* refers to the analogization, not the combination, of sexual orientation with race. Race and ethnicity are essentialized concepts, and racial and ethnic identities are based on the concept of distinct types of persons distinguished by their racial or ethnic heritages. Analogously, an ethnic lesbian or gay identity is an identity based on the concept of a lesbian or gay man as a type of person who is essentially distinct from other types of sexual people, i.e., specifically heterosexuals (bisexual identity was not, and is not, typically ethnicized). The concept of an ethnic lesbian or gay identity does not refer to the racial or ethnic characteristics of lesbians, gay men, or heterosexuals. See chapter 23, note 6, and chapter 27, note 37, for citations to discussions of gay ethnicity and the process of ethnicization.

26. Sampling methods involved a combination of probability sampling and quotas. Full details of the sampling methods are given in Fay et al. (1989). These methods, like full probability sampling methods, produce a sample from which meaningful generalizations to a larger population can be made with an estimable degree of accuracy.

27. In the NABS the question asked of respondents to assess sexual orientation was, "In the past 5 (or 15) years, have you had sex with men only, women only, or to some extent with both men and women?" Respondents under age fifty were asked about the preceding five years, and respondents age fifty or older were asked about the preceding fifteen years on the presumption that the latter had been relatively sexually inactive in their later years.

28. Higher rates of bisexual attraction were found in a representative study of 419 male twins in New South Wales, recruited using the Australian National Health and Medical Research Council Twin Registry. Using an eleven-point scale representing percentages of attraction to the same and the other sex, McConaghy, Buhrich, and Silove (1994) found that 10.4 percent indicated some degree of attraction to both sexes, with three-quarters of these indicating predominantly other-sex attractions; 1.7 percent indicated exclusively homosexual attractions. The difference in rates found by McConaghy, Buhrich, and Silove and the NHSLS could be entirely due to the use of an eleven-point scale by the former and a five-point scale by the latter. If it is assumed that individuals choosing the second and tenth positions of the eleven-point scale would be likely to choose the end-points on a five-point scale, then collapsing points 1 and 2, and points 10 and 11, on McConaghy, Buhrich, and Silove's scale yields findings that 2.4 percent of males were exclusively homosexual and that 4.6 percent were bisexual, estimates that are very similar to NHSLS findings (2.4 percent and 3.9 percent, respectively). Thus, McConaghy, Buhrich, and Silove's finer scale apparently revealed a portion of the population whose bisexuality would not be detected by less sensitive assessment techniques.

29. The work of Freund and colleagues (e.g., 1963; Freund, Watsons, Rienzo 1989) provided contrasting findings. Instead of asking subjects to rate their attractions to males and females, Freund measured sexual responsiveness via genital plethysmography, or "polygraph," a method that is presumed "to bypass an individual's possible attempt to either pretend or mask socially controversial homosexual or bisexual arousal or interest" (Diamond 1998:63). "[Freund's] many investigations in this area lead him to conclude that, while individuals may engage in sexual activity with either males or females or both, very few actually show reflexive responses to both" (Diamond 1998:64), suggesting that bisexual *behavior* is more common than bisexual attractions when measured by polygraph rather than self-report.

30. Regarding representative surveys of particular cities and counties, for example, in a probability sample of 397 men and 458 women in Contra Costa County in California, 97 percent of men and 98 percent of women identified as heterosexual, 2 percent of men and 1 percent of women identified as bisexual, and 1 percent of each gender identified as gay or lesbian (Trocki 1992). The authors noted that an additional three men and three women who reported themselves to be heterosexual had had same-sex contact in the previous year; including these individuals would increase the total percentage of lesbian, gay, and bisexual respondents by 1 percent for each gender. In contrast, in a random sample of 4000 households in San Francisco, yielding a sample of 445 women who are 82 percent white, 8 percent Asian, 4 percent Hispanic, and 3 percent African-American, 85 percent identified themselves as primarily or exclusively heterosexual, 11.7 percent identified themselves as "primarily and exclusively homosexual," and 1.3 percent identified as "bisexual" (Bloomfield 1993). The combined percentage of lesbians and bisexuals—which the author reported as 15 percent—is substantially higher than percentages found in national samples, as might be expected in a geographic location known for its large bisexual, lesbian, and gay population.

Regarding nonprobability samples, Pillard (1990) reported that, among unmarried men and women recruited via newspaper and radio advertisements, the tendency for Kinsey scores to cluster at the extremes (0,6) is stronger among men than women. Pillard also reported that a graduate student who noted the absence of male bisexuals in the sample attempted to recruit male bisexuals but had difficulty; the bisexuals he found tended to be either adolescent, self-identified as "in transition" to homosexuality, or judged by the researchers to be Kinsey 5's or 6's.

31. Tabulated data from the combined NHSLS and GSS surveys in Laumann, Gagnon, Michael, and Michaels (1994) suggest a curvilinear relationship between age and same-gender experience, in which men and women in their 30s are more likely to have had same-gender sexual experience in the past year, past five years, and since age 18 than either older or younger men and women have. For example, 3.2 percent of women aged 30–39, but only 2.5 percent, 1.3 percent, and 0.9 percent of women aged 18–29, 40–49, and 50–59, respectively, had had same-gender sexual experiences. Although Binson et al. (1995) reported no significant correlation with age, tabulated ANOVA results using NABS data show the same pattern. This pattern is also observed in the NHSS study reported by Rogers and Turner (1991), but not in the 1970 Kinsey study nor the 1989 nor the 1990 GSS, also reported by Rogers and Turner (1991).

32. Rogers and Turner (1991) did not report statistics for marital status differences in rates of same-gender contact in the combined 1989 and 1990 GSSs; they reported combined statistics for the 1970 Kinsey Institute Survey and the 1989 and 1990 GSSs. The historical trends uncovered by the recalculations in the current text are obscured by Rogers and Turner's combination of 1970 with 1989 and 1990 data.

33. Reversing percentages in a cross-tabulation is a matter of using cell percentages and marginal totals to calculate cell frequencies (if not already given in the table), and then re-percentaging in the other direction (across rows if the original percentaging was done down columns, or vice versa). Thus, for example, whereas Rogers and Turner (1991) originally provided the percentage of married men with same-gender experience, reversing percentages provides the percentage of men with same-gender experience who were married. Some of the original cross-tabulations (e.g., Binson and colleagues' [1995] cross-tabulations of GSS and NABS data) upon which percentage reversals were performed involve weighted data; in these cases, it is impossible to reverse percentages with complete precision because the weighting process cannot be duplicated without returning to the original dataset used by the authors. In these cases, reversed percentages must be considered estimates.

34. Rogers and Turner (1991) also provided data for widowed, divorced, and separated men; these figures are not repeated here.

35. In this survey, "cohabitation" could be with either a man or a woman.

36. The corresponding percentage for *married* men is 86.6 percent. I do not report this statistic in the main text because it is based on only 5 cases; percentages based on small n's are unreliable. Therefore, I combined married men with separated, divorced, and widowed men (n = 16) to produce the 55.2 percent figure for *ever married* men which is based on 21 subjects and hence more likely to be close to a true population percentage. Using a four-category marital status variable (Married, SDW, Never Married, and Cohabiting), Binson et al. (1995) reported that the correlation between marital status and rates of bisexual behavior among MSM is significant, but pairwise comparisons between the Married category and any of the other three categories produce 2 x 2 cross-tabulations involving chi-square expected cell frequencies of less than 5, making the interpretation of these pairwise comparisons problematic.

37. These statistics were calculated based on tabulated statistics in Billy et al. (1993). See note 21 in this chapter for a description of the method of calculation.

38. Unfortunately, this explanation cannot be tested because we have no data on the relative incidence of bisexuality and homosexuality in urban vs. rural areas. Although Binson et al. (1995) distinguished bisexuals from homosexuals in their analysis of demographic correlates in the NABS subsample data, because the NABS subsample is wholly urban it provides no comparison of urban to other residential areas.

39. Education and income tend to be correlated with each other; Harry (1990) also found that homosexual/bisexual men were underrepresented in the highest income category.

40. Billy et al. (1993), who also found higher rates of same-gender activity among more educated men, found no significant difference in rates of bisexual activity between men (that is, men in general, not only men who have had sex with men as in Binson et al (1995) of different educational levels, suggesting, contrary to Binson and colleagues' (1995) findings, that among men who have sex with men, rates of bisexual behavior decrease with education.

41. Laumann, Gagnon, Michael, and Michaels's (1994) findings regarding same-gender behavior, although insignificant, suggest an interaction in which racial differences exist only among men or among women depending on the length of time in question. Tabulated data regarding the prevalence of same-gender sexual behavior in the past year, in the past five years, and since age eighteen indicate that the longer the time period, the greater the racial difference among women and the smaller the racial difference among men. Specifically, Black women reported greater rates of same-gender sexual behavior than white women only when behavior since age eighteen was considered, whereas the fact that Black men were more likely to have had same-gender experiences than white men in the past year and the past five years washed out when all experiences since age eighteen were considered. If accurate, these findings suggest that the lifetime pattern of same-gender experiences differs for individuals of different race and gender, resulting in racial differences that would show up in a sample depending on the particular gender composition of the sample and the length of the time period in question. However, it would be wrong to make too much of this pattern because some of Laumann, Gagnon, Michael, and Michaels's percentages are based on small numbers of respondents and are therefore not reliable; if, for example, as few as six more Black women respondents had had same-gender experience in the past year, then Laumann, Gagnon, Michael, and Michaels would have found as strong a racial difference in sexual behavior in the past year among women as they did among men. See Laumann, Gagnon, Michael, and Michaels (1994), p. 307, note 26, for a comment about the insignificance of racial differences.

Laumann, Gagnon, Michael, and Michaels (1994) also found higher rates of same-gender attraction among Hispanic and Asian men than among white or Black men, higher rates of same-gender attraction among white women than among Black or Hispanic women, and higher rates of homosexual or bisexual self-identification among white and Hispanic women and men than among Black women and men.

42. The category Hispanic is as problematic as the category nonwhite. Individuals falling into the United States Census Hispanic category belong to a number of different cultural-ethnic groups, including Mexicans, Puerto Ricans, European Spaniards, and South Americans. It is quite likely that rates of same- and other-gender sexual behavior vary greatly among these cultural-ethnic groups, such that an overall rate for Hispanics is virtually as meaningless as an overall rate for nonwhites.

43. Saghir and Robins (1973) reported that "only 10 percent of the homosexual males who had been involved in intercourse were still engaging in it at the time of the interview" (90) and that 48 percent of their male homosexual subjects had ever engaged in heterosexual intercourse. Their male and female homosexual subjects were recruited primarily from homophile organizations in Chicago and San Francisco. The criteria for inclusion were "a self-report of homosexual orientation and a history of repetitive overt homosexual activity continuing beyond the age of 18," "white" race, and an absence of a history of hospitalization for psychiatric disease or incarceration. Their sample includes 104 male and 61 female homosexuals, and a "control" group of 40 male and 44 female heterosexuals. Data were gathered via structured interview.

44. Men were recruited for the African American Men's Health study through bars, baths, erotic bookstores, gay African American organizations, the streets, advertisements in gay and African American newspapers, and health clinics.

45. Statistics on recent heterosexual behavior are also available from studies outside the United States. For example, in a study by Izazola-Licea et al. (1991) of men recruited in six Mexican cities from gay discos, bars, organizations, and a park for the purpose of studying seropositivity and risk behavior, 27 percent reported having had sex with women in the past year and were termed "bisexuals" by the authors. In a study by Griensven et al. (1987) 25 percent of male homosexuals recruited from the "homosexual community" in Amsterdam for a longitudinal study of HIV epidemiology had engaged in heterosexual behavior at least once in the previous six months. Gindorf and Warran (1998) reported that 36 percent of 172 male clients of Germany's only gay professional counseling and research organization had had heterosexual contact during the five years prior to data collection in 1985.

46. As part of an international study of homosexuality in the United States, the Netherlands, and Denmark, Weinberg and Williams mailed questionnaires to people on the mailing lists of homophile organizations in New York and San Francisco and handed out questionnaires in homosexual bars in the same cities to yield a sample of 1,057 male homosexuals. They supplied their respondents with a Kinsey scale and asked, "Do you think of yourself as . . . ?" Half (50.6 percent) described themselves as "exclusively homosexual," 29.8 percent described themselves as Kinsey 5's, 13.1 percent as Kinsey 4's, and 6.5 percent as Kinsey 2's or 3's.

47. Gundlach and Riess recruited 226 self-identified lesbians from a homophile organization and a comparison group of nonhomosexual women matched with the lesbian subjects for age, education, and geographical distribution within the United States.

48. Schäfer's sample consisted of 150 lesbians between 18 and 40 years of age in West Germany in 1972.

49. Sanders, Reinisch, and McWhirter (1990:xxiv).

50. The 85% figure does not appear in Chapman and Brannock (1987); it was calculated by Rust (1992) based on their reported findings. As Rust explained, "Ninety-six percent of the 197 women in Chapman and Brannock's sample were lesbian-identified. Of the 187 women who answered the question 'Have you ever had sexual contact(s) with men?' 88.8 percent said 'yes.' If one assumes that the seven non-lesbian-identified women are among those who answered 'yes,' then an adjusted figure of 85 percent reflects the proportion of lesbian-identified women in that study who had sexual contact with men. Chapman and Brannock did not ask their subjects to distinguish between consensual and nonconsensual heterosexual contact, so it is possible that the figures cited include women whose only heterosexual contact has been nonconsensual" (369, note 4).

51. The authors described the results as an assessment of respondents' "primary sexual orientation." Because the question asked, "How would you classify yourself on the following scale?" does not specify which aspect of sexuality a respondent is supposed to use in rating her or himself, it is likely that each subject used the scale to describe that aspect of her or his sexuality that she or he considered most central to the concept of sexual orientation; for some subjects this might have been sexual behavior, whereas for others it might have been sexual feelings or self-identity. Moreover, among those who interpreted the scale as a reference to behavior or feelings, some might have given answers describing their current behavior or feelings, whereas others might have thought in terms of their entire sexual histories. The mean age of the sample was 29.7 years (SD = 9.22).

52. In 1993 the same authors reported that 132 subjects described themselves as exclusively homosexual, 37 described themselves as bisexual, and 137 described themselves as exclusively heterosexual. Because lesbian/gay respondents were recruited via lesbian and gay social and political groups whereas heterosexual respondents were recruited from an undergraduate psychology class, the ratio of lesbian/gay/bisexual to heterosexual in this sample is meaningless. However, the ratio of bisexual to lesbian/gay respondents, when scores 2–6 are considered bisexual, is 22 percent.

53. In a similar study in which subjects were recruited in only one city, Chicago, a rate

of 27.4 percent bisexual self-identification was found among women (Bailey and Benishay 1993).

54. Respondents were recruited from attendees at events sponsored by the Standing Committee on Lesbian/Gay/Bisexual Awareness in ACPA (American College Personnel Association) and the Network for Gay, Lesbian, and Bisexual Concerns in NASPA (National Association of Student Personnel Administrators) at the annual meetings of ACPA and NASPA. Respondents' mean age was 31.2 years (range 21 to 52 years).

55. D'Augelli (1992) reported the results of a survey based on questionnaires handed out by the members of a college lesbian, gay, and bisexual student association at events organized for lesbians and gay men both on and off campus. Of 170 undergraduates who identified as either lesbian/gay, or as bisexual but primarily lesbian or gay, 17.6 percent were "bisexual but primarily lesbian or gay." If bisexuals who were not primarily lesbian or gay had been retained in the sample, this percentage would undoubtedly be higher, but statistics sufficient to enable calculation of this percentage were not provided.

56. Mays, Beckman, Oranchak, and Harper (1994) studied seventy African American women in alcoholism treatment centers in Los Angeles County. Of the fifty-nine women who identified their sexual orientation, 64 percent identified themselves as heterosexual and 36 percent identified as lesbian or bisexual. Mays and colleagues did not indicate the percentages who identified as lesbian or as bisexual specifically, and attributed the rate of total lesbian and bisexual self-identification to high rates of nonheterosexuality in the southern California population in general. Recall, in comparison, that in a predominantly white random sample drawn in San Francisco Bloomfield (1993) found that 15 percent of women identified themselves as "primarily or exclusively lesbian or bisexual"—a substantially smaller percentage, in a city known for its large lesbian and gay population.

57. In a study of 111 gay and bisexual men aged under twenty-one in the UK, recruited from gay bars, clubs, organizations, and publications, Davies et al. (1992) reported that 45 percent had heterosexual experience, 15.3 percent had had both homosexual and heterosexual contact in the past year, 29.7 percent had some heterosexual feelings, and 8.1 had substantial heterosexual feelings.

58. Rosario et al. (1996) reported finding no ethnic differences in sexual self-identity.

59. Besides MSM, another population of interest in HIV-related epidemiological research is intravenous drug users. Studies of IVDUs sometimes include the gathering of information on sexual contacts and indicate that bisexual and homosexual behavior is more common among illicit drug users than nonusers. For example, Magura, O'Day, and Rosenblum (1992) found that 15 out of 39 female IVDUs in prison reported recent same-sex activity, primarily prior to incarceration. Most had also had heterosexual contact; 80 percent had biological children. In a sample of 1,245 IVDUs in Sydney, Australia, Ross, Wodak, Gold, and Miller (1992, 1998) reported that 13 percent of male and 29 percent of female respondents had had at least one same-gender and one other-gender sexual contact during the previous five years; smaller proportions, 6 percent of males and 3 percent of females, had had only same-gender contacts during the same period. These figures apparently include sexual contact in the context of prostitution, with approximately one-third of bisexually active women and men and one-third of homosexually active men reporting having been paid for sex. See chapter 22, including note 33, on the relationship between bisexual behavior and drug use.

60. Higher rates of bisexual self-description were found in a study done of MSM in Amsterdam, although the difference can be attributed to differences in question wording. In a cohort study of HIV and AIDS among MSM who had had at least two male sex partners in the past six months recruited from the male homosexual community in Amsterdam (see Griensven et al. 1987), Krijnen et al. (1994) reported that when 679 subjects were asked to describe their sexual preference on a five-point scale on which the endpoints represented exclusive heterosexuality and exclusive homosexuality, 26 percent rated themselves as bisexual. (In an earlier stage of this longitudinal study 34 percent of 741 men said they were

not exclusively homosexual on a seven-point scale [Griensven et al. 1987].) Krijnen et al.'s finding is twice as high as the 13 percent found by Wood, Krueger, Pearlman, Goldbaum (1993), who had asked subjects to indicate their self-identity, given response options "gay," "bisexual," and "straight," rather than to describe their sexual preference using scaled response options. Krijnen et al. (1994) also collected data on sexual contact with women for epidemiological purposes. Their subjects reported rates of bisexual behavior that are consistent with those found by Chu et al. (1992) when differences in the length of the time period in question are taken into consideration; Krijnen et al. reported that 55 percent of MSM had had a female partner at least once in their lives and 13 percent had had contact with a woman or women within the last five years. Of the 632 men who had been sexually active in the past 6 months, 4 percent had been active with both women and men and three-quarters of these had had steady female partners. Similar rates were reported in a Canadian sample of 1,295 men drawn from gay bars and baths in Toronto in 1990 for the purpose of studying gay and bisexual men's attitudes toward HIV antibody testing; 48.1 percent reported having had sex only with men, whereas 35.3 percent had had heterosexual experience in their lifetimes and 13 percent had had both homosexual and heterosexual experience within the previous year (Myers, Orr, Locker, Jackson 1993).

61. These recalculations involved, for example, for self-identified straight men: Wood, Krueger, Pearlman, and Goldbaum (1993) reported a seropositivity rate of 7.7 percent among the 457 self-identified straight men, and included 70 self-identified straight men in a table titled "Number of Sex Partners of Uninfected Bisexually Active Men in the Preceding 12 Months, by Stated Sexual Identity and Injection Drug Use." If 7.7 percent of 457 self-identified straight men were seropositive, then 422 of these men were seronegative. If 70 self-identified straight men were seronegative and bisexually active within the past twelve months, then 70/422 = 16.6 percent of self-identified straight seronegative men were bisexually active.

62. Taking a slightly broader view of the population at risk of HIV infection from sexual activity, Chetwynd, Chambers, and Hughes (1992) drew a sample (n = 814) of both men and women consisting of all clients seeking pretest counseling at the Burnett Clinic in Auckland, New Zealand, during a twelve-month period in 1988–1989. Totals given in the authors' table 1 indicate that subjects' "sexual orientations" were as follows. Among men, 25 percent were homosexual, 15.6 percent were bisexual, and 59.3 percent were heterosexual, and among women, 14.2 percent were lesbian or bisexual and 85.8 percent were heterosexual. Although the authors did not define "sexual orientation" or provide the wording of the question that elicited subjects' sexual orientations, they included the sexual orientation category "lesbian/bisexual" in a cross-tabulation of sexual orientation with whether subjects had engaged in anal intercourse. Given that the authors distinguished homosexual from bisexual men in this table, and explained their combining lesbian with bisexual women on the basis of small numbers, this reader is led to assume that subjects were asked to place themselves in sexual orientation categories; hence, data on the sexual orientations of subjects probably reflects sexual self-identification (if sexual orientation were determined on the basis of sexual behavior rather than self-identification and anal intercourse is assumed to involve a penis, lesbians would have been excluded from this table, not combined with bisexual women).

63. Of 634 HIV+ male donors identified, 388 were notified of their seropositivity and agreed to participate, and 215 of these were MSM. The final sample size was 209.

64. The authors did not cross-tabulate same-gender and other-gender experiences but did report that 90 percent and 77 percent, respectively, of males and females were sexually active with other-gender partners, whereas 92 percent and 78 percent, respectively, were active with partners of either gender, suggesting that of the 9 percent and 6 percent with same-gender experience, only 2 percent and 1 percent had no heterosexual experience.

65. The authors noted that this finding of no significant gender difference is consistent with findings of a New York City high school study (Reuben et al. 1988).

66. The authors cited Sonenstein, Pleck, and Ku (1989) and Ku, Sonenstein, and Pleck (1990), who reported findings from the National Survey of Adolescent Males.

67. Gundlach and Riess (1968) found the opposite. Ninety-four percent of their "non-homosexual" women subjects, compared to 75 percent of their self-identified lesbian subjects, had had heterosexual intercourse.

In another study of students—junior and high school students—Remafedi et al. (1992) found that those who had had homosexual experiences were more likely than those who hadn't to have had heterosexual experience (73 percent vs. 61 percent).

68. The low rates might also reflect underreporting. The high rate of exclusion for dishonesty in the McGuire et al. (1992) study suggests that the findings substantially underestimate rates of homosexual and bisexual behavior because it is likely that students who had had same-gender partners were more likely to answer dishonestly.

In comparison to the extremely low rates of same-gender sexual behavior found by McGuire et al. (1992) among American college students, McConaghy, Armstrong, Birrell, and Buhrich (1979) found high rates of homosexual and bisexual feelings among medical students in the late 1970s in New South Wales, Australia. Among 58 female and 138 male medical students who constituted 85 percent of the second-year class, the researchers found that 48 percent of female and 45 percent of male students were currently aware of homosexual feelings, and that 69 percent and 63 percent had been aware of such feelings around the age of puberty. Currently, 19 percent and 22 percent of women and men, respectively, reported that their sexual feelings were 10 percent homosexual/90 percent heterosexual, 20–21 percent of each reported feelings that were 20–50 percent homosexual, and only 3 percent of each reported exclusively homosexual feelings. Replications (McConaghy 1987) in the following two years produced similar results. In a later mailed questionnaire study of 419 Australian male twins that achieved a response rate of 69 percent, McConaghy et al. (1994) found that 1.7 percent reported exclusively homosexual feelings and 10.4 percent reported both homosexual and heterosexual feelings. Both studies confirm Kinsey et al.'s findings that bisexual erotic capacity is more common than exclusively homosexual erotic capacity. McConaghy, Buhrich, and Silove (1994) noted that the former study produced higher rates of both homosexual and bisexual feelings than the latter and argued that the twins, who had been contacted via a twin registry, might have doubted the researchers' promise of anonymity and therefore hesitated to return questionnaires indicating that they had homosexual feelings.

69. Although Freund's findings using genital plethysmography, described in note 29 of this chapter, would suggest that bisexual arousability might be less—not more—common than suggested by behavior or self-reported attractions.

70. Recall that Smith's (1991) estimate of 6.3 percent includes both women and men.

12

Behavior Patterns and Sexual Identity of Bisexual Males

Janet Lever, David E. Kanouse, William H. Rogers,
Sally Carson, Rosanna Hertz

Introduction

THE epidemic spread of human immunodeficiency virus (HIV) in recent years has focused intense scrutiny on people whose behavior places them at especially high risk of acquiring or transmitting infection, including intravenous drug users (IVDUs) and homosexual or bisexual men. Many of the behaviors that pose special risk, and the people who engage in them, are highly stigmatized in mainstream society. As a result, quantitative study of the prevalence and patterning of these behaviors in the general population is difficult. For that reason, much of our scientific knowledge about these behaviors derives from studies of small numbers of subjects, whose typicality is difficult to assess.

The behavioral patterns of bisexual men—men who have sex with both men and women—are especially interesting to epidemiologists concerned with HIV spread, because such men are a potential bridge from the homosexual community to the much larger heterosexual population. Kinsey and associates presented striking data to demonstrate the existence of such a behavioral category, but the data were largely disregarded until AIDS forced a new reckoning. Consequently, little is known about the behavioral patterns of bisexual men. We do not know how many such men there are, how they define themselves, or in what ways their sexual behaviors and relationship choices differ from those of homosexual men on the one hand or heterosexual men on the other.

Bisexuality may be defined and measured in various ways; the way that is chosen in a particular study may have an important bearing on what is found. The two most common ways are based on *self-identity* or on observed or self-reported *behavior*. By the first definition, we might select for study all those men who, given a choice to describe themselves as "heterosexual," "homosexual," or "bisexual," choose the last alternative. By the second definition, we might select for study all those men who respond affirmatively to questions as to whether, within a specified time period, they have had sex with (a) women and (b) other men. It is possible, of course, that the two methods would identify very nearly the same people. But it is also possible that *self-identified* bisexual men and *bisexually experienced* men are rather different sorts of people, in which case it would behoove us to be cautious in drawing from studies of the one to reach conclusions about the other.

The relationship between identity and behavior has not been well studied, however, because the available datasets have generally included measures of only one or the other dimension, or have been based on small samples. The present study addresses this issue with data from a 1982 survey of readers of *Playboy* magazine. The crux of our study is a comparative analysis of men with adult bisexual experience and men who label themselves as bisexual. Because the *Playboy* dataset used in this study contains independent measures of behavior and identity on a very large sample, it is well-suited for this purpose.

In addition, we address a number of related research questions: How do men with adult bisexual experience compare demographically to men who are exclusively heterosexual or homosexual? How do these groups compare in their sexual behavior, including those associated with sexually transmitted diseases (STDs)? What factors predict bisexual identification among those with adult bisexual experience? How does adolescent homosexual experience relate to adult sexual experience and identity? Do the data support the notion of bisexuality as a temporary phase, or do some men seem to settle into a stable long-term pattern?

Background

PROBLEMS OF DEFINITION

Bisexuality is conventionally thought of as sexual attraction and/or relationships with members of both sexes (Warren, 1974, p. 113). Both components, sexual experience and psychic response, were built into the classic seven-point "Kinsey Scale" used to describe an individual's behavior and/or feelings on a continuum ranging from exclusively heterosexual (0) to exclusively homosexual (6) (Kinsey, Pomeroy, and Martin, 1948). Kinsey and associates' landmark study indicated that bisexuals may outnumber homosexuals;[1] nevertheless, there has been little research on bisexuality per se (MacDonald, 1981; Zinik, 1985). Zinik (1985), extrapolating from Kinsey's work and from a more recent study (Gebhard, 1972) estimates that as many as 15 percent of men and 10 percent of women may have bisexual histories.[2] He laments the lack of data to estimate how many of those would actually identify themselves as bisexual.

Estimates of prevalence are confounded by the lack of a single widely accepted definition of bisexuality. Even though sexual identification was not a measure used by Kinsey, contemporary researchers often rely on this social psychological variable to define their sample; others, following the Kinsey tradition, define bisexuality in terms of sexual behavior alone, or in combination with sexual feelings.[3] If persons defined as bisexual via one dimension were congruent with those defined by another dimension, it would not matter which were used, but such is not the case. As Blumstein and Schwartz (1976, p. 342) point out, there may be "little coherent relationship between the amount and 'mix' of homosexual and heterosexual behavior in a person's biography and that person's choice to label himself or herself as bisexual, homosexual, or heterosexual." The literature is sketchy but tentatively supports this conclusion: more people have homosexual feelings than engage in homosexual behavior, and more engage in homosexual behavior than develop lasting homosexual identification (Bell and Weinberg, 1978; Blumstein and Schwartz, 1976).

Previous research provides alternative hypotheses about the antecedents of bisexual behavior compared with bisexual identity. Respondents interviewed by Blumstein and Schwartz (1976), Weinberg (1978), and Hencken (1984) offer their own subjective reasons for the incongruities between their actions and identity, past and present.[4] In contrast, other researchers view the incongruities between behavior and identity as evidence that bisexuality is an inherently unstable and transitory state. In this view, those who have sex with partners of both genders do so not because they eroticize both sexes but because they are attempting to conceal or deny a homosexual preference that they themselves may not yet have accepted, or else for circumstantial reasons (such as partner availability) that temporarily constrain their choices or for experimentation (MacDonald, 1981). Spells of bisexual behavior will, in this view, be relatively brief, followed by exclusively homosexual or heterosexual behavior.

The present study sheds light on several of these issues. We examine what proportion of men who are bisexually experienced also have a bisexual identity and whether the relationship between the two variables is the same across social groups. We examine the extent to which bisexually experienced men are distinctive demographically and/or behaviorally. By comparing adolescent homosexual experience with both adult homosexual experience and current self-identification, we bring data to bear on the question of bisexuality as a "stage" versus a stable characteristic. However, without longitudinal data, we cannot test whether a bisexual identity can be stable over a lifetime.

PROBLEMS OF METHODOLOGY

Other serious problems confound attempts to estimate the prevalence of bisexuality. It may be impossible to find truly representative samples of hard-to-identify populations such as bisexuals and homosexuals. Instead, like virtually all available data on human sexuality, studies have relied on nonprobability "convenience" samples, including patients of STD clinics, members of accessible organizations, persons who frequent public places for sexual contact, and volunteer respondents to magazine and other publicly-announced surveys (Turner, Miller, and Moses, 1989). Other methodological shortcomings of sex research generally include: small sample size, recruitment in one or a few locales, and preponderance of young, white, urban middle-class respondents (Reinisch, Machover, Sanders, and Ziemba-Davis, 1988).

Inaccurate reporting further confounds efforts to quantify bisexual activity. As stigmatizing behavior, homosexuality is likely to be underreported (Fay et al., 1989; Warren, 1974). Most of what little is known about bisexuality is based on empirical studies of homosexual behavior in prisons (Lindler, 1948), in public restrooms and rest stops (Humphreys, 1970; Troiden, 1974), and among male hustlers and clients (Elifson, Boles, Sweat, Darrow, Elsea, and Green, 1989; Reiss, 1961; Waldorf, 1989). These studies are generally of small numbers of men but include significant proportions of men who consider themselves "heterosexual" or "bisexual" and have wives or girlfriends. Excluded are men who think of themselves as "bisexual" but have not acted on their feelings and men who have engaged in homosexual acts but not in the studied locations.

Empirical studies of the gay community also include numbers of men who think of themselves as "bisexual" or who have sexual contact with opposite-sex partners (Bell and Weinberg, 1978; Weinberg and Williams, 1974). These studies very likely overrepresent the bisexual men who are predominantly homosexual. Excluded from these studies are bisexually active men who would not be reached through gay establishments and organizations and those who would not attend to media-based appeals for participation because of their identification as heterosexuals (Blumstein and Schwartz, 1976; Harry, 1986).

The present study examines men who have been underrepresented in previous studies of bisexuality. Drawn from *Playboy* readers, this sample is likely to overrepresent the bisexual men who are predominantly heterosexual. Because of *Playboy*'s media-based recruitment, the survey yields broader representation of high-risk populations than do studies that recruit from identified communities (Harry, 1986). Even so, this study shares the serious flaw that mars virtually all studies of human sexuality: insofar as the sample is not representative of the U.S. population, sample means cannot be extrapolated to that population to estimate the prevalence of male bisexuality.

A broad representation of bisexual men does not yield much insight if these men are not considered separately in analyses. Even previous research that has measured bisexual identity or experience has often failed to distinguish bisexual men from exclusively homosexual men in the rest of the analyses, a practice that limits understanding of bisexuality and, as MacDonald (1981) points out, potentially confounds research on homosexuality.

For the most part, epidemiologists also combine bisexuals with homosexuals in their analyses. The Centers for Disease Control, for example, uses a single transmission category for homosexual/bisexual men in their surveillance reports and most analyses.[5] An unpublished study of HIV-seropositive men is among the few examining both sexual identity and sexual behavior.[6] Among male blood donors who had tested seropositive for HIV infection and who reported having engaged in penetrative sexual intercourse with other men at least once in their lives, there was less concordance between identity and behavior for men identifying themselves as heterosexual or bisexual than as homosexual.

Data and Method

The *Playboy* Reader's Sex Survey is a 133-item questionnaire printed in the January 1982 issue of the magazine. Nearly 100,000 were returned, yielding usable questionnaires from 65,471 men and 14,963 women, which made this the largest sex survey ever conducted and tabulated.[7] We restricted our analysis to 61,229 men who were 18 years or older and who resided in the U.S. We excluded 1,493 men who did not report a sexual identity and 1,123 men who described their identity as "asexual."[8] Our focus is on 6,982 men who reported bisexual experience after adolescence.

The sample poses obvious limitations. *Playboy,* with a circulation of over 5 million at the time of the survey, would be considered a mainstream publication; by comparison, 1981 circulation figures for *Time* and *Newsweek* were 4.4 and 2.8 million, respectively (World Almanac, 1983). *Playboy* readers are not representative of the American adult male population. Respondents, it need be noted, are not necessarily representative of all *Playboy* readers. One hundred thousand questionnaires, while a large return, amounted to only two percent of all questionnaires in circulation. The self-selectivity of the volunteers presents a bias common in sex research. We must presume that those who took the time to fill out the survey were those most interested in the subject matter, they may have differed in their behavior from those who did not respond. In the absence of any comparable dataset, we have tried to make the best use of the Playboy survey while keeping its limitations firmly in mind.

Even though the sample is not representative of the U.S. population, data from this survey are important for several reasons. First, the questionnaire included fairly detailed questions about type and frequency of sexual behavior which, combined with large sample size and demographic information, permits analysis of relationships that have not previously been examined. Second, the sample includes sizable numbers of persons whose sexual behavior puts them in risk categories that are of epidemiological interest. Third, the data were collected in 1982, before public awareness of AIDS effected either a change in behavior or a change in willingness to admit to certain behaviors.

This dataset has other features that make it attractive for analysis. In contrast to the methodological limitations of previous studies, the survey's overall size ensures large numbers of respondents in subgroups defined by gender, age, sexual preference, socioeconomic status, and lifestyle. Ethnic and racial minorities, however, are not well-represented. Not limited to one or a few locales, this survey includes large numbers of respondents from every region of the nation. Furthermore, rural Americans (n = 7,409) and those who live in small towns (n = 16,690) are also better represented here than elsewhere.

The *Playboy* questionnaire elicited responses that allow for classification of bisexuality in terms of either self-identification or self-reported behaviors. In a series of demographic items at the end of the questionnaire, respondents were asked to identify themselves as heterosexual, bisexual, or homosexual. Two earlier items asked about frequency of homosexual experiences during adolescence. Directly following was the question, "Have you had homosexual experiences since adolescence?" Those who answered "yes" were asked to estimate the relative proportion of homosexual and heterosexual behavior. Regardless of sexual identification or adolescent experiences, each respondent was assigned a heterosexual-homosexual rating based on his answers to the two questions about adult behavior:

0 = no homosexual experience = exclusively heterosexual
1 = "rarely" have homosexual experiences = predominantly heterosexual
2 = "sometimes" have homosexual experiences = sometimes homosexual
3 = "usually" have homosexual experiences = predominantly homosexual
4 = "always" have homosexual experiences = exclusively homosexual

Because it is behavior, and not self-image, that determines ones risk of acquiring or transmitting STDs, the data reported here are based on the behavioral definition unless stated otherwise.[9]

Risk factors for STDs, including HIV infection, include both number of sex partners and frequency of anal sex. The association between oral sex and transmission of HIV is less certain, but oral sex poses some risk. By combining questionnaire items, we constructed variables for each of these risk factors.

The "Multiple Partner Index" combines four items that loaded 0.40 or higher on a common factor in a principal components analysis. One item asks, "How many sexual partners have you had?" Midpoint values were calculated for the four categories offering a numerical range; a "0" was assigned for those who indicated "none" and a "51" for those who selected "more then (sic) 50."[10] The other three items indicate whether respondent ever had any of the following sexual experiences: more than one sex partner within a 24-hour period; an extramarital or extrarelational affair; and "sex with more than one person at a time," referred to here as "group sex." These items were weighted equally, combined into an overall index, and standardized to mean = 50, $\sigma = 20.1$.[11]

Measurement of other variables is described in Table 12.1, which also gives means and standard deviations. Means for indicator variables are proportions of respondents who scored "1" on those variables.

Results

Bisexual Identity and Bisexual Experience

One of the main questions addressed by our research concerns the relationship between bisexual identity and bisexual experience. Table 12.2 shows the relationship between self-reported identity and level of homosexual activity for those men in the sample who provided information on both. Not surprisingly, most such men in this sample would be considered heterosexual by either definition: 94 percent reported a heterosexual self-identity and 86 percent reported no adult homosexual experience. Nevertheless, the sample also included substantial numbers of men who could be described as bisexual by one or the other definition: 4.6 percent reported a bisexual self-identity, and 12.5 percent reported adult bisexual experience (neither exclusively heterosexual nor exclusively homosexual).

TABLE 12.1 *Variable Definitions, Means, and Standard Deviations*

Age	Median in years for each of 8 categories ranging from "18–20" to "50 or over," a value of 57 was assigned for the oldest category. Mean = 31.32, S.D. = 9.54.
Education	Years of schooling completed, estimated from respondent's choice of 8 categories ranging from "grade school" (8 Years) to "graduate or professional degree" (19 years). A response of "less than grade school" was treated as missing, because of anomalous patterns of relationships to other item for responses in this category. Mean = 15.30, S.D. = 2.26.
Income	Annual income in $1,000s, estimated using the midpoint of 8 categories ranging form "less than $5000" to "$60,000 or more"; $2500 is lowest and $65,000 the highest value assigned. Mean = 24.073, S.D. = 15.212.
Reside in city	Indicator variable; 1 = respondent lives in city, 0 = suburb, small town, or rural area. Mean = 0.39, S.D. = 0.49.
Reside in metropolis	Indicator variable; 1 = respondent lives in city or suburb, 0 = small town or rural area. Mean = 0.71, S.D. = 0.46.
Ever married	Indicator variable; 1 = respondent describes marital status as married, divorced, widowed, or remarried, 0 = single or cohabiting. (The last response category is not mutually exclusive with the others, but is so treated in the questionnaire and in our coding). mean = 0.57. S.D. = 0.49
Married	Indicator variable; 1 = respondent describes marital status as married or remarried; 0 = single, divorced, widowed, or cohabitating. Mean = 0.43, S.D. = 0.49.
Children	Indicator variable; 1 = respondent has children or stepchildren. Mean = 0.44, S.D. = 0.50.
Anal experience	Indicator variable; 1 = respondent has ever had anal intercourse, Mean = 0.50, S.D. = 0.50.
Anal sex	Experience and frequency of anal intercourse, on a 7-point scale: 0 = has never had anal sex; 1 = has had anal sex, but does not currently engage in it; 2 = has anal sex less than once per month; 3 has anal sex once or twice a month; 4 = has anal sex once a week; 5 = has anal sex a couple of times a week; 6 = has anal sex every time he has sex. Mean = 1.00, S.D. = 1.21.
Sex with a prostitute	Indicator variable; 1 = respondent reports having had sex with a prostitute in the past 5 years. Mean = 0.21, S.D. = 0.41.
Multiple dating Partners	Indicator variable; 1 = respondent describes current social situation as "single and dating around" or "single and dating one person more than others;" 0 = respondent is in a steady relationship or not dating. Mean = 0.34, S.D. = 0.47.
Unfaithful	Indicator variable; 1 = currently in 'open' relationship or unfaithful to partner; 0 = faithful to current partner; missing for those not in a current relationship. Mean = 0.57, S.D. = 0.47.
Masturbation Frequency	Number of times per month, estimated from responses to two items on whether respondent practices masturbation and if so, how frequently. Responses in 5 categories ranging from "once a day" to "less than once a month" were transformed to days/month, with 31 as highest and 0.5 as lowest for those currently engaging in this practice, 0 = does not masturbate. Mean = 11.1, S.D. = 10.9
Intercourse Frequency	Number of times per month, estimated from responses in 8 categories ranging from "at least once a day" to "less than once a month" were transformed to days/month, with 31 as highest and 0.5 as lowest for those currently engaging in this practice, 0 = does not have intercourse. Mean = 9.63, S.D. = 8.42.
Oral sex Frequency	Combines two items on the frequency of performing and receiving oral sex; combined scores range from 0 to 6, responses to the separate items range from "never" (=0) to "every time I have sex" (=3). Mean = 3.1, S.D. = 1.3.
STD history	Indicator variable; 1 = respondent reports having had one or more STDs (e.g., syphilis, gonorrhea, venereal warts) in the past five years. Mean = 0.11, S.D. = 0.32.
Adolescent homosexual experience	Frequency of homosexual experiences during adolescence; 0 = never, 1 = once, 2 = a few times, 3 = frequently. Mean = 0.62, S.D. = 0.90.

| Drugs with sex | Combines two items specifying which drugs, if any, the respondent has used "for sexual stimulation" and/or "to dispel sexual anxiety;" specific drugs listed are marijuana, cocaine, tranquilizers, speed, psychedelics, alcohol, other; value range is from 0 (never used drugs for these purposes) to 7 (used each of these drugs for these purposes). Mean = 1.44, S.D. = 1.72. |

NOTE: A variable describing level of homosexual activity and a "multiple partner index" are described in the text.

The proportion of men who report bisexual experience would be expected to vary with the time frame referred to in the question. The *Playboy* survey asked about homosexual experiences since adolescence. A similar question based on a shorter time frame (e.g., the last year) might yield a much lower proportion of respondents who report bisexual experience. Because the *Playboy* survey did not inquire about gender of partner(s) for current or recent behavior, we have little basis for estimating how many of these men were currently or recently sexually active with both male and female partners. A question that may have an indirect bearing on this, however, is one asking the respondent whether he considers sex with someone of his own sex to be "off limits." Twenty-eight percent of bisexually experienced men answered this question affirmatively.[12] This may provide an indication of how many bisexually experienced men considered their homosexual experiences to be entirely in the past. If so, the data suggest that more than two-thirds of them did not rule out such contacts in the future.

The three middle columns of Table 12.2 show a strong relationship between behavioral rating and self-reported identity. Bisexually identified men, in contrast to their heterosexually identified (but bisexually experienced) peers, are much more likely to report that they have homosexual experiences "sometimes" (51 percent compared with 13 percent) or "usually" (17 percent compared with 3 percent), and correspondingly less likely to report such experiences as occurring only "rarely" (32 percent compared with 85 percent).

Table 12.2 also shows that adult bisexual experience does not necessarily result in acquisition of a bisexual self-identity; most bisexually experienced men in this sample (68.5 percent) labeled themselves as heterosexual. By the same token, adult bisexual experience does not appear to be necessary to have a bisexual identity; 18 percent of those who labeled themselves as bisexual reported no adult homosexual experience whatsoever.[13] Controlling for education did not affect the relationship between bisexual experience and bisexual identity.

CHARACTERISTICS OF BISEXUALLY EXPERIENCED MEN

How do men whose adult sexual experience includes partners of both genders compare with men who are exclusively homosexual or heterosexual in their adult behavior? Tables 12.3 and 12.4 show how groups of men defined by relative proportions of homosexual vs. heterosexual activity compare on a variety of demographic and behavioral characteristics. The large sample size renders even fairly modest differences statistically significant. When we look beyond statistical significance for sizable differences, it is evident that the groups do not differ much on some demographic characteristics, such as age, income, and education, whereas they differ considerably in others, such as urban residence, marital status, and parent-

TABLE 12.2 *Sexual Identity by Behavioral Ratings of Men in the Playboy Readers' Sex Survey, 1982*

Self-reported identity	Behavioral Rating											
	Excl. het.		Pred. het.		Some. hom.		Pred. hom.		Exc. hom.		Total	
	N	%	N	%	N	%	N	%	N	%	N	%
Heterosexual	48.237 (85.2)	98.7	4,049 (7.2)	85.8	603 (1.1)	35.7	133 (0.2)	23.2	152 (0.3)	20.7	53,174	93.9
Bisexual	467 (0.8)	1.0	654 (1.2)	13.9	1,053 (1.9)	62.4	349 (0.6)	60.9	77 (0.1)	10.5	2,600	4.6
Homosexual	180 (0.3)	0.3	19 (.0)	0.4	31 (0.1)	1.8	91 (0.2)	15.9	505 (0.9)	68.8	826	1.5
Total	48,884 (86.4)	100	4,722 (8.4)	100	1,687 (3.1)	100	573 (1.0)	100	734 (1.3)	100	56,600	100

NOTE: Percentages in brackets are of the total sample. Analyses exclude 1,123 men who reported identity as "asexual" and 1,493 men whose sexual identity was unknown. Excluded here, but included in subsequent analyses, are 4,629 men for whom behavioral rating was imputed from sexual identity.

TABLE 12.3 *Demographic Profiles by Men's Heterosexual-Homosexual Rating**

	Excl. Het.	Pred. Het.	Some. Hom.	Pred. Hom.	Excl Hom.	N's
Age (years)	31.0	33.7	32.5	33.0	31.5	61,106
Education (years)	15.3	15.1	15.0	15.3	15.3	55,264
Income ($1000's)	24.1	24.1	24.2	22.0	22.8	60,191
Reside in City (%)	37.6	41.5	43.8	52.7	63.2	60,808
Reside in Metropolis (%)	70.3	71.7	72.2	76.9	78.8	60,808
Ever Married (%)	57.6	61.2	52.8	38.7	23.8	60,917
Married (%)	43.9	40.7	40.0	20.8	14.6	60,917
Children (%)	43.4	50.9	43.7	30.7	17.9	60,593

 * All variables significant at P <.001 level.

TABLE 12.4 *History of Risky Sex Practices and STDs By Behavioral Rating**

	Excl. Het.	Pred. Het.	Some. Hom.	Pred. Hom.	Excl Hom.	N's
Adolescent Homosexual Experience (0 to 3 score)	.5	1.2	1.8	2.0	2.1	60,883
Drugs with Sex (0 to 7 score)	1.4	1.9	1.7	2.0	2.4	61,229
Multiple Partner Index (standardized to mean = .50)	48.3	60.3	61.5	64.1	68.0	61,209
Anal Sex Frequency (0 to 6 scale)	.9	1.4	1.8	2.8	3.2	57,434
Oral Sex Frequency (0 to 6 score)	3.1	3.4	3.4	3.9	4.2	60,009
Anal Experience (%)	46.2	68.3	77.9	85.0	90.1	59,139
Sex with Prostitute (%)	19.3	32.8	33.4	24.6	18.0	60,898
Multiple Dating Partners (%)	33.3	36.5	43.4	50.1	55.2	60,285
Unfaithful (%)	40.2	59.2	69.9	69.8	71.6	47,625[1]
STD (in past 5 years) (%)	9.8	17.6	18.7	22.6	35.0	60,023

 [1] Item restricted to those in relationships
 * All Variables Significant at P <.0001 Level.

hood. For example, bisexually experienced men are much more likely to live in cities than are men with exclusively heterosexual experience, but they are not as concentrated in cities as are exclusively homosexual men.

Bisexually experienced men tend to engage more frequently in various risk behaviors than do men with exclusively heterosexual adult experience, but not as frequently as men with exclusively homosexual experience (Table 12.4). For example, compared with exclusively heterosexual men, bisexually experienced men score higher on the multiple partner index, are more likely to be currently dating multiple partners or to be "unfaithful" to their current partner, are more likely to report anal and oral sexual practices, more likely to report having had sex with a prostitute in the past five years, and more likely to report having had an STD in the past five years (a marker of risk activity). Compared with exclusively homosexual men, however, they exhibit fewer of all these risk behaviors, except for having sex with a prostitute in the last five years.[14]

Men with adult bisexual experience are demographically diverse. Among the subgroups of bisexually experienced men, one of the more interesting is the 29 percent who live in traditional family arrangements—that is, who are currently married and have children. Compared with other bisexually experienced men, this group presents a sharply different demographic profile. It is older (mean age = 39.6 vs. 30.9 years, t = 32.8, p < .0001), more affluent (mean income = $30,100 vs. $21,500, t = 21.7, p < .0001), and more likely to live outside a city (68.3 percent vs. 52.5 percent, t = 12.8, p < .0001).

Behaviorally, this traditional group is somewhat less distinctive, though still meaningfully so. Traditional family men score higher than other bisexually experienced men on the multiple partner index (mean = 62.4 vs. 60.3, t = 4.70, p < .0001), but they report lower levels of risky behavior in other respects: they are less involved in anal intercourse (mean = 1.37 vs. 1.65, t = 8.6, p < .0001), less likely to have had sex with a prostitute in the last five years (28.5 percent vs. 33.4 percent, t = 4.07, p < .0001), less likely to have used drugs in a sexual context (mean = 1.36 vs. 2.09, t = 15.9, p < .0001), and less likely to have had an STD in the previous five years (12.0 percent vs. 20.7 percent, t = 9.6, p < .0001). Their lower risk of STDs undoubtedly reflects their own lesser involvement in high-risk sexual activities and may also reflect their partners' risk characteristics. Only 31.7 percent of the traditional family men live in cities, compared with 47.4 percent of other bisexually experienced men.

Characteristics of Bisexually Identified Men

Among bisexually experienced men, what characteristics distinguish those who label themselves bisexual from those who do not? Table 12.5 summarizes mean demographic and behavioral characteristics for the relevant subgroups in our sample. The groups differ significantly on most measures, but the largest demographic differences are in marital status and parenthood: bisexually identified men are much less likely to have ever married, to be currently married, or to have children.

As seen in Table 12.2, bisexually identified men are more likely than other bisexually experienced men to report their behavior as "sometimes" or "predominantly" homosexual. They show other behavioral differences as well. They are more likely than other bisexually experienced men to have engaged in anal intercourse and to have done so more frequently. They also report masturbating somewhat more frequently. Although they are more likely than other bisexually experienced men to report being in a nonmonogamous relationship, they do not score any higher overall on the multiple partner index. As Table 12.5 shows, however, both groups of men with bisexual experience, regardless of identification, score substantially higher on measures of sexual "risk" behaviors than do men with exclusively heterosexual experience.

One of the strongest predictors of bisexual identification among bisexually experienced men is adolescent homosexual experience. The percentage who consider themselves bisexual increases fourfold from 15.6 to 33.1 to 63.5 for those who report having had homosexual experiences as adolescents no more than once, a few times, or frequently [Ed. note: figure omitted].[15] Adolescent homosexual experience has a strong relationship to identity even after adult homosexual experience has been taken into account. . . . Among those whose adult behavior is entirely heterosexual, the relative odds of a "non-straight" (bisexual or homosexual) identity are more than seven times as great for those with frequent as opposed to no homosexual activity in adolescence (7.3 percent vs. 1.0 percent). Similarly, among those with bisexual adult experience, the odds of a bisexual identity are four times as high for those with frequent vs. no adolescent homosexual activity. [These] strong relationships . . . suggest that both adolescent and adult experience may shape adult sexual identity, and that adolescent homosexual experience may have lasting

TABLE 12.5 *Profiles of Bisexually Experienced Men by Sexual Identity*

	Self-Label	
Demographics	Heterosexual	Bisexual
Age (years)	33.8	32.3
Education (years)	15.2	15.0
Income ($1,000)	24.4	22.9
Reside in City (%)	42.0	44.9
Ever Married (%)	60.6	51.3
Currently Married (%)	41.3	34.9
Children (%)	51.0	40.5
Behavior	Heterosexual	Bisexual
Adolescent Homosexual Experience (0 to 3 score)	1.2	2.1
Multiple Partner Index** (standardized mean = 50)	60.5	61.9
Anal Sex Frequency (0 to 6 score)	1.32	1.87
Oral Sex Frequency (0 to 6 score)	3.3	4.0
Anal Experience (%)	67	81
Sex with Prostitute* (%)	33.4	31.0
Currently in "Open" Relationship or Unfaithful (%)	58.3	73.2
Masturbation Frequency (per month)	12.9	15.5
STD (in past 5 years)* (%)	17.8	19.7

* *Not* statistically significant at P <.01
** Vary on "group sex" but not other 3 variables.

effects of identity even for those who do not follow through in adulthood. Of course, the relationships observed in these cross-sectional data are subject to alternative causal interpretations, and identity may be seen as antecedent or consequent to behavior.[16] . . .

Discussion and Conclusion

IDENTITY AND EXPERIENCE

One of the most striking findings is that approximately two-thirds of the men in this sample who reported bisexual adult experience considered themselves to be heterosexual rather than bisexual. One in eight men in the *Playboy* sample was bisexually experienced, whereas only one in 22 identified himself as bisexual. This suggests that a definition of bisexuality that is based on bisexual identity would fail to capture most of the men who have bisexual experience after adolescence. Given that only 39 percent of the bisexually experienced men who said that sex with a same-gender partner was not "off limits" labeled themselves bisexual, our conclusion that bisexual identity is an imperfect marker for bisexual behavior holds even for those most likely to be currently active. This finding has important implications both for future research on this population and for public health efforts aimed at targeting this population for interventions (e.g., education). Recent changes in targeting "men who have sex with men" rather than "gay and bisexual men" are a step in the right direction.

It is not surprising that among bisexually experienced men, those who label themselves bisexual evince patterns suggesting a relatively higher proportion of bisexual activity. Beyond that key difference, there are few marked behavioral differences associated with identity. Bisexually identified men report greater involvement in anal intercourse and are somewhat more likely to be in a nonmonogamous relationship. But on a variety of other measures, including an index of multiple partners, they score much the same as heterosexually identified men with bisexual experience. Because men who adopt the "bisexual" label exhibit very little more in the way of risky behavior than bisexually experienced men who do not adopt this label, public health outreach effort aimed only at the former may miss a large group that is at similar risk.

LEVEL OF RISK BEHAVIOR

Bisexually experienced men exhibit distinctive patterns of behavior that would place them at intermediate risk of acquiring or transmitting STDs—higher than exclusively heterosexual men but lower than exclusively homosexual men. This receives direct support from data on recent history of STDs, where bisexually experienced men report STDs more frequently than heterosexual men (18 percent vs. 10 percent) but less frequently than exclusively homosexual men (35 percent).

Epidemiological research on HIV transmission suggests a differential risk for insertive vs. receptive anal intercourse (Detels, English, Visscher, Jacobson, Kingsley,

Chmiel, Dudley, Eldred, and Ginzburg, 1989; Kingsley, Detels, Kaslow, Polk, Rinaldo, Chmiel, Detre, Kelsey, Odaka, Ostrow, VanRaden, and Visscher, 1987; Winkelstein et al., 1987), which may apply to certain other STDs as well. The *Playboy* survey did not differentiate between the two. Both the sociological and epidemiological literatures suggest, however, that bisexual- and gay-identified males are likely to take both roles, notwithstanding stereotypes about division of roles (Bell and Weinberg, 1978; Kingsley et al., 1987; McWhirter and Mattison, 1984; Polk, Fox, Brookmeyer, Kanchanaraksa, Kaslow, Visscher, Rinaldo, and Phair, 1987). Meanwhile, ethnographic research suggests that heterosexually identified participants (called "trade") in anonymous homosexual encounters are more likely to engage in oral than anal sex and always to take the insertive role (Humphreys, 1970; Troiden, 1974). This suggests that heterosexually identified bisexual men are at lower risk of STDs than those who are bisexually identified, but we found little difference between the two groups.

Understanding of the epidemiology of HIV transmission highlights the need for future research to pursue a much more detailed inquiry into the sexual behavior of bisexual men. Insofar as unprotected receptive anal intercourse poses the greatest risk of HIV transmission (Turner et al., 1989), it becomes important to know the gender of the partner and, if the partner is male, who takes the receptive role. Regarding sex with prostitutes, we need to know the gender of the prostitute, the acts performed, and the role taken by the respondent. More generally, by underscoring the incidence of homosexual behavior among primarily heterosexual men, these data suggest the importance of routinely inquiring in surveys of sexual behavior about numbers of partners, frequency of contact, and specific sexual practices with partners of each gender.

MALE BISEXUAL BEHAVIOR

Social scientists have not developed formal theories of male bisexual behavior, but their thinking about the phenomena associated with bisexual contact has been guided by certain views and assumptions whose validity or usefulness can be at least partly assessed with these data. Kinsey, challenging the accepted dichotomous characterization of people as either "heterosexuals" or "homosexuals," viewed sexual preferences as a continuum from exclusively heterosexual to exclusively homosexual (Kinsey et al., 1948). Nevertheless, a bipolar model continues to dominate the thinking of scholars and policy makers alike. Even the few researchers who use the Kinsey scale in measurement collapse the categories to form two groups, heterosexual and homosexual (DeCecco, 1990). Underlying the majority view that bisexuality is an inherently unstable state may be the notion that gender preferences (like gender itself) tend to be bimodally distributed, so that relatively few people will choose to be sexually active with partners of both genders over a long period of time.

When respondents to the *Playboy* survey were classified on a behavior rating scale anchored by Kinsey's endpoints, we found that their sexual behavior on a variety of other dimensions was monotonically related to their position on the scale. This recurring pattern illustrates that Kinsey's notion of a preference contin-uum may offer a useful way of organizing and summarizing observations of sex-ual behavior. Kinsey himself would have resisted our use of the label "bisexual" to refer to a third social type, for he viewed intermediates as persons whose sexual histories include a mixture of homosexual and heterosexual acts (Gagnon, 1990). At the same time, it is worth remembering that the notion of a preference contin-uum is not a social psychological variable and has little explanatory value. People do not naturally think of their own sexual behavior as lying on a continuum; they do label themselves in discrete categories, and they are affected by the labels they choose (Gagnon, 1977).

The *Playboy* dataset provides cross-sectional data only on cumulative homo-sexual and heterosexual experience during and after adolescence. Still, our analy-sis reveals a sizable number of males who have an early history of more-than-incidental homosexual activity and who continue to be open to such activity despite their predominantly (but not exclusively) heterosexual histories as adults. For these men, the data suggest a chronically bisexual behavior pattern that is hard to reconcile with the notion of bisexuality as a temporary or transitional state. They suggest that a sizable minority of men genuinely find sex with partners of both genders attractive over a good portion of their lives. That possibility should be seriously considered in future research on male bisexuality.

The data presented here raise the question: How can so many people fit a behav-ioral category without accepting or internalizing the "bisexual" label associated with it? The combination of negatively sanctioned and easily concealed behaviors commonly leads to the situation known as "passing," where a more desirable so-cial identity is assumed. Simply by conforming to prevailing norms in public, the bisexual male is in an excellent position to manage his impression so that others will think more highly of him. The married bisexual man, especially if he is a fa-ther, is above suspicion. Deviant activities can be easily compartmentalized and concealed, even from the self.

But those who "pass" know they are "passing" and recognize the contradiction of their felt identity. In contrast, most of the men who identified themselves as "heterosexual" probably neither think of themselves as "passing" or "in denial" but, rather, chose from a sexual script that offered only two labels the one that fit best. People pigeonhole themselves into socially defined categories, and "bisex-ual" is not one of them.

Without social recognition, there can be no bisexual community, comparable to the gay community with its networks and institutions. And without community, there are no reference groups, supportive norms, or available symbols to counter the pull toward the two extremes of the continuum. Few stereotypes exist for self comparison, except for being sexually avant-garde or voracious, and it is possible that the minority who accept the bisexual label think of themselves in these terms. The discordance noted here between identity and behavior arises from the rare circumstance where social scripts have been so grossly oversimplified that access to a community of similars is precluded, hence the "looking glass self" denied.

Notes

Earlier versions of this paper were presented at the Fifth International Conference on AIDS in Montreal, Quebec, Canada, June 1989, and at a workshop on "Bisexuality and AIDS" held by the Centers for Disease Control (CDC), Atlanta, GA, October 1989. The work was supported by a grant from the American Foundation for AIDS Research and by research funds provided by RAND. The data utilized in this paper were made available by Arthur Kretchmer and *Playboy* magazine. Playboy bears no responsibility for the analyses or interpretations presented here. We are indebted to N. Scott Cardell, E. Michael Gorman, Linda J. Waite, R. Stephen Warner, and CDC workshop participants for comments.

1. Kinsey et al. (1948, pp. 650–51) reported that 37 percent of the male population had "at least some overt homosexual experience to the point of orgasm between adolescence and old age"; 10 percent were "more or less exclusively homosexual" (rating of 5 or 6 for at least three years).

2. Not all studies support this. One recent study (Fay, Turner, Klassen, and Gagnon, 1989), while acknowledging underreporting, sets the lower bound of bisexual preferences at 1.6 percent to 6.7 percent.

3. Klein (1985) calls sexual orientation a multivariable dynamic process and names seven variables (sexual attraction, behavior, fantasies, social preference, emotional preference, self-identification, and hetero/gay lifestyle), each of which is rated by the subject as applying to the present, past, or ideal.

4. The following are examples of conceptualizations of homosexual behavior that may preclude a homosexual or bisexual self-label: performed for money, not pleasure; experimentation; "just a phase"; less enjoyable than sex with someone of opposite gender; only took inserter role (Hencken, 1984).

5. AIDS surveillance data compiled by the Centers for Disease Control do permit disaggregation of cases in the "male homosexual/bisexual contact" category, the largest risk category for adult exposure, into "homosexual" (men who report having sexual relations only with other men) and "bisexual" (men who report having sexual relations with partners of both sexes) Chu, Doll, and Buehler (1989) found that through July 31, 1989, there were 56,110 cases of AIDS in homosexual men and 12,677 cases in bisexual men. The ratio of bisexual to homosexual men (1:4.4) did not change notably over time, but was higher among blacks (1:2) and Hispanics (1:4) than among whites (1:6) The ratio of bisexual to homosexual men among AIDS cases may be different from the ratio in the larger population. In a probability sample of 1,035 single men aged 25–54 in selected areas of San Francisco, 809 (78 percent) were classified as homosexual or bisexual (Winkelstein, Lyman, Padian, Grant, Samuel, Wiley, Anderson, Lang, Riggs, and Levy, 1987); of these, 108 (13 percent) reported having sex with women in the preceding two years (Winkelstein, Wiley, Padian, and Levy, 1986).

6. Doll, Lynda S., and the HIV Blood Donor Study Group. 1990. "Homosexually and Nonhomosexually Identified Male Blood Donors Who Have Sex with Men: A Behavioral Comparison," presented at the Sixth International Conference on AIDS, San Francisco, June 21, 1990.

7. Questionnaires were discarded as unusable if gender was not indicated (N = 211) or if four or more other demographic items were missing. Most of the questionnaires that had to be discarded for this reason were damaged when the heavily-glued answer sheet was opened at the editorial offices. Thus, the high discard rate does not reflect item nonresponse.

8. Virtually all the men whose sexual identification was "asexual" or missing would be classified as heterosexual based on their responses to items about their sexual behavior, but a comparison of conditional means for 40 key behavioral and demographic items showed them to be too atypical to include with other heterosexuals.

9. The data needed to assign a heterosexual-homosexual rating were available for

56,600 (92.4 percent) of our analysis sample. In some of our analyses, we imputed experiential ratings for an additional 4,629 men (7.6 percent) who answered only one of two pertinent behavioral questions or who provided information on identity from which *probable* homosexual-heterosexual experience could be inferred.

10. The literature suggests that the distribution of number of lifetime sex partners will differ by sexual orientation for those with "more than 60" (Bell and Weinberg, 1978). Our procedure for assigning a score of "51" to all persons in that highest category is therefore conservative and has the effect of lowering the mean number of partners across all groups while minimizing differences between groups.

11. Complete data on all four items were available for 93 percent of all male respondents. For another 6.3 percent, information was missing for only one item. In all but 20 cases, we imputed values for missing items by calculating predicted scores from regression equations combining answers to the other questions. The principal components analysis was done with and without first standardizing scores on individual items for the respondent's age, with virtually identical results; we therefore used unstandardized scores in the multiple partner index.

12. Among bisexually experienced men, answers to this question varied sharply with identity. Thirty-nine percent of heterosexually identified men, 5 percent of bisexually identified men and 4 percent of homosexually identified men indicated that they considered same-gender contact off limits.

13. The sample proportions cited above are probably larger than would be found in the population as a whole, given the *Playboy* sample's underrepresentation of men toward the "predominantly homosexual" end of the behavioral continuum.

14. It may be that bisexual men are less likely to satisfy their appetite with noncommercial encounters of the type readily found in the gay subculture. We note, however, that interpretation of this finding is complicated by the fact that the survey question did not specify the gender of the prostitute.

15. The percentages are the same for those reporting no experience or only one experience.

16. Bell et al. (1981) argue from path analytic results that the causal direction may be different for exclusively homosexual men, whose behavior seems to derive from a deep-seated predisposition, and bisexual men, whose behavior may be more influenced by social and sexual learning.

REFERENCES

Bell, A. P., and Weinberg, M. S. (1978). *Homosexualities: A study of diversity among men and women.* New York. Simon and Schuster.

Bell, A. P., Weinberg, M. S., and Kiefer, S. H. (1981). *Sexual preference: Its development in men and women.* Bloomington, IN: Indiana University Press.

Blumstein, P., and Schwartz P. (1976). Bisexuality in men. *Urban Life,* 5, 339–358.

Chu, S. Y., Doll, L. S., and Buehler, J. S. (1989, October). Epidemiology of AIDS in bisexual males, United States. Abstract of presentation at a workshop on Bisexuality and AIDS, Centers for Disease Control, Atlanta.

DeCecco, J. P. (1990). Sex and more sex: A critique of the Kinsey conception of human sexuality. In D. P. McWhirter, S. A. Sanders, and J. M. Reinisch (Eds.), *Homosexuality/heterosexuality: Concepts of sexual orientation,* (pp. 367–386). New York: Oxford University Press.

Detels, R., English, P., Visscher, B. R. Jacobson, L., Kingsley, L. A., Chmiel, J. S., Dudley J. P., Eldred, L. J., and Ginzburg, H. M. (1989). Seroconversion, sexual activity, and condom use among 2915 HIV seronegative men followed for up to 2 years. *Journal of Acquired Immune Deficiency Syndromes,* 2, 77–83.

Elifson, K W., Boles, J., Sweat, M., Darrow, W. W., Elsea, W., and Green, R M. (1989). Seroprevalence of human immunodeficiency virus among male prostitutes. *New England Journal of Medicine*, 321, 832–833.

Fay, R E., Turner, C. F., Klassen, A. D., Gagnon, J. H. (1989). Prevalence and patterns of same-gender contact among men. *Science*, 243, 338–348.

Gagnon, J. H. (1977). *Human sexualities*. Glenview, IL: Scott, Foresman.

Gagnon, J. H. (1980). Gender preference in erotic relations: The Kinsey scale and sexual scripts. In D. P. McWhirter, S. A. Sanders, and J. M. Reinisch (Eds.), *Homosexuality/heterosexuality: Concepts of sexual orientation*, (pp. 177–207). New York: Oxford University Press.

Gebhard, P. H. (1972). Incidence of overt homosexuality in the United States and Western Europe. In *Final report and background papers*, National Institute of Mental Health Task Force on Homosexuality, Washington. DC.: U. S. Government Printing Office.

Harry, J. (1986). Sampling gay men. *Journal of Sex Research*, 22, 21–34.

Hencken, J. D. (1984). Conceptualizations of homosexual behavior which preclude homosexual self-labeling. *Journal of Homosexuality*, 10, 53–63.

Humphreys, L. (1970). *Tearoom trade: Impersonal sex in public places*. Chicago: Aldine.

Kingsley, L. A., Detels, R., Kaslow, R. Polk, B. F., Rinaldo Jr., C. R. Chmiel, J., Detre, K., Kelsey, S. F., Odaka, N., Ostrow, D., VanRaden, M., and Visscher, B. (1987). Risk factors for seroconversion to human immunodeficiency virus among male homosexuals. *Lancet*, 1, 345–349.

Kinsey, A. C., Pomeroy, W. B., Martin, C. E. (1948). *Sexual behavior in the human male*. Philadelphia: W. B. Saunders.

Klein, F. (1985). Sexual orientation: A multi-variable dynamic process. *Journal of Homosexuality*, 11, 36–49.

Lindner, R. (1948). Sexual behavior in penal institutions. In A. Deutsch (Ed.), *Sex habits of American men*, (pp. 201–215). Englewood Cliffs, NJ: Prentice-Hall.

MacDonald, A. P. (1981). A little bit of lavender goes a long way: A critique of research on sexual orientation. *Journal of Sex Research*, 19, 94–100.

McWhirter, D. P., and Mattison, A. M. (1984). *The male couple: How relationships develop*. Englewood Cliffs, NJ: Prentice-Hall.

Polk, B. F., Fox, R. Brookmeyer, R. Kanchanaraksa, S., Kaslow, R. Visscher, B., Rinaldo, C., and Phair, J. (1987). Predictors of the acquired immunodeficiency syndrome developing in a cohort of seropositive homosexual men. *New England Journal of Medicine*, 316, 63–66.

Reinisch, J. M., Sanders, S. A., and Ziemba-Davis, M. (1988). The study of sexual behavior in relation to the transmission of human immunodeficiency virus: Caveats and recommendations. *American Psychologist*, 43, 921–927.

Reiss Jr, A. J. (1961). The social integration of queers and peers. *Social Problems*, 9, 102–120.

Troiden, R (1974). Homosexual encounters in a highway rest stop. In E. Goode and R. Troiden (Eds.), *Sexual deviance and sexual deviants*, (pp. 211–228). New York: William Morrow.

Turner, C. F., Miller, H. G., and Moses, L. E. (Eds.), (1989). *AIDS sexual behavior and intravenous drug use*. Washington, D.C.: National Academy Press.

Waldorf, D. (1989). *Final report of the gay prostitution, IV drug use and AIDS project*. San Francisco: Institute for Scientific Analysis.

Warren, C. A. B. (1974). *Identity and community in the gay world*. New York: John Wiley and Sons.

Weinberg, M. S., And Williams, C. J. (1974). *Male homosexuals: Problems and adaptations*. New York. Oxford University Press.

Weinberg, T. (1978). On "doing" and "being" gay: Sexual behavior and homosexual male self-identity. *Journal of Homosexuality*, 42, 143–156.

Winkelstein Jr., W., Lyman, D. M., Padian, N., Grant, R. Samuel, M., Wiley, J. A., Anderson, R E., Lang, W., Riggs, J., and Levy, J. A. (1987). Sexual practices and risk of infection by the human immunodeficiency virus. *Journal of the American Medical Association*, 257, 321–325.

Winkelstein Jr., W., Wiley, J. A., Padian, N., Levy, J. (1986). Potential for transmission of AIDS-associated retrovirus from bisexual men in San Francisco to their female sexual contacts. *Journal of the American Medical Association*, 255(7), 901 (letter).

World Almanac and Book of Facts. (1983). New York. Newspaper Enterprise Association.

Zinik G. (1986). Identity conflict or adaptive flexibility: Bisexuality reconsidered. *Journal of Homosexuality*, 11, 7–19.

13

On the Diversity of Love Object Orientations Among Women

Sophie Freud Loewenstein

THERE has been strong agreement in the literature on theory of gender identity and gender role that core gender identity is established for boys and girls during a "critical period" of the first two and a half years of life (Stoller, 1974a). Such a core gender identity is linked with parental socialization practices, interacting with a child's developing cognitive skills, such as the acquisition of language and the concept of object constancy. Once a child labels him/herself boy or girl, he or she will seek similarly labeled models for identification, and start to organize his or her sense of self around this presumably enduring label (Stockard and Johnson, 1980).

Similar theoretical certainty does not exist around the establishment of a heterosexual or homosexual love object orientation. Controversies remain on how such an orientation gets established (Loewenstein, 1980a; Stockard and Johnson, 1980), whether it becomes irreversible at a young age or at any other particular age, and whether true bisexuality exists as a valid category.

The Development of Sexual Orientation

Some social scientists connect gender acquisition with love object orientation, while others see them as quite different learning experiences. Money (1975) affirms the former position, linking early programming of sexual orientation to the formation of gender identity as follows:

> Each person's turn-on has rather fixed boundaries which are set before puberty. . . . They were established in childhood as part of the differentiation of gender identity, by the coding of schemas, and by any quirks or oddities that were incorporated into the schemas. Boundaries may first show themselves at puberty,

but they are not set in puberty, and they don't change much, at puberty or later. (p. 164)

Saghir (1973) also views homosexuality or heterosexuality as an early acquired "basic propensity, a result of developmental and/or genetic influences that in turn determine . . . the predominant sexual psychological responses" (p. 45). Saghir's sample included four women who did not "come out" until middle life, thus contradicting his theory:

> In a small proportion of homosexual women early homosexual responses were absent or were not expressed sexually until a delayed age. Frequently these women got married in late adolescence or early adulthood and remained without homosexual contact until the marriage finally deteriorated and broke up. Then a rediscovery or a new awareness of their dormant homosexual responses occurred. (p. 233)

Saghir thus explains late homosexual emergence by assuming *latent* homosexuality. His wording suggests that these women had had unsatisfactory marriages due to their homosexual predisposition. One could also argue that these women simply turn away from men after being disappointed by their husbands. This would then constitute a case of later rather than latent homosexual disposition, an alternate explanation that would fit the data equally well and avoid the questionable device of reconstructing early biographies to fit changing identities (Berger, 1963, pp. 54–65). This theory of an early immutable onset of sexual orientation cuts across sexual politics and is assumed by advocates as well as fervent enemies of the "homosexuality as pathology" position (Klaich, 1974).

Stockard and Johnson (1980) believe that the development of gender identity in women is composed of two parts: a basic nurturant maternalism, and a subsequent heterosexual orientation. Girls and boys, they suggest, acquire a predisposition to be nurturant and socially connected to other human beings in their early relationship with their mother, while it is the father who teaches heterosexuality to his daughter by interacting with her in special ways. Although these authors emphasize early years, they also consider the development of gender identity to be an ongoing learning process that might misfire if fathers are unavailable, repressive or overly seductive. This view is congruent with the early psychoanalytic position of Helene Deutsch (1944) who also stresses the father's role in the girl's acquisition of "proper femininity."

The psychoanalytic position is thus not one of early determinism of love object orientation. Indeed Anna Freud (1965) argues that final love object orientation is not settled until adolescence. Although, like Stoller (1975b), she considers that a person's Oedipal resolution foreshadows future sexual orientation, she also states, partially quoting her father, that:

> the balance between heterosexuality and homosexuality during the whole period of childhood is precarious, and the scales are so readily tipped in one direction or the other by a multitude of influences, that the opinion still holds good that "a person's final sexual attitude is not decided until after puberty." (p. 197)

Henderson (1984), reflecting on the literature and her own clinical experience, discusses the frequent conflicts about sexual orientation among college students. But even this view that sexual orientation is one aspect of a final identity consolidation in adolescence is now in question. Blumstein and Schwartz (1976) found among their 150 gay men and lesbian women a number of women who switched "from heterosexual behavior and identification to homosexual behavior and identification after a very long and quite satisfactory period in the former category" (p. 172). This led them to question "the immutability of sex-object choice" (p. 173). In a similar vein, other sex researchers (Bell and Weinberg, 1979; Kaye, et al., 1967, p. 630; Riess, 1974, pp. 201–202) found that about half of all lesbian women had engaged in heterosexual intercourse and one-third had been married before defining themselves as lesbians.

The Issue of Bisexuality

The label of bisexual is usually reserved for men and women who have concurrent or rapidly alternating sexual relations with men and women, rather than long-term changes of orientation. The original data of Kinsey, Pomeroy and Martin (1948, pp. 650–651) and Kinsey, Pomeroy, Martin and Gebhard (1953, pp. 473–474) showing frequent bisexual behavior among men and women have been repeatedly confirmed. Blumstein and Schwartz (1976) for example, found a variety of bisexual patterns in their sample.

Other sex researchers reject the concept of bisexuality. Thus, Saghir (1973) dismisses sexual behavior that is incongruent with a person's self-definition as contrary to a person's "real" inclinations, calling such behavior "situational" or "limited" experimentation (p. 262). He explains Kinsey's findings of a continuum of sexual behavior in the population by making a "sharp distinction between homosexual and heterosexual behavior and homosexuality and heterosexuality" (p. 44). He believes that the concept of bisexuality lacks psychological credibility and that heterosexual involvements of lesbians are basically ungratifying. He states that "among most homosexuals, heterosexual involvement is not an indication of 'bisexual' psychological tendencies but the result of personal and social expectations" (p. 242). Thus Saghir questions women's capacity for emotional involvement with both men and women, admitting only to a limited physical bisexual willingness for sexual intercourse.

On the other hand Rich (1980) has stated that mother-reared women all had a woman as their first love object and that all women have a core of homosexual potential that patriarchal society tries to combat through its elaborate institutionalized insistence on heterosexuality.

This article examines survey data on the passionate love experiences of women in relation to: (1) the age of establishment of gender love orientation and its reversible or irreversible nature; and (2) the existence of authentic bisexuality. The survey was an exploration of emotional passions, the experience of "falling in love" that may or may not have been accompanied by sexual expression. If it can be demonstrated that some self-defined straight or gay women have a history of falling in love with both women and men, it would suggest that at least some women have the capacity for emotional bisexuality. This would then suggest that Kinsey's continuum of sexual orientation exists not only in the physical and behavioral but also in the emotional realm. The article will also examine, within the limitations of the data, whether women who become lesbians well after adolescence had given any prior evidence of dormant homosexuality, or whether the evidence points to a true change in love object orientation for some women.

Description of the Survey

Seven hundred and three women drawn between 1977 to 1979 from the author's social work classes, evening university classes, lecture audiences and friendship networks, completed an anonymous questionnaire regarding the nature of their major passionate love experiences. Passion was defined as an intense and obsessive emotion of constant yearning for and intense preoccupation with a love object, with or without sexual aspects. Respondents were instructed to count only experiences that had had a significant place in their lives and when a relationship to a real person was involved; but not to include affectionate loving experiences that did not include passion. Reports of strong emotional attraction were studied and differentiated from conventional marriages or sexual experimentation not accompanied by passion.

Subjects were asked for the gender of the person for whom they had felt each passion, the subject's age at that time, the circumstances surrounding the relationship, whether or not the passion had been sexually consummated, and the short- and long-range consequences. Short-range consequences included marriage to the love object, threat to an existing marriage, physical illness, seeking psychiatric help, and a range of emotional reactions. Long-range consequences included continuation of the passion, damaged marriage, improved marriage, loss of self-esteem, greater autonomy, increased compassion, and continuing friendship with the love object. Subjects were also asked for a description of their current or last committed relationship, which they might or might not consider a passion experience.

The questionnaires included both pre-coded and open-ended questions. They were supplemented by 25 individual interviews with selected respondents, in which responses to the questionnaires were amplified.

The ages of the women ranged from 17 to 84, with a mean age of 35. Their education ranged from high-school graduates to Ph.D. degrees, with a preponderance of college-educated women.

Since this was an opportunity sample, no conclusions can be drawn as to the frequency of particular behavior patterns in the larger population. This exploratory study simply identified certain behavior patterns and relied on the respondents' subjective and often vivid and detailed self-reports to illustrate how women make meaning out of their own life experiences.

FINDINGS

The 703 respondent women, by self-definition, fell into the three broad categories of heterosexual, bisexual and lesbian. They are further classified on the basis of their passion experiences.

The 676 heterosexually oriented women varied in their passion experiences as follows:

1. Five hundred and seventy-five had had one or more sexual or non-sexual passions for men, but no passions for women.
2. Sixty-eight had never experienced a passion.
3. Twenty-four had experienced at least one sexual passion for a man and at least one nonsexual passion for a woman.
4. Nine had experienced at least one sexual passion for a man and at least one non-sexual passion for a woman.

Six respondents were women who defined themselves as bisexual. Each had had at least one sexual passion for a person of each gender.

Twenty-one women were self-defined lesbians. Within this group:

1. Eleven had had one or more sexual passions for a woman.
2. Eight had had one or more sexual passions for persons of each gender.
3. Two had had one or more sexual passions for women and a non-sexual passion for a man.

HETEROSEXUAL WOMEN WITH MALE-ONLY PASSION EXPERIENCES

Eight out of ten respondents were in this category. They reported a range of from one to nine passions. The mean and mode were two passions. There were no differences between heterosexual and non-heterosexual women in the number of passion experiences, age at the time of passions, circumstances or consequences.

Intense same-gender friendships in early adolescence are common (Freud, 1965, p. 189). It is possible that many of these women had had such passionate relationships with girlfriends but did not report them in the questionnaire because our heterosexually oriented culture teaches women to discount these experiences. Individual interviews evoked some of these non-sexual adolescent passions, however, giving support to this supposition.

HETEROSEXUAL WOMEN WITHOUT PASSION EXPERIENCES

Sixty-eight women, some married and some unmarried, reported that they were aware of, but had never felt a passion as described in the questionnaire.

HETEROSEXUAL WOMEN WITH NON-SEXUAL PASSIONS FOR WOMEN

Twenty-four heterosexual women reported a non-sexual passion for another woman, and one woman had two such experiences. For two of these women, one aged 25 and the other 19, this had been the only passion of their lives. The others had also had sexual or non-sexual passions for men. Eleven women were less than twenty years old at the time of their woman-oriented passion, the others began their passion from age 25 to 35.

Nine described their passion as a positive experience in which they idolized a teacher, camp counselor or mentor, or loved peers, college roommates or work colleagues. They referred to these relationships as intense friendships. Because western culture permits considerable emotional and physical intimacy between women before labelling it homosexual, these non-sexually expressed passions for women could be integrated into a heterosexual identity without arousing guilt or conflict. These women describe their experiences as joyful, pleasant, confusing, or as having painful memories, but never in more sombre terms.

In contrast, ten others in the group did express considerable emotional turmoil in relation to non-sexual women-oriented passions. Frequently reported short-range consequences included despair, damaged self-esteem, and identity crises. Six of the ten women sought psychiatric help as a direct consequence of the emotional upset arising from their relationship with another woman. This compares with the one-quarter of all women in the sample who sought help in connection with a passion experience. The following examples, with some respondents' occupations modified to disguise their identity, illustrate the kind of distress they suffered.

A 27-year-old married social work student wrote about a four-month passion for a woman. This happened at age 24 while she was still single and working at her first job. She experienced much confusion and "fuller awareness of self and my bisexual nature," leading to a decision to seek psychiatric help.

A 26-year-old woman described her involvement with a heterosexual couple when she was 19. She became more obsessed with the other woman than with the man for whom they were competing. After the triangle dissolved, she felt both rage and despair.

A 53-year-old sociologist described her youthful passion for her female employer, for whom she worked as governess, as having caused her much anguish: "I concealed my feelings and always felt a secret grief."

A 30-year-old married former nun writes of a two-year passionate attraction to another nun that led to her own dismissal from the convent at age 19.

A 55-year-old artist tells of a baffling relationship to a woman mentor when she was 27. She was absorbed by her love for this older woman. Although she defined herself and was seen by others as a loving wife and mother, this relationship overshadowed all others in her life. Her love for this woman had remained undeclared and she became severely depressed.

Heterosexual Women with Sexual Passions for Other Women

Nine women who defined themselves as heterosexual had been involved in a sexually expressed passion for another woman. The ages of the women at the time of the experience ranged from 19 to 38 years. For three women this passion was their first sexual encounter, to be followed later by passionate sexual encounters with men. Four women expressed shame and discomfort about this experience.

A 28-year-old public school teacher explained that her two year long lesbian relationship occurred in college at a time of great loneliness, and disintegrated when her life became fuller and happier. She was, at the time of reporting, enthusiastic about her current committed heterosexual relationship.

A 47-year-old housewife had a three month long passion at age 38 when she was "bored with life—looking for kicks." The relationship left her with intense guilt and she felt used and exploited by the other woman.

Another woman had a year-long sexual passion at age 35 while she was teaching as a nun. The experience was extremely unsettling to her and she sought psychiatric treatment. She describes herself as happily married but with a "sexual hang-up because of my religious background and my first passion experience. . . ."

The fourth woman in this group came to her sexual passion for a woman at age 20 after a non-sexual passion for a man in adolescence and a sexually consummated passion for a man who later rejected her. It was a long and turbulent relationship in which she was never able to accept her lesbian attraction and involvement. Her earlier passionate relationship with a man became important in resolving her lesbian experience.

Three women had sexual passions that ended in friendship. They regarded their involvement primarily as a useful learning experience.

The lesbian passion experiences of the seven primarily heterosexual women described above were secondary and hence might not be described as true bisexuality. The perspective of the two other women in this group is different. Their lesbian passion was a highly positive experience and a major life event.

A 23-year-old dance therapist wrote: "I realized my capacity for passion with a woman is probably greater than with men though I choose to live with a man. I become too dependent on women. The experience of passion for a woman was both the most frightening and in some ways the most fulfilling experience of my life." A 30-year-old nursery school teacher had a devastating lesbian passion, her first love, at age 19. She felt rejected and experienced great despair, leading her to seek psychiatric treatment. In retrospect she felt that the emotional growth had been worth the pain. Her later passion experiences were heterosexual: "The first and last were the most important. The first because I learned there about loving and being loved—that I was capable of both—because it helped me move away from home, because it gave me my first experience of deep friendship."

It would be difficult to determine the fundamental sexual inclination of these two women.

SELF-DEFINED BISEXUAL WOMEN WITH WOMEN- AND MEN-DIRECTED SEXUAL PASSIONS

Six women had alternate or simultaneous love experiences with men and women. They seemed open to both kinds of love relationships and defined themselves as bisexual rather than heterosexual or lesbian. Were these really lesbian women experimenting with heterosexual encounters, or vice-versa? The following brief profiles provide some basis for judgement. The six women ranged in age from 18 to 38. Two were divorced and four had never married.

An 18-year-old college student reported a lesbian passion at age 17, when she was beginning college. The break-up of the relationship after seven months left her with despair and suicidal thoughts. Like most other straight and gay women, she later felt enriched by the experience: "My one passion was one of the most important experiences of my life. I learned a lot about myself and others. I learned that I was capable of loving and being loved. . . . I think I will always cherish this relationship—I hope for another passion in the future with another person. One I can be certain of."

A 23-year-old librarian, reported a one-year-long sexual passion for a man at age 20, followed by an eighteen-month passion for a woman. Her heterosexual passion ended with rage and damaged self-esteem and led her into psychiatric treatment. The lesbian passion appeared to have been less painful.

A 29-year-old clerical worker, described a non-sexual passion for a man at age 21 and a sexual passion for a man a year later, both of them largely positive experiences. At the time of completing the questionnaire, she was involved with both a man and a woman: "My two current relationships are both joyful experiences; I enjoy the freedom these people have taught me."

A 30-year-old social worker wrote of a first heterosexual passion at 22 which made her realize "the height my feelings could reach." She experienced much pain when he rejected her after two years, feeling that it "made marriage to someone else hard." Her subsequent passionless marriage lasted two years. At age 30 she experienced a turbulent and ultimately disappointing eight-month passion for another woman. She writes a year later, "My present relationship is with another woman. I think I am finding over the past two years more possibility for real passion between women than between men and women."

These women have not developed an exclusive sexual inclination to either gender and may continue relationships with both women and men. It would be incorrect to label them as heterosexuals or lesbians as they have the potential for an equally passionate commitment to either a man or a woman. It should also be noted that their relationships are marked by turbulence, distress and confusion as they search for stability and happiness. Whether this is a reflection of their particular psyche or the difficulty in trying to maintain a bisexual position in a society that polarizes people into straight or gay is an open question.

SELF-IDENTIFIED LESBIAN WOMEN WITH HETEROSEXUAL PASSION EXPERIENCES

While many lesbian women have had heterosexual relationships and even marriages, the emotional significance of these experiences has not been clarified. Ten of the 21 lesbian women in this sample reported passionate heterosexual involvements. This group is the counterpart to straight women with lesbian experiences.

Seven of these ten lesbian women had been married and divorced but in no case was their husband the object of their heterosexual passion. Two reported only non-sexual passions with men in early adolescence, one with a classmate and the other with a college professor. Both went on to have much more significant relationships with women.

Four women in this group report experiences with men that were significant and extensive, but without major impact on their lives. Two were divorced professional women. They each described an extended passionate affair during their disappointing marriage. One woman's affair broke up after three years because "he decided he could no longer deal with the intensity of the affair." The other's terminated because "he left when I was serious." Both reported despair, suicidal thoughts and damaged self-esteem as short-range consequences of their heterosexual passions. One also noted emotional illness for which she sought psychiatric help. Both subsequently turned to equally passionate and turbulent relationships with a woman. One wrote: "My most recent relationship lasted five years—[it] was a passionate, intense loving relationship but involved many conflicts and several separations. This was the most satisfying love of my life and also most painful. I now identify as a lesbian as a result of this relationship."

Intensity of emotions is a leitmotif in the lives of lesbian women, and the men in their lives seem unprepared to sustain such intense relationships. Perhaps great intensity in relationships with men is easier to sustain in the realm of passion than in the everyday life of marriage.

Two single respondents reported their first sexual passion with a man, although one had had a prior non-sexual attraction for a woman friend at college that was both turbulent and consuming. Their passions for men, each of several years duration, proved to be highly disappointing and they both subsequently turned to women.

The fifth, a business woman, went through a passionless marriage, followed by a series of four passions during her 30s. The first two were heterosexual, the next two lesbian, each lasting from six months to a year, and all terminated by herself. She felt "a need to combat the chaotic effect of passion on the stable and important parts of my life." Her subsequent relationship with a woman was characterized by "shared affection, ideas and companionship" rather than passion.

The last three women in this group had the most serious involvement with men. One, a psychologist, had at age 34 openly assumed a lesbian identity. She recalled her intense crushes for men and women teachers during adolescence. At age 19 her intimate girl-friendship of many years began to include sexual love and did so for two years. She was not ready to commit herself to a lesbian lifestyle, but when her lover left her, she went into a deep depression and sought psychiatric treatment. She then had a series of sexual affairs with both men and women. At age 24, just before entering graduate school, she fell passionately in love with a young man and was ready to give up professional training in order to travel with him. He simply disappeared one day, and she again became severely depressed. A year later she fell in love with another man whom she hoped to marry. She felt he could not tolerate true intimacy, however, and that he precipitated fights whenever their relationship became too close. She finally terminated the relationship and a sense of relief soon overshadowed her grief. She continued her urgent search for a suitable man to love and marry and had several abortive heterosexual relationships. A year before the interview, at age 33, she started a mutually passionate love relationship with a woman. She then defined herself as a lesbian and established a common household with her lover.

Two other respondents in this group are middle-aged academics. One reported a non-sexual passion for a woman teacher all through high school. Both women fell passionately in love at age 20 with men who eventually rejected them. One recalled despair and emotional illness for which she sought psychiatric treatment. The other was pregnant when she was abandoned and attempted suicide. Both these women later contracted passionless but friendly marriages and went on to have children. Some years later, one at age 33 and the other at 47, each fell in love with a woman. One described this experience as waking up and becoming alive after many years of emotional deadness. The other wrote: "This passion was so overwhelming I hesitate to call previous ones passion. It made me understand what others have felt along that line—I previously had thought it did not exist." These two women were emotionally so shaken by their passions that they could no longer tolerate the devitalized nature of their marriages and they both divorced. One reported: "I'm in the process of getting divorced—our lives, friends, are too disparate; the prospect of remaining together was depressing and of greater weight than the pains of leaving and lessening each of our time with our daughter." Both women subsequently assumed a lesbian lifestyle.

SELF-IDENTIFIED LESBIAN WOMEN

Eleven women in the sample loved women exclusively and reported no passions for men. They ranged in age from 23 to 41. Only one of them had been married but she divorced after 19 years of a "lousy" union. She initiated the divorce when her nine-year-long passion with another married woman terminated.

Although none of the other women in this category had been married, and none had had a heterosexual passion, several reported casual or even prolonged relationships with men. A 29-year-old nurse presented a history of falling in love with girlfriends and women teachers all through her school years. Nonetheless, through junior high school and high school she had longed for a relationship with a boy and felt great anguish about being "unpopular." She started heterosexual dating in college and eventually paired for three years with a young man who was passionately in love with her. The relationship was one of support and affection for her that involved no real passion. She was increasingly alienated by his jealousy, possessiveness, and periodic bouts of depression. Eventually, at age 25, she had an extremely passionate and anguished relationship with a woman and lost interest in maintaining her heterosexual relationship. Henceforth, she defined herself as a lesbian.

A twenty-three-year-old potter who reported only lesbian passions wrote that "I lived for one and one-half years with a man and in the beginning it was a good relationship. I realized through the little problems that I was expecting and wanting a relationship with a woman. The man—with his own problems—was acting as odd as I am sure I was acting and it ended. We are now friends."

In contrast to some of the women described earlier, it is in this group that we find women whose heterosexuality was quite circumscribed and apparently mechanical.

"Coming Out" After Thirty

Among the 21 lesbian women and six bisexual women were seven who had their first love experience with a woman after age 30. It is a temptation to say that the two women academics described above had finally discovered their true sexual inclination, especially in view of their intense emotional responses. If their youthful lovers had not disappointed them, however, their potential for lesbian love might never have emerged.

Another woman who changed from a bisexual to a lesbian identity at age 33 felt that she was open to both kinds of relationships and that either a man or a woman might have met her need for a steady, loving and fulfilling relationship. Labeling her as a basically lesbian woman who finally found herself does not match her own self-evaluation.

Two others also came to lesbianism in their 30s after disappointing relationships with husbands and lovers. Here again, the assumption of a basic lesbian orientation is not supportable. This group of women with delayed passionate involvement with women also includes the social worker who had her first such experience at 30 and still felt open to change, as well as the business woman with four passion experiences in her 30s, including a first involvement with a woman at age 34. In addition there were occasional descriptions of respondents' lovers as late emerging former heterosexual women.

The Nature of Lesbian Passion

The reports of the 21 self-defined lesbian women reveals something about the nature of lesbian passions. Radical feminists have been critical of traditional romantic love between men and women. They suggest that it has been invented to serve "the function of legitimating and reinforcing male hegemony" (Rapaport, 1976, p. 194) and they deplore the dependency relationship set up by romantic love. "There is something wrong with love in addition to sexual oppression. It is a dependency relation which robs the lover of its autonomy" writes Rapaport (1976, p. 190) quoting Atkinson. A radical feminist professor of literature who was a respondent in this study called passion "the most devastating manifestation of bourgeois individualism."

It is interesting, therefore, to point out that the respondents' feelings and comments about their lesbian love were undistinguishable from their emotions about heterosexual love, if personal pronouns were eliminated. There are the same expressions of ecstasy, joy, anguish and suffering regardless of the gender of the love object. Each of the comments made by the exclusively lesbian women about their passions could be matched by a similar comment made by a straight woman about a heterosexual passion.

Discussion of Findings

On Bisexuality

The data on the six women who defined themselves as bisexual, together with a data on the 33 heterosexual women who had experienced sexual or non-sexual passions for women and the ten lesbian women who had had sexual or non-sexual passions for men supports the validity of a bisexual orientation as a category that is different from a purely homosexual orientation. These bisexual women have no clear gender preference in their love affairs, and their passionate relationships to men and women could not be distinguished by personal meaningfulness or emotional significance, or even pure physical pleasure. Their bisexuality transcended mere physical experimentation into the realm of emotional passion.

There would be no good reason to classify a bisexual orientation as one particular form of homosexuality, except for our society's preference for dichotomous categories, even when many people do not fit into them, and for the tendency to assign non-matching, "mixed" people into the "less honorable" category. In the same manner racial categories of black and white have been invented and people of mixed racial heritage have been assigned to the black category. Even if such people "look white" they are known as blacks who "pass as whites." This is a striking analogy to the assignment of bisexual people into the homosexual category.

Personal interviews and a careful reading of the questionnaires of women who showed a shifting unsettled sexual orientation did not suggest that these women were deviant in other ways. The survey data bear out Kinsey's contention that sexual love object orientations exist on a continuum rather than as a dichotomy, making Saghir's distinction between overt behavior and basic predispositions meaningless.

On Changing Love Object Orientation

The data support the position of a number of sex researchers, including Saghir, that it is not unusual for lesbian women to have had a history of heterosexual intercourse. The excerpts from interviews quoted above demonstrate that these heterosexual contacts transcended physical experimentation or conformity to social expectations. They were emotionally meaningful and highly intense passion experiences. The data are consistent with Saghir's observations about the mediocre quality of lesbian women's marriages, but a number of the women in this study who defined themselves as lesbians had significant love relationships with men, albeit outside of marriage. Saghir's contention that lesbians typically have no involvement with men, even if they have a history of sexual contact may apply to some women, but certainly not to all.

There were seven women who had their first lesbian experience after thirty, each of them having already lived through important heterosexual passions before they assumed the identity of lesbian. This phenomenon of change in later years has also been noted by Blumstein and Schwartz (1976). It is also confirmed by anecdotal evidence of midlife divorced or widowed women who create households with women partners that include sexual cohabitation. The data suggest the importance of life circumstances in some of the shifts. A number of late-emerging lesbians had earlier disappointing experiences with men. It remains an open question whether these disappointments were created by an early predisposition for latent homosexuality, or whether the disappointments contributed to their changed self-definition.

The behavioral descriptions of these relationships are more congruent with a genuine shift in love object orientation, suggesting a somewhat fluid gender orientation for women. The data of this survey supports the conclusion that sexual love object orientation is not necessarily a basic propensity that is irreversibly set in infancy or even in adolescence. Some respondents were bona fide heterosexual women who switched in midlife to a lesbian orientation. This leads to the hypothesis that love object orientation is not necessarily a core aspect of female identity.

Conclusion

The diversity of women's lifestyles found in this survey may always have existed in secret, or it may be a new phenomenon. If it is the latter, we can speculate on the reasons. Could it be that the greater diversity of child rearing patterns in our society create more varied personality types? Or is it, more likely, a reaction to the prevailing social climate, outer space creating inner space (Loewenstein, 1979)?

There is evidence (Brim and Kagan, 1980) that there is much less continuity in intelligence or emotional attributes throughout life than used to be assumed, and that, moreover, some of the continuities that are found are located in the sociocultural environment rather than in the individual. This could well be true for gender orientation as well.

Today's protean men and women respond to the rapid cultural changes by adopting more fluid identities. Women and men no longer expect that marriage will necessarily last a lifetime. Careers are now changed in midlife, and sometimes more than once. People take advantage, either deliberately or inadvertently, of new options and opportunities for self-expression and lifestyles that a more diverse society makes available to them. The apparent greater fluidity of love object orientation than has formerly been assumed, challenges early deterministic theories.

The more we learn about people's true private lives, the less do we find that their most intimate personal behavior conforms to conventional societal images. It was not long ago that we were titillated by Eleanor Roosevelt's passionate letters to her friend Lorena Hickok (Faber, 1979). Then we were informed that Margaret Mead led a bisexual life (Bateson, 1984). As we learn more about people's actual lives, we realize that our textbooks give us outdated or false images of human behavior and that the concept of "normality" needs to be expanded and revised. All of us, social workers, academicians, students of human development and enlightened citizens need to heighten our awareness of the great diversity of human behavior and human experience.

REFERENCES

Bateson. M. C. (1984). *With a daughter's eye*. New York: William Morrow.

Bell, A., and Weinberg, M. S. (1978). *Homosexualities*. New York: Simon and Schuster.

Berger, P. (1963). *Invitation to sociology*. Garden City, N.Y.: Anchor Books.

Blumstein, P., and Schwartz, P. (1976). Bisexuality in women. *Archives of Sexual Behavior*. 5, 1971–181.

Brim, O. G., and Kagan, J. (Eds.). (1980). *Constancy and change in human development*. Cambridge, MA: Harvard University Press.

Deutsch, H. (1944). *The psychology of women*. New York: Grune and Stratton.

Faber, D. (1979). *The life of Lorena Hickok: E R.'s friend*. New York: William Morrow.

Freud, A. (1965). *Normality and pathology in childhood*. New York: International Universities Press.

Henderson, A. (1984). Homosexuality in the college years: Developmental differences between men and women. *Journal of American College Health*, 32, 216–219.

Kaye, H. E., Berl, S., Clare, J., Eleston, M. R. Gershwin, B. S., Gershwin, P., Kogan, L. S. and Torda, C. (1967). Homosexuality in women. *Archives of General Psychiatry*, 17, 626–634.

Kinsey, A. C., Pomeroy, W. B., and Martin, C. E. (1948). *Sexual behavior in the human male*. Philadelphia: Saunders.

Kinsey, A. C., Pomeroy, W. B., Martin, C. E., and Gebhard, P. H. (1953). *Sexual behavior in the human female*. Philadelphia: Saunders.

Klaich, D. (1974). *Woman plus woman*. New York: Simon and Schuster.

Loewenstein, S. F. (1979). Inner and outer space in social casework. *Social Casework*, 60, 19–29.

Loewenstein, S. F. (1980). Passion as a mental health hazard. In C. L. Heckerman (Ed.) *The evolving female*. New York. Human Sciences Press.

Loewenstein, S. F. (1980). Understanding lesbian women. *Social Casework*, 61, 29–38.

Money, J., and Tucker, P. (1975). *Sexual signatures*. Boston: Little, Brown.

Rapaport, E. (1976). On the future of love: Rousseau and the radical feminists. In C. Gould and M. Wartofsky (Eds.), *Women and philosophy*. New York. Putnam and Sons.

Rich, A. (1980). Compulsive [sic] heterosexuality and lesbian existence. *Signs*, 5, 631–660.

Riess, B. (1974). New viewpoints on the female homosexual. In V. Franks and V. Burtle (Eds.), *Women in therapy*. New York: Brunner/Mazel.

Saghir, M. T., and Robins, E. (1973). *Male and female homosexuality*. Baltimore: Williams and Wilkins.

Stockard, J., and Johnson, M. (1980). *Sex roles*. Englewood Cliffs, NJH: Prentice-Hall.

Stoller, R. (1974). Facts and fancies: An examination of Freud's concept of bisexuality. In J. Strouse (Ed.), *Women and analysis*. New York: Grossman.

Stoller, R. (1974). *Sex and gender, vol. 1*. New York: Jason Aronson.

PART TWO

From Lesbian Strippers and Prison Punks to Bisexual Subjects: The History of a Research Literature

4
Looking at the Past Through Bi-Colored Glasses

As shown in part 1 of this volume, criticisms of research on sexuality for its neglect of bisexuality arose in the early 1980s, followed by efforts to develop alternatives to the dichotomous model of sexuality that was partially responsible for this neglect and an amassing of statistics on the prevalence of bisexuality for the purpose of stimulating research on the subject. Research on bisexual behavior did occur before the 1980s; it simply was not usually identified as such. Part 2 traces the development of the research literature on bisexuality, from research on "situational homosexuality" in the 1960s and 1970s, and persistent research on "homosexual behavior among heterosexuals" and "heterosexual behavior among gays and lesbians," through the pioneering work on bisexuality in the late 1970s, AIDS-motivated research of the 1980s, and contemporary research on the bisexual experience.

14

Academic Literature on Situational Homosexuality in the 1960s and 1970s

Paula C. Rodríguez Rust

ALTHOUGH bisexuality per se received almost no attention from either theorists or researchers in the United States before the late 1970s, and the contemporary wave of research on bisexuality did not begin until the mid 1980s, many researchers studied bisexual behavior in the 1960s and 1970s under the guise of "situational homosexuality." Because same-sex[1] sexual behavior was still viewed as pathological by some researchers and negative public attitudes kept healthy lesbians and gay men closeted and unavailable as research subjects, sex researchers who were interested in studying same-sex sexual behavior often looked for it—or found it unexpectedly—in unusual social situations such as prisons and the underworld of prostitution. Some of the people studied in these situations were considered homosexual, lesbian, or gay, whereas others were considered heterosexuals who were forced by situational constraints—such as the single sex environment of the prison—to make do with same-sex sexual behavior. In hindsight sex researchers today would consider many of the subjects in these studies technical bisexuals. Although this research would not turn up in a computerized search for literature on "bisexuality," and was not thought of as such by its authors, it is, therefore, a chapter in the history of the study of bisexuality.[2]

Situational Homosexuality in Prisons

Researchers who studied same-sex sexual behavior in prisons, particularly among male prisoners, varied in their conclusions about the prevalence of this behavior among inmates, the degree of coerciveness involved, the motivation for the behavior, and the meaning and implications of prison same-sex experiences for the sexual lives of inmates. For example, one of the most in-depth studies of prison sexuality,

Men Behind Bars: Sexual Exploitation in Prison by Wayne S. Wooden and Jay Parker
(1982), focused primarily on coercive sexual behavior because of the authors' humanitarian concerns about the sexual exploitation of prisoners, thereby highlighting the phenomenon of same-sex sexual behavior among previously heterosexual
prisoners. Leo Carroll (1977), Alan J. Davis (1968, 1970), Daniel Lockwood (1980),
Peter L. Nacci (1978), Nacci and Thomas R. Kane (1984), Michael Schofield (1965a),
Anthony M. Scacco Jr. (1975), and Lee H. Bowker (1980) also focused on this aspect
of male prison sexuality. Schofield wrote that "it is well known that many [non-
homosexual offenders] will take part in homosexual activities" (1965a:158) and
Davis was "struck by the fact that the typical sexual aggressor does not consider
himself a homosexual or even to be engaging in homosexual activity" (1968:37).

   In contrast, Edwin Johnson (1971), writing from his own three years of experience as a maximum security prison inmate, saw homosexuality in prison not as a
disruptive force or a source of violence but as a stabilizing force promoting social
order and "sanity." Johnson reported that an inmate code against homosexual rape
—an imported version of the code against the rape of women in free society—
protects "core" inmates from sexual assault under an inmate-enforced penalty of
death to the aggressor. Only new or young inmates are unprotected by this code
and hence subject to sexual assault. Kinsey, Pomeroy, and Martin (1948), whose
studies of male sexual behavior included the study of sexual behavior among prisoners, and John H. Gagnon and William Simon (1968), whose observations were
also based on research conducted at the (Kinsey) Institute for Sex Research, emphasized the ability of men to adjust to conditions of sexual deprivation such as are
found in a prison by reducing rather than changing their sexual activities. Gagnon
and Simon described prison same-sex rape as "rare" (1973:249). Richard Tewksbury
(1989a, 1989b) and Philip Feldman (1984) downplayed the difference between the
sexual behavior of inmates and that of the general population, including the percentage of inmates who had their first same-sex sexual experience in prison.
Tewksbury accused previous researchers of overemphasizing both the prevalence
of male prison same-sex sexual behavior and its coerciveness at the expense of attention to other sexual activities that occur in men's prisons such as masturbation
and wet dreams.

   The emphasis on sexual assault and on same-sex sexual activity among heterosexual prisoners by some researchers appears largely due to a receptive social and
political climate for this topic in the late 1960s and early 1970s. For example, Davis
(1968) reported that recent publicity surrounding a series of same-sex rapes of men
being transported in sheriff's vans led to his appointment by Judge Barbieri to investigate sexual assault in Philadelphia prisons. Arno Karlen, a journalist whose
goal in publishing *Sexuality and Homosexuality: A New View* in 1971 was to educate a
lay audience about current scientific knowledge about sexuality, likewise attributed researchers' interest in the exploitative side of prison sexuality to journalistic
sensationalism. He recalled that a late 1960s journalistic "exposé of Philadelphia
prisons as 'sodomy factories,'" which followed the "vivid" dramatic production
Fortune and Men's Eyes, had focused national attention on the issue (1971:xv, 554).
In the opening sentence of an article reprinted as chapter 15 in this section George

L. Kirkham also alluded to media publicity (1971:325). Scacco (1975), who provided an extensive review of both academic and popular literature on prison sexuality before 1975, cited several mainstream news stories on the topic, for example, "The terrifying homosexual world of the jail system" by Linda Charlton (1971). A few years later a series of eight inmate murders in the U.S. Penitentiary at Lewisburg between March 1974 and May 1976 led to establishment of a special task force whose findings included a "link" between homosexual activity and prison violence, and a subsequent national investigation by Federal Prison System researchers (Nacci 1978; Nacci and Kane 1983, 1984).

Findings regarding sexual behavior in women's prisons are less controversial. Despite cultural images of the butch lesbian and the aggressive female offender that resonate to produce a racially tinged image of the "aggressive prison lesbian" (Freedman 1996), researchers generally agree that coercion is extremely rare in women's prisons.[3] Accounts of women's prisons universally describe sexual behavior as occurring within the context of complex "fictive kin" relationships that promote social order and cohesion through the establishment of rules for social interaction in women's prisons, an observation conspicuously absent in accounts of men's prisons with the exception of Johnson's (1971) firsthand account. Researchers also agree that a high percentage of previously heterosexual women engage in same-sex sexual behavior and romantic relationships while incarcerated but that most return to a heterosexual existence following release.

Prison Sexual Subculture: A Look at Sexuality in Another World

Understanding the sexual behavior of prisoners requires an understanding of prison sexual subculture. Three of the earliest studies of men's prisons, *The Prison Community* by Donald Clemmer (1958a),[4] *The Society of Captives* by Gresham Sykes (1956),[5] and the aforementioned *Sexual Assaults in the Philadelphia Prison System* by Davis (1968), touched briefly on the subculture that organizes and supports sexual activity in prisons. Drawing on Sykes (1956), Clemmer (1958a), and others, Kirkham (1971) provided a detailed description of the sexual roles and relationships in men's prisons, including a discussion of prison argot and attitudes toward the men who take the various roles. Although lacking a formal recounting of methodology and presentation of findings, Kirkham's article is also informed by his own two years of research at "a major California prison." Also lacking in formal methodology is Johnson's (1971) aforementioned description of the social organization of and circumstances surrounding same-sex prison laiasons; based on his own experience as an inmate, Johnson's account differs dramatically in both content and analysis from the accounts published by social scientific researchers. Published a decade later, Wooden and Parker's (1982) *Men Behind Bars* contains more ethnographic description and quantitative information on prison sexuality than earlier studies. Wooden and Parker drew on information they gathered via questionnaires and interviews conducted in 1979 and 1980 to describe the sexual roles available in male prison subculture.

The sexual subculture in women's prisons has been investigated by David A. Ward and Gene G. Kassebaum (1965, see also 1964), Rose Giallombardo (1966a, see also 1966b), Alice M. Propper (1978, 1981), and Kathryn Watterson Burkhart ([1973] 1996).[6] Ward and Kassebaum (1965) studied the social "types," or roles, in a women's prison, reporting in *Women's Prison: Sex and Social Structure* that the most important social distinctions revolve around involvement in same-sex sexual behavior. They interviewed 45 inmates recruited through quota sampling and referrals, collected 293 questionnaires from 389 randomly selected inmates and 64 questionnaires from staff, and gained access to official inmate records at the California Institution for Women, Frontera, California. Giallombardo, in her classic *Society of Women: A Study of a Women's Prison*, described the Federal Reformatory for Women at Alderson, West Virginia, from a sociological perspective, including the sociosexual roles available in the prison culture. She based her findings on interviews and participant observation research conducted between July 1962 and July 1963.[7] Alice M. Propper began her research on girls in the juvenile justice system in 1971, publishing *Prison Homosexuality: Myth and Reality* in 1981. Propper's findings are based on surveys of the staff and inmate populations of four female and three "coed" institutions or residential training schools chosen through a multistage probability sampling of states and correctional programs. Burkhart's *Women in Prison: Inside the Concrete Womb* was first published in 1973, then revised and republished in 1996 after follow-up research. Prior to the 1973 publication Burkhart visited twenty-one jails and prisons housing women, including county, state, and federal prisons and jails, and some prisons and jails for men and juveniles. She interviewed four hundred women in depth and talked with hundreds more.

Because the Kirkham, Wooden and Parker, Ward and Kassebaum, Giallombardo, and Burkhart studies are all fifteen to thirty years old, their relevance as part of the history of literature on bisexuality might be greater than their value as contemporary descriptions of prison sexual behavior. They might not be entirely antiquated, however; in her research update Burkhart (1996) reported finding that little change had occurred in prison life during the preceding two decades.

In men's prisons men who have sex with men while in prison can be grouped into four categories: the *queen* or *sissy*, the *homosexual* or *gay*, the *kid* or *punk*, and the *jocker* or *stud* (Wooden and Parker 1982).[8] Queens and gays, also called "fags" and "fairies," are self-identified homosexuals or transsexuals who play a range of sexual and gender-typed roles in prison. Punks and jockers, also referred to as "lambs" and "wolves," consider themselves heterosexual, or sometimes bisexual, outside prison but engage in male-male sex within prison.[9] Punks, or "pressure punks," are men who are "turned out" in prison and forced to assume a sexually submissive and socially feminine role. Jockers are men who assume a masculine social and sexual role in prison; they are the ones who turn out the punks. Often, a punk or homosexual will pair or "hook up" with a jocker for protection from the aggressive sexual advances of other inmates, sometimes as the result of a staged gang assault calculated to impress the victim with his vulnerability and need for protection.[10] Other punks become prison "prostitutes," or "canteen punks," who exchange sexual favors with other prisoners for material goods.[11] In chapter 15 of this section Kirkham describes the types of punks and the routes by which an inmate becomes a punk.

Most researchers characterize male prisoners who take the feminine role, whether they be queens, homosexuals, or punks, as "surrogate women" who adopt a socially submissive role in prison analogous to the second-class status of women in free society. Most researchers also describe social relations involving sexual activity between these surrogate women and other male inmates as centrally focused on that sexual activity. Johnson's (1971) description of prison same-sex behavior differs on both counts. He characterized surrogate women as powerful pivotal members of prison society who are accorded respect by other inmates and feared by prison guards. For example, he reported that a raid of prisoners' cells might be followed by retribution on the part of the "broads," who would "club together in a way resembling a homosexual P.T.A. . . . to make life miserable for the guards" (86–87). Johnson also described same-sex behavior among male prisoners as embedded in a context of social relationships, reporting that some liaisons involved dating, courtship, and marriage, complete with printed wedding invitations, wedding gifts, a honeymoon, and a marriage certificate detailing not only the sexual relationship of the partners but also their gendered social roles vis-à-vis each other.

Sociosexual roles are even more elaborate in the culture of women's prisons. As in men's prisons, some women perform crossgender roles, adopting more or less "masculine" demeanors and appearances.[12] These women are called "butches," as opposed to "femmes," who play a feminine social role. Women in prison form "family" relationships including husband and wife, mother or father and son or daughter, cousins, uncle or aunt and niece or nephew, and sometimes grandparents and grandchildren.[13] The family roles available to a given woman depend on her prison "gender" and, in a general way, her age (Giallombardo 1966a). A few researchers have reported that race differences replace sex differences in some prisons, for example, with Black women taking masculine roles and white women taking feminine roles.[14] In prisons where race is used to distinguish gender, the relationship between a husband and a wife is necessarily interracial. In other prisons race is no impediment to the formation of family relationships and a couple and their relatives might be from a variety of racial and ethnic backgrounds. In addition to family relationships, women might also have "rap buddies," "homeys," and "kick partners" (Giallombardo 1966a). These familial and nonfamilial relationships, each of which defines the range of permissible contact two women might have with each other, serve to regulate social and sexual contact between women and stabilize prison society by providing avenues for women to fulfill emotional, social, and sexual needs.

The importance of sexual activity among women prisoners is evidenced by the array of terms used to describe individual women depending on whether they are involved in sexual activity and, if so, in what capacity.[15] One of the most fundamental distinctions is that between the "lesbian," or "true homosexual," who prefers same-sex to other-sex sexual activity and probably engaged in same-sex sexual activity before incarceration, and the "penitentiary turnout," "jailhouse turnout," or "player," who was heterosexual before incarceration and is expected to return to heterosexuality after her release.[16] Among players Giallombardo reported that the idealized sexual pairing is a stable reciprocal relationship based on romantic love that occurs between a feminine and a masculine partner who are referred to respectively as the "femme," "mommy," or "wife" and the "stud broad," "daddy," or "husband." Other sexual roles in women's prison subculture include the "trick," the "commissary hustler," the "chippie," the "cherry," the "punk," and the "square" including the "cube" and the "hip square." A chippie, for example, forms temporary sexual relationships for sexual or material gratification rather than a single stable relationship for love, whereas a commissary hustler forms one stable relationship with a wife while maintaining other relationships with tricks who can provide material favors. Squares do not participate in sexual activity because of lack of socialization to prison sexual subculture, that is, they are not players, whereas cherries do not participate because they have not yet been turned out. Unlike the punk in men's prisons who is a man who was turned out in prison, the punk in women's prisons is a woman who takes the role of a stud but does not succeed in projecting sufficient masculinity. For theoretical discussion of the origins of women's prison families in women's gender socialization outside prison and the prison situation itself, including the history of women's correctional philosophy and prison architecture, and for detailed descriptions of each of the above-mentioned relationships and sociosexual roles, the interested reader is referred to Giallombardo (1966a), Ward and Kassebaum (1965), and Burkhart ([1973] 1996). For a detailed description of sociosexual roles and behaviors among females in juvenile institutions, see Propper (1981). Ward and Kassebaum also provided detailed descriptions of turning out and the course of same-sex relationships among inmates.

Is Situational Homosexuality a Form of Bisexuality?

Of greatest interest to the study of bisexuality are the punks and jockers in men's prisons and the players in women's prisons. Whether these individuals can actually be classified as bisexual depends on which definition of bisexuality is used. If bisexuality is defined behaviorally, then punks, jockers, and players are all bisexual by virtue of their other-sex sexual behavior outside prison and their same-sex sexual behavior inside prison. But, as was shown in part 1 of this volume, bisexual behavior does not always lead to a bisexual self-identity. This is particularly true among male punks and jockers, who generally maintain their heterosexual self-identities for three reasons. First, because pairings between a jocker and a punk are between an active masculine partner and a submissive feminine partner who serves as a surrogate woman, they are coded as heterosexual (Bowker 1980).[17] In fact, contrary to free society, in prison an expression of sexual interest from a feminine male is socially constructed as a testament to a man's masculinity, not an affront to it (Johnson 1971). Second, they are easily attributed to the single-sex environment of the prison (Kirkham 1971) and, in the case of the punk, to coercion rather than to sexual desire for a male on the part of either partner.

Third, in prison subculture the active masculine partner in a male-male encounter is not considered a homosexual (Nacci and Kane 1983).[18] This construction of sexuality at least partially reflects the sexual cultures of the lower class and Latin communities from which prisoners disproportionately come (for example, 20 percent of Wooden and Parker's respondents were Mexican American).[19] In these cultures the unavailability of female sex partners and/or strong taboos against masturbation as well as constructions of the homosexual as the passive partner might encourage men to seek other men for sexual outlet without adopting a homosexual self-identity. Many of the jockers in Wooden and Parker's (1982) study had engaged in similar sexual behavior before incarceration, which they considered to be entirely consistent with their heterosexual self-identities, and only 11 percent considered themselves bisexual at the time of the study.[20] In contrast, Ward and Kassebaum (1965) reported that same-sex relationships do change women inmates' sexual self-identities; they stated categorically that "those women who turn out in prison define themselves as *bisexual*" (76).

If bisexuality is defined in terms of sexual essence or feelings of sexual attraction instead of behavior or self-identity, then the question of whether punks, jockers, and players are bisexual becomes much more complicated. Those who favor this definition would probably not classify most punks, whose male-male experience is sometimes involuntary, as bisexual. They might, however, agree that jockers and players are bisexual; because jockers usually initiate male-male sex and players participate by mutual consent, one could argue that their participation is voluntary and therefore reflects a same-sex desire that arises under sex segregated conditions. Kirkham, for example, cited anecdotal evidence of what he perceived as "latent homosexuality" in some jockers. Note that this line of reasoning leads to the reverse of the conclusion drawn within the lower-class and Mexican cultures that label the submissive effeminate punk the real homosexual partner; Johnson (1971) noted the irony of the fact that, in prison, it is the victim of rape whose participation in the act is involuntary, rather than the rapist whose participation in the act is willful, who is thereafter classified as a homosexual.

But the presumed voluntariness of the jockers' and players' same-sex sexual behavior does not presuppose that the behavior is motivated by homosexual desire. In fact, popular beliefs that prison same-sex sexual activity is encouraged by the absence of opportunity for other-sex sexual relations, exemplified in Kirkham's chapter, rely on the assumption that prisoners' same-sex sexual behavior is not motivated by homosexual desire but by heterosexual desire which, denied other-sex outlet, focuses itself on the nearest available substitute.[21] In the case of male prisoners this substitute is a feminine male or any person capable of receiving the jocker's erect penis. As Schofield wrote, on the basis of interviews with fifty homosexual convicts and fifty nonhomosexual (pedophilic) convicts in three London prisons, "Many of the men who take part in homosexual activities in prison consider this only as a substitute and revert to heterosexual relations as soon as possible" (1965a:159).[22] Giallombardo also clearly ascribed to this explanation, commenting that "the mass of interview data [make it] clear, however, that this mode of adjustment . . . would be repugnant for most prisoners, but the uniqueness of the situation compels the inmate to redefine and attach new meanings to homosex-ual behavior within the prison structure" (1966a:98). It is the belief that same-sex sexual behavior is a simple substitute for unavailable other-sex sexual contact that undergirds proposals to curtail prison same-sex sexual behavior by instituting conjugal visits.[23] If prison same-sex sexual activity is motivated by heterosexual, and not homosexual, desire, then previously heterosexual prisoners are merely ex-pressing their heterosexuality, not their homosexuality, and they cannot be classified as bisexual based on their essence or their feelings of attraction.

However, the question of whether prison same-sex activity is motivated by homosexual or heterosexual desire reflects the same reification of partner sex or gender and dualistic view of sexuality that has repeatedly denied the existence of bisexuality. To what extent can prison same-sex behavior be seen as an expression of *bisexual* desire? Given that not all previously heterosexual inmates engage in same-sex sexual activity, as data presented later in this chapter will demonstrate, the question of what distinguishes those who do from those who don't arises. The case of coercion notwithstanding, if same-sex sexual behavior is a substitute for other-sex sexual behavior, then some inmates apparently find same-sex sexual ac-tivity a more acceptable substitute for other-sex activity than other inmates do. Among those who choose to engage in the activity, enough attraction to the same-sex partner must exist to make the activity preferable to abstinence or masturbation, a threshold that will vary because some class and ethnic cultures proscribe mastur-bation more strongly than others. The fact that it might not be the partner's biologi-cal sex per se that is attractive—it is, after all, the partner's crossgendered social role that allows the individual to consider him a substitute for an other-sexed part-ner—actually strengthens the argument that the sexual desire motivating the activ-ity is best described as bisexual desire. Although heterosexuality and homosexual-ity are necessarily defined in terms of attraction based on partner sex or gender, bisexuality need not be so defined; attraction to an individual that is not based on that individual's biological sex is, therefore, most accurately described as bisexual.

In fact, evidence exists that the same-sex nature of sexual contact between women prisoners might be an integral aspect of this activity. An observation by Giallombardo indicates that a stud's femaleness is not denied but considered an essential aspect of the stud role. She noted that women at Alderson disapproved of studs who carried their masculine role too far by "attempt[ing] to transcend psy-chologically the immutability of anatomy and biological function," for example, by "hitch[ing] up their slacks as if they were manipulating a penis" (1966a:139). If the stud's femaleness is as important as her masculine role, then previously heterosex-ual women prisoners who engage in sexual relations with studs are, in fact, ex-pressing an attraction to femaleness and are, therefore, bisexual in the sense of being capable of attraction to both sexes.

Yet another interpretation of prison same-sex activity, made by most recent au-thors on the subject, is that jockers' and players' sexual activity is not a reflection of sexual desire at all. Instead, among men sexual activity might be a means for establishing status hierarchies, drawing and maintaining territorial boundaries, expressing aggressions including ethnic hostility, demonstrating masculinity in a demasculinizing environment, fulfilling needs for affective social relationships, and resisting the control of the prison administration.[24] For example, arguments made by Bowker (1980) and Scacco (1975) that prison rape is a political act expressive of racial hostility closely parallel contemporaneous feminist arguments about other-sex rape.[25] Citing Susan Brownmiller (1975), Bowker (1980) labeled prison rape a "political act," and Scacco (1975) analyzed the interaction of racism and sexism and argued that prison rape as racial hostility is intimately dependent on coding the victim as woman. Davis (1968) noted that not only is the prison environment demasculinizing but the individuals who populate prisons are generally drawn from lower-class populations who have adopted sexual ways of demonstrating masculinity because they are denied access to middle- and upper-class ways of validating masculinity, such as job success.[26] He clearly distinguished sexual assault from "truly consensual homosexual activity" (4) and argued that the former is an expression of anger and aggression. John A. W. Kirsch and James Eric Rodman (1982) drew a comparison with the use of male-male sexual behavior among nonhuman animals to establish and maintain social hierarchies, and Karlen (1971) commented that the way to reduce the sexual victimization of prisoners would be to provide them with opportunities for establishing "a sense of status and manhood in ways less imitative of hostile primates" (554) in addition to conjugal visits. Johnson's (1971; see also Gagnon and Simon 1968) perspective, once again, is radically different from that of many scientific researchers. Instead of seeing homosexual behavior as a disruptive force in prison life that reflects social tensions and dysfunctions, Johnson argued that prison homosexual liaisons reflect and fulfill needs for social order and cohesion.

Sexual activity among women prison inmates might also not be motivated primarily by sexual desire. Among women, Ward and Kassebaum (1965) asserted that psychological and social needs are more urgent than sexual needs. They argued that women suffer more from separation from their families and disruption of the familial roles on which their identities are more centrally based than men do. Karlen (1971) argued that, like the families women inmates create among themselves, sexual activity between women inmates is an outgrowth of emotional intimacy and serves women's needs for love and affection rather than sexual desire. Giallombardo (1966a) pointed out that the avenues provided by American culture for women to achieve a sense of status are eroticized and that the [heterosexual] woman cut off from men is therefore cut off from those avenues, with the implication that by creating a substitute erotic universe women in prison recreate these avenues for themselves. Being cared about by a partner also gives women a sense of self-worth, counters the depersonalizing effect of institutionalization, and might symbolize rebellion against the conventional norms of a society that imprisoned them or against individuals who failed to prevent their imprisonment (Ward and Kassebaum 1965). Same-sex activity among women prisoners might, therefore, serve as a source of identity, self-esteem, and validation of femininity or as a means of rebellion or of reestablishing disrupted family relationships.

If same-sex sexual activity serves nonsexual needs for previously heterosexual inmates, the implications of this behavior for the study of bisexuality depends on whether one considers the particular need being fulfilled to be an aspect of sexual orientation. Although being heterosexual or lesbian/gay is generally defined primarily in terms of sexual desire, many individuals resist reducing it to sexual desire alone and argue that being heterosexual or lesbian/gay has more to do with whom one loves than whom one sexually desires. In this view an argument can certainly be made that previously heterosexual women prisoners who fulfill each other's need for romantic love and express that love through sexual activity are expressing bisexuality.

Similarly, same-sex activity that is expressive of femininity in women or masculinity in men might not be very different in motivation from much sexual behavior that is considered normally heterosexual in free society. The argument that same-sex activity in prison serves to compensate for the loss of opportunities for validating one's gender in co-ed society assumes that heterosexuality in free society and homosexuality in prison are similarly motivated by gender-related nonsexual needs. For example, in his study of a New Jersey State maximum security prison Sykes (1958) commented that the act of heterosexual intercourse is the primary criterion of masculinity in free society and that prisoners have merely adopted new criteria more suited to the needs of a homosocial society. As John C. Gonsiorek (1982) noted, in a criticism of Ovesey's (1963, 1965) concept of "pseudo homosexuality" as homosexuality motivated by nonsexual needs, heterosexuals as well as homosexuals and bisexuals use sexual expression to meet both nonsexual and sexual needs. Heterosexuals are thought no less heterosexual if their heterosexual activity is not sexually motivated—why should different standards be applied to same-sex activity?

Other motivations for same-sex activity are, however, less convincing. For example, same-sex activity engaged in as an act of rebellion against society or the prison system is not likely to be seen as an expression of underlying sexual orientation. Even more doubtful is the question of whether male prisoners who use sexual activity to fulfill dominance needs or to express ethnic hostility can be described as bisexual; Scacco (1975), again paralleling feminist arguments that other-sex rape is not sexual, explicitly asserted that prison rape cannot be classified as homosexual, with the implication that its existence in an otherwise heterosexual career should not classify the individual as bisexual.

In summary, the question of whether situational homosexuality is an expression of bisexuality is complex. The answer is that sometimes it is and sometimes it isn't, and—as in free society—it depends on which definition of bisexuality is used and what meanings are placed on sexual behavior.

How Common is Situational Homosexuality in Men's and Women's Prisons?

Statistical findings regarding situational homosexuality among prisoners, like any research findings, must be interpreted cautiously. The accuracy of these findings as a description of current prison life is questionable because of changes in the prison environment, the prison population, and societal attitudes toward homosexuality that have occurred since most of this research was done in the 1960s and 1970s, despite Burkhart's ([1973] 1996) claim that not much has changed in prison life. Even as a description of prison sexuality at the time of the research, findings regarding the prevalence of same-sex contact might be biased downward because prison rules proscribe sexual contact and, among male prisoners, cultural proscriptions against unmanliness might have caused subjects to withhold information about certain sexual behaviors, especially submissive ones (Tewksbury 1989a). Ward and Kassebaum (1965) pointed out that estimates of the prevalence of same-sex sexual activity are further complicated by varying definitions of what constitutes such activity. For example, many researchers simply asked respondents whether they had had such experiences, leaving the respondent to use her or his own definition. Ward and Kassebaum explicitly defined same-sex activity as including "kissing and fondling of the breasts, manual or oral stimulation of the genitalia and simulation of intercourse between two women" (1965:80), whereas Kinsey and his associates included psychic responses not involving physical contact.

Some findings regarding the prevalence of situational homosexuality are also confounded by the fact that male-male sexual acts were illegal at the time and place of the research, so some prisoner subjects had been incarcerated for engaging in same-sex sexual acts.[27] For example, Schofield (1965a) estimated that one in sixty of all men in prison at the time were convicted homosexuals. Schofield (1965a) cited Lawrence Zelik Freedman (1961) as reporting that the same amount of same-sex activity occurs among prisoners incarcerated for reasons other than homosexuality as occurs among those convicted for homosexual acts, but, as Tewksbury (1989a) pointed out, in the absence of a comparison to rates of same-sex behavior in the unincarcerated population we cannot draw conclusions regarding the role of the prison environment in encouraging same-sex sexual behavior.[28] Therefore, any estimate of rates of same-sex sexual behavior in prison must be taken within their historical context, adjusted for any overrepresentation of individuals with previous same-sex sexual experience in the prison population, and/or compared to rates in the general population to yield a meaningful understanding of the effect of the prison environment on sexual behavior.

Of course, a comparison to rates in the general population cannot reveal the *nature* of this effect. That is, it cannot tell us whether the prison environment actually *caused* individuals to engage in same-sex sexual behavior and to have the feelings that might lie behind this behavior or whether the prison environment merely caused these individuals to *discover* sexual dispositions they already had but would not have recognized were it not for the facilitating influence of a single-sex environment. Whether prison causes or reveals preexisting same-sex sexual predispositions is a scientifically unanswerable question because it depends on the unmeasurable philosophical concept of "latent homosexuality," that is, it depends on how you look at it.

Comparing the sexual activities of prisoners to those of the general population requires reliable and accurate information about the sexual behavior of the general population. Until recent surveys such as the NHSLS, this information was not available. Different researchers, some more aware of the necessity for a comparison to the general population than others, solved this problem differently. Tewksbury (1989a) and Nacci and Kane (1983) compared their findings to existing information; Tewksbury used Kinsey, Pomeroy, and Martin's (1948) findings, and Nacci and Kane used Hunt's (1974) findings. Kinsey and his associates themselves compared their data on prisoners to their own data on nonprisoners. Paul H. Gebhard, John H. Gagnon, Wardell B. Pomeroy, and Cornelia Christenson (1965), in *Sex Offenders: An Analysis of Types,* solved the problem by comparing prisoners convicted of various sexual offenses to two control groups, one a group of prisoners incarcerated for nonsexual offenses and the other a group of nonprisoners.[29] Gebhard, Gagnon, Pomeroy, and Christenson (1965) also assessed the rate of same-sex sexual activity during incarceration among prisoners whose sexual behavior had been exclusively other-sex prior to incarceration, thereby producing an estimate of the percentage of inmates whose sexual biographies became bisexual during incarceration. Of course, some of these individuals would have engaged in same-sex behavior during that period of time even if they were not incarcerated so this method does not isolate those whose biographies became bisexual *because* of incarceration. Similarly, Wooden and Parker (1982) reported rates of same-sex sexual activity during incarceration among men with different sexual self-identities and compared these to rates for the same men before incarceration. Neither Giallombardo nor Burkhart examined control groups or compared their findings to rates of same-sex sexual activity in the general population, and Ward and Kassebaum relied primarily on inmates' perceptions of the prevalence of first-time same-sex activity among their peers.

Most of this research suggests that rates of same-sex sexual activity among male prisoners are higher than rates of same-sex sexual activity among men in free society.[30] Recall from chapter 11 that NHSLS findings indicate that 9.1 percent of men in the general U.S. population report having engaged in a specific sexual act with another man since puberty, and that only 2.7 percent report having engaged in same-sex activity during the previous year. In comparison, Joseph Fishman (1934) estimated that 30–40 percent of prisoners engage in some same-sex sexual activity, Clemmer (1958b) found that 40 percent of the prisoners he interviewed had had some homosexual experience in prison, Sykes (1958) estimated 35 percent based on observations made by prison guards, and Gagnon and Simon (1973) reported that data at the Institute for Sex Research indicate that 35–40 percent of inmates at long-term felony correctional facilities have ever had a same-sex sexual experience (Fishman 1934).[31] Wooden and Parker (1982) found higher rates; 65 percent of their subjects had engaged in same-sex sexual activity while in prison, including 55 percent of self-identified heterosexual men, and 5–7 percent were "hooked up" in steady relationships with other inmates. Tewksbury (1989a), whose sample of 150 inmates in a men's medium security prison in Ohio overrepresented those who were white, never married, and enrolled in a college program, found substantially lower rates than other researchers. However, his findings are still higher than rates found by the NHSLS in the general population. He found that over 81 percent reported never having engaged in same-sex activites, that 19 percent reported having had sexual contact with another prisoner during the previous year, and that 7.4 percent were currently in a steady sexual relationship. Most who had engaged in same-sex activity had had few partners (2.13, on average). Tewksbury also reported that 67 percent of his respondents said they had never been approached for sex by another prisoner, 93 percent had never been approached in a threatening manner, and none admitted having been raped in prison. Nacci and Kane (1984) found that the prevalence of same-sex behavior depended on the type of institution. In a randomly selected sample of 330 male prisoners in seventeen federal prisons, 12 percent of all inmates surveyed reported having participated in same-sex activity in their current institution, whereas 20 percent of those in federal penitentiaries, which house more dangerous criminals for longer periods of time, had done so, and 30 percent of penitentiary inmates had ever participated in same-sex activity while incarcerated in any prison as an adult. They also reported that 6 percent of nonparticipants, and 22 percent of participants, had been targets of sexual assault by other prisoners (Nacci and Kane 1984).

Estimates of the percentage of male prisoners who engage in same-sex sexual activity for the first time in prison are rare. Among white nonsex offenders over the age of sixteen, Gebhard, Gagnon, Pomeroy, and Christenson (1965) found that up to 88.2 percent of those who engaged in same-sex sexual activities in prison had done so previously and that only 7 percent of the prison population had had their first same-sex sexual experience while in prison.[32] Despite this fairly low rate of first-time experiences, the Gebhard team (1965) also found that lifetime incidence of same-sex sexual activity was much higher among prisoners than among nonprisoners; 33.7 percent of men in their nonprisoner control group had ever had same-sex sexual contact, compared to 60.0 percent of nonsex offender prisoners, indicating that prisoners were 26.3 percent more likely to have had same-sex sexual experiences than men who were never in prison. Combined with their finding that only 7.1 percent of nonsex offender prisoners had had their first same-sex sexual experience while in prison, this suggests that the high overall rates of same-sex sexual activity among male prisoners are due not only to the prison environment but to the nature of the population from which prisoners tend to be drawn. Apparently, those men who ended up in prison were more likely to have engaged in same-sex sexual activity prior to incarceration than were men who would not be imprisoned. The Gebhard team's findings that nonsex offender prisoners (33.8 percent) were more likely than nonprisoners (21.4 percent) to have had their first same-sex experience by age sixteen, and to have a greater frequency of same-sex sexual contact (on average, 8.43 versus 3.37 contacts per year), add further evidence that prisoners and nonprisoners are drawn from populations with different sexual behaviors.

Gebhard, Gagnon, Pomeroy, and Christenson (1965) included control groups in their study expressly to eliminate the inflating effect of the fact that laws against male-male sexual activity caused an overrepresentation of men with previous same-sex sexual experience within the prisoner population. But this procedure could not control for any indirect effects these laws against male-male sexual activity might have had on the composition of the prisoner population; it is possible that these laws, by driving same-sex activity underground, caused a correlation between this form of sexual behavior and other forms of criminal behavior as part of a "deviant subculture," thus increasing the prevalence of same-sex sexual activity among those who would be convicted of nonsexual crimes. Gebhard and colleagues favored this explanation for their findings, arguing that the comparison between prisoners and nonprisoners reflects a difference between the "delinquent and nondelinquent lower socioeconomic" populations (1965:625). Alternatively, these findings could be due to cultural differences between populations with varying rates of incarceration. As mentioned earlier in this chapter and as discussed in chapter 22, different racial and ethnic groups and social classes have different sexual cultures and patterns of sexual behavior. Certain class, racial, and ethnic groups are also more likely than others to be arrested and convicted of crimes for a variety of social and economic reasons.[33] Thus, higher rates of same-sex sexual behavior among prisoners might be due not to the prison environment but to the class, racial, and ethnic composition of the population from which prisoners tend to be drawn and the meanings this behavior holds for inmates within their class, racial, and ethnic cultures of origin.[34]

This latter explanation is supported by Wooden and Parker's (1982) finding of racial and ethnic differences in the sexual behavior of inmates. Wooden and Parker, who classified inmates as heterosexual, bisexual, or homosexual based on their self-identities, found that among heterosexual inmates whites were less likely to have engaged in same-sex sexual activity both before and during incarceration. Prior to incarceration 62 percent of Black heterosexuals, 30 percent of white heterosexuals, and 23 percent of Chicano heterosexuals had had same-sex sexual experiences. While in prison 81 percent of Black, 55 percent of Chicano, and 38 percent of white heterosexuals had engaged in same-sex sexual activity. All bisexual and homosexual inmates, regardless of race or ethnicity, had engaged in same-sex sexual activity in prison. Wooden and Parker found similar racial differences in rates of steady relationships. Among heterosexual inmates 17 percent of Black and 16 percent of Chicano compared to 3 percent of whites were "hooked up" in a steady relationship with another inmate. Among bisexual inmates 78 percent of Blacks, 50 percent of whites, and 33 percent of Chicanos were hooked up. All homosexual inmates, regardless of race or ethnicity, were in steady relationships.

Within sexual encounters and steady relationships the sexual roles played by the inmates studied by Wooden and Parker also reflected racial and ethnic differences. For example, whereas whites were less likely to engage in same-sex sexual activity in the first place, presumably because white and middle-class cultures stigmatize same-sex sexual behavior per se, whites who did engage in such activity were less rigid in their sexual roles than were Blacks or Chicanos, whose ethnic and class cultures involve a more rigid code of machismo and stigmatize effeminacy more than same-sex sexual activity.[35] Blacks and Chicanos avoided effeminate or submissive sexual roles, such as performing fellatio or receptive anal intercourse, whereas whites were more likely to have been forced into a punk role in which they were expected to be the sexually submissive partner. These racial and ethnic differences in sexual role might reflect interracial dynamics as well as cultural differences. For example, Wooden and Parker (1982) reported that Chicanos would not turn out another Chicano but that both Blacks and Chicanos would turn out a white inmate. Scacco (1975) and Bowker (1980), as mentioned earlier in this chapter, explained these racial patterns—at least in the case of sexual assault—in terms of racial hostility rather than cultural differences, and Davis (1968) pointed out that it is safer for any aggressor to assault a member of a numeric minority than a member of a numeric majority. Davis's explanation is consistent with his finding that whites also chose white victims; 15 percent of all rapes he documented in Philadelphia prisons were white on white, and none were white on Black.

Wooden and Parker (1982) found that racial and ethnic sexual role differences were modified among self-identified bisexual inmates. They reported that self-identified bisexual inmates were more likely to play the insertive role in anal intercourse than either heterosexuals or homosexuals and that among bisexuals there were no ethnic differences in the incidence of dominant sexual behaviors, that is, receiving fellatio or insertive anal intercourse. Ethnic differences among bisexuals did appear in the frequency of submissive sexual behaviors, however; only 22 percent of Black bisexuals, compared to 67 percent of Chicano and 90 percent of white bisexuals, had performed fellatio. The authors commented:

> Obviously, in sexual role-playing a bisexual identity has different cultural meanings to this group of blacks than it does to the other bisexuals. For these blacks, to be bisexual means to have sex with other males while still maintaining a traditional, dominant sexual role. For whites, on the other hand, to be bisexual means to be able to reverse sexual roles, to both "pitch" and "catch." . . . For some whites . . . being bisexual not only means engaging in sex with both males and females, but also reciprocating sexually with the male sexual partner. (65–66)

Findings regarding rates of same-sex activity among women inmates are much less detailed than findings regarding men; neither Giallombardo (1966a) nor Burkhart ([1973] 1996) engaged in the collection and analysis of statistical data comparable to that provided by researchers who studied men's prisons. Some conclusions are possible, however. Unlike male prisoners, the population from which women prisoners are drawn does not appear to have more same-sex sexual experience than other female populations. According to the NHSLS, 4.3 percent of women in the general U.S. population have engaged in a specific sexual act with another woman since puberty. In comparison, Giallombardo (1966a) claimed that 5 percent of women at the Federal Reformatory for Women at Alderson, West Viginia, had been homosexual prior to incarceration, and Burkhart ([1973] 1996) reported that prison administrators provided her with an identical estimate.[36] In contrast to adult women prisoners, however, incarcerated juvenile females might be drawn disproportionately from populations with prior same-sex experience. Propper (1981) found that rates of prior homosexual experience ranged from 3 percent to 32 percent at different girls' training schools, with an average of 9 percent, and that half of these juveniles had had their first same-sex experience in another correctional program. Regarding activity during incarceration, Propper (1978) found that 14 percent of juvenile females reported "going with or being married" to another female inmate, 10 percent reported passionate kissing, 10 percent reported writing love letters, and 7 percent reported having sex with another female inmate.

Although adult women prisoners, in contrast to adult men prisoners, might not be drawn from a disproportionately homosexually experienced population, during incarceration rates of same-sex activity might be even higher among women prisoners than among men prisoners. Compared to rates of 30–45 percent found among male prisoners, Giallombardo wrote that "the vast majority of inmates adjust to the prison world by establishing a homosexual alliance with a compatible partner as a marriage unit" (1966a:136).[37] Giallombardo also reported that inmates estimated that 90–95 percent of inmates engage in same-sex sexual activity, whereas the warden estimated 80 percent and the correctional officers estimated 50 or 75 percent. Ward and Kassebaum (1965), combining a 19 percent figure derived from official prison records with inmates' estimates of 60–75 percent, estimated that half of the inmates of the California Institution for Women in Frontera, California had engaged in sexual activity with other women inmates. Ward and Kassebaum's respondents also estimated that 90 percent of those involved had had their first same-sex experience while in prison. Gagnon and Simon (1973) attributed the difference in Giallombardo's and Ward and Kassebaum's estimates of the prevalence of same-sex sexual activity to differences in definition, noting that Ward and Kassebaum included only overt physical contact whereas Giallombardo might have been referring to the proportion of the female inmate population involved in family relationships that *might* have included sexual contact.

If true, the higher rate of same-sex activity found among women prisoners as compared to men prisoners is probably due to the embeddedness of this behavior in the system of family relationships in which the majority of women inmates take part. Whereas Wooden and Parker (1982) found that only 5–7 percent of their male inmates were hooked up with a steady sex partner and that most prisoners who engaged in same-sex activity during incarceration were not in such relationships, Giallombardo found that three-quarters of her women subjects became members of families in prison and that sexual behavior was considered a normal aspect of certain familial relationships.

What effect does same-sex sexual experience during incarceration have on the sexual self-identities and postrelease behavior of those whose sexual activities were exclusively other-sex before incarceration? Do their prison experiences have a lasting effect on their sexual behaviors or self-identities, or, as most expect (Ward and Kassebaum 1965), do they return to exclusively other-sex sexual activity once they have the opportunity? In the past popular belief held that one could become homosexual by contagion and that experiences such as those incurred during imprisonment could turn one homosexual (for example, Plummer 1963; Ibrahim 1974), but evidence bearing on this question is scarce and largely anecdotal (Feldman 1984) or based on extremely small samples. For example, Donald J. West (1967) cited G. Westwood's (1952) anecdotal account of same-sex sexual behavior among previously heterosexual males in prisons and prisoner-of-war camps and suggested that whether men continue to engage in same-sex sexual behavior after release depends on whether or not the sexual gratification was accompanied by emotional gratification. John Money and Carol Bohmer (1980) mentioned the case of a Maryland inmate who "was quite sure" that he had "left" his same-sex activities when he left prison. The authors reported that "his subsequent sexual life on the outside attests to the accuracy of that claim" and characterized his as a case of "situation-specific bisexuality" (265).

Small sample studies on this question include those of Marshall C. Greco and James C. Wright (1944) and Edward Sagarin (1976). On the basis of interviews with ten "chronic homosexual" and ten "nonhomosexual" reform school inmates Greco and Wright (1944) found that all of the former and none of the latter had had early homosexual experiences that were a source of comfort during a period of emotional need, concluding that these early experiences induced a state of "latent chronic homosexuality" and that only individuals so predisposed would become "chronic perverts" as a result of their prison experiences. Sagarin (1976) studied nine ex-prisoners, none of whom had engaged in male-male sex prior to incarceration. Five were aggressors in prison and four were jailhouse turnouts (JTOs). The aggressors all claimed to have returned to heterosexuality, whereas the JTOs had all continued to pursue same-sex activity after their release from prison. Sagarin's attempt to explain this difference by reference to the construction of the JTO but not the aggressor as homosexual in prison culture is seriously undercut by a methodological weakness; the JTOs were recruited for the study through "homosexual social circles," whereas the aggressors were recruited through parole and corrections officers.

The only quantitative evidence bearing on this question suggests that prison sexual experiences do not affect adult prisoners' sexual orientation or self-identity. Tewksbury (1989a) reported that the percentage of his male respondents who considered themselves heterosexual upon entry into prison and at the time of his study were nearly identical (77.6 percent and 76.5 percent) and that most inmates' sexual fantasies during masturbation were exclusively (72.1 percent) or largely (10.9 percent) other-sex. He used this evidence to imply that male inmates retain a heterosexual orientation during incarceration but did not present data regarding inmates' sexual behavior after release. In a study of thirty-nine IVDU women prisoners Stephen Magura, Joanne O'Day, and Andrew Rosenblum (1992) reported that "homosexual relationships were formed and occurred primarily outside of jail" (179), suggesting that incarceration did not increase the prevalence of same-sex experience among female IVDUs. Most of the fifteen homosexually experienced women in the study had no intention of becoming heterosexually involved after their release, but only four identified themselves as gay or bisexual and none identified as lesbian, probably because most had begun same-sex activity recently. Ward and Kassebaum (1965), whose female respondents generally identified themselves as bisexual in prison, asserted that many women become strongly emotionally attached to their partners in prison and are undoubtedly conflicted about giving up these same-sex liaisons. Nevertheless, they asserted that most probably return to heterosexuality upon release for many reasons, including conditions of parole, the resumption of outside family ties including marital and parental ones, and lack of contact with gay groups in free society. In other words, the fact that inmates are released into a social structure that encourages a return to heterosexuality obscures any evidence that might indicate that their sexual experiences during prison had affected their sexual self-perceptions or preferred sexual behaviors. The influence of external social structures might be somewhat weaker for youthful female offenders, thus permitting the continuation of same-sex activity if it was experienced as pleasurable during incarceration; of fifty girls who had kissed or had sex while incarcerated Propper (1981) reported that 69 percent of the thirteen girls who felt more positively than negatively about the experience expected to continue homosexual activity after their release, compared to 18 percent and 0 percent, respectively, of the eleven girls who felt equally positive and negative about the experience and of the twenty-six girls who found it more negative than positive.

Situational Homosexuality in Other Single-Sex Environments

Like prisons, single sex or sex-segregated boarding schools are reputed to foster same-sex activity among their residents. Gay subcultural ideology pinpoints the upper-class English boarding school as a particular haven for youthful same-sex sexual activity.[38] Unfortunately, there is little research on this subject (Feldman 1984), probably because the young age of the individuals involved gives such research a special stigma. Unlike prisoners, youth are culturally constructed as innocent; research on their sexuality, especially their same-sex activities, would challenge this cherished view. Even today, in the midst of several sexual "crises" involving youth such as teenage pregnancy and AIDS, political resistance to the study of the sexuality of minors is strong. Therefore, the lack of publications on same-sex sexual activity in boarding schools during the 1960s and 1970s—the era of research on "situational homosexuality"—is not surprising.

Nevertheless, there is some evidence that same-sex sexual activity is more common among the residents of boarding schools than among their peers. In a study of adolescent sexuality based on a series of random samples totalling 1,873 British youth, Schofield (1965b) found that a higher proportion of individuals who had attended single-sex boarding schools reported "homosexual activities" (28 percent) than did individuals who attended either single-sex or coeducational nonresidential schools (3 percent). There is also some evidence that these boarding school experiences might have an effect on lifetime sexual orientation; A. Kolaszynska-Carr (1970) found that the average length of boarding school attendance was significantly longer for homosexual men than for heterosexual men (eight versus five years).[39] This evidence is suggestive only; it does not demonstrate that the converse—that is, that longer periods of boarding school increase the proportion of bisexuals or homosexuals in a cohort—is true, nor does it establish that the boarding school experience caused a homosexual orientation for any given individual. Kolaszynska-Carr's (1970) finding might also have resulted if parents were more likely to send homosexual, "pre-homosexual," or crossgendered children to boarding school, perhaps in the hope that the school would foster heterosexuality or gender-appropriate behavior in them, or if the boarding school environment merely facilitated the expression of same-sex sexual desire in those students already aware of such desire within themselves.

Whatever the causal connection between same-sex sexual activity and boarding school residence, the correlation is less than perfect; most individuals who attended boarding school live primarily heterosexual lives after boarding school, and among these are undoubtedly some of the individuals who had same-sex experiences during boarding school. Although some of these individuals would have engaged in same-sex sexual activity even if they had not attended boarding school, Schofield's (1965b) finding that same-sex sexual activity is higher among boarding school students suggests that for others the single-sex environment of the boarding school was a contributing factor. For these individuals, as for previously heterosexual prisoners, their experiences with "situational homosexuality" gave them bisexual lifetime biographies that they would not otherwise have had. Unfortunately, because of the lack of data cross-tabulating same-sex sexual experiences during boarding school with postboarding school sexual behavior, we do not know what proportion of former boarding school students have bisexual biographies solely because of boarding school experiences.

Another largely sex-segregated institution is the military. However, the cultural relationship between homosexuality and the military is historically very different from the relationship between homosexuality and other single-sex environments such as prisons and boarding schools. Whereas at various times and places homosexuals were and are purposely sent to prisons, and same-sex sexual activity is studiously overlooked in single-sex boarding schools, in the United States homosexuality has long been seen as antithetical to military service and homosexuals have been actively excluded from military service. Contrary to popular perceptions of men's prisons as "sodomy factories," male military personnel are stereotyped as ideally masculine and undeniably, even promiscuously, heterosexual. Most research on the topic of homosexuality and the military focuses on the question of whether gay men and lesbians should be excluded from miliary service—a particularly hot topic in the 1990s following President Clinton's acknowledgment of the issue—and not on the military as an environment conducive to same-sex sexual activity (e.g., Anderson and Smith 1993). To the extent that military personnel have been seen as including a higher proportion of lesbians and gay men than the general population, this is attributed to a tendency on the part of those already aware of same-sex sexual impulses—primarily lesbians—to gravitate toward military service (Harry 1984). For example, D'Emilio wrote,

> As its official historian ruefully admitted, the WACS labored under a "public impression that a women's corps was the ideal breeding ground" for lesbianism. Ironically, military policy contributed to a situation that it took pains to deny. Recruitment centered on a population group statistically likely to include a disproportionate number of lesbians and women whose sexuality was most malleable: in mid-1943, 70 percent of the women in WACS were single; 83 percent were childless; 40 percent were under twenty-five years of age, and 67 percent

were under thirty. Anxious to counter its reputation of moral laxity, the military sought to avoid unwanted pregnancies by keeping its female personnel segregated, often having women-only nights at canteens or providing separate space for women to socialize. A training manual for officers praised the desire for intense "comradeship" in service as "one of the finest relationships" possible for women. But with emotional attachment serving as a powerful stimulus to female eroticism, such bonding might lead toward unintended results. Taken together, popular stereotypes, army policy, and the special condition of military life may have kept women of confirmed heterosexual persuasion away from enlistment, while drawing in an unusually large proportion of lesbians. (1983:27, citing Treadwell 1954; War Department 1943; and Bérubé 1981)

During World War II the military was also the arena in which many gay men and lesbians found each other for the first time and, along with the Kinsey reports that informed gay men and lesbians that there were others like themselves, is frequently credited with contributing to the transformation of isolated individuals into a lesbian and gay community.[40] D'Emilio, for example, argued that the homosocial and emotionally intense nature of military life made it easier for gay men to identify each other:

> The sex-segregated nature of the armed forces raised homosexuality closer to the surface for all military personnel. . . . Army canteens witnessed men dancing with one another, an activity that in peacetime subjected homosexuals to arrest. Crowded into port cities, men on leave or those waiting to be shipped overseas shared beds in YMCAs and slept in each other's arms in parks or in the aisles of movie theaters that stayed open to house them. Living in close quarters, not knowing whether they would make it through the war, depending on one another for survival, men of whatever sexual persuasion formed intense emotional attachments. In this setting, gay men could find one another without attracting undue attention and perhaps even encounter sympathy and acceptance by their heterosexual fellows. (1983:25–26)

Whether the military environment actually fosters same-sex sexual activity among those whose sexual activities would otherwise be exclusively other-sex is less clear. As with boarding schools, the evidence is largely anecdotal. Donald Vining (1979), excused from service during World War II because of his acknowledged homosexuality, lived in New York City during the war and reported having had sexual relations with both self-acknowledged homosexual and "heterosexually inclined" service members (D'Emilio 1983:27; Vining 1979). Gagnon and Simon (1973) suggested that groups of military personnel, after unsuccessfully seeking heterosexual outlets, might under the right circumstances accept the proposal of a male homosexual. They argued that in such cases the homosexual character of the encounter is neutralized by the group's construction of the event, much as same-sex experiences in other single-sex environments such as prisons and boarding schools are neutralized. On the other hand, Kinsey, Pomeroy, and Martin (1948) found no increase in same-sex sexual behavior during either world war, suggesting that men who engaged in same-sex sexual activity while in the military would have done so anyway (Karlen 1971).

Situational Homosexuality Among Prostitutes

The relationship between prostitution, or sex industry work in general, and homosexuality is as complex as that between the military and homosexuality. Researchers have explored other-sex prostitution as a phenomenon within lesbian and gay subcultures, same-sex prostitution by individuals with both heterosexual and gay self-identities, lesbianism and gayness among prostitutes, and prostitution among gay men and lesbians. Much of the literature on the sex industry and homosexuality will be reviewed in chapter 17, but one segment of it is relevant to the discussion of situational homosexuality; this is the segment in which the world of female sex work is viewed as a social environment that causes women to turn to other women for their own sexual satisfaction.[41] In this view sex work provides an interesting contrast to prison. Whereas prison is a social environment in which men or women turn to their own sex because they are denied sexual contact with the other sex, in sex work men or women have plenty of sexual access to the other sex, but the poor quality of these other-sex contacts causes some to turn to their own sex to look for something better.

For example, in a study of 136 female prostitutes in a large western city, Jennifer James (1976) found that 35.3 percent had experienced a "lesbian relationship," 7.4 percent reported "frequent" same-sex activity, and 6.7 percent were "exclusively lesbian." Although James did not give the wording of the question asked, the implication is that these same-sex experiences were for pleasure and not engaged in as prostitution. She explicitly rejected other theorists' explanations of same-sex activity as stemming from "latent homosexuality" among prostitutes, arguing that such explanations lump prostitution and lesbianism together as related forms of "sexual deviance." Instead she argued that the apparently high incidence of same-sex experience among prostutes might reflect their greater willingness to "admit" their same-sex experiences, the greater feasibility of same-sex activity for prostitutes who operate outside conventional restraints on sexuality and are familiar with a wider variety of sexual techniques, the fact that prostitutes' private lives involve more intimacy with women than men, and a desire for the mutuality of lesbian sexuality in contrast to the unilateral nature of sex in their working lives—in other words, situational factors.

This view is held by some sex workers themselves. Ward and Kassebaum (1965), who discovered in their study of the California Institution for Women, in Frontera, California that inmates who engaged in same-sex activity in prison were twice as likely as inmates who didn't to have engaged in other-sex prostitution outside prison, reported that inmates "interpreted homosexuality as an appropriate and rational reaction to experiences as a prostitute" (129). Their respondents also noted that some prostitutes become involved in same-sex activity because some customers request "a show of that kind" (130) or because they are turned out by other prostitutes. The same opinion was found among strippers by Charles H. McCaghy and James K. Skipper Jr., whose 1969 publication exemplifies this genre of research and is included as chapter 16 in this section. As one of McCaghy and Skipper's informants commented,

Strippers go gay because they have little chance to meet nice guys. They come in contact with a lot of degenerate types. If they do meet a nice guy chances are he will ask them to stop stripping. If he doesn't he's likely to be a pimp. So the girls got to turn to a woman who understands them and their job. (1969:268)

Situational homosexuality, therefore, need not be a negative response to conditions of heterosexual deprivation, but a positive choice in favor of same-sex activities. Certain circumstances offer greater opportunity for sexual activity with members of one's own sex and increase its attractiveness relative to the available heterosexual options, even for people who might arguably otherwise be heterosexual. Such situational homosexuality is, therefore, more than technical bisexuality— it is true bisexuality, motivated either by a disregard for the sex of one's partner or a desire for sexual and emotional intimacy with a member of one's own sex.

Notes

1. In this chapter the terms *same-sex* and *other-sex* are used instead of *same-gender* or *other-gender* to describe sexual activities. This is because in prison subculture as described in this chapter same-sex sexual contacts do not occur between individuals of the same *gender* but between same-sex individuals who have adopted different genders while within prison walls.

2. Perhaps the earliest academic reference to "situational homosexuality" as bisexuality was by Mary McIntosh, whose "The Homosexual Role" was well ahead of its time in many ways. Commenting on a quote from a psychiatrist describing how he diagnoses the condition of homosexuality, McIntosh wrote, "Along with many other writers, he introduces the notion of a third type of person, the 'bisexual,' to handle the fact that behaviour patterns cannot be conveniently dichotomized into heterosexual and homosexual. But this does not solve the conceptual problem, since bisexuality too is seen as a condition (unless as a passing response to unusual situations such as confinement in a one-sex prison). In any case there is no extended discussion of bisexuality; the topic is usually given a brief mention in order to clear the ground for the consideration of 'true homosexuality'" (1968:31). Kirsch and Rodman (1982) took a different point of view, criticizing the acceptance of situational homosexuality as a form of homosexuality, which they defined as an "affective, often erotic interest in the same sex," and referring to "a definitional error that does not make adequate distinction between 'situational homosexuality' (for example, under conditions of deprivation, as in prison or the military) and true substitution of the same sex for the opposite sex in an affective relationship" (184).
Some of the people studied by researchers apparently described their own "situational homosexuality" as bisexuality prior to publication of McIntosh's piece. Ward and Kassebaum (1965) reported that women prisoners who engaged in same-sex behavior preferred to describe themselves and their behavior as bisexual.

3. Giallombardo (1966a; 1966b); Ward and Kassebaum (1965); and Burkhart ([1973] 1996). Researchers also agree that violence associated with same-sex activities in women's prisons is a result of jealousies involving lover's triangles rather than an aspect of the sexual act itself. See Bowker (1980) for a review of literature on assault in women's prisons.

4. Clemmer's findings are not included in the current review because they are encumbered by such outdated and value-laden language as to make the findings themselves difficult to discern. Although, for example, Karlen (1971) cited Clemmer as having found that 10 percent of prisoners were homosexual prior to incarceration and another 30 percent engaged in homosexual activity only or mostly while in prison, what Clemmer actually reported is an estimate that 30 percent of inmates are "quasi-abnormal" whereas 10 percent

are "frankly abnormal." Which category an inmate fell into depended on a combination of factors based on antiquated notions of sexuality. For example, Clemmer commented that "for the adult male in the free community, masturbation is an abnormal act" (1958a:258) and apparently included men who masturbated frequently in the "quasi-abnormal" category. The aggressor in same-sex rape was also only "quasi-abnormal," as compared to the "invert" or "pervert" who commited the sin of caring about his sex partner: "The occasional sodomist who plays the masculine role is placed in this category only if his abnormal behavior is accompanied by ideations of sex contact with a female, and no love reactions exist between him and the person who plays the passive role" (1958a:261).

5. Sykes (1956) is widely cited for his discussion of the "pains of imprisonment," among which he included "the deprivation of heterosexual relationships."

6. See also Halleck and Hersko (1962); Kosofsky and Ellis (1958); and Stockwell (1953).

7. By "participant," Giallombardo meant that she participated in the daily activities of the prison. However, to distinguish herself from both staff and prisoners in an effort to minimize methodological reactivity, she did not live at the prison.

8. See also Davis (1968); Sykes (1958); and Kirkham (1971).

9. Scacco (1975) used the term *punk* differently, that is, as inclusive of prisoners who are forced to submit to same-sex activities *because* other prisoners found out that they were homosexual on the outside.

10. Blake (1956); Devereaux and Moss (1942); Davis (1968); and Karlen (1971). Nacci and Kane (1983, 1984) found that prisoners with homosexual or bisexual self-identities were more likely than those with heterosexual self-identities to be targets of prison sexual assault, although most targets identified as heterosexual and were not otherwise participants in male-male sex while in prison. Nine percent of federal inmates reported having been targets of attempted forced sex.

11. Bowker (1980); Davis (1968); Gagnon and Simon (1973); Johnson (1971). Nacci and Kane (1983) found that 29 percent of federal inmates had been propositioned, but "only 7 percent were 'seduced' by inmates bearing gifts or offering favors" and only 2 percent "had taken money for performing sex" (35).

12. The distinction between masculine and feminine genders is a basic building block in prison relationships, as it is in free society, and women who fail to successfully enact one or the other gender (for example, the punk), or women who switch from one gender to the other (for example, the woman who "drops her belt"), or women who try to play both roles (the turnabout) are criticized.

The role of gender in prisons in the 1960s as described by Giallombardo (1966a, 1966b) or Ward and Kassebaum (1965) or in the early 1970s as described by Burkhart can be compared to the femme-butch gender culture in the lesbian communities of the 1950s and 1960s as described by many authors, including Joan Nestle (e.g., 1989, 1992) and Lillian Faderman (1991). The similarities include the criticism aimed at those who fail to play one of the available gender roles. One difference might be the tendency of prison butches to adopt less extremely masculine appearances to avoid disciplinary action (Ward and Kassebaum 1965). Butch-femme gender roles apparently remained popular in prison subculture after they had fallen out of favor in free lesbian communities; witness Burkhart's respondent Ruth Kelly's comment that lesbians in prison felt disdain for the gender role-playing behavior of "players."

13. Giallombardo referred to the existence of aunts and uncles in women prisoners' prison families, but Burkhart's only mention of this particular familial relationship occurred in a quote by an inmate who reported that it does not exist.

14. Freedman (1996) reviewed this literature. Giallombardo cited Otis (1913) and Ford (1929), who described relationships between Black and white girls in institutions for juvenile delinquents. Giallombardo summarized their findings, reporting that one girl takes the role of wife, and the other the role of husband, although an individual girl's role might be different in concurrent or subsequent relationships—indicating that gender roles are

distinguished by race but not assigned based on race. In contrast, Gagnon and Simon wrote that "in practically all such cases the black females are defined as male and the white females defined as females. . . . This black-white family structure has been observed in training schools in Illinois, in Ohio, California, and New Jersey, and in other institutions across the United States" (1973:257). Unfortunately, this comment regarding assignment of gender role based on race is unreferenced.

15. Ward and Kassebaum (1965), who endeavored to discover the "social types" in women's prisons, reported that they soon discovered the most salient distinction was between those who were involved in same-sex sexual activity and those who were not and, among those involved, between butches and femmes. Sykes (1956) similarly reported that the distinction between "masculinity" and "femininity" in men's prisons overrides all other bases of sexual classification.

16. According to Ward and Kassebaum (1965), true homosexuals are somewhat more likely to be butch than jailhouse turnouts are. These authors also reported that true homosexuals and jailhouse turnouts enact butch and femme roles differently, with true homosexuals being more subdued and jailhouse turnouts, in the eyes of true homosexuals, being overly dramatic, attention-getting, and superficial.

17. For example, Scacco (1975) explored the feminization of the victim in depth and Davis (1968) found that same-sex rape is referred to by inmates as "taking one's manhood" or "making a girl of you," phrases that clearly construct the victim as a woman with the intention of degrading him. Sykes (1956) noted that the "fag" plays the role of a woman socially as well as sexually, whereas the "punk" "has turned himself into a woman . . . by the very act of his submission," but "his forteiture of masculinity is limited to the homosexual act" (96). See also Kirkham (1971), included in this volume. Johnson (1971), who focused on "homosexual" inmates, described them as "surrogate women" but not as victims.

18. Davis (1968), displaying class and racial cultural biases typical of the era, wrote that in his investigation of rape in Philadelphia prisons he was "struck by the fact that the typical sexual aggressor does not consider himself a homosexual, or even to be engaging in homosexual activity. This seems to be based on a startlingly primitive view of sexual relationships which defines as male whichever partner is aggressive and penetrates and as homosexual whichever partner is passive and is penetrated" (37).

19. See Karlen (1971); Kinsey, Pomeroy, and Martin (1948); and note 30 below for references to class differences in attitudes toward masturbation. Kinsey, Pomeroy, and Martin explored the consequences of class differences in sexual mores in the penal system, hypothesizing that a superintendent of a correctional institution might consider masturbation preferable to homosexuality, whereas the prison guards, being from lower-class backgrounds, would probably punish masturbation as severely as homosexual activity. For discussions of Latino constructions of sexuality in which only the passive partner in male-male sex is stigmatized as a homosexual per se, see chapter 22, including note 28. For citations to research demonstrating the disproportionate representation of certain racial, ethnic, and class groups in prison, see note 33 below.

20. This percentage might be different today. Recent research on Mexican and Mexican American men in Mexico and the United States indicates that the spread of European American constructions of sexuality is eroding the distinction between *activos* and *pasivos* and providing Latin men with European American-style sexual identities in which male-male sexual behavior, regardless of sexual role, is a basis for bisexual or gay self-identity (Almaguer 1993; Magaña and Carrier 1991). A similar process of cultural osmosis might be occurring in prisons, leading to greater difficulties in the maintenance of heterosexual self-identities among prisoners.

21. See also Fishman (1934); Plummer (1963); and West (1967) as examples.

22. Schofield (1965a) studied six groups of subjects, homosexual and nonhomosexual convicts and psychiatric patients, and homosexual and nonhomosexual controls. Because he was prohibited from asking convicts who were not incarcerated for homosexual acts

questions about their sexuality, his nonhomosexual convicts consisted of pedophiles who had been classified as homosexual offenders by the prison system but whom Schofield recognized as pedophiles rather than homosexuals. Schofield defined a homosexual as someone who considered himself homosexual and was willing to say so to the interviewer. Writing in 1965, he took a very progressive attitude toward homosexuality, commenting that homosexuals might end up in trouble not because of their homosexuality but because of negative social attitudes.

23. For example, Ibrahim (1974). Although a discussion of the efficacy of conjugal visits in reducing same-sex activity within prisons would speak to the question of whether this activity reflects bisexuality among previously heterosexual prisoners, it is outside the scope of this book. Findings in this area are controversial and conflicting. West (1967) cited Nice (1966) for evidence supporting the claim that conjugal visits reduce same-sex sexual activity, and Shore (1981) provided a bibliography of sixteen articles, chapters, and books on the subject, including Balough (1964); Burstein (1977); Holloway (1974); Hopper (1978); and Johns (1971). More recently, Nacci and Kane (1984) found that participants and nonparticipants in prison homosexual liaisons did not differ on any of a number of variables reflecting access, or expected future access, to heterosexual opportunities, including marital status or other romantic tie to someone outside prison, frequency of outside visitors, furlough eligibility or expectation, or postrelease plans for heterosexual cohabitation.

24. For example, Bowker (1980); Gagnon and Simon (1968, 1973); Karlen (1971); Kirsch and Rodman (1982); Nacci and Kane (1984); and Scacco (1975).

A case cited by Scacco (1975) sheds interesting light on the theory that prison sexual behavior is motivated by nonsexual drives. He noted that in a particular training school Black inmates chose to sexually exploit a white homosexual but not a Black transsexual. The fact that the inmates chose the homosexual over the transsexual calls into question theories about the coding of prison sexuality as heterosexual and the victim as a woman and supports Scacco's own theory that sexual aggression reflects not sexual desire but ethnic hostility. Scacco noted, however, that individual characteristics—the Black transsexual was streetwise and the white homosexual was attractive—could explain the choice in this particular case.

An alternative to the view that prison sexual activity is motivated by either sexual or nonsexual desires is offered by Feldman (1984). In the context of a discussion of single-sex boarding schools Feldman pointed out that same-sex sexual activity among individuals in sex-segregated environments might be at least partially due to role modeling and subcultural encouragement. Because individuals "are rarely isolated completely . . . it is difficult to separate out the effects of isolation from the opportunities to copy [others] who are behaving in a homosexual manner, which they in turn might have acquired from a particular subculture" (29). If prisoners engage in same-sex sexual activity solely as a response to subcultural norms or role modeling, is this behavior therefore not reflective of sexual orientation? Early lesbian feminists argued that allegedly heterosexual women engage in other-sex sexual behavior for such reasons and, although the lesbian feminists therefore concluded that these women were not "really heterosexual," the heterosexual women in question certainly disagreed (Rust 1995a; e.g., Leeds 1981; Rich 1980). The fact that same-sex activity among prisoners might be caused by role modeling and cultural encouragement therefore does not necessarily rule out a bisexual construction of this behavior.

Similarly, Ward and Kassebaum (1965) discussed the process of socialization during which a new inmate is taught that becoming involved in a same-sex relationship makes doing time more bearable and that such relationships are normalized in women's prison subculture. They noted that even prisoners who do not become involved in same-sex sexual activity are immersed in a social world structured around same-sex, not other-sex, relationships.

Earlier literature on the subject of prison sexuality offered explanations for same-sex activity among prisoners that reflect the racist and heterosexist attitudes of the theorists rather than the prisoners. For example, Lindner (1948) argued that homosexuality is a state of sexual immaturity, and that depraved homosexuals, including "'pansy' street nuisances," "in their never ending search for sexual gratification" (203) and amid the "subtle debilitating forces" of prison life, are able to cause other prisoners to regress to homosexual behavior. Judging such explanations to be without merit and therefore their implications for bisexuality worthless, I have chosen not to review literature of this type here.

25. Supporting this argument, Scacco cited findings regarding the racial distribution of prison rapes. Davis (1968) found that 56 percent of rapes in Philadelphia prisons were Black on white, although 80.5 percent of the prisoners were Black and 19.5 percent white. (If 80.5 percent of inmates were Black and rapes were randomly distributed across race, one would expect 80.5 percent of rapes to be committed by Blacks and 80.5 percent of those rapes to involve Black victims. Nineteen point five percent of 80.5 percent, or 15.6 percent, would therefore be by Blacks on non-Blacks, including Black on white rapes.) Jones (1976) found that white inmates reported that most rapes are Black on white; Black inmates disagreed but were unable, according to Jones, to provide examples of other instances of rape. Nacci and Kane (1984) also found "relatively more black assailants" and "a strong tendency for whites to be assault targets" (50). Carroll (1974) showed that the prevalence of Black on white rape is not contingent on a Black majority; in an eastern penitentiary 22 percent of the inmate population was Black, but the racial distribution of rapes was similar to that found by Davis in Philadelphia.

26. See also Sykes (1956) for a discussion of the role of women's presence in providing men with masculine self-images that do not rely on the assumption of other-sex sexual relations. He commented, for example, that "the inmate is shut off from the world of women which by its very polarity gives the male world much of its meaning" (72) and mentioned the importance of the looking-glass self.

27. A comment by Johnson (1971) implies that the prevalence of same-sex activity in prison might be also be increased because some inmates, having established secure homosexual relationships with other prisoners, have been known to commit additional crimes or to refuse parole in an effort to remain in prison.

28. The current author was unable to locate this finding in Freedman (1961). Freedman compared three groups of inmates, "sexual deviates," "aggressive offenders," and "acquisitive offenders," and reported, apparently referring to lifelong sexual behavior, that "more of [acquisitive offenders] had had homosexual relationships than the aggressive subjects, and about the same percentage as the sexual groups" (1961:48).

Compared to the topics covered in other chapters in the current volume, while fact-checking I discovered that there is an unusually high rate of incorrect citations in the literature on same-sex activity in prisons; see, for example, notes 4 and 32 in this chapter. Therefore, in cases in which I was unable to confirm the accuracy of a reference made by an author cited in this chapter, I inserted a textual note or endnote indicating that the reference was not confirmed and I also included a note regarding the citation in the bibliography at the end of this volume. In contrast, when I was unable to confirm sources referenced by authors cited in other chapters in this volume, I indicated this by including a note in the bibliography, the text, *or* the endnotes.

29. Gebhard and colleagues (1965) compared nine categories of sex offenders—distinguished from each other by whether the offending act involved a same- or other-sex partner, the age of that partner, and whether the act was consensual—to these two control groups. The nine categories of sex offenders consisted of 1,356 case histories accumulated by the Institute for Sex Research, the prisoner control group numbered 888 cases, and the nonprisoner control group of 477 men was selected to resemble the low educational attainment level of the convicted subjects. The authors discussed the fact that a certain percentage of the control groups undoubtedly also engaged in the same sexual acts for which members of the other groups were convicted and concluded that the effect on findings would be minimal and the fact of conviction represented an important difference between the groups. The

authors defined homosexual acts as "physical contacts between two persons of the same sex, designed (by at least one of them) to produce sexual arousal and recognized by both as being sexually motivated" (623).

30. Findings by Kinsey, Pomeroy, and Martin (1948) actually suggest that prisoners have lower—not higher—rates of overall sexual outlet than nonprisoners, because most adjust to conditions of sexual deprivation by reducing their sexual activity rather than substituting male partners for female. Kinsey and his colleagues found that although a high percentage of prisoners do engage in same-sex activity in prison, most do not do so until they have been in prison several years and, even then, only a small percentage engage in it frequently. They estimated that in short-term institutions half of the inmates might never engage in same-sex sexual activity. Gagnon and Simon reported that "from a preliminary analysis of the differences between the preinstitutional and institutional sexual outlet of adult male prisoners interviewed by the Institute for Sex Research, the institutional rates are only one-tenth to one-fifth of noninstitutional rates" (1973:242, note 10) and noted "the low order of complaint one hears about sexual deprivation, even when prisoners are presenting a list of grievances after a riot or outbreak of some sort" (242–43).

Kinsey and his associates argued that, because of taboos against masturbation and minimal erotic fantasy activity that reflects a concrete rather than a symbolic orientation to sexual arousal in the lower classes from which many prisoners are drawn, many prisoners find little to arouse them in prison and tend not to substitute masturbation or same-sex activity for other-sex activity. Gagnon and Simon further noted the lack of privacy in prison and argued that heterosexual activity itself has a different meaning for men of different classes. Kinsey and associates' finding that prisoners have lower overall rates of sexual outlet is supported by Wooden and Parker's (1982) finding that self-identified heterosexual men are more likely to have engaged in same-sex sexual activities prior to prison (62 percent) than in prison (55 percent). However, this support is greatly attenuated by the fact that much of the previous experience probably occurred during adolescence. Furthermore, the fact that Kinsey and associates' estimates of rates of same-sex activity in the general population are inflated casts doubt on their findings regarding relative rates among prisoners.

31. Regarding the specific act of sexual assault, the first attempt to estimate a rate in men's prisons was by Davis (1968). Davis interviewed 3,304 inmates and 561 prison employees in the Philadelphia prison system over 26 months. Counting only corroborated reports and including solicitations accompanied by threats as well as actual forced sex acts, he found 156 instances of assault on 97 individuals, leading to an estimate that a total of 1,500 men out of 60,000 prisoners were victimized during the twenty-six months.

32. Tewksbury erroneously concluded from the 7.1 percent statistic that "90–95 percent of those who do engage in same-sex sexual activities in prison have done so prior to being incarcerated" (1989a:35), apparently by subtracting 7.1 percent from 100 percent in ignorance of the fact that the denominator in Gebhard, Gagnon, Pomeroy, and Christenson's (1965) 7.1 percent statistic is the entire nonsex offender prison population, not "those who do engage in same-sex sexual activities in prison." Gebhard, Gagnon, Pomeroy, and Christenson (1965) reported that among the 888 subjects in their nonsex offender prisoner control group 7.1 percent had had their first same-sex experience in prison and 60.0 percent had ever had a same-sex experience either in or out of prison. Minor calculations reveal that 63 men had their first experience in prison and 533 men—including these 63—had ever had same-sex experiences in or out of prison. Because some of these 533 men probably had same-sex contacts *only* outside of prison (for example, during adolescence—evidence presented later in this paragraph in the main text indicates that this number is substantial), some number *less* than 533 of the 888 men had had same-sex contacts while in prison. If 63 out of *less than* 533 men had their same-sex experiences only in prison, then *more than* 11.8 percent of those who have had same-sex experiences had them only in prison, and *less than 88.2 percent*, not 90–95 percent, of men who engage in same-sex sexual activities in prison have done so prior to being incarcerated.

33. Nacci and Kane (1984) reported that, in their representative sample of federal male inmates, 46 percent were Black and 11 percent Hispanic, compared to 11.7 percent Black and 6.5 percent Hispanic in the general U.S. population. Propper's (1981) probability sample of female delinquents was 28 percent Black and 23 percent neither Black nor white; 58 percent had working-class or unemployed parents.

34. See also Gagnon and Simon (1973); Scacco (1975); and Propper (1981). Propper (1981) discussed at length the "import" (nature of prison population) versus "deprivation" (prison environment) theories of same-sex activity. Her own data indicated that differential rates of homosexuality between institutions explains 29 percent of the variation in individual participation in same-sex activity during incarceration among juvenile females. She also found that controlling for homosexual experience prior to incarceration rendered differences in rates of homosexual activity between institutions statistically insignificant and that, once prior homosexual experience was controlled, other background variables including age, race, and social class of parents had no independent correlation with participation in homosexual activity during incarceration. In comparison, thirteen measures of institutional deprivation explained a combined total of only 2.6 percent of the variation in participation in homosexual activity during incarceration.

Compare the argument made by Akers, Hayner, and Gruninger (1974), but note Propper's (1981) criticism of the conclusion that their findings point to the role of prison deprivation in encouraging same-sex activity (page 135, note 1).

35. See also Karlen (1971) and Gagnon and Simon (1973) on sexual roles in prison, and chapter 22, including note 28, for citations to works describing Latin stigmatization of effeminacy and the passive sexual role rather than homosexuality per se.

36. Findings by Magura, O'Day, and Rosenblum (1992) are relevant here. In a random sample of thirty-nine IVDU women prisoners 38 percent reported homosexual behavior during the six months prior to their incarceration. Given research findings of a correlation between drug use and same-sex activity among women reviewed in chapter 22, illicit drug-using prisoners probably are drawn from a population that is disproportionately homosexually experienced. See note 33 in chapter 22 for discussion of the relationship between same-sex or bisexual activity and drug use.

37. Giallombardo (1966a) described sexual activity as an integral part of prison couplings, implying that the "vast majority" are not only involved in same-sex relationships but participate in same-sex sexual activity within those relationships. In contrast, Burkhart ([1973] 1996) reported that many inmates say that some prison couples do not consummate their relationships sexually.

38. Martha Vicinus, a scholar active in the construction of lesbian history, provided a historical treatment of the "crushes" or "raves" of girls at English boarding schools. Although Vicinus did not argue that these friendships involved sexual activity, she described them as based on "what we would now label as sexual desire" and reported that "a woman who loved another girl or woman always spoke of this love in terms that replicated heterosexual love" (1989:213). See also Hickson (1995) and Weinberg's (1967) study of British boarding schools.

39. Kolaszynska-Carr (1970) studied four groups of subjects, male and female heterosexuals and homosexuals. Although the proportion of each group that had attended boarding school ranges from 16 to 31 percent, these differences are not significant. Kolaszynska-Carr also found no significant difference in the average length of boarding school attendance between female heterosexuals and homosexuals. Thus, if boarding school does foster same-sex sexual activity, it appears to be the length of the boarding school experience and not the simple fact of attending a boarding school that is influential, and this influence appears to affect boys only. These findings are described by Feldman (1984); this description was not confirmed by the present author.

40. For example, Adam (1987); D'Emilio (1983); and Marotta (1981). Compare Murray (1996).

41. For example, Gagnon and Simon (1973); Greenwald (1958); and West (1967). A similar argument, albeit without relevance to bisexuality, is that promiscuity is a defense against fear of one's own homosexuality (e.g., Greenwald 1958; Keiser and Schaffer 1949). This explanation for promiscuity, as have approaches that pathologize promiscuity in general, has fallen out of favor in the social sciences. See Ward and Kassebaum (1965) for a review of literature taking this point of view on the relationship between promiscuity or prostitution and homosexuality. The works by Keiser and Schaffer (1949) and Greenwald (1958) are cited by Ward and Kassebaum (1965); these citations were not confirmed by the present author.

As Karlen (1971) pointed out, the argument that prostitutes "turn" to other women for their own sexual satisfaction does not necessarily imply that sex work causes homosexuality, because it "begs the question of why these women chose a life that could offer them only brutalizing relationships with men" (559).

15

Homosexuality in Prison

George L. Kirkham

A NEWSPAPER article or sensational magazine story sometimes focuses brief public attention on the subject of homosexuality in prison. Beyond such ephemeral interest, which usually follows in the wake of a jail or prison scandal, society evinces little interest in the sexuality of those of its members who have been temporarily banished through imprisonment. The entire problem of prison homosexuality thus remains characterized by widespread ignorance and confusion. Even the more basic issue of why the subject warrants being labeled a "problem" is unclear. In an era which witnesses an increasing tolerance of all forms of sexual behavior, it is maintained by some that concern over prison homosexuality derives from nothing more than a residue of Victorian, heterosexual bias; on the other side, moralists and prison reformers attempt to portray American prisons as being "rife with degeneracy." Panaceas, such as "conjugal visitation," are often advocated or opposed with little understanding of the nature of homosexuality in prison. It seems clear that there is a need to objectively examine the entire phenomenon against the unique subcultural backdrop which is represented by the prison.

Basic to any consideration of the structure and dynamics of prison homosexuality is an understanding of the total impact which prolonged confinement in a world without women has upon adult males in our society. Everywhere in the contemporary American prison one finds overwhelming evidence of what Sykes has labeled the "pain of heterosexual deprivation."[1] Perhaps this frustration, which attends the "figurative castration" of prison inmates, is most apparent in the conversation and humor of prisoners. The new employee or visitor to prison is immediately struck by the extent to which "sex" is a dominant motif in the thought and communication patterns of inmates. A rich sexual argot, many terms of which are unintelligible to the outsider, is to be found in all prisons. New words enter the lexicon of both inmates and staff, where they redefine the meaning of sexual phenomena through the subcultural eye of the beholder.

It has been suggested many times that being without women is by far the most difficult aspect of imprisonment for most men. Certainly, the loss of liberty, the requirement to live in a restricted and insecure environment, and the absence of certain goods and services are frustrating to all prisoners; yet, it is the complete unavailability of sexual and social relations with women which is almost intolerable for the average man in prison. As Victor Nelson, a man who spent twelve years in prison, has poignantly written, "But to be starved for month after weary month, year after year . . . this is the secret quintessence of human misery."[2] The prison inmate must somehow adapt to and endure the complete absence of heterosexual intercourse at a social class level where the frequency of marital coitus often averages six or seven times a week.[3] The stoic middle-class ethic of "deferred gratification" finds little acceptance among men whose lives have largely been characterized by an impulsive and hedonistic pursuit of sexual gratification. In addition to facing prolonged—sometimes indefinite[4]—physical frustration, the prisoner must also adjust to what is perhaps an even more painful reality: the complete unavailability of even social contact with women. A man who has become accustomed to validating his masculinity through regular interaction with members of the opposite sex may suddenly find his ego-image in grave jeopardy once a prison sentence consigns him to an all-male world. As Sykes states, "The inmate's self-image is in danger of becoming half complete, fractured, a monochrome without the hues of reality."[5]

As if such sexual and psychological "pain" were not already sufficiently stressful for men whose backgrounds amply attest to an inability to adaptively handle frustration, the memory of woman is kept painfully alive by a multiplicity of stimuli. In addition to the sexual themes so common in prison humor and conversation, and the sub-rosa body of pornographic literature which is always in circulation,[6] the mass media play an important role in aggravating the prisoner's psychosexual condition. Television, radio, newspapers, motion pictures—all combine to provide unrelenting titillation by keeping inmates exposed to the sexually charged atmosphere which characterizes contemporary American society. Mail and visits from wives and girlfriends only exacerbates the frustration which men in prison must endure daily. The result of all this is a kind of green pastures syndrome which engulfs the prison community and serves to keep its members constantly preoccupied with unobtainable sexual objects. Sex, as Tappan notes, "becomes disproportionately important for men in prison."[7]

It is truly paradoxical that the same humanitarian innovations which have improved the overall lot of most prisoners in recent years have also had the dysfunctional effect of intensifying their sexual frustration. Prior to the advent of congregate penology and widespread penal reform, generally wretched physical conditions prevailed in many American prisons. During this period the attention of prisoners was largely focused on the lowest level of what Maslow terms a "natural need hierarchy."[8] Most prisoners were so preoccupied with securing a modicum of edible food, adequate clothing and shelter that "sex" paled to relative insignificance alongside these more prepotent physical needs.

In contemporary American prisons the pendulum of need fulfillment may be said to have come full swing from its position at the turn of the century. The average prisoner, in addition to having most of his important physical needs met, is also provided means for gratifying higher, aesthetic needs. As Lindner observes, "The essential wants and needs, even the basic rights, if there are such things, are satisfied. Food, clothing, shelter, books, movie theatres, recreation, employment—the list is never ending and always on the increase—are obtainable."[9] Prisoners who are cold and hungry are scarcely concerned with sex, but when these same men are given well-balanced meals, comfortable clothing and other creature comforts, they become predictably vulnerable to sexual frustration.

At the same time that prisons were becoming physically less austere places, there was a shift in penal philosophy and practice from the isolation of prisoners from one another—the so-called "separate system"—to congregate confinement: inmates began to work, eat and cell together. With these two developments—improvement of overall physical conditions and the opportunity for interaction among prisoners—the stage was set for the emergence of a complex inmate social system, an important segment of which would center around the problem of adapting to sexual frustration.[10]

Granted the fact of prolonged heterosexual deprivation, there exist only three possible adaptations open to members of the inmate community: sexual abstinence, masturbation, or involvement in institutional homosexuality. The individual reactions of abstinence and masturbation warrant only brief consideration here, since the problems which arise from "sex in prison" are primarily sociological products of the interaction of inmates with one another. Suffice it to say that an inmate may take the ascetic task of complete abstinence during his incarceration, or the more common one of regular or sporadic masturbation. Successful self-imposed continence is usually associated with an extremely short sentence and rigidly internalized notions of the inherent evilness of both masturbation and homosexuality. While it is true that individual differences in age and physiology enable some inmates to serve even long periods of confinement without any sexual outlet, the pressures on the average prisoner are such that he engages in at least periodic masturbation. As Ellis states, "All authorities agree that the great majority of men in prison masturbate."[11]

Homosexuality represents a third possible reaction to the deprivation of heterosexual intercourse. Situational homosexuality is believed by many to be widespread in American prisons, a conviction which is doubtless largely fostered by a tendency on the part of sensational writers to grossly exaggerate the actual incidence of the phenomenon; even veteran prison administrators, such as San Quentin's former Warden Duffy,[12] often argue that the majority of inmates engage in homosexual acts while incarcerated.

Actually, the number of inmates who participate in any form of homosexual behavior while imprisoned is relatively small when compared to the vast majority of prisoners who adapt to sexual frustration by masturbating.[13] However, the constricted microcosm of steel and concrete that is the prison lends such an exaggerated visibility to homosexual activity that both inmates and staff are inclined to misperceive its extensiveness; yet this fact does not diminish its sociological importance. If a sufficient number of men define widespread homosexuality as a reality, the consequences in thought and action will be comparable to those which would obtain if this were really the case. The small number of prisoners who engage in institutional homosexuality comprise a subterranean world, a kind of subculture within a subculture, which has profound consequences for the entire prison community. A homosexually oriented system of values, norms, argot and statuses is so inextricably interwoven with the larger inmate social structure as to render the subject of sex between men an inescapable reality of daily life for all prisoners. Homosexuality in prison becomes something with respect to which every man must constantly define himself as long as he is incarcerated.

A careful definition of terms must precede any serious discussion of homosexuality in prison. This is so because the words "homosexual" and "homosexuality," when used by prison inmates, assume a special subcultural significance. In free society these expressions are highly pejorative and emotionally charged stigma symbols; as such they are often applied indiscriminately and interchangeably to anyone thought to have engaged in erotic activity with a member of his own sex. Most people do not distinguish between individuals in terms of the motives and circumstances which underlie their homosexual acts; rather, all persons are uniformly stigmatized as "homosexuals," or, more colloquially, as "queers" and "fruits."

Homosexuality in prison is quite a different matter. Inmate society makes many complex distinctions between both acts and actors when evaluating any sexual activity which involves two or more prisoners. Like the Eskimo, for whom the word "snow" has little meaning by itself because of so many possible contexts in which it may be employed, "homosexual" must be related to a complex value system in order to acquire meaning to the prison inmate. To categorically label any prisoner who engages in a homosexual act "a homosexual" would seem as absurd to him as the failure to do so would seem to the average person. He would wish to know a great deal about the actors and the act before reaching a conclusion.

Members of inmate society exempt certain of their peers who indulge in homosexuality while incarcerated from the odious ascription of a "homosexual" status. There exist two criteria, both of which must be fulfilled, for an inmate to escape such stigmatization: (1) the homosexual act or acts must represent only a situational reaction to the deprivation of heterosexual intercourse, and (2) such behavior must involve a complete absence of emotionality and effeminacy—both of which are regarded as signs of "weakness" and "queerness." An inmate who engages in homosexual activity must present a convincing façade of toughness and stereotypical "manliness" in order to escape being defined as a homosexual. It is only because of the unrelenting "pain" of being totally deprived of sexual contact with women, something which is felt by all men in prison, that inmates are willing to take into consideration situational determinants of homosexuality. They therefore make a sharp distinction between homosexual behavior which is preferential and that which is believed to be only a substitutive response to heterosexual deprivation.

All inmates who become involved in homosexuality are ascribed particular hierarchical positions in prison life by their peers; predictably, these men reveal in their attitudes and behavior the fulfillment of the role expectations which correspond to such statuses. The tendency for each status to involve a definitive cluster of values, folkways, and mores, which clearly differentiates it from other statuses, has led some writers on the subject to approach it in terms of a tripartite typology of homosexually involved inmates. Expressed in the prison vernacular, these three types of statuses are: (1) The "queen" or "fag," (2) the "punk," and (3) the "wolf" or "jocker."[14] Too often, however, such analyses have taken at most an isolated snapshot of prison homosexuality. An attempt will be made here to link these three argot statuses to the larger inmate substructure and to explain why the phenomenon of homosexuality represents such an important daily reality for the majority of nonhomosexually involved prisoners.

I studied the inmate population of a major California medium security prison—the correctional Training Facility, Soledad—while I was employed there over a two-year period as both a Student Professional Assistant and, later, as a Correctional Counselor. In gathering data for this period, I employed several methods: analysis of case files of homosexually involved inmates; examination of incident reports relating to homosexual acts and actors (many of these yielded information on the subcultural nature of "homosexual violence" and "pressure cliques"); and, thirdly, I developed a forty-three-item questionnaire using a Likert Scale which was designed to tap attitudes of the general inmate population with respect to various kinds of institutional homosexuality, as well as information on masturbation, abstinence, and so forth. This questionnaire was administered to a random sample of 150 Soledad inmates, and I analyzed the responses in terms of racial-ethnic status, marital status, age, offense, time served, and the particular institution—there being three separate prisons at Soledad.

The "Queen" or "Fag": Preferential Homosexuality

The expression "queen" is used by both inmates and staff to refer to the inmate who closely approaches the popular stereotype of the "flaming faggot," the classically effeminate homosexual. It is believed that the queen engages in prison homosexuality solely out of a preference for male sexual partners. The behavior of such an inmate, rather than being rationalized as a situational reaction to being deprived of women, is felt to be merely the logical continuation of a preexisting pattern of "righteous homosexuality." Even if women were available, inmates aver, the queen would continue to play a "passive" homosexual role; nor is his homosexuality felt to derive primarily from either a desire to secure prison amenities, or protection, though these motives are recognized as sometimes being of secondary importance.

While prison queens form the smallest category of homosexually involved inmates, they are quickly identifiable solely on the basis or their overt appearances and mannerisms. Exaggerated limp-wristed effeminacy, a bizarre caricature of real femininity, serves to set them apart from the majority of inmates who engage in homosexuality. In every nuance of appearance, attitude, and behavior, the queen seeks to make "herself" attractive to a heterosexually deprived population of men as the closest approximation to a much desired but unobtainable sexual object:

Woman. Queens, who are usually referred to in the feminine gender by both inmates and staff, usually adopt nicknames which are unequivocally feminine; not infrequently, the selection of names such as Dee-Dee, Chee-Chee, and Peaches, betrays a sardonic mockery of females, which is also apparent in dress and other mannerisms. Even the casual visitor will easily notice the queen's "swishy" gait. If necessity is truly the mother of invention, then the queen has done well in using what the environment offers in approaching a feminine appearance: back pockets are torn out of tight prison denims to make them form-fitting, makeshift cosmetics are fashioned from smuggled medical and food supplies, and jewelry is produced in hobby shops. Hair is grown as long as officials will tolerate, and eyebrows and whiskers often plucked. Like "her" counterpart in free society, the institutional "drag queen" is easily recognized.

The ostensible contempt and ridicule with which members of the inmate population speak of the queen belie the fact that "she" actually enjoys the position of a scarce object of high functional utility; for with the passage of time in prison, the flagrant differences which exist between male and female reach such a point of situational convergence for many sexually deprived men that the queen possesses a very real substitutive appeal. As one inmate confided, "Some of them look and act so damn much like real women!" The queen's effeminacy thus often evokes a memory and longing for females, a longing which sometimes leads otherwise exclusive heterosexual men to seek sexual relief from the queen.

The genesis of the queen's effeminate homosexuality almost always is to be found in events which occurred prior to imprisonment. The noninstitutional etiology of the queen's homosexuality is suggested by the argot saying, "Queens are born. Punks are made."[15] The queen's distinctive effeminacy often involves strong components of narcissism and exhibitionism. This compulsive need to be noticed by others as conspicuously "feminine" is apparent in the following excerpt from a voluminous autobiography entitled *Life History of Lily Bond, The Redhead:*

> I used to dye my hair blonde and let it grow long, just as if I were a real woman. My wardrobe included a mink coat, a choker, a double set of wedding and engagement rings, and a very expensive suit that was more than seventy-five dollars. . . . It hasn't been so awfully long since I was in slacks and blouse, shoes, slip, and panties. . . . I was just wondering what people would say if they could see two or three female "boys" coming from C.I.M. [California Institution for Men] all decked in panties, slip, etc. . . . Lay here on my bunk and wonder why they didn't put two bunks in a cell.

It is common to find strong elements of fetishism and transvestism in the psychopathology of prison queens. Even the more serious gender aberration of transsexualism is sometimes apparent, as suggested in another statement by a queen: "I'd much rather live a girl's life than a man's, because you have much more fun. . . . In fact, if I had the money, I would take the chance of an operation to become a woman. I would give my right leg to be born a girl now." (Author's file).

The queen's scarcity in prison, usually enables her to be highly selective in choosing sexual partners. Exceptions to this occur, however, in the case of older, less attractive queens. One such individual boasted to the writer of having established a sexual liaison with an inmate less than half her age, a claim which was openly and immediately denied by several of her peers, who were present; they derisively maintained that she couldn't find anyone to "go down with," let alone a younger inmate.

Usually the queen will enter into a number of prison sexual liaisons which perhaps are best described as approaching serial monogamy. The use of the term "marriage" to describe these evanescent liaisons is no misnomer, for such relationships often reveal many of the elements common to heterosexual marriage. The queen brings to a marriage a desire for esteem, security, and affection, as well as for sexual gratification. She will usually continue the relationship for only as long as a preponderance of these needs are fulfilled. Like the heterosexual marriage, there is usually a stringent demand for sexual fidelity in such relationships. The violation of this marital form may bring in its wake violence, even murder. It is true that the proclivity for exhibitionism and flirtation which is common among queens has more than once led to institutional homicide, when combined with the strong emotional investment so often found in prison marriages. As one queen, serving a life sentence for murdering her homosexual partner, confided: "No one else had better not interfere, for it is very dangerous."

The following excerpt from a letter written by a queen to her partner illustrates well the charged emotional atmosphere which often exists in prison marriages:

> Dear Danny:
> You see, I have never been able to be a good woman to you because I always knew that you never cared that much for me. I did not know, however, that you did not respect me. That hurts me more than anything. I have read your letter a dozen times, and each time I do I break out crying. I love you and nothing could ever change that. I wish you would give me the chance to be a good woman to you, but I guess it's too late. I pray that you and I can work something out, then, instead of hurting each other. Will you do this for me, darling? Be good, honey, and I do love you.
>
> > *Love Forever and a Day*
> > *Love Always, Johnnie [Author's file]*

Another "kite," or prison note, written by a spurned queen, suggests that dissolution of a marriage may be imminent: "Why did you defy me, Bobby? Why didn't you let me go into the wing? Keep that punk out of your face! You used to tell me how you kept them out of your face, so what's so special about this one?" (Author's file).

Despite the general proscription of infidelity, two marriage partners may arrive at an agreement whereby the queen will prostitute herself to other inmates in return for certain goods and services. One inmate "pimp" exhorts his spouse: "Look sweetheart, I need some cigarettes bad. If this fool doesn't want to play, drop him and find another damn fool. Get busy and get some cigarettes over here because your husband isn't going to smoke that stale shit!" (Author's file). Some prison queens are able to amass considerable institutional affluence through selective prostitution; obviously such activity also may serve the latent function of providing variety in sexual partners as a means of gratifying the queen's narcissism.

The brittle marriage of the queen results from a tacit, symbiotic contract in which she agrees to provide another inmate, usually known in prison parlance as a "wolf" or "jocker," with both sexual gratification and status among his peers as a "daddy." The "jocker," in addition to reciprocating sexual favors, acts as a protector and provides the queen with a measure of security in a highly predatory environment. The symbiosis thus revolves primarily about sex and security. Security, in the form of physical protection, is particularly important to the weak and effeminate queen. It is for this reason that most queens move from marriage to marriage, seldom terminating one relationship unless another is immediately available. By thus remaining always with a strong "daddy," she becomes relatively immune to the institutional phenomenon known as "sex pressuring" (coercion into homosexual activity). An unattached queen is constantly liable to sexual assault by lone predators, gang rape, and coercion into indiscriminate prostitution. Without a protective marriage, as one queen put it, "the traffic gets too heavy to bear." While a married queen may occasionally be "hit on" (approached for sexual favors), the knowledge that any aggressive overture may elicit a reprisal from her "daddy" serves to largely insulate her from the fate which befalls other weak and sexually vulnerable inmates.

The "jocker" or "wolf" who "takes a queen" must be able to convincingly demonstrate toughness and strength to his peers. Most enter such relationships with only the manifest goal of securing substitutive sexual gratification; sometimes, however, an element of latent homosexuality in the "wolf's" personality surfaces, as is suggested in the following excerpt from a letter written by one such inmate to his "wife":

> Darling . . . Angel . . . Sweetheart . . . I need you, baby, and I want you bad. You are making me feel like I do when I am around my wife, Roberta. But I can tell you this, sweetheart, she never made me feel the way I do right at this minute. . . . Sleep tight, my darling, and when you dream, keep everyone out of them but you and me. [Author's file]

As an especially "swishy queen" skips from marriage to marriage, she may leave in her wake a series of beatings and stabbings, spread venereal disease, and occasionally produce riots. Such an inmate, as Lindner states, "is every bit as dangerous as a stray female in prison."[16] It is for this reason that queens who are especially provocative and who fail to settle down in a non-disruptive pattern of serial monogamy are often isolated from the main body of prisoners in a "queen's row" or other specialized unit of an institution; yet, while the queen occasionally creates serious custodial problems, she usually does not produce nearly the volume of trouble that may be attributed to the two other argot types.

The "Punk": Canteen and Pressure

Those members of the inmate community who are regarded by their peers as "punks" occupy a status which is the very nadir of prison life. With the possible exception of the "rat," or informer, the punk is uniformly the most despised of in-mates, a pariah who occupies at most a precarious position on the margin of in-mate society. Unlike the queen who openly chooses a life of passive homosexuality and even embraces the stigma of effeminacy as desirable, the punk is hated be-cause his involvement in prison homosexuality is believed to result from either personal weakness in the face of pressure or from a mercenary willingness to sacri-fice his manhood for certain goods and services. As Sykes states:

> But even though the punk does not exhibit those mannerisms characterized as feminine by the inmate population he has turned himself into a woman, in the eyes of the prisoners, by the very act of his submission. His is an inner softness or weakness; and from the viewpoint of the prisoners, his sacrifice of manhood is perhaps more contemptible than that of the (queen) because he acts from fear or for the sake of quick advantage rather than from personal inclination.[17]

Of perhaps greatest importance in understanding the hostility which is meted out to the punk is the realization that, by failing to live up to the cardinal tenet of the inmate code to "be a man," he raises anxieties in all prisoners over their own ability to successfully resist involvement in prison homosexuality. It is possible to discern two subcategories of institutional punks; in the language of the prison, these are (1) the "canteen punk," and (2) the "pressure punk."

THE CANTEEN PUNK

Inmates who are ascribed membership in this status are believed to engage in homosexual acts out of a desire for personal aggrandizement. They are men whose homosexuality represents an attempt to mitigate the frustration which results from being deprived of certain goods and services; thus canteen punks form a class of prison prostitutes who perform fellatio and submit to pederasty in return for gra-tuities such as candy, cigarettes, money, or personal favors. As such, they represent a sexual outlet which is available to the inmate who desires homosexual release, but who is unable either to win a queen or to successfully coerce a weaker inmate into performing homosexual acts without cost. The "canteen punk's" counterpart in free society is the youthful male prostitute who frequents certain areas of large cities. The canteen punk, like the queen, essentially capitalizes upon his substitu-tive appeal in a world without women. A further point of similarity is the fact that the canteen punk may deal with only particular inmates in return for securing their protection from homosexually aggressive peers.

The number of inmates who elect to engage in such passive homosexuality, without preexisting homosexual tendencies, is indeed small. In most cases, con-finement in prison will eventually bring latent homosexual impulses to the sur-face; often an inmate who is initially raped by a group of predatory peers, or "ripped off," will, as the saying goes, "get to liking it." Such a person may rational-ize future voluntary sexual activity on the ground that, since he has no alternative except to adjust to homosexuality, he may as well profit from it. While effeminacy is seldom apparent in the punk, a few metamorphose into queens with the passage of time in prison.

The Pressure Punk

This category includes most of those who are disparagingly referred to by inmates and staff as punks. The "pressure punk" is one who submits to a homosexually passive role because of either threatened or actual physical force. As a group, such inmates are predominantly younger, less "prisonized"[18] individuals who have been singled out as "weak" by more sophisticated and sexually aggressive peers; usually, such men evince little or no prior history of homosexual behavior.

There exist two subcultural routes to this lowly status in the prison community. Sometimes a man enters prison with a "punk jacket." The dynamics of this process are often as follows: a rumor, often completely false, is circulated by one or more inmates at the institution that a prisoner who is scheduled to arrive has already been "ripped off" or "turned out" at the county jail or the prison transferring him; often this is done with the cooperation of inmate clerks at the other end, who have placed a prearranged pen mark or other symbol on the prisoner's file card to denote that he can probably be successfully "pressured" for sex. Soon word spreads throughout the institution through an amazingly intricate communications system, that the inmate in question is "stuff," or a "broad." By the time the new prisoner arrives, the matter of the truth or falsity of this belief will be sociologically irrelevant. This entire process may be set in motion by nothing more than a "hunch" based upon an inmate's youthful or weak appearance. Sometimes, however, it results from a calculated desire on the part of others to even up a score for some real or imagined wrong committed outside the prison.

Whatever the reason, an inmate defined as amenable to sexual "pressure" will be tested by sexually predatory prisoners for the purpose of verifying his "punk" status as a preliminary to securing homosexual favors. The burden of proving that he is not a "pressure punk" rests entirely with the new inmate.

In other cases, an individual plays a more active role in his own victimization. Prisoners have an expression that "you bring pressure on yourself," by which they mean that failure to meet the normative expectations which attach to "being a man" in prison may render one particularly vulnerable to the sexual aggression of peers. It is because of a lack of "prisonization," acculturation to the complex norms which regulate social behavior in the prison, that the new inmate often inadvertently brings sexual pressure on himself. This is true not only of men who have never before been in prison, but also of the youth facility "graduate"; often such inmates make the grave social error of carrying the swaggering, boisterous actions and "delinquent" appearance—which conferred prestige among a younger group of prisoners—into the quite different milieu of the adult prison. Where the prison social system prescribes serving time quietly, "doing your number by walking slow and drinking plenty of water," the youthful newcomer's loud laughter, horseplay, and "ducktail" haircut makes him stand out like the proverbial sore thumb. It is a deficiency in institutional socialization which makes him ready prey for sexually predatory "wolves" or "jockers."

A very real *rite de passage* confronts all new arrivals at the adult male prison. Unless a man is a well-known returnee or has friends or "homeboys" who will help define him as a "solid con" to other prisoners, he may be in serious trouble. An inmate who lacks such resources, and who does not possess a sufficient level of prisonization to enable him to navigate in a normatively acceptable manner, will very often have to run a terrifying gauntlet of sexual "pressuring" at the hands of other prisoners.

From the moment a new busload of inmates arrives at the prison, institutional "jockers" make a careful review of all "fish," or newcomers, in the hope of discovering which men will likely prove vulnerable to sexual coercion. Inmates who are regarded as potential pressure punks often will be first approached in the yard or cellblock with a friendly offer of goods or services. The new inmate, alone and frightened in a strange environment, is all too eager to accept the offer of assistance, candy or cigarettes, from the man who appears to know his way around. Because of his lack of familiarity with prison life, he does not realize that a "real con" never accepts anything from another prisoner—goods or services—without a clear statement of what is expected in return. He likewise fails to grasp that the acceptance of favors under such circumstances is regarded by those proffering them as tantamount to a willingness to reciprocate in the currency of homosexual behavior.

Another common means of ensnaring the unwary "fish" is the invitation to enter a card game, or other gambling activity—which is predictably crooked—for the purpose of getting him into debt. The "fish," who usually has nothing to gamble with, at first is told that he can owe until canteen draw; however, suddenly he is deeply in debt and his fellow gamblers are no longer willing to wait until commissary time for settlement of the debt. As Lindner states:

> When the showdown arrives and payment is demanded; he [the pressure victim] may be unwilling to come across. Then a startling transformation comes over his benefactor and erstwhile friend, and the harassed neophyte finds himself backed against a wall with a knife pressed to his stomach, and he hears the demand to "fuck or fight."[19]

The approaches of bribery and gambling are often expediently bypassed if an inmate is regarded as especially weak and frightened. Such men are often bluntly informed to submit to homosexual acts or else! One young inmate was approached less than five minutes after his arrival by a prison "jocker" who stated, "Listen, you need a 'daddy' and I'm it!"

Many inmates who capitulate to such demands enter prison as exclusive heterosexuals; however, the fact that a man may have no homosexual tendencies, and may even have a wife and family on the "streets," in no way insulates him from the depredations of prison "pressure artists." The fact that sexually aggressive inmates are often able to back up their demands with impunity is responsible for the "punking" of many such inmates.

Successful homosexual pressuring is made possible by certain tenets of the so-called "inmate code." This system of subcultural folkways and mores is accorded lip support by most inmates in the presence of their peers out of fear of being thought less than a "real con." The code proves singularly dysfunctional for the new and friendless inmate who is not familiar with the nature of prison life. Two maxims of the code, "don't rat" and "do your own time," serve to effectively isolate him from the assistance of either staff or fellow inmates. In the event of "sex pressure," the code, in demanding that such an inmate "be a man" and stand his ground at all costs, proscribes running to other prisoners as "sniveling" and "weak." A "real man" must resist pressure, fight, if necessary, even at the risk of serious injury or death.

Other inmates avoid those of their peers who are being subjected to sex pressuring; they refuse to help either out of fear of suffering the same fate or because of a very real danger of being beaten or even killed for interfering. Nor can the inmate under pressure go to staff for help because of the proscription against "ratting." A man who violates this sacrosanct tenet of the code will be forced to "lock up" in protective custody in order to escape violence at the hands of fellow prisoners. In addition to being called a "p.c. punk," that is, protective custody, such an inmate will suffer the added onus which accompanies the status of "rat." If the punk is jeopardized by the taboo against "ratting," his aggressors are protected by it. "Wolves" and "jockers" are able to wield sanctions ranging from threats to cold-blooded murder with the confidence that virtually no one will inform on them out of fear of being labeled a "rat." The code exhortation to "do your own time" also serves to reinforce the unwillingness of other inmates to become involved in the punk's problem. The subcultural belief that the pressure victim "brings it on himself" out of weakness or stupidity enables other prisoners to rationalize their non-involvement in preventing behavior which they actually disapprove of. Fear, resulting from the well known process of "pluralistic ignorance," effectively keeps prisoners from communicating their real sentiments to one another.

Even inmates who have never been subjected to sexual pressures live in constant fear of being "ripped off" by aggressive peers. Strict public adherence to the inmate code and the formation of a mutual aid pact with a few friends are defensive measures which are employed by most prisoners in the hope of averting "pressure."

The pressure punk is a "situational homosexual" in the strictest sense of the expression. While he typically does not see himself as a "queer," such an inmate faces the formidable task of integrating into his self-image a new identity which has literally been forced upon him. He must somehow deal with the humiliation which attends being passed around like a prostitute among other men, and he must adapt to the derisive remarks which are daily meted out to him by the only reference group on his horizon. His own lower-class socialization, which places a premium on "toughness" and "manliness," condemns him to great inner turmoil. In the eyes of his peers, the punk is little more than an article of commerce. He may not escape from the shackles of this lowly status without incurring the wrath of his masters; indeed, the knowledge that his oppressors stand ready with blade and metal pipe to enforce compliance with their sexual demands keeps the punk trapped in a quagmire of shame and self-hatred. Illustrative of the contempt with which the punk usually comes to regard himself was the statement of one inmate, who, when asked if he would consent to an interview, stated, "No, I don't want anyone to know what I am in here!" Another prisoner, long regarded by his peers as a pressure punk, emotionally burst out during a group therapy discussion, "These people (other inmates) think I'm a sissy, but I'm not. I'm a man."

Pressure punks are usually "owned" by one or more of the predatory groups of "jockers" which exist in prison. In addition to being used for homosexuality by the "pressure clique," the punk is often forced by such groups into prison prostitution or to "burn," that is, rob, the cells of other inmates. These groups of "wolves" or "jockers," each of which may range in size from three or four to twenty or more inmates, divide the proceeds of such activity on a businesslike basis. Sometimes the clique, or one of its members who has come into sole ownership of a "punk," will sell him to another group or individual, a "good punk" bringing perhaps fifteen to twenty cartons of commercial cigarettes. The ignominy of repeatedly being sold is sometimes intolerable for the inmate punk. One such prisoner, revolting against what he called "being sold like an animal," attacked and seriously injured one of his "jockers." Afterward, he confided, "I was afraid they [pressure clique] were going to sell me again, as I was just sold for twelve cartons." Like the queen, a punk may form a symbiotic alliance with a strong "jocker" in the hope of escaping homosexual assaults and control by pressure cliques.

THE "WOLF" OR "JOCKER": LONERS AND PRESSURE CLIQUES

Under certain circumstances a homosexually involved inmate may be defined by his peers as a "wolf," "jocker," or "daddy." These expressions each refer to a single status which involves a minimum of stigmatization. Men who are placed in this category by the inmate community are not regarded as "real homosexuals," since their behavior is felt to be the result of heterosexual deprivation, and conspicuously lacks effeminacy and emotional attachment.

The wolf or jocker plays the stereotyped "male" role in sexual activity. He views himself, and needs to be viewed by his fellow inmates, as "a man"; and within prison to be "a man" and still engage in homosexual acts one must present an image of exaggerated toughness and unequivocal masculinity. The jocker, by consistently wielding force over or raping his sexual partners, maintains for himself and others a perception of his behavior as basically masculine under the circumstances. The more violence that surrounds his sexual acts, the closer the jocker comes to actually engaging in an emotionless act of rape, thereby escaping both homosexual anxiety and the imputation of "queerness" by his peers. Compared to the queen, the wolf represents the opposite side of a coin of bizarre gender caricature: the Marlboro Man juxtaposed against the frail *femme fatale*.

The "jocker's" personality and background are usually characterized by an impulsive and hedonistic concern with securing personal gratification. When combined with the psychopathy which often pervades his personality, imprisonment in a world without women leads him to adopt a "take sex where you can get it" philosophy. While the jocker ostensibly has a strong preference for heterosexual partners, homosexual intercourse means little more to him than the difference between intravaginal and intra-anal penetration. He usually evinces little if any concern for the attitudes or feelings of his partners, whether they are heterosexual or homosexual. The sex history of such an inmate is usually, as Lindner observes, "non-selective, transient, and adventitious."[20] While most prisoners disapprove of his behavior, the jocker usually escapes the public scorn and derision which are meted out to punks and queens. A notable exception to this, however, is the jocker who "takes a queen." Other inmates are aware of the emotional elements likely to be involved in such a relationship, if only because of the nature of queens. Rather than being regarded by peers as consistently playing the masculine sex role, jockers who marry queens are often believed to "flip-flop," that is, sometimes play a passive sex role. Prisoners have a saying, directed toward such liaisons, that "when you make the team, you agree to play any position." One will sometimes hear jibes, such as "Who's playing the daddy tonight?" derisively flung at the jocker who has "courted and married a queen." The possibility of homosexual panic appearing is very real for the would-be masculine jocker who finds himself becoming emotionally involved with a queen.

Prison queens and canteen punks make the sardonic comment that "this year's business is next year's competition," which has reference to the common downward mobility of some wolves or jockers. The jocker is painfully aware that the slightest suggestion of weakness, or emotional involvement in homosexual relations—the smallest chink in his armor of tough masculinity—may instantly topple him to the lowly status of "punk." He constantly must face the possibility that someone will successfully challenge the legitimacy of his claimed status. It is because of this that most prison jockers do not operate as loners; instead, such men usually form predatory alliances with other wolves. The manifest reason for the existence of such groups is the belief that extortion of homosexual favors requires the "muscle" of more than one inmate if it is to be successful; however, the formation of such groups actually serves the latent function of providing security for individuals who often are quite frightened themselves. For the jocker who is running scared, the best defense is a good offense.

The homosexual problem in prison, as Kinsey observes, is largely to be equated with "the control of men who are particularly aggressive in forcing other individuals into homosexual relations."[21] The inability to effectively control prison pressure cliques proves both frustrating and embarrassing to the staff of a correctional institution. The files of many inmates who have been raped, beaten, and even sometimes killed, by groups of pressure "artists," are often filled with letters from the local district attorney's office, the latter declining to prosecute because of the complete unwillingness of inmate witnesses to testify in what would otherwise be prima facie cases. Even in those few instances where a pressure victim initially agrees to testify against his attackers, a sudden "lapse of memory" often occurs just before the case goes to court. Typical of such situations was the statement made by a young inmate who had resisted a group of jockers, only to be knifed by one of their number. He initially agreed to name the inmate who assaulted him, but soon backed down, stating to a prison official from his hospital bed, "You and I both know who 'shanked' [knifed] me, but nothing could make me testify. If I die, my life wouldn't be worth two cents."

The anxiety which prison administrators often feel because of their repeatedly unsuccessful attempts to suppress the formation of pressure cliques is evident in the irate letter of one prison warden to the director of corrections in the wake of a stabbing incident perpetrated by one such group:

> It is indeed a deplorable situation when a young man, helpless and frightened, is nearly murdered four days after his arrival at this institution because he would not submit to the will of a group of criminals. The most unfortunate part of the picture is that it is by no means the first, nor will it be the last such incident. [Author's file]

It is likely that there would be many more injuries and deaths resulting from the aggressiveness of pressure cliques were it not for the willingness of a few inmates to secretly "rat" in order to avert bloodshed.

In addition to often injuring their victims, pressure groups sometimes come into violent conflict with one another, much in the manner of rival delinquent gangs who engage in periodic "rumbles." These incidents, which sometimes escalate into full-scale prison riots, usually arise from an altercation over the ownership of a particular "punk"; sometimes sexual "claim jumping" assumes a racial dimension. This may occur if a Caucasian punk is "ripped off" by a Negro pressure clique, or if a white group begins "burning coal," that is, "punking" a Negro prisoner. The latent racial tensions which characterize contemporary America permeate the walls of this miniature society where they often erupt into internecine violence between white and black prisoners. The following is an account of one such incident:

> The leader of a white pressure clique, who was killed, became involved in an argument with leaders of a Negro clique over the homosexual favors of another Caucasian inmate. This argument resulted in an unexpected attack by the Negroes on Caucasians in the A Wing dayroom on the evening of October 26. During the fight, the Caucasian leader was stabbed to death and several other Caucasian and Mexican inmates were injured by knives and struck by heavy objects. . . . The incident was precipitated by the transfer of a particularly aggressive Caucasian inmate to another prison. This man was feared by all inmates because of his ability to pick out prisoners who would be most vulnerable to pressure. This inmate left behind a homosexual partner who was regarded as one of the more prized "punks" in the prison. A sale of this inmate to a Negro clique promptly followed, but was objected to by many white inmates. Arguments, and meetings with the Negroes in an attempt to nullify the sale, preceded the outbreak of violence. [Author's file]

The author's two-year period of research at a major California prison led him ineluctably to the conclusion that the "homosexual problem" derives largely from the fear and violence which are produced by the attempt of a relatively small number of men to secure substitutive sexual gratification. No attempt has been made here to evaluate the psychological damage which doubtless befalls many men who are sexually victimized by such inmates. It is certainly true, however, that "the impact of incarceration on a man's sex life [is] unquestionably important and must be made the sole subject of an intensive study at some later date."[22] Also beyond the scope of this paper has been a discussion of the numerous proposals which have been advanced as solutions to the problem of prison homosexuality; for example, conjugal visitation, improvements in custody and staffing, isolation of known predatory homosexuals, and architectural changes.

"Homosexuality," as Tappan laconically observes, "is a universal concomitant of sex-segregated living."[22] To reiterate an earlier point, its existence in prison must be constantly dealt with on both a psychological and sociological level by every inmate. The typology of homosexual roles discussed here is certainly neither exhaustive nor immutable; hopefully, however, it provides a reasonably inclusive overview of a highly complex and constantly changing system of social behavior, and will also serve to encourage further research on the subject.

Notes

1. Gresham M. Skyes [*sic*], *The Society of Captives* (Princeton: Princeton University Press, 1958), p. 456.

2. Victor Nelson, *Prison Days and Nights* (Boston: Little, Brown, 1933), p. 143.

3. Alfred C. Kinsey et al., *Sexual Behavior in the Human Male* (Philadelphia: W. B. Saunders, 1948), p. 529.

4. Heterosexual deprivation is perhaps most difficult to endure in those states that employ the so-called indefinite sentence system. Where broad minima and maxima exist in penal statutes, the prisoner is painfully aware that his release could take years; the absence of a clear "definition of the situation" with respect to sentence time leaves him to the capricious whims of his captors.

5. Sykes, *Society*, pp. 71–72.

6. For a discussion of prison pornography and its effects, see Charles E. Smith, "Prison Pornography," *Journal of Social Therapy* I (April 1955): 126–129. and S. B. Zuckerman, "Sex Literature in Prison," *Journal of Social Therapy* I (April 1955): 126–132.

7. Paul W. Tappan. *Crime, Justice and Correction* (Pennsylvania: Maple Press, 1960), p. 678.

8. Abraham H. Maslow. *Motivation and Personality* (New York: Harper and Brothers, 1954) pp. 146–154.

9. Robert M. Lindner, *Stone Walls and Men* (New York: Odyssey Press, 1946) p. 456.

10. The gradual "shift in penal philosophy and practice" from isolating prisoners to permitting increased interaction—which permitted development of a complex inmate social system—was something which paralleled the movement away from the so-called "Pennsylvania or separate system" to the Auburn ("silent system"), or what is known as "congregate confinement" in the United States. The Auburn system involved a radical departure from the old system of complete, round-the-clock separation of prisoners from one another. By permitting congregate or group labor during the day, Auburn opened the door to what has become a steadily increasing level of social interaction between inmates in American prisons. As inmates begin to talk, eat, work, and cell together, a prison subculture emerges—and with it the "homosexual problem." Prior to Auburn, which opened in 1816, the austere "separate system," as its name implies, so isolated men from one another that only the most rudimentary social system may be said to have existed. The history of this gradual shift from isolation to congregate confinement is well documented in Tappan, op. cit., pp. 601–611.

11. Albert Ellis, "Masturbation," *Journal of Social Therapy* I (April 1955): 143.

12. Clinton T. Duffy, *Sex and Crime* (New York: Doubleday and Co., 1965), p. 29.

13. I mean here that not only sensational writers, but professional penologists as well,

misperceive the actual extensiveness of prison homosexuality. One can find in a literature both very high and very low estimates. However, on the basis of questionnaire responses of a stratified random sample of 150 inmates, and the statements of many institutional homosexuals who were in a favorable position to estimate the amount of homosexuality, I conclude that a relatively small number, although a highly visible minority, is actually involved. In my random sample of Soledad's tri-facility (three separate prison units in one compound), 80.7 percent agreed with the statement, "I think that masturbation is far more common in here than sex acts between inmates," 64 percent agreed with the statement, "I would say that very few inmates in here get involved with sex acts with other inmates," while 18.4 percent were undecided and only 17.5 percent disagreed.

14. This typology of homosexually involved inmates is lucidly presented by Sykes, loc. cit.

15. Ibid., p. 96.

16. Lindner, op. cit., p. 464.

17. Sykes, loc. cit.

18. The expression "prisonization" was originated by Donald Clemmer, *The Prison Community* (New York: Holt, Rinehart and Winston, 1958) to denote the extent to which an inmate has taken on or internalized the value system of the prison.

19. Lindner, op. cit., p. 454.

20. Ibid., p. 458.

21. Kinsey et al., loc. cit.

22. Ibid., p. 224.

16

Lesbian Behavior As an Adaptation to the Occupation of Stripping

Charles H. McCaghy and James K. Skipper Jr.

In recent publications Simon and Gagnon (1967a, 1967b) contend that too frequently students of deviant behavior are prepossessed with the significance of the behavior itself and with the "exotic" trappings which accompany it. One finds exhaustive accounts of the demographic characteristics of deviants, the variety of forms their behavior may take, and the characteristics of any subculture or "community," including its argot, which emerge as a direct consequence of a deviant status. Furthermore, Simon and Gagnon chide researchers for being locked into futile searches for ways in which inappropriate or inadequate socialization serves to explain their subjects' behavior.

Simon and Gagnon argue that these research emphases upon descriptions of deviant behavior patterns and their etiology provide an unbalanced and misleading approach to an understanding of deviants. Deviants do or, at least, attempt to accommodate themselves to the "conventional" world, and they play many roles which conform to society's expectations. Yet, for the most part, deviants' learning and playing of nondeviant or conventional roles are either ignored by researchers or interpreted strictly as being influenced by a dominant deviant role. The focus of most research obscures the fact that with few exceptions a deviant role occupies a minor portion of the individuals' behavior spectrums. What is not recognized is the influence which commitments and roles of a nondeviant nature have upon deviant commitments and roles. To illustrate their contention, Simon and Gagnon

This paper is a revised and expanded version of one presented before joint meetings of the Midwest and the Ohio Valley Sociological Societies in Indianapolis May 1–3, 1969. We would like to express our appreciation to David Gray for his assistance during the data collection stage of this research.

discuss how homosexual behavior patterns are linked with the identical concerns and determinants which influence heterosexuals: aging problems, identity problems, making a living, management of sexual activity, etc. The authors argue convincingly for damping concern over ultimate causes of homosexuality and for concentrating on factors and contingencies shaping the homosexual role. In their words: "Patterns of adult homosexuality are consequent upon the social structures and values that surround the homosexual after he becomes, or conceives himself as, homosexual rather than upon original and ultimate causes" (Simon and Gagnon, 1976b:179).

Since past research on homosexuals has been dominated by an emphasis upon the sexual feature of their behavior and its consequences, it is fitting that Simon and Gagnon draw attention to linking deviant with nondeviant behaviors or roles. However, since in their scheme the choice of sexual object is taken as given, a complementary perspective is still needed to gain an understanding of the process by which individuals engage in homosexual behavior. We suggest a structural approach. Because sexual behavior, deviant or not, emerges out of the context of social situations, it would seem that the structure of certain situations might contribute to becoming involved in homosexual behavior and to the formation of a homosexual self-concept. We are not suggesting such structures as "ultimate" causes; rather, we are saying that different social structures may provide conditions, learning patterns, and justifications differentially favorable to the occurrence of homosexual contacts and self-concepts. This is not strictly a matter of etiology, then, but an epidemiological concern over differential incidences of deviance, regardless of how episodic or pervasive homosexual behavior may be for an individual case.

A pertinent, albeit extreme, example here is the incidence of homosexual behavior occurring among incarcerated populations. A large proportion of prisoners can be identified as "jail house turnouts": those whose homosexual behavior is limited to within an institutional setting (Sykes, 1965:72, 95–99; Ward and Kassebaum, 1965:76, 96). Evidence indicates that contingencies and opportunities inherent in the prison setting are related to the onset and possible continuation of homosexual behavior. There is no question that for some prisoners homosexual behavior emerges as an adaptation to the prison structure which not only curtails avenues of heterosexual release, but deprives inmates of meaningful affective relationships they would otherwise have (Gagnon and Simon, 1968b; Giallombardo, 1966:133–157).

We have little reliable information concerning the incidence of homosexuality among various populations outside the setting of total institutions.[1] Most researchers agree that homosexuals will be found across the entire socieconomic [sic] spectrum (Kinsey et al., 1948:639–655; Kinsey et al., 1953; 459–460, 500; Gerassi, 1966; Leznoff and Westley, 1956). There is, however, continual speculation that relatively high proportions of male homosexuals are contained in certain occupational groups such as dancers, hair dressers, etc. Assuming this speculation to be correct it is still unclear which is prior: occupational choice or commitment to homosexual behavior. The sociological literature is replete with examples of how occupation influences other aspects of social life; there is no apparent reason why choice of sexual objects should necessarily vary independently. This is not to say that occupations are as extreme as total institutions in their control over life situations regarding sexual behavior. We do suggest that *some* occupations, like the prison setting, may play a crucial role in providing pressures, rationales, and opportunities leading to involvement in, if not eventual commitment to, homosexual behavior.

In the course of conducting a study of the occupations culture of stripping, we found that homosexual behavior was an important aspect of the culture which apparently stemmed less from any predisposition of the participants than from contingencies of the occupation.

Nature of the Research

The principal research site was a midwestern burlesque theater which employed a different group of four touring strippers each week. With the permission and support of the theater manager, two male researchers were allowed access to the back stage dressing room area during and after afternoon performances. The researchers were introduced to each new touring group by the female stage manager, a person whom the girls trusted. After the stage manager presented them as "professors from the university who are doing an anthology on burlesque," the researchers explained that they were interested in how persons became strippers and what these persons thought about stripping as an occupation. After this, the researchers bided their time with small talk, card playing, and general questions to the girls about their occupation.[2] The purposes of this tactic were to make the girls more comfortable and to allow the researchers to survey the field for respondents.

The primary data were gathered through in-depth interviews with 35 strippers.[3] Although there was no systematic method of selecting respondents from each touring group, an attempt was made to obtain a range of ages, years in the occupation, and salary levels. There were only four cases of outright refusals to be interviewed, one coming after the girl had consulted with a boyfriend. In six cases no convenient time for the interview could be arranged because the potential subjects were "busy." It was impossible in these instances to determine whether the excuses really constituted refusals. In general, the researchers found the girls eager to cooperate and far more of them wanted to be interviewed than could be accommodated.

The interviews, lasting an average of an hour and a half, were conducted in bars, restaurants, and, on occasion, backstage. Although difficult at times, the interviewing took place in a manner in which it was not overheard by others. In all but one case, two researchers were present. Interviews were also conducted with others, both male and female, whose work brought them in contact with strippers: the theater manager, stage manager, union agent, and sales persons selling goods to strippers backstage. The interviews were semi-structured and designed to elicit information on background, the process of entering the occupation, and aspects of the occupational culture.

Incidence of Homosexuality

Ideally, in order to posit a relationship between the occupation and homosexual contacts it would be necessary to establish that the incidence of such behavior is relatively higher among strippers than in other female occupations. However, statistics comparing rates of homosexuality among specific female occupational groups are simply not available. Ward and Kassebaum (1965:75, 148–149) did find as part of female prison lore that lesbianism is prominent among models and strippers. In our research the restricted sample and relatively brief contact with the subjects did not allow us to ascertain directly the extent of homosexual behavior among strippers. We were, however, able to gauge the salience of such behavior in the occupation by asking the subjects to estimate what proportion of strippers had homosexual contacts. Estimates ranged from 15 to 100 percent of the girls currently being at least bisexual in their contacts; most responses fell within the 50 to 75 percent range. We also have evidence, mostly self-admissions, that nine of the thirty-five respondents (26 percent) themselves engaged in homosexual behavior while in the occupation, although in no case did we request such information or have prior evidence of the respondents' involvement. We did make some attempt to include subjects in the sample whom we suspected were maintaining relatively stable homosexual relationships. But these deliberate efforts were futile. In two cases strippers known to be traveling with unemployed and unrelated female companions refused to be interviewed, saying they were "too busy."

Despite our inability to fix an exact proportion of strippers who had engaged in homosexuality, it is clear from the subjects' estimates and their ensuing discussions that such behavior is an important facet of the occupation. The estimates of 50 to 75 percent are well above Kinsey's finding that 19 percent of his total female sample had physical sexual contact with other females by age 40 (1953:452–453). This difference is further heightened when we consider that a large majority of our sample (69 percent) were or had been married; Kinsey found that only three percent of married and nine percent of previously married females had homosexual contacts by age 40 (1953:453–454).

Conditions Contributing to Homosexuality

More relevant to the hypothesis of this paper, however, are the conditions of the occupation which our subjects claimed were related to the incidence of homosexual behavior, whatever its magnitude. It was evident from their discussions that a great part, if not most, of such behavior could be attributed to occupational conditions. Specifically, conditions supportive of homosexual behavior in the strip-

ping occupation can be classified as follows: 1) isolation from affective social relationships; 2) unsatisfactory relationships with males; and 3) an opportunity structure allowing a wide range of sexual behavior.

Isolation from affective social relationships.   Evidence from our research indicates that in general strippers have difficulty maintaining permanent affective
social relationships, judging by their catalogues of marital difficulties and lack of
persons whom they say they can trust. Aside from such basic inabilities, it is apparent that the demands of the occupation as a touring stripper make it exceedingly
difficult for the girls to establish or maintain immediate affective relationships,
even on a temporary basis. The best way to demonstrate this is to describe their
working hours. Generally, strippers on tour spend only one week in each city and
work all seven days from Friday through Thursday evening. They must be in the
next city by late Friday morning for rehearsal. Their working day usually begins
with a show about 1 P.M. and ends around 11 P.M., except on Saturday when there
may be a midnight show. Although the girls' own acts may last only about 20 minutes in each of four daily shows, they also perform as foils in the comedians' skits.
As as a consequence, the girls usually are restricted to the theater every day from 1
to 11 P.M. except for a two and a half hour dinner break. After the last show most either go to a nearby nightclub or to their hotel rooms to watch television. Many girls
spend over 40 weeks a year on tour.

Such working conditions effectively curtail the range of social relationships
these girls might otherwise have. It should not be surprising that a nearly universal
complaint among strippers is the loneliness they encounter while on tour. One girl
claimed: "When you are lonely enough you will try anything." By itself this loneliness is not necessarily conducive to homosexual activities since, aside from other
girls in the troupe, there is isolation from females as well as from males. But strippers find that contacts with males are not only limited but often highly unsatisfactory in content, and homosexuality can become an increasingly attractive alternative.

Unsatisfactory relationships with males.   As stated above, women prisoners claim that lesbianism is very frequent among strippers. Data from our research
tends to confirm this rumor. There is also some evidence that homosexual behavior
is relatively frequent among prostitutes (Ward and Kassebaum, 1965:126–32). It is a
curious paradox that two occupations dedicated to the sexual titillation of males
would contain large numbers of persons who frequently obtain their own gratification from females. Tempting as it may be to turn to some exotic psychoanalytic
explanations concerning latent homosexuality, the reasons may not be so covert.
Ward and Kassebaum (1965:126–132) and others (Benjamin and Masters, 1964:245–
246n) note that among prostitutes homosexual behavior may result less from inclination or predisposition than from continual experiences which engender hostility
toward males in general.

A recurring theme in our interviews was strippers' disillusionment with the
male of the species. This disillusionment often begins on stage when the neophyte

first witnesses audience reactions which prove shocking even to girls who take off their clothes in public. Due to lighting conditions the stripper is unable to see beyond the second row of seats but from these front rows she is often gratuitously treated to performances rivaling her own: exhibitionism and masturbation. There is no question that strippers are very conscious of this phenomenon for they characterize a large proportion of their audience as "degenerates." This term, incidentally, occurred so often in the course of our interviews it could be considered part of the stripper argot. Strippers know that "respectable" people attend their performances, but they are usually out in the dark where they cannot be seen. Furthermore, a sizeable proportion of these "respectables" are perceived by strippers to be "couples," hence most of the unattached male audience is suspect.

There is no indication that strippers on tour have more off-stage contact with their audience than does any other type of performer. But the precedent set by the males in rows one and two persists for strippers even in their off-stage contacts with men. They find that their stage identifications as sex objects are all too frequently taken at face value. Initially, strippers may find this identification flattering but many eventually become irritated by it. As one subject put it:

> If a guy took me out to dinner and showed me a good time, I'd sleep with him. But most of them just call up and say "Let's fuck."

When checking into hotels while on tour most girls register under their real rather than their stage name. Several girls pointed out to us that the purpose of this practice was to eliminate being phoned by their admirers. Furthermore, many of the girls avoid identifying themselves in public as strippers, preferring to call themselves dancers, entertainers, and the like. This enables them not only to steer clear of a pariah label but to minimize unwelcome sexual reactions which they feel the name "stripper" engenders.

When strippers do form relatively prolonged liaisons with males during the course of their stripping career, chances are good that they will result in another embittering experience. In some cases the man will insist that the girl abandon the occupation, something she may not be inclined to do; hence a breakup occurs. But more frequently the girls find themselves entangled with males who are interested only in a financial or sexual advantage. One of our male informants closely connected with the stripping profession claimed, "You know the kind of jerks these girls tie up with? They're pimps, leeches, or weirdos." This, of course is an oversimplification; yet the strippers themselves confirm that they seem to be involved with more than their share of rough, unemployed males who are more than happy to enjoy their paycheck.

Strippers probably are not without fault themselves in their difficulties with heterosexual relationships; in our sample of 35 we found that of the 24 who had ever been married, 20 had experienced at least one divorce. It is evident, however, that their problems are compounded by the exploitive males who gravitate toward them. Under these circumstances contacts with lesbians are often seen as respites from importunate males. One subject claimed that although she did not care to engage in homosexual activities she would frequently go to a lesbian bar where she could "have a good time and not be bothered." Another said that lesbians are the only ones who "treat you like a person." As one reasoned:

> Strippers go gay because they have little chance to meet nice guys. They come in contact with a lot of degenerate types. If they do meet a nice guy chances are he will ask them to stop stripping. If he doesn't he's likely to be a pimp. So the girls got to turn to a woman who understands them and their job. It is very easy for them to listen to the arguments of lesbians who will tell them basically that men are no good and women can give them better companionship.

Our argument should in no way be interpreted to mean that most strippers are anti-male or have completely severed all contacts with males. From our research it appears that the "career" homosexual is the exception among strippers. At best, the majority can be described as bisexual. The point is that experiences gained in the course of their occupation promote the homosexual aspect by generating caution and skepticism where relationships with males are concerned. Limited contacts with males plus the wariness which accompanies these contacts can be instrumental in severely curtailing the sexual activity of strippers outside of prostitution. Thus an opportunity for a warm, intimate relationship unaccompanied by masculine hazards becomes increasingly attractive. According to one of our subjects, when faced by the lesbian ploy, "Men are no good; I can do things for you they can't," many strippers find themselves persuaded, at least temporarily.

Opportunity structure allowing a wide range of sexual behavior.   The final occupational condition contributing to the incidence of homosexual behavior among strippers involves the existence of both opportunities and tacit support for such behavior. As male researchers we found it difficult to fathom the opportunities available for female homosexual activities. Our respondents pointed out, however, that there is no want in this regard. Strippers on tour have easy access to information on the location of gay bars in any city they play; furthermore, the reception strippers receive in these bars is especially hospitable. More immediate opportunities are available, obviously, with the presence of homosexuals in the touring group itself. The group which, of necessity, spends most of the day together provides the novice stripper with at least an opportunity for sexual experimentation without the risks inherent in becoming involved with complete strangers.

There is some indication also that some strippers experienced in homosexual behavior are not particularly quiescent when obtaining partners. One subject informed us that she avoids touring with certain groups simply because homosexual contacts within the group are an expected mode of behavior and noncompliance is punished by ostracism. She claimed that being on tour was boring enough without having the other girls refusing to talk or associate with her. In this same vein, several of our subjects stated that certain older and established women in the occupation actively recruit partners with promises of career rewards. We were at first skeptical of such "casting couch" tactics among strippers, but the same stories and names recurred so often from such diverse sources that the possibility cannot be ignored.

We do not wish to over-dramatize the pressures placed on the girls by others to engage in lesbian practices. No doubt such pressures do occur, but sporadically. More important is the fact that opportunities for homosexual contacts occur in an atmosphere of permissiveness toward sexual behavior which characterizes the workday philosophy of strippers. The strippers' principal salable product is sex; the music, dancing, and costumes are only accessories. The real product becomes, over time, effectively devoid of any exclusiveness and is treated with the same detachment as grocers eventually view their radishes. For some strippers sexual contacts are regarded not only with detachment but with a sense of indifference:

> I usually don't get kicks out of other women, not really, but there are times. Sometimes you come home and you are just too tired to work at it. Then it's nice to have a woman around. You can lay down on the floor, relax, watch T.V. and let her do it.

Add to this a sense of cynicism regarding sexual mores. Sexual behavior is generally not characterized by strippers as right or wrong by any universal standard but in terms of its presumed incidence in the general society; many of our respondents firmly expressed their view that lesbianism and prostitution are easily as common among women outside the occupation as among strippers. One respondent reasoned:

> Strippers are no different in morality than housewives, secretaries, waitresses, or anybody else. There is a certain amount of laxity of behavior which would occur in anybody, but with the occupational hazard of being lonely and moving from town to town, well, that's the reason.

The end effect of such attitudes is that no stigma is attached to either homosexual behavior or prostitution[4] among strippers as long as the participants are discreet, do not bother others, and do not allow their activities to interfere with the stability of the touring group. It appears, then, that strippers work in a situation where opportunities for homosexuality are not only available but where social pressures restricting sexual choice to males are minimal or nonexistent.

Summary

Previous research indicates that most homosexual careers, male or female, begun outside the total institutional setting involve enlistment rather than a system of recruitment through peer group or subcultural pressures (Gagnon and Simon, 1968a:116, 118). As sociologists, however, we must not lose sight of the importance of situational conditions as explanatory variables for understanding rates of deviant behavior. We have attempted to demonstrate how sexual behavior may be an adaptation to social factors immediately impinging upon the actors; specifically, we have argued that the stripping occupation may be analogous to the prison setting in that its structural characteristics contribute to the incidence of homosexual behavior.

Notes

1. Estimates of the proportion of males having homosexual contacts during imprisonment range between 30 and 45 percent, depending on the institution, characteristics of the population, and length of sentences (Gagnon and Simon, 1968b:25). In one women's institution researchers estimated that 50 percent of the inmates had at least one sexual contact during their imprisonment (Ward and Kassebaum, 1965:92).

2. Data concerning stripteasers and the occupation of stripping may be found in a paper by Skipper and McCaghy (1969).

3. The social characteristics of the interviewed sample of strippers are as follows: All were white and ranged in age from 19 to 45, with 60 percent between the ages of 20 and 30. On the Hollingshead (1957) two-factor index of social position, ten came from families in classes I and II, nine from class III, and 12 from classes IV and V. (Family background data were not obtained in four cases.) Their range of education was from seven to 16 years: 22 had graduated from high school, eight of whom had at least one year of college.

4. One perceptive respondent even questioned the rationality of the legal definition of prostitution: "There is a very hazy line between what people call prostitution and just going to bed with a man. What is the difference between taking $50 for it, or receiving flowers, going out to dinner, and then the theater, and then getting laid? One has preliminaries, otherwise there is no difference. There is a payment both ways."

REFERENCES

Benjamin, Harry, and R. E. L. Masters. 1964. *Prostitution and Morality*. New York: Julian Press.

Gagnon, John H. and William Simon. 1968a. "Sexual deviance in contemporary America." *Annals of the American Academy of Political and Social Science*. 376 (March): 106–122.

———. 1968b. "The social meaning of prison homosexuality." *Federal Probation*. 32 (March): 23–29.

Gerassi, John. 1966. *The Boys of Boise: Furor, Vice, and Folly in an American City*. New York: Macmillan.

Giallombardo, Rose. 1966. *Society of Women: A Study of a Woman's Prison*. New York: Wiley.

Hollingshead, August B. 1957. *Two Factor Index of Social Position*. New Haven: Yale University (mimeographed).

Kinsey, Alfred C., Wardell B. Pomeroy, and Clyde E. Martin. 1948. *Sexual Behavior in the Human Male*. Philadelphia: Saunders.

Kinsey, Alfred C., Wardell B. Pomeroy, Clyde E. Martin, and Paul H. Gebhard. 1953. *Sexual Behavior in the Human Female*. Philadelphia: Saunders.

Leznoff, Maurice, and William A. Westley. 1956. "The homosexual community." *Social Problems* 3 (April): 257–263.

Simon, William, and John H. Gagnon. 1967a. "Femininity in the lesbian community." *Social Problems* 15 (Fall): 212–221.

———. 1967b. "Homosexuality: The formulation of a sociological perspective." *Journal of Health and Social Behavior* 8 (September): 177–185.

Skipper, James K., Jr., and Charles H. McCaghy. 1969. "Stripteasers and the anatomy of a deviant occupation." Paper read at American Sociological Association meetings in San Francisco (September, 1969).

Sykes, Gresham M. 1965. *The Society of Captives: A Study of a Maximum Security Prison*. New York: Atheneum.

Ward, David A., and Gene G. Kassebaum. 1965. *Women's Prison: Sex and Social Structure*. Chicago: Aldine.

5
Bisexuality by Another Name

17

Heterosexual Gays, Heterosexual Lesbians, and Homosexual Straights

Paula C. Rodríguez Rust

THE early years of affirmative research on lesbian and gay topics discovered homosexuality in some unexpected places and among some apparently heterosexual people. In "The Social Integration of Queers and Peers" Albert J. Reiss (1961) exposed a world of prostitution in which heterosexually identified adolescent gang members exchange sexual services for payment from older men as part of a lower-class juvenile delinquent subculture. In *Tearoom Trade: Impersonal Sex in Public Places* Laud Humphreys (1970) uncovered the world of men who are married and whose families do not suspect that their apparently conventional husbands and fathers occasionally visit public rest rooms for the purpose of having sex with other men. A decade later, encouraged by gay liberation and fear of AIDS, these men and others who had concealed their same-sex desires began to acknowledge their sexualities to themselves and their families. Many sought psychological counseling during this process. In the 1980s authors like Eli Coleman and Timothy J. Wolf opened the door to the therapist's office and brought to light the issues that arise in marriages in which one partner is bisexual, lesbian, or gay.

Hidden from public view during the 1960s and 1970s, the sexual behaviors of these populations took on added significance once the routes of HIV transmission were discovered (Gagnon 1989). Punk prostitutes and married men who have sex with men, whether found on the streets, in tearooms, or in psychologists' offices, exist at the border between lesbian and gay communities and heterosexual society. They are the conceptual "dirt" (Douglas 1966) that threatens the clarity of the distinction between homosexuality and heterosexuality and shortens the social distance between the lesbian and gay communities on one hand and heterosexual society on the other hand. Fears of HIV and conceptualizations of AIDS as a moral disease because of its association with "dirty" sexual activity resonated with these conceptualizations of border crossers as dirt, leading to the view that these people would be the bridges, or conduits, through which HIV would pass from the marginalized gay population into the "general" heterosexual population (e.g., Shernoff and Palacios-Jimenez 1988). As long as HIV affected mostly gay men, it was popularly viewed as contained and therefore not a real threat; its potential "spread" to heterosexuals would mean that *anyone* could get it. Popular hysteria motivated scientific attention by researchers who varied in the degree to which they shared the popular conception of their subjects as social threats to (heterosexual) society rather than members of an inclusive society that had been among the first to fall victim to a deadly disease.

Male Prostitution

As mentioned in chapter 14, many links between the worlds of prostitution and homosexuality have been studied by social scientists and observed by social commentators. Charles H. McCaghy and James K. Skipper Jr. (1969), in the article reprinted as chapter 16 of section 4, explored same-sex sexual activity among female prostitutes as a consequence of heterosexual sex work. In contrast, the authors reviewed here explored homosexual sex work by gay, bisexual, and heterosexual adults and adolescents. Rather than same-sex sexual behavior being a reaction to the disillusionment of heterosexual prostitution, in this case the prostitution itself is same-sex. This research has focused on male prostitutes; women who have sex with women for money—a phenomenon that is not "sufficiently widespread to be of any social significance"[1]—have largely escaped the attention of researchers. The literature on same-sex male prostitution is relevant to bisexuality because many male prostitutes, regardless of their sexual self-identities, also engage in heterosex for either money or pleasure; these prostitutes are the primary focus here. The reader who is interested in a broader review of the literature on male prostitution is referred to Richard R. Pleak and Heino F. L. Meyer-Bahlburg (1990) and Coleman (1989a) for recent reviews, to Neil R. Coombs (1974) for a review of earlier literature, and to Harry Benjamin and R. E. L. Masters (1964) for a classic historical and sociological examination of male and female prostitution.

Making sense of the research on male prostitution requires recognition that there are several different types of male prostitutes. As among female prostitutes, street prostitutes are the "lowest" class of male prostitute, tending to be young and with few resources for self-protection except the threat of physical retaliation. Prostitutes who solicit in bars or strip clubs, who work as call men or escorts, or who are "kept" typically enjoy safer working environments and higher incomes and can be more selective in choosing clients. Male prostitutes also include those who work part-time while attending college or maintaining regular employment; transvestite, transsexual, or otherwise transgendered prostitutes who tend to work the streets; prison punks whose special circumstances are discussed in chapter 14; gay youths for whom prostitution is a sexual outlet or means of participating in gay male subculture and who tend to be runaways from middle-class homes; and juvenile delinquents for whom prostitution is part of a larger constellation of illicit activities sanctioned by peer subcultures and who tend to be from lower-class homes. Unlike female prostitutes, few male prostitutes work in brothels or for pimps and little research has been conducted on such prostitutes (Coleman 1989a; Waldorf et al. 1990).[2] Descriptions of the distinctions between and psychosocial characteristics of some of these different types of male prostitutes can be found in a number of detailed works on the subject.[3]

The juvenile delinquent male prostitute was the subject of Reiss's (1961) classic study, "The Social Integration of Queers and Peers."[4] Reiss's subjects were adolescent boys whose clients were homosexual men, but who did not identify themselves as bisexual or gay. They were socialized into hustling by their peer groups, who provided the opportunities, rules, and rationale for the behavior. They maintained heterosexual identities by conceptualizing their hustling as one possible income-earning delinquent activity rather than a source of sexual satisfaction. The rules governing the queer-peer transaction—no show of affection by either the boy or his client, no sexual acts other than fellatio, and the necessity of payment—protected this construction of the behavior (see also Hoffman 1972; Visano 1990; Calhoun 1992). The importance of these rules for the maintenance of the boys' heterosexual identities is evidenced by the violence with which they responded when the rules were broken. Although Reiss did not discuss the boys' sexual activities aside from hustling, his anecdotal references to their dating girls imply that they were also sexually active with the other sex and therefore behaviorally bisexual.

More recently, D. Kelly Weisberg (1985; see also Fisher, Weisberg, and Marotta 1982) described changes in the peer delinquent subculture of male prostitution in San Francisco from the 1960s through the 1980s. Reiss's "peers" used violence only when the rules of the transaction were broken, because gratuitous violence would endanger the income potential of hustling. Weisberg made no mention of the use of violence when describing the peer delinquent hustling scene of the 1960s, describing adolescent male prostitutes of the time as "primarily hippies." However, during the 1970s and early 1980s Weisberg reported that peer delinquent male prostitutes became more aggressive, more likely to be drug users, and more heterosexual in their appearance and behavior. By the early 1980s Weisberg found "currents of subsurface hostility" (162) between male adolescent prostitutes and their male customers and Mark-David Janus, Barbara Scanlon, and Virginia Price (1984) described the heterosexual-identified peer delinquent prostitute as more violent than other types of prostitutes.

In contrast to peer delinquents for whom prostitution is a source of income and who use violence to enforce the rules of the transaction, other peer delinquents use prostitution as a ruse for the purpose of theft or violence. H. Laurence Ross's (1959) classic "The 'Hustler' in Chicago" focuses on hustlers whose prostitution was a means to opportunities for pocket picking, extortion, or blackmail. Similarly, Donald M. Allen (1980) described peer delinquents whose rationale for prostitution was the opportunity to assault or rob homosexual customers. Like Reiss's peers, Allen's delinquents identified themselves as heterosexual. They constructed their victimization of gay men as demonstrations of their own masculinity and heterosexuality.

But Allen's findings call these youths' heterosexual identities into question. Based on self-reported feelings of sexual arousal and psychic responses, most of Allen's fourteen peer delinquents (86 percent) received Kinsey ratings of 2–4. None were Kinsey 0's, and only one was a Kinsey 1. Citing one peer delinquent who admitted that his aggressive behavior toward homosexuals was designed to steer suspicion away from himself, Allen implied that this might be true for many or all peer delinquents, especially those who functioned as group leaders. Journalist Arno Karlen was of the same mind, commenting that "it is difficult to believe that some became involved in hustling without some degree of conscious or unconscious interest to begin with" (1971:311). Benjamin and Masters (1964) noted that "there is a kind of proverb in the homosexual world to the effect that today's prostitute is tomorrow's 'score'" (294). They argued that the fact that prostitutes rate customers as more or less desirable on the basis of their appearance, and alter their fees accordingly, suggests a degree of homosexual interest—read bisexuality—on the part of the prostitute (see also Janus, Scanlon, and Price 1984).

Visano (1990) noted that peer delinquent male hustlers and prostitutes probably make up a smaller proportion of the entire male prostitute scene than they did a few decades ago; in a study of male adolescent prostitutes Visano found that only 23 percent identified as heterosexual and belonged to homophobic reference groups, thus fitting the profile described by Reiss, Ross, and Allen. Perhaps growing social acceptance of homosexuality and bisexuality has allowed adolescents who would have been self-identified heterosexual peer delinquents in the past to acknowledge the attractions to men that might partially motivate their behavior and to identify as bisexual or gay.

Pleak and Meyer-Bahlburg also noted that bisexual and homosexual self-identities appear to be increasingly prevalent among male prostitutes. Early studies on male prostitutes characterized most subjects as heterosexual, whereas studies done in the 1970s and 1980s "have found increasing proportions of male prostitutes to be bisexual and homosexual" (1990:577).[5] The authors suggested that this historical trend might be the result of increasing accuracy in researchers' assessments of sexual orientation combined with more inclusive sample selection methods[6] and increasing willingness of prostitutes to identify as bisexual or gay because of changing social attitudes toward homosexuality. Debra Boyer (1989) asserted that earlier researchers and their subjects "agreed upon a mutual denial of homosexuality" (155), a denial that is increasingly unnecessary and untenable.[7] Thus, the significance of prostitution in the study of bisexuality lies not only in the fact that the literature on male prostitution is one genre in which information about bisexuality is found prior to the recent upsurge in scientific attention to bisexuality per se but also in the fact, revealed by increasing social acceptance, that bisexuality might be more common among prostitutes than among nonprostitutes.

Findings regarding the percentages of male prostitutes who identify as bisexual range from 15 percent to 40 percent.[8] For example, among 224 male street prostitutes in Atlanta, Georgia, Jacqueline Boles and Kirk W. Elifson (1994a) found that 35.7 percent identified as bisexual, 17.9 percent as homosexual, and 46.4 percent as heterosexual. Among 79 young male hustlers in five major metropolitan areas

Bruce Fisher, D. Kelly Weisberg, and Toby Marotta (1982) found that 29 percent identified as bisexual, 47 percent as homosexual, 16.5 percent as heterosexual, 8 percent as transvestite, and 4 percent as transsexual. Among 211 male street prostitutes in New Orleans, Edward V. Morse and colleagues (1991) found that 41.2 percent identified as bisexual, 20 percent as exclusively homosexual, and 38.9 percent as heterosexual; among the 56 who were aged eighteen to twenty-three 37.5 percent identified as bisexual, 25 percent as exclusively homosexual, and 37.5 percent as heterosexual (Simon, Morse, Osofsky, and Balson 1994). Rotheram-Borus and colleagues (1994) found that in a sample of 131 gay and bisexual adolescent males in New York City, recruited through a gay-identified social service agency, 26 percent identified as bisexual. In a study of 50 New York City male street and bar/theater prostitutes aged fourteen to twenty-seven, recruited in their places of work or through personal referral by other study participants, Pleak and Meyer-Bahlburg (1990) reported the Kinsey scores and behaviors as well as the self-identities of their subjects. They found that 30 percent identified themselves as bisexual and 34 percent identified themselves as gay. Subjects' reported ratings on Kinsey scales of behavior and fantasy indicated somewhat higher rates of homosexuality and slightly lower rates of bisexuality than their self-identifications would indicate; 50 percent had combined Kinsey scores of 5–6 and 26 percent had combined Kinsey scores of 2–4. Forty-eight percent had had heterosex for pleasure within the previous three months and 32 percent had been involved in other-sex as well as same-sex prostitution. In comparison, Jacqueline Boles, Mike Sweat, and Kirk W. Elifson (1989) found that 13 percent of male prostitutes had engaged in recreational sex with both male and female partners.

Some researchers compared prostitute to nonprostitute samples and found a higher incidence of bisexual and/or homosexual self-identity among prostitutes. Earls and David (1989) recruited fifty male prostitutes from public parks and fifty male nonprostitutes from shopping malls in a major eastern Canadian city, finding that among the prostitutes 18 percent identified as bisexual, 52 percent as homosexual, and 30 percent as heterosexual, whereas 100 percent of the nonprostitutes identified as heterosexual. In a study of male prostitution as an expression of gay self-identity Boyer (1989) found that 19 percent of forty-seven adolescent male street prostitutes in Seattle identified as bisexual and 51 percent identified as homosexual, compared to 0 percent and 4 percent, respectively, of fifty nonprostitute delinquent males. She reported similar striking differences in the Kinsey scores of prostitutes and nonprostitutes; 38 percent of the prostitutes, compared to none of the nonprostitutes, gave their sexual behavior a Kinsey rating of 2, 3, or 4. Jim A. Cates and Jeffrey Markley (1992) interviewed fifteen male hustlers and fifteen male nonhustlers aged sixteen to thirty-four, recruited from "an area known for trade in male prostitution in a midsized midwestern city" (698), and found that among the hustlers four identified as bisexual, four as gay, one as straight, and six as uncertain. Among the nonhustlers two identified as bisexual, one as gay, two as straight, and ten as uncertain. In a study of the health status and HIV risk behaviors of 620 homeless boys and girls aged twelve to twenty-four who visited an outpatient clinic in Los Angeles during 1988–1989 Gary L. Yates, Richard G.

MacKenzie, Julia Pennbridge, and Avon Swofford (1991) found that those who were involved in prostitution were five times more likely than those who weren't to report having bisexual or homosexual self-identities. Among those males and females involved in prostitution 12.4 percent identified themselves as bisexual, 15.7 percent identified as homosexual, and none reported that they were "undecided," compared to 2.5 percent, 2.9 percent, and 2.5 percent, respectively, among those not involved; Yates, MacKenzie, Pennbridge, and Swofford (1991) did not report self-identities separately for males and females.[9]

If bisexual and homosexual self-identities and behavior are higher among male prostitutes than within the general population, this might be a consequence of an increased likelihood that bisexual and gay youths will be rejected by their families and consequently find themselves on the street where they engage in survival sex and, possibly, embark on careers as prostitutes. From one-third to three-fourths of male prostitutes are or were runaways, or "castaways," and Fisher, Weisberg, and Marotta (1982) found that 24 percent in their sample of 79 male runaways cited "family conflict over homosexuality or sexuality" as a reason for running away from home; all of those who cited this reason were gay or bisexual.[10] David F. Luckenbill (1985) found that, among fifteen male hustlers in Chicago who had left home at an average age of fifteen and became involved in prostitution for "defensive" reasons that included financial need, thirteen considered themselves to be homosexual or bisexual. The extent to which bisexual and gay young people are more likely to be cast away from their families than heterosexual young people is a matter of some controversy because of its political implications, but the fact that some families do cast away their children because of homosexuality leads to the conclusion that young people on the street are at least minimally more likely to be bisexual or gay than their peers who remain at home.

Boyer suggested an additional explanation for the prevalence of bisexual and gay self-identities among young male prostitutes. She argued that for some young gay men, who are denied access to gay venues because of their age and who seek validation and expression of their newly recognized gay selves in the face of family rejection and social intolerance, prostitution becomes a way of participating in gay subculture and establishing a gay identity. In this view same-sex interests motivate entry into prostitution for self-expressive, rather than survival, reasons; but, as in the case of survival sex, the ultimate cause of prostitution among these bisexual and gay youth is the lack of social support provided by their families, friends, and society.

As noted above, male prostitutes are not a homogeneous group, and there is evidence that the likelihood of bisexual or gay self-identity varies between the different classes of prostitutes. A comparison of street to bar/theater prostitutes in Pleak and Meyer-Bahlburg's study revealed different biases in self-identification; street prostitutes were more likely than bar/theater prostitutes to score themselves as Kinsey 0–1's (32 percent versus 16 percent) and, even more strongly, to identify themselves as straight (48 percent versus 16 percent). Conversely, street prostitutes were less likely to identify as bisexual (28 percent) than to rate themselves as Kinsey 2–4's (44 percent), whereas bar/theater prostitutes were more likely to identify as bisexual (32 percent) than to rate themselves as Kinsey 2–4's (8 percent) and less likely to identify themselves as gay (48 percent) than to rate themselves as Kinsey 5–6's (76 percent). These findings suggest that street prostitutes are more likely to experience bisexual or heterosexual than homosexual sexual fantasies and behaviors and are biased, relative to their actual behaviors and fantasies, to identify themselves as straight instead of bisexual, whereas bar/theater prostitutes are predominantly homosexual in their fantasies and behaviors but display a bias toward identifying themselves as bisexual rather than gay. Allen (1980), who grouped bar prostitutes with street prostitutes, found that this group tended toward bisexuality whereas call boys and kept boys tended toward homosexuality in their erotic and psychic responses; no subject in either group had Kinsey ratings of 0 or 1, but 78 percent of street/bar prostitutes rated 2–4 and 79 percent of call and kept boys rated 5 or 6. Dan Waldorf and David Lauderback (1992) found that among 552 male sex workers in San Francisco, street hustlers were less likely to identify as gay (31.9 percent versus 61.9 percent) and more likely to identify as bisexual (23.4 percent versus 15.3 percent), heterosexual (12.4 percent versus 1.5 percent), or transsexual (24.8 percent versus 15.9 percent) than call men. In short, there appears to be a correlation between sexual self-identity and the social status of the prostitute, with street prostitutes tending toward heterosexual self-identity and higher social statuses associated with higher Kinsey scores and a higher likelihood of bisexual or gay self-identities.

There are several possible explanations for these status differences in hustlers' sexual self-identities and Kinsey ratings. First, the street prostitutes studied by Yates, MacKenzie, Pennbridge, and Swofford (1991) and Pleak and Meyer-Bahlburg (1990) might include not only gay runaways but also peer delinquents like those studied by Reiss (1961) and Allen (1980) who identify as heterosexual for subcultural reasons. Janus, Scanlon, and Price (1984) explicitly noted the existence of both "permanent street hustlers," who identify as bisexual or as "confused," and peer delinquents, who identify as heterosexual, among teenage prostitutes in Boston and Weisberg (1985) provided an ethnographic comparison of male prostitution in peer delinquent and gay subcultures. Also supporting this explanation, Pleak and Meyer-Bahlburg found that street prostitutes who engage in sex with both men and women were more likely to have engaged in sex with men for money than for pleasure, and in sex with women for pleasure than for money. Bar/theater prostitutes, on the other hand, were as likely to engage in several specific sexual acts with men for pleasure as they were for money. Prostitute's self-identities, then, probably reflect their preferences in pleasure sex; Pleak and Meyer-Bahlburg's subjects might, like Reiss's gang members, discredit sex engaged in for money as a reflection of their sexual orientations.

Second, the bars and theaters frequented by intermediate status hustlers are generally gay bars and theaters, where male customers are most likely to be found. It is not surprising that hustlers operating in gay environments are more likely to identify as bisexual or gay than those operating on the streets. Bisexual or gay identified hustlers are more likely to feel comfortable in these locales and, conversely and in contrast to street subcultures, the subcultures in these locales would support and encourage the adoption of bisexual or gay self-identity. Similarly, call boys and kept boys, because of their longstanding relationships with particular clients, also find themselves in a situation conducive to bisexual or gay self-identity.

Third, bars and theaters have legally mandated age requirements, and street prostitutes who continue hustling often move into these establishments when they reach the required age, as they acquire identification documents, or as they progress in their careers as prostitutes. Luckenbill (1986) reported that male prostitutes tend to move upward in status if they remain in prostitution; those who begin on the street typically spend some months or years on the streets before moving to indoor locales. Thus, hustlers who frequent bars and theaters tend to be older than street hustlers and to have been hustling for longer periods of time.[11] Research findings indicate that increased incidence of bisexuality and homosexuality is associated with age (Visano 1990) and with longer periods of time spent in prostitution (Allen 1980), suggesting that bar and theater prostitutes are more likely to identify as bisexual or gay because they are older and have been involved in prostitution longer.

An unpublished report by R. Furnald (1978) suggests that age or length of time in prostitution and sexual self-identity results in part because the experience of same-sex prostitution affects the prostitute's own sexual self-identity and orientation. Furnald compared the subjects' sexual behaviors and self-concepts before and after they began hustling and found "greater homosexual orientation after the hustling activity began." Allen, noting a similar correlation in his own findings, referred to a "drift toward homosexuality among the young males who continued as prostitutes" (1980:413), implying that prolonged same-sex prostitution contributed to the development of a homosexual orientation. Of course, it is also plausible that the causal order runs in the other direction, with those men who have bisexual or homosexual desires being more likely to continue patterns of same-sex prostitution into their early adult years. Weisberg (1985) reported that "heterosexual" male prostitutes who "closed their eyes and . . . pretended [the homosexual] was a girl" (22) were "situational" hustlers whose involvement in prostitution was temporary, whereas those who remained involved in prostitution tended to have homosexual feelings. Allen alluded to this possibility as well; finding no Kinsey 0's and only one Kinsey 1 among ninety-eight males who had been regularly active as prostitutes for more than six months, Allen concluded that "at the least an incidental homosexual arousal and/or psychic response (Kinsey rating of 1) is present in all males who continue to be active as prostitutes and that almost all . . . have more than an incidental homosexual response" (1980:421). Regardless of whether bisexual and gay self-identities are the cause or the result of lengthy experience as a homosexual prostitute, the result is a greater prevalence of bisexual or gay self-identity among higher status male prostitutes.

The other participant in male prostitution, the customer, has received far less attention than has the prostitute himself. This lack of attention might be due to the fact that customers are a more difficult population to sample and to a tendency to see the prostitute, rather than his customer, as the locus of the problem requiring study. Although not based on data collected directly from customers, earlier studies varied in their characterizations of male prostitutes' customers as primarily homosexual or as primarily married or professional bisexuals who prefer to keep their same-sex sexual activity a secret.[12] Edward V. Morse, Patricia M. Simon, and their colleagues conducted one of few recent studies focusing on the customer, and they succeeded in recruiting only 15 customers (1991, 1992). These customers were recruited while cruising in their cars, through gay-identified social organizations and bars, and through referral by male prostitutes. Whereas male prostitutes estimated that approximately one-third of their customers were heterosexual (11.7 percent) or bisexual (21.5 percent) and that 40 percent of them were married, 14 of the 15 customers identified themselves as either bisexual (53.3 percent) or heterosexual (40 percent). Visano (1990), who succeeded in interviewing 60 customers of hustlers in addition to 120 hustlers, found that 35 percent of the customers identified themselves as gay.

Same-sex prostitution in which either the prostitute or the customer also engages in heterosex has been the subject of increased public concern in the wake of the HIV epidemic. This concern usually centers on the fear that such prostitutes will be a gateway through which HIV passes from the homosexual to the heterosexual population. In some of the research on prostitution that was inspired by HIV epidemiological concerns there is evidence that researchers share this popular conception of male prostitutes' role in the HIV epidemic. For example, Edward V. Morse, Patricia M. Simon, Paul M. Balson, and Howard J. Osofsky (1992) characterized male prostitutes as a "vector for transmission of HIV infection" (348) and presented their finding that the majority of customers are bisexual or heterosexual in behavior as cause for particular concern because they could thus spread HIV "to their female partners and into the more mainstream heterosexual population" (356).

The most obvious alternative to viewing prostitutes as "vectors of transmission" is that HIV-infected male prostitutes are, no less than anyone else, victims of HIV. Like the customer who becomes infected with HIV acquired from a prostitute, and like the customer's other sex partners who in turn acquire HIV, the prostitute himself acquired HIV from either a customer or a sex partner. Only a worldview in which prostitutes are seen as more morally deserving of HIV infection can support a construction of the prostitute as less a victim than any other seropositive person. Female prostitutes rights activists offer yet another alternative view of prostitutes' role in the HIV epidemic, which is that prostitutes have been among the most active inventors of safer sex techniques because their lives and livelihoods depended on it. In fact, prostitutes might be able to instill safer sex practices among populations unreachable by more formal mainstream efforts at safer sex education. In this view prostitutes are not vectors of transmission but sources of safer sex techniques and nexi for safer sex education.

Are male prostitutes protecting themselves and their customers from HIV infection by practicing safer sex? Despite a high level of knowledge about AIDS, Simon, Morse, Osofsky, and Balson (1994) found that most male prostitutes aged eighteen to twenty-three in New Orleans did not report regular condom use during anal sex; among forty-three who reported anal sex, condoms were never used by 23 percent and only sometimes by 37 percent. This was part of a larger study by the same research team in which male prostitutes estimated that 54 percent of their customers did not wear a condom when acting as the insertor in anal sex and 67 percent did not request that the prostitute wear a condom when acting as the insertor (Morse, Simon, Balson, and Osofsky 1992). In contrast, Waldorf and Lauderback (1992), in their study of male sex workers aged eighteen to fifty-four in San Francisco, found that only 1.8 percent had never used a condom and 73 percent had used a condom during the previous week. In their review of existing research Pleak and Meyer-Bahlburg (1990) reported consistent findings that male prostitutes have a higher incidence of HIV seropositivity than the general population.

Although these findings seem to lend credence to the view that prostitutes are vectors of transmission, one might as well focus attention on the customer who fails to practice safer sex or who requests risky sex acts. Furthermore, the appropriate comparison population for male prostitutes might not be the general population but rather all men who have sex with men. In Amsterdam Roel A. Coutinho, Ruud L. M. Van-Andel, and Toine J. Rijsdick (1988) found that 13 percent of male prostitutes were seropositive compared to 31.4 percent of "homosexual" men recruited from sex saunas and baths. This finding suggests that, among men who have multiple male sex partners, prostitutes have a lower rate of HIV infection than nonprostitutes. Coutinho, Van-Andel, amd Rijsdick themselves blamed not prostitutes, but prostitutes' bisexual customers who want to hide their homosexuality, for the HIV transmission to the "general population." The social context of prostitution is very different in Amsterdam than in the United States, so a similar pattern might not exist in the United States. However, the Amsterdam findings and Coutinho, Van-Andel, amd Rijsdick's discussion suggest that the key to preventing HIV transmission via prostitutes in the United States might be a change in social attitudes toward prostitution and bisexuality, not continued criminalization of prostitution and epidemiologic villainization of both prostitutes and bisexuals.

Several studies indicate that condom use and seropositivity are related to sexual orientation self-identity among prostitutes. Waldorf and Lauderback (1992) found that self-identified bisexual and gay sex workers in San Francisco used condoms more frequently than self-identified heterosexual sex workers. Other studies indicate that the seropositivity rates of self-identified bisexual prostitutes fall between the rates of self-identified gay and heterosexual prostitutes. For example, Morse and colleagues (1991) found that 20.7 percent of male street prostitutes in New Orleans who identified as bisexual were seropositive, compared to 33.3 percent of self-identified homosexuals and 6.1 percent of self-identified heterosexuals. In Atlanta Boles and Elifson (1994a) found higher percentages in the same pattern; 36.5 percent of self-identified bisexual prostitutes, compared to 50 percent of self-identified homosexual and 18.5 percent of self-identified heterosexual male prostitutes, were seropositive. However, they also found that when other variables, including participation in receptive anal sex, were controlled, sexual orientation self-identity was not an independent predictor of sexual orientation. Pleak and Meyer-Bahlburg did not find a correlation between condom use and Kinsey score.[13] These findings suggest that it is not sexual orientation self-identity per se but the fact that sexual orientation self-identity reflects differential patterns of sexual behavior that accounts for differential seropositivity rates.

Supporting this interpretation, research findings also indicate that both condom use and seropositivity vary with the gender of the prostitute's customers and recreational sex partners, the status of the prostitute, and participation in receptive anal sex. Pleak and Meyer-Balhburg found, as have several other researchers, that male prostitutes who have sex with both men and women for both money and pleasure were most likely to practice safer sex with their male clients, less likely with their male lovers, and least likely with their female partners.[14] Waldorf and Lauderback (1992) found that male sex workers used condoms more often with male customers than with male intimates and other partners and that call men used condoms more frequently than street hustlers. Julia N. Pennbridge, Thomas E. Freese, and Richard G. MacKenzie (1992) found that male street youth in Hollywood, California, were more likely to always, and less likely to never, use condoms when engaging in a number of different specific sex acts as survival sex than when engaging in the same acts as recreational sex. These patterns appear to reflect male prostitutes' perceptions of their own risk of contracting HIV in each situation as well as a desire to present an image of health and fidelity to their male and female lovers. Regarding seropositivity, in a sample of 961 men and women who attended a New York City sexually transmitted diseases clinic, M. A. Chiasson and colleagues (1988) found that 53 percent of the 32 men who reported prostitution with men, as compared to 10 percent of the 52 men who reported prostitution with women, were seropositive,[15] and Elifson, Boles, and Sweat (1993) found that seropositivity among prostitutes was correlated with having engaged in receptive anal sex with nonpaying partners (see also Morse et al. 1991).

Prostitution is often associated with illicit drug use and, because drug use is a risk factor for HIV infection, studies of male prostitutes often include information about drug use. Pleak and Meyer-Balhburg (1990), for example, reported that almost half of their 50 subjects had been paid for sex with drugs, usually in combination with monetary payment, although only three subjects reported intravenous drug use and none admitted needle sharing. In contrast, Waldorf and colleagues (1990) found that 68 percent of 180 male hustlers in San Francisco were injection drug users, 70 percent of whom reported sharing needles, and Simon, Morse, Osofsky, and Balson (1994) found that 45 percent of male street prostitutes in New Orleans were injection drug users. Research by Boles, Sweat and Elifson (1989) suggests that bisexual prostitutes might be more likely to use drugs than nonbisexual prostitutes; they found that 62 percent of bisexuals, defined as those who engaged in recreational sex with both men and women, had injected drugs, compared to 37 percent of heterosexual and 43 percent of homosexual prostitutes. Other findings among nonprostitutes also show high levels of bisexual behavior among drug users; for example, Sung-Yeon Kang, Stephen Magura, and Janet L. Shapiro (1994) reported that among incarcerated male adolescents in New York City, 5 percent of whom "reported gay or bisexual orientation" (420), those who had used cocaine or crack were "more likely to have frequent sex with girls . . .

[and] to be gay or bisexual" (413). Such findings do not demonstrate that bisexuality increases one's chance of drug use; instead, it probably reflects a tendency for drug users to engage in more frequent and more varied sexual activity than nonusers, either as part of a general pattern of cultural deviance or in exchange for drugs. Possibly, this sexual activity reflects more concern for the drugs, money, or pleasure received in exchange than for the gender of the sex partner. See chapter 22, including note 33, for further discussion of the relationship between drug use and bisexual behavior.

Tearooms and Bath Houses

In the 1990s the fact that some apparently conventional heterosexually married men have sex with other men is common knowledge. The image most likely to come to mind, thanks to media attention in the late 1980s and early 1990s, is of men who sneak around behind their wives' backs, having sex with other men in bath houses and public parks and bringing HIV home to their innocent unsuspecting wives. But in 1970, when Humphreys' classic study *Tearoom Trade: Impersonal Sex in Public Places* was first published, the fact that some men could and did use public rest rooms, or "tearooms," to engage in anonymous sex with other men was a revelation. In the foreword to Humphreys' book Lee Rainwater pointed out that sociologists studying stigmatized behavior generally gain access to the populations they wish to study via their most publicly visible gathering places; in the case of homosexuals in the 1960s entrée to the gay community, for both researchers and gay men alike, was the gay bar. In *Tearoom Trade*, however, Humphreys described a world distinct from the gay community, a world of men looking for sex, not friendship, and for anonymity, not affirmation (cf. Bell and Weinberg 1978).[16] Although some of the men Humphreys found in the tearooms also belonged to the gay community, many did not and most were bisexual in behavior.

Humphreys used research techniques that might have given a Human Subjects Institutional Review Board a moment of pause, despite the precautions he took to protect the identities of the men whose sexual behavior he observed. First, he engaged in covert participant observation in nineteen rest rooms in a particular city. His participation consisted of serving as the "voyeur" or "watchqueen," a tearoom role that allowed him to observe tearoom activities over extended periods of time without either arousing suspicion or participating in sexual acts. Then, in an effort to gather a more systematic sample and more extensive information about the men he observed, he collected license numbers from cars parked outside tearooms, verifying that each belonged to a man who had actually engaged in a sexual act in the tearoom. With the help of "friendly policemen," Humphreys obtained the names and addresses of the men whose licenses he had recorded. He added these men to a sample drawn for a health survey so that he and a trusted graduate student could interview the men, gathering demographic and other information about them without revealing the real reason they had been included in the health survey sample.

Although Humphreys's study is probably best remembered for documenting the fact that the man next door has impersonal sex in rest rooms, its most important findings concern the culture of the tearoom, including its rules, roles, and nonverbal language, and the men's own views of themselves and their behavior. The sex Humphreys observed in these tearooms was intentionally impersonal; usually no words were spoken, much less names exchanged. The men involved were looking for sexual, not social, encounters and sought relative safety in anonymity. Fifty-four percent were married, and these men valued their images as good family men. Whereas married men with middle- or upper-class occupations tended to label themselves bisexual and participate in gay subcultures when they traveled to other cities, those belonging to the lower or working classes tended to see their same-sex sexual activities as an alternate sexual outlet made necessary by unsatisfactory marital sex, and not as an indication of their own sexual orientations. These men neither participated in a gay culture nor saw themselves as anything but heterosexual.[17]

With the advent of AIDS the fact that some married men engage in sex with other men unbeknownst to their wives, like the fact that male prostitutes and their customers engage in heterosex as well as homosex, took on new significance. As described in chapter 27, popular magazine articles such as "The Secret Life of Bisexual Husbands" (Davidowitz 1993) warned women that their husbands might bring HIV home to them and their children. Unfortunately, finer sociological findings regarding the behaviors and self-perceptions of these men were lost on public health officials and moral crusaders who, operating on the assumption that eliminating the location would eliminate the behavior and therefore the risk to heterosexual society, called for a crackdown on tearooms, bath houses, and similar venues. A similar ignorance of sociological findings also impaired the effectiveness of early HIV educational messages, which were aimed at "gay men" and therefore systematically failed to catch the attention of men who had sex with other men but did not identify themselves as gay. Thus, gay men educated themselves about HIV while married men who did not identify themselves as gay—exactly the men heterosexual society feared so much—were overlooked by public safety messages and, simultaneously, threatened with the loss of the only venues through which they could have been targeted by safer sex messages.[18]

In the wake of gay liberation and recent bisexual political activity more and more married and bisexually active men are coming out of the closet and identifying as bisexual or gay. Besides increasing their chances of practicing safer sex, these men are thereby transforming themselves into a new research population known as "married bisexual and gay men."

Heterosexually Married Bisexuals, Gay Men, and Lesbians

The fact that the concept of a "heterosexually married gay man or lesbian" is intelligible reflects the convoluted process of social construction that produced contemporary concepts of sexuality. Recall from chapter 1 that heterosexuality and homosexuality were originally relational terms referring to the similarity or difference between the sexes or genders of two people involved in a sexual or romantic relationship. The concepts were then essentialized such that by the end of the nineteenth century heterosexuality and homosexuality had come to be seen as characteristics of individual persons. Although the evidence of a person's heterosexuality or homosexuality is still to be found in their relationships with others, their hetero- or homosexuality is considered located within themselves and is conceptually independent of its expression in the form of a relationship with another person. Only in the wake of the distinction between and then essentialization of heterosexuality and homosexuality could the concept of bisexuality be born. Now, in the study of heterosexually married nonheterosexuals we are talking about individuals with essential sexualities engaged in relationships with other individuals with essential sexualities, whose respective genders are independent of the nature of their respective essential sexualities. Thus, we can describe relationships, for example, marriages, as heterosexual although the partners in them are bisexual or gay.

The fact that the terms *homosexual* and *heterosexual* can now refer to both individual sexual self-identities and to relationships involving people with such self-identities creates even more of a linguistic nightmare than has heretofore existed. Does *heterosexual* now refer to the similarity or difference between one's own sex and the sex of one's preferred partners, to one's own sexual self-identity or essence, or to the relationship between two people each with their own sexual self-identities based on the sex of the people each is attracted to—which might bear no relation to the sex of the person they are currently involved with? Some authors avoid using the term *heterosexual* in the last sense by using the word *marriage* instead, usually without the qualifier *heterosexual* on the assumption that all marriages are heterosexual. This assumption is legally accurate as of this writing, but it is currently challenged by the fact that more and more same-sex couples are referring to their committed relationships as marriages and the possibility that at least one of the fifty states will eventually begin issuing marriage licenses to same-sex couples—although hopes dimmed in Hawaii and Alaska following the November 1998 approval by voters in both states of measures opposed to same-sex marriage.[19] The linguistic complexities are multiplied when we begin conceptualizing "bisexual relationships" or asking what we should call relationships involving self-identified bisexual people.

Researchers studying married gays, lesbians, and bisexuals have come up with some novel terminology to solve this linguistic problem. Because the concepts of bisexual, gay, and lesbian personhoods are so firmly essentialized, none have sought to substitute other terms to refer to personal sexuality or to use these terms to refer to relationships in preference to personal sexuality. Instead, they have offered new relational terms. Most common is the term *mixed orientation* to refer to a relationship in which the partners have sexual self-identities that differ from each other and in which each partner's personal identity might not be wholly congruent with the sex of their partner in the relationship. For example, Leslie E. Collins and Nathalia Zimmerman (1983) and David R. Matteson (1985) referred to marriages between a woman and a man in which either the woman or the man is bisexual or gay/lesbian and the other partner is heterosexual as mixed orientation marriages. Alternatively, Dorothea Hays and Aurele Samuels (1989) and Frederick Bozett (1982) used the term *heterogenous*. Joan K. Dixon (1984, reprinted in this section as chapter 19; see also 1985), referred to sexual acts between two or more women as *multifemale* rather than *homosexual*. Although these linguistic innovations have not caught on in other areas of research, they are very useful in the study of marriages between a man and a woman in which one spouse is bisexual or gay/lesbian, and the term *mixed orientation* will be employed here.

Research on mixed orientation marriages reached a peak during the 1980s.[20] Between 1978 and 1991 Jane Scott published *Wives Who Love Women* (1978), Rebecca Nahas and Myra Turley published *The New Couple: Women and Gay Men* (1979), Barry Kohn and Alice Matusow published *Barry and Alice: Portrait of a Bisexual Marriage* (1980), John Malone published *Straight Women/Gay Men: A Special Relationship* (1980), Brenda Maddox published *Married and Gay: An Intimate Look at a Different Relationship* (1982), Michael W. Ross published *The Married Homosexual Man: A Psychological Study* (1983), Ivan Hill published *The Bisexual Spouse: Different Dimensions in Human Sexuality* (1987), Jean Schaar Gochros published *When Husbands Come Out of the Closet* (1989), Catherine Whitney published *Uncommon Lives: Gay Men and Straight Women* (1990), and Amity Pierce Buxton published *The Other Side of the Closet: The Coming-Out Crisis for Straight Spouses* (1991).

During the same period approximately twenty journal articles were published on psychosocial issues that arise in mixed orientation marriages. Many were based on subjects who were in therapy or support groups seeking help adjusting to the newly revealed sexual orientation of the nonheterosexual partner and half were published in 1985 in a single issue of the *Journal of Homosexuality*. This special issue of the *Journal* was not devoted to the topic of mixed orientation marriages but to a much broader topic, that is, research and theory on bisexuality. That over one-third of the articles in this issue pertained to the specific topic of mixed orientation marriages apparently reflected a historically located interest in such marriages. At the same time as increasing knowledge of AIDS transmission was generating fear of those who kept one foot in the gay world and the other foot in the heterosexual world, feelings of gay pride generated by gay activists were beginning to reach the homes of people who had married to deny or conceal their gayness or bisexuality. A combination of these factors probably led to many intramarital comings out (Coleman 1985a; Gochros 1985) and subsequent trips to the offices of psychotherapists for couple or individual therapy. In the preface to the special issue of the *Journal* editor John P. De Cecco characterized the eight articles on mixed orientation marriages as a challenge to conventional notions of sexual identity that assume everyone is either heterosexual or homosexual and behaves accordingly; indeed, the marital bedroom was probably one of the places where this challenge was occurring most frequently in the 1980s.

Most research studies focused on marriages in which the husband is bisexual or gay, and many focused on the husband as an individual within those marriages.[21] Other studies focused on the couple as a unit,[22] a few focused on the heterosexual wife or, even more rarely, the heterosexual husband as an individual, or on heterosexual marriages in which it is the woman who is either bisexual or lesbian, and one focused on the couple formed by the lesbian married woman and her same-sex lover.[23] Most of these analyses began with the presumption of monogamous heterosexual marriage and concern subjects who married expecting sexual fidelity, but a few concerned individuals involved in alternative arrangements such as swinging.[24] There is a tendency for the terms *homosexuality* and *bisexuality* to be used interchangeably in this literature (e.g., Gochros 1985) and for subjects to be referred to collectively as "gays and bisexuals."

The research was almost uniformly based on small samples of individuals or couples from whom extensive demographic, psychosocial, and sexual information had been obtained (e.g., Wolf 1985; Coleman 1985a; Bozett 1982). The goal in most studies was to outline the issues facing the partners in mixed orientation couples and to explore the factors that facilitate either the successful continuation of the marriage or, in rare pieces of research, the development of a positive bisexual or gay self-identity in the nonheterosexual partner. Because many samples were clinical, the implicit motivation for discovering these factors was to develop therapeutic techniques for use with such couples and individuals.[25] The focus was generally on the conflicts generated by the disparate sexual orientations of the partners in these marriages, for example, on the conflicts experienced by the bisexual or gay husband between his same-sex impulses and his commitment to a wife who married expecting sexual fidelity and between the gay lifestyle and the life of a "family man." Wolf described his subjects as torn between "the known security of a wife, family, and community support and the unknown attraction to another life-style with a male lover" (1987:163). John J. Brownfain (1985), who recruited a nonclinical sample of sixty married bisexual men through referrals, solicitation at conferences, and a support group for married bisexual men, discussed the difficulties involved in maintaining a heterosexual public identity alongside stigmatized and secret same-sex sexual desires and behaviors and the ethical issues facing men whose wives did not know of their same-sex desires and activities. Coleman (1985a) explored sexual dysfunctioning between these men and their wives. Despite this focus on conflicts generated in mixed orientation marriages, researchers shared the basic assumption that there is no inherent contradiction between marriage on one hand and bisexual or gay self-identity and behavior on the other. Brownfain explained that one's psychosocial and affectional life is distinct from one's erotic and sexual life and that many men whose erotic desires are primarily same-sex nevertheless love their wives and do not wish divorce. Concurring, Wolf (1987) reported that the bisexual men he studied loved their children and wished to remain family men.

The issues identified by these researchers and their prognoses for mixed orientation marriages varied depending on several factors. First, they depended on which partner—the husband or the wife—was bisexual or lesbian/gay. Second, the 1980s was a time of change for bisexuals, because of both increased attention as a result of HIV and growing politicization of bisexuals themselves during that decade. Although authors studying married gay men, lesbians, and bisexuals typically did not report the dates of sample recruitment or data collection, the publication dates of their studies provide an estimate of the chronological order of the studies and reveals a gradual change in researchers' findings over the course of the decade. Third, researchers' findings on mixed orientation marriages depended on characteristics of the sample selected, for example, whether the sample was clinical or nonclinical, whether the nonheterosexual partners in the marriage had known of their same-sex desires prior to marriage, and whether the respondents selected were still married or not.

A comparison of three clinical studies by Coleman illustrates the impact of gender. In the earliest study, which is reprinted as chapter 18 in this section, Coleman (1981/1982) recruited thirty-one male subjects from his own clinical practice. Some of these men were also included in his later (1985a) study of eighteen couples. Most of the men had recognized their same-sex sexual inclinations before marriage, married for a variety of reasons including social pressures, a desire for intimacy they did not believe they would find in the homosexual world, the hope of conquering their same-sex feelings, a desire for children, or love for their spouses, and had not told their wives prior to marriage although they did tell them prior to or during therapy. All of them had entered therapy while married because of concerns about their same-sex feelings and, not surprisingly, had felt guilt and shame over their feelings and tried to eliminate them. The goals of their therapy with Coleman therefore included acceptance of their feelings, and Coleman reported that his clients' Kinsey scores tended to increase over the course of therapy. In contrast, Coleman's (1985b, 1989b) women subjects, whom the author had contacted by asking other therapists to "recruit subjects through their clinical practice and personal contacts and to identify bisexual women who were or had been married" (1985b:89), had entered therapy after leaving their marriages and sought counseling for reasons other than the combination of their marriage and their same-sex feelings.[26] Other clinicians confirmed Coleman's observation that women appear not to enter therapy while still married. Alan P. Bell and Martin S. Weinberg (1978) found that marriages in which the wife was lesbian ended more quickly than those in which the husband was gay, although they also found that homosexual women were more likely to have been married than homosexual men (35 percent versus 20 percent among whites, 47 percent versus 13 percent among Blacks) and that men and women were equally likely to report that their homosexuality had had something to do with the disruption of their marriages.[27] The majority of Coleman's forty-five women subjects reported that they married because they loved their husbands and wanted to be married, not because they were trying to avoid or eliminate their same-sex desires even though half were aware of their same-sex feelings prior to marriage. Other issues facing bisexual and lesbian women who are or have been married concern their relationships with their children, including their roles as mothers and whether to disclose their orientations to their children.

The changes in the issues facing married bisexual and gay men over the course of the 1980s can be seen by comparing Nathaniel McConaghy's (1978) findings to those of Brownfain (1985) and Wolf (1987). McConaghy's 126 "males with homosexual feelings," 44 of whom were married, had all sought therapy for the purpose of reducing or eliminating their homosexual feelings.[28] Most of the men Brownfain studied had not been fully aware of their same-sex sexual desires at the time they married and now faced the difficult question of whether and how to reveal their same-sex sexual involvement to their wives. Some resisted applying a label to their sexual orientations but, when pressed, 50 percent identified themselves as bisexual and 42 percent identified themselves as gay. Unlike McConaghy's subjects, however, they generally felt positively about their bisexual or gay selves, a fact that Brownfain attributed to their having come out in an age of relative tolerance of homosexuality. Some of Brownfain's subjects who married before gay liberation reported that they might make different choices if they were to live their lives over but that they were comfortable with the way things turned out.[29]

In 1987 Wolf reported that the number of men coming to his clinical practice seeking support for their bisexual feelings and behaviors was increasing.[30] They also brought with them a new set of concerns that reflected growing affirmation of bisexuality as a sexual orientation in the late 1980s. This new breed of client sought social contact with other bisexuals in similar situations, support for their bisexuality in the face of biphobia in the gay community and homophobia in heterosexual society, and strategies to deal with their anxieties about HIV. Because Wolf's clients generally valued their relationships with their wives and children, therapy included support in managing their relationships with their wives. Even more recently, Michael F. Myers (1991) focused explicitly on issues that arise in marital therapy with couples in which the husband is bisexual and becomes infected with HIV through same-sex activities. He noted that many married men who become seropositive have avoided acknowledging their bisexuality to themselves or others. Becoming seropositive forces them to confront this aspect of their sexuality and tell their wives about both their bisexuality and their seropositivity.

Issues facing the wives of bisexual and gay men also changed over the course of the decade. Mid-decade, Coleman (1985a) reported that these issues included the difficulty of acknowledging to others that they were married to a bisexual, reluctance to seek psychological support, economic dependence on their husbands, and lowered self-esteem following the discovery of their husband's bisexuality. Six years later the impact of AIDS is evident in Myers's (1991) discussion of bisexual and gay men's wives; he pointed out that these women must simultaneously confront their husband's unfaithfulness and his health prospects as well as the threat to their own health.

Differences in marital outcomes in the men studied by different researchers are generally attributable to differences in the types of men studied or in the treatment approaches used for those in clinical samples. For example, Matteson (1985) attributed the high rate of marital failure in Bozett's (1982) sample—of eighteen men, twelve were divorced and five were separated—to his sampling techniques; most of his subjects were drawn from homosexual groups. Likewise, he attributed the high rate of marital failure in Coleman's (1981/1982) sample to its clinical nature and to Coleman's treatment approach: "By not involving the wives on the very first interview, [Coleman] inadvertently communicated that the man's sexual identity issues were a higher priority than the resolution of the marriage" (151).

In contrast, a high rate of marital success—with success defined in terms of partner happiness within marriage and the continuation of the marriage—existed in

Brownfain's (1985), Wolf's (1985), Matteson's (1985), and Jennifer P. Schneider and Burton H. Schneider's (1990) nonclinical samples. Brownfain's subjects were selected on the basis of characteristics that virtually guaranteed positive findings about combining bisexual or gay self-identity with marital continuation; the sixty men he studied were married at the time of the study, had been married for at least eight years, and were significantly involved in same-sex sexual activities. As reported above, they generally felt positively about their bisexual or gay selves and had come to terms with their married situations, reporting that they were comfortable. The twenty-six couples studied by Wolf (1985) also generally felt positively about their marriages. Two-thirds expected their marriages to last a long time or forever and 62 percent of the husbands and 42 percent of the wives said they would choose "this kind of marriage" (143) again. As in Brownfain's (1985) study, selection criteria are partially responsible for these positive findings; subjects had all been married for at least two years and intended to stay married. The couples were generally of high education and income, were not in therapy at the time of the study although many had received therapy previously, and openly communicated about the husband's sexual activities although they reported intense conflict over these activities. Probably not unrelated to these sample characteristics nor to the positive marital outcomes, Wolf found that two-thirds of the husbands had been aware of their homosexuality at the time of marriage; 38 percent of their spouses entered the marriage knowing of this homosexuality, and a high proportion of the husbands (73 percent) self-identified as bisexual.

Similarly, most of the men in Matteson's (1985) study of forty-one spouses representing thirty marriages were highly educated, were comfortable with either bisexual or gay self-identities, felt positively about their premarital same-sex sexual experiences, and married not to escape their same-sex sexual feelings but because they thought their other-sex sexual feelings were adequate for marital success. Confirming this positive outlook, a follow-up two years after the initial study revealed that 42 percent of marriages in which the husband had disclosed his same-sex activities to the wife were still intact. Schneider and Schneider's (1990) subjects were couples who had joined twelve-step self-help programs in response to what they perceived as the husband's sexually addictive or undesirable homosexual behavior and who had committed to monogamy upon joining the program. Almost all the spouses had college or graduate degrees. At the time of the study the mean duration of the marriages was 18.3 years, and 47 percent rated their marriages as "good" whereas only 16 percent rated their marriages as "bad."

Although comparisons between studies are confounded by sample differences, findings do reveal several factors that are associated with marital success. The most important appears to be open and honest communication, both in general and about the partner's same-sex desires and activities in particular (e.g., Wolf 1985; Coleman 1981/1982, 1985a). Marriages in which both partners love each other, are committed to maintenance of the marriage, and willing to accept extramarital affairs (e.g., Ross 1971; Coleman 1981/1982) are also more likely to succeed. For example, in Wolf's (1985) study of couples who had remained married 76 percent of the wives had come to expect their marriages to be "open"; only 8 percent expected fidelity. This openness did not necessary apply only to the husbands; 54 percent of the wives had had sexual relationships with other men during the marriage and 23 percent currently had such relationships.[31] Other factors include open acknowledgment or partial disclosure of one partner's same-sex desires at the time of marriage (Wolf 1985; Bozett 1982), the husband's having explored his same-sex feelings through same-sex activity before marriage (Matteson 1985), prompt disclosure of same-sex activities when they began or resumed during the marriage (Matteson 1985) or continued secrecy such that a marital crisis had not occurred (Coleman 1981/1982),[32] the way in which the husband informed the wife of his same-sex feelings (Matteson 1985), having been married a long time (Coleman 1985a), a history of marital therapy (Wolf 1985; cf. Coleman 1985a), defining the husband's homosexual activity as "addictive," that is, undesirable but blameless, behavior (Schneider and Schneider 1990), self-esteem and sources of self-worth other than the marriage on the part of the wife (Coleman 1981/1982, 1985a), empathy and capacity for intimacy on the part of the husband (Matteson 1985), resolution of feelings of guilt, blame, and intolerance of one partner's same-sex feelings by both partners (Coleman 1981/1982), and social contact with heterosexuals rather than homosexuals (Wolf 1985). Not surprisingly, Brownfain (1985) found that marriages in which the husband identified as gay were more likely to fail than marriages in which the husband identified as bisexual, although Matteson (1985) reported no correlation between the "level" of the husband's homosexuality and the outcome of the marriage two years later.

In addition to marital continuation, another yardstick for a successful outcome is the development of a positive bisexual or gay self-identity in the spouse who has same-sex desires. Although these goals are not mutually exclusive, the factors found to contribute to the development of a positive bisexual or gay self-identity in the nonheterosexual partner are almost the inverse of those contributing to marital success. Brian Miller (1979) found, for example, that these factors included integrating one's homosexuality into one's life instead of compartmentalizing and hiding it, separating from one's wife, and having social contact with individuals supportive of homosexuality. Coleman (1985a) noted that increased self-esteem and independence for spouses in such marriages might increase the risk of marital failure as spouses are empowered to seek new relationships.

The rate of success of mixed orientation marriages, and the rate at which couples combine marital success with a partner's positive bisexual self-identity, might be increasing. Recall from chapter 11 that, over time, men with same-sex experiences have become less likely to marry, probably because social changes facilitate coming out and reduce pressure on men to marry in an attempt to conceal, deny, or eliminate their same-sex desires. Supporting this argument, Matteson (1985) observed that more recent marriages involving bisexuals are made for positive reasons between partners who acknowledge and accept one partner's bisexuality instead of between one partner who is attempting to escape or deny their homosexuality and another who is unaware or uncomprehending. He found that fewer men are marrying women because they believe intimacy and permanence are unavailable in same-sex relationships. Wolf (1985) also found that younger couples are more likely to have been open about the husband's bisexuality from the beginning and to socialize with homosexuals, whereas older couples tended to socialize more with heterosexuals. Although Wolf also found that socializing with homosexuals was associated with lower rates of marital success, this apparent contradiction is possibly explained by a tendency for younger and older couples to socialize with homosexuals for different reasons. Among the young it might reflect greater acceptance of homosexuality and therefore greater opportunities for positive bisexual and gay self-identities within heterosexual society. Given these trends, it is likely that fewer marriages involving partners with same-sex inclinations will be made in the future but that these marriages will be more successful than those of the past.

Couples who marry expecting fidelity sometimes have to readjust their expectations when one partner comes out as bisexual or gay. As noted above, the marriages that survive often do so by becoming open marriages in which one or both partners, with the knowledge and consent of the other partner, are free to engage in sexual liaisons with other people under agreed-upon conditions. Other couples marry without the expectation of fidelity, that is, the spouses agree from the outset that their marriages will be open or otherwise sexually nonmonogamous. Some of these couples make such an agreement because the bisexuality of one or both partners is known and acknowledged before the marriage, but many other open marriage couples assume that all sexual activity inside and outside the marriage will be other-sex. In these marriages the discovery by one partner of their bisexuality or homosexuality later in the marriage challenges this presumption, as it does in traditional heterosexual monogamous marriages. Joan K. Dixon and Dwight Dixon studied couples who "swing," that is, engage in "mate swapping" with other couples, and in which one partner is bisexual.[33] Joan K. Dixon, author of chapter 19 of this section, studied women who became involved in sexual activity with other women within the context of swinging, and Dwight Dixon compared bisexual to heterosexual men involved in swinging marriages.

The incidence of bisexual behavior among women who swing appears to be higher than among more sexually conventional populations, and higher than among men who swing.[34] Reviewing the literature on the subject, J. K. Dixon (1984, 1985) cited G. C. O'Neill and N. O'Neill's (1970) report that "60 percent of the swinging females in their study engaged in genital sexual activities with other women" (J. K. Dixon 1985:117) and B. G. Gilmartin's (1978) report that 68 percent of swinging women had done so. She also cited G. D. Bartell's (1971) finding that "when two couples swing together [in "open" style] 75 percent of the females engage in sex with each other, while at large parties 92 percent of the females would do so" (J. K. Dixon 1985:117). For her own study, Dixon recruited fifty women aged thirty or more who had engaged in their first sexual contact with another woman during marriage while swinging with their husbands. As described in chapter 19, none had had prior sexual contact with other women and all were enjoying heterosex at the time of their first homosexual contact. Half of Dixon's subjects had their first sexual contact with another woman at a swing party, whereas 32 percent had it in the context of swinging with their husband and another heterosexual couple (J. K. Dixon 1985).

Dixon chose to study bisexual women swingers because she was interested in demonstrating that sexual orientation could change during adulthood and in exploring the factors that facilitate or predict such a change. She collected extensive information regarding her subjects' self-identities, behaviors, and fantasies both before and after their first same-sex encounters. In her 1984 article (chapter 19) she focused on possible predictive factors such as early sexual behavior and facilitative factors including the reasons given by women for their initial sexual contact with another woman and details about the context of this contact. In her 1985 article she reported statistics supporting her contention that these women experienced actual sexual orientation changes from heterosexual to bisexual as opposed to mere changes in behavior. She also reported that the women generally found their initial experiences positive, that they enjoyed their current multifemale activities even more than their initial ones and that, over time, they became more likely to participate actively (as the "oralist") as opposed to only passively (as the "receiver"), to fantasize about women while masturbating, and to engage in multifemale sexual activity in other contexts, for example, with no men present. Most (96 percent) reported that their husbands approved of their sexual activities with women; one-fifth reported that their husbands were also bisexual.

D. Dixon (1985) recruited his fifty bisexual and fifty heterosexual married male swingers at social and educational functions, by answering and placing ads in swingers' publications, and through referrals. Bisexual and heterosexual groups were matched on age, length of current marriage, and socioeconomic status. Bisexual subjects self-identified as bisexual and had sexual experience with both women and men; heterosexual subjects self-identified as heterosexual and had no more than incidental sexual contact with another man. Dixon presented statistics describing the numbers and genders of his subjects' sex partners, frequency and types of sexual activities with and without partners, and sexual satisfaction. Notable comparisons between the two groups of subjects included the finding that bisexual subjects reported more orgasms per week on average (9.3) with female partners than did heterosexual subjects (6.6), and more orgasms per week from masturbation and fantasy. Both bisexual and heterosexual subjects were generally satisfied with their sex lives but, despite the fact that bisexuals reported a greater frequency of orgasms, heterosexuals reported greater overall sexual satisfaction and greater happiness with their current spouse than did bisexuals.

A Concluding Comment

The research on bisexuality among prostitutes and heterosexually married men and women indicates that bisexual behavior sometimes takes different forms among men and women. Insofar as prostitutes are concerned, this gender pattern might be a reflection of the different perspectives that social scientists have brought to bear on the topics of bisexuality among women and men prostitutes as much as it is a reflection of actual gender differences. Among women prostitutes bisexuality is described in the literature as a reaction to negative experiences with men in the context of heterosexual prostitution; one would not know from reading the literature on prostitution that there are women who engage in same-sex sexual activity *as* prostitution because these women have escaped the attention of researchers. In contrast, among men prostitutes those who engage in homosexuality *as* prostitution and who also have heterosex either for money or pleasure are the focus of considerable attention because of concerns about their role in the spread of HIV.

In the literature on married bisexuals, lesbians, and gay men, on the other hand, gender patterns in the expression of bisexuality appear to reflect cultural gender roles. Men, for example, are much more likely to seek anonymous sex with other men in tearooms, as an *extra*marital activity and sometimes without the knowledge of their wives. Women, on the other hand, if they participate in sex with women while married, tend not to do so anonymously; women have nothing analogous to men's tearooms. Instead, they might become involved with another woman in the context of swinging; that is, as part of an activity they engage in *within* their marriages and with the knowledge of their husbands. Those men and women who come out as bisexual or gay while in heterosexual marriages also show different patterns. Men appear more likely to stay married than women—perhaps in this case it is the gender of their partner, as opposed to their own gender, that is the important factor—and more likely to seek therapy for help in maintaining their marriages. These gendered patterns in the expression of bisexuality reflect traditional gender roles in which men are socialized to value sex inside or outside relationships and women are socialized to value relationships and to seek sexual satisfaction within those relationships.

In the 1990s self-identified and politically active bisexuals are challenging these traditional gendered patterns, as they challenge gender itself. The next three sections examine research on bisexuals in their own right, and some of this research explores the effect this challenge is having on gender among bisexuals.

Notes

1. See Benjamin and Masters (1964), who nevertheless are among few researchers who acknowledged the existence of "lesbian brothels." Cross (1956) described a police raid in the early 1960s that discovered an "operation" involving twenty-eight male and nine female prostitutes, three of whom served primarily lesbian customers.

Before the HIV epidemic male-male prostitution also received little attention from researchers; in 1980 Allen reported that a Kinsey Institute for Sexual Research bibliography on male-male prostitution included only fourteen English-language references. Prior to that time research on prostitution was concerned almost exclusively with female prostitutes who have male customers.

2. As of the late 1970s Pittman's (1971) was the only study of a male brothel (Allen 1980). Weisberg (1985) cited Drew and Drake's (1969) description of "peg houses" operating in San Francisco between 1840 and 1910; Salamon (1989) and Luckenbill (1986) described male prostitutes working in "escort agencies."

3. The interested reader is referred to Allen (1980); Boyer (1989); Caukins and Coombs (1976); Fisher, Weisberg, and Marotta (1982); Janus, Scanlon, and Price (1984); Luckenbill (1986); Malone (1980); Visano (1990); and Weisberg (1985).

4. Another early study of contemporary homosexual prostitution is Butts (1947).

5. For examples of early studies that characterized most subjects as heterosexual, see Butts (1947); Churchill (1967); Coombs (1974); Craft (1966); Deisher, Eisner, and Sulzsbacher (1969); Ginsburg (1967); Jersild (1953, 1956); cf. MacNamara (1965). See also Coleman (1989a). For examples of later studies that found subjects increasingly to be bisexual and homosexual, see Allen (1980); Furnald (1978); Lauderback and Waldorf (1989); and Weisberg (1985).

6. More recent studies include male prostitutes who operate in gay settings and "upper class" male prostitutes such as call men and bar prostitutes, who tend to be older men with longer experience as prostitutes. As discussed later in this chapter, increased incidence of bisexuality and homosexuality is associated with longer periods of time spent in male prostitution.

7. Earls and David (1989) suggested the alternate possibility that increasing numbers of gay adolescents are participating in prostitution.

8. Bisexual self-identification appears to be less common among female prostitutes. In a study of female juvenile prostitutes Silbert (1980) found that 72 percent self-identified as heterosexual, 14 percent as asexual, and 14 percent as homosexual or bisexual (Weisberg 1985). In a study of both male and female juvenile prostitutes Harlan, Rodgers, and Slattery (1981) found that 17 percent identified as bisexual and 13 percent identified as gay (Weisberg 1985). As noted in chapter 14, James (1976) found that 35.3 percent of women prostitutes had experienced a "lesbian relationship," whereas only 6.7 percent considered themselves "exclusively lesbian."

9. In Yates, MacKenzie, Pennbridge, and Swofford (1991) the authors did not give the wording of the question(s) they used to assess identity, nor did they mention having assessed the incidence or frequency of same- and other-sex sexual activity among these youths, yet in the discussion they referred to the "greater likelihood of gay or bisexual male involvement." It is, therefore, unclear whether this refers to actual findings regarding the youths' sexual behavior or to a supposition on the part of the authors based on the greater prevalence of homosexual and bisexual self-identification among youths involved in prostitution.

10. Allen (1980) found that one-third of his male prostitute subjects aged fourteen to twenty-four years had been or were runaways; Cohen (1987) estimated that runaway and homeless youth comprise 75 percent of all youth involved in prostitution; and Fisher, Weisberg, and Marotta (1982) found that three-fourths of their sample of juvenile prostitutes ran away from home at an average age of fifteen. Conversely, Rotheram-Borus et al. (1992) reported that estimates of the percentage of runaways who engage in prostitution or other forms of "survival sex" range from 3 percent to 30 percent and that their own research revealed that 22 percent of male and 7 percent of female runaways had exchanged sex for money or drugs.

11. In Pleak and Meyer-Bahlburg's (1990) study, racial and ethnic characteristics of the hustlers might also explain the status differences they found in sexual self-identity. Subjects who were street prostitutes were more likely to be Hispanic, Black, or mixed race (72 percent) than subjects who were bar/theater prostitutes (16 percent) because researchers did not recruit subjects in Black, Hispanic, or Asian hustling bars. Racial and ethnic differences in the cultural construction of sexuality are discussed in chapter 22.

12. For examples of studies that described customers as primarily homosexual, see Perlonger (1985) and Caukins and Coombs (1976). For examples of studies in which customers were characterized as closet bisexuals, see Kamel (1983) and Pittman (1971).

13. Unfortunately, they do not indicate whether condom use was associated with sexual self-identity.

14. Pleak and Meyer-Bahlburg (1990) cited Lauderback and Waldorf (1989) and DiClemente, Forrest, and Mickler (1989) for similar findings on San Franciscan street prostitutes and on Californian college adolescents and Boulton et al. (1989); Gold et al. (1989); and Hooykass et al. (1989) for similar findings in Australia, England, and Amsterdam.

15. This difference in seropositivity rates for male prostitutes with male and female customers is made even more striking by the fact that of the five prostitutes with women customers four had also either used IV drugs or engaged in homosexual activity.

16. In an appendix to *Homosexualities* Bell and Weinberg provided an ethnography in which they described Bay Area gay bars, gay baths, and public places such as streets and rest rooms in which cruising occured as part of the "homosexual scene."

17. More recently, Gindorf and Warran reported that 70 percent of approximately one thousand men seeking anonymous sex at highway rest areas were " 'bisexual' in terms of their sexual preferences and activities" (1998:217) although most identified as heterosexual, were married, had children, and did not participate in gay subculture.

18. Myers (1991) cited a study of the Centers for Disease Control that found 25 percent of male blood donors who were infected with HIV and acknowledged having had sex with other men identified as heterosexual. This finding was reported at the Sixth International AIDS Conference and in the *New York Times*, June 26, 1990, p. C11. Doll, Peterson, Magaña, and Carrier (1991) noted that safer sex education via bathhouses and rest rooms used for sex might be an effective way of reaching this largely inaccessible population. However, Doll et al. (1992) found that most seropositive men they recruited through blood donation centers had not had anonymous male sex partners during the past year and did have at least one steady male partner, suggesting that by the 1990s "key informants" and "peer counselors" might be an effective way of reaching most homosexually active men at risk for HIV.

The situation among women is the reverse. Because of lack of scientific attention to the possibility of woman-to-woman sexual transmission of HIV and institutional denial of this possibility by researchers and policy makers (Cole and Cooper 1990/1991), lesbians have generally considered themselves "safe" from HIV infection. A joke that arose in the 1980s criticizing moralistic interpretations of AIDS illustrates this belief: "If AIDS is God's curse on gay men, then lesbians must be the chosen people." Bisexual women, insofar as they recognize the risk involved in heterosex, might be more aware of their risk and of the need to practice safer sex.

19. The "Defense of Marriage Act," passed by both houses of Congress and signed by President Bill Clinton in fall 1996, stipulates that marriage is defined as a union between a man and a woman. The act is intended to preempt efforts by same-sex couples to claim the legal benefits of marriage should any state begin issuing marriage licenses to same-sex couples. D.O.M.A. and bans on same-sex marriage in twenty-nine states as of October 1998 were a response to the possibility that Hawaii—and later, Alaska—might begin issuing marriage licenses to same-sex couples. However, in the November 1998 elections, voters in Hawaii approved a measure authorizing lawmakers to amend the state's Bill of Rights to limit marriage to other-sex couples, thereby circumventing an expected Hawaii Supreme Court decision upholding a lower court ruling that denying marriage to same-sex couples constituted unjustified sex discrimination and must end. In the same election, voters in Alaska approved a constitutional amendment to define marriage as a relationship between one man and one woman. Both measures passed by more than 2 to 1.

20. Brownfain (1985) reported that the oldest study of bisexual men in marriage is by H. Laurence Ross (1971, 1972), who studied eleven couples in Belgium. Ross (1971) discussed the reasons homosexuals marry (ignorance of their homosexuality, an attempt to overcome their homosexuality, or other priorities such as a desire for children), sources of marital conflict (sexual mismatching, extramarital affective ties on the part of the homosexual partner), and modes of adjustment (separation, platonic marital relations, and innovations such as open marriage). However, earlier studies can be found in citations made by other authors. Collins and Zimmerman (1983) cited an earlier study by Rifkin (1968) and Fox (1996) cited Allen (1961) and Bieber (1969). Michael W. Ross (1983c) described a study of the correlation between degree of homosexuality among men and the success of their marriages (Imielinski 1969) and a study in the Federal Republic of West Germany that noted homosexual men's use of marriage as a means of concealing their homosexuality; the authors

called marriage among homosexuals a "collective neurosis" (Dannecker and Reiche 1974). Additional studies before the 1980s include Latham and White (1978), who studied coping mechanisms in five couples in which the wives were not entirely ignorant of their husbands' homosexuality, and McConaghy (1978), who studied penile responses of married and single men with varying degrees of heterosexual experience. Coleman (1981/1982) and Wolf (1985) cited two early case studies of treatment approaches, Gochros (1978) and Hatterer (1974), and an article by Ross (1979).

A few broader studies conducted before the 1980s also include discussion of the phenomenon of married gays and bisexuals (e.g., Bell and Weinberg 1978; Klein 1978; Masters and Johnson 1979; Saghir and Robins 1973; Tripp 1976), sometimes as part of a study of gay fathers or lesbian mothers who became parents in the context of a heterosexual relationship (e.g., Voeller and Walters 1978; Hatterer 1970; Rand, Graham, and Rawlings 1982; Miller 1979). Hays and Samuels (1989), Ross (1989), and Coleman (1989b) reviewed the literature on married gay men, lesbians, and bisexuals.

More recent studies of "married gays, lesbians, and bisexuals" include Sue Joseph's *She's My Wife, He's Just Sex* (1997), an article by Scott and Ortiz (1996), and Aileen H. Atwood's (1998) sensationalistic, reactionary, and quasi-academic book *Husbands Who Love Men: Deceit, Disease, and Despair.*

21. For example, Bozett (1981, 1982); Brownfain (1985); Coleman (1981/1982); Ross (1983c); and Wolf (1987c). Ross (1983c), who was interested only in men with Kinsey scores of 3 or higher, compared samples of homosexual males who were still married and homosexual males who were separated, divorced, or widowed to homosexual males who had never been married to discover why some men marry while others don't, the process of adjustment for the married homosexual male, and the causes and effects of marriage.

22. For examples of studies on the couple as a unit, see Coleman (1985a); Hill (1987); Kohn and Matusow (1980); Matteson (1985); Myers (1991); Schneider and Schneider (1990); and Wolf (1985).

23. For examples of studies that focused on the heterosexual partner, see Auerback and Moser (1987); Buxton (1991); Gochros (1985); and Hays and Samuels (1989). Because these four studies focused on the heterosexual rather than the bisexual or gay partner in the marriage, they are not reviewed in the main text. Auerback and Moser described seven therapy groups for the wives of gay and bisexual men, including clinical findings regarding issues facing these women and the therapeutic group process. Buxton discussed issues facing heterosexual spouses of both genders, based on five years of discussions with clinical professionals and interviews with "hundreds of straight spouses and gay, lesbian, and bisexual partners" (xviii). Gochros (1985) used snowball sampling and newspaper publicity to recruit a sample of 103 wives, primarily from four major cities in different states, of whom extensive data were collected from thirty-three. Gochros explored factors that affected wives' reactions to their husbands' disclosures of their sexualities (for example, the method of disclosure, availability of social support), issues they faced following disclosure (for example, isolation, feelings of stigmatization, insecurities about their own sexualities), and the stages they went through in coming to terms with the disclosure (for example, cognitive confusion and reintegration). Hays and Samuels (1989) recruited 21 women from support groups in four major cities and through personal networks. Before marriage, most did not know their husbands were bisexual or gay and half were still married, but only three expected their marriages to last. Hays and Samuels explored why these women had chosen the men they married, how they learned of their husbands' gayness or bisexuality and their reactions to this discovery, changes in the quality of the marriage including sexual satisfaction, choices regarding disclosure to persons outside the marriage, and the reactions of their children.

For studies of heterosexual marriages in which the wife is bisexual or lesbian, see Coleman (1985b, 1989b). Maddox studied married homosexual women as well as married homosexual men (1982).

Green and Clunis's (1989) article on the couple formed by two women is not based explicitly on empirical research. Containing such tautological statements as "Married lesbians' relationships come in two forms: either both women are currently married or one is and the other is not, although she may have been previously" (45) and published in the journal *Women and Therapy*, the piece serves more as a sensitizing vehicle for therapists than a substantive report.

24. For studies that concerned alternative marital arrangements, see D. Dixon (1985); J. K. Dixon (1984, 1985); and Smith and Smith (1974).

25. This therapeutic bent is explicit in Collins and Zimmerman (1983), who discussed treatment issues and approaches pertaining to mixed orientation couples. Their article is not included in this review because it makes no claim to being based on empirical research.

26. Coleman (1985b) himself compared this sample of women to his earlier sample of men, taking pains to explain that the samples were drawn differently and differ in their characteristics and therefore must be compared carefully. Because of the lack of representativeness in both samples it is impossible to tell which distinctions between samples reflect sampling differences and which reflect actual gender differences. For example, Coleman interpreted the fact that his women subjects were no longer married whereas his men subjects were to a gender difference, but this could merely be a sampling difference.

27. Bell and Weinberg noted that Saghir and Robins (1973), in contrast, found that the marriages of homosexual men tended to end more quickly than those of lesbians.

28. Similarly, Masters and Johnson (1979) found that none of their "bisexual" subjects, and 17 percent of their "homosexual" male subjects, had been married. Of those homosexual men who had married, 61 percent "had done so in an attempt to reverse their homosexual preferences" (Ross 1983c:23).

29. Brownfain (1985) can also be usefully compared to Coleman (1981/1982). In contrast to Coleman's subjects, who had been married for an average of thirteen years, Brownfain's subjects were an average of six years older and had been married for an average of twenty years. Therefore, although Brownfain's report was published three years after Coleman's, Brownfain's subjects probably married in earlier years than Coleman's did, when social awareness of homosexuality was lower, thus they might have been less likely to have recognized their own homosexuality prior to marriage. Because they came out after marriage, however, they probably came out in later years than Coleman's subjects did, hence their apparent development of more positive bisexual and gay self-identities.

30. In another sign of the times, Wolf's (1987) discussion included men who had never been married but who had been exclusively homosexual in the past and were seeking help in the context of a new heterosexual relationship.

31. Compare Coleman (1985), whose female subjects accepted same-sex activity by their husbands but not by themselves.

32. For example, Matteson (1985) reported a 67 percent two-year marital continuation rate in his sample as a whole, but only a 42 percent rate among those marriages in which the husband had disclosed his same-sex activities to the wife.

33. Ramey (1974a) defined swinging: "Swinging generally involves two or more pair-bonded couples who mutually decide to switch sexual partners or engage in group sex. Singles may be included either through temporary coupling with another individual specifically for the purpose of swinging or as part of a triadic or larger group sexual experience" (116).

34. The incidence of bisexual behavior among men who swing might be substantially lower. Bartell (1974) found that in 75 percent of the cases of "open swinging" the two women engaged in sex with each other, whereas the two men engaged in sex with each other in only 1 percent of cases. Varni (1974) also reported that homosexual behavior among male swingers is rare. Ramey reported that couples who swing with a single third person are more likely to swing with a single woman than with a single man (1974a) and that group marriages might admit a single female but none of eighty group marriages studied had ever

admitted a single man (1974b). Single bisexual men in the current author's research have commented that they find it difficult to find a couple to swing with, in contrast to bisexual women who report unsolicited invitations from swinging couples.

Given the higher rate of same-sex activity among female than male swingers, it is not surprising that some researchers (Cook et al. 1983; Blumstein and Schwartz 1976a) have identified swinging, three-way, or group sex as typical routes to bisexuality for women, but not men. These gendered patterns probably reflect the different views in heterosexual society toward same-sex activity among women and among men. Whereas sex between two women is culturally constructed as sexually exciting for men—it is used as an image in heterosexual men's pornography because it is seen as a prelude to or an extension of heterosexuality—the idea of two men together is culturally threatening.

18

Bisexual and Gay Men in Heterosexual Marriage: Conflicts and Resolutions in Therapy

Eli Coleman

BETWEEN 5 and 10 percent of the population report having predominant same-sex feelings (Hunt, 1974; Kinsey, Pomeroy and Martin, 1948; Kinsey, Pomeroy, Martin, and Gebhard, 1953). A much smaller percentage actually live a life-style congruent with their same-sex preferences. Many men and women marry and attempt to live a life-style more consistent with traditional norms. Until recently, very little has been known about these people.

In their study of homosexuality, Masters and Johnson (1979) were surprised to find that 23 percent of homosexual females and males had previously been married. This statistic is consistent with the finding of the extensive study conducted by Bell and Weinberg (1978) of the Institute for Sex Research. To date, the only systematic study of married men with predominately same-sex feelings is that of 11 couples interviewed in Belgium in 1969–1970 (Ross, 1971). A few case studies of treatment approaches have been reported (e.g., Gochros, 1978; Hatterer, 1974), and very recently a number of books have described bisexual and gay men who are married (Klein, 1978; Kohn and Matusow, 1980; Malone, 1980; Nahas and Turley, 1979). Basically, however, little is known about these men, their wives, or their gay relationships.

The concept that an individual may be married and yet have a significant amount of same-sex feelings seems in particular to have eluded many mental health professionals. For example, in assembling their original heterosexual study group, Masters and Johnson (1966) never considered including individuals who had varying amounts of same-sex experience, and yet when they studied homosexuality, they included individuals with a complete range of heterosexual-homosexual experience (Masters and Johnson, 1979).

This paper describes 31 men who at the time of entering therapy were married and expressing concern about their same-sex feelings and activity. Their beliefs and behaviors before entering group therapy, directly after having completed treatment, and several months after treatment, are compared.

Method

The 31 men in this study came from the author's private practice. Men were selected for a 10-week "bisexuality group" if their clinical needs met the following objectives of the group:

1. To be more comfortable with and accepting of their same-sex feelings.
2. To explore alternative ways of incorporating same-sex and opposite-sex feelings into their lives.
3. To examine myths and stereotypes of homosexuality, bisexuality, and heterosexuality.
4. To create better knowledge and understanding of human sexual functioning.
5. To deal with issues of sexual performance in both same-sex and opposite-sex relationships.

It was intended to accomplish these objectives by:

1. Creating an atmosphere of acceptance for variance in sexual activity.
2. Creating an opportunity for members to share concerns with one another and to receive support from one another.
3. Educating the members on the subject of homosexuality, bisexuality, and heterosexuality
4. Learning the principles of taking responsibility for self in sexual activities.
5. Building assertiveness skills.
6. Creating an atmosphere of experimentation to explore feelings, attitudes, fantasies, and behaviors.
7. Teaching basic sex education on the sexual functioning of men and women.

Through sexual history and clinical observation, information was gathered about reasons for getting married, awareness of same-sex feelings and behaviors, wives' knowledge of husbands' same-sex feelings, marital and sexual conflicts, sexual behavior, extra-marital liaisons, effects upon the children, modes of adjustment, decisions following treatment, and self-esteem. Follow-up questionnaires (designed to assess more of the long-term effects of the therapy), were sent to all the men. The length of time at follow-up varied from a few months to 2-1/2 years after treatment.

Results

ATTITUDES AND BEHAVIOR BEFORE THERAPY

Reasons for Getting Married   Except for one man, all were (to some degree) aware of same-sex feelings, and all but four had acted on these feelings before they were married. Most of this activity could be labeled as normal adolescent exploratory behavior, except that it had a very different *meaning* to these individuals. Very few understood themselves to be "gay"; confusion is a more apt description of their feelings about their same-sex desires. Without exception, they decided to get married because of societal and family pressures and the perceived lack of intimacy in the gay world. Again without exception, they reported that they had married their wives because they loved them. Several men mentioned their interest in having and raising children as one significant motivating factor. Some felt that marriage would help them overcome their same-sex feelings. While the specific reasons varied, the overall motivating factors were love of their wives, societal and family pressures, and negative feelings about "gay life."

Attempts to Eliminate Same-Sex Feelings

All 31 men in the Bisexuality Group reported having previously in some way attempted to eliminate their same-sex feelings, which were a source of intense guilt and shame. Eleven (36 percent) had actually tried to eliminate these feelings and behaviors through psychotherapy with counselors, psychiatrists, or ministers. The length of time spent in therapy varied from 6 months to 17 years. Obviously, not one of these men had been successful in his attempt. Although all the men felt extreme guilt over their feelings and behavior, and many reported having suffered from depression and anxiety over the years, it was clear that except for one man, who had a history of psychiatric hospitalization, none suffered from any serious psychopathology.

The Wives' Knowledge

Only five wives (16 percent) knew of their husbands' same-sex feelings before they were married: In one case, the wife felt that those feelings were normal; in the other four cases, the wife assumed that her husband's same-sex feelings would not be a factor in the relationship. The remaining women did not find out about their husband's feelings until after they were married. Only four wives did not know about their husband's feelings before they entered therapy; all four were told by their husbands during the process of treatment. Most of the wives in this study were unsuspecting at the time of disclosure. Their responses ranged from calm concern, to extreme upset, to revulsion and disgust. It proved just as difficult for the wives to accept their husbands' same-sex feelings as it had originally been for the men.

The scope of this study did not include collecting much information about the wives' histories of reaction or modes of adjustment. Wives were recommended to attend a spouses' support group, but only eight were willing to talk with other wives about their situation. More information needs to be gathered on the spouses of bisexual and gay people.

Sexual Relationship

Sexual problems occurred in 19 (61 percent) of these marriages. There were a number of relationships, however, where there seemed to be satisfactory sexual activity and no reported sexual dysfunctions. Seven men had a history of erectile difficulty (problems with erection more than 50 percent of the time). The remainder of the problems were with frequency of sexual activity and low sexual desire.

Extra-marital Liaisons

All but two men had engaged in sexual activity with other males outside of their marital relationship. The frequency of this activity varied greatly from a single incident to sexual encounters at least once a week. One man had never had a single same-sex experience before or after being married.

After Treatment

Following treatment, 11 of the 31 men (36 percent) decided to end their marriage. (See Table 18.1 for a summary of results.) It should be noted that of these 11 men, 5 had entered treatment already separated or seriously considering separation. The remaining 20 men (64 percent) decided to remain married. Three of these, however, openly admitted that their decision to remain married was temporary and that they would probably eventually leave their wives to pursue same-sex relationships. In other words, 17 (55 percent) of the 31 men decided to re-commit themselves to their relationship. Only five of these men planned a monogamous relationship with their wives. Seven were definitely going to act on their same-sex feelings without the wives' knowledge, two were still undecided whether they would act on their feelings or not, and three men had developed relationships that allowed extra-marital activity by the husband with the wife's knowledge and consent.

Effects of Children   The decision whether or not to leave the marital relationship might have been related to or influenced by the fact that children were involved. Of

TABLE **18.1** *Summary of Data (N = 31)*

	f	%
Average Age	38.58	
Average Length of Marriage (in years)	13.06	
Average Number of Children	2.03	
Awareness of Same-Sex Feelings Prior to Marriage	30	97
Acted on Same-Sex Feelings Prior to Marriage	27	87
Had Had Therapy to Eliminate Same-Sex Feelings	11	36
Wife Knew of Husband's Same-Sex Feelings Prior to Marriage	5	16
Sexual Conflicts Within the Marriage	19	61
Extra-Marital Liaisons	29	94
Commitment Following Treatment		
Marriage	20	64
Divorce	11	36
	31	100
Commitment at the Time of Follow-Up Study		
Marriage	14	45
Divorce	17	55
	31	100

the men studied, 24 (77 percent) had children. All 24 men had truly wished to be fathers and expressed a deep sense of love and admiration for their children. Five of these men had decided to communicate with their children about their same-sex feelings; there was no immediate negative effect reported. In the end, 16 of the 24 men with children decided to stay married.

Follow-Up Results

The 20 men who remained committed to their marriage at the end of the Bisexuality Group have made a number of changes in the months and years since then. Six of these men are now divorced or are in the process of separation or divorce. Of the 14 men still married, three express grave doubts concerning the future of their relationships. Only two men are committed to a monogamous relationship with their wives.

Six married men are pursuing same-sex relationships. Their feeling is that "what my wife doesn't know won't hurt her, me, or our relationship." All of these men originally planned not to get emotionally involved with any of their sexual partners, in order to avoid threats to the primary relationships with their wives. Several men, however, have developed close emotional relationships with males; this causes difficulties in their marriages. Most of the married men continue to keep in contact with other married men with same-sex feelings, for emotional support.

Three men have open-marriage contracts with their wives. In all three cases, the husband has the freedom to seek out sexual partners but the wife has chosen not to do the same. A few other couples have tried this type of arrangement. In the past, this appeared to be a stepping-stone to divorce. It is still uncertain if any of these marriages will last.

A number of married couples have entered a couples' group or have sought marital counseling for additional support in their adjustment. Several of the fathers have joined a "Gay Fathers" group to share similar concerns and to gain support. Several wives have been getting together informally to support each other.

Of the eighteen men who decided to leave their relationship, seven were involved at the time of follow-up in a "steady relationship with another man." Two men were involved in primary relationships with women and continued to have same-sex activity and relationships. The remaining nine men were primarily pursuing same-sex relations; two of these nine expressed an interest in exploring opposite-sex relationships at some future date.

Kinsey-type ratings [A continuum from 0 (exclusive heterosexuality) to 6 (exclusive homosexuality)] of sexual behavior, erotic fantasies, and emotional attachments were obtained from each man as he entered the group and again at the time of follow-up. (See Table 18.2.) A significant change seems to have occurred in terms of increased same-sex sexual behavior (pre-treatment, 2.42; follow up, 4.26). There has been essentially no change in the content of sexual fantasies.

The mean score for *self-esteem* as measured by the Tennessee Self Concept Scale (TSCS) (Fitts, 1965) was 351. This score is within one standard deviation of the

TABLE 18.2 *Changes in Kinsey-Type Ratings (Means)*

	Before Group	Follow-up
Sexual Behavior	2.42	4.26
Erotic Fantasies	4.52	4.67
Emotional Attachment	2.57	3.55

standard mean. It is also consistent with typical post-treatment scores of individuals who have received some type of sexual counseling (e.g., Coleman, 1978). The mean score for *personality integration* as measured by TSCS was 9.07, which is also within one standard deviation of the standard mean and is consistent with post-treatment scores of others seeking sexual counseling (Coleman, 1978).

When the TSCS scores of men who have remained married are compared with those who have separated and divorced, some differences are noticed. The mean self-esteem score for the married men was 346. The mean self-esteem score for the divorced men was 359. This difference does not represent a statistically significant difference.

The results from the sexual behavior survey (Jeddeloh, Aletky, and Coleman [unpub]) provide some additional information. As a group, the men in the sample had had, in the past, more homosexual partners than heterosexual partners. The average number of female partners was between 1 and 5, versus 20 or more male partners. Sixteen reported their only heterosexual partner was their wife. The average frequency of sexual activity with a partner was once a week. These men reported more sexual dysfunction with females than with males, and more anal stimulation with males than females.

Case Studies

The following three case studies illustrate some of the concerns encountered in the process of therapy.

CASE 1
Fred was a 35-year-old man who had been married for 10 years and had two children. He had been aware of his same-sex feelings before he was married but didn't think he would be happy living a gay life-style. He became emotionally involved with a woman when he was 23 and married her.

It was after the birth of their second child that Fred began to feel a greater urge to act on his same-sex feelings. These feelings had never disappeared, but until then he had decided not to act on them. He entered therapy trying to figure out if he should stay with his wife and suppress his homosexual desires, or separate and develop same-sex relationships. His wife was clear. If he decided to pursue same-sex relationships, she wanted a divorce.

In the course of therapy, Fred reported that since his adolescence all his erotic fantasies had been of males. He also was aware of strong emotional attachment to males. He discovered in therapy that his love for his wife was waning. He decided he wanted to pursue same-sex relationships and informed his wife. They discussed this in therapy together, deciding to separate.

CASE 2

Drake was a 39-year-old man who had been married for 15 years and had three children. Drake had been aware of his same-sex feelings since he was very young and had some "exploratory" same-sex experiences in adolescence. He was concerned about these experiences and thought he might be gay. He was somewhat reassured, however, when he developed a loving relationship with his present wife.

For a few months after he was married he thought his same-sex feeling had disappeared, but he soon began to experience the erotic fantasies again and the urge to act on those feelings. He began having sex with men in anonymous situations without his wife's knowledge. He felt extremely guilty about these experiences. Drake maintained this "double life" for most of his marriage.

In the year before entering therapy, he fell in love with another man. This greatly disturbed Drake because up until that point he had never felt emotional attachment to any of his sexual partners. This created the crisis that finally led Drake to therapy.

Over the years as he became more committed to pursuing same-sex relationships, Drake had lost his feelings of love for his wife. However, he feared the reaction of children, family, and people at work to a divorce.

His wife was willing to stay married under any circumstances. There was little pressure for him to make a decision, other than his own guilt and depression. He vacillated back and forth, unable to decide. Although after therapy he decided to remain married, he knew that eventually he would leave.

In the year following treatment there was no change. Drake was still unhappy with his marriage and talked of leaving, but he had made no firm commitment. Meanwhile there was evidence of continued discord and that the children were aware of the uncertain status of the marriage.

CASE 3

Ray was a 50-year-old man who had been married for 25 years. At the time he married, he was aware of his same-sex feelings but thought that marriage would be a "cure." He loved the woman he married and enjoyed their sexual activity, but his interest in sex with men never waned.

He sought out sex in steam baths, bookstores, and restrooms. For twenty-five years, no one knew about this activity. He never knew any of his sexual partners. Ray felt extreme guilt and shame about his behavior but was unable to discontinue it. At one time, he had tried through therapy to eliminate his same-sex thoughts and activity. This therapy was unsuccessful.

Ray entered the Bisexuality Group feeling depressed, guilt-ridden, and lonely. In the course of therapy he developed some of this first male friendships. Ray continued to seek out sexual activity with men, but with less guilt and shame and less compulsively.

While in treatment, he decided to tell his wife about his same-sex feelings. She was shocked but did not reject him. This opened up communication between them and helped to rebuild an intimate relationship. They joined a couples' support group with other couples in similar situations. Ray's wife joined a support group for wives of bisexual and gay men.

His continued sexual activity outside of marriage occurred without his wife's knowledge. She assumed that some activity might be taking place but really did not want to know about it.

Discussion

At present there is no clear model for a married man with same-sex feelings who wishes to maintain his marriage. Based upon clinical experience, here are some of the factors that seem to be important ingredients of successful adjustment.

1. Both people love one another.
2. Both people want to make the relationship work.
3. There is a high degree of communication in the relationship.
4. Both people have resolved feelings of guilt, blame, and resentment.
5. Physical contact is necessary. The husband has to touch, and desire to touch, his wife.
6. The wife has a sense of worth outside the marriage.
7. If there is outside sexual contact, the wife does not know about it, or the husband and wife have worked out an open-marriage contract.
8. The wife is willing to work on understanding and accepting her husband's same-sex feelings.
9. The husband continues to work on his own acceptance of same-sex feelings.

There is now more support available in the gay community for those men who decide to leave their marriages and pursue same-sex relationships. There is also more information on factors for successful adjustment:

1. Acknowledging same-sex feelings to oneself and to significant others (see Hammersmith and Weinberg, 1973). This does not necessarily mean complete public disclosure but, more importantly, self-recognition and the ability to share this fact with someone else (Weinberg and Williams, 1974).
2. Be willing to explore and experiment with the "new" sexual identity. This means developing contacts with other men and women of similar sexual orientations. It also means permitting oneself to be sexual with members of one's own sex, exploring ways of meeting others, and learning new interpersonal skills.
3. Utilizing available support systems, such as friends, gay social groups, church group, political groups, or counseling opportunities.
4. Trying to work on establishing a new relationship with the ex-wife. It is helpful if this relationship is based upon mutual respect and cooperation, especially if children are involved.
5. Look for ways to insure continued parenting of children, possibly considering joint-custody arrangements.
6. During this stage of exploring and experimenting, it is often a mistake to get involved immediately in a long-term committed relationship. This should be an important stage of experimentation, not commitment.
7. When same-sex relationships are explored, some perspective on these relationships is helpful. Learning to be in a same-sex relationship is new for most and often does not work initially. Individuals need to keep this fact in perspective and view "first relationships" as learning experiences.
8. Look for possible support from friends, family, or people at work. This may be difficult to obtain at first; however, it is important not to neglect opportunities for support from these significant people and areas of one's life.

These suggestions have come from 3 years' experience in working with married men with predominantly same-sex sexual preferences. This study represents a beginning in understanding this phenomenon. More information is needed, however; specifically, information about non-patient populations, and about spouses. There is, of course, some question as to whether these findings can be generalized to non-patient populations or even other clinical populations. For example, it would be especially helpful to know about modes of adjustment in marriages wherein both husband and wife express satisfaction with the relationship, and the husband is bisexual.

REFERENCES

Bell, A. P., and Weinberg, M. S. 1978. *Homosexualities: A study of diversity among men and women.* New York: Simon and Schuster.

Coleman, E. 1978. Effects of communication skills training on the outcome of a sex counseling program. Unpublished doctoral dissertation, University of Minnesota.

Fitts, W. H. 1965. *Manual, Tennessee self concept scale.* Nashville: Counselor Recordings and Tests.

Gochros, H. 1978. Counseling gay husbands. *Journal of Sex Education and Therapy,* 4, 6–10.

Hammersmith, S. K., and Weinberg, M. S. 1973. Homosexual identity: Commitment, adjustment, and significant others. *Sociometry,* 36, 56–70.

Hatterer, M. 1974. The problems of women married to homosexual men. *American Journal of Psychiatry,* 131, 275–278.

Hunt, M. 1974. *Sexual behavior in the seventies.* New York: Playboy.

Jeddeloh, R., Aletky, P., and Coleman, E. 1980. A sexual behavior survey. Unpublished manuscript. [Available from the authors at Program in Human Sexuality, 2630 University Ave., S.E., Minneapolis, MN 55414.]

Kinsey, A., Pomeroy, W., and Martin, C. W. 1948. *Sexual behavior in the human male.* Philadelphia: W. B. Saunders.

Kinsey, A., Pomeroy, W. B., Martin, C. W., and Gebhard, P. H. 1953. *Sexual behavior in the human female.* Philadelphia: W. B. Saunders.

Klein, F. 1978. *The bisexual option.* New York. Arbor House.

Kohn, B., and Matusow, A. 1980. *Barry and Alice.* Englewood Cliffs, NJ: Prentice-Hall.

Malone, J. 1980. *Straight women/Gay men.* New York: Dial Press.

Masters, W. H., and Johnson, V. E. 1966. *Human sexual response.* Boston: Little, Brown and Company.

Masters, W. H., and Johnson, V. E. 1979. *Homosexuality in perspective.* Boston: Little, Brown and Company.

Nahas, R., and Turley, M. 1979. *The new couple: Women and gay men.* New York: Seaview Books.

Ross, H. L. 1971. Modes of adjustment of married homosexuals. *Social Problem* 18, 385–393.

Weinberg, M. S., and Williams, C. J. 1974. *Male homosexuals: Their problems and adaptations.* New York: Oxford University Press.

19

The Commencement of Bisexual Activity in Swinging Married Women Over Age Thirty

Joan K. Dixon

CONTROVERSY persists about almost every aspect of bisexuality. If the existence of bisexuality as a discrete sexual orientation is granted or assumed, some fundamental questions about its etiology remain unsettled. For example, scholars such as Ellis (quoted in Clanton, 1979) and Stekel (1950, pp. 27–28) seem to believe that everyone is born bisexual. However, other scholars, like de Saussaure (quoted in Socarides, 1963, p. 399) and Money (1967), feel that there are certain inborn tendencies in only *some* people which lead them at times to desire sex with persons of their own sex. But whereas de Saussaure believed this desire to be the result of a neurosis, Money (1967) said that the desire results when "the social environment happens to provide the right confluence of circumstances" (p. 47). This study examined the "confluence of circumstances" portion of Money's theory.

Also of relevance to this investigation are the behavioral theorists (e.g., Gagnon and Simon, 1973; Kolodny, 1974) who have speculated that, although hormonal and other factors play a part in behavior, choices such as sex object are primarily learned. More specifically, this study sought to put to use the theories of Bacon (1956), Duberman (1974), Ford and Beach (1951), and Stoller (1973) which assert that a bisexual orientation may result from the effects of one's culture and environment acting upon the psyche.

A crucial issue in some theories (e.g., A. Bell, 1980; Duberman, 1974; Fenichel, 1945; SIECUS, 1980; Socarides, 1963) is the matter of timing of influences, for those theories insist that one's sexual orientation, no matter how it is arrived at, is either permanently or very strongly set at an early age, usually at or before puberty. Some authorities (e.g., Silverstein, 1977; Whitam, 1977) hold that sexual orientation is not or may not be subject to any change once it is set. This study tested those theories by examining the sample as to the nature and timing of various psychosexual behaviors relating to the subjects' apparent change in sexual behavior and orientation.

It is not uncommon to find reports of studies which speak of investigating homosexual behavior but whose populations include sizeable proportions of apparently bisexual subjects (e.g., A. P. Bell and Weinberg, 1978; A. P. Bell, Weinberg, and Hammersmith, 1981; Masters and Johnson, 1979; Saghir and Robbins, 1968). Even purely statistical data about bisexual behavior are at times submerged under the heading "homosexual" (Gebhard and Johnson, 1979, p. 611). In those studies and reports, sexual acts engaged in between persons of the same sex are described and listed as "homosexual" acts regardless of whether the persons involved in the acts were of a bisexual or a homosexual orientation.

In an attempt to aid in the contemplation and conceptualization of bisexuality as a sexual orientation distinct from homosexuality, two new terms, "multi-female" and "multi-male," are used in this report to refer to the sex acts engaged in by persons of the same sex. Thus, a sex act involving two or more females or two or more males is not referred to herein as a "homosexual" act; instead, a sex act involving two or more females engaging in sex with each other is referred to as a "multi-female sex act," and a sex act involving two or more males engaging in sex with each other is referred to as a "multi-male sex act."

Mere participation in one or more sexual acts with a same-sex partner by a theretofore heterosexual person does not in itself signify that the actor has incorporated a change in sexual orientation into her or his self-identity (SIECUS, 1980). Blumstein and Schwartz (1976a, 1976b, 1976c, 1976d) recount many instances from their interviews with 75 women where subjects with a considerable number of sexual experiences with partners of each sex did not consider themselves to be "a bisexual." It has also been documented that women who engage in sex acts with other women in correctional institutions (a so-called "situational" experience) do not necessarily alter their sense of sexual orientation as a result (Coles, 1977; Giallombardo, 1966, 1974; Ward and Kassebaum, 1965).

Behavior resulting from a social setting which produces an atmosphere of group approval and encouragement of that behavior is referred to by social psychologists as being the product of "social facilitation." Although social facilitation of multi-female sexual activity is often a very strong influencing factor in female prison situations, it is not sufficient to alter the self-identified sexual orientation of many of the women who experience their first multi-female sexual acts in that environment.

What are the elements which go into the "mix" which is necessary to produce in a woman a self-defined change in sexual orientation from heterosexual to bisexual? Blumstein and Schwartz (1976d) found no answer to that in their study, for they said: "No single or small number of patterns seems to predominate among those who call themselves bisexual, or among those whose behavior might be given that label" (p. 7). They further said, that "one of our most pronounced findings among our female bisexual respondents is the extreme diversity of their lifestyles and sexual histories" (1976a, p. 156).

In the study of behavior causation it is sometimes helpful to examine attributes which are commonly shared by study subjects and which indicate that even before the subjects behaved in a certain way they were predisposed to do so. Stephenson

(1973) has proposed that *conformity* and *variance* may be viewed as generally fixed predispositions and that "for an explanation of [a person's] present behavior or the potentiality for change in it," one must focus on his or her prior states of mind and behavior (p. 183). He argued that the strength of one's socialization contrary to the proposed variant behavior as well as one's past history of toleration of alternatives or of failures to apply personal sanctions in the face of the existence of variant alternatives all would seem to bear on one's predisposition to engage in the variant behavior if the reward for doing so is otherwise sufficient.

Compared to men in our culture, women are generally considered to be more compliant, yielding, and passive—in short, less rigid (Feinman and Rogers, 1974; Michaelson and Aaland, 1976). Further, married women, in general, are said to be culturally scripted to submit to their husbands' desires, to expect the latter to be somewhat more knowledgeable concerning affairs of the world, and to be willing therefore to follow their husbands' wishes (Laws and Schwartz, 1977). If this is true, it would follow that, in general, women would be somewhat predisposed to engage in variant sexual behavior at the behest of or in response to the encouragement of their husbands. Specifically, it would appear that heterosexual married women in our culture might, to some extent, be predisposed to accede to the wishes of their respective husbands if the latter desired that their wives engage in a multi-female sexual act (Fang, 1976). This possibility was examined in this study.

Researchers of other groups have found clues to subsequent sex behavior by examining their subjects' early sex histories (e.g., A. P. Bell et al., 1981; Kinsey, Pomeroy, Martin, and Gebhard, 1953). Thus, one hypothesis of this study was that some clue to the reasons for the commencement of multi-female sexual activity by adult heterosexual females may be found in their early sex histories. It was also speculated that additional insight into the forces at work in the ontogenesis of such a change in sexual behavior might be found in the subjects' later sex and marital histories. For example, there is strong authority for the view that one who has engaged in extramarital sex is likely to have also engaged in premarital sex (Athanasiou, Shaver, and Tavris, 1970; Hamilton, 1929; Kinsey et al., 1953; Levin, 1975; Schupp, 1970; Terman, 1938). Accordingly, the study was designed to conduct a general examination of the entire sex histories and, to a limited extent, the marital histories of the subjects. It was also expected that a high rate of change in sexual orientation from heterosexual to bisexual would be found in the women in this sample.

In order to try to find some pattern in the factors which seem to combine or appear together at the time of such dramatic changes, which would thus appear suggestive of causation, it is helpful to be able to study a population in which such changes in sexual behavior and in sexual orientation are thought to happen at a relatively high rate per capita. It may also be helpful if various members of this population are likely to have in common a number of demographic attributes.

As a way to satisfy both of these requirements, I used a sample of swinging wives. As used in this study, swinging is the term used to refer to the activities of a married couple wherein, with each other's knowledge and consent, the partners engage in sexual activities with another person or persons outside of the marriage.

It is known that the incidence of multi-female sexual activity among women swingers is extremely high when compared to that of other groups of women. This suggests the possibility of a high rate of change in sexual orientation. O'Neill and O'Neill (1970) reported that 60 percent of the females in their study engaged in genital, sexual activities with other women, whereas 68 percent of the women in Gilmartin's (1978, p. 262) study had done so. Bartell (1971, pp. 131–132) reported that any time two couples would swing together, 75 percent of the females would engage in sex with another female, and that at large parties 92 percent of the females would do so. These percentages are substantially higher than the 50 percent of the population reported by Ward and Kassebaum (1965) as engaging in multi-female sexual activity, even though the latter study was conducted among prison women (some of whom, at that, were homosexuals), a subgroup of women known for having a high incidence of such activity.

As a group, swingers (both male and female) *tend* to possess certain attributes in common. Although there are many exceptions, most swinging women are Caucasian, middle-class, married, fairly well educated suburbanites in their mid-twenties to mid-forties (Bartell, 1970, 1971; Gilmartin, 1978; Margolis and Rubenstein, 1972; Smith and Smith, 1970, 1974). As a group they reportedly are neither abnormally neurotic nor variant in other aspects of their lives; rather, they tend to believe in and uphold the most commonly held attitudes and values of American life (Spanier and Cole, 1975).

The use of swinging women as subjects obviates another factor as a consideration, for contrary to situations such as prison, where so-called situational multi-female sex activity by otherwise heterosexual females takes place at times as a result of the lack of male sex partners, women who engage in swinging normally have sexual access to and actually engage in sex with significant numbers of male partners.

To satisfy the research requirement that each member of the sample was heterosexually oriented prior to her first sexual experience with another female and prior to any supposed change to a bisexual orientation, I deemed it desirable to demonstrate that each subject had had a reasonably long history of personally satisfying, exclusively heterosexual sexual activity before her first multi-female sexual activity occurred. To meet this particular requirement, participation in the study was limited to women who reported that they had engaged in sexual activities with another female for the first time (a) at or after the age of 30, (b) while married, (c) while engaged in a swinging lifestyle involving access to and sexual contact with a number of different males, (d) with a current and prior history of a personally satisfying heterosexual sex life, and (e) with no history prior to at least the age of 30 of any conscious sexual desire or significant amount of erotic fantasy involving herself and any other female. Furthermore, participation was limited to those women meeting the above criteria who also were currently engaging in or desirous of engaging in sex with partners of each sex.

Method

SUBJECTS

Subjects were located in several ways: by soliciting volunteer participants at two alternative-lifestyles conventions; by answering ads in swinging publications; by contacting friends and acquaintances; and through referrals from others, including prior participants and operators of "swing-party houses" and swingers' social organizations.

Prospective participants were told that the study would form the basis for a doctoral dissertation; that it was an investigation of women who had experienced sexual activity with other women; and that it would involve a private, personal interview with each subject as the sole means of gathering the data. If the prospective subject agreed to participate, she was then further qualified or rejected by being asked additional questions necessary to determine whether or not she met all of the requirements described above. Only with those women who met all participatory requirements were appointments made to interview them further. In-depth interviews were conducted with the first 50 women who met all the requirements—and these women constitute the sample from which data reported here were derived. All participants were residents of California, Oregon, or Washington.

Because of the difficulties of acquiring a properly randomized sample of underground populations such as sexually variant minorities (A. Bell, 1974, Blumstein and Schwartz, 1976d; Ramey, 1975; Weinberg, 1970), it was decided not to attempt to acquire such a sample for this study. However, I believe the variety of sources from which the sample was gathered includes all major types of sources for such participants in that geographical area. Because no attempt was made to stratify participants by source of contact, it is not claimed that this sample is representative of any larger population. This report is presented only as a descriptive study of the 50 participants, who, nevertheless, were gathered from across the spectrum of available sources.

The participants' ages ranged from 32 to 60, the mean age being 42.9. They were predominantly middle class, and 96 percent were Caucasian. At the time of the interview, 90 percent were married, 4 percent were divorced, 4 percent were widowed, and 2 percent were separated.

INTERVIEWS

I conducted all of the in-depth interviews personally. In all cases except one there were conditions of complete privacy of communication between interviewer and interviewee. In the one exception, the husband of the subject was present at the subject's request. Interviews were usually conducted in or near the subjects' homes or places of work. I assured the women that all information received would be treated as confidential and that the identities of participants would not be divulged.

Interviews were semi-structured around an outline of topics to be covered with each participant. In addition to a section of demographic items, specific topics were placed under the following main headings: preadolescent, postpubertal, marital, extramarital-heterosexual sexuality, same-sex sexuality, and miscellaneous. Items included under these headings were designed to elicit information, where appropriate for the topic and for the purposes of the study, about past and present sociosexual behavior, attitudes, fantasies, dreams, and perceived responses of the subjects and of their sex partners and other persons. Behavior items had, when appropriate, subitems about when, where, how, how often, with whom, and why, the given behavior occurred.

However, as is usual with such an interview technique, there was no rigid order in which items were discussed. Information gathered during each interview was recorded on an interview answer sheet designed by the researcher. The average interview took about 1 hour. Only that portion of the collected data which is relevant to this report is presented here.

Results

No obvious hint that these subjects would at a later time either begin to engage in sex with other females or develop a bisexual orientation appears in their preadolescent or adolescent histories. Most (66 percent) of these women reported that most of their friends during preadolescence were female, and 80 percent reported having had, during adolescence, either an equal number of friends of each gender or a majority of male friends. Sixty percent reported preadolescent crushes on males, and *not one* subject reported having had a crush on a female during either preadolescence or adolescence.

With one exception, none of these subjects reported in their early sociosexual histories any indications of romantic or sexual interest or contact involving other females. The exception involved an occasional fantasy during masturbation by one subject, which involved her imagining the form of a nameless and faceless, large-breasted woman.

Of possible interest as an indicator of a tendency to experiment in the future with sexually variant activity is the finding that 54 percent of these subjects said that they began masturbating before or at the age of 12, compared to only 17 percent of comparably aged Caucasian women reported by Kinsey and associates (in Gebhard and Johnson, 1979, p. 179). Subjects typically experienced their first coitus approximately 7 months after their first date, that first date occurring at about age 15. This may be seen as another early indicator of a tendency to seek one's emotional gratifications from sexual activity.

As expected, a high incidence of premarital coitus among these subjects was confirmed, for 88 percent of them had engaged in it at least once with at least one partner (which, considering the average age of the women, was greater than I had expected). In fact, only 15.9 percent of the subjects with premarital coitus in their histories had had only one premarital coital partner. The average number of premarital coital partners for all subjects who had engaged in that activity was 9 (SD = 10.9), and the number of such partners ranged from 1 to 50. In contrast, only a little more than a third of the married women of comparable age in Hunt's (1974, p. 151) nationwide sample had engaged in premarital coitus, and over half of those had had only one such partner. For subjects in this study with a history of premarital coitus, an average of 5.3 years (SD = 3.8) elapsed between first coitus and first marriage.

The previously noted high incidence of masturbation by these subjects in their youth was a continuing phenomenon in their adulthood. Ninety-six percent, both of the entire sample and of those who were currently married, said that they were currently masturbating to orgasm. This is over double the highest figure reported by Kinsey and his associates (in Gebhard and Johnson, 1979, p. 203) for current masturbation incidence by married women of comparable age groups. The twice weekly active median frequency of current masturbation to orgasm reported by the subjects in this study is 10 times the 0.2 per week median frequency for that activity reported by Kinsey et al. (1953, p. 178) among masturbating married women age 30–60 and also by Hunt (1974, p. 86).

Current marital coital frequency of the 90 percent of subjects in this study who were married and living with their respective husbands was 4.4 per week, a 76 percent increase over the 2.5 times per week cited as a national average (with no age group breakdowns given) by Ramey (1975). That such a high marital coital frequency may not be merely the result of the spouses' influence but may instead be a characteristic of the subjects themselves may be inferred from the marital coitus data of prior marriages given by the subjects (30 percent of the sample) who: (a) were previously married, (b) reported such data, and (c) also were currently married. The weekly mean frequency of coitus in those prior marriages, all of which ended in divorce, was 2.6 (SD = 2.6). That average is almost identical to Ramey's national average and is significantly higher than the mean of 1.0–1.7 times a week for marriages with various problems reported by R. R. Bell and P. L. Bell (1972). It would thus seem that even in marriages which were so unhappy that they ended in divorce the subjects in this study had a much higher frequency of marital coitus than would otherwise be expected.

The mean length of current marriages was over 15 years (SD = 8.5), and the subjects had engaged in swinging for an average of almost 9 years (SD. = 4.2). Still, only 6 percent of these subjects had divorced subsequent to the commencement of swinging, and only 4 percent had divorced subsequent to the commencement of multi-female sexual activity. Sexual satisfaction was rated as excellent or good in 76 percent of current marriages and as fair in 22 percent of them. Marital compatibility was rated excellent or good in 80 percent of them and as fair in another 13 percent.

These subjects typically had had a substantial number of male sex partners. In addition to their spouses and, in most cases, other non-marital, preswinging, male, sex partners, 44 percent of the sample had had between 10 and 99 male swinging partners, 34 percent had had between 100 and 499, and 22 percent had had between 500 and 1000+. The subjects who were currently married and cohabiting with their spouses reported an average of 3.5 swinging occasions per month (SD = 3.2, with a range of 4 per week to 5 per year).

These swinging frequencies, when added to the previously mentioned current masturbation and marital coitus frequencies, indicate a level of sexual-outlet frequency (averaging almost one a day—without yet considering multi-female sexual frequencies) which is the highest rate I have seen recorded for any group of non-prostitute women. It would seem that sexual activity with other women was not resorted to by these subjects because of an actual lack of male partnered or self-stimulative sexual outlets.

The amount of actual involvement of the subjects' husbands in the subjects' swinging activities was inquired into as one measure of the husbands' influence in those activities. Approximately three fourths of the married subjects currently living with their spouses said that the husband was always present when the wife engaged in swinging. Ninety-three percent of married and cohabiting subjects usually or always engaged in "open" swinging (defined here as swinging sexual activity by a couple conducted in the physical presence of each other); none said that the husband was never present.

The subjects had their first multi-female sexual experience at a mean age of 37 (SD 6.5, Range: 30–56). The first experience occurred an average of 2.9 years (SD = 3, Range: 0–11) after the subjects commenced swinging. On the average they had been involved in bisexual activity for 6 years (SD = 3.9, Range: 0– 21) at the time of the interview. The ranges of these three items illustrate the wide breadth of time during which the activities involved may first occur and may continue among swinging wives as well as the impracticality of trying to assemble a control sample of swinging wives who can be counted on to limit their partnered sexual activities to heterosexual experiences only.

The shy and tentative beginnings which the subjects typically made in their initial experiences with multi-female cunnilingus are demonstrated by the roles which they took in those experiences. Because the words "active" and "passive" are not acceptable to some persons who participate in cunnilingus and can be misnomers of what actually takes place, I have chosen to use the terms "oralist" and "receiver" here instead. Of the 50 women interviewed, the vast majority (82 percent) participated only as receivers in their first multi-female sexual experience, whereas 6 percent participated as oralists, and 12 percent participated as both oralists and receivers. In contrast, 80 percent of the women reported current participation as both oralists and receivers, with just 20 percent participating as receivers only, evidencing the subjects' movement toward full participation in multi-female cunnilingus.

The generally positive reactions of these subjects to their first sexual experience with other females after a lifetime of strict heterosexuality is shown in Table 19.1 to have progressed through repeated experience to an overwhelming general rating of excellent. Subsequent to the first multi-female sexual experience, the percentage of subjects who fantasized about anything during masturbation rose from 44.9 percent to 68.8 percent, and the percentage of those whose masturbatory fantasies at times included other females as erotic sex objects rose from 4.5 percent to 61 percent.

TABLE 19.1 *Subjects' Ratings of First and Current Multi-Female Sexual Experiences Compared (N = 50)*

	Excellent	Fair	Neutral	Somewhat Negative	Very Negative
First Experience	16%	36%	24%	14%	10%
Current Experiences	64%	26%	8%	2%	—

The median number of female sex partners was 12; since the range was 3–250, the mean was not useful. Sixty-two percent of the subjects had had over 10 different female sex partners. In contrast, 82 percent of lesbians studied by Hedblom (1973) reported having had 7 or fewer female sex partners, and 58 percent had had 4 or fewer. Of the white female respondents reporting multi-female sexual activity in A. P. Bell and Weinberg's (1978, p. 312) study of "homosexualities" (in which a quarter of an female subjects were self-identified as "bisexual"), 81 percent had had five or fewer different sexual "affairs" with other females. The current mean frequency of multi-female sexual activity of the subjects in this study was 1.5 occurrences per month (SD = 1.8); the median was 1.0 per month. Clearly, these subjects have had ample opportunities to determine their current sexual orientation and to test their original sex-object preference.

At some point in the interview every subject was either specifically asked if she presently considered her sexual orientation to be bisexual or she volunteered the information herself. Every subject self-identified as bisexual. Answers to other questions about their past and current sexual activity with both males and females, their own enjoyment of this activity, and the effects which the subjects perceived that their bisexual orientation had had on their lives clearly indicated that each subject had adopted a bisexual orientation at that time. However, each subject reported that her original overall preference for sex with a male partner had not changed.

FACTORS INVOLVED IN THE BEHAVIOR CHANGE

The main factors that the women reported as contributing to their initial choices to engage in multi-female sex activity are listed in Table 19.2. In order to evaluate the relative importance of the many contributing influences mentioned by the subjects, I asked each woman to discuss in general terms the circumstances of her first multi-female sexual experience and all of the influences she remembered as having led her to it. It should be noted that the categories listed in the table are not mutually exclusive and that the order in which they appear in the table does not indicate the strength of any item as an influence upon the subjects to commence multi-female sexual activity.

As shown in the table, the most commonly mentioned influences were the subjects' spouses, and swinging friends and acquaintances. Although the subjects were not directly asked to identify *the* single most important influence on them to begin multi-female sexual activity, from the tone and content of the subjects' comments the vast majority of them made it clear that they would not have begun either

TABLE 19.2 *Contributing Reasons Given by Subjects for Engaging in First Multi-Female Sexual Activity (N = 50)*

	%
Persons other than spouse encouraged	88
Spouse encouraged	86
Saw other females engaged in such activities	62
Heard such activities discussed	54
Discussed, decided to try, and waited for it to occur	40
Was seduced by another female	38
Spouse pushed subject to try	36
No previous decision to participate, surprise	30
Spur of the moment	24
Spouse arranged for seduction of subject	14
Spouse was supportive only	2

NOTE: Percentages total over 100% because subjects often gave several contributing reasons.

swinging *or* multi-female sexual activity had not their respective spouses suggested it, encouraged them to do so, and convinced them in various ways that they (the spouses) approved of it. The influence of the spouse seemed to be the most crucial factor in almost every instance. No spouse was reported as having disapproved of a subject's commencing to have sex with other females, so the question of whether or not a subject would, as a result of the other enumerated influences, have engaged in such activity and subsequently acquired a bisexual orientation in the face of spousal disapproval is not answered here.

The extensive influence of the husband in this phenomenon among swinging wives in general has been suggested by other observers of the swinging scene and commentators on swinging (Bartell, 1971; Blumstein and Schwartz, 1974, p. 288, 1976c; Fang, 1976; O'Neill and O'Neill, 1970; Ramey, 1972; Symonds, 1971, pp. 96–97), but in no prior study of swinging that this researcher is aware of is the extent of that influence documented by actual declarations of the involved wives. In addition, there was no doubt in many of these subjects' minds that the permissive and encouraging environment toward multi-female sexual activity which is usually found in swinging situations also was a strong factor which facilitated their first and subsequent sexual experiences of this type.

The fear of becoming a lesbian and "giving up men" or of being thought by others to be a lesbian if sex with another female were experienced is a factor which inhibits some females from engaging in such sex (Ziskin and Ziskin, 1974). However, prior to their first multi-female sexual experience, and as a result of swinging, a majority of the subjects (Table 19.2) had seen other females engaged in sexual activities with each other and had heard discussions by others about such activity. From this experience many subjects saw that other women who had sex together did not thereby give up men and become lesbians nor did other group members think them to be lesbians, Thus the combined effect of the swinging peer-group permissiveness regarding multi-female sexuality was instrumental in moving substantial numbers of subjects into the stage which Herold and Goodwin (1981) call "transition-proneness."

Although Blumstein and Schwartz (1976a, p. 156) have indicated that some (no data given) formerly heterosexual females in their study came to bisexuality through the process of prior involvement in the women's movement, no such path was indicated by any subject in this study. In fact, a reverse process was evident. Only 4 percent of subjects were in any way active in the women's movement prior to their involvement in multi-female sexual activity, none of whom ascribed to the former any substantial importance in beginning the latter. However, 22 percent of subjects became active in the women's movement *subsequent* to their first multi-female sexual experience.

The subject-rated assessment of the attitudes of their families of origin toward same-sex sexuality revealed, as expected, a generally negative (70 percent) influence on that activity; only 8 percent of families were rated as supportive or neutral about it, and the feelings of 22 percent were listed as "unknown." Only one subject (2 percent) had a family-of-origin member who was known to be homosexual, and only 18 percent had at least one homosexual friend.

Discussion

The lack of any substantial evidence from this study of either preadolescent or adolescent romantic or erotic attraction by the subjects toward any other females is at odds with the assertion by Landis et al. (1940) that "crushes between adolescent girls constitute part of the normal course of development" (p. 56). Whereas A. Bell (1980) feels that bisexual women must be influenced by childhood homosexual experience, these subjects revealed none. In contrast to Marmor's (reported in Wilson, Strong, Robbins, and Johns, 1977, p. 402) claim of "overwhelming" evidence that the factors which make a child predisposed to homosexuality are probably set in the first 6 years of life, no such evidence as to future bisexuality was found in this study.

Several theories about the nonimmutability of sexual orientation could gain support from the results of this study. The results are consistent with the theory that there is a bisexual potential in at least some people, and that a selectively adequate series of circumstances may activate that potential. Also consistent with the results are the learning or behavior modification theories, which say that at least some people can adapt their sexual orientations (at least from heterosexual to bisexual) to conform with experiences perceived by them as beneficial—and that this adaptation can take place in adulthood.

Of course, one or even more same-sex sexual experiences do not necessarily result in one's adopting a bisexual orientation. Blumstein and Schwartz (1974, 1976a, 1976c) concluded (without giving data) that the amount of overt multi-female sexual behavior by their female subjects was not a reliable predictor of the subjects' actual assumption of a bisexual self-definition. Some of their subjects were said to have had "a great deal of bisexual behavior" (1976a, p. 156) prior to self-labeling themselves bisexual. Other subjects were said to have "adopted an ideological commitment to bisexuality" (1976a, p. 156) *before* having engaged in sex with any other female.

This study did not examine the exact point at which these subjects adopted a bi-sexual label. And it did not address the phenomenon of a change in sex-object "preference" (meaning whether or not one *prefers* to have sex with someone of one's own sex or of the other sex). Accordingly, it would be a mistake to extrapolate from these results a conclusion concerning the alteration of a sex-object preference.

The important distinction between this study, which deals with moving from a heterosexual to a bisexual orientation, and a study or theory which is concerned with changing a heterosexual orientation (which necessarily requires an other-sex preference) to a homosexual orientation (which necessarily requires a same-sex preference), or vice versa, is that the shift to a bisexual orientation involves a *broadening* of sexual interests and an *addition* of a gender which one finds acceptable as a sex partner. In this broadening and adding process, the gender of one's previous sex-object preference may, and perhaps usually does, remain unaffected. It did for all of the subjects in this study. In contrast, when one speaks of a shift from a het-erosexual orientation to a homosexual one, or vice versa, there is a *substitution* and a *replacement* of a gender of preferred sex partner. These are thus two vastly differ-ent concepts and phenomena, and one would expect them to have quite different dynamics.

A. P. Bell et al. (1981) recognized different etiological factors at work in the onto-genesis of bisexual orientations of subjects compared to the factors founds in the ontogenesis of homosexual orientations of subjects. They found that among per-sons with a same-sex preference who also had a bisexual orientation, the bisexual orientation usually appeared at a much later time and was much more likely to be the product of learning from exposure to influences outside the self than was the same-sex preference. In this study, the pattern of a later developing bisexual orien-tation apparently springing forth in response to out-of-self influences is seen among subjects with a previous and on-going *other-sex* preference.

In addition, however, it is noteworthy that A. P. Bell et al. (1981) describe the typical developmental path toward a same-sex *preference* as involving responses to a series of circumstances, each of which predispose the subject to react to sub-sequent circumstances in ways which, taken together, "eventually lead toward the development of a [same-sex] preference" (p. 191). It is striking how similar this process is to the developmental process of an *acquired bisexual orientation*, as found in this study.

It is considered significant as a factor in that developmental path that, as a group, the females in this study revealed such a strong historical pattern of a high level of sexual activity in general and of heterosexual activity in particular (with much of it at variance with societally approved standards of behavior). Taken to-gether, the four factors of high historical level of such sexual activity, strong sexual attraction to males, susceptibility to a sexual partner's (especially a spouse's) influence in sexual matters, and exposure to an encouraging environment seem to have played an important part in the typical case of acquired bisexual orientation in this investigation. It thus seems paradoxical that for some women an affinity for a high level of sexual activity with males may lead to their acquiring an affinity for sexual activities with females.

Because of the bias factors resulting from the subject-selection process and the often subjective nature of the information collection and interpretation methods used in this study, it is presented only as a descriptive study of the sample used. Although the purpose of the inquiry was to gain some insight into the causative factors of the change in sexual behavior, no conclusions of causation should be drawn from any of the findings. On the contrary, it is hoped that the results of this study may be useful in further research into sexual-behavior-change phenomena. A further limitation of this study is that it does not include as subjects women who tried multi-female sexual activity and had at the time of the study stopped engaging in it because of their lack of desire to continue doing it.

Future researchers may find some answers to otherwise unexplained sexual-behavior changes similar to those shown here by looking at physiologically determined predispositions. Speroff (1978) has proposed the likelihood that each person has a "neurohormonally determined predisposition to a particular sexual development which will be expressed if the right social environment is encountered" (p. 74). If this is true it could provide some answers for the unusual cases where a drastic change in sexual attitude and behavior occurs abruptly.

There is a question whether the results of this study (involving former heterosexuals) might apply to some homosexuals. Pflaum (1972) has in fact suggested that something similar to the results in this study might happen involving homosexual couples who together experiment with sharing their sexuality with other-sex partners. A study of the results of situations where one half of a homosexual couple pressed for the other half of the couple to experiment with bisexuality may be extremely difficult to accomplish (for lack of subjects, lack of an encouraging environment of peers, etc.), but might yield valuable findings.

A study of males who begin multi-male sexual behavior well into adulthood would be very useful as a comparison to this study. Actually, age itself may or may not be a factor in one's deciding to engage for the first time in same-sex sexual behavior. If the results shown in this study can occur among women beyond (and at times well beyond) age 30, would not they be even more likely to occur in younger women, raised as many of them have been in a time of freer sexual license and somewhat blurred sex roles? Kelly (1974) and Palson and Palson (1972) thought so, but MacDonald (1977) has argued that acquired bisexuality is more likely to occur later in life. A study of younger women subjected to influences similar to the women in this study would help answer that question.

REFERENCES

Athanasiou, R., Shaver, P., and Tavris, C. (1970, July). *Psychology Today*, pp. 37–52.
Bacon, C. L. (1956). A developmental theory of female homosexuality. In S. Lorand and M. Balint (Eds.), *Perversions: psychodynamics and therapy* (pp. 131–160). New York: Random House.
Bartell, G. D. (1970). Group sex among the mid-Americans. *Journal of Sex Research, 6,* 113–130.
Bartell, G. D. (1971). *Group sex.* New York: Peter H. Wyden.

Bell, A. (1974). Homosexualities: Their range and character. In J. K. Cole and R. Dienstbier (Eds.), *Nebraska symposium on motivation: 1973* (pp 1–26). Lincoln, NE: University of Nebraska Press.

Bell, A. (1980, October). Untitled address presented and video taped at the Institute for Advanced Study of Human Sexuality, San Francisco.

Bell, A. P., and Weinberg, M. S. (1978). *Homosexualities: A study of diversity among men and women*. New York: Simon and Schuster.

Bell, A. P., Weinberg, M. S., and Hammersmith, S. F. (1981). *Sexual preference: Its development in men and women*. Bloomington, IN: Indiana University Press.

Bell, R. R., and Bell, P. L. (1972, December). Sexual satisfaction among married women. *Medical Aspects of Human Sexuality*, pp. 136–144.

Blumstein, P. W., and Schwartz, P. (1974). Lesbianism and bisexuality. In E. Goode and R. R. Troiden (Eds.) *Sexual deviance and sexual deviants* (pp. 278–295). New York: William Morrow.

Blumstein, P. W., and Schwartz, P. (1976a). Bisexual women. In J. P. Wiseman (Ed.), *The social psychology of sex* (pp. 154– 162). New York: Harper and Row.

Blumstein, P. W., and Schwartz, P. (1976b, October). Bisexuality in men. *Urban Life*, pp. 339–358.

Blumstein, P. W., and Schwartz, P. (1976c). Bisexuality in women. *Archives of Sexual Behavior*, 5, 171–181.

Blumstein, P. W., and Schwartz, P. (1976d, August). Bisexuality: Some social psychological issues. Revised version of paper presented at the annual meeting of the American Sociological Association, New York.

Clanton, G. (1979). A conversation with Albert Ellis. *Alternative Lifestyles*, 2, 243–253.

Coles, F. S. (1977, December). Sex in women's prisons. *Medical Aspects of Human Sexuality*, pp. 67–68.

Duberman, M. (1974, June). The bisexual debate. *New Times*, pp. 35–41.

Fang, B. (1976). Swinging: In retrospect. *Journal of Sex Research*, 12, 220–237.

Feinman, S.. and Rogers J. D. (1974). Sex differences in psychological rigidity. *Perceptual and Motor Skills*, 39, 1337–1338.

Fenichel, O. (1945). *The psychoanalytic theory of neurosis*. New York: Norton.

Ford, C. S., and Beach, F. A. (1951). *Patterns of sexual behavior*. New York: Harper and Brothers/Hoeber.

Gagnon, J. H., and Simon, W. (1973). *Sexual conduct. The social sources of human sexuality*. Chicago: Aldine.

Gebhard, P. H., and Johnson, A. B. (1979). *The Kinsey data. Marginal tabulations of the 1938–1963 interviews conducted by the Institute for Sex Research*. Philadelphia: W. B. Saunders.

Giallombardo, R. (1966). *Society of women*. New York: Wiley.

Giallombardo, R. (1974). *The social world of imprisoned girls*. New York: Wiley.

Gilmartin, B. G. (1978). *The Gilmartin report*. Secaucus, NJ: Citadel.

Hamilton, G. V. (1929). *A research in marriage*. New York: Albert and Charles Boni.

Hedblom, J. H. (1973). Dimensions of lesbian sexual experience. *Archives of Sexual Behavior*, 2, 329–341.

Herold, E. S., and Goodwin, M. S. (1981). Adamant virgins, potential nonvirgins and non-virgins. *Journal of Sex Research*, 17, 97–113.

Hunt, M. (1974). *Sexual behavior in the 1970's*. Chicago: Playboy Press.

Kelly. G. F. (1974). Bisexuality and the youth culture. *Homosexual Counseling Journal*, 1, 16–25.

Kinsey, A. C., Pomeroy, W. B., Martin, C. E., and Gebhard, P. H. (1953). *Sexual Behavior in the human female*. Philadelphia: W. B. Saunders.

Kolodny, R. (1974). Depression of plasma testosterone levels after chronic marihuana use. *New England Journal of Medicine*, 290, 872–874.

Landis, C., Landis, A. T., Boles, M. M., Metzger, H. F., Pitts, M. W., D'esopo, D. A., Moloy,

H. C., Kleegman, S. J., and Dickinson, R. L. (1940). *Sex in development. A study of the growth and development of the emotional and sexual aspects of personality together with physiological, anatomical, and medical information on a group of 153 normal women and 142 female psychiatric patients.* New York: Hoeber.

Laws, J. L., and Schwartz P. (1977). *Sexual Scripts: The social construction of female sexuality.* Hinsdale, IL: Dryden.

Levin, R J. (1975, October). The Redbook report on premarital and extramarital sex: The end of the double standard? *Redbook,* pp. 38–44, 190–192.

Macdonald, A. P., Jr. (1977). Bisexuality: What do we know about it? Unpublished manuscript, University of Massachusetts.

Margolis, H. F., and Rubenstein, P. M. (1972). *The groupsex tapes.* New York: Paperback Library.

Masters, W. H., and Johnson, V. E. (1979). *Homosexuality in perspective.* Boston: Little, Brown.

Michaelson, E. J., and Aaland, L. A. (1976). Masculinity, femininity, and androgyny. *Ethos,* 4, 251–270.

Money, J. (1967). Sexual dimorphism and homosexual gender identity. Working paper prepared for the NIMH Task Force on Homosexuality.

O'Neill, G. C., and O'Neill, N. (1970). Patterns in group sexual activity. *Journal of Sex Research,* 6, 101–112.

Palson, C., and Palson, R. (1972, February). Swinging in wedlock. *Society,* 9, 28–37.

Pflaum, J. H. (1972). *Delightism.* New Jersey: Prentice-Hall.

Ramey, J. W. (1972). Emerging patterns of behavior in marriage: Deviations or innovations? *Journal of Sex Research,* 8, 6– 30.

Ramey, J. W. (1975). Intimate groups and networks: Frequent consequence of sexually open marriage. *Family Coordinator,* 24, 515–530.

Saghir, M. T., and Robbins, E. (1968, November–December). Lesbian study upsets notion one is dominant, the other passive. *Psychiatric Progress,* 4, 214–221.

Schupp, C. E. (1970). An analysis of some social-psychological factors which operate in the functioning relationship of married couples who exchange mates for the purpose of sexual experience. *Dissertation Abstracts International,* 31A:2524A.

SIECUS (1980, January). Uppsala principles basic to education for sexuality. *SIECUS Report,* pp. 8–9.

Silverstein, C. (1977), Homosexuality and the ethics of behavioral intervention: Paper 2. *Journal of Homosexuality,* 2, 205–211.

Smith, J. R., and Smith, L. G. (1970). Co-marital sex and the sexual freedom movement. *Journal of Sex Research,* 6, 131– 142.

Smith, L. G., and Smith, J. R. (1974). Co-marital sex: The incorporation of extramarital sex into the marriage relationship. In J. R. Smith and L. G. Smith (Eds.), *Beyond monogamy: Recent studies of sexual alternatives in marriage* (pp. 84–102). Baltimore, MD: Johns Hopkins University Press.

Socarides, C. W. (1963). The historical development of theoretical and cynical concepts of overt female homosexuality. *Journal of the American Psychoanalytic Association,* 21, 386–414.

Spanier, G. B., and Cole, C. L. (1975). Mate swapping: Perceptions, value orientations, and participation in a Midwestern community. *Archives of Sexual Behavior,* 4, 143–159.

Speroff, L. (1978). Is there a biologic basis for homosexuality? *Contemporary OB/GYN,* 12, 65–74.

Stekel, W. (1950). *Bi-sexual love.* (J. S. Van Teslaar, Trans.). New York: Emerson Books.

Stephenson, R. M. (1973). Involvement in deviance: An example and some theoretical implications. *Social Problems,* 21, 173– 190.

Stoller, R. J. (1973). The "bedrock" of masculinity and femininity: Bisexuality. In J. B. Miller (Ed.), *Psychoanalysis and women* (pp. 245–258). New York: Brunner/Mazel.

Symonds, C. (1971). Sexual mate-swapping: Violations of norms and reconciliation of guilt. In J. M. Henslin (Ed.), *Studies in the sociology of sex* (pp. 81–109). New York: Appleton-Century-Crofts.

Terman, L, M. (1938). *Psychological factors in marital happiness.* New York: McGraw-Hill.

Ward, D. A., and Kassebaum, G. G. (1965). *Women's prison: Sex and social structure.* Chicago. Aldine.

Weinberg, M. S. (1970). Homosexual samples: Differences and similarities. *Journal of Sex Research, 6,* 312–325.

Whitam, F. L. (1977). The homosexual role: A reconsideration. *Journal of Sex Research,* 13, 1–11.

Wilson, S., Strong, B., Robbins, M., and Johns, T. (1977). *Human sexuality.* New York: West.

Ziskin, J., and Ziskin, M. (1974, January). Three in a bed, the new thrill seekers. *Sexology,* pp. 30–34.

6
A Topic in Its Own Right

20

Pioneers in Contemporary Research on Bisexuality

Paula C. Rodríguez Rust

THE pioneers in modern social scientific research and thinking on bisexuality are Fritz Klein, author of *The Bisexual Option,* the research team of Philip Blumstein and Pepper Schwartz, and Janet Bode, author of *View from Another Closet: Exploring Bisexuality in Women.*[1] During the 1970s these scholars displayed a level of theoretical sophistication well ahead of the time, although not unprecedented, arguing that sexuality is "fluid," that same- and other-sex sexual desires are not mutually exclusive or opposite phenomena, and that sexual self-identity, sexual feelings, and sexual behaviors are often not "congruent" with each other. Predating A. P. MacDonald Jr., Jay P. Paul, and other authors whose critiques of the research literature were published in the 1980s, Klein recognized the depth of the threat that bisexuality poses to dichotomous constructions of sexuality, to the social structures based on this dichotomy, and to the heterosexuals, lesbians, and gay men who inhabit these social structures. Writing at length on the cultural denial of the existence of bisexuality, Klein noted that "a threat is best dealt with if it is dismissable" (1978:9). Similarly, Blumstein and Schwartz pointed out that scientists had been blinded by dichotomous thinking about sexuality, neglecting bisexuality because it "does damage to an otherwise neat and uncomplicated conceptual apparatus" (1976b: 340). They argued that bisexuality exists as a form of sexuality that merits study on a par with lesbian, gay, and heterosexual forms of sexuality, and they conducted social scientific research on bisexual women and men themselves. Janet Bode (1976) was more charitable in her criticism of scientific research, asserting that "the scientific community has quietly recognized bisexuality for some time, but it has seldom been discussed as a possible alternative to heterosexuality or homosexuality" (18). In her introduction she provided a history of scientific perspectives on bisexuality including the affirming work of Margaret Mead, Wilhelm Stekel, Charlotte Wolff, Clellan S. Ford and Frank A. Beach, and Alfred Kinsey and his colleagues.

Blumstein and Schwartz interviewed 156 women and men who had had "more than incidental sexual experience with members of both sexes" (1976b:342). The interviews were conducted between 1973 and 1975, largely in Seattle, New York, Berkeley, and San Francisco. Based on these interviews, Blumstein and Schwartz wrote several articles and chapters on bisexuality in the mid to late 1970s. Primarily concerned with documenting the bisexual experience and characterizing the forms bisexuality could take, in these publications Blumstein and Schwartz provided qualitative descriptions of the variations that exist among individuals with both same- and other-sex sexual experience. They analyzed the social, cultural, and political context in which bisexuals find themselves with an insight that would not be demonstrated by most other social scientists for another decade. They also discussed topics that would not be studied again for nearly two decades, such as the pressure to identify as lesbian or gay that bisexuals experience in lesbian and gay communities and the discrediting constructions of and political interpretations given to bisexual behavior in those communities.

For example, in a pair of articles on bisexuality in women and men Blumstein and Schwartz discussed bisexual behavior in self-identified bisexuals, self-identified homosexuals, and self-identified heterosexuals (1976a, 1976b). They described the variety of social contexts in which individuals had their first same- or other-sex sexual experiences, such as the gradual intensification and sexualization of a close friendship between women or a recognition of continued other-sex attraction following the adoption of gay self-identity in men. They analyzed the interpretations individuals put on their sexual behavior that either lead to a change in sexual self-identity or permit maintenance of an existing sexual self-identity. In particular, they noted the factors that encouraged individuals to either adopt or reject a bisexual self-identity.

Blumstein and Schwartz also described the various forms bisexual "careers" could take. These include tearoom activity among married men, initiation to same-sex activity via group sex or swinging among women and men or during prostitution or incarceration among women, homosexual activity during adolescence followed by heterosexual marriage and renewed homosexual activity later in life, consistent heterosexuality until a certain age followed by a change to homosexual behavior and self-identification, simultaneous relationships with both men and women, same-sex sexual contacts concurrent with a committed other-sex relationship, or bisexual self-identity maintained for political reasons in the absence of significant same-sex sexual experience. The emphasis in their work, as seen in the overview of their research and thinking about bisexuality that is included in this section as chapter 21, was on the variety of patterns of same-sex and other-sex behavior and sexual self-identity that could be considered bisexual, that is, on the heterogeneity and complexity of bisexuality.

Fred Klein, who later published as Fritz Klein, also emphasized diversity among bisexuals. However, his primary focus in *The Bisexual Option* was to weave the concept of bisexuality into popular thinking about sexuality, breaking down the belief that everyone must be either heterosexual or homosexual. He presented the Kinsey scale to a lay audience and explained the distinction between gender and sexual orientation. He discussed the slippery distinction between emotional intimacy and sexual intimacy, arguing that hetero- and homophobia result in part from fear that emotional intimacy will grow into sexual intimacy. Calling bisexuality a "concept of one hundred percent intimacy," he characterized bisexuals as people with a healthy ability to experience the full range of emotional intimacy as a result of overcoming their fears of sexual intimacy. By drawing on historical and crosscultural anecdotes, presenting personal and engaging stories of individual bisexual people, and describing the results of a survey of 144 people who visited the Bisexual Forum in New York City in 1976–1977, Klein sought to introduce bisexuality to a skeptical audience and win the empathy and understanding of that audience.

In contrast, Janet Bode did not spend much energy convincing her readers of the authenticity of bisexuality. In her introductory chapter she simply stated, nondefensively, "I think bisexuality is a viable life-style," and then quickly moved beyond the question of authenticity: "I am a feminist and want to aid in the process of women's understanding of each other. This book is not a scientific study with control groups and extensive charts. It is the recorded experiences and philosophies of bisexual women. By speaking for themselves, they provide a view from another closet" (1976:33). That closet has two doors, and Bode provided views through both doors; she recorded bisexual women's experiences both in heterosexual society and within feminist and lesbian communities. By doing so she joined Blumstein and Schwartz in exploring politics within sexual minority communities. In comparison to Klein, for whom the development of a theoretical perspective on bisexuality was a primary concern, Bode refused to impose a theoretical framework on her subjects' stories. At the end of *View,* she wrote, "Conclusions about bisexual women and their life-styles are for the reader to make. . . . The women interviewed for this book ask only that they, and all people, be accorded the freedom of emotional and sexual interaction" (240).

After the 1970s both Philip Blumstein and Pepper Schwartz turned their attention to other matters, although Schwartz has continued to include bisexuality in her research and writing. Janet Bode remained a prolific nonfiction writer through the 1980s and 1990s, although the topic of bisexuality was superseded by the problems of children and adolescents including sibling and peer relations, eating disorders, and teen pregnancy. In his work Fritz Klein has maintained a strong focus on bisexuality, developing the Klein Sexual Orientation Grid (KSOG) in the mid-1980s, coediting a special issue of the *Journal of Homosexuality* on bisexuality in 1985, personally encouraging others' research on bisexuality, participating in the growth of a bisexual community and movement, and, as of this writing, preparing to edit the new *Journal of Bisexuality* scheduled to begin publication in 2000. Once the flood of social scientific theory and research on bisexuality began in the 1980s, citations to Blumstein and Schwartz's work and to Klein's *The Bisexual Option* were virtually mandatory for social scientists writing about bisexuality up through the early 1990s. Bode's work was also often cited as pioneering, although it was rarely used by social scientists as a significant source of ideas because of its lack of theory. Contemporary authors now have a wealth of theory and research on bisexuality to cite—including a revised edition of *The Bisexual Option* and more recent publications based on Blumstein and Schwartz's work (e.g., Schwartz and Blumstein 1998)—but the early works of Blumstein and Schwartz, Janet Bode, and Fritz Klein have earned their places in the history of the modern study of bisexuality.

Note

1. There are other authors who wrote about bisexuality in the 1970s, but for various reasons I do not include them as pioneers in the modern social scientific study of bisexuality. These include some of the works reviewed in sections 4 and 5, particularly those on "Married gays and lesbians," surveys conducted in the Kinseyan tradition, and the work of Charlotte Wolff and Shere Hite. Researchers whose work is reviewed in sections 4 and 5 generally did not conceptualize the topic of their research as "bisexuality," and surveys of sexual behavior typically included bisexuality only as one aspect of sexuality in general and usually conceptualized it as a "degree" of homosexuality.

Although Charlotte Wolff's criticism (1977) of the view that bisexuality is "deviate" and her recognition of bisexuals' social oppression reflect modern scientific thinking about bisexuality, I do not include her work among the pioneers of modern social scientific research on bisexuality because her conceptualization of bisexuality resembles earlier concepts of degrees of homosexuality. A psychiatrist by training, her thinking is also rooted in theories of homosexuality as gender inversion. Although explicitly critical of earlier theorists' conflation of androgyny and bisexuality, she herself frequently failed to distinguish the concepts, using the term *bisexuality* to refer to biological, social, sexual, and psychological behaviors and states of being without consistently recognizing distinctions between biological sex, gender identity, gender role, and sexual orientation. She commented, for example, that "[previous authors] omitted to investigate a possible correlation between bisexuality (androgyny) and sexual orientation" (66), and "Even if it is not obvious in their day-to-day living and attitudes, all bisexual people are aware of their male/female gender identity, and therefore retain, consciously or unconsciously, a spark of the androgynous magic of love so beautifully illustrated in the legend of Hermaphroditus" (200). Wolff also differed from the pioneers in the modern study of bisexuality because she lacked a critical view of dualistic models of sexuality. Although she pointed out that "society has categorized people according to their sexual orientation, and has never understood that there is only human sexuality with manifold expressions" (1971:109), she also asserted that "a comparison of bisexual subjects with 'normal' controls would be nonsensical because of their own heterosexual side. The same holds good for homosexual controls as homosexuality is also part of bisexuality" (67–68).

Shere Hite (1976), who was not as constrained as Wolff (1977) by cultural concepts of sexuality, boldly asserted that "it must be clear by now that female sexuality is physically 'pansexual,' or just 'sexual' "; Hite also thought that "as we move toward a more equitable view of life, [women's] right to love other women will be taken for granted" (257). Although acknowledging bisexuality as an authentic form of sexuality, her research emphasized heterosexuality and her findings regarding same-sex and bisexual activity are presented in a chapter on "lesbianism."

21

Bisexuality: Some Social Psychological Issues

Philip W. Blumstein and Pepper Schwartz

THE scientific study of human sexuality has not reached a stage of conceptual maturity. Any scientific endeavor must, as an important early step, develop a workable number of abstractions to simplify a complex universe of phenomena. The study of sexuality has had little success at such a task because it has failed to address an even more fundamental problem, i.e., to recognize and map the complexity and diversity of the very sexual phenomena under scrutiny. It is not difficult to understand why sex research is replete with oversimplifications masquerading as scientific abstractions. By and large, investigators working with sexual data have accepted uncritically the pervasive cultural understandings of sexuality, and have assumed there to be a simple and "correct" conceptual scheme readily modifiable to the requirements of scientific rigor. As a result of our continuing study of sexual identity we have been led to quite the opposite view, and have become disaffected with scientific conceptions that simply reflect the prejudices of folk wisdom. Indeed, the most fundamental conclusion from our research has been that the closer we probe such questions as how people come to define themselves sexually or how their erotic and affectional biographies are structured, the more—not less—the data defy organization in terms of the classical simplicities.

Escaping scientists' borrowed conceptions of sexuality is difficult indeed, because these lay notions, we feel, play a very important part in shaping the actual sexual data themselves. We take the simple position that personal views about sexuality in the abstract reflect wider cultural understandings, and affect, in turn, the concrete constructions people place on their own feelings and experiences, and thereby affect their behavior. So it is essential to accept cultural understandings of sexuality as crucial data, while at the same time rejecting the scientific validity of their underlying premises.

Guiding our primary cultural understandings concerning sexuality are three related dichotomies: gender (female versus male), sex role (feminine versus masculine), and affectional preference (homosexual versus heterosexual). Although departures from these dichotomies can be accommodated (e.g., trans-sexualism has been allowed to emerge as both a concept and as an empirical reality), the very extraordinariness that accompanies such departures reflects and reinforces the cultural simplifications.

Bisexuality is another conceptual loose-end which has been forced by recent media events into a precarious niche in an otherwise neat conceptual apparatus. There is certainly nothing new in the fact that some people do not limit their lifetime of sexual experiences to one sex or the other. In fact, sex researchers over the years have presented compelling evidence of bisexuality in both our own culture and elsewhere around the world (Ford and Beach, 1951). Nevertheless it seems clear that such behavior has been seen as a curiosity, and no attempt has been made to integrate the occasional data on bisexuality into any coherent scientific view of sexuality, nor to modify the hegemony of dichotomous concepts.

As far back as 1948, Kinsey admonished sex researchers to think of sexuality in general, and sex-object choice in particular, in terms of a continuum rather than as a rigid set of dichotomous categories (Kinsey, Pomeroy, and Martin, 1948). His studies found that "37 percent of the total male population had had at least some overt homosexual experience to the point of orgasm between adolescence and old age," and that between 8 percent and 20 percent of females (depending on marital status and education) had made at least incidental homosexual responses or contacts in each of the years between 20 and 35 years of age (Kinsey, Pomeroy, Martin, and Gebhard, 1953). These data, as revolutionary as they were, need to be contrasted with the findings that only 4 percent of Kinsey's white males and between 0.3 percent and 3 percent of his females were exclusively homosexual after the onset of adolescence. The inescapable—but often escaped—conclusions from Kinsey et al.'s findings are that a mix of homosexual and heterosexual behaviors in a person's erotic biography is a common occurrence, and that it is entirely possible to engage in anywhere from a little to a great deal of homosexual behavior without adopting a homosexual lifestyle.

The implications of viewing human sexuality as being plastic and malleable have never really been exploited. Even the word *bisexuality* gives a misleading sense of fixedness to sex-object choice, suggesting as it does a person in the middle, equidistant from heterosexuality and from homosexuality, equally erotically disposed to one gender or the other. Our data show that exceedingly few people come so neatly packaged, thus if we were to be really true to Kinsey's idea of a sexual continuum, we would instead use the preferable term, *ambisexuality*, connoting some ability for a person to eroticize both genders under some circumstances. However, *bisexuality* seems to have already become entrenched in our language, and we will have to settle for it, rather than the term Kinsey would have preferred. Indeed, even though we are indebted to Kinsey for his insistence on a homosexual/heterosexual continuum, we must emphasize that this view also misleads by focusing on the individual, with his or her sexual "place" as a unit of conceptualization, rather than on the sexual behavior (with all of its antecedents and subjective meanings) as a unit for theorizing.

Kinsey et al.'s data were not the only ones indicating that homosexual and heterosexual behavior could be incorporated in a single sexual career. Other studies have pointed to a bisexual phenomenon, although they have never dealt with the question of bisexuality per se. McCaghy and Skipper (1969), for example, argued that because of the social organization of the occupation of striptease, many of the women become involved in homosexual relationships, although they often continue to have heterosexual involvements. Furthermore, it has been well documented that women in correctional institutions commonly develop homosexual relationships within a well-articulated, quasi-kinship system (Giallombardo, 1966, 1974; Ward and Kassebaum, 1965). While the homosexual liaisons seem to be very important for the psychological well-being of the inmates and serve as a major foundation for the social organization of the institutions, the homosexuality is for most inmates situational. Most of those women and girls who were committed to a heterosexual lifestyle before incarceration return to the same pattern upon release.

The existence in our society of bisexuality in males has received somewhat greater documentation. Studies of prisoners (Kirkham, 1971; Lindner, 1948; Sykes, 1958) have repeatedly shown a fair incidence of homosexual behavior and the development of homosexual liaisons among men who had no prior homosexual experience and who would return to exclusive heterosexuality upon release. A study of brief homosexual encounters in public restrooms (Humphreys, 1970) demonstrated that a sizeable number of men who take part in "tearoom" activities are heterosexually married and do not consider themselves to be homosexual. Ross (1971) has reported that some of the men in his sample of self-identified homosexual men who were married to women had ongoing sexual relationships with their wives. Reiss (1961) interviewed teenage male prostitutes who engaged in homosexual relations with adult men, while maintaining a heterosexual self-perception and an otherwise heterosexual career. Reiss viewed this duality as a reflection of the legitimizing effects of peer group norms, the depersonalized nature of the sexual relations, and the financial gain that could be used as a neutralization technique.

What has been obscured in all of this haphazard treatment of bisexuality is that these sexual data can be used to address more general questions of theoretical importance. Bisexuality illustrates and illuminates important facets of processes of self-labeling, of the plasticity of human sexuality, and of the differences between the erotic and emotional socialization of men and women in our society.

The Present Study

In our study of bisexuality, we were interested in four major questions. First, in deference to Kinsey et al.'s observation of sexual fluidity, we were particularly interested in how sexual object choice develops, and how this development fits into the life experiences of the individual. Is bisexuality, for example, a continuous theme throughout a person's life, foreordained by events occurring in childhood and adolescence—as much of psychosexual theory (e.g., Fenichel, 1945) would argue—or does it emerge and change with the buffeting of events and circumstances throughout the life cycle? Second was the question of self-definition. When does a pattern of sexual or other social behaviors give rise to a person's sense of his or her sexual identity, and when are they simply behaviors with no further implications? Our third concern was with the circumstances and conditions that either encourage or allow, discourage or prevent, the development of bisexual behavior. And finally, our fourth interest was in how these three things—continuity, self-definition, and causal factors—would differ between males and females in our society. What might a comparison of the processes of becoming a bisexual woman and the processes of becoming a bisexual male tell us about male and female sexuality in general?

Our observations in response to these four questions are based on lengthy semi-structured interviews with 156 people (equally divided between men and women), who had had more than incidental sexual experience with both men and women. We also interviewed a number of persons who had strong feelings about bisexuality as it pertained either to their own lives or to groups to which they belonged. The interviews were conducted in Seattle, New York, Berkeley, San Francisco, and a few other locations between 1973 and 1975. The respondents ranged in age from 19 to 62, and reflected a broad spectrum of occupations, educational levels, and sexual histories. Most of those interviewed were recruited through advertisements in taverns, restaurants, churches, universities, voluntary associations, and even a few embryonic bisexual rap groups. A large number of respondents were from a "snowball" sample or were personal contacts of the authors. The interviews generally lasted between 1–1/2 and 3 hours and were tape-recorded. They covered the following areas of the respondents' lives: sexual and romantic history, family relationships and background, preferred sexual behaviors and fantasies, and most important, critical events in the formation of a sexual identity and the development of a sexual career. These interviews were conducted against a backdrop of several years of formal and informal observation and interviews with self-identified male and female homosexuals.

While our respondents constitute a very diverse and heterogeneous group, they are certainly not representative of anything but themselves. It is quite inappropriate to think in terms of random sampling of a specifiable universe of persons when dealing with underground populations or sexual minorities (Bell, 1974; Weinberg, 1970), and it was our intention to find any bisexuals we could and explore with them any themes that they might have shared in their socio-sexual development. Because the sample was heterogeneous we are quite confident that we are not simply describing the idiosyncrasies of a unique set of persons, and that we are able to suggest some regularities that exist among a broad group of people in the present cultural and historical context. But we also feel that to place great stock in the frequencies of response patterns would give a misleading sense of concreteness to what we have observed. Therefore we have chosen to present data only when patterns occurred with sufficient regularity to deserve interpretation, and to present data in the form of verbatim responses that represent (perhaps with a prejudice to more articulate statements) a class of responses that were found among a sizeable number of respondents. In this paper we present a general discussion of how our interview data were used to address the four guiding questions outlined above. (For other treatments of this material see Blumstein and Schwartz, 1976a, 1976b, 1976c.

The Erotic Biography of Respondents

We found no such thing as a prototypic bisexual career. This is not to say there are no patterns to the lives of our respondents, but rather no single or small number of patterns seems to predominate among those who call themselves bisexual, or among those whose behavior might be given that label. For example, a sizeable number of male respondents and the majority of the females had no homosexual experiences prior to adulthood. Furthermore, the occurrence of family patterns often claimed to predict a nonheterosexual adaptation (e.g., boys with weak distant fathers and overwhelming mothers) was quite rare. A few respondents had early sexual experiences that might be termed traumatic, but their adult lives had very little else in common. Major themes in psychosexual theory were of little utility in understanding our respondents.

Perhaps the most interesting finding was that many respondents, who had once seemed well along the road to a life of exclusive heterosexuality or of exclusive homosexuality made major changes in sex-object choice. For example, early in the study we interviewed a young professional woman who referred to herself as "purely and simply gay," even though she had had sexual experience with men. In recounting her life history she mentioned that at the age of 7 or 8 she habitually initiated sexual contacts with her friends at pajama parties. Eventually one girl's mother learned about it, and our respondent was castigated by her friends' families, her friends, and her own family. If that stigmatizing experience were not enough to plant the seeds of a deviant self-definition, in adolescence she was the victim of a brutal sexual assault by a group of boys. She pointed to both of these experiences as reasons she had become a lesbian 10 years prior to the interview. We found her analysis convincing since it was so consistent with prevailing views on the psychodevelopment of lesbianism (e.g., Wilbur, 1965). Then, a year later she wrote to tell us she was in love with a man and they planned to marry.

Clearly, this woman's early experiences, as well as her 10 years of lesbian relationships and her active adherence to a lesbian self-label, did not guarantee that she would not experience a significant change in her life. Other interviews like this one, some starting with homosexual identification, some with heterosexual, suggested to us that while childhood and adolescent experiences do have a place in developing sexuality, their effects are far from immutable. For the majority of respondents, pivotal sexual experiences occurred in adulthood, and those whose experiences or fantasies stemmed from adolescence or childhood were no more or less likely to make a subsequent change than the larger group.

We were continually surprised at how discontinuous our respondents' erotic biographies could be. For example, a number of men who had decided they were homosexual at an early age and lived in almost exclusively homosexual networks later met women with whom they had sexual relationships for the first time in their lives. A very large number of both male and female respondents had made at least one full circle—an affair with a man, then one with a woman, and finally back to a man, or vice versa. For example, one woman of about 45 had been married and had three children. After divorcing and having several heterosexual relationships, she fell in love with another woman of her own age, and they began the first homosexual relationship that either of them had experienced. Neither had ever had any homosexual fantasies prior to their meeting. After a three-year relationship, they broke up and our respondent had a number of brief affairs with both women and men. Our interview captured her at this point in her life, but she reflected that in each of her relationships she considered herself to *be* what was implied by the gender of the person with whom she was amorously involved: homosexual when with a woman, heterosexual when with a man. She wondered aloud whether perhaps *bisexual* might be a more appropriate term.

It is clear from these cases that it was crucial for us to have the respondent's retrospective report as well as some longitudinal data. Fortunately, we were able to retain contact after the interview with about a quarter of our sample. It is misleading to try to understand anything about the achievement of sexual identity or about the importance of sexual events in a person's life without longitudinal observation. Speaking to respondents more than once was important, too, because they often tended to see more continuity in their lives than we found. It was very common for them to say that prior changes in sex-object choice were part of a past history of self-misperception, and that they had finally found their sexual "place." A follow-up interview often contradicted their assertions.

Our conclusion was that classical notions of the immutability of adult sexual preference are an overstatement and often misleading. Because of the unrepresentativeness of our sample, we cannot speculate about how widespread such erotic malleability is in our society. Perhaps there are many people who have undergone major life changes. The ease with which we found respondents with such a background suggests that it is more than a rare occurrence. Perhaps there are many people who could experience such monumental changes if they were not insulated from precipitating circumstances; or perhaps the vast majority would not be subject to such changes under any circumstances. If future research proves bisexual potential to be relatively rare, then classic developmentalist approaches that view childhood socialization to be all-important will be vindicated. If, on the other hand, the potential is not uncommon, then approaches that emphasize the situational emergence of human behavior will be supported. From our data, we conclude that (a) sex-object choice and sexual identification can change in many ways and many times over the lifecycle, (b) the individual is often unaware of his or her ability to change, and (c) childhood and adolescent experiences are not the final determinants of adult sexuality.

SEXUAL BEHAVIOR AND SEXUAL IDENTITY

In our early interviews it became clear that people often adopted homosexual or bisexual self-identifications without having any homosexual experience. It was equally clear that, for many people, extensive homosexual experience had no effect on their heterosexual identity. For example, one male respondent recalled:

> I had this affair with a gay guy for almost a year. We were good friends and we became identified as a couple after a while. I think he basically saw me as a straight person who was kind of stepping over the imaginary line for a while. I was also sleeping with a woman, and, while I liked them both, I thought I was heterosexual as a person.

Another female respondent recalled her first homosexual encounter:

> It was a great experience. I think everyone should have it. Before this happened, I was really hung up. When I got involved with another woman, I realized how nice it was. It was really enlightening. I think heterosexually though, so I don't feel any big drives to repeat it. But I probably will if the opportunity comes along.

Still other respondents could have a single erotic encounter with a person of either the same or opposite gender and decide unequivocally what they "really were." As one woman reported:

> The first time Linda touched me, I went weak. The men I had made love with were so clumsy and awkward by comparison. I just realized who I was, that I was gay, and men were OK, but not the main thing.

On the other hand, experience with both genders could be seen as confirmation of a bisexual identity. One respondent told us how it had seemed reasonable to him:

> "Well," I thought as this guy climbed in my bed, "What the hell? Why shouldn't I? There's no reason why I should cut off my nose to spite my face. It's going to be fun; it's been fun before, and why can't I have the best of both possible worlds?" Bisexuality seemed like me.

We feel that certain conditions were significant in making a sexual event either crucial or irrelevant in the process of assuming a sexual identity.

Labelling.   Consistent with what sociologists have noted in regards to other self-definitions (Becker, 1973), events or behaviors that produced a public reaction or otherwise affected the reactions other people made to our respondents were important in providing a bisexual self-definition (or homosexual or heterosexual). Such events were particularly significant during adolescence, when peer-group definitions have tremendous power over people. Several male respondents, who had been labelled the "class sissy," had felt that surely they must be sexually odd, and that their oddness was recognized by their peers. They had believed that their peers knew more about them than they had known themselves, and this was often self-fulfilling when it came to sex-object choice. Interestingly, such labelling processes seemed to be more important for males than females in the assumption of a homosexual or bisexual identity in adulthood. In contrast, boys and girls who escaped such labelling, even though some of their behavior might be homosexual, seemed somewhat less apt to apply deviant labels to themselves. For example, we interviewed two men who had been successful high school athletes. They shared a sexual relationship throughout high school and also had sexual relations with girls. They were never ridiculed or stigmatized in high school, even though their inseparability was well-known. Because so much of these men's behavior was considered sex-role appropriate, they escaped a homosexual label from others who might suspect their relationship. The two continued their homosexual activities into adulthood, one finally deciding he was homosexual, the other preferring to be bisexual.

Conflicting events.   The ability to perform sexually with a person of the opposite gender was not sufficient to inhibit the adoption of a homosexual identity, nor was it necessary for a bisexual identification. But it did seem to increase the likelihood of the latter. Many respondents seemed to be caught up in dichotomous thinking about sexuality, and struggled to resolve conflicting events (sexual experiences, attraction, or fantasies directed at both genders) by emphasizing one set of events as more plausible than the other. Commonly, one set of explanatory events was adduced for one's heterosexual behavior and a completely different set for one's homosexual behavior. For example, a male respondent reported:

> I'm straight, but I need outlets when I'm away from home and times like that. And it's easier to get with men than women. So I go into the park, or at a rest station on the highway and get a man to blow me. I would never stay the night with one of them, or get to know them. It's just a release. It's not like sex with my wife. It's just a way to get what you need without making it a big deal. And it feels less like cheating.

While attempts to balance the two sets of conflicting information might have offered the chance of deciding one was bisexual, for most of our respondents (especially men) fairly strong heterosexual feelings and a good deal of heterosexual experience from an early age were necessary for a bisexual identification to compete with a homosexual identity. Our cultural logic holds that it is almost impossible to have only some homosexual feelings. The idea is seldom questioned that a single homosexual act or strong homosexual feelings reveal the "true person." Hence, since we have no imagery for partial states of being, the individual often reinterprets past events as further confirmation of his or her undeniable homosexuality. As one respondent said:

> I was married for four years when I started to have these fantasies about a guy I worked with. I would get these fantasies and I would have to masturbate. I think that this was just the most mature crush I had, because when I think back on it, there had been lots of others, although I didn't know what they were then. I began to think I was homosexual about this time, even though I was still sleeping with my wife and enjoying it. But I felt guilty, and I was worried she would find out what I really was.

Of course, interpretations of respondents' erotic recollections are indeed risky, and commonly the present shapes the past more than the reverse. Nevertheless, it seemed clear that most respondents actively searched their memories for significant events that would help confirm their lay hypotheses concerning present events and feelings.

Among our interviewees, it seems that sexual attraction, as well as enjoyable sexual experience with both genders, helped people adopt a bisexual identity. Another factor was the emotional response to persons of either gender. Whom a person loved seemed to have an impact somewhat independent of whom that person eroticized. This was particularly true of women, since love and sexuality are customarily such interwoven themes in female erotic socialization. But it was also true of a sizeable number of males. It was not uncommon for a nonsexual but deeply emotional attachment between two people of the same gender who had no prior homosexual feelings to develop into a sexual relationship, and sometimes a shift to a bisexual identification for both partners. On the other hand, if a person (mostly men) could relate sexually to men and women but could only love one or the other, then that person would not likely assume a bisexual label.

Reference group contact.   Sexual behavior and sexual identification both seem to vary by whether the respondent was a social isolate, was involved in an ongoing relationship, or was part of a sexual community. By the latter we mean subcultural groups that have formed and organized around members' sexual similarities, e.g., the various gay subcultures. So, for example, some respondents were strongly committed to particular homosexual relationships for a number of years without assuming a homosexual identity if they were not involved in the gay community. When most of their friends were homosexual, respondents were likely to be treated as homosexual and come to define themselves as such.

Our conclusion, after noticing the regularity in the differences of sexual identity depending on subculture membership and involvement, was that the social ratification of identities provided by such groups can be very powerful (Berger and Luckmann, 1966). Respondents who were ambivalent or questioning about their bisexual attractions or behaviors often encountered people in the gay world who could provide easy vocabularies for interpreting these feelings and acts (Blumstein and Schwartz, 1976a, 1976b). Sometimes they were told that heterosexual attractions were only a cop-out or an aspect of false consciousness, that the respondent was really denying his or her true sexuality, being unwilling to come to grips with being a homosexual. After varying amounts of personal struggle, some respondents found this explanation plausible and moved toward adoption of a homosexual identity, developed a gay lifestyle, and concentrated on homosexual relationships. Others, finding the gay world unsympathetic or incredulous when it came to their bisexuality, either left the community for periods of time or kept their bisexual feelings private. For example, one woman who had a lesbian identification fell in love with a man and felt compelled to leave her women's collective because the other members would not grant support or legitimacy for her new relationship and asserted that it was simply "neurotic acting out."

We do not mean to paint the homosexual communities as villains in thwarting people's bisexuality. Indeed, respondents were much more likely to report hostility to their lifestyles among heterosexuals (who could not appreciate the distinction between bisexual and homosexual) than among homosexuals, and many reported a great deal of support for a bisexual identification among homosexual friends. But in both the straight and gay communities, the fact that respondents had had homosexual relationships tended to define an identity for them, while their heterosexual relationships were considered somehow irrelevant or a passing fancy.

The final step, we began to see, especially in the San Francisco area, was a deliberate attempt to create a bisexual community, where members could come together to give mutual support and to share with one another a collective wisdom for developing a bisexual lifestyle. Although it is premature to know, it seems very likely that such institutions as bisexual rap groups will increasingly support people's assumption of a bisexual identification.

CIRCUMSTANCES CONDUCIVE TO BISEXUALITY

While there is a wide array of situations or conditions that serve to introduce people to novel sexual experiences, we found three themes to be particularly prevalent among our respondents. The first of these was experimentation in a friendship context. Many respondents (especially women) progressed to a sexual involvement from an intense emotional attachment with a person of the gender they had never before eroticized. A male with a homosexual identification might develop a casual experimental heterosexual relationship with a close woman friend at a point in his life where he seemed perfectly comfortable with his homosexuality. Several previously heterosexual men who came to a bisexual identity in their 30s reported they had had early homosexual experiences with close teen-age friends when heterosexual relations were somewhat limited. They had treated these experiences as irrelevant teen-age play, until adult experiences precipitated reconsideration. A few respondents with no previous homosexual experience reported that they were able to eroticize adult male friendships. A few lesbians reported being able to develop sexual involvements with male friends, especially homosexual men whose sexual politics they found less objectionable. The most common finding, however, was that previously heterosexual women who developed deep attachments to other women, e.g., as college roommates or later in life when involved in the women's movement, ultimately shifted these feelings into the erotic arena and began long-term homosexual relationships.

Bisexual encounters also emerged frequently in such liberal hedonistic environments as group sex, "three ways," and other combinations. These often proved a less threatening arena for sexual experimentation for heterosexuals than would a dyadic homosexual encounter. Females found these experiences less difficult than males, who were customarily the instigators of the event. These occurrences were understood to be pleasure seeking in a diffuse sense, rather than a specific act with stigmatizing implications for one's sexual identity. Focus was on the good feelings rather than on the gender of the person providing them.

The third pattern was supported by a number of erotically based ideological positions. For example, some people came to a bisexual identification (occasionally without any corresponding behavior) because of adherence to a belief in humanistic libertarianism. They felt that everyone should be free and able to love everyone in a perfect erotic utopia. For them, love meant sex, which was seen as a means of communication and "becoming human." Encounter groups or group massages often progressed to a sexual stage. As one respondent explained, "It only made sense. We had all been psych majors, and every psych major learns that we are all inherently bisexual." How much of this ideology preceded the behavior and how much provided post hoc legitimacy is, of course, difficult to assess.

Many of the women in our study decided to experiment with homosexual relationships because they felt encouraged by the tenets of the women's movement to examine their feelings towards other women and to learn to be close to them. The movement had encouraged them to respect and like other women, and for many this novel feeling was closely akin to the feelings they had felt with those men whom they had eroticized. Sometimes these women instigated sexual encounters for ideological rather than erotic reasons, but soon developed erotic responses and became more generally physically attracted to other women. In some cases the homosexual attraction became a dominating force in the women's lives; in other cases it coexisted with heterosexual responses; and in still other cases it never established any prominence and homosexual behavior was discontinued (although a political bisexual self-identification was sometimes retained).

Differences Between Women and Men

There were a great many differences in the bisexual behavior of male and female respondents, which seemed quite consistent with what we know about general patterns of male and female sexuality (Gagnon and Simon, 1973). Most prominently, men and women differed in the ease with which they incorporated homosexual activity into their lives. Women found initial experiences much less traumatic than men, and they were less likely to allow a single experience or a few experiences to lead them to an exclusive homosexual identification. Women often felt that such activities were a natural extension of female affectionate behavior and did not have implications for their sexuality. Men, on the other hand, were much more preoccupied with what the experience meant for their masculinity, sometimes fearing that they might never again be able to respond erotically to a woman. Some men insulated themselves from the homosexual implications of homosexual behavior by exclusively engaging in either impersonal sex, as in public restrooms (Humphreys, 1970), or in homosexual acts where they took what they considered to be the masculine role, i.e., the insertor role in fellatio or sodomy. As one man recounted, "There are four kinds of men: men who screw women, men who screw men and women, men who screw men, and then there are the queers [i.e., the ones who *get* screwed]."

For men, both their first heterosexual and first homosexual experience were very likely to be with strangers (prostitutes, "bad girls," homosexual tricks), whom they would probably never see again. The predominant pattern among women was for sex to occur with a close friend, and this to them was a natural and logical outgrowth of a strong emotional attachment. The realization that they were in love with a person (of the same or opposite gender) was often a prerequisite for sexual attraction, sexual behavior, or a change in sexual identity.

Males reported much more difficulty coping with homosexual behavior and developing a homosexual identification than women. We attribute this to the stigma attached to homosexuality among American men (more than among women). Masculinity is a major element in men's sense of self-worth, and homosexuality, in the popular imagination, implies impaired masculinity.

Conclusion

This study has been part of our ongoing research on sexual identity and how it reflects the interaction of social forces, cultural perspectives, and psychological processes. We chose bisexuality as a vehicle of inquiry because we feel it has a strategic capacity for illuminating more general issues in the study of human sexuality. We view our research as exploratory, but we feel that when more investigators have addressed themselves to the phenomenon of bisexuality the accumulated evidence will help transform the way science views human sexuality. We anticipate that the perspective which emerges will reflect a number of thematic questions. What is the nature of the relationship between people's sexual experiences and the ways they make sense of their sexuality? How do cultural and subcultural understandings regarding sexuality affect sexual experience and sexual identification? How much of sexuality can be understood by focusing on the continuities among males and the continuities among females, irrespective of affectional preference or sexual lifestyle? How much of adult sexuality is determined by socialization experiences and how much reflects adult experiences and events? And finally, what do the answers to these questions tell us about the variability and plasticity of sexual behavior and sexual definitions?

REFERENCES

Becker, H. S. 1973. *Outsiders: Studies in the sociology of deviance* (Rev. ed.). New York: Free Press.

Bell, A. P. 1974. Homosexualities: Their range and character. In *Nebraska Symposium on Motivation*. Lincoln: University of Nebraska Press.

Berger, P. L., and Luckmann, T. 1966. *The social construction of reality: A treatise in the sociology of knowledge*. Garden City, N.Y.: Doubleday.

Blumstein, P. W., and Schwartz, P. 1976a. Bisexuality in women. *Archives of Sexual Behavior*, 5, 171–181.

Blumstein, P. W., and Schwartz, P. 1976b. Bisexuality in men. *Urban Life*.

Blumstein, P. W., and Schwartz, P. 1976c. Bisexuality. Paper presented at the meeting of the America Sociological Association, New York, August.

Fenichel O. 1945. *The psychoanalytic theory of neurosis*. New York: Norton.

Ford, C. S., and Beach, F. A. 1951. *Patterns of sexual behavior*. New York: Harper and Row.

Gagnon, J. H., and Simon, W. 1973. *Sexual conduct: The social sources of human sexuality*. Chicago: Aldine.

Giallombardo, R. 1966. *Society of women.* New York: Wiley.

Giallombardo, R. 1974. *The social world of imprisoned girls.* New York: Wiley.

Humphreys, L. 1970. *Tearoom trade: Impersonal sex in public restrooms.* Chicago: Aldine.

Kinsey, A. C., Pomeroy, W. B., and Martin, C. E. 1948. *Sexual behavior in the human male.* Philadelphia: W. B. Saunders.

Kinsey, A. C., Pomeroy, W. B., Martin C. E., and Gebhard, P. H. 1953. *Sexual behavior in the human female.* Philadelphia: W. B. Saunders.

Kirkham, G. L. 1971. Homosexuality in prison. In J. M. Henslin (Ed.), *Studies in the sociology of sex.* New York: Appleton-Century-Crofts.

Lindner, R. 1948. Sexual behavior in penal institutions. In A. Deutsch (Ed.), *Sex habits of American men.* New York: Prentice-Hall.

McCaghy, C. H., and Skipper, J. K., Jr. 1969. Lesbian behavior as an adaptation to the occupation of stripping. *Social Problems,* 17, 262–270.

Reiss, A. J., Jr. 1961. The social integration of queers and peers. *Social Problems,* 9, 102–120.

Ross, H. L. 1971. Modes of adjustment of married homosexuals. *Social Problems,* 18, 385–393.

Sykes, G. 1958. *The society of captives.* Princeton, N. J.: Princeton University Press.

Ward, D. A., and Kassebaum, G. G. 1965. *Women's prison: Sex and social structure.* Chicago: Aldine.

Weinberg, M. S. 1970. Homosexual samples: Differences and similarities. *Journal of Sex Research,* 6, 312–325.

Wilbur, C. B. 1965. Clinical aspects of female homosexuality. In J. Marmor (Ed.), *Sexual inversion: The multiple roots of homosexuality.* New York: Basic Books.

7

Attention for All the Wrong, and All the Right, Reasons

22
Bisexuality in HIV Research

Paula C. Rodríguez Rust

From the Shadows to the Spotlight: The Changing Role of Bisexual Men in HIV-Related Research in the United States

Since the mid 1980s most of the publications that turn up in a literature search of social scientific journals for research on bisexuality report research on samples of "gay and bisexual men" or "homosexual/bisexual men" and focus on the epidemiology of HIV infection or the psychosocial effects of HIV and fear of HIV. Earlier publications on HIV epidemiology generally refer to "gay men;" the increasing reference to "and bisexual" men in the mid to late 1980s reflected growing awareness among AIDS researchers and educators that sexual behavior and self-identity are not always congruent and that many men who engage in male-male sex do not identify as gay; it did not reflect interest in bisexual men or bisexuality in particular.[1] Both gay and bisexual men were considered to be epidemiologically interesting for what they presumably have in common—sexual contact with other men—and not for anything that would differentiate one from the other, such as sexual self-identity or other-sex activity.[2]

Therefore, in most of this research bisexual men were not distinguished from gay men, although a few authors reported the percentages of their samples that were bisexual by either behavior or self-identity before lumping them together with gay men for the purpose of data analysis.[3] Some authors who provided detailed data about their respondents' sexual activities explicitly limited their reports to male-male sex acts, but—oddly—other authors did not mention the sex of subjects' sex partners, leaving the reader to assume that only male-male sex acts were being reported.[4] This latter practice constructed these men's heterosexual activities, and therefore their bisexuality, as not only irrelevant but as so obviously irrelevant that their exclusion required no comment, let alone explanation. In many articles the phrase "gay and bisexual men" is used interchangeably with "gay men," or combined with references to the "gay community," further evidence that bisexuals were included in this research only because they have sex with men and not because of their bisexuality per se.[5] For example, under the subheading "Presumptions About *Gay* Men," Walter F. Batchelor wrote, "Much of AIDS research has focused on *gay and bisexual* men. . . . A pervasive ignorance of *gay* life and *gay* sex has made much of the research designs, and consequent findings, questionable" (1984:1281, emphasis added). The same comment could be made regarding researchers' early ignorance and neglect of the importance of bisexual life and sexual activity in the epidemiology of AIDS.

In 1986 the Centers for Disease Control (CDC) changed its emphasis in discussions of HIV risk from *who* was at risk to what *behaviors* placed a person at risk.[6] Concurrently and thereafter, in the 1980s and early 1990s, epidemiological researchers gradually replaced the phrase "gay and bisexual men" with the descriptor "men who have sex with men" (MSM). The latter phrase more accurately describes the population in question, reflecting the fact that these men are considered to be at risk for HIV infection because they engage in male-male sexual behavior and not because they identify as either gay or bisexual. The term *MSM* remains in common usage in HIV epidemiological and psychosocial research.[7]

Also during the late 1980s and early 1990s, as mentioned in chapter 17, fears about HIV being transmitted to the heterosexual population via bisexuals raised epidemiological concerns about bisexual men in particular. This fear was fueled by growing recognition that HIV educational messages aimed at gay men or communicated through gay community networks might not have effectively reached MSM who identify as bisexual or heterosexual or who do not participate in gay communities, and that these men might require different kinds of HIV education because they have different risk factors.[8] These concerns led researchers to reconsider the importance of sexual self-identity and of heterosexual behavior among MSM, an importance that was also recognized by the World Health Organization (WHO). In December 1992 a consultation was held at WHO in Geneva to collect information about the role of bisexuality in HIV epidemiology and to explore intervention strategies. Participants noted that bisexual behavior is "of direct relevance to HIV/AIDS transmission" and that bisexual self-identity, which "does not coincide entirely" with either behavior or sexual preference, is "important to consider in the development of appropriate HIV/AIDS prevention messages" (2). In response to this growing awareness, some researchers collected extensive descriptive data regarding the other-sex or bisexual as well as the same-sex activities of their subjects, whereas others distinguished their homosexual from their bisexual subjects, on the basis of either behavior or self-identity, and compared them to each other.

An example of the first approach is a study by Mary Jane Rotheram-Borus and colleagues (1994), who collected extensive data on the same-sex and other-sex contacts of a sample of predominantly Black (31 percent) and Hispanic (50 percent) youths recruited through a gay-identified social service agency.[9] The authors reported detailed statistics regarding the AIDS-relevant characteristics of each type of sexual activity, such as rates of condom use, but they did not cross-tabulate same-sex activities with other-sex activities. Thus, the sex act rather than the sexual career was the unit of analysis and same-sex and other-sex activities were treated as distinct forms of sexual activity, each with separate relevance for HIV epidemiology, with no attention paid to the patterns of sexual activity in individual subjects' careers.[10] This approach is in line with the recommendation of Philip Blumstein and Pepper Schwartz (1977), who advised researchers to focus on the sex act in preference to the essentialized sexual individual.

An example of the second approach is a study by Lynda S. Doll and colleagues (1992), who recruited 209 white (41 percent), Black (35 percent), and Hispanic (23 percent) HIV seropositive (HIV+) MSM through ten Red Cross and ten community or hospital-based blood donation centers. They questioned these respondents extensively about their other-sex and same-sex activities, their sexual self-identities, and their social activities, including ties to the gay community. Throughout the analysis the authors compared bisexual- , homosexual- , and heterosexual-identified men to each other. In comparison to the approach used by the Rotheram-Borus research team, which was based on recognition of the separate roles of same-sex and other-sex contacts in HIV epidemiology, the approach used by the Doll research team was motivated by recognition that different intervention strategies would be necessary for men with different combinations of sexual behavior, sexual self-identity, and social networks.

A third approach used by researchers in response to concern about the role of bisexuals and bisexual behavior in the transmission of HIV is to study samples consisting entirely of bisexual men. These studies tend to focus on the sexual behaviors, safer sex practices, and seropositivity rates of bisexual men and on the question of the risk posed to women who have sex with bisexual men. Some researchers, for example, David J. McKirnan, Joseph P. Stokes, and their colleagues (e.g., McKirnan, Stokes, Doll, and Burzette 1995; Stokes, McKirnan, and Burzette 1993; Stokes, McKirnan, Doll, and Burzette 1996; Stokes, Taywaditep, Vanable, and McKirnan 1996) were primarily concerned about bisexual men's own risk of HIV infection. Other researchers were primarily concerned about the risk bisexual men might pose to their female partners and not about bisexual men themselves; Robert W. Wood, Leigh E. Krueger, Tsilke Pearlman, and Gary Goldbaum (1993), for example, wrote, "because bisexual men are increasingly likely to contribute to human immunodeficiency virus (HIV) infections in women, we sought to further characterize the risk of HIV infection for men who have sex with men and to identify the risk such men pose to women" (1757). Demonstrating similar emphasis on bisexual men's role in transmission rather than bisexual men's health, Mary Boulton, G. Hart, and R. Fitzpatrick (1992) stressed the importance of the percentage of bisexual men who had had unprotected penetrative sex with *both* male and female partners within the previous year as a method of assessing the efficacy of bisexuality as a "bridge." The risk of transmission to women and the need for more effective HIV education among bisexual men were also primary concerns of the research teams of Susan Y. Chu and Maria L. Ekstrand (Chu et al. 1992; Ekstrand et al. 1994).[11] In most of these studies the emphasis is on the epidemiological importance of behavioral bisexuality; a small study by the McKirnan and Stokes team (Stokes, McKirnan, and Burzette 1993) was one of the few to compare the epidemiologically relevant characteristics of the behaviorally bisexual population to those of the self-identified bisexual population.

Many of the samples used for HIV research are drawn from populations that are available to researchers for HIV-related reasons, for example, men seeking testing for HIV antibodies, men and women already participating in AIDS research, injection drug users, seropositive men, and men with AIDS diagnoses.[12] As such, the bisexuals included in these samples are not representative of all bisexuals because they are likely to differ in important ways from bisexuals who do not seek HIV antibody testing or respond to solicitations for AIDS research subjects, are seronegative, or do not have AIDS diagnoses. HIV research samples that are not drawn from populations defined by HIV-related characteristics are often drawn from gay-related venues.[13] For example, Timothy G. Heckman and colleagues (1995) recruited their subjects at gay bars. Bisexuals in these samples are also not representative of all bisexuals; Boulton, Hart, and Fitzpatrick (1992) pointed out that such samples would underrepresent behavioral bisexuals who identify as heterosexual, who are secretive, and who lack ties to gay networks. Findings from such samples must be interpreted carefully if they are to be used to yield information about bisexuals in general.[14]

A notable exception to these criticisms is the sample used by the McKirnan and Stokes research team (1995).[15] They recruited behaviorally bisexual men who had had both same-sex and other-sex contacts within the previous three years through a multipronged method that has been shown to produce samples approximating random representative samples.[16] The four recruitment methods used included ads in "White- and Black-oriented media targeting 'Men who have sex with men and women' " (68), outreach into areas frequented by bisexually active men such as sexual pick-up areas, clubs, and organizations, outreach into gay and mixed bars, and snowball sampling. The resulting sample consisted of 536 men aged eighteen to thirty years old, 66 percent of whom placed themselves in the middle three categories of a Kinsey scale and 59 percent of whom self-identified as bisexual. Compared to other samples of bisexual or "gay and bisexual" men recruited via AIDS-related sources or gay community networks, this sample included a higher percentage of Black (52 percent) men and probably included a wider variety of bisexual men, particularly behaviorally bisexual men without gay or bisexual self-identities and without connections to a gay community. In other reports by the same research team, this sample of behaviorally bisexual men is compared to a sample of men who had had sex only with men during the previous three years (Stokes, Taywaditep, Vanable, and McKirnan 1996; Stokes, Vanable, and McKirnan 1997). By using the McKirnan and Stokes research team's findings as a benchmark and triangulating findings from other samples with differing types of sampling bias, we can use HIV-related research to shed light on the social and sexual lives of bisexual men.

With Whom and How Often? HIV-Relevant Sexual Behaviors Among Bisexual Men

HIV research has provided data on the numbers and types of male and female sex partners, the frequencies of same- and other-sex contacts, and incidence rates for specific sex acts reported by behaviorally bisexual or self-identified bisexual men. In general, these findings indicate that within a given time period bisexual men are more likely to have, and to have more, male than female partners. For example, the McKirnan and Stokes research team (1995) discovered that among men aged eighteen to thirty who had had penetrative sex with both a man and a woman in the previous three years 90 percent had had male partners (30 percent had had only male partners), 70 percent had had female partners, and 60 percent had had both male and female partners in the previous six months. Regarding numbers of partners, they had had an average, or *mean*, of 4.7 male and 1.8 female partners during these six months, with most male partners being casual partners (3.6) rather than steady partners (0.63) or friends (1.09), and female steady partners (0.45) nearly as common as male steady partners (cf. Weatherburn et al. 1998). Wold et al. (1998) found that among MSM in Boston, those who had also had sex with women (MSMW) during the previous six months had had means of twenty-four male and seventeen female partners in their lifetimes and means of 8.5 males and 4.2 female partners in the previous year.

Wold et al. (1998) also reported that their behaviorally bisexual male respondents had had *medians* of seven male and five female partners during their lifetimes.[17] The fact that these medians are substantially lower than the *means* these researchers reported for the same respondents indicates the existence of a small proportion of respondents who had had extremely large numbers of partners. Because of this skewed pattern, in which a few men with large numbers of partners elevate the mean for the population as a whole, the median is a better indication of the number of partners reported by the "middle of the road" or "typical" individual. Incidentally, among "gay and bisexual youths," recruited through a gay-identified social service agency in New York City, Rotheram-Borus and colleagues (Rotheram-Borus et al. 1994) found even greater skew. In their lifetimes these youths had had median numbers of partners similar to those reported by the Wold team's adult respondents, specifically, 7.0 male and 2.0 female lifetime partners. However, the mean numbers of male partners reported by the youths studied by the Rotheram-Borus research team far exceeded the number reported by the adults studied by the Wold research team; the youths had had an average of 70.1 male and 5.9 female partners during their short lifetimes.

Contrary to the stereotype that bisexuality is a transitional form of sexuality, the McKirnan and Stokes team (1995; see also Stokes, Damon, and McKirnan 1997) observed considerable stability of bisexual behavior over time; 65 percent of those whose bisexuality began at least five years prior to the study reported both same-sex and other-sex activity within the previous six months. This pattern was more pronounced among Black (71 percent) than white (47 percent) respondents, with white respondents being more likely to have gravitated toward exclusively same-sex behavior (41 percent versus 20 percent).[18] In a related study of Asian Americans using similar sampling methods and inclusion criteria, David R. Matteson (1997) found that only 35 percent of thirty-one men who had been bisexually active within the previous three years were currently bisexually active, suggesting that Asian American men are more likely than either Black or white men to gravitate over time toward monosexual behavior.

Boulton, Hart, and Fitzpatrick (1992) drew a sample using similar selection criteria in Britain and reported comparable results regarding the numbers and genders of bisexual men's sex partners. In their study of sixty British men, 95 percent of whom were white and 5 percent of whom were Afro-Caribbean and all of whom had had both same-sex and other-sex contacts within the previous five years, they found that 80 percent had had at least one male partner and 73 percent had had at least one female partner in the previous year. Despite the longer time period assessed (one year versus six months), these figures are slightly lower than the rates found in the McKirnan and Stokes study (1995) for prevalence of same-sex contact and identical to those for prevalence of other-sex contact. Findings regarding numbers of male partners are substantially different, however; the Boulton research team reported that those subjects who had had any male or female partners in the previous year had had a mean of twenty male and two female partners (ranges: 1–100 and 1–24). These means are higher than those found in the McKirnan and Stokes study, partially because, in addition to using the longer time period of a year, the Boulton researchers excluded respondents who had had no partners of a particular sex when calculating the means.[19] However, these methodological differences do not appear to completely explain the difference in findings, suggesting that there might be racial or national differences in sexual behavior, with British white men reporting more male partners than American Black and white men.[20] Among the Boulton team's respondents 58 percent had "regular" male and 47 percent had "regular" female partners, rates higher than those reported by McKirnan, Stokes, and colleagues (1995) for "committed relationships." Despite the difference in actual figures, the Boulton findings confirm the McKirnan and Stokes findings that behaviorally bisexual men are more likely to have, and have more, male than female partners (cf. Weatherburn et al. 1998).[21]

Among men who were not only behaviorally bisexual but had also sought HIV testing Wood and colleagues (Wood, Krueger, Pearlman, and Goldbaum 1993) found numbers of partners similar to those found in the McKirnan and Stokes and the Wold studies. The Wood research team's subjects included 5,480 men who had had sex with men since 1977, recruited via HIV testing services of the AIDS Prevention Project of the Seattle-King County Department of Public Health. Those who were seronegative and had been bisexually active during the previous year had had a mean of 7.7 male and 2.8 female partners; these figures are slightly lower than the annual means of 8.5 and 4.2 reported by Wold et al. (1998) among serologically mixed behaviorally bisexual men and only slightly higher than the six-month figures produced if the McKirnan and Stokes figures are adjusted to exclude those who had had no male (5.2) or no female (2.6) partners in the previous six months. If decisions to seek HIV testing are at least partially correlated with actual or realistically perceived risk of infection, a supposition examined later in this chapter, then one might have expected the Wood respondents to report much higher numbers of partners, especially male partners, than the McKirnan and Stokes or the Wold respondents. John L. Martin and Laura Dean's (1990) finding that gay men recruited from STD clinics are less likely to be coupled with a lover than gay men recruited from other sources would also lead to this expectation. However, the fact that the Wood team's findings were based on those men whose test results were negative might have attenuated this effect.

Given the stability of bisexual behavior over time discovered by the McKirnan and Stokes team (1995), to define bisexuality in terms of behavior over a three- or five-year period, as McKirnan, Stokes, and colleagues (1995), Matteson (1997), Boulton, Hart, and Fitzpatrick (1992), Weatherburn and colleagues (1998), and Wood, Krueger, Pearlman, and Goldbaum (1993) did, virtually guarantees that high proportions of bisexuals will have engaged in both same- and other-sex behavior in the previous six months or the previous year. In contrast, among men classified as bisexual on the basis of their self-identities, Ekstrand and colleagues (1994) found much lower rates of recent bisexual behavior, due in particular to much lower rates of other-sex contact. Among 119 self-identified bisexual men aged twenty-five to fifty-four years recruited as part of the San Francisco Men's Health Study, they found that 91 percent had had same-sex contact (65 percent exclusively), 32 percent had had other-sex contact, 26 percent had had both same- and other-sex contact, and 5 percent were celibate during the year 1984–1985. Five years later in 1988–1989, after half a decade of AIDS awareness education programs, those who had been bisexually active in 1984–1985 had shifted either to celibacy or to exclusively same- or exclusively other-sex contact; in that year 77 percent had had same-sex contact (70 percent exclusively), 17 percent had had other-sex contact, 7 percent had had both same- and other-sex contact, and 13 percent were celibate. The Ekstrand team also found that bisexuals had fewer sex partners by the end of the decade; 54 percent, down from 74 percent, had multiple male partners and 5 percent, down from 14 percent, had multiple female partners in 1988–1989.[22]

Although comparisons between the Ekstrand and the McKirnan and Stokes findings would be enlightening, in making these comparisons the reader should remember not only that the two studies used different definitions of bisexuality but that the McKirnan and Stokes sample was drawn via multipronged sampling methods in Chicago, whereas the Ekstrand sample was drawn via probability methods in San Francisco. One might be tempted to conclude from a comparison of these two studies that the stability of bisexual behavior discovered among behaviorally bisexual individuals by the McKirnan and Stokes team exists alongside a more general social trend toward decreasing bisexual behavior among self-identified bisexuals, and that the preponderance of male over female partners is greater among bisexual men defined by self-identity than among bisexual men defined behaviorally. But an earlier study by the McKirnan and Stokes research team suggests that much of the difference between their findings and the Ekstrand findings is due to the geographic contrast rather than the distinction between behavioral bisexuals and self-identified bisexuals. Among 105 men recruited through an advertisement targeting "bisexuals" in a free weekly newspaper, this earlier study (Stokes, McKirnan, and Burzette 1993) found that in the past six months 76 percent had had male partners (24 percent exclusively) and 68 percent had had female partners (14 percent exclusively). In other words, these men, whose response to the ad indicates a minimum of bisexual self-identification or, more accurately, *self-perception*, were as likely as the behavioral bisexuals this research team studied a few years later to have had heterosexual contact in the past six months and, unlike the Ekstrand team's self-identified bisexuals, did not display markedly different rates of same- and other-sex contact. A strong preponderance of male over female partners, and dramatic decreases rather than stability in rates of bisexual behavior, therefore, might be characteristic of self-identified bisexual men only in cities like San Francisco with high HIV awareness and prevalence.

Considering definitions based on self-identity and sexual behavior simultaneously leads to further findings regarding the sexual behavior of bisexual men. Wood, Krueger, Pearlman, and Goldbaum (1993) found that among behaviorally bisexual men, and MSM in general, sexual self-identity is related to numbers of male and female partners and to the incidence of specific sex acts. Among men who were seronegative and bisexually active in the previous year, the 277 who identified as bisexual had an average of 7.9 male and 2.6 female partners in the preceding twelve months, compared to an average of 2.8 male and 3.8 female partners among those who identified as straight and 9.9 male and 2.3 female partners among those who identified as gay. Thus, it appears that higher numbers of male than female partners are found specifically among behaviorally bisexual men who identify as either gay or bisexual and not among those who identify as straight. In terms of total number of sex partners, male and female, self-identified bisexuals fell between gay-identified behavioral bisexuals and straight-identified behavioral bisexuals, more closely resembling gays than straights (10.5 versus 12.2, 6.6).

Given that having male sex partners and having large numbers of sex partners increases one's risk of HIV infection, one would expect men who are HIV infected to be more likely to have had male partners and to have had more male, and more total, partners than those who are seronegative. Doll and colleagues (1992) reported incidence rates for same- and other-sex contact, including numbers of male and female partners, for seropositive men who had ever had sex with men in their lifetimes. The respondents were recruited to the study upon learning of their seropositivity, presumably before they had made modifications to their sexual behavior motivated by knowledge of their serologic status. Of the sixty-two men who rated themselves as Kinsey 3–5's, 34 percent had had only male partners, 5 percent had had only female partners, 52 percent had had both male and female partners, and 10 percent had been celibate in the previous year. The total incidence rate of 86 percent for same-sex activity among these self-rated bisexual seropositive MSM is similar to the rates found in the serologically mixed samples used in the McKirnan and Stokes, the Boulton, and the Weatherburn studies (McKirnan, Stokes, Doll, and Burzette 1995; Boulton, Hart, and Fitzpatrick 1992; Weatherburn et al. 1998; respectively, 90 percent, 80 percent, and 92 percent) and higher than that of Ekstrand and colleagues' serologically mixed self-identified bisexual men in late-1980s San Francisco (77 percent). The total incidence rate of 57 percent for other-sex contact is lower than that reported for serologically mixed behavioral bisexuals (70 percent, 73 percent, 95 percent) and higher than that reported for serologically mixed self-identified bisexuals (32 percent). Unfortunately, because these studies used different definitions of bisexuality—Kinsey ratings, behavior, and self-identification, respectively—the fact that similar rates of same-sex behavior were found among seropositive and serologically mixed samples does not indicate conclusively that seropositive men are not more likely to have male partners.

Comparisons of findings regarding numbers of partners of seropositive and seronegative men are also made difficult by methodological differences between the studies. Doll and coauthors used the median as a summary statistic in their research report, whereas the Wood and the McKirnan and Stokes research reports used the mean, Wold reported medians for lifetime behavior only, and, in a study of men with AIDS diagnoses, Theresa Diaz and coauthors who include Susan Y. Chu (1993) provided neither summary statistic. Furthermore, even though the Doll (1992) and the Boulton (1992) teams both presented medians, these medians are not comparable to each other because of sampling differences and because the one-year medians of six male (one female) partners reported by Boulton, Hart, and Fitzpatrick exclude subjects with no male (female) partners; these differences in sampling and statistical procedure could account for the fact that these medians are higher than those Doll and colleagues found among seropositive men (cf. Weatherburn et al. 1998).

Despite these differences in statistical presentation and the resulting incomparability, however, findings by both the Doll and Diaz research teams indicate that seropositive men, like the seronegative or serologically mixed behaviorally bisexual men studied by the research teams of Wood, Krueger, Pearlman, and Goldbaum; McKirnan, Stokes, and colleagues; and Boulton, Hart, and Fitzpatrick have more male than female partners. Doll and colleagues (1992) reported that seropositive self-rated bisexual MSM had medians of 7.5 male and 6 female lifetime partners, with medians of 2 male and 1 female partners (range 0–15 and 0–29) in the previous year.[23] Diaz and colleagues (1993) found that 34.8 percent of men with AIDS who had had both male and female sex partners in the previous five years had had ten or more male partners, three times the percentage (11.2 percent) who had had ten or more female partners during that time period.[24]

Because different racial and ethnic groups have different rates of HIV infection, some HIV research has explored racial and ethnic differences in sexual behavior. This research shows that bisexual men belonging to different racial and ethnic groups vary in their sexual practices and sexual self-identities because of culturally based preferences for particular sex acts and cultural differences in the meaning of homosexuality.[25] Regarding sexual practices, anal intercourse appears to be rare among men of some Asian ethnic groups, including Chinese Canadians and Vietnamese Americans (Kapac 1992; Carrier, Nguyen, and Su 1992).[26] This preference is influenced by acculturation to white American culture; Joseph Carrier, Bang

Nguyen, and Sammy Su (1992) found that more acculturated Vietnamese Americans were more likely to engage in anal intercourse. In contrast, Latino men are culturally encouraged to find sexual pleasure in anal or vaginal, but not oral, sex (Magaña and Carrier 1991; Carrier 1985) and Black/African American men are less likely than white men to practice oral sex (McKirnan, Stokes, Doll, and Burzette 1995) and more likely than white men to practice anal intercourse, particularly insertive anal intercourse.[27] In their classic study *Homosexualities: A Study of Diversity Among Men and Women* Alan P. Bell and Martin S. Weinberg (1978) found that among Black homosexual men in the San Francisco Bay Area half preferred insertive anal intercourse and one-fifth preferred receiving fellatio, whereas these two activities were equally popular among white homosexual men (26 percent and 27 percent), although both groups actually engaged in fellatio more than in any other specific activity.

Homosexuality has different meanings in different cultures because sexuality is conceptualized differently, and homosexuality defined differently, in different cultures. Although ethnic and national differences exist within racial groups, East Asian and Latin cultures—like earlier Western culture—generally consider the role taken during the sex act to be equally or more important than the sex of the sex partner.[28] In these cultures a homosexual is defined as a man who takes the receptive role in penetrative sex. Seen as taking the woman's role in the sex act, such a man is also ascribed a feminized social gender. A heterosexual plays the insertive role in sexual contact and might do so with either female or male partners. The fact that some of his partners are male is not considered contrary to his masculinity or his heterosexuality. Because this construction of homosexuality is best known in anthropological literature as a characteristic of Latin (specifically, Mexican) cultures, it is sometimes referred to as "Latin homosexuality," even when it occurs among individuals from non-Latin cultures, and even though the concept has been criticized because it glosses over important cultural differences among Latinos of varying nationalities and ethnicities (Kurtz 1997). In contrast, in contemporary Anglo-American culture both receptive and insertive same-sex activities are considered homosexual and stereotypically associated with effeminacy. As a result, whereas white MSM generally take both receptive and insertive roles in anal sex, alternating roles with different partners or within a single sexual encounter, men of some Asian American and Latino ethnicities tend to take either one or the other role consistently with all their sex partners.[29] Asian Americans and Latinos who take both roles tend to be those who are more assimilated to mainstream white culture; in Mexican Spanish they are called *internacionales* (Almaguer 1993; Carrier 1992; Magaña and Carrier 1991).

The distinction between Latin homosexuals and other Latino MSM was described ethnographically by Alex Carballo-Diéguez and Curtis Dolezal (1994; see also Cáceres and Cortiñas 1996; Carballo-Diéguez 1995; Zamora-Hernández and Patterson 1996), who recruited 182 Latino MSM in New York City from a number of gay- and nongay-identified locations, organizations, and events for a study of risk behaviors. All subjects had had at least one male partner within the previous year; 10 percent self-identified as straight or heterosexual, 20 percent as bisexual (or as *hombres modernos*), 65 percent as gay, and 4 percent as drag queens. Self-identified gay and bisexual men were much more likely than self-identified heterosexual men to have engaged in receptive anal sex (74 percent and 50 percent versus 10 percent) or receptive oral sex (95 percent and 71 percent versus 21 percent), undoubtedly because of the Latin cultural association between sexual receptivity, femininity, and homosexual status. In contrast, the researchers found very little difference in the practice of insertive anal sex, which was reported by 86 percent of gay self-identified, 89 percent of bisexual self-identified, and 79 percent of heterosexual self-identified Latinos. Those who identified as straight explained that their same-sex behavior was a source of income or other nonsexual satisfaction rather than an expression of homosexuality. Those who identified as bisexual tended, along with those who identified as straight, to have less education and lower incomes than those who identified as gay. Although the authors did not discuss the possibility, this class difference might reflect a higher rate of assimilation to or familiarity with Anglo culture, which makes gay self-identity more available among men of higher socioeconomic classes.

One result of racial and ethnic differences in concepts of homosexuality is that bisexual behavior is more common among men of some racial and ethnic groups than others.[30] Cultures with Latin-type constructions of homosexuality also tend to be cultures that place a strong emphasis on the obligation of the individual to the family and view the family as the source of individual identity and purpose. In these cultures, because insertive same-sex activity among men is not contrary to heterosexual identity or heterosexual activity, and because one's obligation to the family includes marriage and procreation, rates of bisexual behavior are typically higher than in cultures with gender-based concepts of homosexuality and more individualistic conceptions of selfhood.[31] In some Latin cultures the unavailability of women as sex partners prior to marriage also contributes to same-sex behavior among those who will also have female partners during their lifetimes.

Like bisexual behavior, bisexual self-identity is more common among some racial and ethnic groups than others, but not necessarily those with the highest rates of bisexual behavior. Whereas Latinos have high rates of bisexual behavior, they have low rates of bisexual self-identification, African American men have high rates of both bisexual behavior and self-identity, and whites have low rates of bisexual behavior and even lower rates of bisexual self-identification. Doll and colleagues (1990, see also 1992) found that, among behaviorally bisexual men, Latino men were more likely to identify as heterosexual, whereas Blacks tended to identify as bisexual and whites as homosexual. McKirnan, Stokes, Doll, and Burzette (1995) also reported higher rates of bisexual self-identification among Blacks than whites (67 percent versus 52 percent) and Bell and Weinberg (1978) found that more white than Black "homosexuals" described their sexual feelings as exclusively homosexual (58 percent versus 45 percent). Taywaditep and Stokes (1998) found racial differences between "subtypes" of behaviorally bisexual men; a gay-identified subtype was predominantly Caucasian and two bisexual-identified subtypes were predominantly African American. The prevalence of heterosexual self-identity among Latinos is attributable to the fact that other-sex activity is culturally consistent with male-male activity as long as it is insertive; hence behaviorally bi-sexual Latinos are typically those who engage in insertive sex and identify as het-erosexual. The greater popularity of bisexual self-identity among Blacks has been attributed to homophobia in the Black community (Peterson 1995; Diaz et al. 1993; cf. Wright 1993), conversely, the greater popularity of homosexual self-identity among whites has been attributed to biphobia in the white community (Rust 1996a). The possibility that there are racial and ethnic differences in the acceptance of same-sex activity and bisexuality are explored in chapter 23 and further findings regarding racial and ethnic differences in the prevalence of bisexual behavior and self-identity are reviewed in chapter 11.

Racial and ethnic differences in the incidence of bisexuality show up among men diagnosed with AIDS. Using national surveillance data on AIDS cases re-ported to the Centers for Disease Control (CDC) between June 1981 and January 1988, Richard M. Selik, Kenneth G. Castro, and Marguerite Pappaioanou (1988) found that the proportion of behaviorally bisexual men among "homosexual and bisexual" men aged sixteen years or older was lower in whites (14 percent) than in Blacks (30 percent) or Hispanics (20 percent). Using CDC data on a slightly differ-ent population—cases of PWAs thirteen years or older who had had sex with men since 1977 and whose AIDS diagnoses were reported between June 1981 and June 1990—Chu and colleagues (1992) found higher percentages in a similar pattern (21 percent versus 41 percent and 31 percent).[32] These studies are representative of in-dividuals with AIDS diagnoses nationally and their findings regarding racial and ethnic differences in rates of behavioral bisexuality among MSM agree with find-ings from general population studies, including findings by Diane Binson and col-leagues (1995) and Bell and Weinberg (1978) reported in chapter 11.

Neither Black nor Latino populations are ethnically homogeneous, and findings by Diaz and colleagues (1993) indicate that the proportion of bisexuals among men with AIDS varies not only between white, Black, and Latino men but also among Blacks and among Latinos. Based on interviews with PWAs recruited with the co-operation of eleven states and local health departments, the Diaz team (1993) found higher rates of bisexual behavior among Latino men born outside the United States with ten or fewer years of residence in the United States (38 percent) than among those born in the United States (16 percent) or with more than ten years' residency (25 percent) and, conversely, among Black men born in the United States (20 percent) than among those born elsewhere (3 percent). Although these findings could reflect different HIV infection risk ratios for bisexual versus gay men within each ethnic group, rather than different rates of bisexuality between ethnic groups, Diaz and colleagues interpreted them as indicating ethnic differences in rates of bisexuality. Their explanations for these ethnic differences mirror the explanations given by other authors for differences between Blacks, whites, and Hispanics; they suggested that the higher rates among Latinos born outside the United States are due to the cultural construction of sexuality in Latin countries along sexual role rather than gender lines, with lower rates among Latinos in the United States reflecting acculturation to Anglo sexuality, and that the higher rates among U.S. born African Americans are due to homophobia which discourages exclusive homosexuality. Rates of bisexuality did not differ appreciably between white men born inside and outside the United States (15 percent). The rates found in the Diaz study are based on PWA populations including men who had had exclusively other-sex contacts, and are not, therefore, directly comparable to the findings of Selik, Castro, and Pappaioanou (1988) and Chu and colleagues (1992), whose percentages are based on MSM PWAs.

Bisexuality and Condom Use

In addition to statistics on the numbers and types of partners and sex acts reported by bisexuals, HIV research has provided a wealth of complex and conflicting information regarding rates of risky sexual practices among bisexuals, such as rates of condom use and nonuse.[33] Statistics regarding condom use must be interpreted carefully, because they are rarely adjusted for the facts that some subjects have not engaged in an act during which a condom could be used and that some subjects engage in the act more frequently, or with more partners, than others. Because of the complexity and political sensitivity of statistics in this area, reviewers of this research disagree on the degree to which bisexual men practice safer sex and on whether bisexual men are more or less conscientious about safer sex than gay or heterosexual men. For example, Boulton, Hart, and Fitzpatrick (1992) characterized behaviorally bisexual men as having a high rate of condom use—twice that reported in studies of gay men—and a relatively low rate of penetrative sex. S. M. Adib and D. G. Ostrow (1991), on the other hand, citing findings by G. W. Rutherford, J. L. Barnhardt, and G. F. Lemp (1988) that bisexuals are more likely to practice unsafe sex than strictly homosexual men, listed bisexuals as a special at-risk subgroup of "homosexual and bisexual men" that has received less attention and education and hence displays less behavioral change than gay men.

Two research reports that can be used to illustrate how the same statistics on condom use can be interpreted in very different ways are the Doll team's (1992) research comparing condom use among self-identified bisexual, heterosexual, and homosexual men and the Rotheram-Borus team's (1994) research comparing condom use by bisexual youth with their male and female partners. One might conclude from the Doll team's finding—"Overall, more than twice as many homosexually (73 percent) and bisexually (62 percent) identified men reported engaging in unprotected anal sex [in the previous year] with male partners as did heterosexually identified men (29 percent)" (9–10)—that men who identify as heterosexual are more likely to practice safer sex with their male partners than men who identify as bisexual or homosexual. However, the authors go on to report that, *among men who had had male sex partners in the previous year,* 72 percent of bisexual- , 82 percent of homosexual- , and 100 percent of heterosexual-identified men had had unprotected anal sex, revealing that bisexuals were in fact the most likely and heterosexuals the least likely to always use a condom when they had sex with a man.[34] The original finding that heterosexual self-identified men practiced the least unprotected male-male sex is based on *simple* rates unadjusted for the percentages of men who had actually had sex with a man and reflects the fact that heterosexuals were least likely to have male-male sex at all, not that they were more likely to use condoms when they did have male-male sex.[35] The latter set of statistics is *adjusted* for the fact that bisexual, homosexual, and heterosexual men were not equally likely to have had male-male sex within any given time period.

The two sets of statistical findings reported by Doll and coauthors are not contradictory; they merely reflect different aspects of condom use. Because few people are statistically knowledgeable, statistics like these can easily be used by individuals with political motivations for presenting bisexuals as either sexually responsible or sexually irresponsible—statistics don't lie, but they are easy to spin. In the absence of a political agenda the choice between these two sets of statistics depends on one's purpose. If one wanted to find out which risky behaviors were most common in a particular population so as to design an HIV education program that would target the areas with the most potential for a reduction in HIV transmission, then one would want simple unadjusted rates of condom use. But if one were interested in determining which areas of sexual behavior had been poorly addressed by previous educational efforts and therefore carry the greatest potential for future change, then one might be more interested in adjusted rates of condom use.

The study by Heckman and colleagues (1995) cut through these statistical complexities by reporting, in addition to adjusted condom use rates, the average number of partners with whom their respondents had had unprotected sex.[36] Their research demonstrated that bisexual men practice more unsafe sex, with more partners, than gay men during oral, but not anal, sex. Based on a survey of 1,316 men recruited upon their entry into gay bars in sixteen U.S. cities, they found that men who had had at least one male and one female partner within the previous two months were more likely to have had unprotected oral sex (60.3 percent) during that period than were men who had had only male partners (46.6 percent). The behaviorally bisexual men had also had unsafe oral sex with more partners, more frequently; they had had unprotected oral sex with an average of 2.25 male partners on an average of 4.04 occasions during that time period, compared to an average of 1.53 partners and 2.44 occasions among exclusively homosexual men. These findings are heightened by the fact that the behaviorally bisexual respondents studied by the Heckman team had had fewer male partners than their exclusively homosexual respondents; thus, their higher incidence of unsafe oral sex cannot be explained as a result of larger numbers of partners. Regarding anal intercourse, one-third of these behaviorally bisexual men had had unprotected anal intercourse, with an overall average of 0.9 partners and 1.49 occasions. This resembles a finding by the McKirnan and Stokes team (Stokes, Taywaditep, Vanable, and McKirnan 1996) that 35 percent of behavioral bisexuals reported having had unprotected anal intercourse in the previous six months. Like the Heckman team, the McKirnan and Stokes team found no difference in rates of condom use in anal sex between behaviorally bisexual and exclusively homosexual men—even when rates were adjusted for the different rates of same-sex activity in the two populations.

The second statistical complication in interpreting condom use rates can be illustrated using a study by Rotheram-Borus and colleagues (1994) on condom use rates with male versus female partners. These authors reported only rates adjusted for the percentage of the sample that had actually engaged in the relevant sexual behavior and found that 52 percent of heterosexually active youths recruited through a gay social service agency had "never" used a condom with a female partner, whereas 12 percent of homosexually active youths had "never" used a condom with a male partner. On the surface, the finding seems to indicate that these youths were engaging in more unsafe sex with female than with male partners. But to describe oneself as having "never" (or "always") used a condom with a partner of a particular sex, one has to have not used (or used) a condom with all of one's partners of that sex; the more partners of a given sex one has had, the more demanding this requirement.[37] Also, the fact that the Rotheram-Borus team (1994) reported that their subjects typically began condom use in conjunction with particular acts some time after beginning to engage in the act virtually guaranteed that those who had engaged in an act with a partner of a particular sex only a small number of times would generally fall into the "never used" category regardless of what their condom use rate would turn out to be on future occasions. Therefore, given that research cited earlier in this chapter, including the Rotheram-Borus team's (1994) own study, indicates that behaviorally bisexual males typically have greater numbers of male than female sex partners, rates of never (or always) having used condoms cannot be used as a way to compare rates of condom use with male versus female partners. Even if this problem were avoided by using the more robust categories of "rare," "sometimes," or "usual" to measure rates of condom use (which Rotheram-Borus and coauthors also reported), and it were still found that bisexuals' rates of condom use were higher with male than female partners, the fact that they have more male than female partners still leaves open the possibility that these individuals are engaging in unsafe sex with more male than female partners. In fact, some of the Rotheram-Borus findings do suggest that bisexual youths practice safer sex with female than male partners. When those who never used a condom were excluded, rates of consistent ("always") condom use were higher with female (27 percent) than with male (15 percent) partners.[38] The authors also reported that the delay between one's first sexual experience and the initiation of condom use was longer in male-male anal sex (1.3 years on average) or oral sex (1.8 years) than in vaginal sex (1.1 years). Thus, a closer look casts substantial doubt on the initial conclusion a reader might draw, that is, that the Rotheram-Borus subjects were more attentive to safer sex guidelines with their male than with their female partners; their findings can easily be spun to indicate the opposite.

Notwithstanding the difficulties involved in comparing condom use rates with male and female partners, researchers generally agree that bisexuals practice safer sex with their male than their female partners. For example, the McKirnan and Stokes team (1995; see also Wold et al. 1998) reported that 42 percent of men who had been bisexually active in the past three years had engaged in unprotected vaginal or anal penetration with a female partner in the past six months, with 28 percent reporting that they had done so three or more times. Rates of unprotected sex with female partners were higher among men with only a high school education than among men with college education (53 percent versus 31 percent). In comparison, 31 percent of the McKirnan and Stokes subjects reported having engaged in unprotected anal sex with a male partner in the previous six months (19 percent receptively, 28 percent insertively), with 22 percent having done so three or more times. Rates of unprotected oral sex with male partners were much higher; 62 percent receptively and 72 percent insertively.[39] Rates of unprotected sex with male partners did not differ by education. When these figures are adjusted to reflect percentages of only those subjects who had engaged in each specific sexual activity within the previous six months, they yield estimates that 63 percent of those who had had vaginal intercourse, 47 percent of those who had had anal intercourse with a female partner, 40 percent (42 percent) of those who had had receptive (insertive) anal intercourse with a male partner, and 87 percent (87 percent) of those who had had receptive (insertive) oral intercourse with a male partner had done so without a condom.[40] An earlier report by the McKirnan research team on a different sample indicates that rates of consistent condom use in oral sex are even lower with female than with male partners.[41] Therefore, these findings indicate that bisexuals are more likely to practice unprotected sex with female than male partners, regardless of the type of sexual activity. Lower rates of condom use with female than male partners have also been found among behaviorally bisexual Asian American men (Matteson 1997) and British men (Boulton, Hart, and Fitzpatrick 1992; Weatherburn et al. 1998).[42]

This pattern of practicing safer sex with male than with female partners apparently developed during the late 1980s, a time of intense safer sex education in the gay community, as bisexual men increased their use of condoms with male, but not female, partners. In their five-year longitudinal study of men in San Francisco Ekstrand and colleagues (1994) found that 65 percent of seronegative self-identified bisexual men reported unprotected anal sex with male partners during the 1984–1985 year, dropping to an annual rate of 20 percent five years later. Rates of unprotected vaginal sex began at much lower levels and dropped less precipitously from 35 percent to 20 percent annually in five years.[43] However, fewer seronegative men had sexual contact with women (25 percent) than with men (76 percent) in 1988–1989; adjusting for this factor, Ekstrand and colleagues reported that in 1988–1989 26 percent of those who had male partners had unprotected anal intercourse, whereas 80 percent of those who had female partners had unprotected vaginal intercourse during that year.[44]

There are a few possible explanations for bisexuals' greater increase of condom use with male than female partners during the safer sex educational campaigns of the 1980s. Matteson (1997) argued that AIDS education, which focused on male-male sex, was inappropriate to the needs of bisexual men, leading bisexual men to associate HIV risk with homosexual but not heterosexual behavior. In contrast, Boulton, Hart, and Fitzpatrick's (1992) respondents felt that using condoms with male but not female partners was a way of protecting their female partners from HIV. Boulton and colleagues noted that such a strategy would also conveniently enable MSM to keep their same-sex activities secret from their female partners by avoiding the need to explain their condom use to those female partners. Along quite different lines, Boulton, Hart, and Fitzpatrick also suggested that behaviorally bisexual men's greater condom use with male than female partners might reflect the facts that they are more likely to use condoms with casual than regular partners and that they—particularly those who self-identify as heterosexual—tend to lack regular male partners. Research by Wold et al. (1998) suggests that this is only a partial explanation; they found that among men who had had sex with both women and men in the previous six months the odds ratio of having had unprotected sex with female versus nonsteady male partners while sober was 12.0 whereas the odds ratio of having had unprotected sex with female versus steady male partners while sober was 4.0—smaller, but still substantial.

A comparison between the rates of unprotected anal sex found by the McKirnan and Stokes team (1995) among serologically mixed men (40 percent/42 percent) and those found by the Doll team (1992) among seropositive men (72 percent) also show predictably higher rates of unsafe sex among the latter. However, seropositivity is not the only difference between the two research samples that could explain the difference in findings. First, Doll subjects were bisexual self-identified MSM, whereas the selection criterion for McKirnan subjects was behavioral bisexuality. Second, the McKirnan and Stokes team assessed behavior over a period of six months, whereas Doll and colleagues assessed behavior over a period of one year. Third, the McKirnan sample was 52 percent Black and 48 percent white, whereas the Doll sample was 41 percent white, 35 percent Black, and 23 percent Hispanic.

Some studies have shown that there are racial and ethnic differences in rates of condom use. McKirnan, Stokes, and their coauthors (1995) reported that white behaviorally bisexual men had more oral sex with men overall, including more unprotected receptive oral sex, than Black men (74 percent versus 53 percent in the previous six months). Black and white men did not differ in rates of unprotected anal sex, commonly considered the riskiest sexual behavior, but the Asian American behaviorally bisexual men described by Matteson (1997) had lower rates of unprotected anal sex (17 percent) than the Black and white respondents (31 percent) in the McKirnan and Stokes study. Rotheram-Borus, Reid, and Rosario (1994) reported that rates of unprotected anal and oral sex with male partners among Hispanic "gay and bisexual" male adolescents were initially similar to those among African American youths in a longitudinal study, although African Americans reduced their rates of unprotected sex as a result of educational intervention more than Hispanics or whites. Patterns of condom use were different with female partners, with Black men more likely than white men to report unprotected sex (49 percent versus 32 percent) and Asian American men falling in between (37 percent; McKirnan, Stokes, Doll, and Burzette 1995; Matteson 1997). The difference in rates of unprotected vaginal sex between Black and white men withstood controls for sociodemographic variables but not limitation of the analysis to men who had had sex with women in the previous six months, leading McKirnan, Stokes, and coauthors to conclude that "Black and White respondents were equally likely to have unprotected sex with a woman if they had any sex with a woman, but Black men were more likely to have had sex with a woman" (71).[45]

There are several factors that increase or decrease the chance that an individual bisexual man will use condoms during any given sexual contact. One of the most important factors is his relationship with his sex partner; condom use is less likely with regular sex partners than with casual partners, and most research indicates that this is true for both male and female partners. Boulton, Hart, and Fitzpatrick (1992) found that behaviorally bisexual men were more likely to have unprotected receptive anal sex with regular male partners (29 percent) than with casual male partners (11 percent) and less likely to always use condoms with regular female partners (14 percent) than with casual female partners (36 percent).[46] Self-identified bisexual men in San Francisco told Ekstrand's research team (1994) that they were less likely to use a condom when their sex partner was their lover, or if they were in love with him or her, and reported to Martin S. Weinberg, Colin J. Williams, and Douglas W. Pryor, authors of *Dual Attraction: Understanding Bisexuality* (1994), that they were less likely to use condoms with primary partners (40 percent always did) than with secondary partners (50 percent) and most likely to use them with casual or anonymous partners (87 percent and 83 percent). The McKirnan and Stokes team (Stokes, McKirnan, and Burzette 1993) found, however, that condom use rates depended on the type of relationship only in the case of vaginal intercourse. Their self-perceived bisexual men used condoms 74 percent of the time in vaginal intercourse with friends and casual partners, compared to only 35 percent of the time with steady partners, but were equally likely to use condoms with friends, casual partners, and steady partners when they engaged in oral or anal sex with either male or female partners.

The Importance of Connections: AIDS Awareness Among Bisexual Men

As mentioned earlier in this chapter, HIV epidemiological research on bisexuality was motivated by concerns that AIDS educational messages aimed at or communicated through the gay community were not reaching bisexuals and that bisexuals therefore did not consider themselves at risk and were not following safer sex guidelines. Fueling this concern, research findings suggest that bisexual men are less connected to gay community networks through which they might receive AIDS educational messages. For example, Doll's research team (1992) found that 5 percent of bisexual self-identified men compared to 19 percent of homosexual self-identified and 2 percent of heterosexual self-identified men had ever belonged to a gay organization. The McKirnan and Stokes team (Stokes, McKirnan, and Burzette 1993) found that only 3 percent of men who responded to an ad soliciting "bisexuals" currently belonged to a gay or lesbian organization and 30 percent had no gay men, lesbians, or bisexuals among the ten most important people in their lives, although 81 percent had read a gay- or lesbian-oriented paper or magazine at least once and 30 percent went to a gay bar more than once a month. The McKirnan and Stokes team (1995) also found low rates of participation in the gay community among their behaviorally bisexual respondents, who typically had only two gay friends, had had no contact with gay organizations in the previous year (60 percent), and went to a gay bar once a month or less (47 percent). Kalichman, Roffman, Picciano, and Bolan (1998) found lower rates of subscription to gay literature, attendance at gay marches, and patronage of gay bars and clubs among behaviorally bisexual men (MSMW) than among men who had sex with men only (MSMO) during the previous year. Even among men who do visit gay bars, those who have sexual contact with women as well as men do so less frequently; Heckman and colleagues (1995) reported that men who had been behaviorally bisexual during the previous two months, and who were surveyed upon entry into a gay bar, had visited gay bars an average of 8.32 times during those months compared to an average of 10.55 visits among men whose sex partners had been exclusively male. The behaviorally bisexual men in the Heckman study were also less likely to perceive social approval and encouragement of safer sex among their friends, indicating that whatever social networks these men did belong to were not as conducive to condom usage as the networks to which the exclusively homosexual men belonged to.

If bisexual men in general are at greater risk than gay men because of a lack of connection to gay community networks, Black, Asian American, and Latino bisexual men might be at even greater risk of missing messages aimed at a predominantly white gay male population. In the McKirnan and Stokes study, (1995; see also Stokes, Vanable, and McKirnan 1996) Black bisexually active men were less connected than white bisexually active men to gay communication networks; 33 percent of Black respondents, compared to 58 percent of white respondents, read a gay-oriented newspaper more than once a month. The researchers suggested that this finding might reflect racial differences in general reading volume, but it is also possible that it reflects social distance on the part of African American bisexuals and other bisexuals of Color from a gay community that is predominantly white in composition, culture, and sociopolitical concerns. Either way, the result is that Black bisexual men are less likely to encounter safer sex messages in gay publications. There is also evidence that Asian American and Latino men became aware of AIDS and routes of HIV transmission more slowly than white men.[47]

Other evidence that lack of connection to a gay community leads to a lack of AIDS awareness and high rates of unsafe sex includes W. Palmer's (1989) finding that "married homosexual and bisexual men who called a telephone counselling service in Melbourne, Australia displayed lower levels of knowledge of safe sex than was found within the local gay community" (Boulton, Hart and Fitzpatrick 1992:166), William L. Earl's (1990) finding that among ninety-four men recruited at anonymous sex sites and compared to a cohort of fifty gay and bisexual men, married men were three times more likely than other men not to use a condom, and Kalichman, Roffman, Picciano, and Bolan's (1998) finding that behaviorallly bisexual men perceived safer sex as less normative than men who had had only male sex partners within the previous year.[48] Among seropositive men who had ever had sex with men Doll and colleagues (1992) found that 27 percent of those who rated themselves as Kinsey 1's or 2's (heterosexual) had had an anonymous male partner within the previous year, compared to 2 percent of those rating themselves as homosexual and 7 percent of those rating themselves as bisexual. Also, men closely associated with the gay community are likely to have friends with AIDS; in the Heckman study (1995) behaviorally bisexual men had fewer seropositive friends than exclusively homosexual men (2.25 versus 4.99 on average), and the National Survey of Men revealed that men in general are more likely to use condoms with male partners if they know someone with AIDS (Tanfer, Grady, Klepinger, and Billy 1993).

Bisexuals, and nongay self-identified MSM in general, are consistently found to have low perceptions of their risk of HIV infection, another factor that has been attributed to lack of connection to gay networks and blamed for high rates of unsafe sex. Among Doll and colleagues' (1992) respondents 77 percent of self-identified bisexual, compared to 65 percent of self-identified homosexual and 98 percent of self-identified heterosexual men, had low perceptions of their risk of HIV infection before learning their serologic status, with 17 percent of self-identified bisexual compared to 8 percent of self-identified homosexual and 28 percent of self-identified heterosexual men believing that they were not in a risk group. Among Boulton, Hart, and Fitzpatrick's (1992) behaviorally bisexual male respondents, 59 percent felt there was virtually no chance that they were seropositive. These men's estimates of their risk were especially low with regard to female partners; 81 percent felt that the risk of infection from female partners was negligible, and they were primarily concerned about the risk to themselves from female partners, not the risk they might pose to their female partners. The implication that bisexuals' low perception of risk is related to lack of connection to gay communities is supported by the McKirnan and Stokes finding that bisexual men whose social lives were more gay oriented "had a more positive attitude toward condom use [and] tended to deny AIDS risk to a lesser extent" (Stokes, McKirnan, and Burzette 1993: 208).

Low perceptions of risk might lead not only to low rates of safer sex but also to low rates of HIV testing. Ted Myers, Kevin W. Orr, David Locker, and Edward A. Jackson (1993; see also Godin, et al 1997) studied factors affecting the decision to seek HIV testing in a sample of 1,295 gay and bisexual men recruited using quota and systematic selection techniques from gay-identified bars and bathhouses in Toronto. Forty-eight percent of the men had had exclusively same-sex contact in their lifetimes, 35 percent had had other-sex contact in their lifetimes, and 13 percent had had both same-sex and other-sex contact within the past year. Defining this last group as bisexual, the authors reported that 41.5 percent of bisexual men compared to 55.7 percent of gay men had been tested for HIV antibodies and that perceived risk of infection was one of the factors associated with the decision to be tested. Myers and colleagues' statistical findings agree with the Heckman team's (1995) finding that gay male bar patrons who had had at least one male and one female partner in the previous two months were less likely (62.5 percent) to have been tested for HIV than those who had had only male partners (71.4 percent). They are also similar to Boulton, Hart, and Fitzpatrick's (1992) finding that 45 percent of British men who had engaged in both same- and other-sex behavior in the previous five years had been tested. Kalichman, Roffman, Picciano, and Bolan (1998) found that, among high-risk MSM, 80 percent of those who had had sex with women in the previous year compared to 93 percent of those who had not had been tested. But a finding by the McKirnan and Stokes team (1995; see also Evans, Bond, and MacRae 1998) contradicts evidence that bisexuals—particularly those without ties to gay communities—are unconcerned about HIV and unlikely to be tested; in a sample that undoubtedly included a higher proportion of bisexuals not connected to gay communities because of broad sample recruitment methods, McKirnan, Stokes, and their colleagues found that 74 percent of behavioral bisexuals had been tested.

Bisexual men's lack of contact with the gay community is often assumed to flow from a lack of acceptance of their same-sex impulses; in fact, the choice of bisexual self-identity over gay self-identity is sometimes interpreted as evidence that one is denying one's "true" sexual orientation because of internalized homophobia. Some AIDS educators worry that homophobic self-denial prevents bisexuals, particularly married men, from recognizing the personal relevance of safer sex messages, from seeking HIV testing that would constitute an acknowledgment of their homosexual activity, and from adopting safer sex practices out of self-hatred even if they do recognize the relevance of these messages (e.g., Myers, Orr, Locker, and Jackson 1993; see Rust 1996d). Lending credence to these concerns, Myers and colleagues found that behaviorally bisexual men were more likely than exclusively homosexual men to say that concerns about anonymity and self-assessed good health were reasons for not being tested. Concerns about anonymity are also higher among men who are bisexual by self-identity; Susan M. Kegeles and colleagues (1990) found that self-identified bisexual men expressed less willingness than heterosexual men or women or homosexual men to be tested for HIV if the names of those testing positive would be reported to public health officials. African American MSM told Stokes and Peterson (1998) that they perceived a link between internalized homophobia and HIV risk behaviors, and Stokes, McKirnan, and Burzette (1993) found that bisexual men with more gay-oriented social lives have lower levels of self-homophobia. Additional findings that bisexuals are generally more closeted and less comfortable with their sexuality than gay men are reviewed in chapter 23.

However, research bearing more directly on this point indicates that neither the adoption of a self-identity that does not reflect the extent of one's same-sex activities, nor the choice to conceal these activities from others or to maintain distance from the gay community necessarily indicates either a lack of self-acknowledgment of the activity or a tendency to engage in unsafe sex. Matteson (1997) found no correlation between levels of homophobia, acculturation to gay subculture, connections to gay social networks, or gay self-identity with risk taking among Asian Americans; Stokes, McKirnan, Doll, and Burzette (1996) found that a correlation between homophobia and nondisclosure to female partners disappeared when it was controlled for other psychosocial variables; and R. B. Hays, S. M. Kegeles, and T. J. Coates (1991) found a positive correlation between levels of unsafe sex and self-acceptance.[49] Kalichman, Roffman, Picciano, and Bolan (1998) found that behaviorally bisexual men with high-risk sexual behavior were more, not less, connected to a gay community than behaviorally bisexual men with low-risk sexual behavior. Regarding the implications of self-acknowledgment for safer sex behavior, McKirnan, Stokes, Doll, and Burzette (1995) directly tested the supposition that men whose sexual self-identities do not fully reflect their participation in same-sex activity, and men who perceive themselves as bisexual but are closeted, are more likely to engage in risky sex than men whose self-identities more accurately reflect their behavior (according to Anglo conceptions of sexuality). Contrary to expectations, these researchers found that men whose behavior was more male oriented than their self-identification (heterosexual self-identity with any male partners or bisexual self-identity with only male partners) were *less* likely to have engaged in unprotected anal sex than those whose self-identities and behaviors were consistent with each other. This finding is weakened by the fact that the latter group had had more male partners; the authors note this but do not present findings adjusted for number of male partners. In an earlier study the same research team (Stokes, McKirnan, and Burzette 1993) found that among men who responded to an ad seeking bisexual study participants those who were more closeted tended to have lower (unadjusted) rates of unprotected sex with male partners. Taywaditep and Stokes (1998) found that the level of risk for HIV infection in each of their eight subtypes of behaviorally bisexual men could not have been predicted from the men's sexual self-identities. For example, among the subtypes with the highest levels of HIV risk with women were one straight-identified subtype and two bisexual-identified subtypes; other subtypes characterized by the same identities but differing in their behavioral profiles engaged in less risk behavior.

One reason the expected differences in risky sex practices were not found might be that, among men with connections to the gay community, greater opportunities for male-male sex might offset the effects of greater exposure to safer sex messages, greater likelihood of knowing someone with AIDS, and increased rates of condom use. In their early study the McKirnan and Stokes team (Stokes, McKirnan, and Burzette 1993) found that self-described bisexuals who were more "gay-involved" had more—not less—unprotected oral sex with men, and less unprotected vaginal sex with women, although they did not differ from less gay-involved men in rates of unprotected anal sex with men and women. Their later study (McKirnan, Stokes, Doll, and Burzette 1995) found that respondents recruited for their research through print ads were more likely to have engaged in unprotected sex with female partners (55 percent) than respondents recruited from networks or bars (40 percent) or community settings (30 percent), although rates of unsafe sex with male partners did not differ by recruitment source. These findings suggest that involvement in the gay community might lead to more exposure to safer sex messages but also to greater opportunities for (unprotected) sexual contact with men— and to fewer opportunities for (unprotected) sex with women.

Boulton, Hart, and Fitzpatrick's (1992) research also bears directly on the question of whether contact with a gay community in fact reduces risk for HIV infection. They distinguished their behaviorally bisexual subjects according to their "social contexts."[50] Those who belonged to organized bisexual groups were classified as living in a bisexual context. Those who were married, living with a female partner, or heterosexually self-identified were classified as living in a heterosexual context and those with "significant involvement" in the organized gay community were classified as living in a gay context. Arguments that self-identified and

behaviorally bisexual men are less likely than gay men to have heard and responded to safer sex messages transmitted through gay networks lead to the expectation that behaviorally bisexual men living in heterosexual or bisexual contexts would engage in higher levels of risky sex than those living in a gay context.
Contrary to this expectation, Boulton, Hart, and Fitzpatrick (1992) found that, in
the previous year, those living in a bisexual context tended not to have had unprotected sex with either males or females, whereas those living in a gay context had
almost universally had unprotected sex with females if at all and were evenly split
in terms of their sexual contact with males, and those living in a heterosexual context had had unprotected sex with women and either no male partners or no unprotected sex with male partners. In other words, bisexuals living in a bisexual
context were the only ones tending to practice safer sex with both males and females, indicating that HIV education has been more, not less, effective at reaching
this group. It appears that bisexuals living in bisexual contexts not only received
safer sex information but received information that was more pertinent to their
lives as bisexuals than the education received by behavioral bisexuals who got
their information through gay community networks. The fact that the pattern of
safer sex with male but not female partners was most characteristic of heterosexual-identified behavioral bisexuals indicates that the barrier to safer sex with female partners is neither behavioral bisexuality, nor bisexual self-identity, nor lack
of contact with a gay community, but heterosexual self-identity combined with bisexual behavior and lack of contact with a bisexual community.

The importance of bisexual community in mediating bisexuals' responses to the
AIDS epidemic is evident in Weinberg, Williams, and Pryor's study of bisexuals recruited through the Bisexual Center in San Francisco. Interviewed in both 1983 and
1988, these bisexual men and women were clearly living in a "bisexual context,"
and the influence of this context is evident in the changes they reported making in
their sexual and social lives in response to the AIDS epidemic during the interven-
ing years. Many had lost friends and lovers to AIDS, learned to associate sex with
death, and reconsidered the meaning of a bisexual identity that they once associated with sexual liberation and validated with bisexual behavior. Whereas monogamy had previously been considered sexually restrictive and "at odds with a bisexual identity," some bisexuals now considered having multiple sex partners
"passé" and had adopted monogamous or "bi-monogamous" (simultaneous fidelity to one woman and one man) relationship patterns. Both women and men had
begun to avoid men—especially bisexual men—as sex partners and had high rates
of condom use by 1988. Among men the percentage with no male partners increased from 14.3 percent to 32.1 percent and the percentage with fifteen or more
decreased from 21.4 percent to 10.7 percent. Much smaller decreases were seen in
numbers of female partners. In 1988 54 percent of women and 78 percent of men
said that they always used condoms with male partners. These findings are consistent with the Ekstrand (Ekstrand et al. 1994) finding that bisexuals in San Francisco
substantially changed their behavior during the second half of the 1980s and pinpoint involvement in a bisexual community as an important factor in this behavior
change.

Unlike the self-identified bisexual men and women studied by Weinberg, Williams, and Pryor and by Boulton, Hart, and Fitzpatrick, most bisexuals do not live in bisexual contexts. Most live in isolation without connection to either a gay or bisexual community and are therefore less likely than gay men to have been exposed to safer sex education. However, the Boulton and the Weinberg findings indicate that those few bisexuals who are connected to a bisexual community do receive information about safer sex and support for sexual behavior change through that community. Bisexual organizations, whose numbers have mushroomed since the early 1990s, are therefore a key vehicle for AIDS education among bisexuals. In reaction to charges that bisexuals are a gateway for HIV transmission from the gay to the straight population, some bisexual activists describe bisexuals as a gateway for safer sex information. Bisexuals are in a unique position to transmit safer sex knowledge to both men and women, and to lesbians, gay men, and heterosexuals. Through the efforts of bisexual organizations to educate their members, bisexuals might well be pivotal in turning the tide of the epidemic.

Risk Denial or Real Safety? Seropositivity Rates Among Bisexual Men

The argument that nonuse of condoms among bisexuals results from lack of AIDS awareness or lack of self-acknowledgment makes the assumption that gay men, in contrast, generally have a more educated and realistic response to the AIDS epidemic. It is possible, however, that bisexuals' perceptions that they are at low risk of HIV infection are accurate. Research suggests that HIV seropositivity rates, unlike rates of other STDs, are in fact lower among bisexuals than among gay men.[51] Wood, Krueger, Pearlman, and Goldbaum (1993) reported that seropositivity among self-identified bisexual men was intermediate (12 percent) to that among self-identified heterosexual (8 percent) and gay (27 percent) men, and 6.9 percent of the McKirnan and Stokes team's behaviorally bisexual men who had sought testing were seropositive. Lower rates were found by the Heckman research team (1995) among men entering gay bars; only 1.6 percent of those who had had sex with both a woman and a man in the previous two months, compared to 6.3 percent of those who had had sex only with men, reported being seropositive. Boulton, Hart, and Fitzpatrick, who found a seropositivity rate of 15 percent among British behaviorally bisexual men, attributed bisexuals' low seropositivity to high rates of safer sex. On the other hand, if literature reviewers such as Adib and Ostrow (1991) are correct in their conclusion that bisexual men practice low rates of safer sex, then we must entertain the possibility that these low rates of safer sex are a result of a realistic perception of low risk, and not an unrealistic perception resulting from either self-denial or social isolation from gay communities. Of course, over time, continued practice of risky sex would lead to increasing seropositivity rates or, as found by Torian et al. (1996), slower decreases in seropositivity rates among bisexual men. The Ekstrand (Ekstrand et al. 1994) and the Weinberg, Williams, and

Pryor (1994) findings that bisexual men in San Francisco, an area heavily saturated with AIDS education, increased their practice of safer sex over the course of the late 1980s holds out hope that bisexuals in other geographic areas will also respond to increasing risk with increasingly safer sex.

Among bisexual men, as in the general United States population, rates of HIV infection and AIDS differ between racial and ethnic groups, with Blacks and Hispanics having higher rates than whites. Using data reported to the CDC, Selik, Castro, and Pappaioanou (1988) found that among bisexual men the relative risk of AIDS was 3.6 and 2.5 times as great in Black and Hispanic men, respectively, as in white men. The McKirnan and Stokes team found that 10.5 percent of Black compared to 2.9 percent of white behaviorally bisexual men were seropositive and Susan B. Manoff, Helene D. Gayle, Mitzi A. Mays, and Martha F. Rogers (1989) reported that a higher percentage of adolescent infections were attributable to same-sex contact among Blacks (44 percent) than among Hispanics (29 percent) or whites (24 percent). There are many possible reasons for the higher relative risks and seropositivity rates of Black and Hispanic bisexual men, including weaker connections to predominantly white organizations through which AIDS education might be obtained as well as factors that operate among Blacks and Hispanics of all sexual orientations, such as higher rates of drug use and lower quality health care.

Women, Bisexuality, and HIV/AIDS

Several research studies have shown that women who have sex with women (WSW) are more likely than exclusively heterosexual women to be seropositive.[52] These reports were initially surprising to epidemiologists because female-female contact is not believed to transmit the HIV virus as efficiently as male-female contact, leading to the assumption that WSW are at less risk for HIV than heterosexual women. The explanation for the finding lies not only in the fact that many WSW also have sex with men, i.e., they are bisexual, but also in the fact that WSW —especially bisexual women—have higher rates of other risk factors than exclusively heterosexual women.

For example, using New York City Department of Health data on 4,585 clients of an STD clinic—a population that undoubtedly overrepresents individuals with high risk for HIV infection—Pamela Jean Bevier, Mary Ann Chiasson, Richard T. Heffernan, and Kenneth G. Castro (1995) found that 17 percent of WSW, compared to 11 percent of women who had had only male sex partners, were seropositive.[53] A more representative sample of women who had had sex with women or who self-identified as either lesbian or bisexual was recruited by George F. Lemp and colleagues (1995) from clubs, bars, community events, and street corners in San Francisco and Berkeley. The seropositivity rate in this sample was a more modest 1.2 percent, which is nevertheless three times higher than the rate for women in general in San Francisco.[54] The seropositivity rate is even lower among lesbian and bisexual women in smaller cities in other areas of the United States. In a survey of 1,057 lesbian and bisexual women surveyed as they entered gay bars in sixteen small cities, Ann Duecy Norman and colleagues (1996) found only 5 women infected with HIV, constituting a rate of 0.5 percent.

Further findings by Bevier, Chiasson, Heffernan, and Castro (1995) demonstrate that the higher rates of seropositivity among WSW are due partially to high levels of sexual activity relative to exclusively heterosexual women; 38 percent of WSW, compared to 13 percent of exclusively heterosexual women, reported three or more sex partners in the previous three months, and WSW had a median of fourteen partners, compared to four partners for heterosexual women. These findings are consistent with other research on levels of sexual activity among bisexuals compared to monosexuals that are discussed in chapter 23, including findings that WSW have paradoxically higher rates of sexual contact with men than exclusively heterosexual women do. In the Bevier study WSW also had higher rates of exchanging sex for money or drugs (48 percent versus 12 percent), having sex partners who used injection drugs (45 percent versus 21 percent) or who were bisexual men (19 percent versus 5 percent), engaging in oral-penile and anal intercourse with these male partners, and using injection drugs (31 percent versus 7 percent) or crack cocaine (37 percent versus 15 percent) themselves. Similarly, Rebecca M. Young, Gloria Weissman, and Judith B. Cohen (1992) found that WSW were twice as likely to have used injection drugs (76 percent versus 42 percent) and to have engaged in anal intercourse with a male partner (33 percent versus 19 percent) than women who had had only male sex partners.[55] Of course, these findings do not mean that having sex with women leads to drug use (or to sex with men, for that matter); the correlation might be due to a proportion of the population for whom a permissive approach to life leads to both drug use and socially proscribed sexual behaviors, to drug use lowering inhibitions regarding socially proscribed sexual behaviors including same-sex activity, or to sexual activity being used as a method for obtaining drugs.[56] Regression analysis demonstrated that the higher seropositivity rates among the WSW studied by Bevier, Chiasson, Heffernan, and Castro are entirely explained by factors other than the fact of having had sex with women; after controlling for these other risk factors, having had sex with another woman is negatively associated with seropositivity. The scientific consensus remains that female-to-female HIV transmission is exceedingly rare.[57]

Among WSW, behaviorally bisexual women appear to have slightly higher seropositivity rates than exclusively homosexual women, although there are few data bearing directly on this question.[58] In one of the few studies to distinguish bisexual women from lesbians in reporting seropositivity rates, Scott B. McCombs and colleagues (1992) found that 2.8 percent of women who had had sex with both men and women since 1978 were seropositive, compared to 0 percent of women who had had only female partners, although this difference is not statistically significant. Because the McCombs research team used data reported to the CDC on the sexually active clients of sexually transmitted disease clinics and women's health clinics, 2.8 percent is probably an overestimate of the seropositivity rate for bisexual women in general.[59] In the Bevier study (1995) cited above, 18 percent of bisexual women and 0 percent of exclusively homosexual women were seropositive; this difference is also statistically insignificant, probably because of the small numbers of exclusively homosexual women (n = 10) in the study. In other studies bisexual women were not distinguished from lesbians, but because most of the women in these studies had had sex with men as well as women the figures given for "lesbians and bisexual women" can be taken as close approximations of the seropositivity rates for bisexual women. These include more representative samples that provide lower estimates of the seropositivity rate among "lesbian and bisexual women," for example, the 1.2 percent and 0.5 percent rates found in the Lemp and Norman studies cited above.

In these last two studies lesbian and bisexual women were sampled at least partially on the basis of their self-identities rather than solely on their sexual behavior as was the case in the McCombs and Bevier studies. When bisexual women and lesbians are distinguished by self-identity rather than sexual behavior there is likely to be less difference in seropositivity rates between lesbian and bisexual women because many self-identified lesbians are behaviorally bisexual. This is especially true when lifetime behavior, or behavior since 1978, is taken into account as is usually the case in HIV research. One study even suggested that the direction of the difference is reversed; Young, Weissman, and Cohen (1992) found higher seropositivity rates among self-identified lesbians than among self-identified bisexual women (15 percent versus 13 percent).[60] This might be an anomalous finding, however, because the weight of the evidence indicates that even when defined by self-identity, bisexual women engage in more risk behaviors than lesbians.

The higher risk of self-identified bisexual women stems from factors similar to those contributing to the higher risk of WSW in general, that is, higher rates of heterosexual activity and the types of men with whom bisexual women, as compared to lesbians, have sexual contact. Based on a survey of 1,086 bisexual (6.5 percent) and lesbian (84.9 percent) women recruited through women's festivals, bars, and organizations, Lena Einhorn and Michael Polgar (1994) found that 90 percent of self-identified bisexuals, compared to 53 percent of self-identified lesbians, had had heterosexual contact since 1978. Among those who did, 47 percent of bisexual women compared to 25 percent of lesbians had had sex with at least one man whom they knew or suspected was bisexual or gay and 14 percent of bisexuals compared to 6 percent of lesbians had had sex with a man who was an injection drug user.[61] In their survey of lesbian and bisexual women in small cities the Norman research team (1996) found that women who placed themselves in the middle three categories of a five-point Kinsey-type scale had high rates of sexual contact with bisexual men (39 percent) and injection drug users (20 percent). A study by the San Francisco Department of Public Health AIDS Office (SFDPH 1993a) of 483 self-identified lesbian and bisexual women recruited from "street and community locations in San Francisco" (8) found that 34 percent of self-identified bisexual women, compared to 5 percent of self-identified lesbian women, had had sex with a gay or bisexual man in the previous three years. This study also found that 14 percent of bisexuals and 1.6 percent of lesbians had had sex with a known or suspected male IDU. In the Einhorn and Polgar study Black women were more likely to report injection drug use themselves than white women (8 percent versus 2 percent), but neither Einhorn and Polgar nor the Norman team found any difference between lesbian and bisexual women in drug use.[62] Einhorn and Polgar concluded that bisexual women were twice as likely as lesbians (49 percent versus 21 percent) to report high-risk behavior.

In addition to having more sex with at-risk male partners, bisexual women are more likely than lesbians to have unprotected sex with their male partners. The Norman team (1996) found that 16.5 percent of bisexual women compared to 0.5 percent of lesbians had had unprotected vaginal or anal sex with a male partner during the previous two months. The SFDPH study (1993a) found that 42 percent of self-identified bisexual women, compared to 53 percent of self-identified lesbians, said that they always used condoms with male sex partners. The Lemp team (1995) found that 71 percent of self-identified bisexuals, compared to 19.8 percent of self-identified lesbians, reported having had unprotected sex with a male partner in the previous three years. Figures from these studies are not adjusted for the fact that bisexuals were more likely to have had a male sex partner, and they do not tell us whether bisexual women were also less likely to use latex barriers with their female partners, but they do provide estimates of the percentages of bisexual women who are at risk for infection from male partners.

Other research indicates that rates of latex use among "lesbian and bisexual women" with both female and male partners are very low. Patricia E. Stevens (1994) reported that 15 percent of a sample of "lesbian and bisexual women" "volunteered that they regularly had sex with men without using barriers" (1569), that half regularly had sex with women without using barriers, and an additional 25 percent had "semi-safe" sex or inconsistent use of barriers with male and female partners. The SFDPH AIDS Office study (1993a) found that among self-identified lesbian and bisexual women 70 percent had had unprotected vaginal sex with male primary partners and 43 percent had done so with male secondary partners in the previous three years. The Lemp team found that 92 percent of women who had had sex with women in the previous three years had had unprotected oral sex and 25 percent reported unprotected vaginal fisting. Einhorn and Polgar (1994) likewise reported low levels of safer sex among lesbian and bisexual women; they found that only 6 percent "always" and 15 percent "sometimes" practiced safer sex with their female partners. Even among those who believed that they might be HIV infected themselves, only 8 percent "always" and 15 percent "sometimes" practiced safer sex with female partners. Moreover, when asked what their safer sex practices were, it turned out that even fewer were actually practicing safer sex.

Rates of latex use among both bisexual women and lesbians are probably low because women who have sex with women do not perceive themselves as being at risk for HIV infection. Young, Weissman, and Cohen (1992) pointed out that the perception of low risk among WSW is supported by institutional neglect of research on female-to-female transmission and lack of AIDS educational efforts aimed at this population. Likewise, Stevens (1994) discussed the "cultural construction of immunity" that occurs among lesbians and bisexual women, and Norman and coauthors (1996) referred to the "false sense of security" that WSW might have as a result of being "told repeatedly that they are not at risk for HIV"

(351).[63] The perception of safety might be more pronounced among lesbians than among bisexual women; Martin, Seifen, and Maloney (1993) suggested that lesbians avoid acknowledging their own risk by blaming HIV transmission on bisexual women, and Einhorn and Polgar reported that bisexual women were much more likely to have been tested for HIV (48 percent) than lesbians (26 percent), suggesting that bisexual women perceive themselves to be at greater risk for infection than lesbians. This concern, however, does not appear to have been translated into action; if AIDS educational efforts have been slow to reach bisexual men, it appears that they have been even less effective at encouraging bisexual women to adopt safer sex practices.

But Weinberg, Williams, and Pryor's (1994) findings that in the San Francisco bisexual community bisexual women as well as bisexual men made behavioral changes during the late 1980s holds out hope that continuing growth of bisexual community networks, and increased attention to the need for safer sex education among WSW, will eventually spread knowledge about safer sex and an awareness of its importance to bisexual women elsewhere. In *Dual Attraction* these authors described how women, like men, responded to the AIDS epidemic by reducing their numbers of partners, especially male partners, and increasing their use of condoms. Among the bisexual women interviewed by Weinberg, Williams, and Pryor, the percentage with no male sex partners in the previous twelve months increased from 7.4 percent in 1983 to 33.3 percent in 1988, and the percentage with fifteen or more male partners decreased from 22.2 percent to 3.7 percent. By 1988 54 percent claimed that they always practiced safe sex with male partners and 47 percent claimed to do so with female partners—the former figure is slightly higher than that found a few years later by the SFDPH AIDS Office. The SFDPH study also found that 62 percent of self-identified lesbian and bisexual women reported that they had heard safer sex messages addressing sex between women, indicating these messages were being received by this population in San Francisco and might be at least partly responsible for the behavioral changes observed by Weinberg, Williams, and Pryor.

In the above discussion sex with a bisexual man is characterized as a risk factor for women. Although this is generally believed to be the case, such an assumption should not pass without examination, especially given the difficulties involved in interpreting rates of condom use described earlier in this chapter. Several researchers have produced data bearing on the question of the risk to heterosexually active women from bisexual male partners. Some approached the problem of estimating this risk by using data on the numbers of female partners potentially exposed to HIV by seropositive MSM. Ekstrand and colleagues (1994) found reason for alarm in the facts that 5 percent of single men in the San Francisco Men's Health Study were both bisexual and seropositive and that these men had had an average of 2.9 female partners during the previous two years (Winkelstein, Wiley, and Padian 1986). Wood, Krueger, Pearlman, and Goldbaum (1993) reported that among 457 straight-identified MSM seeking HIV testing 7.7 percent were seropositive and 12 of these men had had a total of 32 female partners, whereas of 711 self-identified bisexual MSM 12.4 percent were seropositive, 31 of whom had had a total of 116 partners, and of 4,226 self-identified gay MSM 26.6 percent were seropositive, 18 of whom had had a total of 32 female partners. Thus, taking into account the different rates of seropositivity and the different numbers of female partners of men with different sexual self-identities, but not taking into account different rates of condom use, 63 percent of the female partners of seropositive men in their sample had been potentially exposed to HIV by self-identified bisexual men, although self-identified bisexual men comprised only 13 percent of the sample. The implication is that, among MSM, those who identify as bisexual potentially expose more women to HIV than do those who don't, resulting from a combination of more female partners than either self-identified heterosexual or gay MSM and higher seropositivity rates than self-identified hetrosexual MSM. However, if the analysis is restricted to the 61 men who were seropositive and behaviorally bisexual, then the findings indicate that the percentage of women potentially exposed to HIV by those who are bisexually self-identified (64 percent) is more proportionate to the percentage of such men in the sample (51 percent).

Other researchers used data on rates of unprotected sex rather than seropositivity to estimate the risk posed by bisexual men to their female partners. Although separate rates of unprotected sex with male and with female partners are relevant, the combined rate of unprotected sex with both male and female partners provides a more accurate estimate of the possibility that bisexual men will become HIV infected via same-sex activity and subsequently infect their female partners. The Stokes and McKirnan research team (Stokes, McKirnan, Doll, and Burzette 1996) found that 23 percent of behaviorally bisexual men reported having had unprotected sex with at least one woman and one man during the previous six months, and Boulton, Hart, and Fitzpatrick (1992) found that 22 percent of behaviorally bisexual men—36 percent of those who had been behaviorally bisexual in the previous year—had had unprotected sex with at least one male and at least one female partner in the previous year. The two research teams reacted to these similar findings very differently, however. Whereas Stokes, McKirnan, and colleagues found the 23 percent semiannual figure cause for concern and called bisexual activity "potentially an important HIV transmission route" (281), Boulton, Hart, and Fitzpatrick used their 22 percent annual figure to call into question the characterization of bisexuals as a bridge "between gay men and the rest of the population" (173). The McKirnan and Stokes team (1995) reported that behaviorally bisexual Black men were more likely than white men to report at least one instance of unprotected penetrative sex with both a man and a woman in the previous six months (21 percent versus 10 percent) and Matteson (1997) argued that behaviorally bisexual Asian American men's sexual behavior patterns placed them at less risk of transmitting HIV from their male to their female partners than other groups of bisexuals.

But neither seropositivity rates alone nor rates of unprotected sex alone provide reasonable estimates of the potential for HIV transmission from bisexual men to their female partners; in the absence of either factor, transmission is either impossible or much less likely. Therefore, more accurate estimates of the potential for HIV transmission from bisexual men to their female partners require simultaneous consideration of both seropositivity rates and condom use rates. The Ekstrand research team (1994), whose findings are discussed in detail earlier in this chapter, found that rates of condom use, particularly with female partners, increased more dramatically among seropositive than seronegative self-identified bisexual men in San Francisco over the course of the late 1980s. In 1988–1989 only 2 percent of seropositive self-identified bisexual men had unprotected sex with both men and women during the year, a figure much lower than the 10 percent to 23 percent annual and semiannual rates found among bisexuals of mixed serologic status by the Boulton and the McKirnan and Stokes research teams (Boulton, Hart, and Fitzpatrick 1992; Stokes, McKirnan, Doll, and Burzette 1996; McKirnan, Stokes, Doll, and Burzette 1995). Of course, even a small rate of unprotected sex when one partner is seropositive puts the other partner's health and life at risk, and the degrees of behavior change among bisexual men elsewhere in the country are probably more modest than those found by Ekstrand and colleagues in a city saturated by AIDS education. However, the differential increase in use of condoms by seropositive and seronegative men found by the Ekstrand team suggests that the risk of transmission from bisexual men to women is much smaller than estimated by other researchers on the basis of either rates of condom use or rates of seropositivity alone. Taking into account rates of seropositivity, condom use, and numbers and types of female partners among bisexual men, Kahn et al. (1997) used NABS data to estimate that HIV transmission from bisexual men to female sex partners accounts for only 1 percent of all new infections annually.

Another approach to assessing HIV transmission to women via bisexual men is analysis of existing data on individuals with AIDS diagnoses. Chu and co-authors (1992) reported that among 3,555 women who had acquired HIV through heterosexual contact within the United States 11 percent reported that their only risk factor was sexual contact with a bisexual man, and a 1994 CDC report put the figure at 15 percent.[64] The risk of infection from bisexual men varies by race and ethnicity; among Black and Hispanic women the Chu study (1992) found that the proportion whose only risk factor was sex with a bisexual man was five and three times larger, respectively, than the proportion among white women. Similarly, Selik, Castro, and Pappaioanou (1988) reported that the relative risk of AIDS among women with bisexual sex partners was 4.6 and 3.6 times greater in Black and Hispanic women than in white women, and that among women with AIDS who had had bisexual male sex partners 48 percent were Black or Hispanic.

The fact that Black and Hispanic women are at greater risk from bisexual men than are white women has many possible explanations, including higher rates of bisexual behavior among Black and Hispanic men than white men (assuming predominantly intraracial sexual contact), higher rates of bisexual self-identification among Black men than white men (McKirnan, Stokes, Doll, and Burzette 1995), higher proportions of female relative to male partners and higher rates of unprotected sex with female partners among Black bisexual men (McKirnan, Stokes, Doll, and Burzette 1995), higher rates of seropositivity among bisexual Black and Hispanic men, and lower rates of infection by alternate routes among Black and Hispanic than among white women.

The degree to which Black and Latina women are at greater risk from bisexual men than white women might be even greater than indicated by the findings of the Chu and Selik studies (Chu et al. 1992; Selik, Castro, and Pappaioanou 1988). Many women are unaware of the bisexual experience of their male partners and are therefore not classified in AIDS surveillance data as having this source of risk. Black or African American and Latina women are more likely than white women to be unaware, as indicated by findings by N. S. Padian (1989) and by the McKirnan and Stokes team (McKirnan, Stokes, Doll, and Burzette 1995; Stokes, McKirnan, Doll, and Burzette 1996). The McKirnan and Stokes team found that Black bisexually active men were less likely to disclose their bisexual activity to their female partners, compared to white bisexually active men. Of those who had had female partners within the previous six months, nearly two-thirds of African American men, compared to slightly less than half of white men, reported that none of these female partners knew, before sexual contact, that they also had sex with men (61 percent versus 46 percent). When asked whether they had told their steady female partners of their same-sex activities, the racial difference was even more striking; of those with steady female partners 75 percent of African American men compared to 36 percent of white men had not told those partners; rates of nondisclosure to wives might be even higher (Earl 1990).[65] The racial difference is more than a simple one in which African American men are less likely to disclose; these figures also indicate racial differences in patterns of disclosure, with African American men less likely to tell steady partners than casual partners and white men conversely more likely to tell steady partners than casual partners. Padian's (1989) unpublished findings are even more ominous; only 20 percent of African American and 22 percent of Latina women were aware of their sex partners' bisexuality, compared to 80 percent awareness among white women.[66]

These statistics paint a grim picture of the risk to bisexual women from bisexual men. One more statistic will put this risk in perspective, however. National surveillance data indicate that among women diagnosed with AIDS who had had male in addition to female partners, i.e., behaviorally bisexual women, most infections (79 percent) could be attributed to injection drug use and not to sex with a man, whether bisexual or not (Chu, Buehler, Fleming, and Berkelman 1990).[67]

Notes

As in the rest of this volume, my focus here is on research conducted within the United States. Although I note references to research studies conducted in other countries when they bear directly on a particular point, readers who are interested in a more international perspective toward research on bisexuality and HIV are referred to two excellent anthologies: *Bisexuality and HIV/AIDS*, edited by Tielman, Carballo, and Hendricks (1991), and *Bisexualities and AIDS*, edited by Aggleton (1996).

1. The transformation from the focus on "gay" men to a focus on "gay and bisexual men," including the shift from viewing status as a risk factor to viewing behavior as a risk factor, can be seen nicely in the text of Donlou, Wolcott, Gottlieb, and Landsverk (1985). These researchers collected their data in 1982 but published in 1985. Reading the report, one observes the authors struggling to use mid 1980s language to present data collected at a time when sexual transmission routes for HIV were only beginning to be understood and when

essentialized "homosexual men" were considered a risk group. See also Shernoff and Palacios-Jimenez, who, writing in 1988, still felt the need to impress on their readers the fact that risk is caused by one's behavior, not by membership in a risk group. See Adib and Ostrow (1991) for an overview of HIV/AIDS research from 1981–1991 in which these trends are described and documented.

An exception to the absence of interest in bisexual men as bisexuals is Silvestre et al. (1986), who commented that the fact that 32 percent of their sample of "gay and bisexual men" characterized themselves as bisexual "has significant epidemiological implications" (231), although they did not explore these epidemiological implications in their report.

2. Usage of the term *homosexual/bisexual* is taken to an extreme by Singer et al. (1990), who—admittedly drawing on CDC usage at the time—referred to the "male homosexual/bisexual contact" exposure category, apparently in reference to individuals classified as having become HIV-infected via male-male sexual contact. See also Thomas and Hodges (1991) for usage of the term *homosexual/bisexual contact.*

3. Examples of research in which bisexual and gay men were not distinguished: Chuang, Devins, Hunsley, and Gill (1989) studied psychosocial distress in 65 HIV+ "gay or bisexual men" who were "homosexual and/or bisexual in orientation and practice." Kaslow et al. (1987) reported on the Multicenter AIDS Cohort Study (MACS) of nearly 5,000 "homosexual men," also described by the authors as a "prospective study in a population of homosexual or bisexual men" (311). The MACS sample (or portions of it) was also described by Phair et al. (1992) and Joseph, Adib, Koopman, and Ostrow (1990; see also O'Brien, Wortman, Kessler, and Joseph 1993) as a sample of "homosexual/bisexual men," by Kass, Faden, Fox, and Dudley (1992), Lyter et al. (1987), Silvestre et al. (1986), and Schneider, Taylor, Kemeny, and Hammen (1991) as a sample of "gay and bisexual men," and by Ostrow et al. (1989) as a sample of "homosexual men," "homosexually active men," or "homosexual or bisexual men." Kaslow et al. (1987) reported detailed information about these subjects' specific "homosexual" behaviors but made no mention of the possibility that some were also heterosexually active. The San Francisco Men's Health Study (SFMHS) utilized a systematic sample of single men aged twenty-five to fifty-five years old and included 799 "homosexual/bisexual men" and 204 "heterosexual men" (Winkelstein et al. 1987a; Winkelstein et al. 1988; Winkelstein et al. 1987b), and the San Francisco Young Men's Health Study sample of single men aged eighteen to twenty-nine included 428 who self-identified as "homosexual/bisexual or reported sexual intercourse with a male in the previous 5 years" (Osmond et al. 1994:1934). Lifson et al. (1990) referred consistently to the San Francisco City Clinic Cohort as "homosexual and bisexual men." Siegel, Bauman, Christ, and Krown (1988) studied changes in the (same-sex) sexual practices of 162 asymptomatic "gay and bisexual men." Peterson, Ostrow, and McKirnan (1991) provided a review of literature on behavior change among "homosexual/bisexual men." Stevens (1994) reported findings on a sample of "lesbian and bisexual women."

Examples of authors who distinguished between "bisexual" and "gay" subjects: Rotheram-Borus and her colleagues routinely include a breakdown of their sample by either sexual self-identity or sexual behavior along with other descriptive information about their sample, even when this distinction is irrelevant to their research questions and is not utilized in data analysis. In a report on the sexual behaviors of a sample of "homosexual and bisexual male adolescents who were predominantly Black and Hispanic" (Rotheram-Borus et al. 1994:47; see also Rotheram-Borus and Koopman 1991; Rotheram-Borus, Hunter, and Rosario 1994) recruited via a gay-identified agency in New York City, Rotheram-Borus and her colleagues reported that 69 percent labeled themselves gay, 26 percent labeled themselves bisexual, and 5 percent did not label themselves. In a study of AIDS knowledge and psychosocial characteristics including attitudes about condoms, Peterson et al. (1992) selected their 250 "gay and bisexual African-American men" aged eighteen or older on the basis of their gay or bisexual self-identities but did not report the percentages of men with each self-identity in their sample. Instead, they reported two Kinsey ratings representing sexual experiences and sexual fantasies during the previous two years. Thirty-five percent were Kinsey 1–5's based on their sexual experiences, and 47 percent were Kinsey 1–5's based on their fantasies. Only data on the respondents' same-sex activities were reported by the authors, who referred consistently to their sample as "gay and bisexual men" and included one paragraph specifically about bisexual men in which they suggested that "bisexual activity may be an important source of HIV transmission" and that bisexual men might require different intervention strategies than exclusively homosexual men. (See also Adib and Ostrow 1991. Only three years earlier in 1988, Shernoff and Palacios-Jimenez had also made the point that prevention programs should target specific audiences, but they listed "gay and bisexual men" as one of those specific audiences.) Thomas and Hodges (1991) described the "sexual preferences" of their subjects, eighteen out of ninety-one of whom had had vaginal sex in the previous twelve months, as "gay or homosexual" in 76.4 percent of cases, "bisexual" in 20.2 percent, and "heterosexual" in 2.2 percent. Twenty-three of Kooperman's (1994) "older gay and bisexual men" identified as bisexual, and 168 identified as gay, whereas 32 percent of Silvestre et al.'s (1986) Pittsburgh MACS sample characterized themselves as bisexual. Similarly, McCusker, Zapka, Stoddard, and Mayer (1989), whose selection criteria included recent homosexual activity, reported that 83 percent of their subjects were "exclusively homosexual" and 17 percent were "bisexual" in their "sexual orientation" and Westermeyer, Seppala, Gasow, and Carlson (1989) reported that the "sexual preferences" of their subjects in a study of issues that arise in treatment of homosexual and bisexual male substance abusers were "bisexual" in six cases and "homosexual" in twelve cases but did not indicate how they assessed or defined sexual preference. In none of these studies was the distinction between gay or homosexual men and bisexual men carried through into data analysis (in the case of Silvestre et al. [1986] there was no data analysis).

A few authors of reports on "gay and bisexual men" not only distinguished between their gay and bisexual subjects but provided comparisons between them. Examples include distinctions based on self-reported Kinsey scores by Ostrow et al. (1989) and distinctions made on the basis of behavior by Selik, Castro, and Pappaioanou (1988).

4. For examples of reports limited to male-male sex, see McCusker, Zapka, Stoddard, and Mayer (1989) and Peterson et al. (1992).

Siegel, Bauman, Christ, and Krown (1988) nowhere specified that they would focus only on same-sex activities, nor did they mention the sex of subjects' partners in specific sex acts, leaving the reader to assume that their data refer to male-male sex acts only. For example, they reported incidence data for "monogamy" but did not indicate whether female sex partners were included. If any of these "gay and bisexual men" were currently involved with one woman, were they classified as "monogamous" or as "celibate"? Other examples include Osmond et al. (1994), who referred to the nongender-specific anal and oral sex "partners" of their respondents, whom the reader is left to assume are all male; Thomas and Hodges (1991), who specified that the partner in one sex act was female, leaving the reader to assume that all other activities described were with male partners; Kooperman (1994), who did not specify partner gender and appeared to be operating on the assumption that the partners were male, except that his list of sex acts included "vaginal intercourse," and Westermeyer, Seppala, Gasow, and Carlson (1989), who referred to gender-unspecified "sex partners" in their text, although they also presented case material in which information about partner gender was given. Sullivan (1996) reported that 53 percent of sixty male street youths in Hollywood, California, "practiced anal or vaginal intercourse without a condom" (63), never indicating the percentages that practiced anal intercourse with male versus female partners. Stokes, Taywaditep, Vanable, and McKirnan (1996), who cited Chetwynd, Chambers, Hughes (1992); Lever et al. (1992); and Ross, Wodak, Gold, and Miller (1992), expressed surprise at the number of research reports that do not specify the sex of the partner.

5. Kramer, Aral, and Curran (1980) made this usage explicit: "Eighty-two per cent of homosexual or bisexual (hereafter referred to as 'gay') male patients were White"

(1980: 997). Kaslow et al. (1987) referred to their subjects as "homosexual men" more often than as "homosexual or bisexual men" and described recruiting the sample via the "gay press," "gay medical practices," "gay activists," etc. Siegel, Bauman, Christ, and Krown (1988) referred to their sample of "gay and bisexual men" as "gay men" and, in the introduction and discussion of their article, to "gay men" in general. Wolcott et al. (1986) likewise referred to their sample as "50 homosexual or bisexual men" in the abstract, but as "50 gay men" in the body of their article, even though 4 percent of the sample was "married." Stall, Coates, and Hoff (1988) reviewed the literature on health-related behavior among "gay and bisexual men" but were inconsistent in the use of this phrase. For example, they referred to the MACS sample as a sample of "self-identified gay men," and, with the exception of the article's title and abstract, habitually referred to "gay men." Other examples of the interchangeable use of the terms *gay and bisexual* or *homosexual and bisexual* with *gay* or *homosexual* include Valdiserri et al. (1987); McKusick, Horstman, and Coates (1985); Levin, Berger, Didona, and Duncan (1992); Quadland (1985); and Quadland and Shattls (1987). Gorman (1991), who also used both "gay and bisexual men" and "gay men," in his review of anthropological aspects of the HIV epidemic, was more cognizant than most of the implications of this terminology.

6. See Weinberg, Williams, and Pryor (1994) for discussion of this change in perspective.

7. In 1994 Carballo-Diéguez and Dolezal described usage of the term *MSM* as "popular" in "epidemiological parlance."

8. For example, Matteson (1997); Anderson and May (1992); Crawford et al. (1992); Doll and Beeker (1996); Doll et al. (1991); Earl (1990); McKirnan, Stokes, Doll, and Burzette (1995); Lifson (1992). See Doll and Beeker (1996) for a detailed discussion of the various psychosocial contexts of bisexuality and their relationship to HIV risk, with specific recommendations for intervention in four high-risk contexts: male prostitution, injecting drug use, sexual identity exploration, and racial/ethnic subcultures with particular constellations of gender roles and norms.

9. Compare to Rotheram-Borus and Koopman 1991; Rotheram-Borus, Reid, Rosario, and Kasen 1995; and Rotheram-Borus, Rosario, Reid, and Koopman 1995, in which the authors reported their respondents' sexual self-identities and three-month incidence rates for same-sex and other-sex activity and then explicitly limited the rest of the report to same-sex activity.

See also Meyer-Bahlburg et al. (1991) for detailed descriptions of both same-sex and other-sex activities of 205 HIV+ and HIV- gay and bisexual men in New York City. The numbers of female partners among the men in this sample were too small to enable researchers to provide statistically reliable comparisons of safer sex rates either between exclusively homosexual and bisexual men or between same-sex and other-sex sex acts.

10. Except in the last sentence of the article in which the researchers recommended tailoring HIV prevention programs to "each youth's sexual history" (1994:55).

11. Similarly, describing the "background and objectives" of their 1994 report on a study of homosexual and bisexual men in Amsterdam, Krijnen, van den Hoek, and Coutinho (1994) wrote, "to assess the potential role of bisexual men in the transmission of HIV to women" (24).

12. See, for examples of samples drawn from men seeking testing, Chetwynd, Chambers, and Hughes (1992); Hernandez et al. (1992); Landis, Earp, and Koch (1992); and Wood, Krueger, Pearlman, and Goldbaum (1993). For examples of samples drawn from men and women already involved in AIDS research, see Krijnen, van den Hoek, and Coutinho (1994); Ostrow et al. (1989); and Young, Weissman, and Cohen (1992). For a sample drawn from a population of injection drug users, see Ross, Wodak, Gold, and Miller (1992). For on a sample of seropositive men, see Doll et al. (1992). See, for examples of samples drawn from men already diagnosed with AIDS, Chu et al. (1992); Diaz et al. (1993); and Selik, Castro, and Pappaiaonou (1988).

13. In a review of the public health literature Sell and Petrulio (1996) found that researchers studying homosexuals, lesbians, gays, and/or bisexuals rarely discussed their conceptual definitions of sexual orientation and often relied on respondents' self-reported identities or recruitment settings to determine respondents' sexual orientations. Researchers who studied bisexuals were more likely than others (100 percent versus 80–93 percent) to describe their operational methods of identifying subjects and least likely (24 percent versus 32–53 percent) to assume subjects' sexual orientations based on recruitment setting.

14. See Stokes, Taywaditep, Vanable, and McKirnan (1996) for a discussion of methodological issues in HIV research, including sampling and generalizability issues.

15. Other exceptions are the samples used by Boulton, Hart, and Fitzpatrick (1992); Carballo-Diéguez and Dolezal (1994); Myers, Orr, Locker, and Jackson (1993); Stokes, McKirnan, and Burzette (1993); and Weatherburn et al. (1998). Matteson (1997) used a sample drawn via methods analogous to McKirnan, Stokes, Doll, and Burzette's (1995).

16. Martin and Dean (1990) tested the efficacy of multipronged sampling by drawing a sample of "gay men" in New York City via gay organizations, unsolicited volunteers who learned of the study through news reports, referrals from participants in a pilot study, gay pride festival participants, clients of sexually transmitted disease clinics, and five generations of snowballing originating with the respondents recruited by each of these five recruitment methods. They detailed the differences in the types of respondents recruited through each method and compared the overall sample to two probability samples of gay men in San Francisco (Research and Decisions Corporation 1984; Winkelstein et al. 1987a). The New York City sample resembled the two San Francisco samples in terms of race, age, and degree of closetedness. They differed most strongly on education, with 77 percent of the New York City sample but just over half of each San Francisco sample having completed four years of college or more. Martin and Dean (1990) also found that gay men recruited from STD clinics were younger, less educated, had lower annual incomes, were less likely to belong to a gay organization, and were primarily Black or Hispanic.

17. The median is the midpoint of a distribution. For example, to say that Wold et al.'s respondents had a median of seven male partners means that if all their respondents were lined up in order of the number of male partners they had had, the man in the exact center of that line would have had seven male partners; half of the respondents would be standing to his left, and half to his right, and everyone on one side would have had seven or fewer male partners whereas everyone on the other side would have had seven or more male partners.

18. The 71 percent and 47 percent figures, unlike the 65 percent reported in the previous sentence, are based on the entire (Black/white) sample and not only on those subjects whose bisexuality began at least five years prior to the study. The comparable percentage not broken down by race is 60 percent.

In an earlier research report on a small sample of men recruited via newspaper ads aimed at bisexuals, the same research team (Stokes, McKirnan, and Burzette 1993) reported almost identical results. Of thirty men who participated in a follow-up interview nine to thirteen months after the initial interview, 53 percent had not changed their self-rated sexual orientation, 40 percent had moved toward a homosexual orientation, and 7 percent had moved toward a heterosexual orientation. Sixty-two percent of the original sample of 105 men was white, and the authors indicated no significant difference in racial distribution between those who did and those who did not participate in the follow-up interview.

19. McKirnan, Stokes, Doll, and Burzette (1995) did not explicitly say that those with no male or female partners in the previous year were included in the calculation of these respective averages, but n's given in tabulated data indicate that they were.

20. They do not completely explain the difference because, doubling the adjusted means (given two paragraphs hence in the main text) for McKirnan, Stokes, Doll, and Burzette's respondents, to produce a probable overestimate of the average number of male partners these respondents would have had in a full year, yields an estimate of 10.4 male partners—still much lower than Boulton et al.'s average of twenty.

21. A more recent study of British behaviorally bisexual men produced very different findings. Weatherburn et al. (1998) found that among 745 men who had had sex with both men and women in the previous five years, 91.9 percent had had at least one male partner and 94.7 percent had had at least one female partner in the previous year. Apparently not excluding those with no partners in the previous year, the researchers found that these men had had means of 3.75 male and 3.22 female partners, and medians of two male and two female partners. At the time of the interview 71.3 percent had regular female partners, whereas 31.5 percent had regular male partners. The most dramatic difference between the Weatherburn findings and the findings of other research on behaviorally bisexual men, including both the Boulton and the McKirnan findings, is the fact that men in the Weatherburn sample were not more likely to have male than female partners and did not have more male than female partners.

22. The figures given in the text were calculated by the current author based on data published by Ekstrand et al. (1994). Ekstrand et al. presented separate data for seronegative and seropositive men. Because the sample included nearly equal numbers of seronegative and seropositive men, the average of the percentages reported for each of these two groups estimates the percentage of the overall sample. Specifically, Ekstrand et al. reported that during 1984–1985 86 percent of seropositive and 63 percent of seronegative men had multiple male partners and 7 percent of seropositive and 21 percent of seronegative men had multiple female partners, whereas during 1988–1989 58 percent of seropositive men and 51 percent of seronegative men had multiple male partners and 2 percent of seropositive men and 8 percent of seronegative men had multiple female partners.

23. In comparison, self-identified homosexual men had had 2 male and 0 female (range 0–805 and 0–3) partners and self-identified heterosexual men had had 0 male and 2 female partners (range 0–6 and 0–50) in the previous year. See Doll et al. (1992).

24. These percentages are calculations based on figures provided by Diaz et al. (1993). The authors presented percentages separately for those who had and those who had not used injected drugs; recalculation involved regaining frequencies, combining the frequencies for injecting drug users and nonusers, and calculating new percentages.

25. To the extent that the sexual cultures of racial and ethnic groups in the United States reflect the sexual cultures of Americans' countries of origin, studies of international diversity in bisexuality can shed light on racial and ethnic differences in the United States. See Aggleton (1996); Tielman, Carballo, and Hendriks (1991); and World Health Organization (1992) for descriptions of the conceptualization of sexuality and the social context of bisexual behavior in various countries.

26. This might not be true of all Asian ethnic groups; Matteson found that only 20 percent of the Chinese American, Filipino American, and Korean American men in his original sample were eliminated by a requirement that subjects have engaged in penetrative sex with both a man and a woman in the previous three years.

27. Stokes, Taywaditep, Vanable, and McKirnan (1996) found that 90 percent of behaviorally bisexual African American men, compared to 68 percent of behaviorally bisexual white men, had had anal intercourse in the previous six months, entirely the result of a difference in rates of insertive anal sex.

28. Matteson (1997); Magaña and Carrier (1991);, Almaguer (1993); Alonso and Koreck (1993); Carballo-Diéguez (1989); Carballo-Diéguez and Dolezal (1994); Carrier (1976, 1985, 1992); and Ross (1991); compare Vazquez (1979). See also Carrier (1995) on homosexuality among Mexican men, several chapters on Latinos in Aggleton (1996) and Tielman, Carballo, and Hendriks (1991), and González and Espín (1996) on various cultural factors affecting sexuality in Latino cultures.

29. Matteson (1997), for example, found that some of his Filipino American, Chinese American, and Korean American respondents restricted themselves to either the receptive or the insertive role and adopted either feminine or masculine gender styles accordingly.

30. See Manalansan (1996) for descriptions of Black, Asian, and Latin sexual cultures with a focus on the implications for the practice and cultural role of bisexuality.

31. Evidence of higher rates of bisexuality in men of these cultures is reviewed in chapter 11 of this volume and include the NHSLS finding of an insignificantly higher rate of same-sex behavior among Blacks than whites (Laumann, Gagnon, Michael, and Michaels 1994); Billy, Tanfer, Grady, Klepinger's (1993) finding that same-sex experience, exclusively same-sex experience, and bisexual experience are more common among Hispanic than non-Hispanic men; and Binson et al.'s (1995) finding that among MSM higher percentages of Black men than of white and Hispanic men have also had sex with women. Findings by Kumar and Ross (1991) indicate that among MSM the proportion who also have sex with women is higher among Asian Indian men than among Australian men. In their classic study Bell and Weinberg (1978) found that 74 percent of white "homosexual" men, compared to 62 percent of Black "homosexual" men, described their current behavior as exclusively homosexual and that whites were less likely to have had female sex partners (14 percent versus 22 percent) in the previous year or in their lifetimes (64 percent versus 73 percent).

Kramer, Aral, and Curran (1980) analyzed records of all men and women attending the Columbus Health Department STD Clinic in 1977. Among the subjects were 1,107 "homosexual or bisexual" men, and of these 47 percent of the Black men and 27 percent of the white men "classified themselves as bisexual" (997). The authors did not indicate the basis on which these men were classified as homosexual or bisexual, nor did they give the wording of the question in response to which some men classified themselves as bisexual, although Chu et al. (1992) either knew or assumed that the men were classified on the basis of their sexual contacts. Kramer, Aral, and Curran's finding occurred within the context of their broader finding that 17.5 percent of whites were "homosexual/bisexual" as compared to 6.0 percent of Blacks. Thus, whites were more likely than Blacks to be "homosexual/bisexual," but among "homosexual/bisexuals" Blacks were more likely than whites to classify themselves as bisexual. The fact that Kramer, Aral, and Curran's (1980) findings conflict with national probability samples in which Blacks have higher rates of same-gender experience than whites is probably the result of the specific population being sampled. Note that the figures 17.5 percent and 6.0 percent do not appear in Kramer, Aral, and Curran's article. The article presents the percentage of homosexual or bisexual men who are white/Black rather than the reverse. Fortunately the authors provided the cell frequencies so that their percentages could be reversed.

In Doll et al.'s (1992) study of seropositive men who had ever had sex with other men, Hispanics were less likely than Blacks and whites to have had a male sex partner in the year prior to participation in the study (66 percent versus 76–78 percent), and Blacks were most likely to have had a female partner during that year (48 percent versus 33–36 percent).

32. Centers for Disease Control data showing higher proportions of bisexually active men among Latinos and Blacks than whites were also reported by the Centers for Disease Control (1990) and by Rogers and Williams (1987). The number of cases in Selik, Castro, and Pappaioanou's (1988) study is 50,830 and the number in Chu et al.'s (1992) study is 65,389. Information was gathered from completed CDC AIDS case report forms that included questions about sexual relations with male and female partners since 1977.

In the Chu study, among men of all racial/ethnic groups with AIDS who had had sex with men since 1977 the proportion who had also had sex with women had increased slightly over time, from 23 percent in 1983 to 26 percent in 1989, and increased with age after age thirty. The authors noted that the increase over time could be a statistical artifact resulting from question wording; those whose AIDS cases were reported more recently had had a longer time period since 1977 within which to acquire both same- and other-sex experience. If not an artifact, this finding that the proportion of bisexuals with AIDS increased over time might be evidence of the lesser effectiveness of HIV educational efforts in reaching bisexual than gay men. Artifact or not, in light of the Chu research team's inclusion of two and a half more recent years' worth of PWAs, this pattern—plus the different lower age boundaries used by the two sets of researchers—might partially explain the higher rates of bisexual behavior in each racial/ethnic group found in the Chu study (1992) compared to the Selik study (1988).

33. Several studies also explored rates of sex with anonymous partners, injection drug use, and exchanging sex for money or drugs. Doll et al. (1992) reported that 7 percent of bisexual self-identified men, compared to 2 percent of homosexual self-identified and 27 percent of heterosexual self-identified men, had had oral or anal sex with an anonymous male partner in the previous year. Weinberg et al. (1994) reported that self-identified bisexuals had had more anonymous sex partners than heterosexuals; bisexual men had had fewer than gay men and bisexual women had had more than lesbians.

Among behaviorally bisexual men McKirnan, Stokes, Doll, and Burzette (1995) found that 25 percent had received money or money plus drugs in exchange for sex from a man during their lifetime (compared to 11 percent from a female partner, 8.5 percent to a male partner, and 9 percent to a female partner) and 15 percent had done so in the previous six months. Among Latinos Carballo-Diéguez and Dolezal (1994) found that 88 percent of MSM who identified as "drag queens," compared to 74 percent of "straights," 58 percent of "bisexuals," and 16 percent of "gays," had been paid for sex in the previous twelve months. The strong correlation between sexual self-identity and the exchange of sex for money among Latinos was due to the fact that those who did not identify as gay considered payment their motivation for same-sex activity.

Several studies show injection drug use to be higher among bisexual than homosexual men. Diaz et al. (1993), reporting the results of a research group also including Susan Y. Chu, found that among men with AIDS diagnoses bisexual men (defined as men who had had sex with both men and women in the previous five years) were more likely than homosexual men (12 percent versus 6 percent, $p < 0.05$) to have injected drugs in the previous five years and more likely than either homosexual or heterosexual men to have exchanged money for sex. Among noninjection drug users 13 percent of bisexuals, compared to 10 percent of homosexuals and 37 percent of heterosexuals, had paid money or drugs for sex; 9 percent, 4 percent, and 3 percent, respectively, had received money for sex. Subjects in this sample were recruited from PWA populations served by state and local health departments in collaboration with the CDC. See also Chu et al. (1992) for a finding that bisexual men with AIDS are twice as likely as homosexual men to report use of intravenous drugs. When defined by sexual self-identity, bisexual men also appear more likely to use injection drugs than gay men. Wood, Krueger, Pearlman, and Goldbaum (1993) found that, in a sample of men seeking HIV testing, 20 percent of the self-identified bisexual men, as compared to 11 percent of the self-identified gay men and 34 percent of the self-identified heterosexual men, had used injection drugs. See also Ross, Wodak, Gold, and Miller (1992) for detailed statistics on the incidence of specific HIV risk practices associated with drug use among behaviorally homosexual, bisexual, and heterosexual men and women in Australia.

Higher rates of drug use among bisexuals than among gay men does not necessarily mean that bisexuality causes drug use; it could, conversely, reflect higher rates of bisexuality among drug users who, in connection with their drug use, engage in more sex in general than nonusers. For example, Wood, Krueger, Pearlman, and Goldbaum (1993) found that (bisexual) male injection drug users reported having five (two) times the average number of female partners in the previous year than did (bisexual) nonusers, a finding consistent with the interpretation that drug use might lead to greater sexual activity in general, or greater other-sex activity in particular, and hence to higher rates of bisexual behavior. Also supporting this interpretation, in a nonprobability sample of 427 incarcerated male adolescents in New York City Kang, Magura, and Shapiro (1994) discovered that current cocaine/crack use was correlated with a number of sociopathological indicators and with more frequent heterosexual sex as well as homosexuality/bisexuality. Both studies are also consistent with the possibility that both drug use and bisexual behavior reflect an underlying willingness to defy social conventions.

Findings that illicit drug use is more prevalent among women who have had sex with other women—although not necessarily more prevalent among bisexual than lesbian women—are presented later in this chapter; findings that illicit drug use might be more prevalent among bisexual prostitutes than other prostitutes are presented in chapter 17; findings that bisexuality might be more prevalent among illicit drug users are presented in note 59 of chapter 11.

34. These findings can be compared to those of Chetwynd, Chambers, and Hughes (1992) in Auckland and Ross, Wodak, Gold, and Miller (1992) in Australia. For example, among 1,245 injection drug users Ross, Wodak, Gold, and Miller found that "sexual HIV risk behaviours were lowest for homosexual men, intermediate for bisexual men, and highest for heterosexual men in the case of condom use: however, for numbers of partners, seroprevalence, and anal sex the trends were reversed" (139). The authors provided detailed data regarding sexual practices, sex partners, drug use, and condom use for heterosexual, bisexual, and homosexual men as defined by the sex of their sex partners over the past five years.

Wood, Krueger, Pearlman, and Goldbaum (1993) reported that among 451 HIV seronegative men who had had sex with both men and women in the previous year, 277 identified as bisexual and "these bisexual men reported always using condoms only 12 percent of the time, and 30 percent reported never using condoms" (1758). The authors provided neither tabulated data nor information about assessment that would allow the reader to deduce whether this comment refers to male, female, or male and female partners or what the authors meant by "always using condoms 12 percent of the time." However, slightly later in the article the authors stated that "men who have sex with men, both HIV seropositive and seronegative, had a low rate of consistent condom use during vaginal sex (12 percent)" (1758), and the current author wonders whether this is the same 12 percent as previously reported.

35. In the Doll et al. (1992) study both simple and adjusted rates indicate that bisexuals have lower rates of unprotected sex than homosexuals; Stokes, Taywaditep, Vanable, and McKirnan (1996), who reviewed research on this issue, including research done in Australia and New Zealand, cited two other studies in which simple rates of condom use indicated lower rates of unprotected sex among bisexual than homosexual men (Hood et al. 1994; Ross, Wodak, Gold, and Miller 1992) and two studies in which adjusting for the percentage of men who had actually had anal sex produced the opposite finding, that bisexual men have higher rates of unprotected sex (Chetwynd, Chambers, and Hughes 1992; Kippax, Crawford, Rodden, and Benton 1994)

36. Heckman et al. (1995) also asked respondents to indicate the strength of their intentions to use condoms in their next sexual encounter. When describing their results, they reported that men who had been behaviorally bisexual during the previous two months had weaker intentions to use condoms in the future than did men who had been exclusively homosexual. Indeed, in the accompanying table the average score for bisexuals is higher than that for exclusive homosexuals and a footnote indicates that "lower values indicate stronger intentions." That is, in fact, how the measure of intention was originally scored, but when the authors initially presented this measure they stated that scoring on the measure was reversed such that higher scores indicated stronger intentions. Although this finding would be very useful and relevant, it is not reported in the main text here because of this ambiguity.

Findings by Kalichman, Roffman, Picciano, and Bolan (1998) can be usefully compared to Heckman et al.'s (1995) findings. The Kalichman subjects were men who had had three instances of unprotected sex with men within the previous three months, with bisexuals defined as those who had also had sex with a female partner during the previous year. Rates of unprotected sex in the previous four weeks, apparently unadjusted for four-week incidence of sexual contacts, indicate that homosexual and bisexual men did not differ in the number of instances of unprotected anal intercourse with male partners (2.6 versus 3.2, n.s.) but that homosexual men reported more instances of unprotected oral intercourse with male partners (12.6 versus 11.0). The two groups did not differ in the percentage of their oral or anal sex acts with male partners that were protected. Stokes, Vanable, and McKirnan (1997) reported higher rates of unprotected receptive anal sex among MSMO than among MSMW.

In his research on Asian American men Matteson (1997) reported that bisexuals were more likely to have engaged in risky sex than gay men, although he did not fully present the data underlying this conclusion.

37. The use of self-reported rates of condom use raises the question of respondent honesty. Thirteen percent of Rotheram-Borus et al.'s subjects reported "always" using a condom in sex with a male. In comparison, 34 percent reported that their male partners always use condoms. Although Rotheram-Borus et al. (1994) did not comment on the inconsistency between subjects' reports of their own and their partners' rates of condom use, one wonders whether a sample of these individuals' partners would provide a converse, or an identical, estimate of their own and their partners' rates of condom usage. In other words, do Rotheram-Borus et al.'s subjects really demand condom use of their partners more often than they use condoms themselves, or are these self-reported data affected by a tendency on the part of these respondents to either underestimate their own condom use or to overestimate their partners' condom use?

Incidentally, respondents were just as likely to report "always" using a condom in sex with a female (13 percent) as with a male partner. Similarly, Wood, Krueger, Pearlman, and Goldbaum (1993), based on a sample of men seeking HIV testing, reported that 12 percent of men who had had sex with men consistently used condoms during vaginal sex.

38. This point was not made by Rotheram-Borus et al. (1994). The last two percentages reported were obtained via the current author's recalculations of data presented by Rotheram-Borus et al.

39. Stokes, McKirnan, and Burzette (1993) reported that 16 percent of self-described bisexuals had had unprotected insertive or receptive anal sex with a male partner in the previous six months and that 38 percent had had unprotected insertive or receptive oral sex with a male partner in the previous six months. Although it is tempting to compare these findings to those of McKirnan, Stokes, Doll, and Burzette (1995) and conclude that unadjusted rates of unprotected sex with male partners are lower among men who are bisexual by self-identity than among men who are behaviorally bisexual—possibly because of lower rates of same-sex activity—this interpretation is challenged by higher rates of unprotected anal sex found among self-identified bisexuals by Doll et al. (1992; 62 percent in the previous year) and by Ekstrand et al. (1994; baseline 1984–1985 rates of 65–89 percent).

40. These figures were calculated by the current author based on McKirnan, Stokes, Doll, and Burzette's (1995) reported rates of each behavior and rates of condom use in the entire sample.

41. Of 105 men who responded to a newspaper ad soliciting "bisexual" men "to be interviewed as part of a study of men's social and sexual behavior," Stokes, McKirnan, and Burzette (1993:204) reported that 47 percent of those who had had vaginal intercourse in the past month said that they had used condoms every time they had vaginal intercourse, compared to rates of invariable condom use of 78 percent (71 percent) among those who had had receptive (insertive) anal intercourse with a male partner, 0 percent among those who had had anal intercourse with a female partner, and 22 percent (24 percent) among those who had had receptive (insertive) oral sex with a male partner, and—a behavior not reported by McKirnan, Stokes, Doll, and Burzette (1995)—6 percent among those who had had insertive oral sex with a female partner.

42. Boulton, Hart, and Fitzpatrick (1992) reported that 30 percent of British behaviorally bisexual men had had unprotected penetrative sex with a male partner in the previous year (38 percent of those who had had a male sex partner during that year) and 57 percent had had unprotected penetrative sex with a female partner in the previous year (77 percent of those who had had a female sex partner during that year). Using a sample of MSM from the

Boston area, Wold et al. (1998) found that 25.5 percent of men who had been behaviorally bisexual during the previous six months had had anal sex with male partners without a condom, whereas 42.6 percent had had vaginal sex without a condom. Kalichman, Roffman, Picciano, and Bolan (1998) reported that behaviorally bisexual men had had more instances and higher rates of unprotected oral and anal sex with male than female partners, but these findings artifactually reflect that only men who reported having had at least three instances of unprotected sex with men during the previous three months were included in the study.

43. Citing an earlier report by Ekstrand, Coates, Lang, and Guydish (1989) in comparison to three other studies and their own data, Boulton, Hart, and Fitzpatrick (1992) also concluded that bisexual men have changed their behavior vis-à-vis male, but not female, partners: "In an early analysis of data on 58 bisexual men in the San Francisco Men's Health study, Ekstrand, Coates, Lang, and Guydish (1989) found that only a very small proportion (5 percent) engaged in unprotected vaginal sex. However, two more recent studies carried out in the UK (Fitzpatrick, Hart, and Boulton 1989; Fitzpatrick, Boulton, and Hart 1989) and Australia (Bennett, Chapman, and Bray 1989) found that unprotected vaginal sex was the common practice amongst bisexual men. This study provides further evidence that the shift to safer sex which has occurred with male partners has not occurred to the same extent with female partners. Virtually all the men who had female partners had penetrative sex with them and two-thirds had unprotected penetrative sex. Nevertheless, the proportion always using condoms with their female partners was higher in this study than in a study of men attending an STD clinic, where less than 10 percent of men always used condoms (Sonnex et al. 1989)" (172).

44. Among seropositive self-identified bisexual men, rates of unprotected anal sex began higher and dropped lower (89 percent to 18 percent) than among seronegative men, and rates of unprotected vaginal sex began lower and dropped to negligible levels (16 percent to 2 percent). In addition to the fact that behavior changes occurred among both seronegative and seropositive men, these figures indicate that men who subsequently became seropositive initially engaged in more unprotected same-sex behavior than men who remained seronegative, a factor that undoubtedly contributed to their seropositivity. They also indicate that seropositive men made more dramatic strides toward safer sex practices than seronegative men.

Although these findings suggest that seropositive men's more dramatic behavioral changes were motivated by their discovery or knowledge of their seropositivity, the authors reported that "previous analyses have shown that knowledge of antibody status did not influence risk behaviors in this cohort" (916). These analyses can be found in Coates, Ekstrand, Kegeles, and Stall (1989).

Compare Ekstrand et al.'s (1994) findings of dramatic change in rates of unprotected sex to those of Landis, Earp, and Koch (1992). Landis, Earp, and Koch's sample consisted of 235 men and women tested at two anonymous HIV testing sites in North Carolina. Their primary research goal was the assessment of behavioral change between the initial assessment, which took place subsequent to testing but prior to learning test results, and the follow-up assessment one year later. They found very little behavior change in numbers of sex partners, condom use, and rates of other safer sex practices. Landis, Earp, and Koch (1992) reported data on rates of condom use comparatively for anal, vaginal, and oral sexual contact, but because these authors did not differentiate rates for male and female subjects nor for male and female partners—factors that, according to other research, are associated with substantial differences in rates of condom use—the findings are of limited utility to the question of whether safer sex is practiced with male or with female partners.

45. The National Survey of Men, a representative sample of men aged twenty to thirty-nine, also provided data regarding demographic, including racial and ethnic, differences in condom use. Because these findings were not cross-tabulated with sexual orientation or partner gender (only 41 of 2,607 respondents were "bisexual or homosexual"), they are not reported in the current volume, but the interested reader is referred to a report by Tanfer,

Grady, Klepinger, and Billy (1993). Briefly, condom use increased with education, especially among white men, decreased with age, and was higher among single men, even those with regular partners, than among married or cohabiting men. The study found that Hispanics were more likely to use condoms than men of other racial or ethnic groups; the authors asserted that this reflects their higher rates of participation in risky sexual behaviors. Consistent with other researchers' findings that behavioral bisexuality is more prevalent among Blacks than whites, Tanfer, Grady, Klepinger, and Billy reported that Blacks were more likely than whites to use condoms (38 percent versus 25 percent) and twice as likely as whites to use condoms for both birth control and STD prevention, whereas whites were three times more likely than Blacks to use condoms only for birth control.

46. However, Boulton, Hart, and Fitzpatrick (1992) cited Fitzpatrick et al. (1990) for a finding of no difference in condom use among men with regular versus casual female partners.

47. Matteson (1997), who cited Albrecht et al. (1989); DiClemente (1987); Strunin (1991); and Horan and DiClemente (1993).

48. Findings by O'Brien, Wortman, Kessler, and Joseph (1993) shed a different light on the relationship between social connections and safer sex. Contrary to expectations, they found that "gay and bisexual" men who felt a high degree of validation, i.e., feeling that others would accept one for oneself, showed less decrease in risky sexual behaviors over time than men who felt less validated. The authors of this study, which began in 1984, suggested that those men who first adopted safer sex practices were, at the time, pioneers who were instrumental in promoting safer sex norms. Prior to the acceptance of these new norms by others, these men might not have felt a great deal of validation for their beliefs and practices, thus producing a negative correlation between feelings of validation and increased safer sex. The authors suggested that this correlation might be altering as safer sex becomes normative in the gay community.

49. Matteson hypothesized that the process of acculturation to white gay culture for Asian Americans might involve both an introduction to anal penetrative sex and an introduction to gay community norms regarding the practice of safer sex. Whereas the first might increase risky behavior among Asian Americans, the latter would offset that increase. Matteson's (1997) study has been criticized for small sample size and sampling biases (Chng, Wong, and Chen 1997; Hagland 1997).

See Sandfort (1995) for a review of research findings on the relationship between unsafe sex and acceptance of one's homosexuality, openness, and gay community involvement. For pertinent findings based on samples of men in the U.S., see Emmons et al. (1986) and Siegel, Mesagno, Chen, and Christ (1989).

50. The notion of bisexuals living in sexual "social contexts" is attributable to Gagnon (1989).

51. Among members of the bisexual community in San Francisco Weinberg, Williams, and Pryor (1994) found much higher rates of STDs than among heterosexuals and homosexuals recruited via similar community networks. Three-quarters (77 percent) of bisexual men, compared to 46 percent of heterosexual men and 73 percent of homosexual men, and 61 percent of bisexual women, compared to 45 percent of heterosexual women and 37 percent of homosexual women, had ever had an STD. About a quarter of bisexual men and women had had STDs four times or more, compared to 8 percent of heterosexual women and 2 percent of heterosexual men.

Tables summarizing research on HIV seropositivity rates in several countries compiled by Boulton (1991) and Stokes, Taywaditep, Vanable, and McKirnan (1996) show that bisexuals generally have lower seropositivity rates than homosexual men in most Pattern I countries. For example, Ross, Wodak, Gold, and Miller (1992) found that seropositivity rates were 35 percent among homosexual men, 12 percent among bisexual men, and 3 percent among heterosexual men in Australia. In exception to the general pattern, Lemp et al. (1994) found insignificantly higher seropositivity rates among self-reported bisexual (11.1 percent) than homosexual (9.5 percent) men in San Francisco and Berkeley, and Wold et al. (1998)

found no difference in seropositivity rates between men who had had sex with both men and women during the previous six months and men who had only had sex with men.

52. Some data to the contrary exist. Among women participating in an AIDS research program (see note 60 in this chapter), Young, Weissman, and Cohen (1992) found that women who had had female sex partners were less, not more, likely to be seropositive than women who had not had female sex partners (15 percent versus 10 percent).

Bevier, Chiasson, Heffernan, and Castro (1995) also pointed out that national survey data indicate that 2–4 percent of women are lesbian or bisexual, whereas such women represented only 2 percent of female AIDS cases as of September 1989 (also Chu et al. 1990). Although this would apparently indicate that the overall incidence of AIDS among lesbian and bisexual women is lower than among heterosexual women—a conclusion contradicted by Bevier, Chiasson, Heffernan, and Castro's own findings—the difference might be due to different criteria for classifying women as "lesbian and bisexual."

53. Bevier, Chiasson, Heffernan, and Castro (1995) found no significant differences in the overall seropositivity rates of white (3.0 percent), Black (2.4 percent), and Hispanic (0.0 percent) WSW, although this lack of significance might have been due to small numbers of women.

54. Stevens (1994), citing SFDPH (1993b).

55. Studies of injection drug using populations, for example, the National AIDS Demonstration Research Project, have found that even among illicit drug users WSW have higher rates of other risk factors than exclusively heterosexual women (Stevens 1994, who also cited Case et al. 1988 and Ross et al. 1991) and WSW have higher seropositivity rates than exclusively heterosexual women (Friedman 1992; Friedman et al. 1992; Young, Weissman, and Cohen 1992).

56. See note 33 in this chapter.

57. Rila (1996) noted that there have only been two reported cases of female-to-female transmission of HIV (i.e., only two cases in which the newly infected woman had no other risk factors), that Raiteri, Fora, and Sinicco (1994) studied eighteen serologically mixed lesbian couples and found that none of the seronegative partners seroconverted after six months despite high-risk sexual contacts within the couples, and that Cohen, Marmor, Wolfe, and Ribble (1993) searched for evidence of female-to-female transmission and found none.

58. Weinberg, Williams, and Pryor (1994) found that bisexual women have higher rates of STDs than either heterosexual or homosexual women. See note 51 in this chapter for details.

59. McCombs et al.'s (1992) sample consisted of 15,685 women who visited clinics in 1989–1991, 3.3 percent of whom had had sex with another woman since 1978. Of these, 92 percent had also had sex with men since 1978 and were defined by the authors as bisexual. The proportion of "bisexuals" among WSW in general was lower among subjects recruited from women's health clinics than among those recruited from STD clinics (77.8 percent versus 95.0 percent).

60. Young, Weissman, and Cohen (1992) studied 711 women who were participants in the Association for Women's AIDS Research and Education (AWARE) research program on drug use and sexual behavior in San Francisco and Alameda counties in California. That study also found a rate of 11 percent seropositivity among self-identified heterosexual women. In addition to Young, Weissman, and Cohen (1992), see Rila (1996) for methodological details.

61. All these figures are recalculations based on data presented by Einhorn and Polgar (1994), who reported that 13 percent of 922 lesbians and 42 percent of 71 bisexuals had had sex with a known or presumed gay or bisexual man, and that 3 percent of lesbians compared to 13 percent of bisexuals had had sex with a male IVDU. Subtracting the 47 percent (n = 433) of lesbians and 10 percent (n = 7) of bisexuals who had not had sex with a man, recalculation of these percentages produces the figures given in the text.

62. Lemp et al. (1995) also found no significant difference in drug use between self-identified lesbian and bisexual women, possibly because of small numbers of IVDUs in their community-based sample.

63. To the extent that lesbians do perceive themselves as at risk, bisexual women are sometimes accused of being the sources of that risk—a paradoxical mirror of the blame placed on bisexuals for spreading HIV from gay men to heterosexuals (Danzig 1990).

64. Krijnen, van den Hoek, and Coutinho (1994) reported that AIDS registration data show that of seventy-three female PWAs reported in Amsterdam as of July 1993, twenty-eight had been infected through heterosexual contact, five of whose male partners were bisexual, for a rate of 6.8 percent.

65. Earl (1990) did not provide a breakdown by race, but in a sample of seventy-nine men recruited from sites of anonymous sexual activity, 68 percent of whom were white and 12.6 percent of whom were married, only 14.3 percent of the married men had "informed their female sex partner(s) of the risk to which they had been exposed." In comparison, 58 percent of a cohort of fifty gay and bisexual men "reported sharing their HIV status with their partners" (254).

66. In a study of 138 seropositive men, 75 percent of whom were Hispanic and all of whom were recruited in a clinic waiting room in Los Angeles, Marks, Richardson, and Maldonado (1991) found no ethnic (Hispanic versus non-Hispanic) difference in rates of disclosure. Ninety percent of the men identified as homosexual or bisexual, but the authors did not present seropositivity data broken down by sexual orientation or by sex of the sex partner. However, rates of disclosure among bisexual men were not significantly different for partners in vaginal intercourse as compared to anal intercourse.

67. In comparison, among exclusively homosexual women, who by definition had not had male partners, thus eliminating sex with at-risk men as a source of infection, 93 percent of AIDS cases were attributed to injection drug use and 7 percent to blood transfusions.

8
Coming Out and Coming of Age

23

The Biology, Psychology, Sociology, and Sexuality of Bisexuality

Paula C. Rodríguez Rust

THE growing inclusion of bisexuals in HIV research and growing awareness of the existence of bisexuality and its relevance to research on sexuality in general have led to an increasing mention of bisexuality in non-HIV research.[1] In some of this research, however, as was the case in much mid to late 1980s HIV research, bisexuals are not distinguished from gay men or lesbians.[2] In some studies this is because the reference to bisexuality merely constitutes an acknowledgment that, given the sample selection methods, some respondents might be or are bisexual rather than gay or lesbian—a fact that was equally true though unacknowledged in most earlier research on "lesbian" and "gay" samples.[3] In other studies it is because the term *bisexual* was added as if to a grocery list, without any thought given to the changes in the author's argument that would ensue from the actual and purposeful inclusion of bisexuals.[4] This practice might reflect growing fashionability of the phrase "lesbian, gay, and bisexual"—or, in what is colloquially referred to as alphabet soup style, "LGB" or "LGBT" (*T* = "transgender")—instead of "lesbian and gay" as a way to describe the sexual orientation minority population, and it adds little to our knowledge of bisexuality. Some authors and editors have shown a sincere interest in being inclusive of bisexuality in more than name, but the dearth of information about bisexuality has proven to be an impediment. For example, in the introduction to *Beyond Tolerance: Gays, Lesbians, and Bisexuals on Campus* Nancy J. Evans commented that she and her coeditor developed an "unanticipated concern" when they noticed that few of the chapters submitted to them paid more than lip service to bisexuality. To help compensate for this neglect of bisexuality, they included a chapter focusing specifically on bisexuality, which, at eight pages, is the shortest chapter in the book.

But the number of studies in which bisexuality is not only acknowledged but taken seriously is slowly climbing. In addition to journal articles and chapters in books on sexuality, several book-length works focusing on bisexuality in the social sciences and humanities have been published since 1990, including *Bisexuality and HIV/AIDS: A Global Perspective*, edited by Rob Tielman, Manuel Carballo, and Aart Hendriks (1991), *Bisexuality in the Ancient World*, by Eva Cantarella (1992), a new edition of *The Bisexual Option*, by Fritz Klein (1993), *Dual Attraction: Understanding Bisexuality*, by Martin S. Weinberg, Colin J. Williams, and Douglas W. Pryor (1994), *Vice Versa: Bisexuality and the Eroticism of Everyday Life*, by Marjorie Garber (1995), *Bisexuality and the Challenge to Lesbian Politics: Sex, Loyalty, and Revolution*, by Paula C. Rust (1995), *Bisexuality: The Psychology and Politics of an Invisible Minority*, edited by Beth Firestein (1996), *RePresenting Bisexualities: Subjects and Cultures of Fluid Desire*, edited by Donald E. Hall and Maria Pramaggiore (1996), *Hybrid: Bisexuals, Multiracials, and Other Misfits Under American Law*, by Ruth Colker (1996), *Bisexualities and AIDS: International Perspectives*, edited by Peter Aggleton (1996), *Lesbian and Bisexual Identities: Constructing Communities, Constructing Selves*, by Kristin G. Esterberg (1997), *Bisexual Characters in Film: From Anaïs to Zee*, by Wayne M. Bryant (1997), *The Bisexual Imaginary: Representation, Identity, and Desire*, edited by Phoebe Davidson, Jo Eadie, Clare Hemmings, Ann Kaloski, and Merl Storr (1997), *Bisexualities: The Ideology and Practice of Sexual Contact with Both Men and Women*, edited by Erwin J. Haeberle and Rolf Gindorf (1998), and *Sexual Pathways: Adapting to Dual Sexual Attraction*, by Mark J. K. Williams (1999).[5] From these studies we can learn something about bi-biology, bi-psychology, bi-sociology, as well as bi-sexuality— but, most of all, we learn how much we have yet to find out about bisexuality.

Bisexuality and Biology

Research on biology and sexual orientation is generally driven by the desire to pinpoint a biological cause for sexual orientation. Although researchers have sought a biological cause for more than a hundred years, the motivations underpinning this research have changed over time. Much early research was driven by a desire to find a "cure" for homosexuality. In contrast, the modern wave of biological research is more often driven by the hope that the discovery that sexual orientation is inborn, not chosen, will lead to greater tolerance for homosexuality and bisexuality (De Cecco and Parker 1995a, 1995b). This hope is in keeping with the ethnicization of the modern lesbian and gay movement and, in fact, many researchers who have contributed to the modern wave of biological research are self-identified gay men and lesbians.[6] Like many gay and lesbian activists, these researchers reason that if sexual orientation is a matter of biology then sexual orientation becomes analogous to race, with the implication that individuals cannot be blamed for their sexual orientation and should not be disliked or discriminated against for it. Ironically, some contemporary homophobes, like early scientists, also hope for evidence that sexual orientation is biologically based so that a biological cure can be found. Because both sides in this political struggle have imbued biological research findings with moral meaning, the popular media tend to seize on these findings, proclaiming over and over that new research has "proven" that homosexuality is biologically caused.[7]

These media reports gloss over what scientists in this area know; that biological research on sexual orientation does not actually test the question of whether there is a biological factor in the etiology of sexual orientation. Instead, most of this research seeks to detect either biological differences between people of different sexual orientations or to determine whether sexual orientation tends to run in families. If biology were a factor in determining sexual orientation, we would expect to find such biological differences and familial patterns, but the converse is not true. First, biological differences—with the notable exception of chromosomal differences—could be a consequence of sexual orientation rather than a cause. As Bailey (1995) incisively pointed out, "There must be relevant brain differences between . . . people who have learned the quadratic theorem and [people who have not]" (104), because memory recall, like all behavior, must ultimately be grounded in brain states; this does not mean that some people are born knowing the theorem. Second, as Anne Fausto-Sterling and Evan Balaban (1993) pointed out, any causal connection between genetics and sexual orientation might be indirect. For example, a gene influencing the tendency for siblings to psychologically identify with each other could produce concordance along a number of traits, including sexual orientation and other socially significant characteristics. Third, familial patterns could be due to environmental similarities rather than biological similarities. For example, siblings raised together not only have some genetic, and therefore biological, similarity, but are also raised in similar environments; any similarity among them in sexual orientation might result from either factor. Angela M. L. Pattatucci and Dean H. Hamer (1995) pointed out that "last names and religious affiliation run in families but are not genetic" (417). Even studies of monozygotic (identical) twins raised apart would be subject to this criticism; because of intracultural consistencies in the way people tend to react to others' physical appearances, twins' similar physical appearances might lead to similar treatment even if they are raised in different families. These and other issues pertinent to the biological study of sexual orientation are discussed at length in several comprehensive reviews of the literature written by researchers active in this field.[8]

Much research on the biological differences between people of different sexual orientations is based on the assumption that gay men are "like women" and lesbians are "like men" (cf. the concepts of androphilia and gynephilia).[9] Thus, the biological characteristics most frequently studied are those already known to differentiate males and females and believed to underlie sex-differentiated sexual role behavior, such as pre- and postnatal levels of androgens and estrogens, chromosomes, and brain structures. This assumption dates back to the concept of homosexuality as inversion and has been criticized by several authors who point out that much of this research has confused sexual role behavior with the gendered attractions considered definitive of sexual orientation in Anglo culture.[10] It also imposes a heterosexual construction on homosexuality by assuming that people can only sexually desire members of their own sex if they are themselves cross-sexed; in other words, the desire itself is still heterosexual. Bailey (1995), who provided a carefully worded nonheterosexist explanation of the logic behind neuroendocrine research into sex-typed bases for sexual orientation, nevertheless revealed the heterosexism of the genre when, two pages later, he referred to the process by which heterosexual men and lesbians come to be attracted to women by the standard term *masculinization* (109).

In keeping with the hypothesis that same-sex behavior is caused by cross-sexed biology, bisexuals would be expected to fall between homosexuals and heterosexuals in terms of their biological sex characteristics (Snyder, Weinrich, and Pillard 1994; Bailey 1995; Garber 1995). However, as in research on other topics, in most biological research bisexuals are either ignored or grouped with lesbians and gay men, despite considerable awareness among recent researchers of the complexity of sexuality and the existence of bisexuality. For example, in a study that received widespread popular attention in 1991 for allegedly having discovered a biological basis for sexual orientation, Simon LeVay reported a difference in the size of INAH-3 nuclei in the hypothalami of homosexual as compared to heterosexual men.[11] LeVay, whose detailed criticisms of his own study and cautious interpretation of the finding escaped most popular news reports, grouped his one bisexual subject with his homosexual subjects.[12]

Dean H. Hamer and colleagues (1993a) conducted an analysis of the DNA of gay men and their families, producing some of the most compelling findings to date on the possibility of a genetic factor in the etiology of sexual orientation. Nevertheless, these authors used the opportunity to note that sexual orientation is unlikely to have a single cause and is likely the result of complex genetic, biological, and environmental factors, a view articulated in the 1960s by Milton Diamond (1965) and accepted by most researchers in the field today. Unfortunately, the Hamer study yielded no information on the possibility of a genetic basis for bisexuality as distinct from heterosexuality and homosexuality; finding that 90 percent of subjects and their family members scored themselves as Kinsey 0's, 1's, 5's, or 6's on scales measuring self-identification, sexual attraction, fantasy, and behavior, the researchers deemed it appropriate to treat sexual orientation as dimorphic for their purposes and classified bisexuals with heterosexuals as "nonhomosexuals."

Studies of concordance rates between lesbians and gay men and their siblings also provide evidence consistent with a genetic factor. In a series of studies J. Michael Bailey and colleagues found that 20–25 percent of the brothers of gay men are gay, compared to 4–6 percent of the brothers of heterosexual men. However, after initially distinguishing bisexuals from homosexuals and heterosexuals among their subjects (i.e., "probands") and among the probands' twin and adopted siblings, J. Michael Bailey and Richard C. Pillard (1991; see also Bailey and Benishay 1993) grouped bisexuals with homosexuals for the purpose of assessing rates of sexual orientation concordance between subjects and their siblings, so again no information about bisexuality can be extracted from the findings. However appropriate or necessary it might have been to group bisexuals with gay men in each of these studies, the result is that we have little information on the biology of bisexuality.

Some researchers do incorporate concepts of scalar or trichotomous sexuality into their analyses, but for various reasons have produced few findings pertinent to the heritability of bisexuality specifically. Frederick L. Whitam, Milton

Diamond, and James Martin (1993), for example, recruited male and female twins through ads in the gay press and referrals. They rated probands and their twins as concordant, partially concordant, or discordant depending on whether the degree of difference between their Kinsey scores was 0–1 points, 2–3 points, or 4 or more points. The researchers found a 65.8 percent concordance rate among thirty-four male and four female monozygotic (identical) twins and a rate of 30.4 percent among twenty-three pairs of dizygotic twins. The authors did not address the question of the linearity of concordance rates across the range of the Kinsey scale, and tabulated data on the monozygotic twins shows that very few had Kinsey scores of 2–4 (cf. Bailey and Bell 1993). Although the results are therefore most accurate in describing individuals at the ends of the Kinsey scale, Diamond later found the fact that "when the brothers were concordant for sexual orientation, they were usually so within one rating on the Kinsey scale," which indicated that homosexuals typically had either homosexual or heterosexual, and not bisexual, brothers, to be "of interest" to the study of bisexuality. He wondered,

> Why, among monozygotic twin brothers who are not concordant for homosexuality, do only a minority show bisexual behavior whilst the majority are heterosexual (K=0) instead? Intuitively one might expect a higher ratio of bisexuals to heterosexuals. Indeed, it may be that bisexuality is related to homosexuality and heterosexuality but quite different in its developmental pattern. (1998:72)

In a study of familiality of sexual orientation among women, Pattatucci and Hamer (1995) provided great detail regarding the distinction between lesbianism and bisexuality among the relatives of heterosexual and nonheterosexual women. They recruited a sample of 358 women through announcements in local homophile organizations, social groups, and women's studies programs in the Washington, D.C. area. These women were asked to rate themselves on four seven-point Kinsey scales representing self-identity, sexual/romantic attraction, sexual/romantic fantasy, and sexual behavior, and these four scores were averaged. They were also asked to assess the sexual orientations of several of their family members, and these assessments were confirmed in selected cases by interviews with the family members themselves. Rates of concordance between probands' and their relatives' sexual orientations were calculated in two ways; first, by grouping Kinsey 2–4's with Kinsey 5–6's to produce a rate of concordance for "nonheterosexuality," and second by grouping Kinsey 2–4's with Kinsey 0–1's to produce a rate of concordance for more exclusive homosexuality. Subjects whose own Kinsey ratings were 0 or 1 (effectively, K = 0 – 1.49 because of previous rounding) were classified as heterosexual and used to establish baseline rates of familial nonheterosexuality; among these subjects' relatives 1.2 percent of the women and 2.1 percent of the men were nonheterosexual (lesbian, gay, or bisexual). Baseline rates of familial homosexuality (K = 5,6) for nonhomosexual subjects (K = 0–3) were 0.85 percent for female relatives and 1.8 percent for male relatives. The researchers found that rates of nonheterosexuality among certain relatives of nonheterosexual women, and rates of homosexuality among certain relatives of lesbians, were elevated. In both cases elevation occurred among daughters, sisters, brothers, and the female cousins of paternal uncles. Despite their careful attention to the fact that sexuality is not dichotomous, because Pattatucci and Hamer did not present correlational data between the degree of homosexuality of their subjects and their subjects' relatives, nor distinguish Kinsey 2–4's from 0–1's and 5–6's simultaneously except when presenting frequency data, their findings as presented do not bear directly on the question of whether the role of bisexuality in familial patterns of sexual orientation is different from the role of exclusive homosexuality.

But another study of familiality of sexual orientation in women does provide evidence bearing on the familiality of bisexuality as distinct from homosexuality. Bailey, Pillard, Neale, and Agyei (1993; see also Pillard 1990; Hershberger 1997) discovered that although monozygotic twins of nonheterosexual women displayed an increased likelihood of nonheterosexuality themselves, there was no significant correlation between nonheterosexual twins' degrees of homosexuality or choices of identifying as bisexual as opposed to lesbian. These findings suggest that it might be appropriate for researchers to group bisexuals with homosexuals because the distinction between bisexuality and homosexuality appears biologically unimportant compared to that between exclusive heterosexuality and nonexclusive homosexuality.

However, Paul H. Van Wyk and Chrisann S. Geist (1995) combed the research literature for glimpses into the biology of bisexuality and found evidence suggesting that—contrary to the conclusion based on the Bailey findings—bisexuals do differ from homosexuals as well as from heterosexuals and should be studied as a group distinct from both heterosexuals and homosexuals. Furthermore, the difference is not one of simply falling between homosexuals and heterosexuals. Specifically, Van Wyk and Geist found evidence that prenatal hormonal masculinization of females appears to produce bisexuality, not homosexuality, and that bisexual men might be equally or more, not less, hormonally masculine than heterosexual men.[13] Further evidence of the possible existence and complexity of biological correlates is provided by Peter J. Snyder, James D. Weinrich, and Richard C. Pillard (1994). In their study of lipid levels, unique in its focus specifically on the question of whether and how bisexual men differ biologically from homosexual and heterosexual men, self-identified bisexuals resembled self-identified homosexuals and differed from self-identified heterosexuals on levels of HDL ("good cholesterol"), but resembled heterosexuals more than homosexuals on triglyceride levels.

In short, the only conclusions possible at this point are those cautiously drawn by Van Wyk and Geist (1995), who asserted that "bisexuals differ from both heterosexuals and homosexuals" (358), advised further study of bisexuals as a distinct group, and reminded us that cognitive, cultural, and subcultural factors must also be taken into account when attempting to trace the etiology of sexual orientation.

Bisexuality and Gender Roles

Lesbians and gay men are commonly stereotyped as acting like the other gender; that is, lesbians are stereotyped as masculine and gay men are stereotyped as effeminate. Stereotypes regarding the gender traits of bisexuals tend to focus on bisexuals' potential for other-sex attraction and hence characterize bisexuals as traditionally gendered. For example, bisexual women have been depicted in fictional literature and in sexual psychopathological literature as "more feminine" and more amenable to "treatment" than lesbians.[14]

Whereas researchers studying biological correlates of sexual orientation sometimes incorporate crossgender stereotypes into their own hypotheses, researchers studying the relationship between sexual orientation and gender roles often study the stereotypes themselves.[15] Michael G. Shively, James R. Rudolph, and John P. De Cecco (1978), for example, documented the existence of stereotypes of lesbians and gay men by studying their respondents' perceptions of homosexuality as a cross-gendered personality trait. Asking three hundred individuals to "list specific, observable characteristics that people expect (a) a masculine man, (b) a feminine woman, (c) a feminine man, and (d) a masculine woman to have" (228), they reported that masculine men and feminine women tended to be perceived as heterosexual whereas feminine men and masculine women tended to be perceived as homosexual. These authors, who would play a central role in the renewed challenge to simplistic and essentialist dichotomous conceptions of sexuality a decade later, provided information regarding the percentage of their sample that was heterosexual, bisexual, and homosexual in terms of physical sexual activity, close relationships, and erotic fantasies. Unfortunately, because this detailed information was not utilized in the data analysis, the report provides no insight into the extent to which bisexuals might differ from lesbians, gay men, and heterosexuals in the degree to which they perceive homosexuality as crossgendered or the extent to which bisexuality is similarly stereotyped.

Other researchers study whether crossgendered stereotypes are true or not.[16] Some explore the gender traits displayed during childhood by individuals who will subsequently be identified as heterosexual or lesbian or gay, and, in rare cases, bisexual, whereas others explore the gender traits of adult bisexuals, heterosexuals, lesbians, and gay men. Research on childhood gender traits, like research on biological differences, usually involves the question of causality either implicitly or explicitly; evidence that prehomosexual or prebisexual children display crossgendered traits would suggest that such traits are precursors or early signs of homosexual tendencies, although it is equally possible that it is the expectation that crossgendered children will become homosexual that in fact subtly encourages these children to adopt lesbian, gay, or bisexual self-identities as adults.

The greatest weakness of research on the relationship between childhood gender traits and adult sexuality is that it tends to be retrospective, a fact acknowledged by most researchers in this area. For example, Gabriel Phillips and Ray Over (1995) asked adult heterosexual, bisexual, and lesbian women to "[recall] the extent to which they had engaged in gender conforming (female-stereotypic) behaviors and gender nonconforming (male-stereotypic) behaviors in childhood" (1). Such retrospective accounts are likely to be biased by subjects' own expectations that bisexual, lesbian, and gay people are crossgendered. Any findings that bisexual, lesbian, or gay individuals recall being crossgendered in childhood, therefore, could be artifacts of memory bias and not evidence that prebisexual or prehomo-sexual children are actually more likely to exhibit crossgender traits than pre-heterosexual children.[17] Only prospective studies, such as those done by Richard Green (1987) and Bernard Zuger (1978), can determine whether there is any rela-tionship between actual childhood gender traits and adult sexual orientation.[18]

Although there is a great body of literature regarding the relationship between childhood gender traits and adult sexual orientation, few studies make note of bisexuality. Even those in which sexuality is assessed with Kinsey scales treat bisex-uality as a form of homosexuality. J. Michael Bailey, Joseph S. Miller, and Lee Wil-lerman (1993), for example, dichotomized subjects into "heterosexual" and "ho-mosexual and bisexual" categories based on their Kinsey scores, excluding Kinsey 2's because of "problems in classifying their orientations" (462). Fortunately, Green's study, in which both sexual fantasy and behavior were assessed using Kinsey scales, is an exception; Green trichotomized his subjects into heterosexuals (0–1), bisexuals (2–4), and homosexuals (5–6).

The few studies of childhood gender traits in which bisexuality is acknowledged suggest that, to the extent that adult sexual orientation is related to childhood gen-der, the differences involve bisexuals as much as they involve heterosexuals, les-bians, and gays. Green (1987) found that both bisexuality and homosexuality were far more common among men who had been gender nonconforming (that is, femi-nine) as boys than among men who had been masculine as boys. Van Wyk and Geist (1984) did not distinguish bisexuals from lesbians and gay men, but they did study correlations between Kinsey scores and gender-related variables. They dis-covered that, among females, greater "degrees" of homosexuality were associated with having fewer female companions at age ten. Among males greater "degrees" of homosexuality were associated with fewer male companions at ages ten and sixteen, more female companions at age ten, and less participation in sports, espe-cially contact sports. To the extent that these correlations are linear, these findings suggest that bisexuals' friendship patterns and levels of sports involvement fall between those of lesbians and gay men on one hand and heterosexuals on the other hand. Alan P. Bell, Martin S. Weinberg, and Sue Kiefer Hammersmith (1981), using path modeling, found that childhood gender nonconformity was a more important factor in the development of women whose adult sexual feelings and behaviors were exclusively homosexual (Kinsey 6's) than in the development of bisexual women (Kinsey scores = 2–4).[19]

The study by Phillips and Over (1995), conducted in Australia, is one of the few to distinguish bisexuals categorically.[20] They found that lesbians recalled more gender nonconforming than conforming behaviors whereas the reverse was true for heterosexual women; bisexual women, defined as women with Kinsey scores of 1–5 or orgasmic contact with both women and men since age eighteen, were in-termediate but more similar to heterosexual women than to lesbians in recalled childhood experiences. When bisexual women were defined more narrowly as women with Kinsey scores of 2–4 regardless of orgasmic experience, they fell more clearly in between lesbian and heterosexual women, reporting equal numbers of conforming and nonconforming behaviors: more of the former than lesbians, but more of the latter than heterosexual women. In an earlier study (1992) these researchers had found that bisexual men were similarly intermediate to heterosexual and gay men in their recall of childhood gender. In discussing their findings, the authors stressed the diversity of gender experiences within sexual orientation groups; although bisexual, lesbian/gay, and heterosexual women and men differed from each other in general, individuals within each category ranged broadly from gender conformity to nonconformity.

Research on the relationship between adult gender traits and sexual orientation is less subject to recall or other perceptive bias, but findings in this area are mixed.[21] Using the masculinity and femininity subscales of the Personal Attributes Questionnaire (Spence and Helmreich 1978), Michael D. Storms (1980) found no evidence that 185 self-identified homosexual, bisexual, and heterosexual male and female midwestern university students displayed different gender traits.[22] Similarly, Kirk Stokes, Peter R. Kilmann, and Richard L. Wanlass (1983) found "no significant support" (427) for cross-gender stereotypes when they administered the Bem Sex Role Inventory to 186 male and female homosexual, bisexual, and heterosexual people residing in the southeastern United States. In this study subjects were recruited through community networks rather than university courses and organizations, and special attention was given to the recruitment of bisexuals. The authors reviewed earlier research that found some truth to crossgender stereotypes of gay men and lesbians and explored possible explanations for their own negative findings. These possibilities include their small sample size, the possibility that the BSRI does not measure the particular gender traits that differentiate bisexuals, lesbians, gay men, and heterosexuals, the possibility that Southern culture repressed crossgender expression in their respondents, and the possibility that their sample was more representative than those of other researchers because they actively recruited respondents instead of waiting for volunteers to respond to general solicitations.

One study that found some truth to crossgender stereotypes and included bisexuals is by Ronald A. LaTorre and Kristina Wendenburg (1983).[23] This study is also one of the few studies done in the United States to put into practice the observation that sexual orientation consists of several dimensions that are not necessarily congruent with each other—an observation made repeatedly by theorists discussed in chapter 4 of this volume but given little more than lip service by most researchers.[24] LaTorre and Wendenburg not only assessed sexual orientation in multiple ways, but carried the distinction between these different dimensions of sexual orientation through data analysis. To assess sexual orientation they asked 125 female students at the University of British Columbia for their self-identities, whether they preferred sex with men or with women, and for information regarding their same- and other-sex sexual experiences. Twenty-two of the subjects labeled themselves bisexual, and eighteen self-identified bisexuals, five self-identified heterosexuals, and one self-identified lesbian expressed no preference for either men or women over the other. Thus finding 89.6 percent agreement between the first two methods of assessing sexual orientation, LaTorre and Wendenburg proceeded to compare bisexual, homosexual, and heterosexual subjects to each other as variously defined by these different dimensions.

LaTorre and Wendenburg's findings differed depending on which aspect of sexual orientation they used to classify subjects' sexual orientations. For example, sexual self-identity but not erotic preference was significantly associated with gender traits. Specifically, they found that when women were classified as bisexual or homosexual based on their self-identities, bisexual and homosexual women were less likely to be "feminine" than heterosexual women, with bisexual women particularly likely to be "masculine." However, the same could not be said when women were classified as bisexual or lesbian on the basis of their expressed preferences for sex with women versus men. Regarding the former finding, the authors theorized that the masculine traits of self-identified bisexual and lesbian women enable them to stand up to a society whose sexual mores are inhospitable to them and that whereas lesbians might avoid "unmitigated agency (i.e., masculinity)" (95) for fear of the "butch" label, the bisexual woman is "allowed expression of masculine ascendancy because this is balanced, in society's eyes, by her sexual involvement with men" (95–96). The findings that bisexual women are more, rather than less, masculine than lesbians directly contradicts the stereotype that bisexual women are more traditionally gendered than lesbians.

Biphobia, Heterosexism, and Monosexism: Attitudes About Bisexuality

Negative attitudes about bisexuality exist in both heterosexual society and lesbian and gay communities. In the eyes of heterosexual society, bisexuality is tantamount to homosexuality; in lesbian and gay communities bisexuality is only halfway there. Bisexual activist Robyn Ochs (1996), writing for an academic audience, discussed the "double oppression" of biphobia (monosexism) and analyzed its relationship to homophobia (heterosexism).[25] She argued that heterosexism affects bisexuals as well as lesbians and gay men and that bisexuals also experience forms of oppression that are unique to bisexuals. Foremost in Ochs's list of oppressions is the denial of the very existence of bisexuality, which results from the culturally dominant conception of sexuality as dichotomous, that is, binary. She outlined a vicious circle in which the monosexist belief that bisexuality does not exist results in bisexual invisibility—as when a person involved in a monogamous relationship is assumed to be either heterosexual or homosexual, depending on their partner's gender—which in turn leaves monosexism unchallenged. Ochs traced biphobia in heterosexual society to the challenge bisexuality poses to deeply embedded tendencies toward binary thinking in Western culture and to fears that bisexuals will spread AIDS to the heterosexual population.[26] She attributed biphobia in lesbian and gay communities to the need of oppressed people to distinguish between us and them for reasons of safety; bisexuals challenge the division between the heterosexual oppressor and the lesbian and gay oppressed, thus threatening the safety of lesbians and gay men within their own communities. Similarly, Joshua Gamson (1995) argued that bisexuality threatens the naturalized gender and sexual binaries that underlie traditional lesbian and gay identities and quasi-ethnic political strategies, Clare Hemmings (1993) argued that the bisexual is distrusted and debased as a "double agent," Jo Eadie (1993) analogized bisexuality and racial miscegenation, and Rebecca Shuster (1987) pointed out that bisexuality reopens the issue of choice and undermines beliefs in the immutability of sexual identity, thus challenging politically advantageous and psychologically reassuring analogies between sexual orientation and ethnicity or race. Weinberg, Williams, and Pryor (1994) documented bisexuals' experiences of rejection from both heterosexual and lesbian/gay communities and by potential lovers of both sexes.

Bisexuality is particularly controversial in lesbian communities, in which sexual identity is highly politicized as a result of the lesbian feminist movement of the 1970s and political gains are more recent and therefore less secure.[27] For some lesbians, lesbian self-identity reflects a political and social commitment to women and feminism at least as much as it reflects sexual interest in other women. Bisexual self-identity, therefore, is seen as reflecting a lack of commitment. Lesbian attitudes toward bisexuality have been interpreted as an effort to neutralize the threat posed by bisexuality to lesbian identity, community, and political strength (Rust 1993b; Ault 1994; see also Heldke 1997; O'Connor 1997). Amber Ault (1994; cf. Wilkerson 1997) perceives a similarity in the attitudes of lesbian feminists and of the radical right, both of which construct bisexuals as "stigmatized others"; she locates lesbian neutralizing discourse within broader discourses on gender and race and in the Western cultural search for security in binary classification systems.

Some of the earliest descriptions of antagonism toward bisexuality in lesbian and gay communities were written by Philip Blumstein and Pepper Schwartz, for example, in the 1977 article reprinted as chapter 21 of this volume, and by Barbara Ponse (1978), Deborah G. Wolf (1979), and Carol A. B. Warren (1974) in their ethnographies of lesbian and gay communities. More recently, Esterberg (1997) described relations between lesbians and bisexual women, and lesbian and bisexual identities, based on participant observation and interviews in a small eastern community. Also, Rust (1993b) conducted a survey of self-identified lesbian and bisexual women's attitudes about bisexuality; a report of this study is reprinted in this section. More personal perspectives are offered by Michelle T. Clinton (1996), who discussed her own experiences as a bisexual woman confronting negative attitudes from lesbians and trying to assimilate into a lesbian community, and by Jan Clausen (1990a), who analyzed the political dynamics behind her "fall from grace" in the lesbian community when she became involved with a man.

Among the attitudes described in these studies of lesbian and gay communities are the beliefs that bisexuality is a transitional form of sexuality or a transitional identity adopted by some lesbians and gay men as a temporary stage in coming out and that bisexual self-identity is a way for lesbians and gay men to deny their true sexual orientation to themselves or to others. Bisexuals are also believed to be better at passing as heterosexual and thereby avoiding the full force of the oppression that lesbians and gay men experience, to be capable of "becoming" heterosexual when being lesbian or gay is too hard for social or political reasons, to be more likely to leave a same-sex lover for a socially approved other-sex lover and the social privileges of a heterosexual life, and to be less committed than lesbians and gay men in the struggle for sexual freedom and sexual minority civil rights. Bisexuals are considered fence-sitters who want the best of both worlds or are too indecisive or confused to figure out whether they are lesbian/gay or straight. They are also accused of being unable to practice monogamy, usually because they are thought to require two lovers—a woman and a man—for satisfaction or because they are believed to be as indecisive or noncommittal toward their lovers as they are regarding the question of whether they are lesbian/gay or straight.

As Ochs argued, many of these attitudes can be attributed to the cultural construction of sexuality as binary, which leads not only to the belief that bisexuality does not exist but also to a concept of bisexuality—existent or not—as a hybrid form of sexuality. If bisexuality is nonexistent, then the fact that some people identify themselves as bisexual, behave bisexually, and claim to be attracted to both women and men needs to be explained. Beliefs that bisexuality is transitional, a denial of one's true sexuality, or a reflection of indecisiveness or confusion explain that those who appear to be bisexuals are really lesbian or gay (or heterosexual), thus preserving the belief that bisexuality does not exist. The concept of bisexuality as a hybrid form of sexuality leads to the beliefs that bisexuals—whether they are "really" bisexual or not—can switch to heterosexuality when it is personally or politically expedient and that bisexuals are political fence-sitters whose commitment to lesbian and gay rights is watered down by their "heterosexual half." The belief that bisexuality is tantamount to nonmonogamy also follows from the hybrid conception of bisexuality. The cultural logic is as follows: if a heterosexual needs a lover of the other sex to be satisfied, and a lesbian or gay man needs a lover of the same sex to be satisfied, then someone who is half-heterosexual and half-lesbian/gay must need lovers of both sexes. Any single lover would be able to satisfy only one of the bisexual's two desires. The flaw in this logic is most easily seen by analogy; if a person were capable of being attracted to both green-eyed and brown-eyed people, we would probably not assume that she needed two lovers, one with each eye color, but rather that she could be satisfied by one lover with either eye color. In truth, many bisexuals can also be satisfied with a single lover. As will be seen later in this chapter, a minority of bisexuals have had partners of both sexes in the recent past, and even fewer have male and female partners simultaneously; even bisexuals with multiple partners often have partners of only one sex.

Bisexuals are also stereotyped as having more active sex lives than either heterosexuals or lesbians and gay men and are sometimes accused of having become bisexual for the purpose of increasing their sexual opportunities. Joseph Istvan (1983), for example, in an article reprinted as chapter 25 in this section, found that bisexuals with predominantly homosexual experience are stereotyped as more sexually active than exclusive heterosexuals. Like other stereotypes, this one results at least partly from the conceptualization of bisexuals as hybrid homo-heteros, with its implication that bisexuals have twice the sexual opportunities or twice the sexual drive as either heterosexuals or lesbians and gay men. It might also be a result of the process of sexualization that many minorities have gone through; African Americans and other racial and ethnic minorities, as well as lesbians and gay men, have been sexualized in the public eye. This process might be particularly influential in the case of bisexuals, who are defined primarily by their sexuality. Other minorities who are defined primarily by their sexuality, for example, lesbians and gay men, have succeeded somewhat in countering these stereotypes by presenting the public with more well-rounded and politicized images of themselves, but bisexuals, at this early stage of the effort to reshape public opinion, are still perceived largely in sexual terms.

To what extent does social disapproval of bisexuality translate into discrimination against bisexuals? In lesbian and gay communities discrimination against bisexuals often takes the form of exclusion, or a lack of recognition, in lesbian and gay events and organizations. In 1989 Gary North surveyed the attitudes of national gay and lesbian leaders on the question of "bisexuals in the gay rights movement" and found opinions ranging from acceptance and inclusion to the view that bisexuals should form their own movement. Controversies over the exclusion or inclusion of bisexuals are often reflected in controversies about whether the word *bisexual* should be included in the titles of events and organizations. Sometimes the word is added one year, only to be removed the next. For example, in January 1990 organizers voted to remove the word *bisexual*—which had been added the previous year—from the name of the Northampton, Massachusetts "Lesbian and Gay Pride March." The decision touched off a firestorm of controversy in the local lesbian, gay, and bisexual media over the relationship of bisexuals to the "lesbian and gay" community and the place of bisexuals in the "lesbian and gay" political movement. Similarly, the first three annual "Lesbian and Gay Studies" conferences were followed by a fourth "Lesbian, Bisexual, and Gay Studies" conference in 1991, and then by a fifth "Lesbian and Gay Studies" conference. After much lobbying, bisexuals celebrated the inclusion of *Bi* in the title of the 1993 March on Washington, but wondered whether they should take the use of the prefix instead of the whole word as an attempt to desexualize bisexuality for public consumption.[28]

In general, heterosexuals who are unfamiliar with the identity politics that are so important to lesbians, gay men, and bisexuals tend to lump bisexuals with lesbians and gay men. Therefore, among heterosexuals bisexuals tend to suffer from the same heterosexism and homophobia that affects lesbians and gay men. As Ochs wrote, "We don't lose only half our children in custody battles. When homophobia hits, we don't get just half fired from our jobs. . . . We, too, get discriminated against *because we are gay*" (1990:2). Supporting this claim, Eliason (1997) found that the majority of heterosexual college students agreed that "bisexual rights are the same as gay and lesbian rights." Also, Istvan (1983; reprinted as chapter 25, this volume) found that bisexuals who were less than 50 percent homosexual were only slightly more disliked than exclusive heterosexuals, whereas bisexuals who were 50 percent or more homosexual were just as disliked as exclusive homosexuals and considered equally undesirable as coworkers. However, Eliason's (1997) research suggests that bisexuals also experience prejudice specific to their bisexuality. She found that heterosexual college students were less likely to rate bisexual men and women than lesbians and gay men as "very acceptable" and that bisexual men were most often rated as "very unacceptable." Spalding and Peplau (1997) found that heterosexuals perceive bisexuals to be more likely than either heterosexuals or gays and lesbians to give an STD to a sex partner. Heterosexual behavior provides no exemption to this biphobia; Spalding and Peplau also found that heterosexuals distrusted bisexuals in male-female relationships as much as they distrusted bisexuals in same-gender relationships.

Discrimination on the basis of sexual orientation is illegal in a handful of states and many cities.[29] But even where it is illegal it still occurs, and evidence of this discrimination is difficult to produce, as any political activist who has tried to convince a legislature of the need for laws against sexual orientation discrimination can attest. Individuals who have suffered discrimination are often reluctant to speak of it for fear of further reprisals, and individuals who haven't experienced outright discrimination have often avoided it by remaining closeted—a form of discrimination that policy makers, who are accustomed to thinking in terms of the forms of discrimination experienced by visibly identifiable racial and ethnic minorities, have trouble understanding.

Compounding the problem of demonstrating the need for antidiscrimination laws, citizens allied with antilesbigay agendas provide policy makers with statistics purporting to demonstrate that lesbians and gay men have higher annual incomes than heterosexuals and therefore have not suffered from economic discrimination (Badgett 1996). The statistics usually provided are those collected by Overlooked Opinions, a gay-identified polling organization whose respondents were recruited via methods that disproportionately drew upper-class lesbians and gay men. Contrary to the Overlooked Opinions findings, evidence from the nationally representative General Social Survey (GSS) indicates that, in fact, gay and bisexual men earn 11 percent to 27 percent less than heterosexual men, even when education and occupation are controlled, and that lesbian and bisexual women might earn 12 percent to 30 percent less than heterosexual women (Badgett 1995).[30]

Unfortunately, in this report on GSS data bisexuals were not distinguished from lesbians and gay men.[31] They were distinguished in another much smaller (n = 348) and nonrepresentative survey of student affairs professionals attending events sponsored by a Lesbian, Gay, and Bisexual organization (Croteau and von Destinon 1994). In this study, although fewer self-identified bisexuals reported having experienced discrimination (21 percent) than did lesbians (28 percent) or gay men (26 percent), the difference is not statistically significant. Given the findings of other research reviewed later in this chapter that bisexuals are less likely to disclose their sexual orientation, if bisexuals do experience less discrimination it might be because they are more likely to be closeted. In other words, their less frequent experience of discrimination should not be taken as evidence that employers and coworkers are less prejudiced against bisexuals or less disposed to discriminate against them. The findings by Eliason (1997), Istvan (1983), and Spalding and Peplau (1997) cited above suggest that, when they do come out in the workplace, bisexuals face a risk as great as that faced by lesbians and gay men.

Sexual Activity and Romantic Desire: Is Bisexuality the Best of Two Worlds or a World of Its Own?[32]

Contrary to stereotypes that paint a narrow portrait of what bisexuals are like sexually, there are many ways to be bi*sexual*. In an effort to make sense of the sexual diversity found among bisexuals, some researchers have developed typologies of bisexuality. For example, Klein (1978, 1993) distinguished transitional, historical, sequential, and concurrent bisexuality. Transitional bisexuality is a stage some people go through while coming out as lesbian or gay or while changing from a lesbian or gay orientation to a heterosexual one; a person who has had both male and female sex partners in their lifetimes is a historical bisexual; serial relationships with both men and women, but with partners of only one gender at a time, constitutes sequential bisexuality. These forms of bisexuality are distinct from concurrent bisexuality, which involves simultaneous relationships with both women and men. A. P. McDonald Jr. (1982) distinguished between transitory and transitional bisexuality, and distinguished these from enduring bisexuality. Mary Boulton (1991) distinguished bisexuality, which she defined as the choice of a bisexual lifestyle, bisexual self-identity, and participation in self-defined bisexual groups, from "adolescent bisexuality," "married homosexual men," "prostitution," and "situational homosexuality." Stokes and Miller (1998) classified behavioral bisexual men as "men in transition," "experimenters," "opportunity-driven men," or "men with dual involvement." Taywaditep and Stokes (1998) used cluster analysis to identify eight subtypes among behaviorally bisexual men. Two types are characterized by gay self-identity, two by straight self-identity, and four by bisexual self-identity, differing in each case from each other in terms of the content of their sexual fantasies, the numbers of their male and female sex partners, and their histories of relationships with either women or men.

Diamond (1998) discussed the difference between primary and secondary bisexuality, wherein primary bisexuality is defined in terms of erotic psychological arousal by both sexes regardless of sexual behavior and secondary bisexuality includes bisexual behavior unaccompanied by actual erotic response to both sexes. This distinction presents an interesting theoretical shift from the distinction between primary and secondary homosexuality, wherein secondary homosexuality is usually defined with reference to bisexual behavior. Weinberg, Williams, and Pryor (1994) classified bisexuals according to their "degrees" of bisexuality. Using averaged Kinsey scores representing sexual feelings, sexual behaviors, and romantic feelings, they distinguished the pure type of bisexual, who scores a perfect 3 on all three dimensions, from the mid type who scores a 3 on one dimension and 2–4 on the other two dimensions. The heterosexual-leaning and homosexual-leaning types are those who score themselves as K = 0–2 or K = 4–6, respectively, on all three dimensions, and the "varied" category encompasses those whose three scores are too disparate to fit into any of the other categories.

Bisexuals have also been classified according to their social contexts. John H. Gagnon (1989), for example, distinguished "persons having sex with both men and women" in various contexts, including the marginal demimonde of male prostitutes and the heterosexual social worlds of married men. Lynda S. Doll, John Peterson, J. Raul Magaña, and Joe M. Carrier (1991) further divided behaviorally bisexual men embedded in heterosexual networks into those who had primary heterosexual relationships, those who had no primary heterosexual relationships, and those without access to women such as men in prison. Taking a more cross-cultural view, Michael W. Ross (1991a) identified defense bisexuality in cultures where homophobia discourages self-identification as gay, Latin bisexuality in cultures in which insertive sex with a partner of either sex is consistent with hetero-sexual self-identity, ritual bisexuality in cultures that prescribe same-sex activity for some individuals at certain life stages and do not consider the activity a reflec-tion of an essential homo- or bisexuality, married bisexuality in cultures in which marriage is obligatory for most individuals and same-sex activity occurs extramar-itally, experimental and secondary bisexuality when same-sex behavior occurs in people who are otherwise heterosexual, equal bisexuality among people who are truly attracted to both sexes or who feel attracted to people regardless of their sex, and technical bisexuality when a sex partner is not of the sex they appear to be (cf. Herdt and Boxer [1995] on "paradigms"). To this list, McKenna (1995) added "cul-tural situational homosexuality" as a form of bisexuality occuring in cultures in which men's sexual access to women is restricted.

In contemporary Western culture the archetypal bisexual is a person who is equally attracted to men and women or who is simultaneously involved with both male and female sex partners. However, a great deal of research—some of which is reviewed in chapters 11 and 22—has shown that equal attractions are rare, that people who identify as bisexual range from almost exclusively homosexual to al-most exclusively heterosexual in their attractions, and that very few are simultane-ously involved in both other-sex and same-sex relationships. Weinberg, Williams, and Pryor (1994) found that, among self-identified bisexuals included in their 1984–1985 survey, only 7 percent of men and under 4 percent of women were "pure" bisexuals.[33] Of the men one in five (19.8 percent) gave their romantic feel-ings a rating of "3," and the same proportion (19.8 percent) gave their sexual feel-ings a rating of "3." Of the women one in five (19.1 percent) gave their romantic feelings a rating of "3," and a larger proportion (29.5 percent) gave their sexual feelings a rating of "3." Whereas most bisexual men and women said that their sex-ual feelings fell within the 2–4 range (71 percent and 73 percent), romantic feelings were often directed strongly toward one sex or the other; just over half of the men (54 percent), and just under half of the women (46 percent), rated their romantic feelings as almost exclusively or exclusively hetero- or homosexual. Klein (1978) found that only 35 percent of the men and 40 percent of the women attending the Bisexual Forum in New York City in 1976–1977 said that they preferred sex with males and females "equally"; men with a preference tended to favor females, and women with a preference tended to favor males. Rust (1992) found that self-identified bisexual women recruited largely through lesbian and feminist social and political networks ranged from 10 percent to 90 percent attracted to men, with 61 percent reporting more attraction to women than to men and only 17 percent reporting equal attraction to men and women. Mary Boulton, G. Hart, and

R. Fitzpatrick (1992) found that among behaviorally bisexual men, 56 percent of whom described their private sexual identity as bisexual, 93 percent indicated some degree of both same-sex and other-sex attraction, with 65 percent reporting equal or almost equal degrees of attraction.

Very few bisexuals are simultaneously involved with both men and women; few have even had partners of both sexes in the recent past.[34] For example, Maria L. Ekstrand and colleagues (1994) found that only 7 percent of self-identified bisexual men in San Francisco had had sex with both men and women during the 1988–1989 year, and Norman and colleagues (1996) found that 6.9 percent of bisexual women surveyed in gay bars had had both male and female partners within the previous two months. Among the self-identified bisexual women in Rust's (1992) sample 16.7 percent were simultaneously involved in relationships with both men and women; 38.1 percent were involved with one or more women only and 23.8 percent were involved with one or more men only. Joseph P. Stokes, David J. McKirnan, and Rebecca G. Burzette (1993) found that only 4 percent of self-perceived bisexual men were involved in relationships with both a man and a woman simultaneously and 28 percent rated themselves overall as "equally homosexual and heterosexual." Klein (1978) found higher rates among people at the Bisexual Forum, three quarters of whom considered themselves bisexual; 26 percent of the men and 14 percent of the women in his survey said that they had been "involved in sexual activity with two or more other people at the same time" in the previous month and 48 percent and 40 percent, respectively, had been so involved in the previous year. Only one in ten of Weinberg, Williams, and Pryor's bisexual women, and one in eight bisexual men, gave their sexual behavior a rating of "3"; in fact, two-thirds of the women and over half the men rated themselves outside the 2–4 bisexual range (66 percent and 58 percent). One-third of Weinberg, Williams, and Pryor's bisexuals were in both same- and other-sex relationships, one in ten were involved in multiple other-sex relationships only, and approximately 3 percent were involved in multiple same-sex relationships only. Women, more than men, tended toward almost exclusive, or exclusive, heterosexual behavior (56.6 percent, 35.8 percent). Bisexual women also tended more strongly toward exclusive heterosexual behavior in a representative survey of the populations of four cities; Daniel C. Berrios and colleagues (1992) found that most individuals who had ever had both male and female sex partners had had only other-sex (41 percent of men; 53 percent of women) or only same-sex (32 percent of men; 26 percent of women) partners in the previous year. Among behaviorally bisexual men in David J. McKirnan, Joseph P. Stokes, Lynda Doll, and Rebecca Burzette's (1995) sample, 3 percent were involved in committed relationships with both men and women at the time of the study; 24 percent were involved in a relationship with a man only, and the same percentage were involved in a relationship with a woman only. David Matteson (1997) found that 55 percent of behaviorally bisexual Asian American men currently had more than one sex partner, but only 35 percent had sex partners of both sexes.

In short, few bisexuals actually have quintessential bisexual feelings or engage in quintessential bisexual behavior. Most women and men who identify as bisexual do so because they feel attracted to both women and men in some unequal or variable degrees or because they feel they have the capacity to be sexually active with either women or men, not because they feel equally attracted to women and men or because they engage in concurrent heterosex and homosex. In fact, some identify as bisexual without ever having same- and/or other-sex experience; Schwartz and Blumstein (1998) found that 19 percent of males and 27 percent of females who had had adult same- and other-sex experience had not yet had both types of experience when they began identifying as bisexual. Conversely, many self-identified heterosexuals, lesbians, and gay men have bisexual feelings and engage in bisexual behavior, resulting in considerable overlap in the actual sexual experiences of individuals who identify themselves as bisexual, lesbian or gay, and heterosexual. Recall from chapter 11, for example, that the SFDPH AIDS Office Survey found that 22 percent of lesbians, like 71 percent of bisexual women, had had sex with men as well as women in the previous three years (1993a) and that Susan D. Cochran and Vickie M. Mays (1988) found that 12 percent of lesbians, like 65 percent of bisexual women, had had heterosexual coitus within the previous year.[35] One-third of Weinberg, Williams, and Pryor's (1994) self-identified heterosexual men and almost half of self-identified heterosexual women said that their sexual feelings were not exclusively heterosexual, and identical percentages of self-identified gay men and lesbians, respectively, said that their sexual feelings were not exclusively homosexual. Smaller percentages, approximately one in ten in each group, rated their sexual behaviors as nonexclusive. Pattatucci and Hamer (1995) found that, among women whose averaged Kinsey scores indicated predominant or exclusive lesbianism, 45.3 percent reported that they had ever been romantically or sexually attracted to men, compared to 85.2 percent of Kinseyan bisexual women and 100 percent of Kinseyan heterosexual women. Rust (1992) found that 65 percent of lesbians reported being attracted to men as well as women and that these two-thirds of lesbians covered the same range of attractions (60–90 percent attracted to women) as did a very similar proportion (61 percent) of self-identified bisexual women. Findings regarding inconsistencies between sexual self-identity and both sexual behavior and feelings of sexual attraction are, however, heavily dependent on how sexual self-identity is measured; Rust (1999) found that different methods of assessing "lesbian self-identity" produced estimates of the proportion of lesbians who acknowledge that 20 percent or more of their attractions are toward men ranging from 24 percent to 70 percent, and estimates of the proportion who were currently heterosexually active ranging from 5 percent to 28 percent.

Many of the beliefs and stereotypes about bisexuals discussed earlier in this chapter pertain to bisexuals' sexuality, for example, the belief that bisexuals have difficulty forming commitments and are unable to be monogamous—either because of their inability to commit or because they need both male and female sex partners—and the stereotype of bisexuals as very sexually active. The stereotype that bisexuals have difficulty forming romantic commitments is contradicted by evidence that bisexual women and men do have long-term committed relationships and that bisexual women take their current relationships just as seriously as lesbians. Lauren C. Bressler and Abraham D. Lavender (1986) found that, on average, self-identified bisexual women had actually had more relationships lasting over six months (3.22) than either heterosexual (2.60) or homosexual (2.96) women.[36] The bisexual men in Stokes, McKirnan, and Burzette's (1993) study also demonstrated the capacity for enduring relationships; among those who had ever been married, the mean length of their marriages was almost eight years. Weinberg, Williams, and Pryor (1994) found that, among both men and women, the longest relationships were reported by heterosexuals, followed by bisexuals, and then lesbians and gay men—a pattern that points to the importance of social validation and support in maintaining a relationship. Approximately one-third of bisexual men and women (37.1 percent, 31.3 percent) reported their longest relationship to have lasted ten or more years; for both men and women this relationship had usually been with an other-sex partner. Higher percentages (54.8 percent, 59.2 percent) said they expected their current relationship to last more than ten years, and the majority did not feel that their sexual preference had had any negative effect on their ability to sustain a long-term relationship. Among Rust's (1992) respondents bisexual women and lesbians were equally likely to describe their current relationships as serious, committed, or marriagelike, and 81 percent of bisexuals reported that they had had or were currently in a serious relationship with or marriage to a man.

But committed long-term relationships are not necessarily monogamous, and a handful of studies have shown that self-identified bisexuals are, consistent with the stereotype, somewhat less likely than self-identified monosexuals to be involved in monogamous relationships. Lena Einhorn and Michael Polgar (1994) reported that bisexuals were significantly less likely than lesbians to be involved in a monogamous relationship (40 percent versus 63 percent), and, in a sample of men and women with bisexual experience or bisexual attractions, Rust (1996b) found that those who identified as bisexual were less likely to be in a monogamous relationship than those who identified as lesbian or gay (16.4 percent versus 28 percent). Among individuals who took part in their 1984–1985 questionnaire study Weinberg, Williams, and Pryor (1994) found that almost half of bisexual men and women (48.7 percent and 45.8 percent), compared to one-third of heterosexual and gay men (31.7 percent and 32.2 percent), a quarter of heterosexual women (22.8 percent), and only one in ten lesbians (10.9 percent) were involved in multiple "significant" relationships. They also found that bisexuals were less likely to practice sexual fidelity vis-à-vis their significant relationships, whether they had one or more than one such relationships. For example, among bisexuals who had only one significant relationship, 45.9 percent of the women and 45.0 percent of the men were nonmonogamous, compared to 12.5 percent of lesbians, 14.9 percent of heterosexual women, 36.8 percent of gay men, and 11.4 percent of heterosexual men. In the 1982 *Playboy* survey one-third of self-identified bisexual women and less than one-quarter of the self-identified bisexual men said they were faithful to their partners, compared to "most" of the lesbians and straight women; 22 percent of bisexual women said they "try to be" faithful. Given that some bisexuals are monogamous and practice sexual fidelity, the higher rate of nonmonogamy among bisexuals cannot be attributed—as the stereotype would have it—to an inherent contradiction between bisexuality and monogamy. Instead, as shown below in this chapter, it is due to a conscious rejection by some bisexuals of the cultural ideal of monogamy in favor of other forms of sexual and romantic relating.

The stereotype that bisexuals have higher levels of sexual activity and fantasy than lesbians, gay men, or heterosexuals appears to contain a grain of truth, although, like all stereotypes, it overlooks the great diversity among bisexuals. Research by Storms (1980) actually supports the notion that bisexuals—*in general*—resemble homosexuals in their levels of same-sex fantasy and heterosexuals in their levels of other-sex fantasy, as if a bisexual experiences the combined fantasy lives of a heterosexual and a homosexual. Using a sample of 185 men and women university students, Storms found that those who self-identified as bisexual, on average, were "indistinguishable" from self-identified gays and higher than self-identified heterosexuals in the frequency of their same-sex fantasies, and that they were identical to heterosexuals and higher than homosexuals in the frequency of their other-sex fantasies. Similarly, Stokes, Burzette, and McKirnan (1991) found that bisexual men reported more male and more female partners, and more frequent sexual activity, than "a combined sample of exclusively gay and exclusively heterosexual men" (Heckman et al. 1995:505).

Other research supports the belief that bisexuals in general have higher levels of sexual fantasy or experience—except, perhaps, in comparison to gay men—but not because they live a double sex life. For example, Bressler and Lavender (1986) found that self-identified bisexual women had more orgasms per week on average than either self-identified heterosexual or self-identified homosexual women, but less than the combined number of orgasms of heterosexuals and homosexuals (8.8 compared to 4.7 and 6.2, respectively). Although these researchers did not report how many of these orgasms were with male and how many with female partners, other research in which partner sex is taken into account shows that the pattern of same-sex and other-sex activity is not a simple combination of the patterns found among heterosexuals and lesbians or gay men. This research, much of which is HIV-related and is reviewed in chapter 22, shows that bisexuals have levels of same-sex activity that fall between those of heterosexuals and lesbians or gay men and levels of other-sex activity that are higher than those of lesbians and gay men. Some studies show that bisexuals have levels of other-sex activity that are lower than heterosexuals, but others show that bisexuals have, paradoxically, more heterosex than heterosexuals.[37] In general, research indicates that bisexuals are more sexually active than other sexual orientation groups, although some studies found that gay men have larger total numbers of partners because of larger numbers of male partners.[38] Most of this research also shows that both bisexual men and bisexual women have more male than female partners.[39]

Recall from chapter 22, for example, that Pamela Jean Bevier, Mary Ann Chiasson, Richard T. Heffernan, and Kenneth G. Castro (1995) found that a community-based sample of WSW had had a median of 14 sex partners in the previous three months, compared to 4 partners among exclusively heterosexual women. Among self-identified bisexual seropositive MSM Doll and colleagues (1992) found medians of 7.5 male and 6 female lifetime partners, whereas homosexual self-identified MSM had medians of 20 male and 2 female partners and heterosexual self-identified MSM had medians of 2 male and 9.5 female partners. Among male PWAs whose behavior had been bisexual during the previous five years, Theresa Diaz and colleagues (1993) found that 34.8 percent had had 10 or more male partners and 11.2 percent had had ten or more female partners, whereas 43.7 percent of exclusively homosexual men had had ten or more male partners and 38.4 percent of exclusively heterosexual men had had ten or more female partners.[40] Wold et al. (1998) found that among MSM, those who had also had sex with women during the previous six months had means of twenty-four male and seventeen female and medians of seven male and five female partners during their lifetimes, compared to means of sixty-two male and three female and medians of twelve male and two female partners among men who had had sex with men only during the previous six months. Recall also that Robert W. Wood, Leigh E. Krueger, Tsilke Pearlman, and Gary Goldbaum (1993) found that men who both identified as bisexual and were bisexually active during the year previous to the survey reported averages of 7.9 male and 2.6 female partners during that year whereas behaviorally bisexual "gays" reported averages of 9.9 male and 2.3 female partners and "straights" reported 2.8 male and 3.8 female partners. One HIV-related study that found that bisexuals had more heterosex than heterosexuals is by Stokes, McKirnan, and Burzette (1993) who found that, among self-perceived bisexual men, those who had had sex with both men and women in the previous six months reported 2.0 female partners during those six months compared to 1.3 among men who had had only female partners during that period.[41]

Non-HIV related research shows the same patterns. For example, Cochran and Mays (1988) found that Black bisexual women reported medians of seven female and nine male sex partners in their lifetimes, whereas Black lesbians reported eight female and five male partners in their lifetimes. In a sample of Hispanic (37 percent), Black (35 percent), and white (22 percent) youth aged fourteen to twenty-one Margaret Rosario and colleagues including Heino F. L. Meyer-Bahlburg (1996) found that twenty-four self-identified bisexual females reported a median of one female and eight male partners in their lifetimes, whereas fifty-one self-identified lesbians reported a median of four female and three male partners. The twenty-five self-identified bisexual males in this study reported a median of five male and three female partners, whereas fifty-two self-identified gay males reported a median of five male and no female partners.[42] In another study of gay and bisexual male youth, Ritch C. Savin-Williams (1995a) found that male youth who rated their current sexual orientations as 2–4 (bisexual) on the Kinsey scale (14 percent of the sample) had had more sexual contact with female partners than the 86 percent of the sample who rated themselves as Kinsey 5's or 6's (gay).

Weinberg, Williams, and Pryor (1994) found that bisexual men reported fewer same-sex partners than gay men, similar rates of heterosex compared to heterosexuals, and a predominance of male over female partners. Similar patterns were found for women, with the exception that bisexual women reported more other-sex partners than heterosexual women did. Specifically, the researchers found that bisexual men in their 1984–1985 survey had a median of three male partners in the previous twelve months, compared to six among gay men, and that bisexual men had a median of 30 male partners in their lifetimes, compared to 100 among gay men. Regarding lifetime heterosexual activity among bisexuals and heterosexuals, they found that, among men, bisexuals and heterosexuals both reported a median of 20 other-sex partners and that, among women, bisexuals reported 30, compared to 25 reported by heterosexuals. The predominance of male over female partners was more pronounced among bisexual women (30 male versus 7 female lifetime) than among bisexual men (30 male versus 20 female lifetime). Bisexual women and men had also had more male than female partners in the previous twelve months, and Weinberg, Williams, and Pryor made similar findings in the other phases of their research. Klein (1978), in his survey of 144 people attending the Bisexual Forum in New York City, found that men had had an average of 12.9 male and 9.2 female partners, whereas women had had an average of 4.7 male and 3.0 female partners in the previous year.

In addition to Stokes, McKirnan, and Burzette's (1993) findings on men and Weinberg, Williams, and Pryor's finding on women, other studies indicating that either bisexual men or women have more heterosex than heterosexuals include Erich Goode and Lynn Haber (1977), Marcel T. Saghir and Eli Robins (1973), and Alex Carballo-Diéguez and Curtis Dolezal (1994). Details of these studies are reviewed in chapter 11. An interesting contrast to Goode and Haber's study of women university students is provided by another study of university students by Stephen N. Haynes and L. Jerome Oziel (1976). Whereas Goode and Haber found a higher incidence of heterosexual experience, and higher levels of heterosexual activity, among women who had had sex with another woman than among women without same-sex experience, Haynes and Oziel found no correlation between frequency of same-sex activity and frequency of heterosexual intercourse. Haynes and Oziel asserted, therefore, that rates of heterosexual activity do not differ between those who are, and those who are not, involved in homosexual activity, although they did not provide statistics reflecting this categorical comparison nor give any indication of whether there might be a nonlinear correlation between same- and other-sex activity. It is possible, therefore, that a curvilinear relationship existed or that low rates of heterosexual experience among exclusive homosexuals in the study counterbalanced a higher rate of heterosex among bisexuals, thus producing the finding of no difference. If the Goode and Haber and the Haynes and Oziel studies contained different proportions of exclusive homosexuals, this could explain the difference in their findings regarding the relationship between same-sex and other-sex experience. Nevertheless, Haynes and Oziel's findings, like Goode and Haber's, demonstrate that—contrary to popular belief—same-sex and other-sex activities are not opposite or contrary experiences and more of one does not imply less of the other.

Several other studies provide additional evidence that bisexual men's levels of same-sex activity are lower than gay men's but higher than heterosexual men's. For example, among men who had been behaviorally bisexual during the previous two months, Timothy Heckman and colleagues (1995) found an average of 2.92

male partners during that period, compared to an average of 3.36 male partners among those whose partners had been exclusively male. Stokes, Taywaditep, Vanable, and McKirnan (1996) also found fewer lifetime male partners among men who had been behaviorally bisexual during the previous three years than among men who had had only male partners during the previous three years. Janet Lever and colleagues (1992) found that behaviorally bisexual men were more likely than exclusively heterosexual men and less likely than exclusively homosexual men to be dating multiple partners (43 percent versus 33 percent and 55 percent), and Norman Breslow, Linda Evans, and Jill Langley (1986) found that, among male sadomasochists, on average bisexuals reported more sex partners in the previous year than heterosexuals but fewer than gay men (10.6 versus 3.4 versus 15.0).

However, one study (Lewis and Watters 1994) found no difference in the prevalence of multiple male partners reported by bisexual and homosexual IDUs, and the difference between bisexual and homosexual men in general tends to be minimized when certain restrictions are applied (Stokes, Taywaditep, Vanable, and McKirnan 1996). For example, S. Kippax, J. Crawford, P. Rodden, and K. Benton (1994) found no difference when only casual partners in the previous six months were counted and Doll and colleagues (1992) found no difference in the median number of partners in the previous year, although differences emerged when longer time periods were considered. Stokes and colleagues (Stokes, Taywaditep, Vanable, and McKirnan 1996; see also Stokes, McKirnan, and Burzette 1993) found that the difference between behaviorally bisexual and homosexual men disappeared when only partners in the previous six months were counted, although they did find differences in the types of partners reported by bisexual and homosexual men during that period. Homosexual men were more likely to have had lovers or steady partners, whereas bisexual men had had more casual or anonymous partners.

Some research suggests that the predominance of male over female partners among bisexuals is minimized or reversed under certain conditions. Research by Stokes, McKirnan, and Burzette (1993) suggests that self-labeled bisexual men have more male than female partners only in the short term; they found a difference in the average number of male and female (2.1 and 1.2, respectively) partners in the previous six months but no difference in the number of male and female lifetime partners (23.3 and 22.5, respectively). Another study suggests that the ratio of male to female partners among women might depend on exactly which portion of the bisexual population is studied. Norman and colleagues (1996), who recruited women as they entered gay bars in sixteen cities in the United States, classified as bisexual those who rated themselves on a five-point scale as being "bisexual," "primarily heterosexual," or "primarily homosexual." They found that these bisexual women were much more likely to have had a female (89.4 percent) than a male (17.5 percent) partner in the previous two months. The fact that these women were sampled in gay bars undoubtedly contributed to the preponderance of recent female partners; those with more, or only, male partners in the recent past would probably have been less likely to visit a gay bar at that point in their lives.

It is important to remember that research findings regarding the sexual activity levels of bisexuals and monosexuals are based on means and medians—summary statistics that gloss over individual differences. Like monosexuals, bisexuals vary greatly in their levels of sexual activity. Not all bisexuals are more active than all monosexuals; in fact, some bisexuals are not sexually, or not romantically, active at all. Thirteen percent of Ekstrand's self-identified bisexual men were celibate, Rust (1992) found that 21.4 percent of bisexual women—incidentally, the same percentage as found among lesbians (23.5 percent)—were not involved in any kind of relationship, even a casual dating relationship, and McKirnan, Stokes, Doll, and Burzette (1995) found that 49 percent of men who had been behaviorally bisexual within the previous three years were not in relationships.

An interesting finding by Stokes, McKirnan, and Burzette (1993) sheds light on the patterns of sexual diversity among bisexuals. They found a correlation between number of lifetime male partners and number of lifetime female partners, indicating that bisexuals who have large numbers of male partners also tend to have large numbers of female partners—that is, some bisexuals are very active with both men and women and some are not very active with either men or women. This finding undermines the conceptualization of heterosexuality and homosexuality as opposite forms of sexuality—a conceptualization incorporated into Kinsey-type scales on which hetero- and homosexual attractions and behaviors are counterposed at opposite ends of a continuum. Stokes, McKirnan, and Burzette's finding—along with Haynes and Oziel's (1976) finding of no inverse correlation between frequency of same-sex and other-sex activities and findings that bisexuals might be more heterosexually active than heterosexuals—suggests that heterosexual and homosexual activities are not contrary to each other. In fact, at least among bisexuals, they appear to be complementary, with both reflecting a common underlying level of sexual interest that is expressed not toward *either* men or women but toward *both* or *neither*.

Counting the number of sex partners bisexuals have reveals only part of the story of bisexuals' sex lives. What about the *quality* of bisexuals' sexual experiences? Some research suggests that bisexuals, especially bisexual women, are more satisfied with their sex lives than heterosexual women, and at least as satisfied as lesbians. Bressler and Lavender (1986) found that bisexual women and lesbians were more likely to describe their orgasms as "strong" than heterosexual women were (86 percent and 80 percent compared to 48 percent, respectively). In their sample of 125 women university students, LaTorre and Wendenburg (1983) found that women who had had both male and female sex partners were more satisfied with their sexual activities than women who had had only male partners. The 1983 *Playboy* sex survey found that 70 percent of bisexual women reported happy sex lives, although it also found that almost half of male bisexuals—more than any other group in the study—were unsatisfied. One explanation offered by *Playboy* author Kevin Cook for this finding is the ease with which bisexual women can find compatible sex partners compared to the difficulties bisexual men have. For example, bisexual men typically reported that their most intense orgasms occurred during fellatio. However, bisexual men also reported that most of their sex was with straight women, and straight women reported the lowest preference for oral sex of all groups of women surveyed. Thus, the mismatch between their own and their sex partners' desires would leave bisexual men unsatisfied.[43] Research findings regarding satisfaction among bisexual women and men are not all in agreement, however; Gary A. Zinik (1985) cited two unpublished studies (Saliba 1982; Zinik 1983) that found no difference in sexual satisfaction reported by bisexual, heterosexual, and homosexual individuals, and a finding by Paula S. Nurius (1983) that bisexuals were more sexually satisfied than lesbians and gay men was rendered insignificant when background characteristics were controlled.

If bisexual women are more satisfied with their sex lives than heterosexual women it might not be because their sex lives are objectively better but because their sexual expectations are less rigid and they place less emphasis on the sexual component of a relationship. David G. Daniel, Virginia Abernethy, and William R. Oliver (1984) studied bisexual and heterosexual feminists' reactions to male sexual dysfunction. They found that bisexual women had had more experience with male sexual dysfunction than heterosexual women and were more tolerant of it. Specifically, bisexual women were less threatened by the sexual dysfunction of their male partners, less likely to disparage their partners for sexual dysfunction, and more direct and honest in their responses to it than heterosexual feminists. Bisexual women also rated sexual satisfaction as less important in evaluating the overall quality of a relationship. In other words, bisexual women seem better able to enjoy whatever transpires sexually, compared to heterosexual women who are more likely to find satisfaction, both sexual satisfaction and satisfaction with a relationship as a whole, only when a stereotypical sexual script is successfully enacted.

Research by John W. Engel and Marie Saracino (1986), Rust (1996b), and Weinberg, Williams, and Pryor (1994) also suggests that bisexuals have slightly different priorities and requirements vis-à-vis their sexual and romantic partners than heterosexuals, lesbians, and gay men. Engel and Saracino (1986) asked self-identified bisexuals, heterosexuals, and gays/lesbians to rate the importance of a number of "love object characteristics," that is, characteristics that a romantic partner might have. Overall, bisexuals, heterosexuals, lesbians, and gay men considered many of the same things important; most people, regardless of sexual orientation, wanted a partner who shares their interests, values, and religious beliefs and who is intelligent, honest, affectionate, physically attractive, and dependable, with whom they could have a committed relationship involving emotional intimacy and intensity, physical intimacy, fun, and respect. But when asked about the sexual component of a relationship, bisexuals again expressed less rigid expectations.

Specifically, bisexuals were less concerned about jealousy within a relationship. Only 63 percent of Engel and Saracino's bisexuals, compared to 92 percent of heterosexuals and 91 percent of lesbians and gay men, considered it important that a relationship be "free of jealous feelings." Engel and Saracino explained the finding by suggesting that "bisexuals have a larger pool of eligibles to select love objects from, and therefore are less concerned about jealousy" (247). But research by Rust (1996b) and Weinberg, Williams, and Pryor (1994) suggests instead that bisexuals' relative lack of concern about jealousy reflects an entirely different view of what a sexual or romantic relationship should be like. Both Rust and Weinberg, Williams, and Pryor found that many bisexuals reject the cultural ideal of monogamy in favor of other types of relationships. In Rust's study only 29.5 percent of bisexual women and 15.4 percent of bisexual men said that their dream was to have a lifetime committed monogamous relationship, compared to 46.7 percent of lesbians and 75.9 percent of gay men.[44] Instead of monogamy, many bisexuals said that they would prefer to have an "open" primary relationship with secondary romantic relationships or sexual encounters, serial monogamy, lifetime polyfidelity, or multiple simultaneous primary or secondary relationships. Dual primary or simultaneous primary and secondary relationships were also the most popular ideals among the bisexual individuals interviewed by Weinberg, Williams, and Pryor in 1983. These ideals largely coincide with reality; the most common arrangement among Weinberg, Williams, and Pryor's bisexual subjects was a primary heterosexual relationship with or without secondary same- or other-sex liaisons. Similarly, in the 1983 *Playboy* survey 20 percent of bisexual men said that their primary sexual relationships were "open," and "almost half again" as many bisexual women reported being in open relationships. Engel and Saracino (1986) themselves found that only 26 percent of bisexuals, compared to 74 percent of heterosexuals and 62 percent of homosexuals, felt that "sexual fidelity is very important in a love relationship." However, the threat of AIDS has apparently changed some bisexuals' ideals regarding sexual fidelity, if not monogamy; Weinberg, Williams, and Pryor found that by 1988 sexual fidelity—with one partner in monogamy or more than one partner in polyfidelity—had become a much larger component of many bisexuals' ideal relationships.

The findings that bisexuals are less likely than lesbians, gay men, and heterosexuals to value monogamy in a relationship dovetail neatly with the fact that bisexuals are less likely to be involved in monogamous relationships than monosexuals are. In other words, bisexuals' lower rates of monogamy are not due to inability to commit or to practice fidelity, as is stereotypically assumed, but to positive choices in favor of other types of romantic and sexual relationships that might, in fact, be more effective and stable ways of fulfilling sexual and emotional needs for some people (Rust 1996b). In *Dual Attraction* Weinberg, Williams, and Pryor discussed at length the various ways in which bisexuals organize their romantic and sexual lives and the issues that arise for bisexuals who choose nonmonogamous relationships.

Engel and Saracino also found that bisexuals, along with lesbians and gay men, were less concerned that their partner be of their own social class and ethnic background than heterosexuals.[45] They suggested that heterosexuals might be more influenced by parental expectations regarding the type of person they should marry than bisexuals and homosexuals who cannot marry their same-sex partners. Bisexuals, lesbians, and gay men in Engel and Saracino's study were somewhat more likely to consider physical intimacy important than heterosexuals (95 percent and 100 percent compared to 89 percent, $p < .01$) and more likely to believe that "you should share your most intimate thoughts and feelings with the person you love" (95 percent and 95 percent compared to 76 percent). The authors noted that different characteristics are important at different stages of romantic relationships and suggested that some of the differences found in bisexuals', heterosexuals', and

homosexuals' ideals might have resulted from bisexuals and homosexuals thinking in terms of new or short-term relationships whereas heterosexuals thought in
terms of more mature relationships. It is also plausible, however, that the different
levels of social sanction given same-sex and other-sex relationships, and the fact
that heterosexual relationships are more heavily socially scripted and assumed to
produce children, influences the types of partners and relationships that bisexuals
and homosexuals, compared to heterosexuals, seek.

Bisexuals are in a unique position to compare the experiences of sexual contact
and romance with men and with women. Both autobiographical comments by
some bisexuals and social scientific findings suggest that for many bisexuals these
experiences are different. For example, Clausen (1990a)—who described herself as
a "technical" bisexual engaged in identity resistance—wrote that "my desire is always for a specifically sexed and gendered individual. When I am with a woman, I
love as a woman loves a woman, and when I am with a man, I love as a woman
loves a man" (454). Zinik (1983) found that self-identified bisexual men and women
reported that they were similarly sexually aroused by men and by women but that
they received more emotional satisfaction from their female partners and fell in
love with women more often than with men. Similarly, Weinberg, Williams, and
Pryor (1994) reported that bisexual men and women find it easier to have sex with
men but easier to fall in love with women, and Taywaditep and Stokes (1998) concluded, on the basis of a cluster analysis of bisexual men's self-identities, erotic fantasies, and sexual and relationship histories, that "sex with men seemed to be less
bound to relationships than sex with women" (35). Recall from chapter 22 that
McKirnan, Stokes, Doll, and Burzette (1995) found that most of behaviorally bisexual men's male partners were casual and that bisexuals tended to have more male
than female sex partners. Relationships with men tend to be shorter and more centered on sexuality than relationships with women; Charlotte Wolff (1977) found
that bisexual men's same-sex relationships were shorter and more sexual than
their other-sex relationships, whereas bisexual women's same-sex relationships
were fewer and longer lasting than their other-sex relationships. Stokes, McKirnan,
and Burzette (1993) found that most bisexual men who had had heterosex had had
it with steady partners (62 percent), whereas those who had had homosex had usually had it with casual partners or friends (57 percent, 50 percent).[46] They also
found that bisexual men were twice as likely to be living with a female spouse or
lover than with a "gay male roommate" (19 percent versus 8 percent) and were
more likely to be in a steady heterosexual than a steady homosexual relationship
(27 percent versus 8 percent; 4 percent had both).

Given gender role socialization that encourages men more than women to engage in sexual activity, and to do so without the trappings of romance, these findings are not surprising. Gender socialization would lead bisexuals to view women
as more appropriate partners for serious relationships and to draw sharper distinctions between sex and commitment with regard to male partners than with regard
to female partners (Stokes, McKirnan, and Burzette 1993). Weinberg, Williams, and
Pryor (1994) pointed out that the types of same- and other-sex activities one engages in also depend on one's sexual opportunities and that sexual opportunities

are gendered; impersonal sexual interactions between men are facilitated by cruising areas and other sex-focused venues that have little counterpart among women. They noted the irony in the fact that bisexuals—who, unlike monosexuals, do not discriminate exclusively against either gender in their sexual attractions and choice of partners—nevertheless organize their sexual and romantic activities along traditional gender lines. They argued that bisexuals, like monosexuals, learn traditional gender schemas and that the process of eroticizing both genders does not erase what one has learned regarding the differences between men and women.

If the actual experiences of most bisexual people are gendered, then is the concept of bisexuality as a gender-independent form of sexuality merely a heuristic tool for social scientists and a political tool for the bisexual movement? The simple answer is no; some individual bisexuals do describe their sexual and emotional feelings for others as depending primarily on characteristics other than gender. However, a more complete understanding of the role of gender in the experience of bisexuality requires more than a "most do, some don't" answer; it requires challenging the assumptions underlying the question of whether gender is important. One assumption is that the possibilities are binary, that is, that gender is either important or not important, with importance perhaps varying in degree. Through her hypothetical character "Cloe," Elisabeth D. Däumer challenged this assumption by suggesting that the two positions are not irreconcilable. Referring to conceptions of bisexuality as either "neatly divided between or integrating heterosexuality and homosexuality" (1994: 103), Cloe

> finds it impossible to say, with the absolute certainty that such definitions of bisexuality imply, that she loves men and women differently; and although she finds it equally impossible to say that she loves them the same, she is reluctant to ascribe the difference in these encounters—whether imaginary or real—to gender alone. . . . What if, by mistake, one forgot that the person holding one's hand was a man—or a woman—and if one, equally by mistake, were to slip into a heterosexual relationship with a woman, a lesbian relationship with a man? (104)

How could one forget? In the abstract the possibility might be inconceivable to nonbisexuals, but Ann Kaloski described an environment in which even monosexuals might understand the possibilities. She noted that in the flesh-free environment of virtual reality, or cyberspace, "bodies, genders, sex-acts, and sexualities can be reformulated through language" and asked, "What does bisexuality signify in a space where sex/gender is mutable, and your female lover might be a man in real life?" (1997:49–50). The question of whether gender is important subtly assumes that gender is immutable and essential; if it is mutable and socially inscribed, then it can be simultaneously important and not important.

The question of whether gender is important is also usually assumed to refer to traditional dichotomous gender, i.e., to the distinction between men and women, who are also correspondingly males and females. Theoretical dismantling of dichotomous sex and gender by sexologists is discussed in chapter 4; might nonbinary models help increase our understanding of the gendering of bisexual experience? Research by Rust (1995b, 1995c) suggests that they would. She found that, among individuals who had either been attracted to or sexually active with both men and women, those who identified as bisexual made a sharper distinction between biological sex and gender than did those who identified as lesbian or gay. Both sex and gender were important to lesbians and gay men, whereas gender but not sex was important to bisexuals, especially bisexual women. When asked to use a seven-point scale to rate the importance of a person's biological sex in determining how strong their attractions were to that person, only 12 percent of bisexual women and 28 percent of bisexual men said that sex is very or extremely important compared to 64 percent of lesbians and 86 percent of gay men. When asked to rate the importance of a person's gender, 44 percent of bisexual women and 50 percent of bisexual men, compared to 42 percent of lesbians and 59 percent of gay men, said that gender is very or extremely important. When asked, if gender were important to them, *which* genders they preferred, half of bisexual men and only 17 percent of bisexual women checked "masculinity" and/or "femininity"; 39 percent of the women and 24 percent of the men preferred "androgyny" or "gender blending" forms of gender, and others described a variety of unique gender styles, including "butch women who are obviously women" and "masculine personality, but feminine appearance." Thus it appears that gender does matter to most bisexuals, but *gender* does not necessarily refer to the dichotomous distinction between male men and female women.

Dual Challenges to Duality: Bisexuality Among Transgenderists

Like bisexuality, transgenderism involves a potential challenge to simplistic binary notions of gender. Because the cultural distinction between heterosexuality and homosexuality assumes that all people are either male or female and men or women, individuals who are not simply men or women—that is, transgenderists and transsexuals—sometimes have difficulty fitting themselves into these monosexual categories. If one is not clearly a man or a woman oneself, on what basis can one label one's relationship with another person heterosexual, lesbian, or gay, regardless of the gender of that other person? Some researchers have bypassed the complexities involved in this question by asserting a specific definition of sexual orientation. For example, in keeping with traditional psychiatric nomenclature, Ray Blanchard wrote, "The terms *homosexual* and *heterosexual* are applied to gender dysphorics (including pre- and postoperative transsexuals) exactly as they are to other individuals, to refer to erotic attraction to members of the same or the opposite chromosomal sex" (1989:316).[47] Such definitions have been criticized by other authors as androcentric, and Eli Coleman, Walter O. Bockting, and Louis Gooren (1993) pointedly disagreed with authors like Blanchard, writing, "With transsexualism, the complexities and inadequacies in defining sexual orientation on the basis of biological sex become more obvious" (38). Instead of hiding the definitional dust under a black-and-white rug, authors such as Coleman, Bockting, and Gooren (1993), Dallas Denny and Jamison Green (1996), Weinberg, Williams, and Pryor (1994), Clare Hemmings (1996), and Holly Devor (1993) see transsexualism as an opportunity to explore these complexities and inadequacies. Denny and Green provided a review of scientific views of the sexuality of transsexuals and other transgenderists with a special focus on bisexuality among transgenderists and Weinberg, Williams, and Pryor (1994) explored transsexualism among bisexuals. Hemmings used an interview with Bet Power, curator of the Sexual Minorities Archives and a female-to-male nonoperative transsexual, as a take-off point for theorizing bisexuality and transgenderism in relation to each other, and Devor conducted a study of the pre- and post-transition sexual experiences of forty-five female-to-male (FTM) transsexuals.

Devor found that most FTM transsexuals were attracted to women both before and after transition (96 percent, 90 percent) and that many (56 percent) were also attracted to straight men before, but not after (3 percent), their transition. After transition, those who were attracted to men were generally attracted to gay men (28 percent). Devor outlined the various sexual orientation self-identities her respondents adopted pre- and post-transition, describing the various bases they used to build these self-identities. For example, prior to transition some respondents who had sexual contact with women labeled themselves lesbian women based on their physical beings, whereas others identified themselves as straight based on the social meanings they gave these sexual relations. Although more than half were attracted to both women and men before transition, only 10 percent identified themselves as bisexual men and 5 percent as bisexual women. It seems that, as in the nontranssexual population, bisexual self-identity is rarer than bisexual feelings or behaviors.[48] Using transsexuals' identity struggles to point out the inadequacies of cultural sexual orientation categories, Devor characterized these struggles as a more "stark" version of a process that "most members of society go through" as they seek to form sexual self-identities using available cultural categories (314). It is to this process of sexual identity formation, and the particular difficulties that bisexuals have in forming sexual self-identities, that I now turn.

Coming Out and Staying Out: Bisexual Identity

Bisexuals face many issues when coming out, some similar to those faced by lesbians and gay men and others unique to bisexuals. Like lesbians and gay men, bisexuals are usually raised with a default heterosexual identity and must, at some point, question that identity. Unlike lesbians and gay men, bisexuals must question the even deeper assumption that there are only two authentic forms of sexuality and that sexual expression must be directed toward either one gender or the other. Like lesbians and gay men, most bisexuals come to recognize within themselves feelings of sexual and romantic attraction toward members of their own sex and have to come to terms with general social attitudes, which they might share as a result of socialization, that these feelings are not as acceptable as heterosexual feelings. Unlike lesbians and gay men, bisexuals must also recognize their feelings of attraction for the other sex, which, if they have been previously involved in lesbian or gay subculture, they might have learned to devalue in the process of developing "gay pride." Some bisexuals have to come out twice, once as lesbian or gay within the context of heterosexual society, and a second time as bisexual within the context of lesbian and gay society. Like lesbians and gay men, bisexuals must confront people who would prefer they be heterosexual, or at least act heterosexual. Unlike lesbians and gay men, bisexuals often find that they first have to convince these people that bisexuality exists before they can persuade them to tolerate or accept it. Gay men and lesbians, although they might come out in isolation, often find a supportive gay or lesbian community. Bisexuals, even after they come out, might find it difficult to locate a bisexual community. Many seek support in lesbian and gay communities that sometimes provide little validation for bisexual self-identity. Although bisexual organizations are multiplying at a phenomenal rate, exist in many large cities, and are nationally and internationally networked, the size, cultural development, and resources of this bisexual network are incomparable to those of 'lesbian and gay' communities.

Because of the cognitive and social difficulties in developing and maintaining a bisexual self-identity, many bisexual individuals seek other solutions to the problem of self-identification. Some individuals switch between bisexual, heterosexual, and lesbian or gay self-identities, depending on the gender of their current sex partners or other social factors, rather than maintain a continuous self-identity as bisexual. Others adopt a stable self-identity as lesbian, gay, or heterosexual. Margaret Nichols (1988) characterized gay as a residual category in which anyone with any measure of homosexual interest might place themselves—a sexual version of the racist one drop rule that is encouraged by both a heterosexual society that seeks to purify itself of all homosexuality and by lesbian and gay subcultures that tend to discredit the other-sex portion of bisexual behavior as the ego-dystonic result of socialization. But evidence presented in chapters 14 and 17 regarding heterosexual self-identified men and women who have same-sex experiences in the context of anonymous cruising, swinging, prostitution, or prison indicates that much bisexual experience is also hidden behind heterosexual self-identities. Some individuals adopt what Ault (1996) called "fractured" identities, for example "bi-dyke" or "lesbian-identified bisexual," usually as a way of identifying their own sexuality while seeking to retain their membership in lesbian or gay communities and politics. Finally, some individuals do identify as bisexual, but this might be a private identity maintained alongside a more public lesbian or gay identity used to gain acceptance in lesbian or gay communities (Golden 1987). Even among those who are out as bisexual, Däumer noted that many conceptualize this bisexuality as a hybrid form of sexuality composed of parts heterosexuality and parts homosexuality or an integration of heterosexuality and homosexuality. Thus dichotomous social constructions of sexuality assert and reassert themselves at the psychological, social, and political levels as bisexuals seek to identify themselves in a culture that expects each individual to possess a sexual identity.

Bisexuals themselves discuss the difficulties of developing and maintaining bisexual self-identity, and the political implications of the various self-identities that result, in the numerous popular publications that have appeared "by and for" bisexuals in the late 1980s and 1990s (e.g., Hutchins and Ka'ahumanu 1991). For example, activist Lucy Friedland (1989) described the tendency for individuals with bisexual experiences or feelings to identify as either lesbian/gay or heterosexual and coined this "BLAS"—Bisexual Label Avoidance Syndrome. These politicized discussions of identity occasionally surface in the social scientific literature. For example, Ault (1996) charged that "fractured identities" erase bisexual experience and produce fractured communities, thwarting bisexual activists' views of bisexuality as a challenge to binary gender. Däumer argued that concepts of bisexuality as a combination or integration of heterosexuality and homosexuality are a form of false consciousness that counteracts the subversive potential of bisexuality.

In the past most social science research on sexual identity neglected bisexual identity entirely, and some researchers—and mental health clinicians, who would be in a position to support the formation of healthy bisexual self-identities—have explicitly discounted the possibility of an authentic bisexual identity (e.g., Schäfer 1976). Those few social scientists who acknowledged the possibility of bisexual self-identity usually characterized it as a transitional phase or stepping stone on the way to a lesbian or gay self-identity (e.g., Chapman and Brannock 1987; cf. Bell, Weinberg, and Hammersmith 1981)—a characterization that reflects popular beliefs that bisexuality is a transitional and inauthentic form of sexuality and sexual identity. However, a recent survey of 207 psychiatrists and 63 sex therapists, conducted by the Opinion Research Corporation, suggests that many mental health professionals are no longer as quick to discredit bisexual self-identity; 63 percent of psychiatrists and 82 percent of sex therapists indicated that they believed bisexuality to be a "bona fide classification" (Hill 1987). In each group approximately half the remainder indicated that they were "not sure." Publications urging clinicians to recognize bisexuality as authentic and educating them about issues pertinent to bisexual clients have begun to appear (e.g., Davies 1996; Deacon, Reinke, and Viers 1996; Douce 1998; Firestein 1996; Hawkins 1998; Matteson 1995, 1996a, 1996b; Morrow 1998; Paul 1996; Phillips and Fischer 1998; Smiley 1997; Weasel 1996).

Reflecting the growing acknowledgment of bisexuality as an authentic orientation, a few researchers added bisexual self-identity as an alternate outcome to models designed primarily to describe coming out among lesbians and gay men.[49] These models of lesbian and gay self-identity formation, developed in the post-1960s initial blush of affirmative research on sexual orientation and before researchers turned their attention to AIDS in the 1980s, cast coming out as a linear developmental process consisting of a series of milestone events.[50] As noted by Esterberg (1997) in *Lesbian and Bisexual Identities* and by Rust (1993a) in an article reprinted as chapter 26 in this section, the coming out process described by these models is one of psychological and social maturation beginning with a default, and perhaps unrecognized, heterosexual self-identity and ending with the achievement of a positive self-conscious gay or lesbian self-identity. The milestone events occurring along the way include, for example, an individual's first experience of feeling sexual attraction to a member of their own sex, their first suspicion that they might not be heterosexual, their first same-sex experience, and their initial adoption of a nonheterosexual self-identity. Although these linear developmental models were initially intended as simple descriptions of the coming out process, they acquired a moral prescriptive quality in which achieving a positive lesbian or gay self-identity came to be seen as healthy and normal and "failure" to do so—including the adoption of a bisexual self-identity instead of a lesbian or gay one—was attributed to internalized homophobia or some other social or psychological barrier (Rust 1996d).

By simply adding bisexuals to these models, rather than studying the process of coming out as bisexual per se, researchers blind themselves to the unique issues faced by bisexuals (Rust 1996d). For example, the assumption that coming out begins with a default heterosexual identity in the context of heterosexual society conceals the issues faced by individuals who have already come out as lesbian or gay and whose process of coming out as bisexual begins with a questioning of lesbian or gay identity within the context of a lesbian or gay community.[51] Although research suggests that most bisexuals do first eroticize the other sex and identify as heterosexual because of the societal preference for and assumption of heterosexuality,[52] the growing visibility and cultural influence of the lesbian and gay community might be increasing the number of individuals who identify as lesbian or gay first and then come out a second time as bisexual. Among the particular issues faced by these individuals are confusion and fear upon (re)recognition of their sexual and emotional attractions toward people of the other sex (A. Fox 1991). This confusion and fear results from biphobia or heterophobia that they internalized while struggling to maintain a lesbian or gay self-identity in the face of their bisexual feelings and experiences. Individuals who became involved in lesbian or gay communities might also face antagonism from some lesbians and gay men who consider bisexuals political traitors or cowards, accuse them of indecisiveness, and tell them that they are denying their "true" lesbian or gay sexuality and that their bisexuality is a transitional phase.

Linear models designed to describe lesbian and gay self-identity development also assume that coming out ends with the acquisition of a self-identity that accurately reflects the individual's "true" sexual orientation. This assumption is based on the belief that individuals "inherently strive for congruence between [their] sexual feelings, activities, and identities" and that congruence is the mark of true identity (Golden 1987:31). But for bisexuals, who arrive at a bisexual self-identity only to experience continued pressure to "decide" whether they are gay or straight, this process of self-discovery might be followed by another process of renewed self-denial as they attempt to fit themselves into socially acceptable monosexual categories. Matteson (1997, see also 1996a), for example, reported that "the move of some bisexuals to solely heterosexual or solely homosexual relationships was not necessarily an indication that bisexuality was not 'real' for these men, but that social supports and personal resources to handle the complexity were lacking" (98). Thus, one might be moving away from, rather than toward, a true self-identity.

Alternatively, one might abandon the concept of true identity altogether. Joan Sophie (1986) found that some women who had been in the process of developing a lesbian self-identity and then reacknowledged attractions to men dealt with this by shifting not from one fixed self-identity to another, but from a fixed identity to a flexible sexual identity. The concept of flexible identity might be especially applicable to women. As discussed in chapter 11, several researchers have found that women's sexuality is more "fluid," or variable, than men's and that there is less internal consistency among women's than among men's sexual self-identities, feelings, and behaviors (e.g., Laumann, Gagnon, Michael, and Michaels 1994; Storms 1978; Weinberg, Williams, and Pryor 1994). Pillard (1990) commented that his research team found it more difficult to assign Kinsey ratings to women than to men because women seemed to experience greater changes in their sexual lives even as adults and because their sexual feelings were more influenced by situational factors such as their current sex partner (see also Schwartz and Blumstein 1998). Nichols (1985, 1990) found that "gays and lesbians, but particularly lesbians, showed little internal consistency" in Kinsey-style ratings of their behaviors, fantasies, and emotional attractions. Carla Golden (1987) noted that the women she interviewed were markedly undisturbed by discrepancies between their own self-identities and behaviors and discussed the fluidity of women's sexuality at length.

Several explanations have been offered for the internal inconsistencies in women's sexuality. Most social theorists argue that, whereas men might base their sexual self-identities directly on the evidence of their sexual feelings and experiences, women's sexual self-identities are influenced by myriad social and political factors. For example, general social repression of women's sexuality inhibits women from expressing their feelings through behavior, resulting in discrepancies between their feelings, behaviors, and self-identities. The situational dependence of women's sexual self-identities might be due to socialization that teaches women to draw their identities from their relationships with others, thus leading to greater variability in women's self-identities as these relationships change. Within sexual minority communities antipathy toward bisexuality and the politicization and desexualization of lesbian identity by the lesbian feminist movement of the 1970s (discussed earlier in this chapter) means that for many women the choice to self-identify as a lesbian—or as a bisexual—reflects one's personal politics at least as much as it reflects one's sexual feelings and behaviors. One's self-identity might, therefore, be "inconsistent" with one's actual sexual experiences.

In an effort to more accurately describe the experience of coming out as bisexual, Weinberg, Williams, and Pryor (1994) formulated a linear model of bisexual self-identity development based on their research with bisexual women and men in San Francisco.[53] The stages of their model are initial confusion, finding and applying the bisexual label to oneself, settling into the bisexual self-identity, and—in contrast to other linear models, which end with the acquisition of a "true" identity—continued uncertainty regarding this self-identity. In explaining both the initial confusion and the continuing uncertainty reported by their bisexual respondents, Weinberg, Williams, and Pryor stressed the role of lack of social validation for bisexual self-identity. A. X. van Naersson (1998), who also sought to make sense of the process of sexual identity formation among bisexuals, found confusion among ten adolescent males with bisexual erotic feelings and suggested that confusion might not be particular to bisexuals but rather a normal aspect of the human condition.

Researchers working with an understanding of coming out as a linear developmental process often ask their respondents about the ages at which they experienced particular milestone events. They then average respondents' answers to produce a portrait of the "typical" coming out experience.[54] Weinberg, Williams, and Pryor (1994), for example, discovered that the bisexual women they interviewed in 1983 had their first heterosexual attraction at an average age of 11.6 years, three years before their first heterosexual experience at the average age of 14.7 years, and that homosexual attraction and experience occurred later, at the average ages of 16.9 and 21.4 years. Men also experienced heterosexual attractions first at an average age of 11.7 years but had their first heterosexual experience (17.3 years) after their first homosexual attraction and experience (13.5 and 16.3 years). Women first labeled themselves bisexual at an average age of 26.8 years, and men did so at an average age of 27.2 years. Based on these findings that other-sex milestones generally occurred before same-sex ones, the researchers characterized bisexuality as the result of "adding on" homosexuality "to an already developed heterosexual interest" (1994:43).

Most other research studies in which adult bisexual men's and/or women's same-sex and other-sex milestones were compared also found that other-sex milestones typically occur before same-sex milestones.[55] For example, Klein found that women attending the Bisexual Forum first realized their other-sex feelings at an average age of 11.3 years and their same-sex feelings at 17 years, and had their first sexual experience with a man at age 15.5 years, five years before their first experience with a woman at age 23 years. Men realized their other-sex feelings at an average age of 13.1 years and their same-sex feelings at 16 years, and had their first sexual experience with a woman at age 16 years, almost two years before their first experience with a man at 17.8 years old. The women in this survey first identified themselves as bisexual at 24.4 years, compared to 24.1 years among men. On the other hand, in a general population sample including heterosexuals Van Wyk and Geist (1984) found that those who had had same-sex orgasms did so first at younger ages than those who had had other-sex orgasms; 66 percent of females and 71 percent of males had coital orgasms at average first ages of 23.1 and 19.6 respectively, whereas 11 percent of females and 32 percent of males had homosexual orgasms at average first ages of 20.5 and 15.0 respectively.

Research in which bisexuals are compared with lesbians and gay men suggests that bisexuals recognize the same-sex aspects of their sexuality at later ages than lesbians and gay men do and, once having felt same-sex attraction, take longer to adopt a nonheterosexual self-identity. For example, in a 1984–1985 survey that included heterosexuals and homosexuals as well as bisexuals in San Francisco, Weinberg, Williams, and Pryor (1994) found that bisexual women first felt homosexual attraction at the average age of 18.5 years and had their first homosexual experience five years later at 23.5 years, compared to average ages of 16.4 and 20.5 years for homosexual women. Both groups had their first heterosexual attraction and experience prior to their first homosexual ones—among bisexual women, at average ages of 10.9 and 15.1 years, respectively. The researchers also found that bisexual men first felt homosexual attraction at the average age of 17.1 years and had their first homosexual experience almost simultaneously at 17.2 years, compared to average ages of 11.5 and 14.7 years for gay men. Bisexual men experienced their other-sex milestones prior to their same-sex ones, with heterosexual attraction and experience occurring at averages ages of 12.8 years and 15.9 years respectively, whereas gay men experienced them in the opposite order. Bisexual women and bisexual men first identified themselves as bisexual or homosexual at the average ages of 27.0 and 29.0 years; this was 8.5 and 11.9 years, respectively, after they first felt same-sex attractions. In comparison, homosexual women and men first identified themselves at average ages of 22.5 and 21.1 years, only 6.1 and 9.6 years, respectively, after first feeling same-sex attractions (see also Kooden et al. 1979).

Pattatucci and Hamer (1995) also found evidence of these patterns in their research on women. They discovered that women with Kinsey scores of 2–4 first felt a romantic or sexual attraction to another female at an average age of 12.6 years, three years after they first felt attracted to a male (9.5 years) and two years later than more exclusively homosexual women (10.6 years; Kinsey 5–6's) first felt attracted to a female. Bisexual women acknowledged their sexual orientations to themselves at an average age of 21.4 years, one year later than more exclusively homosexual women (20.4 years), although this latter difference is not statistically significant. Noting that many lesbian and heterosexual women, like bisexuals, had had both same- and other-sex milestone experiences, and that lesbians experienced their same-sex milestones before their other-sex milestones whereas heterosexuals experienced their other-sex milestones first, Pattatucci and Hamer characterized bisexual women as following a path of development intermediate to that of lesbian and heterosexual women in terms of the timing of their milestone events.[56] Also supporting the claim that bisexuals come out later in life than lesbians and gay men is Bell, Weinberg, and Hammersmith's (1981) finding that bisexual women exhibited more discrepancy between their adolescent and adult sexualities than lesbians did and Gary Remafedi, Michael Resnick, Robert Blum, and Linda Harris's (1992) finding that high school students who were "unsure" of their sexual self-identity were more likely than students with sexual self-identities to report feeling bisexual attractions. For a complete summary of average age data on the milestone event experiences of lesbians, gay men, and bisexuals from over two dozen research studies, arranged in tabulated format to facilitate comparisons, see Ronald C. Fox (1995, also 1996).

Research on lesbian, gay, and bisexual youths yields findings that differ from adult samples. Some of these studies suggest that youths experience same-sex milestones before other-sex milestones—the reverse of the pattern found among bisexual adults. Savin-Williams (1995a) and Mary-Jane Rotheram-Borus and colleagues, including Margaret Rosario, Helen Reid, Cheryl Koopman, Heino F. L. Meyer-Bahlburg, and Joyce Hunter (Rotheram-Borus, Hunter, and Rosario 1994; Rotheram-Borus, Reid, and Rosario 1994; Rotheram-Borus et al. 1994; Rotheram-Borus, Reid, and Rosario, and Kasen 1995; Rotheram-Borus, Rosario, Reid, and Koopman 1995; Rotheram-Borus et al. 1995), studied gay and bisexual males aged

17 to 23 years and 14 to 19 years, respectively, Margaret Rosario and colleagues, including Heino F. L. Meyer-Bahlburg and Joyce Hunter (Rosario et al. 1996), studied both gay and bisexual males and lesbian and bisexual females aged 14 to 21, and Anthony R. D'Augelli and Scott L. Hershberger (1993) studied lesbian, gay, and bisexual youths aged 21 or younger.[57] The first two studies found that male youths had their first same-sex experiences before their first other-sex experiences.[58] Savin-Williams found that the first "gay feelings" occurred at the average age of 7.4 years, that the 94 percent who had had "homosexual experience" first did so at the average age of 14.2 years, and that the 55 percent who had had "heterosexual experience" first did so at the average age of 15.5 years (no average age for first heterosexual feelings was reported). The authors noted that the time gap between first same-sex and first other-sex contact was 1.5 years among those individuals who had had both same- and other-sex contact but did not provide average ages for this bisexually experienced portion of the sample. Rotheram-Borus and colleagues (Rotheram-Borus et al. 1994) asked more specific questions about particular forms of same-sex and other-sex contact, discovering that, among those who had had each experience, manual sex occurred at an average age of 12.4 years with male partners (92 percent) and 13.1 years with female partners (52 percent), oral sex at an average age of 13.5 years with male partners (86 percent) and 14.3 years with female partners (30 percent), penile-vaginal sex at an average age of 13.8 years (48 percent), anal sex at an average age of 14.0 years with male partners (80 percent) and 14.4 years with female partners (6 percent), and anilingus with male partners at an average age of 15.3 years (49 percent).

Rosario and colleagues, who reported average ages for the initiation of various specific sexual practices as well as same- and other-sex milestones in general, found smaller differences in the opposite direction. They found that gay and bisexual male respondents first became aware of same-sex attractions at an average age of 10.8 years, and the 58 percent who reported other-sex attractions first became aware of them at an average age of 10.6 years. Ninety-five percent had same-sex contacts at an average first age of 13.3, and 56 percent had other-sex contacts at an average first age of 11.9. D'Augelli and Hershberger (1993) found no difference in the timing of same- and other-sex experiences; for males both occurred at an average first age of 15 years. They became aware of their same-sex feelings at an average age of 9.8 years and self-labeled at an average age of 14.8 years. Neither the Rotheram-Borus and Rosario team nor D'Augelli and Hershberger provided average ages or data regarding time gaps between these experiences specific to the bisexually experienced portions of their samples, although Rosario and colleagues (1996) did report that the 48 males who had ever thought that they were really bisexual did so first at an average age of 14.7 years.

Among "lesbian and bisexual" females, Rosario and colleagues found that same-sex attractions occurred before other-sex attractions, but same-sex contact occurred after other-sex contact. Their female respondents first became aware of same-sex attractions at an average age of 10.5, and the 71 percent who were also aware of other-sex attractions became aware of them at an average age of 11.5. Eighty-eight percent of females had same-sex contacts at an average first age of

14.0, and 80 percent had other-sex contacts at an average first age of 13.1. Compared to males in this study, therefore, females were more likely to have had other-sex contacts, less likely to have had same-sex contacts, and had other-sex contacts at older ages; the difference in age at initial same-sex contact is not statistically significant. The forty-seven females who had thought that they were really bisexual did so first at an average age of 15.3 years. D'Augelli and Hershberger (1993) also found, on average, that other-sex contact (12 years) occurred before same-sex contact (14.6 years) for lesbian and bisexual females aged 21 or younger. These young women first became aware of same-sex feelings at an average age of 11.1 years and first self-labeled at an average age of 14.6 years.

Aside from a possible difference in the order of same- and other-sex events, the most striking difference between the findings of research on youths and on adults is that the average ages at which youths experienced many milestones are substantially lower than those at which adults experienced them, especially among males. For example, Weinberg, Williams, and Pryor's adult bisexual and gay men first experienced same-sex feelings of attraction at 17.1 years and 11.5 years, respectively, compared to 7.4 years among Savin-Williams' gay and bisexual male youths, 9.8 years among D'Augelli and Hershberger's male youths, and 10.8 among Rosario and colleague's gay and bisexual male youths. The average ages at which these youths first experienced other-sex attractions are also lower, although not as dramatically so. The average ages at which lesbian, gay, and bisexual adults first identified themselves as nonheterosexual range from 20.4 years among Pattatucci and Hamer's lesbian women to 29.0 years among Weinberg, Williams, and Pryor's bisexual men, whereas male and female youths first identified themselves as gay, lesbian, or bisexual at approximately 15 years old. Noting that the average ages at which their young respondents experienced milestone events are low in comparison to other researchers' findings on older respondents, Rosario and colleagues suggested the possibility of generational differences between their subjects who were adolescent in the 1990s and other researchers' subjects who were adults in the 1970s and 1980s (see also Fox 1995). That earlier generations came out later in life would seem to be a reasonable conclusion, because earlier generations grew up in more homophobic and biphobic times.

However, this might be an erroneous conclusion because a great deal, if not all, of the difference might be an artifact of sample selection bias. The fact that Savin-Williams, the Rotheram-Borus and Rosario team, and D'Augelli and Hershberger purposefully recruited samples of lesbian, gay, and bisexual *youths* guaranteed that their subjects would have recognized their same-sex attractions at younger ages than most people do; they had to have come out at young enough ages to qualify as "lesbian, gay, and bisexual youths" and be included in these studies. Their peers who will come out later in life—and would be included in later studies of "lesbian, gay, and bisexual adults"—still identified themselves as heterosexual at the times of these studies and so, of course, were not included in them. Later research on the same generation would include those who will come out later, and would therefore find older average ages. Youths who come out early—for whatever reason—represent a special segment of the population that will eventually become lesbian, gay, and bisexual adults. Findings among such youth accurately reflect the youths' own experiences. However, these findings cannot be generalized to adults nor compared to findings made on older samples because the average ages at which youth experience coming out milestones are biased downward, relative to the ages at which adults have experienced these milestones, by their very youth.

Unlike the studies by Savin-Williams, the Rotheram-Borus and Rosario team, and D'Augelli and Hershberger, most studies include people of varying ages, compounding the statistical problem of greater downward bias in average ages among younger respondents. Older respondents in such studies will have lived a greater proportion of their lives and will, everything else equal, therefore be more likely to have had a given experience before the time of the survey and to have done so at a higher average age. This would make it appear that older generations experienced each milestone event at older ages, that is, that they came out later in life. But, as in the comparison between studies of youth with studies of adults, different average ages for different generations in a single study could result from the fact that average ages for older generations include the older ages of those members of that generation who did come out later in life—older ages that are excluded from the averages calculated for younger generations. Short of surveying people on their deathbeds, there are statistical procedures that can correct this problem, but they have rarely, if ever, been used in coming out research.

Another statistical problem involved in studying the average ages at which individuals experience any given event arises when average ages for different events or different populations are compared to each other, as when the fact that bisexual women first experienced heterosexual attraction at the average age of 11.6 years and homosexual attraction at the average age of 16.9 years is interpreted as indicating that bisexuals women typically recognize their heterosexual prior to their homosexual attractions, or when the fact that bisexual women first felt attracted to women at an average age of 12.6 years compared to 10.6 years among lesbians is interpreted as indicating that bisexuals typically come out later than lesbians. Actually, that the average age of one event, for example, first other-sex attraction, is lower than the average age of another event, for example, first same-sex attraction, does not indicate that everyone first felt other-sex attraction prior to same-sex attraction or even that this was the experience of the majority. For example, although Klein (1978) found that bisexual men had had their first other-sex experience an average of 1.8 years prior to their first same-sex experience, only 47 percent of individual men had actually had their first sex with a woman at a younger age than their first sex with a man. Thus the order of milestone events indicated by average ages might not be the "typical" order in which individuals experience these events at all.

Most researchers who study the coming out process acknowledge the fact that not all individuals experience coming out milestone events in the same order. For example, Vivienne Cass (1979, 1990) noted that each event might be followed by "foreclosure" rather than by the next event in the sequence, and Gary J. McDonald (1982) observed that some people do not "move predictably" (40) through milestone events. But these researchers conceptualized these possibilities as deviations from a fundamentally ordered and sequential process and based their discussions of the issues faced by individuals at each stage of the process on their findings regarding the order in which these events "typically" take place, as indicated by comparisons of average ages. Given that individuals who experience events in different orders might face very different issues during coming out—for example, individuals who come out as bisexual first, then lesbian or gay compared to individuals who come out as lesbian or gay first, and then bisexual—these researchers' conclusions reflect the experiences and issues faced by only those individuals who experience these events in the order suggested by the average ages.

Rust (1993a; reprinted as chapter 26, this volume) gave an example of the way in which comparisons of average ages distort the process of coming out as experienced by bisexuals. The findings cited above that bisexuals come out more slowly than lesbians were founded on the assumption that individuals typically experience same-sex attraction before self-identifying as lesbian or bisexual—an assumption made because the average age of the former was lower than the average age of the latter. Rust discovered, however, that one quarter of lesbians identified themselves as lesbian prior to feeling attraction for another woman. There was no similar pattern among bisexuals, and Rust suggested that these lesbians might be the "political lesbians" of the 1970s who identified as lesbian for political, not sexual, reasons.[59] Whatever the reason, the inclusion of these lesbians in the calculation of average ages had raised the average age of first same-sex attraction and lowered the average age of first self-identification as lesbian, thus decreasing the average time gap between these experiences among lesbians. When these lesbians were excluded from the analysis a new comparison between lesbians and bisexual women who had experienced same-sex attraction before identifying themselves as bisexual or lesbian revealed that bisexual women had actually questioned their heterosexual self-identities following the experience of same-sex attraction *more quickly*, not more slowly, than lesbians.

Recognizing the fact that individuals experience coming out events in differing orders—not as deviations from a unilinear process but as variations from each other—leads to interesting findings regarding the coming out experiences of bisexuals and the role of bisexual self-identity in coming out among lesbians and gay men. The most consistent findings are that many bisexuals, lesbians, and gay men change sexual self-identities more than once and that many people experience shifts over time in their Kinsey scores. Among men and women with more than incidental adult same- and other-sex contact, Schwartz and Blumstein found that recent identity changes were most common among self-identified lesbian and bisexual women, among whom 33 percent and 15 percent, respectively, had changed identities within the past year. In chapter 26 Rust (1993a) documented the large percentage of currently self-identified lesbians (41 percent) who, either before or after initially adopting a lesbian self-identity, identified themselves as bisexual. Lesbians who self-identified as bisexual before coming out as lesbian often look back at their own lives and describe their bisexual identity as a transitional phase during which they were in denial regarding their true sexual identity. As shown by

Rust in another article reprinted in this section as chapter 24 (1993b), these lesbians are especially likely to doubt other women's bisexual self-identities because they suspect the other women are likewise denying their true lesbian sexuality. Ironically, many bisexual women could look back at their own lives and say that lesbian self-identity was a transitional phase for them; 27 percent of the currently self-identified bisexual women in Rust's study identified as lesbian before coming out as bisexual, and a total of 76 percent had identified as lesbian at some time in their lives.

Even at a young age some bisexuals, lesbians, and gays have already experienced multiple self-identity changes. In a study of eighty males and seventy females aged fourteen through twenty-one years recruited from five community- or university-based organizations for gay and lesbian youth in New York City, Rosario and colleagues (1996) found that 31 percent identified themselves as bisexual at the time of the interview. Among the females, two-thirds of those who did not currently identify as bisexual had thought in the past that they might be bisexual, and two-thirds of those who currently identified as bisexual had thought in the past that they might be lesbian. Among the males, 58 percent of those who did not currently identify as bisexual had thought in the past that they might be bisexual, and 57 percent of those who did not currently identity as gay, most of whom currently self-identified as bisexual, had thought in the past that they might be gay.[60]

Another consistent finding is that, although bisexual self-identity is stable for a substantial proportion of the bisexual population, those who identify as bisexual at any given point in time have generally experienced greater variability in their Kinsey ratings and sexual self-identification than those who identify as lesbian or gay at that same point in time. Rust (1993a) found that self-identified bisexual women were more likely than lesbians to have changed their sexual self-identities multiple times in the past, and the studies by Weinberg, Williams, and Pryor (1994) and by Pattatucci and Hamer (1995) revealed greater—although limited—variability over time in the sexualities of bisexual women than lesbian or heterosexual women. Weinberg, Williams, and Pryor asked their respondents to rate themselves currently, and as they would have three years previously, on three Kinsey scales representing sexual feelings, romantic feelings, and sexual behaviors.[61] They also asked them to recall the largest shift in sexual feelings they had ever experienced. They found that about half of self-identified bisexual men and women reported that their sexual feelings were different than they had been three years previously, although a third had shifted by only one Kinsey scale point. In comparison, about 80 percent of self-identified heterosexual men and women and gay men, and 75 percent of lesbians, reported no change in their sexual feelings. They also found that lesbians were most likely to have experienced a change of at least three Kinsey scale points at some time in their lives (50 percent), followed by bisexual women and men (35 percent, 18 percent). Most of lesbians' major changes occurred in their twenties, whereas major changes in bisexuals' sexual feelings were more spread out across the lifespan, and for all groups the vast majority of changes were in the homosexual direction.

Pattatucci and Hamer reinterviewed 175 of their heterosexual, bisexual, and lesbian women respondents twelve to eighteen months after the initial interview. The women were asked to rate themselves each time on Kinsey scales representing sexual behavior and self-identification. By averaging the behavior and identity ratings, rounding to the nearest whole score, and comparing each woman's scores at the two points in time, they found the greatest change over time occurred among those who were Kinsey 2's and 4's at the initial interview. Nineteen percent of Kinsey 0–1's, 33 percent of Kinsey 2's, 24 percent of Kinsey 3's, 42 percent of Kinsey 4's, and 15 percent of Kinsey 5–6's changed Kinsey scores. All but one respondent moved only one degree, and most Kinsey 2–4's changed to another score within the 2–4 range. Stokes, Damon, and McKirnan (1997) reinterviewed 216 behaviorally bisexual men one year after the initial interview. Thirty-four percent had experienced a shift toward greater homosexuality and 17 percent had experienced a shift toward greater heterosexuality in their sexual feelings. Those who experienced a homosexual shift had begun heterosexual activity at later ages, had had fewer female sex partners, and reported lower levels of depression and anxiety and higher self-esteem in the initial interview than men who did not. In contrast to Weinberg, Williams, and Pryor (1994), who used their findings to emphasize the degree to which sexuality can change over the life course, Pattatucci and Hamer, like McKirnan, Stokes, Doll, and Burzette (1995), used their findings to emphasize the stability of bisexuality as a sexual orientation, at least among some bisexuals. Stokes, Damon, and McKirnan (1997) focused on factors predicting whether a behaviorally bisexual individual would shift toward homosexuality or heterosexuality.

Because linear developmental models characterize coming out as a goal-oriented process of maturation leading to a single self-identity, the identity changes that some individuals experience repeatedly are interpreted as indications of developmental immaturity, i.e., signs that one has not yet achieved one's final true sexual identity (Esterberg 1997; Golden 1987, 1994; Rust 1993a, 1996d)—an interpretation that is reflected in bisexuals, lesbians, and gay men's own accounts of their coming out processes.[62] Because bisexuals are more likely than lesbians or gay men to undergo repeated self-identity changes, such models therefore imply that bisexuals tend to be developmentally immature. But self-identity changes do not necessarily indicate developmental immaturity, especially among bisexuals, nor do they indicate that one has not yet achieved a true sexual identity. Instead, they might reflect changes in one's true sexuality or in the behavior one uses to express one's sexuality. Weinberg, Williams, and Pryor (1994) found that some individuals changed their self-identities because of a deepening relationship with either a man or a woman or in response to fluctuations in their degrees of attraction to women and men, sometimes as a result of increased contact with a lesbian, gay, or heterosexual community. Some men moved in a heterosexual direction, seeking greater intimacy in their relationships or to avoid HIV infection; some women moved in a homosexual direction because of HIV or increasing involvement in the women's movement. Findings by many researchers that sexual self-identity correlates with behavior in the last year much better than with earlier behavior indicates that many individuals change self-identities as the gender of their sex partners changes.[63] Rust found that, despite their more frequent self-identity changes, bisexual women were no more likely than lesbians to be dissatisfied with their current sexual self-identity. This finding suggests that bisexual women change their self-identities frequently not because they are engaged in a constant struggle to find a satisfactory, or true, identity but rather because they find different sexual self-identities satisfying, or true, at different times. Such identity changes reflect not developmental immaturity among bisexuals but the constraints imposed on bisexuals by monosexist concepts of sexuality.

Recognizing self-identity change as a normal part of mature sexuality—especially among bisexuals in a monosexual world—is facilitated by the use of nonlinear, nondevelopmental models of sexual identity formation. Several alternatives to linear developmental conceptualizations of the process of self-identity formation have been suggested. Alica Twining (1983) suggested that "bisexual identity development seems to call for a task model rather than a phase or stage model" (158). Such a model would focus, for example, on self-acceptance as a task facing bisexuals rather than as a stage to be passed through. Judith Butler (1990), referring primarily to lesbian identity, characterized identity as "performative." In other words, identity is created and recreated through symbolic representations of the self. In effect, a woman does not come out as a lesbian—or as a bisexual—but rather becomes a lesbian or a bisexual by portraying herself as a lesbian or bisexual to herself and others. Her identity *is* her performance of that identity and, presumably, changes as her performance of it changes. Schwartz and Blumstein (1998) argued that individuals impute or construct their own sexual essences by examining their sexual histories and that, more important, the sexual identities based on these imputations thenceforth shape, but do not determine, ensuing sexual history. Michele J. Eliason (1996), Rust (1993a, 1996c, 1996d), and Esterberg (1997) argued that an understanding of bisexual identity requires recognition of the social and political context not as it facilitates or hinders the process of individual "development" but as it creates the possibility and meaning of bisexual identity. Eliason suggested conceptualizing bisexual, lesbian, and gay "not as autonomous, stable persons, but as subject positions from which to speak" (55), and Rust (1993a; chapter 26, this volume) suggested replacing the concept of identity development with a concept of ongoing *identity maintenance* in which psychologically mature individuals continue to undergo identity change as the language and sociocultural landmarks they use to construct their self-identities change (see also Rust 1996c).

Research on coming out has been criticized for its inattention to the ways in which race, class, and other social dimensions affect sexual self-identity. In a detailed review of various models of sexual self-identity formation, Eliason (1996) pointed out that "the vast majority of research on lesbian, gay, and bisexual people has been on white, middle class, well-educated samples" (53).[64] A few researchers have used race as a background, or predictor, variable in their statistical analyses of milestone ages. For example, Rosario and colleagues (1996) found no significant differences in the ages at which Black, Hispanic, and white youths experienced coming out milestones, whereas Matteson (1997) found that Asian American men came out an average of 2.5 years later than behaviorally bisexual white and Black men.

But the most important racial, ethnic, and class differences in coming out will not be found in average ages. They exist in the different meanings that members of different cultural groups attribute to these coming out milestones and in the issues they face at each stage of coming out. Most editors and authors of recent books on or including bisexuality have shown a sincere desire to include racial and ethnic, and sometimes social class, cultural diversity in their work. This is particularly true of the editors of books by and for bisexuals, who typically include writing by authors from a variety of cultural backgrounds. For example, the editors of *Plural Desires: Writing Bisexual Women's Realities* were committed to producing a book that was at least half-written and edited by Women of Color. Most recent academic anthologies and single-author books have included chapters examining bisexuality among minoritized racial, ethnic, and class groups. For example, Esterberg (1997) included a chapter on "Race, Class, Identity," Firestein included a chapter on "Managing Multiple Identities" (Rust 1996a), Ritch C. Savin-Williams and Kenneth M. Cohen included a chapter on Latino, Black, and Asian MSM (Manalansan 1996), and Brett Beemyn and Mickey Eliason included a chapter on Asian and Asian American lesbian and bisexual women (Lee 1996).

One of the most fundamental cultural differences is the fact that the very idea of basing one's personal identity on one's sexual feelings or behaviors is specific to Anglo or "Western" cultures.[65] In many other cultural communities, for example, some Latin, Asian American, and Arab cultures, one's role in the family is the primary source of one's identity.[66] In such communities forming a self-identity based on one's sexuality requires some assimilation to Anglo culture and might be interpreted by one's ethnic peers as a rejection of one's family and one's ethnicity (Tremble, Schneider, and Appathurai 1989). Assumptions, made on the basis of linear models of coming out, that the formation of a sexual self-identity reflects a healthy acknowledgment of one's sexuality and, conversely, that failure to do so reflects denial of one's sexuality are unfair to individuals whose cultures do not expect sexual inclinations to be reflected in personal identity (Rust 1996a).

Different ethnic cultures also have different norms regarding sexuality and different concepts of personhood that create culturally specific issues for individuals attempting to form sexual identities. For example, many Asian American cultures draw a sharp distinction between private and public spheres. Sexuality belongs in the private sphere, and shame arises not so much from sexuality itself as from public acknowledgment of sexuality. The adoption of a self-identity based on one's sexuality is shameful because it represents a public announcement of that which should be kept private.[67] Furthermore, because one is seen primarily as a family member, one risks shaming not only oneself but also one's family.[68] In many cultures the difficulty is compounded for women, for whom the declaration of bisexual or lesbian identity means overcoming cultural denial that women have a sexuality independent of male arousal or procreation.[69] Cross-cultural variation in the concept of homosexuality also creates different possibilities for self-identity development for individuals in different ethnic cultures; recall from chapter 22, for example, that in some Latin cultures heterosexual self-identity is available to men who engage in insertive sex with both male and female partners, whereas in Anglo culture such men are expected to identify as gay or bisexual.

Bisexuals belonging to different racial and ethnic communities might also face different levels of cultural acceptance of bisexuality and homosexuality as they come out. African American culture is often characterized as more accepting of bisexuality than of homosexuality relative to white culture. As shown by evidence reviewed in chapters 11 and 22, bisexual behavior and self-identity are more common among African Americans than among white Americans.[70] White gays and lesbians have generally construed this as evidence of homophobia among African Americans that causes many to deny their true lesbian or gay identity, as have some researchers (Diaz et al. 1993; Doll, Peterson, Magaña, and Carrier 1991; cf. Wright 1993). Some researchers cite Judeo-Christian religious traditions and traditional views of gender roles in African American communities as the sources of this homophobia and the lack of a strong Black gay subculture as the reason Black gay men respond to this homophobia by adopting bisexual self-identities (Jones and Hill 1996; Klassen, Williams and Levitt 1989; Mays and Cochran 1987; Peterson et al. 1992; Stokes and Peterson 1998; cf. Wekker 1993). However, McKirnan, Stokes, Doll, and Burzette's (1995; see also Doll, Peterson, White, and the HIV Blood Donor Study Group 1990) finding that this racial difference in rates of bisexual self-identification existed among behaviorally bisexual men suggests to the current author that the pattern is caused instead by biphobia among white Americans whose European traditions rely heavily on dualistic thinking and cause pressure on white women and men to choose between heterosexual and lesbian or gay self-identities. Bell, Weinberg, and Hammersmith (1981), to explain differences in the developmental patterns of Black and white men, hypothesized that Black men acted on their homosexual inclinations at a younger age than white men because the Black community is less sexually restrictive than the white community.[71] Doll and colleagues (1991), however, argued that the sexual permissiveness of the Black community extends only to heterosex and that Black homophobia leads Black men to engage in both same- and other-sex activity while retaining a heterosexual self-identity.[72]

Other than anecdotal accounts of acceptance or condemnation in African American communities, there is little research on the question of whether African American and white American communities differ in their levels of acceptance of bisexuality and homosexuality. Stokes, McKirnan, Doll, and Burzette (1996; see also Taywaditep and Stokes 1998) found that, in a sample of 350 behaviorally bisexual men aged eighteen to thirty, African American men rated their network members, friends, and neighbors as less accepting of their homosexual activity than white men rated theirs. In this study there were no racial differences among the men themselves in levels of self-homophobia, self-acceptance of homosexual behavior, or perceived acceptance of their homosexual behavior by family members, although in a later study Stokes and Peterson (1998) did find evidence that negative attitudes had been internalized by African American MSM. A study by Melissa L. Smith and Christine A. Smith (1994) found no significant differences in the attitudes of African American and Caucasian high school students, and a study by Louis Bonilla and Judith Porter (1990) found that Blacks were more favorable to lesbian and gay civil rights but less morally tolerant of homosexuality than Latinos. F. A. Ernst, R. A. Francis, H. Nevels, and C. A. Lemeh (1991) found that Blacks were more likely than whites to endorse negative statements about homosexuals. They found that the racial difference was due primarily to negative attitudes on the part of Black females, and hypothesized that Black females were reacting to a dearth of marriageable Black men caused by a variety of other social factors.

Whether or not different racial and ethnic groups have different levels of biphobia and homophobia, these attitudes take different forms in different cultural communities. In minoritized racial and ethnic groups biphobia and homophobia are sometimes motivated by a desire to protect ethnic identity and preserve ethnic culture by defending traditional values, such as the cultural preference for heterosexuality. As Tremble, Schneider, and Appathurai (1989) put it, "One can abandon traditional values in Portugal and still be Portuguese. If they are abandoned in the New World, the result is assimilation" (255).[73] The irony is that in many of these cultures it is the biphobia and homophobia, not the bisexuality and homosexuality, that was imported from Anglo culture. For example, the Chinese term *cut sleeve*, derived from a story about the Han emperor, Ai-di, who cut his sleeve rather than wake his male lover who was sleeping on it, carries the connotation of tolerance that characterized Chinese culture before the influence of Western religion.[74] Some traditional Native American cultures not only tolerate diversity, but celebrate it in the form of *two spirit* people.[75] Two spirit people are neither men nor women, but a third gender often seen as a bridge between the masculine and feminine spheres. Because in some tribes two spirit people traditionally take partners of their own biological sex, contemporary bisexual, lesbian, and gay Native Americans look to these traditions to find pride in the face of the homophobia that was encouraged among First Nations peoples by European immigrants.

Finally, coming out among bisexuals who are members of minoritized racial or ethnic groups is complicated by multiple marginalization.[76] Bisexuals of Color are marginalized from mainstream society because of both their ethnic and sexual identities, from their ethnic communities because of their sexuality, and from predominantly white lesbian and gay communities because of their ethnicity and bisexuality. None of these communities offer them role models for the integration of ethnic identity with bisexual identity; the images offered in the lesbian and gay community are white images and those offered in ethnic communities are heterosexual. The prospect of this multiple marginalization prevents some members of minoritized racial and ethnic groups from coming out as bisexual. However, Rust (1996a) reported that others find the skills they developed in response to racial or ethnic marginalization can be adapted to handle sexual marginalization. She also found that some biracial individuals feel a comfortable resonance between their mixed cultural heritage and their bisexuality. She quoted an Asian-European American woman who wrote:

Being multiracial, multicultural has always made me aware of nonbipolar thinking. I have always been outside people's categories, and so it wasn't such a big leap to come out as bi, after spending years explaining [my racial and cultural] identity rather than attaching a single label [to it]. (70)

Being In and Being Out: Psychological and Social Closets

Given the difficulties involved in identifying as bisexual or engaging in bisexual behavior in a culture that denies the possibility and political legitimacy of bisexuality, it would not be surprising to find that bisexuals display some symptoms of psychological distress. A long tradition of research literature has examined the extent to which social prejudice against homosexuality has impacted the self-conceptions and psychological health of lesbians and gay men; how much more damaging might the denial of one's very existence be for bisexuals?[77] There is a small but growing clinical literature addressed to therapists regarding the issues that arise for bisexual individuals. Therapists are advised, for example, that bisexuals need affirmation that bisexuality exists and bisexual self-identities are legitimate, support in the face of potential rejection from both lesbians/gays and heterosexuals, and education to overcome stereotypes of bisexuals that might either prevent them from identifying as bisexual or, once identified, engaging in stereotypical but ego-dystonic and potentially dangerous sexual behaviors. Because most of this literature is based on the clinical experiences of the authors rather than on systematic research, and because this literature has been extensively reviewed elsewhere, I will not present a thorough treatment of it here. Instead, I limit myself to empirical research on the social and psychological characteristics of bisexuals not geared specifically toward therapeutic applications. Readers interested in literature on therapy with bisexual clients are referred to Firestein (1996).[78]

The particular difficulties facing bisexuals were acknowledged as early as 1963, by Donald Webster Cory and John P. LeRoy. Seeking to affirm homosexuality in the face of popular and professional characterization of homosexuality as a mental illness, however, they displaced the specter of mental illness onto bisexuality. Thus, they attributed bisexuals' difficulties to psychological immaturity, describing the bisexual as "peculiarly pathetic" because "he" is "an overgrown young adolescent" who "lacks above all a sense of identity, a feeling of group identification" (1963:61).

A decade later Martin S. Weinberg and Colin J. Williams (1974) refocused attention on the lack of social support bisexuals experience, rather than on any inherent psychological defect in bisexuals, and studied the degree to which bisexual men were actually psychologically affected by this lack of social support. Defining bisexuals as those who rated themselves as Kinsey 2–4's, they found that bisexual men anticipated more discrimination, were more concerned with passing as heterosexual, and were more closeted than Kinsey 5's and 6's. However, overall they did not find bisexuals to be any more confused about their sexual self-identities or otherwise adversely affected psychologically except that bisexuals reported more "guilt, shame, or anxiety over being *homosexual*" (211; emphasis added). The authors commented that the lack of psychological damage they found attests to the human ability to adapt and compartmentalize oneself when necessary to preserve psychological health.

Weinberg and Williams's findings, of course, must be interpreted both in terms of the researchers' methods and in terms of the time period. First, as the authors pointed out, their sampling procedures recruited bisexuals with some involvement in gay male subculture but excluded men without ties to that community. It is entirely possible that men without the support of this community would have shown more adverse psychological effects. Second, bisexuals were asked to state their feelings about their *homosexuality*, not their bisexuality; therefore, their greater expressions of guilt indicate that they felt more guilty about the homosexual component of their sexuality than more exclusive homosexuals, not that they felt more guilty about their *bisexuality* than homosexuals did about their homosexuality. Although seemingly a matter of trivial semantics, this is an important point. In the 1970s homosexuality was the problematized sexuality and the source of sexual shame; bisexuality was seen as a degree of homosexuality—see, for example, John H. Gagnon and William Simon (1973), who admonished other researchers to recognize variations in sexuality *among* homosexuals. Therefore, if bisexuals felt guilty, that guilt was over their homosexuality. Even if Weinberg and Williams had asked these men about their feelings regarding their bisexuality, they would probably have understood it as a reference to the homosexual "component" of their sexuality.[79]

Therefore, Weinberg and Williams's finding is not that *bisexuals* felt more guilty about their sexuality than exclusive homosexuals did but that men whose homosexual feelings were accompanied by substantial heterosexual ones felt more guilty about their homosexual feelings than men whose homosexual feelings were more exclusive. In fact, contemporaneous findings by Jerrold S. Greenberg (1973) suggest that, among bisexuals, *stronger* heterosexual feelings were associated with *more* guilt about homosexual feelings; Greenberg found that bisexuals who were predominantly heterosexual had lower self-esteem than either exclusive homosexuals or bisexuals who were predominantly homosexual, and he hypothesized guilt as the cause of this self-deprecation. Given that Weinberg and Williams found that their bisexual subjects were more socially involved with heterosexuals, less socially involved with homosexuals, and less acculturated to gay subculture than their exclusively homosexual subjects, these bisexual respondents—particularly those who were predominantly heterosexual—probably experienced greater guilt because they were more socially embedded in heterosexual cultural devaluation of homosexuality and less familiar with gay cultural values that would reverse this devaluation. Self-acceptance is more difficult for men who live in heterosexual worlds; recall, for example, the discussion of "married gay men" in chapter 17 of this volume and the difficulties these men had informing their wives of their same-sex activities.

In contrast to Greenberg's (1973) findings that bisexuals experienced more negative psychological effects, findings reported by Gagnon and Simon (1973) suggest that prior to gay liberation bisexuals experienced fewer social difficulties. Among 550 white males with extensive homosexual histories who were interviewed by Kinsey and his associates in the years 1940–1956, Gagnon and Simon reported that 31 percent of exclusive homosexuals, compared to 22 percent of those with mixed homosexual and heterosexual experiences, had had trouble with the police. Also, 25 percent of the former, compared to 16 percent of the latter, had had trouble with their families of origin.

More recent studies focusing on bisexuals as bisexuals rather than as partial homosexuals confirm Weinberg and Williams's (1974) finding that bisexual women and men are more concerned than lesbians and gay men with passing. Two studies of women show that bisexuals are more closeted and less likely to disclose their bisexuality to health care practitioners than lesbians. In a study of predominantly white (94 percent) self-identified bisexual and lesbian women's attitudes and experiences with health care professionals, Elaine M. Smith, Susan R. Johnson, and Susan M. Guenther (1985) found that bisexual women were twice as likely as lesbians to prefer not to disclose their sexual orientation to a physician and were in fact less likely to have disclosed this information, especially to physicians who had not asked for it. Twenty-two percent (22.2 percent) of bisexual women (n = 387) had told a physician about their sexual orientation even when not asked, 37.2 percent had not disclosed their orientation but wanted to, and 30.5 percent preferred not to disclose and had not done so. Comparable figures for lesbians were 36.9 percent, 36.4 percent, and 15.5 percent (n = 1,811). These women were recruited for the study while attending "week-long cultural events for women." Incidentally, Smith, Johnson, and Guenther also found that bisexual women were more likely to receive routine gynecological care (59 percent) than lesbians, who tended to seek care only in response to gynecologic problems (58 percent). In a different study Cochran and Mays (1988) found that among Black women recruited via gay organizations, gay newspapers, and lesbian bars bisexuals were also less likely than lesbians to disclose their orientation and that rates of self-disclosure were similar to those found by Smith, Johnson, and Guenther. Sixty-six percent of Black bisexual women (n = 65), compared to 45 percent of Black lesbians (n = 529), said that their physician did not know of their orientation and 18 percent of bisexual women, compared to 33 percent of lesbians, had explicitly discussed the topic with their physicians.

Several studies indicate that self-identified bisexuals and heterosexuals are less likely than gay self-identified people to disclose to relatives, friends, colleagues, and female sex partners. Twenty-four percent of Doll et al.'s (1992) self-identified bisexual respondents and 40 percent of their self-identified heterosexual respondents, compared to only 7 percent of their self-identified homosexual respondents, had never disclosed their same-sex activity to relatives, heterosexual friends, or colleagues. Among the men recruited by Stokes, McKirnan, and Burzette (1993) through an ad targeting bisexuals, 19 percent said they believed that none of the ten most important people in their lives knew they were attracted to men, and 72 percent believed that their female spouse or lover did not know; overall disclosure rates did not differ depending on whether these self-perceived bisexual men had actually had both male and female sex partners in the previous six months. Among McKirnan, Stokes, Doll, and Burzette's (1995) behaviorally bisexual respondents a full third had disclosed to only one person or to no one, among Wold et al.'s (1998) behaviorally bisexual respondents 54 percent had not told their female sex partners that they had also had sex with men during the previous year, and among Boulton, Hart, and Fitzpatrick's (1992) British behaviorally bisexual men over half of self-identified bisexual men compared to only a third of self-identified gay men maintained a public heterosexual identity. Among Kalichman, Roffman, Picciano, and Bolan's (1998) MSM, those who had also had sex with women were much less likely to have disclosed their homosexual behavior to close and casual friends and to parents than those who had had only male sex partners. Martin F. Manalansan IV (1996) cited an unpublished report by the National Task Force on AIDS Prevention, a project of the National Association of Black and White Men Together, that found that, of 952 Black males, 74 percent identified as gay or homosexual and 18 percent identified as bisexual in private but only 48 percent and 13 percent, respectively, publicly acknowledged these private identities. Recall also findings by Ted Myers, Kevin W. Orr, David Locker, and Edward A. Jackson (1993) and Susan M. Kegeles et al. (1990), reported in chapter 22, that bisexual men were more concerned than gay men and heterosexual men and women with anonymity and privacy in HIV testing and by Earl (1990) that married MSM were less likely to inform their wives "of the risk to which they had been exposed" (254) than gay and bisexual men were to inform their sex partners of their HIV status (14 percent versus 58 percent). Ironically, but consistent with Greenberg's (1973) finding that degree of homosexuality is associated with degree of closetedness, Stokes and colleagues (Stokes, McKirnan, and Burzette 1993; see also Stokes, McKirnan, Doll, and Burzette 1996) found that bisexual men who rated themselves as "more homosexual" on a five-point scale were less closeted than those who placed themselves nearer the heterosexual end of the scale.

Nondisclosure among bisexual men and self-identified heterosexual MSM might reflect internalized homophobia or biphobia. Stokes, McKirnan, Doll, and Burzette (1996) found that internalized homophobia and the perceived homophobia of friends and family members were among the best predictors of nondisclosure in their sample of behaviorally bisexual men, although closeted men did not show decreased psychological well-being in other areas such as self-esteem. Doll et al. (1992) found that 31 percent of self-identified bisexual MSM and 44 percent of self-identified heterosexual MSM, compared to 6 percent of self-identified homosexual men, were "moderately to very" uncomfortable with their sexual attraction to men. The same pattern has been found among Latino men; Carballo-Diéguez and Dolezal (1994) found that Latino MSM who identified as heterosexual or, to a lesser extent, bisexual, had higher levels of homophobia than those who identified as gay. Wold et al. (1998) found that men who had had sex with both men and women during the previous six months had lower scores on a measure of self-acceptance of homosexuality than men who had sex with men only during that period (see also Stokes, Vanable, and McKirnan 1997). The threat of HIV has also made some bisexuals more hesitant to disclose their sexual identities; when they reinterviewed their bisexual respondents five years after their initial 1983 study, Weinberg, Williams, and Pryor (1994) found that 40 percent said they were more wary of disclosing their bisexuality than they had been before, whereas only 20 percent said that they had become less wary.

Another recent finding, however, suggests that bisexuals are no more concerned about others' reactions to their sexuality than lesbians and gay men are. Lynn R. Anderson and Lori Randlet (1994) studied self-monitoring among 155 bisexuals, lesbians, and gay men recruited through gay and lesbian organizations. Self-monitoring refers to the process of shaping one's own behavior in response to "group norms and the behavior of others" (790); high self-monitors are more attuned to situational cues and more flexible in adapting their behavior in response to these cues. Anderson and Randlet argued that bisexuals, lesbians, and gay men can practice varying degrees of self-monitoring in managing information about their sexuality and hypothesized that those who engage in high degrees of self-monitoring would find coming out a more pleasant experience and would be more satisfied with their lives as bisexuals, lesbians, and gay men than those who self-disclose with little regard for situational considerations. In preparation for testing these hypotheses, the researchers compared levels of self-monitoring and difficulties in coming out among bisexuals versus lesbians and gay men, with bisexuals defined as those sixteen female and fourteen male respondents who rated themselves as Kinsey 3–5's. They found no significant difference, suggesting that bisexuals find coming out no more or less difficult, and do not pay any more or less attention to situational cues when disclosing information about their sexuality, than lesbians and gay men.[80] The former finding is consistent with a finding by Rotheram-Borus and colleagues, including Margaret Rosario (Rotheram-Borus et al. 1995), that self-identified bisexual male youths experienced the same level of "gay-related stress" as self-identified gay youths.[81] The latter finding does not necessarily contradict other researchers' findings that bisexuals are more closeted than lesbians and gay men,[82] but it does suggest that bisexual men and women are no more preoccupied with others' reactions to their sexuality than lesbians and gay men.

Notwithstanding the fact that Anderson and Randlet's (1994) bisexual respondents engaged in no more or less self-monitoring and recalled coming out as no more or less painful than their lesbian and gay respondents, self-monitoring was more strongly and significantly related to painfulness of coming out among bisexual than among lesbian and gay respondents. Attempting to explain this finding, Anderson and Randlet suggested that "bisexuality may be a notably more complicated orientation to enact in contemporary society compared to mono-sexual orientations. There may be an even greater need for the thoughtful, situation-specific tactics of self-disclosure" (798). In other words, bisexuals in general might find coming out no more painful than lesbians and gay men, but the degree to which a bisexual individual self-monitors during that process is more important in minimizing her or his pain than it would be for a lesbian or gay individual.

Anderson and Randlet (1994) also asked their respondents a series of five questions regarding their satisfaction with their lives as bisexuals, lesbians, and gay men and discovered that bisexuals were significantly less satisfied than lesbians and gay men.[83] This finding provides an interesting comparison to Bressler and Lavender's (1986) and LaTorre and Wendenburg's (1983) findings suggesting that bisexuals have more satisfying sex lives. Anderson and Randlet's five questions focused on the psychosocial aspects of life, indicating that although bisexuals might be sexually more satisfied the difficulties they face in a society that does not authenticate bisexuality compromise their more general satisfaction with their lives as bisexuals.

Despite this dissatisfaction, and in contrast to "partially homosexual" men in the 1970s, in the 1980s and 1990s bisexual men and women might be slightly less depressed[84] and have higher self-esteem than lesbians and gay men. Nurius (1983) classified her 689 respondents, most of whom were students in college and graduate social science courses and 67.5 percent of whom were female, as asexual (8.2 percent), homosexual (1.2 percent), ambisexual (16.5 percent), or heterosexual (74.2 percent) based on their responses to the Sexual Activity and Preference Scale (SAPS). She also administered a Sexual Attitude Scale, a Generalized Contentment Scale measuring depression, an Index of Self-Esteem, an Index of Marital Satisfaction wherein the concept of marriage was broadened to include any "ongoing intimate dyadic relationship" (124), and an Index of Sexual Satisfaction. The four sexual orientation groups differed significantly although minimally in depression, self-esteem, and sexual satisfaction, with the asexual group displaying the most depression and the lowest self-esteem and sexual satisfaction, followed by homosexuals, then ambisexuals, and finally heterosexuals. When background characteristics were controlled, the correlations with self-esteem and sexual satisfaction became insignificant, leaving only the correlation with depression.[85] A similar finding by Rotheram-Borus and colleagues (Rotheram-Borus et al. 1995) that self-identified bisexual male youths had significantly higher self-esteem than self-identified gay youths, as measured by the Rosenberg Self-Esteem scale, also disappeared when subjected to further testing.[86] Rotheram-Borus, Hunter, and Rosario (1994) also found that those youths who had attempted suicide and those who had not were equally likely to identify as bisexual, suggesting that self-identified bisexual youths are no more nor less likely to attempt suicide than self-identified gay youths. Neither the Rotheram-Borus (Rotheram-Borus et al. 1995) nor the Nurius (1983) findings regarding differences between bisexuals' and lesbians' or gay men's levels of depression and self-esteem should be overstated. In the Rotheram-Borus study the researchers found the difference between bisexual and gay respondents so inconsequential that they did not incorporate it into further data analyses, and in the Nurius study the actual differences between sexual orientation groups were very small. In contrast to the youths studied by Rotheram-Borus, Hunter, and Rosario (1994), 39 percent of whom had attempted suicide, the members of all four of Nurius's sexual orientation groups covered a broad range of psychological health, with a "lack of marked disturbance" in all four groups (129), and Nurius herself characterized her findings as having "quite limited" (132) clinical relevance.

Three other findings regarding variations in self-esteem among bisexuals cannot be so easily dismissed. A finding by Marguerite (Maggi) Rubenstein (1982) that the longer an individual has identified as bisexual the higher his or her self-esteem suggests that, over time, individuals develop the ability to defend themselves psychologically against social disapproval—or that those who are unable to defend themselves give up the effort to maintain a bisexual self-identity. Stokes, McKirnan, and Burzette (1993) found that, among men who volunteered for a research study on bisexuals, those who had had both male and female partners during the previous six months had higher self-esteem and were less depressed than those who had not. There are several possible interpretations for this finding. The authors offer the possibilities that consistency of self-identity and behavior might lead to greater mental health, or that greater mental health enables men to be more sexually assertive, or that psychological well-being is enhanced when bisexuals are able to express "both major components of [their] sexuality" (211). Taywaditep and Stokes (1998) found differences in psychological distress, self-esteem, and other psychological characteristics (although not self-homophobia) between subtypes of behaviorally bisexual men. Subtypes characterized by large numbers of partners tended to have more psychological problems than those characterized by current romantic involvements.

Bisexual women might have healthier body images and gender self-concepts than heterosexual women, and bisexual men might have healthier body images than homosexual men. LaTorre and Wendenburg (1983), in their study of 125 women university students, found that women who had had both same- and other-sex contact were "more satisfied with their bodies and its functions, more satisfied with both their sexual activities and their biological sex, and more satisfied with themselves and their abilities than were women who only reported opposite-sexual experiences" (87). It should be noted that all LaTorre and Wendenburg's respondents had had sexual experiences with men, hence it cannot be determined whether the critical factor in this finding is having had sex with women or having had sex with both women and men. French et al. (1996), however, distinguished self-identified bisexual women and men from self-identified heterosexual and homosexual women and men. Bisexual and homosexual women were more likely than heterosexual women to perceive their weight as "about right" and to have positive body images, whereas bisexual and heterosexual men were more likely than homosexual men to perceive their weight as about right and less likely to have negative body images than homosexual men. In short, bisexuals do not display the patterns of increased negative body image found among heterosexual women and homosexual men.[87]

Lavender and Bressler (1981) provided a refreshing break from the debate over which sexual orientation minority experiences the most psychological damage by posing a question regarding cognitive differences between bisexuals and monosexuals. Agreeing with Martin Duberman (1977), Vern L. Bullough and Bonnie Bullough (1977), and Richard J. Hoffman (1984) that the hegemonic distinction between lesbian/gay and heterosexual persons is grounded in Western dualistic thinking, these researchers hypothesized that bisexuals are more nondualistic, or "Eastern," in their thinking than heterosexuals and homosexuals. They conducted extensive interviews with seventy women, making an effort to interview equal numbers of self-identified heterosexual, bisexual, and homosexual women. They found that bisexual women were much more likely than heterosexual women to reject the concept of a traditional Western dualistic God who "divides behavior into dichotomous good-or-bad categories" (161; 64 percent versus 26 percent) and much more likely to reject Western organized religion (91 percent versus 39 percent). Homosexual women were almost as likely as bisexual women to reject a dualistic God (52 percent) and Western organized religion (68 percent). Conversely, bisexual women were more likely than either heterosexuals or homosexuals to believe in nondualistic Eastern concepts such as "reincarnation, different levels of existence, and living in harmony with nature and holistic principles" (160; 55 percent versus 13 percent and 28 percent). In other words, women who break from dualistic thinking regarding sexuality to identify themselves as bisexuals also tend to reject dualistic thinking in their broader worldviews. Adding their voices to the critics of dichotomous models of sexuality, Lavender and Bressler used their findings to suggest that the neglect of bisexuality in Western culture is not an isolated phenomenon but a reflection of a broader cultural tendency toward dualistic thought. The growing bisexual community and political movement, which will be explored in the next section, presents a direct challenge to this culturally ingrained dualism.

Notes

1. The role of HIV research in encouraging the inclusion of bisexuals in research on other topics is seen clearly in studies that use samples collected for the purpose of HIV research to study other research questions. For example, Becker et al. (1992) used the MACS sample to study the correlation between handedness and sexual orientation, concluding that "there was a small but significant elevation in left-handedness among gay/bisexual men compared to available normative data" (229). Gay and bisexual men were not distinguished from each other in this study.

2. MacDonald's 1983 review of the literature, reprinted in chapter 3, found that bisexuals were usually excluded or lumped together with lesbians and gay men in research on sexual orientation. Research by Doll (1997) suggests that many researchers still lump bisexuals with gay men. Specifically, Doll found that most of 166 peer-reviewed articles published in the United States that mentioned bisexual men lumped gay and bisexual men together. Eight articles gave information exclusively about bisexual men, and twenty-one compared bisexual and gay men; 34 percent of these twenty-nine articles pertained to HIV risk behaviors. Of sixty-one articles mentioning bisexual women, more than half lumped bisexual women and lesbians together, three gave information exclusively about bisexual women, and twenty-two compared bisexual women and lesbians.

Two other recent reviews of empirical research on lesbians, gay men, and bisexuals have been published by Chung and Katayama (1996) and Sell and Petrulio (1996). Chung and Katayama reviewed 144 articles appearing in volumes 1–24 (1974–1993) of the *Journal of Homosexuality*; therefore, their findings are heavily influenced by editorial decisions made by the board of the *Journal*, such as the decision to publish special issues on bisexuality in the mid 1980s. Chung and Katayama found a peak in the number of studies including bisexual subjects in the middle of each decade. These peaks correspond with the three eras of popular attention to bisexuality described in chapter 27: the "bisexual chic" of the mid 1970s, the HIV panic of the mid 1980s, and the growth of the bisexual movement since the late 1980s and into the 1990s. Only the mid 1980s peak, which included special issues on bisexuality in volume 11, included articles based entirely on bisexual samples; before and after that period bisexuals were included in samples of lesbians and/or gay men but not studied alone. Over the entire time span bisexual men were included in 16.7 percent of the studies and bisexual women were included in 13.2 percent of the studies.

Sell and Petrulio reviewed only public health articles published during the years 1990–1992. Their review therefore cannot reveal any trends over time nor provide evidence that researchers outside the field of public health, a field directly affected by fears that bisexuals are a gateway for HIV transmission, are becoming more inclusive of bisexuality in their research. They found that 13.2 percent of the 152 articles they identified were studies of bisexual men and 3.3 percent were studies of bisexual women.

See Eadie (1993) for an analysis of the submergence of bisexuality in modern scholarly discourse.

3. Research on samples of "gays/lesbians and bisexuals," in which gay or lesbian and bisexual subjects are not distinguished from each other and the bisexuality of some subjects is not treated as relevant to the research—sometimes to the point that the subjects are collectively referred to as gay—include Becker et al. (1992); Holtzen (1994); Kruks (1991); and Laner (1977). Some researchers engaged in minimal discussion of the existence of bisexuals among their subjects, or presented data regarding the percentage of their sample that was bisexual by either behavior or self-identity, before combining bisexual with gay or lesbian respondents for the purpose of data analysis. These include, for example, Bloomfield (1993); D'Augelli (1989, 1992); Franke and Leary (1991); Hershberger and D'Augelli (1995); Mays, Beckman, Oranchak, and Harper (1994); Proctor and Groze (1994); Remafedi, Farrow, and Deisher (1991); Rotheram-Borus, Hunter, and Rosario (1994); and Uribe and Harbeck (1991). Of these Bloomfield (1993) appeared the most cognizant of bisexuals as a distinct population and engaged in the most extensive discussion of her justifications for grouping bisexual women with lesbians. D'Augelli (1992) and Hershberger and D'Augelli (1995) excluded bisexuals who were "predominantly heterosexual" but included bisexuals who were "mostly lesbian or gay" or "equally lesbian or gay and heterosexual" with their gay and lesbian respondents.

4. For example, Coleman and Remafedi (1989) discussed concerns affecting "gay, lesbian, and bisexual" adolescents and the role of counselors in addressing these concerns. However, all the concerns discussed affect gays and lesbians; no concerns particular to bisexuals were discussed. Other examples include D'Augelli (1993) and Herek, Kimmel, Amaro, and Melton (1991).

In some articles the term *bisexual* is included only occasionally, amid numerous references to gays and lesbians. Paul, Stall, and Bloomfield's (1991) discussion of alcoholism follows this pattern with the exception of two references to bisexuals as a distinct population of interest, i.e., a comment regarding the importance of addressing internalized biphobia as well as homophobia in the maintenance of sobriety and a comment that, in addition to problems shared with gays and lesbians, bisexuals also experience "pressure to conform to either an exclusively heterosexual or exclusively homosexual lifestyle" (154). The first author of this article is Jay P. Paul, whose criticism of the neglect of bisexuality in research on sexual orientation is reprinted as chapter 2 of this volume.

5. The study described in *Dual Attraction* is a longitudinal in-depth study of the bisexual community in San Francisco. After four months of intensive participant observation in the bisexual community, Weinberg and colleagues interviewed 100 bisexuals recruited via the Bisexual Center in 1983. Then, in 1984–1985, they conducted a questionnaire study of 96 bisexual women, 116 bisexual men, 105 heterosexual women, 85 heterosexual men, 94 lesbians, and 186 gay men recruited through the Bisexual Center, the Pacific Center (a lesbian and gay organization), the Institute for Advanced Study of Human Sexuality, and the San Francisco Sex Information service. In 1988, interested in the effect that AIDS had had on the bisexual community, they returned to reinterview 61 of the original bisexual interviewees.

6. Recall from note 25 in chapter 11 that "ethnic" refers to the analogization, not the combination, of sexual orientation with race; an ethnic lesbian or gay identity is an identity

based on the concept of a lesbian or gay man as a type of person who is essentially distinct from other types of sexual people, specifically heterosexuals.

See Adam (1979, 1987) and Epstein (1987), for discussion of gay quasi ethnicity, and Faderman (1991) and Voeller (1990), on the conscious borrowing of ethnic political strategies by lesbian and gay activists. See also Altman (1982); Berlant and Freeman (1993); D'Emilio (1983); and Seidman (1993). See note 37, chapter 27, for a quote from Voeller (1990) on this point. See Eadie (1993) for an analogy between bisexuality and racial miscegenation.

See Somerville (1996) for a different perspective on the relationship between essentialized race and essentialized sexual orientation. Whereas other theorists see contemporary efforts to essentialize sexual orientation as being based on an already essentialized concept of race, Somerville argued that both classifications were essentialized during the same historical period, in part because of medical discourse, and that these processes were mutually reinforcing and associated with the pathologization of both the nonwhite and the nonheterosexual body.

7. See, for example, De Cecco and Parker (1995b) for a review and discussion of media publicity surrounding LeVay's (1991) research report. Hamer et al.'s (1993a) report in *Science* touched off a similar debate about the political sensitivity of research into the etiology of sexual orientation among readers of this scholarly scientific publication. See, for example, Risch, Squires-Wheeler, Keats (1993); Fausto-Sterling and Balaban (1993); Diamond (1993); and Hamer et al. (1993b). See Haeberle (1998) for a critical discussion of the view that the discovery of a biological basis for sexual orientation would precipitate change in moral attitudes toward homo- and bisexuality.

8. For additional reviews, discussions, and critiques of this literature, see Bailey (1995); Bancroft (1990); Byne (1988); Byne and Parsons (1993); De Cecco and Parker (1995a, 1995b); Diamond (1995, 1998); Ellis (1996a, 1996b); Feldman (1984); Gooren (1990); Hamer and Copeland (1994); LeVay (1996); Lidz (1993); Meyer-Bahlburg (1984, 1997b); Money (e.g., 1990b); Pillard and Bailey (1995); and the works listed in note 10, this chapter. For examples of this literature, see Allen and Gorski (1992); LeVay (1991); Bailey, Pillard, Neale, and Agyei (1993); Bailey and Pillard (1991); Dörner (Dörner et al. 1975; Dörner 1976); Hamer et al. (1993a); Kolodny et al. (1971, 1972); and Swaab and Hoffman (1990).

Evidence that male and female homosexuals differ from heterosexuals in the sex ratios of their own siblings and parental siblings is also consistent with biological theories of the etiology of sexual orientation. This branch of biological research is not discussed in this volume, but reviews of it can be found in the works cited above. Although studies of twins reared apart would be best suited for distinguishing biological from environmental factors, current social preferences for the preservation of sibling groups makes such twins difficult to find. Eckert, Bouchard, Bohlen, and Hesten (1986) were able to find six pairs of monozygotic twins reared apart (Diamond 1995).

9. See note 13, chapter 4.

10. Early criticisms of this aspect of biological research were made by Kinsey, Pomeroy, and Martin (1948); Ford and Beach (1951); and by Churchill (1967), who cautioned against confusing "inversion" of sexual role—such as female-typical sexual presenting, or lordosis, among male animals—with "homosexuality." More recently, Whalen, Geary, and Johnson (1990) commented that "we do not conclude that neonatally androgenized female hamsters, which do show male-typical mounting responses when given testosterone in adulthood, are homosexual, even though our treatment clearly 'masculinized' their behavior" (64).

But that is exactly what many researchers have done. Ironically, John Money, who was central in developing the distinction between biological sex, gender identity, and gender role (1955, 1990b; see also an earlier distinction between sex-role identification, sex-role preference, and sex-role adoption in Lynn [1959]) which was later elaborated by other theorists, and who continues to critique the concepts of masculinity and femininity (1990b:50), wrote: "the brains and behavior of ewe lambs, independently of their bodies, can be masculinized in utero by implanting the pregnant mother with testosterone. . . . The lamb grows up to be a lesbian ewe. Its brain is so effectively masculinized that its mating behavior . . . is exactly like that of a ram. . . . Moreover, the normal rams and ewes of the flock respond to the lesbian ewe's masculinized mating behavior as if it were that of a normal ram" (1990b:49).

Researchers who produce cross-sex sexual behavior, e.g., mounting in females or lordosis in males, do in fact frequently observe females mounting other females or males lordosing to males. Such behavior would be described as homosexual. However: 1. It is homosexual on the part of *both* animals involved, not only the one displaying cross-sex behavior; if the lordosing male's and mounting female's "homosexual" behavior is explained by virtue of hormonal manipulation, how is the homosexual behavior of their sex partners to be explained? 2. What has been altered is not the hormonally manipulated animal's object choice, but their sexual role. The female mounts another female not because she desires a female, but because she desires to mount; because other females are more likely to be receptive to her mounting behavior than males, her search for a sex partner is more likely to end by mounting a female than a male. 3. If hormonal manipulation that caused cross-sex sexual behavior were the explanation for homosexuality, then the ideal case would be sex between two hormonally manipulated animals, because both animals would be "homosexual." A moment's thought, however, leads to the conclusion that such sex would occur between a mounting female and a lordosing male—under the common European American understanding of human sexual orientation, this would constitute heterosexual, not homosexual, behavior. Heterosexual behavior does not become homosexual just because the woman is on the top instead of on the bottom. At best, this theory might come closest to explaining homosexuality as conceptualized in Mexican culture, in which taking the insertive role in male-male anal sex is considered compatible with heterosexual status, and only the receptive partner bears stigma as a homosexual per se. See chapter 22, for discussion of "Latin" constructions of sexuality.

Money is cognizant of criticisms regarding the confounding of the various components of sex, gender, and sexuality and seeks to reassert his own conceptualization of the relationships among these components. For example, he wrote, "in popular and in scientific usage, gender role and gender identity have become separated, whereas they are really two sides of the same coin. Other people infer your private and personal gender identity from the public evidence of your gender role. You alone have intimate access to your gender identity. The acronym G-I/R (gender-identity/role) unifies identity and role into a singular noun" (1990b:52).

Other authors have analyzed other assumptions typically made in research on the biology of sexual orientation. De Cecco and Parker (1995a, 1995b); Gooren (1990); Van Wyk and Geist (1995); Ricketts (1984); Byne and Parsons (1993); and Byne (1997) pointed out that biological research assumes that homosexuality is an essential characteristic and that homosexuals and heterosexuals are distinct "species" of humans, an assumption called into question by social scientific research demonstrating the historical and cultural specificity of the concept of a "homosexual person." They also pointed out methodological flaws typical of particular genres of biological research or particular studies. De Cecco and Parker's review focuses on describing historical trends in biological research and the social context surrounding those trends such as the political climate and media reactions. They summarized the most well-known studies in the area, including Dörner's research on prenatal hormones (Dörner et al. 1975; Dörner 1976); genetic research by Pillard and Weinrich (1986) and Hamer et al. (1993a); brain research by Swaab and colleagues (e.g., Swaab and Hofman 1990); LeVay (1991); and Allen and Gorski (1992); and twin research by Bailey and Pillard (1991).

11. See note 7, this chapter.

12. Garber (1995:273–277) discussed LeVay's treatment of bisexuality at length. Similarly, Meyer-Bahlburg (1997a) used the SERBAS to assess sexual orientation, thus measuring several aspects of sexual orientation including fantasies, attractions, dreams, etc., but dichotomized the resulting K scores in his presentation of findings.

13. Van Wyk and Geist reviewed research on women with adrenogenital syndrome by Ehrhardt, Evers, and Money (1968); Lev-Ran (1974); and Money (1985; see also Ehrhardt et al. [1985] and Money, Schwartz, and [Lewis] [1984]); and research on women prenatally exposed to diethylstilbestrol (DES) by Ehrhardt et al. (1985), noting the "high incidence of bisexuality . . . and the relative dearth of predominant or exclusive homosexuality" in these studies. Specifically, among twenty-two women, four reported bisexual behavior, none reported exclusive homosexual behavior, and ten reported bisexual fantasies (Ehrhardt, Evers, and Money 1968); of twenty-three women, eleven reported bisexual behavior and fantasy, six rated themselves as bisexual, and five rated themselves as predominantly or exclusively homosexual (Money 1985); and of twenty-nine women, four were bisexual and one was exclusively homosexual in lifetime sexual behavior (Ehrhardt et al. 1985). Comparing these findings to their own finding (1984) that 0.7 percent of women and 1.2 percent of men were behaviorally bisexual (K = 2.00 – 4.00 since age eighteen) whereas 1.8 percent of women and 4.7 percent of men were predominantly or exclusively homosexual, the authors concluded that behavioral bisexuality—not homosexuality—is unusually prevalent among women prenatally exposed to high levels of masculinizing hormones. In terms of total prevalence of same-sex experience since age eighteen, Van Wyk and Geist's (1984) own findings are substantially in agreement with more recent national population studies, for example, the GSSs in which, after adjustment for household sampling bias, 4.8 percent of men had been behaviorally bisexual and 0.7 percent had been exclusively homosexual since age eighteen (Rogers and Turner 1991). See also Swaab et al. (1995) for evidence that pre- and postnatal treatment with ATD (1,4,6-androstatrienne-3,17-dione) produces bisexual rather than homosexual partner preference among male rats.

When injected with estrogen, Dörner's bisexual male subjects displayed a more "masculine" hormonal response than heterosexual men (Van Wyk 1984).

14. See, for example, a discussion of the relationship between femininity and perceptions of sexual orientation in Lee (1996) and a discussion of cultural images of bisexuality in Michel (1996).

15. Research on childhood crossgendered behavior is an exception. Paul (1993) argued that this research typically assumes that childhood crossgendered behavior is an early sign of homosexuality, with both the crossgender behavior and the homosexuality thought to be caused by a common, presumably biological, precursor. Paul therefore criticized research on childhood crossgender behavior for many of the same reasons De Cecco and Parker (1995a, 1995b) and others have criticized biological research.

16. See, for example, Bailey (1996) and Bailey and Zucker (1995) for reviews of this literature.

17. Bailey (1996) discussed this possible bias and suggested that it is also possible for gay men to underreport their degree of childhood femininity.

Bailey, Miller, and Willerman (1993) attempted to assess the role of recall bias in mothers' reports of their adult homosexual and heterosexual sons' and daughters' childhood gender behaviors. Homosexual subjects were asked the extent of their mothers' knowledge of their sexual orientation. The correlation between mothers' knowledge and ratings of childhood gender behavior was significant among female subjects but not among male subjects, suggesting a role for recall bias in the finding of crossgendered behavior in mothers' reports of the childhoods of lesbians but not gay men. This strategy can assess the degree of recall bias but cannot eliminate it where it exists as could be done in a prospective study. It also cannot eliminate the possibility that adult sons, knowing of their own nonheterosexuality, engaged in a process of reconstructing their childhoods with their mothers even though the mothers were unaware of their sons' adult sexual orientations. Furthermore, the fact that mothers' knowledge was assessed through sons' reports leaves open the possibility that mothers are consciously or unconsciously aware of their sons' sexual orientations even though their sons believe them to be unaware.

18. See Zucker (1990) for a review of prospective studies of childhood gender and sexual

orientation in males. Bailey (1996) noted that no prospective studies have been done on females.

19. Bailey (1996) cited Bell, Weinberg, and Hammersmith (1981) for finding that bisexual women reported less childhood gender nonconformity than homosexual women; I could not confirm this citation.

20. Phillips and Over (1995) is also one of the few studies in which sexual orientation was measured in multiple ways, with data from multiple assessments carried through data analysis. Phillips and Over classified their subjects in three different ways. First, they distinguished Kinsey 0–1's from Kinsey 2–4's and Kinsey 5–6's; second, they distinguished Kinsey 0's and Kinsey 6's from Kinsey 1–5's; and third, they combined Kinsey scores with information regarding the women's orgasmic experiences since age eighteen.

21. Findings by Ross (1983a) regarding the relationship between gender and sexual orientation in Australian compared to Swedish and Finnish men shed some light on the conflicting findings regarding North Americans. At the time of Ross' study homosexual acts were criminal in Victoria and Queensland in Australia, whereas Sweden was both more accepting of homosexuality and supportive of equality between the sexes and Finland was sexually egalitarian but more antihomosexual than Sweden. Ross found that masculinity, as measured by the Bem Sex Role Inventory, was correlated with Kinsey score among Australian men, whereas no significant correlations were found between Kinsey score and either masculinity or femininity in either Sweden or Finland. These findings suggest that heterosexism promotes crossgender behavior among gay men, perhaps because the stereotypes are self-fulfilling prophecies that create, rather than reflect, actual crossgender behavior. This could explain differences in findings among North Americans because of varying levels of heterosexism in different North American populations. Because Ross used Kinsey ratings to produce correlation coefficients rather than trichotomizing subjects into sexual orientation classes, specific findings regarding bisexuality cannot be gleaned from his research although recognition of the existence of bisexuality is integral to Ross's analysis.

22. Storms asked his subjects both to self-identify as either "straight," "bisexual," or "gay" and to rate themselves on the Kinsey scale. For the purpose of comparison, however, subjects were classified according to their sexual self-identity only. Nine men and 15 women, out of a total of 185 subjects, were thereby classified as bisexual.

23. LaTorre and Wendenburg did not find significant differences between sexual orientation groups when mean masculinity and femininity scores were compared; the differences showed up only when subjects were classified, on the basis of their combined masculinity and femininity scores, into the four gender categories described by Bem (1974): masculine, feminine, androgynous, and undifferentiated. Given the fact that Storms found no such significant difference, it is worth noting that LaTorre and Wendenburg used the masculinity and femininity subscales of the EPAQ (Spence, Helmreich, and Holohan 1979), a revised version of the PAQ used by Storms (1980). The difference in findings is easily explained by the fact that Storms, however, examined only mean M and F scores.

24. See also note 20, this chapter.

25. Homophobia means fear of homosexuals, and it is a component of heterosexism. Heterosexism is a broader term referring to any aspect of the structural and cultural conditions that privilege heterosexuality over homosexuality. For example, the fact that the Defense of Marriage Act prohibits federal recognition of same-sex marriages is an instance of heterosexism, not homophobia, although it was certainly enacted in part because of homophobia. Biphobia means fear of bisexuals, and monosexism refers to any structural or cultural condition that privileges monosexism—heterosexuality and/or homosexuality, or the idea that sexuality must be directed toward one gender or the other—over bisexuality. In both popular and academic usage, the terms *homophobia* and *biphobia* are often used to refer to heterosexism and monosexism.

26. For discussion of bisexuality, as well as multiraciality and other challenges to binary/categorical Western thought, and the sanctions imposed by a society determined to

preserve its familiar categories, see Colker (1996). See also Klein's *The Bisexual Option* ([1978] 1993).

27. For discussions of lesbian feminist reconstruction of lesbian identity, including the politicization and desexualization of lesbian identity and its consequences for the politics of bisexuality, see Rust (1995a); Ochs (1996); Däumer (1994); Echols (1984); Esterberg (1997); Faderman (1991); Golden (1994, 1996); Hollibaugh and Moraga ([1981]1983); Kaplan (1992); King (1986); Udis-Kessler (1996); Young (1992); and Weise (1992).

On political gains, see Gamson (1995).

28. See Garber (1995); Rust (1995a); and vol. 4, no. 1 of *North Bi Northwest*, newsletter of the Seattle Bisexual Women's Network, for details about these particular events and others.

29. See Badgett (1996) for an overview of employment discrimination on the basis of sexual orientation.

30. Badgett (1995) found that the difference between bisexual/lesbian and heterosexual women was not consistently statistically significant and, unlike the difference between bisexual/gay men and heterosexual men, decreased when controlled for occupation and adjusted for other factors. The authors suggested that the lack of consistent significance could be due to the small number of lesbians in this nationally representative sample (n = 34, compared to n = 47 for bisexual and gay men, n = 698 for heterosexual women, and n = 901 for heterosexual men).

31. Taylor and Raeburn (1995) explicitly included bisexuals in their study of the career consequences of lesbian, gay, and bisexual identity among sociologists. However, they did not distinguish the experiences of bisexuals from those of lesbians and gay men in their analysis, with the exception of a quote from a bisexual respondent who noted that when she married and suddenly began to receive social invitations she realized the extent of the social discrimination she had experienced previously because of her sexual orientation. Krieger and Sidney (1997) also explicitly included subjects who had had at least one same-sex partner and subjects who had had sex partners of both sexes, but grouped them together when presenting rates of reported sexual orientation discrimination.

32. This section focuses largely on bisexuals' sexual and romantic relationships with women and men. Some of the research studies cited herein provide much more detailed data on specific sexual practices, and the reader who is interested in this detail is referred to them. Also, two studies of sadomasochists, one of women and one of men, have explored sexual differences between bisexual and monosexual sadomasochists. Although data are scarce, the proportion of bisexuals in the sadomasochistic population appears to run 16–20 percent among women and 40 percent among men (Breslow, Evans, and Langley 1985, 1986; see also Levitt, Moser, and Jamison 1994); this provides an interesting contrast to swingers, among whom bisexuality is more common among women than men. In their study of men Breslow, Evans, and Langley (1986) found that bisexuals resembled gay men in terms of their route of entry into sadomasochistic practice but resembled heterosexual men in the degree to which they had friends and acquaintances who also practiced S&M. Specifically, bisexuals and gay men were less likely than heterosexuals to have become interested via pornography and more likely to have been introduced to the practice by a sex partner, and bisexuals and heterosexuals were much less likely than gay men to have friends who practiced S&M. Bisexuals were also more likely than heterosexuals or gay men to contact sex partners through ads, whereas gay men were more likely to find partners in S&M bars or clubs and heterosexuals used private introductions. The researchers also asked their respondents about their level of commitment to S&M, i.e., whether they considered it merely a form of foreplay or a lifestyle. Bisexuals were more likely than gay men or heterosexuals to respond that they considered it both. However, when asked whether they preferred the dominant or the submissive role in S&M, bisexuals were ironically less likely than gay men or heterosexuals to say that they were "versatile"—apparently, among these sadomasochists, those who were more versatile regarding the sex of their partner were less versatile regarding the role that partner played during sex.

33. In general, the self-identified bisexuals who participated in the earlier interview phase of the Weinberg, Williams, and Pryor (1994) study tended more strongly toward the center of the Kinsey scale than did the bisexuals in their 1984–1985 survey, perhaps because the former were more strongly associated with the Bisexual Center through which they were recruited for this phase of the study.

34. Some research focuses on either heterosexual or homosexual behavior rather than the simultaneity of heterosexual and homosexual behavior. For example, Cochran and Mays (1988) found that 44 percent of self-identified bisexuals were not currently heterosexually active, much less concurrently involved with same- and other-sex partners. Among self-defined bisexuals in the *Playboy* survey (Cook et al. 1983), 19 percent of males and 18 percent of females reported no homosexual experience at all as adults.

35. Bisexual women's heterosexual relationships have been more recent than lesbians', however. Cochran and Mays (1988) found that bisexual women had had their most recent heterosexual experience a median of seven months previously, compared to sixty-seven months among lesbians. The modal bisexual woman in Rust's (1992) study had had a heterosexual relationship within the past year, whereas the modal lesbian had had her last heterosexual involvement six years previous.

36. This finding could be interpreted as either supporting or contradicting the stereotype; the authors did not provide enough evidence to determine which interpretation is correct. On one hand, such findings could result if bisexuals' relationships are, in fact, longer on average than heterosexuals' or homosexuals' relationships, such that the ratio of long to short relationships is higher for bisexuals than for heterosexuals or homosexuals. On the other hand, the finding that bisexuals have more long relationships might simply reflect a tendency for bisexuals to have more relationships overall, including more short as well as more long relationships. If that were the case, it is possible that the average length of bisexuals' relationships is shorter, not longer, than the average length of heterosexuals' or homosexuals' relationships. Also, the finding that bisexuals have more long-term relationships could be artifactually produced by the six-month definition of *long-term,* if heterosexuals' and homosexuals' fewer long-term relationships are long*er* term than bisexuals' long-term relationships.

Wold et al. (1998) described MSMW and MSMO as "similar" in the proportions that had only steady, only nonsteady, or both steady and nonsteady sex partners. However, statistics embedded in the text do differ somewhat—for example, 23 percent versus 31 percent had only steady partners—and it is unclear which set of statistics describes which group because the order of reference varies throughout the paragraph in question. The most recent reference is to "homosexual and bisexual groups," suggesting that the 23 percent refers to MSMO.

37. According to research by Van Wyk and Geist (1984), patterns of same- and other-sex desire among bisexuals follow similar patterns, relative to same- and other-sex behavior. They found that homosexual masturbation fantasies and arousal were linearly correlated with adult Kinsey sexual behavior scores for both men and women, indicating that those with intermediate Kinsey behavioral scores had levels of same-sex masturbation fantasies that fell between those of men and women with high (homosexual) and those with low (heterosexual) Kinsey scores. However, they found curvilinear relationships for other-sex desire; individuals whose overt behavior fell between 2.0 and 4.0 on the Kinsey scale "had more heterosexual fantasy than did either behaviorally exclusive heterosexuals or predominant or exclusive behavioral homosexuals" (Van Wyk and Geist 1995:365) and "bisexual and predominantly heterosexual males and females [showed] more heterosexual arousal than either exclusively heterosexual or predominantly or exclusively homosexual subjects" (Van Wyk and Geist 1984:528).

38. See, for example, Wold et al. (1998). Findings from the French National Survey on Sexual Behavior, a large-scale random sample telephone survey of 4,820 adults in France, also showed that bisexuals fall between heterosexuals and homosexuals in terms of levels of

homosexual activity. Messiah, Mouret-Fourme, and the French National Survey on Sexual Behavior Group (1995) reported that French bisexual men, defined as men who had had both male and female sex partners in the previous year, had an average of 7.0 sex partners in the previous five years compared to 16.2 among homosexual men and 2.9 among heterosexual men. In the past year bisexuals had an average of 2.8 partners, including 1.2 "new" partners, compared to 4.1 partners (3.3 new) partners among homosexual men, and 1.3 partners (0.3 new) partners among heterosexual men.

39. HIV-related studies showing that bisexuals have more male than female partners include McKirnan, Stokes, Doll, and Burzette (1995); Boulton, Hart, and Fitzpatrick (1992); Rotheram-Borus et al. (1994); Wood, Krueger, Pearlman, and Goldbaum (1993); Doll et al. (1992); Wold et al. (1998); and Diaz et al. (1993). Studies showing that bisexuals are more likely to have male than female partners include McKirnan, Stokes, Doll, and Burzette (1995); Boulton, Hart, and Fitzpatrick (1992); Ekstrand et al. (1994); Stokes, McKirnan, and Burzette (1993); and Doll et al. (1992). See details of these studies in chapter 22.

40. These percentages are calculations based on figures provided by Diaz et al. (1993). The authors presented percentages separately for those who had and those who had not used injected drugs; recalculation involved regaining frequencies, combining the frequencies for IDUs and non-IDUs, and calculating new percentages.

41. Stokes, McKirnan, and Burzette (1993) found that unconventional heterosex might also be more common among bisexuals. They noted that rates of oral sex with female partners among their bisexual respondents were higher than rates found in a nationally representative survey of men aged twenty to thirty-nine by Billy, Tanfer, Grady, and Klepinger (1993).

42. The difference between bisexuals and lesbians or gay men, and the preponderance of male over female partners among bisexuals, was even more striking when Rosario et al. (1996) counted numbers of sexual occasions rather than numbers of sex partners. They reported that bisexual women had had 3 occasions of sex with women and 100 occasions of sex with men, whereas lesbians had had 116 occasions of sex with women and 8 occasions of sex with men. Bisexual men had had 12 occasions of sex with men and 8 occasions of sex with women, whereas gay men had had 53 occasions of sex with men and none with women.

43. See also note 34, chapter 17.

44. This study used a sample of over 900 men and women from various English-speaking countries who had ever felt attracted to both men and women, ever had sexual contact with both men and women, or ever identified themselves as bisexual. The sample was recruited primarily via bisexual social and political organizations, gay and lesbian organizations, conferences on sexuality, the internet, and ads in bisexual and mainstream publications.

45. The finding regarding social class is not statistically significant.

46. These percentages were not reported as such in Stokes, McKirnan, and Burzette (1993). The authors reported that 30 percent (n = 28) of all respondents had had heterosex with a steady female partner. They also reported that forty-five of the ninety-four respondents who were asked about female partners reported heterosex, leading to the conclusion that 62 percent (28/45) of those who had had heterosex had it with a steady female partner. Similar recalculations led to the 57 percent and 50 percent reported in the text here.

47. Finding that, unlike "homosexual transsexuals," heterosexual, asexual, and bisexual transsexuals displayed high rates of "crossgender fetishism," i.e., sexual arousal associated with crossdressing, Blanchard concluded that bisexual and asexual transsexualism are actually subtypes of heterosexual transsexualism and that heterosexual and homosexual transsexualism constitute the two basic types of transsexualism. He characterized "bisexual gender dysphorics" as those in which "autogynephilic disorder gives rise to some secondary erotic interest in males that coexists with the individual's basic attraction to females," with autogynephilia defined as "love of oneself as a woman" (1989:323).

48. Coleman, Bockting, and Gooren (1993), in a small sample of nine Dutch FTM trans-sexuals with homosexual or bisexual self-identities, found that four identified themselves as bisexual and five identified themselves as predominantly or exclusively homosexual in response to the self-identification subscale of the Klein Sexual Orientation Grid.

49. For example, Coleman and Remafedi (1989). See Fox (1996) for a detailed review of the role given bisexuality in various theorists' self-identity development models.

50. For example, Cass (1979); Coleman (1982); and McDonald (1982). More recently, Cass has placed her linear model of lesbian, gay, and bisexual self-identity formation within a social constructionist framework. Arguing that "psychological functioning and human behavior is specific to the sociocultural environment in which people live" (1996:229) and that there is an "indigenous psychology" in each sociocultural setting, she argued that her model reflects lesbian, gay, and bisexual self-identity formation as it occurs in Western culture.

The work of Bell, Weinberg, and Hammersmith (1981) is a notable exception amid the linear models of coming out proposed before the 1980s. These researchers looked for predictive childhood experiences rather than milestone events. Using path analyses conducted separately for bisexuals and homosexuals, they found a weaker relationship between childhood sexual feelings and adult sexual preference and a stronger relationship between homosexual genital activities in childhood and adult sexual preference among bisexual men. This led the authors to the intriguing conclusion that "exclusive homosexuality tends to emerge from a deep-seated predisposition, while bisexuality is more subject to influence by social and sexual learning" (201), which reinforces the view that homosexuality is the more "authentic" sexuality. Research by Storms (1978) suggests a different interpretation. Among those with substantial homo- and heteroeroticism, he found that sexual fantasies did not predict self-label (see chapter 11). Thus, the findings of Bell, Weinberg and Hammersmith might not reflect a lack of continuity between adolescent and adult feelings but a more general lack of "consistency" between the components of sexuality among individuals whose sexual feelings and experiences don't fit neatly into cultural categories.

See Levine and Evans (1991) for a comprehensive and concise overview of the literature on the linear development of lesbian and gay self-identity and its neglect of bisexual self-identity.

51. Cass (1990) acknowledged that it is "theoretically possible to develop an alternative identity that . . . replaces an existing one" (255), that is, to come out more than once.

52. Zinik (1985) cited the findings of Bell, Weinberg, and Hammersmith (1981); Bode (1976); Klein (1978); and Zinik (1983), which, with the exception of Zinik (1983), are described elsewhere in this volume. See also note 55 in this chapter and findings by Weinberg, Williams, and Pryor (1994) and Pattatucci and Hamer (1995), which are presented later in this chapter, regarding the relative ages at which other-sex and same-sex milestones are experienced. Schwartz and Blumstein (1998), using 1970s data, found that 58 percent of male and 67 percent of female self-identified bisexuals had previously identified as heterosexual; only 16 percent of males and 18 percent of females had come out as bisexual from a homosexual, lesbian, or gay identity.

53. Cass (1990) also recognized the development of bisexual self-identity as a developmental process distinct from that leading to lesbian or gay self-identity but did not propose a model for bisexual self-identity development.

54. Instead of (or in addition to) calculating average ages for comparison between sexual orientation groups, some researchers calculated correlations between actual ages—or other dimensions of the coming out experience—and respondents' scaled Kinsey scores. This procedure implicitly acknowledges the existence of bisexuality but does not produce findings that can be used to describe the experience of coming out for bisexuals. For example, Van Wyk and Geist (1984) explored the relationship between early sexual experiences and adult sexual orientation using the original Kinsey interviews conducted between 1938 and 1963. They discovered that "degree" of homosexuality in adulthood was associated with the number of years of prepubertal involvement in homosexual "play" for males, but not for

females. In other words, the longer a male had been homosexually active prior to puberty, the higher his adult Kinsey score. Although reflecting the existence of bisexuality, this finding does not provide a description of the types or degrees of prepubertal homosexual play characterizing bisexuals except to imply that it is intermediate to that characterizing heterosexuals and homosexuals. Van Wyk and Geist also found that the degree of participation in postpubertal heterosexual activities was more strongly related to adult Kinsey scores among men than women, suggesting that men are more likely than women to express the strength of their heterosexual preferences through behavior. Among women the frequency of orgasmic homosexual contacts during the first year of such experiences was associated with higher Kinsey scores.

55. These include Harris (1977); Klein (1978); Morse (1989); Rust (1993a); and Fox (1993). See Fox (1995, 1996) for a summary. See also note 52, this chapter.

56. Both Weinberg, Williams, and Pryor (1994) and Pattatucci and Hamer (1995) reported average ages for both same-sex and other-sex milestones for heterosexual respondents—Pattatucci and Hamer noted that two-thirds of their "heterosexual" women had ever felt romantically or sexually attracted to a female.

57. Savin-Williams (1995a) recruited 83 respondents via solicitation in classes, bars, restaurants, and newspaper advertisements, whereas Rotheram-Borus and colleagues (1994) recruited via a gay-identified social service agency in New York City. Rosario et al. (1996) studied 76 lesbian and bisexual and 80 gay and bisexual youths recruited from "community-based or college organizations for lesbian/gay youths in New York City" (113). D'Augelli and Hershberger (1993) studied 194 "lesbian, gay, and bisexual youth aged twenty-one and younger who attended programs in [lesbian/gay] community centers" in fourteen metropolitan areas (421).

58. This finding might seem counterintuitive; given that heterosexuality, not homosexuality, is culturally encouraged, one might expect youths to recognize and act on their other-sex attractions first. Savin-Williams did find other evidence that the patterns of sexual development of these youths had been affected by the cultural encouragement of heterosexuality. Comparing his gay and bisexual respondents to a sample of heterosexual males, he discovered that the onset of puberty (biological age) was correlated with the beginning and frequency of homosexual but not heterosexual activity, whereas the onset and level of heterosexual activity was correlated with chronological age. Savin-Williams argued that the cultural preference for heterosexuality encourages young men to begin heterosexual activity at a particular age regardless of the strength of their other-sex attractions, in contrast to homosexual activity, which would be more directly related to pubertal awakening of same-sex sexual feelings. Similarly, Van Wyk and Geist (1984) found that adult Kinsey scores were more strongly correlated with degree of postpubertal homosexual activity than postpubertal heterosexual activity among both men and women, suggesting a closer relationship between adolescent behavior and adult preferences when those behaviors are homosexual than when they are heterosexual.

59. Reseach by Diamond (1998) suggests that similar differences do not exist among contemporary young adults; among women aged sixteen to twenty-three she found that self-identified lesbians were not more likely to report having questioned their sexual orientation prior to experiencing same-sex attractions. Diamond found a general lack of difference in the milestone experiences of self-identified lesbian and bisexual women. Golden (1996) describes interviewing bisexual women who were attracted to bisexuality as an intellectual idea prior to experiencing bisexual feelings.

60. Rosario et al. (1996) also explored the relationship between young men's and women's self-identity histories and sexual experiences. In general, among those who currently identified as lesbian or gay, those who had ever wondered if they were bisexual were more bisexual in their sexual experiences than those who had never wondered if they were bisexual, whereas among those who identified as bisexual those who ever wondered if they were lesbian or gay were more homosexual in their sexual experiences than those who had

never wondered if they were lesbian or gay. More specifically, among women who currently identified as lesbians, those who had ever thought they might be bisexual had first thought that they might be lesbian or that they were lesbian at older ages and had had more other-sex sex partners and sexual contacts than those who had never considered the possibility that they were bisexual. Conversely, among those who currently identified as bisexual, those who had ever thought that they might be lesbian had had more same-sex partners and same-sex contacts than those who had not. Similarly, among men who currently identified as gay, those who had ever thought they might be bisexual had first thought that they might be gay or that they were gay at older ages and had had more other-sex sex partners and other-sex contacts than those who had never considered the possibility. They also reported more same-sex partners and contacts.

61. Weinberg, Williams, and Pryor (1994) also collected longitudinal data on this question from the bisexuals they interviewed in 1983 and reinterviewed in 1988.

62. Esterberg (1997) and Weinberg, Williams, and Pryor (1994) noted that their respondents tended to perceive their current sexual self-identity as their single "true" identity, commenting that they had always known, deep down, that they were "really" [whatever their current identity was]. They tended to perceive their own previous self-identity changes in the way that social scientists using linear models do, i.e., as immature stages of development. Esterberg (1997) argued that social scientific perceptions of coming out have filtered into popular circles, causing individuals to experience their own self-identity histories as linear processes ending with their current sexual self-identities. Esterberg noted that her lesbian and bisexual respondents might, if they had been interviewed at different times in their lives when they had different sexual self-identities, have told different stories about the process of their self-identity formation. At each point in life they would have "interpreted their histories through their present understandings of themselves" (8), thus producing a "true self narrative" (57), i.e., a linear account of progression toward a "true" identity that accurately reflects their "essential" sexuality, which, not coincidentally, would be their current self-identity. See also Cass on the "indigenous psychology" of coming out, note 50, this chapter.

63. For studies finding sexual self-identity correlating to recent behavior, see Rust (1992); Nichols (1985, 1990); Laumann, Gagnon, Michael, and Michaels (1994).

64. Research and theory reviewed by Eliason (1996) include Altman (1971); Plummer (1975); Moses (1978); Ponse (1978); Cass (1979); Ettorre (1980); Minton and McDonald (1984); Chapman and Brannock (1987); Kitzinger (1987); Troiden (1988); and Rust (1992, 1993a).

65. Matteson (1997) and Katz (1995).

66. For details regarding the role of the family in these cultures, including pressures to marry, resources for personal identity, and resilience of family ties, see Afshar (1994); Almaguer (1993); Atkinson, Morten, and Sue (1993); Augustin (1993); Cabaj and Stein (1996); Carballo-Diéguez (1989); Chan (1989, 1992); Espin (1987); Greene (1994); H. (1989); Icard (1986); Helie-Lucas (1994); Matteson (1997); Morales (1989); Thiam (1986); Tremble, Schneider, and Appathurai (1989); Sue (1981); and Vazquez (1979). For further summary of these factors and their effects, see Rust (1996a).

67. Matteson (1997) and Chan (1992). This is not to say, however, that biphobia and homophobia are unknown in Asian American cultures, and that shame would not also follow from the fact that this public identity is a bisexual or gay one. See Wooden, Kawasaki, and Mayeda (1983) and Carrier, Nguyen, and Su (1992) on heterosexism among Japanese Americans and Vietnamese Americans.

68. Matteson (1997), Roland (1988).

69. For discussion of Mexican repression of women's sexuality and concepts of Chicana womanhood, see Almaguer (1993); Moraga (1983); Greene (1994); and Trujillo (1991).

70. Bisexual self-identity is especially common among African American men with strong ties to the African American heterosexual community. Johnson (1982) found that among self-identified bisexual and gay Black men those who saw themselves as gay tended

to identify more strongly with the gay community, whereas those who saw themselves as bisexual tended to identify more with the Black community.

71. The actual empirical finding concerned a difference between path models predicting adult homosexual orientation among Blacks and among whites. Preadult homosexual activity was a more important precursor of adult homosexual orientation among Blacks, whereas preadult homosexual feelings were more important among whites.

72. Citing Klassen, Williams, and Levitt (1989), who found that Blacks were slightly less approving of homosexuality but much more tolerant of premarital sex than whites. See also a report by Francis, Ernst, Devieux, and Perkins (1995) comparing a study of Black and white attitudes toward specific sexual behaviors in which Blacks were found less likely than whites to prefer anal sex and oral sex. Subjects were not asked about their sexual orientations; most subjects were probably answering with regard to *heterosexual* anal or oral sex.

73. For discussion of the concept of homosexuality as a "white thing" or as Western behavior among Asian Americans, Latinos, and African Americans, see Chan (1989); Espín (1987); H. (1989); Icard (1986); Matteson (1997); Morales (1989, 1990); Wooden, Kawasake, and Mayeda (1983); Carrier, Nguyen, and Su (1992).

74. Hinsch (1990) and Lau and Ng (1989).

75. The term *two spirit* has been adopted by some Native Americans as a pan-Indian term for the third and fourth gender roles found in many tribes. The roles vary from tribe to tribe, e.g., the Navajo *nadle* is different from the Lakota *winkte*. The term *two spirit* is preferred over the earlier anthropological term *berdache*, which is offensive because of its origin in a Persian term meaning "kept male" or "slave" and because it was imposed by non-Natives (Red Earth 1994; Tafoya and Rowell 1988).

For descriptions of two-spirit traditions and their resurgence as a source of pride for contemporary lesbian and gay Native Americans, see Blackwood (1984); Roscoe (1988, 1997); Tafoya and Wirth (1996); Trumbach (1997); Williams (1986); and Whitehead (1981). See Herdt (1997) and Nanda (1997) for descriptions of third-gender roles in many other cultures.

Although some anthropological reports indicate that two-spirit traditions succumbed to European Christian efforts to eradicate them, Williams (1993) reported that they continue to exist but Native Americans informants conceal them from white anthropologists from whom they expect disapproval.

76. For discussion of the ways in which individuals respond to this multiple marginalization, see Espín (1987); Johnson (1982); and Morales (1989, 1992), and for further discussion of antagonism between ethnic and gay communities and its effect on sexual minority individuals, see Conerly (1996); Gutiérrez and Dworkin (1992); and Icard (1986). For an analysis of the advantageous epistemologic position of biraciality and bisexuality as forms of marginality, see Kich (1996).

77. The part of this literature that has received the most popular and political attention pertains to suicide rates among gay, lesbian, and bisexual youths. The oft-cited statistics that "gay and lesbian youths are two to three times more likely to commit suicide than other youths, and 30 percent of all completed youth suicides are related to issues of sexual identity" (Proctor and Groze 1994:504) come from a U.S. Department of Health and Human Services (DHHS) study (Gibson 1989) whose statistical methods have been called into question (e.g., Richardson 1995). Unfortunately, bisexuals are usually not distinguished from lesbian and gay youth in this literature, hence nothing can be said about bisexuals' position in this well-publicized issue. For example, Hershberger and D'Augelli (1995) excluded bisexual respondents who described themselves as predominantly heterosexual and then combined the remaining bisexual youths with lesbian and gay youths (see also Proctor and Groze 1994; Remafedi, Farrow, and Deisher 1991).

Rotheram-Borus, Hunter, and Rosario (1994) reported that 25 percent of the "gay and bisexual" youths they sampled from a gay-identified youth social service agency in New York City self-identified as bisexual and that there were no differences in sexual self-identification between those adolescents who had attempted suicide (39 percent) and those who had not. In another report on gay and bisexual male youths Rotheram-Borus et al. (1995) found that, compared to rates found for general youth populations by other researchers, gay and bisexual youths did not differ appreciably in drinking, drug use, conduct problems, or emotional distress, and had less contact with the criminal justice system but, in confirmation of the DHHS finding, were more likely to attempt suicide. Unfortunately, although these researchers distinguished self-identified gay and bisexual youths in other portions of the study (finding no durable significant differences), they did not present separate data for the two populations regarding these measures of social distress.

For reviews of the literature on suicide, "gay-related stressors," and other indicators of social distress among "lesbian, gay, and bisexual" youths, see Proctor and Groze (1994); Hartstein (1996); and Savin-Williams (1994). See also Remafedi, Farrow, and Deisher (1991).

78. Other works on this topic include Deacon, Reinke, and Viers (1996); Lourea (1985); Matteson (1995); Paul (1996); Smiley (1997); and Weasel (1996). Schaefer, Evans, and Coleman (1987), who discussed biphobia as well as homophobia, advised therapists who treat chemically dependent individuals that sexual orientation is not dichotomous and that bisexuals are "often most cautious and confused about their sexual feelings, since they have been raised with the belief they must choose between being straight or gay/lesbian" (133).

79. Klein (1978) did ask his respondents about the degree to which they had disclosed their bisexuality to others. Because they were recruited through the Bisexual Forum in New York City, his respondents probably did understand the question to be about bisexuality and not homosexuality. The highest rate of disclosure was to friends and the lowest was to siblings and parents; 62.2 percent said that their friends knew they were bisexual, 10.2 percent said their parents knew, and 7.9 percent said their sibling(s) knew.

80. Interestingly, the above-mentioned study by Smith, Johnson, and Guenther (1985) found that "among lesbians, but not bisexuals, the use of a non-private practice source was correlated with the belief that physician awareness of their sexual orientation would hinder the quality of health care" (1066). This would seem to indicate that lesbians were more concerned with the influence of context on others' reactions to their sexuality, even though the same study showed that bisexuals were less likely overall to disclose their sexual orientation. Thus, high self-monitoring does not necessarily imply low rates of self-disclosure and the difference between bisexual women and lesbians is not a simple matter of a difference in degree of closetedness.

81. Rotheram-Borus et al. (1995) measured "gay-related stress" with seven items including the disclosure of "one's homosexuality to family and friends, having one's homosexuality discovered by them, and being ridiculed or harassed for being gay" (78).

82. Because self-monitoring refers to the degree of variation in self-disclosure across situations, and not to degree of self-disclosure, this finding could result if bisexuals were simply more closeted across the board, with no more variation in degree of closeting across situations than that displayed by lesbians and gay men. See note 80 in this chapter for evidence that high self-monitoring does not necessarily imply greater closetedness.

83. Respondents used seven-point scales to answer the following five statements: "I am not happy being a gay man/lesbian/bisexual," "I expect being gay/lesbian/bisexual will make my life more difficult as I grow older," "In general I feel that my loved ones have supported my being gay/lesbian/bisexual," "At present I am glad I am gay/lesbian/bisexual," "Compared to other lesbian/gay/bisexual people I know, I am more frustrated with my life and lifestyle" (Anderson and Randlet 1994:793–94, note 2)

84. Findings from two studies in specific bisexual populations suggest that the opposite might be true regarding depression. In a study of male sadomasochists, Breslow, Evans, and Langley (1986) found that bisexual sadomasochists were less likely than heterosexual or gay male sadomasochists to say that they rarely or never felt depressed for a week or longer (55.6 percent vs. 73.5 percent and 76.1 percent). In a study of psychological functioning, including AIDS-related stress, among men at risk for AIDS but without an AIDS diagnosis,

Ostrow et al. (1989) reported that "subjects reporting a substantially bisexual orientation (Kinsey score = 3–6) had higher mean CES-D scores than those endorsing an 'exclusively homosexual' orientation" (739; *sic*, Kinsey = 6 usually indicates "exclusive homosexuality"). The authors did not discuss the finding and therefore gave no opinion regarding whether the greater depression found among Kinsey bisexuals was due to greater AIDS-related stress or to other aspects of bisexuality. The sample used by Ostrow et al. was the MACS sample, and both HIV+ and HIV- men without AIDS diagnoses were included in the analysis. In a study of HIV+ and HIV- African American men without AIDS diagnoses, CES-D scores did not differ for self-identified gay and bisexual men although bisexual men reported more negative life events than gay men (Peterson, Folkman, Blakeman 1996). A stratified random sample of men in Calgary, Canada showed no difference in the CES-D scores of MSMO, MSWO, and MSMW; mean scores for all groups were 13.7–15.7, indicating lack of clinical depression (Bagley and Tremblay 1998).

85. The background characteristics controlled were age, sex, ethnicity, education, marital status, number of marriages, number of children, number in household, and sexual attitudes. The authors did not provide detailed data regarding which background characteristics explained the first two correlations.

86. In the Rotheram-Borus et al. (1995) study the correlation with self-esteem disappeared when subjected to a Bonferroni correction. The researchers conducted multiple bivariate analyses, and the Bonferroni correction is designed to correct significance levels for the fact that the chances of a false positive finding increase with the number of significance tests done.

87. The lack of research on body image among nonheterosexual women, especially bisexual women who have been excluded even from studies of lesbians (e.g., Striegel-Moore, Tucker, and Hsu 1990) and from studies of the relationship between sexual orientation and body image (e.g., Brand, Rothblum, and Solomon 1992) is a focus of Atkins (1998).

24

Neutralizing the Political Threat of the Marginal Woman: Lesbians' Beliefs About Bisexual Women

Paula C. Rust

ONE might expect lesbian and bisexual women to form a strong alliance because of their common marginalization in a heterosexist and sexist society. As noted by Simmel (1923/1955), a common external threat often causes those under siege to cohere. But Simmel also noted that as the besieged close ranks in defense, differences among them become potential sources of weakness. Ironically, therefore, although external threat might have the effect of causing a group to cohere more tightly, it might also have the effect of exacerbating internal divisions. For this reason, relations between politically dissimilar minority members are often more problematic than relations between minority members and dominants and constitute a special case in the study of intergroup relations (Robb, 1978).

Tension has existed between lesbian and bisexual women since at least the early 1970s, shortly after the lesbian feminist movement broke away from the feminist movement (Faderman, 1991; Radicalesbians, 1972). Based on interviews with bisexual and lesbian women in the 1970s, Blumstein and Schwartz (1974) reported that bisexual women faced hostility and suspicion in most lesbian communities and that radical lesbian feminists considered bisexuality dangerous and contrary to gay liberation. Other researchers reported that some segments of the lesbian community, particularly radical lesbian feminists, considered bisexuality a

This research was conducted in partial fulfillment of requirements for a Ph.D. at the University of Michigan with the guidance of Mary Jackman, Mayer Zald, Beth Reed, and Mark Chesler. Portions of these data were presented at the 1991 Annual Meeting of the American Sociological Association, Cincinnati, Ohio, and at the 1991 Annual Lesbian and Gay Studies Conference, Rutgers University, New Brunswick, New Jersey. This research was funded in part by a grant from the Horace H. Rackham School of Graduate Studies of the University of Michigan, Ann Arbor, Michigan.

personal, social, and political threat (Altman, 1982; Klein, 1978; Ponse, 1978). Ethnographers (e.g., Ponse, 1978, 1980) provided information about the content of lesbians' beliefs about bisexual women in the 1970s. Recent bisexual writers have described similar attitudes (Udis-Kessler, 1990; Wittstock, 1990), providing anecdotal evidence that lesbians continued to perceive bisexuality as a threat in the 1980s and early 1990s. But, despite the increasing significance of bisexuality and the intensification of sexual identity politics in the wake of the AIDS crisis, no research has been published on this topic since the early 1980s.

The research reported in this article builds on earlier research by updating it and by supplementing anecdotal information with quantitative data on the prevalence, strength, and correlates of lesbians' attitudes toward bisexual women. I interpret these data within the wider framework of intergroup relations theory, in an attempt to show that intraminority relations—relations between groups within a minority—can be fruitfully viewed as a special case of intergroup relations. Jackman and Senter (1983) argued that attitudes between racial, gender, and social class groups reflect the political relationships between the groups. I argue that the same is true of lesbians' attitudes toward bisexual women, that lesbians' attitudes can be understood within the context of the political relationship between lesbians and bisexual women, and that lesbians' attitudes will change as the political status of bisexual women in the lesbian community changes.

INTERGROUP RELATIONS AND THE LESBIAN-BISEXUAL CONTEXT

Most researchers on intergroup relations have explored relations between dominant social groups and traditional minorities, for example, whites and Blacks, Anglos and other white ethnic groups, men and women, and different socioeconomic classes. Early studies explored intergroup attitudes by presenting members of the dominant group with trait checklists (e.g., Katz and Braly, 1933; Gilbert, 1951), a method of stereotype measurement that has been criticized for lacking validity. A common criticism is that it measures "cultural consensus" (Brigham, 1971, p. 30) rather than "personal stereotypes" (Karlins, Coffman, and Walters, 1969, p. 15). Brigham (1971) noted that the checklist failed to measure the degree to which people generalize about a target group. He reported that when respondents were asked what percentage of the target group was described by the traits they had selected on the checklist, their answers ranged from 10 percent to 100 percent. The trait checklist also failed to assess the degree to which respondents believed that the traits typical of subordinates actually differentiated subordinates from dominants.

Later researchers developed improved methods of measuring intergroup attitudes. Sherriffs and McKee (1957) asked respondents to indicate, for each of 200 adjectives, "whether it is more true of men or women." This measure detected the existence of trait differentiation but neither the degree of differentiation nor the degree of generalization. Kammeyer (1966) measured the degree of trait differentiation by providing respondents with four-point scales on which they could agree or disagree with statements such as "women are more emotional then men."

Building on this approach, Jackman and Senter (1983) used pairs of questions of the form "How many poor people would you say are lazy?" and "How many working class people would you say are lazy?" followed by 9-point scales. Each question provided a measure of the degree to which respondents generalized about the target group, and the arithmetic difference between respondents' answers to the two questions provided a measure of the existence and size of the trait distinctions made by respondents. Jackman and Senter's measurement technique was adapted for use in the study reported in this article.

Using this technique, Jackman and Senter studied the reciprocal intergroup attitudes of women and men, Blacks and whites, and people of different social classes. They found that the gender context was characterized by an "amicable consensus" (1983, p. 329) in which a substantial percentage of men asserted the existence of moderate trait differences between men and women that were socially meaningful but not intentionally pejorative, and women shared these beliefs. In contrast, attitudes in the racial context were characterized by disagreement both among and between Blacks and whites. The percentage of people who perceived trait differences in the race context was smaller than in the gender context, and these differences were perceived to be small, but they carried evaluative overtones. The members of each racial group were divided between those who considered Blacks and whites equal and those who believed that their own racial group possessed more desirable traits.

Interpreting these findings, Jackman and Senter (1983) suggested that dominant groups maintain the most effective control over subordinates through ideology that asserts that the two groups are benignly different, hence suited to different social roles. In the "paternalistic" stage of political relations between dominants and subordinates, subordinates accept this ideological justification of the status quo, and beliefs about trait differences are widespread and largely uncontroversial among both dominants and subordinates. When subordinates begin to challenge the status quo, consensus breaks down among dominants. Whereas some dominants are persuaded to adopt more egalitarian belief systems, others adopt a defensive posture in which they cling to beliefs that justify their superior status by derogating subordinates.

Do relations within subordinate groups follow patterns that are similar to those found between dominants and subordinates? Higgins' (1979) analysis of the deaf community suggests that differences of opinion over relations with the dominant outgroup can create a hierarchy within a minority group and that relations between different levels of this hierarchy resemble relations between dominant and subordinate groups. The deaf community is divided into speakers and signers, a division imbued with political importance because of the history of the deaf experience in a society that values auditory communication. In the past, hearing teachers with assimilationist philosophies and paternalistic attitudes prohibited deaf students from using sign language. As a result, in the contemporary deaf community, signing symbolizes commitment to the community and an affirmation of deafness (Higgins, 1979). Persistent use of speech and lipreading symbolizes a lack of commitment and pride in one's deaf self. Although both signers and speakers are subordinated in a predominantly hearing society, speakers are tainted by their closer association with the dominant hearing outgroup and their apparent acceptance of the auditory values of this dominant group. Thus, within the deaf community, signers occupy a higher moral status and sometimes marginalize speakers because of their different symbolic relationship with the dominant group (Higgins, 1979).

Similarly, both lesbian and bisexual women are subordinated in a predominantly heterosexual society. But within the sexual minority community lesbians occupy a higher moral status than bisexual women because of bisexual women's closer relationships with *two* dominant outgroups, men and heterosexuals. Bisexual women, by virtue of their bisexuality, are presumably more likely than lesbians to engage in close relationships with members of the male dominant outgroup. Blumstein and Schwartz found that lesbian feminists reported feeling that bisexuals were "consorting with the enemy" (1974, p. 291). Moreover, by engaging in heterosexual relationships with men, bisexual women behave heterosexually and therefore resemble members of the dominant heterosexual outgroup. Notwithstanding the fact that lesbians also engage in heterosexual relationships (Chapman and Brannock, 1987; Rust, 1992), bisexual status symbolizes a different relationship to dominant outgroups than does lesbian status, a difference that causes tension between lesbian and bisexual women and marginalizes bisexual women in the sexual minority community.

Lesbians also possess a well-developed social structure and subculture (Faderman, 1991) that places them in a dominant position vis-à-vis bisexual women. Local and national organizations provide lesbians with information, social support, legal aid, and political leverage. Social events facilitate contact between potential friends and romantic partners. Until the late 1980s, bisexual women lacked a community of their own, and to the extent that they desired social support for and the expression of their interests in other women, were largely dependent upon the institutions and networks established by lesbians. Since the late 1980s, bisexual groups have multiplied rapidly, but the structural and cultural resources of the bisexual women's community still do not approach those of the lesbian community. One might argue that bisexual women have access to resources offered by heterosexual society and are therefore in less need of alternative resources. Notwithstanding this argument, and in fact precisely because bisexuals' needs have been perceived as less urgent, within the sexual minority community lesbians control the greater share of resources, and bisexual women are subordinated by their dependence on structures designed to meet the needs of lesbians.

Bisexual women have only recently begun to protest their marginalization in the lesbian community (Hutchins and Kaahumanu, 1991b). I expected, therefore, that the bisexual movement does not yet constitute a threat to the lesbian community and that lesbians have not yet have adopted a defensive posture toward bisexuals. If this were the case, then the pattern of lesbians' attitudes toward bisexual women should reflect the juvenile stage of the political relationship between lesbian and bisexual women. More specifically, according to the model of intergroup relations developed by Jackman and Senter (1983), I expected that beliefs that bisexual women differ from lesbians in moderate but socially meaningful ways would be widespread among lesbians and that there would be little evidence of extreme reactionary attitudes or disagreements over bisexuals' traits.

LESBIANS' BELIEFS ABOUT BISEXUAL WOMEN

Previous researchers (e.g., Blumstein and Schwartz, 1974; Bode, 1976; MacDonald, 1981; Ponse, 1978, 1980) and self-identified bisexual authors (e.g., Geller, 1990; Hutchins and Ka'ahumanu, 1991a; Weise, 1992) have provided information about the content of lesbians' beliefs about bisexual women that I used to develop the questions I asked respondents in my study. For example, Blumstein and Schwartz (1974), MacDonald (1981), and Ponse (1980) reported the beliefs that bisexuals are in transition between heterosexuality and lesbianism and that bisexuals are really lesbians who are claiming to be bisexual to avoid homosexual stigma. Both beliefs cast doubt on the authenticity of bisexuality, but they have different moral implications. Bisexual identification is widely recognized among lesbians as an acceptable stage in the process of coming out as a lesbian (Ponse, 1980). A woman who has recently begun to come out is allowed to call herself bisexual because she is assumed to be in transition to a lesbian identity. If she fails to adopt a lesbian identity within a reasonable period of time, she will begin to attract criticism (Ponse, 1980) from lesbians who suspect that she is "selling out," that is, denying her true self and her political obligation to the lesbian community to avoid stigma and preserve her privileged position within a heterosexist society.

Blumstein and Schwartz (1974) and Ponse (1978) also reported that lesbians doubt bisexual women's political and personal loyalties. Lesbians worried that bisexual women will abandon their lesbian lovers for heterosexual lovers, abandon lesbian lifestyles for heterosexual lifestyles, conceal their true sexuality by passing as heterosexual, and harbor political allegiances to the heterosexual majority. Similarly, lesbians have sometimes accused bisexual women of purposefully avoiding a commitment to one side or the other, either by being "fencesitters" or by trying to get "the best of both worlds" without having to pay the price of either (Ponse, 1978). Many of these attitudes are described by Sumpter (1991) in a list entitled "Myths/realities of bisexuality," and several other bisexual authors have reported encountering these attitudes during their interactions with lesbian women, especially lesbian feminists (e.g., Queen, 1991; Young, 1992).

Despite this evidence of the existence of these attitudes among lesbians, many questions remain unanswered. Are these attitudes widespread, or are they held by a few vocal and articulate lesbians who provide quotable material for researchers and ammunition for bisexual political activists? Do lesbians of different ages, races, social classes, and sexual backgrounds have different beliefs about bisexual women, or do beliefs about bisexual women crosscut demographic and sexual differences among lesbians? Before principles of intergroup relations can be used to interpret lesbians' attitudes toward bisexual women, the popularity and distribution of these attitudes among lesbians must be more fully described.

Method

SUBJECTS

A total of 427 usable questionnaires were collected from respondents who self-selected on the basis of sexual identity. Eighty-one percent, or 346, of the respondents identified themselves as lesbians, dykes, or gay or homosexual women. Fourteen percent, or 60, of the respondents identified themselves as bisexual or as heterosexual with bisexual tendencies. Five percent, or 21, reported that they did not know what their orientation was or declined to label themselves. Calculation of an accurate response rate is impossible because some questionnaires probably never reached eligible respondents and some probably passed through the hands of eligible nonrespondents before reaching a respondent. However, based on the number of questionnaires that left the investigator's hands, 427 represents an estimated response rate of 45 percent.

This article is based on the responses of only the 346 women who identified themselves as lesbians, dykes, gays, or homosexuals. In the interest of brevity, these women will be referred to henceforth as "lesbians" or the "lesbian sample."

MEASURES

Questionnaire.   All data reported in this article were collected via self-administered questionnaire. The questionnaire was developed following a pilot study and one pre-test involving unstructured and structured face-to-face interviews with a total of 35 self-identified lesbian and bisexual women. The questionnaire was pretested a second time on a new sample of 10 women. Six trained lesbian and bisexual female interviewers and the investigator conducted the interviews during the first pre-test, and comments from these interviewers and from the women who participated in the second pre-test were solicited and incorporated into the final draft of the questionnaire.

Demographics and sexual experiences.   Demographic information was collected at the beginning and the end of the questionnaire. At the beginning of the questionnaire, respondents were asked for their date of birth; the name of the city, town, or suburb and state in which they lived; and their race or ethnicity. Respondents were also asked to which of five social class categories they belonged: poor, working, middle, upper middle, and upper. At the end of the questionnaire, they were asked about their romantic status, number of children, number of years of formal education completed, employment status, and annual household income. The question about romantic status included several response options that ranged from "not involved with anyone by choice" through dating and casual relationships to serious relationships and "marriage" and included both homosexual and heterosexual relationships. Respondents were instructed to "check all that apply."

Following the demographic and ice-breaking questions at the beginning of the questionnaire, respondents' feelings of sexual attraction were measured by asking respondents to place themselves on a single 11-point scale ranging from "100 percent sexually attracted to women / 0 percent attracted to men" through "0 percent attracted to women / 100 percent attracted to men." The use of a single bipolar scale was not meant to imply that homosexual and heterosexual feelings are opposite or contrary experiences, nor that gender is the sole criterion of sexual attraction, nor that respondents do not differ on other dimensions of sexual feeling, such as libido strength. Ideally, gender-directed sexual feelings should be measured with separate scales representing homosexual and heterosexual feelings, but given constraints on questionnaire length, the single scale was judged sufficient for the purposes of the current research.

Immediately after describing their feelings of sexual attraction, respondents answered the question about sexual self-identity that was used to select the lesbian sample, "when you think about your sexual orientation, what word do you use most often to describe yourself?" Respondents chose from among the following responses: lesbian; gay; dyke; homosexual; bisexual; mainly straight or heterosexual but with some bisexual tendencies; I am not sure what my orientation is (I do not know, I haven't decided, or I am still wondering); and I prefer not to label myself. Respondents who answered that they preferred not to label themselves were directed to the follow-up question, "if you had to choose one term to describe your orientation, which would come closest to the way you feel?" and offered the following responses: lesbian/gay/homosexual, bisexual, I really can't choose. Each response to the initial and the follow-up questions was followed by instructions to skip certain subsequent questions. A small number of respondents failed to check a response to the questions about sexual self-identity; the sexual identities of these respondents were inferred from the instructions they chose to follow.

Respondents then encountered a series of questions about their sexual identity histories and their previous heterosexual experiences. Among the former were questions about the age at which a respondent first identified herself as a lesbian, whether she had ever identified herself as a bisexual and if so, at what ages she first and last identified herself as a bisexual, and the number of times she had either given up a lesbian identity for a bisexual identity or vice versa. Among the latter were questions about whether she had ever dated a man or had a romantic relationship with a man. Respondents who had been heterosexually involved were asked how long ago the last time they were romantically involved with a man was and whether they had ever been married or involved in a serious, committed, nonmarital relationship with a man. If so, they were asked how long ago this marriage or serious relationship was.

Beliefs about trait differences between lesbians and bisexual women.   The Appendix presents the measures that were used to assess respondents' beliefs about trait differences between lesbian and bisexual women. Some measures consisted of a single question in which respondents were asked for a direct comparison between lesbians and bisexual women. Other measures consisted of pairs of questions. In each such pair, one question asked for a response to a statement about bisexuals, whereas the other question asked for a response to a similar statement about lesbians.

Some of these question pairs were worded symmetrically and presented together in the questionnaire so that their paired nature was obvious to the respondent. Other pairs were distinguished by asymetrical wording and separate placement in the questionnaire. The latter technique was used when presenting respondents with quoted statements; the elimination of the need for symmetrical wording allowed each statement in a pair to be worded to sound like the comments some lesbian and bisexual women made in the pilot and pre-test phases of this research. Each of the paired statements was worded as naturally as possible while retaining as fully as possible the objective equivalence in meaning of the paired statements. Thus, the use of asymetrical wording in these particular questions served not only to make the questions realistic and relevant but also to disguise the comparative purpose of the questions.

The variety in the formats of these measures had both advantages and disadvantages. The foremost disadvantage was that findings regarding the prevalence and strength of different beliefs had to be compared to each other carefully, with appropriate allowances made for the effects of differences in measurement format. The advantage was that each measure could be designed for the sole purpose of accurately assessing a particular belief.

Respondents' acceptance of beliefs that cast doubt on the authenticity of bisexual identity were assessed with two pairs of asymetrical questions. In the first pair, the statement "women who say they are bisexual will eventually realize that they are lesbians" reflects a belief often expressed by lesbians about bisexuals, whereas the statement "some women who claim to be lesbians will eventually find out that they actually are bisexual or straight" expresses the same idea about lesbians. The first statement asserts that bisexual women are in transition to lesbianism, and the second statement asserts that lesbians are in transition to bisexuality or heterosexuality. The degree to which a respondent gives higher estimates of the likelihood of the first phenomenon than the second is a measure of the degree to which she believes bisexual identity is more likely to be transitional.

In the second pair, the statement "society makes it difficult to be a lesbian, so some women claim to be bisexual when they are really lesbians who are afraid to admit it" reflects a belief often expressed by lesbians about bisexual women, whereas the statement "some lesbians really are somewhat attracted to men, but they are afraid to express these feelings because other lesbians would not approve of them" expresses a similar idea about lesbians. The first statement asserts that women who are really lesbian will call themselves bisexual because of social pressure, whereas the second statement asserts that women who are really bisexual will call themselves lesbian because of social pressure. The degree to which a respondent agrees with the first statement more than she agrees with the second is a measure of the degree to which she is more likely to believe that bisexual-identified women are denying their true sexuality.

Lesbians' beliefs about bisexuals' tendency to pass as heterosexual were assessed with two pairs of symmetrically worded questions. These questions were designed to distinguish clearly the ability to pass from the desire to pass, a distinction that had not been made in previous research, because of the different moral implications of these two qualities. One's ability to pass is largely a function of the characteristic one is attempting to conceal and of the circumstances in which one is attempting to conceal it. For example, being Black is difficult to conceal in the United States because of the visibility of skin color and North Americans' heightened awareness of race. Sexual orientation per se is an invisible characteristic, but pre-test respondents explained that bisexuality is easier to conceal than lesbianism because bisexual women appear to be heterosexual when they are with male lovers or when they talk about male lovers. The desire to pass, on the other hand, is a function of the individual; despite the fact that this desire arises within a set of social circumstances, the desire itself is internal to the individual. An individual might not be responsible for the circumstances that make it possible for her to pass as heterosexual, but she can be held responsible for her desire to pass. The operational distinction between these two qualities made it possible to determine whether the belief that bisexuals are more likely than lesbians to pass is merely a belief that bisexual women's circumstances make passing more likely for bisexuals, rather than a belief that bisexuals lack loyalty to lesbianism and lesbian politics.

Finally, lesbian respondents were asked to make direct comparisons between bisexuals' and lesbians' loyalties. Lesbians who participated in the pilot and pre-test stages of this research often unhesitatingly made strongly worded statements criticizing bisexual women for a lack of loyalty, and the two questions about bisexual women's loyalties were developed by paraphrasing these statements. The first question put the issue of loyalty in a personal light, referring to lesbians' ability to trust their bisexual friends to remain personally committed to them as friends. The second question put the issue in a more political light; the phrases "when the going gets rough" and "stick around and fight it out" imply a group struggle against an enemy.

PROCEDURES

It is impossible to obtain a representative sample of an invisible and secretive population (Gonsiorek, 1982; Morin, 1977; Weinberg, 1970), but sample bias can be reduced by sampling methods designed to ensure the inclusion of individuals most likely to be underrepresented. The ethnographic and personal interview methods of research usually used to study the lesbian population typically produce samples that underrepresent secretive and less sociopolitically active lesbians. To overcome the bias against secretive lesbians, I collected data via anonymous self-administered questionnaires that bore the ambiguous title, "A Study of Women's Attitudes Toward Sexual Orientations." To overcome the bias against less sociopolitically active lesbians, the questionnaire was designed to be completely self-contained so that copies could be passed from hand to hand within the lesbian and bisexual population, reaching sociopolitically peripheral women whom I would not have been able to reach via more direct or formal methods. Each questionnaire contained a self-addressed business reply mail (postage paid) return envelope, and the cover of the questionnaire contained a letter addressed to potential respondents that explained the purpose of the study and the eligibility requirements for participation.

In the letter, I described the survey as a study of "women who consider themselves to be lesbian or bisexual, or who choose not to label their sexual orientation, or who are not sure what their sexual orientation is." I asked eligible individuals to participate in the study and ineligible individuals to give the questionnaire to an eligible friend. Because individuals reading the letter judged for themselves whether they were eligible to participate, the sample obtained is self-selected on the basis of sexual self-identity.

To maximize sample diversity, I distributed the questionnaire by several methods. I set up displays on literature tables at conferences on women's, lesbian, and gay topics and handed out questionnaires to conference attendees; I attended meetings of some gay, bisexual, and lesbian social and political organizations to distribute questionnaires to members, and I recruited members of other organizations to distribute questionnaires within their organizations on my behalf, I placed announcements of the study in gay and lesbian newsletters and sent questionnaires to individuals who responded; and I distributed questionnaires through lesbian and bisexual friendship networks. I encouraged each person with whom I had personal contact at conferences, meetings, etc., to take multiple copies of the questionnaire to distribute among their own friends and the members of organizations to which they belonged in an effort to broaden further the spectrum of potential respondents. The interviewers who had assisted in the first pre-test, who represented different political, social, and sexual segments of lesbian and bisexual society, also helped to distribute the questionnaire within the organizations and friendship networks to which they belonged.

This multi-pronged sampling method produced a snowball sample containing women from many segments of the lesbian and bisexual population. Details about the response rates and types of respondents obtained via the various methods used to distribute the questionnaire are presented in a manuscript that is in preparation. Aggregate demographic data about the lesbian sample are provided in this article.

Results

DEMOGRAPHICS

The sample resembled earlier samples of the lesbian population in overrepresenting white and well-educated women, but the distributions of income, employment status, and age were less skewed. Three percent of the sample were Black and 4 percent were Arab, Indian, Native American, Greek, or Latina/Hispanic. The remaining 93 percent were white. More than 16 years of formal schooling had been completed by 46 percent of lesbian respondents, but the median household income was only $20,000. Eighty-nine percent were employed, one quarter of whom were also students. An additional 6 percent were non-employed students, and 3 percent were unemployed or retired. One out of two lesbians described herself as middle class; the remainder were almost equally divided between the working class and the upper middle class. The women ranged in age from 18 to 67; 46 percent were in their 20s, 38 percent were in their 30s, and 11 percent were in their 40s. Ninety-three percent lived in Midwestern states.

Respondents reported a variety of romantic and sexual experiences. Only 22 percent were romantically unattached at the time of the study; 55 percent were involved in serious relationships with other women, 8 percent were involved in casual relationships with women, and 15 percent were dating women. Most (91 percent) had had heterosexual relationships in the past, but only 15 percent had been married to men, and 29 percent had had serious, non-marital relationships with men. Fourteen percent had children. Thirty-six percent reported that their feelings of sexual attraction were exclusively homosexual, 40 percent reported that 10 percent of their feelings of sexual attraction were heterosexual, and the remainder reported that up to half of their feelings were heterosexual.

Forty percent of lesbian respondents had identified themselves as bisexual in the past. Of those who had ever identified themselves as bisexual, 54 percent (or 20 percent of all lesbian respondents) came out as bisexual before or in the same year that they came out as lesbian and, after coming out as lesbian, never again considered themselves bisexual. In retrospect, bisexual identity might have served a transitional role in these women's lives. The other 46 percent (or 17 percent of all lesbian respondents) had identified themselves as bisexual after they came out as lesbian; for them, bisexual identity was temporary but not transitional. One third (36 percent) of the women who had ever identified as bisexual had switched between lesbian and bisexual identities multiple times; in retrospect, these women had experienced both lesbian and bisexual identities as temporary. Further details about the sexual and romantic experiences and identity histories of the lesbians in this sample are presented in Rust (1993).

BELIEFS ABOUT TRAIT DIFFERENCES BETWEEN LESBIAN AND BISEXUAL WOMEN

The degree to which lesbians held different beliefs about bisexual women and lesbians was calculated by taking the arithmetic difference between respondents' responses to the two questions in each question pair. On the resulting 13-point scales, positive scores indicated differentiation in the expected direction, that is, acceptance of a belief about bisexuals that had been reported by previous researchers. The significance of the difference between lesbians' responses to the two questions in each pair was tested by a one-tailed matched pairs *t*-test.

One of the sharpest and most prevalent beliefs among lesbians was that pertaining to transitional identity (see Figure 24.1). Although a large majority of lesbian respondents believed that it is possible for both lesbians and bisexual women to realize eventually that they have mislabeled their own sexuality, they believed that this is far more likely to occur among bisexual women than among lesbians. Most lesbians (67 percent) expected at least half of bisexual women to realize that they are lesbian, whereas an even greater percentage (91 percent) believed that only a few lesbians, at most, will eventually come out as bisexual or straight. A one-tailed matched pairs *t*-test indicated that the lesbians' responses to the two questions differed, $t(334) = 26.00$, $p > .0001$. Difference scores indicated that 79 percent of lesbians believed that bisexual identity is more likely than lesbian identity to be transitional and that the degree of this perceived difference was moderate, with a mean difference score of 2.10 (see Table 24.1).

Lesbians were also more likely to suspect that bisexuals deny their true sexuality than they were to believe that lesbians do the same (see Figure 24.2). Denial was perceived to be possible among both lesbians and bisexual women; most lesbians (83 percent) agreed that "some women claim to be bisexual when they are really lesbians who are afraid to admit it," and a smaller majority (69 percent) agreed that "some lesbians really are somewhat attracted to men, but they are afraid to express these feelings." Difference scores indicated that half (50 percent) of lesbians were more suspicious of bisexual identity than they were of lesbian identity, whereas only 22 percent were equally suspicious and 28 percent were more suspicious of lesbian identity than bisexual identity (refer to Table 24.1). Lesbians' responses to the two questions differed, $t(339) = 6.08$, $p < .0001$. On average, lesbians were only slightly more suspicious of bisexual women than of lesbian women; the mean difference score was 0.77.

When asked how easy it is for bisexuals and lesbians to pretend they are straight (see Figure 25.3), lesbians leaned toward believing that passing is somewhat to very easy for bisexuals but somewhat difficult for lesbians; 71 percent answered that passing is easy for bisexual women, but only 31 percent believed that it is easy for lesbians. Taking the difference between these two measures showed that a large majority of lesbians (82 percent) believed that bisexuals find it easier to pass as straight than do lesbians, and 17 percent felt lesbians and bisexuals find it equally easy or difficult (refer to Table 24.1). The difference was significant, $t(335) = 23.79$,

Figure 24.1: Lesbians' Beliefs About the Likelihood that Bisexual and Lesbian Identities are Transitional

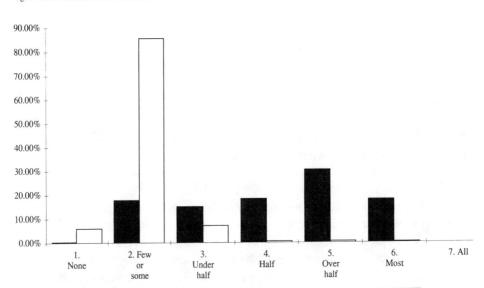

Bisexuals will realize that they are lesbians, mean = 4.15, sd = 1.38 □ Lesbians will realize that they are bisexual, mean = 2.05, sd = .50

TABLE 24.1 *The Degree to Which Lesbians' Beliefs About Bisexual Women Differ from Their Beliefs About Lesbians*

Transitional

Lesbian identity is more likely to be transitional <-------------------> Bisexual identity is more likely to be transitional

	−6	−5	−4	−3	−2	−1	0	1	2	3	4	5	6
Difference score													
%	0	0	0	0	0.3	0.9	19.4	14.6	18.8	27.2	16.7	2.1	0
(n)	(0)	(0)	(0)	(0)	(1)	(3)	(65)	(49)	(63)	(91)	(56)	(7)	(0)

Denial

Stronger suspicion that lesbians are denying heterosexual feeling <-------------------> Stronger suspicion that bisexuals are denying their lesbianism

	−6	−5	−4	−3	−2	−1	0	1	2	3	4	5	6
Difference score													
%	0.3	0.6	2.4	2.6	8.5	13.2	22.1	19.1	10.3	5.6	6.8	5.9	2.6
(n)	(1)	(2)	(8)	(9)	(29)	(45)	(75)	(65)	(35)	(19)	(23)	(20)	(9)

Passing ability

Passing is easier for lesbians <-------------------> Passing is easier for bisexuals

	−6	−5	−4	−3	−2	−1	0	1	2	3	4	5	6
Difference score													
%	0	0	0	0	0	0.9	16.7	25.9	26.5	14.6	8.6	6.0	0.9
(n)	(0)	(0)	(0)	(0)	(0)	(3)	(56)	(87)	(89)	(49)	(29)	(20)	(3)

Passing desire

Lesbians are more likely to want to pass <-------------------> Bisexuals are more likely to want to pass

	−6	−5	−4	−3	−2	−1	0	1	2	3	4	5	6
Difference score													
%	0	0	0	0	0.6	4.8	29.5	25.9	19.3	10.4	7.7	1.5	0.3
(n)	(0)	(0)	(0)	(0)	(2)	(16)	(99)	(87)	(65)	(35)	(26)	(5)	(1)

Personal commitment

'Bisexuals are not as committed to other women as lesbians are . . .'

Disagree <-------------------> Agree

	1	2	3	4	5	6	7
Original score							
%	11.2	11.8	4.4	12.4	21.2	24.7	14.4
(n)	(38)	(40)	(15)	(42)	(72)	(84)	(49)

Political trustworthiness

'It can be dangerous for lesbians to trust bisexuals too much, because . . .'

Disagree <-------------------> Agree

	1	2	3	4	5	6	7
Original score							
%	11.8	12.1	8.0	15.6	23.9	21.2	7.4
(n)	(40)	(41)	(27)	(53)	(81)	(72)	(25)

Figure 24.2: Lesbians' Beliefs About Bisexual and Lesbian Identities as Denial of True Sexuality

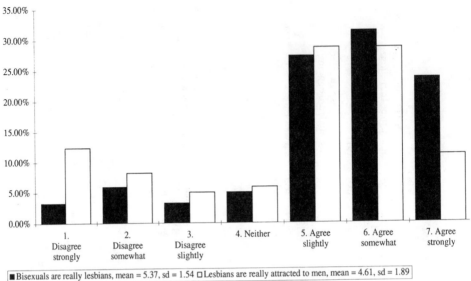

Bisexuals are really lesbians, mean = 5.37, sd = 1.54 □ Lesbians are really attracted to men, mean = 4.61, sd = 1.89

Figure 24.3: Lesbians' Beliefs About Bisexual Women's and Lesbians' Abilities to Pass as Heterosexual

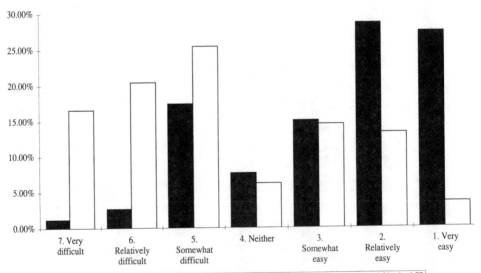

Bisexuals' ability to pass as heterosexual, mean = 2.72, sd = 1.59 ■Lesbians' ability to pass as heterosexual, mean = 4.64, sd = 1.77

$p > .0001$, but the degree to which lesbians believed passing is easier for bisexuals than lesbians was moderate; the mean difference score was 1.91.

When asked what proportion of bisexuals and lesbians want to pretend that they are straight, lesbians tended to say that more than half of bisexuals want to pass but that fewer than half of lesbians want to pass (see Figure 24.4). Difference scores show that 65 percent of lesbians believed that bisexuals are more likely than lesbians to want to pass and that 30 percent believed that bisexuals and lesbians are

Figure 24.4: Lesbians' Beliefs about Bisexual Women's and Lesbians' Desires to Pass as Heterosexual

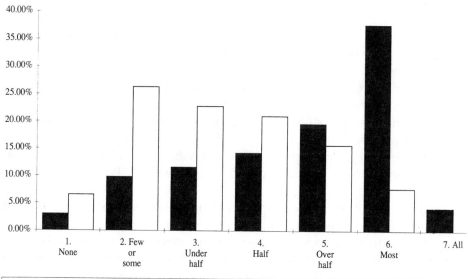

equally likely to want to pass (refer to Table 24.1). Again, this difference was significant, $t(335) = 16.56$, $p < .0001$, but the average lesbian did not believe that this difference is extreme; the mean difference score was 1.30.

A majority of lesbians (60 percent) agreed that bisexuals are "not as committed to other women as lesbians are," and a smaller majority (53 percent) agreed that "when the going gets rough, [bisexuals] are not as likely to stick around," although few expressed very strong agreement with either statement (refer to Table 24.1). Agreement with the first statement was slightly stronger and more widespread than agreement with the latter statement, suggesting that lesbians doubted bisexuals' personal commitment more than they doubted their political trustworthiness. More than one quarter (27 percent, 32 percent respectively) disagreed with each statement, indicating that they did not believe that bisexuals are less personally or politically loyal than lesbians. The mean scores are 4.52 and 4.21, respectively.

CORRELATES OF LESBIANS' BELIEFS ABOUT BISEXUAL WOMEN

Pearson correlation coefficients were used to test for differences in the beliefs of respondents with varying incomes and ages. ANOVAs were used to test for differences in the beliefs of white respondents and respondents of Color and for differences in the beliefs of respondents with different educational levels, social classes, romantic statuses, previous heterosexual experiences, sexual feelings, and identity histories. Associations with significance levels exceeding $p = .05$ were judged nonsignificant. Because of the large number of bivariate analyses performed, there was a high probability of Type I errors. Therefore, significant bivariate associations that did not appear to be part of a larger pattern of findings are reported but were not considered substantively meaningful. Finally, standard multiple regression analysis was used to detect overlap in the variances explained by significant independent variables.

Demographics.   The degree to which lesbians held beliefs about bisexual women that differed from their beliefs about lesbians was not significantly associated with their age, race, educational status, or income (data not shown). Two significant differences did exist between lesbians of different social classes. The average working class lesbian believed more strongly than the average middle or upper middle class lesbian that bisexuals have a greater desire than lesbians to pass as heterosexual, $F(2,332) = 6.92$, $p = .001$, but she was also relatively less suspicious that bisexual identity reflects a denial of lesbianism, $F(2,336) = 3.37$, $p = .04$. These differences fit no discernible pattern and are probably Type I errors.

Romantic and sexual experiences.   Lesbians' beliefs were not associated with their own romantic experiences, but lesbians with different sexual feelings and different sexual identity histories did express different beliefs about bisexual women. Data not reported indicated that the beliefs of lesbians who had been involved in serious heterosexual relationships did not differ from those of lesbians who had had only casual heterosexual relationships nor from those of lesbians who had never had heterosexual relationships. Similarly, there were no systematic differences between the beliefs of lesbians who were currently romantically uninvolved with other women and lesbians who were involved in lesbian relationships of varying seriousness.

Lesbians whose sexual feelings were exclusively homosexual held beliefs that differentiated between bisexual women and lesbians more sharply than those of women who report that they experienced heterosexual feelings (see Table 24.2). Associations significant at the $p = .01$ level were found between the exclusivity of lesbians' homosexual feelings and their beliefs that bisexuals deny their true sexuality, wish to pass, and lack political trustworthiness. Associations significant at the $p = .05$ level were found with the beliefs that bisexuals are able to pass and lack personal commitment. Moreover, among lesbians who reported having heterosexual feelings, the strength of these heterosexual feelings was negatively associated with the degree to which lesbians believed bisexual women are more likely to deny their sexuality and to lack political trustworthiness. But even lesbians who experienced substantial heterosexual feelings differentiated between bisexual and lesbian women in favor of lesbians to some extent. They agreed with other lesbians that bisexual women are more likely to be in transition and more able and willing to pass as heterosexual, although they rejected the beliefs that bisexual identity is a denial of lesbianism and that bisexuals lack personal and political loyalty.

Some of lesbians' beliefs depended on the role played by bisexual identity in their own lives (refer to Table 24. 2). Lesbians who had identified themselves as bisexual in the past were less likely to believe that bisexuals deny their true sexuality than lesbians who had never had a bisexual identity were. Among those who had identified themselves as bisexual, however, those whose own bisexual identities preceded their coming out as lesbians were more suspicious of others' bisexual

TABLE 24.2 *Differences in Beliefs About Bisexual Women Between Lesbians with Different Sexual Feelings and Identity Histories*

	(N)	Mean Difference Scores				Mean Original scores	
		Transitional	Denial	Passing ability	Passing desire	Personal commitment	Political trustworthiness
Feelings of Sexual Attraction							
Exclusively Homosexual	(118)	2.2	1.4	2.2	1.6	4.8	4.6
Ninety % Homosexual	(129)	2.2	0.6	1.8	1.2	4.4	4.1
Eighty % Homosexual	(55)	2.1	0.5	1.9	1.1	4.3	4.1
Seventy % Homosexual	(15)	1.7	−0.4	1.7	0.9	3.9	3.6
≤Sixty % Homosexual	(8)	1.6	−1.3	1.6	1.0	3.7	2.7
Significance:							
All categories							
F (df) =		0.73 (4,323)	5.36 (4,328)	1.36 (4,324)	1.79 (4,324)	1.69 (4,328)	3.89 (4,327)
p =		n.s.	.0003	n.s.	n.s.	n.s.	.004
Exclusively vs.≤90%							
F (df) =		0.31 (1,326)	12.44 (1,331)	5.07 (1,327)	6.70 (1,327)	4.76 (1,331)	9.54 (1,330)
p =		n.s.	.0005	.025	.01	.03	.002
Identity History							
Never identified as bisexual	(196)	2.0	1.1	1.9	1.4	4.7	4.4
Identified as bisexual before coming out	(65)	2.4	0.5	2.0	1.3	4.5	4.4
Identified as bisexual since coming out	(53)	2.0	−0.1	1.8	1.0	4.2	3.6
Significance:							
All categories							
F (df) =		1.35 (2,312)	6.63 (2,317)	0.53 (2,313)	1.90 (2,315)	1.22 (2,317)	4.55 (2,316)
p =		n.s.	.002	n.s	n.s.	n.s.	.01
Never identified vs. Identified							
F (df) =		0.86 (1,328)	11.48 (1,333)	0.44 (1,329)	5.40 (1,330)	3.71 (1,333)	5.12 (1,332)
p =		n.s.	.0008	n.s.	.02	n.s.	.02

NOTES: Difference scores are based on a 13-point scale on which a score of 0 indicates a lack of differentiation between beliefs toward bisexual women and lesbians and positive scores indicate beliefs that differentiate between bisexual women and lesbians in the expected direction. Original scores are based on 1–7 scales on which a score of 4 indicates a lack of differentiation and higher scores indicate beliefs that differentiate in the expected direction.

Cases with missing data were excluded only from analyses containing the variables for which data was missing. Therefore, actual Ns vary somewhat. The minimum number of cases used in the calculation of all six means for each indicated category are given in the table; actual Ns for each mean were never more than four cases larger than the stated Ns.

identities than were those who had entertained the idea of bisexuality since coming out as lesbians. In fact, the average member of this latter group believed that lesbians are just as likely to deny their bisexuality as bisexuals are to deny their lesbianism. Similar patterns were found with respect to lesbians' beliefs about bisexuals' desire to pass and lack of political trustworthiness.

To test the mutual independence of the findings that lesbians' sexual feelings and identity histories were associated with their beliefs about bisexual women, standard multiple regression analyses were performed. Each attitudinal measure was regressed simultaneously over three dichotomous variables: whether a lesbian respondent's sexual feelings were exclusively homosexual; whether she had ever identified herself as bisexual; and whether bisexual identity had played a transitional role in her life, that is, whether she had identified herself as bisexual prior to coming out as a lesbian and never again identified herself as bisexual after coming out as a lesbian. The results of these analyses are presented in Table 24.3 and show that exclusivity of homosexual feelings and a history of bisexual identification were independently significant predictors of the belief that bisexuals deny their sexuality. All three variables were significant predictors of the belief that bisexuals lack political trustworthiness, and exclusivity of homosexual feelings was the only significant predictor of the belief that it is easier for bisexuals to pass. None of the variables was a predictore of the beliefs that bisexuality is more likely to be transitional, that bisexuals have a greater desire than lesbians to pass, or that bisexuals are less personally committed.

Discussion

MEASUREMENT ISSUES

Because a variety of measurement formats were used to assess lesbians' beliefs, the current research provides some exploratory findings regarding the methodology of lesbian attitude measurement. Because the differences between measurement formats are confounded by differences in the beliefs being measured, these findings are preliminary at best, but it is hoped that they will provide suggestions for future researchers.

In general, when respondents were asked to make indirect comparisons between lesbian and bisexual women by responding to symmetrical or asymmetrical question pairs, they differentiated between lesbians and bisexual women more sharply than they did when they were asked to make direct comparisons. Given that the beliefs measured by means of direct comparison questions were those that were expressed most frequently and most enthusiastically by pilot and pre-test respondents, this finding suggests that the measurement of lesbians' beliefs about bisexual women is subject to reactivity because of a desire on the part of lesbians to appear unprejudiced. But symmetrical question pairs whose comparative purposes should also have been obvious to respondents detected as much differentiation as asymmetrical question pairs whose comparative purposes were disguised. This might be because of the content of the beliefs being measured, or it might indi-

TABLE 24.3 *Regression Coefficients for Lesbians' Beliefs About Bisexual Women*

	Transitional		Denial		Passing ability		Passing desire		Personal commitment		Political trustworthiness	
	b	(se)	b	(se)	b	(se)	b	(se)	b	(se)	b	(se)
Presence of heterosexual feelings 0 = No, 1 = Yes	-0.207	(.18)	-0.637*	(.28)	-0.366*	(.18)	-0.315	(.18)	-0.356	(.24)	-0.492*	(.22)
Ever identified as bisexual 0 = No, 1 = Yes	0.022	(.24)	-1.031**	(.36)	-0.053	(.24)	-0.288	(.23)	-0.354	(.31)	-0.617*	(.28)
Identified as bisexual before coming out as lesbian (transitional bisexual) 0 = No, 1 = Yes	0.367	(.28)	0.656	(.42)	0.186	(.28)	0.234	(.27)	0.251	(.36)	0.747*	(.33)
Multiple R-squared	.013		0.58		0.15		.021		.016		.043	
n	309		314		310		312		314		313	

*$p<.05$
**$p<.005$

cate that although lesbians were reluctant to agree with direct comparisons that derogate bisexual women, they were willing to express differential beliefs indirectly.

Despite these differences in the apparent sensitivity of different measurement formats, all measures detected differentiation of beliefs in at least half of lesbian respondents. Hence, although some lesbians might have been reluctant to appear prejudiced against bisexual women, most displayed considerable willingness to draw trait distinctions between bisexual women and lesbians.

THE PATTERN OF LESBIANS' BELIEFS ABOUT BISEXUAL WOMEN

The overall pattern of lesbians' beliefs about bisexual women suggests that most lesbians in this sample believed that there are differences between lesbians and bisexual women, but that these are differences of degree rather than kind and that the degree of these differences is moderate. For example, most lesbians believed that both lesbians and bisexual women are capable of passing, denying their true sexuality, and lacking awareness of their own sexuality, but that bisexual women are more likely than lesbians to possess these characteristics. Lesbians' beliefs about trait differences between lesbian and bisexual women cut across age, racial, class, and educational differences. These results suggest that the beliefs that previous researchers found among lesbians are not confined to a small percentage of the lesbian community but instead represent widespread subcultural attitudes about bisexuality.

Lesbians were more likely to make morally neutral trait distinctions than they were to make invidious comparisons between themselves and bisexual women. For example, lesbians were more likely to agree that bisexual women are in transition —an acceptable phase in the process of coming out as a lesbian—than they were to agree with the more invidious belief that bisexuals are denying their true sexuality; more than twice as many lesbians rejected the latter belief than rejected the former. The same pattern was found between lesbians' beliefs about bisexuals' relative ability and desire to pass as heterosexual. Thirty-five percent disagreed with the assertion that bisexual women are more likely to want to pass than lesbians, but only 17 percent disagreed with the assertion that bisexual women are more able to pass.

THE RELATIONSHIP BETWEEN LESBIANS' OWN EXPERIENCES AND THEIR BELIEFS ABOUT BISEXUAL WOMEN

The role played by bisexual feelings and identities in individual lesbians' own lives was associated with the strength of some of their beliefs about bisexual women. Lesbians who experienced both heterosexual and homosexual feelings themselves or who had identified themselves as bisexual in the past were less suspicious of others' bisexual identities and less doubtful of bisexuals' loyalty. Conversely, lesbians whose own feelings were exclusively homosexual or whose brush with bisexual identity had been transitional had more trouble believing that others' bisexuality is authentic, perhaps because their own experiences did not contradict subcultural wisdom that teaches that bisexuality does not really exist.

Invidious beliefs tended to be associated with lesbians' own experiences of heterosexual feelings or bisexual identities, whereas morally neutral beliefs were not. For example, the belief that bisexuals are really lesbians who are denying their sexuality was associated with lesbians' experiences, but the degree to which lesbians believed that bisexuals are in transition was not. Similarly, the belief that bisexuals have a greater desire to pass was more closely associated with lesbians' experiences than the belief that bisexuals find it easier to pass. In other words, lesbians who had personal experience of bisexuality agreed with lesbians who had not that bisexuals differ from lesbians in sociopolitically important but morally neutral ways, but they were less inclined to derogate bisexual women.

If lesbians who had heterosexual feelings or a history of bisexual identification were less inclined to derogate bisexual women, then one would expect lesbians who had had actual heterosexual experiences to be similarly inclined. But unlike sexual feelings and identities, sexual experience was not associated with lesbians' beliefs about bisexual women. Lesbians who had had previous heterosexual relationships were no less suspicious of others' bisexuality than were lesbians who had never been heterosexually involved. This apparently anomalous finding is easily explained, however. Previous heterosexual experience is almost universal among lesbians. In the current study, 91 percent of lesbian respondents had had heterosexual relationships, and this figure is similar to that reported by other researchers (Chapman and Brannock, 1987; Hedblom, 1973; Saghir and Robins, 1973). The ubiquity of previous heterosexual experience among lesbians has generated numerous subcultural explanations for these experiences. For example, lesbians frequently explain that their previous heterosexual behavior was a test of their lesbianism, a response to social pressure, or a result of socialization that temporarily obscured their true sexuality. Subcultural ideology and social pressure within lesbian society encourage the use of such explanations to nullify the implications of heterosexual experiences for one's own sexuality (Blumstein and Schwartz, 1977; Ponse, 1978; Udis-Kessler, 1990, 1991), and it is therefore not surprising to find that actual heterosexual experiences fail to correlate with lesbians' beliefs about bisexuality.

LESBIANS' BELIEFS ABOUT BISEXUAL WOMEN AS A REFLECTION OF LESBIAN-BISEXUAL INTERGROUP RELATIONS

The pattern of beliefs found among lesbians in this study is similar to that found by Jackman and Senter (1983) among the members of dominant groups whose dominance has not yet been threatened by subordinate protest. Lesbians' attitudes do not display the patterns that would be expected of a dominant group that is defending itself against a serious antagonist. It appears that the bisexual movement has not yet become strong enough to cause either a backlash among lesbians or a schism among lesbians over how to respond to the demands of the bisexual movement.

These findings do not imply that bisexuality per se is not a threat to lesbians, the lesbian community, and lesbian politics. On the contrary, bisexuality is perceived as a threat because of bisexuals' close relationships with men and resemblance to heterosexuals, as argued previously. The current findings suggest that the beliefs that many lesbians hold about bisexual women are part of a lesbian subcultural ideology that, thus far, has effectively contained the threat of bisexuality.

To understand the manner in which lesbians' beliefs contain the threat of bisexuality, one must examine the specific content of these beliefs. I argue that lesbians' beliefs about bisexuals fall into two general categories that reflect two different ideological responses to the threat of bisexuality. The belief that bisexuals are in transition and the belief that bisexuals are really lesbians claiming to be bisexual are "explanatory" beliefs. These beliefs cast doubt on the existence of authentic bisexual experience and identity by providing alternative explanations for apparent bisexuality. These beliefs contain the threat of bisexuality by trivializing it as a temporary state or a façade. Even though few lesbians hold extreme forms of this belief—that is, few lesbians believe that all bisexual women are in transition or denial—the effect is to cast doubt on every bisexual woman's claim to bisexual identity.

The second category of beliefs, "depoliticizing" beliefs, includes beliefs that acknowledge bisexual experience and identity but pinpoint bisexuals as political risks. This category includes the belief that bisexuals lack loyalty to the lesbian movement and the beliefs that this lack of loyalty is reflected in a greater propensity for passing as heterosexual, abandoning female lovers for male lovers, abandoning a lesbian lifestyle for a heterosexual lifestyle, and harboring loyalty to a heterosexual society from which bisexuals derive benefits that are denied lesbians. These beliefs are based on the assumption that bisexuals' interests are reducible to a combination of lesbian interests and heterosexual interests—in fact, they are based on a concept of bisexuality as a hybrid form of sexuality that combines homosexuality and heterosexuality. It follows from this conceptualization of bisexual interests that insofar as bisexuals lack loyalty to lesbian politics, they must be allied with heterosexual politics. These beliefs dismiss bisexuals as confused individuals, traitorous lesbians, or interloping heterosexuals; they are not subordinates with unique political interests and needs of their own that might differ from both lesbians' and heterosexuals' interests. By "depoliticizing" bisexuality, lesbians' beliefs about bisexuality defuse a potential political challenge from within their own community.

Bisexuals have recently begun to assert that they do have unique interests and needs that are not met by either heterosexual society or lesbian society. The bisexual movement began and is most active in the major coastal cities that have historically been the focal points for the lesbian and gay liberation movements, that is, San Francisco and New York (Faderman, 1991) and in Boston, Chicago, and Washington, DC (Hutchins and Ka'ahumanu, 1991b). Small bisexual groups have existed since the 1970s, and several local political organizations such as the Boston Bisexual Women's Network were founded in the early 1980s. The number of bisexual groups multiplied rapidly during the very late 1980s and early 1990s, and many of these groups now publish newsletters. A national bisexual network was established at the BiPOL conference in San Francisco in June 1990, the first international bisexual conference was held in Amsterdam in October 1991, and the third international bisexual conference was held in Washington, DC in April 1993. The October 1992 edition of the *International Directory of Bisexual Groups* listed 31 bisexual social and political organizations in the Bay Area of California, 10 in New York City, six in Boston and Cambridge, and 15 in Washington, DC (Ochs, 1992). In contrast, there has been much less activity in the Midwestern states in which most lesbians who participated in this study lived; the *Directory* listed six groups in Chicago and an average of only 3.4 groups per Midwestern state. Most of these groups were support groups; few were political.

If the bisexual movement continues to grow and becomes a major political force, lesbians' attitudes toward bisexual women are likely to change. If lesbian-bisexual relations continue to follow the pattern that characterizes dominant-subordinate relations as described by Jackman and Senter, then lesbians' widespread beliefs that there are moderate differences between lesbian and bisexual women will be replaced by greater disagreement among lesbians over the characteristics of bisexual women and by stronger adherence to beliefs that are morally unfavorable to bisexual women. But lesbian and bisexual women differ from the groups studied by Jackman and Senter because they are both subordinate groups relative to the dominant heterosexual outgroup. It is therefore possible that the development of relations between lesbian and bisexual women will follow a pattern that is modified by their intraminority context. For example, lesbian and bisexual women might develop distinct communities and movements that will then ally in common struggle against a heterosexist society. Changes might already be taking place in San Francisco, New York, Boston, Chicago, and Washington, DC. Whether these changes will follow the typical dominant-subordinate pattern, or whether they develop a different pattern characteristic of intraminority relations, is a question for future research.

REFERENCES

Altman, D. (1982). *The homosexualization of America*. New York: St. Martin's Press.

Blake, T., and Dennis, W. (1943). The development of stereotypes concerning the Negro. *Journal of Abnormal and Social Psychology, 38*, 525–531.

Blumstein, P. W., and Schwartz, P. (1974). Lesbianism and bisexuality. In E. Goode (Ed.), *Sexual deviance and sexual deviants* (pp. 278–295). New York: Morrow.

Blumstein, P. W., and Schwartz, P. (1977). Bisexuality: Some social psychological issues. *Journal of Social Issues, 33*(2), 30–45.

Bode, J. (1976). *View from another closet: Exploring bisexuality in women*. New York: Hawthorn Books.

Brigham, J. C. (1971, July). Ethnic stereotypes. *Psychological Bulletin, 76*, 15–38.

Chapman, B. E., and Brannock, J. C. (1987). Proposed model of lesbian identity development: An empirical examination. *Journal of Homosexuality, 14*(3/4), 69–80.

Faderman, L. (1991). *Odd girls and twilight lovers*. New York: Columbia University Press.

Geller, T. (Ed.) (1990). *Bisexuality: A reader and sourcebook*. Navato, CA: Times Change Press.

Gilbert, G. M. (1951). Stereotype persistence and change among college students. *Journal of Abnormal and Social Psychology, 46*, 245–254.

Gonsiorek, J. C. (1982). Introduction. In W. Paul, J. D. Weinrich, J. C. Gonsiorek, and M. E. Hotvedt (Eds.), *Homosexuality: Social, psychological, and biological issues* (pp. 57–70). Beverly Hills, CA: Sage.

Hedblom, J. H. (1973). Dimensions of lesbian sexual experience. *Archives of Sexual Behavior, 2*, 329–341.

Higgins, P. C. (1979). Outsiders in a hearing world. *Urban Life: A Journal of Ethnographic Research, 8*, 3–22.

Hutchins, L., and Kaahumanu, L. (Eds.) (1991a). *Bi any other name: Bisexual people speak out.* Boston: Alyson Publications.

Hutchins, L., and Kaahumanu, L. (1991b). Political activism: A brief history. In L. Hutchins and L. Kaahumanu (Eds.), *Bi any other name: Bisexual people speak out* (pp. 359–367). Boston: Alyson Publications.

Jackman, M. R., and Senter, M. S. (1983). Different, therefore unequal: Beliefs about trait differences between groups of unequal status. *Research in Social Stratification and Mobility, 2*, 309–335.

Kammeyer, K. (1966). Birth order and the feminine sex role among college women. *American Sociological Review, 31*, 508–515.

Karlins, M. T., Coffman, T. L., and Walters, G. (1969). On the fading of social stereotypes: Studies in three generations of college students. *Journal of Personality and Social Psychology, 13*, 1–16.

Katz, D., and Braly, K. W. (1933). Racial stereotypes in 200 college students. *Journal of Abnormal and Social Psychology, 28*, 280–290.

Klein, F. (1978). *The bisexual option: A concept of one hundred percent intimacy.* New York: Arbor House.

MacDonald, A. P., Jr. (1981). Bisexuality: Some comments on research and theory. *Journal of Homosexuality, 6*(3), 21–35.

Morin, S. F. (1977). Heterosexual bias in psychological research on lesbianism and male homosexuality. *American Psychologist, 32*, 629–637.

Ochs, R. (1992). *International directory of bisexual groups.* Boston: East Coast Bisexual Network.

Ponse, B. (1978). *Identities in the lesbian world: The social construction of self.* Westport, CT: Greenwood Press.

Ponse, B. (1980). Finding self in the lesbian community. In M. Kirkpatrick (Ed.), *Women's sexual development: Explorations of inner space* (pp. 181–200). New York: Plenum.

Queen, C. A. (1991). The queer in me. In L. Hutchins and L. Kaahumanu (Eds.), *Bi any other name: Bisexual people speak out* (pp. 17–21). Boston: Alyson Publications.

Radicalesbians. (1972). The Woman-identified woman. *Ladder, 14*, 6–8.

Robb, J. H. (1978). A theoretical note on the sociology of inter-group relations. *Ethnic and Racial Studies, 1*, 465– 473.

Rust, P. C. (1993). 'Coming out' in the age of social constructionism: Sexual identity formation among lesbian and bisexual women. *Gender and Society, 7*, 50–77.

Rust, P. C. (1992). The politics of sexual identity: Sexual attraction and behavior among lesbian and bisexual women. *Social Problems, 39*, 366–386.

Rust-Rodríguez, P. C. (1989). When does the unity of a 'common oppression' break down? Reciprocal attitudes between lesbian and bisexual women. *Dissertation Abstracts International, 50*, 08A, 268. (University Microfilms No. 9001704).

Saghir, M. T., and Robins, E. (1973). *Male and female homosexuality: A comprehensive investigation.* Baltimore: Williams and Wilkins.

Scott, W. A. (1965). Psychological and social correlates of international images. In H. C. Kelman (Ed.), *International behavior: A social psychological analysis* (pp. 71–105). New York: Holt, Rinehart, and Winston.

Sherriffs, A. C., and McKee, J. P. (1957). Qualitative aspects of beliefs about men and women. *Journal of Personality*, 25, 451–464.

Simmel, G. (1955). *Conflict and the web of group-affiliations*. (K. H. Wolff and R. Bendix, Trans.) New York: Free Press. (original work published in 1923).

Sumpter, S. F. (1991). Myths/realities of bisexuality. In L. Hutchins and L. Kaahumanu (Eds.), *Bi any other name: Bisexual people speak out* (pp. 12–13). Boston: Alyson Publications.

Udis-Kessler, A. (1990). Bisexuality in an essentialist world. In T. Geller (Ed.), *Bisexuality: A reader and sourcebook* (pp. 51–63). Novato, CA: Times Change Press.

Udis-Kessler, A. (1991). Present tense: Biphobia as a crisis of meaning. In L. Hutchins and L. Kaahumanu (Eds.), *Bi any other name: Bisexual people speak out* (pp. 350–358). Boston: Alyson Publications.

Weinberg, M. S. (1970). Homosexual samples: Differences and similarities. *Journal of Sex Research*, 6, 312–325.

Weise, E. R. (Ed.) (1992). *Closer to home: Bisexuality and feminism*. Seattle: Seal Press.

Williamson, J. B. (1974). Beliefs about the motivation of the poor and attitudes toward poverty policy. *Social Problems*, 21, 634–648.

Wittstock, M. (1990). The best of both worlds and still nothing. In T. Geller (Ed.), *Bisexuality: A reader and sourcebook* (pp. 26–33). Novato, CA: Times Change Press.

Young, S. (1992). Breaking silence about the "b-word": Bisexual identity and lesbian-feminist discourse. In E. R. Weise (Ed.), *Closer to home: Bisexuality and feminism* (pp. 75–87). Seattle: Seal Press.

Appendix: Measures Used to Assess Lesbians' Beliefs About Bisexual Women and About Lesbians

A. Transitional identity

a. "Women who say they are bisexual will eventually realize that they are lesbians." What proportion of women who say they are bisexual do you think will eventually realize that they are lesbian?

b. "Some women who claim to be lesbians will eventually find out that they actually are bisexual or straight." What proportion of women who say they are lesbians do you believe will eventually realize that they are bisexual or straight?

7. All	6. Most	5. Over Half	4. Half	3. Under Half	2. Few/some	1. None

B. Denial of true sexuality

a. "Society makes it difficult to be a lesbian so some women claim to be bisexual when they are really lesbians who are afraid to admit it." How strongly do you agree or disagree with this statement?

b. "Some lesbians really are somewhat attracted to men, but they are afraid to express these feelings because other lesbians would not approve of them." How strongly do you agree or disagree with this statement?

7. Agree Strongly	6. Agree Some	5. Agree Slightly	4. Neither	3. Disagree Slightly	2. Disagree Some	1. Disagree Strongly

C. Ability to pass as heterosexual

a. In general, if a lesbian/gay woman *wanted* to pretend that she was straight in order to avoid the prejudice some people have against lesbians/gay women, do you think this would be easy or difficult for her to do?

b. In general, if a bisexual woman *wanted* to pretend that she was straight, how easy or difficult do you think pretending to be straight would be?

1. Very easy	2. Relatively easy	3. Somewhat easy	4. Neither	5. Somewhat difficult	6. Relatively difficult	7. Very difficult

D. Desire to pass as heterosexual
a. Now imagine that it is *very easy* for all lesbians/gay women to pretend that they are heterosexual. What proportion of lesbians/gay women do you believe *would want* to pretend they're heterosexual?

b. Imagine that it is *very easy* for all bisexuals to pretend that they are heterosexual. What proportion of bisexual women do you think *would want* to pretend they're heterosexual?

Same response format as Question Pair A

E. Personal commitment
"Bisexuals are not as committed to other women as lesbians are; they are more likely to desert their female friends." How strongly do you agree or disagree with this statement?

Same response format as Question Pair B

F. Political Trustworthiness
"It can be dangerous for lesbians to trust bisexuals too much, because when the going really gets rough, they are not as likely to stick around and fight it out." How strongly do you agree or disagree with this statement?

Same response format as Question Pair B

Notes

In the case of question pairs, the same response scale was used for both questions in the pair.

Respondents were instructed at the beginning of the questionnaire to read questions containing the word "lesbian" as if they contained instead whichever synonym (e.g., gay, homosexual, dyke) the respondent preferred to use herself.

The questions appeared in the questionnaire in the following order: Ca, Cb, Da, Db, Aa, Bb, E, Ba, F, Aa. The first four questions were presented in sequence. The latter six questions were presented as part of a longer series of questions about lesbians' attitudes on various issues, and were interspersed among questions about issues other than bisexuality.

Coding for questions Ca and Cb were reversed prior to statistical analysis so that respondents whose beliefs about bisexual women corresponded with those reported by previous researchers would have higher scores than respondents who rejected these beliefs or who held converse beliefs on all measures.

25

Effects of Sexual Orientation on Interpersonal Judgment

Joseph Istvan

SEXUAL attitudes have been the object of continuing interest by American social scientists over the past several decades (e.g., Bauman and Wilson, 1976; Bromley and Britten, 1938; Reiss, 1960, 1967). One trend suggested by much of this research is that, over a period of years, sexual attitudes in the United States have grown increasingly liberal or permissive (Christensen and Gregg, 1970: Finger, 1975; Hunt, 1974). One sexual attitude that seems to have experienced little overall change, however, is acceptance of homosexuals and/or homosexual activities. For example, a National Opinion Research Center (NORC) survey conducted in 1970 and utilizing a representative sample of adult Americans found that 72 percent of the respondents believed that homosexual relations were "always wrong" (Levitt and Klassen, 1974). Remarkably, follow-up surveys conducted by the NORC in 1974 and 1977 found that exactly the same percentage of respondents agreed with this item (Glenn and Weaver, 1979; Nyberg and Alston, 1976). Thus, during a period marked by the liberalization of other sexual attitudes, approval of homosexual activities remained virtually unchanged. Similar expressions of disapproval and rejection have been found in recent laboratory investigations (Elman, Killebrew, and Oros, 1978; Krulewitz and Nash, 1980; SanMiguel and Millham, 1976).

One significant issue, however, has not been addressed in studies examining reactions to homosexuality—the majority of individuals with homosexual experience also have extensive heterosexual histories. Kinsey and his associates (Kinsey, Pomeroy, and Martin, 1948; Kinsey et al., 1953), for instance, found that some 37 percent of males and 13 percent of females had engaged in some form of homosexual activity to the point of orgasm. Although it appears that the proportion of males with some homosexual experience in Kinsey et al.'s (1948) survey was probably an overestimate (Pomeroy, 1972), a more recent survey has found that 25 percent to 30 percent of adult males and 10 percent to 15 percent of adult females have had some homosexual experience, whereas only 2 percent to 3 percent of males and 1 percent to 2 percent of females are exclusively homosexual (Hunt, 1974). Extrapolation from these data suggests that some 80 percent to 90 percent of individuals with homosexual experience also have histories of heterosexual orgasm. Despite the presence of substantial proportions of individuals with bisexual histories, the majority of both survey and laboratory investigations have assessed reactions to identified homosexuals (Cuenot and Fugita, 1982; Elman, Killebrew, and Oros, 1978; Karr, 1978; Krulewitz and Nash, 1980; SanMiguel and Millham, 1976; Storms, 1978) and/or to homosexual behavior itself (e.g., Levitt and Klassen, 1974; MacDonald and Games, 1974; Millham, SanMiguel, and Kellogg, 1976).

Although there are no empirical data regarding the reactions of heterosexuals to individuals with mixed homosexual-heterosexual histories, Kinsey et al. (1953) have speculated that:

> Legal penalties, public disapproval, and ostracism are likely to be leveled against a person who has had limited homosexual experience as quickly as they are leveled against those who have had exclusive experience. (p. 469)

The knowledge of homosexual behavior in an individual's past, thus, results in a form of "spoiled identity" (Goffman, 1963). Based on this notion, it seems reasonable that there should be marked differences between the evaluations received by heterosexuals in comparison to individuals of varying degrees of bisexuality and exclusive homosexuality, whereas there should be little if any difference between responses to those persons with any proportion of homosexual experience. Kinsey et al. (1953), however, presented no data to support this hypothesis.

Another notion regarding reactions to individuals with homosexual experience has been popularized by Gagnon and Simon (1973). These authors have asserted that, since homosexuals are defined by their sexual orientation, others come to regard this defining feature as being the central focus of their lives. Thus, heterosexuals would be expected to perceive homosexuals as obsessively concerned with sexual matters, and as pervasively "sexual" beings. However, no suggestions were offered concerning reactions to persons with both homosexual and heterosexual experience, nor has the accuracy of this notion been examined with respect to perceptions of exclusive homosexuals only.

It was the purpose of the present study, thus, to examine the reactions of heterosexuals to both same- and opposite-sex stimulus persons of varying proportions of bisexuality in contrast to their responses to both exclusive homosexuals and exclusive heterosexuals. Based on previously discussed notions, several possible hypotheses seemed tenable: (a) Stimulus persons with any homosexual experience (whether bisexual or exclusively homosexual) would be evaluated more negatively than heterosexual stimulus persons; (b) homosexual and bisexual stimulus persons would be evaluated similarly; (c) homosexual (and possibly bisexual) stimulus persons would be seen as more "sexual" than heterosexual stimulus persons.

Method

Subjects

The subjects were 212 (102 males and 110 females) undergraduate students at a large northeastern state university. Since the goal of the experiment was to examine heterosexuals' evaluations of homosexuals, those individuals who indicated a substantial proportion of homosexual fantasy and/or experience were not included in subsequent statistical analyses. The criterion for exclusion was a score of 2 or above on a self-report version of the Kinsey et al. (1948) heterosexual-homosexual continuum (to be described below). On this basis, 15 subjects were eliminated from the study, leaving a total sample of 197 subjects.

Design

The design of the experiment was a 2 x 2 x 5 between-subjects factorial, with sex of subject, sex of stimulus person, and the stimulus person's sexual orientation as independent variables. Levels of the last factor included exclusive heterosexual experience, three proportions of bisexual experience, and exclusive homosexual experience.

Procedure

Subjects were recruited for an experiment entitled "Sexual Experiences and Interpersonal Perceptions." All subjects participated in small same-sex groups. Upon arrival for the experimental session, subjects initially completed a modified version of the Brady and Levitt (1965) Sexual Experience Inventory and provided self-ratings of their sexual orientation.

Following completion of these scales, subjects were told that the second part of the experiment would involve making judgments concerning some of the personal characteristics of another individual based upon examination of his (or her) responses to some of the same questionnaires the subjects themselves had just completed. Subjects were then given a Sexual Experience Inventory and sexual orientation self-rating which had ostensibly been completed by an anonymous same- or opposite-sex individual of approximately the same age as the subject. The sexual orientation of this bogus stimulus person was manipulated by varying both the endorsement of items on the Sexual Experience Inventory and the bogus subject's self-rating on the heterosexual-homosexual continuum.

After examining these responses, the subjects were asked to indicate their impressions of the stimulus person on five items from Byrne's (1971) Interpersonal Judgment Scale (IJS) and to rate the person on a Personality Impressions Scale consisting of 36 bipolar items designed to assess a variety of sex-related and evaluative responses. After the completion of these scales, all subjects were informed regarding the goals of the experiment and were asked to indicate with a written "yes" or "no" if they had any suspicions that the questionnaires they examined were bogus.

Following the assessment of subject suspicion, all subjects were pledged to secrecy and dismissed.

INDEPENDENT VARIABLE MEASURES

The modified Brady and Levitt (1965) scale asked subjects to indicate in a "yes-no" format their experience with seven heterosexual activities and four homosexual activities. Eliminated from the original scale were items that were not potentially orgasmic or were not applicable to both sexes (e.g., homosexual anal intercourse). In addition, mutual oral-genital contact with a member of the opposite sex was added as an item. The wording of heterosexual items differed somewhat for males and females. Thus, the first item was "manual manipulation of a female's nude genitals" for males, and "manual manipulation of your nude genitals by a male" for females. The heterosexual activities contained in the questionnaire were (a) manual manipulation of nude female genitals, (b) oral contact with nude male genitals, (c) manual manipulation of nude male genitals, (d) face-to-face sexual intercourse, (e) oral contact with nude female genitals, (f) rear vaginal entry heterosexual intercourse, and (g) mutual oral-genital contact with member of opposite sex. The homosexual activities were (a) manual manipulation of your nude genitals by a member of the same sex, (b) manual manipulation of the nude genitals of a member of the same sex; (c) oral contact with your nude genitals by a member of the same sex, and (d) oral contact with the nude genitals of a member of the same sex.[1]

The heterosexual-homosexual self rating requested subjects to indicate their sexual orientation by circling one of seven response alternatives: (0) All my sexual fantasies and overt sexual activities are heterosexual, (1) 90 percent of my sexual fantasies and overt sexual activities are heterosexual, and 10 percent are homosexual, (2) 75 percent of my sexual fantasies and overt sexual activities are heterosexual, and 25 percent are homosexual, (3) 50 percent of my sexual fantasies and overt sexual activities are heterosexual, and 50 percent are homosexual, (4) 75 percent of my sexual fantasies and overt sexual activities are homosexual, and 25 percent are heterosexual, (5) 90 percent of my sexual fantasies and overt sexual activities are homosexual and 10 percent are heterosexual, and (6) All my sexual fantasies and overt sexual activities are homosexual.

The sexual orientation of the bogus stimulus person was manipulated by varying both the yes-no endorsement of items on the Sexual Experience Inventory and the bogus same- or opposite-sex subject's self-rating on the heterosexual-homosexual continuum. These responses reflected a sexual history which was either exclusively heterosexual, 75 percent heterosexual/25 percent homosexual, 50 percent heterosexual/50 percent homosexual, 75 percent homosexual/25 percent heterosexual, or exclusively homosexual. The exclusive heterosexual stimulus person indicated "yes" for all heterosexual items on the Sexual Experience Inventory and "no" for all homosexual items, the 25 percent homosexual/75 percent heterosexual indicated "yes" for all heterosexual items and "yes" for the first homosexual item, the 50 percent homosexual/50 percent heterosexual indicated "yes" for all heterosexual and "yes" for the first two homosexual items, the 75 percent homosexual/25 percent heterosexual indicated "yes" for all heterosexual items and "yes" for the first three of four homosexual items, and the exclusive homosexual indicated "no" for all heterosexual items and "yes" for all four homosexual items. In addition, the exclusive heterosexual had circled the 0 point on the heterosexual-homosexual continuum, the three bisexual stimulus persons the second, third, and fourth points respectively, and the exclusive homosexual stimulus person the sixth and the last point on the scale.

DEPENDENT MEASURES

The five IJS items included among the dependent measures required subjects to indicate their evaluations of the stimulus person's intelligence, morality, adjustment, likability, and desirability as a work partner on 7-point scales. Higher scores on these scales indicate greater attributed intelligence, morality, adjustment, likability, and work partner desirability, respectively. The Personality Impressions Scale contained 36 6-point semantic-differential type items designed to tap both global impressions of sexuality and positive-negative evaluative reactions. Following a factor analysis (to be described in the Results section), further use of this scale was in terms of derived factor scores.

Results

ASSESSMENT OF SUBJECT SUSPICION

Overall, 51 percent of the subjects responded affirmatively to the suspicion item. The proportion of subjects indicating suspicion in each of the stimulus person sexual orientation conditions was: exclusive heterosexual = 38 percent, 25 percent homosexual/75 percent heterosexual = 55 percent, 50 percent homosexual/50 percent heterosexual = 37 percent, 75 percent homosexual/25 percent heterosexual = 58 percent, and exclusive homosexual 68 percent.

In order to assess the effect of suspicion on subjects' judgments, the "yes-no" rating of suspicion was included as an additional between-subjects factor in analyses of variance of all IJS items and the two primary factor scores obtained from Personality Impressions Scale ratings. In each of these analyses, there were a total of eight effects involving suspicion as a factor. For all seven variables, the only significant effects were three three-way interactions, each for a different variable and none readily interpretable. Although it should be emphasized that lower rates of subject suspicion would have been desirable, these analyses would seem to indicate that suspicion was not a potent determinant of subjects' responses.

STIMULUS PERSON EVALUATIONS

All IJS ratings were examined in a 2 (sex of subject) x 2 (sex of stimulus person) x 5 (stimulus person sexual orientation) analysis of variance. Significant main effects for stimulus person sexual orientation appeared for all five IJS items: likability,

$F(4, 177) = 18.95, p < .001$, work partner desirability, $F(4, 177) = 13.97, p < .001$, intelligence, $F(4, 177) = 2.55, p < .05$, morality, $F(4, 177) = 5.34, p < .001$, and adjustment, $F(4, 177) = 10.78, p < .001$. Means for ratings in each stimulus person sexual orientation condition and results of Newman-Keuls comparisons between conditions are presented in Table 25.1.

These comparisons generally showed that the exclusive heterosexual targets and, to some extent, the 25 percent homosexual/75 percent heterosexual targets were regarded more favorably than all other stimulus persons. Thus, the exclusive heterosexual stimulus persons were seen as more likable than all other stimulus persons, whereas the 25 percent homosexual/75 percent heterosexual stimulus persons were seen as more likable than those with a greater proportion of homosexual experience or a history of exclusive homosexuality. Those stimulus persons with a total sexual outlet 50 percent or more homosexual were not seen as differentially likable.

Comparisons of ratings of stimulus person work partner desirability revealed that the exclusive heterosexual and 25 percent homosexual/75 percent heterosexual persons were regarded as similar in desirability as a work partner, whereas stimulus persons with a greater proportion of homosexual experience were all seen as less desirable work partners and received generally similar ratings.

Evaluations of stimulus person morality and adjustment showed essentially the same pattern of results: Exclusive heterosexual targets were seen as both more moral and well-adjusted than all remaining stimulus persons, whereas those with any proportion of homosexual experience were not evaluated differently. Finally, all comparisons of ratings of stimulus person intelligence were nonsignificant.

The only remaining significant effect uncovered by analyses of the IJS was a sex of subject x sex of stimulus person interaction for ratings of the stimulus person's likability, $F(4, 177) = 12.50, p < .001$. The source of this interaction appeared to be the higher regard male subjects had for female stimulus persons ($M = 4.51$) than male stimulus persons ($M = 3.71$) whereas female subjects did not evaluate the male and female stimulus persons differently ($M = 4.40$ and $M = 4.18$, respectively).

It will be recalled that according to Kinsey et al.'s (1953) notion, the presence of any homosexual experience in any individual's background is sufficient to evoke

TABLE 25.1 *Mean Interpersonal Judgment Scale Responses as a Function of Type of Stimulus Person Sexual Orientation*

	0% Hom'l/ 100% Het'l	25% Hom'l/ 75% Het'l	50% Hom'l/ 50% Het'l	75% Hom'l 25% Het'l	100% Hom'l/ 0% Het'l
Likability	5.43_a	4.60_b	3.90_c	3.61_c	3.44_c
Work Partner Desirability	5.14_a	4.69_a	3.73_b	3.56_b	3.61_b
Intelligence	4.59_a	4.79_a	4.15_a	4.56_a	4.12_a
Morality	4.41_a	3.71_b	3.39_b	3.44_b	3.29_b
Adjustment	5.00_a	3.90_b	3.51_b	3.28_b	3.12_b

NOTE: All ratings were made on 7-point scales. Higher scores indicate greater attributed likability, work partner desirability, intelligence, morality, and adjustment. Means sharing a common subscript are not significantly different at the .05 level in a Newman-Keuls test.

TABLE 25.2 *F Values for Analyses of Trend in Main Effect for Stimulus Person Sexual Orientation—All Interpersonal Judgment Scale Items*

	F for Linear Trend	F for Quadratic Trend
Likability	70.27**	6.18**
Work Partner Desirability	48.20**	6.32*
Intelligence	3.80	.08
Morality	16.49**	4.08*
Adjustment	36.84**	5.77*

* p < .05.
** p < .001.

the negative reactions usually associated with exposure to exclusive homosexuality. The results of post hoc comparisons of IJS responses would seem to support this view, at least partially.

One further means of examining this hypothesis is by performing a trend analysis on the main effect for stimulus person sexual orientation for each of the evaluative ratings. A trend analysis, when performed on a quantitative independent variable with equal intervals between levels, will provide information about the form of the relationship between the independent and dependent variables. If evaluations of individuals differing in terms of sexual orientation were a simple linear function of proportion of homosexual/heterosexual experience, this effect should be revealed by a significant linear component in analyses of trend, and the absence of a significant quadratic trend component (i.e., a nonlinear function with one "bend"). However, if subjects tended to regard the homosexual and bisexual persons similarly, a significant quadratic component would be present following the test for linear trend. *F* values for analyses of linear and quadratic trend for each IJS item are listed in Table 25.2. Significant linear and quadratic effects were present for ratings of the stimulus person's likability, desirability as a work partner, morality, and adjustment. The only other significant trend component for all IJS items was a significant quartic effect for ratings of intelligence, $F(1, 177) = 5.71$, $p < .05$.

SEXUALITY IMPRESSIONS

All Personality Impressions Scale ratings provided by subjects were initially subjected to a principal components factor analysis followed by a varimax orthogonal rotation. Three interpretable factors appeared as a result of this analysis. The first seemed to reflect the stimulus person's perceived sexual desirability, the second general likability,[2] and the third the stimulus person's attributed sexual activity. These three factors accounted for 53 percent, 14 percent, and 8 percent of the total common item variance, respectively.

Factor scores were obtained for the sexual desirability and sexual activity factors by summing subjects' ratings for each item loading > + .50 on these factors.[3] Items contributing to the sexual desirability factor score were *attractive*-unattractive (.66),[4] *stimulating*-unstimulating (.61), *sexy*-not sexy (.78), *popular*-unpopular (.56), *sexually desirable*-sexually undesirable (.79), and *seductive*-nonseductive (.67), whereas items contributing to the sexual activity factor were retiring-*outgoing* (.62), *willing*-unwilling (.56), *active*-passive (.54), *sexually experienced*-sexually inexperienced (.69), and *sexually responsive*-sexually unresponsive (.64). Analyses of variance of subjects' scores on each of these dimensions revealed a significant stimulus person sex orientation main effect for both sex desirability, $F(4, 177) = 17.46$, $p < .001$, and sex activity, $F(4, 177) = 18.87, p < .001$. Newman-Keuls tests for each of these main effects disclosed a somewhat different pattern of results. Means for each stimulus person sex orientation condition and results of pairwise comparisons are displayed in Table 25.3.

In contrast to all persons with any proportion of homosexual experience, exclusive heterosexuals were regarded as possessing greater sexual desirability. However, among those with homosexual experience, 25 percent homosexual/75 percent heterosexual and 50 percent homosexual/50 percent heterosexual persons were seen as having greater sexual desirability than 75 percent homosexual/25 percent heterosexual and exclusive homosexual persons.

Comparisons of impressions of stimulus persons' sexual activity showed that targets with a sexual history 50 percent or more heterosexual were rated higher on this factor than those persons with a greater degree of homosexual experience. The 75 percent homosexual/25 percent heterosexual persons, however, were seen as more sexually active than exclusive heterosexuals.

Discussion

The results of the present experiment clearly show that reactions to persons with bisexual histories are complex and unlike responses to those with either exclusive homosexual or heterosexual histories. Furthermore, these responses were found to vary with both the nature of the dimension being assessed and the stimulus person's proportion of homosexual/heterosexual experience. Thus, those with exclusive heterosexual experience were seen as more likable, moral, and well-adjusted than persons with any proportion of homosexual experience, and as more desirable work partners than all but the 25 percent homosexual/75 percent heterosexual stimulus persons. These latter targets were seen as more likable and as more ac-

TABLE 25.3 *Mean Ratings of Stimulus Person Sexual Desirability and Sexual Activity as a Function of Type of Stimulus Person Sexual Orientation*

	0% Hom'l/ 100% Het'l	25% Hom'l/ 75% Het'l	50% Hom'l/ 50% Het'l	75% Hom'l 25% Het'l	100% Hom'l/ 0% Het'l
Sexual Desirability	37.68_a	33.29_b	31.59_b	27.92_c	25.27_c
Sexual Activity	25.32_a	25.36_a	25.68_a	23.25_b	10.05_c

NOTE: Scores could potentially range from 6 to 36 for the Sexual Desirability factor and 5 to 30 for the Sexual Activity factor. Higher scores indicate greater perceived sexual desirability and sexual activity. Means sharing a common subscript are not significantly different at the .05 level in a Newman-Keuls test.

ceptable work partners than others with homosexual experience, but not as more moral or well-adjusted.

Kinsey et al. (1953) seem to have been at least partially correct in asserting that heterosexuals would be as condemning of individuals with both heterosexual and homosexual experience as they are of persons with exclusive homosexual experience, the major exception being responses to stimulus persons with 25 percent homosexual/75 percent heterosexual histories. Although the reasons for this inconsistency are unclear, it might be noted that responses to the 25 percent homosexual/75 percent heterosexual person were most similar to those of other persons with homosexual experience for ratings that assessed perceptions of "character" (morality and adjustment) and different from these persons for evaluations of more general favorability-unfavorability (likability and desirability as a work partner).

Ratings of stimulus person sexuality, further, did not resemble findings for IJS evaluative responses. An initial factor analysis of items contained on the Personality Impressions Scale yielded two interpretable factors that seemed to be related to perceptions of sexuality. The first of these factors seemed to represent impressions of the stimulus person's sexual desirability, and the second seemed to represent impressions of stimulus person sexual activity.[5] Analysis of variance of subjects' factor scores for stimulus person sexual desirability showed that exclusive heterosexuals were seen as more sexually desirable than those with any homosexual experience, whereas those with up to half of their total outlet being homosexual outlet were regarded as more sexually desirable than stimulus persons with a greater proportion of homosexual experience. Exclusive heterosexuals, and those with up to half of their total sexual outlet being homosexual outlet were seen as equally sexually active; those with 75 percent total homosexual outlet, and, most particularly, stimulus persons with exclusive homosexual outlet, were seen as less sexually active. If it can be assumed that this second dimension taps the sort of perceptions that Gagnon and Simon (1973) have suggested, their notion that homosexuals are regarded as having greater eagerness and interest in sexual activity than heterosexuals was not supported.

It should be mentioned that it does not seem plausible that the lower sexual activity ratings of exclusive homosexuals were due to the fact that the exclusive homosexual stimulus persons had indicated less affirmative responses to the Sexual Experience Inventory than persons with any heterosexual experience. The 75 percent homosexual/25 percent heterosexual persons had the greatest number of affirmative responses of any stimulus persons yet their sexual activity ratings were lower than those of persons with more heterosexual experience. Failure to find confirming evidence for attribution of greater sexual activity to homosexuals, thus, must rest with some other factors.

First, it seems quite possible that heterosexuals' conception of being sexual is embedded in their conception of heterosexuality. There would seem to be substantial public exposure to expressions of heterosexuality, whereas there is not the same general exposure to expressions of homosexuality. Homosexual portrayals in the entertainment media, for instance, typically do not depict any but the most fleeting physical contact between same-sex individuals (e.g., the television film *That Certain Summer*). If global judgments of sexuality are at least partially determined by the accessibility of such behavioral referents, the attribution of less sexual interest and desire to homosexuals would be understandable.

Second, lower sexual activity ratings of exclusive homosexuals and 75 percent homosexual/25 percent heterosexual persons may have been a consequence of threat induced in subjects by acknowledging the sexuality of those with homosexual experience. Although the concept of latent homosexuality—unconscious homosexual desires that exist behind a veneer of superficial heterosexuality—is not generally popular in contemporary personality theory and research, it may well remain a widespread social belief. Avoiding acknowledgment of the sexual activity of persons with homosexual experience may have been a means of avoiding thoughts concerning the potential for homosexual behavior in one's self. However, why persons with half or less total homosexual outlet received sexual activity ratings similar to exclusive heterosexuals is unclear.

The present data are inconsistent with some previous research which has found greater same-sex than opposite-sex derogation of homosexual targets and/or greater derogation by males than females (e.g., Millham et al., 1976; Minnigerode, 1976; Steffensmeier and Steffensmeier, 1974). The only subject or stimulus person sex difference found in the present study was that male subjects expressed greater liking for female targets over male targets than female subjects did for male targets over female targets. Conceivably, one explanation for this general lack of sex differences is that the impact of stimulus person sexual orientation was attenuated by the presence of targets with mixed homosexual/heterosexual histories. However, analyses of variance performed on all IJS items and the sexual activity and sexual desirability summed scores including only the exclusive heterosexual and the exclusive homosexual stimulus persons produced no significant effects involving either sex of subject or sex of stimulus person.[6] Failure to find these differences, thus, shows that including bisexual stimulus persons in the present experiment did not play a role in the absence of sex effects. However, the sample of subjects utilized in this study (young and college educated) comes from a group identified in previous research as having relatively tolerant attitudes toward homosexuality (Nyberg and Alston, 1976). This generally high level of acceptance of homosexuality may well have "washed out" any weak sex of subject or stimulus person effects that would otherwise have been present. Also, data to support the presence of more negative reactions to same than opposite-sex homosexuals is far from conclusive. Recent research employing both same- and opposite-sex targets and subjects found little evidence that same-sex homosexual targets received less favorable sociometric ratings than opposite-sex homosexual targets (Gross, Green, Storck, and Vanyur, 1980), or that males were more rejecting than females of homosexual targets overall (Cuenot and Fugita, 1982).

An additional point regarding the operationalization of the stimulus person's sexual orientation should be noted. One of the measures used to manipulate perceptions of the stimulus person's sexual activities—the Sexual Experience Inventory—contained a series of items that required simple "yes-no" ratings to indicate experience (or lack of experience) with a particular behavior. Also, this scale contained fewer homosexual items than heterosexual items. Although the stimulus person's actual degree of heterosexual-homosexual orientation was provided by a self-rating on the Kinsey et al. (1948) sexual orientation continuum, it would have been desirable, nonetheless, to have equated the frequency and variety of homosexual and heterosexual behaviors on the Sexual Experience Inventory. Investigation of issues involving both the characteristics of persons with bisexual experience and the manner in which they are viewed by heterosexual individuals would greatly benefit if a scale that thoroughly assesses experience with both homosexual and heterosexual activities were to be developed.

Subject suspicion, although not found to differentially affect subjects' interpersonal judgments, should nonetheless be a matter of some concern. Institutional procedures required that information concerning the use of sexual materials and the general goals of the study be provided to subjects prior to their participation. Since subjects were made aware that reactions to the sexual experiences of another were the central concern of the investigation, their attention was understandably focused on those aspects of the procedure that might well have appeared bogus. However, the high rates of suspicion found in the present study must also be viewed in the context of prior research. In other studies examining responses to individuals with varying sexual orientations, there is either no report that suspicion was assessed (Cuenot and Fugita, 1982; Elman, Killebrew, and Oros, 1978; Gross et al., 1980; Karr, 1978; SanMiguel and Millham, 1976), mention that subjects were questioned regarding suspicion, but no information concerning the proportion of subjects indicating suspicion and whether or not these subjects were dropped from the study (Krulewitz and Nash, 1980), or a brief statement that subjects who indicated suspicion during debriefing were eliminated, with no further description of the manner in which information regarding suspicion was obtained from subjects (Gurwitz and Marcus, 1978). One might suspect that if a rigorous method of assessing suspicion had been used in these studies, there might well have been a substantial proportion of subjects who would have expressed doubts regarding the authenticity of the investigative procedures. In a relatively sophisticated subject population, such suspicions might well be unavoidable. In future research, it would seem prudent that attempts be made to include a thorough technique of probing for subject suspicion. In the event suspicion cannot be eliminated, one might at least systematically examine its impact on the outcome of an investigation.

A few further cautions should be noted regarding the generalizability of these results. Given the general goal of examining reactions to others differing in their proportion of heterosexual/homosexual experience, the bogus stranger technique used in this study provided the only feasible method of examining these issues. Obviously, however, in everyday social interaction one seldom becomes aware of the sexual experiences of another in a similar fashion. An alternative technique for manipulating perceived sexual orientation employed in several studies (e.g. Cuenot and Fugita, 1982; Elman, Killebrew, and Oros 1978; Gurwitz and Marcus, 1978) is to have subjects evaluate either an experimental confederate or a symbolically represented stimulus person who has spontaneously provided information concerning his/her sexual orientation (typically, either through use of a "Gay Lib" lapel button or avowed membership in a gay rights organization or social group). In some sense, such a manipulation might provide a greater degree of verisimilitude than the methodology used in the present study. However, the majority of individuals who engage in non-normative sexual activities do not offer unelicited proclamation of their sexual preferences. It would not be unreasonable to assume that the manner in which subjects respond to a stimulus person using a manipulation of this sort is to some degree a function of their reactions to an individual who would freely provide information regarding their participation in activities which generally earn societal disapproval, rather than being a consequence of the stimulus person's sexual orientation per se. In the present study, instructions provided to subjects made it clear that information regarding the stimulus person's sexual experiences had been obtained anonymously and, of course, had also been explicitly requested. The nature of the information provided by these varying methodologies regarding reactions of heterosexuals to others with homosexual experience might well be quite different.

Finally, in the present experiment, subjects were provided with specific information concerning the sexual experiences *and* self-identified sexual orientation of another individual. In all cases, the stimulus person's sexual orientation self-rating and actual sexual experiences corresponded in a predetermined manner. Blumstein and Schwartz (1977) however, found that many individuals with mixed homosexual/heterosexual histories considered one form of outlet experimental, less valued, or to be engaged in only when their primary outlet was not available. Despite more than incidental levels of sexual experience at variance with their self-identified sexual orientation, these individuals maintained a conception of themselves as "homosexual" or "heterosexual." The actual co-occurrence of mixed homosexual-heterosexual histories and the self-identified label of "bisexual," thus, might be far from perfect.

Notes

1. An analysis of variance of subjects' responses to the heterosexual items on the Sexual Experience Inventory showed that males were somewhat more heterosexually experienced than females, $F(1, 195) = 7.25$, $p < .01$. Males indicated an average of 5.47 affirmative responses and females an average of 4.46, An analysis of subjects' responses to the homosexual experience items yielded no significant effects.

2. Since analyses of this likability factor yielded results which were essentially redundant with those provided by IJS items, it will not be discussed further.

3. Summed raw scores were used for ease of interpretability. Averaged across sex orientation conditions using Fisher's r to Zr transformation (McNemar, 1969), the summed scores for sexual desirability and sexual activity were correlated with normalized exact procedure factor scores .90 and .85, respectively.

4. The italicized item of each pair was scored 6 and the non-italicized item was scored 1. Also, all factor loadings were positive.

5. In interpreting differences in ratings received by stimulus persons for these two factors, one matter that should be kept in mind is the substantially greater percentage of

common item variance accounted for by the sexual desirability factor in contrast to the sexual activity factor (53 percent to 8 percent). Much previous research has demonstrated that interpersonal assessment is dominated by evaluative dimensions (cf. Osgood, 1962), of which the sexual desirability factor would be an example. The lesser proportion of variance associated with the sexual activity factor can be attributed to the fact that ratings of stimulus person sexual activity are not as clearly evaluative in character.

6. In these analyses, significant main effects for stimulus person sexual orientation appeared for the IJS items likability, work partner desirability, morality, and adjustment, and the two summed sexuality scores. Details of these analyses are available from the author.

REFERENCES

Bauman, K. E., and Wilson, R. R. 1976. Premarital sexual attitudes of unmarried university students: 1968 vs. 1972. *Archives of Sexual Behavior*, 5, 29–37.

Blumstein, P. W., and Schwartz, P. 1977. Bisexuality: Some social psychological issues. *Journal of Social Issues*, 33(2), 30–45.

Brady, J. P., and Levitt, E. E. 1965. The scalability of sexual experiences. *Psychological Record*, 15, 275–279.

Bromley, D. D., and Britten, F. H. 1938. *Youth and sex: A study of 1300 college students*. New York: Harper and Row.

Byrne, D. 1971. *The attraction paradigm*. New York: Academic Press.

Christensen, H. T., and Gregg, C. F. 1970. Changing sex norms in America and Scandinavia. *Journal of Marriage and the Family*, 32, 616–627.

Cuenot, R. G., and Fugita, S. S. 1982. Perceived homosexuality: Measuring heterosexual attitudinal and nonverbal reactions. *Personality and Social Psychology Bulletin*, 8, 100–106.

Elman, D., Killebrew, T. J., and Oros, C. 1978. How sexual orientation and physical attractiveness affect impressions of males. Paper presented at the annual meeting of the American Psychological Association, Toronto, August.

Finger F. W. 1975. Changes in sex practices and beliefs of male college students over 30 years. *Journal of Sex Research*, 11, 304–317.

Gagnon, J. H., and Simon, W. 1973. *Sexual conduct: The social sources of human sexuality*. Chicago: Aldine Publishing.

Glenn, N. D., and Weaver, C. N. 1979. Attitudes toward premarital, extramarital, and homosexual relations in the U.S. in the 1970s. *Journal of Sex Research*, 14, 108–118.

Goffman, E. 1963. *Stigma: Notes on the management of spoiled identity*. Englewood Cliffs, N.J.: Prentice-Hall.

Gross, A. E., Green, S. K., Storck, J. T., and Vanyur, J. M. 1980. Disclosure of sexual orientation and impressions of male and female homosexuals. *Personality and Social Psychology Bulletin*, 6, 307–314.

Gurwitz, S. B., and Marcus, M. 1978. Effects of anticipated interaction, sex, and homosexual stereotypes on first impressions. *Journal of Applied Social Psychology*, 8, 47–56.

Hunt, M. 1974. *Sexual behavior in the 1970's*. Chicago: Playboy Press.

Karr, R. G. 1978. Homosexual labeling and the male role. *Journal of Social Issues*, 34, (3) 73–83.

Kinsey, A. C., Pomeroy, W., and Martin, C. 1948. *Sexual behavior in the human male*. Philadelphia: Saunders.

Kinsey, A. C., Pomeroy, W., Martin, C., and Gebhard, P. 1953. *Sexual behavior in the human female*. Philadelphia: Saunders.

Krulewitz, J. E., and Nash, J. E. 1980. Effects of sex role attitudes and similarity on men's rejection of male homosexuals. *Journal of Personality and Social Psychology*, 38, 67–74.

Levitt, E., and Klassen, A. 1974. Public attitudes toward homosexuality: Part of the 1970 national survey by the Institute for Sex Research. *Journal of Homosexuality*, 1, 29–43.

MacDonald, A. P., and Games, R. G. 1974. Some characteristics of those who hold positive and negative attitudes toward homosexuals. *Journal of Homosexuality*, 1, 9–27.

McNemar, Q. 1969. *Psychological statistics*. New York: John Wiley and Sons.

Millham, J., SanMiguel, C. L., and Kellogg, R. 1976. A factor-analytic conceptualization of attitudes toward male and female homosexuals. *Journal of Homosexuality*, 2, 3–10.

Minnigerode, F. A. 1976. Attitudes toward homosexuality: Feminist attitudes and sexual conservatism. *Sex Roles*, 2, 347–352.

Nyberg, K. L., and Alston, J. P. 1976. Analysis of public attitudes toward homosexual behavior. *Journal of Homosexuality*, 2, 99–107.

Osgood, C. E. 1962. Studies on the generality of affective meaning systems. *American Psychologist*, 17, 10–28.

Pomeroy, W. B. 1972. *Dr. Kinsey and the Institute for Sex Research*. New York: Harper and Row.

Reiss, I. L. 1960. *Premarital sexual standards in America*. New York: Free Press.

Reiss, I. L. 1967. *The social context of premarital sexual permissiveness*. New York: Holt, Rinehart and Winston.

SanMiguel, C. L., and Millham, J. 1976. The role of cognitive and situational variables in aggression toward homosexuals. *Journal of Homosexuality*, 2, 11–27.

Steffensmeier, D., and Steffensmeier, R. 1974. Sex differences in reactions to homosexuals: Research continuities and further developments. *Journal of Sex Research*, 10, 52–67.

Storms, M. D. 1978. Attitudes toward homosexuality and femininity in men. *Journal of Homosexuality*, 3, 257–263.

26

"Coming Out" in the Age of Social Constructionism: Sexual Identity Formation Among Lesbian and Bisexual Women

Paula C. Rust

SOCIAL sexologists became interested in homosexual identity development in the 1970s. This interest arose as attempts to discover the etiology of homosexuality gave way to efforts to understand the lives of lesbians and gay men, a shift that occurred in response to social and political changes in society at large. Social and political circumstances continued to change, and during the 1980s researchers once again shifted their attention toward more contemporary topics such as acquired immune deficiency syndrome (AIDS).

Meanwhile, sexological theory progressed as social constructionists carefully exposed and challenged essentialist assumptions. This scrutiny changed scientific understandings of sexuality, sexual identity, sexual politics, and the history of sexuality. But sexologists have not yet fully reexamined the process of sexual identity formation. The result is a disjunction between contemporary concepts of sexual identity and available models for describing sexual identity formation. This disjunction magnifies some of the conceptual problems in the existing literature on sexual identity formation and highlights the need to reconceptualize the process.

One problem is the linearity of most available models. Homosexual identity formation is not orderly and predictable; individuals often skip steps in the process, temporarily return to earlier stages of the process, and sometimes abort the process altogether by returning to a heterosexual identity. Recognizing this shortcoming, earlier theorists modified linear models by introducing feedback loops, alternate routes, and dead ends. These efforts produced linear models with ample room for deviation rather than models that effectively describe the formation of sexual identity. What is needed is a completely new model.

This research was supported in part by a grant from the Horace H. Rackham School of Graduate Studies of the University of Michigan, Ann Arbor, Michigan.

Earlier work on the coming out process also neglects bisexual identity. Despite ample evidence of prevalent bisexual behavior and frequent theoretical admonishments for ignoring this evidence (e.g., MacDonald 1981, 1983; Paul 1985), few researchers in the 1970s and 1980s gave bisexuality more than a passing nod. Because prevailing models of sexuality were either dichotomous (Paul 1985; Ross 1984) or scalar (e.g., Bell and Weinberg 1978; Kinsey, Pomeroy and Martin 1948; Kinsey, Pomeroy, Martin, and Gebhard 1953; Shively and De Cecco 1977), bisexuality was either considered non existent or conceptualized as an intermediate state between heterosexuality and homosexuality. Bisexual identity, therefore, might be adopted as a stepping stone on the way to homosexual identity (e.g., Chapman and Brannock 1987), but was not considered an end in itself.

Recent constructionist criticism of the dichotomous and scalar models of sexuality has paved the way for the recognition of bisexuality as an authentic form of sexuality. Coincidently, the AIDS epidemic and the increasing politicization of bisexual people have called attention to the practical and theoretical importance of bisexuality. A few recent studies explicitly and intentionally include bisexuals. Many of these studies explore AIDS-related issues within samples of gay and bisexual men (e.g,. Lyter et al. 1987; McCusker et al. 1989; Siegel et al. 1988; Winkelstein et al. 1987). But AIDS researchers are not concerned about bisexuality per se and rarely distinguish between gay and bisexual subjects. Other studies focus on clinical issues raised by heterosexually married bisexual, lesbian, and gay psychotherapy clients or compare bisexuals to heterosexuals, gays and lesbians on a variety of health, personality, attitudinal, and behavioral variables (e.g., Daniel, Abernethy and Oliver 1984; Engel and Saracino 1986; LaTorre and Wendenberg 1983; Nurius 1983; Smith, Johnson and Guenther 1985; Stokes, Kilmann and Wanlass 1983). Despite the increased interest in bisexuality, research that focuses on bisexual identity remains scarce.

The present research renews empirical investigation into the coming out process in an effort to develop a nonlinear model of identity formation that treats bisexual identity and homosexual identity as equally valid alternatives to heterosexual identity. The inquiry begins by recognizing that women who are raised to assume heterosexual identities nevertheless adopt both lesbian and bisexual identities. The identity history patterns of women who currently possess lesbian and bisexual identities are compared to each other, and then individual variations in identity histories are examined. Observations about individual differences serve as a springboard for a constructionist critique of existing models of identity formation and a reconceptualization of the process.

Previous Literature

In scientific literature and popular lesbian and gay literature, the term *coming out* refers to processes as well as particular events within these processes. Early researchers typically defined coming out as a single event, usually first identification of oneself as homosexual (e.g., Cronin 1974; Dank 1971; Hooker 1967). More recent theorists conceptualize coming out as a process, and many have proposed developmental models of this process. Working within the developmental paradigm, some researchers document the order and nature of milestone events in individuals' lives (e.g., Coleman 1982; Hencken and O'Dowd 1977; Lee 1977; McDonald 1982; Schäfer 1976; Troiden and Goode 1980), whereas others discuss the psychological changes that occur during and between these events (e.g., Cass 1979, 1990; Fein and Nuehring 1982). Each author chooses a particular point as the beginning of the process and a particular point as its termination. Some discuss the assumptions that underlie these choices (e.g., Cass 1984), but few question the assumptions that underlie the developmental paradigm itself.

These assumptions are numerous. First, a developmental process is linear and unidirectional, with a positive value assigned to later stages in the process. The process has a beginning stage and an end stage, connected to each other by a series of intermediate and sequential steps. Persons are expected to move from each step to the next in the sequence, with progress defined as movement from earlier steps to later steps and maturity defined as achievement of the end stage. Movement in the other direction is defined as regression. The end stage becomes the goal of the process, and all activity taking place prior to achievement of this stage is presumably directed toward this goal. This activity is expected to cease upon achievement of the end stage, and continued activity is taken as a sign of immaturity.

As applied to homosexual identity formation, the developmental model defines progress as the replacement of a heterosexual identity with a homosexual identity. The privileged status given homosexual identity as the goal of this process is justified by the assumption that this identity is an accurate reflection of the essence of the individual.[1] In other words, coming out is a process of discovery in which the individual sheds a false heterosexual identity and comes to correctly identify and label their own true essence, which is homosexual.

The assumptions of linearity and stage-sequentiality are evident in the writings of early coming out theorists. For example, Troiden and Goode (1980: 387) assert that their one hundred fifty gay male respondents "did embrace the components of the gay experience in a specific sequence," and describe this process as a series of five milestone events. The sequence starts when one first suspects that one might be homosexual and ends with one's first homosexual relationship. Coleman (1982) also identified five steps, beginning with childhood feelings of being different and ending with the integration of public and private identity, whereas McDonald (1982) prefers an expanded series of nine milestone events. De Monteflores and Schultz (1978) argue that individuals first recognize their homosexuality and then integrate this knowledge into their lives, implying a stepwise progression toward greater personal integrity.

Several theorists acknowledge that the linear processes they describe do not accurately reflect the experiences of some subjects. McDonald observes that some of his subjects did not "move predictably" (1982: 40) through the five steps he outlines, and Coleman (1982) acknowledges that not all individuals follow the stages of coming out in sequential order. Cass (1979, 1990) asserts that each stage of coming out might be followed by "foreclosure," or termination of the process, instead of the next step in the process. Nevertheless, these theorists present linear, stage-sequential models of coming out, revealing their assumption that coming out is fundamentally a linear and orderly process. Normal and expected though they are, complexities like sequential disorder and foreclosure are understood as deviations from the underlying linear process of coming out.

Research conducted under the developmental model provides information about the average ages at which lesbians and gay men experience the stages of coming out. Despite the fact that this research spans a decade during which the relaxation of social attitudes toward homosexuality should have eased the coming out process, different researchers report remarkably similar findings. Most lesbians who have ever experienced homosexual arousal recall having such feelings around the age of twelve or thirteen, but they typically did not become aware of their sexual feelings toward other women until ages fourteen through nineteen. Women begin suspecting that they are lesbian at an average age of eighteen, but they do not define themselves as lesbian until a few years later at an average age of twenty one to twenty three, with 77 percent having done so by age twenty three. Research on gay men indicates that they experience these events at younger ages and more rapidly than lesbians (Bell, Weinberg, and Hammersmith 1981; Califia 1979; Cronin 1974;, Jay and Young 1979; Kooden et al. 1979; McDonald 1982; de Monteflores and Schultz 1978; Riddle and Morin 1977; Schäfer 1976; Troiden 1988).

Bisexual women experience each milestone at older ages than lesbians. On average, bisexual women become aware of homosexual feelings at age sixteen and define themselves as homosexual at age twenty-eight (Kooden et al. 1979). Bisexual women also exhibit more discrepancy between adolescent and adult sexuality than homosexual women, suggesting that the preferences of bisexual women might become established later in life (Bell, Weinberg, and Hammersmith 1981).

The developmental paradigm has been challenged by symbolic interactionists who view sexual identity formation as a process of creating an identity through social interaction rather than a process of discovering identity through introspection. Interactionists vary in the degree to which they discuss the effect of contextual factors on this interactive process; some describe particular social situations that are conducive to the creation of gay identity (e.g., Dank 1971) whereas others examine the constraints imposed the process by socially constructed conceptions of sexuality.

Plummer's (1975) description of the process of "becoming homosexual" is one of the earliest interactionist analyses of sexual identity formation. His four-stage model begins with the "sensitization" stage, during which one has experiences that later acquire sexual meaning. These experiences, for example, same-sex childhood fantasies or close friendships, become part of the coming out process only after one comes out and retrospectively reinterprets them as early evidence of homosexuality. Thus the sensitization stage is not a particular pre-homosexual state of being, and homosexuality is not an essential characteristic awaiting discovery. Rather, homosexual identity is socially created, and the coming out process itself is retrospectively constructed. Despite these insights, Plummer nevertheless describes coming out as a goal-oriented process that culminates with the acquisition and stabilization of homosexual identity.

In a series of publications on bisexual behavior and identity, Blumstein and Schwartz (1974, 1976, 1977, 1990) emphasize the mutability of human sexuality and sexual identity as well as the normalcy of incongruence between an individual's sexual identity and sexual behavior. They describe subjects who exhibit various combinations of identity and behavior, for example, women who identify themselves as lesbians but engage in bisexual behavior. In so doing, Blumstein and Schwartz treat these combinations as phenomena worthy of explanation in their own right rather than as temporary transitional states or unstable deviations from a hypothetical normal state in which identity accurately reflects essence. They explain these phenomena by asserting that identity formation is a process of creation (1990) that is influenced by social factors such as dichotomous thinking about sexuality, antagonism toward bisexuality (especially among lesbians), political ideologies, and gender role expectations (1974, 1977). For example, dichotomous thinking about sexuality inhibits bisexual identification by encouraging individuals to emphasize either their homosexual or their heterosexual experience and to produce a consistent account of either homosexual or heterosexual identity by reinterpreting past events (1977). Such assertions extend the interactionist insights of Plummer (1975) into a recognition of the impact of social constructs upon self identity.

Since the publication of Blumstein and Schwartz's work in the late 1970s, several researchers have confirmed the finding that incongruities between sexual identity and sexual experience are commonplace (e.g., Klein, Sepekoff, and Wolf 1985; LaTorre and Wendenburg 1983; Loewenstein 1985; Nichols 1988). The work of Blumstein and Schwartz remains pivotal, however, because the investigation of incongruities between identity and behavior is not the central research question in most of these recent studies, and few of these authors discuss the social and political factors that influence sexual identity.

Richardson and Hart (1981) argue that any sexual identity is the product of an ongoing process of dynamic social interaction. An individual's sexual identity may therefore change at any stage of the life cycle, and the meaning of a given sexual identity may differ among individuals and over time. Moreover, identity stability is no less a dynamic product than identity change. By applying interactionist principles to identity stability as well as identity change, Richardson and Hart finalize the divorce between sexual identity and sexual essence, reconceptualize identity as a process rather than a goal, and produce a fully interactionist account of sexual identity. Richardson and Hart agree with Blumstein and Schwartz that the lack of social validation for bisexual identity makes the maintenance of bisexual identity difficult, and they argue that a woman who has adopted a lesbian identity on the basis of her sexual experiences with other women might not have done so if she lived in a society in which sex of partner was not considered an indication of essential sexual orientation. These ideas have not been fully developed into a social constructionist account of sexual identity formation.

Methods and Measures

The difficulties inherent in collecting a sample of an undocumented, invisible, and stigmatized population are well known. The sample selection and data collection methods used in the current study were designed to maximize coverage of the target population. In order to reach secretive lesbian-identified and bisexual-identified women, data were collected via self-administered questionnaires and postage-paid return envelopes, thus guaranteeing complete anonymity for respondents. Questionnaires were distributed by several methods, including booths at lesbian, gay, and women's conferences and through lesbian, gay, and bisexual social and political organizations, friendship networks, and newsletter advertisements.

The cover of the questionnaire presents the survey as a study of "women who consider themselves to be lesbian or bisexual, or who choose not to label their sexual orientation, or who are not sure what their sexual orientation is," thus defining the sample population as all women who have questioned or rejected heterosexual identity. The majority of the respondents are currently self-identified lesbians, dykes, gay or homosexual women[2] (n = 346 or 81 percent), and a minority are self-identified bisexuals or "straights with bisexual tendencies" (n = 60 or 14 percent). In the interest of brevity, these two groups of respondents will henceforth be called *lesbians* and *bisexuals* respectively; these terms refer to current self-identity only, and imply neither that self-identity reflects essence nor that it is static. The findings will show that many individuals, especially those who currently identify themselves as bisexual, frequently switch back and forth between identities. Bearing this in mind, the current sample is a "snapshot" of respondents' sexual identities at a particular point in time.

Twenty-one respondents indicated that they do not know their sexual orientation, that they are still wondering, or that they prefer not to label themselves. These women, who might possess sexual self-representations that are not organized into sexual identities, will be called *not sexually identified*. Because an understanding of women who have not created sexual identities is relevant to the larger question of sexual identity formation, some data about the identity histories of these twenty-one women are presented.

The sample is predominantly young, white, well educated and employed, but with low income. Respondents range in age from 16 to 78, with the majority in their twenties (45 percent), thirties (38 percent), or forties (12 percent). Two-thirds are involved in serious or marital relationships with either women or men, and fifteen percent have children. Four percent of the sample is African-American and two percent is Arab, Asian, Indian, Native American, or Latina/Hispanic. The remaining 94 percent is white. Thirty-four percent of respondents have 18 or more years of formal education, 25 percent have completed college, and only 7 percent have no schooling beyond high school. Despite this high level of education, the median household income is $20,000. Eighty-nine percent are employed, one quarter of whom are also students. An additional 7 percent are non employed students, and 4 percent are unemployed or retired. Most (84 percent) currently reside in a single midwestern state, although twenty-four states are represented in the sample.

Respondents answered a series of questions about their sexual identity histories. These questions asked whether each of several psychological events had taken place in their lives and, if so, at what age. Some of the events are milestones that were reported in previous research on coming out as a developmental process, whereas others are events that have not been previously studied, such as changes in identity that occur subsequent to initial identification as either lesbian or bisexual. The former include a respondent's first awareness of homosexual attraction, first questioning of heterosexual identity, and first self-identification as lesbian. The latter include first self-identification as bisexual, the last time a self-identified lesbian wondered whether she was bisexual or identified herself as bisexual, the last time a self-identified bisexual wondered whether she was lesbian or identified herself as lesbian, and whether a respondent has switched between lesbian and bisexual self-identities zero, one, or more times.[3] Respondents who do not currently identify themselves as either lesbian or bisexual were asked whether they had ever wondered if they were lesbian or bisexual or identified themselves as lesbian or bisexual and, if so, at what age they last did so. Whenever the word *lesbian* appeared in a question, it was accompanied by the alternative terms *gay*, *homosexual* and *dyke*. Respondents were instructed to read the question using the word with which they felt most comfortable.

Findings

The average lesbian and the average bisexual woman experienced the psychological events in almost identical order, although the average bisexual experienced each event at an older age than did the average lesbian (see Table 26.1). Lesbians first felt sexually attracted to women at an average age of 15, whereas bisexual women did not experience these feelings until an average age of 18. Slightly less than two years after this experience, respondents in both subsamples began questioning their heterosexual identities. It then took another five years for the average lesbian or bisexual woman to first adopt the identity she now has; the average lesbian was nearly twenty-two years old at this time, and the average bisexual was age twenty-five. Among those who also at some point adopted the other identity, both lesbian and bisexual respondents did so slightly prior to adopting their current identity. The average lesbian first called herself a bisexual shortly before her twenty-first birthday, and the average bisexual first called herself a lesbian as she approached her twenty-fifth.

Within each subsample, the average respondent continued to wonder about her identity even after adopting her current identity. Those lesbians who ever wondered if they were bisexual did so for an average of almost four years after adopting a lesbian identity, and those who ever thought of themselves as bisexual gave up this bisexual identity for the last time at the average age of twenty-five. Those bisexuals who ever wondered or identified themselves as lesbians continued to do so for a similar period of time following their adoption of bisexual identity, until an average age of almost thirty.

TABLE 26.1 *Average Ages at which Events in Respondents' Identity Histories Occurred*

	Average Age		
Milestone	Lesbian Identified	Bisexual Identified	Not Sexually Identified
Current age	31.2 (n = 342)	32.5 (n = 60)	29.9 (N = 20)
First homosexual attraction	15.4 (n = 329)	18.1 (n = 56)	20.2*** (N = 21)
First questioning of heterosexual identity	17.0 (n = 339)	20.0 (n = 60)	20.9** (N = 20)
First lesbian identification	21.7 (n = 331)	24.5* (n = 44)	—
First bisexual identification	20.9 (n = 133)	25.0*** (n = 55)	—
First identification as either lesbian or bisexual, whichever came first	20.9 (N = 331)	23.4* (N = 55)	—
Last wondered about bisexual identity	25.4 (n = 208)	—	27.2 (N = 16)
Last bisexual identification	25.1 (N = 125)	—	26.2 (N = 11)
Last wondered about lesbian identity	—	29.6 (n = 45)	27.2 (N = 18)
Last lesbian identification	—	28.8 (n = 33)	25.5 (N = 13)

*p ≤ .01 **p ≤ .005 ***p ≤ .001

The difference between the ages at which lesbian and bisexual respondents experienced each milestone increases steadily with each successive milestone. The average bisexual was 2.7 years older than the average lesbian when she first felt attracted to a woman, 3.0 years older when she realized that she might not be heterosexual, 3.3 years older when she first adopted the identity she currently possesses, and 4.2 years older when she stopped wondering whether she should have chosen the other identity. Thus the process not only occurred at an older age for the average bisexual than for the average lesbian but also happened more slowly.

But these figures conceal much variation in the coming out process among lesbian and bisexual women. For example, not all lesbians have ever identified themselves as bisexual, not all bisexuals have ever identified themselves as lesbian, and not all individuals experience the events in the same order or at the same ages. Some respondents change identities frequently, whereas others, after questioning their original heterosexual identity, adopted the identity they now have and maintained it ever since.

Figure 26.1 is a flowchart of the patterns of identity change reported by lesbian and bisexual respondents. Fewer than half of lesbian-identified respondents have ever identified themselves as bisexual, although nearly two thirds have wondered if they were bisexual. In contrast, most bisexuals have not only wondered if they were lesbian but have identified themselves as lesbians in the past. Bisexuals are no more likely than lesbians to be wondering about their sexual identity at the current time, however. Most respondents who report no current sexual identity (not shown in Figure 26.1) have identified as both lesbian and bisexual in the past (80 percent and 74 percent respectively); in fact, most are currently wondering

Figure 26.1: Flowchart of Lesbian and Bisexual Respondents' Identity Histories

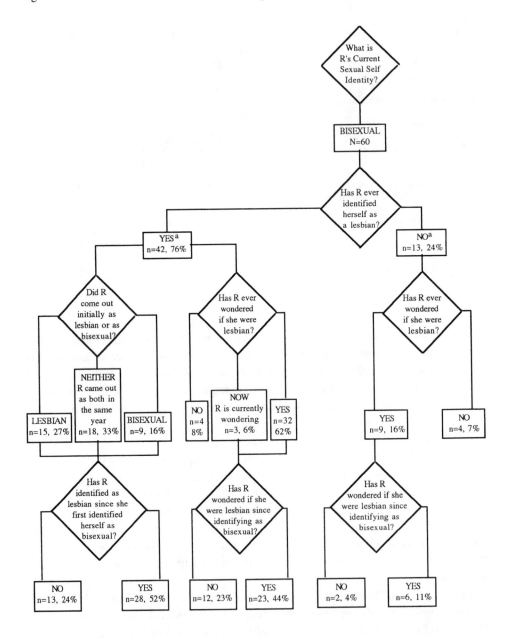

Notes:
a. Cases with missing data are deleted stepwise. Therefore, the total number of respondents at each level of the flowchart may be smaller than the total number of respondents at higher levels.
b. Percentages given in each cell of the flowchart represent the percentage of the total lesbian or bisexual subsample which falls in that cell. Percentages are calculated based upon the total number of respondents for whom relevant data are nonmissing.

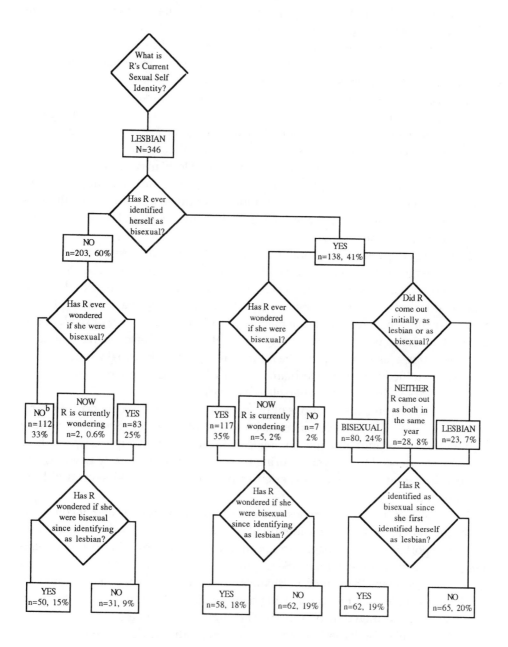

whether or not they are lesbian or bisexual (74 percent and 70 percent respectively). Bisexual women report switching between lesbian and bisexual identities more frequently than lesbian women; 58 percent of bisexual women and 14 percent of lesbian women report switching identities two or more times.

The order in which respondents adopted lesbian and bisexual identities also varies among both lesbians and bisexual women, although certain patterns are prevalent within each subsample. Bisexuals were much less likely than lesbians to come out initially as lesbians; 27 percent of bisexuals compared to 66 percent of lesbians initially identified themselves as lesbians. The difference is not accounted for by a complementary tendency among bisexuals to come out initially as bisexual; fewer than half of the respondents who now consider themselves bisexual adopted this identity in the first place. Twenty-four percent of lesbians came out as bisexual at least one year prior to adopting a lesbian identity, a finding that might account for the role of bisexual identity as a transitional identity in developmental theories of lesbian identity development, as well as the lesbian subcultural belief that bisexuality is a phase in the process of coming out as a lesbian.

Even after adopting the identities they possess today, many respondents continued to undergo periods of alternative identification or uncertainty about their sexual identities. One of five lesbians has experienced a period of bisexual identification since first adopting a lesbian identity, and one of three has wondered if she were bisexual since identifying herself as a lesbian. In fact, most of the lesbian-identified women who report ever wondering if they were bisexual have done so since adopting a lesbian identity. The figures are higher for bisexual women; one of two has identified herself as a lesbian, and one of two has wondered if she were a lesbian since she first identified herself as a bisexual.

Table 26.2 presents distributions of the ages at which each event occurred in respondents' lives. The first events in most respondents' lives were becoming aware of homosexual feelings and questioning their heterosexual identities. Two of three women experienced these events during their teenage years or early twenties, but many other women had these experiences prior to puberty, and several did not have them until their 30s or 40s.

For most respondents, awareness of homosexual feelings preceded or coincided with questioning heterosexual identity, but a substantial minority of each subsample reported that they began to question their heterosexuality before experiencing attraction to other women (See Figure 26.2). This latter pattern is more common among lesbians than among bisexuals; one in four lesbians began to question her heterosexuality before experiencing homosexual feelings, whereas only one in seven bisexual women did so ($p < .05$). The number of years that passed between these two events also varies considerably among individuals. Some respondents did not question their heterosexual identities until as many as 26 years after first experiencing homosexual feelings, whereas others experienced homosexual feelings as many as 15 years after questioning their heterosexual identity. Such lengthy periods are rare, however, especially among bisexual women; 52 percent of bisexual women, 31 percent of lesbians, and 40 percent of sexually unidentified women reported that these events occurred within a single year of each other.

TABLE 26.2 *Incidence of Milestone Events and the Ages at Which They Occurred (Percentages)*

Age	First homosexual attraction	First questioning of hetero-sexual identity	First self-identification as either lesbian or bisexual	Last bisexual identification (excludes bisexual Rs)	Last lesbian identification (excludes lesbian Rs)	Last wondered if bisexual (excludes bisexual Rs)	Last wondered if lesbian (excludes lesbian Rs)
Preschool, 0–4	2.5% (N = 10)	2.6% (N = 11)	0.5% (N = 2)	0.0% (N = 0)	2.2% (N = 1)	0.4% (N = 1)	0.0% (N = 0)
Child, 5–9	9.6% (N = 39)	6.7% (N = 28)	0.3% (N = 1)	0.0% (N = 0)	0.0% (N = 0)	0.0% (N = 0)	0.0% (N = 0)
Preteen, 10–12	15.5% (N = 63)	13.1% (N = 55)	5.2% (N = 20)	0.0% (N = 0)	2.2% (N = 1)	0.4% (N = 1)	1.6% (N = 1)
Young teen, 13–15	23.6% (N = 96)	16.0% (N = 67)	9.6% (N = 37)	2.2% (N = 3)	0.0% (N = 0)	1.3% (N = 3)	0.0% (N = 0)
Old Teen, 16–19	28.3% (N = 115)	29.4% (N = 123)	31.3% (N = 121)	14.0% (N = 19)	4.3% (N = 2)	15.2% (N = 34)	4.8% (N = 3)
Young adult 20–24	11.3% (N = 46)	17.7% (N = 74)	28.2% (N = 109)	41.9% (N = 57)	30.4% (N = 14)	37.1% (N = 83)	27.0% (N = 17)
25–29	4.7% (N = 19)	7.4% (N = 31)	13.7% (N = 53)	19.1% (N = 26)	23.9% (N = 11)	20.5% (N = 46)	25.4% (N = 16)
Adult 30–34	1.7% (N = 7)	4.1% (N = 17)	4.4% (N = 17)	11.8% (N = 16)	10.9% (N = 5)	12.9% (N = 29)	19.0% (N = 12)
35–39	1.5% (N = 6)	1.9% (N = 8)	3.9% (N = 15)	3.7% (N = 5)	19.6% (N = 9)	5.8% (N = 13)	11.1% (N = 7)
40–44	1.0% (N = 4)	1.2% (N = 5)	2.3% (N = 9)	6.6% (N = 9)	4.3% (N = 2)	4.0% (N = 9)	6.3% (N = 4)
45+	0.3% (N = 1)	0.0% (N = 0)	0.6% (N = 2)	0.7% (N = 1)	2.2% (N = 1)	2.2% (N = 5)	4.8% (N = 3)
Range: (Total):	0–46 (N = 406)	0–42 (N = 419)	4–50 (N = 386)	14–45 (N = 136)	3–45 (N = 46)	4–50 (N = 224)	11–50 (N = 63)

The difference between bisexual women and lesbians is statistically significant (p = .03).

These findings contrast sharply with the finding in Table 26.1 that the average bisexual woman experiences the coming out process more slowly than the average lesbian. Figure 26.2 shows, on the contrary, that, once bisexual women become aware of their homosexual feelings, they begin to question their heterosexuality more quickly than lesbians. The former finding is an artifact of the fact that bisexual women become aware of their homosexual feelings at older ages than lesbians and the fact that lesbians are more likely than bisexual women to question their heterosexuality prior to experiencing feelings of sexual attraction to other women.

After experiencing feelings of homosexual attraction and questioning their prescribed heterosexual identities, most respondents eventually adopted either a lesbian or a bisexual identity. Approximately one in four women did so immediately, and another one in four did so within five years, although others took up to 35 years to do so. There is no significant difference between lesbian and bisexual women in the time lag between these two events. For most respondents, these events occurred in their late teens or early twenties (See Table 26.2).

Among those respondents who have changed identities since first adopting a lesbian or bisexual identity, bisexuals typically did so more quickly than lesbians

(See Figure 26.3). Two-fifths of bisexual women changed identities within the first year of coming out, but only one-fifth of lesbians did so. A substantial number of lesbians who came out initially as bisexual took up to ten years to adopt a lesbian identity.

As reported above, many lesbian and bisexual respondents continued to consider alternative identities even after adopting their current identities. There are no striking differences between lesbians and bisexual women in the length of time that passed before they ceased to question their sexual identities; periods of up to a decade are not uncommon within either subsample. There is a difference in the ages at which lesbian and bisexual women ceased considering alternative identities, however; most lesbians gave up their bisexual identity by age 25, whereas bisexuals last identified themselves as lesbians at older and more varied ages (See Table 26.2).

The variation in ages at which bisexuals last identified themselves as lesbians is explained by the fact that most (54 percent) bisexuals last identified themselves as lesbian within the past year. Respondents who are not currently sexually identified are even more likely than bisexuals to have recently possessed a different sexual identity; 73 percent have identified as lesbian and 92 percent have identified as bisexual within the past year. In contrast, only 18 percent of lesbians have identified themselves as bisexual within the past year; the modal lesbian has not identified herself as bisexual for over five years.

In summary, there is considerable variation among lesbian-identified, bisexual-identified, and sexually unidentified women, and this variety overshadows the

Figure 26.2: Time Lapse between First Awareness of Attraction to Women and First Realization that One Might Not Be Heterosexual

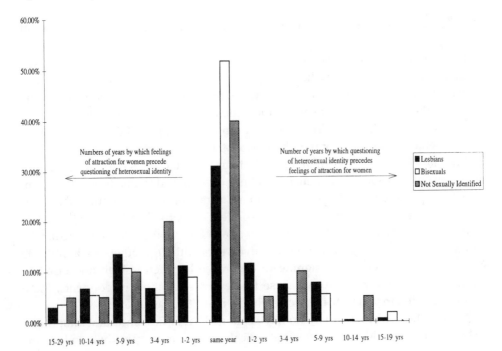

Figure 26.3: Time Lapse between Initial Lesbian or Bisexual Identification and Subsequent Change in Sexual Identification

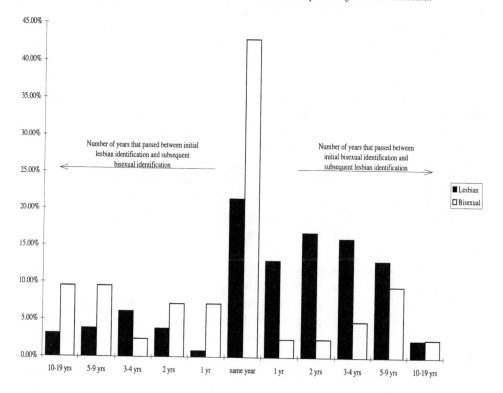

average differences between women with different sexual identities that are presented in Table 26.1. There is, however, one consistent difference between the patterns found among bisexual women and those found among lesbians; on almost every measure, bisexual women describe less "stable" identity histories than lesbians. Most lesbians initially adopted a lesbian identity and have maintained it ever since. Bisexual women, on the other hand, are more likely to wonder about or change their sexual identities, and they change identities more rapidly and more frequently than lesbians.

Discussion

Previous authors' descriptions of sexual identity formation as a developmental process were based upon the calculated average ages at which various milestone events occurred in subjects' lives. When presented in this form, the current findings also suggest that coming out is an orderly, stage-sequential process. The average ages at which lesbians in the current study first experienced homosexual attraction, first questioned their heterosexual identities, and first identified themselves as lesbians are consistent with the findings of previous research. Also consistent with previous research, bisexuals in the current study apparently came out more slowly and at older ages than lesbians.

But the statistical distributions behind these averages tell a different story. Most individuals do not progress through stages in an orderly sequence. On the contrary, as first noted by Blumstein and Schwartz (1976, 1977), individuals often switch back and forth between sexual identities. Women in the current study also experience periods of ambivalence during which they wonder about their sexual identities and periods during which they have no particular sexual identity. Different individuals experience different events in different orders; in fact, with the exception of questioning heterosexual identity and the near exception of experiencing homosexual feelings, none of the assessed events was experienced by all of the women in the current study. Although some women do progress from awareness of homosexual feelings to questioning heterosexual identity and then to ultimate and permanent identification as a lesbian, this pattern is by no means universal. Variations on this experience are too common to be considered deviations from the norm. The developmental model must be replaced by a social constructionist model of sexual identity formation in which variation and change are the norm.

Social constructionism teaches that self identity is the result of the interpretation of personal experience in terms of available social constructs. Identity is therefore a reflection of sociopolitical organization rather than a reflection of essential organization, and coming out is the process of describing oneself in terms of social constructs rather than a process of discovering one's essence. By describing oneself in terms provided by one's social context, one locates oneself within this social context and defines one's relations to other individuals, groups, and sociopolitical institutions in this context. For example, a woman may adopt lesbian identity as a representation of her relationship to her woman lover and the differential romantic potential of her relationships with women and men in general, as well as her structural location vis-à-vis sociopolitical institutions such as the lesbian movement, legal marriage, Judeo-Christian religions, and the tax and social welfare structures. Heterosexual identity would imply a very different set of structural relations to these individuals, groups, and institutions.

Unlike individual essences, social contexts are constantly changing. Within the developmental model of coming out, changes in self-identity are considered indicative of immaturity, that is, signs that one is still in the process of development. The achievement of homosexual identity signals the achievement of maturity, and, once achieved, this identity is expected to be permanent. In contrast, within the social constructionist model of identity formation, changes in self-identity may in fact be necessary in order to maintain an accurate description of one's social location within a changing social context; hence changes in self-identity are to be expected of psychologically and socially mature individuals.

There are many types of changes in social context that may lead to changes in one's sexual self-identity. First, the social constructs that provide a language for the description of social location change over time. Historical changes in the conceptualization of sexuality change the meaning of existing constructs and generate new constructs. As an example of the former, although the homosexual construct has existed since the late 1800s, it has changed from a descriptive clinical category to a pejorative psychoanalytic category to a category imbued with myriad positive social and political meanings. Such changes in meaning are often symbolized by changes in terminology. For example, Ulrichs' urnings became yesterday's homophiles and today's gay men, and yesterday's gay girls are today's lesbian feminists. Changes in meaning are not always symbolized by changes in terminology, however; for example, a lesbian feminist identity represented a very different relationship to the feminist movement in 1972 than it did in the late 1970s. In response to changes in the meanings of constructs and the terminology used to represent them, individuals must sometimes update the language they use to describe their own social locations or risk misrepresenting themselves to others.

As an example of the latter, contemporary academic and political discourse on sexuality is constructing bisexuality. As this discourse continues, the bisexual construct will take shape and become increasingly available as a category for the description of social location. As it does, the homosexual and heterosexual constructs must also change to accommodate it, and some individuals will modify their language of self-description. For example, a woman who was heterosexually married prior to her current union with another woman could comfortably call herself a lesbian during the late 1970s and 1980s, when the lesbian construct did not imply the absence of previous heterosexual relations. During the 1990s, however, it will become increasingly difficult for her to maintain this lesbian identity as the bisexual construct becomes the accepted descriptor for a mix of homosexual and heterosexual relations. At some point, she might find that the term *lesbian* no longer accurately describes her social location because it denies the fact that she has an ex-husband.

Second, social constructs vary cross-(sub)culturally. Some of this variation reflects the fact that historical changes occur more quickly in some cultural pockets than others, and some reflects racial-ethnic, class, generational, geographic, and political differences in the social construction of sexuality. An individual might use different constructs to accurately describe her social location within different cultural contexts. For example, a woman who occupies a progressive position vis-à-vis lesbian and gay political institutions might call herself a lesbian when speaking to her parents but call herself a queer when she attends a planning meeting for a Lesbian and Gay Pride March. Her parents have never heard of Queer Nation and would not understand the reference to this branch of sexual politics, whereas her co-planners would underestimate her affinity for other sexual and genderal minorities if she identified herself as a lesbian to them. Even though this woman presents herself differently within these different contexts, she probably does not feel that she is misrepresenting herself to either audience. On the contrary, she is merely using the language that most accurately describes herself within each context.

Third, the sociopolitical landscape upon which one locates oneself can change. As new political movements emerge, develop, and change, new social and political institutions are built, and new social and political positions are created. In other words, old landmarks disappear and new ones appear. Language that locates oneself in relation to old landmarks becomes meaningless as these landmarks fade; eventually, such language locates one within a historical context but can not accurately describe one's location within the contemporary sociopolitical context.

Finally, one's own location within a sociopolitical context can change. As one develops new relationships with other individuals, groups, and sociopolitical institutions, new self-descriptions become necessary. For example, when a woman who identified herself as a homosexual because she read the word *homosexual* in a book from the HQ section of her local library discovers and joins the lesbian community, she may begin to call herself lesbian instead of homosexual. Her new lesbian identity represents her membership in this community. Then, when she falls in love with a man, she may begin to call herself a bisexual in order to acknowledge this relationship. When she is told by other lesbians that it is OK for her to sleep with a man, but that she should still call herself a lesbian in order to protest heterosexism, she may begin to call herself a lesbian again. Her renewed lesbian identity represents a commitment to the lesbian political movement.

But individuals themselves generally do not experience their sexual identities as socially constructed and variable descriptions of their social locations. They experience their own sexuality as stable (Blumstein and Schwartz 1977; Richardson and Hart 1981) and essential (Hart 1984; Ponse 1978, 1980; Richardson 1981; Warren 1974, 1980), and they retrospectively perceive changes in their sexual identities as part of a goal-oriented process of discovering and accepting this essential sexuality. Popular essentialism is an integral part of the social context within which individuals seek to locate themselves. If a social constructionist model of sexual identity formation is to be useful, it must account for the fact that the process is understood as a goal-oriented process of essential discovery by those who experience it (cf. Epstein 1987). This is accomplished by recognizing that goals themselves are constructed. In short, the social constructionist must avoid incorporating essentialist goals into theories of sexual identity formation, but allow for the possibility that individuals who are creating their own identities will introduce their own goals.

Individuals choose their goals from the options they perceive, and these options are defined by the available social constructs. As a result, most individuals who are searching for sexual identity perceive heterosexual identity and homosexual identity as the two possible options. Because bisexuality is still not considered an authentic form of sexuality in popular discourse, few perceive bisexual identity as a valid, permanent option. The goal introduced into the coming out process by the identity-seeking individual, then, is to discover whether her essence is really heterosexual or homosexual. This determination is made through the observation of evidence that is believed to reflect essence—her own sexual thoughts, feelings, and behaviors. The catch is that for many individuals, this evidence is neither consistently heterosexual nor consistently homosexual. The result is that people whose experience of sexuality is highly varied try to fit themselves into a dichotomous model of sexuality.

Heterosexual and homosexual constructs are not equally matched players in this game, however. Because individuals are raised to assume heterosexual identities, the development of non heterosexual identity requires the perception of a contradiction between one's initial heterosexual identity and one's own psycho-sexual experience. Much experience goes unacknowledged and uncodified, particularly experience that does not fit into an existing perceptual schema or that is socially disapproved (Plummer 1984). Heterosexual identity serves as a perceptual schema that filters and guides the interpretation of experience; experiences are given meanings that are consistent with heterosexual identity. Same sex attractions and intimate relationships that might otherwise be viewed as homosexual can be interpreted as platonic or transitory or attributed to nonessential causes, such as drunkenness or situational constraints, whereas comparable other sex attractions and relationships are interpreted as reflections of heterosexual essence.

It follows that the likelihood that one will perceive a contradiction depends on the capacity of the heterosexual construct to provide credible meanings for same sex experiences, the degree to which one's same sex experiences challenge this capacity, and the availability of non-heterosexual constructs. Generally speaking, the heterosexual construct provides meanings for a wide range of psycho-social experiences and owes its persistence to this ability to "co-opt" potentially challenging experiences. There is, however, no monolithic heterosexual construct; the construct varies in breadth and rigidity across social contexts. A heterosexual identity that is grounded in a rigid and narrow concept of heterosexuality is more easily broken than one that is more flexible. Because male heterosexuality is more rigidly defined and more exclusive of intimate same sex interaction than female heterosexuality, men tend to come out at earlier ages and more rapidly than women.

Even female heterosexuality is incapable of providing meanings for all same-sex experience, however. Although much same-sex hugging and kissing and even sexual contact can be reconciled with heterosexual identity under the rubric of "practice for the real thing," ongoing homosexual relationships and postadolescent experiences present a greater challenge. Women whose experiences are more challenging to the heterosexual construct are more likely to search for alternative sources of meaning for these experiences, and to do so with less delay than women whose experiences are readily interpretable within the heterosexual construct. Moreover, because constructs capable of accounting for both heterosexual and homosexual experience are largely unavailable, experiences cannot be given homosexual meaning without calling into question the heterosexual meanings that have already been given to other experiences. Thus women whose histories are heavily invested with heterosexual meaning or whose other sexual experiences have no credible interpretation within the homosexual construct are less likely to attribute homosexual meanings to same-sex experiences. Furthermore, if and when these women begin to reinterpret these experiences, they will do so more gradually if only because of the sheer volume of heterosexual meaning which must be reexamined. Some of these women may eventually hit on the bisexual construct as a suitable framework for the interpretation of their experience, but this process will also be delayed by the relative unavailability of the bisexual construct.

Therefore, women with more heterosexual and less homosexual experience are expected to retain heterosexual identity more effectively and for longer periods of time than women with less heterosexual and more homosexual experience. The finding that bisexual-identified women became aware of their homosexual feelings and questioned their heterosexual identities at older ages than lesbian-identified women supports this argument; if those who now call themselves bisexual experience higher ratios of heterosexual: homosexual experience,[4] then they were able to maintain heterosexual identities for longer periods of time.

One might expect that individuals who come out at older ages would continue to exhibit greater "inertia" once they did come out. In fact, however, the current findings indicate that once bisexual-identified women begin to come out they do so more quickly than lesbians and subsequently exhibit less, not more, identity stability than lesbian-identified women. Social interactionists have argued that the greater instability of bisexual identity is attributable to dichotomous thinking about sexuality and the lack of social support for bisexual identity—the same factors that delay the coming out process among bisexuals. They suggest that bisexuals change identities and wonder if they have adopted the right identity frequently because they are trying to fit themselves into a typology that does not describe their experience of themselves. Lesbians, on the other hand, exhibit more stable identity histories because the dichotomous typology provides a more adequate fit for their experience.

But this argument rests upon the questionable assumption that the bisexual construct remains unavailable to an individual even after she has adopted a bisexual identity and implies that bisexual women are engaged in a constant search for a satisfying sexual identity. It is quite possible that, at any given moment, women who switch back and forth between different sexual identities feel that the identity they currently possess is entirely satisfactory. Although the bisexual women in the current study are more likely than lesbians to have ever wondered about their identities and very likely to have done so within the past year, they are no more likely than lesbians to be wondering about their sexual identity at the current time. Presumably, therefore, they are momentarily satisfied with the bisexual identity they currently possess. What changes cause these women to become dissatisfied with a previously satisfactory identity more frequently than currently lesbian-identified women do?

One's self-identity is a description of one's social location. Changes in identity are to be expected of mature individuals and reflect changes in these individuals' social locations or in the language used to describe social location. But change is as socially constructed as the constructs that are being exchanged. One cannot cross a fence that has not been built no matter how many times one walks across the field; similarly, one cannot "change" if categories of meaning have not been constructed on the experiential space one traverses. Conversely, the construction of categories creates the possibility of change. In particular, the construction of sexual categories based on partner gender creates a boundary that bifurcates sexual experiential space. A woman who repeatedly crosses this boundary as she accumulates psychosexual experience, that is a "*bisexual*," gives the appearance of sexual mutability and inconsistency. In contrast, a woman whose sexual experience consistently lies on one side of this boundary gives the appearance of greater sexual constancy—

unless and until she, too, crosses the boundary. The former woman may adopt bisexual, lesbian, or heterosexual identities at different points in time depending on the particular constellations of relationships represented by her sexual identity at these different times, whereas the latter woman will probably maintain a consistent lesbian or a consistent heterosexual identity.

Both lay and scientific authors frequently confuse the concepts of bisexuality and sexual mutability because of a failure to recognize the constructed nature of change. Bisexuality is perceived as sexual mutability only because the observer perceives sexuality in terms of the dichotomous constructs, heterosexuality and homosexuality. Perceived without benefit of this dichotomous framework, the bisexual is a person who is consistently open to having lovers of either gender, or to whom gender is as irrelevant as eye color. The bisexual is not more essentially or socially mutable than is the lesbian or the heterosexual; the appearance of greater change is a product of the socially constructed context within which the bisexual is beheld.

Descriptions of bisexuality as sexual mutability are often associated with an idealized conception of bisexuality as the most open form of sexuality. In this view, bisexuals are seen as individuals who have overcome repressive sexual scripts to enable themselves to experience the whole range of their human sexual emotions or as individuals who are uniquely nondiscriminatory in their lovemaking. These appealing images of bisexuality are merely euphemistic variations on earlier stereotypes of bisexuals as indecisive, promiscuous, and fickle. Both conceptions of bisexuality ultimately rest on an outdated dichotomous conception of sexuality that reifies the importance of gender as a criterion in the choice of sexual partners.

Changes in the conceptualization of sexuality must be accompanied by parallel changes in models of sexual identity formation. Outdated developmental models can be replaced by an understanding of sexual identity formation as an ongoing dynamic process of describing one's social location within a changing social context. Identity change should no longer be understood as a sign of immaturity but as a normal outcome of the dynamic process of identity formation that occurs as mature individuals respond to changes in the available social constructs, the sociopolitical landscape, and their own positions on that landscape.

Notes

1. The positive value assigned to homosexual identity by developmental theorists was at least in part a reaction to the negative value assigned to homosexuality by the illness model of homosexuality (Coleman 1982). Whereas the illness model presented heterosexual identity as the desirable goal of a process of treatment for homosexuality, developmental theorists presented homosexual identity as the desirable goal of a process of essential self-discovery.

Ironically, the assumption of homosexual essence is based on the privileged status accorded heterosexuality in society. Because homosexuality is suppressed in a heterosexually dominated society, an individual who displays any evidence of homosexuality is suspected of being homosexual despite concurrent evidence of heterosexuality. Evidence of heterosexuality is easily dismissed as an attempt to conceal one's homosexuality, whereas evidence of homosexuality can only be explained as a reflection of the essence of the individual (Zinik 1985, 10).

2. Sexual self-identity was assessed with the question "when you think about your sexual orientation, what word do you use most often to describe yourself?" a question designed to elicit expressions of self-identity rather than presented or perceived identity. Respondents chose from among the following responses: lesbian, gay, dyke, homosexual, bisexual, mainly straight or heterosexual but with some bisexual tendencies, unsure (don't know, undecided, or still wondering), and "I prefer not to label myself."

3. Respondents were not asked whether they had ever returned to a heterosexual identity. Future research in this area should include this question as well as other more detailed questions about the sequence and circumstances surrounding identity changes.

4. The psychosocial experiences of the lesbian-identified and bisexual-identified women in this study have been described elsewhere (Rust-Rodríguez 1989) and are consistent with this argument. Bisexual respondents have higher ratios of heterosexual: homosexual feelings of sexual attraction and report having more recent and more serious heterosexual relationships than do lesbian respondents. Some of this difference may be due to differential interpretation of experience in retrospect. The fact of marriage, however, is not subject to interpretation; bisexual respondents are more likely to have been married than lesbian respondents.

References

Bell, Alan P., and Martin S. Weinberg. 1978. *Homosexualities: A study of diversity among men and women.* New York: Simon and Schuster.

Bell, Alan P., Martin S. Weinberg, and Sue Kiefer Hammersmith. 1981. *Sexual preference: Its development in men and women.* Bloomington: Indiana University Press.

Blumstein, Philip, and Pepper Schwartz. 1974. Lesbianism and Bisexuality. In *Sexual deviance and sexual deviants,* edited by Erich Goode. New York: Morrow.

—— 1976. Bisexuality in Men. *Urban Life* 5(3):339–358.

—— 1977. Bisexuality: Some Social Psychological Issues. *Journal of Social Issues* 33(2):30–45.

—— 1990. Intimate Relationships and the Creation of Sexuality. In *Homosexuality/heterosexuality: Concepts of sexual orientation,* edited by David P. McWhirter, Stephanie A. Sanders, and June Machover Reinisch. New York: Oxford University Press.

Califia, Pat. 1979. Lesbian Sexuality. *Journal of Homosexuality* 4(3):255–266.

Cass, Vivienne C. 1979. Homosexual Identity Formation: A Theoretical Model. *Journal of Homosexuality* 4(3):219–235.

——. 1984. Homosexual Identity: A Concept in Need of Definition. *Journal of Homosexuality* 9(2,3):105–125.

—— 1990. The Implications of Homosexual Identity Formation for the Kinsey Model and Scale of Sexual Preference. In *Homosexuality/heterosexuality: Concepts of sexual orientation,* edited by David P. McWhirter, Stephanie A. Sanders, and June Machover Reinisch. New York: Oxford University Press.

Chapman, Beata E., and JoAnn C. Brannock. 1987. Proposed Model of Lesbian Identity Development: An Empirical Examination. *Journal of Homosexuality* 14(3/4):69–80.

Coleman, Eli. 1982. Developmental Stages of the Coming Out Process. *Journal of Homosexuality* 7:31–43.

Cronin, Denise M. 1974. Coming Out Among Lesbians. In *Sexual deviance and sexual deviants,* edited by Erich Goode and Richard R. Troiden, 268–277. New York: Morrow.

Daniel, David G., Virginia Abernethy, and William R. Oliver. 1984. Correlations between Female Sex Roles and Attitudes toward Male Sexual Dysfunction in Thirty Women. *Journal of Sex and Marital Therapy* 10(3):160–169.

Dank, Barry M. 1971. Coming Out in the Gay World. *Psychiatry* 34:180–197.

de Monteflores, Carmen, and Stephen J. Schultz. 1978. Coming Out: Similarities and Differences for Lesbians and Gay Men. *Journal of Homosexuality* 34(3):59–72.

Engel, John W., and Marie Saracino. 1986. Love Preferences and Ideals: A Comparison of Homosexual, Bisexual, and Heterosexual Groups. *Contemporary Family Therapy* 8(3): 241–250.

Epstein, Steven. 1987. Gay Politics, Ethnic Identity: The Limits of Social Constructionism. *Socialist Review* 17(3/4):9–53.

Fein, Sara Beck, and Elane M. Nuehring. 1982. Intrapsychic Effects of Stigma: A Process of Breakdown and Reconstruction of Social Reality. *Journal of Homosexuality* 7(1):3–13.

Hart, John. 1984. Therapeutic Implications of Viewing Sexual Identity in Terms of Essentialist and Constructionist Theories. *Journal of Homosexuality* 9(4):39–51.

Hencken, Joel D., and William T. O'Dowd. 1977. Coming Out as an Aspect of Identity Formation. *Gai Saber* 1(1):18–22.

Hooker, Evelyn. 1967. The Homosexual Community. In *Sexual deviance,* edited by John H. Gagnon, and William Simon. New York: Harper and Row.

Jay, K., and A. Young (eds.) 1979. *The gay report: Lesbians and gay men speak out about sexual experiences and lifestyles.* New York: Simon and Schuster.

Kinsey, Alfred Charles, W. B. Pomeroy, and C. E. Martin. 1948. *Sexual behavior in the human male.* Philadelphia: W. B. Saunders.

Kinsey, Alfred Charles, W. B. Pomeroy, and Paul H. Gebhard. 1953. *Sexual behavior in the human female.* Philadelphia: W. B. Saunders.

Klein, Fritz, Barry Sepekoff, and Timothy J. Wolf. 1985. Sexual Orientation: A Multi-Variable Dynamic Process. In *Two lives to lead: Bisexuality in men and women,* edited by Fritz Klein and Timothy Wolf. New York: Harrington Park Press.

Kooden, H. D., S. F. Morin, D. I. Riddle, M. Rogers, B. E. Sang, and F. Strassburger. 1979. Removing the Stigma: Final Report of the Board of Social and Ethical Responsibility for Psychology's Task Force on the Status of Lesbian and Gay Male Psychologists. Washington, DC: American Psychological Association. September.

LaTorre, Ronald A., and Kristina Wendenburg. 1983. Psychological Characteristics of Bisexual, Heterosexual and Homosexual Women. *Journal of Homosexuality* 9(1):87–97.

Lee, John Alan. 1977. Going Public: A Study in the Sociology of Homosexual Liberation. *Journal of Homosexuality* 3(1):49–79.

Loewenstein, Sophie Freud. 1985. On the Diversity of Love Object Orientations Among Women. *Journal of Social Work and Human Sexuality* 3(2/3):7–24.

Lyter, David W., Ronald O. Valdiserri, Lawrence A. Kingsley, William P. Amoroso, and Charles R. Rinaldo. 1987. The HIV Antibody Test: Why Gay and Bisexual Men Want or Do Not Want to Know Their Results. *Public Health Reports* 102:468–474.

McCusker, Jane, Jane G. Zapka, Anne M. Stoddard and Kenneth H. Mayer. 1989. Responses to the AIDS Epidemic Among Homosexually Active Men: Factors Associated with Preventive Behavior. *Patient Education and Counseling* 13:15–30.

MacDonald, A. P., Jr. 1981. Bisexuality: Some Comments on Research and Theory. *Journal of Homosexuality* 6(3):21–35.

—— 1983. A Little Bit of Lavender Goes a Long Way: A Critique of Research on Sexual Orientation. *Journal of Sex Research* 19(1):94–100.

McDonald, Gary J. 1982. Individual Differences in the Coming Out Process for Gay Men: Implications for Theoretical Models. *Journal of Homosexuality* 8(1):47–60.

Nichols, Margaret. 1988. Bisexuality in Women: Myths, Realities, and Implications for Therapy. *Women and Therapy* 7(2/3):235–252.

Nurius, Paula S. 1983. Mental Health Implications of Sexual Orientation. *Journal of Sex Research* 19(2):119–136.

Paul, Jay P. 1985. Bisexuality: Reassessing Our Paradigms of Sexuality. In *Two lives to lead: Bisexuality in men and women,* edited by Fritz Klein and Timothy Wolf. New York: Harrington Park Press.

Plummer, Kenneth. 1975. *Sexual stigma: An interactionist account*. London: Routledge and Kegan Paul.

Plummer, Kenneth. 1984. Sexual Diversity: A Sociological Perspective. In *The psychology of sexual diversity*, edited by Kevin Howells. New York: Blackwell.

Ponse, Barbara. 1978. *Identities in the lesbian world: The social construction of self*. Westport: Greenwood.

—— 1980. Lesbians and Their World. In *Homosexual behavior: A modern reappraisal*, edited by Judd Marmor. New York: Basic Books.

Richardson, Diane. 1981. Lesbian Identities. In *The theory and practice of homosexuality*, edited by John Hart and Diane Richardson. London: Routledge and Kegan Paul.

Richardson, Diane, and John Hart. 1981. The Development and Maintenance of a Homosexual Identity. In *The theory and practice of homosexuality*, edited by John Hart and Diane Richardson. London: Routledge and Kegan Paul.

Riddle, D., and S. Morin. 1977. Removing the Stigma: Data from Institutions. *APA Monitor* November: 16–28.

Ross, Michael W. 1984. Beyond the Biological Model: New Directions in Bisexual and Homosexual Research. *Journal of Homosexuality* 10(3/4):63–70.

Rust-Rodríguez, Paula C. 1989. *When does the unity of "common oppression" break down: Reciprocal attitudes between lesbian and bisexual women*. Ph.D. diss., University of Michigan, Ann Arbor.

Rust, Paula C. 1992. The Politics of Sexual Identity: Sexual Attraction and Behavior among Lesbian and Bisexual Women. *Social Problems* 39: 366–86.

Schäfer, Siegrid. 1976. Sexual and Social Problems of Lesbians. *Journal of Sex Research* 12(1):50–69.

Shively, Michael G., and John P. De Cecco. 1977. Components of Sexual Identity *Journal of Homosexuality* 3:41–48.

Siegel, Karolynn, Laurie J. Bauman, Grace H. Christ, and Susan Krown. 1988. Patterns of Change in Sexual Behavior among Gay Men in New York City. *Archives of Sexual Behavior* 17(6):481–497.

Smith, Elaine M., Susan R. Johnson, and Susan M. Guenther. 1985. Health Care Attitudes and Experiences During Gynecologic Care Among Lesbians and Bisexuals. *American Journal of Public Health* 75(9):1085–1087.

Stokes, Kirk, Peter R. Kilmann, and Richard L. Wanlass. 1983. Sexual Orientation and Sex Role Conformity. *Archives of Sexual Behavior* 12(5):427–433.

Troiden, Richard R. 1988. *Gay and lesbian identity: A sociological analysis*. Dix Hills, NY: General Hall.

Troiden, Richard R., and Erich Goode. 1980. Variables Related to the Acquisition of a Gay Identity. *Journal of Homosexuality* 5(4):383–392.

Warren, Carol A. B. 1974. *Identity and community in the gay world*. New York: John Wiley.

—— 1980. Homosexuality and Stigma. In *Homosexual behavior: A modern reappraisal*, edited by Judd Marmor. New York: Basic Books.

Winkelstein, Warren, David M. Lyman, Nancy Padian, Robert Grant, Michael Samuel, James A. Wiley, Robert E. Anderson, William Lang, John Riggs, and Jay A. Levy. 1987. Sexual Practices and Risk of Infection by the Human Immunodeficiency Virus. *Journal of the American Medical Association* 257(3):321–325.

Zinik, Gary. 1985. Identity Conflict or Adaptive Flexibility? Bisexuality Reconsidered. In *Two lives to lead: Bisexuality in men and women*, edited by Fritz Klein and Timothy Wolf. New York: Harrington Park Press.

9

From Bisexual Chic to Bisexual Activism

27

Popular Images and the Growth of Bisexual Community and Visibility

Paula C. Rodríguez Rust

IN JULY 1995 *Newsweek* announced that bisexuality had emerged as a "new sexual identity."[1] But self-identified bisexuals and bisexual organizations were not new. Social groups for bisexuals existed in the 1970s and bisexuals were active in the sexual liberation and early gay liberation movements when the modern popular press proclaimed that bisexuality was chic. Bisexual organizations multiplied in the 1980s when the popular press warned heterosexual women that their husbands might be secret bisexuals who would bring HIV home to them. So, when *Newsweek* announced the appearance of bisexuality in 1995, many bisexuals commented that it was not new at all for them. But there was something different about bisexuality in the mid-1990s. A growing political self-consciousness and formalized networking among bisexual organizations distinguished bisexuality in the 1990s from bisexuality in previous decades. As the 1990s progressed, bisexuality became more visible and bisexuals created a community and a political movement that was unprecedented. This chapter explores the growth of that community and the changes that occurred in popular images of bisexuality during the 1970s, 1980s, and 1990s.

Bisexual Chic: The 1970s

"Everybody does bisexuality now. It's really big," commented a nineteen-year-old Vassar sophomore in the pages of *Newsweek* in 1974.[2] And why shouldn't they? Celebrities like Kate Millett, David Bowie, Janis Joplin, and Joan Baez were doing it, and Mick Jagger was singing love songs to his drummer. "It has become very fashionable in elite and artistically creative subgroups to be intrigued by the notion of bisexuality," said psychiatrist Norman Fisk of the Gender Dysphoria Program at Stanford University Medical School, according to *Time Magazine*.[3] In the *New York*

Times Jane E. Brody reported that "experts" had noticed a "definite increase" among women in this "age-old but still largely mysterious lifestyle." *Cosmopolitan* asked readers, "Could *you* be ready for a lesbian encounter? Well, a surprising number of perfectly 'normal' man-loving females *are*" (Margold 1974:189). *Time* attributed the fashionability of bisexuality to the feminist movement's promotion of "sisterly love" and the "invention of mass birth control." The *New York Times* cited Richard Green's and Pepper Schwartz's theories of the role of cultural femininity and the feminist movement in facilitating lesbian experiences among women who might otherwise be heterosexual. *Newsweek* pointed to growing acceptance of homosexuality and the rise of unisex styles that blurred the "line between the sexes until they overlapped [and] the only thing left to swap was sex itself" (see chapter 28, this volume).

Bisexuality's sudden burst into public view in the 1970s probably had as much to do with the vagaries of publicity as with any real increase in bisexuality. By proclaiming bisexuality a chic new sexual trend, popular magazines helped create the very fashionability they were reporting. The public was treated to a flurry of articles bearing names like "The New Bisexuals" (*Time*, May 13, 1974), "Bisexual Chic" (*Oui*, February 1974), "Bisexual Chic: Anyone Goes" (*Newsweek*, May 27, 1974), and "Bisexuality: The Newest Sex-Style" (*Cosmopolitan*, June 1974).[4] These articles characterized bisexuality as a new form of sexual openness and a healthy social trend. *Time* was particularly enthusiastic about the "new bisexuals," noting the possibility that bisexuality is the "best of both worlds," sympathically reporting Blumstein and Schwartz's work on the lack of acceptance that bisexuals face among gay men and lesbians, and relegating the "other side of the story"—psychoanalyst Natalie Shainess's view that bisexuals are even more psychologically damaged and unbalanced than homosexuals—to the last paragraph. *Newsweek*, although generally positive about bisexuality, was somewhat less enthusiastic about its alleged growth in popularity. *Newsweek* empathized with the wives of bisexual men and with college students who felt threatened by the trend, and gave a fairly prominent position to Dr. Charles Socarides's view that bisexuality is a cultural disaster; this article is reprinted as chapter 28 in this section. Jane Margold, writing in *Cosmopolitan*, prefaced her exploration of the emotional, personal, and (feminist) political complexities of bisexuality with a defensive emphasis on the "many of us [who] *do* manage to resist [the radical psychosexual climate]" (189). Seeking the middle ground, the *New York Times*'s article "Bisexual Life-style Appears to Be Spreading and Not Necessarily Among Swingers" cited Blumstein and Schwartz's research on the fluidity of sexuality and quoted Shainess and half a dozen other professionals representing various positions in the debate over the "normality" and "health" of bisexuality.

A few social scientists wrote articles for the popular press arguing for the normalization and acceptance of bisexuality and applauding the growing cultural view that sexual openness is healthy and liberatory (cf. Duberman 1974).[5] *Ms. Magazine* published "Bisexuality: Where Love Speaks Louder Than Labels" by Pepper Schwartz and Philip Blumstein and *Redbook* published "Bisexuality: What's It All About?" by Margaret Mead.[6] Blumstein and Schwartz portrayed bisexuals as "caught in the middle." They explored cultural discomfort with people who do not fit easily into sexual categories, and sought acceptance for bisexuality by emphasizing the normality of sexual change over a lifetime. Margaret Mead wrote, "The time has come, I think, when we must recognize bisexuality as a normal form of human behavior." She commented on the new gay liberation movement, observing that "there is not, and it seems unlikely that there will be, a bisexual liberation movement. For the truth is, bisexual men and women do not form a distinct group, since in fact we do not really recognize bisexuality as a form of behavior, normal or abnormal, in our society. Instead we tend to divide people into two groups" (1975: 29). She explored "our" cultural denial of bisexuality's existence and used her anthropological knowledge of historical and cross-cultural diversity in sexual attitudes and practices to encourage her readers to "free men and women alike to live as persons" (31).

Bisexual chic was not confined to the popular magazine market; a number of books on bisexuality also appeared in the 1970s bearing titles like *Loving Them Both: A Study of Bisexuality*, by Colin MacInnes, *Total Sexuality*, by John Warren Wells, *The Bisexuals*, by Bernhardt J. Hurwood, *Bisexuality: Confessions of Bisexual Men and Women*, by Jason Douglas, and, of course, *The Bisexual Option: A Concept of One-Hundred Percent Intimacy*, by Fred (Fritz) Klein.[7] Many books, like Klein's *The Bisexual Option* and Wells's *Total Sexuality*, relied heavily on personal vignettes of individual bisexuals to convince a skeptical public that bisexuality exists and that it can be a healthy lifestyle—possibly healthier than strict hetero- or homosexuality.[8] In *Barry and Alice: Portrait of a Bisexual Marriage* authors Barry Kohn and Alice Matusow documented their own relationship, including both its challenges and rewards. They stressed the importance of being honest with oneself and one's partner, discussed the negative effects of secrecy and sexual shame, and lauded the sexual liberation movement for freeing people from rigid sexual and gender roles and rules.

Other authors were more clinical in their use of bisexuals' personal stories. Although these authors ranged in the degree to which they attributed bisexual behavior to pathological psychological traits, many encouraged the liberalization of public opinion by rejecting earlier professional characterizations of bisexuality as "deviate."[9] For example, in *Bisexual Living* Julius Fast and Hal Wells (1975) presented synopses of interviews with several bisexuals, each followed by an analysis written by Dr. Wells, a clinical psychologist.[10] Although Wells tended to attribute bisexuality to unresolved childhood issues, experimentation or rebelliousness, a need for acceptance grounded in low self-esteem, a last-ditch attempt to save a failing marriage, fear of the opposite sex, or homosexual denial, he also clearly stated that true bisexuality does exist.[11] He looked favorably on the increasing social acceptance of bisexuality and explored theoretical questions that contemporary sexual theorists still discuss. For example, he mused about the definition of bisexuality (how much sex with each sex does one have to have to be a bisexual?), the relationship between sex and love and the possibility of loving two people at the same time, the normalcy of jealousy, whether prostitution is really any different from many other forms of earning a living ("How many men do we know who are in the jobs they are in because they truly like them?" (113), and the implications of binary ("right-wrong") thinking versus moral relativity for the social acceptance of bisexuality. Similarly, in *Strange Loves: The Human Aspects of Sexual Deviation*, Eustace Chesser (1971) discussed bisexuality in the course of essays on sadism, nymphomania, satyriasis, prostitution, and other sexual behaviors. Chesser philosophically concluded that "I have come to realise that many of the problems which seemed at times intractable are not genuine problems at all. They are difficulties of our own making. It has become clear to me that the only rational and humane line to draw in passing judgment on any sort of conduct is between what is anti-social and what harms no one" (24).

Bisexuality, the HIV Gateway: The 1980s

In the context of newly awakened fears of the connection between death and sexuality, the moral admonition to accept behaviors that harm no one carried very different implications for bisexuality in the 1980s than Chesser intended upon writing it in 1971. Initially complacent about the spread of HIV because it was believed to be a "gay disease," policy makers and the general heterosexual population became horrified when they realized—for the second time in as many decades—that homosexual behavior is not limited to "homosexuals," but is practiced by a number of people who also engage in heterosexual behavior. Even more terrifying was the realization that many of these people identify as and appear to be heterosexual. Accordingly, the public response to bisexuality in the 1980s was dramatically different than it had been in the 1970s—bisexuals had fallen from the height of sexual fashionability to become the "ultimate pariahs of the '80s" (Gelman 1987:44, in *Newsweek*; reprinted as chapter 29 in the volume).

The most threatening bisexual figure in the 1980s was the invisible bisexual man—the bisexual man who passed as a heterosexual. He was, in effect, seen as a stealth weapon, carrying the HIV virus into the heterosexual population by infecting his unsuspecting female sex partners. The evil of the bisexual, and the innocence of his female partner, were most dramatic—and made the best copy—when the female partner herself was morally blameless. To be morally blameless, a sexually active woman must be a wife, having sex with her husband. Accordingly, the public was treated to a series of magazine articles in the 1980s and early 1990s warning wives of the prevalence and invisibility of bisexuality among men—particularly among their own apparently heterosexual husbands. *Mademoiselle* asked readers, "Is there a man in your man's life? What every girl should know about the bisexual guy" (Heller 1987). *Redbook* played up the fear of the unknown in "The secret life of bisexual husbands," asserting that "He may be a great husband and a loving father. Yet he could be making love to a man . . . and his wife will be the last to know" (Davidowitz 1993:114; ellipses in original), and *New Woman* told readers that "no woman is safe" (Avery 1991). *Cosmopolitan* authors Susan Gerrard and James Halpin fanned these fears by asserting that "bisexuals are better than other men at hiding infidelities" (1989:204) in their article "The Risky Business of

Bisexual Love." Citing Pepper Schwartz, they gave women signs to look for: "Be suspicious if he seems intensely interested in how other men dress. . . . If he looks into another man's eyes for even a microsecond longer than it takes to make socially acceptable eye contact, beware. Heterosexual men do not do it" (204). *Newsweek*, described bisexuality as "A Perilous Double Love Life" (Gelman 1987; reprinted as chapter 29 in this section). *Ebony* warned African American women in "The Hidden Fear: Black Women, Bisexuals, and the AIDS Risk" (Randolph 1988), and *Essence* columnist Dr. Gwendolyn Goldsby Grant echoed these fears in "Loving a Bisexual Man" (1986). Concerns about bisexuals and HIV were also addressed and sensationalized in newspapers and talk shows. The *Boston Globe,* for example, reported epidemiological research on HIV and bisexuality conducted by the California Department of Health Services and by Nancy Padian of the University of California under the title "Bisexuals Put Women at Risk, Studies Say."[12] Ann Landers warned readers that "married bisexuals, when presented with a choice, invariably go for members of their own sex. Furthermore, when the proclivity is present, they can be expected to wander off occasionally," and Phil Donahue, in a show titled "A Husband's Secret Sex Life," interviewed "Tom Smith," whose "wife does not know."[13]

Meanwhile, bisexuality was also receiving attention in the lesbian and gay press, although for different reasons. The threat posed by bisexuality to lesbians and gay men was not the threat of HIV infection; gay men had been constructed as the source from which bisexual men would get the HIV that they would give to their heterosexual partners, and lesbians perceived themselves to be safe from HIV infection because of the lack of evidence that HIV could be transmitted through sexual contact between women.[14] Bisexuals were psychologically and socially threatening to lesbians and gay men because they blurred the distinction between straight and lesbian/gay, thus undermining the basis for lesbian and gay identities and quasi-ethnic lesbian and gay political movements. This threat underlay the hostility of lesbians and gay men toward bisexuals that was described in the 1970s by researchers Blumstein and Schwartz, and it found expression in the lesbian and gay press of the 1980s.

The threat of bisexuality to lesbian and gay identities and politics is most effectively neutralized by reinforcing the authenticity and clarity of the distinction between heterosexuality and lesbianism/gayness, and this was the approach generally taken in the gay and lesbian press of the 1980s. Few articles during this period actually mentioned *bisexuality*; instead, the discussion typically revolved around the issue of lesbians having sex with men or gay men having sex with women—constructions of the issue that reimpose dichotomous understandings of sexuality on the experience of bisexuality. For example, the *Advocate* published "Gay Men, Lesbians and Sex" by Pat Califia in July 1983, "Yes, I'm Still a Lesbian—Even Though I Love a Man" by Harriet Laine in July 1986, and "Unresolved Harmonies: The Ups and Downs of Not Quite Coming Out" by Mark Chaim Evans in November 1989. Although all these authors discussed their sexual desires or contacts with both men and women, none felt that the term *bisexual* described their experiences and only Califia affirmed the existence of bisexuality. The letters to the editor following these articles indicated that the *Advocate*'s readers accepted the issue as concerning heterosex among lesbians and gay men; none reframed the issue in terms of bisexuality (Rust 1995a). Similarly, in 1983 the second issue of *Lesbian Contradiction* included, "Many Lesbians Are Going Straight Now . . .—A Conversation," consisting of thirteen comments written on a women's bathroom wall, and in 1988 and 1989 the same newspaper published "Desire and Consequences: Sleeping with a Strange Man" by Juana Maria Paz, "A Second Coming Out" by Stephanie Sugars, and "I'm Still a Lesbian" by Jane Dwinell.[15] Readers generally blasted the authors, especially Paz and Dwinell, for using lesbian space to discuss their heterosexuality and for failing to recognize their heterosexual privilege, not for their bisexuality.

When bisexuality was mentioned explicitly in the lesbian and gay press, its political, if not its experiential, reality was often questioned, and individuals who called themselves bisexual or behaved bisexually were typically characterized as fence-sitters who could not be trusted to remain faithful lovers or loyal comrades in the struggle against heterosexism. In "Thinking About Bisexuality," for example, Marilyn Murphy and Irene Weiss asserted the political nonexistence of bisexuality, arguing that bisexual women are the only true "heterosexual" women because they are the only women who knowingly choose heterosexuality with full knowledge of the alternative.[16] In the 1983 April Fool's issue, the *Gay Community News* (*GCN*) published a cartoon that soon became infamous among bisexuals. The cartoon depicted a lesbian whose bisexual lover had just left her, and the punch line concerned the need for "bisexual insurance."

The rejection of the lesbian and gay communities and the finger pointing of the mainstream press spurred bisexuals—who had already formed organizations in many major cities—into a new wave of political organizing.[17] For example, the Bivocals, a bisexual women's discussion group, had been meeting at the Cambridge Women's Center for several months when the bisexual insurance cartoon appeared in *GCN*. In response to the cartoon, the Bivocals, including Lisa Orlando, called a women's bisexual support network meeting in June 1983. The meeting led to the formation of the Boston Bisexual Women's Network (BBWN), which became one of the most long-standing and politically active local bisexual organizations in the United States.[18] Marcia Deihl (1989) later analogized the cartoon's role in the development of the bisexual movement to the role of the 1969 police raid of the Stonewall Bar in the development of the gay liberation movement. Before long BBWN began publishing *Bi Women*, which celebrated its fifteenth year of publication in 1997. Later in the 1980s other bisexual organizations began publishing newsletters; notable among them is the Seattle Bisexual Women's Network, which celebrated its tenth year of publishing *North Bi Northwest* in 1997.

Newly politicized bisexual individuals and newly formed bisexual political organizations responded to unflattering coverage of bisexuality in both the lesbian and gay and the mainstream presses. Readers of lesbian and gay publications protested the denial of bisexuality's existence as an authentic sexuality. For example, in 1985 a female reader asked the *Advocate* why the word *bisexual* had been put in quotation marks in a paragraph about Elton John and a male reader questioned the magazine's characterization of Jacob Holdt as a heterosexual who had had sexual experience with a man.[19] Bisexual activists also wrote letters to popular magazine editors, protesting stereotypical characterizations of bisexuals as HIV carriers and secretive adulterers. For example, following their articles on bisexual transmission of HIV to women, *Cosmopolitan, Newsweek,* and *Ebony* received letters to the editor written by bisexual men and women and their allies. Some of these letters, such as one from Robyn Ochs objecting to *Newsweek*'s characterization of bisexuals as more sexually irresponsible than heterosexuals, in "A Perilous Double Love Life," and a multiauthored letter to *Ms.* commenting on the "undertone" blaming bisexuals for the spread of AIDS in an article on AIDS and women, were published by the magazines in question, but other letters never reached the eyes of the articles' original audiences.[20] Some of these letters were published in the gay press or in bisexual newsletters; *Gay Community News,* which had become more bi-sensitive since 1983, published several such letters.[21] The Bisexual Archives, maintained by the Bisexual Resource Center (formerly the East Coast Bisexual Network) in Boston, collects both published and unpublished letters to the editor sent to mainstream publications in response to their coverage of bisexuality. This collection includes letters from Barbara Smith to *Ebony,* from Lucy Friedland to *Newsweek,* and from Pamela Lipshutz and the Bisexual Committee Engaging in Politics (BiCEP) and the Bay Area Bisexual Network to *Cosmopolitan.*[22]

Bisexuals did not remain reactive for long; in the hope of influencing public images of bisexuality and discouraging its stereotypical coverage by the press, bisexual activists made themselves available for interviews with journalists. Articles giving voice to bisexuals and focusing on bisexuals' own concerns, instead of on lesbians', gays', and heterosexuals' concerns about bisexuality, began to appear in gay, lesbian, and other alternative and progressive publications. As early as 1983 the *San Francisco Chronicle* described "How Bisexuals Face a Hostile World" (Sylvia Rubin), featuring cofounders of the San Francisco Bisexual Center David Lourea, who had recently appeared on Phil Donahue's talk show, and Maggi Rubenstein, who would be the New York City Gay and Lesbian Pride March's "first bisexual grand marshal" in 1992.[23] In the same year the *Boston Globe* published "Bisexuality: Toward a New Understanding of Men, Women, and Their Feelings" in which author Arthur Kroeber gently rejected stereotypes of bisexuals as people who are really gay or lesbian or who are confused and unable to commit to long-term relationships. A letter by Lucy Friedland and Liz Nania encouraging bisexuals to be visibly present at the 1987 March on Washington for Lesbian and Gay Rights appeared in *In These Times.*[24] The *Weekly Tab* interviewed activists Lucy Friedland and Robyn Ochs for "Double Perspective" (Ertel 1989). In 1990 Holly Near's "misunderstood sexuality" was the subject of Carol Stocker's article in the *Boston Globe,* and Lani Ka'ahumanu told *Utne Reader* readers that "Bisexuals Battle for Acceptance: Both Heterosexuals and Gays Seem Threatened by the 'Third Category.' " Wayne Scott (1992) told *Changing Men* readers his bisexual coming out story in "Coming Out Both Ways." The *Boston Phoenix* explored relations between bisexuals and the lesbian, gay, and feminist communities and movements in "The Bisexuality Debate: A Struggle for Recognition—and Differentiation" (Tait 1991), and June Jordan (1991) affirmed her bisexuality and argued in the *Progressive* that the "New Politics of Sexuality" was politicizing the "Middle Ground: Bisexuality." In 1992 Kristen Stuenkel told readers of the *Washington Peace Letter* about the Alliance of Multicultural Bisexuals (AMBi), and in 1993 Washington's free weekly, the *City Paper*, published Liza Mundy's cover story, "Black and Bi," profiling School of Divinity Professor Elias Farajajé-Jones.

Bisexuals were not the only ones to express dissatisfaction with traditional sex and gender categories during the 1980s and early 1990s; transgender and queer activism also emerged. Transgenderists questioned traditional therapies designed to reconcile mind and body into conventional male/man or female/woman categories, began opting out of sex reassignment surgery, and shed the clinical term *gender dysphoric* in favor of affirming self-identities as transgenderists. Queer activism emerged in response to the increasingly conventional appearance of the lesbian and gay movement, the slow pace of civil rights advances, and a sex-phobic society's reaction to the deadly disease AIDS. Queer politics, "although given organized body in the activist group Queer Nation, operates largely through the decentralized, local, and often anti-organizational cultural activism of street postering, parodic and non-conformist self-presentation, and underground alternative magazines ('zines')" (Gamson 1995:393).

Because both the bisexual and the transgenderist movements find themselves caught between the desire to deconstruct categories of sex and gender and the desire to develop positive identities in a discourse of identity politics that has thus far excluded them, both bear an ambiguous relationship to the queer movement whose central theme is the "disruption of sex and gender identity boundaries and deconstruction of identity categories" (Gamson 1995:390; cf. "pomosexuality," e.g., Queen and Schimel 1997). This ambiguous relationship is further complicated by the multiple political meanings of *queer* within the context of sexual politics. On one hand, queer as an anti-identity exists outside and in partial conflict with conventional identity-based movements such as the lesbian and gay political movements and with bisexual and transgenderist impulses to build collective identities. On the other hand, *queer* is also used as a new umbrella term to refer to all sexual and gender minorities. As an alternative to the alphabet soup method of naming, it avoids the need to rename organizations and design new pride march banners each year as new minorities appear—"lesbian and gay (LB) . . . and bisexual (LGB) . . . and transgender (LBGT). . ."—and it helps avoid politically incorrect faux pas by eliminating the need either to remember every minority or to reveal whom one would exclude. In this usage bisexuals and transgenderists are the unnamed constituents who are implicitly included when *lesbian and gay* is broadened to *queer*. Some lesbians and gay men object to being swept into a new political category called *queer* because of the pejorative history of the term; Joshua Gamson (1995) argued that underneath these objections is a discomfort with bisexuals and transgenderists in particular because of the challenge they pose to the binary categories of sex and gender upon which lesbian and gay identities depend—in other words, because of the other meaning of the word (see also Humphrey 1999).

Against this queer backdrop, as the 1990s progressed bisexuality received increasingly prominent and favorable coverage in the lesbian and gay press, although debates about queerness and the inclusion of bisexuality—and transgenderism—in the "lesbian and gay" movement continued. Jan Clausen's 1990 *Out/Look* article, "My Interesting Condition," in which the author described herself as a self-identified lesbian woman who became involved with a man and explicitly discussed her refusal to identify as bisexual, touched off a firestorm of letters to the editor that lasted a full year.[25] In spring 1992 the same magazine featured bisexuality, with fifteen pages of cartoons and a selection of articles titled "What Do Bisexuals Want?" "Just Add Water: Searching for the Bisexual Politic," "Strangers at Home: Bisexuals in the Queer Movement," and "Love and Rockets."[26] The editors received such a "striking number of responses" from "bisexuals who felt uncomfortable with the constraints of a 'debate' around bisexuality as we had posited it" that in the next issue they printed a dialogue between three bisexual writers/activists, Amanda Udis-Kessler, Elizabeth Reba Weise, and Sarah Murray, with excerpts from readers' letters in a sidebar.[27] *Lesbian Contradiction* explored the politics of bisexuality in a favorable way and questioned cultural "gender-fetishism" in "Sisterhood Crosses Gender Preference Lines" by Dajenya (1990), "Some Thoughts on Bisexuality" by Jane Litwoman (1990), and "Heads or Tails" by Alena Smith (1993).[28] In June 1991 the *Advocate* published a one-page article by bisexual activists Lani Ka'ahumanu and Loraine Hutchins pointing out that arguments over whether bisexuals should be included in the gay and lesbian movement were specious because bisexuals had always been involved in the so-called lesbian and gay movement.[29] In July 1992 the *Advocate* published Lily Braindrop's description of the growth of the bisexual movement and community and bisexual inclusion in the lesbian and gay movement in "Bi and Beyond." By the early 1990s bisexuality was no longer merely a matter of heterosex among lesbians and gay men, nor merely an "issue" for lesbians and gay men; bisexuals had found their own voice and become a constituency in the lesbian, gay, *and bisexual* movement as well as a political movement of their own.

Bisexuality, a Revolutionary New Political Identity: The 1990s

Bisexuals' political voices also broke the sound barrier between alternative communities and mainstream society in the early 1990s, when the mainstream press discovered bisexuality once again. *Time* was among the first popular magazines to rediscover bisexuality, publishing Anastasia Toufexis's "Bisexuality: What Is It?" in 1992. This time around, however, bisexuality was touted as a "new sexual identity," and a new political movement, that would revolutionize sexuality in the United States. Unlike the 1970s, when popular magazines described bisexuality as a trendy sexual behavior that heterosexuals—and sometimes lesbians and gay men—were enjoying in increasing numbers, or the 1980s, when they described bisexuals as threats to the health of the nation, in the 1990s bisexuality was portrayed as a revolution not in sexual behavior but in the conceptualization of sexuality.[30]

This was bisexual chic personified and with a political edge. In a *Newsweek* article titled "Bisexuality Emerges as a New Sexual Identity" and reprinted in this section as chapter 30, author John Leland characterized 1970s bisexual chic as an "offshoot of the sexual revolution; it was straight, with a twist" whereas "the current bisexual moment [*sic*] rises from the gay and feminist movements" (1995:47) and is therefore more political in character. Journalists interviewed bisexuals themselves and presented bisexuality to the nation through the eyes of bisexual activists and their allies. Leland, for example, cited Rebecca Kaplan, Melissa Merry, William Wedin, Marjorie Garber, Elias Farajajé-Jones, Paula C. Rust, and Martin Weinberg, among others.

Leland exemplified the political characterization of bisexuality by focusing on the cultural challenge posed by bisexual visibility in the 1990s. He pointed out that the existence of bisexuality "makes many people uncomfortable [because] it suggests that all sexual identity might be subject to change." He asserted that "to a social order based on monogamy, bisexuality looms as a potent threat" (47), while it paradoxically also undermines the dichotomous distinction between gay and straight that underlies the association between bisexuality and nonmonogamy in the public mind. Similarly, in "Bisexuality Out of the Closet," Allison Abner (1992) quoted bisexual activist Lani Ka'ahumanu who said that "bisexuality shakes up the rigid assumption that there is only heterosexuality and homosexuality." Incidentally, Abner's article, published in *Essence* six years after that magazine joined the furvor over bisexual husbands, also presented *Essence* columnist Gwendolyn Goldsby Grant's view that lesbian sex was becoming more common among previously heterosexual African American women—along with her theory that African American women were turning to women because of the dearth of eligible Black men.

The political focus of bisexuality in the 1990s was even evident in articles with sexually suggestive titles; in contrast to articles published in the 1970s such as *Cosmopolitan*'s "Bisexuality: The Newest Sex-Style" (Margold 1974), in the 1990s *Lear's* "Bisexuality: Having It All" (1992) and *Vogue*'s "Sex: Going Both Ways" (1995) stopped far short of proclaiming a new era of sexual freedom. Both *Lear's* author Susan Barron and *Vogue* author Robert S. Boynton caught their readers' attention by beginning with anecdotal and sexually focused descriptions of bisexual individuals but quickly moved on to discussions of the challenge posed by bisexuality to familiar, dichotomous sexual categories—in both cases, by the end of the first column. Boynton concluded, "The demise of artificially secure identities is nothing to regret; it is, in fact, a success that we can celebrate" (143).

The focus on politics reflected the centrality of bisexual political activists' voices in the publicity afforded bisexuality in the 1990s, and the fact that the breaking news about bisexuality did indeed concern bisexual politics and not bisexual sexuality. In the late 1980s and early 1990s bisexual organizing, led by activists experienced in feminist, gay and lesbian, and left-wing political movements, had spread rapidly from the local to the national and the international levels. In June of 1990 the North American Multicultural Bisexual Network, later renamed the Bisexual Network of the USA, or BiNet USA, was founded at the BiPOL conference in San

Francisco.[31] Shortly thereafter the scores of local bisexual newsletters that had begun publication during the 1980s were joined by a few national publications, including the short-lived *Bisexuality: News, Views, and Networking,* edited by Gary North, BiNet's national newsletter, titled *BiNet News,* and the first national bisexual magazine, *Anything That Moves,* published by the Bay Area Bisexual Network (BABN). In October 1991 the First International Bisexual Conference was held in Amsterdam, in June 1994 the Third International Conference Celebrating Bisexuality was held in New York City simultaneous with the twenty-fifth anniversary of the Stonewall rebellion, and in May 1996 the Fourth International Bisexual Symposium was held in Berlin.[32] In April 1993 bisexuals marched in the National March on Washington for Lesbian, Gay *and Bi* Rights and Liberation. The *International Directory of Bisexual Groups,* whose first edition listed forty organizations, was expanded by editor Robyn Ochs and renamed the *Bisexual Resource Guide* in 1995. The third edition of the new *Guide,* published in 1999, includes twenty-one hundred bisexual and bisexual-inclusive organizations in fifty-five countries, plus electronic resources, a bi-bliography, and a film guide.

As the 1990s began, books by and for bisexuals also began to appear; Thomas Geller's *Bisexuality: A Reader and Sourcebook* was published in 1990, and Loraine Hutchins and Lani Ka'ahumanu's landmark anthology, *Bi Any Other Name: Bisexual People Speak Out,* written by and for bisexuals, was published in 1991.[33] Containing over seventy poems, personal stories, and essays on bisexual oppression, politics, and spirituality, *Bi Any Other Name* quickly found its way onto the shelves of thousands of bisexuals seeking a way out of isolation. Aimed at a more specific audience, Elizabeth Reba Weise's anthology, *Closer to Home: Bisexuality and Feminism* (1992), explored the relationship between sexuality, sexual behavior, and feminist politics, motivated partially by the need to build a bisexual feminist identity and politics in the face of lesbian feminist criticism of heterosexuality and bisexuality. By the mid 1990s the market for books by and for bisexuals was growing, and the pace of publication stepped up accordingly. Sue George's *Women and Bisexuality* was published in 1993, Naomi Tucker's *Bisexual Politics: Theories, Queries, and Visions* and the Bisexual Anthology Collective's *Plural Desires: Writing Bisexual Women's Realities* appeared in 1995, *Bisexual Horizons,* edited by Sharon Rose and Cris Stevens, was published in London in 1996, and in 1997 Brett Beemyn published *Creating a Place for Ourselves: Lesbian, Gay, and Bisexual Community Histories.*

The rise of bisexual—and transgendered and queer—activism was closely linked to the contemporaneous surge in academic attention to bisexuality in particular and queer theory in general. In part the close link between activism and academia in the bisexual movement is due to the fact that many prominent bisexual activists and political allies are also graduate students, instructors, faculty members, or administrators at colleges and universities. Among bisexual political activists with national reputations in the bisexual community and links to academia are Robyn Ochs, Elias Farajajé-Jones, Brett Beemyn, Fritz Klein, and Maggi Rubenstein. Robyn Ochs designed and taught one of the first college courses on bisexuality. Elias Farajajé-Jones is on the faculty of Howard University. Brett Beemyn coedited *Queer Studies: A Lesbian, Gay, Bisexual, and Transgender Anthology* with Mickey Eliason. Fritz Klein, a psychiatrist and lead developer of the Klein Sexual Orientation Grid, heads a funding organization interested in providing money to promote both scientific research on bisexuality and bisexual community development. Maggi Rubenstein is dean of students at the Institute for the Advanced Study of Human Sexuality in San Francisco.

The link between activism and academia is further strengthened by the fact that many leading bisexual activists, including those who are not academics themselves, pay attention to the theoretical and empirical works of academics.[34] Many academics who publish books on bisexuality intentionally target both academic and popular bisexual audiences, and each new research study on bisexuality becomes a focus of discussion in bisexual electronic mail discussion groups and at bisexual group meetings and conferences. The strengths and weaknesses of the methodology and findings reported in *Dual Attraction: Understanding Bisexuality* (1994), based on research by Martin S. Weinberg, Colin J. Williams, and Douglas W. Pryor, were extensively discussed among bisexual activists. Marjorie Garber's *Vice Versa: Bisexuality and the Eroticism of Everyday Life,* despite its postmodernist jargon and daunting length, also received considerable attention from bisexual activists upon its publication in 1995. Both of these books also received attention from the mainstream press; Marjorie Garber spent some time on the talk show circuit and *Dual Attraction* was reviewed by the *Nation* (Stroud 1994), among other publications. *Bisexuality and the Challenge to Lesbian Politics* brought its author, Paula C. Rust, to the attention of the journalistic mainstream, while the book itself received attention from bisexuals. Other books that grew out of increased bisexual activism, contributed to the growth of bisexual communities and politics, or were discussed on bisexual electronic listserves, although aimed primarily at academic or professional audiences, include Beth A. Firestein's *Bisexuality: The Psychology and Politics of an Invisible Minority* (1996) and Donald E. Hall and Maria Pramaggiore's *RePresenting Bisexualities: Subjects and Cultures of Fluid Desire* (1996). As of this writing, Brett Beemyn and Erich Steinman are in the process of compiling *Facts and Fictions: Experiencing Male Bisexuality* and Haworth Press is preparing to publish the *Journal of Bisexuality,* edited by Fritz Klein, in 2000.

Bisexuals who do not read academic literature are also exposed to academic findings because several bisexual anthologies, edited by bisexuals and intended for the popular bisexual audience, include chapters written by academics. Geller's *Bisexuality: A Reader and Sourcebook* (1990) includes a three-chapter section titled "Academia looks at bisexuality," with chapters by Amanda Udis-Kessler, Fritz Klein, Barry Sepekoff, and Timothy J. Wolf, and Albert Richard Allgeier and Elizabeth Rice Allgeier. Hutchins and Ka'ahumanu's landmark *Bi Any Other Name* includes several chapters by graduate students, college professors, and university administrators. Most of these chapters are personal in orientation, and most authors' academic affiliations are underplayed or even hidden, but Amanda Udis-Kessler's "Present tense: Biphobia as a crisis of meaning" aims to explain the academic essentialist-constructionist debate, and its implications for bisexual politics, to a lay audience. Weise's *Closer to Home* includes chapters by academics Stacey

Young on the construction of bisexual identity in lesbian feminist discourse, Amanda Udis-Kessler on bisexual feminism and hetero/sexism, and Paula C. Rust on the conceptualization and sociopolitical construction of bisexuality, as well as Rebecca Kaplan's reanalysis of Adrienne Rich's famous essay "Compulsory Heterosexuality," titled "Compulsory Heterosexuality and the Bisexual Existence." Nearly one-third of the authors in Tucker's *Bisexual Politics* were graduate students or instructors at the college level.

This blurring of the distinction between academia and activism has resulted in a resonance between academic theorizing about sexuality and bisexual political theory (e.g., Young 1997). Academic queer theory, postmodernism applied to the theoretical understanding of sexuality, has had an immense impact on queer politics generally and on bisexual activist political theory in particular; queer and bisexual politics have, in turn, enriched the development of queer theory. Queer theory is a challenge to traditional scientific and humanistic understandings of sexuality, including but not limited to challenging the distinction between and the essentialization of other-sex and same-sex love, affection, and sexuality, and the cultural presumption of heterosexuality. Just as lesbianism was redefined by early 1970s lesbian feminists as the perfect experiential vehicle for feminism, bisexuality (and transgenderism) in the 1990s is constructed by both activists and academics as a real life analog for queer philosophy.[35] Like queer theory, bisexuality challenges the dichotomy between and essentialization of straight and gay, it undermines and reconstructs gender differences and reinterprets the relationship between gender and biological sex, and it calls into question the boundaries between the sexual, the sensual, and the platonic. It reinterprets texts and historical events, previously interpreted only in light of a heterosexual presumption, by revealing or constructing same-sex or bisexual subtexts. Queer theory gives social and cultural meaning to bisexuality, and bisexuality demonstrates the real-life utility of queer theory.

Early leaders of the modern gay and lesbian liberation movements initially held a vision that would be familiar in its content, if not its jargon, to many bisexual activists and queer theorists today. For example, the Radicalesbians saw gender itself as oppressive and argued for a "cultural revolution" in which all people would "achieve maximum autonomy in human expression" via the elimination of prescribed gender (1970:55). Martha Shelley and Rita Mae Brown were among those who recognized that the elimination of gender would also eliminate the distinction between heterosexuality and homosexuality, thus eliminating sexual identities based on this distinction.[36] Marilyn Frye's (1983) conceptualization of lesbians as women who can see through, and therefore disrupt, male-defined Reality resembles Elisabeth D. Däumer's (1994) more recent suggestion that bisexuality be conceptualized as a "vantage point" rather than an identity. However, in the face of very real economic, legal, and social discrimination the gay and lesbian movements' emphasis on cultural reconstruction soon gave way to a struggle for civil and legal equality and an ethnic model of political action more suited to these goals (Voeller 1990; Faderman 1991).[37] Some contemporary gay and lesbian activists, notably Urvashi Vaid, in *Virtual Equality: The Mainstreaming of Gay and Lesbian Liberation*, argue for a return to cultural reconstructionism, but the actual strategies used by the mainstream gay and lesbian movement—pursuit of same-sex marital rights, antidiscrimination laws, and hate crimes laws, to name a few—reflect an ethnicized view of same-sex oppression.

In contrast, many leading bisexual activists in the 1990s, especially bisexual women activists, actively reject the ethnic model of political action as antithetical to queer philosophy (Rust 1995a; Ault 1994; Morris and Storr 1997).[38] Although a quasi-ethnic bisexual identity would have psychological benefits for many individual bisexuals, they argue that the political potential of bisexuality to undermine and deconstruct traditional distinctions between genders and sexes would be thwarted by the development of such a bisexual identity (e.g., Däumer 1994; Eadie 1993). For example, if bisexuality were to become merely a third form of sexuality, with bisexual identity taking a place next to gay, lesbian, and heterosexual identities, then it would have been co-opted into the traditional sex/gender system. Alternatively, if the gay/straight distinction is replaced with a bisexual/monosexual distinction, then binary thinking is preserved and bisexuality merely becomes part of a new hegemonic construction of sexuality (Ault 1996). Either way, concepts of essential sexual categories and sexual immutability—the roots of sexual oppression—are left intact. Therefore, although there is a great deal of discussion among bisexual activists about bisexuality and its expression, there is also a great resistance toward efforts to define bisexuality and to develop a universal bisexual identity.

Efforts by bisexual activists to avoid defining bisexuality to preserve its radical political potential imply that, if bisexual essentialization and identification can be avoided, bisexuality will in fact undermine contemporary cultural constructions of sexuality. Bisexual activists who advocate this strategy hope to prevent the bisexual movement from making what they see as the mistakes that led to the co-optation of the lesbian and gay movement into a reformed hegemonic sexual culture. But there is concern among some bisexual academics that this strategy might simply lead bisexuals to a different political dead end. Sharon Morris and Merl Storr (1997; see also Hemmings 1993), for example, argue that bisexual activists' vision of bisexuality as a radical challenge to Western sexual culture is untenable and that by making grandiose claims bisexual activists are setting themselves up for failure. They worry that bisexual politics will be abandoned in a few years when the revolution fails to materialize.

The central truth amid the debates about strategy is that there will never be, as suggested rhetorically by Rust (1995a), a "final revolution in the wheel of sexual identity politics." Change and conflict are inherent in complex cultures, and some of us will always be engaged in a struggle against prevailing cultural constructions of sexuality regardless of the content of those constructions. The "impulse to build a collective identity" is the flip side of the impulse to destroy identity categories (Gamson 1995:391); together they produce a dynamic tension, not a tendency toward resolution. The contributions of the lesbian and gay movement, the contributions of the bisexual movement, and the contributions of every other political movement should not be measured by the ability of that movement to survive in a single form, to achieve a specific goal, or to end the need for further struggle. The contributions of a political movement should be measured by the hope it generates and by the improvements it makes in people's lives; success sometimes brings longevity and it sometimes brings irrelevance, but almost invariably it brings change. Those of us who celebrate the process of change—whether as activists or as academics, or both—are fortunate because political movements do not die; they metamorphose.

Notes

1. Leland (1995).
2. Author unknown.
3. Author unknown.
4. The authors of these four articles are, in order: unknown, Carroll, unknown, and Margold. This attitude lasted into the early 1980s. See, for example, "Bisexuality in the Women's Movement" by Beth Mudd, published in *Plexus* in 1982.
5. Not all social scientists welcomed bisexual chic as an aspect of sexual liberation, however. Duberman was skeptical: "I'm less sure than they of everyone's 'innate' bisexual nature, and I'm worried that that assumption—though seemingly on the side of liberation— could prove tyrannical, could become the latest in a long series of 'scientific' party lines used to whip deviants—in this case exclusive homosexuals *or* heterosexuals—into line" (1977:199)
6. A few years later, in 1979, *Time* informed their readers about Masters and Johnson's research on homosexuality, including the finding that " 'ambisexuals,' Masters and Johnson's term for their admittedly small sampling of twelve bisexuals who are equally attracted to both sexes, have few sex fantasies and rarely fantasize about real people" (77).
7. Some books on bisexuality published in the 1970s or late 1960s are no longer in print and either not held by lending libraries or not permitted to circulate, and so are not included in the text. They include Jim Curry's *Jet-Set Bisexuals* (1978), David Lynne's *The Bisexual Woman* (1967), Richard Spellman's *The Bisexual Male* (1968), and Preston Harriman's *Bisexuality: Normal or Not?* (1969).
   Examples of the genre of popular literature on bisexuality herein described as characteristic of the 1970s can also be found in the 1980s. For example, Arno Karlen's (1988) *Threesomes: Studies in Sex, Power, and Intimacy* advocated sexual liberation and presented sexual experimentation and variation as healthy. See also note 33, this chapter.
8. The personal story approach can also be seen in Orlando's article, "Bisexuality: A choice not an echo?" published in *Ms.* in 1978. Anecdotal stories of bisexuals are also used by Hurwood in *The Bisexuals* and by John Warren Wells in *Total Sexuality*.
9. Compare this to the unabashedly pathologizing treatment of bisexuality by George Bishop in *The Bisexuals*, published a decade earlier in 1964. In a chapter on "Dual sexuality and crime," for example, Bishop wrote "The bisexual deviate occupies a unique niche in the annals of sexual crime. The confused passions aroused by his double deviation make him an all the more dangerous killer, when the delicate balance that contains his mental aberration within reasonable bounds becomes tipped toward the side of psychopathic criminality" (90).
10. Similarly, Roger Blake (1968) provided a "psychological comment" on each of the individual "case histories" presented in *The Bi-sexual Female*.
11. Jason Douglas's ([1967]1970) approach in *Bisexuality* was similar but lacked the lengthy philosophical analysis provided by Fast and Wells. Douglas promoted cultural images of bisexuals as oversexed creatures motivated by unresolved childhood needs and fears. He included chapters on bisexual nymphomaniacs and bisexual satyrs, although he denied any "necessary connection" between bisexuality and either nymphomania or satyriasis, explicitly rejected the characterization of bisexuality as a deviation, and asserted that "all men and women are, to a certain extent, bisexual" (7).

12. Knox, exact date unknown.

13. Ann Landers, July 1985. Similarly, seven years later, Landers warned readers, "If a man tells you he doesn't know if he's straight or gay, it means he has had at least one sexual encounter with another male. If you are sleeping with him, you are at risk for AIDS" (September 1992).

14. Later in the 1980s lesbian and gay coverage of bisexuality did include discussion of HIV. For example, the *Advocate* used AIDS as a hook for an article on "Women who marry gay men," although in this article author Brian Miller (1989) actually emphasized the rarity of HIV transmission between gay husbands and their wives and focused instead on the psychological characteristics and concerns of women who find themselves married to gay men.

15. Juana Maria Paz, "Desire and consequences: Sleeping with a strange man," *Lesbian Contradiction*, no. 21 (Winter 1988); Stephanie Sugars, "A second coming out," *Lesbian Contradiction*, no. 26 (Spring 1989): and Jane Dwinell, "I'm still a lesbian," *Lesbian Contradiction*, no. 27 (Summer 1989).

16. Marilyn Murphy and Irene Weiss, "Thinking about bisexuality," *Lesbian Contradiction*, no. 17 (Winter 1987).

17. For descriptions of the bisexual "scenes" in New York City, San Francisco, and Chicago in the mid-1980s, see Mishaan (1985); Paul (1998); Rubenstein and Slater (1985); Barr (1985). For a history of bisexual organizations, see Liz Highleyman's entry in the *Encyclopedia of Homosexuality*. See Hutchins (1996) for a detailed account of the development of bisexual politics, community, and literature during the 1970s, 1980s, and 1990s.

18. Marcia Deihl, "A Stonewall within a Stonewall," *Bi Women*, vol. 7, no. 3 (June-July 1989).

19. Letters by Young and by Goodkin, *Advocate*, no. 412.

20. Letter by Ochs in *Newsweek*, August 3, 1987; and letter by Elisa Arespacochaga, Susan Goldstine, and Tim Pierce, Lesbian, Bisexual, Gay Alliance, Amherst College, Amherst, Mass., in *Ms.*, June 1991, p. 7.

21. For example, letters from Robyn Ochs and Lucy Friedland to *Newsweek*, GCN August 9–15, 1987; from Barbara Smith to *Ebony*, GCN April 17–23, 1988; from the Bisexual Committee Engaging in Politics (BiCEP) to *Cosmopolitan*, GCN October 29-November 4, p. 5, 1989; and from Marcia Deihl to the *Boston Globe*, GCN August 11–17, p. 5, 1991. Such letters were also published by *Bay Windows, San Francisco Bay Times*, and other publications.

22. Letters to *Cosmopolitan* from Pamela Lipshutz, and BiCEP, dated December 4, 1989, and from BABN, published in the *San Francisco Bay Times*, November 1989. Collection also includes a multi- and anonymously authored letter in response to Richman's "A dating dilemma" in the *Boston Globe;* the letter is dated August 1984, and a notation indicates that it was typeset but never printed by the *Boston Globe*. See note 21, this chapter, regarding letters from Barbara Smith and Lucy Friedland.

23. As reported by wire services, June 1992.

24. October 7–13, 1987.

25. Jan Clausen, "My interesting condition", *Out/Look*, no. 7 (January 1990)

26. Authors Wilson, Queen, and Stevens, respectively.

27. Compiled by Roberta Gregory.

28. Dajenya, "Sisterhood crosses gender preference lines," *Lesbian Contradiction*, no. 29 (Winter 1990); Jane Litwoman, "Some thoughts on bisexuality," *Lesbian Contradiction*, no. 29 (Winter 1990); and Alena Smith, "Heads or tails," *Lesbian Contradiction*, no. 44 (Fall 1993).

29. Lani Ka'ahumanu and Loraine Hutchins, "Do bisexuals have a place in the gay movement?" *Advocate*, no. 578 (June 1991).

30. Cf. Wilkinson (1996), who sees greater similarity between 1970s and 1990s bisexual visibility. In "Bisexuality 'a la mode,'" she argued that "bisexuality is being marketed—both to lesbians and to heterosexual women—as the latest fashion trend" and observed "a return to sexual hedonism, with sexual desire clearly privileged over political analysis" (293).

31. The movement also experienced some early factionalism; the BiCentrist Alliance, led

by Robin Margolis, split off from the BiNetwork of Washington, D.C., in 1991 to focus on the quasi-ethnic goal of developing a bisexual culture, while other organizations adhered to a more "liberationist" philosophy.

32. See Roberts (1997) for an overview of the Fourth Bisexual Symposium.

33. In Britain *Bisexual Lives* was published by the Off Pink Collective in 1988. During these same years books addressed to the general heterosexual public also continued to appear. For example, Tom Smith's autobiographical *Half Straight: My Secret Bisexual Life* appeared in 1992. Beginning with the comment, "I had to let the world know what bisexuality has done to me. . . . it is my hope that this book will be perceived by many not as a self-incriminating disclosure but rather as a cultural revolution" (13), this autobiographical account is reminiscent of the confessional style used by Jason Douglas in his 1967 publication *Bisexuality: Confessions of Bisexual Men and Women* to gain the sympathy often afforded blameless victims. The tone of *Half Straight* stands in striking contrast to the self-affirmation characterizing other writings by and for bisexuals during the 1990s.

34. The interest in research on bisexuality extends overseas as well; when journalist Sue George's book *Women and Bisexuality*, based on her research on bisexual women in the United Kingdom, appeared in 1993, interest by bisexuals in the United States exceeded the distributor's expectations and copies were temporarily in short supply.

35. See Ault (1996); Däumer (1994); Hemmings (1996); and Gamson (1995) for discussions of the challenge posed by bisexuality to gender and the relationship between bisexuality and queerness. Eadie (1993) pointed out that even the concept of *queer*ness can be used to submerge bisexuality; the newly acknowledged phenomenon of sex between lesbians and gay men is not constructed in terms of bisexuality, but as an expression of lesbian and gay queerness.

36. In fact, Goodman, Lakey, Lashof, and Thorne (1983) saw the goal of lesbian liberation as being the elimination of heterosexuality and lesbianism. See discussion of the views of early lesbian feminists in Adam (1987); Echols (1984); Evans (1993); Faderman (1991); Marotta (1981); Rust (1995a); and Seidman (1993). See also the writings of Gore Vidal, "rebel son of Kinsey" (Katz 1990:22), who argued against the concepts of homosexual and heterosexual persons because they enable the sexual "ruling class to rule" (Vidal 1985:48).

37. Voeller (1990) recounted the intentional ethnicization of gayness by gay activists. He wrote, "without the notion of 'gay,' we could not gain the support of our own people or create a gay civil rights agenda based on accessing the legitimacy of the existing civil rights movement of other minorities and women. Thus, sadly, we too became exclusive in terms of sexual orientation rather than inclusive. . . . Unfortunately, a large number of us have subscribed to our own rhetoric. But our movement will only be successful when the distinction no longer has significance to anyone" (36).

38. See also Rust's (1995a) analysis of the various political traditions, including the ethnic model and the feminist-inspired choice model, that feed into bisexual politics.

28

Bisexual Chic: Anyone Goes

Newsweek

THERE is a new vibration to spring this year. While the birds and the bees are striking up their vernal hum, so are the boys and girls, the boys and the boys, and the girls and the girls. Bisexuality is in bloom.

On some college campuses, prom queens are dancing with other prom queens while their kings are smoothing on eye shadow in the men's room. In the May issue of Vogue, an interviewed trio of two lads and a lass caress each other through a six-page display of swim wear, while in Glamour, a Mary Quant cosmetics ad features a poutingly pretty boy and girl in matching glitter makeup. The news media have become a confessional for celebrities who are rushing out of their closets to join the new cult of bisexual chic. "One of the nicest—whatever you want to call it—loves of my life was a woman," confided folk heroine Joan Baez in an interview last year.

It was probably inevitable. As his-and-her clothes, hair styles and role assignments blurred the line between the sexes until they overlapped, the only thing left to swap was sex itself. Homosexuals have become so accepted in some circles that the American Psychiatric Association recently decided to drop homosexuality from its list of mental illnesses—though most therapists continue to treat it as a disorder. In the women's liberation movement, some politicized sisters have been establishing lesbian relaitonships, which they see as almost obligatory. "Why should we be restricted from sleeping with half the human race?" asks one feminist lawyer. "But that doesn't mean we don't sleep with men too."

Shift: Not surprisingly, students who passed through puberty watching rock star Mick Jagger sing love songs to his drummer are pushing hardest at the perimeters of sexuality. "All my friends are into it," confides Sharon, a pre-sex junior at a Los Angeles high school. "There have been times when I've been afraid to go into the girl's room." The sexual shift was more traumatic for Sue McGovern, a 19-year-old Vassar sophomore who came at it from the other side. After four years of lesbian relationships, the avid feminist recently proclaimed her bisexuality by taking up with a man. "Coming out into the straight world blew my mind," she says. "But everybody does bisexuality now. It's really big."

Despite the ruling of its official representatives, the psychiatric community is far from phlegmatic about anyone-goes sex. "Bisexuality is a disaster for culture and society," claims Dr. Charles Socarides, a New York psychiatrist. "They're selling a phony sexual utopia in which the kingdom of the orgasm will supposedly replace the house of the ego." But other psychiatrists like Dr. Judd Marmor, president-elect of the American Psychiatric Association, take exception to such blanket condemnations. "It is getting to the point," he says, "where heterosexuality can be viewed as a hangup. The new bisexual consciousness, besides being viewed as a rebellion against puritanism, may also be conveying a feeling of universality among men and women."

Perhaps, but only a tiny minority, even among the most sexually liberated, are ready to accept the message. After seven years of a marriage and two children, a highly successful New York dress designer finally left her bisexual husband. "I could not live with it anymore," she explains. "All day I live the executive life of a man of 45. At night I need five minutes to be a woman."

Race: But the bisexual beat goes on. Hot-blooded rock groupies let go at Max's Kansas City in New York, where a male model named Cyrk appears in androgynous attire and boasts: "We're the new race. I'm somewhere else and in between." In Chicago, more than 10,000 boy/girls and girl/boys wedge weekly into The Bistro, a gay discotheque, to dance, drink and glitter. In Paris, sexual experimenters from the international set make the his-and-her scene at Le Bronx, a freaked-out boite on the Rue Ste. Anne. "People aren't hiding themselves any more," shrugs one male couturier. "They don't give a damn."

Certainly few give a damn at Le Jardin, an ultra-in gay discotheque in New York where the banquettes swarm with sexual permutations. "We have homosexuals, bisexuals and trisexuals," chuckles owner John Addison. "They'll try anything." The sequin-bedecked regulars at Le Jardin are luring droves of straight couples who come to gape but are sometimes drawn into the bisexual cavorting in spite of themselves. "I'm from Montclair," confided a wide-eyed New Jersey matron. "But don't tell anyone."

29

A Perilous Double Love Life

David Gelman with Lisa Drew, Mary Hager, Monroe Anderson, George Raine, and Sue Hutchison

AC/DC AM/FM. The double-gaited set. The nicknames have always been a little nasty. One view commonly held by therapists and gay activists is that bisexuals are merely self-deceived homosexuals, "fence sitters" unwilling to face up to their same-sex perference. Heterosexuals tend to think of "bi's" as the ultimate libertines, the ones most determined to "have it all." As one bisexual once put it, "Why should we be restricted from sleeping with half the human race?" There is now a very short answer to that question, a four-letter word that explains why bisexuals are becoming the ultimate pariahs of the 80's. That word is AIDS.

Very little is known about the numbers and habits of bisexuals—especially males who keep their dual activites secret from female lovers. But the available evidence suggests that these male bi's could represent a new dimension in the deadly epidemic. Many doctors consider them among the most likely potential conduits for the spread of AIDS to heterosexuals—who may bed them or, as often happens, marry them, never suspecting that their partners are leading a dangerous double love life.

So far, there has been no evidence that bisexuals are passing the disease from the gay to the straight community at anything like an overwhelming rate. About 2 to 3 percent of AIDS patients are women thought to have contracted the disease from male lovers, and some of those men were intravenous-drug users. But the fears about bisexuals are not unfounded. In theory, bisexual husbands and bachelors can spread the infection that ultimately afflicts their wives and children, or their straight girlfriends, who in turn may infect other boyfriends.

Bedroom Behavior: How many bisexuals are out there? No major study of sexual mores has been undertaken since Alfred C. Kinsey published his landmark survey of (white) male and female bedroom behavior in 1948 and '53. Rather than work from fixed categories, Kinsey posited a heterosexual-to-homosexual scale of 0 to 6, with the lower number indicating undiluted heterosexuality and the higher one signifying extreme "gayness." Most people, he found, fell between 1 and 5. The survey also found that 18 percent of males were equally involved with men and women for at least three years between the ages of 16 and 55, and an additional 13 percent tended to be more homosexual than heterosexual. For women, the figures were about half those of men.

On the subject of bisexuals in the era of AIDS, however, Dr. June Reinisch, the current director of the Kinsey Institute, says simply that "we don't have enough data." Researchers are only now beginning to get some hint of the size of the bisexual population because of the growing numbers coming in for help after testing positive for the AIDS antibodies. In Minnesota, the Department of Health estimates that 35 percent of the state's AIDS cases are bisexual men. In Chicago, health officials say the chances that a bisexual man will be exposed to AIDS may soon approach the 50–50 mark.

It is clear from those scattered studies that most bisexual men are probably still undercover, agonizing over what they should do. Experts worry that bisexuals' lack of organizational ties—and their fear of losing their wives and children—may make them the hardest to reach of the potential AIDS-carrying groups. Says June Osborn, dean of the University of Michigan School of Public Health: "These people are not going to come forward under any circumstances."

We are just beginning to understand how bisexuality develops. Sigmund Freud believed firmly in "the original bisexuality of the individual." We all begin with the bisexual potential, he wrote. As children, we are "polymorphous perverse," knowing no sexual barriers. Where we go from there may depend on the quality of relations with the male or female parent, or other early objects of love.

In the decades since the founder of psychoanalysis first put forth those ideas, we have learned that like some homosexuals, bisexual men frequently report having had distant, unsympathetic fathers. "James," a Louisiana civic leader who had his first homosexual experience three years after he married, recalls feeling insufficiently loved by his father. Still married, he began to find gratification with partners he picked up in bathhouses and service-station lavatories, continuing a double life for 12 years until his wife found out and issued an ultimatum. James thinks he was acting partly in rage against his father. "I remember gritting my teeth a lot," he says.

Emotions and Romance: Not all bisexuals harbor such feelings. Francis Giambrone, a Boston psychotherapist who says he has treated hundreds of bisexuals, divides them into three categories. "One type," he says, "is the person who's transitional; he's essentially gay but he needs to identify as a bisexual to come out to others. Then there are hundreds of men and women who are genuinely erotically and emotionally attracted to both sexes." A third group, he adds, is drawn erotically to the same sex but emotionally to the opposite sex. Others agree that the emotional component is important in understanding the inner workings of people who find themselves attracted to both sexes. Bisexuality begins in the imagination, "where there is a fantasy life involving both sexes, be it of a romantic or sexual kind," observes Manhattan-based therapist Bill Wedin. "There's a problem in thinking of this exclusively in sexual terms when in fact it's as much emotional and romantic as sexual."

For "Henry," a New York therapist who treats many gay men, it was clearly both. Although he loved his second wife, he nevertheless found his erotic feelings for his own sex so powerful that for a time he engaged in anonymous, furtive homosexual encounters. Finally he told his wife, who did not want to lose him. The marriage survived, and he found a male lover with whom he formed such a strong attachment that he calls him a "second spouse." Years later, he still divides his time between his two partners, who accept the arrangement. "I wanted a relationship with a man," Henry explains. "It was not simply a sexual thing, not something that could be satisfied through an occasional one-night stand. It represented a broader emotional need of which sex was merely the expression."

The erotic factor alone can be overpowering. "Even faced with a miserable, awful death, the sex drive is a strong drive," said one Washington, D.C., man who resumed homosexual contracts after 30 years of heterosexual marriage. Despite all the public discussion about AIDS, male bisexuals tend to have multitple partners, sometimes engaging in sex without even speaking. Roadside rest areas have become a popular locale for cruising. "A man leaves his house to get the paper, has sex and returns to his wife," says Gary Drake, a gay therapist in Brookline, Mass. Men and women bisexuals alike often talk of the "intense" arousal, the "different energy" they experience with their own sex. James remembers it as being "like sky diving. It was intoxicating, a high."

Many bisexuals seem reluctant or unable to deny themselves the exotic other side of sex. The right to have it both ways was a recurring theme at a recent conference on bisexuality that drew participants from 16 states to a weekend-long series of workshops in New York. The keynote speaker was Maggi Rubenstein, a 56-year-old nurse, counselor, and mother of two grown children who is the duenna of San Fransisco's bisexual community. "I'm proud to love both sexes," says Rubenstein. "The world says you have to choose, but I never have."

Despite the generally self-assured tone of the conference, there was abundant evidence of the new uneasiness about AIDS. Along with a workshop on "Erotic Imagery" and "Bisexuality 101," there were such others as "The Joy of Safe Sex" and "Building Your Immune System." AIDS consciousness is hitting bisexuals with increasing force. "These are tortured souls in a wretched situation," says Dr. Thomas Wise of Fairfax Hospital in northern Virginia. "They have to make sure the wife is not infected and then risk the whole revelation of their other life." Doctors first try to help such patients discuss the AIDS test with their wives. The next stop is trying to develop a support relationship between the two through couples therapy. But "when the wife is infected, too, we also have to deal with her rage," Wise adds. If both partners are infected and they have young children, the situation becomes even more tragic. He imagines worse scenarios: a young bride unknowingly infected by a bisexual boyfriend before she married, for example, who then infects her husband and, at the same time, becomes pregnant, posing a threat to the unborn child.

Sex Therapy: Faced with such horror stories, more bisexuals are seeking to change. Dr. Mark Schwarts, a Masters and Johnson consultant who runs a sex-therapy clinic in New Orleans, says that in the past year he has been overwhelmed by bisexuals hoping to go "straight," among them, doctors, lawyers, and "high officials." He claims a 70 percent success rate with such patients.

Such claims of success in altering sexual orientation are hotly disputed. Many people in the pyschiatric community believe that an individual's sexual orientation is already set by the time of adolescence. "There's no evidence at all that the object of desire has ever been changed by any form of treatment," says Michael Shernoff, a New York therapist. "What therapist consider a success is changing who patients can function with, not who they are aroused by."

Therapist who work with bisexuals are advocating, if not change, at least "openness." If bisexuals have no choice, they argue, then at least their partners should have one. Bisexuals are increasingly coming to terms with that obligation. Arlene Krantz, a 47-year-old mother of two who lives in San Francisco, says that even though there are almost no known cases of lesbians transmitting AIDS to each other, she now tells any prospective partner she is bisexual and whether she is currently involved in a relationship. "I expect the same in return," she says. "We are talking about life and death, not some little disease."

Some bisexuals stress that they are not apologizing for their behavior. They are celebrating themselves in gay-pride parades and protesting the attitude of straights and gays alike—that coolness that often makes bisexuals feel, says Robyn Ochs, who cofounded a women's bisexual support group in Boston, "that you don't exist at all." Any thaw in relations is not likely to happen in the current climate, though—not so long as many straights and gays are discussing AIDS candidly with their partners while bisexual men often don't tell the truth—even to themselves.

30

Bisexuality Emerges as a New Sexual Identity

John Leland with Steve Rhodes, Peter Katel, Claudia Kalb, Marc Peyser, Nadine Joseph, Martha Brant

STEVEN and Lori are what you might call the marrying type. They met on the first day of freshman orientation at the University of Chicago in 1988. By Thanksgiving, she was taking him home to meet her family; the following year they got engaged. This May they celebrated their first wedding anniversary.

In their one-bedroom apartment in Hyde Park, a collegiate affair down to the cinderblock bookshelves, Steven and Lori, now both 24, have developed an almost telepathic relationship. If anyone tells one of them anything, they joke, the other knows about it immediately. But during their freshman year, Steven says, he used to go off on his own every so often. "I think I told you I was going to a Democratic Socialist meeting," he recalls to Lori. He was really going to a campus gay and lesbian support group. Steven had come to college with a "practically nonexistent" romantic life, but a clear attraction to both men and women. After one of the group meetings, he decided to come clean to Lori.

STEVEN:
[I said] Lori, I have something to tell you.

LORI:
At which point, I thought he had cancer.

STEVEN:
And I told her, and her response was "Oh, is that all?"

LORI:
Yeah, it's not like cancer, after all. After that big buildup, it's like, gee, that's not a
   big deal.

When the couple got married at city hall last year, perhaps the most relieved person in the Midwest was Lori's mother. "Now she thinks I'm going to behave," says Lori. She says this with a playful smirk. In the years before their marriage—during their engagement—Lori had a serious relationship with another woman, and Steven had one with another man. Their marriage now is a home invention that they describe as "body-fluid monogamous." In conversation, they discuss condoms as matter-of-factly as the weather. Lori has an on going sexual relationship with another man and is looking for another woman; Steven has a friendship with a man that is sometimes sexual. Lori says, "At the time that I was coming out I was more interested in men, and now I'm more interested in women." Steven is "much more interested" in men right now. He still has sex with his wife, but he now identifies himself as gay, though he also calls himself a "once and future bisexual."

Bisexuality is the hidden wild card of our erotic culture. It is what disappears when we divide desire into gay and straight, just as millions of Americans of various ethnic origins disappear when we discuss race in terms of black and white. Now, in scattered pockets, bisexuality is starting to become more visible. Bisexual characters have popped up in TV series like "Roseanne" and "Melrose Place" and in films like "Three of Hearts" and "Threesome." Two decades after Mick Jagger and David Bowie flaunted thier androgynous personas, pop stars like Michael Stipe, Courtney Love and Sophie B. Hawkins and model Rachel Williams have discovered anew that there's more to life than when a man loves a woman. As Stipe told *Newsweek*, promoting R.E.M.'s latest album, "I've always been sexually ambiguous in terms of my proclivities; I think labels are for food." MTV and fashion advertising, pumping out fetishized images of men and women, have created a climate that Harvard professor Marjorie Garber, author of the provocative new book "Vice Versa: Bisexuality and the Eroticism of Everyday Life," calls "virtual bisexuality": the only way to watch these naked torsos, male and female alike, is erotically. Many college students, particularly women, talk about a new sexual "fluidity" on campus. And most significantly, the Internet has emerged as a safe harbor where users can play fluidly with gender, both their own and that of their virtual partners. As Garber puts it, "We are in a bisexual moment."

In the splintered multiculturalism of the 1990s, an independent bisexual movement is starting to claim its own identity. The Bisexual Resource Guide lists 1,400 groups spread throughout the United States and abroad, including Bi Women of Color, Bi Adult Children of Alcoholics, Bi Star Trekkies. There are bi cable shows, bi web sites, bi newsletters and magazines. "We are taught we have to be one thing," says Howard University divinity professor Elias Farajajé-Jones. "Now people are finding out that they don't have to choose one thing or another. That doesn't mean they are confused."

The bridge: Freud called bisexuality a universal "disposition"; he believed that we all have male and female sides, each heterosexually attracted to people of the opposite gender, but that most of us repress one side. For him, it was exclusive *heterosexuality* that was "a problem that needs elucidating" (unfortunately, he never got around to it). Alfred Kinsey, in his famous 1948 report, mapped human sexuality on a scale of zero to 6, with zero representing exclusively heterosexual behavior and 6 exclusively homosexual behavior; bisexuality was the bridge that held the poles together. The anthropologist Margaret Mead urged in 1975 that we "come to terms with the well-documented, normal human capacity to love members of both sexes." And in 1995, "Adam," a bisexual teen in Oakland, Calif., says bisexuality is no guarantee of a date on Saturday night: "A bisexual," he says, "doesn't have any more sex than the captain of the football team."

After a brief vogue during the sexual revolution—"Bisexual Chic: Anyone Goes," chortled *Newsweek* in 1974—it moved back underground in the 1980s, pushed by fears of AIDS and by gay identity politics. Nobody knows how many bisexuals there are in the country, or just how bisexuality should be defined. Its existence alone makes many people uncomfortable; it suggests that all sexual identity might be subject to change or expansion, and that we may not ever really be able to fulfill our partners or be fulfilled ourselves. "I'll put it this way," says Faune, a bi New York grad student who asked to be identified by his online handle. "You're attracted to only one sex and you don't feel there's anything missing. To me that would be hell."

In a culture organized, however precariously, around monogamy, bisexuality lurks as a rupture in the social structure, conjuring fears of promiscuity, secret lives and instability. It can make the knotty issues of human relationships—jealousy, fidelity, finances, parental roles, custody—even more complex. And with these uncertainties comes an increased threat of AIDS. Failed monogamy is already a principal source of pain in this country; bisexuality suggests that nonmonagamy, or "polyamory," is an accepted part of life. Not for nothing does one bisexual journal call itself, with mock derision, Anything That Moves. In practice promiscuity is not an article of faith for all bisexuals; it's an option. Many bis are monogamous for all or parts of their lives. The sociologist Paula Rust, in the upcoming book, "Bisexuality: The Psychology and Politics of an Invisible Minority," explains the paradox this way: "Imagine concluding that a person who finds both blue and brown eyes attractive would require two lovers, one with each eye color, instead of concluding that this person would be happy with *either* a blue-eyed or a brown-eyed lover."

Mostly, though, we'd rather not think about bisexuality. When Rolling Stone publisher Jann Wenner left his wife this spring for another man, bisexuality was the possibility missing from most accounts. Bisexuality has been written out of our literature: early publishers simply rewrote the genders of male love objects in Plato's "Symposium" and some of Shakespeare's sonnets; more often schools just teach around them. Bisexuality even disappears from many sex surveys, which count people with any same-sex behavior as homosexual. And yet it has had a tremendous impact on our culture. Many of the men who have taught us to be men—Cary Grant, James Dean—and the women who've taught us to be women—Billie Holiday, Marlene Dietrich—enjoyed sex with both men and women.

The bisexual blip of the 70's was an offshoot of the sexual revolution: it was straight, with a twist. By contrast, the current bisexual moment arises from the gay and feminist movements. For a generation that came of age during the gay-rights movements, same-sex relationships or experiments no longer carry the stigma they once did. More and more of us—at work, at school, in our families and in our entertainments—move comfortably between gay and straight worlds. "Those of us who are younger," says Rebecca Kaplan, 24, a psychology major at MIT, "owe a great deal to gays, lesbians and bisexuals who came out before us. Because of them I was able to come out as a bisexual and not hate myself." Feminism has also made romantic attachments between two women—either provisional or lasting—more acceptable, even privileged. As president of the National Organization for Women, Patricia Ireland sets a quiet example: she has both a husband and a female companion. Nearly every college or university in the country, and some high schools, now have gay and lesbian student centers; sex with one's own gender, for anyone who's curious, is now a visible and protected part of campus culture. Queer studies and gender studies are now a part of the national curriculum. A popular T shirt, spotted recently in a Connecticut high school, puts it this way: DON'T ASSUME I'M STRAIGHT. As one 17-year-old bi says, "It's not us-versus-them anymore. There's just more and more of us."

Tim Horing, 21, a sophomore at City College in San Francisco, describes himself as "typical of bisexual youth. We just refuse to label ourselves as any of the five food groups. . . . [We] revel in the fuzziness, in the blurred images." Working-class, Roman Catholic, son of a retired New York narcotics cop, Höring had his first sexual fantasies about Wonder Woman and the Bionic Woman. Then in his teens he admitted to himself, in a series of difficult steps, that he was also attracted to men. He came out to a few friends in high school; at his graduation, when his name was called, the last six rows in the auditorium mischievously yelled out, "the bisexual" (this news came as a surprise to his parents). For the most part he has been in monogamous relationships, usually with men—though now he is dating two gay men and a bisexual woman. "I never wanted a white picket fence," he says, "but I do want someone I can settle down with and raise my Benetton kids." His partner may be a man or a woman. "I don't feel forced to choose," he says. "I don't have to make any tough choices."

Softening tensions: For many bisexuals, it hasn't been that easy. "When I came out in '88," says Melissa Merry, 31, an energetic Chicagoan who calls herself Mel, "I was told by people from [local lesbian] support groups not to come out as bisexual or I'd be asked to leave." Many gays and lesbians, she says, dismissed bisexuals as fence sitters, unwilling to give up a "phase" they themselves had outgrown. As a college student in Michigan, Merry remembers, she went to a singles-heavy bar one night. "And I saw this woman across the room and I thought, `She is just so attractive.' I thought, `Where did that come from?' I was involved with a guy, we were going to get married, and then all of the sudden that didn't make sense anymore." Now Merry works in two organizations for bis, but says tensions between bis and gays have softened. After years of resistance, gay and lesbian organizations have started to add bisexuality to their banners. As for the lesbian groups that shunned her, Merry says, "I can't think of any . . . that I can't go to now."

Many bis, though, still feel rejected on two fronts: by straights for being too gay, and by gays for not being gay enough. During the late 80's, bisexual men—espe-

cially married men who stepped out with other men—were painted as stealth as-
sassins bringing AIDS to their unsuspecting wives. As Cosmopolitan warned in
1989, "If a man's eyes follow other men, be very cautious." This fear has cooled
somewhat, particularly among younger women—both because of the availability
of condoms, and because AIDS never swept through the heterosexual population,
except around IV drug use. Of women who contract AIDS sexually, the portion
who get it from bisexual males remains at 10 to 20 percent: 80 to 90 percent get it
from drug users, Centers for Disease Control and Prevention estimates. Still, for
many women this is reason enough to worry. The bisexual response: it is unprotected sex, not bisexuality, that transmits AIDS.

Luis, 36, has felt pressures from both gays and straights. A marine biologist by
training, Luis now runs a Miami prescription drug service for patients with HIV.
For the last 5 1/2 years, he has been involved with a bi woman; recently, he invited
a gay man into their relationship and home. Luis is HIV-positive; his parents are
not. "My first lover and first relationship was with a [gay] man, Juan." says Luis. "I
learned a lot from him, but there was this other part of me that needed to be expressed. Juan would tell me, `You're just trying to conform and go back into the
closet.' I didn't mind being called gay, but that's not all of who I am. I'm as queer as
they come and as straight as they come. I'm 200 percent." Luis remembers once
telling a man he'd slept with that he also had sex with a woman. "He got up in the
middle of the meal and walked out," Luis says. The prejudice is no more palatable
when it comes from straights. Shopping at a northwest Miami mall with his male
lover recently, Luis found himself assaulted with anti-gay slurs. "How did the guy
know about us?" asks Luis, who does not dress outrageously. "We don't have any
stickers on the car."

These dual pressures push some to lead bifurcated lives. William Wedin, a psychologist and director of the Bisexual Information and Counseling Service, says
that most of the bisexuals he sees would rather remain in the closet. "Sometimes
they will lead separate lives where they are known as gay to one group of friends
and seen as straight by another group of people. Sometimes they will go to two
doctors: one who deals with medical problems, another who deals with sexually
transmitted diseases. They will create separate worlds."

Amid these fears and prejudices, scholars and researchers are looking for ways
to rethink bisexuality: how to make sense of the millions of Americans, maybe tens
of millions, who over the course of their lifetimes have sex with both men and
women. Many, even most, don't call themselves bisexual. According to sex researcher Martin Weinberg of Indiana University, the majority of men who engage
in sex with both men and women label themselves "heterosexual." Conversely,
Paula Rust, in a 1992 survey of women who identified themselves as lesbians,
found that two-thirds of them said they were attracted to men, and 90 percent had
been in sexual relationships with men. Further, most bisexuals are not attracted
equally to men and women. Where do you draw the line? Should fantasy and desire count, even if they aren't acted upon? And what about married people who
later come to recognize themselves as gay? "I don't have a definition [of bisexual-
ity]," says John O. G. Billy, lead author of the 1991 study "The Sexual Behavior of

Men in the United States," "because I'm not sure there is any one standard definition." The number of Americans who have sex with both men and women concurrently is very small. According to the University of Chicago's massive 1992 "Sex in America" study, about .7 percent of American men, and .3 percent of American women report having both male and female sexual partners in the last 12 months. Most of the self-identified bisexuals interviewed for this article would not qualify under these terms.

Erotic patterns: In practice, bisexuality has come to describe an incredibly broad range of erotic patterns: some monogamous, some polyamorous, some fleeting and some wholly fantastic. Indigo Som, 28, a paper artist currently in a monogamous relationship with another woman, considers the word bisexual far too vague to describe her life. "My sexual orientation," she says, "is toward creative people of color who can cook."

So who are bi, and how did they get that way? Are they really different from everybody else? "Some people say everyone has the biological potential for bisexuality, but that's untestable," says Weinberg, who led one of the few major studies of bisexuals (published last year as "Dual Attraction: Understanding Bisexuality"). "The answer is, we don't know." Weinberg conceives of bisexuality as often being an "add-on"—we commonly develop one orientation first, usually straight, and then "add-on" an attraction to the other gender. "Learning bisexuality," he writes, is a matter of "failing to unlearn the desirable aspects of one's own gender."

J. Michael Bailey, a sociologist at Northwestern University, says bisexuality is in the genes. In a study of sexual orientation in nearly 5,000 Australian twins, he found that identical twins were more likely both to have bisexual feelings than fraternal twins, suggesting bisexuality might have a genetic basis. "I conceptualize bisexuality this way," he says: "if somebody has enough of the relevant genetic factors, they'll be homosexual. If they don't have enough, they'll be bisexual." His data are still preliminary and have not been subjected to peer scrutiny.

At bottom, though, bisexuality simply does not reduce neatly. There are no bisexual acts nor bisexual desires, only bisexual histories. Bisexuality is less a root than a construction—different in each individual—of passions and actions we are accustomed to calling heterosexual or homosexual. In its ambiguities, it calls into question the certainties of both gay and straight identities. Pushed far enough, it absorbs both.

Matthew Ehrlich, 25, argues that his own desire has nothing to do with gender. Ehrlich, managing editor of VH1 Online in New York, said he was attracted to both men and women once he "started smooching at age 14." He came out as gay at Williams College, he says, because he saw a lot of abusive heterosexual relationships around him; for the last five years he has identified himself as bi though he prefers the term queer. "There are some times that I want a certain kind of hair at the back of someone's neck, a look in their eyes, the way they hold their mouth, but it's not necessarily limited to one gender," he says. "It's often much stronger that I want to run my hands through short hair at the back of the neck than that it's a man or woman's hair." Ehrlich says some of his partners don't understand this, which leads to problems of trust or jealousy. "[They'll say], `How can you be sure you de-sire me when I'm only one gender?'" he says. But this is not the point. "I don't de-sire a gender, I desire a person."

Many orientations: This remains the unresolved paradox of bisexuality: that in its most individuated moments, it is most indistinguishable from homosexuality or heterosexuality. Desire is desire. John Cheever, who described the breadth of his passions in his journals, deemed bisexuality a pitifully narrow way to look at human attraction. "To interrogate oneself tirelessly on one's sexual drives," he wrote, "seems to me self-destructive. One can be aroused, for example, by the sight of a holly leaf, an apple tree, or a male cardinal bird on a spring morning." As Garber argues, we all have mainfold orientations: to green eyes, say, or to money or power. But deep down we remain defiantly attracted to individuals.

In San Francisco recently, Tom Höring was telling his friends about how he changed his approach to picking up boys. He used to say, "Are you queer?" Then he switched to, "Do you like boys?" Now his favorite line is "Do you like me?" As he sees it, "I've gone from the political to the historical attraction to the very per-sonal. All that really matters is if they like me." This is the new bisexual moment in a nutshell: hard fought, hard thought, and distinctly individual. It is a thorny nar-rative, fraught with questions of identity and belonging. And in the end, it is really about the simple, mysterious pull between warm human bodies when the lights go out.

Bibliography

Abner, Allison. 1992. Bisexuality out of the closet. *Essence* 23 (October 6): 61, 62, 130–132.

Adam, Barry D. 1979. A social history of gay politics. In Martin P. Levine, ed., *Gay Men: The Sociology of Male Homosexuality*, pp. 285–300. New York: Harper and Row.

—— 1987. *The Rise of a Gay and Lesbian Movement*. Boston: Twayne.

Adib, S. M. and D. G. Ostrow. 1991. Trends in HIV/AIDS behavioural research among homosexual and bisexual men in the United States: 1981–1991. *AIDS Care* 3, 3: 281–287.

Afshar, Haleh. 1994. Fundamentalism and women in Iran. Pp. 276– 294 in Oliver Mendelsohn and Upendra Baxi, eds., *The Rights of Subordinated Peoples*. Delhi: Oxford University Press.

Aggleton, Peter, ed. 1996. *Bisexualities and AIDS: International Perspectives*. Bristol, Pa.: Taylor and Francis.

Akers, Ronald L., Norman S. Hayner, and Werner Gruninger. 1974. Homosexual and drug behavior in prison: A test of the functional and importation models of the inmate system. *Social Problems* 21, 3: 410–422.

Albrecht, G. L., J. A. Levy, N. M. Sugure, T. R. Prohaska, and D. G. Ostrow. 1989. Who hasn't heard about AIDS? *AIDS Education and Prevention* 1(Winter): 261–267. [Cited by Matteson 1997.]

Allen, C. 1961. When homosexuals marry.In I. Rubin, ed., *The Third Sex*, pp. 58–62. New York: New Book. [Cited by Fox 1996.]

Allen, Donald M. 1980. Young male prostitutes: A psychosocial study. *Archives of Sexual Behavior* 9, 5: 399–426.

Allen, Laura S. and Roger A. Gorski. 1992. Sexual orientation and the size of the anterior commissure in the human brain. *Proceedings of the National Academy of Science* 89: 7199–7202.

Almaguer, Tomás. 1993. Chicano men: A cartography of homosexual identity and behavior. In Henry Abelove, Michèle Aina Barale, David M. Halperin, eds., *The Lesbian and Gay Studies Reader*, pp. 255–273. New York: Routledge.

Alonso, Ana Maria and Maria Teresa Koreck. 1993. Silences: "Hispanics," AIDS, and sexual practices.In Henry Abelove, Michèle Aina Barale, David M. Halperin, eds., *The Lesbian and Gay Studies Reader*, pp. 110–126. New York: Routledge.

Altman, Dennis. 1971. *Homosexual Oppression and Liberation*. New York: Outerbridge and Dienstfrey. Rpt. 1973. New York: Avon.

—— 1982. *The Homosexualization of America and the Americanization of the Homosexual*. New York: St. Martin's.

Altshuler, Kenneth Z. 1984. On the question of bisexuality. *American Journal of Psychotherapy* 38, 4: 484–493.

American Psychiatric Association. 1994. *Diagnostic and Statistical Manual of Mental Disorders*. 4th ed. Washington, D.C.: American Psychiatric Association.

Anderson, Clinton W. and H. Ron Smith. 1993. Stigma and honor: Gay, lesbian, and bisexual people in the U.S. military. In Louis Diamant, ed., *Homosexual Issues in the Workplace*, pp. 65–89. Washington, D.C.: Taylor and Francis.

Anderson, Lynn R. and Lori Randlet. 1993. Self-monitoring and life satisfaction of individuals with traditional and nontraditional sexual orientations. *Basic and Applied Social Psychology* 14, 3: 345–361.

—— 1994. Self-monitoring, perceived control and satisfaction with self-disclosure of sexual orientation. *Journal of Social Behavior and Personality* 9, 4: 789–800.

Anderson, R. M. and R. M. May. 1992. Understanding the AIDS pandemic. *Scientific American* 266, 5: 20–27. [Cited by Matteson 1997.]

Atkins, Dawn. 1998. *Looking Queer: Body Image and Identity in Lesbian, Bisexual, Gay, and Transgender Communities*. New York: Haworth.

Atkinson, D. R., G. Morten, and D. W. Sue. 1993. *Counseling American Minorities: A Cross-cultural Perspective*, 4th ed. Madison, Wis.: Brown and Benchmark.

Atwood, Aileen H. 1998. *Husbands Who Love Men: Deceit, Disease and Despair*. Providence, Utah: AMI.

Augustin, Ebba, ed. 1993. *Palestinian Women: Identity and Experience*. London: Zed.

Auerback, Sandra and Charles Moser. 1987. Groups for the wives of gay and bisexual men. *Social Work* 32 (July/August): 321–325.

Ault, Amber. 1994. Hegemonic discourse in an oppositional community: Lesbian feminists and bisexuality. *Critical Sociology* 20, 3: 107–122.

—— 1996. Ambiguous identity in an unambiguous sex/gender structure: The case of bisexual women. *Sociological Quarterly* 37, 3: 449–463.

Avery, C. S. 1991. AIDS: Why no woman is safe. *New Woman* (January): 96–98.

Badgett, M. V. Lee. 1995. The wage effects of sexual orientation discrimination. *Industrial and Labor Relations Review* 48, 4: 726–739.

—— 1996. Employment and sexual orientation: Disclosure and discrimination in the workplace. In Alan L. Ellis and Ellen D. B. Riggle, eds., *Sexual Identity on the Job: Issues and Services*, pp. 29–52. New York: Harrington Park.

Bagley, Christopher and Pierre Tremblay. 1998. On the prevalence of homosexuality and bisexuality, in a random community survey of 750 men aged 18 to 27. *Journal of Homosexuality* 36, 2: 1–18.

Bailey, Derrick Sherwin. 1955. *Homosexuality and the Western Christian Tradition*. London, New York: Longmans, Green. Rpt. 1975. Hamden, Conn.: Archon.

Bailey, J. Michael. 1995. Biological perspectives on sexual orientation. In Anthony R. D'Augelli and Charlotte J. Patterson, eds., *Lesbian, Gay, and Bisexual Identities Over the Lifespan: Psychological Perspectives*, pp. 102–135. New York: Oxford University Press.

Bailey, J. Michael. 1996. Gender identity. In Ritch C. Savin-Williams and Kenneth M. Cohen, eds., *The Lives of Lesbians, Gays, and Bisexuals: Children to Adults*, pp. 71–93. New York: Harcourt Brace.

Bailey, J. Michael and Alan P. Bell. 1993. Familiality of female and male homosexuality. *Behavior Genetics* 23, 4: 313–322.

Bailey, J. Michael and Deana S. Benishay. 1993. Familial aggregation of female sexual orientation. *American Journal of Psychiatry* 150, 2: 272–277.

Bailey, J. Michael, Joseph S. Miller, and Lee Willerman. 1993. Maternally rated childhood gender nonconformity in homosexuals and heterosexuals. *Archives of Sexual Behavior* 22, 5: 461–469.

Bailey, J. Michael and Richard C. Pillard. 1991. A genetic study of male sexual orientation. *Archives of General Psychiatry* 48 (December): 1089–1096.

Bailey, J. Michael, Richard C. Pillard, Michael C. Neale, and Yvonne Agyei. 1993. Heritable factors influence sexual orientation in women. *Archives of General Psychiatry* 50, 3 (March): 217–223.

Bailey, J. Michael and Kenneth J. Zucker. 1995. Childhood sex-typed behavior and sexual orientation: A conceptual analysis and quantitative review. *Developmental Psychology* 31: 43–55. [Cited by Bailey 1996.]

Balough, Joseph K. 1964. Conjugal visitations in prisons: A sociological perspective. *Federal Probation* 28, 3 (September): 52–58. [Cited by Shore 1981.]

Bancroft, John. 1990. Commentary: Biological contributions to sexual orientation. In David P. McWhirter, Stephanie A. Sanders, and June Machover Reinisch, eds., *Homosexuality/Heterosexuality: Concepts of Sexual Orientation*, pp. 101–111. New York: Oxford University Press.

Bancroft, John, ed., 1997. *Researching Sexual Behavior: Methodological Issues*. Bloomington: Indiana University Press.

Barr, George. 1985. Chicago Bi-Ways: An informal history. In Fritz Klein and Timothy J. Wolf, eds., *Two Lives to Lead: Bisexuality in Men and Women*, pp. 231–234. New York: Harrington Park.

Barron, Susan. 1992. Bisexuality: Having it all. *Lear's* 5, 3 (May): 55+.

Bartell, G. D. 1971. *Group Sex*. New York: Peter H. Wyden. [Cited by J. K. Dixon 1985.]

—— 1974. Group sex among the mid-Americans. In James R. Smith and Lynn G. Smith, eds., *Beyond Monogamy*, pp. 185–201. Baltimore: Johns Hopkins University Press.

Batchelor, Walter F. 1984. AIDS: A public health and psychological emergency. *American Psychologist* 39, 11: 1279–1284.

Becker, James T., Sue M. Bass, Mary Amanda Dew, Lawrence Kingsley, Ola A. Selnes, and Kathleen Sheridan. 1992. Hand preference, immune system disorder and cognitive function among gay/bisexual men: The Multicenter AIDS Cohort Study (MACS). *Neuropsychologia* 30, 3: 229–235.

Beemyn, Brett., ed. 1997. *Creating a Place for Ourselves: Lesbian, Gay, and Bisexual Community Histories.* New York: Routledge.

Beemyn, Brett and Mickey Eliason, eds. 1996. *Queer Studies: A Lesbian, Gay, Bisexual, and Transgender Anthology.* New York: New York University Press.

Bell, Alan P. 1975. Research in homosexuality: Back to the drawing board. *Archives of Sexual Behavior* 4, 4: 421–431.

Bell, Alan P. and Martin S. Weinberg. 1978. *Homosexualities: A Study of Diversity Among Men and Women.* New York: Simon and Schuster.

Bell, Alan P., Martin S. Weinberg, and Sue Kiefer Hammersmith. 1981. *Sexual Preference: Its Development in Men and Women.* Bloomington: Indiana University Press.

Bem, Sandra L. 1974. The measurement of psychological androgyny. *Journal of Consulting and Clinical Psychology* 42, 2: 155–162.

Benjamin, Harry. and R. E. L. Masters. 1964. *Prostitution and Morality: A Definitive Report on the Prostitute in Contemporary Society and an Analysis of the Causes and Effects of the Suppression of Prostitution.* New York: Julian.

Bennett, G., S. Chapman, and F. Bray. 1989. A potential source for the transmission of the human immunodeficiency virus into the heterosexual population: Bisexual men who frequent "beats." *Medical Journal of Australia* 151: 314–318. [Cited by Boulton, Hart, and Fitzpatrick 1992.]

Bentler, P. M. 1968. Heterosexual behavior assessment I: Males. *Behaviour Research and Therapy* 6: 21–5.

Bergler, Edmund. [1956] 1962. *Homosexuality: Disease or Way of Life?* New York: Hill and Wang.

Berk, Richard A. 1983. An introduction to sample selection bias in sociological data. *American Sociological Review* 48 (June): 386–398.

Berlant, Lauren and Elizabeth Freeman. 1993. Queer nationality. In Michael Warner, ed., *Fear of a Queer Planet: Queer Politics and Social Theory,* pp. 193–229. Minneapolis: University of Minnesota Press.

Berrios, Daniel C., Norman Hearst, Laura L. Perkins, Gregory L. Burke, Stephen Sidney, Heather E. McCreath, Stephen B. Hulley. 1992. HIV antibody testing in young, urban adults. *Archives of Internal Medicine* 152: 397–402.

Bérubé, Allan. 1981. Marching to a different drummer: Coming out during World War II. Paper presented at the December 1981 annual meeting of the American Historical Association, Los Angeles.

Bevier, Pamela Jean, Mary Ann Chiasson, Richard T. Heffernan, and Kenneth G. Castro. 1995. Women at a sexually transmitted disease clinic who reported same-sex contact: Their HIV seroprevalence and risk behaviors. *American Journal of Public Health* 85, 10: 1366–1371.

Bhugra, Dinesh and Padmal De Silva. 1998. Dimensions of bisexuality: An exploratory study using focus groups of male and female bisexuals. *Sexual and Marital Therapy* 13, 2: 145–157.

Bieber, I. 1969. The married male homosexual. *Medical Aspects of Human Sexuality* 3, 5: 76–84.

Billy, John O. G., Koray Tanfer, William R. Grady, and Daniel H. Klepinger. 1993.

The sexual behavior of men in the United States. *Family Planning Perspectives* 25, 2: 52–60.

Binson, Diane, Stuart Michaels, Ron Stall, Thomas J. Coates, John H. Gagnon, and Joseph A. Catania. 1995. Prevalence and social distribution of men who have sex with men: United States and its urban centers. *Journal of Sex Research* 32, 3: 245–254.

Birke, Lynda. 1982. Cleaving the mind: Speculations on conceptual dichotomies. In Steven Rose and the Dialectics of Biology Group, eds., *Against Biological Determinism*, pp. 60–78. New York: Allison and Busby.

Bisexual Anthology Collective (Leela Acharya, Nancy Chater, Dionne Falconer, Sharon Lewis, Leanna McLennan, and Susan Nosov), eds. 1995. *Plural Desires: Writing Bisexual Women's Realities.* Toronto: Sister Vision.

Bishop, George. 1964. *The Bisexuals.* Los Angeles: Century.

Blackford, Lara, Shannon Doty, and Robert Pollack. 1996. Differences in subjective sexual arousal in heterosexual, bisexual, and lesbian women. *Canadian Journal of Human Sexuality* 5, 3: 157–167.

Blackwood, Evelyn. 1984. Sexuality and gender in certain Native American tribes: The case of cross-gender females. *Signs: Journal of Women in Culture and Society* 10, 1: 27–42.

Blake, James. 1956. Letters from an American prisoners. *Paris Review* 13: 8–44. [Cited by Gagnon and Simon 1973.]

Blake, Roger. 1968. *The Bi-sexual Female.* Cleveland: Ambassador.

Blanchard, Ray. 1985. Typology of male-to-female transsexualism. *Archives of Sexual Behavior* 14, 3: 247–261.

—— 1989. The classification and labeling of nonhomosexual gender dysphorias. *Archives of Sexual Behavior* 18, 4: 315–334.

Bloomfield, Kim. 1993. A comparison of alcohol consumption between lesbians and heterosexual women in an urban population. *Drug and Alcohol Dependence* 33, 3: 257–269.

Blumstein, Philip W. and Pepper Schwartz. 1974. Lesbianism and bisexuality. In Erich Goode and Richard Troiden, eds., *Sexual Deviance and Sexual Deviants*, pp. 278–295. New York: Morrow.

—— 1976a. Bisexuality in women. *Archives of Sexual Behavior* 5, 2: 171–181.

—— 1976b. Bisexuality in men. *Urban Life* 5, 3: 339–358.

—— 1976c. Bisexual women. In Jacqueline P. Wiseman, ed., *The Social Psychology of Sex*, pp. 154–162. New York: Harper and Row.

—— 1977. Bisexuality: Some social psychological issues. *Journal of Social Issues* 33, 2: 30–45.

—— 1983. *American Couples: Money, Work, Sex.* New York: William Morrow.

—— 1990. Intimate relationships and the creation of sexuality. In David P. McWhirter, Stephanie A. Sanders, and June Machover Reinisch, eds., *Homosexuality/Heterosexuality: Concepts of Sexual Orientation*, pp. 307–320. New York: Oxford University Press.

Bode, Janet. 1976. *View from Another Closet: Exploring Bisexuality in Women.* New York: Hawthorn.

Boles, Jacqueline and Kirk W. Elifson. 1994a. Sexual identity and HIV: The male prostitute. *Journal of Sex Research* 31, 1: 39–46.

—— 1994b. The social organization of transvestite prostitution and AIDS. *Social Science and Medicine,* 39, 1: 85–93.

Boles, J., K. Elifson, and M. Sweat. 1989. Male prostitutes and their customers and lovers. One hundred forty-second meeting of the American Psychiatric Association, San Francisco, May 6–11, abstract no. 92D. [Cited by Pleak and Meyer-Bahlburg 1990.]

Boles, J., M. Sweat, and K. Elifson. 1989. Bisexuality among male prostitutes. Paper presented at CDC workshop on bisexuality and AIDS, Atlanta, Georgia. [Cited by Ross, Wodak, Gold, and Miller 1992; Ross 1991.]

Bonilla, Louis and Judith Porter. 1990. A comparison of Latino, Black, and non-Hispanic white attitudes toward homosexuality. *Hispanic Journal of Behavioral Sciences* 12, 4 (November): 437–452.

Boswell, John. 1980. *Christianity, Social Tolerance, and Homosexuality: Gay People in Western Europe from the Beginning of the Christian Era to the Fourteenth Century.* Chicago: University of Chicago Press.

—— 1982. Revolutions, universals, and sexual categories. *Salmagundi. Homosexuality: Sacrilege, Vision, Politics* nos. 58–59 (Fall 1982–Winter 1983): 89–113.

—— 1990. Sexual and ethical categories in premodern Europe. In David P. McWhirter, Stephanie A. Sanders, and June Machover Reinisch, eds., *Homosexuality/Heterosexuality: Concepts of Sexual Orientation,* pp. 15–31. New York: Oxford University Press.

Boulton, M. 1991. Review of the literature on bisexuality and HIV transmission. In Rob A. P. Tielman, Manuel Carballo, and Aart C. Hendriks, eds., *Bisexuality and HIV/AIDS: A Global Perspective,* pp. 187–209. Buffalo, N.Y.: Prometheus.

Boulton, M., R. Fitzpatrick, G. Hart, J. Dawson, and J. McClean. 1989. High risk sexual behavior and condom use in a sample of homosexual men in England. Fifth International Conference on AIDS, Montreal, Quebec, June 4–9, abstract no. M.D.P.15. [Cited by Pleak and Meyer-Bahlburg 1990.]

Boulton, M., G. Hart, and R. Fitzpatrick. 1992. The sexual behaviour of bisexual men in relation to HIV transmission. *AIDS Care* 4, 2: 165–175.

Bowker, Lee H. 1980. *Prison Victimization.* New York: Elsevier.

Boyer, Debra. 1989. Male prostitution and homosexual identity. *Journal of Homosexuality* 17, 1/2: 151–184.

Boynton, Robert S. 1995. Sex: Going both ways. *Vogue* 185, 6 (June): 132, 143.

Bozett, Frederick. 1981. Gay fathers: Identity conflict resolution through integrative sanctioning. *Alternative Lifestyles* 4, 1: 90–107.

—— 1982. Heterogeneous couples in heterosexual marriages: Gay men and straight women. *Journal of Marital and Family Therapy* 8, 1 (January): 81–89.

Braindrop, Lily. 1992. Bi and beyond. *Advocate* (July).

Brand, Pamela A., Esther D. Rothblum, and Laura J. Solomon. 1992. A comparison of lesbians, gay men, and heterosexuals on weight and restrained eating. *International Journal of Eating Disorders,* 11(3): 253–259. [Cited by Atkins 1998.]

Bray, A. 1982. *Homosexuality in Renaissance England.* London: Gay Men's.

Breslow, Norman, Linda Evans, and Jill Langley. 1985. On the prevalence and roles of females in the sadomasochistic subculture: Report of an empirical study. *Archives of Sexual Behavior* 14: 303–317. [Cited by Levitt, Moser, and Jamison 1994.]

—— 1986. Comparisons among heterosexual, bisexual, and homosexual male sado-masochists. *Journal of Homosexuality* 13, 1: 83–107.

Bressler, Lauren C. and Abraham D. Lavender. 1986. Sexual fulfillment of heterosexual, bisexual, and homosexual women. *Journal of Homosexuality* 12, 3/4 (May): 109–122.

Brierley, Harry. 1984. Gender identity and sexual behavior. In Kevin Howells, ed., *The Psychology of Sexual Diversity*, pp. 63–88. New York: Basil Blackwell.

Bristow, Joseph and Angelia R. Wilson, eds., 1993. *Activating Theory: Lesbian, Gay, Bisexual Politics*. London: Lawrence and Wishart.

Brody, Jane E. 1974. Bisexual life-style appears to be spreading and not necessarily among "swingers." *New York Times*, March 24, p. 37.

Brownfain, John J. 1985. A study of the married bisexual male: Paradox and resolution. *Journal of Homosexuality* 11, 1/2. Rpt. 1985. In Fritz Klein and Timothy J. Wolf, eds., *Two Lives to Lead: Bisexuality in Men and Women*, pp. 173–188. New York: Harrington Park.

Brownmiller, Susan. 1975. *Against Our Will*. New York: Simon and Schuster.

Bryant, Wayne M. 1997. *Bisexual Characters in Film: From Anaïs to Zee*. New York: Haworth.

Bullough, Vern L. 1976. *Sexual Variance in Society and History*. Chicago: University of Chicago Press.

—— 1979. *Homosexuality: A History*. New York: New American Library.

—— 1990. The Kinsey scale in historical perspective. In David P. McWhirter, Stephanie A. Sanders, and June Machover Reinisch, eds., *Homosexuality/Heterosexuality: Concepts of Sexual Orientation*, pp. 3–14. New York: Oxford University Press.

Bullough, Vern and Bonnie Bullough. 1977. *Sin, Sickness, and Sanity: A History of Sexual Attitudes*. New York: New American Library.

Burch, Beverly. 1993. Heterosexuality, bisexuality, and lesbianism: Rethinking psychoanalytic views of women's sexual object choice. *Psychoanalytic Review* 80, 1 (Spring): 83–99.

—— 1997. *Other Women: Lesbian/Bisexual Experience and Psychoanalytic Views of Women*. New York: Columbia University Press.

Burkhart, Kathryn Watterson. [1973] 1996. *Women in Prison: Inside the Concrete Womb*. Boston: Northeastern University Press.

Burstein, Jules Quentin. 1977. *Conjugal Visits in Prison: Psychological and Social Consequences*. Lexington, Mass.: Lexington. [Cited by Shore 1981.]

Butler, Judith. 1990. *Gender Trouble: Feminism and the Subversion of Identity*. New York: Routledge.

Butts, W. M. 1947. Boy prostitutes of the metropolis. *Journal of Clinical Psychopathology* 8: 674–681. [Cited by Pleak and Meyer-Bahlburg 1990; Coombs 1974.]

Buxton, Amity Pierce. 1991. *The Other Side of the Closet: The Coming-Out Crisis for Straight Spouses*. Santa Monica, Cal.: IBS.

Byne, William. 1988. Science and social values II. A critique of neuroendocrinological theories of the origin of sexual preference. *Einstein Quarterly Journal of Biology and Medicine* 6: 64–70.

—— 1997. LeVay's thesis reconsidered. In Martin Duberman, ed., *A Queer World: The Center for Lesbian and Gay Studies Reader*, pp. 318–327. New York: New York University Press.

Byne, William and Bruce Parsons. 1993. Human sexual orientation: The biologic theories reappraised. *Archives of General Psychiatry* 50 (March): 228–239.

Cabaj, Robert P. and Terry S. Stein, eds., 1996. *Textbook of Homosexuality and Mental Health*. Washington, D.C.: American Psychiatric.

Cáceres, Carlos F. and Jorge I. Cortiñas. 1996. Fantasy island: An ethnography of alcohol and gender roles in a Latino gay bar. *Journal of Drug Issues* 26, 1: 245–260.

Calhoun, Thomas C. 1992. Male street hustling: Introduction processes and stigma containment. *Sociological Spectrum* 12: 35–52.

Califia, Pat. 1983. Gay men, lesbians and sex: Doing it together. *Advocate* (July): 24–27. [Cited in Gagnon 1990.]

—— [1979] 1994. A secret side of lesbian sexuality. Pp. 157–164 in *Public Sex: The Culture of Radical Sex*. San Francisco: Cleis.

Cantarella, Eva. 1992. *Bisexuality in the Ancient World*. New Haven: Yale University Press. Rpt. 1988 *Secondo Natura*. Rome: Editori Riuniti

—— 1995. The sexual identity and behavior of Puerto Rican men who have sex with men. In Gregory M. Herek and Beverly Greene, eds., *AIDS, Identity, and Community: The HIV Epidemic and Lesbians and Gay Men*, pp. 105–114. Thousand Oaks, Cal.: Sage.

Carballo-Diéguez, Alex. 1989. Hispanic culture, gay male culture, and AIDS: Counseling implications. *Journal of Counseling and Development* 68, 1: 26–30.

Carballo-Diéguez, Alex and Curtis Dolezal. 1994. Contrasting types of Puerto Rican men who have sex with men (MSM). *Journal of Psychology and Human Sexuality* 6, 4: 41– 67.

Carrier, Joseph M. 1976. Cultural factors affecting urban Mexican male homosexual behavior. *Archives of Sexual Behavior* 5, 2: 103–124.

—— 1985. Mexican male bisexuality. In Fritz Klein and Timothy J. Wolf, eds., *Two Lives to Lead: Bisexuality in Men and Women*, pp. 75–85. New York: Harrington Park.

—— 1992. Miguel: The sexual life history of a gay Mexican American. In Gilbert Herdt, ed., *Gay Culture in America: Essays from the Field*, pp. 202–224. Boston: Beacon.

—— 1995. *De Los Otros: Intimacy and Homosexuality Among Mexican Men*. New York: Columbia University Press.

Carrier, Joseph, Bang Nguyen, and Sammy Su. 1992. Vietnamese American sexual behaviors and HIV infection. *Journal of Sex Research* 29, 4 (November): 547–560. [Cited by Matteson 1997.]

Carroll, Jon. 1974. Bisexual chic. *Oui Magazine* (February): 48, 115–118, 120.

Carroll, Leo. 1974. Race and sexual assault in a prison. Paper presented at the annual meeting of the Society for the Study of Social Problems.

—— 1977. Humanitarian reform and biracial assault in a maximum security prison. *Urban Life* 5: 417–437. [Cited by Long 1993.]

Case, P., M. Downing, B. Fergusson, J. Lorvick, and L. Sanchez. 1988. The social context of AIDS risk behavior among intravenous drug using lesbians in San Francisco. Paper presented at the Fourth International Conference on AIDS, June, Stockholm, Sweden. [Cited by Stevens 1994.]

Cass, Vivienne C. 1979. Homosexual identity formation: A theoretical model. *Journal of Homosexuality* 4: 219–35.

Cass, Vivienne C. 1990. The implications of homosexual identity formation for the Kinsey model and scale of sexual preference. In David P. McWhirter, Stephanie A. Sanders, and June Machover Reinisch, eds., *Homosexuality/ Heterosexuality: Concepts of Sexual Orientation*, pp. 239–266. New York: Oxford University Press.

—— 1996. Sexual orientation identity formation: A western phenomenon. In Robert P. Cabaj and Terry S. Stein, eds., *Textbook of Homosexuality and Mental Health*, pp. 227–251. Washington, D.C.: American Psychiatric.

Catania, Joseph A., Thomas J. Coates, Ron Stall, Heather Turner, John Peterson, Norman Hearst, M. Margaret Dolcini, Estie Hudes, John Gagnon, James Wiley, Robert Groves. 1992. Prevalence of AIDS-related risk factors and condom use in the United States. *Science* 258 (November 13): 1101–1106.

Cates, Jim A. and Jeffrey Markley. 1992. Demographic, clinical, and personality variables associated with male prostitution by choice. *Adolescence* 27, 107: 695–706.

Caukins, Sivan E. and Neil R. Coombs. 1976. The psychodynamics of male prostitution. *American Journal of Psychotherapy* 30: 441–451.

Centers for Disease Control. 1990. *HIV/AIDS Surveillance Report*. Atlanta: Centers for Disease Control.

—— 1994. *HIV/AIDS Surveillance Report*, 5, 4: 8. [Cited by McKirnan, Stokes, Doll, and Burzette 1995.]

Chan, Connie S. 1989. Issues of identity development among Asian-American lesbians and gay men. *Journal of Counseling and Development* 68, 1: 16–21.

—— 1992. Cultural considerations in counseling Asian American lesbians and gay men. In S. Dworkin and F. Gutiérrez, eds., *Counseling Gay Men and Lesbians*, pp. 115–124. Alexandria, Va.: American Association for Counseling and Development.

Chapman, Beata E. and JoAnn C. Brannock. 1987. Proposed model of lesbian identity development: An empirical examination. *Journal of Homosexuality* 14, 3/4: 69–80.

Charlton, Linda. 1971. The terrifying homosexual world of the jail system. *New York Times*, April 25.

Chauncey, George Jr. 1982/1983. From sexual inversion to homosexuality: Medicine and the changing conceptualization of female deviance. *Salmagundi* 58–59: 114–146.

Chesser, Eustace. 1971. *Strange Loves: The Human Aspects of Sexual Deviation*. New York: William Morrow.

Chetwynd, Jane, Angus Chambers, and Anthony J. Hughes. 1992. Condom use in anal intercourse amongst people who identify as homosexual, heterosexual, or bisexual. *New Zealand Medical Journal* 105, 937: 262–264.

Chiasson, M. A., A. R. Lifson, R. L. Stoneburner, W. Ewing, D. Hildebrandt, and H. W. Jaffe. 1988. HIV-1 seroprevalence in male and female prostitutes in New York City. Fourth International Conference on AIDS, June, Stockholm, Sweden, abstract no. 4116. [Cited by Pleak and Meyer-Bahlburg 1990.]

Chng, Chwee Lye, Frank Wong, and Jarvis Chen. 1997. Response to bisexual and homosexual behavior and HIV risk among Chinese-, Filipino-, and Korean-American men. *Journal of Sex Research* 34, 4: 423–424.

Chu, Susan Y., James W. Buehler, Patricia L. Fleming, Ruth L. Berkelman. 1990. Epidemiology of reported cases of AIDS in lesbians: United States, 1980–89. *American Journal of Public Health* 80, 11: 1380–1381.

Chu, Susan Y., Thomas A. Peterman, Lynda S. Doll, James W. Buehler, and James W. Curran. 1992. AIDS in bisexual men in the United States: Epidemiology and transmission to women. *American Journal of Public Health* 82, 2: 220–224.

Chuang, Henry T., Gerald M. Devins, John Hunsley, and M. John Gill. 1989. Psychosocial distress and well-being among gay and bisexual men with human immunodeficiency virus infection. *American Journal of Psychiatry* 146, 7: 876–880.

Chung, Y. Barry and Motoni Katayama. 1996. Assessment of sexual orientation in lesbian/gay/bisexual studies. *Journal of Homosexuality* 30, 4: 49–62.

Churchill, Wainwright. 1967. *Homosexual Behavior Among Males: A Cross-Cultural and Cross-Species Investigation*. New York: Hawthorn. [Cited by Pleak and Meyer-Bahlburg 1990.] Rpt. 1968.

Clausen, Jan. 1990a. My interesting condition. *Journal of Sex Research* 27, 3: 445–459.

—— 1990b. My interesting condition. *Out/Look* no. 7 (Winter).

Clemmer, Donald. 1958a. *The Prison Community*. New York: Holt, Rinehart.

—— 1958b. Some aspects of sexual behavior in the prison community. *Proceedings of the American Correctional Association*. [Cited by Gagnon and Simon 1973.]

Clinton, Michelle T. 1996. Almost a dyke: In search of the perfect bisexual. In Meg Daly, ed., *Surface Tension: Love, Sex, and Politics Between Lesbians and Straight Women*, pp. 160–165. New York: Simon and Schuster.

Coates, T. J., M. L. Ekstrand, S. M. Kegeles, and R. D. Stall. 1989. HIV antibody status and behavior change in two cohorts of gay men in San Francisco. Paper presented at the Fifth International Conference on AIDS, June, Montreal, Canada. [Cited by Ekstrand et al. 1994.]

Coates, Thomas J., Ron D. Stall, Joseph A. Catania and Susan M. Kegeles. 1988. Behavioral factors in the spread of HIV infection. *AIDS* 2(supp. 1):S239–S246.

Cochran, Susan D. and Vickie M. Mays. 1988. Disclosure of sexual preference to physicians by black lesbian and bisexual women. *Western Journal of Medicine* 149, 5: 616–619.

Cochran, William G., Frederick Mosteller, and John W. Tukey. 1953. Statistical problems of the Kinsey Report. *Journal of the American Statistical Association* 48, 264: 673–716.

Cohen, H., M. Marmor, H. Wolfe, and D. Ribble. 1993. Risk assessment of HIV transmission among lesbians. *Journal of Acquired Immune Deficiency Syndromes* 6: 1173–1174. [Cited by Rila 1996.]

Cohen, M. 1987. *Identifying and combating juvenile prostitution.* Washington, D.C.: National Association of Counties Research. [Cited by Yates, MacKenzie, Pennbridge, and Swofford 1991.]

Cole, Rebecca and Sally Cooper. 1990/1991. Lesbian exclusion from HIV/AIDS education: Ten years of low-risk identity and high-risk behavior. *SIECUS Report* 19, 2 (December/January): 18–23.

Coleman, Eli. 1981/1982. Bisexual and gay men in heterosexual marriage: Conflicts and resolutions in therapy. *Journal of Homosexuality* 7, 2/3: 93–103.

Coleman, Eli. 1982. Developmental stages of the coming out process. *Journal of Homosexuality* 7: 31–43.

—— 1985a. Integration of male bisexuality and marriage. *Journal of Homosexuality* 11, 1/2. Rpt. 1985. In Fritz Klein and Timothy J. Wolf, eds., *Two Lives to Lead: Bisexuality in Men and Women*, pp. 189–207. New York: Harrington Park.

—— 1985b. Bisexual women in marriages. *Journal of Homosexuality* 11, 1/2. Rpt. 1985. In Fritz Klein and Timothy J. Wolf, eds., *Two Lives to Lead: Bisexuality in Men and Women*, pp. 87–99. New York: Harrington Park.

—— 1987. Assessment of sexual orientation. *Journal of Homosexuality* 14, 1/2: 9–24.

—— 1989a. The development of male prostitution activity among gay and bisexual adolescents. *Journal of Homosexuality* 17, 1/2: 131–149.

—— 1989b. The married lesbian. *Marriage and Family Review* 14, 3/4: 119–135.

—— 1990. Toward a synthetic understanding of sexual orientation. In David P. McWhirter, Stephanie A. Sanders, and June Machover Reinisch, eds., *Homosexuality/Heterosexuality: Concepts of Sexual Orientation*, pp. 267–276. New York: Oxford University Press.

—— 1998. Paradigmatic changes in the understanding of bisexuality. In Erwin J. Haeberle and Rolf Gindorf, eds., *Bisexualities: The Ideology and Practice of Sexual Contact with Both Men and Women*, pp. 107–112. New York: Continuum.

Coleman, Eli, Walter O. Bockting, and Louis Gooren. 1993. Homosexual and bisexual identity in sex-reassigned female-to-male transsexuals. *Archives of Sexual Behavior* 22, 1: 37–50.

Coleman, Eli, Louis Gooren, and Michael Ross. 1989. Theories of gender transpositions: A critique and suggestions for further research. *Journal of Sex Research* 26, 4: 525–538.

Coleman, Eli and Gary Remafedi. 1989. Gay, lesbian, and bisexual adolescents: A critical challenge to counselors. *Journal of Counseling and Development* 68 (September/October): 36–40.

Colker, Ruth. 1996. *Hybrid: Bisexuals, Multiracials, and Other Misfits Under American Law.* New York: New York University Press.

Collins, Leslie E. and Nathalia Zimmerman. 1983. Homosexual and bisexual issues. *Family Therapy Collections*, pp. 82–100.

Conerly, Gregory. 1996. The politics of Black lesbian, gay, and bisexual identity. In Brett Beemyn and Mickey Eliason, eds., *Queer Studies: A Lesbian, Gay, Bisexual, and Transgender Anthology,* pp. 133–145. New York: New York University Press.

Converse, Jean, and S. Presser. 1986. *Survey Questions: Handcrafting the Standardized Questionnaire,* Beverly Hills, Cal.: Sage.

Cook, Kevin, in collaboration with Arthur Kretchmer, Barbara Nellis, Janet Lever, and Rosanna Hertz. 1983. The Playboy readers' sex survey: Part three. *Playboy* (May): 126, 128, 136, 210–212, 215–216, 219–220.

Coombs, Neil R. 1974. Male prostitution: A psychosocial view of behavior. *American Journal of Orthopsychiatry* 44, 5: 782–789.

Coons, Frederick W. 1972. Ambisexuality as an alternative adaptation. *Journal of the American College Health Association* 21: 142–144.

Cory, Donald Webster and John P. LeRoy. 1963. *The Homosexual and His Society.* New York: Citadel.

Coutinho, Roel A., Ruud L. M. Van Andel, and Toine J. Rijsdijk. 1988. Role of male prostitutes in spread of sexually transmitted diseases and human immuno-deficiency virus. *Genitourinary Medicine* 64, 3: 207–208. [Cited by Morse, Simon, Balson, and Osofsky 1992.]

Craft, M. 1966. Boy prostitutes and their fate. *British Journal of Psychiatry* 112: 1111. [Cited by Allen 1980.]

Crawford, J., G. W. Dowsett, S. Kippax, R. W. Connell, D. Baxter, et al. 1992. *Bisexual and Gay: The Sexual Behaviour of Men Who Have Sex with Men and Women in an Australian Sample of Gay and Bisexual Men.* Study A—Report no. 8, Social Aspects of the Prevention of AIDS Project, Macquarie University, Sydney, Australia. [Cited by Matteson 1997.]

Cross, Harold H. V. 1956. *The Lust Market.* New York: Citadel. [Cited by Benjamin and Masters 1964.]

Croteau, James M., and Mark von Destinon. 1994. A national survey of job search experiences of lesbian, gay, and bisexual student affairs professionals. *Journal of College Student Development* 35, 1: 40–45.

Curry, Jim. 1978. *Jet-set Bisexuals.* New York: Midwood.

Dajenya. 1990. Sisterhood crosses gender preference lines. *Lesbian Contradiction* no. 29 (Winter).

Daniel, David G., Virginia Abernethy, and William R. Oliver. 1984. Correlations between female sex roles and attitudes toward male sexual dysfunction in thirty women. *Journal of Sex and Marital Therapy* 10, 3: 160–169.

Dannecker, M. and R. Reiche. 1974. *Der Gewöhnliche Homosexuelle: Eine Soziologische Untersuchung uber Mannliche Homosexuelle in der Bundesrepublik.* Frankfurt am Main: Fischer Verlag. [Cited by Ross 1983c.]

Danzig, Alexis. 1990. Bisexual women and AIDS. In ACT UP/New York Women and AIDS Book Group, Marion Banzhaf et al., eds., *Women, AIDS, and Activism,* pp. 193–198. Boston: South End.

D'Augelli, Anthony R. 1989. Lesbians' and gay men's experiences of discrimination and harassment in a university community. *American Journal of Community Psychology* 17, 3: 317–321.

—— 1992. Lesbian and gay male undergraduates' experiences of harassment and fear on campus. *Journal of Interpersonal Violence* 7, 3 (September): 383–395.

—— 1993. Preventing mental health problems among lesbian and gay college students. *Journal of Primary Prevention* 13, 4: 245–261.

D'Augelli, Anthony R. and Scott L. Hershberger. 1993. Lesbian, gay, and bisexual youth in community settings: Personal challenges and mental health problems. *American Journal of Community Psychology* 21, 4: 421–448.

Däumer, Elisabeth D. 1994. Queer ethics; or, the challenge of bisexuality to lesbian ethics. In Claudia Card, ed., *Adventures in Lesbian Philosophy*, pp. 98–111. Bloomington: Indiana University Press. Rpt. from *Hypatia* 7, 4 (Fall 1992), pp. 91–105

Davidowitz, Esther. 1993. The secret life of bisexual husbands. *Redbook* 181, 5 (September): 114–117, 135.

Davidson, Phoebe, Jo Eadie, Clare Hemmings, Ann Kaloski, and Merl Storr, eds., 1997. *The Bisexual Imaginary: Representation, Identity and Desire*. London: Cassell.

Davies, Dominic. 1996. Working with people coming out. In *Pink Therapy: A Guide for Counsellors and Therapists Working with Lesbian, Gay, and Bisexual Clients*, pp. 66–85. Bristol, Pa.: Open University Press.

Davies, P. M., P. Weatherburn, A. J. Hunt, F. C. I. Hickson, T. J. McManus, and A. P. M. Coxon. 1992. The sexual behaviour of young gay men in England and Wales. *AIDS Care* 4, 3: 259–272.

Davis, Alan J. 1968. *Report on Sexual Assaults in the Philadelphia Prison System and Sheriff's Vans*. Philadelphia: Philadelphia District Attorney's Office. Rpt. Sexual assaults in the Philadelphia prison system and sheriff's vans. *Trans-Action* 6, 2 (December): 8–17.

—— 1970. Sexual assaults in the Philadelphia prison system. In J. H. Gagnon and W. Simon, eds., *The Sexual Scene*. New York: Aldine. [Cited by Tewksbury 1989b.]

Davis, J. A. and T. W. Smith. 1994. *General Social Surveys, 1972–1993*. Chicago: National Opinion Research Center, producer; Storrs, Conn.: Roper Center for Public Opinion Research, University of Chicago, distributor. [Cited by Binson et al. 1995.]

Deacon, Sharon A., Laura Reinke, and Dawn Viers. 1996. Cognitive-behavioral therapy for bisexual couples: Expanding the realms of therapy. *American Journal of Family Therapy* 24, 3 (Fall): 242–258.

Deb, Subimal. 1979. On bisexuality: An overview. *Samiksa* 33, 2: 53–57.

De Cecco, John P. 1981. Definition and meaning of sexual orientation. *Journal of Homosexuality* 6, 4 (Summer): 51–67.

—— 1985. Preface. In Fritz Klein and Timothy J. Wolf, eds., *Two Lives to Lead: Bisexuality in Men and Women*, pp. xi–xiii. New York: Harrington Park.

—— 1990. Sex and more sex: A critique of the Kinsey conception of human sexuality. In David P. McWhirter, Stephanie A. Sanders, and June Machover Reinisch, eds., *Homosexuality/Heterosexuality: Concepts of Sexual Orientation*, pp. 367–386. New York: Oxford University Press.

De Cecco, John P. and David Allen Parker. 1995a. The biology of homosexuality: Sexual orientation or sexual preference? *Journal of Homosexuality* 28, 1/2: 1–27.

—— 1995b. *Sex, Cells, and Same-Sex Desire: The Biology of Sexual Preference.* Binghamton, N.Y.: Haworth.

De Cecco, John P. and Michael G. Shively. 1983/1984. From sexual identity to sexual relationships: A contextual shift. *Journal of Homosexuality* 9, 2/3 (Winter/ Spring): 1–26.

DeHart, Dana D. and John C. Birkimer. 1997. Trying to practice safer sex: Development of the sexual risks scale. *Journal of Sex Research* 34, 1: 11–25.

Deihl, Marcia. 1989. A Stonewall within a Stonewall. *Bi Women* 7, 3 (June–July).

Deisher, Robert, V. Eisner, and S. I. Sulzsbacher. 1969. The young male prostitute. *Pediatrics* 43: 936–941. [Cited by Deisher, Robinson, and Boyer 1982.]

Deisher, Robert, Greg Robinson, and Debra Boyer. 1982. The adolescent female and male prostitute. *Pediatric Annals* 11, 10 (Ocrober): 819–825.

D'Emilio, John. 1983. *Sexual Politics, Sexual Communities: The Making of a Homosexual Minority in the United States, 1940–1970.* Chicago: University of Chicago Press.

Denny, Dallas and Jamison Green. 1996. Gender identity and bisexuality. In Beth A. Firestein, ed., *Bisexuality: The Psychology and Politics of an Invisible Minority,* pp. 84–102. Thousand Oaks, Cal.: Sage.

Devereaux, George and M. C. Moss. 1942. The social structure of prisons and the organic tensions. *Journal of Criminal Psychopathology* 4 (October): 306–324. [Cited by Gagnon and Simon 1973.]

Devor, Holly. 1993. Sexual orientation identities, attractions, and practices of female-to-male transsexuals. *Journal of Sex Research* 30, 4: 303–315.

Diamond, Lisa M. 1998. Development of sexual orientation among adolescent and young adult women. *Developmental Psychology* 34, 5 (September): 1085–1095.

Diamond, Milton. 1965. A critical evaluation of the ontogeny of human sexual behavior. *Quarterly Review of Biology,* 40: 147–175.

—— 1993. Homosexuality and bisexuality in different populations. *Archives of Sexual Behavior* 22, 4: 291–310.

—— 1995. Biological aspects of sexual orientation and identity. In Louis Diamant and Richard D. McAnulty, eds., *The Psychology of Sexual Orientation, Behavior, and Identity,* pp. 45–80. Westport, Conn.: Greenwood.

—— 1998. Bisexuality: A biological perspective. In Erwin J. Haeberle and Rolf Gindorf, eds., *Bisexualities: The Ideology and Practice of Sexual Contact with Both Men and Women,* pp. 53–80. New York: Continuum.

Diamond, Rochelle. 1993. Letter to the editor. *Science* 261 (September 3): 1258–1259.

Diaz, Theresa, Susan Y. Chu, Margaret Frederick, Pat Hermann, Anna Levy, Eve Mokotoff, Bruce Whyte, Lisa Conti, Mary Herr, Patricia J. Checko, Cornelis A. Rietmeijer, Frank Sorvillo, and Quaiser Mukhtar. 1993. Sociodemographics and HIV risk behaviors of bisexual men with AIDS: Results from a multistate interview project. *AIDS* 7, 9: 1227–1232.

DiClemente, R. J. 1987. The association of gender, ethnicity, and length of residence in the Bay Area to adolescents' knowledge and attitudes about acquired immune deficiency syndrome. *Journal of Applied Social Psychology* 17: 216–230. [Cited by Matteson 1997.]

DiClemente, R. J., K. Forrest, and S. Mickler. 1989. Differential effects of AIDS knowledge and perceived susceptibility on the reduction of high-risk sexual behaviors among college adolescents. Fifth International Conference on AIDS, Montreal, Quebec, June 4–9, abstract no. T.D.P.92. [Cited by Pleak and Meyer-Bahlburg 1990.]

Dixon, B. W., E. J. Streiff, A. H. Brunwasser, C. E. Haley, A. Freeman, and H. G. Green. 1991. Pilot study of a household survey to determine HIV seroprevalence. *Morbidity and Mortality Weekly Report* 40, 1:1–3.

Dixon, Dwight. 1985. Perceived sexual satisfaction and marital happiness of bisexual and heterosexual swinging husbands. *Journal of Homosexuality* 11, 1/2. Rpt. 1985. In Fritz Klein and Timothy J. Wolf, eds., *Two Lives to Lead: Bisexuality in Men and Women*, pp. 209–222. New York: Harrington Park.

Dixon, Joan K. 1984. The commencement of bisexual activity in swinging married women over age thirty. *Journal of Sex Research* 20, 1 (February): 71–90.

—— 1985. Sexuality and relationship changes in married females following the commencement of bisexual activity. *Journal of Homosexuality* 11, 1/2. Rpt. 1985. In Fritz Klein and Timothy J. Wolf, eds., *Two Lives to Lead: Bisexuality in Men and Women*, pp. 115–133. New York: Harrington Park.

Doll, Lynda S. 1997. Sexual behavior research: Studying bisexual men and women and lesbians. In John Bancroft, ed., *Researching Sexual Behavior: Methodological Issues*, pp. 145–182. Bloomington: Indiana University Press.

Doll, Lynda S. and Carolyn Beeker. 1996. Male bisexual behavior and HIV risk in the United States: Synthesis of research with implications for behavioral intervention. *AIDS Education and Prevention* 8, 3: 205–225.

Doll, Lynda, Ted Myers, Meaghan Kennedy, and Dan Allman. 1997. Bisexuality and HIV risk: experiences in Canada and the United States. *Annual Review of Sex Research VII*, pp. 102–147.

Doll, Lynda S., L. Peterson, C. W. White, and HIV Blood Donor Study Group. 1990. HIV-1 seropositive blood donors: A multi-center analysis of who they are and why they donate blood. Manuscript. [Cited by Doll, Peterson, Magaña, and Carrier 1991.]

Doll, Lynda S., John Peterson, J. Raul Magaña, and Joe M. Carrier. 1991. Male bisexuality and AIDS in the United States. In Rob Tielman, Manuel Carballo, and Aart Hendriks, eds., *Bisexuality and HIV/AIDS: A Global Perspective*, pp. 27–39. Buffalo, N.Y.: Prometheus.

Doll, Lynda S., Lyle R. Petersen, Carol R. White, Eric S. Johnson, John W. Ward, and the Blood Donor Study Group. 1992. Homosexually and nonhomosexually identified men who have sex with men: A behavioral comparison. *Journal of Sex Research* 29, 1: 1–14.

Donlou, John N., Deane L. Wolcott, Michael S. Gottlieb, and John Landsverk. 1985. Psychosocial aspects of AIDS and AIDS-related complex: A pilot study. *Journal of Psychosocial Oncology* 3, 2: 39–55.

Donahue, Phil. 1992. A husband's secret sex life. Donahue transcript no. 3442, April 9.

Donoghue, Emma. 1993. *Passions Between Women: British Lesbian Culture, 1668–1801.* Great Britain: Scarlet. Rpt. 1995. New York: Harper Collins.

Dörner, Günter. 1976. *Hormones and Brain Sexual Differentiation.* Amsterdam: Elsevier Scientific.

Dörner, Günter, Wolfgang Rohde, Fritz Stahl, Lothar Krell, and Wolf-Günther Masius. 1975. A neuroendocrine predisposition for homosexuality in men. *Archives of Sexual Behavior* 4, 1: 1–8.

Douce, Louise A. 1998. Can a cutting edge last twenty-five years? *Counseling Psychologist* 26, 5 (September): 777–785.

Douglas, Jason. [1967] 1970. *Bisexuality.* London: Canova. Rpt. 1997. Random House.

Douglas, Mary. 1966. *Purity and Danger.* London: Routledge.

Drew, Dennis and Jonathan Drake. 1969. *Boys for Sale: A Sociological Study of Boy Prostitution.* New York: Brown.

Duberman, Martin. 1974. The bisexual debate. *New Times,* June 28.

Duberman, Martin, ed. 1997. *A Queer World: The Center for Lesbian and Gay Studies Reader.* New York: New York University Press.

Duberman, Martin, Martha Vicinus, and George Chauncey, Jr., eds., 1989. *Hidden from History: Reclaiming the Gay and Lesbian Past.* New York: Meridian. Rpt. 1990.

Dwinell, Jane. 1989. I'm still a lesbian. *Lesbian Contradiction* no. 27 (Summer).

Eadie, Jo. 1993. Activating bisexuality: Towards a bi/sexual politics. In Joseph Bristow and Angelia R. Wilson, eds., *Activating Theory: Lesbian, Gay, Bisexual Politics,* pp. 139–170. London: Lawrence and Wishart.

—— 1997. Living in the past: *Savage Nights,* Bisexual times. *Journal of Gay, Lesbian, and Bisexual Identity* 2, 1: 7–26.

Earl, William L. 1990. Married men and same sex activity: A field study on HIV risk among men who do not identify as gay or bisexual. *Journal of Sex and Marital Therapy* 16, 4 (Winter): 251–257.

Earls, Christopher M. and Hélène David. 1989. A psychosocial study of male prostitution. *Archives of Sexual Behavior* 18, 5: 401–419.

Echols, Alice. 1984. The taming of the id: Feminist sexual politics, 1968–83. In Carole S. Vance, ed., *Pleasure and Danger: Exploring Female Sexuality,* pp. 50–72. London: Routledge. Rpt. 1989. London: Pandora.

Eckert, E., T. Bouchard, J. Bohlen, and L. Heston. 1986. Homosexuality in monozygotic twins reared apart. *British Journal of Psychiatry* 148: 421–425. [Cited in Diamond 1995.]

Ehrhardt, A. A., K. Evers, and J. Money. 1968. Influence of androgen and some aspects of sexually dimorphic behavior in women with the late-treated adrenogenital syndrome. *Johns Hopkins Medical Journal* 123, 3: 115–122. [Cited by Meyer-Bahlburg 1977b.]

Ehrhardt, Anke A., Heino F. L. Meyer-Bahlburg, Laura R. Rosen, Judith F. Feldman, Norma P. Veridiano, I. Zimmerman, and Bruce S. McEwen. 1985. Sexual orientation after prenatal exposure to exogenous estrogen. *Archives of Sexual Behavior* 14, 1: 57–75. [Cited by Meyer-Bahlburg 1977.]

Einhorn, Lena and Michael Polgar. 1994. HIV-risk behavior among lesbians and bisexual women. *AIDS Education and Prevention* 6, 6: 514–523.

Ekstrand, Maria L., Thomas J. Coates, Joseph R. Guydish, Walter W. Hauck, Linda Collette, and Stephen B. Hulley. 1994. Are bisexually identified men in San Francisco a common vector for spreading HIV infection to women? *American Journal of Public Health* 84, 6: 915–919.

Ekstrand, M., T. Coates, S. Lang, and J. Guydish. 1989. Prevalence and change of AIDS high risk sexual behaviour among bisexual men in San Francisco: The San Francisco Men's Health Study, abstract no. MDP31. Fifth International Conference on AIDS, June, Montreal, Canada. [Cited by Boulton, Hart, and Fitzpatrick 1992.]

Eliason, Michele J. 1996. Identity formation for lesbian, bisexual, and gay persons: Beyond a "minoritizing" view. *Journal of Homosexuality* 30, 3: 31–58.

—— 1997. The prevalence and nature of biphobia in heterosexual undergraduate students. *Archives of Sexual Behavior* 26, 3: 317–326

Elifson, Kirk W., Jacqueline Boles, and Mike Sweat. 1993. Risk factors associated with HIV infection among male prostitutes. *American Journal of Public Health* 83, 1: 79–83.

Elifson, K., J. Boles, M. Sweat, and W. Darrow. 1989. Risk factors for HIV infection among male prostitutes in Atlanta. V International Conference on AIDS, June 4–9, Montreal, Quebec, abstract no. W.A.P.38. [Cited by Pleak and Meyer-Bahlburg 1990.]

Elifson, Kirk W., Jackie Boles, Mike Sweat, William W. Darrow, William Elsea, and R. Michael Green. 1989. Seroprevalence of human immunodeficiency virus among male prostitutes. *New England Journal of Medicine* 321, 12: 832–833. [Cited by Pleak and Meyer-Bahlburg 1990.]

Elise, Dianne. 1997. Primary femininity, bisexuality, and the female ego ideal: A reexamination of female developmental theory. *Psychoanalytic Quarterly* 66: 489–517.

—— 1998. Gender repertoire: Body, mind, and bisexuality. *Psychoanalytic Dialogues* 8, 3: 353–371.

Ellis, Havelock. [1897] 1915, *Studies in the Psychology of Sex. Vol II, Sexual Inversion.* Philadelphia: F. A. Davis.

—— 1928. *Studies in the Psychology of Sex. Vol. VII, Eonism and other supplementary studies.* Philadelphia: Davis.

Ellis, Lee. 1996a. Theories of homosexuality. In Ritch C. Savin-Williams and Kenneth M. Cohen, eds., *The Lives of Lesbians, Gays, and Bisexuals: Children to Adults*, pp. 11–34. New York: Harcourt Brace.

—— 1996b. The role of perinatal factors in determining sexual orientation. In Ritch C. Savin-Williams and Kenneth M. Cohen, eds., *The Lives of Lesbians, Gays, and Bisexuals: Children to Adults*, pp. 35–70. New York: Harcourt Brace.

Ellis, Lee, Donald Burke, and M. Ashley Ames. 1987. Sexual orientation as a continuous variable: A comparison between the sexes. *Archives of Sexual Behavior* 16, 6: 523–529.

Emmons, C.-A., J. G. Joseph, R. C. Kessler, C. B. Wortman, S. B. Montgomery, and D. G. Ostrow. 1986. Psychosocial predictors of reported behavior change in homosexual men at risk for AIDS. *Health Education Quarterly* 13: 331–345. [Cited by Sandfort 1995.]

Engel, John W. and Marie Saracino. 1986. Love preferences and ideals: A comparison of homosexual, bisexual, and heterosexual groups. *Contemporary Family Therapy* 8, 3 (Fall): 241–250.

Epstein, Steven. 1987. Gay politics, ethnic identity: The limits of social constructionism. *Socialist Review* 17: 9– 54.

Ernst, F. A., R. A. Francis, H. Nevels, and C. A. Lemeh. 1991. Condemnation of homosexuality in the black community: A gender-specific phenomenon? *Archives of Sexual Behavior* 20: 579–585. [Cited by Francis et al. 1995.]

Ertel, Chris. 1989. Double perspective. *Weekly Tab*, May 2.

Espín, Oliva M. 1987. Issues of identity in the psychology of Latina lesbians. In Boston Lesbian Psychologies Collective, eds., *Lesbian Psychologies: Explorations and Challenges*, pp. 35–51. Urbana, Ill.: University of Illinois Press.

Esterberg, Kristin G. 1997. *Lesbian and Bisexual Identities: Constructing Communities, Constructing Selves.* Philadelpha: Temple University Press.

Ettorre, E. M. 1980. *Lesbians, Women, and Society.* London: Routledge.

Evan, Derek and Antonette M. Zeiss. 1985. Catastrophe theory: A topological reconceptualization of sexual orientation. *New Ideas in Psychology* 2, 3: 235–251.

Evans, B. A., R. A. Bond, and K. D. MacRae. 1998. Heterosexual behaviour, risk factors, and sexually transmitted infections among self-classified homosexual and bisexual men. *International Journal of STD and AIDS* 9: 129–133.

Evans, David T. 1993. *Sexual Citizenship: The Material Construction of Sexualities.* New York: Routledge.

Evans, Mark Chaim. 1989. Unresolved harmonies: The ups and downs of not quite coming out. *Advocate* (November).

Evans, Nancy J. and Vernon A. Wall. 1991. *Beyond Tolerance: Gays, Lesbians, and Bisexuals on Campus.* Alexandria, Va.: American College Personnel Association.

Faderman, Lillian. 1981. *Surpassing the Love of Men: Romantic Friendship and Love between Women from the Renaissance to the Present.* New York: William Morrow.

—— 1991. *Odd Girls and Twilight Lovers: A History of Lesbian Life in Twentieth-Century America.* New York: Columbia University Press.

Fast, Julius and Hal Wells. 1975. *Bisexual Living.* New York: Evans.

Fausto-Sterling, Anne. 1993. The five sexes; Why male and female are not enough. *Sciences* 33, 2 (March/April): 20–25.

Fausto-Sterling, Anne and Evan Balaban. 1993. Letter to the editor. *Science* 261 (September 3): 1257.

Fay, Robert E., Charles F. Turner, Albert D. Klassen, and John H. Gagnon. 1989. Prevalence and patterns of same-gender sexual contact among men. *Science* 243 (January 20): 338– 347.

Feldman, Philip. 1984. The homosexual preference. In Kevin Howells, ed., *The Psychology of Sexual Diversity*, pp. 5–41. New York: Basil Blackwell.

Feldman, Philip and M. J. MacCulloch. 1971. *Homosexual Behavior: Therapy and Assessment*. Oxford: Pergamon.

Feldman, M. P., M. J. MacCulloch, V. Mellor, and J. M. Pinschof. 1966. The application of anticipatory avoidance learning to the treatment of homosexuality III: The sexual orientation method. *Behaviour Research and Therapy* 4: 289–99.

Ferguson, Ann. 1981. Patriarchy, sexual identity, and the sexual revolution. Published as part of Ann Ferguson, Jacquelyn N. Zita, and Kathryn Pyne Addelson. On "Compulsory heterosexuality and lesbian existence": Defining the issues. *Signs* 7, 1: 158–199.

Firestein, Beth A., ed. 1996. *Bisexuality: The Psychology and Politics of an Invisible Minority*. Thousand Oaks, Cal.: Sage.

Fisher, Bruce, D. Kelly Weisberg, and Toby Marotta. 1982. *Report on Adolescent Male Prostitution*. San Francisco: Urban and Rural Systems Associates.

Fishman, Joseph. 1934. *Sex in Prison*. New York: National Library Press.

Fitzpatrick, Ray, Mary Boulton, and Graham Hart. 1989. Gay men's sexual behaviour in response to AIDS: Insights and problems. In Peter Aggleton, Graham Hart, and Peter M. Davies, eds., *AIDS: Social Representations, Social Practices*, pp. 127–146. London: Falmer. [Cited by Boulton, Hart, and Fitzpatrick 1992.]

Fitzpatrick, R., G. Hart, M. Boulton et al. 1989. Heterosexual sexual behaviour in a sample of homosexually active men. *Genito-Urinary Medicine* 65: 259–262. [Cited by Boulton, Hart, and Fitzpatrick 1992.]

Fitzpatrick, R., J. McLean, M. Boulton, G. Hart, and J. Dawson. 1990. Variation in sexual behaviour in gay men. In P. Aggleton, P. Davies, and G. Hart, eds., *AIDS: Individual, Cultural and Policy Dimensions*. London: Falmer. [Cited by Boulton, Hart, and Fitzpatrick 1992.]

Ford, Charles A. 1929. Homosexual practices of institutionalized females. *Journal of Abnormal and Social Psychology* 23 (January–March): 442–449. [Cited by Giallombardo 1966.]

Ford, Clellan S. and Frank A. Beach. 1951. *Patterns of Sexual Behavior*. New York: Harper and Row.

Foucault, Michel. 1979. *The History of Sexuality, I: An Introduction*. London: Allen and Lane. Rpt. 1990. Vintage.

Fox, Ann. 1991. Development of a bisexual identity: Understanding the process. In Loraine Hutchins and Lani Ka'ahumanu, eds., *Bi Any Other Name: Bisexual People Speak Out*, pp. 29–36. Boston: Alyson.

Fox, Ronald C. 1993. Coming out bisexual: Identity, behavior, and sexual orientation self-disclosure. Ph.D. diss., California Institute of Integral Studies, San Francisco. [Cited by Fox 1995.]

—— 1995. Bisexual identities. In Anthony R. D'Augelli and Charlotte J. Patterson, eds., *Lesbian, Gay, and Bisexual Identities Over the Lifespan: Psychological Perspectives*, pp. 48–86. New York: Oxford University Press.

—— 1996. Bisexuality in perspective: A review of theory and research. In Beth A.

Firestein, ed., *Bisexuality: The Psychology and Politics of an Invisible Minority*, pp. 3–50. Thousand Oaks, Cal.: Sage.

Francis, Rupert A., Frederick A. Ernst, Jessy G. Devieux, and Joyce Perkins. 1995. Race and sexuality in the United States: Sexuality and sexual preference in the African-American population. In Louis Diamant and Richard D. McAnulty, eds., *The Psychology of Sexual Orientation, Behavior, and Identity*, pp. 384–397. Westport, Conn.: Greenwood.

Franke, Rachel and Mark R. Leary. 1991. Disclosure of sexual orientation by lesbians and gay men: A comparison of private and public processes. *Journal of Social and Clinical Psychology* 10, 3: 262–269.

Freedman, Estelle B. 1996. The prison lesbian: Race, class, and the construction of the aggressive female homosexual, 1915–1965. *Feminist Studies* 22 (Summer): 397–423.

Freedman, Lawrence Zelik. 1961. Sexual, aggressive, and acquisitive deviates. *Journal of Nervous and Mental Diseases* 132: 44–49.

Freimuth, Marilyn J. and Gail A. Hornstein. 1982. A critical examination of the concept of gender. *Sex Roles* 8, 5: 515–532.

French, Simone A., Mary Story, Gary Remafedi, Michael D. Resnick, Robert W. Blum. 1996. Sexual orientation and prevalence of body dissatisfaction and eating disordered behaviors: A population-based study of adolescents. *International Journal of Eating Disorders* 19, 2: 119–126.

Freud, Sigmund. [1905] 1962. *Three Essays on the Theory of Sexuality*. Trans. James Strachey. New York: Basic.

—— [1920] 1955. The psychogenesis of a case of female homosexuality. *The Standard Edition of the Complete Psychological Works of Sigmund Freud*, vol. 7. Ed. and trans. James Strachey. London: Hogarth. [Cited by Freimuth and Hornstein 1982.]

—— [1937] 1964. Analysis terminable and interminable. *The Standard Edition of the Complete Psychological Works of Sigmund Freud*, vol. 23. Ed. and trans. James Strachey. London: Hogarth. [Cited by Freimuth and Hornstein 1982.]

Freund, Kurt. 1963. A laboratory method for diagnosing predominance of homo- and hetero-erotic interest in the male. *Behaviour Research and Therapy* 1, 1: 85–93. [Cited by Diamond 1998.]

Freund, Kurt, Robin Watsons, and Douglas Rienzo. 1989. Heterosexuality, homosexuality, and erotic age preference. *Journal of Sex Research* 26, 1: 107–117. [Cited by Diamond 1998.]

Friedland, Lucy. 1989. Are you suffering from the BLAS? New disease discovered in bi population: The Bisexual Label Avoidance Syndrome. *Bi Women: The Newsletter of the Boston Bisexual Women's Network* 7, 5: 1, 3, 7.

Friedman, Robert M. 1986. The psychoanalytic model of male homosexuality: A historical and theoretical critique. *Psychoanalytic Review* 73, 4: 483–519.

Friedman, Samuel R. In press, 1992. HIV seroconversions among out-of-treatment drug injectors in fourteen United States Cities. *Proceedings of the Third National AIDS Demonstration Research Conference*. Rockville, Md.: National Institute on Drug Abuse. [Cited by Young, Weissman, and Cohen 1992.]

Friedman, Samuel R., D. C. Des Jarlais, S. Deren et al. In press, 1992. HIV seroconversion among street-recruited drug injectors: A preliminary analysis. *Proceedings of the Third National AIDS Demonstration Research Conference.* Rockville, Md.: National Institute on Drug Abuse. [Cited by Young, Weissman, and Cohen 1992.]

Frye, Marilyn. 1983. *The Politics of Reality: Essays in Feminist Theory.* Trumansburg, N.Y.: Crossing.

Furnald, R. 1978. Male juvenile prostitution. Master's thesis. University of Southern California, Los Angeles. [Cited by Coleman 1989a.]

Gagnon, John H. 1977. *Human Sexualities.* Glenview, Il.: Scot, Foresman. OR Gagnon, John H. (Ed.) 1977. *Human Sexuality in Today's World.* Boston: Little, Brown.

Gagnon, John H. 1989. Disease and desire. *Daedalus* 118, 3: 47–77.

—— 1990a. Gender preference in erotic relations: The Kinsey scale and sexual scripts. In David P. McWhirter, Stephanie A. Sanders, and June Machover Reinisch, eds., *Homosexuality/Heterosexuality: Concepts of Sexual Orientation,* pp. 177–207. New York: Oxford University Press.

—— 1990b. The explicit and implicit use of the scripting perspective in sex research. *Annual Review of Sex Research* 1: 1–43.

Gagnon, John H. and William Simon. 1968. The social meaning of prison homosexuality. *Federal Probation* 32, 1: 23– 29.

—— 1973. *Sexual Conduct: The Social Sources of Human Sexuality.* Chicago: Aldine.

—— 1987. The sexual scripting of oral genital contacts. *Archives of Sexual Behavior* 16, 1: 1–25.

Gamson, Joshua. 1995. Must identity movements self-destruct? A queer dilemma. *Social Problems* 42, 3: 390–407. Rpt. in Steven Seidman. 1996. *Queer Theory/ Sociology.* Cambridge: Blackwell, pp. 395–420.

Garber, Marjorie. 1995. *Vice Versa: Bisexuality and the Eroticism of Everyday Life.* New York: Simon and Schuster.

Gebhard, Paul 1972. Incidence of overt homosexuality in the United States and Western Europe. In John M. Livingood, ed., *National Institute of Mental Health Task Force on Homosexuality: Final Report and Background Papers,* pp. 22–29. DHEW Publication no. (ADM) 76—357. U.S. Department of Health, Education, and Welfare Public Health Service Alcohol, Drug Abuse, and Mental Health Administration. National Institute of Mental Health. Washington, DC: US. Government Printing Office.

Gebhard, Paul. H. 1978. Preface. In Alan P. Bell and Martin S. Weinberg, *Homosexualities: A Study of Diversity Among Men and Women,* pp. 9–11. New York: Simon and Schuster.

Gebhard, Paul H., John H. Gagnon, Wardell B. Pomeroy, and Cornelia V. Christenson. 1965. *Sex Offenders: An Analysis of Types.* New York: Harper and Row.

Geller, Thomas, ed., 1990. *Bisexuality: A Reader and Sourcebook.* Ojai, Cal.: Times Change.

Gelman, David, with Lisa Drew, Mary Hager, Monroe Anderson, George Raine, and Sue Hutchison. 1987. A perilous double love life. *Newsweek* (July 13): 44–46.

George, Sue. 1993. *Women and Bisexuality*. London: Scarlet Press.

Gerrard, Susan and James Halpin. 1989. The risky business of bisexual love. *Cosmopolitan* (October): 203–205.

Giallombardo, Rose. 1966a. *Society of Women: A Study of a Women's Prison*. New York: Wiley.

——— 1966b. Social roles in a prison for women. *Social Problems* 13, 3: 268–288.

Gibson, P. 1989. Gay male and lesbian youth suicide. In M. Feinleib, ed., *Prevention and Intervention in Youth Suicide*, pp. 110–142. Report to the Secretary's Task Force on Youth Suicde, vol. 3. Washington, D.C.: U.S. Department of Health and Human Services. [Cited by Proctor and Groze 1994.]

Gilmartin, B. G. 1978. *The Gilmartin Report*. Secaucus, N.J.: Citadel. [Cited by Dixon 1984.]

Gindorf, Rolf and Alan Warran. 1998. Bisexualities: Heterosexual contacts of "gay" men, homosexual contacts of "straight" men. In Erwin J. Haeberle and Rolf Gindorf, eds., *Bisexualities: The Ideology and Practice of Sexual Contact with Both Men and Women*, pp. 213–220. New York: Continuum.

Ginsburg, Kenneth N. 1967. The "meat-rack": A study of the male homosexual prostitute. *American Journal of Psychotherapy* 21: 170–185.

Gochros, H. 1978. Counseling gay husbands. *Journal of Sex and Marital Therapy* 5: 142–151. [Cited by Coleman 1981/1982.]

Gochros, Jean S. 1985. Wives' reactions to learning that their husbands are bisexual. *Journal of Homosexuality* 11, 1/2. Rpt. 1985. In Fritz Klein and Timothy J. Wolf, eds., *Two Lives to Lead: Bisexuality in Men and Women*, pp. 101–113. New York: Harrington Park.

——— 1989. *When Husbands Come Out of the Closet*. New York: Harrington Park.

Godin, G., T. Myers, J. Lambert, L. Calzavara, and D. Locker. 1997. Understanding the intention of gay and bisexual men to take the HIV antibody test. *AIDS Education and Prevention* 9, 1: 31–41.

Gold, J., L. Griggs, M. Toomey, D. L. Alan, P. Turbitt, M. Anns, and P. R. McElwee. 1989. The development of a street based outreach programme to reach young male, female, and transsexual, street based prostitutes in Sydney, Australia. Fifth International Conference on AIDS, June 4–9, Montreal, Quebec, abstract no. M.D.O. 12. [Cited by Pleak and Meyer-Bahlburg 1990.]

Golden, Carla. 1987. Diversity and variability in women's sexual identities. In Boston Lesbian Psychologies Collective, ed., *Lesbian Psychologies: Explorations and Challenges*, pp. 19–34. Chicago: University of Illinois Press.

——— 1994. Our politics and choices: The feminist movement and sexual orientation. In Beverly Greene and Gregory Herek, eds., *Lesbian and Gay Psychology: Theory, Research, and Clinical Applications*, pp. 54–70. Thousand Oaks, Cal.: Sage. [Cited by Esterberg 1997.]

——— 1996. What's in a name? Sexual self-identification among women. In Ritch C. Savin-Williams and Kenneth M. Cohen, eds., *The Lives of Lesbians, Gays, and Bisexuals: Children to Adults*, pp. 229–249. New York: Harcourt Brace.

Goldsby Grant, Gwendolyn. 1986. Loving a bisexual man, letter. *Essence* (November): 12.

Gómez, Cynthia A. 1995. Lesbians at risk for HIV: The unresolved debate. Pp. 19–31 in Gregory M. Herek and Beverly Greene, eds., *AIDS, Identity, and Community: The HIV Epidemic and Lesbians and Gay Men*. Thousand Oaks, Cal.: Sage.

Gonsiorek, John C. 1982. Part II: Mental Health. Introduction. In William Paul, James D. Weinrich, John C. Gonsiorek, and Mary E. Hotvedt, eds., *Homosexuality: Social, Psychological, and Biological Issues*, pp. 57–70. Beverly Hills: Sage.

Gonsiorek, John C., Randall L. Sell, and James D. Weinrich. 1995. Definition and measurement of sexual orientation. *Suicide and Life-Threatening Behavior* 25 (Supplement): 40–51.

González, Francisco J. and Oliva M. Espín. 1996. Latino men, Latina women, and homosexuality. In Robert P. Cabaj and Terry S. Stein, eds., *Textbook of Homosexuality and Mental Health*, pp. 583–601. Washington, D.C.: American Psychiatric.

Goode, Erich and Lynn Haber. 1977. Sexual correlates of homosexual experience: An exploratory study of college women. *Journal of Sex Research* 13, 1: 12–21.

Goodman, Gerre, George Lakey, Judy Lashof, and Erika Thorne. 1983. *No Turning Back: Lesbian and Gay Liberation for the Eighties*. Philadelphia: New Society.

Gooren, Louis. 1990. Biomedical theories of sexual orientation: A critical examintion. In David P. McWhirter, Stephanie A. Sanders, and June Machover Reinisch, eds., *Homosexuality/Heterosexuality: Concepts of Sexual Orientation*, pp. 71–87. New York: Oxford University Press.

Gooren, Louis and Peggy T. Cohen-Kettenis. 1991. Development of male gender identity/role and a sexual orientation towards women in a 46,XY subject with an incomplete form of the androgen insensitivity syndrome. *Archives of Sexual Behavior* 20, 5: 459–470.

Gorman, E. Michael. 1991. Anthropological reflections on the HIV epidemic among gay men. *Journal of Sex Research* 28, 2: 263–273.

Gosselin, Chris and Glenn Wilson. 1984. Fetishism, sadomasochism and related behaviours. In Kevin Howells, ed., *The Psychology of Sexual Diversity*, pp. 89–110. New York: Basil Blackwell.

Greco, Marshall C. and James C. Wright. 1944. The correctional institution in the etiology of chronic homosexuality. *American Journal of Orthopsychiatry* 14, 2: 295–307.

Gregory, Roberta. 1992. "Bi way of response . . ." *Out/Look* no. 17 (Summer): 6–9.

Green, G. Dorsey and D. Merilee Clunis. 1989. Married lesbians. *Women and Therapy. Lesbianism: Affirming Nontraditional Roles* 8, 1/2 (special issue): 41–49.

Green, Richard. 1987. *The "Sissy Boy Syndrome" and the Development of Homosexuality*. New Haven: Yale University Press.

Greenberg, Jerrold S. 1973. A study of the self-esteem and alienation of male homosexuals. *Journal of Psychology* 83: 137–143.

Greene, Beverly. 1994. Ethnic-minority lesbians and gay men: Mental health and treatment issues. *Journal of Consulting and Clinical Psychology* 62, 2: 243–251.

Greenwald, Harold. 1958. *The Call Girl*. New York: Ballantine. [Cited by West 1967; Ward and Kassebaum 1965.]

Griensven, Godfried J. P. van, Robert A. P. Tielman, and Jaap Goudsmit, Jan van der Noordaa, Frank de Wolf, Ernest M. M. de Vroome, Roel A. Coutinho. 1987. Risk factors and prevalence of HIV antibodies in homosexual men in the Netherlands. *American Journal of Epidemiology* 125, 6: 1048–1057.

Guastello, Stephen J. 1987. A butterfly catastrophe model of motivation in organizations—academic-performance. *Journal of Applied Psychology* 72, 1: 165–182.

Gundlach, Ralph H. and Bernard F. Riess. 1968. Self and sexual identity in the female: A study of female homosexuals. In Bernard F. Riess, ed., *New Directions in Mental Health*, pp. 205–231. New York: Grune and Stratton.

Gutiérrez, Fernando J. and Sari H. Dworkin. 1992. Gay, lesbian, and African American: Managing the integration of identities. In Sari H. Dworkin and Fernando Gutiérrez, eds., *Counseling Gay Men and Lesbians: Journey to the End of the Rainbow*, pp. 141–155. Alexandria, Va.: American Association for Counseling and Development.

H., Pamela. 1989. Asian American lesbians: An emerging voice in the Asian American community. In Asian Women United of California, eds., *Making Waves: An Anthology of Writings by and About Asian American Women*, pp. 282–290. Boston: Beacon.

Haeberle, Erwin J. 1998. Bisexuality: History and dimensions of a modern scientific problem. Erwin J. Haeberle and Rolf Gindorf, eds., *Bisexualities: The Ideology and Practice of Sexual Contact with Both Men and Women*, p. 13–51. New York: Continuum.

Haeberle, Erwin J. and Rolf Gindorf, eds., 1998. *Bisexualities: The Ideology and Practice of Sexual Contact with Both Men and Women.* New York: Continuum.

Hagland, Paul EeNam Park. 1997. Response from Hagland to Matteson. *Journal of Sex Research* 34, 4: 424.

Hall, Donald E. and Maria Pramaggiore, eds., 1996. *RePresenting Bisexualities: Subjects and Cultures of Fluid Desire.* New York: New York University Press.

Halleck, Seymour L. and Marvin Hersko. 1962. Homosexual behavior in a correctional school for adolescent girls. *American Journal of Orthopsychiatry* 23: 911–917. [Cited by Gagnon and Simon 1973.]

Halperin, David M. 1993. Is there a history of sexuality? In Henry Abelove, Michèle Aina Barale, and David M. Halperin, eds., *The Lesbian and Gay Studies Reader*, pp. 416–431. New York: Routledge.

Hamer, Dean and Peter Copeland. 1994. *The Science of Desire: The Search for the Gay Gene and the Biology of Behavior.* New York: Simon and Schuster.

Hamer, Dean H., Stella Hu, Victoria L. Magnuson, Nan Hu, and Angela M. L. Pattatucci. 1993a. A linkage between DNA markers on the X chromosome and male sexual orientation. *Science* 261 (July 16): 321–327.

—— 1993b. Response to letters to the editor. *Science* 261 (September 3): 1259.

Hansen, Charles E. and Anne Evans. 1985. Bisexuality reconsidered: An idea in pursuit of a definition. *Journal of Homosexuality* 11, 1/2: 1–6.

Harbison, J. J., P. J. Graham, J. T. Quinn, H. McAllister, and R. A. Woodward. 1974. A questionnaire measure of sexual interest. *Archives of Sexual Behavior* 3: 357–66.

Harlan, Sparky, Luanna L. Rodgers, and Brian Slattery. 1981. *Male and Female Adolescent Prostitution: Huckleberry House Sexual Minority Youth Services Project.*

Washington, D.C.: Youth Development Bureau, U.S. Department of Health and Human Services. [Cited by Weisberg 1985.]

Harriman, Preston. 1969. *Bi-sexuality, Normal or Not?* North Hollywood, Cal.: Dominion.

Harris, D. A. I. 1977. Social-psychological characteristics of ambisexuals. Ph.D. diss., University of Tennessee. *Dissertation Abstracts International*, 39, 2: 574A. [Cited by Fox 1996.]

Harry, Joseph. 1984. Homosexual men and women who served their country. *Journal of Homosexuality* 10, 1/2: 117–125.

—— 1990. A probability sample of gay males. *Journal of Homosexuality* 19, 1: 89–104.

Hart, John and Diane Richardson, eds. 1981. *The Theory and Practice of Homosexuality*. Boston: Routledge and Kegan Paul.

Hartstein, Norman B. 1996. Suicide risk in lesbian, gay, and bisexual youth. In Robert P. Cabaj and Terry S. Stein, eds., *Textbook of Homosexuality and Mental Health*, pp. 819–837. Washington, D.C.: American Psychiatric.

Hatterer, L. 1970. *Changing Homosexuality in the Male.* New York: McGraw-Hill. [Cited by Hays and Samuels 1989.]

Hatterer, M. 1974. The problems of women married to homosexual men. *American Journal of Psychiatry* 131: 257–278.

Hawkins, Robert O. Jr. 1998. Educating sexuality professionals to work with homoerotic and ambierotic people in counseling and therapy: A voice from the trenches. *Journal of Sex Education and Therapy* 23, 1: 48–54.

Haynes, Stephen N. and L. Jerome Oziel. 1976. Homosexuality: Behaviors and attitudes. *Archives of Sexual Behavior* 5, 4: 283–289.

Hays, Dorothea and Aurele Samuels. 1989. Heterosexual women's perceptions of their marriages to bisexual or homosexual men. *Journal of Homosexuality* 18, 1/2: 81–100.

Hays, R. B., S. M. Kegeles, and T. J. Coates. 1991. Understanding the high rates of HIV risk-taking among young gay and bisexual men: The Young Men's Survey. Paper presented at the 7th International Conferences on AIDS, Florence, Italy, June. [Cited by Sandfort 1995.]

Heckathorn, Douglas D. 1997. Respondent-driven sampling: A new approach to the study of hidden populations. *Social Problems* 44, 2: 174–199.

Heckman, Timothy G., Jeffrey A. Kelly, Kathleen J. Sikkema, Roger R. Roffman, Laura J. Solomon, Richard A. Winett, L. Yvonne Stevenson, Melissa J. Perry, Ann D. Norman, Laurie J. Desiderato. 1995. Differences in HIV risk characteristics between bisexual and exclusively gay men. *AIDS Education and Prevention* 7, 6: 504–512.

Hedblom, Jack H. 1973. Dimensions of lesbian sexual experience. *Archives of Sexual Behavior* 2, 4: 329–341.

Heldke, Lisa. 1997. In praise of unreliability. *Hypatia* 12, 3 (summer): 174–182.

Helie-Lucas, Marie-Aimee. 1994. Strategies of women and women's movements in the Muslim world vis-à-vis fundamentalisms: From entryism to internationalism. In Oliver Mendelsohn and Upendra Baxi, eds., *The Rights of Subordinated Peoples*, pp. 251–275. Delhi: Oxford University Press.

Heller, A. C. 1987. Is there a man in your man's life? What every girl should know about the bisexual guy. *Mademoiselle* 93: 134–135, 153–154.

Hemmings, Clare. 1993. Resituating the bisexual body: From identity to difference. In Joseph Bristow and Angelia R. Wilson, eds., *Activating Theory: Lesbian, Gay, Bisexual Politics*, pp. 118–138. London: Lawrence and Wishart.

—— 1996. From lesbian nation to transgender liberation: A bisexual feminist perspective. *Journal of Gay, Lesbian, and Bisexual Identity* 1, 1: 37–59.

—— 1997. Bisexual theoretical perspectives: Emergent and contingent relationships. In Phoebe Davidson, Jo Eadie, Clare Hemmings, Ann Kaloski, and Merl Storr, eds., *The Bisexual Imaginary*, pp. 14–37. London: Cassell.

Herdt, Gilbert 1984. A comment on cultural attributes and fluidity of bisexuality. *Journal of Homosexuality* 10, 3/4: 53–61.

—— 1988. Cross-cultural forms of homosexuality and the concept "gay." *Psychiatric Annals* 18, 1: 37–39.

—— 1990. Developmental discontinuities and sexual orientation across cultures. In David P. McWhirter, Stephanie A. Sanders, and June Machover Reinisch, eds., *Homosexuality/Heterosexuality: Concepts of Sexual Orientation*, pp. 208–236. New York: Oxford University Press.

—— 1997. Third genders, third sexes. In Martin Duberman, ed., *A Queer World: The Center for Lesbian and Gay Studies Reader*, pp. 100–107. New York: New York University Press.

Herdt, Gilbert and Andrew Boxer. 1995. Bisexuality: Toward a comparative theory of identities and culture. In Richard G. Parker and John H. Gagnon, eds., *Conceiving Sexuality: Approaches to Sex Research in a Postmodern World*, pp. 69–83. New York: Routledge.

Herek, Gregory M., Douglas C. Kimmel, Hortensia Amaro, and Gary B. Melton. 1991. Avoiding heterosexist bias in psychological research. *American Psychologist* 46, 9: 957–963.

Hernandez, M., P. Uribe, S. Gortmaker, C. Avila, L. Elena De Caso, N. Mueller, and J. Sepulveda. 1992. Sexual behavior and status for human immunodeficiency virus type 1 among homosexual and bisexual males in Mexico City. *American Journal of Epidemiology* 135, 8: 883–894.

Hershberger, Scott L. 1997. A twin registry study of male and female sexual orientation. *Journal of Sex Research* 34, 2: 212–222.

Hershberger, Scott L. and Anthony R. D'Augelli. 1995. The impact of victimization on the mental health and suicidality of lesbian, gay, and bisexual youths. *Developmental Psychology* 31, 1: 65–74.

Hewitt, Christopher. 1998. Homosexual demography: Implications for the spread of AIDS. *Journal of Sex Research* 35, 4: 390–396.

Hickson, Alisdare. 1995. *The Poisoned Bowl: Sex, Repression, and the Public School System*. London: Constable.

Hill, Ivan. 1987. *The Bisexual Spouse: Different Dimensions in Human Sexuality*. McLean, Va.: Barlina.

Hinsch, Bret. 1990. *Passions of the Cut Sleeve: The Male Homosexual Tradition in China*. Berkeley: University of California Press.

Hirschfeld, Magnus. 1896 [1902]. *Sappho und Sokrates: Wie erklärt sich die Liebe der Männer und Frauen zu Personen des eigenen Geschlechts?* (Sappho and Socrates: How is the love of men and women to persons of their own sex to be explained?) Leipzig: Max Spohr. [Cited by Haeberle 1998.]

—— 1938. *Sexual Anomalies and Perversions.* London: Encyclopaedic.

Hite, Shere. 1976. *The Hite Report: A Nationwide Study on Female Sexuality.* New York: Macmillan.

—— 1987. *Women and Love: A Cultural Revolution in Progress.* New York: Knopf.

Hoffman, Martin 1972. The male prostitute. *Sexual Behavior* 2, 8: 16–21.

Hoffman, Richard J. 1984. Vices, gods, and virtues: Cosmology as a mediating factor in attitudes toward male homosexuality. *Journal of Homosexuality* 9, 2/3: 27–44.

Hollibaugh, Amber and Cherríe Moraga. [1981] 1983. What we're rollin around in bed with: Sexual silences in feminism. In Ann Snitow, Christine Stansell, and Sharon Thompson, eds., *Powers of Desire: The Politics of Sexuality,* pp. 394–405. New York: Monthly Review. Rpt. from. *Heresies* 12.

Holloway, Louis X. 1974. Sex at Parchman: Conjugal visiting at the Mississippi State Penitentiary. *New England Law Review* 10, 1: 143–155. [Cited by Shore 1981.]

Holtzen, David W. 1994. Handedness and sexual orientation. *Journal of Clinical and Experimental Neuropsychology* 16, 5: 702–712.

Hood, D., G. Prestage, J. Crawford, T. Sorrell, and C. O'Reilly. 1994. *Report on the B.A.N.G.A.R. Project: Bisexual Activity/Non-gay Attachment Research.* Darling-hurst, Australia: National Centre in HIV Epidemiology and Clinical Research. [Cited by Stokes, Taywaditep, Vanable, McKirnan 1996.]

Hooykaas, C., J. Van der Pligt, G. J. J. Van Doornum, M. D. Van der Linden, and R. A. Coutinho. 1989. High risk heterosexuals: Differences between private and commercial partners in sexual behavior and condom use. Fifth International Conference on AIDS, June 4–9, Montreal, Quebec, abstract no. T.A.P.14. [Cited by Pleak and Meyer-Bahlburg 1990.]

Hopper, Columbus B. 1978. Conjugal visiting. In Norman Johnston and Leonard D. Savitz, eds., *Justice and Corrections.* New York: Wiley. [Cited by Shore 1981.]

Horan, P. F. and R. J. DiClemente. 1993. HIV knowledge, communication, and risk behaviors among White, Chinese-, and Filipino-American adolescents in a high-prevalence AIDS epicenter: A comparative analysis. *Ethnicity and Disease* 3: 97–105. [Cited by Matteson 1997.]

Humphrey, Jill C. 1999. To queer or not to queer a lesbian and gay group? Sexual and gendered politics at the turn of the century. *Sexualities* 2, 2: 223–246.

Humphreys, Laud. 1970. *Tearoom Trade: Impersonal Sex in Public Places.* Chicago: Aldine.

Hunt, Morton. 1974. *Sexual Behavior in the 1970s.* Chicago: Playboy.

Hurwood, Bernhardt J. 1974. *The Bisexuals.* Greenwich, Conn.: Fawcett.

Hutchins, Loraine. 1996. Bisexuality: Politics and community. In Beth A. Firestein, ed., *Bisexuality: The Psychology and Politics of an Invisible Minority,* pp. 240–259. Thousand Oaks, Cal.: Sage.

Hutchins, Loraine and Lani Ka'ahumanu, eds. 1991. *Bi Any Other Name: Bisexual People Speak Out.* Boston: Alyson.

Ibrahim, Azmy Ishak. 1974. Deviant sexual behavior in men's prisons. *Crime and Delinquency* 20, 1: 38–44.

Icard, Larry. 1986. Black gay men and conflicting social identities: Sexual orientation versus racial identity. *Journal of Social Work and Human Sexuality* 4, 1/2: 83–92.

Imielinski, K. 1969. Homosexuality in males with particular reference to marriage. *Psychotherapy and Psychosomatics* 17, 2: 126–132. [Cited by Ross 1983c.]

Istvan, Joseph. 1983. Effects of sexual orientation on interpersonal judgment. *Journal of Sex Research* 19, 2: 173–191.

Izazola-Licea, Jose A., Jose L. Valdespino-Gomez, Steven L. Gortmaker, John Townsend, Julie Becker, Manuel Palacios-Martinez, Nancy E. Mueller, and Jaime Sepulveda Amor. 1991. HIV-1 seropositivity and behavioral and sociological risks among homosexual and bisexual men in six Mexican cities. *Journal of Acquired Immune Deficiency Syndromes* 4, 6:614–622.

Jacobs, Sue-Ellen and Jason Cromwell. 1992. Visions and revisions of reality: Reflections on sex, sexuality, gender, and gender variance. *Journal of Homosexuality* 23, 4: 43–69.

James, Jennifer. 1976. Motivations for entrance into prostitution. In Laura Crites, ed., *The Female Offender,* pp. 177–198. Lexington, Mass.: Lexington.

Janus, Mark-David, Barbara Scanlon, and Virginia Price. 1984. Youth prostitution. In Ann Wolbert Burgess, with Marieanne Lindeqvist Clark, eds., *Child Pornography and Sex Rings,* pp. 127–146. Lexington, Mass.: Lexington.

Janus, Samuel S. and Cynthia L. Janus. 1993. *The Janus Report on Sexual Behavior.* New York: Wiley.

Jeffreys, Sheila. 1985. *The Spinster and Her Enemies: Feminism and Sexuality, 1880–1930.* London: Zed.

Jersild, J. 1953. *Den Mandlige prostitution—årsager, omfang, følger.* Copenhagen: Dansk Videnskabs Forlag. [Cited by Pleak and Meyer-Bahlburg 1990.]

—— 1956. *Boy Prostitution.* Copenhagen: G. E. C. Gad. [Cited by Allen 1980; Pleak and Meyer-Bahlburg 1990.]

Johns, Donald R. 1971. Alternatives to conjugal visiting. *Federal Probation* 35, 1: 48–51. [Cited by Shore 1981.]

Johnson, Edwin. 1971. The homosexual in prison. *Social Theory and Practice* 1, 4: 83–95. Rpt. 1977. In R. Leger and J. Stratton, eds., *The Sociology of Corrections: A Book of Readings,* pp. 254–255. New York: Wiley.

Johnson, J. 1982. The influence of assimilation on the psychosocial adjustment of Black homosexual men. Ph.D. diss., California School of Professional Psychology, Berkeley, California. [Cited by Morales 1989.]

Jones, Billy E. and Marjorie J. Hill. 1996. African American lesbians, gay men, and bisexuals. In Robert P. Cabaj and Terry S. Stein, eds., *Textbook of Homosexuality and Mental Health,* pp. 549–561. Washington, D.C.: American Psychiatric.

Jones, David A. 1976. *The Health Risks of Imprisonment.* Lexington, Mass.: Heath.

Jordan, June. 1991. A new politics of sexuality. *Progressive* 55 (July): 12–13.

Joseph, Jill G., S. Maurice Adib, James S. Koopman, and David G. Ostrow. 1990. Behavioral change in longitudinal studies: Adoption of condom use by homosexual/bisexual men. *American Journal of Public Health* 80, 12: 1513–1516.

Joseph, Sue. 1997. *She's My Wife: He's Just Sex.* Sydney: Australian Centre for Independent Journalism, University of Technology.

Ka'ahumanu, Lani. 1990. Bisexuals battle for acceptance. *Utne Reader* no. 42 (November/December): 21–22.

Ka'ahumanu, Lani and Loraine Hutchins. 1991. Do bisexuals have a place in the gay movement? *Advocate* no. 578 (June).

Kahn, James G., Jill Gurvey, Lance M. Pollack, Diane Binson, and Joseph A. Catania. 1997. How many HIV infections cross the bisexual bridge? An estimate from the United States. *AIDS* 11:1031–1037.

Kalichman, Seth C., Roger A. Roffman, Joseph F. Picciano, and Marc Bolan. 1998. Risk for HIV infection among bisexual men seeking HIV-prevention services and risks posed to their female partners. *Health Psychology* 17, 4: 320–327.

Kaloski, Ann. 1997. Bisexuals making out with cyborgs: Politics, pleasure, con/fusion. *Journal of Gay, Lesbian, and Bisexual Identity* 2, 1: 47–64.

Kamel, H. 1983. *Downtown Street Hustlers: The Role of Dramaturgical Imaging Practices in the Social Construction of Male Prostitution.* University of California, San Diego. [Cited by Morse, Simon, Balson, and Osofsky 1992.]

Kang, Sung-Yeon, Stephen Magura, and Janet L. Shapiro. 1994. Correlates of cocaine/crack use among inner-city incarcerated adolescents. *American Journal of Drug and Alcohol Abuse* 20, 4 (November): 413–429.

Kapac, J. S. 1992. Chinese male homosexuality: Sexual identity formation and gay organizational development in a contemporary chinese population. Ph.D. diss., University of Toronto. [Cited by Matteson 1997.]

Kaplan, Gisela T. and Lesley J. Rogers. 1984. Breaking out of the dominant paradigm: A new look at sexual attraction. *Journal of Homosexuality* 10, 3/4: 71–75.

Kaplan, Rebecca. 1992. Compulsory heterosexuality and the bisexual existence: Toward a bisexual feminist understanding of heterosexism. In Elizabeth Reba Weise, ed., *Closer to Home: Bisexuality and Feminism*, pp. 269–280. Seattle: Seal.

Karlen, Arno. 1971. *Sexuality and Homosexuality: A New View.* New York: Norton.

—— 1988. *Threesomes: Studies in Sex, Power, and Intimacy.* New York: William Morrow.

Kaslow, Richard A., David G. Ostrow, Roger Detels, John P. Phair, B. Frank Polk, Charles R. Rinaldo, Jr. 1987. The Multicenter AIDS Cohort Study: Rationale, organization, and selected characteristics of the participants. *American Journal of Epidemiology* 126, 2: 310–318.

Kass, Nancy E., Ruth R. Faden, Robin Fox, and Jan Dudley. 1992. Homosexual and bisexual men's perceptions of discrimination in health services. *American Journal of Public Health* 82, 9: 1277–1279.

Katz, Jonathan Ned. 1976. *Gay American History: Lesbians and Gay Men in the U.S.A.* New York: Harper and Row.

—— 1983. *Gay/Lesbian Almanac: A New Documentary.* New York: Harper and Row.

—— 1990. The invention of heterosexuality. *Socialist Review* 20: 7–34.

—— 1995. *The Invention of Heterosexuality.* New York: Dutton. [Cited by Matteson 1997.]

—— 1997. "Homosexual" and "heterosexual": Questioning the terms. In Martin Duberman, ed., *A Queer World: The Center for Lesbian and Gay Studies Reader,* pp. 177–180. New York: New York University Press.

Kauth, Michael R. and Seth C. Kalichman. 1995. Sexual orientation and development: An interactive approach. Louis Diamant and Richard D. McAnulty, eds., *The Psychology of Sexual Orientation, Behavior, and Identity,* p. 81–103. Westport, Conn.: Greenwood.

Kegeles, Susan M., Joseph A. Catania, Thomas J. Coates, Lance M. Pollack, and Bernard Lo. 1990. Many people who seek anonymous HIV antibody testing would avoid it under other circumstances. *AIDS* 4, 6: 585–588.

Keiser, Sylvan and Dora Schaffer. 1949. Environmental factors in homosexuality in adolescent girls. *Psychoanalytic Review* 36: 283–295. [Cited by Ward and Kassebaum 1965.]

Kertbeny, Karoly Maria (as anonymous author). 1869. Section 143 of the Prussian Penal Code of April 14, 1851, and its upholding of Paragraph 152 in the draft of a penal code for the North German Confederation. Open, expert letter to His Excellence Herr Dr. Leonhardt, Royal Prussian Minister of State and Justice, Berlin 1869. Reprint in the *Jahrbuch für sexuelle Zwischenstufen* (Yearbook for sexual intermediate stages) 7:1. [Cited by Haeberle 1998.]

Kessler, Suzanne J. and Wendy McKenna. 1978. *Gender: An Ethnomethodological Approach.* New York: Wiley.

Kich, George Kitahara. 1996. In the margins of sex and race: Difference, marginality, and flexibility. In Maria P. P. Root, ed., *The Multiracial Experience: Racial Borders as the New Frontier,* pp. 263–276. Thousand Oaks, Cal.: Sage.

King, Katie. 1986. The situation of lesbianism as feminism's magical sign: Contests for meaning and the U.S. women's movement, 1968–1972. *Communication* 9, 1 (Fall): 65–91.

Kinsey, Alfred C., Wardell B. Pomeroy, and Clyde E. Martin. 1948. *Sexual Behavior in the Human Male.* Philadelphia: Saunders.

Kinsey, Alfred C., Wardell B. Pomeroy, Clyde E. Martin, and Paul H. Gebhard. 1953. *Sexual Behavior in the Human Female.* Philadelphia: Saunders.

Kippax, S., J. Crawford, P. Rodden, and K. Benton, 1994. *Report on Project Male-Call: National Telephone Survey of Men Who Have Sex with Men.* Canberra: Australian Government Publishing Service. [Cited by Stokes, Taywaditep, Vanable, McKirnan 1996.]

Kirkham, George L. 1971. Homosexuality in prison. In J. M. Henslin, ed., *Studies in the Sociology of Sex,* pp. 325–349. New York: Appleton-Century-Crofts.

Kirsch, John A. W. and James Eric Rodman. 1982. Selection and sexuality: The Darwinian view of homosexuality. In William Paul, James D. Weinrich, John C. Gonsiorek, and Mary E. Hotvedt, eds., *Homosexuality: Social, Psychological, and Biological Issues,* pp. 183–195. Beverly Hills: Sage.

Kitzinger, Celia. 1987. *The Social Construction of Lesbianism.* London: Sage. Rpt. 1989.

—— 1995. Social constructionism: Implications for lesbian and gay psychology. In Anthony R. D'Augelli and Charlotte J. Patterson, eds., *Lesbian, Gay, and Bisexual Identities Over the Lifespan: Psychological Perspectives*, pp. 136–161. New York: Oxford.

Klassen, A. D., C. J. Williams, and E. E. Levitt. 1989. *Sex and Morality in the U.S.* Middletown, Conn.: Wesleyan University Press.

Klein, Fred. 1978. *The Bisexual Option: A Concept of One-Hundred Percent Intimacy.* New York: Arbor House.

Klein, Fritz. 1990. The need to view sexual orientation as a multivariable dynamic process: A theoretical perspective. In David P. McWhirter, Stephanie A. Sanders, and June Machover Reinisch, eds., *Homosexuality/Heterosexuality: Concepts of Sexual Orientation*, pp. 277–282. New York: Oxford University Press.

—— 1993. *The Bisexual Option.* 2d ed. New York: Harrington Park.

Klein, Fritz, Barry Sepekoff, and Timothy J. Wolf. 1985. Sexual orientation: A Multivariable dynamic process. *Journal of Homosexuality* 11, 1/2: 35–49. Rpt. 1985. In Fritz Klein and Timothy J. Wolf, eds., *Two Lives to Lead: Bisexuality in Men and Woman*, pp. 35–49. New York: Harrington Park.

Klitzman, Robert, J. Alexander Bodkin, and Harrison G. Pope Jr. 1998. Sexual orientation and associated characteristics among North American academic psychiatrists. *Journal of Sex Research* 35, 3 (August): 282–287.

Knox, Richard A. N.d. [post-1988]. Bisexuals put women at risk, studies say. *Boston Globe.*

Koch, Nadine S. and H. Eric Schockman. 1998. Democratizing internet access in the lesbian, gay, and bisexual communities. In Bosah Ebo, ed., *Cyberghetto or Cybertopia? Race, Class, and Gender on the Internet*, pp. 171–184. Westport, Conn.: Praeger.

Koertge, Noretta. 1990. Constructing concepts of sexuality: A philosophical commentary. In David P. McWhirter, Stephanie A. Sanders, and June Machover Reinisch, eds., *Homosexuality/Heterosexuality: Concepts of Sexual Orientation*, pp. 387–397. New York: Oxford University Press.

Kohn, Barry and Alice Matusow. 1980. *Barry and Alice: Portrait of a Bisexual Marriage.* Englewood Cliffs, N.J.: Prentice-Hall.

Kolaszynska-Carr, A. 1970. Ph.D. diss., University of Birmingham. [Cited by Feldman 1984.]

Kolodny, R. C., L. S. Jacobs, W. H. Masters et al. 1972. Plasma gonadotrophins and prolactin in male homosexuals. *Lancet* 2: 18–20.

Kolodny, R. C., W. H. Masters, J. Hendryx et al. 1971. Plasma testosterone and semen analysis in male homosexuals. *New England Journal of Medicine* 285: 1170–1174.

Kooden, Harold D., Stephen F. Morin, Dorothy I. Riddle, Martin Rogers, Barbara E. Sang, and Fred Strassburger. 1979. *Removing the Stigma: Final Report of the American Psychological Association's Board of Social and Ethical Responsibility for Psychology's Task Force on the Status of Lesbian and Gay Male Psychologists.* Washington, D.C.: American Psychological Association.

Kooperman, Leonard. 1994. A survey of gay and bisexual men age fifty and older: AIDS related knowledge, attitude, belief, and behavior. *AIDS Patient Care* 8, 3: 114–117.

Kosofsky, Sidney and Albert Ellis. 1958. Illegal communications among institutionalized female delinquents. *Journal of Social Psychology* 48 (August): 155–160. [Cited by Gagnon and Simon 1973.]

Kramer, Mark A., Sevgi O. Aral, and James W. Curran. 1980. Self-reported behavior patterns of patients attending a sexually transmitted disease clinic. *American Journal of Public Health* 70, 9: 997–1000.

Krieger, Nancy and Stephen Sidney. 1997. Prevalence and health implications of anti-gay discrimination: A study of black and white women and men in the CARDIA cohort. *International Journal of Health Services* 27, 1: 157–176.

Krijnen, Pieta, J. Anneke R. van den Hoek, Roel A. Coutinho. 1994. Do bisexual men play a significant role in the heterosexual spread of HIV? *Sexually Transmitted Disease* 21, 1: 24–25.

Kroeber, Arthur. 1983. Bisexuality: Toward a new understanding of men, women, and their feelings. *Boston Globe* (October 10): 52, 54.

Kruks, Gabe. 1991. Gay and lesbian homeless/street youth: Special issues and concerns. *Journal of Adolescent Health* 12, 7: 515–518.

Ku, Leighton C., Freya L. Sonenstein, and Joseph H. Pleck. 1990. Patterns of AIDS-related risk and preventive behaviors among teenage men in the U.S.A. Paper presented at the Sixth International Conference on AIDS, San Francisco, CA. [Cited by Rotheram-Borus et al. 1992.]

Kuhn, Thomas S. 1970. *The Structure of Scientific Revolutions.* Chicago: University of Chicago Press. 2d ed. Rpt. 1962.

Kumar, Bhushan and Michael W. Ross. 1991. Sexual behaviour and HIV infection risks in Indian homosexual men: A cross-cultural comparison. *International Journal of STD and AIDS* 2: 442–444.

Kurtz, Steven P. 1997. Teaching sexuality in a multicultural environment. In Paula C. Rust, ed., *The Sociology of Sexuality and Sexual Orientation: Syllabi and Teaching Materials,* pp. 165–167. Washington, D.C.: American Sociological Association Teaching Resources Center.

Laine, Harriet. 1986. Yes, I'm still a lesbian—Even though I love a man. *Advocate* (July).

Landis, Suzanne E., JoAnne L. Earp, and Gary G. Koch. 1992. Impact of HIV testing and counseling on subsequent sexual behavior. *AIDS Education and Prevention* 4, 1: 61–70.

Laner, Mary Riege. 1977. Permanent partner priorities: Gay and straight. *Journal of Homosexuality* 3, 1: 21–39.

Latham, J. D. and G. D. White. 1978. Coping with homosexual expression within heterosexual marriages: Five case studies. *Journal of Sex and Marital Therapy* 4: 198–212. [Cited by Brownfain 1985.]

LaTorre, Ronald A. and Kristina Wendenburg. 1983. Psychological characteristics of bisexual, heterosexual, and homosexual women. *Journal of Homosexuality* 9, 1: 87–97.

Lau, M. D. and M. L. Ng. 1989. Homosexuality in Chinese culture. *Culture, Medicine, and Psychiatry* 13:465–488.

Lauderback, D. and D. Waldorf. 1989. Male prostitution and AIDS: preliminary findings. *Focus: A Guide to AIDS Research* (January): 3–4. [Cited by Pleak and Meyer-Bahlburg 1990.]

Laumann, Edward O., John H. Gagnon, Robert T. Michael, and Stuart Michaels. 1994. *The Social Organization of Sexuality: Sexual Practices in the United States.* Chicago: University of Chicago Press.

Lavender, Abraham D. and Lauren Bressler. 1981. Nondualists as deviants: Female bisexuals compared to female heterosexuals-homosexuals. *Deviant Behavior: An Interdisciplinary Journal* 2: 155–165.

Laws, D. R. 1984. The assessment of diverse sexual behaviour. In Kevin Howells, ed., *The Psychology of Sexual Diversity,* pp. 177–218. New York: Basil Blackwell.

Lee, JeeYeun. 1996. Why Suzie Wong is not a lesbian: Asian and Asian American lesbian and bisexual women and femme/butch/gender identies. In Brett Beemyn and Mickey Eliason, eds., *Queer Studies: A Lesbian, Gay, Bisexual, and Transgender Anthology,* pp. 115–132. New York: New York University Press.

Leeds Revolutionary Feminist Group. 1981. Political lesbianism: The case against heterosexuality. *Love Your Enemy? The Debate between Heterosexual Feminism and Political Lesbianism,* pp. 5–10. London: Onlywomen. Previously presented at "a conference" in 1979 and published in *Wires* 81.

Leland, John with Steve Rhodes, Peter Katel, Claudia Kalb, Marc Peyser, Nadine Joseph, and Martha Brant. 1995. Bisexuality emerges as a new sexual identity. *Newsweek* (July 17): 44–50.

Lemp, George F., Anne M. Hirozawa, Daniel Givertz, Giuliano N. Nieri, Laura Anderson, Mary Lou Lindegren, Robert S. Janssen, and Mitchell Katz. 1994. Seroprevalence of HIV and risk behaviors among young homosexual and bisexual men: The San Francisco/Berkeley Young Men's Survey. *Journal of the American Medical Association* 272, 6: 449–454.

Lemp, George F., Melissa Jones, Timothy A. Kellogg, Giuliano N. Nieri, Laura Anderson, David Withum, and Mitchell Katz. 1995. HIV seroprevalence and risk behaviors among lesbians and bisexual women in San Francisco and Berkeley, California. *American Journal of Public Health* 85, 11: 1549–1552.

Lesbian Contradiction. 1983. Many lesbians are going straight now: A conversation. *Lesbian Contradiction,* no. 2 (Spring).

LeVay, Simon. 1991. A difference in hypothalamic structure between heterosexual and homosexual men. *Science* 253 (August 30): 1034–1037.

—— 1996. *Queer Science: The Use and Abuse of Research into Homosexuality.* Cambridge: The MIT Press.

Lever, Janet. 1994. Sexual revelations: The 1994 Advocate survey of sexuality and relationships: The men. *Advocate* nos. 661–662 (August 23).

Lever, Janet, David E. Kanouse, William H. Rogers, Sally Carson, and Rosanna Hertz. 1992. Behavior patterns and sexual identity of bisexual males. *Journal of Sex Research* 29, 2: 141–167.

Levin, Bonnie E., Joseph R. Berger, Toni Didona, and Robert Duncan. 1992.

Cognitive function in asymptomatic HIV-1 infection: The effects of age, education, ethnicity, and depression. *Neuropsychology* 6, 4: 303–313.

Levine, Heidi and Nancy J. Evans. 1991. The development of gay, lesbian, and bisexual identities. In Nancy J. Evans and Vernon A. Wall, eds., *Beyond Tolerance: Gays, Lesbians and Bisexuals on Campus*, pp. 1–24. Alexandria, Va.: American College Personnel Association.

Levitt, Eugene E., Charles Moser, and Karen V. Jamison. 1994. The prevalence and some attributes of females in the sadomasochistic subculture: A second report. *Archives of Sexual Behavior* 23, 4: 465–473.

Lev-Ran, A. 1974. Sexuality and educational levels of women with late-treated adrenogenital syndrome. *Archives of Sexual Behavior* 3, 1: 27–32.

Lewis, Diane K. and John K. Watters. 1994. Sexual behavior and sexual identity in male injection drug users. *Journal of Acquired Immune Deficiency Syndromes* 7: 190–198.

Lidz, Theodore. 1993. Reply to "A genetic study of male sexual orientation." *Archives of General Psychiatry* 50 (March): 240.

Lifson, Alan R. 1992. Men who have sex with men: Continued challenges for preventing HIV infection and AIDS. *American Journal of Public Health* 82, 2: 166–167.

Lifson, Alan R., Mark Stanley, Jim Pane, Paul M. O'Malley, Judith C. Wilber, Allyson Stanley, Beverly Jeffery, George W. Rutherford, and Paul R. Sohmer. 1990. Detection of human immunodeficiency virus DNA using the polymerase chain reaction in a well-characterized group of homosexual and bisexual men. *Journal of Infectious Diseases* 161, 3: 436–439.

Lindner, Robert M. 1948. Sexual behavior in penal institutions. In Albert Deutsch, ed., *Sex Habits of American Men: A Symposium on the Kinsey Report*, pp. 201–215. New York: Prentice-Hall.

Litwoman, Jane. 1990. Some thoughts on bisexuality. *Lesbian Contradiction* no. 29 (Winter).

Lockwood, Daniel. 1980. *Prison Sexual Violence*. New York: Elsevier. [Cited by Tewksbury 1989b.]

Loewenstein, Sophie Freud. 1984/85. On the diversity of love object orientation among women. *Journal of Social Work and Human Sexuality* 3, 2–3:7–24.

Long, Gary Thomas. 1993. Homosexual relationships in a unique setting: The male prison. In Louis Diamant, ed., *Homosexual Issues in the Workplace*, pp. 143–159. Washington, D.C.: Taylor and Francis.

Lorber, Judith. 1994. *Paradoxes of Gender*. New Haven: Yale University Press.

—— 1996. Beyond the binaries: Depolarizing the categories of sex, sexuality, and gender. *Sociological Inquiry* 66, 2 (May): 143–159.

Lothane, Zvi. 1992. The human dilemma: Heterosexual, homosexual, bisexual, holosexual? *Issues in Ego Psychology* 15, 1: 18–32.

Lourea, David N. 1985. Psycho-social issues related to counseling bisexuals. In Fritz Klein and Timothy J. Wolf, eds., *Two Lives to Lead: Bisexuality in Men and Women*, pp. 51–62. New York: Harrington Park.

Luckenbill, David F. 1985. Entering male prostitution. *Urban Life* 14, 2: 131–153.

—— 1986. Deviant career mobility: The case of male prostitutes. *Social Problems* 33, 4: 283–296.

Lynn, D. B. 1959. A note on sex differences in the development of masculine and feminine identification. *Psychological Review* 66: 126.

Lynne, David. 1967. *The Bisexual Woman*. New York: Midwood.

Lyter, David W., Ronald O. Valdiserri, Lawrence A. Kingsley, William P. Amoroso, and Charles R. Rinaldo. 1987. The HIV antibody test: Why gay and bisexual men want or do not want to know their results. *Public Health Reports* 102, 5: 468–474.

McCaghy, Charles H. and James K. Skipper, Jr. 1969. Lesbian behavior as an adaptation to the occupation of stripping. *Social Problems* 17: 262–270.

McCombs, Scott B., Eugene McCray, Deborah A. Wendell, Patricia A. Sweeney, and Ida M. Onorato. 1992. Epidemiology of HIV-1 infection in bisexual women. *Journal of Acquired Immune Deficiency Syndromes* 5, 8: 850–852.

McConaghy, Nathaniel. 1978. Heterosexual experience, marital status, and orientation of homosexual males. *Archives of Sexual Behavior* 7, 6: 575–581.

—— 1987. Heterosexuality/homosexuality: Dichotomy or continuum. *Archives of Sexual Behavior* 16, 5: 411–424.

McConaghy, N. and M. S. Armstrong. 1983. Sexual orientation and consistency of sexual identity. *Archives of Sexual Behavior* 12, 4: 317–327.

McConaghy, N., M. S. Armstrong, P.C. Birrell, and N. Buhrich, 1979. The incidence of bisexual feelings and opposite sex behavior in medical students. *Journal of Nervous and Mental Disease* 167, 11: 685–688.

McConaghy, Nathaniel, Neil Buhrich, and Derrick Silove. 1994. Opposite sex-linked behaviors and homosexual feelings in the predominantly heterosexual male majority. *Archives of Sexual Behavior* 23, 5: 565–577.

McCusker, Jane, Jane G. Zapka, Anne M. Stoddard, and Kenneth H. Mayer. 1989. Responses to the AIDS epidemic among homosexually active men: Factors associated with preventive behavior. *Patient Education and Counseling* 13: 15–30.

MacDonald, A. P. Jr. 1981. Bisexuality: Some comments on research and theory. *Journal of Homosexuality* 6, 3: 21–35.

—— 1982. Research on sexual orientation: A bridge that touches both shores but doesn't meet in the middle. *Journal of Sex Education and Therapy* 8: 9–13. [Cited by Evans 1991.]

—— 1983. A little bit of lavender goes a long way: A critique of research on sexual orientation. *Journal of Sex Research* 19, 1 (February): 94–100.

McDonald, Gary J. 1982. Individual differences in the coming out process for gay men: Implications for theoretical models. *Journal of Homosexuality* 8: 47–60.

McGuire, Edward III, Judith Shega, Glenn Nicholls, Patrick Deese, and C. Seth Landefeld. 1992. Sexual behavior, knowledge, and attitudes about AIDS among college freshmen. *American Journal of Preventive Medicine* 8, 4: 226–234.

MacInnes, Colin. 1973. *Loving Them Both: A Study of Bisexuality and Bisexuals*. London: Martin Brian and O'Keeffe.

McIntosh, Mary. 1968. The homosexual role. *Social Problems*, 16, 2: 182–192. Rpt. 1981. In Kenneth Plummer, ed., *The Making of the Modern Homosexual*, pp. 30–49. Totowa, N.J.: Barnes and Noble.

McKenna, Neil. 1995. Men loving men: Towards a taxonomy of male-to-male sexualities in the developing world. *Perversions* 5 (Summer): 54–101.

McKirnan, David J., Joseph P. Stokes, Lynda Doll, and Rebecca G. Burzette. 1995. Bisexually active men: Social characteristics and sexual behavior. *Journal of Sex Research* 32, 1: 65–76.

McKusick, Leon, William Horstman, and Thomas J. Coates. 1985. AIDS and sexual behavior reported by gay men in San Francisco. *American Journal of Public Health* 75, 5: 493–496.

MacNamara, Donal E. J. 1965. Male prostitution in American cities: A socioeconomic or pathological phenomenon? *American Journal Orthopsychiatry* 35: 204.

McWhirter, David P., Stephanie A. Sanders, and June Machover Reinisch, eds. 1990. *Homosexuality/Heterosexuality: Concepts of Sexual Orientation.* New York: Oxford University Press.

Maddox, Brenda. 1982. *Married and Gay: An Intimate Look at a Different Relationship.* New York: Harcourt Brace Jovanovich.

Magaña, J. R. and J. M. Carrier. 1991. Mexican and Mexican American male sexual behavior and spread of AIDS in California. *Journal of Sex Research,* 28, 3: 425–441.

Magura, Stephen, Joanne O'Day, and Andrew Rosenblum. 1992. Women usually take care of their girlfriends: Bisexuality and HIV risk among female intravenous drug users. *Journal of Drug Issues* 22, 1: 179–190.

Malone, John. 1980. *Straight Women/Gay Men.* New York: Dial. [Cited by Coleman 1981/1982; Wolf 1985.]

Manalansan IV, Martin F. 1996. Double minorities: Latino, Black, and Asian men who have sex with men. In Ritch C. Savin-Williams and Kenneth M. Cohen, eds., *The Lives of Lesbians, Gays, and Bisexuals: Children to Adults,* pp. 393–415. New York: Harcourt Brace.

Manoff, Susan B., Helene D. Gayle, Mitzi A. Mays, and Martha F. Rogers. 1989. Acquired immunodeficiency syndrome in adolescents. Epidemiology, prevention, and public health issues. *Pediatric Infectious Diseases Journal* 8: 309–314.

Margold, Jane. 1974. Bisexuality: The newest sex-style. *Cosmopolitan* (June), 189–192.

Marks, Gary, Jean L. Richardson, and Norma Maldonado. 1991. Self-disclosure of HIV infection to sexual partners. *American Journal of Public Health* 81, 10: 1321–1322.

Martin, Angela K., Dorothee Seifen, and Mary Maloney. 1993. Lesbians, bisexual women, and perceptions of risk in the bluegrass. *Practicing Anthropology* 15, 4: 48–51.

Martin, John L. and Laura Dean. 1990. Developing a community sample of gay men for an epidemiologic study of AIDS. *American Behavioral Scientist* 33, 5: 546–561.

Marotta, Toby. 1981. *The Politics of Homosexuality: How Lesbians and Gay Men Have Made Themselves a Political and Social Force in Modern America.* Boston: Houghton Mifflin.

Masters, William H. and Virginia E. Johnson. 1979. *Homosexuality in Perspective.* Boston: Little, Brown.

Matteson, David R. 1985. Bisexual men in marriage: Is a positive homosexual identity and stable marriage possible? *Journal of Homosexuality,* 11, 1/2. Rpt. 1985. In Fritz Klein and Timothy J. Wolf, eds., *Two Lives to Lead: Bisexuality in Men and Women,* pp. 149–171. New York: Harrington Park.

—— 1995. Counseling with bisexuals. *Individual Psychology* 51, 2: 144–159.

—— 1996a. Psychotherapy with bisexual individuals. In Robert P. Cabaj and Terry S. Stein, eds., *Textbook of Homosexuality and Mental Health,* pp. 433–450. Washington, D.C.: American Psychiatric.

—— 1996b. Counseling and psychotherapy with bisexual and exploring clients. In Beth A. Firestein, ed., *Bisexuality: The Psychology and Politics of an Invisible Minority,* pp. 185–213. Thousand Oaks, Cal.: Sage.

—— 1997. Bisexual and homosexual behavior and HIV risk among Chinese-, Filipino-, and Korean-American men. *Journal of Sex Research* 34, 1: 93–104.

Mays, Vickie M. and Susan D. Cochran. 1987. Acquired immunodeficiency syndrome and Black Americans: Special psychosocial issues. *Public Health Reports* 102, 2 (March/April): 224–231.

Mays, Vickie M., Linda J. Beckman, Eric Oranchak, and Bridget Harper. 1994. Perceived social support for help-seeking behaviors of Black heterosexual and homosexually active women alcoholics. *Psychology of Addictive Behaviors* 8, 4: 235–242.

Mead, Margaret. 1949. *Male and Female: A Study of the Sexes in a Changing World.* New York: William Morrow. [Cited by Bode 1976.]

Mead, Margaret. 1975. Bisexuality: What's it all about? *Redbook* (January): 29–31.

Messiah, Antoine, Emmanuelle Mouret-Fourme, and the French National Survey on Sexual Behavior Group. 1995. Sociodemographic characteristics and sexual behavior of bisexual men in France: Implications for HIV prevention. *American Journal of Public Health* 85, 11: 1543–1546.

Meyer-Bahlburg, Heino F. L. 1984. Psychoendocrine research on sexual orientation: Current status and future options. *Progress in Brain Research* 61: 375–398.

—— 1997a. The role of prenatal estrogens in sexual orientation. In L. Ellis and L. Ebertz, eds., *Sexual Orientation: Toward Biological Understanding,* pp. 41–51. Westport, Conn.: Praeger.

—— 1997b. Psychobiologic research on homosexuality. In Martin Duberman, ed., *A Queer World: The Center for Lesbian and Gay Studies Reader,* pp. 285–297. New York: New York University Press.

Meyer-Bahlburg, Heino F. L., Anke A. Ehrhardt, Theresa M. Exner, M. Calderwood, and Rhoda S. Gruen. 1988. Sexual Risk Behavior Assessment Schedule— Adult, Baseline Interview for Gay Men (SERBAS-A-HOM-1). Manuscript. Columbia University, Department of Psychiatry. [Cited by Meyer-Bahlburg et al. 1991.]

Meyer-Bahlburg, Heino F. L., Theresa M. Exner, Gerda Lorenz, Rhoda S. Gruen, Jack M. Gorman, Anke A. Ehrhardt. 1991. Sexual risk behavior, sexual functioning, and HIV-disease progression in gay men. *Journal of Sex Research* 28, 1: 3–27.

Michael, Robert T., John H. Gagnon, Edward O. Laumann, and Gina Kolata. 1994. *Sex in America.* Boston: Little, Brown.

Michael, R. T., E. O. Laumann, J. H. Gagnon, T. W. Smith. 1988. *Morbidity and Mortality Weekly Report* 37, 37: 565–567.

Michel, Frann. 1996. Do bats eat cats? Reading what bisexuality does. In Donald E. Hall and Maria Pramaggiore, eds., *RePresenting Bisexualities: Subjects and Cultures of Fluid Desire*, pp. 55–69. New York: New York University Press.

Miller, Brian. 1979. Unpromised paternity: The lifestyles of gay fathers. In Martin Levine, ed., *Gay Men: The Sociology of Male Homosexuality*, pp. 239–252. New York: Harper and Row. [Cited by Wolf 1985; Matteson 1985.]

—— 1989. Women who marry gay men. *Advocate*, no. 523 (May 9): 22–30.

Miller, Neil. 1995. *Out of the Past: Gay and Lesbian History from 1869 to the Present.* New York: Vintage.

Minton, Henry L. and Gary J. McDonald. 1984. Homosexual identity formation as a developmental process. *Journal of Homosexuality* 9, 2/3: 91–104.

Mishaan, Chuck. 1985. The bisexual scene in New York City. In Fritz Klein and Timothy J. Wolf, eds., *Two Lives to Lead: Bisexuality in Men and Women*, pp. 223–225. New York: Harrington Park.

Money, John. 1955. Hermaphroditism, gender, and precocity in hyperadreno-corticism: Psychologic findings. *Bulletin of the Johns Hopkins Hospital* 96: 253–264.

—— 1984. Paraphilias: Phenomenology and classification. *American Journal of Psychotherapy* 38, 2: 164–179.

—— 1985. Pediatric sexology and hermaphroditism. *Journal of Sex and Marital Therapy* 11, 3: 139–156.

—— 1986. *Lovemaps: Clinical Concepts of Sexual/Erotic Health and Pathology, Paraphilia, and Gender Transposition in Childhood, Adolescence, and Maturity.* New York: Irvington.

—— 1987. Sin, sickness, or status? Homosexual gender identity and psychoneu-roendocrinology. *American Psychologist* 42, 4 (April): 384–399.

—— 1990a. Androgyne becomes bisexual in sexological theory: Plato to Freud and neuroscience. *Journal of the American Academy of Psychoanalysis* 18, 3: 392–413.

—— 1990b. Agenda and credenda of the Kinsey scale. In David P. McWhirter, Stephanie A. Sanders, and June Machover Reinisch, eds., *Homosexuality/ Heterosexuality: Concepts of Sexual Orientation*, pp. 41–60. New York: Oxford University Press.

—— 1998. Homosexuality, Bipotentiality, terminology, and history. Erwin J. Haeberle and Rolf Gindorf, eds., *Bisexualities: The Ideology and Practice of Sexual Contact with Both Men and Women*, pp. 118–129. New York: Continuum.

Money, John and Carol Bohmer. 1980. Prison sexology: Two personal accounts of masturbation, homosexuality, and rape. *Journal of Sex Research* 16, 3: 258–266.

Money, John and Margaret Lamacz. 1989. *Vandalized Lovemaps.* Buffalo, N.Y.: Prometheus.

Money, J., M. Schwartz, and V. G. Lewis. 1984. Adult erotosexual status and fetal hormonal masculinization and demasculinization. *Psychoneuroendocrinology* 9: 405–414. [Cited by Bailey 1995.]

Money, J. and P. Tucker. 1975. *Sexual Signatures: On Being a Man or a Woman*. Boston: Little, Brown.

Moraga, Cherríe. 1983. *Loving in the War Years: Lo Que Nunca Pasó por Sus Labios*. Boston: South End.

Morales, Edward S. 1989. Ethnic minority families and minority gays and lesbians. *Marriage and Family Review* 14, 3/4: 217–239.

—— 1990. HIV infection and Hispanic gay and bisexual men. *Hispanic Journal of Behavioral Sciences* 12, 2: 212–222.

—— 1992. Counseling Latino gays and Latina lesbians. In Sari H. Dworkin and Fernando Gutiérrez, eds., *Counseling Gay Men and Lesbians: Journey to the End of the Rainbow*, pp. 125–139. Alexandria, Va.: American Association for Counseling and Development.

Morris, Sharon and Merl Storr. 1997. Bisexual theory: A bi academic intervention. *Journal of Gay, Lesbian, and Bisexual Identity* 2, 1: 1–6.

Morrow, Susan L. 1998. Toward a new paradigm in counseling psychology training and education. *Counseling Psychologist* 26, 5: 797–808.

Morse, C. R. 1989. Exploring the bisexual alternative: A view from another closet. Master's thesis, University of Arizona. *Master's Abstracts* 28, 2: 320.

Morse, Edward V., Patricia M. Simon, Paul M. Balson, Howard J. Osofsky. 1992. Sexual behavior patterns of customers of male street prostitutes. *Archives of Sexual Behavior* 21, 4: 347–357.

Morse, Edward V., Patricia M. Simon, Howard J. Osofsky, Paul M. Balson, and H. Richard Gaumer. 1991. The male street prostitute: A vector for transmission of HIV infection into the heterosexual world. *Social Science and Medicine* 32, 5: 535–539.

Moses, A. E. 1978. *Identity Management in Lesbian Women*. New York: Praeger.

Mudd, Beth. 1982. Bisexuality in the women's movement. *Plexus* (June).

Mundy, Liza. 1993. Black and Bi. *Washington City Paper* 13, 5 (February 5–11): 28–35.

Murphy, Marilyn and Irene Weiss. 1987. Thinking about bisexuality. *Lesbian Contradiction* no. 17 (Winter).

Murphy, Timothy F. 1983/1984. Freud reconsidered: Bisexuality, homosexuality, and moral judgment. *Journal of Homosexuality* 9, 2/3 (Winter/Spring): 65–77.

Murray, Stephen O. 1984. *Social Theory, Homosexual Realities*. New York: Gai Sabre.

—— 1996. *American Gay*. Chicago: University of Chicago Press.

Myers, Michael F. 1991. Marital therapy with HIV-infected men and their wives. *Psychiatric Annals* 21, 8, August): 466–470.

Myers, Ted, Kevin W. Orr, David Locker, and Edward A. Jackson. 1993. Factors affecting gay and bisexual men's decisions and intentions to seek HIV testing. *American Journal of Public Health* 83, 5: 701–704.

Nacci, Peter L. 1978. Sexual assault in prisons. *American Journal of Correction* 40 (January–February): 30–31.

Nacci, Peter L. and Thomas R. Kane. 1983. The incidence of sex and sexual aggression in Federal prisons. *Federal Probation* 47 (December): 31–36.

—— 1984. Sex and sexual aggression in Federal prisons. *Federal Probation* 48 (March): 46–53.

Naerssen, A. X. van. 1998. Bisexuality during the teenage years: A theoretical model and several clinical experiences in confused identity. In Erwin J. Haeberle and Rolf Gindorf, eds., *Bisexualities: The Ideology and Practice of Sexual Contact with Both Men and Women*, pp. 229–233. New York: Continuum.

Nahas, Rebecca and Myra Turley. 1979. *The New Couple: Women and Gay Men.* New York: Seaview.

Nanda, Serena. 1997. The hijras of India. In Martin Duberman, ed., *A Queer World: The Center for Lesbian and Gay Studies Reader*, pp. 82–86. New York: New York University Press.

Nestle, Joan. 1989. The fem question. In Carol Vance, ed., *Pleasure and Danger: Exploring Female Sexuality*, pp. 232–241. London: Pandora. Rpt. 1984. Routledge.

—— 1992. *The Persistent Desire: A Femme-Butch Reader.* Boston: Alyson.

Newsweek. 1974. Bisexual chic: Anyone goes. *Newsweek* 83 (May 27): 90.

Nice, R. W. 1966. The problem of homosexuality in corrections. *American Journal of Corrections* 28: 30–32. [Cited by West 1967.]

Nichols, Margaret. 1985. Relationships between sexual behavior, erotic arousal, romantic attraction, and self-labeled sexual orientation. Paper presented at SSSS Conference, September, San Diego, California. [Cited by Nichols 1990.]

—— 1988. Bisexuality in women: Myths, realities, and implications for therapy. *Women and Therapy* 7, 2/3: 235–252.

—— 1990. Lesbian relationships: Implications for the study of sexuality and gender. In David P. McWhirter, Stephanie A. Sanders, and June Machover Reinisch, eds., *Homosexuality/Heterosexuality: Concepts of Sexual Orientation*, pp. 350–364. New York; Oxford University Press.

Norman, Ann Duecy, Melissa J. Perry, L. Yvonne Stevenson, Jeffrey A. Kelly, Roger A. Roffman, HIV Prevention Community Collaborative. 1996. Lesbian and bisexual women in small cities— At risk for HIV? *Public Health Reports* 111 (July/Aug): 347–52.

North, Gary. 1989. Drawing a fine line: How gay and lesbian leaders feel about bisexuals and bisexuality in the gay rights movement and organizations. *Bisexuality: News, Views, and Networking.*

Nurius, Paula S. 1983. Mental health implications of sexual orientation. *Journal of Sex Research* 19, 2: 119– 136.

Nurius, Paula S. and Walter W. Hudson. 1988. Sexual activity and preference: Six quantifiable dimensions. *Journal of Sex Research* 24: 30–46.

O'Brien, Kerth, Camille B. Wortman, Ronald C. Kessler, and Jill G. Joseph. 1993. Social relationships of men at risk for AIDS. *Social Science and Medicine* 36, 9: 1161–1167.

Ochs, Robyn. 1990. Gay liberation is our liberation. In Thomas Geller, ed., *Bisexuality: A Reader and Sourcebook*, p. 2. Ojai, Cal.: Times Change.

—— 1996. Biphobia: It goes more than two ways. In Beth A. Firestein, ed., *Bisexual-*

ity: The Psychology and Politics of an Invisible Minority, pp. 217–239. Thousand Oaks, Cal.: Sage

Ochs, Robyn, ed. 1999. *The Bisexual Resource Guide.* 3d ed. Boston: Bisexual Resource Center.

O'Connor, Peg. 1997. Warning! Contents under heterosexual pressure. *Hypatia* 12, 3: 183–188.

Off Pink Collective. 1988. *Bisexual Lives.* London: Off Pink.

O'Neill, G. C. and N. O'Neill. 1970. Patterns in group sexual activity. *Journal of Sex Research* 6: 101–112. [Cited by Dixon 1984.]

"Orlando." 1978. Bisexuality: A choice not an echo? A very personal confession by "Orlando." *Ms.* (October): 60–62, 70–75.

Osmond, Dennis H., Kimberly Page, James Wiley, Karen Garrett, Haynes W. Sheppard, Andrew R. Moss, Lewis Schrager, and Warren Winkelstein. 1994. HIV infection in homosexual and bisexual men eighteen to twenty-nine years of age: The San Francisco Young Men's Health Study. *American Journal of Public Health* 84, 12: 1933–1937.

Ostrow, David G., Andrew Monjan, Jill Joseph, Mark VanRaden, Robin Fox, Lawrence Kingsley, Janice Dudley, and John Phair. 1989. HIV-related symptoms and psychological functioning in a cohort of homosexual men. *American Journal of Psychiatry* 146, 6: 737–742.

Otis, Margaret. 1913. A perversion not commonly noted. *Journal of Abnormal Psychology* 8 (June–July): 113–116. [Cited by Giallombardo 1966.]

Ovesey, Lionel, and Willard Gaylin. 1965. Psychotherapy of Male Homosexuality: Prognose, Selection of Patients, Technique. *American Journal of Psychotherapy* 19, 3: 382–396.

Ovesey, Lionel, Willard Gaylin, and Herbert Hendin. 1963. Psychotherapy of Male Homosexuality: Psych-dynamic formulation. *Archives of General Psychiatry* 9, 1: 19–31.

Padgug, Robert A. 1979. Sexual matters: On conceptualizing sexuality in history. *Radical History Review* 20: 3–23.

Padian, N. S. 1989. Female partners of bisexual men. Paper presented at the CDC Workshop on Bisexuality and AIDS, October, Atlanta, Georgia. [Cited by Chu et al. 1992.]

Paitich, D, R. Langevin, R. Freeman, K. Mann, and L. Handy. 1977. The Clarke SHQ: A clinical sex history questionnaire for males. *Archives of Sexual Behavior* 6, 5: 421–436.

Palmer, W., 1989. Accessing, educating and researching married homosexual and bisexual men, abstract no. MEP43. Fifth International Conference on AIDS, June, Montreal, Canada. [Cited by Boulton, Hart, and Fitzpatrick 1992.]

Pattatucci, Angela M. L. and Dean H. Hamer. 1995. Development and familiality of sexual orientation in females. *Behavior Genetics* 25, 5: 407–420.

Paul, Jay P. 1983/1984. The bisexual identity: An idea without social recognition. *Journal of Homosexuality* 9, 2/3 (Winter/Spring): 45–63.

—— 1985. Bisexuality: Reassessing our paradigms of sexuality. *Journal of Homosexuality* 11 , 1/2 (Spring): 21–34. Rpt. in Fritz Klein and Timothy J. Wolf, eds.,

Two Lives to Lead: Bisexuality in Men and Woman, pp. 21–34. New York: Harrington Park.

—— 1993. Childhood cross-gender behavior and adult homosexuality: The resurgence of biological models of sexuality. *Journal of Homosexuality* 24, 3/4: 41–54.

— 1996. Bisexuality: Exploring/Exploding the boundaries. In Ritch C. Savin-Williams and Kenneth M. Cohen, eds., *The Lives of Lesbians, Gays, and Bisexuals: Children to Adults*, pp. 436–461. New York: Harcourt Brace.

—— 1998. San Francisco's Bisexual Center and the emergence of a bisexual movement. In Erwin J. Haeberle and Rolf Gindorf, eds., *Bisexualities: The Ideology and Practice of Sexual Contact with Both Men and Women*, pp. 130–139. New York: Continuum.

Paul, Jay P., Ron Stall, and Kim A. Bloomfield. 1991. Gay and alcoholic: Epidemiologic and clinical issues. *Alcohol Health and Research World* 15, 2: 151–160.

Paz, Juana Maria. 1988. Desire and consequences: Sleeping with a strange man. *Lesbian Contradiction* no. 21 (Winter).

Pennbridge, Julia N., Thomas E. Freese, and Richard G. MacKenzie. 1992. High-risk behaviors among male street youth in Hollywood, California. *AIDS Education and Prevention* 4, 3 (supplement): 24–33.

Peplau, Letitia Anne and Susan D. Cochran. 1990. A relational perspective on homosexuality. In David P. McWhirter, Stephanie A. Sanders, and June Machover Reinisch, eds., *Homosexuality/Heterosexuality: Concepts of Sexual Orientation*, pp. 321–349. New York: Oxford University Press.

Perlongher, Nestor O. 1985. O contrato da prostituicao virile [On the "virile prostitution" contract]. *Arquivos Brasileiros de Psicologia* 37, 2: 94–105. [Cited by Morse, Simon, Balson, and Osofsky 1992.]

Peterson, John L. 1995. AIDS-related risks and same-sex behaviors among African American men. In Gregory M. Herek and Beverly Greene, eds., *AIDS, Identity, and Community: The HIV Epidemic and Lesbians and Gay Men*, pp. 85–104. Thousand Oaks: Sage.

Peterson, John L., Thomas J. Coates, Joseph A. Catania, Lee Middleton, Bobby Hilliard, and Norman Hearst. 1992. High-risk sexual behavior and condom use among gay and bisexual African-American men. *American Journal of Public Health* 82, 11: 1490–1494.

Peterson, John L., Susan Folkman, and Roger Blakeman. 1996. Stress, coping, HIV status, psychosocial resources, and depressive mood in African American gay, bisexual, and heterosexual men. *American Journal of Community Psychology* 24, 4: 461–487.

Peterson, Peggy L., David G. Ostrow, and David J. McKirnan. 1991. Behavioral interventions for the primary prevention of HIV infection among homosexual and bisexual men. *Journal of Primary Prevention* 12, 1: 19–34.

Phair, John, Don Hoover, Jay Huprikar, Roger Detels, Richard Kaslow, Charles Rinaldo, and Alfred Saah. 1992. The significance of Western Blot Assays indeterminate for antibody to HIV in a cohort of homosexual/bisexual men. *Journal of Acquired Immune Deficiency Syndrome* 5 (Sept.): 988–992.

Phillips, Gabriel and Ray Over. 1992. Adult sexual orientation in relation to memories of childhood gender conforming and gender nonconforming behaviors. *Archives of Sexual Behavior* 21, 6: 543–558.

—— 1995. Differences between heterosexual, bisexual, and lesbian women in recalled childhood experiences. *Archives of Sexual Behavior* 24, 1: 1–20.

Phillips, Julia C. and Ann R. Fischer. 1998. Graduate students' training experiences with lesbian, gay, and bisexual issues. *Counseling Psychologist* 26, 5 (September): 712– 734.

Pillard, Richard C. 1990. The Kinsey scale: Is it familial? In David P. McWhirter, Stephanie A. Sanders, and June Machover Reinisch, eds., *Homosexuality/ Heterosexuality: Concepts of Sexual Orientation*, pp. 88–100. New York: Oxford University Press.

Pillard, Richard C. and J. Michael Bailey. 1995. A biologic perspective on sexual orientation. *Clinical Sexuality* 18, 1: 71–84.

Pillard, Richard C. and James D. Weinrich. 1986. Evidence of familial nature of male homosexuality. *Archives of General Psychiatry* 43: 808–812.

—— 1987. The periodic table model of the gender transpositions: Part I. A theory based on masculinization and defeminization of the brain. *Journal of Sex Research* 23, 4: 425–454.

Pittman, D. J. 1971. The male house of prostitution. *Trans-Action* (March/April). [Cited by Allen 1980; Morse, Simon, Balson, and Osofsky 1992.]

Playboy readers sex survey. 1983. *Playboy Magazine* (May): 126, 128, 136, 210–212, 215–216, 219–220. [Cited by Zinik 1985.]

Pleak, Richard R. and Heino F. L. Meyer-Bahlburg. 1990. Sexual behavior and AIDS knowledge of young male prostitutes in Manhattan. *Journal of Sex Research* 27, 4 (November): 557–587.

Plummer, Douglas. 1963. *Queer People: The Truth About Homosexuals*. London: Allen.

Plummer, Kenneth. 1975. *Sexual stigma: An interactionist account*. London: Routledge and Kegan Paul.

—— 1981a. Homosexual categories: Some research problems in the labelling perspective of homosexuality. In Kenneth Plummer, ed., *The Making of the Modern Homosexual*, pp. 53–75. London: Hutchinson.

—— 1981b. Going gay: Identities, life cycles and lifestyles in the male gay world. In John Hart and Diane Richardson, eds., *The Theory and Practice of Homosexuality*, pp. 93–110. Boston: Routledge and Kegan Paul.

—— 1984. Sexual diversity: A sociological perspective. In Kevin Howells, ed., *The Psychology of Sexual Diversity*, pp. 219–253. New York: Basil Blackwell.

Pomeroy, Wardell B. 1972. *Dr. Kinsey and the Institute for Sex Research*. New York: Harper and Row.

Pomeroy, W. B., C. C. Flax, and C. C. Wheeler. 1982. *Taking a Sex History*. New York: Free.

Ponse, Barbara. 1978. *Identities in the Lesbian World: The Social Construction of Self*. Westport, Conn.: Greenwood.

—— 1980. Lesbians and their worlds. In Judd Marmor, ed., *Homosexual Behavior: A Modern Reappraisal*, pp. 157–175. New York: Basic.

Proctor, Curtis D. and Victor K. Groze. 1994. Risk factors for suicide among gay, lesbian, and bisexual youths. *Social Work* 39, 5 (September): 504–513.

Propper, Alice M. 1978. Lesbianism in female and coed correctional institutions. *Journal of Homosexuality* 3, 3: 265–274.

—— 1981. *Prison Homosexuality: Myth and Reality*. Toronto: Lexington.

Quadland, Michael C. 1985. Compulsive sexual behavior: Definition of a problem and an approach to treatment. *Journal of Sex and Marital Therapy* 11, 2: 121–132.

Quadland, Michael C. and William D. Shattls. 1987. AIDS, sexuality, and sexual control. *Journal of Homosexuality* 14, 1/2: 277–298.

Queen, Carol A. 1992. Strangers at home: Bisexuals in the queer movement. *Out/Look* no. 16 (Spring): 23, 29–33.

Queen, Carol and Lawrence Schimel. 1997. *Pomosexuals: Challenging Assumptions About Gender and Sexuality*. San Francisco: Cleis.

Radicalesbians. 1970. The woman-identified woman. *Come Out! Selections from the Radical Gay Liberation Newspaper*, pp. 49–55. New York: Times Change.

Rado, Sandor. 1965. A critical examination of the concept of bisexuality. In Judd Marmor, ed., *Sexual Inversion: The Multiple Roots of Homosexuality*, pp. 175–189. New York: Basic.

Raiteri, R., R. Fora, and A. Sinicco. 1994. No HIV-1 transmission through lesbian sex, letter. *Lancet* 344: 270. [Cited by Rila 1996.]

Ramey, James W. 1974a. Emerging patterns of innovative behavior in marriage. In James R. Smith and Lynn G. Smith, eds., *Beyond Monogamy*, pp. 103–137. Baltimore: Johns Hopkins University Press.

—— 1974b. Communes, group marriage, and the upper middle class. In James R. Smith and Lynn G. Smith, eds., *Beyond Monogamy*, pp. 214–229. Baltimore: Johns Hopkins University Press.

Rand, C., D. L. R. Graham, and E. I. Rawlings. 1982. Psychological health and factors the court seeks to control in lesbian mother custody trials. *Journal of Homosexuality* 8, 1: 27–39. [Cited by Coleman 1985b.]

Randolph, L. B. 1988. The hidden fear: Black women, bisexuals, and the AIDS risk. *Ebony* (January).

Red Earth, Michael (Dakota). 1994. Two spirit versus berdache: Challenging the stereotypes of academia. Paper presented at the Sixth North American Lesbian, Gay, and Bisexual Studies Conference, Nov. 17–20, University of Iowa, Iowa City.

Reinisch, June Machover. 1976. Effects of prenatal hormone exposure on physical and psychological development in humans and animals: With a note on the state of the field. In E. J. Sacher, ed., *Hormones, Behavior, and Psychopathology*, pp. 69–94. New York: Raven. [Cited by Sanders, Reinisch, and McWhirter 1990.]

Reinisch, June Machover and Stephanie A. Sanders. 1987. Behavioral influences of prenatal hormones. In Charles B. Nemeroff and Peter T. Loosen et al. eds., *Handbook of Clinical Psychoneuroendocrinology*, pp. 431–448. New York: Guilford. [Cited by Sanders, Reinisch, and McWhirter 1990.]

Reinisch, June Machover, Stephanie A. Sanders, and Mary M. Ziemba-Davis. 1988. The study of sexual behavior in relation to the transmission of Human

Immunodeficiency Virus: Caveats and recommendations. *American Psychologist* 43, 11: 921–927. [Cited by Sanders, Reinisch, and McWhirter 1990.]

—— 1995. Self-labeled sexual orientation and sexual behavior: Considerations for STD-related biomedical research and education. In Marvin Stein and Andrew Baum, eds., *Chronic Diseases*, pp. 241–257. Mahwah, N.J.: Lawrence Erlbaum.

Reiss, Albert J. Jr. 1961. The social integration of queers and peers. *Social Problems* 9, 2 (Fall): 102–120. Rpt. 1967. In John H. Gagnon and William Simon, eds., *Sexual Deviance*, pp. 197–228. New York: Harper and Row.

Remafedi, Gary. 1994a. Predictors of unprotected intercourse among gay and bisexual youth: Knowledge, beliefs, and behavior. *Pediatrics* 94, 2: 163–168.

—— 1994b. Cognitive and behavioral adaptations to HIV/AIDS among gay and bisexual adolescents. *Journal of Adolescent Health* 15: 142–148.

Remafedi, Gary, James A. Farrow, and Robert W. Deisher. 1991. Risk factors for attempted suicide in gay and bisexual youth. *Pediatrics* 87, 6 (June): 869–875.

Remafedi, Gary, Michael Resnick, Robert Blum, and Linda Harris. 1992. Demography of sexual orientation in adolescents. *Pediatrics* 89, 4 (April): 714–721.

Research and Decisions Corporation. 1984. *Designing an Effective AIDS Prevention Campaign Strategy for San Francisco*. Report for the San Francisco AIDS Foundation. [Cited by Martin and Dean 1990.]

Reuben, N., K. Hein, E. Drucker, L. Bauman, and J. Lauby. 1988. Relationship of high-risk behaviors to AIDS knowledge in adolescent high school students. Paper presented at the Annual Research Meeting of the Society for Adolescent Medicine, New York City. [Cited by Rotheram-Borus et al. 1992, who found it cited by Miller, Turner, and Moses 1990.]

Rich, Adrienne. 1980. Compulsory heterosexuality and lesbian existence. *Signs: Journal of Women in Culture and Society*, 5, 4. Rpt. 1983. In Ann Snitow, Christine Stansell, and Sharon Thompson, eds., *Powers of Desire: The Politics of Sexuality*, pp. 177–205. New York: Monthly Review.

Richardson, Diane. 1981. Theoretical perspectives on homosexuality. In John Hart and Diane Richardson, eds., *The Theory and Practice of Homosexuality*, pp. 5–37. London: Routledge and Kegan Paul.

—— 1984. The dilemma of essentiality in homosexual theory. *Journal of Homosexuality* 9, 2/3 (Winter/Spring): 79–90.

Richardson, Justin. 1995. The science and politics of gay teen suicide. *Harvard Review of Psychiatry* 3: 107–110.

Richman, Alan. 1984. A dating dilemma. *Boston Globe* (July 26).

Ricketts, Wendell. 1984. Biological research on homosexuality: Ansell's cow or Occam's razor? *Journal of Homosexuality* 9, 4: 65–93.

Rifkin, H. A. 1968. Homosexuality in marriage. In E. S. Rosenbaum and I. Alger, eds., *The Marriage Relationship*. New York: Basic. [Cited by Collins and Zimmerman 1983.]

Rila, Margo. 1996. Bisexual women and the AIDS crisis. In Beth A. Firestein, ed., *Bisexuality: The Psychology and Politics of an Invisible Minority*, pp. 169–184. Thousand Oaks, Cal.: Sage.

Risch, Neil, Elizabeth Squires-Wheeler, Bronya J. B. Keats. 1993. Technical comment: Male sexual orientation and genetic evidence. *Science* 262 (Dec. 24): 2063–2064.

Roberts, B. C. 1997. "The many faces of bisexuality": The 4th International Bisexual Symposium. *Journal of Gay, Lesbian, and Bisexual Identity* 2, 1: 65–76.

Robinson, Paul. 1976. *The Modernization of Sex: Havelock Ellis, Alfred Kinsey, William Masters, and Virginia Johnson.* New York: Harper and Row.

Rogers, Martha F., and Walter W. Williams. 1987. AIDS in Blacks and Hispanics: Implications for prevention. *Issues in Science and Technology* 3, 3: 89–94.

Rogers, Susan M., and Charles F. Turner. 1991. Male-male sexual contact in the U.S.A.: Findings from five sample surveys, 1970– 1990. *Journal of Sex Research* 28, 4 (November): 491–519.

Roland, A. 1988. *In Search of Self in India and Japan: Toward a Cross-cultural Psychology.* Princeton: Princeton University Press. [Cited by Matteson 1997.]

Rosario, Margaret, Heino F. L. Meyer-Bahlburg, Joyce Hunter, Theresa M. Exner, Marya Gwadz, and Arden M. Keller. 1996. The psychosexual development of urban lesbian, gay, and bisexual youths. *Journal of Sex Research* 33, 2: 113–126.

Roscoe, Will. 1997. Gender diversity in Native North America: Notes toward a unified analysis. In Martin Duberman, ed., *A Queer World: The Center for Lesbian and Gay Studies Reader,* pp. 65–81. New York: New York University Press.

Roscoe, Will., ed., 1988. *Living the Spirit: A Gay American Indian Anthology.* New York: St. Martin's.

Rose, Sharon, Cris Stevens (Off Pink Collective), eds. 1996, *Bisexual Horizons: Politics, Histories, Lives.* London: Lawrence and Wishart.

Ross, H. Laurence. 1959. The 'hustler' in Chicago. *Journal of Student Research* 1: 13–19.

—— 1971. Modes of adjustment of married homosexuals. *Social Problems* 18, 3: 385–393.

—— 1972. Odd couples: Homosexuals in heterosexual marriage. *Social Problems* 2: 42–49. [Cited by Wolf 1985.]

Ross, Michael W. 1979. Heterosexual marriage of homosexual men: Some associated factors. *Journal of Sex and Marital Therapy* 5: 142–151. [Cited by Wolf 1985.]

—— 1983a. Femininity, masculinity, and sexual orientation: Some cross-cultural comparisons. *Journal of Homosexuality* 9, 1: 27–36.

—— 1983b. Societal relationships and gender role in homosexuals: A cross-cultural comparison. *Journal of Sex Research* 19, 3: 273–288.

—— 1983c. *The Married Homosexual Man: A Psychological Study.* London: Routledge and Kegan Paul.

—— 1984. Beyond the biological model: New directions in bisexual and homosexual research. *Journal of Homosexuality* 10, 3/4: 63–70.

—— 1989. Married homosexual men: Prevalence and background. *Marriage and Family Review* 14, 3/4: 35– 57.

—— 1991. A taxonomy of global behavior. In Rob Tielman, Manuel Carballo, and Aart Hendriks, eds., *Bisexuality and HIV/AIDS: A Global Perspective,* pp. 21–26. Buffalo, N.Y.: Prometheus.

Ross, Michael W., Julian Gold, Alex Wodak, and M. E. Miller. 1991. Sexually transmissible diseases among injecting drug users. *Genitourinary Medicine* 67, 1 (February): 32–36. [Cited by Stevens 1994.]

Ross, Michael W. and Jay P. Paul. 1992. Beyond gender: The basis of sexual attraction in bisexual men and women. *Psychological Reports* 71: 1283–1290.

Ross, M. W., A. Wodak, J. Gold, and M. E. Miller. 1992. Differences across sexual orientation on HIV risk behaviours in injecting drug users. *AIDS Care* 4, 2: 139–148.

—— 1998. Differences in sexual orientation in relation to HIV-risk behavior among intravenous drug addicts. Erwin J. Haeberle and Rolf Gindorf, eds., *Bisexualities: The Ideology and Practice of Sexual Contact with Both Men and Women*, pp. 234–242. New York: Continuum.

Rotheram-Borus, Mary Jane, and Cheryl Koopman. 1991. Sexual risk behavior, AIDS knowledge, and beliefs about AIDS among predominantly minority gay and bisexual male adolescents. *AIDS Education and Prevention* 3, 4: 305–312.

Rotheram-Borus, Mary Jane, Joyce Hunter, and Margaret Rosario. 1994. Suicidal behavior and gay-related stress among gay and bisexual male adolescents. *Journal of Adolescent Research* 9, 4: 498–508.

—— 1995. Coming out as lesbian or gay in the era of AIDS. Gregory M. Herek and Beverly Greene, eds., *AIDS, Identity, and Community: The HIV Epidemic and Lesbians and Gay Men*, pp. 150–168. Thousand Oaks, Cal.: Sage.

Rotheram-Borus, Mary Jane, Heino F. L. Meyer-Bahlburg, Cheryl Koopman, Margaret Rosario, Theresa M. Exner, Ronald Henderson, Marjory Matthieu, and Rhoda S. Gruen. 1992. Lifetime sexual behaviors among runaway males and females. *Journal of Sex Research* 29, 1 (February): 15–29.

Rotheram-Borus, Mary Jane, Helen Reid, and Margaret Rosario. 1994. Factors mediating changes in sexual HIV risk behaviors among gay and bisexual male adolescents. *American Journal of Public Health* 84, 12: 1938–1946.

Rotheram-Borus, Mary Jane, Helen Reid, Margaret Rosario, and Stephanie Kasen. 1995. Determinants of safer sex patterns among gay/bisexual male adolescents. *Journal of Adolescence* 18, 1: 3–15.

Rotheram-Borus, Mary Jane, Margaret Rosario, Heino F. L. Meyer-Bahlburg, Cheryl Koopman, Steven C. Dopkins, and Mark Davies. 1994. Sexual and substance use acts of gay and bisexual male adolescents in New York City. *Journal of Sex Research* 31, 1: 47–57.

Rotheram-Borus, Mary Jane, Margaret Rosario, Helen Reid, and Cheryl Koopman. 1995. Predicting patterns of sexual acts among homosexual and bisexual youths. *American Journal of Psychiatry* 152, 4: 588–595.

Rotheram-Borus, Mary Jane, Margaret Rosario, Ronan Van Rossem, Helen Reid, and Roy Gillis. 1995. Prevalence, course, and predictors of multiple problem behaviors among gay and bisexual male adolescents. *Developmental Psychology* 31, 1: 75–85.

Rowland, David L. 1995. The psychobiology of sexual arousal and behavior. Louis Diamant and Richard D. McAnulty, eds., *The Psychology of Sexual Orientation, Behavior, and Identity*, pp. 19–42. Westport, Conn.: Greenwood.

Rubenstein, Marguerite. 1982. An in-depth study of bisexuality and its relation to self-esteem. Ph.D. diss., Institute for Advanced Study of Human Sexuality, San Francisco. [Cited by Zinik 1985.]

Rubenstein, Maggi and Cynthia Ann Slater. 1985. A profile of the San Francisco Bisexual Center. In Fritz Klein and Timothy J. Wolf, eds., *Two Lives to Lead: Bisexuality in Men and Women*, pp. 227–230. New York: Harrington Park.

Rubin, Gayle. 1975. The traffic in women: Notes on the "political economy" of sex. In Rayna Rapp Reiter, ed., *Toward an Anthropology of Women*, pp. 157–210. New York: Monthly Revew. Rpt. in Karen V. Hansen and Ilene J. Philipson. 1990. *Women, Class, and the Feminist Imagination: A Socialist-Feminist Reader*, pp. 74–113. Philadelphia: Temple University Press.

Rubin, Sylvia. 1983. How bisexuals face a hostile world. *San Francisco Chronicle* (September 2).

Rust, Paula C. 1992. The politics of sexual identity: Sexual attraction and behavior among lesbian and bisexual women. *Social Problems* 39, 4: 366–386.

—— 1993a. "Coming out" in the age of social constructionism: Sexual identity formation among lesbian and bisexual women. *Gender and Society* 7, 1: 50–77.

—— 1993b. Neutralizing the political threat of the marginal woman: Lesbians' beliefs about bisexual women. *Journal of Sex Research* 30, 3: 214–228.

—— 1995a. *Bisexuality and the Challenge to Lesbian Politics: Sex, Loyalty, and Revolution*. New York: New York University Press.

—— 1995b. Bisexual experiences, identities, and politics. Paper presented at the International Academy of Sex Research annual meeting, September 23, Provincetown, Massachusetts.

—— 1995c. Hybrid or whole: The politics of defining bisexuality into existence. Paper presented at the Department of Psychology Colloquium Series, April 21, University of Vermont.

—— 1996a. Managing multiple identities: Diversity among bisexual women and men. In Beth A. Firestein, ed., *Bisexuality: The Psychology and Politics of an Invisible Minority*, pp. 53–83. Thousand Oaks, Cal.: Sage.

—— 1996b. Monogamy and polyamory: Relationship issues for bisexuals. In Beth A. Firestein, ed., *Bisexuality: The Psychology and Politics of an Invisible Minority*, pp. 127–148. Thousand Oaks, Cal.: Sage.

—— 1996c. Sexual identity and bisexual identities: The struggle for self-description in a changing sexual landscape. In Brett Beemyn and Mickey Eliason, eds., *Queer Studies: A Lesbian, Gay, Bisexual, and Transgender Anthology*, pp. 64–86. New York: New York University Press.

—— 1996d. Finding a sexual identity and community: Therapeutic implications and cultural assumptions in scientific models of coming out. In Esther D. Rothblum and Lynne A. Bond, eds., *Preventing Heterosexism and Homophobia*, pp. 87–123. Thousand Oaks, Cal.: Sage.

—— 1999. Lesbianism and bisexuality: Cultural categories and the distortion of human sexual experience. Paper presented at the twenty-fifth annual meeting of the International Academy of Sex Research, June 25, Stony Brook, New York.

Rutherford, G. W., J. L. Barnhardt, and G. F. Lemp. 1988. The changing demographics of AIDS in homosexual and bisexual men in San Francisco. Paper presented at the Fourth International Conference on AIDS, Stockholm. [Cited by Coates, et al. 1988, who are cited by Adib and Ostrow 1991.]

Ryan, Rosemary, John F. Longres, and Roger A. Roffman. 1996. Sexual identity, social support, and social networks among African-, Latino-, and European-American men in an HIV prevention program. *Journal of Gay and Lesbian Social Services* 5, 3: 1–24.

Saewyc, Elizabeth M., Carol L. Skay, Linda H. Bearinger, Robert W. Blum, Michael D. Resnick. 1998. Demographics of sexual orientation among American-Indian adolescents. *American Journal of Orthopsychiatry* 68, 4: 590–600.

Sagarin, Edward. 1976. Prison homosexuality and its effect on post-prison sexual behavior. *Psychiatry* 39 (August): 245–257.

Saghir, Marcel T. and Eli Robins. 1973. *Male and Female Homosexuality: A Comprehensive Investigation.* Baltimore: Williams and Wilkins.

Salamon, Edna D. 1989. The homosexual escort agency: Deviance disavowal. *British Journal of Sociology* 40, 1: 1–21.

Saliba, P. 1982. Research project on sexual orientation. *Bi-monthly Newsletter of the Bisexual Center of San Francisco* 6, 5: 3–6. [Cited by Zinik 1985.]

Salzman, Leon. 1965. "Latent" homosexuality. In Judd Marmor, ed., *Sexual Inversion: The Multiple Roots of Homosexuality,* pp. 234–247. New York: Basic.

Sanders, Stephanie A., June Machover Reinisch, and David P. McWhirter. 1990. Homosexuality/Heterosexuality: An overview. In David P. McWhirter, Stephanie A. Sanders, and June Machover Reinisch, eds., *Homosexuality/ Heterosexuality: Concepts of Sexual Orientation,* pp. xix–xxvii. New York: Oxford University Press.

Sandfort, Theo G. M. 1995. HIV/AIDS prevention and the impact of attitudes toward homosexuality and bisexuality. Gregory M. Herek and Beverly Greene, eds., *AIDS, Identity, and Community: The HIV Epidemic and Lesbians and Gay Men,* pp. 32–54. Thousand Oaks, Cal.: Sage.

San Francisco Department of Public Health (SFDPH). AIDS Office, Prevention Services Branch. 1993a. *Health Behaviors Among Lesbian and Bisexual Women: A Community-based Women's Health Survey.* San Francisco: SFDPH.

—— Surveillance Branch, AIDS Office. 1993b. *HIV Seroprevalence and Risk Behaviors Among Lesbians and Bisexual Women: The 1993 San Francisco/Berkeley Women's Survey.* San Francisco: SFDPH.

Savin-Williams, Ritch C. 1994. Verbal and physical abuse as stressors in the lives of lesbian, gay male, and bisexual youths: Associations with school problems, running away, substance abuse, prostitution, and suicide. *Journal of Consulting and Clinical Psychology* 62, 2: 261–269.

—— 1995a. An exploratory study of pubertal maturation timing and self-esteem among gay and bisexual male youths. *Developmental Psychology* 31, 1: 56–64.

—— 1995b. Lesbian, gay male, and bisexual adolescents. Pp. 165–189 in Anthony R. D'Augelli and Charlotte J. Patterson, eds., *Lesbian, Gay, and Bisexual Identities Over the Lifespan.* New York: Oxford University Press.

Savin-Williams, Ritch C. and Kenneth M. Cohen., eds., 1996. *The Lives of Lesbians, Gays, and Bisexuals: Children to Adults.* New York: Harcourt Brace.

Scacco, Anthony M. Jr. 1975. *Rape in Prison.* Springfield, Ill.: Thomas.

Schaefer, Susan, Sue Evans, and Eli Coleman, Eli. 1987. Sexual orientation concerns among chemically dependent individuals. *Journal of Chemical Dependency Treatment* 1, 1: 121–140.

Schäfer, Siegrid. 1976. Sexual and social problems of lesbians. *Journal of Sex Research* 12: 50–69.

Schneider, Jennifer P. and Burton H. Schneider. 1990. Marital satisfaction during recovery from self-identified sexual addiction among bisexual men and their wives. *Journal of Sex and Marital Therapy* 16, 4: 230–250.

Schneider, Stephen G., Shelley E. Taylor, Margaret E. Kemeny, and Constance Hammen. 1991. AIDS-related factors predictive of suicidal ideation of low and high intent among gay and bisexual men. *Suicide and Life-Threatening Behavior* 21, 4: 313–328.

Schofield, Michael. 1965a. *Sociological Aspects of Homosexuality: A Comparative Study of Three Types of Homosexuals.* Boston: Little, Brown/London: Longmans, Green.

Schofield, Michael. 1965b. *The Sexual Behaviour of Young People.* London: Longmans, Green.

Schwartz, Pepper and Philip Blumstein. 1976. Bisexuality: Where love speaks louder than labels. *Ms.* 3 (November): 80–81.

—— 1998. The acquisition of sexual identity: Bisexuality. Erwin J. Haeberle and Rolf Gindorf, eds., *Bisexualities: The Ideology and Practice of Sexual Contact with Both Men and Women*, pp. 182–212. New York: Continuum.

Scott, Jane. 1978. *Wives Who Love Women.* New York: Walker.

Scott, Patrick Ross and Elizabeth Thompson Ortiz. 1996. Marriage and coming out: Four patterns in homosexual males. *Journal of Gay and Lesbian Social Services* 4, 3: 67–79.

Scott, Wayne. 1992. Coming out both ways: The search for acceptance in a gay/straight culture. *Changing Men* 24 (Summer/Fall): 36–39.

Sedgwick, Eve Kosofsky. 1990. *Epistemology of the Closet.* Berkeley: University of California Press.

Seidman, Steven. 1993. Identity and politics in a "postmodern" gay culture: Some historical and conceptual notes. In Michael Warner, ed., *Fear of a Queer Planet: Queer Politics and Social Theory*, pp. 105–142. Minneapolis: University of Minnesota Press.

Selik, Richard M., Kenneth G. Castro, and Marguerite Pappaioanou. 1988. Racial/ethnic differences in the risk of AIDS in the United States. *American Journal of Public Health* 78, 12: 1539–1545.

Sell, Randall L. 1997. Defining and measuring sexual orientation: A review. *Archives of Sexual Behavior* 26, 6: 643–658.

Sell, Randall L. and Christian Petrulio. 1996. Sampling homosexuals, bisexuals, gays, and lesbians for public health resarch: A review of the literature from 1990 to 1992. *Journal of Homosexuality* 30, 4: 31–48.

Sell, Randall L., James A. Wells, and David Wypij. 1995. The prevalence of homosexual behavior and attraction in the United States, the United Kingdom, and France: Results of national population-based samples. *Archives of Sexual Behavior* 24, 3: 235–248.

Shernoff, Michael and Luis Palacios-Jimenez. 1988. AIDS: Prevention is the only vaccine available: An AIDS prevention educational program. *Journal of Social Work and Human Sexuality* 6, 2: 135–150.

Shively, Michael G. and John P. De Cecco. 1977. Components of sexual identity. *Journal of Homosexuality* 3, 1: 41–48.

Shively, Michael G., Christopher Jones, and John P. De Cecco. 1983/84. Research on sexual orientation: Definitions and methods. *Journal of Homosexuality* 9, 2/3 (Winter/Spring): 127–136.

Shively, Michael G., James R. Rudolph, and John P. De Cecco. 1978. The identification of the social sex-role stereotypes. *Journal of Homosexuality* 3, 3 (Spring): 225–233.

Shore, David A. 1981. *Sex-related Issues in Institutional Settings: A Classified Bibliography.* Chicago: Playboy Foundation.

Shuster, Rebecca. 1987. Sexuality as a continuum: The bisexual identity. In Boston Lesbian Psychologies Collective, ed., *Lesbian Psychologies,* pp. 56–71. Chicago: University of Illinois Press.

Siegel, Karolynn, Laurie J. Bauman, Grace H. Christ, and Susan Krown. 1988. Patterns of change in sexual behavior among gay men in New York City. *Archives of Sexual Behavior* 17, 6: 481–497.

Siegel, K., P. F. Mesagno, J.-Y. Chen, and G. Christ. 1989. Factors distinguishing homosexual males practicing risky and safer sex. *Social Science and Medicine* 28: 561–569. [Cited by Sandfort 1995.]

Silbert, Mimi H. 1980. *Sexual Assault of Prostitutes: Phase One.* Washington, D.C.: National Institute of Mental Health, National Center for the Prevention and Control of Rape. [Cited by Weisberg 1985.]

Silvestre, Anthony, David W. Lyter, Charles R. Rinaldo Jr., Lawrence A. Kingsley, Randall Forrester, and James Huggins. 1986. Marketing strategies for recruiting gay men into AIDS research and education projects. *Journal of Community Health* 11, 4: 222–232.

Simon, Patricia M., Edward V. Morse, Howard J. Osofsky, and Paul M. Balson. 1994. HIV and young male street prostitutes: A brief report. *Journal of Adolescence* 17: 193–197.

Simon, William and John H. Gagnon. 1987. Sexual scripts: Permanence and change. *Archives of Sexual Behavior* 15, 2: 97–120.

Singer, Merrill, Candida Flores, Lani Davison, Georgine Burke, Zaida Castillo, Kelley Scanlon, and Migdalia Rivera. 1990. SIDA: The economic, social, and cultural context of AIDS among Latinos. *Medical Anthropology Quarterly* 4, 1: 72–114.

Smiley, Elizabeth B. 1997. Counseling bisexual clients. *Journal of Mental Health Counseling* 19, 4 (October): 373–382.

Smith, Alena. 1993. Heads or tails. *Lesbian Contradiction* no. 44 (Fall).

Smith, Elaine M., Susan R. Johnson, and Susan M. Guenther. 1985. Health care attitudes and experiences during gynecologic care among lesbians and bisexuals. *American Journal of Public Health* 75, 9: 1085–1087.

Smith, James R. and Lynn G. Smith, eds. 1974. *Beyond Monogamy*. Baltimore: Johns Hopkins University Press.

Smith, Melissa L. and Christine A. Smith. 1994. Attitudes toward gay men and lesbians: What do high school students think? Poster presented at the Thirty-seventh Annual Meeting of the Society for the Scientific Study of Sex, November 3–6, Miami.

Smith, Tom W. 1991. Adult sexual behavior in 1989: Number of partners, frequency of intercourse and risk of AIDS. *Family Planning Perspectives* 23, 3 (May/June): 102–107.

—— 1992. *Half Straight: My Secret Bisexual Life*. Buffalo, N.Y.: Prometheus.

Smith-Rosenberg, Carroll. 1975. The female world of love and ritual: Relations between women in nineteenth-century America. *Signs* 1, 1: 1–29.

Snyder, Peter J., James D. Weinrich, and Richard C. Pillard. 1994. Personality and lipid level differences associated with homosexual and bisexual identity in men. *Archives of Sexual Behavior* 23, 4: 433–451.

Somerville, Siobhan. 1996. Scientific racism and the invention of the homosexual body. In Brett Beemyn and Mickey Eliason, eds., *Queer Studies: A Lesbian, Gay, Bisexual, and Transgender Anthology*, pp. 241–261. New York: New York University Press.

Sonenstein, Freya L., Joseph H. Pleck, and Leighton C. Ku. 1989. Sexual activity, condom use, and AIDS awareness among adolescent males. *Family Planning Perspectives* 21: 152–159. [Cited by Rotheram-Borus et al. 1992.]

Sonnex, C., G. Hart, P. Williams, and M. Adler. 1989. Condom use by heterosexuals attending a department of genito-urinary medicine: Attitudes and behaviour in light of HIV infection. *Genito-Urinary Medicine* 65: 248–251. [Cited by Boulton, Hart, and Fitzpatrick 1992.]

Sophie, Joan. 1986. A critical examination of stage theories of lesbian identity development. *Journal of Homosexuality* 12, 2: 39–51.

Spalding, Leah R. and Letitia Anne Peplau. 1997. The unfaithful lover: Heterosexuals' perceptions of bisexuals and their relationships. *Psychology of Women Quarterly* 21: 611–625.

Spellman, Richard. 1968. *The Bisexual Male*. Canoga Park, Cal.: Viceroy.

Spence, J. T. and R. Helmreich. 1978. *Masculinity and Femininity: Their Psychological Dimensions, Correlates, and Antecedents*. Austin: University of Texas Press. [Cited by Storms 1980.]

Spence, J. T., R. L. Helmreich, and C. K. Holohan. 1979. Negative and positive components of psychological masculinity and femininity and their relationships to self-reports of neurotic and acting out behaviors. *Journal of Personality and Social Psychology* 37: 1673–1682. [Cited by LaTorre and Wendenburg 1983.]

Spence, J. T., R. Helmreich, and J. Stapp. 1974. The personal attributes questionnaire: A measure of sex-role stereotypes and masculinity-femininity. *JSAS Catalog of Selected Documents in Psychology* 4: 43–44, MS 617. [Cited by Whalen, Geary, and Johnson 1990 etc.]

Spira, Alfred, Nathalie Bajos, André Béjin, Nathalie Beltzer et al. Analyse des

Comportements Sexuels en France [ACSF] Investigators. 1992. AIDS and sexual behaviour in France. *Nature* 360 (December 3): 407–409.

Stall, Ron D., Thomas J. Coates, and Colleen Hoff. 1988. Behavioral risk reduction for HIV infection among gay and bisexual men. *American Psychologist* 43, 11: 878–885.

Stevens, Patricia E. 1994. HIV prevention education for lesbians and bisexual women: A cultural analysis of a community intervention. *Social Science and Medicine* 39, 11: 1565–1578.

Stevens, Robin. 1992. Love and rockets. *Out/Look* no. 16 (Spring): 32–35.

Stocker, Carol. 1990. So near, yet so far. *Boston Globe,* (August 27): 30, 32.

Stockwell, Spencer. 1953. Sexual experiences of adolescent delinquent girls. *International Journal of Sexology* 7: 25–27. [Cited by Gagnon and Simon 1973.]

Stokes, Kirk, Peter R. Kilmann, and Richard L. Wanlass. 1983. Sexual orientation and sex role conformity. *Archives of Sexual Behavior* 12, 5: 427–433.

Stokes, Joseph P. and Robin L. Miller. 1998. Toward an understanding of behaviourally bisexual men: The influence of context and culture. *Canadian Journal of Human Sexuality* 7, 2:101–113.

Stokes, Joseph P. and John L. Peterson. 1998. Homophobia, self-esteem, and risk for HIV among African American men who have sex with men. *AIDS Education and Prevention* 10, 3: 278–292.

Stokes, Joseph P., Rebecca G. Burzette, and David J. McKirnan. 1991. Bisexual men: Social characteristics and predictors of AIDS-risk behavior. Poster presented at Seventh International Conference on AIDS, June, Florence, Italy. [Cited by Heckman et al. 1995.]

Stokes, Joseph P., Will Damon, and David J. McKirnan. 1997. Predictors of movement toward homosexuality: A longitudinal study of bisexual men. *Journal of Sex Research* 34, 3: 304–312.

Stokes, Joseph P., David J. McKirnan, and Rebecca G. Burzette. 1993. Sexual behavior, condom use, disclosure of sexuality, and stability of sexual orientation in bisexual men. *Journal of Sex Research* 30, 3: 203–213.

Stokes, Joseph P., David J. McKirnan, Lynda Doll, and Rebecca G. Burzette. 1996. Female partners of bisexual men: What they don't know might hurt them. *Psychology of Women Quarterly* 20: 267–284.

Stokes, Joseph P., Kittiwut Taywaditep, Peter Vanable, and David J. McKirnan. 1996. Bisexual men, sexual behavior, and HIV/AIDS. In Beth A. Firestein, ed., *Bisexuality: The Psychology and Politics of an Invisible Minority,* pp. 149–168. Thousand Oaks, Cal.: Sage.

Stokes, Joseph P., Peter A. Vanable, and David J. McKirnan. 1996. Ethnic differences in sexual behavior, condom use, and psychosocial variables among black and white men who have sex with men. *Journal of Sex Research* 33, 4: 373–381.

—— 1997. Comparing gay and bisexual men on sexual behavior, condom use, and psychosocial variables related to HIV/AIDS. *Archives of Sexual Behavior* 26, 4: 383–397.

Storms, Michael D. 1978. Sexual orientation and self-perception. In P. Pilner,

K. Blankstein, and I. Spiegel, eds., *Advances in the Study of Communication and Affect: Perception of Emotion in Self and Others*, pp. 165–180. New York: Plenum.

—— 1980. Theories of sexual orientation. *Journal of Personality and Social Psychology* 38, 5: 783–792.

—— 1981. A theory of erotic orientation development. *Psychological Review* 88, 4: 340–353.

Storr, Merl. 1993. Psychoanalysis and lesbian desire: The trouble with female homosexuals. Joseph Bristow and Angelia R. Wilson, eds., *Activating Theory: Lesbian, Gay, Bisexual Politics*, pp. 53–69. London: Lawrence and Wishart.

Striegel-Moore, Ruth H., Naomi Tucker, and Jeanette Hsu. 1990. Body image dissatisfaction and disorder eating in lesbian college students. *International Journal of Eating Disorders* 9(5): 493–500. [Cited by Atkins 1998.]

Stroud, Irene Elizabeth. 1994. Out of the straight jacket [review of *Dual Attraction*]. *Nation* (July 4): 27–28.

Strunin, L. 1991. Adolescents' perceptions of risk for HIV infection: Implications for future research. *Social Science Medicine* 32: 221–228. [Cited by Matteson 1997.]

Stuenkel, Kristen. 1992. Honoring bisexual identity. *Washington Peace Letter* (April).

Sugars, Stephanie. 1989. A second coming out. *Lesbian Contradiction* no. 26 (Spring).

Sudman, Seymour and Graham Kalton. 1986. New developments in the sampling of special populations. *Annual Review of Sociology* 12: 401–429.

Sue, Derald Wing, ed. 1981. *Counseling the Culturally Different: Theory and Practice.* New York: Wiley.

Sullivan, T. Richard. 1996. The challenge of HIV prevention among high-risk adolescents. *Health and Social Work* 21, 1: 58–65.

Suppe, Frederick, 1981. The Bell and Weinberg Study: Future Priorities for Research on Homosexuality. *Journal of Homosexuality* 6, 4: 69–97.

—— 1984. In defense of a multidimensional approach to sexual identity. *Journal of Homosexuality* 10, 3/4 (Winter): 7–14.

Swaab, D. F. and M. A. Hofman. 1990. An enlarged suprachiasmatic nucleus in homosexual men. *Brain Research* 537, 1/2 (December 24): 141–148.

Swaab, D. F., A. K. Slob, E. J. Houtsmuller, T. Brand, J. N. Zhou. 1995. Increased number of vasopressin neurons in the suprachiasmatic nucleus (SCN) of "bisexual" adult male rats following perinatal treatment with the aromatase blocker ATD. *Developmental Brain Research* 85:273–279.

Sykes, Gresham M. 1958. *The Society of Captives: A Study of a Maximum Security Prison.* Princeton: Princeton University Press.

Tafoya, Terry and Ron Rowell. 1988. Counseling gay and lesbian Native Americans. In Michael Shernoff and William A. Scott, eds., *The Sourcebook on Lesbian/Gay Health Care*. Washington, D.C.: National Lesbian/Gay Health Foundation.

Tafoya, Terry and Douglas A. Wirth. 1996. Native American two-spirit men. *Journal of Gay and Lesbian Social Services* 5, 2/3:51–67.

Tait, Vanessa. 1991. The bisexuality debate: A struggle for recognition—and differentiation. *Boston Phoenix* (August 16): 6–7.

Tanfer, Koray, William R. Grady, Daniel H. Klepinger, and John O. G. Billy. 1993. Condom use among U.S. men, 1991. *Family Planning Perspectives* 25, 2: 61–66.

Taylor, Verta and Nicole C. Raeburn. 1995. Identity politics as high-risk activism: Career consequences for lesbian, gay, and bisexual sociologists. *Social Problems* 42, 2: 252– 273.

Taywaditep, Kittiwut Jod and Joseph P. Stokes. 1998. Male bisexualities: A cluster analysis of men with bisexual experience. *Journal of Psychology and Human Sexuality* 10, 1: 15–41.

Terman, Lewis M. 1948. Kinsey's "Sexual Behavior in the Human Male": Some comments and criticisms. *Psychological Bulletin* 45: 443–459.

Tewksbury, Richard. 1989a. Measures of sexual behavior in an Ohio prison. *Sociology and Social Research* 74, 1: 34–39.

—— 1989b. Fear of sexual assault in prison inmates. *Prison Journal* 69: 62–71.

Thiam, Awa. 1986. *Black Sisters, Speak Out: Feminism and Oppression in Black Africa.* Concord, Mass.: Pluto. Rpt. 1991.

Thomas, Stephen G. and Bonnie Hodges. 1991. Assessing AIDS knowledge, attitudes, and risk behaviors among Black and Hispanic homosexual and bisexual men: Results of a feasibility study. *Journal of Sex Education and Therapy* 17, 2: 116–124.

Thorne, F. C. 1966. The sex inventory. *Journal of Clinical Psychology* 22: 367–74.

Tielman, Rob, Manuel Carballo, and Aart Hendriks, eds. 1991. *Bisexuality and HIV/AIDS: A Global Perspective.* Buffalo, N.Y.: Prometheus.

Time. 1974. The new bisexuals. *Time* (May 13).

— 1979. Masters and Johnson on homosexuality. *Time* (April 23): 77–78.

Torian, Lucia V., Isaac B. Weisfuse, Hadi A. Makki, Deborah A. Benson, Linda M. DiCamillo, Priti R. Patel, and Francisco E. Toribio. 1996. Trends in HIV seroprevalence in men who have sex with men: New York City Department of Health sexually transmitted disease clinics, 1988–1993. *AIDS* 10: 187–192.

Toufexis, Anastasia. 1992. Bisexuality: What is it? *Time* (August 17): 49–51.

Treadwell, Mattie E. 1954. *The Women's Army Corps.* Washington, D.C. [Cited by D'Emilio 1983.]

Tremble, Bob, Margaret Schneider, and Carol Appathurai. 1989. Growing up gay or lesbian in a multicultural context. *Journal of Homosexuality* 17, 1–4: 253–267.

Tripp, C. A. 1976. *The Homosexual Matrix.* New York: New American Library. [Cited by Hays and Samuels 1989.]

Trocki, Karen F. 1992. Patterns of sexuality and risky sexuality in the general population of a California county. *Journal of Sex Research* 29, 1: 85–94.

Troiden, Richard R. 1988. *Gay and Lesbian Identity: A Sociological Analysis.* Dix Hills, N.Y.: General Hall.

Trujillo, C., ed. 1991. *Chicana Lesbians: The Girls Our Mothers Warned Us About.* Berkeley: Third Woman.

Trumbach, Randolph. 1977. London's sodomites: Homosexual behavior and Western Culture in the eighteenth century. *Journal of Social History* 2: 1–33.

—— 1997. Are modern Western lesbian women and gay men a third gender? In Martin Duberman, ed., *A Queer World: The Center for Lesbian and Gay Studies Reader,* pp. 87–99. New York: New York University Press.

Tucker, Naomi, ed., 1995. *Bisexual Politics: Theories, Queries, and Visions*. Binghamton, N.Y.: Haworth.

Turner, Charles F., Heather G. Miller, and Lincoln E. Moses. 1989. Sexual behavior and AIDS. In C. Turner, H. Miller, and L. Moses, eds., *AIDS, Sexual Behavior, and Intravenous Drug Use*, pp. 73–185. Washington, D.C.: National Academy.

Twining, Alice. 1983. Bisexual women: Identity in adult development. Ph.D. diss., Boston University School of Education. *Dissertation Abstracts International*, 44, 5, 1340A. [Cited by Fox 1996.]

Udis-Kessler, Amanda. 1996. Identity/Politics: Historical sources of the bisexual movement. In Brett Beemyn and Mickey Eliason, eds., *Queer Studies. A Lesbian, Gay, Bisexual, and Transgender Anthology*, pp. 52–63. New York: New York University Press.

Ulrichs, Karl Heinrich. 1864 [1889]. *Inclusa*. [Cited by Haeberle 1998.]

Uribe, Virginia and Karen M. Harbeck. 1991. Addressing the needs of lesbian, gay, and bisexual youth: The origins of PROJECT 10 and school-based intervention. *Journal of Homosexuality* 22, 3/4: 9–28.

Vaid, Urvashi. 1995. *Virtual Equality: The Mainstreaming of Gay and Lesbian Liberation*. New York: Anchor.

Valdiserri, Ronald O., David W. Lyter, Lawrence A. Kingsley, Laura C. Leviton, Janet W. Schofield, James Huggins, Monto Ho, and Charles Rinaldo. 1987. The effect of group education on improving attitudes about AIDS risk reduction. *New York State Journal of Medicine* 87, 5: 272–278.

Valverde, Mariana. 1985. Bisexuality: Coping with sexual boundaries. *Sex, Power, and Pleasure*, pp. 109–120. Toronto: Women's.

Van Wyk, Paul H. 1984. A critique of Dörner's analysis of hormonal data from bisexual males. *Journal of Sex Research* 20: 412–414.

Van Wyk, Paul H. and Chrisann S. Geist. 1984. Psychosocial development of heterosexual, bisexual, and homosexual behavior. *Archives of Sexual Behavior* 13, 6: 505–544.

—— 1995. Biology of bisexuality: Critique and observations. *Journal of Homosexuality* 28, 3/4: 357–373.

Varni, Charles A. 1974. An exploratory study of spouse swapping. In James R. Smith and Lynn G. Smith, eds., *Beyond Monogamy*, pp. 246–259. Baltimore: Johns Hopkins University Press.

Vazquez, Elisa. 1979. Homosexuality in the context of the Mexican-American culture. In Dale Kunkel, ed., *Sexual Issues in Social Work: Emerging Concerns in Education and Practice*, pp. 131–147. Honolulu: University of Hawaii.

Vicinus, Martha. 1989. Distance and desire: English boarding school friendships, 1870–1920. In Martin Duberman, Martha Vicinus, and George Chauncey Jr., eds., *Hidden from History: Reclaiming the Gay and Lesbian Past*, pp. 212–229. New York: Meridian. Rpt. 1990.

Vicinus, Martha. 1992. "They wonder to which sex I belong": The historical roots of the modern lesbian identity. *Feminist Studies* 18, 3: 467–497.

Vidal, Gore. 1985. "Someone to laugh at the squares with" [Tennesee Williams],

New York Review of Books, June 13. Repr. *At Home: Essays, 1982–1988*. New York: Random House, 1988. [Cited by Katz 1990.]

Vining, Donald. 1979. *A Gay Diary, 1933–1946*. New York.

Visano, Livy Anthony. 1990. The impact of age on paid sexual encounters. *Journal of Homosexuality* 20, 3/4: 207–226.

Voeller, Bruce. 1990. Some uses and abuses of the Kinsey scale. In David P. McWhirter, Stephanie A. Saunders, and June Machover Reinisch, eds., *Homosexuality-Heterosexuality: Concepts of Sexual Orientation*, pp. 32–38. New York: Oxford University Press.

Voeller, Bruce and James Walters. 1978. Gay fathers. *Family Coordinator* (April): 149–157.

Waldorf, Dan and David Lauderback. 1992. The condom use of male sex workers in San Francisco. *AIDS and Public Policy Journal* 7, 2: 108–119.

Waldorf, Dan, Sheigla Murphy, David Lauderback, Craig Reinarman, Toby Marotta. 1990. Needle sharing among male prostitutes: Preliminary findings of the Prospero Project. *Journal of Drug Issues* 20, 2: 309–334.

Wallis, W. Allen. 1949. Statistics of the Kinsey Report, *Journal of the American Statistical Association* 44, 248: 463–484.

War Department. 1943. *Sex Hygiene Course: Officers and Officer Candidates, Women's Army Auxiliary Corps*, pamphlet no. 35-1. Washington, D.C. [Cited by D'Emilio 1983.]

Ward, David A. and Gene G. Kassebaum. 1964. Homosexuality: A mode of adaptation in a prison for women. *Social Problems* 12, 2: 159–177.

—— 1965. *Women's Prison: Sex and Social Structure*. Chicago: Aldine.

Warren, Carol A. B. 1974. *Identity and Community in the Gay World*. New York: Wiley.

Watters, John K. and Patrick Biernacki. 1989. Targeted sampling: Options for the study of hidden populations. *Social Problems* 36, 4: 416–430.

Weasel, Lisa H. 1996. Seeing between the lines: Bisexual women and therapy. *Women and Therapy* 19, 2: 5–16.

Weatherburn, P., F. Hickson, D. S. Reid, P. M. Davies, and A. Crosier. 1998. Sexual HIV risk behaviour among men who have sex with both men and women. *AIDS Care* 10, 4: 463–471.

Weeks, Jeffrey. 1977. *Coming Out: Homosexual Politics in Britain, from the Nineteenth Century to the Present*. London: Quartet. Rpt. 1979.

—— 1981a. Discourse, desire and sexual deviance: Some problems in a history of homosexuality. In K. Plummer, ed., *The Making of the Modern Homosexual*. London: Hutchinson.

—— 1981b. *Sex, Politics and Society: The Regulation of Sexuality Since 1800*. Essex: Longman.

—— 1982. The development of sexual theory and sexual politics. In M. Brake, ed., *Human Social Relations: A Reader*. Harmondsworth: Penguin.

—— 1985. *Sexuality and Its Discontents*. London: Routledge and Kegan Paul.

—— 1986. *Sexuality*. New York: Tavistock.

Weinberg, Ian. 1967. *The English Public Schools: The Sociology of Elite Education*. New York: Atherton. [Cited by Propper 1981.]

Weinberg, Martin S. and Colin J. Williams. 1974. *Male Homosexuals: Their Problems and Adaptations*. New York: Oxford University Press.

Weinberg, Martin S., Colin J. Williams, and Douglas W. Pryor. 1994. *Dual Attraction: Understanding Bisexuality*. New York: Oxford University Press.

Weinrich, James D. 1988. The periodic table model of the gender transpositions: Part II. *Journal of Sex Research* 24: 113–129.

Weinrich, James D., Peter J. Snyder, Richard C. Pillard, Igor Grant, Denise L. Jacobson, S. Renée Robinson, and J. Allen McCutchan. 1993. A factor analysis of the Klein Sexual Orientation Grid in two disparate samples. *Archives of Sexual Behavior* 22, 2: 157–168.

Weisberg, D. Kelly. 1985. *Children of the Night: A Study of Adolescent Prostitution*. Lexington, Mass.: Lexington.

Weise, Elizabeth Reba. 1992. *Closer to Home: Bisexuality and Feminism*. Seattle, Wash.: Seal.

Wekker, Gloria. 1993. Mati-ism and black lesbianism: Two idealtypical expressions of female homosexuality in Black communities of the diaspora. *Journal of Homosexuality* 24, 3/4. Rpt. 1997. *Journal of Lesbian Studies* 1, 1: 11–24.

Wells, John Warren. 1974. *Total Sexuality*. New York: Warner.

West, Donald J. 1967. *Homosexuality*. Chicago: Aldine.

Westermeyer, Joseph, Marvin Seppala, Shelly Gasow, and Gregory Carlson. 1989. AIDS-related illness and AIDS risk in male homo/bisexual substance abusers: Case reports and clinical issues. *American Journal of Drug and Alcohol Abuse* 15, 4: 443–461.

Westphal, Carl. 1870. Die conträre Sexualempfindung, Symptom eines neuropathischen (psychopathischen) Zustandes. (Contrary sexual feeling: Symptom of a nuropathic (psychopathic) condition. *Archiv für Psychiatrie und Nervenkrankheiten* (Archives of psychiatry and nervous diseases) 2:1: 73–108. [Cited by Haeberle 1998.]

Westwood, G. 1952. *Society and the Homosexual*. London: Gollancz.

Whalen, R. E. 1974. Sexual differentiation: Models, methods, and mechanisms. In R. C. Friedman, R. M. Richart, and R. L. Vande Wiele, eds., *Sex Differences in Behavior*, pp. 467–481. New York: Wiley. [Cited by Whalen, Geary, and Johnson 1990.]

Whalen, Richard E., David C. Geary, and Frank Johnson. 1990. Models of sexuality. In David P. McWhirter, Stephanie A. Sanders, and June Machover Reinisch, eds., *Homosexuality/Heterosexuality: Concepts of Sexual Orientation*, pp. 61–70. New York: Oxford University Press.

Whitam, Frederick L., Milton Diamond, and James Martin. 1993. Homosexual orientation in twins: A report on sixty-one pairs and three triplet sets. *Archives of Sexual Behavior* 22, 3: 187–206.

Whitehead, Harriet. 1981. The bow and the burden strap: A new look at institutionalized homosexuality in Native North America. In Sherry B. Ortner and Harriet Whitehead, eds., *Sexual Meanings: The Cultural Construction of Gender and Sexuality*, pp. 80–115. New York: Cambridge University Press.

Whitney, Catherine. 1990. *Uncommon Lives: Gay Men and Straight Women*. New York: Plume.

Wilkerson, Abby. 1997. Ending at the skin: Sexuality and race in feminist theorizing. *Hypatia* 12, 3 (Summer): 164–173

Wilkinson, Sue. 1996. Bisexuality "a la mode." *Women's Studies International Forum* 19, 3: 293–301.

Williams, Mark J. K. 1999. *Sexual Pathways: Adapting to Dual Sexual Attraction.* Westport, Conn.: Praeger.

Williams, Walter L. 1986. *The Spirit and the Flesh: Sexual Diversity in American Indian Culture.* Boston: Beacon.

—— 1993. Being gay and doing research on homosexuality in non-Western cultures. *Journal of Sex Research* 30, 2: 115–120.

Wilson, Ara. 1992. Just add water: Searching for the bisexual politic. *Out/Look* no. 16 (Spring): 22, 24–28.

Winkelstein, Warren, David N. Lyman, Nancy Padian, Robert Grant, Michael Samuel, James A. Wiley, Robert E. Anderson, William Lang, John Riggs, and Jay A. Levy. 1987a. Sexual practices and risk of infection by the Human Immunodeficiency Virus: The San Francisco Men's Health Study. *Journal of the American Medical Association* 257, 3: 321–325.

Winkelstein, Warren, Michael Samuel, Nancy Padian, James A. Wiley, William Lang, Robert E. Anderson, and Jay A. Levy. 1987b. The San Francisco Men's Health Study: III. Reduction in human immunodeficiency virus transmission among homosexual/bisexual men, 1982–86. *American Journal of Public Health* 76, 9: 685–689.

Winkelstein, Warren, James A. Wiley, and Nancy Padian. 1986. Potential for transmission of AIDS-associated retrovirus from bisexual men in San Francisco to their female sexual contacts. *Journal of the American Medical Association* 255: 901. [Cited by Ekstrand et al. 1994.]

Winkelstein, Warren, James A. Wiley, Nancy Padian, Michael Samuel, Stephen Shiboski, Michael S. Ascher, and Jay A. Levy. 1988. The San Francisco Men's Health Study: Continued decline in HIV seroconversion rates among homosexual/bisexual men. *American Journal of Public Health* 78, 11: 1472– 1474.

Wire service. 1992. Gays and lesbians celebrate pride with parades in NYC, across nation. June.

Wolcott, Deane L., Sheila Namir, Fawzy I. Fawzy, Michael S. Gottlieb, and Ronald T. Mitsuyasu. 1986. Illness concerns, attitudes towards homosexuality, and social support in gay men with AIDS. *General Hospital Psychiatry* 8: 395–403.

Wold, Cheryl, George R. Seage III, William R. Lenderking, Kenneth H. Mayer, Bin Cai, Timothy Heeren, and Robert Goldstein. 1998. Unsafe sex in men who have sex with both men and women. *Journal of Acquired Immune Deficiency Syndromes and Human Retrovirology* 17: 361–367.

Wolf, Deborah Goleman 1979. *The Lesbian Community.* Berkeley: University of California Press. Rpt. 1980

Wolf, Timothy J. 1985. Marriages of bisexual men. *Journal of Homosexuality,* 11, 1/2. Rpt. 1985. In Fritz Klein and Timothy J. Wolf, eds., *Two Lives to Lead: Bisexual in Men and Women,* pp. 135–148. New York: Harrington Park.

—— 1987. Group counseling for bisexual men. *Journal for Specialists in Group Work* 12, 4 (November): 162–165.

Wolff, Charlotte. 1971. *Love Between Women*. New York: Harper and Row.

—— 1977. *Bisexuality: A Study*. London: Quartet. [Cited by Zinik 1985.]

Wood, Robert W., Leigh E. Krueger, Tsilke Pearlman, and Gary Goldbaum. 1993. HIV transmission: Women's risk from bisexual men. *American Journal of Public Health* 83, 12: 1757–1759.

Wooden, Wayne S., Harvey Kawasake, and Raymond Mayeda. 1983. Lifestyles and identity maintenance among gay Japanese-American males. *Alternative Lifestyles* 5: 236–243. [Cited by Matteson 1997.]

Wooden, Wayne S. and Jay Parker. 1982. *Men Behind Bars: Sexual Exploitation in Prison*. New York: Plenum.

World Health Organization. 1992. Information consultation on interventions to prevent HIV transmission among behaviorally bisexual men, December 7–9, Geneva.

Wright, Jerome W. 1993. African-American male sexual behavior and the risk for HIV infection. *Human Organization* 52, 4: 421–431.

Yates, Gary L., Richard G. MacKenzie, Julia Pennbridge, and Avon Swofford. 1991. A risk profile comparison of homeless youth involved in prostitution and homeless youth not involved. *Journal of Adolescent Health* 12: 545–548.

Young, Rebecca M., Gloria Weissman, and Judith B. Cohen. 1992. Assessing risk in the absence of information: HIV risk among women injection-drug users who have sex with women. *AIDS and Public Policy Journal* 7, 3 (Fall): 175–183.

Young, Stacey. 1992. Breaking silence about the "B-word": Bisexual identity and lesbian-feminist discourse. In Elizabeth Reba Weise, ed., *Closer to Home: Bisexuality and Feminism*, pp. 75–87. Seattle, Wash.: Seal.

Young, Stacey. 1997. Dichotomies and displacement: Bisexuality in queer theory and politics. In Shane Phelan, ed., *Playing with Fire: Queer Politics, Queer Theories*, pp. 51–74. New York: Routledge.

Zamora-Hernández, Carlos E. and Davis G. Patterson. 1996. Homosexually active Latino men: Issues for social work practice. *Journal of Gay and Lesbian Social Services* 5, 2/3: 69–91.

Zinik, Gary A. 1983. The relationship between sexual orientation and eroticism, cognitive flexibility, and negative affect. Ph.D. diss., University of California, Santa Barbara. [Cited by Zinik 1985.]

—— 1985. Identity conflict or adaptive flexibility? Bisexuality reconsidered. *Journal of Homosexuality* 11, 1/2: 7–19. Rpt. 1985. In Fritz Klein and Timothy J. Wolf, eds., *Two Lives to Lead: Bisexuality in Men and Women*, pp. 7–19. New York: Harrington Park.

Zucker, K. J. 1990. Gender identity disorders in children: Clinical descriptions and natural history. In R. Blanchard and B. W. Steiner, eds., *Clinical Management of Gender Identity Disorders in Children and Adults*, pp. 1–23. Washington, D.C.: American Psychiatric. [Cited by Bailey 1996.]

Zuger, Bernard. 1978. Effeminate behavior present in boys, from childhood: Ten additional years of follow-up. *Comprehensive Psychiatry* 19, 4: 363–369.

Name Index

In the case of empirical research reports, **bold type** indicates pages or notes in which research methodology or sampling techniques are described. Chapters 2, 3, 5–10, 12, 13, 15, 16, 18, 19, 21, and 24–26 are previously published articles, reprinted in this volume with their original bibliographies intact. Citations made in these chapters are neither indexed here nor included in the bibliography at the end of this volume.

Subject Index

In the case of empirical research reports, **bold type** indicates pages or notes in which research methodology or sampling techniques are described.

Copyright Acknowledgments

Between Men ~ Between Women

Lesbian and Gay Studies

Lillian Faderman and Larry Gross, Editors

Terry Castle, *Noel Coward and Radclyffe Hall: Kindred Spirits*

Kath Weston, *Render Me, Gender Me: Lesbians Talk Sex, Class, Color, Nation, Studmuffins . . .*

Ruth Vanita, *Sappho and the Virgin Mary: Same-Sex Love and the English Literary Imagination*

renée c. hoogland, *Lesbian Configurations*

Beverly Burch, *Other Women: Lesbian Experience and Psychoanalytic Theory of Women*

Jane McIntosh Snyder, *Lesbian Desire in the Lyrics of Sappho*

Rebecca Alpert, *Like Bread on the Seder Plate: Jewish Lesbians and the Transformation of Tradition*

Emma Donoghue, editor, *Poems Between Women: Four Centuries of Love, Romantic Friendship, and Desire*

James T. Sears and Walter L. Williams, editors, *Overcoming Heterosexism and Homophobia: Strategies That Work*

Patricia Juliana Smith, *Lesbian Panic: Homoeroticism in Modern British Women's Fiction*

Dwayne C. Turner, *Risky Sex: Gay Men and HIV Prevention*

Timothy F. Murphy, *Gay Science: The Ethics of Sexual Orientation Research*

Cameron McFarlane, *The Sodomite in Fiction and Satire, 1660–1750*

Lynda Hart, *Between the Body and the Flesh: Performing Sadomasochism*

Byrne R. S. Fone, editor, *The Columbia Anthology of Gay Literature: Readings from Western Antiquity to the Present Day*

Ellen Lewin, *Recognizing Ourselves: Ceremonies of Lesbian and Gay Commitment*

Ruthann Robson, *Sappho Goes to Law School: Fragments in Lesbian Legal Theory*

Jacquelyn Zita, *Body Talk: Philosophical Reflections on Sex and Gender*

Evelyn Blackwood and Saskia Wieringa, *Female Desires: Same-Sex Relations and Transgender Practices Across Cultures*

William L. Leap, ed., *Public Sex/Gay Space*

Larry Gross and James D. Woods, eds., *The Columbia Reader on Lesbians and Gay Men in Media, Society, and Politics*

Marilee Lindemann, *Willa Cather: Queering America*

George E. Haggerty, *Men in Love: Masculinity and Sexuality in the Eighteenth Century*

Andrew Elfenbein, *Romantic Genius: The Prehistory of a Homosexual Role*

Gilbert Herdt and Bruce Koff, *Something to Tell You: The Road Families Travel When a Child Is Gay*

Richard Canning, *Gay Fiction Speaks: Conversations with Gay Novelists*

Laura Doan, *Fashioning Sapphism: The Origins of a Modern English Lesbian Culture*